Contents

HIGHWAYS

THE ISLANDS

MAJOR ATTRACTIONS

MAJOR CITIES

GENERAL INFORMATION

Northwest Mileposts®

Managing Editor, Kris Graef
Graphic Designer, Beth L. Atkins
Copy Editor, Caryn Mohr
Field Editors: Tina L. Boyle, Liz Bryan, Melissa Bryan, Dennis M. Carpenter, Michele Andrus Dill, Susan Dunn, Charles M. Gordon, Sam Smith, Linda Thielke
Editorial Assistants: Andrew Boynton, Heidi Roe
Production Manager, Jon Flies
Production Coordinator, Alexa Peery
Cartography: David Ranta, Trevor Vernon
Fulfillment Manager, Tina L. Boyle
Associate Publisher, Michele Andrus Dill
Publisher, Geoffrey P. Vernon

COVER: Mount Rainier is Washington's highest peak and one of its best-known landmarks. (© John Barger)
Cover Design: Beth L. Atkins

ISBN 1-878425-80-3
Key Title: Northwest Mileposts
Printed in the U.S.A. on recycled stock

Vernon Publications Inc.
3000 Northup Way, Suite 200
Bellevue, WA 98004
(206) 827-9900
1-800-726-4707
Fax (206) 822-9372

Publishers of:
The MILEPOST®
The ALASKA WILDERNESS GUIDE
ALASKA A to Z
The MILEPOST® Souvenir Log Book
Northwest Mileposts®

Fifth Edition

Vernon Publications Inc.
Geoffrey P. Vernon,
Chairman, President & CEO
Michele Andrus Dill, Vice President
Judy Vernon, Secretary
Fred W. Gallimore, Treasurer

Bill R. Vernon, Chairman Emeritus

0Field Editor Report

Between the time of our field editors' surveys and the time of our readers' trips, changes may take place along the highway routes covered in *Northwest Mileposts®*. A sincere effort is made to give you a complete, accurate and up-to-date guidebook, but travelers may nonetheless find changes in hours of operation, prices, road conditions, and services and facilities available. In all such cases the publisher will not be held responsible.

We would appreciate hearing from you, our readers, about any inaccuracies or changes that have taken place that need to be corrected or included in the next edition of *Northwest Mileposts®*. We would also like to hear about new attractions, or old attractions we may have missed, that you wish to see included in *Northwest Mileposts®*, and any suggestions you may have on how we can improve or expand our coverage of the Northwest.

Please drop us a note or use the Field Editor Report form on page 304 to let us know what you discover while traveling the Northwest with *Northwest Mileposts®*.

Photo Contribution

Northwest Mileposts® invites Northwest travelers and residents to submit photographs for consideration in future editions of the book. Copies of photo submission guidelines must be requested before submitting photos. Send guidelines request and a postpaid return envelope to Editor, *Northwest Mileposts®*, P.O. Box 96043, Bellevue, WA 98009-9643. Vernon Publications Inc. assumes no responsibility for unsolicited materials.

Thanks

The editors of *Northwest Mileposts®* would like to acknowledge their appreciation to the many staff members of the U.S. National Park Service, the U.S. Forest Service and other federal agencies; the state and provincial divisions of tourism, parks, fish and game, fish and wildlife, and transportation; and the many local chambers of commerce, tourist bureaus, and countless individuals who have contributed information and ideas to *Northwest Mileposts®*.

Key to Highways in Northwest Mileposts.

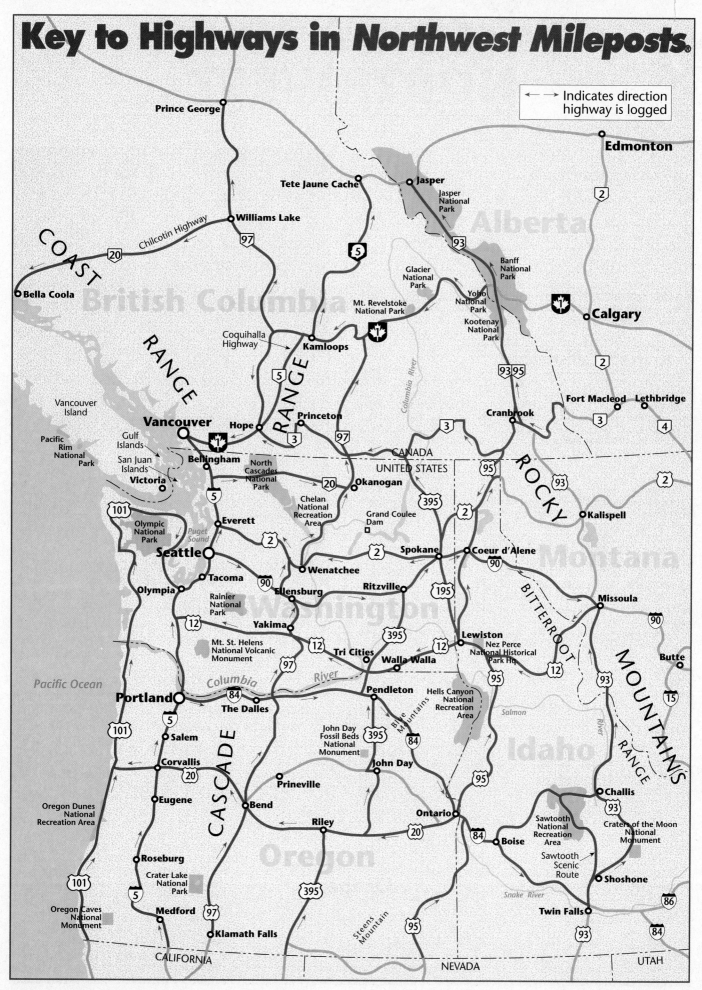

Indicates direction highway is logged

WELCOME TO THE NORTHWEST

Following are brief sketches of the states and the province that make up the Pacific Northwest, as defined in *Northwest Mileposts®*. Most of the features of this region can be found along the highways and in the cities and national parks of British Columbia, Idaho, Oregon and Washington. Read through the individual highway logs, the MAJOR CITIES section and the MAJOR ATTRACTIONS section to learn more about this diverse and historic part of the country.

British Columbia

Population: 3,282,061
Capital: Victoria
Area: 365,900 square miles/947,800 square km
Provincial Flower: Dogwood
Provincial Motto: *Splendor Sine Occasu* (Splendour Without Diminishment)

Canada's most western—and third largest—province, British Columbia stretches 813 miles/1,300 km from its southern border with the United States to the north boundary with Yukon Territory. It is bounded on the east by Alberta and the Rocky Mountains, and on the west by the Pacific Ocean. Victoria, the capital city, is located on Vancouver Island. Vancouver, on the mainland, is the province's largest city. Approximately half the province's population resides in the Victoria–Vancouver area.

British Columbia entered the dominion of Canada on July 20, 1871, as the sixth province. An important region in the early fur trade, expansion of the province came with the 1860s Cariboo gold rush, followed by the completion of Canada's first transcontinental railway—the Canadian Pacific. Today, the province has a diverse economy based on agriculture, fishing, forestry, manufacturing, mining and services.

Idaho

The Gem State

Population: 1,011,986
Capital: Boise
Area: 83,574 square miles
State Bird: Mountain bluebird
State Motto: *Esto Perpetua* (Let it be perpetual)
State Song: Here We Have Idaho
State Tree: White pine

Carved out of Washington Territory in 1863, Idaho is an integral part of the Pacific Northwest, although it is also considered a Rocky Mountain state. It is bordered to the west by Washington and Oregon, to the east by Montana and Wyoming, to the south by Utah and Nevada, and to the north by British Columbia. It measures 483 miles from south to north at its greatest length (the Panhandle), and 316 miles from east to west at its greatest width.

Idaho has been an important crossroads in the path of westward migration. Lewis and Clark crossed this country in 1804–1806, following the Lochsa and Snake rivers. Immigrants followed the Oregon Trail through southern Idaho.

The Snake River is the major river system in the state. (The Snake River and Hells Canyon form much of the state's border with Oregon.) Tributaries of the Snake include the Middle Fork of the Salmon River, a wild and scenic river famous for its commercial river running. Lake Pend Oreille is Idaho's largest lake.

Major mountain ranges in Idaho include the Bittterroot Range, which forms the Idaho–Montana border, and the Coeur d'Alene, Clearwater, Salmon River and Sawtooth mountains.

Dramatic scenery and pristine wilderness attract many visitors, and tourism comprises a significant percentage of the state's services industry. Also contributing to the state's economy are agriculture (beef cattle, potatoes, milk, hay, wheat, barley, sugar beets), mining (silver, phosphate rock, gold) and manufacturing.

Idaho became the 43rd state on July 3, 1890. Slightly more than half of the state's population resides in urban areas. Its capital and largest city is Boise.

Oregon

The Beaver State

Population: 2,853,733
Capital: Salem
Area: 97,052 square miles

Lower Proxy Falls cascades over moss-covered rocks in the Three Sisters Wilderness of Oregon's central Cascade Mountains. (© John Barger)

State Bird: Western meadowlark
State Flower: Oregon grape
State Motto: The Union
State Song: Oregon, My Oregon
State Tree: Douglas fir

Oregon is bounded to the north by the Columbia River; to the west by the Pacific; to the northeast by Hells Canyon and the Snake River; to the southeast by high desert plateau; and to the southwest by the Siskiyou Mountains of California.

The original Oregon Country stretched from Mexican California to Russian Alaska and from the crest of the Rockies to the Pacific. Fur traders worked the mountain valleys for beaver, and fur-trading companies established the first settlements. Fur traders were followed by land-hungry settlers, who came over the Oregon Trail to the rich Willamette River valley of western Oregon in the mid-1800s.

Oregon's major cities, including Portland (the largest) and Salem (the capital), are located in the Willamette Valley. Interstate 5 is the major corridor through western Oregon, one of the state's 2 major economic regions. Many manufacturing and service industries are concentrated in the Willamette Valley of western Oregon. Oregon's great forests, which cover almost half the state and represent about 10 percent of the nation's timber resources, feed the state's main manufacturing activity—wood processing

The Cascade Range divides western Oregon from drier and less populated eastern Oregon. Chief products in this half of the state include cattle, wheat and potatoes.

Oregon's dramatic coastline is a major tourist attraction. Other scenic wonders are the Columbia River Gorge, Hells Canyon National Recreation Area, John Day Fossil Beds National Monument, Oregon Caves National Monument and Crater Lake National Park.

Washington

The Evergreen State

Population: 4,887,941
Capital: Olympia
Area: 68,126 square miles
State Bird: Willow goldfinch
State Flower: Western rhododendron
State Motto: Alki (by and by)
State Song: Washington, My Home
State Tree: Western hemlock

Like other Northwestern states, Washington has a striking dichotomy of climate, terrain and population: The western half is green, wet and populous; the eastern half is drier and flatter and a little bit lonelier. Eastern Washington has warmer summers, but colder winters, than western Washington (although residents in the eastern half claim it

Alpenglow—the reddish glow sometimes seen on mountain summits at sunrise or sunset—on Mount Adams in the Cascade Mountains of southern Washington.
(© John Barger)

actually "feels" colder west of the Cascades).

The drier Yakima, Wenatchee and Okanogan districts east of the Cascades produce the majority of Washington's apples. Eastern Washington also produces wheat, the state's most valuable field crop.

A major portion of the state's economy depends on services and industries such as manufacturing, most of them centered along the Interstate 5 corridor in western Washington. The Boeing Co., a major manufacturer, is headquartered in Seattle. Seattle is Washington's largest city, with the greater Puget Sound area accounting for about half of the state's population. The importance of Puget Sound as

a safe harbor along the Pacific coast was first noted by the Wilkes Expedition in 1841–42. Today, it is a major shipping center.

Another important shipping lane is the Columbia River, which forms Washington's southern border with Oregon. One of the longest rivers in the United States, the Columbia drains more than half of Washington.

The state is perhaps best defined by its natural features, which attract thousands of visitors each year. Olympic National Park, North Cascades National Park, Mount Rainier National Park and Mount St. Helens National Volcanic Monument preserve much of the unique and natural beauty of Washington.

Pronunciation Guide

The following is a phonetic pronunciation guide for some of the most commonly mispronounced place names in the Northwest.

Agassiz—AG-a-see
Arimo—AIR-i-mo
Boise—BOY-see
Bruneau—BREW-no
Camano—kuh-MAY-no
Cathlamet—kath-LAM-ett
Celilo—se-LIE-lo
Chehalis—che-HAY-liss
Chelan—sh-LAN
Chewelah—che-WEE-la
Clatskanie—KLAT-skuh-neye
Cle Elum—clee-ELL-lum
Coeur d'Alene—CORR-duh-LANE
Copalis—Coe-PAY-liss
Coquihalla—COE-kwi-HALL-a
Dalles—DALZ
Dubois—DEW-boyce
Enumclaw—EE-num-claw
Galiano—GALL-ee-ANN-o
Hoquiam—HO-kwee-um
Ilwaco—ill-WAU-co
Kalaloch—KA-LAY-lock
Kamiah—KAMM-ee-eye
Kananaskis—KANNA-nas-kiss
Keremeos—KAIR-e-mose
Kittitas—KITT-i-tass
Kooskia—KOOS-kee
Kootenai—KOOT-nee or KOOT-nay
Lapwai—LAP-way
Lilliwaup—LILL-lih-wop
Lillooet—LIL-loo-et or lil-LUTE
Lummi—LUHM-ee

Memaloose—MEMM-a-loos
Methow—MET-how
Mukilteo—MUK-il-TEE-o
Multnomah—mult-NO-mah
Naches—nat-CHEESE
Nanaimo—nuh-NEYE-moe
Naselle—nay-SEL
Neah—NEE-uh
Nespelem—nes-PEE-lem
Nez Perce—nez purse
Nisqually—nih-SQUALL-lee
Okanagan—OH-kuh-NAW-gun
Onalaska—Ohn-uh-LAS-kuh
Orovada—ORR-uh-VADD-uh
Osoyoos—oh-SOY-youss
Oswego—os-WEE-go
Owyhee—oh-WHY-ee
Palouse—puh-LOOS
Pe Ell—pay-ELL
Pend Oreille—pon-doe-RAY
Pocatello—POKE-a-TELL-o
Poulsbo—PALZ-boh
Puyallup—pew-AL-up
Pysht—PISHT
Quilcene—KWIL-seen
Quilchena—kwill-CHEE-na
Quillayute—KWIL-uh-yute
Samish—SAM-ish
Sappho—SAFF-o
Sekiu—SEE-que
Sequim—SKWIM
Siskiyou—SISS-que or SISS-sk'ewe
Siuslaw—sigh-OOS-law
Skagit—SKAE-jit
Skamania—skuh-MAY-nee-uh
Skamokawa—skuh-MAH-kuh-way

Skykomish—sky-KO-mish
Snoqualmie—snow-KWALL-mee
Soleduck (Sol Duc)—SAWL-duhk
Spokane—spoh-KAN
Stehekin—ste-HEE-kin
Steilacoom—STILL-uh-come
Taholah—tuh-HOH-luh
Teanaway—tee-ANN-a-way
Tenino—te-NINE-o
Terrebonne—TERR-e-bon
Tete Jaune Cache—tee-john-cash
Tofino—tuh-FEE-no
Tonasket—tuh-NASS-kett
Tsawwassen—tuh-WAH-sen
Tualatin—too-AL-i-ton
Tukwila—tuck-WILL-a
Tulalip—too-LAY-lip
Tyee—TEYE-ee
Ucluelet—you-CLU-let
Uintah—you-INN-ta
Vashon—VASH-on
Wahkuakum—wuh-KEY-uh-kuhm
Waiilatpu—why-LAT-poo
Walhachin—wall-LAW-chin
Wallowa—wall-LAU-wa
Washougal—WAW-shoo-guhl
Washtucna—wawsh-TUHK-nuh
Wawawai—wuh-WAH-ee
Wenatchee—wuh-NATCH-ee
Wetaskiwin—wi-TASS-ke-win
Willamette—will-LAM-met
Willapa—WILL-aw-pa
Wyeth—WHY-eth
Yachats—YAH-hots
Yakima—YAK-ih-ma
Yaquina—yah-KEE-na

PLANNING YOUR TRIP WITH NORTHWEST MILEPOSTS®

Northwest Mileposts® covers the major highways of British Columbia, Idaho, Oregon and Washington. These mile-by-mile logs provide a detailed account of what you will see along the roads. Major metropolitan areas are included in the MAJOR CITIES section, and details on national parks, monuments and recreation areas are covered under MAJOR ATTRACTIONS. In addition, THE ISLANDS section covers the San Juan Islands, Gulf Islands and Vancouver Island, and includes details on the region's ferry systems. Additional subjects of interest to Northwest travelers are detailed in the GENERAL INFORMATION section.

How to Read a Highway Log

U.S. highways are logged east to west and interstates are logged west to east in *Northwest Mileposts®*. All south-north routes are logged south to north. (Travelers headed in the opposite direction of the log should read the log back to front.)

Each highway log in *Northwest Mileposts®* is based on a beginning and ending destination, indicated in boldfaced text at the beginning of the highway log; e.g. **Seattle** and **Missoula** in the Interstate 90 log. Each individual log entry is preceded by a boldfaced **Mile** followed by distance in miles from the beginning destination and—in parenthesis—distance in miles from the ending destination. For example, Fourth of July Summit at **Mile 328 (153)** on Interstate 90 is 328 miles from Seattle and 153 miles from Missoula.

In Canada, the equivalent distances in kilometres follow the miles and are indicated by **Km.** Miles and kilometres in *Northwest Mileposts®* highway logs are rounded off to the whole or half mile.

To determine driving distance between 2 points, simply subtract the mileage figure for point 1 from the mileage figure for point 2. For example, Moses Lake is at **Mile 176.5** and Coeur d'Alene is at **Mile 311** on Interstate 90: The distance between these 2 points is 134.5 miles. Mileages are also included on the highway strip maps accompanying each highway section.

Physical mileposts—where they exist—are indicated in the logs after the abbreviation MP. Interstate exit numbers are given in log entries after EXIT. These exit numbers usually reflect the milepost. In addition, icons at the end of each log entry indicate camping, fishing, picnic areas, hiking trails, downhill ski areas, handicap-accessible facilities and special attractions: ♿☝ⵗ☂⛵▲★.

Crossing the Border

Travel to and from Canada is usually a fairly straightforward procedure, but Northwest travelers should be aware of customs requirements before starting out. Following is some general information on crossing the border. Contact customs offices directly for more information: Canada customs in Vancouver, BC, phone (604) 666-0545, or U.S. customs in Seattle, WA, phone (206) 553-4676.

BORDER CROSSINGS
You cannot cross the border unless the customs office for the country you are entering is open. Severe fines are levied for crossing without clearing customs. Following are the locations and hours of operation for customs offices located in British Columbia along the U.S. border. In addition, customs is available at all ports.

Location	Hours of Operation
Aldergrove–Lynden, WA	8 a.m.–midnight
Boundary Bay–Point Roberts, WA	24 hours a day
Carson–Danville, WA	8 a.m.–midnight
Cascade–Laurier, WA	8 a.m.–midnight
Chopaka–Nighthawk, WA	9 a.m.–5 p.m.
Douglas–Blaine, WA	24 hours a day
Flathead–Trail Creek, MT	9 a.m.–5 p.m., June 1–Oct. 31
Huntingdon–Sumas, WA	24 hours a day
Kingsgate–Eastport, ID	24 hours a day
Midway–Ferry, WA	9 a.m.–5 p.m.
Nelway–Boundary Dam, WA	8 a.m.–midnight
Osoyoos–Oroville, WA	24 hours a day
Pacific Highway	24 hours a day
Paterson–Frontier, WA	8 a.m.–midnight
Roosville–Port of Roosville, MT	24 hours a day
Rykerts–Porthill, ID	8 a.m.–midnight from last Sun. in Oct. to last Sat. in April; 7 a.m.–midnight the rest of the year (Mountain standard time)
Waneta–Boundary, WA	9 a.m.–5 p.m.

A vineyard in Oregon's Tualatin Valley. (Steve Terrill, courtesy of Oregon Tourism Division)

Special Offer for
Northwest Mileposts® Readers!

Photo: Earl L. Brown

Subscribe now to **RV West**, the magazine serving RVers in the Western United States, and receive **53%** off the cover price, plus an additional three issues FREE, giving you 15 issues for the price of 12. It's a $37.50 value for just $13.99! (See other side of this page for more information.)

Photo: Sharon Paul Nault.

Name _____

Address _____

City _____ State _____ ZIP_____

Payment enclosed for $_____ Bill me for $_____

Charge my   ❑ VISA   ❑ MasterCard for $_____

Credit Card Number _____ Expiration Date _____

Signature _____

(We cannot charge your credit card without a signature.)

Just $13.99 for 15 issues. Please allow 4 to 6 weeks for your subscription to begin.

If at any time you are not completely satisfied with your subscription to *RV West*, you may cancel your subscription for a refund on all remaining issues.

ORDER TODAY!
CALL TOLL FREE
1-800-700-6962
Fax: 206-822-9372

OR MAIL TO:

RVWest

Vernon Publications Inc.
3000 Northup Way, Ste. 200
Bellevue, WA 98004

ENTRY INTO CANADA FROM THE U.S.

Citizens or permanent residents of the United States can usually cross the U.S.–Canada border either way without difficulty. They do not require passports or visas. However, to assist officers of both countries in speeding the crossing, native-born U.S. citizens should carry some identifying paper that shows their citizenship, just in case they are asked for it. This could include a driver's license and voter's registration (together), passport with photo, or some employment cards with description and photo. Social security cards or driver's licenses alone are not positive identification. Birth certificates of children are sometimes required. Proof of residence may also be required. Naturalized U.S. citizens should carry a naturalization certificate or some other evidence of citizenship. Permanent residents of the United States who are not U.S. citizens are advised to have their Resident Alien Card (U.S. Form 1-151 or Form 1-551).

All persons other than U.S. citizens or legal residents, and residents of Greenland, require a valid passport or an acceptable travel document.

Visitors to the United States who have a single-entry visa to the U.S. should check with an office of the U.S. and Naturalization Service to make sure that they have all the papers they need to get back into the United States.

Persons under 18 years of age who are not accompanied by an adult should bring a letter with them from a parent or guardian giving them permission to travel into Canada. Officials at Canadian customs are concerned about child abductions. If you are traveling with children, remember to bring identification for them. A divorced parent traveling with their young child may find a copy of the divorce/custody papers helpful.

U.S. motorists planning to travel in Canada are advised to obtain a Canadian Nonresident Interprovincial Motor Vehicle Liability Insurance Card, which provides evidence of financial responsibility. This card is available only in the United States through U.S. insurance companies or their agents. All provinces in Canada require visiting motorists to produce evidence of financial responsibility should they be involved in an accident. Financial responsibility limits vary by province.

All national driver's licenses are valid in Canada.

Entry by private boat: Visitors planning to enter Canada by private boat should contact customs in advance for a list of ports of entry that provide customs facilities and their hours of operation. Immediately upon arrival, visitors must report to customs and complete all documentation. In emergency situations, visitors must report their arrival to the nearest regional customs office or office of the RCMP.

Baggage: The necessary wearing apparel and personal effects in use by the visitor are admitted free of duty. Up to 50 cigars, 200 cigarettes (1 carton) and 14 ounces of manufactured tobacco and up to 40 ounces of spiritous liquor or wine or 24 12-ounce cans or bottles of beer or ale may be allowed entry in this manner. Additional quantities of alcoholic beverages up to a maximum of 2 gallons may be imported into Canada (except the Northwest Territories) on payment of duty and taxes plus charges for a provincial permit at port of entry. To import tobacco products a person must be 18 years of age or over, and to import alcoholic beverages the importer must have reached the legal age established by authorities of the province or territory into which the alcoholic beverages are being entered.

Firearms: Firearms are divided into 3 categories—prohibited, restricted and long guns. Nonresidents arriving at Canada customs port must declare all their firearms. Anyone who illegally carries a firearm into Canada is subject to a number of penalties, including seizure of the weapon and the vehicle in which it is carried.

Plants, fruit and vegetables: House plants may be imported without a permit. Some fruits and vegetables may be restricted entry into Canada and all are subject to inspection at the border.

Animals: Dogs and cats (over 3 months of age) from the United States must be accompanied by a certificate issued by a licensed veterinarian of Canada or the United States certifying that the animal has been vaccinated against rabies during the preceding 36 months; such a certificate shall describe the animal and date of vaccination and shall be initialed by inspectors and returned to the owner.

Up to 2 pet birds per family may be imported into Canada. Birds of the parrot family and song birds may be admitted when accompanied by the owner, if the owner certifies in writing that, upon entering the country, the birds have not been in contact with any other birds during the preceding 90 days and have been in the owner's possession for the entire period. All birds of the parrot family, except budgies, cockatiels and Rose-ringed parakeets, are on the CITES endangered species list and require special permits.

RE-ENTRY INTO THE U.S.

It is, of course, the responsibility of the traveler to satisfy U.S. immigration authorities of his right to re-enter the United States.

Canadian immigration officers may caution persons entering from the United States if they may have difficulty in returning.

Re-entry to the United States can be simplified if you list all your purchases before you reach the border, keep sales receipts and invoices handy, and pack purchases separately.

Within 48 hours: Residents of the United States visiting Canada for less than 48 hours may take back for personal or household use merchandise to the fair retail value of $200, free of U.S. duty and tax. Any or all of the following may be included, as long as the total value does not exceed $200: 50 cigarettes, 10 cigars (non-Cuban in origin), 4 ounces/150 ml of alcoholic beverages or alcoholic perfume.

If any article brought back is subject to duty or tax, or if the total value of all articles exceeds $200, no article may be exempted from duty or tax. Members of a family household are not permitted to combine the value of their purchases under this exception.

Persons crossing the international boundary at one point and re-entering the United States in order to travel to another part of Canada should inquire at U.S. customs regarding special exemption requirements.

After more than 48 hours: U.S. residents returning from Canada may take back, once every 30 days, merchandise for personal or household use to the value of $400 free of U.S. duty and tax, provided they have remained in Canada 48 hours. The exemption will be based on the fair retail value of the article acquired and goods must accompany the resident upon arrival in the United States. Members of a family household traveling together may combine their personal exemptions—thus a family of 5 could be entitled to a total exemption of $2,000. Up to 100 cigars (non-Cuban in origin) per person may be imported into the United States by U.S. residents, and up to 200 cigarettes, and 1 liter of alcoholic beverages if the resident has reached the age of 21 years.

Animals, including those taken out of the country and being returned, must have a valid veterinarian health certificate. Particularly, dogs must have proof of rabies vaccination.

Sandstone formation catches the evening light at Arcadia Beach along Oregon's northern coast. (© John Barger)

Driving Information

For complete information on state and provincial driving laws, contact the addresses below or consult AAA's *Digest of Motor Laws*. Keep in mind that being an out-of-state/province driver does not generally exempt you from local driving laws. Regulations common to British Columbia, Idaho, Oregon and Washington include: Right turn on red permitted after complete stop unless prohibited by signs; riding in towed trailer prohibited, riding in pickup camper permitted; and camping in rest areas prohibited.

Phone the road-condition-report phone numbers listed here for 24-hour recorded information on highway and winter driving conditions, including pass reports.

BRITISH COLUMBIA

Superintendent, Motor Vehicle Branch, 2631 Douglas St., Victoria, BC VBT 5A3; phone (604) 387-3140.

Road Condition Report: provincewide (toll free in Canada) 1-800-663-4997; Vancouver (604) 525-4997; Victoria (604) 380-4997.

Minimum driver's age: Driver's license divided into 6 classes—age 19 for classes 1, 2 and 4; 18 for class 3; 16 for classes 5 and 6.

Rest area camping: Not permitted.

Seat belts: Seat belts are mandatory for driver and all passengers. Child restraints are mandatory for children under 6 years. Applies to out-of-state/province drivers.

Studded tires: Legal between Oct. 1 and April 30.

CB Radio: Not monitored for emergencies.

Alcohol: Open container in vehicle is illegal.

Firearms: All rifles and shotguns must be declared at the border. Pistols are prohibited; strictly enforced.

IDAHO

Transportation Dept., P.O. Box 7129, Boise, ID 83707-1129; phone (208) 334-8800.

Road Condition Report: Boise (208) 336-6600; Coeur d'Alene (208) 772-0531; Lewiston (208) 746-3005.

Minimum driver's age: 16; restricted license for age 14 or 15 after completion of approved driver's education course.

Seat belts: Mandatory for all front seat occupants in passenger vehicles. Applies to out-of-state drivers. Child restraints mandatory for children under 4. Does not apply to out-of-state drivers.

Studded tires: Legal between Oct. 1 and April 15.

CB Radio: State police may monitor Channel 19.

Alcohol: Open container in vehicle is illegal.

OREGON

Driver and Motor Vehicle Services, Dept. of Transportation, 1905 Lana Ave. NE, Salem, OR 97314; phone (503) 945-5000.

Road Condition Report: Statewide (503) 889-3999; Portland (503) 222-6721.

Minimum driver's age: 16; special conditions permit issued at 14.

Seat belts: Seat belts are mandatory for driver and all passengers. Child restraints mandatory for children under 4 years or 40 lbs.

Studded tires: Legal from Nov. 1 to April 30. Chains are required where posted.

CB Radio: Monitor Channel 9 (emergency).

Alcohol: Open container in vehicle is illegal.

Firearms: All weapons must be unloaded and in view. No concealed weapons are permitted.

NOTE: Self-service gas is not available in Oregon; only full service. Do not attempt to pump your own gas.

WASHINGTON

Dept. of Licensing, 1125 Washington St. SE, Olympia, WA 98504-8001; phone (360) 902-3900.

Road Condition Report: Bellingham (360) 738-6215; Everett (360) 658-1345; Seattle (206) 455-7900; Spokane (509) 456-2872; Tacoma (206) 593-2157; Tri-Cities (509) 783-6105; Vancouver (360) 690-7100; Wenatchee (509) 662-0431; Yakima (509) 457-7100.

Minimum driver's age: 16 with driver training course, otherwise 18.

Seat belts: Washington has a mandatory seat-belt law. Drivers are responsible for seeing that all passengers use seat belts. Child restraints mandatory for children under 3 years.

Studded tires: Legal from Nov. 1 to April 1. Chains required where posted (unless 4-wheel drive with approved traction devices for all 4 wheels).

CB Radio: Monitor Channel 9 (emergency).

Alcohol: Open container in vehicle is illegal. Chartered buses, motorhomes and camper living exempt.

Firearms: Permits, which are good statewide, are required to carry a concealed weapon. Unloaded shotguns and rifles may be carried in the vehicle.

Insurance: Mandatory Liability Insurance Law. Motorists must carry proof of auto insurance. $475 fine.

Metric System

Canada has converted to the metric system. Inches have been replaced with centimetres, feet and yards with metres, miles with kilometres and Fahrenheit with Celsius. Logs of Canadian highways in *Northwest Mileposts®* include metric conversion in the miles, elevations and temperatures. See the accompanying chart for liters to gallons conversion.

LITERS TO GALLONS CONVERSION TABLE

Liters	Gallons	Liters	Gallons	Liters	Gallons
1	.3	21	5.5	41	10.8
2	.5	22	5.8	42	11.1
3	.8	23	6.1	43	11.4
4	1.1	24	6.3	44	11.6
5	1.3	25	6.6	45	11.9
6	1.6	26	6.9	46	12.2
7	1.8	27	7.1	47	12.4
8	2.1	28	7.4	48	12.7
9	2.4	29	7.7	49	12.9
10	2.6	30	7.9	50	13.2
11	2.9	31	8.2	51	13.5
12	3.2	32	8.5	52	13.7
13	3.4	33	8.7	53	14.0
14	3.7	34	9.0	54	14.3
15	4.0	35	9.2	55	14.5
16	4.2	36	9.5	56	14.8
17	4.5	37	9.8	57	15.0
18	4.8	38	10.0	58	15.3
19	5.0	39	10.3	59	15.6
20	5.3	40	10.6	60	15.9

For more precise conversion: 1 liter equals .2642 gallons; 1 gallon equals 3.785 liters.

Spring tulips in Oregon's Willamette Valley. Both Oregon and Washington are major producers of flower bulbs. (© John Barger)

A CHRONOLOGY O NORTHWEST HISTO[

The Pacific Northwest was one of the last major areas of the American West to be explored and developed. The first prehistoric inhabitants of the Northwest lived here some 10,000 years ago, but recorded history of the region begins with Spanish explorer Bartolome Ferello in 1543.

The following chronology of significant events in the history of the Northwest is intended to give a brief overview of this region's rich and diverse history.

1543—Spanish explorer Bartolome Ferello sails north along the coast of modern day Oregon.

1592—A greek named Apostolos Valerianos (Juan de Fuca) claims discovery for Spanish of the Strait of Anian (the Spanish designation for the legendary Northwest Passage).

1741—Danish Capt. Vitus Bering, and Aleksei Chirikov of the Russian Imperial Navy, explore the coast of Alaska. Bering is shipwrecked on what is now called Bering Island; he and half his crew perish.

1765—First known use of the name Oregon, spelled Ouragon.

1774—Juan Perez explores the coast as far north as the Queen Charlotte Islands for Spain. Perez anchors at Nootka Sound on the northwest coast of Vancouver Island and also names Mount Olympus on Washington's Olympic Peninsula.

1776—Declaration of Independence, July 4.

1778—Capt. James Cook explores much of the Northwest Coast between California and Alaska. Called his "last voyage," Cook was killed by natives in the Hawaiian Islands.

1787—Capt. Charles W. Barkley of England finds and names the Strait of Juan de Fuca, after its presumed discoverer.

1789—Nootka Sound controversy. A Spanish expedition takes possession of Nootka Sound, the center for the maritime fur trade, and seizes an English ship. Spain eventually yields territorial claims to England. George Washington becomes first president of the United States.

1792—Capt. Robert Gray, an American, discovers Grays Harbor—which is named for him—and the Columbia River, which he names for his ship, the *Columbia*. (The *Columbia*, in 1790, was the first U.S. vessel to circumnavigate the globe.) George Vancouver circumnavigates and names Vancouver Island. Vancouver also explores Puget Sound and names Admiralty Inlet, Dungeness, Hood Canal, Port Orchard, Port Discovery, Possession Sound, Restoration Point,

Deception Pass, Bellingham Bay, Whidbey and Vashon islands, the Gulf of Georgia, and Mounts Baker and Rainier.

1793—Alexander Mackenzie completes the first overland crossing of the North American continent to the Pacific Ocean. Mackenzie reaches the Pacific on July 22 at Bella Coola, BC.

1803—President Thomas Jefferson engineers the Louisiana Purchase. For $15 million, the United States buys Louisiana Territory from France, which includes all of the land west of the Mississippi drained by it and its tributaries.

1804-06—Financed by President Jefferson and Congress as an exploration up the Missouri River and west to the Pacific Ocean, Lewis and Clark commence their journey from winter camp near Saint Louis on May 14, 1804. In 1805, an interpreter named Toussaint Charbonneau, his Shoshone woman Sacajawea, and their baby, Baptiste, join the expedition. The party crossed present-day Idaho via the Bitterroot Mountains and continued down the Clearwater, Snake and Columbia rivers to the Pacific, arriving on Nov. 7, 1805. Their return journey began March 23, 1806, and they arrived in Saint Louis on Sept. 13, 1806.

1805-06—Simon Fraser explores New Caledonia (British Columbia), establishing fur-trading posts for the North West Co.

1807—David Thompson explores British Columbia, Idaho and Montana for the North West Co., establishing fur-trading posts at Kullyspell House in northern Idaho (1809) and Spokane House (1810) in Washington.

1808—Simon Fraser explores and names the Fraser River in British Columbia.

1810-11—John Jacob Astor creates the Pacific Fur Co., a subsidiary of his American Fur Co. The *Tonquin* sails from New York with men and materials in Sept. 1810 under Capt. Jonathan Thorn, and arrives at the mouth of the Columbia River in March 1811 to establish Fort Astoria. Several crewmen are lost while exploring sandbars at the mouth of the Columbia River for safe passage. (The *Tonquin* is then dispatched to Nootka Sound under Capt. Thorn and never returns. It is believed that captain and crew were killed by natives except for 1 crew member, who managed to blow up the ship by setting off the tons of gun powder in the hold.) An overland expedition led by Wilson Price Hunt departs Saint Louis in Oct. 1810 for Fort

Astoria.

1812—Hunt party arrives at Fort Astoria in January. The Astorians establish Fort Okanogan (the first American structure in the future state of Washington) and Fort Spokane, next to the North West Co.'s Spokane House. A Pacific Fur Co. trader named Robert Stuart discovers South Pass through the Rocky Mountains, the route followed by the Oregon Trail. War of 1812.

1813—British North West Co. buys out interests of the American Pacific Fur Co. in the Columbia River valley. In December, a British warship occupies Fort Astoria and renames it Fort George.

1818—Fort Nez Perce (Fort Walla Walla) is constructed by the North West Co. Treaty is signed by United States and Great Britain agreeing that the Northwest will remain under the joint control of both nations, pending the final settlement of the question of sovereignty.

1819—Adams-Onis Treaty: Spain cedes all land claims north of 42nd parallel (present Oregon–California border) to the United States.

1821—A union is forced between North West Co. and Hudson's Bay Co. under the name of Hudson's Bay Co.

1824—Hudson's Bay Co. establishes Fort Vancouver on the north bank of the Columbia River (site of present-day Vancouver, WA). Dr. John McLoughlin, "the Father of Oregon," is chief factor of the Hudson's Bay Co.'s Columbia District from 1824 to 1846. Peter Skene Ogden leads the Snake brigades, trapping the Snake River country. Jedediah Smith crosses South Pass (in present-day Wyoming) through the Rocky Mountains.

1825—Russia cedes all land claims south of 54°40' to the United States and Great Britain. British and U.S. citizens retain free access to the Oregon Country, which stretches from the boundary of Mexican California to Russian Alaska and encompasses the future states of Washington, Oregon and Idaho, plus western Montana and Wyoming, and southern British Columbia. Hudson's Bay Co. establishes Fort Colville.

1828—British abandon Fort George (formerly Fort Astoria).

1832—First crossing of the Rocky Mountains by wagons over South Pass by Capt. Benjamin L.E. Bonneville, leading 110 men to Fort Walla Walla and Fort Vancouver.

1833—First school in the Pacific Northwest is founded at Fort Vancouver. Hudson's Bay Co. establishes Fort

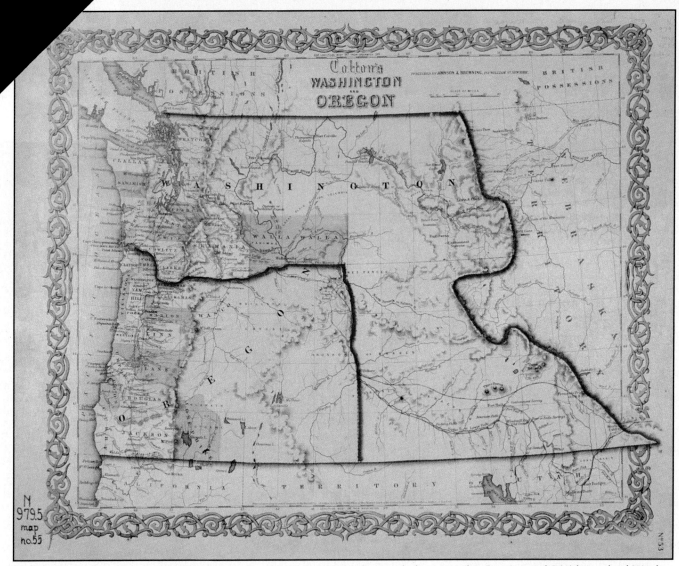

Prior to becoming a state in 1859, Oregon Territory's border had extended east to the Continental Divide, as had Washington Territory's. But Oregon ceded its eastern reach to Washington Territory as seen here. Washington gave up much of this new land when Idaho Territory was created in 1863. (Courtesy of Special Collections, University of Washington Libraries)

Nisqually.

1834—Nathaniel Wyeth establishes Fort Hall near present-day Pocatello. Hudson's Bay Co. establishes Fort Boise.

1836—Wyeth sells Fort Hall to the Hudson's Bay Co. Presbyterian missionaries Marcus and Narcissa Whitman and Henry and Eliza Spalding arrive in Fort Vancouver. The Whitmans establish a mission near Fort Walla Walla on a site called Waiilatpu by the local Cayuse Indians. The Spaldings establish a mission at Lapwai among the Nez Perce. The *Beaver,* the first steam boat on the Pacific Ocean, arrives at Fort Vancouver.

1839—Hudson's Bay Co. forms the Puget Sound Agricultural Co. to farm at Fort Nisqually and Fort Colville, reinforcing British territorial claims in the Oregon Country. The first printing press in the Northwest is brought from Hawaii to Lapwai in Idaho by Henry Spalding. The missionaries use it to produce a Nez Perce primer, the first book published in the Pacific Northwest.

1841—Ships of the United States Exploring Expedition led by Lieutenant Charles Wilkes arrive off the Oregon Coast. The expedition names more than 250 landmarks in present-day Washington and explores Puget Sound and the interior of Oregon Country. Value of Puget Sound as a safe harbor is noted.

1842—Founding of the Oregon Institute—now Willamette University—in Salem, the first university in the Pacific Northwest.

1843—Nearly 900 white immigrants accompany Marcus Whitman from Missouri to the Columbia River. Beginning of heavy migration on the Oregon Trail from Independence, MO (later Council Bluffs, IA). The Oregon Trail crosses what will be Wyoming and Idaho, entering the future state of Oregon near Fort Boise. Provisional government established at Champoeg.

1844—The Democratic party nominates James K. Polk as president on an expansionist platform with the slogan "Fifty-four Forty or Fight," referring to the northernmost boundary —

54°40'—of Oregon Country, currently claimed by the British.

1845—First American settlers on Puget Sound reach Tumwater. Hudson's Bay Co. decides to move its regional headquarters to Vancouver Island.

1846—The United States and Great Britain agree that the international boundary between the U.S. and Canada will be along the 49th parallel from the Rocky Mountains to the middle of the Strait of Georgia. The Senate ratifies the treaty in June. The first newspaper in the Oregon Country, the *Oregon Spectator,* is published in Oregon City.

1847—Annual migration along the Oregon Trail established, with 5,000 white immigrants crossing the Blue Mountains on their way to the Willamette Valley. A measles and dysentery epidemic brought to the Waiilatpu Mission by settlers kills half of the Cayuses. On Nov. 29, the Cayuse attack the mission, killing Marcus and Narcissa Whitman and 11 other whites.

1848—Oregon Territory is created by a congressional act on Aug. 14. The territory includes the present-day states of Oregon and Washington and most of Idaho. Joseph Lane is appointed first governor of Oregon Territory.

1849—Many immigrants cut off from the Oregon Trail in southeastern Idaho for the California goldfields. Fort Steilacoom (in Washington) is established by the U.S. Army. Pacific University in Forest Grove (Oregon) is established.

1850—Five Cayuses who took part in the "Whitman Massacre" are tried and hung in Oregon City. Donation Land Claim Act allows white male citizens of 18 years or older to acquire 320 acres of land if single, an additional 320 if married, in the wife's name.

1851—The city of Portland is incorporated. The schooner *Exact* brings the first members of the Denny Party to Alki Point in present-day Seattle.

1853—Congress approves legislation to divide Oregon Territory at the Columbia River, creating Washington Territory, named for George Washington. Isaac Stevens is appointed first territorial governor. The new territory, with Olympia as capital, includes the present-day state of Washington, most of present-day Idaho, and western Montana and Wyoming. Table Rock Treaty sets aside reservation lands for Rogue River Indians to quell dispute with gold seekers on the Rogue River.

1855—So-called Yakima Indian war erupts when upper Columbia River gold rush brings white gold seekers across Yakima Indian lands.

1856—Gen. John E. Wool, U.S. Army regulars and volunteers defeat Rogue River Indians and Chief Kamiakin of the Yakimas.

1858—Col. Edwart Steptoe and U.S. Army soldiers are defeated by combined force of Spokans, Yakimas, Coeur d'Alenes and Palooses. Col. George Wright returns with 600 well-armed regulars and hangs 24 chiefs and others.

1859—Oregon becomes the 33rd state in the Union. The Fraser River gold rush begins in present-day British Columbia, and gold strikes are made in eastern Washington and in Idaho. Construction begins on the Mullan Road from Fort Walla Walla in Washington to Fort Benton in Montana. Pig War erupts on San Juan Island between British and American residents.

1860—Gold discovered at Orofino Creek in Idaho. Franklin, Idaho's first permanent settlement, is founded north of the Utah border on April 14. Daily stagecoach service is initiated between Portland and Seattle.

1861—Lewiston is established as a distribution center for local mining camps and the town has the first newspaper to be published in the present-day state of Idaho, the *Golden Age*. In Seattle, the Territory University—now the University of Washington—opens its doors. The Civil War begins.

1862—Gold strikes along the Salmon River and in the Boise basin in Idaho.

1863—Congress creates the new territory of Idaho out of parts of Washington, Nebraska and Dakota territories. Idaho Territory encompasses present-day Idaho, Montana and most of Wyoming. President Abraham Lincoln appoints William H. Wallace as Idaho's first executive. Battle of Bear River in Idaho: California volunteers massacre an estimated 400 men, women and children, mostly Shoshone.

1864—Montana Territory is created, contracting Idaho's boundaries. The first "Mercer Girls" are brought to Seattle by Asa Mercer to supply wives for the local unmarried men. Salem is made the capital of Oregon. The first transcontinental telegraph lines are completed.

1865—Boise is made capital of Idaho Territory. The Civil War ends.

1867—The United States purchases Alaska from Russia for $7.2 million ("Seward's Folly").

1869—The first transcontinental railroad is completed, with the driving of the golden spike at Promontory Summit in Utah on May 10.

1871—British Columbia enters the Confederation of Canada.

1872—Congress establishes Yellowstone as first national park. U.S.–Canada international boundary fixed. Modoc Indian War, Oregon–California border.

1876—George Armstrong Custer and his men are killed at the Battle of the Little Bighorn in Wyoming. University of Oregon opens.

1877—Nez Perce Indian War. Nez Perce refuse to move to the Clearwater River reservation, and 800 men, women and children flee 1,700 miles across the Bitterroot Mountains to Montana and the Canadian border. On Sept. 30, Chief Joseph and 480 remaining Nez Perce surrender to Col. Nelson Miles just 40 miles from the border.

1878—Bannock Indian uprising in south-central Idaho quelled by Gen. Oliver O. Howard.

1879—Sheepeaters, a Shoshone band, surrender to Gen. Howard and are moved to Fort Hall Reservation.

1880—Population of Oregon—174,768; Washington Territory—75,116; Idaho Territory—32,619.

1883—Completion of the Northern Pacific Railroad.

1889—Washington is admitted as the 42nd state.

1890—Idaho is admitted as the 43rd state into the Union. Population of Oregon—317,704; Washington—337,232; Idaho—88,548.

1892—University of Idaho opens.

1893—Great Northern Railway reaches Seattle.

1897-98—Klondike gold rush begins.

1899—Mount Rainier National Park created.

1900—Population of Oregon—413,536; Washington—518,103; Idaho—161,772.

1905—Lewis and Clark Centennial Exposition held in Portland.

1909—Alaska–Yukon–Pacific Exposition held in Seattle.

1910—Population of Oregon—672,765; Washington—1,141,990; Idaho—325,594.

1912—Women's suffrage enacted in Oregon.

1916—First transcontinental telephone service to Seattle. The "Everett Massacre" of 5 Wobblies takes place on Nov. 5 in Everett, WA. Wobblies were members of IWW (Industrial Workers of the World), which formed in 1905.

1917—United States enters WWI.

1918—WWI ends.

1921—First airplane service between Seattle and Vancouver, BC.

1922—Radio station KGW, the first commercial broadcasting station in Oregon, goes on the air.

1927—"Oregon, My Oregon" is adopted as the official Oregon state song.

1929—Stock market crashes, Great Depression begins.

1931—"Here We Have Idaho" is adopted as the official Idaho state song.

1933—The Tillamook Burn, one of the worst forest fires in recorded history, destroys hundreds of thousands of acres of Oregon. Construction begins on Bonneville Dam.

1934—Construction begins on Grand Coulee Dam.

1937—President Roosevelt dedicates Timberline Lodge on Mount Hood.

1938—U.S. Highway 95 in Idaho is paved. Bonneville Dam is completed.

1940—Tacoma Narrows Bridge "Galloping Gertie" collapses in windstorm within 4 months of its completion.

1941—Grand Coulee Dam is completed. Called the "eighth wonder of the world," it is the largest concrete dam in the world. Japanese attack Pearl Harbor on Dec. 7.

1942—Farragut Naval Training Station is established at Lake Pend Oreille as part of the war effort.

1945—WWII ends.

1948—Tragic Memorial Day flood destroys Vanport, OR.

1950—Northgate—the first American regional shopping center—opens in Seattle.

1955—First public test flight of the Boeing 707 jet aircraft in Seattle.

1959—Brownlee Dam on Snake River completed.

1962—"Century 21," Seattle World's Fair.

1966—Official completion of Interstate 5 between Washington and California.

1971—Oregon's "Bottle Bill" is passed, first such legislation in the United States.

1972—91 miners die in Sunshine Mine disaster in Idaho.

1974—Spokane hosts EXPO 74 world exposition.

1979—Hood Canal Bridge sinks on Feb. 13. Ferry service moves people and vehicles between the Kitsap and Olympic peninsulas until the new bridge is completed in 1982.

1980—Eruption of Mount St. Helens on Sunday, May 18.

1986—Vancouver, BC, is site of EXPO 86 world exposition.

1989—City of Portland bans styrofoam.

1990—Population of Oregon—2,853,733; Washington—4,887,941; Idaho—1,011,986. Seattle hosts the Goodwill Games. Lacey V. Murrow I-90 floating bridge sinks during November storm.

1993—President Clinton and world leaders meet in Seattle in November for Asia Pacific Economic Cooperation (APEC) conference.

CALENDAR

Following are some of the annual events celebrated throughout the Northwest. The exact dates for events are not given, but the approximate time periods are noted as follows: Early—the 1st-10th, Mid—the 11th-23rd, and Late—the 24th-31st. Call for exact dates and more information; phone numbers listed are either for the local chamber of commerce, the local visitor center or the event office.

JANUARY

British Columbia: *Early*—Brackendale Annual Bald Eagle Festival, Squamish, (604) 892-9244. *Mid*—Kelowna Snow Festival, (604) 861-1515.

Idaho: *Late*—Kellogg Winter Games, (208) 784-0821; Sandpoint Winter Carnival, (800) 800-2106 or (208) 263-2161.

Washington: *Mid*—Freeze Yer Buns Run, Twisp, (509) 997-2926; The Great Bavarian Ice Fest, Leavenworth, (509) 548-5807.

FEBRUARY

British Columbia: *Early*—Cariboo Cross-Country Ski Marathon, 100 Mile House, (604) 791-6212; Vernon Winter Carnival and Hot-Air Balloon Fiesta, (604) 545-2236.

Idaho: *Early*—Boulder Mountain Cross-Country Ski Tour and Race, Ketchum, (800) 634-3347 or (208) 726-3423; McCall Winter Carnival, (208) 634-7631; U.S. Pacific Coast International Sled Dog Racing Championships, Priest River, (208) 443-2512.

Oregon: *Mid*—Beginning of Oregon Shakespeare Festival (continues to late Oct.), Ashland, (503) 482-4331. *Late*—Newport Seafood & Wine Festival, (503) 265-8801.

Washington: *Early*—Smelt Derby, La Conner, (360) 466-4778; Upper Skagit Bald Eagle Festival, Concrete, Rockport and Marblemount, (360) 853-7009.

MARCH

British Columbia: *Mid*—Beginning of Pacific Rim Gray Whale Festival (continues to early April), Tofino and Ucluelet, (604) 725-3414.

Idaho: *Early*—Moscow Mardi Gras and Beaux Arts Ball, (208) 634-7631. *Mid*—Dodge National Circuit Finals Rodeo, Pocatello, (208) 233-1546.

Oregon: *Early*—All-Northwest Barbershop Ballad Contest, Forest Grove, (503) 357-3006.

Washington: *Mid*—Old Time Music Festival, Tenino, (360) 264-5075.

APRIL

British Columbia: *Mid*—Victoria Jazz Festival, (604) 381-5277.

Idaho: *Late*—Dogwood Festival, Lewiston, (800) 473-3543 or (208) 743-3531.

Oregon: *Early*—Pear Blossom Festival, Medford, (503) 779-4847 or 734-PEAR. *Mid*—Annual Tulip Festival, Portland, (503) 228-5108. *Late*—Great Astoria Crab Feed and Seafood Festival, (503) 325-6311; Hood River Valley Blossom Festival, (800) 366-3530 or (503) 386-2000.

Washington: *Early*—Beginning of Puyallup Valley Daffodil Festival (continues to late April), Puyallup and surrounding communities, (800) 634-2334 or (206) 845-6755; Skagit Valley Tulip Festival, Mount Vernon, (360) 428-8547. *Late*—Ragtime Rhodie Dixieland Jazz Festival, Long Beach, (800) 451-2542 or (360) 642-2400; Spring Barrel Tasting, Yakima Valley, (509) 786-2163; Beginning of Washington State Apple Blossom Festival (continues to early May), Wenatchee, (509) 662-3616; Lilac Festival (or early May), Hulda Klager Lilac Gardens, Woodland, (360) 225-8996.

MAY

British Columbia: *Late*—May Day Celebration, New Westminster, (604) 521-7781; Swiftsure Lightship Classic Sailing Races, Victoria, (604) 592-2441.

Idaho: *Early*—Apple Blossom Festival, Payette, (208) 642-2362; Kamloops and Kokanee Days, Sandpoint, (800) 800-2106 or (208) 263-2161. *Mid*—Depot Days, Wallace, (208) 752-0111. *Late*—Fred Murphy Days, Coeur d'Alene, (208) 664-0587.

Oregon: *Mid*—All Indian Rodeo, Tygh Valley, (503) 544-3371; Beachcomber Days, Waldport, (503) 563-2133; Rhododendron Festival, Florence, (503) 997-3128. *Late*—Azalea Festival (Memorial Day weekend), Brookings, (800) 535-9469 or (503) 469-3181; Boatnik Festival (Memorial Day weekend), Grants Pass, (800) 547-5927 or (503) 476-7717.

Washington: *Early*—Opening Day of Yachting Season (1st Saturday), Seattle; Holland Days Festival, Lynden, (360) 354-5995; Lilac Bloomsday Run, Spokane, (509) 325-8747; Lilac Festival (or late April), Woodland, (360) 225-9552; Sequim Irrigation Festival, (360) 683-6197; Victorian Homes Tour, Port Townsend, (360) 385-2722. *Mid*—'49er Days (featuring Mountain Man Days and the Washington State Chili Cook-off), Winthrop, (509) 996-2125; Lilac Festival, Spokane, (509) 326-3339; Maifest, Leavenworth, (509) 548-5807; Norwegian Constitution Day, Seattle, (206) 461-5840; Rhododendron Festival, Port Townsend, (360) 385-2722; Seattle International Children's Festival, (206) 684-7200; University District Street Fair, Seattle, (206) 461-5840; Viking Fest, Poulsbo, (360) 779-4848. *Late*—Northwest Folklife Festival, Seattle, (206) 684-7300; Ski to Sea Festival, Bellingham, (360) 671-3990; Spring Festival, Moses Lake, (509) 765-7888; Winthrop Rodeo (there is also one held in early Sept.), (509) 996-2125.

JUNE

British Columbia: *Mid*—International Dragon Boat Festival, Vancouver, (800) 663-6000; Sam Steele Days, Cranbrook, (604) 426-5914. *Late*—Victoria Folkfest, (604) 382-2127; Williams Lake Stampede, (604) 392-5025.

Idaho: *Early*—Timberfest, Sandpoint, (800) 800-2106 or (208) 263-2161. *Mid*—Cherry Festival, Emmett, (208) 365-3485; Beginning of Idaho Shakespeare Festival (continues to mid-Sept.), Boise, (208) 336-9221; Old-time Fiddlers Contest, Weiser, (208) 549-0452. *Late*—Idaho Regatta, Burley, (208) 436-4793.

Oregon: *Early*—Obsidian Days, Hines, (503) 573-2636; Beginning of Portland Rose Festival (continues to mid-July), (800) 962-3700 or (503) 275-9750; Strawberry Festival, Lebanon, (503) 258-7164. *Mid*—Cascade Festival of Music, Bend, (503) 382-3221; Beginning of Peter Britt Festivals (continues to early Sept.), Jacksonville, (800) 88-BRITT or (503) 773-6077; Rockhound Pow Wow, Prineville, (503) 447-6304. *Late*—Beginning of Oregon Bach Festival (continues to early July), Eugene, (800) 457-1486.

Washington: *Early*—Founders Day Rodeo, Tonasket, (509) 826-1880; Salty Sea Days, Everett, (206) 339-1113; Speelyi-Mi Arts and Crafts Festival, Toppenish, (509) 865-3262; Yakima International Air Fair, (509) 248-0246. *Mid*—Berry-Dairy Days, Burlington, (360) 755-9382; Peace Arch Celebration, Blaine, (360) 332-6484; Strawberry Festival, Marysville, (360) 659-7664; World's Longest Beach Run and Walk, Long Beach, (800) 451-2542 or (360) 642-2400.

JULY

British Columbia: *Early*—Annual International Pow Wow, Mission, (604) 826-6914; Bluegrass and Country Music Fest, Burns Lake, (604) 692-3773; Old Time Accordion Championships, Kimberley, (604) 427-3666. *Mid*—Billy Barker Days, Quesnel, (604) 992-8716; Great

OF EVENTS

International Nanaimo Bathtub Race, (604) 754-8474; Kelowna Regatta, (604) 861-1515; Vancouver Folk Music Festival, (604) 683-2000; Vancouver Sea Festival, (604) 683-2000. *Late*—Beginning of Great Cariboo Ride (continues to early Aug.), 100 Mile House, (604) 395-5353; Parksville Sand Castle Contest, Parksville, (604) 248-3613.

Idaho: *Early*—Salmon River Days, (208) 756-2100. *Mid*—Broiler Festival, Springfield, (503) 484-5307; Snake River Stampede, Nampa, (208) 466-4641. *Late*—Beginning of Festival at Sandpoint (continues to late Aug.), (800) 800-2106 or (208) 263-2161; Beginning of Idaho International Folk Dance Festival (continues to early Aug.), Rexburg, (208) 356-5700.

Oregon: *Early*—July Smelt Fry Festival, Yachats, (503) 547-3530; Old-fashioned July 4th Food and Fireworks Celebration, Ashland, (503) 779-4847; Waterfront Blues Festival, Portland, (800) 962-3700 or (503) 222-2223; World Championship Timber Carnival, Albany, (800) 526-2256 or (503) 928-0911. *Mid*—Miss Oregon Pageant, Seaside, (800) 444-6740 or (503) 738-6391; Salem Art Fair & Festival, (800) 874-7012 or (503) 581-4325. *Late*—Bach Festival, Mount Angel, (503) 845-9440; Broiler Festival, Springfield, (503) 484-5307.

Washington: *Early*—Loggerodeo, Sedro Woolley, (360) 855-1841. *Mid*—Bite of Seattle, Seattle, (206) 461-5840; Capitol Lakefair, Olympia, (360) 943-7344; July Rhythm and Blues Festival, Winthrop, (509) 996-2125; Kla Ha Ya Days, Snohomish, (360) 568-2526; Lake Chelan Rodeo, Chelan, (800) 4-CHELAN or (509) 682-3503; Beginning of Seafair (continues to early Aug.), Seattle, (206) 461-5840; Whidbey Island Race Week, (360) 675-3535. *Late*—Columbia Gorge Bluegrass Festival, Stevenson, (509) 427-8911; Port Townsend Jazz Festival, (360) 385-2722; Sand Castle Contest, Long Beach, (800) 451-2542 or (360) 642-2400; San Juan Islands Jazz Festival, (360) 468-3663; Tri-Cities Water Follies, (509) 547-2203.

AUGUST

British Columbia: *Early*—Benson and Hedges International Fireworks Competition, Vancouver, (604) 683-2000; Golden Rodeo, (604) 344-7125; World's Invitational Gold Panning Championships, Taylor, (604) 785-6037. *Mid*—Abbotsford International Airshow, (604) 859-9651; Beginning of Pacific National Exhibition (continues to early Sept.), Vancouver, (604) 683-2000; Peach Festival, Penticton, (604) 493-4055. *Late*—Blackberry Festival, Powell River, (604) 485-4701; Bulkley Valley Exhibition, Smithers, (604) 847-5072; Ironman Canada Triathlon, Penticton, (604) 493-4055.

Idaho: *Early*—Shoshone-Bannock Indian Festival, Fort Hall, (208) 238-2301. *Mid*—Caldwell Night Rodeo, (208) 459-7493; The Crossing, Glenns Ferry, (208) 366-2394. *Late*—Twin Falls County Fair, (208) 733-3974.

Oregon: *Early*—Many fairs offered throughout the state; Mount Hood Festival of Jazz, Gresham, (503) 232-3000. *Mid*—Astoria Regatta, (503) 325-6311; The Bite, Portland, (800) 962-3700 or (503) 222-2223. *Late*—Filbert Festival, Springfield, (503) 484-5307; Beginning of Oregon State Fair (continues to early Sept.), Salem, (800) 874-7012 or (503) 581-4325.

Washington: *Early*—Arts & Crafts Festival, Anacortes, (360) 293-3832; Beginning of Renton River Days (continues to mid-Aug.), (206) 235-2587; Torchlight Parade (part of Seafair), Seattle, (206) 461-5840. *Mid*—Coupeville Arts & Crafts Festival, (360) 678-5434; International Folk Dance Festival, Ferndale, (360) 384-3042; Morton Loggers Jubilee, (360) 496-6086; Omak Stampede & Suicide Race, (800) 225-6625 or (509) 826-4218; Prosser Wine and Food Fair, (509) 786-3177; Taste of Edmonds, (206) 776-6711; Beginning of Washington International Kite Festival (continues to late Aug.), Long Beach, (800) 451-2542 or (360) 642-2400. *Late*—Beginning of Evergreen State Fair (continues to early Sept.), Monroe, (206) 883-8033; National Lentil Festival, Pullman, (800) 365-6948 or (509) 334-3565; Sagebrush Loggers Tourney, Tonasket, (509) 826-1880.

SEPTEMBER

British Columbia: *Early*—Alpine Folk Dance Festival, Kimberley, (604) 427-3666; Classic Boat Festival, Victoria, (604) 382-2127; Molson Indy, Vancouver, (604) 683-2000; Nicola Valley Rodeo and Fall Fair, Merritt, (604) 378-2281.

Idaho: *Early*—Art in the Park, Boise, (208) 344-7777; Eastern Idaho Fair, Blackfoot, (208) 785-2480; Lewiston Roundup, (800) 473-3543 or (208) 743-3531. *Mid*—Clearwater County Fair and Lumberjack Days, Orofino, (208) 476-4335; Idaho Spud Day, Shelley, (208) 357-7662.

Oregon: *Early*—Numerous fairs throughout the state. *Mid*—Autumn Festival & Sand Castle Contest, Rockaway Beach, (503) 355-8108; Oktoberfest, Mount Angel, (503) 845-9440; Pendleton Round-Up, (800) 45-RODEO or (503) 276-2553. *Late*—Alpenfest, Wallowa Lake, (503) 432-4704.

Washington: *Early*—Bumbershoot Festival (Labor Day weekend), Seattle, (206) 461-5840; Ellensburg Rodeo, (503) 925-3138; Kelso Hilander Summer Festival, (360) 577-8058; Loggers Play Day, Hoquiam, (800) 321-1924 or (360) 532-

1924; Sausage Festival, Vancouver, (360) 696-4407; Western Washington State Fair (Puyallup Fair), Puyallup, (206) 845-1771; Winthrop Rodeo (there is also one held in late May), (509) 996-2125; Wooden Boat Festival, Port Townsend, (360) 385-2722. *Mid*—Interstate Fair, Spokane, (509) 535-1766; Victorian Historical Homes Tour, Port Townsend, (360) 385-2722; Winthrop Antique Auto Rally, (509) 996-2125. *Late*—Autumn Leaf Festival, Leavenworth, (509) 548-5807; Central Washington Fair, Yakima, (509) 452-0889.

OCTOBER

Idaho: *Early*—Idaho State Draft Horse International, Sandpoint, (800) 800-2106 or (208) 263-2161. *Mid*—Sandpoint Oktoberfest, (800) 800-2106 or (208) 263-2161; Sun Valley Swing 'n' Dixie Jazz Jamboree, (800) 634-3347 or (208) 726-3423.

Oregon: *Early*—Alsea Bay Salmon Derby, Waldport, (503) 563-2133; Octoberfest, Bend, (503) 385-5366. *Mid*—Hood River Valley Harvest Fest, (503) 386-2000; Oregon Dixieland Jubilee Jazz Festival, Seaside, (800) 444-6740 or (503) 738-6391.

Washington: Oktoberfest celebrations in several communities. *Early*—Harvest Festival, Lynden, (360) 354-5995; Oysterfest, Shelton, (360) 426-8678. *Mid*—Country Collection Craft & Antique Show, Lynden, (360) 966-5573.

NOVEMBER

Idaho: *Early*—Beginning of Festival of Trees (continues to late Nov.), Boise, (208) 344-7777. *Late*—Beginning of Idaho Festival of Lights (continues to early Jan.), Preston, (208) 852-0155.

Oregon: *Early*—Kraut and Sausage Feed and Bazaar, Verboort, (503) 359-5425.

Washington: *Early*—Dixieland Jazz Festival, Ocean Shores, (360) 289-2451; Northwest Wine Festival, Pasco, (800) 666-1929. *Late*—Christmas at the End of the Road, Winthrop, (509) 996-2125.

DECEMBER

British Columbia: *Mid*—Christmas Carol Ship Parade, Vancouver, (604) 683-2000.

Idaho: *Early*—Arts for Christmas Fair, Boise, (208) 344-7777.

Oregon: *Mid*—Dickens Christmas Feast, Ashland, (503) 488-1115.

Washington: *Early*—Christmas Cruise, Seattle, (206) 461-5840; Town Christmas Lighting Festival, Leavenworth, (509) 548-5807.

TRANS-CANADA HIGHWAY 1

Alberta–British Columbia Border to Vancouver, BC
(See maps, pages 16, 19 and 23)

Trans-Canada Highway 1 is the world's longest national highway, stretching nearly 5,000 miles/8,047 km from St. Johns, NF, on the Atlantic Coast, to Victoria, BC, on Vancouver Island on the Pacific Coast.

Northwest Mileposts® logs Trans-Canada Highway 1 west from the Alberta–British Columbia border to Vancouver, BC, perhaps the most scenic 500 miles in all of Canada. The highway climbs through the Rocky, Selkirk and Purcell mountains, crossing British Columbia to the Coast Mountains and then the flatlands of the Fraser River.

CAUTION: Signs along the highway warn of the danger of feeding bears. Black bears are numerous in the mountains, regular pests in camp and picnic sites, and they often stroll down the highway. Stop at safe distances only, with windows closed. Do not feed the bears! Stay in your vehicle!

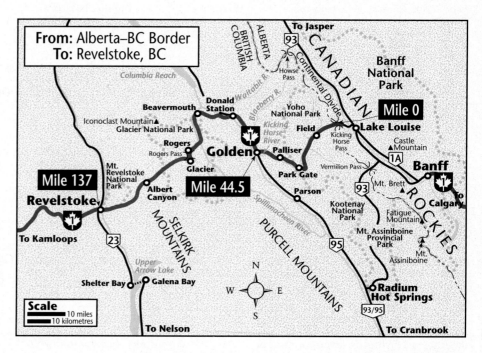

From: Alberta–BC Border
To: Revelstoke, BC

Trans-Canada Highway 1 Log

Distance in miles from the Alberta–British Columbia border is followed by distance in miles from Vancouver, BC. Equivalent distances in kilometres are indicated by Km.

Mile 0 (527.5) Km 0 (849): Kicking Horse Pass (elev. 5,333 feet/1,625m) lies south along Highway 1A, the original road. Along Highway 1 there is a gravel turnout but no official marker. The pass marks the boundary between Alberta and British Columbia and between Banff and Yoho national parks. In 1881, railway surveyors chose this route over the Continental Divide for Canada's first transcontinental railway, the Canadian Pacific. The Alberta–British Columbia border marks the time zone change from Mountain to Pacific.

Mile 0.5 (527) Km 1 (848): Sink Lake picnic area. The lake has no visible outlet; it is believed to drain underground, perhaps into the Kicking Horse River. ⋒

Mile 1.5 (526) Km 2.5 (846.5): Junction with Highway 1A to Lake Louise. Great Divide picnic area and limited access road (8 miles/13 km) to Lake O'Hara Campground and lodge (open all year, winter access by

skis). The campground is open from late June to Sept., has 30 walk-in campsites, and reservations are required. Fee is $5. Area is very popular—reserve at least 60 days in advance. The lake is surrounded by a network of scenic hiking trails. Hikers may use the road or arrange transportation by bus; phone (604) 343-6324. ⋒⋒⋒▲

Mile 3 (524.5) Km 5 (844): Wapta Lake picnic area, lodge and gas station adjacent. The lake, which holds its ice into late May, is the source of the Kicking Horse River, which was named for Sir James Hector of the 1857–60 Palliser Survey Expedition, who was killed by a kicking pack horse. A trail leads from the picnic area 1.8 miles/3 km to Sherbrooke Lake and 2.2 miles/3.6 km to Paget Lookout. ⋒⋒⋒

Mile 4 (523.5) Km 6.5 (842.5): Old railway bridge on Big Hill right-of-way is adjacent to the highway. This section of rail was abandoned after the spiral tunnels were built. The Big Hill was at one time the steepest railway grade in North America, with a 4.5 percent grade. The railbed was later used for the highway.

Mile 5 (522.5) Km 8.5 (840.5): Viewpoint of the Lower Spiral railway tunnel in Mount Ogden. A display explains the history and present operation of the 2 tunnels (the other is in Cathedral Mountain to the south).

Mile 6.5 (521) Km 10.5 (838.5): Viewpoint, Mount Stephen and old tunnel entrance to abandoned lead, zinc and silver mine on the mountain slope. To find the tunnel, look below and to the right of the hanging glacier.

Mile 7.5 (520) Km 12.5 (836.5): Junction with Yoho Valley Road north 10 miles/16 km to spectacular Takakkaw Falls, which drop 1,248 feet/380m from a limestone cliff. Access to Kicking Horse picnic area at highway junction with exhibit on the fossil beds (the Burgess Shale) on nearby Mount Stephen, a world heritage site. (Conducted hikes to the fossil beds available by reservation at park office. Hikes are strenuous.) Picnic area is a good place to see mountain goats, which come down from the bluffs in early evenings; best in early summer and fall. Trailers are not allowed on the road beyond the picnic area because of steep grades and tight switchbacks. Takakkaw Falls Campground at road's end offers 35 walk-in tent sites only. ⋒⋒⋒▲★

Mile 10 (517.5) Km 16 (833): Alberta and British Columbia Travel offices and Yoho National Park information office and picnic area. Turnoff here for **FIELD**, east across the river, a small settlement under the shadow of Mount Stephen. Field began as a railway construction camp and is still a railway division plant. Food, lodging and gas are available. ⋒

Mile 10.5 (517) Km 17 (832): Rest area by a

small lake in the glacial river flats.

Mile 11.5 (516) Km 18.5 (830.5): Turnoff for Natural Bridge and Emerald Lake. The Kicking Horse River gouged the natural bridge out of the rocks. The road also goes to animal salt licks frequented by moose. Hiking trails to Burgess and Yoho passes and Hamilton Lake Falls. There are tourist facilities at Emerald Lake, including a 1902 heritage lodge and tearoom. Horses and boats are available for hire.

Mile 15.5 (512) Km 25 (824): Trailhead parking area; access to several popular trails, including Ottertail Pass and Lake O'Hara.

Mile 16 (511.5) Km 26 (823): Ottertail viewpoint and picnic area. Heavily braided river formations are due to heavy silts carried by the glacially fed river and its tributaries.

Mile 20.5 (507) Km 33 (816): Finn Creek picnic area. (Limited access eastbound.)

Mile 21 (506.5) Km 34 (815): Misko lookout over the valley to the peaks of Vaux, Hunter and King. Sign explains effect of glaciation. Look at the rocks on the west side of the road for glacial scratches.

Mile 23 (504.5) Km 37 (812): Faeder Lake picnic area; avalanche nature trail leads through the forest to the edge of a large avalanche slope on the side of Mount Vaux. (Limited access eastbound.)

Mile 23.5 (504) Km 38 (811): Hoodoo Creek Campground, open late June to Labour Day; 106 campsites, 4 kitchens, sani-station. Short, steep trail to the hoodoos, which are eroded towers of boulder clay topped by harder rocks. Beaver Pond nature trail; Deerlodge trail to the first warden cabin; and trail access to Beaverfoot Valley and Ice River, where the largest outcropping of igneous rock in the Rockies contains veins of blue sodalite. Cross-country ski trails in winter.

Mile 24 (503.5) Km 39 (810): Turnoff to Chancellor Peak campground (0.5 mile/1 km) on Kicking Horse River; open May to Oct.; 64 campsites, kitchen shelters.

Mile 24.5 (503) Km 40 (809): Wapta Falls Road leads south 1.5 miles/2.5 km through Leanchoil Marsh to parking area; 2.5-mile/4-km trail to falls. The falls are 200 feet/60m wide and more than 90 feet/27m high.

On the north side of the highway a trail takes off for Mount Hunter Lookout (2.2 miles/3.5 km), which provides a grand panoramic view of the mountains.

Mile 26 (501.5) Km 42 (807): Leanchoil picnic area and viewpoint for Mount Vaux (elev. 10,892 feet/3,320m). Watch for elk crossing the highway.

Mile 27.5 (500) Km 44.5 (804.5): Eastbound traffic only: park information office, picnic tables and route map of road through Yoho Park. Sign identifies Mount Hunter (elev. 8,661 feet/2,640m).

Mile 28 (499.5) Km 45.5 (803.5): Western entrance to Yoho National Park.

Mile 29 (498.5) Km 47 (802): Beaverfoot Road to lodge; accommodations, trail rides.

Mile 29.5 (498) Km 48 (801): Viewpoint with picnic tables.

Mile 34 (493.5) Km 55 (794): Brake check point. Highway begins steep, winding descent westbound. Narrow road, watch for rocks.

Mile 36 (491.5) Km 58 (791): Park Bridge over Kicking Horse Canyon; railway below.

Mile 36.5 (491) Km 59 (790): Yoho rest area and highway map.

Trans-Canada Highway 1 descends westward from Rogers Pass Summit. (Liz Bryan)

Mile 44 (483.5) Km 71 (778): Viewpoint to south with stop of interest sign about the town of Golden. This is a good view over the Rocky Mountain Trench, the geological fault line that divides the Rocky Mountains on the east from the Columbia Mountains on the west. The Kicking Horse River cuts a canyon far below the road.

Mile 44.5 (483) Km 71.5 (777.5): Junction with Highway 95 South to Radium Hot Springs (63.5 miles/102 km) on Highway 93. (See Highway 95 side road log on page 30 in the CANADA HIGHWAY 93 section.)

Entering **GOLDEN** (pop. 3,500), all visitor facilities. Golden began life as a Canadian Pacific Railway construction camp and boomed when the railway came through. Golden became primarily a logging community in the 1880s. Around the turn of the century, when the railway began advertising the Alpine charms of Glacier National Park, Swiss guides were brought here to lead the tourists. The guides were housed in the Swiss-style chalets of Edelweiss Village northeast of town.

Today, whitewater rafting on the Kicking Horse and Blaeberry rivers is gaining popularity here. The town is also a mecca for outdoor mountain activities. Summer tourist information office in cedar-shake teepee on highway.

Mile 50.5 (477) Km 81 (768): Old community of **MOBERLY**; rail station, pub.

Mile 52.5 (475) Km 84.5 (764.5): Stop of interest marker commemorates Walter Moberly, the first surveyor of the railway route through the mountains. To the west lies Moberly Marsh, a wildlife preserve donated to British Columbia by pioneers Burges and James Gadsden, now a provincial park. Look for muskrat lodges, osprey and bald eagles. The marsh is accessible from the old Moberly railway station. Dyke trail leads along the riverbank for about 2.2 miles/3.5 km.

Mile 54 (473.5) Km 87.5 (761.5): Blaeberry River bridge. The river was named by explorer David Thompson, who crossed the Rockies via Howse Pass in 1807 and followed the river down to the Columbia Valley where he founded Kootenae House, a fur-trapping post beside Lake Windermere (see CANADA HIGHWAY 93). The river is turbulent and discharges much silt and gravel into the Columbia; its delta is a maze of sloughs and marshy ponds. Blaeberry School Road, 0.5 mile/1 km west, follows the river upstream for nearly 30 miles/50 km. Past Mummery Creek Forestry Recreation Area follow signs to trail that leads 3 miles/5 km up to the toe of the Mummery Glacier. At road end a hiking trail continues over Howse Pass across the Continental Divide to Banff.

Mile 56.5 (471) Km 91 (758): Doyle Creek rest area; picnic tables under the trees.

Mile 60 (467.5) Km 97 (752): Small sawmill community of **DONALD STATION** just off highway; no services. Old Big Bend Highway to north, once the only auto route through the rugged Columbia Mountains, provides access to Columbia Reach, Bush Arm and Kinbasket Lake.

Mile 61.5 (466) Km 99.5 (749.5): Highway and railway cross the Columbia River.

Mile 68 (459.5) Km 110 (739): Redgrave picnic areas on both sides of the road. ⋔

Mile 83 (444.5) Km 133.5 (715.5): East boundary of Glacier National Park. Mountain–Pacific time zone change: Eastbound travelers move watches ahead 1 hour, westbound travelers set watches back 1 hour.

Heather Hill lookout and mountain panorama, with signposts.

Mile 84 (443.5) Km 135.5 (713.5): Mountain Creek Campground; 306 campsites, kitchen shelters. Trestle hiking trail, a 20-minute walk up to the modern rail bridge that replaced the wooden trestle bridge over Mountain Creek. ⋔▲

Mile 85 (442.5) Km 137 (712): East entrance to Glacier National Park. Travelers who plan to stop overnight in any of the mountain national parks are required to buy auto permits: $5 for 1 day; $10 for 4 days; $30 for 1 year, good in all national parks in Canada.

Mile 87.5 (440) Km 141 (708): Viewpoint over Beaver Valley.

Mile 88.5 (439) Km 143 (706): East entrance to Rogers Pass, viewpoint and rest area.

Lots of rainfall helps create lush vegetation and giant cedars in Glacier National Park. (Courtesy of Parks Canada)

Mile 89 (438.5) Km 144 (705): East end of the first of 5 snowsheds westbound. *WARNING*: Obscured vision, speed 35 mph/60 kmph in tunnels. Near here the Canadian Pacific Railway enters the long Connaught Tunnel, which bypasses its earlier route over the pass and most of the avalanche hazards, and the recently completed Mount MacDonald Tunnel, the longest rail tunnel in North America (more than 9 miles/14.7 km).

Mile 94.5 (433) Km 152 (697): Tractor Shed rest area at the west end of the snowsheds westbound. Picnic area with exhibit explaining avalanche control. Travelers can see several active avalanche paths, a gun emplacement (for triggering avalanches) and an old railway snowshed. A short 1-mile/1.6-km walk along the Sir Donald Trail leads to

an avalanche path strewn with the debris from a 1972 avalanche. ⋔

Mile 95.5 (432) Km 153.5 (695.5): **ROGERS PASS** tourist service area; lodge with restaurant, store and gas station. Park headquarters south side of highway. Just west of the lodge is the Rogers Pass Interpretation Centre, built of massive timbers to resemble an old-time railway snowshed, complete with sod roof.

From the center a 0.5-mile/1.2-km trail traces the abandoned railway route through the pass, leading to abandoned snowsheds. Expect snow on trail (and roadsides) well into May. ⋔▲

Mile 96 (431.5) Km 154.5 (694.5): Rogers Pass Summit (elev. 4,347 feet/1,325m) marker arch. Turnouts with picnic tables on both sides of the highway. The views are great, particularly of Mounts Rogers and Sir Donald.

The pass was named for its discoverer, Major A.B. Rogers, a railway engineer in charge of the Canadian Pacific Railway route-finding expedition in 1882. Good view westbound of huge Illecillewaet Glacier. ⋔

Mile 97.5 (430) Km 157 (692): Access road to Illecillewaet Campground; 59 campsites,

kitchen shelters, open July to mid-Sept. Trail from campground to the site of Glacier House, a major Canadian Pacific Railway hotel at the turn of the century. Also trailheads here for several strenuous day hikes up to some of the glaciers.

Westbound travelers watch for the eastern portal of the disused Connaught Tunnel north of the highway. ⋔▲

Mile 98.5 (429) Km 158.5 (690.5): Large turnout and viewpoint of the mammoth stone pillars (60 feet/18m high) that once carried the railway across the creek, bypassing an earlier long loop. A scenic 1-mile/1.6-km trail follows the abandoned railway loop to Brook Campground. From the trail there are stunning views of the north face of Mount Bonney, hung with glaciers. ⋔

Mile 99.5 (428) Km 160 (689): Loop Brook Campground; open mid-July to mid-Sept., 20 campsites, kitchen shelter. ▲

Mile 100 (427.5) Km 161 (688): Illecillewaet River bridge; picnic tables and viewpoint of Mount Sir Donald (elev. 10,817 feet/ 3,297m), the park's highest peak. ⋔

Mile 102 (425.5) Km 164 (685): Large turnout. South of highway look for west portal of the Mount MacDonald rail tunnel.

Mile 106.5 (421) Km 171.5 (677.5): Bostock Creek bridge and the west gateway of Glacier National Park. Picnic tables are located on the north side of the highway. ⋔

Mile 108.5 (419) Km 175 (674): First of 3 avalanche sheds eastbound. Use headlights. Heavy snowfall and steep mountain terrain make this one of the most active avalanche areas in the world.

Mile 111 (416.5) Km 179 (670): Juniper Creek rest area and brake check.

Mile 115 (412.5) Km 185.5 (663.5): **ALBERT CANYON** road to Canyon Hot Springs; campground, restaurant, store; hot pool and cooler swimming pool; trails to Albert Canyon ghost town, trail rides. Open summer only. ⋔▲

Mile 118 (409.5) Km 190.5 (658.5): Woolsey Creek. Eastern boundary of Mount Revelstoke National Park.

Mile 119 (408.5) Km 191.5 (657.5): Giant Cedars picnic area. Short interpretive trail along a boardwalk through Interior rain forest typical of wet valley bottoms in the Columbia Mountains. ⋔⋔

Mile 120.5 (407) Km 194 (655): Skunk Cabbage picnic area and 1/2-hour nature trail along a boardwalk through Illecillewaet River swamplands. Good bird watching; watch for dippers in trailhead creek. ⋔⋔

Mile 125.5 (402) Km 202 (647): West boundary, Mount Revelstoke National Park. Only the northeast corner of the park is accessible along Trans-Canada Highway 1. The major portion is accessed at **Mile 136.5**.

Mile 127.5 (400) Km 206 (643): Eastbound traffic only: Illecillewaet rest area with cairn commemorating the opening of the Rogers Pass Highway in 1962. This route over the Selkirks was pioneered by the railway builders of the Canadian Pacific Railway (CPR) in the 1800s.

Mile 129.5 (398) Km 208.5 (640.5): Rest area overlooking Revelstoke.

Mile 135.5 (392) Km 219 (630): Secondary access road to Revelstoke city centre; good view southwest to snowy Mount Begbie, which overlooks the city. The mountain was named for Judge Begbie, known throughout British Columbia at the time of the Cariboo gold rush as the Hanging Judge.

Mile 136.5 (391) Km 220 (629): **Junction** with scenic Summit Drive, which leads north into Mount Revelstoke National Park. Open from late June to early Sept., this well-maintained gravel road switchbacks 16

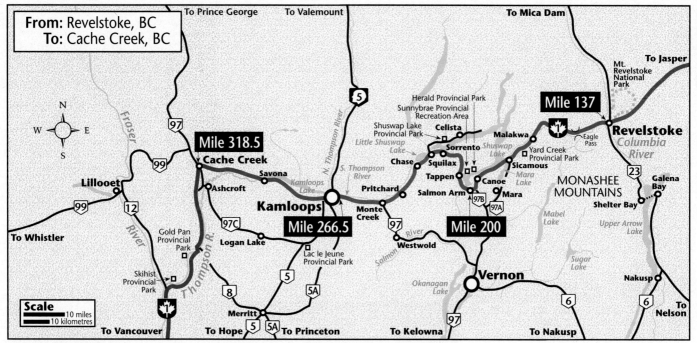

From: Revelstoke, BC
To: Cache Creek, BC

To Prince George · To Valemount · To Mica Dam

To Jasper

Mt. Revelstoke National Park

Mile 137

Revelstoke
Columbia River

To Whistler · To Vancouver · To Hope · To Princeton · To Kelowna · To Nakusp · To Nelson

Mile 318.5 — Cache Creek

Mile 266.5 — Kamloops

Mile 200

Scale
10 miles
10 kilometres

---

miles/26 km up to high alpine lakes and meadows. The Mountain Meadows Interpretive Trail (a 0.5-mile/1-km round-trip) begins at Heather Lake parking lot at road's end and is highly recommended. An easily accessible, spectacular mountain area not to be missed! ⚘★

Mile 137 (390.5) Km 220.5 (628.5): Main entrance to city of Revelstoke (to south) and **junction** with Highway 23 north to Revelstoke and Mica Creek dams (see feature this page). Summer tourist information office has old loaded logging truck nearby.

REVELSTOKE (pop. 8,500) lies at the confluence of the Illecillewaet and Columbia rivers. Originally an Indian trading centre, the city saw fur trading and gold rush activities, though the main impetus for its growth was the construction of the Canadian Pacific Railway. Later, highway construction and the building of 2 large dams on the Columbia added to its importance.

Today, tourism is playing an increasingly important part in the city's economy, both in summer (hiking, boating, fishing, swimming) and in winter (alpine and cross-country skiing, snow-cat and heli-skiing, plus ice-fishing, snowmobiling). The city's downtown core has recently been revitalized, with restoration of all the major heritage buildings and shop fronts and the construction of Grizzly Plaza, a pedestrian area with huge sculptures of grizzly bears and a bandstand; evening entertainment in summer, farmers' market on Saturday. Attractions include the restored heritage courthouse, open to the public (subject to use); the railway museum, with steam engines and rail cars; and a piano museum in a huge heritage home, which is also open for bed and breakfast. Full tourist facilities. Public campgrounds north of town on Highway 23; private campgrounds east and west of town on Highway 1.

Hydroelectric dams on the Columbia have created Lake Revelstoke, above the Revelstoke Dam; Lake Kinbasket above the Mica Dam; and the Arrow Lakes above the Hugh Keenleyside Dam near Castlegar. All of these provide good fishing for rainbow, ling, Dolly Varden and mountain whitefish. ⇐▲

Mile 137.5 (390) Km 221.5 (627.5): Columbia River bridge. The river was named by David Thompson, first man to map the river, after the ship of Robert Gray, the first independent trader on the north Pacific Coast. Picnic area on east side.

Highway 23 North

Highway 23 North leads up the eastern shore of Lake Revelstoke to Revelstoke and Mica dams.

Mile 0 Km 0: **Junction** of Highway 1 and Highway 23 North.

Mile 2.5 Km 4: Canada's highest concrete dam, Revelstoke Dam rises 575 feet/175m above the canyon floor. Year-round tours include elevator to the dam crest lookout and views of the main powerhouse gallery, tailrace and control room. Open 8 a.m. to 8 p.m., mid-June to mid-Sept.; 9 a.m. to 5 p.m. rest of year. Tours are free, self-guided, though tour guides are on hand. Just below the dam is Columbia View Provincial Park picnic area and playground.

Mile 10 Km 16: Martha Creek Provincial Park; 26 campsites, swimming beach, fishing and boat launch. Trail to Martha Lakes (5 hours round-trip).

Mile 17 Km 27: Lake Revelstoke Resort on La Forme Creek; camping, boat launch. Lake access also at Carnes and Mars Creek, to the north.

Mile 36 Km 58: Downie Creek Provincial Park on a sheltered bay that is the drowned lower section of the creek; 22 campsites, picnic shelter, swimming, fishing, boat ramp. Good view of nearby glaciers.

Mile 52 Km 85: Gravel road east to the Noranda Mine and access to a popular canoe route on the Goldstream River.

Mile 71 Km 115: Lake access at the mouth of Bigmouth Creek

Mile 80 Km 130: Pitt Creek Forestry Recreation Site; 18 campsites, maintained June 1 to Sept. 30.

Mile 83.5 Km 135: Mica Village, home base for dam workers. Store with basic supplies and gas (no propane or diesel). Just north is a hiking trail up Fred Laing Ridge, 1.6 miles/2.6 km round-trip (great views).

Nearby is the drowned historic site of Boat Encampment where explorer David Thompson built canoes to carry him and his party down the Columbia to the Pacific. An important depot of the fur-brigade, goods traveled up the Columbia in boats, were transferred here to packhorses for the journey over Athabasca Pass.

Mile 88 Km 142: Mica Dam, North America's largest earth-filled dam, more than 800 feet/250m high. Daily 90-minute guided tours 11 a.m. and 2 p.m., mid-June to early Sept. North lies one of the arms of sprawling Kinbasket Lake reservoir and a forestry campsite and boat launch at the mouth of Potlatch Creek. The road is unpaved and used by logging trucks: Drive with caution.

WARNING: Boaters on both Revelstoke and Kinbasket lakes are warned of sudden gusting winds, icy water, unstable shoreline and the presence of debris and deadheads. Night boating is not advised. Boaters on Revelstoke Lake just south of the Mica Dam are advised to keep well away from the spillway and racehouse.

Just west of the bridge, Trans-Canada Highway 1 **junctions** with Highway 23 south to Shelter Bay (30 miles/50 km) on Arrow Lakes for Galena Bay ferry. From Galena Bay, highways 23 and 6 continue south beside Arrow and Kootenay lakes to Crowsnest Highway 3 at Castlegar. The ferry runs on the half hour from Shelter Bay and makes 20-minute runs. ⚓

Mile 145 (382.5) Km 233.5 (615.5): Summit Lake, the divide between the Fraser and Columbia watersheds. Good view of rail tunnels.

Mile 146 (381.5) Km 235.5 (613.5): Provincial park picnic area by Victor Lake; good swimming. Stop of interest sign describes how railway surveyor Walter Moberly found Eagle Pass through the Monashee Mountains (the route of the highway) by watching flying eagles. ⚓

Mile 148.5 (379) Km 239.5 (609.5): THREE VALLEY GAP at the eastern end of Three Valley Lake. Resort motel adjacent to an excellent relocated ghost town village with heritage buildings brought in from outlying areas. Restaurant and gas station. Note avalanche sheds protecting railway on the steep north bank of the lake.

Mile 150 (377.5) Km 242 (607): South Pass rest area. A rough gravel road from Monashee Pass on Highway 6 east of Vernon **junctions** with Highway 1 here. Springwater bottling plant.

Mile 154 (373.5) Km 248 (601): Griffin Lake, south of highway. West of the lake is the Enchanted Forest tourist attraction.

Mile 158 (369.5) Km 254.5 (594.5): Rest area; short shady walk to Kay Falls.

Mile 160.5 (367) Km 258.5 (590.5): Eagle River Fish Hatchery raises chinook and coho salmon; picnic area, self-guided tours, open daily all year. Best time to visit is Aug. to Nov. Just to the west is Beardale Castle tourist attraction, a miniature medieval town and a prairie town. ⚓

Mile 165 (362.5) Km 265.5 (583.5): Large rest area and stop of interest sign commemorating the driving of the last spike on Canada's first transcontinental railway, the Canadian Pacific. The railway whistle stop here is Craigellachie, part of the battle cry of the Grant clan. (Most of the CPR hierarchy at that time were of Scottish descent.) In a historic telegram from London in 1884, "Stand fast, Craigellachie!" was used as a code signifying the successful completion of a loan that guaranteed the railway's completion. Information cabin and gift shop open in summer.

Mile 167 (360.5) Km 269 (580): Eagle River bridge. The Eagle River offers good family canoeing and fishing for Dolly Varden and rainbow trout and char. ⚓

Mile 170 (357.5) Km 274 (575): Access road to small community of **MALAKWA**; limited services.

Mile 171.5 (356) Km 276.5 (572.5): Yard Creek Provincial Park, one of the most popular stopping places on the Trans-Canada

Highway; 90 campsites in the rain forest with sani-station; fishing in the creek, mushrooms in fall. ⚓▲

Mile 172.5 (355) Km 278 (571): Eagle River Nature Park. Hiking/ski trails in old-growth forest. ⚓

Mile 173.5 (354) Km 280 (569): Access road to small communities of Solsqua and Cambie.

Mile 177 (350.5) Km 285 (564): Access to the "D" Dutchman's Dairy, which features fresh dairy products of all kinds, including homemade cheese and incredibly good ice cream. Free children's zoo with exotic petting animals, including llamas and camels. It is well worth a stop. ★

Mile 180 (347.5) Km 290 (559): Junction with Highway 97A to Enderby (20 miles/33 km), Armstrong (28 miles/46 km) and Vernon (38 miles/62 km) on Highway 97.

CP Rail crossing at Shuswap Narrows. (Liz Bryan)

Mile 187 (340.5) Km 301 (548): Bridge over Shuswap Narrows; west access to **SICAMOUS** (pop. 3,000), all tourist services. Originally a railway construction depot, Sicamous is now primarily a resort community strategically located on a narrow neck of water separating Shuswap and Mara lakes. It calls itself the "Houseboat Capital of Canada" because of the number of houseboats (more than 300) available for rent here.

From Sicamous public dock (turn south just east of the river bridge), the Shuswap Lake ferry provides service to the northern reaches of enormous Shuswap Lake, its final destination the old gold camp at the head of Seymour Arm. There are round-trip mail-run sailings Monday, Wednesday and Friday in summer, twice weekly in winter. Ferry maintains 2 boats—the MV *Phoebe Ann* is a sternwheeler with snack bar and room for 40 passengers and is also used for lake cruises. The MV *Stephanie* is the lake workhorse, a steel tug that pushes a barge, accommodates 9 cars and 18 passengers, plus freight. From the docks, where many houseboats are moored, you can walk under the highway bridge to Finlayson Park for swimming, sunning and boating in Shuswap Lake.

Mile 188 (339.5) Km 303 (546): Rest area above Shuswap Lake with stop of interest marker about the lake and the local Shuswap Indians. Shuswap Lake is huge, with 190 miles/300 km of shoreline, and it's popular with sailors and windsurfers because of its high winds.

Mile 192.5 (335) Km 310 (539): Shady and cool creekside rest area.

Mile 196.5 (331) Km 316 (533): Junction with road north to small community of **CANOE** and public beach and boat launch.

Mile 197.5 (330) Km 318 (531): Junction of Highway 97B, which connects with Highway 97A south to the Okanagan Valley. Take 97B south 2.5 miles/4 km for R.J. Haney Heritage House and park, with restored church, schoolhouse and farm. Also access to Larch Hills cross-country ski area. Its 93 miles/150 km of trails provide good summer hikes. ⚓

Mile 200 (327.5) Km 322 (527): SALMON ARM (pop. 11,900) lies at the southern tip of the southeastern arm of Shuswap Lake. It takes its name from the salmon in nearby Salmon River that were once so prolific at spawning time that pioneer farmers shoveled them onto the fields for fertilizer. Today the city is a busy supply centre for surrounding farms where fruit, berries and dairy products are the mainstay. The wood industry and tourism are also important to the economy. Highway 1 goes beside McGuire Lake, the city's main park.

The city provides full tourist services. Visitor information office at the junction of Highway 1 and Hudson Street. Main summer activities centre around the lake for swimming, boating and fishing. There is a waterfront marina with pier and moorings for houseboats and other craft. Lakefront west of the government wharf to the Salmon River delta and beyond is a winter refuge and spring nesting area for waterfowl.

Mile 202 (325.5) Km 325.5 (523.5): Silver Creek Road south to Gort's Gouda Farm for flavored gouda and quark. Salmon River back road nearby connects with Highway 97 near Falkland.

Mile 205.5 (322) Km 331 (518): Small community of **TAPPEN**; gas and groceries available.

Mile 206.5 (321) Km 333 (516): Canoe Point Road leads north to Sunnybrae (3.5 miles/6 km distance) and Herald (7 miles/12 km), both provincial parks on the lakeshore. Sunnybrae has lakeside picnic areas, swimming beaches and fishing. Herald has 51 campsites, picnicking, swimming and a boat launch. A short trail leads from Herald park to Margaret Falls on Reinecker Creek. West of the creek are circular depressions, the remains of Indian kekuli, which were circular, semi-underground winter homes up to 30 feet in diameter. Also in the park are remains of the pioneer Herald family farm buildings.

Mile 209.5 (318) Km 337 (512): East access road to Little White and White Lake (3.5 miles/6 km); excellent rainbow fishing by fly or troll. Also hiking, canoeing and cross-country skiing. The marsh between the lakes is popular with birders.

Mile 211.5 (316) Km 341 (508): Balmoral general store and road south to old railway settlement of Notch Hill. Notch Hill Road follows the railway and returns to Highway 1 at Sorrento, 10 miles/16 km west.

West access road to White Lake on north side of highway.

Mile 214.5 (313) Km 345.5 (503.5): Turnoff north to lakeshore resort communities of Blind Bay and Eagle Bay.

Mile 220 (307.5) Km 354 (495): **SORRENTO**, a resort community with motels, store, restaurants, gas; tourist information on Notch Hill Road. The community is known for its Arts Festival held in July. Restored heritage St. Mary's Church on highway.

Mile 222 (305.5) Km 357.5 (491.5): Turnout with viewpoint of Shuswap Lake.

Mile 225 (302.5) Km 362.5 (486.5): Picnic area on lakeside.

Mile 226.5 (301) Km 364.5 (484.5): Small community of **SQUILAX** (Indian word for "bear"), at the junction with road overpass and bridge north to Adams River, Adams Lake and Shuswap Lake Provincial Park. Also access to the resort communities of Scotch Creek, Celista and Anglemont.

The whole of the lower Adams River has been set aside as the Roderick Haig-Brown Conservation Area, named after the famous conservationist. Adams River sockeye salmon spawn along here in October, and it is a great tourist spectacle. The runs peak every 4 years: 1994, 1998, etc. Roderick Haig-Brown Park, 3 miles/5 km north of Highway 1, has picnic sites, interpretive trails and viewing platforms (handicap-accessible).

Adams Lake Provincial Recreation Area, 9 miles/15 km from highway, on south end of lake, has 15 campsites, swimming and fishing.

Shuswap Lake Provincial Park, 12 miles/20 km north of Highway 1 on the north shore, has 265 campsites, a sani-station, swimming, boat launch, visitor centre, interpretive programs, and fishing for large lake and rainbow trout, kokanee and whitefish. Camping fee.

Mile 230.5 (297) Km 371.5 (477.5): Jade Mountain lookout with a good view of Little Shuswap Lake, headwaters of the South Thompson River, and Chase Indian village. The short stretch of water between Shuswap and Little Shuswap lakes is known as Little River. It offers excellent trout fishing in February, March and October.

Mile 232 (295.5) Km 373.5 (475.5): Chase Creek Falls rest area. Watch for bighorn sheep on the bluffs south of the highway. A small band of sheep, brought in from Banff, lives on nearby Squilax Mountain and often comes to the lake for water.

Mile 232.5 (295) Km 374.5 (474.5): Junction with a loop road to **CHASE** (pop. 1,850), a small village dependent on the lumber industry, situated on the western end of Little Shuswap Lake. Fishing for rainbow, lake trout, Dolly Varden and kokanee. All visitor facilities. Watch for osprey nests in snags overlooking the river. There is a boat launch at the government wharf and picnic areas in the community parks. Popular launch spot for canoe trip down Thompson River to Kamloops.

Chase bridge crosses the Thompson River and provides access to Niskonlith Lake Provincial Recreation Area, 5 miles/8 km north, which has 30 campsites and good fishing for large rainbow. In May and June, the spring flower displays here are wonderful.

Mile 236 (291.5) Km 380 (469): Gravel road south up Chase Creek to Pillar Lake and Falkland on Highway 97. Pillar is an 82-foot/25-m tower of glacial conglomerate topped by a giant boulder. Pillar Lake has rainbow to 3 lbs.

Mile 244 (283.5) Km 393 (456): Turnoff to **PRITCHARD** (pop. 459), a small community on the South Thompson River. Good fishing for spring salmon here. Bridge crosses river at Pritchard to a network of good gravel roads leading along the north bank of the Thompson to Kamloops and Chase, and back into the hills to several good fishing lakes.

Near north side of bridge at Gore Creek, archaeologists recently discovered the earliest human remains in British Columbia, those of a man believed to have been trapped and drowned in a mud flow some 8,500 years ago.

Mile 246.5 (281) Km 397 (452): Good view of high clay banks on the north side of the river, remnants of glacial lake beaches eroded into hoodoos. Ginseng farm nearby; plants grow under sheets of black plastic mesh.

Mile 250 (277.5) Km 403 (446): **MONTE CREEK**, store and gas station at **junction** with Highway 97 South to Vernon and the Okanagan Valley (see **Mile 165** in the CANADA HIGHWAY 97 section for log of that route). Highways 1 and 97 share a common alignment west from here to Cache Creek. A road south of the highway leads steeply up to tiny St. Peter's Church, built in 1926.

Mile 254.5 (273) Km 409.5 (439.5): Stop of interest on a gravel turnout on north side of the highway, near Monte Creek railway station, explains the "Great Train Robbery." The robbery took place near here in 1906. Bill Miner and his gang held up a Canadian Pacific Railway express but netted only $15. Miner was successfully tracked by a mounted police posse and sent to jail for life. His story was made into a movie, *The Grey Fox.*

Mile 255 (272.5) Km 410.5 (438.5): Kamloops city limits, B.C. Livestock Auction yards.

Mile 255.5 (272) Km 411.5 (437.5): Highway overpass to wildlife park and museum. More than 60 species of birds and animals inhabit the park. There is a petting farm for youngsters, hiking trails, miniature railway, picnic areas and playground. The park is open daily in summer from 8 a.m. until 6 p.m. Waterslide and RV park adjacent.

Eroded columns of rock—called hoodoos—north of the Thompson River near Kamloops. (Liz Bryan)

Above—Kamloops, at the confluence of the South and North Thompson rivers, is the 5th largest city in the province.

Right—Murray Creek Falls at Mile 348.

(Photos by Liz Bryan)

Mile 266.5 (261) Km 429 (420): Westbound exit for Kamloops (description follows) and exit for Highway 5 north to Tete Jaune Cache (see HIGHWAY 5 section for log). From here to **Mile 273.5**, highways 1, 97 and 5 share a common alignment on controlled-access freeway.

KAMLOOPS (pop. 67,000), established by fur traders as Fort Kamloops in 1811, is located at the confluence of the North and South Thompson rivers. (David Thompson, the explorer, never saw the river that bears his name. It was named for him by Simon Fraser.) In 1862, the Overlanders, a group of immigrants who had set out from the prairies to travel to the goldfields by land, rafted down the North Thompson from Tete Jaune Cache. They arrived at Fort Kamloops in time for the only woman among them, Catherine Schuman, to deliver the 1st white girl born in the British Columbia Interior. Several of the Overlanders settled in Kamloops. One of them, William Fortune, built British Columbia's first flour mill.

Kamloops boomed with the arrival of the Canadian Pacific Railway in 1885. Today it is British Columbia's 4th largest settlement, a bustling city with excellent shopping and tourist facilities at the crossroads of 2 major tourist routes: Trans-Canada Highway 1 and Highway 5. Travel information centre at 10 10th Ave. is open daily June to Sept.; phone (604) 374-3377.

Its economy is based on primary and secondary manufacturing, with a copper smelter, 2 plywood plants and a pulp mill. The tall stack of Weyerhaeuser Canada's mill carries effluent (and odor) high above the city. Only rarely do climatic conditions force it down. Daily tours of the mill available May to Sept. Cattle ranching continues to be a mainstay along with mining and tourism.

Attractions include a good museum and art gallery, Secwepemc Native heritage park and Riverside Park, with its replica of old Fort Kamloops.

There are 2-hour river cruises on the paddle wheeler MV *Wanda Sue*, which depart from the river dock near the Travel Information Centre, May to Sept. The 200 lakes around Kamloops make the city a magnet for fishermen. Local rainbow trout, known as Kamloops trout, have a reputation as wily fighters; 5- to 6-pounders are not uncommon.　　　　　↩

Mile 269 (258.5) Km 433.5 (415.5): Summit Drive and east exit for Kamloops; Exit 370 westbound, Exit 369 eastbound.

Mile 270 (257.5) Km 434.5 (414.5): **Junction** of Highway 5A South to Merritt and Princeton. This is now one of the least traveled highways in southern British Columbia, having been supplanted by the Coquihalla section of Highway 5. Exit 368 eastbound, Exit 367 westbound.

Mile 271 (256.5) Km 436 (413): Copperhead Drive leads south 18 miles/29 km to Lac le Jeune Provincial Park; 144 campsites, swimming and fishing.　　　↩▲ EXIT 366

Mile 273.5 (254) Km 440 (409): **Junction** with Highway 5 to Merritt and Hope (see HIGHWAY 5 section). Freeway ends. Kamloops western city limits.　　　EXIT 362

Mile 276 (251.5) Km 444 (405): Tailings of the Afton copper mine are visible on the south side of the highway. Mining operations are spread for some distance along the highway. On the north side of the highway, notice the range rehabilitation project in which sagebrush semidesert has been cultivated and seeded to grass.

Mile 279 (248.5) Km 449 (400): Greenstone Mountain Road leads to several high fishing lakes.

Mile 282.5 (245) Km 455 (394): Cherry Creek ranch, one of the pioneer ranches in the area. More ginseng plantations.

Mile 291.5 (236) Km 469.5 (379.5): Turnout and viewpoint over Kamloops Lake (a widening of the Thompson River). Geologists believe that the lake may be an ancient volcanic crater, the source of the area's lava outcrops. Stop of interest sign here recalls the days of lake steamboats, and a display board illustrates the types of Indian shelters on the interior Plateau. Sign identifies the different types of noxious knapweed, which in areas of British Columbia are taking over the rangeland.

Across the lake are Battle Bluffs, their red color attributed to legendary blood stains from an Indian battle fought on top.

Mile 293.5 (234) Km 472.5 (376.5): Turnoff north to Savona Provincial Park for swimming and picnicking. **SAVONA** is a small trading community at the narrow west end of Kamloops Lake; limited facilities.　　　　　⚓

Mile 296.5 (231) Km 477.5 (371.5): Bridge over the Thompson River.

Mile 298.5 (229) Km 480.5 (368.5): Bridge over Deadman River. Pacific salmon spawn here in the fall. The river was named for an early Hudson's Bay Co. trader who was found murdered here.

Mile 299.5 (228) Km 482 (367): Turnoff on gravel road north to Deadman River valley, an attractive ranch valley with a spectacular multicolored volcanic canyon (good rock-hounding for agates and petrified wood) and rock hoodoos (ask for permission and directions at Deadman Creek Ranch). Also access to Vidette Lake and gold mine.

Mile 304.5 (223) Km 490 (359): Turnoff south to a bridge over the Thompson River and the small community of **WALHACHIN**. When nearby orchards flourished, so did Walhachin; today a desert of prickly pear cactus and sagebrush has ousted the fruit trees and the settlement is almost a ghost town. No services available.

Mile 307 (220.5) Km 494 (355): Road to Juniper Beach Provincial Park on Thompson River; 30 campsites, sani-station, fishing. An oasis in the dry belt desert. Remains of an irrigation flume are visible on the north side of the highway.　　　　↩▲

Mile 308.5 (219) Km 496.5 (352.5): Stop of interest sign commemorates the orchard settlement of Walhachin. On the river flats east of here pioneers planted apple orchards, building dams in the hills and miles of irrigation flumes to bring water. By 1913, these dry benches were covered with sturdy young trees. But when all but 10 of the eligible males of the area enlisted for service in

WWI, the irrigation flumes were breached by floods and landslides and the thirsty orchards shriveled. Today there are still a few phantom trees among the sagebrush and cactus. The flumes are merely rotting streaks of wood along the hillsides.

The climate, too dry for orchards, is ideal for cattle but few are to be seen from June to Sept. because they are sent to the high forested hills to graze. There are huge cattle feeding stations just east of Cache Creek.

Mile 318.5 (209) Km 513 (336): Junction of Trans-Canada Highway 1 and Highway 97 at CACHE CREEK (pop. 1,200). Travel Information Centre just north of highway intersection. The settlement grew up around the confluence of the creek (named after a reputed cache of gold) and the Bonaparte River. The Hudson's Bay Co. opened a store to benefit from trade at the intersection of trails east and north. Cache Creek became a major supply point on the Cariboo Wagon Road. Today, the junction is still very much a traveler's way station. Gas stations, motels and restaurants line both sides of the highway. The area is famous for jade (nephrite). Visit the Cariboo Jade Shop to see this stone being cut and polished.

Travelers continuing north on Highway 97 turn to **Mile 232.5** in the CANADA HIGHWAY 97 section for log of that route. Trans-Canada Highway 1 swings south from Cache Creek for Vancouver-bound travelers.

Mile 319 (208.5) Km 513.5 (335.5): Bonaparte River bridge at south edge of Cache Creek. The river flows into the Thompson River at Ashcroft.

Mile 319.5 (208) Km 514 (335): Junction with road to **ASHCROFT,** a small village with full tourist facilities just east of the highway. Attractions include a lively museum, a restored stagecoach depot and a "wild West" ambiance. Also **junction** with Highway 97C to the mining community of Logan Lake and to Merritt.

Mile 325 (202.5) Km 523 (326): Stop of interest sign describes Ashcroft Manor and roadhouses built in 1864 by the 2 Cornwall brothers, Clement and Henry, who brought fox hunting and horse racing to the Canadian frontier. The manor burned in 1943 but the roadhouse remains, one of the few left on the Cariboo Wagon Road. Today it houses several shops selling antiques, memorabilia and British Columbia crafts. Behind the manor a cedar building houses an English-style tearoom that serves afternoon tea and cakes as well as lunches and dinners. Open March to Nov. Well worth a stop. ★

Mile 328.5 (199) Km 528.5 (320.5): Hat Creek Road to Cornwall Forestry Lookout, 12 miles/19 km west. The road is narrow and rough and the climb to the lookout is steep, but Alpine meadows and the view are worth the trip. Road continues to Highway 99 and Highway 97 north of Cache Creek.

Mile 329.5 (198) Km 530.5 (318.5): Rest area on the east side of the highway beneath Red Hill. A side road 2 miles/3 km south turns west to Venables Valley. Up this narrow, winding road 1.5 miles/3 km are 3 mineral lakes, heavily encrusted with white salts of magnesium sulphate, which were mined sporadically for epsom salts. An interesting excursion.

Mile 336.5 (191) Km 541.5 (307.5): Excellent viewpoint of the Thompson River valley. The broad river benches are evidence of temporary lakes created during periods of glaciation. Stop of interest sign commemorates the driving of the last spike in 1915 of Canada's third transcontinental railway, the Canadian Northern Pacific, now the Canadian National Railway.

Mile 343.5 (184) Km 553 (296): Watch for bighorn sheep on the road. A small band of sheep live on the rocky bluffs west of the highway and come down to the river for water. They are fed in winter beside the highway. On the east side of the river is a huge talus or scree slope. This feature was noted on early maps as "the great rock slide."

Mile 345 (182.5) Km 555.5 (293.5): Side road down to the river at the Canadian Pacific Railway flagstop of Spatsum. The name is derived from Indian spep-sum, meaning "place where milkweed grows." Milkweed is abundant in the dry interior of British Columbia, along with the monarch butterfly, whose larvae feed on the leaves. This is the northern extremity of the monarch's range. The sand beach at Spatsum is a good place for picnics; rafts for river float trips are often put into the water here. Across the river lies the tiny Indian settlement of Spatsum with its wooden church.

Mile 347 (180.5) Km 559 (290): North access road to Spences Bridge and Highway 8 to Merritt. SPENCES BRIDGE (pop. 300) lies at the confluence of the Nicola and Thompson rivers. The first settlement was known as Cook's Ferry because of the ferry crossing here, but the name was changed in 1864 when Thomas Spence built a toll bridge. An important stop on the Cariboo Road, Spences Bridge used to be known for some of the best steelhead fishing in British Columbia, but today the Thompson River is subject to intense regulation.

Mile 348 (179.5) Km 560.5 (288.5): Junction with Highway 8 East to Merritt along the Nicola River. This is also the south access to the community of Spences Bridge. Old church and graveyard at junction. A stop of interest sign nearby commemorates the great mudslide of 1905, which dammed the Thompson River for 5 hours. Across the river, Murray Creek Falls tumbles over the lip of a narrow red-walled canyon into an inviting pool, a popular rest stop for whitewater rafters.

Mile 351.5 (176) Km 565.5 (283.5): Community of Big Horn. Fruit stands. River access.

Mile 355 (172.5) Km 571.5 (277.5): Goldpan Provincial Park is located on the narrow flats beside the river; 14 campsites, picnic area,

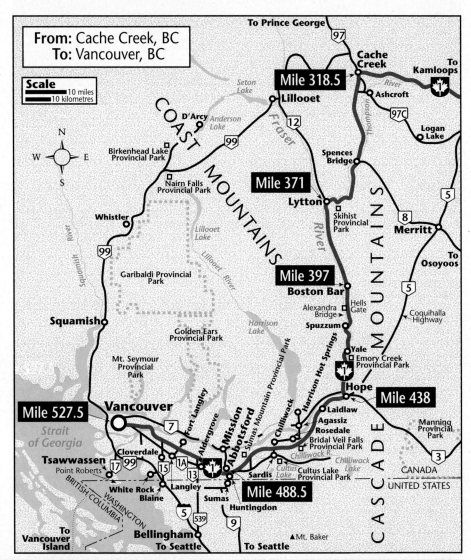

From: Cache Creek, BC
To: Vancouver, BC

Scale
10 miles
10 kilometres

fishing, river rafting. The park is usually full from mid-Oct. to Dec. with steelhead fishermen. Gold can be panned from the river gravels here. 🏕🛶▲

Mile 355.5 (172) Km 572 (277): Shaw Springs, a small community on the river bench where mule and oxen teams once pastured overnight.

Mile 357 (170.5) Km 574.5 (274.5): Highway winds along river level on steel retaining walls; this section of road cost $1 million a mile to build. Good close-up view of river rapids and migrating salmon in the fall. Excellent fishing spot during low water when trout may be taken on a fly. 🛶

dredge gold from submerged bars failed. A Hudson's Bay Co. post, Fort Dallas, was established nearby, and the later settlement was named for Sir Edward Bulwer Lytton, secretary of state for the British Colonies. The town provides full tourist services and is headquarters for river raft trips. Travel information office is on Fraser Street, downtown. One of the local sights is the confluence of the turbulent coffee-colored Fraser River and the sparkling green Thompson River. It is best observed from south of the ferry terminal on the west side of the river, or from the railway bridge over the Thompson on Highway 12. The ferry here is one of few remaining current-driven ferries in British Columbia and has been operating since 1894. It provides

way climbs up and over Jackass Mountain, the steepest hill on the old wagon road, so named because many mules slipped to their deaths on the narrow, tortuous track. Viewpoint and stop of interest plaque on west side of highway.

Mile 385 (142.5) Km 620 (229): Shady rest area by waterfall.

Mile 387 (140.5) Km 623 (226): An Indian cemetery is visible on the hillside. Both sides of the canyon are sprinkled with small Indian reserves. The Salish population was large at one time, but the Indians succumbed quickly to the diseases of the white pioneers. Just to the south, a steep road leads eastward onto a forested shelf where Blue Lake resort provides boating, swimming, horseback riding, meals and accommodations.

Mile 388.5 (139) Km 625.5 (223.5): Boothroyd airstrip.

Mile 391.5 (136) Km 630 (219): Highway crosses Ainslie Creek canyon. Nine Mile Lookout nearby.

Mile 397 (130.5) Km 639 (210): BOSTON BAR (pop. 885), named for the many Americans (called Boston Men by the Indians) who came to seek gold in the Fraser River gravel bars. Unique aerial car ferry to North Bend on the river's west bank was replaced by a bridge in the spring of 1986. The old cable cage is on display at the bridge's north side. The main industry here is logging and a large sawmill operation occupies one of the river benches. All services are available. Boston Bar/North Bend's annual May Day celebrations are among the province's oldest. They include old-fashioned English Maypole dancing.

NORTH BEND is a fascinating old railroad community, complete with storage sheds and roundhouse and a picturesque old station. Today it is still a Canadian Pacific divisional point, but acts mainly as a dormitory community for Boston Bar. From North Bend, drive 9 miles/15 km north to logging road up Nahatlatch River to chain of lakes; forestry campsites, fishing. 🛶▲

Mile 398.5 (129) Km 641.5 (207.5): Anderson Creek bridge. Private campground. ▲

Mile 402.5 (125) Km 648 (201): China Bar Tunnel, almost 2,300 feet/700m long, one of the longest in North America. The tunnel curves and should be driven with extreme care. A stop of interest sign at the south end of the tunnel quotes from the writings of Simon Fraser, the 1st white man to descend the river that now bears his name: "We could scarcely make our way. ... We had to pass where no human being should venture."

Mile 403.5 (124) Km 650 (199): Entrance to Hells Gate for southbound travelers.

Mile 404.5 (123) Km 651 (198): Entrance for northbound traffic to parking lot and pedestrian overpass to Hells Gate. Here, where the Fraser River is at its narrowest, are fish ladders built in 1913–14 by the International Fisheries Commission to enable spawning salmon to overcome a blockage in the river caused by railway construction. Two 28-pas-

The blue-green Thompson River meets the brown Fraser River at Lytton. The town is headquarters for river rafters. *(Liz Bryan)*

Mile 360 (167.5) Km 579.5 (269.5): Little Hells Gate rapids on the Thompson River, a good place to watch spawning salmon in the fall. The rapids are also one of the thrills of a ride downriver in an inflatable raft. There are several companies operating on the river, with trips from a few hours to several days.

Mile 365.5 (162) Km 588.5 (260.5): Skihist Provincial Park. Picnic area on west side of highway provides spectacular view over the Thompson River canyon; good place to watch the trains go by. (Both Canadian Pacific and Canadian National rail lines pass through the canyon.) On the east side of the highway are 68 shaded campsites, sani-station and hiking trails. Fee charged from June to Sept. Keep a lookout for elk: An introduced herd thrives in this dry belt country. 🏕🏕▲

Mile 369 (158.5) Km 594.5 (254.5): North access road to town of Lytton and **junction** with Highway 12 to Lillooet. Native graveyard of Klickumsheen by town and river overlook.

Mile 371 (156.5) Km 597.5 (251.5): Lytton pioneer cemetery and south access road to **LYTTON** (pop. 400). At the confluence of the Thompson and Fraser rivers, Lytton was called Camchin by the Indians and The Forks by explorers. Sandbars above and below the settlement yielded much gold but attempts to

access for 2 vehicles or 20 passengers at a time to the west side of the Fraser River.

Three miles/5 km of river frontage in Lytton have been set aside as a gold-panning recreational reserve. Only hand-panning is permitted. Ask for directions at the travel office. An Environment Canada weather station is located here and tours can be arranged. Lytton has recorded the highest temperature in British Columbia (111°F/ 44°C).

Mile 374 (153.5) Km 602.5 (246.5): Skupper rest area and viewpoint.

Mile 376.5 (151) Km 606 (243): Siska Siding road and viewpoint down the Fraser River at the point where 2 rail bridges cross. The Canadian Pacific Railway reached here 1st and crossed here by choice, seeking the easiest route through the canyon. Thirty years later, the Canadian National also came this way and was forced to cross here because there wasn't room for 2 tracks on the same side of the river.

Mile 379 (148.5) Km 610.5 (238.5): KANAKA BAR, restaurant. The river bar below was worked by Kanakas, natives of Hawaii, who were probably brought over from the Hudson's Bay Co. post in Honolulu. 🏕

Mile 382 (145.5) Km 615 (234): The high-

senger aerial trams take tourists 500 feet/153m down across the river to a restaurant, shops and other attractions. Footbridge across the river provides view of fish ladders and access to fisheries displays. Trams operate daily, April to Nov.

If you want some exercise, there is a trail down to the fish ladders. It starts from the southern end of the river viewpoint. The trail is steep. Allow about an hour for the return trip.

Hells Gate was well named. Construction of the railways through this narrow gap was hazardous and many workers lost their lives here. To haul supplies for the railway upstream of Hells Gate, railroad builder Andrew Onderdonk ordered a stern-wheeler steamer to be built at Yale. The gallant little *Skuzzy* miraculously made its way upstream through the terrifying waters of Hells Gate in 1882, hauled by ropes attached to the canyon walls by bolts. Estimated speed of the river through Hells Gate is 17 mph/28 kmph.　▲★

Mile 406 (121.5) Km 653.5 (195.5): Ferrabee and Hells Gate tunnels (both 328 feet/100m long).

Mile 407.5 (120) Km 656 (193): Rest area by Copper Creek, a leafy grotto, east of highway.

Mile 408.5 (119) Km 657.5 (191.5): Alexandra Tunnel (nearly 984 feet/300m long).

Mile 410.5 (117) Km 660.5 (188.5): Historic Alexandra Lodge is the last surviving original roadhouse on the Cariboo Wagon Road. Just north of the lodge a section of the 1848 Hudson's Bay Co. trail from Yale to Kamloops that leads east to a high valley above the river. The 8-mile/13-km hike ends at a small lake where the brigade once camped. ▲

Mile 411 (116.5) Km 661.5 (187.5): Alexandra Bridge Provincial Park picnic area with interpretive displays on both sides of highway. Trail from park leads to the old wagon road alignment across the rail tracks to the now-abandoned suspension bridge, built in 1926 on the same abutments of an earlier structure built in 1863.　▲⊼

Mile 411.5 (116) Km 662.5 (186.5): Stop of interest at the south end of the Alexandra Bridge, built in 1962, more than 1,640 feet/500m long, the 2nd largest fixed arch span in the world.

Mile 414 (113.5) Km 666.5 (182.5): **SPUZZUM**, a small community with gas and food. The Hudson's Bay Co. maintained a fur depot here and it was a toll station on the wagon road. Before the building of the Alexandra Bridge, a ferry took travelers across the river here.

Highway crosses Spuzzum Creek canyon.

Mile 416 (111.5) Km 670 (179): Sailor Bar Tunnel (nearly 984 feet/300m long).

Mile 420 (107.5) Km 676.5 (172.5): Saddle Rock Tunnel (480 feet/146m), named after a saddle-shaped rock in the river, an early landmark.

Mile 421 (106.5) Km 678 (171): Turnout and stop of interest sign for the Cariboo Wagon Road, built by Royal Engineers from England in 1861–63. Up this 20-foot-/6-m-wide road hacked out of the wilderness came men and supplies bound for the gold rush boom towns of the Cariboo.

Mile 423.5 (104) Km 681.5 (167.5): Yale Tunnel. The huge dark rock in the river north of the tunnel was named after the wife of arctic explorer Sir John Franklin, who disappeared while searching for the Northwest Passage in 1845. Lady Franklin, refusing to believe her husband was dead, came to British Columbia in search of him.

Mile 424 (103.5) Km 682.5 (166.5): **YALE** (pop. 500), a small community on the river bench. Founded in 1847 as a fur-trading post of the Hudson's Bay Co., the fort was named after trader James Yale.

The discovery of gold in the Fraser catapulted the small settlement into a boom town with 3,000 miners eager to spend their pokes of gold dust in the saloons and dance halls. Yale was head of navigation on the Fraser, and paddle-steamers arrived almost daily from the coast during gold rush days. When gold was discovered upriver in the creeks of the Cariboo, Yale became the southern terminus of a wagon road. (Highway 1 follows much of the general route of, and sometimes the same roadbed as, the historic road.) It experienced a second boom with the construction of the Canadian Pacific Railway, but today it is a quiet little place, dependent on lumber, mining and tourism. All services are available. Tourist infocentre on highway, open June to Sept.

Yale is the home of the St. John of the Divine Church, built in 1859, the oldest Anglican church in British Columbia still on its original site. It is just east of the highway in the town centre. Beside it is the museum, housed in an 1868 heritage house; open daily June to Sept. Visit the pioneer cemetery with gravestones dating back to 1850, and Foreshore Park where you can pan for gold. On Front Street (Highway 1) there are monuments to the Cariboo Wagon Road and to Barnard's Express.

Mile 424.5 (103) Km 683.5 (165.5): Trail to Spirit Cave starts on the east side of the highway and climbs steeply up the mountain to the cave mouth. One-hour hike to viewpoint.▲

Mile 428.5 (99) Km 689.5 (159.5): Turnoff for Emory Creek Provincial Park with 34 shaded campsites; gold panning and fishing in the creek mouth. Camping fee May to Oct.

The gold rush settlement of Emoryville grew into a lusty town with 9 saloons, a brewery and the mainland's first newspaper. When the gold on the river bars was gone, the town was abandoned. A nearby stop of interest sign commemorates Chinese immigrants who came with the gold rush and stayed on to help build the Cariboo Wagon Road, then the railway.　◄▲

Mile 430 (97.5) Km 692 (157): Dogwood Valley Community.

Mile 431.5 (96) Km 695 (154): Texas Creek bridge. Road west to B.C. Nickel Mine.

Mile 435.5 (92) Km 701 (148): Lake of the Woods (officially Schkam Lake) rest area; good swimming and fair fishing for cutthroat and rainbow trout. Restaurant and motel at north end of lake. *NOTE*: Northbound travelers have no direct access to the rest area. To use the site, turn around at the motel entrance.　◄

Mile 437 (90.5) Km 703.5 (145.5): **Junction with Highway 7**, a more leisurely route to the coast along the north side of the Fraser River to Agassiz, the resort town of Harrison Hot Springs, and Mission to Vancouver. Highway 1 between Hope and Vancouver is a 4-lane freeway.

Mile 438 (89.5) Km 705 (144): Two-lane double-deck bridge over the Fraser River. The upper deck (metal surface) carries the road and the lower deck used to carry the track of the now defunct Kettle Valley Railway. Park at the large turnout on the north side of the bridge if you want to cross the bridge on the pedestrian footpath for a close-up view of the churning river beneath.

South of the bridge is the town of **HOPE** (pop. 6,500), at the confluence of the Fraser and Coquihalla rivers. At Hope, the Fraser River leaves the rugged confines of the canyon and becomes wide, flat and pastoral. Hope is overlooked by the Coast Mountains on the north and the Cascade Mountains to the south and east. In 1848, the Hudson's Bay Co. built a fur-trading post here. When 10 years later gold was discovered on the river bars, 30,000 miners converged on the tiny settlement. Royal Engineers surveyed a townsite in 1859. When gold was discovered in the Cariboo, Hope was bypassed as a supply centre in favor of Yale, head of navigation, farther upriver.

Today, Hope is a bustling little town strategically located at the junction of several travel routes: highways 1, 3, 5 and 7. All services are available. Tourist Information Office and museum at the corner of Hudson Bay Street and Water Avenue. Outside the museum is the impressive, fully restored gold mill concentrator from the Home Gold Mining Co.'s Pipestem Mine in the Coquihalla area. Inside, the museum presents 6 displays of pioneer life. Open 8 a.m. to 8 p.m., daily, July and Aug.; 9 a.m. to 5 p.m., May, June and September; weekdays, 10 a.m. to 4 p.m., rest of year. City Center Memorial Park has a bandstand for summer entertainment and tree stumps carved into animal forms. Adjacent is the Japanese Garden, dedicated to the displaced coastal Canadians of Japanese background who were interned at Tashme (east of Hope on Highway 3). Christ Church here, built in 1859, is one of British Columbia's oldest churches.

Tourist highlight of the town is Coquihalla Canyon Provincial Recreation Area, where you can walk the abandoned tracks of the Kettle Valley Railway through 3 of the famous Quintette tunnels and cross a bridge over the foaming river. (See also CANADA HIGHWAY 5 section.) To reach the tunnels, take Kawkawa Lake Road north from town.

Just across Coquihalla River bridge on Kawkawa Lake Road is Kawkawa Creek Salmon Enhancement Site with boardwalk trails and a viewing area. Chum salmon spawn here in late September, coho in late October. In odd-numbered years, heavy runs of pink salmon also clog the channels. Municipal campgrounds nearby provide full facilities and space for 95 RVs and 22 tents. Farther along the road is Kawkawa Lake itself with a provincial park at its southern end, a popular spot for swimming, fishing, picnics and boating (no camping).

If Hope and Coquihalla Canyon seem

vaguely familiar, you may have seen them before in the movies, including *First Blood*, *Shoot to Kill* and *Fire with Fire*. 🏕🛶⛵★

Mile 439 (88.5) Km 706.5 (142.5): Freeway overpass; **junction** with Highway 3 and access to Flood/Hope Road. Travelers heading east on Highway 3 turn to the end of the CROWSNEST HIGHWAY 3 section and read log back to front. **Junction** with Coquihalla Highway 5 lies a short distance to the east (see CANADA HIGHWAY 5 section). Highway 1 westbound enters the freeway at the junction. At the junction, a 1914 railway station has been restored as a teahouse and centre for local arts and crafts. The freeway westbound is 4 lanes, maximum speed 60 mph/100 kmph.

Mile 440.5 (87) Km 709 (140): Silverhope Creek exit for eastbound travelers. Access to RV park. Also access to the Skagit Valley. Provincial Recreation Area and Silver Lake Provincial Park; primitive camping. ▲ EXIT 168

Mile 443.5 (84) Km 714 (135): Exit to Flood/Hope Road, business route to Hope for eastbound travelers and access to Hope airport. Access to RV park. Gliders enjoy mountain thermals and soar high above the river. They can be seen here most weekends. Mount Hope is visible to the east. ▲ EXIT 165

Mile 446 (81.5) Km 718 (131): Hunter Creek rest area, public phone and summer Tourist Information trailer. Eastbound access to Laidlaw. EXIT 160

Mile 448.5 (79) Km 722 (127): Exit to small residential community of **LAIDLAW** (no services) and road to Jones Lake (officially Wahleach Lake), 7 miles/11 km of rough road; fishing for rainbow, kokanee and cutthroat in glacially fed hydro reservoir. Highway runs beside the Fraser River; good views; watch for bald eagles in trees in the winter; also for remains of gold dredge, visible at low water. 🛶 EXIT 153

Mile 454.5 (73) Km 731.5 (117.5): Exit to Herrling Island (no access, no services), a cottonwood tree farm (visible from highway). Good views westbound of Mount Cheam and Mount Welch. EXIT 146

Mile 461 (66.5) Km 742 (107): Exit to Popkum Road for Bridal Veil Falls Provincial Park, the small community of **POPKUM** and various roadside highway attractions, including waterslide, Sandstone Gallery rock and gem museum, Flintstones amusement park, restaurant, motel and gas station. The provincial park provides excellent picnic facilities in meadows at the base of aptly named Bridal Veil Falls, an exquisite tumble of water 200 feet/60m high. Short trail leads to base of falls. 🏕 EXIT 138

Mile 461.5 (66) Km 742.5 (106.5): Exit to Highway 9 east for Rosedale, Agassiz, Harrison Hot Springs and alternate route Highway 7 to Hope and Vancouver; this is the recommended route for eastbound travelers on Highway 1 who wish to bypass Hope. This is also the west exit for Bridal Veil Falls.

On Highway 9 at the intersection is Minter Gardens, which rivals Victoria's famous Butchart Gardens for beauty. It features seasonal floral displays, trails, topiary, a maze, fountains, streams, gazebos, a restaurant and gift shop. Gardens are open daily mid-June to mid-Sept.; weekends only late May to mid-June. 🏕★ EXIT 135

Mile 470 (57.5) Km 756.5 (92.5): Prest Road exit north to Rosedale, south to the small mountain community of Ryder Lake. EXIT 123

A field of flowers in the Fraser Valley. Outside of Greater Vancouver, much of the valley is rolling farmland. (Liz Bryan)

Mile 470.5 (57) Km 757.5 (91.5): Field of hop vines on the north side of the highway and on the south 2.5 miles/4 km west. The Fraser Valley is British Columbia's biggest producer of hops, used in the brewing of beer. Good view to the south of Mount Slesse, a giant sawtooth, and Mount Tomahoy, a snowy ridgeback tent.

Mile 471 (56.5) Km 758 (91): Exits 119A and B south to Sardis and Vedder Crossing, north to Chilliwack and Chilliwack airport. **SARDIS** is the centre of a hop-growing industry and home of the native Salish weavers who spin and weave traditional Indian baskets. **VEDDER CROSSING** is the site of the Canadian Forces Base Camp and Royal Engineers Military Museum. (Kids will love the outdoor displays of tanks and a bailey bridge.)

Access to Cultus Lake resort area (10 miles/16 km south), which has full tourist facilities, including a giant waterslide and a provincial park with 300 campsites. Continue southeast 27 miles/44 km via partly rough road to Chilliwack Lake Provincial Park; 100 campsites, picnicking, swimming, fishing, boating and mountain scenery.

CHILLIWACK (pop. 50,000) is a large city, primarily a trading centre for the surrounding dairy farmers and vegetable growers. Excellent tourist facilities. It is an old community that began life as a busy steamboat landing and transshipment point during the gold rush era of the 1880s and grew to city stature in 1908. Many heritage buildings remain, including the old city hall, now a national historic site and used as the city museum. 🏕🛶▲ EXIT 119

Mile 474 (53.5) Km 763 (86): Lickman Road exit; access to tourist information centre,

open daily in summer, weekdays the rest of the year. Behind the infocentre is Chilliwack Antique Powerland, where old farm machinery, including steam-driven tractors, is restored and displayed in a working museum, complete with busy blacksmith. Annual old-time threshing bee is held here early August and plowing match in April. EXIT 116

Mile 477.5 (50) Km 769 (80): Vedder Canal, built in 1920 to drain Sumas Lake and reclaim large areas of floodlands for agriculture.

Mile 481 (46.5) Km 774 (75): Exit south to **YARROW**, a small farming community founded by Mennonites. Access to Cultus Lake and Chilliwack Lake provincial parks for eastbound travelers (see **Mile 471**). EXIT 104

Mile 484.5 (43) Km 780 (69): Eastbound access to rest area beside Sumas River. Stop of interest marker tells of the reclamation of 33,000 acres from shallow Sumas Lake in 1924 by a system of stream diversions, dams, dikes, canals and pumps. EXIT 99

Mile 485.5 (42) Km 781.5 (67.5): Exit to Whatcom Road. Wonderland Amusement Park and westbound access across highway to rest area (see **Mile 484.5**). Access to Sumas Mountain Provincial Park. No camping but there are hiking trails with great views. 🏕 EXIT 95

Mile 487 (40.5) Km 784 (65): The Lucky Four group of mountains is visible to eastbound travelers.

Mile 488.5 (39) Km 786 (63): Exit for Highway 11 South to Huntingdon–Sumas border crossing (open 24 hours a day) and highway north to **ABBOTSFORD** (pop. 60,400), all services, and bridge over the Fraser River to Mission and Highway 7 to Harrison Hot Springs. Major attraction at **MISSION** (pop. 28,800), located on the Fraser River, is Westminster Abbey, a Benedictine monastery built in 1961.

Drive south on Highway 11 for Fraser Valley Trout Hatchery, British Columbia's largest, which raises rainbow, cutthroat and

steelhead. One entire floor of the building is allocated to public displays, viewing walkways and a theatre. The garden area around outdoor rearing ponds provides excellent views of Mount Baker and the valley.
EXITS 90 and 92

Mile 491.5 (36) Km 791 (58): Exit to **CLEARBROOK**, a fruit and vegetable processing community and centre of a raspberry growing area. Some raspberry fields are visible to the south.
EXIT 87

Mile 494 (33.5) Km 795 (54): Exit for Highway 1A, Mount Lehman Road to Aldergrove and Abbotsford airport. Abbotsford International Air Show, largest in Canada, is held here every August. The 3-day event attracts 100,000 spectators. Around Mount Lehman, fields are planted with daffodils and the community of **BRADNER** holds an annual Daffodil Festival and flower show every April.
EXIT 83

Mile 495.5 (32) Km 798 (51): A good view (best eastbound) of Mount Baker and the other snowcapped peaks of the Cascade Range in Washington. Mount Baker (elev. 10,778 feet/3,285m) is a dormant volcano; it last erupted in 1881 and still belches sulfurous fumes.

Mile 497 (30.5) Km 800 (49): Exit westbound traffic only to rest area and Tourism B.C. visitor centre.

Mile 497.5 (30) Km 801 (48): Good view north of Mount Judge Howay.

Mile 499.5 (28) Km 804.5 (44.5): Exit to Highway 13 South to the U.S.–Canada customs at Aldergrove/Lynden, open 8 a.m. to midnight, and the Vancouver Game Farm. The game farm houses more than 60 species of animals from all parts of the world in large paddocks. The site may be toured by car or on foot. There are picnic areas, a gift shop and food available.
⚲ EXIT 73

Mile 504.5 (23) Km 812.5 (36.5): Exit to Highway 10 to **CLOVERDALE**, known for its annual Victoria Day Rodeo (end of May) and for harness racing (Oct. through April), and access to Langley and Fort Langley. Historic Transportation Centre, south on Highway 10, displays more than 100 antique cars, trucks and planes. Open daily in summer; Tuesday to Saturday rest of year.
EXIT 66

Mile 506 (21.5) Km 814.5 (34.5): Good view of Mount Baker.

Mile 508.5 (19) Km 819 (30): Exit on 200th Street to **LANGLEY** (area pop. 66,000) and **FORT LANGLEY** (pop. 16,000). The fort at Fort Langley is a national historic park. A Hudson's Bay Co. fur-trading post was built here in 1827 just downstream and was rebuilt at its present location in 1840. It served for many years as the fur company's headquarters on the West Coast. In 1868 the mainland of British Columbia was declared a crown colony here and Sir James Douglas

was proclaimed the colony's 1st governor. To commemorate this event, the British Columbia Cabinet meets here every Nov. 19.

Langley is a fast-growing trading centre of the lower Fraser Valley and provides good shopping and full tourist facilities.
EXIT 58

Mile 512 (15.5) Km 824 (25): Exit to Highway 15 South to Cloverdale and the U.S. border at Douglas (customs open 24 hours); north to Barnston Island. Barnston Island (follow 176th Street until it hits 104th Avenue, then turn north) is accessible by a free ferry; its encircling dike makes a bracing 2- to 3-hour walk.
EXIT 53

Mile 514 (13.5) Km 827 (22): Westbound-only exit for Surrey City Centre, and B.C. Ferries Tsawwassen terminal for Vancouver Island and Gulf Island service. (For descriptions of ferries and islands, see THE ISLANDS section.) Also access to Vancouver International Airport.
EXIT 50

Mile 515.5 (12) Km 829.5 (19.5): Eastbound-only exit for **SURREY** (pop. 240,000), which includes the communities of Whalley, South Surrey, Cloverdale, Newton and Guildford. Tourist Information Centre on 105th Avenue is open year-round.
EXIT 48

Mile 516.5 (11) Km 831.5 (17.5): Port Mann Bridge over the Fraser River.

Mile 517.5 (10) Km 833 (16): Exit for Highway 7, which goes east along the north side of the Fraser River through Maple Ridge and Mission to Harrison Hot Springs and Hope. Also exit here for the Greater Vancouver suburbs of Coquitlam and Port Coquitlam.
EXIT 44

Mile 520 (7.5) Km 837 (12): Exit to New Westminster, Coquitlam and Maillardville. The highway parallels the Canadian National Railway. **NEW WESTMINSTER** (pop. 40,000) was designed to be the capital of

British Columbia. Its site was chosen and surveyed in 1858 and Queen Victoria bestowed its name in 1859, but the capital later went to Victoria, for mostly political reasons.

The city has some colorful traditions, including a 100-year-old May Day celebration and the Hyack Anvil Battery, which fires a 21-gun salute in honor of the queen each May 24, using blacksmith anvils and gunpowder instead of cannons.
EXIT 40

Mile 523 (4.5) Km 842 (7): Exit Gaglardi Way to Cariboo Road. Access to private RV park. Also access to Simon Fraser University, atop Burnaby Mountain, which features spectacular architecture and views and an excellent Museum of Archaeology and Ethnology (open daily).
▲ EXIT 37

Mile 524.5 (3) Km 844 (5): Exit Kensington Avenue South for Deer Lake Park, **BURNABY** (pop. 158,000), New Westminster and Highway 99A, which crosses the Fraser on Pattullo Bridge and connects to Highway 99 South, Highway 1A East. Visit Burnaby Heritage Village, 30 buildings depicting pioneer life.
EXIT 33

Mile 525 (2.5) Km 845 (4): Exit to the visitor information centre, Sprott Street and Sperling Avenue, in Burnaby. Go north on Sprott, then east to Burnaby Lake Regional Park; hiking trails, canoeing.
⚲ EXIT 32

Mile 527 (0.5) Km 848 (1): Willingdon Road exit.
EXIT 28A

Mile 527.5 (0) Km 849 (0): **VANCOUVER** city boundary at Grandview Highway. Canada's third largest city, with half the province's population, Vancouver occupies a spectacular setting between the Straight of Georgia and the Coast Mountains. For more information on Greater Vancouver, see the MAJOR CITIES section.
EXIT 28B

Minter Gardens, at Mile 461.5, rivals Victoria's famous Butchart Gardens. Its 27 acres of floral displays feature 11 themed gardens, topiary figures and a rare collection of Chinese Penjing Rock Bonsai. (Liz Bryan)

U.S. HIGHWAY 2

Montana–Idaho Border to Everett, WA
(See maps, pages 28 and 31)

Highway 2 is the last of the U.S. transcontinental highways, a thin ribbon of road, often 2-lane, crossing the northern tier of the country from the Atlantic to the Pacific. *Northwest Mileposts* logs Highway 2 from the Montana–Idaho border west to Interstate 5 at Everett, WA.

The route is rich with history, scenery and wildlife. There is much to see and it's advisable to allow ample travel time for spontaneous side trips. One of the most prominent attractions along Highway 2 is the world's largest hydroelectric dam at Grand Coulee.

Travel on this highway is much slower and decidedly more scenic than in the fast lane of the east-west interstate highways. Travelers should be prepared for ice and snow in fall and winter. As a rule, the highway is a well-maintained all-season route. Chains may be required in winter crossing Stevens Pass in the Cascade Mountains, approximately 67 miles east of I-5. In winter, phone the Washington State Patrol for current pass conditions. Gas stations, modern motels and the usual highway service facilities are numerous and convenient.

In Idaho, physical mileposts on U.S. 2 indicate distance from the Washington–Idaho border, except for a 37-mile section between Sandpoint and Bonners Ferry, where U.S. 2 shares a common alignment with U.S. 95 and mileposts reflect distance from the Washington–Idaho border via U.S. 95. Mileposts in Washington reflect distance from the U.S. Highway 2 junction with I-5 at Everett.

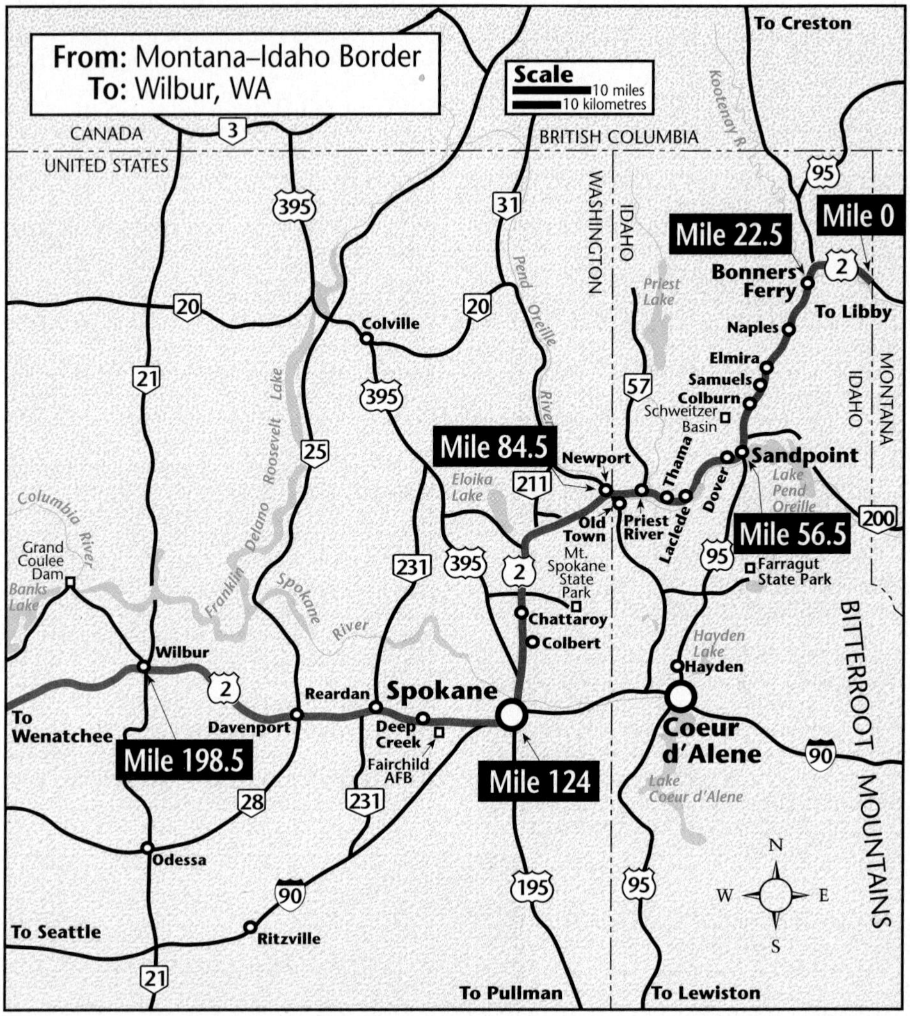

From: Montana–Idaho Border
To: Wilbur, WA

Scale 10 miles / 10 kilometres

[Map showing U.S. Highway 2 from Montana–Idaho Border to Wilbur, WA, with locations including Mile 0, Mile 22.5, Mile 56.5, Mile 84.5, Mile 124, Mile 198.5; towns including Bonners Ferry, Naples, Elmira, Samuels, Colburn, Sandpoint, Dover, Priest River, Old Town, Newport, Chattaroy, Colbert, Spokane, Reardan, Davenport, Wilbur, Odessa, Ritzville, Coeur d'Alene, Hayden, Colville; routes 3, 95, 31, 20, 395, 57, 211, 231, 2, 21, 25, 28, 195, 90; features Grand Coulee Dam, Banks Lake, Columbia River, Priest Lake, Lake Pend Oreille, Hayden Lake, Lake Coeur d'Alene, Franklin Delano Roosevelt Lake, Kootenay River, Pend Oreille River, Spokane River, Farragut State Park, Mt. Spokane State Park, Fairchild AFB, Deep Creek, Eloika Lake, Schweitzer Basin, Bitterroot Mountains; directional references To Creston, To Libby, To Wenatchee, To Seattle, To Pullman, To Lewiston; Canada/United States border, British Columbia, Washington, Idaho, Montana]

U.S. Highway 2 Log

Distance from Montana–Idaho border is followed by distance from Everett, WA.

Mile 0 (415.5): Montana–Idaho state border. Mountain–Pacific time zone line. Pacific time is 1 hour earlier than Mountain. Restaurant, bingo parlor, gas and phone.   MP 80

Mile 3.5 (412): Side road leads 2 miles north to Herman Lake in Kaniksu National Forest. There is a resort on Herman Lake with rental boats, swimming area and an excellent largemouth bass potential. This is moose country, and the largest of North America's deer family are frequently visible from the road.

Mile 10 (405.5): MOYIE SPRINGS (pop. 415). Gas and grocery. An overlook on the outskirts of town has a view down into a deep gorge and the town. Private campground resort (open May to Oct.) with shaded tent and RV sites along the Moyie River; turn south at east end of bridge. Moyie River Road (gravel) leads north along the Moyie River to the spectacular Moyie Falls and dam and also campgrounds. The Moyie is a whitewater stream with a local reputation for rafting thrills and producing pan-sized trout when fly-fishing.   ▲ MP 70

Mile 16 (399.5): Junction of U.S. Highway 2 with U.S. Highway 95; turn to **Mile 630.5** in the U.S. HIGHWAY 95 section for log of that route. (Highways 2 and 95 share a common alignment south to Sandpoint.)

County airport, several service stations and a hotel are located at this intersection.

Mile 18.5 (397): Historical marker commemorating David Thompson's passage. The famous map maker and trader for the North West Co. explored this area in 1808.

Mile 20.5 (395): Start of 1.5 miles of 6 percent downhill grade westbound to the Kootenai River.

Mile 22.5 (393): BONNERS FERRY (pop. 2,600) and Kootenai River bridge. All services, including motels, restaurants, gas stations, pharmacy, hardware stores and supermarket. Here, in 1808, trappers David Thompson and Finan McDonald established a fur-trading post. It was not until 1864, though, that a permanent settlement was founded, named after E.L. Bonner's ferry, which carried gold miners headed to the Canadian Wild Horse lode. Bonners Ferry is the county seat of Boundary County and its economy is dependent on farming and lumber. Tree farming and nursery stock has become a major new industry here. Visitor services are limited and hunting and fishing are the major recreational opportunities. Bonners Ferry ranger station has information and maps on Kaniksu National Forest.

Bonners Ferry is a mecca for wildlife photographers and wildlife viewing. Kootenai National Wildlife Refuge is 5 miles from the Kootenai River bridge. There is a loop auto tour along the refuge's dike system for viewing mallards, pintails, Canada geese, swans, great blue herons, sandpipers and other marsh and shorebirds. MP 506

Mile 26.5 (389): Geologic and historic site. Parts of 1864–65 gold rush trail can be seen. Sign explains glacial lake formation during ice age.

Mile 29.5 (386): Start of 5 percent downgrade for next 1.5 miles westbound.

Mile 30 (385.5): Pleasant Valley.

Mile 32 (383.5): Blue Lake private campground. Winter snowmobile recreation area trailhead 3 miles west. ▲

Mile 33 (382.5): NAPLES is a small community with a general store and gasoline pumps.

Mile 37 (378.5): Sportsman's access to Kaniksu National Forest, Kootenai National Wildlife Refuge and McArthur Lake Farm Management Area. The highway runs the eastern edge of the popular bass, perch and crappie lake. ◄

Mile 37.5 (378): Small town of **ELMIRA**. Gas and food available. MP 490

Mile 41.5 (374): Small community of **SAMUELS**. No services. MP 486

Mile 42 (373.5): Bridge crosses the Pack River, a major tributary of giant Lake Pend Oreille. Above the bridge the Pack is small and fair to good for trout fishing with light tackle and is accessible from gravel Forest Service road. Downstream from Highway 2 the Pack River is broad, slow and not a significant contributor to the regional fishery. ◄

Mile 44.5 (371): COLBURN. Service station, groceries, bar and cafe. MP 483

Mile 53.5 (362): The northern edge of Sandpoint and **junction** with the road to Schweitzer ski area (11 miles). Schweitzer Mountain Resort has 1 high-speed quad and 5 double-chair lifts, with 2,300 acres of skiing. The resort has a lodge with food service, ski school, rentals, slope-side accommodations and groomed cross-country ski trails. Phone (208) 263-9555; snow conditions (208) 263-9562. In summer, a chair lift remains open for mile-long, 45-minute round-trip rides up the mountain. Stunning view of Lake Pend Oreille. The summer chair lift ride operates daily 11:30 a.m. to 5:30 p.m., mid-June through Labor Day. Also access to Bonner County Fairgrounds. ◄

Mile 54.5 (361): Junction with Idaho Highway 200.

Mile 55 (360.5): Chamber of Commerce information center. The friendly and helpful staff here provide maps and travel information.

Mile 56.5 (359): SANDPOINT (pop. 6,500) has all tourist facilities, including some top hotels and restaurants along Lake Pend Oreille. Of interest is the Cedar Street bridge shopping center, a 2-story, rough-lumber-and-glass series of boutiques. The Vintage Wheel Museum, on Cedar Street and 3rd Avenue, displays carriages, steam engines, and automobiles dating from early 1900s to a 1962 Rolls Royce Silver Cloud 2; admission charge.

Sandpoint is situated on Lake Pend Oreille, which is 43 miles long, 6 miles wide, has a shoreline of 111 miles and is up to 1,150 feet deep. It is one of the most popular fishing lakes in the state. Guides and rental boats are available along with first-class boat ramps and moorage facilities. Fishing is concentrated on kokanee salmon and kamloops rainbow, and is celebrated with Kamloops and Kokanee Days early in May each year. This lake is large, confusing and can be dangerous in stormy weather. Newcomers are urged to check with sporting goods stores in Sandpoint for fishing maps of the lake, current catch conditions and guide service.

U.S. Highway 2 **junctions** with U.S. Highway 95 at Sandpoint and the 2 highways follow a common alignment north to Bonners Ferry. See **Mile 594** in the U.S. HIGHWAY 95 section for log of that highway.

Westbound, U.S. Highway 2 follows the Pend Oreille River to the Idaho–Washington border. ◄

Mile 59 (356.5): DOVER (pop. 294). No services. MP 26

Priest Lake

Often called "a sapphire set on an emerald," Priest Lake is one of the Northwest's most visited year-round destinations. Demand is so great at resorts that summer accommodations sometimes require reservations a year in advance. The town of Priest River on U.S. Highway 2 is the gateway to the Priest Lake Recreation Area. The lake is 25 miles north of Priest River via Idaho Highway 57 (turnoff at **Mile 79**).

Despite its popularity, Priest Lake exudes solitude. It is still a place where deer cross front lawns and moose feed in shoreline shallows. Known for its clear waters, 19-mile-long Priest Lake is connected to 2½-mile-long Upper Priest Lake by a 2-mile channel. Upper Priest Lake is not accessible by road.

Except for a small town and a golf course, Priest Lake and its facilities are completely hidden from Highway 57. Along the shores are condominiums, waterfront resorts, bed and breakfasts, 18 campgrounds and several marinas. Water-skiers and jet-skiers predominate, but the bright sails of windsurfers also decorate the lake's surface.

In summer, these lakes offer some of Idaho's best trout fishing. Anglers use everything from surface, leaded, and steel line for jig and fly-fishing.

Hiking trails provide good opportunities to see wildlife as well as enjoy the pine-scented outdoors. Watch for nesting osprey along the lake. Other summer lakeside activities are tennis, horseshoes, volleyball, and swimming in heated pools. Several northshore beaches are favorites of sunbathers. Virtually any and all sport equipment may be rented locally.

Many visitors elect to experience Priest Lake from an island campsite. Kalispell Island's waterfront campsites and large, sandy beaches are often filled with swimmers and sunbathers. Bartoo Island has primitive camping areas and is also known for its large beaches. Four Mile and Eight Mile islands make up in solitude and scenery what they lack in beach area.

For details on Priest Lake campgrounds, and reservations, contact the U.S. Forest Service, Priest Lake Ranger Station, at (208) 443-2512.

In winter, it is usually either sunny or snowing at Priest Lake. With more than 400 miles of groomed trails, winter brings droves of snowmobilers along with ice skaters and ice fishermen. Winter festivities center around the winter carnival, guided winter photo tours, and the Snowlympics held on President's Day. Another Priest Lake tradition is the annual Snowshoe Softball tournament. It is held in conjunction with the U.S. Pacific Coast International Sled Dog Racing Championships. The 2-day event attracts about 75 teams annually from the Western states and Alaska. Hill's Resort (208/443-2551), a popular summer resort, also offers a variety of winter events.

Swimming beach at Luby Bay campground on Priest Lake. (L. Linkhart)

Above—The Pend Oreille River north of Newport, WA. The river flows to the Canadian border and into the Columbia River. *Right*—Sunset on Diamond Lake. (Photos by L. Linkhart)

Mile 69.5 (346): Historic marker commemorating ancient Indian crossing and camp. MP 15

Mile 70.5 (345): LACLEDE. A small community with a tavern and store. Riley Creek Recreation Area is a mile south; 68 campsites, 45 picnic tables, swim beach, boat launch and drinking water. One of the nicest campsites along the river. The river here is part of the Hoodoo Game Management Unit. ⚲▲ MP 14

Mile 78 (337.5): Priest River Recreation Area; 17 campsites, water, swim beach, boat launch and picnic shelter. ⚲▲ MP 7

Mile 79 (336.5): Junction with Highway 57, which leads 25 miles north to Priest Lake at **PRIEST RIVER** (pop. 1,561). Most services are available in Priest River, including gas, food, and public and private campgrounds. The town is at the junction of the Pend Oreille and Priest rivers, and was built by workers on the Great Northern Railroad during the early part of the 1890s. Fishermen will find boat launches at the city park and city dock, boat rentals, a marina and commercial outfitters. Local sporting goods outlets can provide current hunting and fishing information. Priest Lake to the north is a popular destination offering watersports, fishing, resorts and camping (see feature on page 29). ⟋▲★

Mile 80.5 (335): Public golf course. MP 4

Mile 82.5 (333): Albeni Dam Visitor Center and viewpoint. Albeni Cove Campground; 13 sites, picnic facilities, boat launch and swim beach. ⚲▲ MP 2

Mile 84.5 (331): OLD TOWN, ID (pop. 151), and **NEWPORT,** WA (pop. 1,745). These towns straddle the state borderline and the Pend Oreille River. The towns have modest tourist facilities (gas, supermarket), most of which are on the Washington side. **Junction** with Idaho Highway 415 to Spirit Lake and Coeur d'Alene, and with Washington Highway 20 west to Cusick and Metaline Falls.

Mile 93.5 (322): DIAMOND LAKE, a resort area popular with Spokane residents, has cutthroat trout fishing, boat launch, rentals and gas station. ⟋

Mile 98 (317.5): Junction with Washington Highway 211, which goes due north to join Highway 20 at Usk. Access

to Kalispell Indian Reservation, Pend Oreille River Recreation Area and Metaline Falls.

Mile 101 (314.5): A 6-mile stretch of 4-lane highway begins southbound. Access to Sacheen Lake and Pend Oreille County Park, which has a trailer park, hiking and horseback riding. 🚶

Mile 105 (310.5): Turnoff west for road to Eloika Lake, which has camping, service stations and is one of the best largemouth bass and crappie lakes in this region. There are resort facilities, boat rentals and boat launches at the lake. Good duck and white-tailed deer hunting in the fall. ⟋▲

Mile 109 (306.5): Community of **RIVERSIDE;** gas and food.

Mile 110.5 (305): Junction with all-weather road west to Deer Park on U.S. Highway 395. Bear Lake County Park with swimming and picnic areas. ⚲

Mile 111 (304.5): CHATTAROY, an unincorporated town with limited services. The road bridges the Little Spokane River, which flows mostly through private ranch property, but can provide fair trout fishing for rainbow and brookies if you ask permission. There is a

small campground (4 sites) 4 miles northeast of Chattaroy accessible from Bruce Road. ⟋▲

Mile 120 (295.5): Junction with Highway 206, which leads east about 20 miles to Mount Spokane State Park (12 tent sites) and the downhill ski area. Mount Spokane (elev. 5,878 feet) rises abruptly on the eastern horizon. Gas and food at intersection. Mount Spokane ski area has 5 double-chair lifts. Season is mid-Nov. to mid-April; night skiing. Phone (509) 238-6281. ⛷▲

Mile 124 (291.5): SPOKANE (pop. 177,200) city limits. See the MAJOR CITIES section for detailed information on Spokane.

Mile 126.5 (289): Junction of U.S. Highway 395 and U.S. Highway 2. The highways merge to become Division Street, a heavily traveled thoroughfare lined with shopping malls and other services.

Mile 128.5 (287): Junction with Highway 291 to Nine Mile Falls, Tum Tum and Riverside State Park, which has 101 campsites and a boat launch. ▲

Mile 132.5 (283): Junction with Interstate 90. U.S. Highway 2 merges with Interstate 90 for 4 miles westbound. Travelers continuing on Interstate 90 in either direction turn to **Mile 281** in the INTERSTATE 90 section for log.

Mile 134.5 (281): Exit to U.S. Highway 195 south to Colfax and Pullman. EXIT 279

Mile 136.5 (279): Exit to Spokane Falls Community College, Spokane Airport. **Junction** of Interstate 90 and U.S. Highway 2 west.
EXIT 277

Mile 141.5 (274): Community of **AIRWAY HEIGHTS;** gas and restaurants.

Mile 144 (271.5): FAIRCHILD AIR FORCE BASE (pop. 4,000); the largest refueling wing in the world.

Mile 145.5 (270): Fairchild Hospital.

Mile 146.5 (269): Junction with Highway 902 South to Medical Lake.

Mile 147.5 (268): Community of **DEEP CREEK**.

Mile 150.5 (265): Historical marker commemorating the explorers, fur traders, soldiers, missionaries and pioneers who forged the Colville Walla Walla Road in 1811.

Mile 153.5 (262): Junction with road that leads south 8 miles to Waukon.   MP 265.5

Mile 155.5 (260): REARDAN (pop. 510). This small incorporated town is at the intersection of U.S. Highway 2 and Washington Highway 231 north to Long Lake Dam and Springdale.   MP 262

Mile 158.5 (257): Junction with Highway 231 south to Edwall and Sprague.

Mile 169 (246.5): DAVENPORT (pop. 1,505) is the county seat of Lincoln County, and the intersection of U.S. Highway 2 and Washington highways 28 and 25. Lincoln County is the largest wheat-producing county in the nation. The county fair is held here the last weekend in August. Lincoln County Museum, 1 block south of Highway 2 in Davenport, is open daily in summer.

Highway 28 leads to Harrington. Highway 25 leads north to Coulee Dam National Recreation Area (see MAJOR ATTRACTIONS section), following Lake Roosevelt north to the Canadian border. Franklin D. Roosevelt Lake impounds the Columbia River behind Grand Coulee Dam.

There are Coulee Dam National Recreation Area campgrounds 20 miles north of Davenport at Porcupine Bay (29 campsites, swimming, boating and picnic facilities) and 23 miles north at Fort Spokane (67 campsites, handicap-accessible facilities, swimming, boating and picnic facilities). Established in 1880 at the confluence of the Spokane and Columbia rivers, Fort Spokane was the last of the frontier Army posts to be established in the Pacific Northwest. A visitor center at the fort is open 9 a.m. to 6 p.m. daily, May through Sept.; phone (509) 633-3836.   ᴦᴬ▲

Mile 182 (233.5): Rest area with handicap-accessible facilities on the south side of the highway. This part of the region is notable for the number of lava outcroppings seen along the highway, which make farming difficult because they can't be easily and cheaply moved, so equipment has to be driven around them. This area is generally known as the Big Bend because the Columbia River takes a big southward swing to the west well beyond Grand Coulee Dam.   ᴦᴬ MP 238

Mile 187 (228.5): Junction with north road to Fort Spokane (18 miles) and Kettle Falls (76 miles).

Mile 189.5 (226): CRESTON, a small town (pop. 245) with gas and restaurants. Creston is famous for the arrival of Harry Tracy in August 1902. He was a hard-case criminal who had escaped from an Oregon penitentiary with another prisoner, and they went through Washington robbing and shooting. Tracy was cornered in a field near town, but he committed suicide rather than surrender.   MP 230

Mile 194 (221.5): Access road north to Sherman (5 miles).   MP 226

Mile 198.5 (217): WILBUR (pop. 870) is a major intersection with the east-west Highway 2 being principal and Highway 21 running south-north from Interstate 90 across the Columbia River and into the Colville Indian Reservation. Also, Highway 174 leads northwest from Wilbur to Grand Coulee Dam.

Wilbur was named for Samuel Wilbur Condit, the first homesteader in the area. He was known as "Wild Goose Bill" because he once shot into what he thought was a flock of wild geese and downed a tame goose belonging to a settler. Thus, until it was platted in 1889, the community was called Goosetown. Wilbur's Big Bend Museum, located 1 block off Main Street, is open Saturdays, June to Aug., from 2 to 5 p.m. Highway 21 north from Wilbur leads to a tiny auto ferry, referred to as the Keller Ferry, that crosses Lake Roosevelt. Keller Ferry Campground; 55 sites, open all year. The crossing is free and quite an experience.   ▲ MP 222

Mile 203.5 (212): Road to the community of GOVAN, 1 mile off the highway.

Mile 210 (205.5): ALMIRA (pop. 305) is mainly an agricultural community. Gas, food and lodging.   MP 210

Mile 218.5 (197): HARTLINE (pop. 180) is another incorporated farming town; restaurant. Many towns in this area were established first as railroad sidings with elevators built by the railroads to stimulate business.   MP 202

Mile 229 (186.5): COULEE CITY (pop. 598), just west of the **junction** of U.S. Highway 2 and Washington Highway 155. Highway 155 follows the east shore of Banks Lake north to Grand Coulee Dam (see GRAND COULEE SIDE TRIP this section). Coulee City has all services. Camping at Coulee City Park on Banks Lake and 16 miles north on Highway 155 at Steamboat Rock State Park (handicap-accessible facilities). Coulee City is one of a trio of towns with names that confuse visitors, the other 2 being Coulee Dam and Grand Coulee some 25 miles north. Banks Lake is a major recreation area for boaters and fishermen.   ⬤◀▲★ MP 192

Mile 233 (182.5): Junction with Highway 17, which leads south 2 miles to Dry Falls State Park, a spectacular ancient waterfall, and 4 miles to Sun Lakes State Park, a popular camping and watersports area. Handicap-accessible facilities at park. (See GRAND COULEE SIDE TRIP this section.)   ᴦ◀▲★

Mile 234.5 (181): Junction with Highway 17 north to Bridgeport and Chief Joseph Dam.

Mile 249 (166.5): Winding descent westbound to the floor of Moses Coulee. This is one of the longest of the coulees in the region, running from Grimes and Jameson lakes to the north, southwest to the Columbia River a few miles downstream from Wenatchee. Most of the coulee floor is irrigated farming now, and less than a mile south of Highway 2 is a unique suspended irrigation system. The basalt walls are fairly narrow here and sheer, so the farmer strung steel cables back and forth between the walls and hung irrigation sprinklers from them, making it

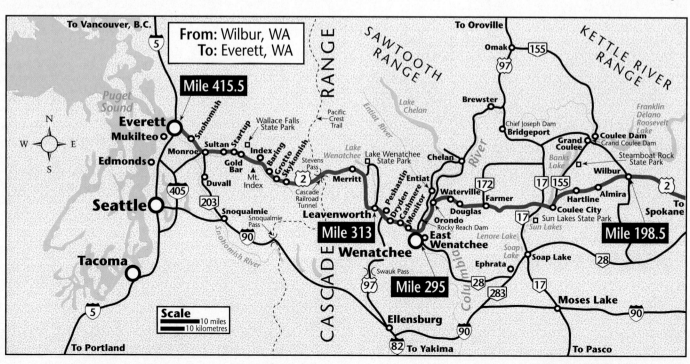

unnecessary to move the sprinklers.

There are resorts on Jameson Lake, which in the spring is considered one of the best rainbow trout producers in the state. Grimes Lake is a highly alkaline lake that has been stocked with Lahontan cutthroat, imported from Nevada's Pyramid Lake and growing to 10 or 12 lbs. No facilities on Grimes, but boat rentals can be arranged at Jameson Lake Resort. Turnoff for Jameson Lake to north.
⬤ MP 173

Mile 251 (164.5): Road leads 8 miles south to Rimrock.

Mile 258 (157.5): Washington Highway 172 leads north to Mansfield.

Mile 267 (148.5): DOUGLAS, former county seat of Douglas County before they lost it to Waterville, is a tiny but picturesque village in a small coulee.

Mile 271 (144.5): WATERVILLE (pop. 1,015) is the county seat of Douglas County. Limited services. Waterville's business district contains 17 historic brick buildings constructed in the late 1800s. The town has a small museum on Walnut Street that contains pioneer relics and a large rock collection, including the 73-lb. iron and nickel Waterville meteorite discovered in 1917, the first recovered in the state.   MP 150

Mile 274 (141.5): The highway drops rapidly westbound, from the 2,800-foot Waterville plateau down the picturesque Pine Canyon to the Columbia River valley, which is 700 feet above sea level here. A small ski area has been developed at the head of the canyon. Watch for turnoff to Badger Mountain ski area, open weekends for 3 months in winter.

This is a popular spot with local residents. There are rope tows, snowmobiling, sledding and cross-country skiing (no groomed trails). The lodge serves hamburgers. It's a good place for kids to learn how to ski. No rentals. Walk-in about ¼ mile to ski area; phone (509) 745-8541 for more information.   ⬤

Mile 281 (134.5): Junction with Highway 97 at Orondo. Travelers continuing on Highway 97 to Chelan, turn to **Mile 482** in the U.S. HIGHWAY 97 section for log. Southbound Highway 97 merges with Highway 2 for the next several miles.

ORONDO was named for Indians of the same name who worked the copper mines near Lake Superior. It is a major orchard town and you will see thousands of trees—apple, cherry, peach, etc.—along the roadside, stands selling the fresh fruit and fresh vegetables in season, and mountains of pick-

Grand Coulee Side Trip
Washington Highways 155 and 17

Two interesting side trips from U.S. Highway 2, one 30 miles north on Washington Highway 155, and the other 20 miles south on Highway 17, offer an introduction to Grand Coulee country. See also Coulee Dam National Recreation Area in the MAJOR ATTRACTIONS section.

Following are logs of both these routes, showing distance measured from the junction with U.S. Highway 2.

HIGHWAY 155

Mile 0: Highway 155 **junctions** with U.S. 2 just east of Coulee City, **Mile 229.** This route parallels 27-mile-long Banks Lake, which was formed by Grand Coulee Dam and is used as a reservoir for irrigation water. Along the first 10 miles there are many dirt roads leading from the highway to the water's edge; trailers and motorhomes cluster at the lakeside for tailgate fishing, picnicking and informal camping.

Mile 9: Public fishing area and boat launch.

Mile 16: Steamboat Rock State Park (phone 509/633-1304). Steamboat Butte rises 700 feet above Banks Lake, and was used as a reference point by Indians and pioneers. It's still used as a visual reference by pilots. A hiking trail leads to the top, where there are panoramic views of the surrounding area. Situated on a peninsula in Banks Lake, Steamboat Rock attracts fishermen drawn to the lake's walleye, crappie and rainbow trout. Many largemouth and smallmouth bass tournaments are held here. The park has more than 100 full-hookup campsites, tent areas, handicap-accessible facilities, boat launch and concessions.

Mile 18: Historical marker tells of Indians, fur traders, military expeditions and settlers who traveled this route.

Mile 19: Steamboat Rock rest area and boat launch. Informal camping.

Mile 25: ELECTRIC CITY (pop. 915) is primarily a residential community for Grand Coulee Dam employees. All services available, including airport.

MILE 25.5: City of GRAND COULEE (pop. 1,010). All services available.

Mile 28: City of COULEE DAM (pop. 1,087) and Grand Coulee Dam Visitor Center. Grand Coulee Dam is the world's largest concrete structure. Visitor center displays highlight the project's history and technology. A self-guided tour brochure covers the visitor center, pump-generator plant, spillway and power plants. From Memorial Day through Labor Day, Grand Coulee tops off the evening with an after-dark laser light show. Visitor center hours are 8:30 a.m. to the end of the laser light show in summer, 9 a.m. to 5 p.m. the rest of the year. Self-guided tours available daily in summer. Laser light show at 10 p.m. May 27 through July, 9:30 p.m. in August and 8:30 p.m. in September. Phone the visitor center at (509) 633-9265 for more information.

One block east of Highway 155 in Coulee Dam is the Colville Confederated Tribes Museum, featuring murals and dioramas.

HIGHWAY 17

Mile 0: Highway 17 **junctions** with U.S. Highway 2 at **Mile 233.**

Mile 2: Dry Falls Visitor Center (handicap-accessible); phone (509) 632-5214. Open 10 a.m. to 6 p.m. daily in summer. Centuries ago, Dry Falls was the largest waterfall on earth. It equaled 5 Niagaras in width, was 2½ times its height and 100 times more powerful. The wall of water dropped 400 feet over a double crescent 3 miles wide. In the visitor center are geologic time charts and relief maps that interpret the formation of Grand Coulee County and Dry Falls. A path leads 400 feet down to the falls base and a small cave. On the floor of the falls are Deep Lake, Perch Lake and Dry Falls Lake. All are accessible by car from Sun Lakes State Park.

Mile 4: Sun Lakes State Park (phone 509/632-5583) sprawls over 4,000 acres of desert with most of it sandwiched between 400- to 800-foot cliffs. Inside are 10 small lakes, several natural springs, 17 miles of trails and 12 miles of equestrian trails. It also has a 9-hole

A popular attraction at Coulee Dam is the nightly laser light show in summer. (Courtesy of Grand Coulee Dam Area Chamber of Commerce)

ing bins. The rugged hill to the east of the highway is Badger Mountain (elev. 3,500 feet), a landmark for the Wenatchee area.

MP 140

Mile 288.5 (127): Lincoln Rock State Park and Rocky Reach Dam. The park offers 66 RV and 28 tent sites, picnic areas, boat launch and handicap-accessible facilities. Steelhead and trout are fished along the bank at Rocky Reach Dam. (The Rocky Reach Dam visitor center and museum are accessible only from the west side of the river via Highway 97 Alternate.) ⚿⚐⚑▲

Mile 293 (122.5): Junction with Washington Highway 28 (Sunset Highway), which leads south 4 miles to East Wenatchee. Access to central Wenatchee via Columbia River bridge from East Wenatchee. Continue west on Highway 2 to bypass city.

Mile 294 (121.5): Junction with Highway 97 Alternate, which follows the west side of Lake Entiat north to Chelan.

Mile 295 (120.5): Junction with Wenatchee Avenue and access south to **WENATCHEE** (pop. 22,710) city center. Wenatchee is the center of the fruit growing industry in central Washington, and its name is synonymous with apples. The major event each year is the Apple Blossom Festival held from the last weekend in April through the first weekend in May, with the Grand Parade (and big crowds) taking place the last weekend. Phone 1-800-57-APPLE for more information. Shopping at Valley North Mall at the north end of town, downtown and in East Wenatchee. Major motels are located along Wenatchee Avenue. All visitor services are available.

A major attraction here is Ohme Gardens

County Park, located 3 █████ off Highway 97 Alternate ████ overlooks the Wenatche ████ Columbia River and features g███ from alpine to tropical. Open ███ sion fee.

The North Central Washington ███ in downtown Wenatchee at 127 Sou██ sion, has displays depicting pioneer life██ natural history and Native culture of ██ region. Open daily, admission fee; phon██ (509) 664-5989.

North of town 7 miles on Highway 97 Alternate is Rocky Reach Dam, with a visitor center, excellent museum, fish ladder and grassy picnic area. Open daily, free; phone (509) 663-7522.

South of town 13 miles is Mission Ridge, a popular ski resort with 4 double-chair lifts, 2 rope tows and 33 groomed ski runs. Ski school, rentals, open daily, free transportation from Wenatchee. Phone the resort at (509) 663-7631; ski conditions 1-800-374-1693. Near Mission Ridge is Squilchuck Recreation Area with 20 campsites. ⚲▲

Mile 299 (116.5): Small town of **MONITOR**. Camping at Wenatchee River County Park south of highway along the river; 40 full hookups, 24 with water and electricity, restrooms, picnic tables and shelter. Nice view of the Wenatchee River, which is fished in summer for trout and in the fall and early winter for steelhead and salmon.

⚐⚑▲ MP 115

Mile 303 (112.5): CASHMERE (pop. 2,560) has a motel, bed and breakfast, several restaurants, a pharmacy, hardware store and shopping. Cashmere is probably best known as the home of Aplets and Cotlets, a confection that has been described as a sweetmeat flavored with apple or apricot juice and enriched with walnuts and spices. Free tours of the candy kitchen at Liberty Orchards (117–123 Mission Street) are offered daily from May to Dec., and most weekdays from Jan. through April. Phone (509) 782-2191 for more information. The Chelan County Museum and Pioneer Village here is noted for the quality reconstruction of the village buildings and the Indian artifact collection. Open daily, admission fee; phone (509) 782-3230. The Chelan County fairgrounds are located at the west end of town. MP 111

Mile 306.5 (109): Peshastin Pinnacles State Park, a popular spot with rock climbers. Picnic tables. ⚐

Mile 308 (107.5): DRYDEN is a small fruit town with gas, food and groceries available.

Mile 308.5 (107): Crossing the Wenatchee River. This section of the river is one of the most popular in the state with river runners.

Mile 310 (105.5): Junction with U.S. Highway 97, which leads south over Blewett Pass (actually named Swauk Pass, but engraved in all Northwesterners' memories as Blewett, the original tortuous pass that was abandoned in favor of the lower and straighter Swauk Pass) to Interstate 90, a distance of 50 miles. For Highway 97 log south from here, turn to **Mile 449** in the U.S. HIGHWAY 97 section and read that log back to front.

Mile 311 (104.5): PESHASTIN, unincorporated, is primarily a sawmill town just across

Sun Lakes State Park, 4 miles south of Highway 2, has camping and swimming.

(L. Linkhart)

golf course, heated swimming pool, environmental learning center, handicap-accessible facilities and 4 boat launches. From opening day of fishing season to Labor Day, the lakes are prime fishing spots for rainbow, eastern brook and German brown trout. Sunbathers, boaters and swimmers take over during July and August when temperatures soar into the 90s and 100s. Sun Lakes has 181 campsites.

Mile 6.5: Private campground with store.

Mile 7: Rest area.

Mile 9: Blue Lake Resort and historical marker at site of an ancient Indian campground and Caribou Cattle Trail Crossing. Blue Lake is an excellent rainbow fishery.

Mile 10.5: Popular public fishing area.

Mile 12: Access to Lake Lenore Caves via a 0.4-mile good gravel road. A moderately steep 0.7-mile hiking trail leads from the parking area to the shelters.

Mile 15: Lake Lenore produced Washington's record Lahontan cutthroat trout. Fish taken from here average 16 to 20 inches. The lake is open year-round to artificial flies and lures and single pointed barbless hooks only. Catch limit is 1 fish daily.

Mile 20.5: SOAP LAKE (pop. 1,100). Indians camped at Soap Lake for centuries to use its healing waters, and they actually called it Smoki-am, which means "healing waters." Cowboys and settlers learned of the healthlike quality from Indians. White men named it Soap Lake because of the soapy feel of the water and the "suds" that formed along the shore.

The lake's water contains 17 minerals and an ishthyol-like oil. Visitors have claimed its waters have helped relieve arthritis, psoriasis, acne and Buergers disease. A city park on the lakeshore has a campground with playground equipment. The lake is used by windsurfers, water-skiers and swimmers.

From Soap Lake, travelers have the option of backtracking to U.S. Highway 2 or continuing south to Interstate 90.

... e highway. This ... heading areas ... th boat launch

... **LEAVEN-** ... or facilities ... tels, restau- ... nworth was ... s; it decid- ... the 1960s ... ng and the ... coming a ghost ... n has frequent festivals, ... ing Maifest (early May), the Autumn Leaf Festival (October) and the Christmas Lighting Festival (early December). Throughout the summer, arts and crafts events are held. Rafting the Wenatchee River to Monitor is very popular, with several whitewater outfitters operating here in season. Leavenworth is also a popular destination with cross-country skiers during the winter.

★ MP 100

Mile 314 (101.5): Icicle Creek Road west of town leads southwest to hiking trails and Forest Service campgrounds up Icicle Canyon, a popular rock climbing practice area. Icicle Creek is also a popular rainbow trout stream. 🏕🛶▲ MP 99

Mile 314.5 (101): East end of Tumwater Canyon, one of the prettiest drives in Washington, which goes 10 miles west from here along the Wenatchee River through a sheer canyon with lots of waterfalls and rapids. The canyon is famous for its fall colors, and tour companies run dozens of buses over to Leavenworth with an emphasis on the canyon. The Wenatchee River heads near the west end of the canyon at Lake Wenatchee and flows east to join the Columbia River at the town of Wenatchee. It is one of the best rivers for river runners in the Washington Cascades, although the Tumwater Canyon section of the river is generally considered unrunnable. Commercial raft trips on the Wenatchee are run from Leavenworth to Cashmere or Monitor. Inquire in Leavenworth. The Wenatchee is a rough, complicated river and should not be attempted by novice floaters. In summer this area is heavily stocked with fat rainbow, and fishing can be good with bait, flies or spinners. 🛶★

Mile 318 (97.5): Swiftwater Forest Service campground, with 76 sites, tables. This is one of the very few places in the narrow canyon where you can safely pull off the highway. The river near the campground is stocked during the summer with rainbow trout. 🛶▲ MP 93

Mile 319.5 (96): Tumwater Forest Service campground with 80 sites and picnic tables, and Wenatchee River bridge at the head of the canyon. Access to state fish hatchery. 🏕▲

Mile 328 (87.5): Coles Corner; restaurants and service stations. **Junction** with Highway 207, which leads to Lake Wenatchee State Park (3 miles north) and Fish Lake. Lake Wenatchee is 2,445 acres and 5 miles long. The state park campground is one of the most popular in the state, with 199 sites, handicap-accessible facilities, showers and swim beach. Several resorts also service the lake, the largest of which is the Cougar Inn on the lake's northwest shore. Anglers troll

for rainbow, cutthroat, kokanee and sometimes, depending on seasonal restrictions, Dolly Varden and sockeye salmon.

Additional and more primitive camping can be found in several Wenatchee National Forest campgrounds above the lake by following roads up the Little Wenatchee River, which also offers fair to good light spin and fly-fishing action for rainbow and brook trout. Fish Lake, 1 mile north of Lake Wenatchee, has resort facilities with boat rentals, and is a good rainbow and brown trout fishery, with excellent yellow perch catches reported.

Trailheads take off from the Little Wenatchee to Pacific Crest Trail hiking areas and alpine fishing lakes, with backpack access to the Glacier Peak Wilderness Area, dominated by 10,541-foot Glacier Peak, visible from Glacier View Forest Service campground on the lake's south side. There is a ranger station on Highway 207 where maps and local mountain information are available. ♿🏕🛶▲

Mile 328.5 (87): Nason Creek Campground; 76 sites, tables, stocked rainbow trout in the stream. 🛶▲

Mile 331.5 (84): Highway rest area with handicap-accessible facilities; the last one westbound for many miles. ♿

Mile 333 (82.5): MERRITT, a 1-store town, and a road leading to a Forest Service campground and trailheads. This is a chain-up area for pass traffic. 🏕▲

Mile 334.5 (81): White Pine Road and Cascade Meadows.

Mile 337 (78.5): Mount Lake Trail. MP 76

Mile 342.5 (73): Stevens Pass Nordic Center.

Mile 343.5 (72): Bygone Byways Interpretive Trail.

Mile 344 (71.5): Sno-Park parking south of highway.

Mile 348 (67.5): Summit of Stevens Pass (elev. 4,061 feet). Stevens Pass is a popular ski resort with Puget Sound residents. The resort offers a quad, 4 triple-chair lifts and 6 double-chair lifts. Operates days and evenings from late Nov. through early April. Ski school, rentals, restaurants and lounges, cafeteria, Nordic Center with groomed cross-country skiing trails. Phone Stevens Pass ski

Bavarian-style village of Leavenworth at Mile 313. (L. Linkhart)

area at (360) 973-2441; snow conditions (206) 634-1645. Much of the mountain country south of the pass almost to Interstate 90 is part of the Alpine Lakes Wilderness Area. ↙

Mile 354 (61.5): The western portal of the railroad tunnel beneath Stevens Pass. At 7.8 miles long, it is one of the longest in the world. It is not unusual to spot the creamy white form of mountain goats on the surrounding peaks, and black-tailed deer are frequently seen from the highway.

Mile 356 (59.5): Winter chain-up area for eastbound travelers.

Mile 357 (58.5): Deception Falls south of highway. Picnic area and nature trail north of highway. 🏕🍴

Mile 364 (51.5): Tye River.

Mile 365 (50.5): Skykomish ranger station with a small store and gas pumps nearby. Recreational maps of the Mount Baker/Snoqualmie National Forest and Skykomish Ranger District are available here. Beckler River Forest Service campground 1 mile north. ▲ MP 50

Mile 366 (49.5): SKYKOMISH (pop. 265) city limits. All services are available on the highway. This is primarily a logging town built right on the Skykomish (nicknamed the "Sky") River to the south of the highway. Many river runners put their kayaks and inflatable rafts in the river at Skykomish to drift the upper portions well above the waterfalls and Class VI rapids that characize much of the Skykomish farther west. In this area the Skykomish and a major tributary, the Beckler River, are fished primarily for resident rainbow and cutthroat trout. Downstream the Skykomish is one of the most productive Puget Sound salmon and steelhead streams. ↩

Mile 369 (46.5): Money Creek Forest Service campground with 13 RV and 6 tent sites. Miller River campground, 3.5 miles south, has 18 sites. ▲ MP 46

Mile 374 (41.5): GROTTO, unincorporated, was formerly a town built around a cement plant. Snohomish/King County line. MP 41

Mile 375 (40.5): BARING was named for the nearby mountain of the same name. Limited services. The prominent peak to the southwest is Mount Index (elev. 5,979 feet) and due north is Gunn Peak (elev. 6,245 feet).

Mile 377.5 (38): Mount Baker/Snoqualmie National Forest boundary.

Mile 379.5 (36): Junction with road to **INDEX** (pop. 140), a small town 1 mile north on the North Fork Skykomish River with restaurants, a small hotel and a hardware store. Mount Index looms over the town and the whole area. Its north face is one of the great challenges for rock climbers in the region, and a favorite with photographers.

The high bridge carrying Highway 2 across the Skykomish River marks the beginning of the most popular steelhead and salmon fishing waters. Upstream from the bridge the river is extremely dangerous for float fishermen, and not recommended for novice boatmen. ↩

Mile 384.5 (31): Public fishing access. ↩

Mile 386.5 (29): GOLD BAR (pop. 1,140) is an incorporated town named by an early prospector who found promising "colors" in the river here. It has all visitor services. Just east of town is the road leading to Wallace Falls State Park, 2 miles away, which offers 6 tent sites and handicap-accessible facilities. At the foot of the falls is a trail that leads 2.5 miles to the summit with an excellent view from the 250-foot-high falls. ♿☆▲

Mile 388 (27.5): State salmon hatchery; in the fall you can sometimes see the biologists taking eggs from the salmon.

Mile 389 (26.5): STARTUP, unincorporated, has all services. It originally was named Wallace but after its mail kept going to Wallace, ID, it was renamed in honor of a local sawmill manager named George S. Startup (not, as some suggest, because it is where you start up the mountains). The Wallace River joins the Skykomish River near here.

Mile 390 (25.5): Covered picnic area on riverbank south of highway. ⛱

Mile 393 (22.5): SULTAN (pop. 2,293) began as a rip-snorting frontier mining town, but over the years calmed down to a pleasant little town where the Sultan and Skykomish rivers join. There is a pleasant little park near the Sultan River confluence where steelheaders frequently launch McKenzie-style drift boats and there are tables for picnicking. A road runs north along to the Sultan/Pilchuck Multiple Use Area, 62,000 acres of recreation land, which includes numerous small trout lakes, hiking trails, stream fishing access sites and campgrounds. ♿⛱↩▲

Mile 394 (21.5): Covered picnic area with 1,000-year-old Douglas fir. Lodging. ⛱

Mile 394.5 (21): Wayside chapel.

Mile 400 (15.5): Access north to Monroe public golf course. Crossing Woods Creek.

Mile 402 (13.5): MONROE (pop. 4,970) is probably best known as the home of the state reformatory, but it is also well known as the home of the Evergreen Fairgrounds, located at the west end of town, site of the Evergreen State Fair (held the last week of Aug. through Labor Day). All visitor facilities available, including motels, major fast-food outlets and gas.

Junction with Highway 203, south to Duvall (10 miles) and Fall City (25 miles), and Highway 522, south to Interstate 405 (13 miles). Washington Highway 203 runs south from Monroe, crossing the Skykomish River at the Lewis Street bridge (one of the most popular steelhead and salmon fishing areas on the river), through the scenic Snoqualmie River valley to join Interstate 90 at North Bend (33 miles).

The Duvall–Fall City Road (Highway 203) also provides access to **CARNATION** (pop. 1,100) and the 1,000 acre Carnation Farm overlooking the Snoqualmie Valley. The farm offers self-guiding tours of a milking parlor, maternity barn, calf nursery, dog and cat kennels, and extensive gardens. Started by E.A. Stuart, founder of the Carnation Co., the farm was the site of nutrition testing for Friskies petfood products for many years. Open Monday through Saturday, 10 a.m. to 3 p.m., April through Oct.; phone (206) 788-1511. Carnation Farm is located approximately 17 miles south of Monroe via Highway 203; watch for turnoff to west for farm. Recommended for children and adults! ★

Mile 404.5 (11): Junction with access road to **SNOHOMISH** (pop. 6,650), one of the most historic towns in the region, with much of the original Victorian architecture surviving. The town was founded in 1854. Once a shipping center on the Snohomish River, it now is best known for its antique shopping center. Follow signs for historic district, which is where most of the antique shops are located. Snohomish has bed-and-breakfast accommodations, restaurants, major fast-food outlets, gas stations and supermarkets.

Mile 405 (10.5): Rest area. MP 10

Mile 407.5 (8): Access north to Snohomish public golf course and south to Snohomish.

Mile 408.5 (7): Pilchuck River.

Mile 410 (5.5): Junction with Highway 9 north to Arlington (17 miles) and south to Highway 522 to Bothell (17 miles). MP 4

Mile 412.5 (3): Junction with Highway 204 north to Lake Stevens. Start of the 2-mile-long Snohomish River bridge and causeway that protects the highway from the annual floods that are part of life in the flood plain.

Mile 415.5 (0): Junction of U.S. Highway 2 and Interstate 5. End of U.S. Highway 2 log. Turn to **Mile 502** in the INTERSTATE 5 section for log of that highway.

Landmark statue at Carnation Farm commemorates one of its greatest milk-producers.
(Courtesy of Carnation Farm)

CROWSNEST HIGHWAY 3

Alberta–British Columbia Border to Hope, BC
(See maps, pages 37 and 39)

Crowsnest Highway 3 is a scenic route that snakes its way west from Medicine Hat, AB, to Hope, BC. *Northwest Mileposts*® logs Highway 3 from the Alberta–British Columbia border to Hope.

Highway 3 crosses historic Crowsnest Pass, from which it derives its name, in the Rocky Mountains. Continuing west, the highway crosses 3 other high mountain passes—through the Selkirks, Monashees and Cascades—before dropping into the Fraser River valley at Hope. From Cranbrook to Hope, the highway follows the Dewdney Trail, forced through the wilderness in the 1800s by Edgar Dewdney to provide access to the gold diggings of the southern interior of British Columbia.

Crowsnest Highway 3 Log

Distance in miles from the Alberta–British Columbia border is followed by distance in miles from Hope, BC. Equivalent distances in kilometres are indicated by Km.

Mile 0 (534) Km 0 (859.5): Alberta–British Columbia border at Crowsnest Pass on the Continental Divide. The pass is one of the lowest in the Rockies (elev. 4,534 feet/ 1,382m). Below lies Summit Lake. The old railway community at the east end of the lake has a thriving pub.

Mile 2.5 (531.5) Km 4 (855.5): Crowsnest Provincial Park; overnight parking for 25 vehicles, picnic tables, and interpretive display of human and natural history of pass area. ⊼

Mile 6 (528) Km 9.5 (850): Road south to Byron Creek collieries.

Mile 9 (525) Km 14.5 (845): Michel Hotel, still in operation, is the only building left of the towns of Michel and Natal. Residents of both communities moved into the new towns when strip-mining operations began. A short distance west, old brick colliery buildings date from 1909.

Mile 10 (524) Km 16.5 (843): Road passes through Elkview Coal Corp. headquarters.

Mile 12.5 (521.5) Km 20.5 (839): Junction with Highway 43, which leads north 8 miles/13 km to Crowsnest Resources Line Creek open-pit coal mine and 22 miles/35 km to community of **ELKFORD** (pop. 3,000), one of the new mining towns built near 2 large metallurgical coal operations—Fording Coal and Westar/Greenhills.

Mile 13 (521) Km 21 (838.5): Access north to **SPARWOOD** (pop. 4,000); all tourist facilities. Sparwood was built in 1968 when Kaiser Resources opened its open-pit coal mine on Harmer Ridge. The mine was bought by the B.C. government in 1980 and operates today as Westar. Daily tours of Canada's largest open-pit coal mine, Balmer, in July and August; visitors can watch the 350-ton Titan Terex truck in action. For tour information, contact the Tourist Information booth on Highway 3 (look for statue of coal miner in front).

Mile 20 (514) Km 32.5 (827): Elk Valley Provincial Park picnic area. ⊼

Mile 21 (513) Km 34 (825.5): Olson rest area. Picnic tables. ⊼

Mile 24 (510) Km 39 (820.5): All that is left of the once-thriving mine settlement of Hosmer is the big old Elk River Inn, still in operation.

Mile 31 (503) Km 49.5 (810): Tourist office on outskirts of Fernie. The oil derrick and drilling equipment displayed outside are reproductions of machinery used in the Flathead Valley southeast of Fernie between 1914 and 1920.

Mile 31.5 (502.5) Km 50.5 (809): Elk River bridge and eastern city limits of **FERNIE** (pop. 5,000); good tourist facilities. One of the earliest of the Crowsnest settlements, Fernie depended on the mines at Coal Creek. Coking ovens, at one time more than 400 of them, were located around the town. But the mine that gave Fernie life also brought a series of disastrous explosions and fires between 1902 and 1917. In 1957 the coal mines closed and Fernie seemed doomed. But the recent opening of large open-pit coal mines has revitalized the town and the area. Fernie retains many of the solid brick buildings of its earlier prosperity, most notably the courthouse, city hall and the Historical Museum (open 1–5 p.m. weekdays in July and August). Heritage walking tour maps are available at the tourist office. Today the city is a popular winter sports centre.

Mile 32.5 (501.5) Km 52.5 (807): Fernie west city limits at Elk River bridge.

View of Mount Hosmer, elev. 8,221 feet/2,505m, in the Rocky Mountains east of Fernie.
(Liz Bryan)

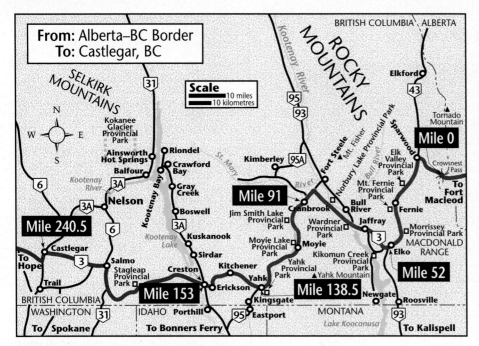

From: Alberta–BC Border
To: Castlegar, BC

Scale
10 miles
10 kilometres

BRITISH COLUMBIA · ALBERTA

SELKIRK MOUNTAINS

ROCKY MOUNTAINS

Kootenay River

Elkford

31

95
93

43

Tornado Mountain

Kokanee Glacier Provincial Park

Ainsworth Hot Springs
Riondel
Crawford Bay
Balfour
Gray Creek

Mile 0

St. Mary River

Fort Steele
Mt. Fisher
Kimberley   95A

Elk Valley Provincial Park
Sparwood
Crowsnest Pass

Kootenay River

6
3A
Nelson
3A
Boswell

Mile 91
Cranbrook

Norbury Lake Provincial Park
Mt. Fernie Provincial Park

Bull River
Jaffray
Fernie
To Fort Macleod

Mile 240.5

Kootenay Lake

Kuskanook

Jim Smith Lake Provincial Park
Wardner Provincial Park

Morrissey Provincial Park
MACDONALD RANGE

6
Castlegar
3
Salmo
Stagleap Provincial Park
Creston
Sirdar
Kitchener
Yahk
Moyie Lake Provincial Park
Moyie

Kikomun Creek Provincial Park
Yahk Provincial Park
Yahk Mountain

Elko

Mile 52

To Hope
Trail

Mile 153
Erickson
Kingsgate
Mile 138.5
Newgate
Roosville

BRITISH COLUMBIA
WASHINGTON
IDAHO
Porthill
Eastport
95
MONTANA
Lake Koocanusa
93

To Spokane   31
To Bonners Ferry
To Kalispell

Mile 34 (500) Km 55 (804.5): Mount Fernie Provincial Park, open June to Sept.; 38 campsites, camping fee, picnic area beside tumbling Lizard Creek. Fishing in the Elk River for cutthroat, Dolly Varden and brook trout.

Mile 36 (498) Km 58 (801.5): Junction with the road to Fernie Snow Valley Recreation Area. Downhill ski resort and cross-country trails.

Mile 42.5 (491.5) Km 68 (791.5): Morrissey Provincial Park beside Elk River offers shaded picnic areas and fishing. History buffs can look for nearby old coke ovens.

Mile 44.5 (489.5) Km 72 (787.5): Highway goes through short rock tunnel. *CAUTION:* Watch for bighorn sheep on road.

Mile 52 (482) Km 84 (775.5): Community of ELKO, named for the Elk River, on which it is situated. Limited services available.

Mile 53 (481) Km 85.5 (774): Junction with Highway 93, which leads south 25 miles/40.5 km to the U.S. border and customs post at Roosville (open 24 hours).

Travelers headed south on Highway 93 turn to the end of the U.S. HIGHWAY 93 section and read the log back to front.

Highways 3 and 93 share a common alignment the next 34.5 miles/55.5 km westbound.

Mile 54 (480) Km 87 (772.5): Road south to Baynes Lake (2.5 miles/4 km); fishing for eastern brook trout. The road also goes to Kikomun Creek Provincial Park (7 miles/11 km) on the east shore of Lake Koocanusa, a large reservoir formed by the Libby Dam on the Kootenai River in Montana; 104 campsites, camping fee, sani-station, picnicking, swimming, fishing and boat launch. Within the park are 2 small lakes, Surveyor's and Hidden (no powerboats). Fishing in Koocanusa for cutthroat, Dolly Varden and whitefish; Surveyor's Lake for eastern brook, rainbow, Dolly Varden, and kokanee in September. One of the largest concentrations of turtles in North America exists here.

Badgers are also abundant.

Mile 57 (477) Km 92 (767.5): Caithness Creek rest area.

Mile 61 (473) Km 98.5 (761): Sawmill community of GALLOWAY.

Mile 63.5 (470.5) Km 102.5 (757): Gravel road to Rosen Lake (north of highway); rainbow and cutthroat trout.

Junction with 2.5-mile/4-km road to Tie Lake Regional Park; day-use only. Gas and food at junction. Also access south to Kikomun Creek Provincial Park and Baynes Lake (see **Mile 54**).

Mile 64.5 (469.5) Km 103.5 (756): Community of Jaffray south of highway.

Mile 71 (463) Km 114 (745.5): Junction with Wardner–Fort Steele Road, which leads north 4 miles/6.5 km to Kootenay trout hatchery. About 6 million rainbow, eastern brook, kokanee, lake and yellowstone cutthroat trout are raised here annually for stocking lakes in the Kootenay and Cariboo region. An aquarium features local fish. Open 8 a.m. to 4 p.m. year-round.

The road also provides access to Norbury Lake Provincial Park, 10 miles/16 km north; 46 campsites, picnic area, fishing, swimming, boat launch (no powerboats) and interpretive display. Picnic tables also at the park's smaller Peckham's Lake under towering crags of The Steeples, part of the Rockies' Hughes Range.

The side road continues north to junction with highways 93/95 at Fort Steele.

Mile 71.5 (462.5) Km 115 (744.5): Kootenay River bridge at north end of Lake Koocanusa. West of the bridge a side road leads 1 mile/2 km to the small community of **WARDNER** and Wardner Provincial Park on Lake Koocanusa; picnicking, swimming and fishing for Dolly Varden, cutthroat trout and whitefish.

Mile 76.5 (457.5) Km 123.5 (736): Stop of interest marker commemorating the Koote-

nay steamboats. Good view of the Kootenay River. In the mining boom days of the 1890s, a fleet of stern-wheelers ran from Fort Steele to Jennings, MT. *NOTE:* This stop is safely accessible only for westbound traffic.

Mile 85 (449) Km 137 (722.5): Rampart rest area.

Mile 87.5 (446.5) Km 141 (718.5): Junction with Highways 93/95 to Fort Steele and Radium Hot Springs. Travelers headed north on Highway 93 turn to **Mile 60** in the CANADA HIGHWAY 93 section. Tourist route map just east of junction.

Highway 3 shares a common alignment eastbound for 34.5 miles/55.5 km with Highway 93, and a common alignment with Highway 95 westbound for the next 51 miles/82 km.

Mile 91 (443) Km 146.5 (713): Junction with Highway 95A for Kimberley (see feature page 38) and Cranbrook airport. Eastern city limits of **CRANBROOK** (pop. 16,000). Highway 3 bypasses the downtown area (for downtown, turn south on Victoria Avenue). Tourist information office on highway is open all year. The main shopping and distribution centre for the East Kootenays, Cranbrook is a thriving city well endowed with tourist facilities. Settled in 1885, Cranbrook was located between the rich gold mines of Moyie to the west and Wildhorse to the east. When the Canadian Pacific Railway's Crowsnest line came through in 1888, it stimulated an instant boom. But unlike many other towns that rose to glory in the 19th century, Cranbrook has retained its ascendancy, though the mines are played out. Several outstanding heritage homes and buildings are in the downtown area. Ask at the visitor centre for tour maps. The Canadian Museum of Rail Travel is not to be missed. Located on Van Horne (bypass route) and Baker streets, it comprises 9 restored cars of the Trans-Canada Limited, one of the great trains of the Canadian Pacific Railway's heyday of the 1920s, plus the original Elko station. Visitors can take tea and crumpets in the dining car while they wait for a guided tour. Open daily 9 a.m. to 8 p.m. June to Aug.; afternoons only the rest of the year. ★

Mile 95 (439) Km 152.5 (707): Western city limits of Cranbrook. Visitor information office (open May to Sept.) on south side of highway by Elizabeth Lake Wildlife Sanctuary. The lake has nesting islands for waterfowl, hiking trails and picnic tables. The 250-acre marsh is an important stop along the Rocky Mountain Trench migration corridor.

Just west of Elizabeth Lake, a side road leads north 2.5 miles/4 km to Jim Smith Lake Provincial Park; 28 campsites, camping fee, picnic area, fishing, boat launch (no powerboats), swimming.

Mile 104 (430) Km 167.5 (692): Access road (0.5 mile/1 km) to Moyie Lake Provincial Park with 104 campsites, camping fee, picnic area, fishing, hiking, swimming, boat launch and sani-station. Popular summer spot, particularly for sailing and windsurfing.

Mile 114 (420) Km 183.5 (676): Viewpoint over Moyie Lake. Sign commemorates David Thompson, the 1st white man to find this route through the Purcell Mountains.

Kimberley

Bavarian Alpine village of Kimberly is about a half-hour's drive north from Cranbrook. (Liz Bryan)

From Cranbrook, **Mile 91** on Crowsnest Highway 3, travelers may head north via Highway 95A to the old mining town of Kimberley, now nicely revamped in Bavarian style. It is 20.5 miles/31 km to Kimberley from Cranbrook.

In 1892, 3 tremendous deposits of galena (silver/lead) were staked in the mountains near Kimberley. One of these became the famous North Star Mine, whose ores were shipped down the Kootenay River to a smelter at Jennings, MT. While the ores were rich, the quantity was limited, and the North Star was soon played out. But the 2 other deposits—Shylock and Hamlet—eventually became the Sullivan mine. Put into production in 1909, the Sullivan became one of the largest lead-zinc mines in the world. Now, its ores are almost depleted, and the mine will close in the year 2000.

Though Kimberley was founded and sustained on mining, the settlement today presents a startling new face as a Bavarian Alpine village, as befits the highest city in Canada (elev. 3,652 feet/1,113m). The town centre has become the Platzl, an L-shaped pedestrian area with tiled walkways, streams, fountains, trees and flower beds, and the world's largest cuckoo clock (it yodels on the hour). The shops and open-air restaurants have Black Forest facades, with window boxes, steeply gabled roofs and hand-painted murals. In summer, a wandering minstrel plays the accordian.

Attractions include the Bavarian City Mining Railway, a train that once hauled ore underground and now takes visitors on a scenic parkland loop. The ski area chair lift operates in summer for great views of the area. There are also thrills on the Alpine bob slide and wet bumper boats. Foot path leads from the Platzl to Cominco Gardens, featuring beautiful flower displays and a tea garden. Two golf courses.

Events in Kimberley include an accordian championship in July and an Alpine folk dance festival in September. In winter, Kimberley comes into its own as a destination ski resort on the slopes of North Star Mountain.

For travelers continuing north from Kimberley to Highways 93/95, it is 16.5 miles/27 km to the junction.

ates, but today produces mainly pine fence posts. The name Yahk is a Kootenai Indian word meaning "river bend" or "bow."

Mile 136 (398) Km 219 (640.5): Yahk Provincial Park with 24 campsites and picnic tables on Moyie River. Camping fee. Good fall fishing for rainbow and cutthroat trout. Open May to Sept.
CAUTION: Watch for deer.

Mile 138.5 (395.5) Km 223 (636.5): **Junction** with Highway 95, which leads south 7.5 miles/12 km to the border crossing at Kingsgate, BC (open 24 hours a day). Travelers headed south on U.S. Highway 95 turn to the end of the U.S. HIGHWAY 95 section and read log back to front.
Eastbound, Highway 3 shares a common alignment with Highway 95 for 51 miles/82 km.

Mile 141 (393) Km 227 (632.5): Kidd Creek rest area. Rock shop opposite the rest area.

Mile 144 (390) Km 231.5 (628): Meadow Creek bridge. Side road south to small community of **KITCHENER**; store, pub, restaurant.

Mile 147.5 (386.5) Km 237.5 (622): Goat River bridge. **ERICKSON**, a farm community surrounded by orchards; many fruit stands. Visit Wayside Gardens and Arboretum, open May to Oct.; roses, rhododendrons and 200 other species of trees and shrubs are featured.

Mile 150.5 (383.5) Km 242 (617.5): Bridge over Goat River to orchard communities of Canyon and Lister. Scenic drive rejoins Highway 3 at Creston.

Mile 153 (381) Km 246.5 (613): **Junction** at Creston with Highway 21 south to U.S. border at Rykerts and Porthill, ID. Customs open daily 8 a.m. to 11 p.m.
CRESTON (pop. 4,200) is primarily a farming town surrounded by fruit orchards and grain and hay fields. There are 2 grain elevators at the west end of town, a sight more familiar on the prairies. The highway east of town is lined with fruit stands, open most of the summer starting with strawberries in June through to apples in the fall. Creston also has several large sawmills and Columbia Brewing Co. (tours available in summer). Tourism is becoming increasingly important. Look for the log cabin Tourist Information Centre on the south side of the highway near town centre. Creston has a wide variety of tourist accommodations and buildings decorated with murals.
Attractions include the Creston Valley Museum on Devon Road, open 10 a.m. to 4 p.m. in summer months, which features a replica of Kootenay "sturgeon-nose" canoe.
The Kootenay Candle Factory, just off Highway 3 south of the junction with Highway 3A, is known for its beeswax creations. Tours Monday to Saturday, 9 a.m. to 5 p.m., from May 15 to Oct. 15.

Mile 157 (377) Km 253 (606.5): **Junction** with Highway 3A, which loops north along the east side of Kootenay Lake to ferry crossing and back to Highway 3 at Castlegar. See feature this section.
★

Mile 159 (375) Km 256 (603.5): Crossing Kootenay River. The wide, flat river valley is diked to prevent floods.

Mile 114.5 (419.5) Km 184.5 (675): Old mining community of **MOYIE** (pop. 200), notable for its elegant Roman Catholic church and picturesque wooden fire hall, which date from the turn of the century. Gas, general store and pub.

Mile 115.5 (418.5) Km 185.5 (674): Stop of interest sign on lakeside near the site of the St. Eugene Mine, once the largest silver/lead mine in Canada. The deposits were discovered by Pierre, a Kootenai Indian from Father Coccola's St. Eugene mission near Fort Steele. The priest and Pierre sold their claims to miner James Cronin. Today, a large colorful pyramid of slag, mine-building relics and pioneer cemetery recall the past.

Mile 127 (407) Km 204 (655.5): Pacific/ Mountain time zone line. Westbound travelers set their watches back 1 hour; ahead 1 hour for eastbound travelers, but only in summer. Yahk, Kitchener and Creston stay on Mountain standard time all year. (In winter this is the same as Pacific daylight saving time.)

Mile 131 (403) Km 211 (648.5): Ryan rest area beside Moyie River.

Mile 135 (399) Km 217.5 (642): Small community of **YAHK** (pop. 170) with a general store, motels and gas station. A pub operates in the grand old hotel here. Yahk was a major supplier of railway ties for the Canadian Pacific Railway until the 1940s. The mill still oper-

Mile 159.5 (374.5) Km 257 (602.5): Road to Creston Valley Wildlife Interpretation Centre, open May 1 to Oct. 31, from 9 a.m. to 5 p.m. (extended hours July and August); weekdays only the rest of the year. The centre, where bird books and binoculars may be borrowed, is built on stilts in the middle of Corn Creek marsh, outside valley dikes. Several self-guided nature trails. Naturalists also lead nature excursions on foot and by canoe in the marsh or along nearby mountainsides. Wildlife ranges from the moose to the tiny Calliope hummingbird, though the emphasis is on water birds and marsh life. An osprey nest is in view on the mountainside behind the centre. Best times are mid-March for spring migration of whistling swans and others; October for fall migration. 🏕

Mile 161.5 (372.5) Km 259.5 (600): Creston Valley Wildlife Management Area Summit Creek Campground; camping (July and August only, fee charged), picnicking, children's play area, nature programs and walks.

Pedestrian suspension bridge crosses Summit Creek to connect with a restored section of the Dewdney Trail. Great views across valley. Osprey nests are visible. 🏕⛺▲

Mile 169.5 (364.5) Km 273 (586.5): Blazed Creek rest area. Highway climbs steadily, westbound, up Summit Creek valley.

Mile 184.5 (349.5) Km 297 (562.5): Kootenay Pass, also known as Stagleap Summit and the Skyway (elev. 5,823 feet/1,775m), one of the highest road passes in Canada. Stagleap Provincial Park on Bridal Lake; hiking and picnicking. Section of Dewdney Trail along north side of lake. Park is named for small herd of woodland caribou that migrates through the area. Mountain route is prone to closure because of avalanches. Avalanche-triggering cannon stations are along west side of pass. 🏕⛺

Mile 197.5 (336.5) Km 318 (541.5): Lost Creek rest area.

Mile 198.5 (335.5) Km 319.5 (540): Junc-

tion with Highway 6 south to border crossing at Nelway (open daily 8 a.m. to midnight).

Highways 3 and 6 share a common alignment for the next 9 miles/14.5 km westbound.

Mile 202 (332) Km 325 (534.5): Junction north side with road to Salmo airport and golf course. Nearby Sheep Creek Road (south side) leads to abandoned mines.

Mile 206 (328) Km 331.5 (528): Junction with road to Salmo Ski Hill.

Mile 207.5 (326.5) Km 334 (525.5): SALMO (pop. 1,000), at the **junction** with Highway 6 north to Nelson, was named for the fish in the Salmo River, a tributary of the Columbia River. (Columbia dams ruined the salmon runs.) Full tourist facilities. An old mining town, today forestry and sawmills support this tidy little town with its spruced-up 1930s architecture embellished with fine mosaic murals done by students at the local school of stone masonry. The local golf course is also the airport; locals call it a golfport. Visitor information office on Highway 3 is open daily May to Sept.

Mile 210 (324) Km 338 (521.5): Erie Lake rest area.

Mile 224.5 (309.5) Km 361.5 (498): Junction with Highway 3B to Trail. Highway 3 swings sharply north across Beaver Creek bridge.

Mile 232 (302) Km 373.5 (486): Bombi Summit (elev. 3,983 feet/1214m). Brake check area for steep descent westbound.

Mile 237 (297) Km 381.5 (478): Rest area and viewpoint over the confluence of the Columbia and Kootenay rivers. Nature trail around Champion Pond. 🏕

Mile 239.5 (294.5) Km 385.5 (474): Junc-

Castlegar lies at the confluence of the Columbia and Kootenay rivers. (Liz Bryan)

tion with Highway 3A to Nelson and Kootenay Lake communities (see feature this section). Turn here for airport and access to Doukhobor Historic Village (opposite the airport). A model communal settlement, it was built to show the way of life of the early Russian settlers. A large portion of the village was destroyed by fire in 1985, but much of interest remains. Adjacent is the Cultural Education Centre, which serves authentic Doukhobor foods. Just to the west is Kinnaird Bridge over the Columbia River.

Mile 240.5 (293.5) Km 387 (472.5): Exit north for Highway 22 along the Columbia River, and for the city of CASTLEGAR (pop. 7,500), at the confluence of the Kootenay

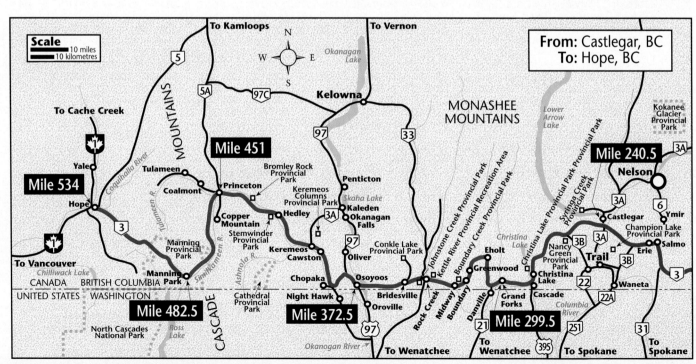

Scale
10 miles
10 kilometres

From: Castlegar, BC
To: Hope, BC

To Kamloops To Vernon

To Cache Creek

MONASHEE MOUNTAINS

Okanagan Lake

Kelowna

COQUIHALLA MOUNTAINS

Lower Arrow Lake

Kokanee Glacier Provincial Park

To Vancouver

Yale

Mile 534

Hope

Tulameen

Coalmont

Princeton

Copper Mountain

Stemwinder Provincial Park

Manning Provincial Park

Mile 451

Bromley Rock Provincial Park

Keremeos Columns Provincial Park

Hedley

Keremeos

Cawston

Mile 482.5

Manning Park

CANADA BRITISH COLUMBIA

UNITED STATES WASHINGTON

Cathedral Provincial Park

Chopaka

Night Hawk

Mile 372.5

North Cascades National Park

Ross Lake

CASCADE

Penticton

Skaha Lake

Kaleden

Okanagan Falls

Oliver

Osoyoos

Bridesville

Oroville

To Wenatchee

Okanogan River

Conkle Lake Provincial Park

Johnstone Creek Provincial Park

Kettle River Provincial Recreation Area

Boundary Creek Provincial Park

Eholt

Greenwood

Midway

Rock Creek

Boundary

Danville

Grand Forks

To Wenatchee

Christina Lake Provincial Park

Christina Lake

Nancy Green Provincial Park

Christina Lake

Cascade

Columbia River

To Spokane

Syringa Creek Provincial Park

Mile 240.5

Nelson

Castlegar

Champion Lake Provincial Park

Trail

Waneta

Mile 299.5

Ymir

Salmo

Erie

To Spokane

Nelson

and Columbia rivers; full tourist facilities. It's a thriving community whose livelihood is largely based on lumber and a big pulp mill. Many residents work at nearby Trail's big lead-zinc smelter.

Visit Zuckerberg Island Heritage Park, once home to Doukhobor teacher Alexander Zuckerberg, who built Chapel House there in 1931. The park is accessible by a pedestrian suspension bridge. Just outside of town on the road to Robson is the tomb of Peter Verigin, the Doukhobor's spiritual leader who led his people here from Russia in 1908.

Northwest of town is the Hugh Keenleyside Dam. Built in 1965, the 164-foot-/50-m-high earthfill and concrete structure impounds the waters of Arrow Lakes reservoir (the Columbia River). Beyond the dam is Syringa Creek Provincial Park, with 60 campsites, picnic tables, boat launch, sanistation, swimming, boating and fishing. Camping fee.

Westbound from Castlegar, Highway 3 climbs steeply and steadily up Blueberry Creek.

Mile 257.5 (276.5) Km 414 (445.5): Junction with Highway 3B south to Rossland (description follows). In summer, a small tourist information trailer is parked here. Also at the junction is Nancy Greene Provincial Park with 10 campsites, picnic area, swimming, fishing, boat launch and nature trails. Camping fee. The lake was named in honour of Rossland resident Nancy Greene, who won Canada a gold medal for alpine skiing in the 1968 Olympics. There are almost 50 km of hiking and cross-country ski trails around the lake and near the summit.

ROSSLAND (pop. 3,400), an old mining town 17 miles/28 km south from the junction that is well worth a visit, particularly if you have children. Here you can tour the only hard-rock gold mine in Canada that's open to the public, the famous Le Roi mine. Guided tours (with hard hats) from mid-May to mid-Sept. Gold panning outside mine entrance. Museum and tearoom adjacent. Tourist information at museum. The town itself, in a dramatic alpine setting (elev. 3,412 feet/1,040m), has 30 heritage buildings, full tourist facilities and a well-known

Alpine ski area at Red Mountain, site of Canada's first chair lift. Red Mountain has the highest ratio of advanced and expert terrain of any resort in the province. There is 1 triple chair, 2 double chairs and a T-bar; phone (604) 362-7700.

Mile 260.5 (273.5) Km 419.5 (440): Rest area at Sheep Creek, north of the highway. Side road leads south to Blueberry/Paulson cross-country ski area, home of some of the best cross-country ski trails in the southern Interior.

Mile 264 (270) Km 425 (434.5): Bonanza Pass (elev. 5,036 feet/1,535m). Brake check area for steep descent westbound.

Mile 267 (267) Km 430 (429.5): Walker Creek rest area.

Mile 270.5 (263.5) Km 435.5 (424): Paulson bridge over deep McRae Canyon. The suspension bridge is 295 feet/90m high with an arch span of 590 feet/180m. Sharp curve in narrow highway at east end of bridge.

Highway 3A Loop
Creston to Castlegar

This slow and scenic alternate route between Creston and Castlegar is only 12 miles/19 km longer than Highway 3, but much longer in terms of time. The road is narrow, winding along the shore of giant Kootenay Lake, and there's a 40-minute ferry crossing (the longest free ferry ride in North America). However, it leads through some interesting old mining towns.

Mile 0 Km 0: Junction with Highway 3 just west of Creston at **Mile 157.** The Kootenay Lake ferry schedule is posted here. Nearby ranch breeds Norwegian Fjord horses. Mountain Stream Trout Farm offers fishing, hiking, barbecues.

Mile 2 Km 3: Large viewpoint with picnic shelter overlooking the Kootenay Valley. Stop of interest marker describes 1880s reclamation efforts.

Mile 3 Km 5: Grain elevator at small community of Wynndel.

Mile 8 Km 12.5: Gravel turnout by Washout Creek. Below the highway is shallow Duck Lake, part of Creston Valley Wildlife Management Area. There are gravel roads and dikes for walking and bird watching.

Mile 10.5 Km 17: Small community of **SIRDAR,** once the site of an old B.C. Southern Railway roundhouse and turntable. A visit to the Sirdar store and post office, built in 1913, is well worthwhile. Nextdoor is the Sirdar Pub. Access to Duck Lake boat launch.

Mile 12.5 Km 20: Access to Duck Lake and Creston Valley Wildlife Area trails.

Mile 14 Km 23: South end of Kootenay Lake.

Mile 15 Km 24: Kuskanook rest

area with picnic tables and boat launch on the site of railway roundhouse. The art gallery beside the road occupies the 1903 station house.

Mile 19 Km 30.5: Twin Bays loop road to public beach and rest area.

Mile 21.5 Km 35: Sanca Creek and small resort community of Sanca, once the mining town of Granite Creek, destroyed by fire in 1900.

Mile 24 Km 38.5: Community of **BOSWELL,** known for its Glass House, a private home constructed from 500,000 square glass bottles that once held embalming fluid. (The builder was a retired mortician.) Open to the public, admission fee. Boswell hosts East Shore Craft Fair in August. Store, restaurant.

Mile 26 Km 42: Good viewpoint of lake. Destiny Bay, a private resort, is to the north. Store, post office and gas station beside highway.

Mile 28.5 Km 66.5: Boat launch.

Mile 29 Km 47: Road west to Lewis Bay, a public pebble beach.

Mile 32 Km 51.5: Lockhart Beach Provincial Park; 12 campsites, picnic tables, beach, boat launch, fishing. Trail leads up Lockhart Creek 8 miles/12 km to Baker Lake, a popular fishing hole. Private marina, resort and restaurant nearby.

Mile 33 Km 53.5: La France Creek. Several resorts, restaurants, marina, RV campground and residential area.

Mile 35.5 Km 57.5: Public lake access with small beach.

Mile 37 Km 69: GRAY CREEK, a thriving resort community overlooking Crawford Bay. The old-fashioned general store has been in business since 1913, and the hand-hewn log community

hall, built in 1912, still stands. All tourist services; public beach. Just south of community, forest road leads over Baker Pass to Kimberley. Good gravel road, okay for trailers. Road is passable June through Oct.

Mile 43.5 Km 70: CRAWFORD BAY (pop. 300) is the largest community on Kootenay Lake's eastern shore. Cottage industries here include Crawford Bay Clothing, the North Woven Broom Co. and Kootenay Forge. All tourist services are available. Of interest architecturally is the Wedgwood Manor, a splendid Victorian bed-and-breakfast originally built as a private home by a British naval commander.

Mile 47.5 Km 76.5: Stop of interest sign about the Bluebell Mine at Riondel which closed in 1972. The village of Riondel is mostly a retirement community today with store, pub, restaurant and golf course. Walkway through old mine site and museum (open daily July and August).

Mile 48 Km 77.5: Kootenay Lake ferry terminal at **KOOTENAY BAY,** a small community with a post office, bank, accommodations and restaurant. Rest area and tourist information office by the ferry terminal. Two boats operate on this 40-minute free crossing: the MV *Balfour* and the MV *Anscomb.*

Pilot Bay road leads south 3 miles/5 km from Kootenay Bay to historic Pilot Point Lighthouse (reached by a short trail). The Lighthouse, built in 1905, is a federal park and is open to the public. Great views from the top of the tower.

Mile 48 Km 77.5: Kootenay Lake ferry terminal at **BALFOUR,** on the

Mile 272 (262) Km 438 (421.5): McRae Creek rest area.

Mile 278.5 (255.5) Km 448 (411.5): Rest area. Highway descends westbound with views of Christina Lake.

Mile 280 (254) Km 451 (408.5): Exit for Texas Creek Provincial Park on Christina Lake; 33 campsites, camping fee, fishing, picnicking, boat launch, sandy beach and hiking.

Mile 282 (252) Km 454 (405.5): CHRISTINA LAKE (pop. 1,500) resort community with full tourist facilities. This 12-mile-/19-km-long lake is clear, shallow and warm, offering good fishing and swimming. It is a popular sailing and windsurfing spot. Christina Lake Provincial Park, at the south end of the lake, has an extensive beach, change rooms, picnic tables, children's play area and boat launch.

Mile 285 (249) Km 459 (400.5): *CAUTION:* Watch for mountain sheep on road.

Mile 288 (246) Km 463.5 (396): Junction with Highway 395 south to border crossing at Cascade, open daily 8 a.m. to midnight. (Just south of this junction there is a good viewpoint of the Cascade River gorge.)

Travelers heading south on U.S. Highway 395 turn to the end of the U.S. HIGHWAY 395 section and read log back to front.

Mile 299.5 (234.5) Km 482 (377.5): Bridge over Granby River, just north of its confluence with the Kettle River. Pleasant, well-preserved city of **GRAND FORKS** (pop. 3,500), incorporated in 1897. A road east of the bridge leads north to the site of the famous Granby copper smelter, at one time the 2nd largest in the world, which operated from 1900 to 1919. Today, Grand Forks is known for its potatoes. The local honey, made mostly from alfalfa and knapweed, is excellent.

Municipal park by the river has a playground, swimming and 28 campsites with hookups.

Boundary Museum, on Highway 3 and 5th Street, displays the history of the area.

Tourist information office is adjacent. Ask at the office for a walking tour map of heritage sites, and scenic drive maps.

The Doukhobor community here is well established (about half the city's population is Doukhobor). Russian is taught in the schools and many restaurants serve Russian food. ▲

Mile 301.5 (232.5) Km 485 (374.5): Exit on 19th Street for Mountain View Doukhobor Museum 3 miles/5 km north; open 9 a.m. to 7 p.m. daily, June to Sept.

Westbound travelers watch for pioneer flour mill south of Highway 3. Built in 1915, it is still in operation. Its "Pride of the Valley" flour is sold locally.

Mile 303 (231) Km 488 (371.5): Junction with Highway 41 to Carson/Danville border crossing, open daily 8 a.m. to midnight. Highway 3 westbound climbs into Monashee Mountains.

Mile 310 (224) Km 499 (360.5): Road to Phoenix Mountain Ski Area; 9 runs, nordic trails, open weekends, weeknights and holidays. Phone (604) 442-2813.

Small ferry accesses Procter and Harrop on west arm of Kootenay Lake. Highway 3A travelers must make the crossing between Kootenay Bay and Balfour. (Liz Bryan)

west side of Kootenay Lake, a resort community with all tourist services. Pleasant beachside rest area.

Junction with Highway 31, which provides access to Ainsworth Hot Springs Resort (9 miles/14.5 km), Cody Caves Provincial Park (20.5 miles/33 km) and the historic old mining town of Kaslo (22 miles/35.5 km), site of the SS *Moyie*, the last stern-wheeler to ply the Kootenay.

Mile 52 Km 84: Small 10-car cable ferry to Procter and Harrop.

Mile 56 Km 90: Kokanee Creek Provincial Park; 112 campsites, picnic areas, great sandy beaches, boat launch, playground, visitor centre. Tours of nearby Redfish Creek Spawning Channel. Area has high population of osprey. Look for their nests on old lake pilings. On mountain to the north is Kokanee Glacier Provincial Park, accessible by rough gravel road to Gibson Lake. Alpine hiking, wilderness camping.

Mile 63 Km 101: Blalocks estate, huge Tudor mansion, built in 1930s; now condominiums.

Mile 65 Km 104.5: Upper saloon and wheelhouse of old stern-wheeler, the MV *Nasookin*, now a private house on the west side of the road.

Mile 66.5 Km 107.5: Bridge across Kootenay Lake to city of **NELSON** (pop. 9,000), an old mining city with a considerable heritage of elegant turn-of-the-century architecture. Of particular note are the courthouse, city hall, and British Columbia's only operating streetcar, No. 23, which makes city-long trips along the lakeshore. The Steve Martin movie *Roxanne* was filmed

here. A thriving commercial and lumbering centre. Full tourist facilities.

Mile 72.5 Km 117: Grohman Narrows Provincial Park; picnicking, hiking trail.

Mile 74.5 Km 119.5: Kootenay River bridge and the community of Taghum.

Mile 79 Km 127.5: Viewpoint of the Kootenay River. Four hydro dams owned by West Kootenay Power make use of the 360-foot/200-m drop between Kootenay Lake and the Columbia River.

Mile 81 Km 130: Viewpoint of Bonnington Falls and stop of interest marker about West Kootenay Power. The 1st hydroelectric plant was built at the falls here in 1898 to generate power for the mines at Rossland.

Mile 84.5 Km 136: Junction with

Highway 6 at South Slocan. Highway goes north to New Denver and Nakusp Hot Springs.

Mile 86 Km 138: Road leads south 2 km to free cable ferry across Kootenay River to community of Glade Runs, daily, 5 a.m. to 2:30 a.m.

Mile 87.5 Km 141: Small community of Tarrys.

Mile 91.5 Km 147.5: Brilliant rest area.

Mile 92 Km 148: Viewpoint of Lower Bonnington Dam.

Mile 93 Km 149.5: Viewpoint of Brilliant Dam just north of Kootenay River bridge at Brilliant. Access to Hugh Keenleyside Dam on Lower Arrow Lake.

Mile 95 Km 153: Junction with Highway 3 just east of Castlegar, **Mile 239.5.**

Mile 316.5 (217.5) Km 509.5 (350): Rest area beside small Wilgress Lake, known locally as Loon Lake.

Mile 324 (210) Km 521.5 (338): Boundary Creek Road and **junction** with road to Jewel Lake fishing camp and cross-country ski trails. There is also a provincial park day-use area with swimming, fishing for rainbow and trails to old mine sites. No park services.

Mile 325 (209) Km 523 (336.5): Eastern limits of **GREENWOOD** (pop. 1,000), just west of old highway tunnel. Motels, restaurants, several stores and a pleasant creekside municipal campground. Greenwood was incorporated in 1899 when it was the centre of a rich copper-mining area with a population of 2,500. When the ore bodies diminished in the 1920s, the smelters closed and Greenwood's population dwindled. However, it still boasts a magnificent courthouse, gothic-spired Catholic church and 20 heritage buildings. Greenwood Museum contains excellent memorabilia of the city's mining days; tourist office adjacent. And not to be missed is a visit to the smelter site in Lotzgar Park. ▲

Mile 328.5 (205.5) Km 529 (330.5): Western edge of Greenwood with a stop of interest marker commemorating the Greenwood smelter. Black heap of slag rises above Boundary Creek, north side of highway.

Mile 330.5 (203.5) Km 531.5 (328): Boundary Creek Provincial Park with 18 campsites and fishing. Camping fee. To the west, the site of Boundary smelter. ⛱▲

Mile 331 (203) Km 533 (326.5): Boundary Creek bridge at Boundary Falls, site of a former power plant, and marker commemorating the building of the Dewdney Trail from Hope to the Kootenays in 1865.

Mile 335 (199) Km 539.5 (320): **MIDWAY** (pop. 650), so named because it is midway between the Rockies and the Pacific Ocean and the halfway point on the Dewdney Trail from Hope to Wildhorse. All services available. The road through the village leads south to the border crossing of Midway (open daily 9 a.m. to 5 p.m.). When Midway was founded, settlers believed it to be in Washington state. When the boundary was resurveyed in 1861, the settlement was found to be just north of the boundary line. Indians living north of the line were given a choice: to remain in Canada or to move south to Colville. Most chose to move south, but before they went, one of them twined 2 sapling pines as a symbol of the continuing unity of the divided tribe. These entwined trees, today a larger symbol of the friendship between the United States and Canada, grow in the park beside the museum. There are several picnic tables in the park.

The Midway courthouse has memorabilia of the B.C. Provincial Police Force. There are 2 old railways to explore in the Midway area: the Kettle Valley and the Vancouver, Victoria and Eastern. Ask at the museum.

Municipal park in town beside the Kettle River provides 12 campsites. Good place for a swim. ⛽▲

Mile 335.5 (198.5) Km 540 (319.5): Stop of interest sign at restored Midway station, built in 1900, terminus of Kettle Valley Railway. New Midway Museum adjacent (open daily July and August) has fine collection of Kettle Valley pioneer artifacts. Museum also houses tourist infocentre.

Mile 337.5 (196.5) Km 543 (316.5): Pope and Talbot sawmill, major employer of the area.

Mile 341 (193) Km 549 (310.5): Bridge over the Kettle River. West of the bridge is a war memorial cairn.

Mile 346.5 (187.5) Km 558 (301.5): Bridge over Kettle River. Community of **ROCK CREEK** has a general store and post office, medical clinic, 2 gas stations, a motel, 2 restaurants and the oldest continuously operating hotel in British Columbia. It has become famous for its 2-day fall fair held in mid-September.

In Olsen Park, east of the bridge, a stop of interest sign commemorates the finding of gold in the creek in 1859. The ensuing gold rush led to the building of the Dewdney Trail. Trail up creek leads to boulder fields from hydraulic mining.

Junction with Highway 33 to Kelowna. Kettle River Provincial Recreation Area, 3 miles/5 km north on Highway 33, is an attractive riverside spot with 49 campsites, picnicking, fishing, swimming and hiking. Camping fee. A popular summer pursuit is floating downriver to the Rock Creek bridge on air mattresses or inner tubes.

West of Rock Creek, the highway climbs steeply with a severe hairpin bend, to reach the shoulders of the plateau. Good view of Kettle Valley. ⛱⛽▲

Mile 351 (183) Km 565 (294.5): Johnstone Creek Provincial Park with 16 campsites; camping fee. Small waterfall where Johnstone Creek enters Rock Creek. ▲

Mile 355 (179) Km 571.5 (288): Bridge over Rock Creek canyon, 328 feet/100m above the river. Junction with gravel road to Mount Baldy Ski Area (12 miles/19 km); 15 runs, 2 T-bars, day lodge, ski school and ski rental. Open Friday to Monday and holidays; phone (604) 498-2262.

Mile 356 (178) Km 573 (286.5): **BRIDESVILLE**, limited services. Town was named for David McBride, who cornered the local market on land when the Vancouver, Victoria and Eastern Railway built here and he agreed to sell only if the town was named after him. He built a hotel here in 1910, and in it he installed the mahogany bar from Camp McKinney's Bucket of Blood Saloon.

Mile 358.5 (175.5) Km 577 (282.5): Anarchist Summit (elev. 4,435 feet/1,352m). The mountain was named for Richard Sidley, who settled here in 1889 and lost his job as local justice of the peace because of his extremist political views.

Good gravel turnouts on both sides of highway. Excellent view west of the Cascade Mountains in Cathedral Park.

Mile 359.5 (174.5) Km 578.5 (281): Sidley Mountain loop. Returns to highway 3 miles/5 km west.

Mile 360.5 (173.5) Km 580 (279.5): Wagon Wheel Ranch has fallow deer herd. Road north leads to mohair goat farm. Both open to public.

Mile 367.5 (166.5) Km 591.5 (268): Anarchist Mountain rest area in yellow pine forest. A good spot to watch for the rare white-headed woodpecker.

CAUTION: Steep downgrades and hairpin turns, westbound.

Osoyoos, at Mile 377.5, spans the narrows of Osoyoos Lake. It is a farming and tourism centre. (Liz Bryan)

Mile 352 (182) Km 566.5 (293): Rough gravel road (not suitable for trailers) leads north 16 miles/26 km to Conkle Lake Provincial Park. The park has 24 campsites, a picnic area, a boat launch, swimming and fishing for rainbow. Camping fee. Alternate park access via Highway 33. ⛱⛽▲

Mile 371.5 (162.5) Km 597.5 (262): Viewpoint for westbound travelers of Osoyoos Lake and the town of Osoyoos.

At the next hairpin turn there is a large viewpoint at Eddy's Point, with a stop of interest sign about Southern Crossroads; accessible for eastbound travelers only.

Mile 377.5 (156.5) Km 607.5 (252): **OSOYOOS** (3,000) has an annual precipitation of less than 8 inches and summer temperatures as high as 111°F/44°C. Surrounding it is an arid biotic zone, though much of the semi-desert has been transformed by irrigation into orchards and vineyards. There is even a banana farm, the only one in Canada.

Lake Osoyoos, which straddles the international boundary, is Canada's warmest freshwater lake, and its sandy beaches make it a popular summer playground. Water sports are the chief attraction in this desert hot spot.

The town architecture has been renovated in a Spanish motif. The co-op fruit packing shed has been decorated with murals by artist Jack Campbell. Osoyoos has full tourist facilities.

Just east of the town centre is Canada's only fully operational Dutch windmill, a faithful replica of an 1816 building where the owners live and grind flour the old-fashioned way. Stone-ground whole-wheat bread and flour, and other tempting baked goods, are for sale in the bakery. Open for tours daily early May to late Sept., Monday to Saturday only the rest of the year.

Mile 378.5 (155.5) Km 609 (250.5): **Junction** with Highway 97, which leads 2.5 miles/4.5 km south to border crossing at Oroville, WA (open 24 hours a day), and north to Oliver and Penticton. B.C. government information trailer at intersection open mid-May to mid-Sept.

Travelers headed north on Highway 97 turn to CANADA HIGHWAY 97 section for log. If southbound on Highway 97, turn to the end of the U.S. HIGHWAY 97 section and read log back to front.

Mile 382 (152) Km 615 (244.5): Viewpoints of south end of Okanagan Valley and Osoyoos Lake. Stop of interest sign about irrigation.

Mile 383 (151) Km 616 (243.5): Old Richter Pass road (original Dewdney Trail route) and road south to Blue and Kilpoola lakes.

Mile 384 (150) Km 618 (241.5): Spotted Lake (private property). High concentrations of magnesium and sodium create white spots on this alkali lake, although in years of high rainfall the water is relatively clear. Indians used the lake water for its curative properties.

Mile 386.5 (147.5) Km 622 (237.5): Richter Pass summit (elev. 2,231 feet/680m). The road leads north to the site of a proposed observatory on top of Mount Kobau. Construction was suspended because of high costs. The road gives access to alpine meadows. Good birding.

Mile 393 (141) Km 632.5 (227): Large turnout at junction with road south to U.S. border crossing near Nighthawk, WA (open 9 a.m. to 5 p.m. daily). Highway enters the valley of the Similkameen River.

The only operational water-powered gristmill in British Columbia is located at Keremeos. (Liz Bryan)

Mile 396 (138) Km 637 (222.5): Dankoe silver mine, still in operation, was originally worked in 1901 as the Horn mine.

Mile 397 (137) Km 639 (220.5): Bridge over Similkameen leads to Indian village of Chopaka and border crossing (open 9 a.m. to 5 p.m. daily).

Mile 405 (129) Km 651.5 (208): **CAWSTON**, a small fruit-growing community with packing plant. Site of Hudson's Bay Co. store in 1860. First homesteaded in 1865 by Frank Richter, who wintered cattle here. There are many fruit stands in season along the highway here.

Mile 405.5 (128.5) Km 652.5 (207): Becks Road leads north 2.5 miles/4 km to restored Keremeos gristmill built in 1877.

Mile 406.5 (127.5) Km 654.5 (205): St. Laszlo Vineyard Estate Winery. Tasting room and store open 9 a.m. to 9 p.m. daily year-round.

Mile 408 (126) Km 656.5 (203): **Junction** with Highway 3A to Penticton. This road passes close to Keremeos Columns Provincial Park, with its cliffs of gigantic basaltic columns; no road access, hike in.

Mile 408.5 (125.5) Km 657.5 (202): **KEREMEOS** (pop. 850), a small supply centre for surrounding orchardists and ranchers. All services available. Public campgrounds are located by the river. Tourist information office in the park on main street.

The grassy river benches of the Similkameen River are covered with fruit trees, mostly early ripening apricots, cherries and peaches. The highway on both sides of town is lined with fruit stands.

On Keremeos Creek just north of the town centre is British Columbia's only fully operational water-powered gristmill, still with its original machinery. Built in 1877, the mill has been fully restored as a provincial historic site. The grounds are open year-round. The mill is open from mid-May to mid-Sept., 9 a.m. to 4 p.m. Guided tours, flower gardens, tea house. A great place for a picnic.

Visit the South Similkameen Museum in an old police office and jail, on side street just north of highway. ▲

Mile 411 (123) Km 661.5 (198): Gravel side road crosses Similkameen River (covered railway bridge) and follows the Ashnola River 13.5 miles/22 km southwest to Cathedral Provincial Park boundary. Park accessible on foot or by prearranged 4-wheel-drive transport to private lodge in park centre. The heart of Cathedral Park is a ring of 7,000-foot/2,100-m alpine lakes.

Mile 411.5 (122.5) Km 662.5 (197): Rest area and picnic site beside river. Stop of interest sign about the covered railway bridges built by the Vancouver, Victoria and Eastern Railway, which serviced the mines at Hedley and Princeton. Watch for mountain goats on cliffs north of road. ⚑

Mile 413 (121) Km 665 (194.5): Standing Rock, a prominent glacial erratic on the north side of the highway, is an ancient Indian trail marker and pictograph rock. Indian craft shop on opposite side of highway.

Mile 414.5 (119.5) Km 667 (192.5): Large turnout and viewpoint with sign about California bighorn sheep transplanted to this area.

Mile 417 (117) Km 671 (188.5): Viewpoint, junction of Ashnola and Similkameen rivers. Westbound, watch for collection of hubcaps (thousands of them) at roadside ranch.

Mile 422 (112) Km 679 (180.5): Watch for Indian grave marked by pickets in the middle of field south of the highway. Park off highway near here for a short walk to Indian pictographs. (Climb steep road embankment north of highway then head northwest across pine-clad bench to base of white cliffs.) Pictographs are in good condition, painted in red and black.

Mile 424 (110) Km 682.5 (177): Renovated St. Ann's Catholic Church, built of logs on a glacial ridge above the river, and the nearby Indian village of Snazaist in the Chuchuawaa Indian Reserve. "Corkscrew Road" (4-wheel drive only) to abandoned Nickel Plate townsite and open-pit gold mine turns north off highway opposite Indian village.

Mile 425 (109) Km 684 (175.5): Tailings from Candorado Gold Mine operations beside Hedley cemetery. Company is extracting gold from previously discarded tailings.

Mile 426.5 (107.5) Km 686.5 (173): HEDLEY village lies just to the north of the highway in the valley of 20 Mile Creek. Named after the man who had grubstaked many of the prospectors, Hedley flourished with the mines, but faded when the mines closed. Fires in 1956 and 1957 destroyed much of the old town. Visit Heritage House, a modern building displaying Hedley's past. Service station, general store, restaurants,

A field of lupine in Manning Provincial Park.
(Liz Bryan)

bed-and-breakfast accommodation in historic Colonial Inn; private campgrounds on highway. Picnic at Woodley Park, in town behind the church.

Rock cliff to the west of the Hedley townsite shows good examples of deeply folded rock strata. The Indians called this the Striped Rock, or Snazaist.

Stop of interest sign west of town commemorates the rich gold finds from the Nickel Plate Mine above the town of Hedley. From 1903 to 1955, more than $47 million in gold was taken out of the mountain and brought down by aerial tramway to a reduction mill. Old mine buildings are visible on the rock ridge high above town. Recently, gold mining activity has begun again at Hedley, with the Candorado Mine in operation.   ▲

Mile 429 (105) Km 690.5 (169): Ginseng field. Hot valley provides ideal climate, but crop must grow in the shade—hence the covers of black plastic mesh.

Mile 430 (104) Km 692 (167.5): Stemwinder Provincial Park on riverbank with 23 campsites and picnic tables. Camping fee. The park is named for the stemwinder snake. The Similkameen River flows swiftly here; recommended for very strong swimmers only. Indian pithouse depression inside park. Watch for poison ivy.   ⋔▲

Mile 431 (103) Km 694 (165.5): Highway crosses Similkameen River. Old Hedley Road follows river's north bank to Princeton.

Mile 437 (97) Km 703.5 (156): Bromley Rock Provincial Park with 17 campsites, picnic area, swimming and fishing. Camping fee. The river here forms a large, deep pool overhung by Bromley Rock, an excellent summer swimming hole with small sandy beaches. Fishing for rainbow trout.

⋔ ⊷▲

Mile 448.5 (85.5) Km 722 (137.5): Darcy Mountain Road; access to Princeton Country Club and Amber Ski Hill.   ⚲

Mile 450 (84) Km 724 (135.5): Copper Mountain Road to ghost town of Allenby and open-pit mines (restricted access). Good birding route.

Mile 450.5 (83.5) Km 725 (134.5): Bridge over Similkameen River. **Junction** with Highway 5A north to Merritt. Tourist information centre at east end of bridge. Access to Princeton Airport, home of the Princeton Cadet Glider School.

Mile 451 (83) Km 726 (133.5): PRINCETON (pop. 4,000); all services available. Princeton is located at the confluence of the Similkameen and Tulameen rivers. Tulameen is the local Indian name for "red earth" and refers to the nearby bluffs of red ochre. The first white settlement here in the 1850s was known as Vermilion Forks, but in 1860 when the Royal Engineers surveyed the road through the valley, a townsite was laid out and renamed after Edward, Prince of Wales, who was visiting eastern Canada.

Princeton was an important centre for coal mining, which reached its peak here in the 1920s. The hills are riddled with old workings. Today the town is a supply centre for surrounding ranches, the nearby copper mine and lumber companies.

Tourist information in the old rail caboose on Vermilion Avenue; museum adjacent. Fishing in the rivers and many small lakes in the surrounding hills is the main recreational attraction here. Others include rockhounding and exploring the back roads and ghost towns of the mining areas. Take the back road northwest of Princeton up the Tulameen River to the coal mining towns of Coalmont and Tulameen, and the old gold camp of Granite Creek.

Notice bright yellow sandstone forma-

tions behind the bus depot, west edge of town, just before highway climbs a steep hill into the Cascade Mountains.   ⊷

Mile 458.5 (75.5) Km 738 (121.5): Bridge over Whipsaw Creek and stop of interest sign for yellow or Ponderosa Pine Ecological Reserve. Old Hope Pass Trail (1861), which follows the creek, has been restored as a hiking and horse trail. It extends 16 miles/26 km into Manning Provincial Park (see **Mile 507.5**). *CAUTION:* 8 percent downgrade for westbound traffic, trucks use lower gear. Watch for hairpin turn and narrow bridge over Copper Creek at bottom of hill.   ⋘

Mile 461 (73) Km 741.5 (118): Similco Mine (closed). Copper ores were mined in open pits across the valley, concentrated here for shipment.

Mile 468.5 (65.5) Km 754 (105.5): Large gravel turnout and brake testing area for eastbound traffic. Map shows hairpin turns and steep downgrades.

Mile 472 (62) Km 760 (99.5): Sunday Summit (elev. 4,596 feet/1,401m). The mountains nearby are covered with lodgepole pine, the first evergreen to grow back after a forest fire.

Mile 479.5 (54.5) Km 772 (87.5): Highway goes through narrow river canyon. Watch for rock fall. View south to Similkameen Falls; limited parking at bend in highway east of falls.

Above canyon, highway becomes 4-lane.

Mile 481.5 (52.5) Km 775 (84.5): Upper Pasaylen River road.

Mile 482.5 (51.5) Km 776.5 (83): MANNING PARK, east gate of Manning Provincial Park; gas station, small store. The big carved wooden bear by the sign is a popular background for family photos. (Bears are common in the park.)

Mile 484 (50) Km 778.5 (81): McDiarmid Meadows picnic area.   ⋔

Mile 486.5 (47.5) Km 783 (76.5): Mule Deer Campground with 34 sites (some on river). Camping fee. Mule deer are common on the east side of the Cascades, black-tailed deer on the west side.   ▲

Mile 489.5 (44.5) Km 788 (71.5): Blowdown picnic area beside river. On the opposite side of the highway is Hampton Campground with 80 sites. Camping fee.   ⋔▲

Mile 490 (44) Km 788.5 (71): Castle Creek Trail to Boyd's Meadows and Monument 78 on Canada–U.S. boundary, the start of the Pacific Crest Trail. Also trail to Monument 83.

⋘

Mile 491.5 (42.5) Km 791 (68.5): Road south to parking lot for Beaver Pond nature trail. Several varieties of birds can be seen here, as well as beaver, muskrat and mule deer. Windy Joe Mountain trailhead.   ⋘

Mile 492 (42) Km 792 (67.5): Manning Provincial Park Visitor Center; sani-station. Road north to Cascade Lookout and Alpine meadows; good views, wildflowers, nature walks.

Visitors to Coquihalla Canyon Provincial Recreation Area walk through old rock railway tunnels. (Liz Bryan)

Mile 492.5 (41.5) Km 793 (66.5): Road south to Manning Park Lodge, trail rides, Gibson Pass Ski Area, Lightning Lakes and Strawberry Flats. Swimming, canoeing on lakes, camping and hiking in summer, skiing in winter. Gibson Pass has 2 double chairs, a T-bar, 24 runs and extensive nordic trails; phone (604) 840-8822.

Mile 494 (40) Km 795 (64.5): Coldspring Campground with 67 sites and picnic tables beside the Similkameen River. Camping fee. Nature trail.

Mile 496.5 (37.5) Km 799 (60.5): Cambie Creek Cross-country Ski Area. Brake check for eastbound trucks.

Mile 498 (36) Km 801.5 (58): Summit of Allison Pass (elev. 4,403 feet/1,342m). The pass was named for John Fall Allison, Princeton's first settler, who pioneered this route through the mountains. Near the summit, B.C. Highways has a road maintenance depot; emergency phone. West of the pass, Highway 3 follows the Skagit River in a swift descent to the Fraser Valley.

Mile 502.5 (31.5) Km 809 (50.5): Remains of old forest fire. In 1945 fire swept through the area, destroying nearly 1.2 million acres of forest. Hillsides still bear scars despite reforestation.

Mile 507.5 (26.5) Km 817 (42.5): Cayuse Flats rest area. Beginning of Hope Pass Trail, which goes north up Skaist River.

Mile 509.5 (24.5) Km 820 (39.5): Highway threads around sheer Skagit Bluffs. Watch for rock fall.

Mile 511 (23) Km 822.5 (37): Snass Creek (Indian word for "rain"). Just east of the bridge, a stop of interest sign describes the Dewdney Trail, built from Hope to Rock Creek in 1860–61 and completed to the Kootenays 4 years later. To the west, access and parking for Cascade Provincial Recreation Area, which protects 3 heritage trails: Dewdney, Whatcom and Hope Pass. These trails were the 1st routes through the Canadian Cascades. Horse and hiking trail up Snass Creek to Dewdney Trail, which connects to Whatcom Trail.

Mile 512 (22) Km 824 (35.5): Rhododendron Flats rest area and nature trail. Here is one of the few places where the red rhododendron grows wild on the British Columbia mainland. The shrubs provide a colorful display in June. The red rhododendron is protected; do not pick or uproot.

Mile 513 (21) Km 825.5 (34): Sumallo Grove picnic area in a stand of old cedars beside the Sumallo River. The Whatcom Trail follows the Skagit River southwest from here to Skagit Valley south of Hope. A good, easy hike, but long (9 miles/15 km).

Mile 513.5 (20.5) Km 826.5 (33): Old buildings of former Foundation Mines to east.

Mile 516 (18) Km 830.5 (29): Stop of interest. In 1860, a platoon of 80 Royal Engineers from England replaced the Dewdney Trail with a wagon road. They completed 34 miles/55 km from Hope but were called off the job because of more urgent work in the Cariboo, where a gold rush was in full swing. A well-preserved section of the old road lies just north of the highway.

Mile 518 (16) Km 833.5 (26): West gate of Manning Provincial Park is marked by large carving of a hoary marmot. Rest area, picnic tables and short loop trail to section of Engineer's Road. Well worth a lengthy stop. Just outside the park gates is a lodge with restaurant and gas station.

Mile 520 (14) Km 837 (22.5): Small vacation community of **SUNSHINE VALLEY** beside the Sumallo River. On nearby Trites Ranch property was Tashme Camp where some 3,500 Japanese were interned during WWII.

Mile 523.5 (10.5) Km 842.5 (17): Rest area and viewpoint of Hope Slide. In January 1965 a minor earthquake triggered a gigantic rock fall. Tons of rock, earth and snow slid from Johnson's Peak north of the highway, killing 4 people and burying miles of the road and adjacent Outram Lake.

CAUTION: 7 percent downgrade westbound; trucks stop here to check brakes.

Mile 527.5 (6.5) Km 849 (10.5): Nicolum River Provincial Park; 9 campsites, picnic area. Good fishing for cutthroat, coho and squawfish.

Mile 528.5 (5.5) Km 850.5 (9): **Junction** with Coquihalla Highway 5 to Merritt and Kamloops. See the CANADA HIGHWAY 5 section.

Mile 532.5 (1.5) Km 857 (2.5): Exit to Hope business route. Hope has all visitor services. See description of Hope in the TRANS-CANADA HIGHWAY 1 section.

The main attraction in the Hope area is the Coquihalla Canyon Provincial Recreation Area, the focus of which is the Othello Quintette Tunnels. The 5 rock tunnels that cut throught the tortuous canyon were part of the Kettle Valley Railway. This stretch of railway has been restored as a walking trail through the tunnels and across bridges. The tunnels are accessible from downtown Hope via Kawkawa Lake Road and Othello Road, about a 10-minute drive.   EXIT 173

Mile 534 (0) Km 859.5 (0): Exit to Hope town centre and **junction** with Trans-Canada Highway 1. Turn to **Mile 439** in the TRANS-CANADA HIGHWAY 1 section.

EXIT 170

INTERSTATE 5

California–Oregon Border to Canadian Border
(See maps, pages 47, 52 and 59)

Interstate 5 is a 4- to 6-lane divided highway that cuts an almost straight line from the southern to the northern border of the United States. In the Northwest it passes through Oregon and Washington. It's the most important north-south shipping and travel route on the West Coast, heavily traveled day and night, especially in the metropolitan areas.

While not generally regarded as a scenic route, Interstate 5 climbs through the steep green canyons of the Siskiyou Mountains, divides agricultural farms in the Willamette Valley and crosses the historically rich Columbia River (10th longest river in the country at 1,214 miles). It skirts the western edge of the Cascade Range and the eastern shore of sprawling Puget Sound. It passes next to vast fields of tulips and daffodils in the Skagit Valley and enters Canada in the beautifully landscaped flower gardens at the Peace Arch Park in Blaine, WA.

There are many attractions along the interstate easily accessible to motorists who take the time to pull off the highway for an hour or more. Food, gas and lodging are readily available, with major hotels, restaurants and gas stations at most major exits. Travelers overnighting along the way are advised to call ahead for motel accommodations in summer. Well-maintained highway rest areas, with restrooms and pay phones, are located along the interstate.

Exit numbers and physical mileposts along I-5 in Oregon reflect distance from the California–Oregon border. Mileposts and exit numbers in Washington reflect distance from the Oregon– Washington border. The *Northwest Mileposts* log reflects cumulative mileages from the California–Oregon state border to the Canadian border.

Interstate 5 Log

Distance from California–Oregon border is followed by distance from the Canadian border.

Mile 0 (584.5): California–Oregon border. Mileposts and exit numbers on Interstate 5 in Oregon reflect distance from here. There are no self-serve gasoline stations in Oregon. Attendants must pump gasoline. The highway climbs a 6 percent grade the next 5 miles northbound.

Mile 1 (583.5): Exit (northbound only) Siskiyou Summit.   EXIT 1

Mile 2 (582.5): On a clear day southbound travelers can see the top of Mount Shasta to the northeast.

Mile 4.5 (580): Siskiyou Summit (elev. 4,310 feet) in the Siskiyou Mountains. Trucks turn off at the road cut here to test their brakes before beginning the descent either north- or southbound. There is a truck escape ramp northbound.

Road conditions can be hazardous on this stretch of highway anytime during the year in wet or cold weather. There is a 6 percent downgrade for the next 7 miles northbound. Watch for slow-moving trucks, and be alert for deer. Black-tailed deer frequently wander onto the freeway in this area and can be a hazard during low light situations, late evening and early morning.

Mile 5.5 (579): Exit to Mount Ashland and access to Mount Ashland Ski Area: 4 chair lifts, 23 runs plus open bowl skiing, ski school, rentals, lodge with cafeteria. Skiing from Nov. to April, open daily; night skiing Thursday, Friday and Saturday. For snow condition, phone (503) 482-2754.   EXIT 6

Mile 8 (576.5): View to the east of Emigrant Lake (accessible from Exit 14) and the foothills of the Cascade Range.

Ashland's 100-acre Lithia Park offers many hiking trails. (L. Linkhart)

Mile 10 (574.5): Rest area (northbound) with information center, handicap-accessible restrooms and pay phones.   &

Mile 11 (573.5): Exit (northbound only) to Siskiyou Boulevard and Highway 99 in Ashland. For more direct access to downtown Ashland, northbound travelers should take Exit 14.   EXIT 11

Mile 14 (570.5): Exit to **ASHLAND** (pop. 17,320), Klamath Falls, Southern Oregon State College and Oregon Highway 66. Easy access to major-chain motels and restaurants, fast-food outlets, gas and campgrounds at exit. Ashland offers 22 motels and hotels, 66 restaurants and 40 bed and breakfasts. For local information and city center, head west 1.3 miles to Highway 99 north (1-way); turn and follow signs another 1.7 miles to the information center at E. Main and Pioneer. Motels, shopping center and other services are available along Highway 66 west.

Ashland is well known to theater lovers for the Oregon Shakespeare Festival, which features works of Shakespeare and other playwrights. Plays are performed from late Feb. through Oct. at the indoor 600-seat Angus Bowmer Theatre, and at the smaller indoor Black Swan. In June through Oct. plays are performed in the outdoor Elizabethan Theatre. Contact Oregon Shakespeare Festival, P.O. Box 158, Ashland, OR 97520; (503) 482-4331.

The new (1994) Pacific Northwest Museum of Natural History, located near Southern Oregon State College, re-creates ecosystems of the Northwest. Walk-through lava tube with Indian cave paintings, brown bats and a lava flow. Interactive exhibits and educational programs. Phone (503) 488-1084 for more information.

For camping, swimming and boating, head east at Exit 14 on Highway 66 (a winding 2-lane road) through a rural residential area. There is a private campground 3 miles east of Exit 14. Emigrant Lake Jackson County Park is 3.5 miles from the exit; tent and RV campsites, day-use area for picnicking, swimming, showers and boat ramp.

Approximately 1 mile east of Interstate 5 on Highway 66, turn off on Dead Indian Road (paved) and drive 20 miles northeast to Howard Prairie Reservoir, a major recreation site for the Ashland area. Four campgrounds on the lake offer 84 tent sites, 195 trailer/RV sites, plus resort facilities where rental boats, bait and fishing information are available. It's open year-round; a good fishing lake for rainbow trout, use flies, trolling tackle or bait.

⚓☂▲★ MP 14 EXIT 14

Mile 17 (567.5): View of Ashland immediately to the west and the forested Klamath Mountains in the distance. Southbound travelers should be able to see Horn Peak behind 7,523-foot Mount Ashland in the Siskiyou Mountains directly to the south.

Mile 18 (566.5): Weigh station (southbound).

Mile 19 (565.5): Exit (southbound only) to Ashland (see city description at **Mile 14**). Most direct access to Ashland city center for southbound travelers. From this exit it is approximately 2 miles via Highway 99 to Ashland city center. Medford is also accessible from this exit via Highway 99. Easy access to services, motels, hospital and Shakespearean Center.   EXIT 19

Mile 21 (563.5): Exit to **TALENT** (pop. 3,830), a residential area. There is an RV park on the west side of the interstate. ▲ EXIT 21

Mile 22.5 (562): Southbound rest area (handicap-accessible) and Bear Creek. A tributary of the Rogue River, Bear Creek flows through the city of Medford and meanders across the interstate 4 times during the next 9 miles. Orchards seen on either side of the interstate produce pears, this area's primary fruit crop.   ♿

Mile 24 (560.5): Exit to **PHOENIX** (pop. 3,190). Motel with 24-hour restaurant, gas station and RV park; truck stop with diesel.
▲ EXIT 24

Mile 27 (557.5): Exit to Medford, Jacksonville National Historic Landmark and Barnett Road. Easy access to food, gas and lodging at this exit; South Gateway shopping mall just east of exit. For visitor information, take Stewart Avenue to Maple Grove Drive for Log Cabin Information Center. Call or write the Medford Visitors and Convention Bureau, 101 E. 8th, Medford, OR 97501; phone (503) 779-4847. This is the northbound access to Medford city center and riverside motels. Travelers may note the large building on the hill to the east: It is a retirement home.

MEDFORD (pop. 49,900) is a sprawling service center for this area's agriculture and tourism industries, with 27 motels (including major chains), family restaurants and fast-food establishments, gas, diesel and other facilities.

The city began in the 1880s as a train depot for the newly established Oregon–California Railroad line. Since its modest inception, Medford has grown to be the largest city in southern Oregon. To view some of Medford's history, drive down Oakdale Avenue, where many of the city's original homes are located. Also stop by the Southern Oregon Historical Society's History Center, located at 106 N. Central Ave. (phone 503/773-6536).

Medford is also home to Harry & David's, the world's largest mail-order fruit-packing business and home of the Fruit-of-the-Month Club. Tours of the packing plant and the Jackson and Perkins rose gardens are available daily. Tours are free but fill up

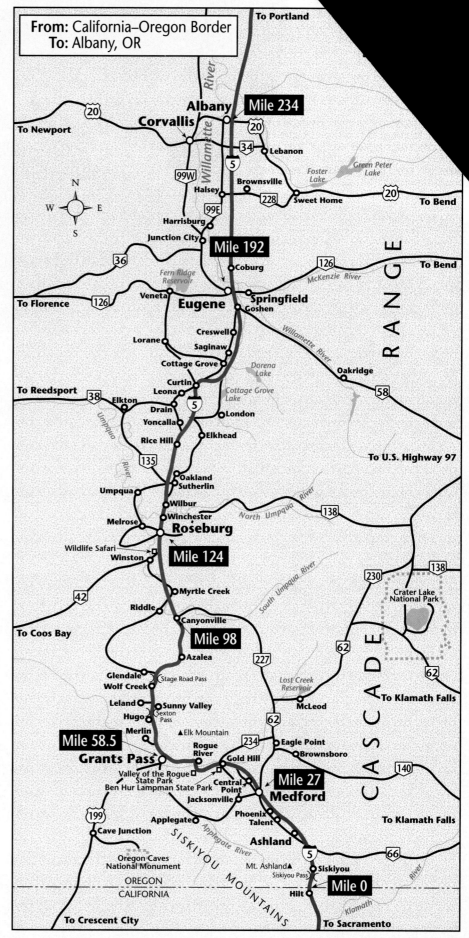

From: California–Oregon Border
To: Albany, OR

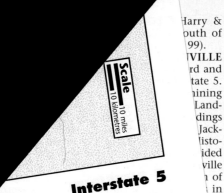

Scale
10 miles
10 kilometres

Interstate 5

Harry &
...outh of
...99).

...VILLE
...rd and
...tate 5.
...mining
...Land-
...dings
...Jack-
...listo-
...ided
...ville
...n of
...in
...ate July
...ontact Peter Britt Festivals,
...box 1124, Medford, OR 97501; phone
(503) 773-6077 or 1-800-882-7488.
★ MP 28 EXIT 27

Mile 30 (554.5): Exit to Medford, Crater Lake, Oregon Highway 62, Rogue Valley Mall and Klamath Falls. Easy access to food, gas and lodging at this exit; 24-hour restaurant and truck stop with diesel. This is the southbound access to Medford's city center and riverside major-chain motels, northbound access to Medford airport. Highway 62 provides the most direct access to Crater Lake National Park for northbound Interstate 5 motorists. Crater Lake is approximately 75 miles from Medford via this route. There are several campgrounds along Highway 62. (See description of Crater Lake in the MAJOR ATTRACTIONS section.)
▲ MP 31 EXIT 30

Mile 32 (552.5): Exit for **CENTRAL POINT** (pop. 8,195), Medford airport and Jackson County Exposition Park. Easy access to gas stations with diesel and family restaurant at this exit. MP 33 EXIT 32

Mile 33 (551.5): Northeast of the highway is distinctive Table Rock. On a clear day, travelers may see the top of cone-shaped Mount McLoughlin (elev. 9,495 feet) in the distance directly to the east. Northbound, the highway leaves the flat valley and enters the mountains. It is a winding road with steep grades from here to Canyonville (next 70 miles).

Mile 35 (549.5): Exit for northbound access to Blackwell Road, southbound access to Highway 99, Central Point, North Medford and Jacksonville. Restaurants and gas stations are at this exit. EXIT 35

Mile 40 (544.5): Exit to Gold Hill, Jacksonville, highways 99 and 234. Access to Ben Hur Lampman State Park on the northeast side of the interstate (follow signs), a day-use area on the Rogue River with picnicking and swimming.

The community of **GOLD HILL** (pop. 1,175) is about a mile northeast from the interstate. All services available including gas, groceries, deli and campground. This is the location of the Oregon Vortex, a natural phenomenon of magnetic forces that affects the perception of height, among other things. Follow the signs from the interstate approximately 5 miles for House of Mystery/Oregon Vortex.

Gold Hill, originally on the south bank of the Rogue River opposite the current townsite, was the location of an early gold discovery in Oregon. The Old Oregon Historical Museum, on the road to the Oregon Vortex,

Jacksonville is a restored 1800s gold-mining town 5 miles west of Medford.
(© Lee Foster)

has an excellent gun and Indian artifacts collection. ⊼▲ EXIT 40

Mile 43 (541.5): Exit for Rogue River Route (Oregon Highway 99) to Rock Point and Highway 234 to Gold Hill and Crater Lake Highway (Highway 62). Gas, food, lodging and camping. ▲ MP 44 EXIT 43

Mile 45 (539.5): Exit 45A Rogue River Route (Oregon Highway 99), Savage Rapids Dam with fish ladders; steelhead and salmon viewing in season. There is a gas station with diesel east off the exit.

Highway 99 follows the Rogue River to junction with U.S. Highway 199 (Redwood Highway) just west of Grants Pass. The Rogue River heads in the Cascade Range and flows west into the Pacific Ocean at Gold Beach. It is well known throughout the country for its fishing and whitewater rafting. It was named for the fierce Indians in the area, whom the French called *Les Coquins*, "the rogues."

Exit 45B, just north, is the access to Valley of the Rogue State Park Campground and highway rest area, both located just off the interstate to the west. Restrooms (handicap-accessible) and pay phones at rest area. Paved loop road through shaded camping area along Rogue River; 22 tent and 100 RV sites, full hookups, dump station and showers.
ﾖ▲ MP 46 EXIT 45

Mile 48 (536.5): Exit to **ROGUE RIVER** (pop. 1,815) and South Grants Pass via Highway 99. All services are available. Easy access to gas, diesel east off this exit. The town was originally called Woodville, but changed its name to that of the river in 1912. Western author Zane Grey (1875–1939), who had a cabin along the Rogue, helped popularize the river in his novels. Access to Rogue River jet boat excursion operator. MP 49 EXIT 48

Mile 55 (529.5): Exit to East Grants Pass, U.S. Highway 199 (Redwood Highway) to Cres-

cent City, CA. Rogue Community College, fairgrounds, gas, major motel and fast-food outlets at this exit. Also northbound access to Rogue River jet boat rides. Take Redwood Spur to Grants Pass Parkway and turn right on M Street, then left on 8th Street; watch for Hellgate Excursion signs. Phone ahead for reservations, 1-800-648-4874.

Highway 199 leads southwest 34 miles to **CAVE JUNCTION** (pop. 1,200), gateway to Oregon Caves National Monument. Located in the Illinois Valley, Cave Junction has all visitor services, including restaurants, gas stations, lodging, grocery, shopping and an airport. Oregon Caves National Monument, located 19 miles from Cave Junction, has a picturesque chateau offering lodging and daily tours of the magnificent Oregon Caves (see MAJOR ATTRACTIONS section). A highly recommended side trip. ★ EXIT 55

Mile 58.5 (526): Exit to Grants Pass, Highway 99 and U.S. Highway 199, Oregon Caves and Redwood Highway. Easy access to major-chain lodging, 24-hour major-chain restaurants, fast-food outlets, gas, diesel, hospital and state police at this exit. Grants Pass city center is to the south.

GRANTS PASS (pop. 18,120) is headquarters for Rogue River outfitters. For information on rafting trips down the Rogue, contact the U.S. Forest Service office for Siskiyou National Forest in Grants Pass (phone 503/471-6516) or Grants Pass Visitors and Convention Bureau, 1-800-547-5927. Visitor information is also available at the chamber of commerce visitor center at 1501 NE 6th St., downtown; phone (503) 476-7717. Southbound access to Hellgate Excursion jet boat rides: follow 6th Street to M Street, turn left and continue to 8th.

The Rogue River above Grants Pass is heavily fished during the summer for rainbow with seasonal runs of chinook to 40 lbs., steelhead and fall salmon. Numerous boat launches, guide services, parks and fishing resorts are available. Sporting goods stores in Grants Pass are good sources of current fishing conditions and guide-trip information. ➤▲ EXIT 58

Mile 61 (523.5): Exit to **MERLIN** (unincorporated), which has a gas station with diesel. Access to airport and Hog Creek boat launch on the Rogue River (8 miles west of exit on Merlin-Galice Road). Continue past boat launch for river overlooks and Hellgate Canyon view. EXIT 61

Mile 61.5 (523): Louse Creek.

Mile 62.5 (522): Rest area with handicap-accessible facilities. ♿ MP 63

Mile 65 (519.5): Jumpoff Joe Creek.

Mile 66 (518.5): Exit to Hugo (unincorporated). Lodging and RV park. ▲ EXIT 66

Mile 69 (515.5): Summit of Sexton Mountain Pass (elev. 1,960 feet) and beginning of 6 percent downgrade for 3 miles.

Mile 71.5 (513): Exit to Sunny Valley (unincorporated) and LeLand. This village used to go by the name Grave Creek, but the locals thought the name was too morbid, so they selected the name Sunny Valley because the area is often free of the low fogs that hang in adjacent valleys. Motel, food, gas, campground. ▲ EXIT 71

Mile 74 (510.5): Smith Hill Summit (elev. 1,730 feet). MP 74

Rafting on the Rogue River is a popular activity.
(© Lee Foster)

Mile 76 (508.5): Exit to **WOLF CREEK** (unincorporated); food, gas, lodging and camping available. Easy on-off access to this small community and historic Wolf Creek Tavern, less than a mile west of the interstate.

Wolf Creek Tavern was 1 of 60 stage stops on the Portland–Sacramento stage route where travelers could get a night's rest

and meals and where new horses and drivers took over. It remained in almost continuous operation between 1868 and 1873. Wolf Creek Tavern was restored in 1979 and today offers food and lodging as it did in the 1800s. It is well worth a stop. There is a general store across the street and a family restaurant and gas station with diesel nearby. Drive to the end of Main Street (follow signs) for Wolf Creek Josephine County Park; 18 tent/RV campsites. ▲ MP 77 EXIT 76

Mile 78 (506.5): Exit (southbound only) to Speaker Road. EXIT 78

Mile 79.5 (505): Summit of Stage Road Pass (elev. 1,830 feet). MP 80

Mile 80.5 (504): Leaving Josephine County, entering Douglas County, northbound. Douglas County produces more sheep than any other county in Oregon. Lumbering and sawmilling are the principal industries.

Mile 81 (503.5): Exit to **GLENDALE** (pop. 710); family restaurant, drive-in, gas and camping. ▲ EXIT 80

Mile 82 (502.5): Rest area with pay phones and restrooms (handicap-accessible). ♿ MP 82

Mile 83 (501.5): Exit to Barton Road (northbound only). EXIT 83

Mile 86 (498.5): Exit to Quines Creek Road and Barton Road. There is a gas station with diesel and convenience store east of this exit; also a 24-hour cafe and an RV park. ▲ EXIT 86

Mile 88 (496.5): Exit to **AZALEA** (unincorporated) and Galesville Reservoir; gas available. The town was named for the abundance of azalea plants that grow in the area. MP 88 EXIT 88

Mile 90 (494.5): Summit of Canyon Creek Pass (elev. 2,020 feet).

Mile 95 (489.5): Exit to Canyon Creek. North to Roseburg, Interstate 5 is roughly paralleled by the South Fork Umpqua River, a fine fishing stream. ➤ MP 96 EXIT 95

Mile 98 (486.5): Exit to Canyonville and Days Creek and Oregon Highway 227. Highway 227 junctions with Highway 62 to Crater Lake. Easy access to food, gas and information center at this exit. **CANYONVILLE** (pop. 1,220) has all services available. Canyonville is situated at the north end of Canyon Creek canyon, the area that offered so much trouble for immigrants en route to the Willamette Valley in 1846. The total descent from the pass at the head of Canyon Creek to Canyonville is nearly 1,300 feet. EXIT 98

Mile 99 (485.5): Exit to North Canyonville. Southbound to Crater Lake and Highway 227. Easy access to lodging and truck stop with diesel at this exit. Information center.

Northbound access to Charles V. Stanton Douglas County Park on the east side of the interstate (follow signs); 40 tent/RV campsites, picnic tables, restrooms and showers. ⛺▲ MP 100 EXIT 99

Mile 100.5 (484): South Umpqua River.

Mile 101 (483.5): Exit for **junction** with Highway 99 west to Riddle, site of the Hanna Nickel Mine. Southbound access for county park campground. See **Mile 99**. EXIT 101

Mile 101.5 (483): South Umpqua River. Interstate 5 parallels the South Umpqua north to Roseburg, where it meets the North Umpqua at River Forks.

Mile 102 (482.5): Exit to Gazley Road. RV park. ▲ MP 102 EXIT 102

Mile 102.5 (482): Wide gravel turnout (southbound only) next to the Umpqua River. MP 103

Mile 103 (481.5): Exit to Tri City and Highway 99 to Riddle. Easy access to gas stations, diesel, restaurant and fast-food outlet at this exit. MP 104 EXIT 103

Mile 105.5 (479): South Umpqua River.

Mile 106 (478.5): Exit to Weaver Road. MP 107 EXIT 106

Mile 108 (476.5): Exit for **junction** with Highway 99 to **MYRTLE CREEK** (pop. 3,095). All services available. The town, established in 1854, was named for the groves of Oregon myrtle that grow in the area. MP 109 EXIT 108

Mile 110 (474.5): Exit to Boomer Hill Road. MP 110 EXIT 110

Mile 111 (473.5): Weigh station (northbound).

Mile 111.5 (473): Rest area with handicap-accessible facilities (southbound access). ♿ MP 112

Mile 112 (472.5): Rest area with handicap-accessible facilities (northbound access) and **junction** with Highway 99 to Dillard and Winston (see **Mile 119**) and Highway 42 to Coos Bay. ♿ EXIT 112

Mile 112.5 (472): South Umpqua River.

Mile 113 (471.5): Exit to Round Prairie and Clarks Branch Road. Motel. EXIT 113

Mile 119 (465.5): Exit for **junction** with Highways 99 south and 42 west to Winston (4 miles) and Coos Bay (75 miles). This is the access to the 600-acre Wildlife Safari reserve, a drive-through wild animal park, located a few miles west of the interstate; open year-round. See feature on page 50. ▲★ MP 120 EXIT 119

Mile 120 (464.5): Exit for **junction** with Highway 99 north to the Green District, Roseburg. For Roseburg city center, use Exit 124 (see **Mile 124**). Lodging and camping. ▲ EXIT 120

Mile 120.5 (464): South Umpqua River.

Mile 121 (463.5): Exit to McLain Avenue in Roseburg.   MP 122 EXIT 121

Mile 123 (461.5): Exit to Umpqua Park, Douglas County Fairgrounds and museum in Roseburg. Camping.   ▲ EXIT 123

Mile 124 (460.5): Exit to Roseburg city center, Diamond Lake and the **junction** with Oregon Highway 138 (North Umpqua Highway). Food and gas are available at this exit. **ROSEBURG** (pop. 17,910) city center is to the east; all services available with 15 motels and 70 restaurants including major-chain 24-hour restaurants and fast-food outlets. Information center.

Aaron Rose chose this location to settle in 1851, after filing for land under the Land Claim Act of 1850. Rose donated land for a public school and gave free lots to several persons wishing to establish commercial outlets. Rose wanted his city to be selected as the county seat and generously extended the hospitality of his tavern for outlying settlers who wished to stop by and vote. His generosity worked and the town became the county seat. Rose donated land for the courthouse.

The Rogue River Indian Wars of 1855–56 brought hundreds of soldiers into the area, which helped the local businesses prosper. In 1857, the town was renamed Roseburg in honor of Aaron Rose.

Roseburg touts itself as the "Timber Capital of the World," and the community offers historical displays, excellent fishing and hunting and wineries.

Highway 138 follows the North Umpqua River east. This is a scenic route to Crater Lake National Park (approximately 100 miles) and Diamond Lake. The North Fork Umpqua is one of the finest fishing streams in Oregon. Sporting goods dealers in Roseburg can provide current fishing information.   ↜ EXIT 124

Mile 125 (459.5): Exit to Roseburg, Garden Valley Boulevard. Easy access to restaurants and fast-food outlets, major-chain lodging, gas and diesel. Airport to east of freeway. Roseburg city center is approximately 2 miles east (follow signs).

Private campground and River Forks Park are located 6.5 miles west from this exit. Head west on Garden Valley Road (follow signs for camping) 4.6 miles; turn left at llama farm and continue 1.9 miles for private campground and River Forks Douglas County Park. River Forks Park has picnicking and a playground; no dogs allowed May to Sept. It was named for the spectacular meeting of the North and South Umpqua rivers here.   ⛽▲ EXIT 125

Mile 128.5 (456): North Umpqua River.

Mile 129 (455.5): Exit to Winchester, North Roseburg and Highway 99 to Wilbur. This is the access to Umpqua Community College and Amacher Park. Amacher Douglas County Park has 30 tent/RV campsites, full hookups, restrooms and showers. The campground is located 0.5 mile south of Winchester on Highway 99.

WINCHESTER is the town that paid the price of Roseburg's success. It had been the county seat and a prospering community until Aaron Rose promoted Roseburg. The town was named after the Winchester brothers, who were part of a San Francisco explor-

Wildlife Safari

The rhino stood a few feet from the edge of the road and stared at the motorhome brought to a halt by the ostriches. One ostrich was in the middle of the road, inches from the front bumper. The other was face-to-face with the driver, separated only by the vehicle's window.

This is Wildlife Safari, where 550 birds and animals—85 species—roam over 600 acres. Motorists on the 1½-hour auto tour will travel through the Asian section, filled with cheetahs and tigers, past ape and elephant islands to the North American compound, where Roosevelt elk, brown and black bears, and bison roam. In the African section are hippo ponds, lions, white-bearded gnus and zebras.

Southern Oregon's climate is moderate and closely resembles many habitats and areas of Africa. With plenty of open space and a hospitable environment, Wildlife Safari has become a prime breeding ground for many animals. (The endangered cheetahs have reproduced 117 cubs here.) Unlike many zoos and wild animal parks where species are represented by 1 or 2 animals, herds of animals roam here, increasing the possibility of reproduction.

In addition to the auto tour, there is Safari Village, where attractions include flamingo ponds, bear and timber wolf

compounds, and a children's zoo. There are elephant rides, or visitors may board a narrow-gauge train for a short ride by the bear exhibit. Live animal programs are presented several times daily. Visitor facilities include a restaurant, gift shop, RV park for self-contained vehicles, picnic area and pet kennels (pets are not allowed on the auto tour).

Wildlife Safari is located 6 miles south of Roseburg, OR, and 4 miles west of Exit 119 on Interstate 5 (**Mile 119**). It is open year-round. Summer hours are: 8:30 a.m. to 8 p.m., daily. Admission is $1 per vehicle plus $9.95 adults; $8.50 over 65 years; $6.75 ages 4 to 12; 3 and under, free. Admission includes 2 drive-throughs on the same date, plus Safari Village attractions. Safari Village-only admission: $2 adults, $1 children.

ing expedition on the Umpqua River in the 1850s.   ▲ EXIT 129

Mile 130 (454.5): Weigh station (southbound) with phone.   MP 130

Mile 131 (453.5): Sutherlin Creek.

Mile 135 (449.5): Exit to **WILBUR** and northbound access to Sutherlin. Wilbur was named for James H. Wilbur, D.D., known as Father Wilbur, who was one of Oregon's best-known Methodist ministers and who founded several educational institutions.   EXIT 135

Mile 136 (448.5): Exit to **SUTHERLIN** (pop. 5,155) and **ELKTON** (pop. 180) via Highway 138. Access to Oregon beaches. Gas, fast-food outlets, restaurants, lodging and camping. Information center. Sutherlin has all services available.   ▲ EXIT 136

Mile 138 (446.5): Northbound exit to Oakland Historic District, an easy and worthwhile side trip. Head east on paved 2-lane winding road through a rural area and follow signs 1.6 miles to **OAKLAND** (pop. 855). Food service available.

Settled in the 1850s, Oakland prospered first as a trading center and mail point for the surrounding area; then as a shipping center on the railroad between Portland and San Francisco; and finally as a turkey ranching and shipping center in the 1900s. The

present-day economy is based on farming, cattle and sheep ranching. Many of the town's early structures remain and house local businesses. The area is noted for its covered bridges.

Follow north-south signs from Oakland to continue on the interstate.   ★ EXIT 138

Mile 138.5 (446): Calapooya Creek.

Mile 140.5 (444): Southbound exit to Oakland Historic District (see **Mile 138**) and Highway 99.   EXIT 138

Mile 142 (442.5): Exit to Metz Hill.   EXIT 142

Mile 142.5 (442): Rest area with handicap-accessible restrooms and pay phone.   ♿

Mile 146 (438.5): Exit to Rice Valley and northbound access to Rice Hill (food, gas, diesel, lodging). Rice Hill was named for I.F. Rice who settled here in 1850, and the hill that presented a problem for pioneer travelers and railroad construction crews.   EXIT 146

Mile 148 (436.5): Exit to Rice Hill; easy access to food, gas, diesel and lodging east of the interstate.   MP 149 EXIT 148

Mile 150 (434.5): Exit to **YONCALLA** (pop. 940), Drain and Red Hill; Highway 99 heads north to junction with Highway 38 to Reedsport. Yoncalla is an Indian word meaning "home of the eagles," and refers to the mountain near this town.

DRAIN (pop. 1,105) was named for a pioneer settler, Charles Drain, who donated 60 acres to the railroad for a total sum of $1, "in consideration of establishing a station and laying out a town to be called Drain." He and his son, J.C. Drain, served terms on the Oregon Legislature, and the younger Drain became speaker of the house. A Queen Anne-style house here, built in 1893, is on the National Register of Historic Places. RV park, motel.   ▲ EXIT 150

Mile 154 (430.5): Exit to Scotts Valley, Yoncalla and Elkhead.   EXIT 154

Mile 156 (428.5): Elk Creek.

Mile 156.5 (428): Curtis Creek.

Mile 159 (425.5): Exit to Elk Creek and Cox Road.   EXIT 159

Mile 160 (424.5): Exit to Salt Springs Road.
                    MP 160 EXIT 160

Mile 161 (423.5): Exit (northbound only) to Anlauf and Lorane. Both were railroad towns during their founding.   EXIT 161

Mile 162 (422.5): Exit to Drain and Elkton; Highway 99 heads south to junction with Highway 38 to Reedsport and Coos Bay.
                    EXIT 162

Mile 163 (421.5): Exit to Curtin, Lorane and Pass Creek Park. There are gas stations, diesel, truck stop, a motel and a 24-hour restaurant at this exit.   EXIT 163

Mile 169.5 (415): Martin Creek.

Mile 170 (414.5): Northbound exit for junction with Highway 99 to London Road and Cottage Grove Lake.   EXIT 170

Mile 171.5 (413): Coast Fork Willamette River. Northbound travelers may note the change in vegetation as the interstate enters the Willamette River valley.

Mile 174 (410.5): Exit to COTTAGE GROVE (pop. 7,200) and Dorena Lake. All services are available in Cottage Grove, including major-chain motels, restaurants, fast-food outlets, a hospital, 5 banks and information center. Wood products and manufacturing power the local economy, with Weyerhaeuser, Willamette Industries and Georgia-Pacific represented here.

Lane County has the greatest number of covered bridges of any county west of the Mississippi, and many of them are located in Cottage Grove. Maps to area bridges are available at the information center off this exit.

There is access to Baker Bay Lane County Park on Dorena Lake, 8 miles east on a county road; swimming, boating, fishing and camping.   ◄▲ EXIT 174

Mile 174.5 (410): Row River.

Mile 176 (408.5): Exit to Saginaw, named after the town in Michigan. Vehicles with loads more than 12 feet wide must use this exit.   EXIT 176

Mile 178 (406.5): Rest area with handicap-accessible restrooms, phones and travel information. Brown Creek is just south and Gettings Creek is just north of the rest area.   ♿

Mile 180 (404.5): Coast Fork Willamette River. Northbound, the highway cuts a flat, straight line up the Willamette Valley. The Coast Range is to the west and the Cascade Range is to the east.   MP 180

Mile 182 (402.5): Exit to CRESWELL (pop. 2,430), easy access to gas, diesel, fast-food outlets, motel, campground, information center, west off the exit.   ▲ EXIT 182

Mile 183.5 (401): Creswell airstrip to the east.

Mile 185 (399.5): Camas Swale Creek.

Mile 185.5 (399): Exit (northbound only) to Goshen.   EXIT 186

Mile 188 (396.5): Exit 188A is the junction with Oregon Highway 58 (Willamette Highway) to Oakridge, Klamath Falls and Highway 99 to Goshen. Exit 188B is the junction with Highway 99 south to Goshen. Gas is available at Exit 188A.   EXIT 188

Mile 189 (395.5): Exit to 30th Avenue in Eugene, access to Lane Community College and South Eugene. Camping.   ▲ EXIT 189

Mile 191 (393.5): Exit to Glenwood, Springfield and East Eugene. Easy access to food, gas and major-chain lodging west off this exit.   MP 192 EXIT 191

Mile 192 (392.5): Northbound-only exit for junction with Highway 99 to Eugene and access to the city center via highways 99/126 (Franklin Boulevard). Exit here for northbound access to major-chain motels.

EUGENE (pop. 118,370) is a major wood products center and site of the University of Oregon, which serves some 16,500 students. All services are available in Eugene. Special events are held at the Hult Center for the Performing Arts, located downtown adjacent the hotel-conference complex. The 5th Street Public Market offers unique shopping opportunities. Eugene has an extensive system of bicycle and jogging trails and more than 70 parks.

The University of Oregon is nationally known for its School of Architecture and prides itself on the architectural diversity of its campus, which spans the years from historic Villard Hall, constructed in the late 1800s, to the modern architectural wonder of Streisinger Hall Science Complex.   EXIT 192

Mile 193 (391.5): Willamette River.

Mile 194 (390.5): Exit to junction of Highway 126 and Interstate 105 to Eugene and Springfield. Exit 194A is access to Springfield east and McKenzie River. Southbound Exit 194B permits access to University of Oregon, city center, major-chain motels and Valley River Center (the largest shopping center in the southern Willamette Valley) located off I-105.

SPRINGFIELD (pop. 45,765), east of Interstate 5, is the fourth largest city in Oregon; all services available. Major attractions include the Springfield Museum on Main Street and the restored Springfield Train Depot. The town hosts 2 festivals: the Broiler Festival in July and the Filbert Festival, which celebrates the town's favorite nut, on Labor Day weekend. Contact the visitors

The Cottage Grove area has many covered bridges. (Sam Smith)

bureau at (503) 484-5307 for details.

Access to the McKenzie River via Highway 26 east. The McKenzie is almost 90 miles long, and is where the McKenzie-style river drift boat originated. The double-ended, rocker-bottomed craft, built to float on just an inch or so of water yet safely ride out the wildest white water, is the standard for river fishing craft throughout the West. Now known as drift boats, the craft were originally called McKenzies after this river. The McKenzie River is best known as a trout stream, generously endowed with campsites, boat launches and access areas. Local tackle shops can recommend fishing and white-water guides.

Twelve miles west on Highway 126 is Fern Ridge Reservoir, the most popular water recreation area near Eugene. The Long Tom River impoundment has 6 launch ramps, picnic sites and a campground. The lake is good for waterskiing and fishing. It's open year-round. No boat rentals.

                    ♨ ◄▲ EXIT 194

Mile 195 (389.5): Exit 195 is the northbound access to Florence, North Springfield, Junction, Gateway Mall and Eugene airport. Southbound Exit 195A provides access to Springfield and Gateway Mall. Exit 195B leads to Santa Clara and Florence. There is easy access to family and fast-food restaurants, diesel and gas, and major-chain lodging at these exits. Armitage State Park, with picnicking, fishing, boating and handicap-accessible facilities, is located on Coburg Road to the west.   ♿◄ EXIT 195

Mile 197 (387.5): McKenzie River.

Mile 199 (385.5): Exit to COBURG (pop. 750), a national historic district. Easy access to food, lodging, gas and diesel at this exit. Campground.   ▲ MP 200 EXIT 199

Mile 206 (378.5): Rest area with handicap-accessible restrooms and phone.   ♿ MP 206

Mile 209 (375.5): Exit to Harrisburg and Junction City. There is easy access to gas at the exit.   EXIT 209

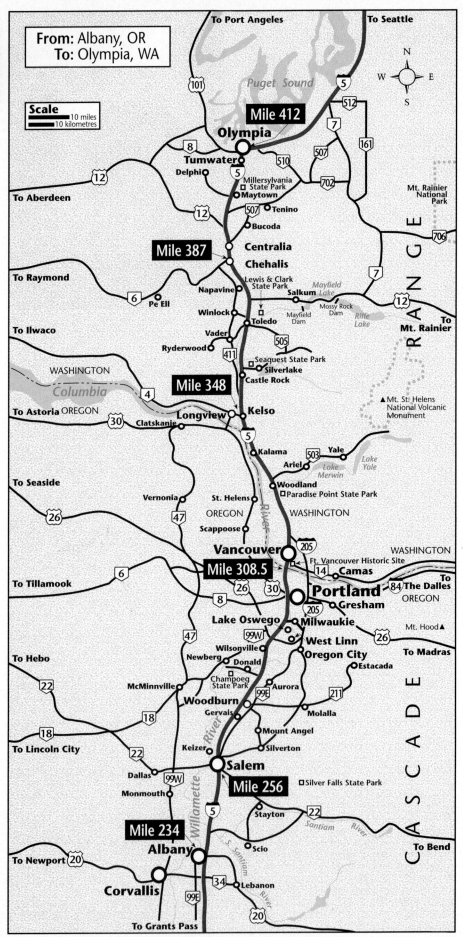

From: Albany, OR
To: Olympia, WA

Scale
10 miles
10 kilometres

Mile 214 (370.5): After the long, flat drive through the Willamette Valley, southbound travelers will notice the hump-shaped Coburg Hills to the east.

Mile 216 (368.5): Exit to Halsey, Harrisburg, Junction City and Highway 228 to Brownsville. This is the access to the Linn County Historical Museum. Food, gas, diesel, lodging and market are available east off this exit.   EXIT 216

Mile 217 (367.5): Crossing Calapooya River.

Mile 222.5 (362): Butte Creek.

Mile 228 (356.5): Exit for **junction** with Highway 34 to Corvallis, Lebanon and Sweet Home. There is easy access to gas, diesel, campground and a 24-hour restaurant at this exit. Corvallis, about 10 miles west, is the site of Oregon State University. ▲ EXIT 228

Mile 230.5 (354): Oak Creek.

Mile 233 (351.5): Exit for **junction** with U.S. Highway 20 (Santiam Highway) to Albany, Lebanon and Sweet Home. (Turn to **Mile 371** in the U.S. HIGHWAY 20 section for log.) Northbound access to Albany city center via Highway 20 west and Pacific Boulevard. Family restaurants, lodging, gas, diesel.   EXIT 233

Mile 234 (350.5): Exit 234A east to municipal airport and Knox Butte. Exit 234B is the **junction** with Highway 99 east to Albany. Easy access to restaurants, fast-food outlets, gas, diesel and lodging at this exit. Information center. Just west of the interstate exit is Waverly Lake Park, where there is a small lake stocked with panfish and restricted to anglers under 18 years old.

Drive west 2 miles on Highway 99 east/Pacific Boulevard for downtown **ALBANY** (pop. 34,125) and historic district (follow signs). Fast-food outlets, shopping and gas stations are located along Highway 99 east/Pacific Boulevard. Albany offers 10 motels, a bed and breakfast and 71 restaurants.

Albany's historic districts (Hackleman, Monteith and downtown) are well known for the varied architectural styles of their buildings, constructed between the 1840s and 1920s. The buildings are detailed in a guide available from the Albany Visitors Assoc., 300 2nd Ave. SW, Albany, OR 97321; phone (503) 928-0911. A guide to covered bridges in the area is also available from the Visitors Assoc.

Albany was named after Albany, NY, by its founders who purchased the land for the city for $400 and a horse. Some 500 Chinese workers, who had been brought to the valley to work on the railroad, dug the Santiam Canal, bringing water and hydropower to the city.

Albany hosts one of the only Veterans Day Parades in the country that is recognized by the American military as an official celebration. All branches of the military are represented as the parade marches down Highway 20 to downtown Albany.

Oregon's logging industry is celebrated in early July with the World Championship Timber Carnival. This event features competitions in ax throwing and tree topping among other skills.

Albany is the retail center of the mid-Willamette Valley and touts itself as the

"Ryegrass Capital of the World." It is the center of the world's foremost grass seed regions. ⊷ EXIT 234

Mile 235 (349.5): Exit to Viewcrest and **MILLERSBURG** (pop. 708), site of 2 wood-processing plants, which sometimes give off a noxious odor. MP 236 EXIT 235

Mile 236.5 (348): Southbound exit to Viewcrest. EXIT 237

Mile 238 (346.5): Exit to Scio (pop. 630) and Jefferson. EXIT 238

Mile 239 (345.5): Exit to Dever and Conner. EXIT 239

Mile 240 (344.5): Exit to Hoefer Road. Gas and diesel available. MP 240 EXIT 240

Mile 240.5 (344): Santiam River. The North and South forks of the Santiam meet a few miles north of Albany and create one of the most productive fishing streams in the state. The North Fork is paralleled by Highway 22 and the South Fork by Highway 20. ⊷

Mile 241 (343.5): Rest area with handicap-accessible restrooms and pay phone. ♿

Mile 242 (342.5): Exit to Talbot Road. MP 242 EXIT 242

Mile 243 (341.5): Exit to Ankeny Hill and Jefferson. No services, but easy access to Ankeny National Wildlife Refuge; a good opportunity for bird watching and seeing area farms (follow signs). MP 244 EXIT 243

Mile 244 (340.5): Exit to Jefferson. *NOTE:* Because of overpass construction, easier access to Jefferson at Exit 243. EXIT 244

Mile 248 (336.5): Exit to Sunnyside and Turner. There is a gas station with diesel west of the exit. This is the access to the Enchanted Forest theme park and RV park east of the interstate. Enchanted Forest offers storybook characters and settings, a haunted house and summer theatre. Open daily, mid-March through Sept.; admission fee; phone (503) 363-3060. Major-chain fast-food outlets. ▲ MP 249 EXIT 248

Mile 249 (335.5): Exit (northbound only) to Salem, Western Oregon State College and museum via Highway 99. EXIT 249

Mile 251 (333.5): Exit to Kuebler Boulevard. Gas, food and lodging. MP 251 EXIT 252

Mile 252 (332.5): Mill Creek.

Mile 253 (331.5): Exit for **junction** with Oregon Highway 22 (North Santiam Highway) east to Stayton and Detroit Lake, and west (via Mission Street) to the airport, downtown Salem and Willamette University. Major-chain motels, family restaurant, campground. Access to Mission Mill Village, a 5-acre park featuring retail shops, historic homes, a textile museum and the Salem visitor center; phone (503) 585-7012. Open daily, admission fee.

Stayton, 17 miles east via Highway 22, is the site of a historic woolen mill (still operating).

Silver Falls State Park, 25 miles east via Highways 22 and 214, offers 10 waterfalls and riding and hiking trails in a lush, narrow canyon. It is Oregon's largest state park and has 53 RV sites with electrical hookups, 51 tent sites, showers, dump station, picnicking and handicap-accessible restrooms. A scenic park, worth the drive.
♿🏕🏞▲ EXIT 253

Mile 256 (328.5): Exit to Market Street, access to downtown **SALEM** (pop. 115,000), Lancaster shopping mall and state fairgrounds. Easy access to gas, major-chain lodging, family and 24-hour restaurants, fast-food outlets at this exit. Salem is the capital of Oregon and the site of Willamette University, which has an enrollment of more than 2,500 students. Scheduled tours of the capitol building weekdays in summer. Salem offers 17 motels and 195 restaurants.

Salem is the second largest city in Oregon and is the center of the fertile Willamette Valley between Portland and Eugene. The 4 biggest industries in Salem are government, food processing, light manufacturing and wood products. Boise Cascade has a fine paper and container plant here.

Willamette Valley is also home to 69 wineries. Several of these are located near Salem and offer tours. Maps are available at the Mission Mill Village visitor center (follow signs from Exit 253), or by writing to the Oregon Wine Advisory Board at 1200 NW Front Ave., Suite 400, Portland, OR 97209; phone (503) 228-8403. (See also Wineries in the GENERAL INFORMATION section.)

Salem offers several parks: Mission Mill Village on Mill Street SE (Exit 253) is a 5-acre park featuring the Thomas Kay Woolen Mill, Marion Museum, John D. Boone House and Jason Lee House; Deepwood Estate on Mission Street SE (Highway 22) is a Queen Anne-style home located in a 6-acre garden; and Bush House, located in the 89-acre Pasture Park on Mission Street SE, was built in 1877. The state capitol on Court Street also has extensive grounds.
MP 256 EXIT 256

Mile 258 (326.5): Exit (northbound only) for **junction** with Highway 99 east (Salem Parkway) to Salem and access to Chemeketa Community College plus Salem historic museums, fairgrounds and state capitol. Gas and lodging available.
MP 259 EXIT 258

Mile 259.5 (325): Sign marks the 45th parallel, halfway between the equator and the North Pole. MP 260

Mile 260 (324.5): Keizer (unincorporated).
Southbound Exit 260A le... Parkway Business 99E and We... State University; Exit 260B to... Chemawa Road and Chemeketa Comm... College. Fast-food restaurant. EXIT 26...

Mile 262.5 (322): Commercial flower fields either side of highway.

Mile 263 (321.5): Exit to Brooks (unincorporated), a small farming community, and access to **GERVAIS** (pop. 1,030). There is a truck stop with diesel west of the exit and food east of the exit. Drive west approximately 6 miles to Maud Williamson and Willamette Mission state parks (day use only) and Wheatland ferry. EXIT 263

Mile 271 (313.5): Exit to Woodburn, Silverton and Oregon Highway 214 to St. Paul, Hubbard and Mount Angel; and Oregon Highway 219 west to Newberg. Family restaurants and fast-food outlets, motels, gas, diesel and RV park are available.

MOUNT ANGEL (pop. 2,930) is the home of the Benedictine Mount Angel Abbey. Mount Angel's Oktoberfest, held in September, is a popular annual event. A Bach Festival is held in July.

The abbey is a monastery of Benedictine monks founded by Fr. Adelelm Odermatt and a group of monks from the Abbey of Engelberg in Switzerland. The main work of

South Falls is one of 10 waterfalls in Silver Falls State Park, located 25 miles east of Exit 253. (L. Linkhart)

Interstate 5

Northbound access to the Salem...
...eads to the Salem
...western Oregon
...Keizer

rs has been
...en for the
...urch, retreat
to guests and
...ormation, write
...ary, St. Benedict,

...4,005) was named
...rew out of control.
...ay passed through a
...he trees were felled to
...he tracks. The crews
waited ... to burn the slash and
dead trees, ... fire went out of control
and destroyed the standing timber as well as
the felled trees. Woodburn is now a busy
agricultural community with all services
available. ▲ EXIT 271

Mile 274 (310.5): Southbound weigh station.

Mile 278.5 (306): Exit to **DONALD** (pop. 370) and Aurora. There is a truck stop with diesel on the west side of this exit, an RV park on the east side.

AURORA (pop. 620), located 3 miles east of the interstate, is a National Historic Landmark District. Founded as a religious colony in the 1850s and named after the daughter of the founder, Dr. William Keil, many of the original buildings of the Aurora Colony now house antique stores. Arts and crafts are preserved at the Ox Barn Museum. A walking tour of the Aurora Colony takes visitors past 33 historic homes and several antique shops. Maps are available at the visitor center.

Drive 6 miles west on a winding 2-lane road through farming area for Champoeg State Park (follow signs). The park has a visitor center, museum, large picnic area on the Willamette River and a 48-site campground with electrical hookups, 6 tent sites, shower and dump station. All park facilities are handicap-accessible. Champoeg was the site of the first Hudson's Bay Co. warehouse and was later a shipping point for Willamette Valley wheat. A provincial government was established at Champoeg in 1843 but the town was destroyed by a flood in 1861. An outdoor historical pageant is presented Friday, Saturday and Sunday nights in July.

The town of **NEWBERG** (pop. 13,735), site of Herbert Hoover's boyhood home, is 7 miles northwest of Champoeg. Hoover was the only president to have lived in Oregon. Newberg was settled by Quakers.
♿🏕▲ MP 279 EXIT 278

Mile 281.5 (303): Rest area with handicap-accessible facilities and travel information center. ♿

Mile 283 (301.5): Exit to the Charbonneau District and **CANBY** (pop. 9,565). Canby has 15 restaurants and a motel.

Southbound Exit 282A is the access to Canby, Hubbard and Aurora Airport; Exit 282B to the Charbonneau District and Aurora, family restaurants. EXIT 282

Mile 283.5 (301): Willamette River. Exit to **WILSONVILLE** (pop. 9,255). Easy access to

family restaurants, fast-food outlets, major-chain motel, gas stations, hospital and information center. MP 283 EXIT 283

Mile 286 (298.5): Exit to Stafford, North Wilsonville and Boones Ferry Road. Hotels, major-chain 24-hour restaurants, gas, diesel. EXIT 286

Mile 288 (296.5): Exit for **junction** with Interstate 205 to **WEST LINN** (pop. 17,645), Oregon City and Interstate 84 to Portland International Airport. Located in West Linn are the Willamette Falls Locks, which opened navigation of the upper Willamette River. Food, gas, lodging, campground and hospital.

OREGON CITY (pop. 16,810) was the first incorporated city west of the Mississippi River. It was the end of the Oregon Trail and the first territorial capital of Oregon. It is a city of firsts: It had the West's first government, newspaper, library, Protestant church, mint, water-powered industry, Catholic archdiocese, Masonic lodge and first court of record.

The Oregon Trail Interpretive Center, located at 5th and Washington Street, has artifacts and displays on the Oregon Trail. Open daily, admission charged. Phone (503) 657-9336.

Mount Hood, easily reached from Portland, offers year-round recreation. (© Lee Foster)

Other points of interest include the Municipal Free Elevator, located at 7th Street and Railroad Avenue, which lifts pedestrians 90 feet up the face of a cliff to a residential-business district and observation deck with a view of downtown and Willamette Falls. The Mountain View Cemetery on Hilda Street has the grave of Peter Skene Ogden, a British fur trader who explored the West in the 1820s.

I-205 is a 4- to 6-lane divided highway that bypasses downtown Portland and rejoins Interstate 5 at **Mile 315** in Washington. This 37-mile route is somewhat longer than I-5, but may be less congested during peak traffic times. (See ALTERNATE ROUTE INTERSTATE 205 log opposite page.) ▲ EXIT 288

Mile 289 (295.5): Exit to **TUALATIN** (pop. 16,640) and **SHERWOOD** (pop. 3,635). Major-chain motels and restaurants, gas, trailer park and hospital. ▲ MP 289 EXIT 289

Mile 289.5 (295): Tualatin River.

Mile 290 (294.5): Exit to **DURHAM** (pop. 800) and Lake Oswego. Family restaurants and fast-food outlets, gas and diesel available at this exit. EXIT 290

Mile 291 (293.5): Exit to Carman Drive, King City (pop. 2,010) and access to Oregon Business Park with all services available. EXIT 291

Mile 292 (292.5): Exit for **junction** with Highway 217 to the Portland suburb of **LAKE OSWEGO** (pop. 31,885), and to Beaverton and the Sunset Highway.

The large spired building seen from the freeway approaching Exit 292 is the Portland, OR, temple of the Church of Jesus Christ of Latter-day Saints (Mormon). The gold-leaf angel atop the tallest spire on the east side represents an angel declaring the gospel of Christ to the world. Dedicated in 1989, the 70,000-square-foot temple is open only to members of the church. There is no visitor center, but non-members are free to walk the beautifully landscaped grounds. No picnicking is allowed. Go east off Exit 292, and look for the "Portland LDS Temple" sign. From the exit, take Kruse Way to Kruse Oaks Blvd., and turn left on Kruse Oaks. The temple is at the end of the street. EXIT 292

Mile 293 (291.5): Exit to Haines Street, Portland Community College and Sylvania. EXIT 293

Mile 294 (290.5): Exit to **TIGARD** (pop. 31,265), Newberg and Highway 99 west. All services available. This is the access to Highway 18 to McMinnville and Lincoln City. Northbound access to Barbur Boulevard. Motels and fast-food outlets. EXIT 294

Mile 295 (289.5): Exit to Capitol Highway and access to food, gas, lodging, Sylvania, Portland Community College and Taylor's Ferry Road. EXIT 295

Mile 296 (288.5): Exit 296B (southbound only) to Multnomah Boulevard. Exit 296A (southbound only) to Barbur Boulevard; all services available. EXIT 296

Mile 297 (287.5): Exit to Terwilliger Boulevard S., Washington Highway 10, Bertha Boulevard and access to Lewis and Clark College and Oregon Health Sciences University. Lewis and Clark College is a private 4-year institution. This exit is closed to trucks more than 15 tons. EXIT 297

Mile 298.5 (286): Exit to Corbett Avenue and John's Landing (northbound only). EXIT 298

Mile 299 (285.5): Exit to Lake Oswego via Highway 43 (SW Macadam Street). Ross Island Bridge and John's Landing. EXIT 299A

Mile 299.5 (285): Northbound exit on west side of freeway to city center, Beaverton, Interstate 405 and U.S. Highway 26. EXIT 299B

Mile 300 (284.5): Exit to Portland city center, U.S. highways 26 and 99 east to Oregon City and **MILWAUKIE** (pop. 19,550). Also access to Central Eastside Industrial District and the Oregon Museum of Science and Industry, which features interactive displays, national touring shows and the 5-story domed screen Omnimax Theater. Handicap-accessible. Exit 300B northbound is access to Water Avenue.   ♿ EXIT 300B

Mile 300.5 (284): The Marquam Bridge spans the Willamette River. **PORTLAND** (pop. 458,275) lies on either side of the Willamette River. The city center is on the west side. (See description of Portland in the MAJOR CITIES section.)

Mile 301 (283.5): Exit for **junction** with Interstate 84 and U.S. Highway 30E to Mount Hood and Gresham. I-84 is the scenic route east up the Columbia River Gorge. Turn to the INTERSTATE 84 section for log. EXIT 301

Mile 302 (282.5): Exit 302A is access to Portland city center and Broadway Bridge, the Memorial Coliseum, Lloyd Center (shopping) and hospital.

Just north is Exit 302B, the **junctions** of Interstate 405 and U.S. Highway 30 to Beaverton, Oregon beaches and **ST. HELENS** (pop. 7,700). Exit 302C northbound is to Swan Island. EXIT 302

Mile 303 (281.5): Exit to Alberta Street and Swan Island, Killingsworth, Interstate Avenue. Hospital. EXIT 303

Mile 304 (280.5): Exit to Portland Boulevard, access to University of Portland. EXIT 304

Mile 304.5 (280): Exit 305A to Lombard Street east; U.S. Highway 30 bypass, and Portland International Airport (northbound only); Exit 305B (northbound only) to U.S. 30 bypass and Lombard Street west. EXIT 305

Mile 306 (278.5): Exit 306B southbound to Interstate Avenue, U.S. Highway 30 bypass, Delta Park and Lombard Street. It is also the access to Portland Meadows, Portland International Raceway and Multnomah Kennel Club's greyhound race track, the only greyhound race track in the Northwest. Major-chain pancake restaurant and fast-food outlets. Exit 306A northbound is to Columbia Boulevard. Exit 306B northbound is access to Delta Park and Expo Center. EXIT 306

Mile 307 (277.5): Exit to Martin Luther King Jr. Boulevard, Union Avenue, Marine Drive, the Rivergate area, shipping terminals T4, T5 and T6 and the **junction** with Highway 99 east. Truck stop. EXIT 307

Mile 308 (276.5): Exit to turnoff for Jantzen Beach; shopping mall. All services available. PUC permits. Major-chain motel, fast-food outlets, gas. EXIT 308

Mile 308.5 (276): Columbia River, the border between Oregon and Washington. Northbound travelers are entering Vancouver, WA.

Mile 309 (275.5): Exit 1A is the **junction** with Washington Highway 14 east to Yakima and Camas. Just north is Exit 1B to Fort Vancouver National Historic Site, Clark College, city center, Mill Plain Boulevard and 4th Plain Boulevard. Exit 1C is southbound exit to Fort Vancouver and Mill Plain Boulevard and provides access to Pearson Air Museum (Pearson is the country's oldest operating airfield). North of this exit is Exit 1D, which is to E. 4th Plain Boulevard, west to Fort Vancouver, and the **junction** with Highway 501.

Highway 14 parallels the north bank of the Columbia River through the famed Columbia Gorge and junctions with Interstate 82 180 miles east from here.

VANCOUVER (pop. 64,350) is the oldest continuous settlement in the Northwest and the 7th largest city in Washington. It was founded in 1824 as Fort Vancouver by the Hudson's Bay Co. In the 1860s, the town thrived from the gold rushes to eastern Washington and Idaho. Over the next century the town continued to grow with increased river traffic and connections with the Northern Pacific Railroad Line, creating a busy shipping center in the town. Today, it is an important navigation center as the terminus of the Columbia channel at the Pacific Ocean. It is

Alternate Route Interstate 205

Travelers passing through Portland, OR, on their way south or north may wish to avoid the heavy traffic of Interstate 5 by taking Interstate 205.

This short highway log is an alternate route through Portland that leaves Interstate 5 at **Mile 288** and rejoins the main highway at **Mile 315** in Washington.

In terms of distance, the route is longer, but it may be quicker during heavy traffic hours and is a thoroughfare for north-south travelers passing through Portland. It also provides easier access to travelers intending to use Interstate 84 east.

This log begins at **Mile 288** and continues north 37 miles to the junction with I-5 in Washington.

Mile 0 (37): South **junction** with Interstate 5.

Mile 3 (34): Exit 3 to Stafford Road and access to Lake Oswego. Hospital.

Mile 4 (33): Tualatin River.

Mile 6 (31): Exit 6 to 10th Street. Gas, food.

Mile 7 (30): Viewpoint (northbound) of snowcapped Mount Hood (elev. 11,235 feet), Oregon's only active volcano.

Mile 8 (29): Exit 8 to Highway 43, West Linn, Clackamas History Museum and Lake Oswego.

Mile 9 (28): Exit 9 is the **junction** with Highway 99 east to Oregon City, Gladstone and access to McLoughlin House Historic Site.

Mile 10 (27): Exit 10 to Oregon City, Highway 213, Parkplace, Molalla, Clackamas Community College and access to Oregon Trail Visitor Center. Gas, food.

Mile 11 (26): Exit 11 to Gladstone.

Mile 12 (25): Exit 12 to Estacada, Mount Hood, Oregon highways 212 and 224 east; all services available.

Mile 13 (24): Exit 13 to 82nd Avenue, Milwaukie, Johnson City, highways 213 and 224, and access to Clackamas Town Center shopping mall. All services available.

Mile 14 (23): Exit 14 to Sunnyside Road. Fast food, gas, lodging and hospital.

Mile 16 (21): Johnson Creek Boulevard.

Mile 17 (20): Exit 17 to Foster Road.

Mile 19 (18): Exit 19 to Highway 26, Powell Boulevard W., Division Street E. and Eastport Plaza.

Mile 20 (17): Exit 20 to Washington Street, Stark Street and shopping mall.

Mile 21 (16): Exit 21A to Glisan Street. Exit 21B to Interstate 84W and Highway 30 to Portland.

Mile 22 (15): Exit 22 to Interstate 84, U.S. Highway 30, Mount Hood, Columbia River Gorge and The Dalles. Travelers headed east on I-84 should take this exit and turn to the INTERSTATE 84 highway log.

Mile 23 (14): Exit 23A to U.S. Highway 30 east bypass and Sandy Boulevard.

Just north is Exit 23B to U.S. Highway 30 west and Columbia Boulevard.

Mile 24 (13): Exit 24A to Portland International Airport. Just north is Exit 24B to 122nd Avenue and Airport Way E.

Mile 25 (12): Columbia River crossing via Glenn Jackson Bridge marks the border between Oregon and Washington.

Mile 27 (10): Exit 27 to Vancouver, Camas and Washington Highway 14.

Mile 28 (9): Exit 28 to Mill Plain Road.

Mile 30 (7): Exit 30 to Orchards, Vancouver, Washington Highway 500 and Vancouver Mall.

Mile 32 (5): Exit 32 to NE 83rd Street, Andresen Road and access to Battle Ground.

Mile 36 (1): Exit 36 to NE 134th Street and NE 20th Avenue.

Mile 37 (0): North **junction** with Interstate 5 at **Mile 315**.

the gateway for oceangoing vessels headed to ports in Washington, Oregon and Idaho via the Columbia and Snake rivers.

Among the many attractions in Vancouver is the Clark County Historical Museum, located at 1511 Main St., phone (360) 695-4681; the Grist Mill on Cedar Creek, north of Vancouver (believed to be the only remaining 19th century grist mill in the state); and Fort Vancouver National Historical Site, located at 1501 E. Evergreen Blvd., phone (360) 696-7655.   EXIT 1

Mile 310 (274.5): Exit for **junction** with Washington Highway 500 east to Orchards and 39th Street, northbound.   MP 2 EXIT 2

Mile 311 (273.5): Exit to Main Street and access to hospital facilities. This is the northbound access to Hazel Dell and NE 99th Street.   EXIT 3

Mile 311.5 (273): Burnt Bridge Creek.

Mile 312.5 (272): Exit to NE 78th Street. Easy access on either side of this exit to motels, major-chain 24-hour restaurants, fast-food outlets and gas.   EXIT 4

Mile 315 (269.5): Exit for **junction** with Interstate 205 (see **Mile 288** and ALTERNATE ROUTE INTERSTATE 205 log on page 55). It also leads to Highway 14, Interstate 84 and north to NE 134th Street and Hazel Dell. Hospital, motels, fast-food outlets and RV park.   ▲ EXIT 7

Mile 317 (267.5): Exit to NE 179th Street, Clark County Fairgrounds and Washington Highway 502 to Battle Ground Lake State Park; 35 campsites, handicap-accessible toilets and showers, swimming beach and boat launch on lake. Battle Ground Lake is stocked with trout and heavily fished. Gas, diesel, 24-hour family restaurant and pizza parlor at exit. ⑤◄▲ EXIT 9

Mile 319 (265.5): Rest area (northbound) with handicap-accessible restrooms and dump station.   ⑤ MP 11

Mile 321 (263.5): Rest area (southbound) with handicap-accessible restrooms and dump station.   ⑤

Mile 322 (262.5): Exit to NW 269th Street, Ridgefield, Washington Highway 501 west; southbound access to **BATTLE GROUND** (pop. 4,244) and Battle Ground Lake State Park (see **Mile 317**). Handicap-accessible facilities. There are gas stations and a restaurant at this exit.   ⑤▲ MP 14 EXIT 14

Mile 323 (261.5): Weigh station with pay phone (northbound).   MP 15

Mile 324.5 (260): Exit to NW 319th Street and **LaCENTER** (pop. 504). Gas, food, 24-hour food mart, phone and diesel 2 miles east of exit. Access to Paradise Point State Park. For the state park, follow signs 1.1 miles north to entrance; 70 campsites in grassy area on east side of Interstate 5. Ranger in residence. There is a small day-use area 0.7 mile from the park entrance (follow signs), with a dirt turnaround and some picnic tables beside the East Fork Lewis River underneath the highway bridge. ⊼▲ EXIT 16

Mile 326.5 (258): The East Fork Lewis River is one of Washington's premier steelhead and salmon streams with year-round runs. ◄

Mile 328 (256.5): The North Fork Lewis River is not as productive as the East Fork, but does offer steelhead and salmon in summer and winter.   ◄ MP 20

Mile 329 (255.5): Exit to **WOODLAND** (pop. 2,500) and the **junction** with Washington Highway 503 east to Cougar and Mount St. Helens. Motels, fast-food outlets, deli and 24-hour restaurant, gas, diesel and RV park at this exit. This is the access to Hulda Klager Lilac Gardens (1.5 miles west, follow signs). Hulda Klager gained fame in the early 1900s for her work hybridizing apples. When her attention turned to lilacs, the gardens surrounding her home began bursting with the colors of new strains of the

flowering plants that she had developed herself. These gardens are now open to the public year-round. Her turn-of-the-century home is open for tours during late April, when the lilacs are in full bloom. Admission fee $1; phone (360) 225-8996. Highway 503 leads east to the Yale Information Station at the southwest corner of Mount St. Helens National Volcanic Monument. (For more information on Mount St. Helens National Volcanic Monument, see the MAJOR ATTRACTIONS section.)

Highway 503 also provides access to the 3-lake chain of Merwin, Yale and Swift Creek reservoirs on the North Fork Lewis River. Good for rainbow and kokanee with a few stray cutthroat and Dolly Varden. ◄▲ EXIT 21

Mile 330 (254.5): Exit to Dike Access Road. RV park.   ▲ MP 23 EXIT 22

Mile 333 (251.5): View of Columbia River to the west. Logs are often stockpiled along the river here, bound for the shipping docks at Longview. Excellent bass fishing near log rafts and pilings and some sturgeon fishing.   ◄

Mile 335 (249.5): Exit to Todd Road, access to Port of Kalama; truck stop and food.   EXIT 27

Mile 338 (246.5): Exit to **KALAMA** (pop. 1,225). Founded in the 1840s, the town was named for John Kalama, who settled in the area after his marriage to the daughter of a Nisqually chief. Kalama boasts a 140-foot single-tree totem pole in Marine Park and the first fish hatchery in the state. All services available including antique shopping malls, campgrounds and a park and marina on the Columbia River. 24-hour cafe, family restaurant and food mart; motel, gas.   ▲ MP 31 EXIT 30

Mile 338.5 (246): Kalama River.

Mile 340 (244.5): Exit to Kalama River Road. There is an RV park and small gas station east of this exit. The Kalama River is a premium steelhead river. The river road parallels the water upstream, leading to several boat launches and access points. Camp Kalama Campground, with 30 tent sites and 84 RV sites, is just above the Interstate 5 bridge.   ◄▲ MP 32 EXIT 32

Mile 344 (240.5): Exit for **junction** with Highway 432 west to Washington Highway 4, Cowlitz County Fairgrounds, the Kelso–Longview industrial area and Oregon Highway 433 to U.S. Highway 30, which parallels the Columbia River west to Astoria and south to Portland. Also access to Carrolls, state patrol, hospital and Port Longview at this exit. The odor in this area comes from the pulp and paper mills, visible to the west. Exit here for the Trojan Nuclear Power Plant; follow signs to Lewis and Clark Bridge across the Columbia River. Head east on Highway 30 for 7 miles to Trojan power plant. The visitor center is open Wednesday through Sunday, 9:30 a.m. to 5 p.m.; phone (503) 556-3751 or 226-8510. Trailer and RV park 3 miles west of this exit.   ▲ MP 37 EXIT 36

Mile 346.5 (238): Highway crosses Coweeman River, excellent Aug. to Nov. producer of sea-run cutthroat; winter steelheading. ◄

Mile 347 (237.5): Exit for **junction** with

Western rhododendrons, the official flower of Washington state, bloom in a variety of colors. (© Lee Foster)

Washington Highway 4 west to **KELSO** (pop. 11,820) and the Long Beach Peninsula. This is also the access to Lower Columbia College, Three Rivers Mall, Kelso city center and the Cowlitz County Historical Museum. Easy access on the east side of the highway to major-chain motels, fast-food outlets, family restaurants and gas. The Kelso Chamber of Commerce Volcano Tourist Information Center is across from the bowling alley on the east side of the interstate. Stop here for information on the park and photos of the Mount St. Helens eruption; phone (360) 577-8058.

Highway 4 parallels the north bank of the lower Columbia and provides access to coastal highways. Good sturgeon, salmon and steelhead fishing from the sandbars near Stella, Cathlamet and Megler. Kelso was named by Peter Crawford for his home town

A view of of Mount St. Helens crater from the Windy Ridge viewpoint. The mountain erupted on May 18, 1980. (© John Barger)

in Scotland, and this Scottish heritage is shown during the Kelso Hilander Summer Festival held during the 2nd weekend in September. The area's history is portrayed in several exhibits at the Cowlitz County Historical Museum (360/577-3119), located on Allen Street. The museum is open daily except Mondays and is free. Because of the Cowlitz River smelt run in January and February, Kelso touts itself as the "Smelt Capital of the World."   ← EXIT 39

Mile 348 (236.5): Exit to N. Kelso Avenue, Cowlitz County Fairgrounds, Highway 431 and access to **LONGVIEW** (pop. 32,300) via the Cowlitz River bridge. Longview is the first planned city in the Northwest, named for its founder, R.A. Long. The Port of Longview is the third largest port in Washington and the seventh largest on the West Coast. Access south to Kelso, Lower Columbia College and Long Beach via highways 4 and 431. Gas, food, lodging and hospital.   EXIT 40

Mile 350.5 (234): Exit to Ostrander Road and Pleasant Hill Road.   EXIT 42

Mile 352 (232.5): Weigh station and phone (southbound).

Mile 354 (230.5): Exit to Headquarters Road. Pleasant Hill Road. Campground. ▲ EXIT 46

Mile 357 (227.5): Exit to **CASTLE ROCK** (pop. 2,075) and Washington Highway 504 (Spirit Lake Memorial Highway) to Mount St. Helens National Volcanic Monument visitor centers and Seaquest State Park. Follow Highway 504 east 5 miles for Seaquest State Park and Mount St. Helens National Volcanic Monument Visitor Center, which is nearest of the 2 centers to the interstate. Seaquest State Park has 92 campsites and is open from May 1 through Labor Day weekend. The Mount St. Helens visitor center, on the shore of Silver Lake, is open daily and has a model of volcano, interpretive display,

films and a viewpoint of Mount St. Helens. The visitor center is free; phone (360) 274-6644 or 274-4038. Highway 504 parallels the Toutle River east for 27 miles and ends at Mount St. Helens National Volcanic Monument. Continue east 43 miles on Highway 504 for the Coldwater Ridge Visitor Center. For travelers with more time, the 43-mile trip to Coldwater Ridge offers several dramatic viewpoints of Mount St. Helens. (For a quick side trip, the Mount St. Helens Visitor Center at Silver Lake offers a modest view of the mountain and focuses primarily on the prelude to the eruption.) The newer Coldwater Ridge Visitor Center focuses on the eruption and the region's recovery, along with offering breathtaking views of Mount St. Helens and Coldwater Lake. A gift shop, bookstore and restaurant are located at Coldwater Ridge. Guided tours and fishing in Coldwater Lake available. The center is open daily and is free; phone (360) 274-2131.

Also access at this exit to Cinedome Theater, which shows "The Eruption of Mount St. Helens" daily on a panoramic screen. Admission fee, phone (360) 274-8000 for more information.

Access to Castle Roc ▓ motels, family restaur ▓ outlet, food mart, priva ▓ Castle Rock Exhibit Hall ▓ Rock features interpret ▓ Cowlitz River, Mount ▓ impact of the mountain ▓ town. Open daily in sur ▓ 274-6603. The exhibit ▓ mile southwest of the inte▓▓▓ ▓▓▓.
     ←▲ MP 50 EXIT 49

Mile 360 (224.5): The Toutle River. Dredging operations continue on the Toutle River and there is quite a deposit of volcanic ash along its banks. The river, once a premier steelhead and salmon fishing stream, was completely washed out by the 1980 eruption of Mount St. Helens. The gray ash being dredged out here originated on the volcano and was washed down by torrential floods unleashed by the melting glacier and the collapse of Spirit Lake on the flanks of the volcano.

Incredibly, steelhead and salmon are again returning to the silt-laden Toutle, and some spawning is taking place in upstream tributaries.

Mile 360.5 (224): Exit to Barnes Drive and Toutle Park Road. Gas, phone and campground.   ▲ EXIT 52

Mile 362.5 (222): Toutle River rest areas with restrooms and often free coffee.

Mile 365 (219.5): Exit to the Jackson Highway and Barnes Drive. Truck stop; food and camping.   ▲ MP 57 EXIT 57

Mile 367 (217.5): Crossing the Cowlitz River. Exit to **VADER** (pop. 425), Ryderwood and Washington Highway 506. Northbound-only access to an RV park, gas station, diesel, mini-market and fast-food outlet on the east side of the highway. Southbound-only access to a gas station and cafe on the west side of the highway.   ▲ MP 59 EXIT 59

Mile 368 (216.5): Exit to **TOLEDO** (pop. 600) on Highway 505, which junctions with Highway 504 13 miles east of Toledo.
     MP 61 EXIT 60

Mile 371 (213.5): Exit to **WINLOCK** (pop. 1,060), access to Toledo and **junction** with Washington Highway 505. Motel, gas, food and RV park.   ▲ MP 63 EXIT 63

Mile 376 (208.5): Exit for **junction** with U.S. Highway 12 east to Mossy Rock and Yakima; access to Morton and Mount Rainier National Park. (See U.S. HIGHWAY 12 section for log of that highway and MAJOR ATTRACTIONS for description of Mount Rainier National Park.) RV park, 24-hour gas, diesel, family restaurant at exit.

For an interesting side trip, drive 2 miles east on U.S. Highway 12, then turn south on the Jackson Highway, which parallels the old Oregon Trail. One mile south of the U.S. Highway 12 junction is the John R. Jackson House. Built in 1848, this renovated log cabin was the 1st American pioneer home north of the Columbia River. Directly south of the cabin is Lewis and Clark State Park with 25 campsites, a marked nature trail and juvenile fishing for stocked trout. A good viewpoint for Mount St. Helens is 600 feet south of the park.
     ▲←▲ MP 68 EXIT 68

Left—The Olympia Brewing Co., at Exit 103 in Tumwater, offers free tours daily. *Above*—The Washington state capitol building in Olympia was completed in 1928. (Photos by L. Linkhart)

Mile 379 (205.5): Exit to **NAPAVINE** (pop. 770) to the west and Washington Highway 508 east to Onalaska. There are a gas station, truck stop and store, diesel and a family restaurant east of the exit.   EXIT 71

Mile 379.5 (205): Newaukum River. Fly-fishermen like this small brushy stream for steelhead, cutthroat and rainbow.   🐟

Mile 380 (204.5): Exit to Rush Road and Napavine. Family restaurant, drive-in, and gas and diesel east of exit.   EXIT 72

Mile 384 (200.5): Exit to 13th Street, Chehalis industrial area. Major-chain 24-hour restaurant, gas, mini-market and major-chain lodging east of this exit. RV park and hospital access. ▲ MP 76 EXIT 76

Mile 385 (199.5): Exit for **junction** with Washington Highway 6 west 20 miles to Pe Ell (pop. 560) and 46 miles to Raymond (pop. 2,870) on U.S. Highway 101. Rainbow Falls State Park is 16 miles west. The park offers 47 tent sites and rainbow trout fishing. Easy access to gas station, drive-in, food mart and lodging at this exit.
&🐟▲ MP 78 EXIT 77

Mile 387 (197.5): Exit to Chamber Way, National Avenue, Chehalis city center and access to Lewis County museum and fairgrounds. **CHEHALIS** (pop. 6,670) is the seat of Lewis County and is located halfway between Portland and Seattle. It is the home of the Claquato Church, located on Stern Road, one of the oldest territorial churches still standing. The bronze bell in the church's belfry was cast in Boston in 1857 and shipped around Cape Horn. Food, gas and lodging available.   MP 79 EXIT 79

Mile 388 (196.5): Salzer Creek.

Mile 389 (195.5): Exit to Mellen Street, Cen-

tralia, **junction** with Washington Highway 507 to Bucoda (pop. 535) and access to Centralia College. Easy access to motel, family restaurants, gas, RV park and hospital east of the exit. **CENTRALIA** (pop. 12,330) was founded in 1875 by George Washington, a black man born into slavery 50 years before the end of the Civil War. He was adopted by a white family and moved west in 1852. It is the home of the largest coal-burning plant in the West, the Centralia Steam-Electric Plant. In spite of the vast amounts of coal burned, you won't see a sign of emission from either of the 400-foot stacks. Tours of the facility are available.

The Fort Borst Blockhouse in Centralia was constructed in the 1850s as a defense against hostile natives. The natives weren't hostile and the fort was used only to store grain.

All services are available. Downtown's Centralia Square Antique Mall offers some 100 antique shops; open daily, phone 1-800-831-5334.   ▲ EXIT 81

Mile 389.5 (195): Skookumchuck River, a small river fished primarily for winter steelhead in March and April.   🐟 MP 82

Mile 390 (194.5): Exit to Centralia and access to Centralia College. Easy access to major-chain motel, fast-food outlets, cafe and family restaurants, RV park. Factory outlet mall at exit.   ▲ EXIT 82

Mile 396 (188.5): Exit 88B is the **junction** with U.S. Highway 12 west to Rochester and Aberdeen. All services available. Just north is Exit 88A, the **junction** of Highway 507 east 8 miles to **TENINO** (pop. 1,315) and access to the South Sound Speedway. Tenino has gas and a deli, no lodging. Wolf Haven is located 5 miles north of town; see **Mile 407** (Exit 99).   EXIT 88

Mile 398 (186.5): Rest area (northbound) with restrooms (handicap-accessible). &

Mile 401.5 (183): Rest area (southbound) with restrooms (handicap-accessible). &

Mile 403 (181.5): Exit to Little Rock, Maytown and **junction** with Washington Highway 121. Access to Millersylvania State Park (open May 1 through Labor Day weekend): Follow signs east 2.4 miles on 2-lane paved road; turn left on Tilley Road and continue 0.5 mile to the state park entrance. Millersylvania has 135 tent sites, 52 RV sites with hookups, all shaded, dump station; good swimming beach and restrooms (handicap-accessible). Boat rentals are available from Deep Lake Resort adjacent the state park; phone (360) 352-7388. Deep Lake is stocked each spring with rainbow. There is a Game Dept. boat launch. Fast-food drive-in west of exit.   &🐟▲ MP 95 EXIT 95

Mile 407 (177.5): Exit to 93rd Avenue, Scott Lake and Washington Highway 121 south. Southbound access to Tenino. Family restaurant, truck stop and gas. Private campgrounds 0.5 and 1.5 miles from highway.

Access this exit to Wolf Haven International, a wolf sanctuary offering narrated tours daily year-round, with "howl-ins" on Fridays and Saturdays in summer. To reach Wolf Haven, go east on 93rd to T junction and turn south on Old Highway 99; continue south about 4 miles past old railroad overpass, then turn left on Offut Lake Road and drive approximately ¹/₃ mile to entrance. Admission charged, phone (360) 264-4695 for more information.
▲ MP 99 EXIT 99

Mile 409 (175.5): Exit to Airdustrial Way and Olympia airport. Southbound access to private campground on 83rd Avenue.
▲ MP 101 EXIT 101

Mile 410 (174.5): Exit to South Tumwater, Black Lake, Trosper Road and access to the Olympia airport. Major-chain motel, fast-food outlets and gas are available at this exit. Southbound access to Evergreen State College, South Puget Sound Community College and Tumwater parks east off exit via Trosper Road to Capitol Boulevard. Black Lake (to the west) is an outstanding year-round lake with rental boats and resorts, providing rainbow, cutthroat, large-mouth bass, bluegills, perch, crappie and bullhead catfish.　　　　　� EXIT 102

Mile 410.5 (174): Exit to **TUMWATER** (pop. 10,000), Deschutes Parkway, 2nd Avenue, and access to the courthouse and Olympia Brewing Co. east off exit. Tumwater, founded in 1845, was the first American settlement north of Fort Vancouver. Some of the area's earliest homes are preserved in the historic district at Grant Street and Deschutes Way. Nearby are Tumwater Historical Park (picnicking, fishing, trails) and Tumwater Falls Park (walking path along river and falls). Contact the Greater Olympia Area Visitor and Convention Bureau, 316 Schmidt Place, Tumwater, WA 98501, phone (360) 357-3370, for more information. The Olympia Brewing Co. (a division of Pabst) was founded here in 1896. Free tours of the brewery are offered daily, 8 a.m. to 4:30 p.m.; phone (360) 754-5177. This exit also leads to Evergreen State College and South Puget Sound Community College. The Deschutes River, visible between the freeway and the brewery, is fished for winter steelhead in December, January and February. Above the brewery it is stocked with rainbow and supports a native cutthroat population. ⚓A⬤ EXIT 103

Mile 411 (173.5): Exit to Capitol Mall (shopping center) on Black Lake Boulevard and West Olympia via U.S. Highway 101. Visitor information; hospital. **Junction** with U.S. Highway 101 to Shelton, Aberdeen and Port Angeles. Travelers headed north on U.S. 101 turn to the end of the U.S. HIGHWAY 101 section and read log back to front.

MP 104 EXIT 104

Mile 412 (172.5): Exit to **OLYMPIA** (pop. 33,900) is the northbound access to Henderson Boulevard, city center, the state capitol and museum and Port of Olympia. The capitol building is visible from the interstate. Tours of the Legislative Bldg. are offered daily 10 a.m. to 3 p.m. Olympia offers major-chain motels and numerous restaurants.

Washington was made a territory in 1853. Olympia, originally called Smithfield but renamed in honor of the mountains to the west, was designated the state capital in 1854. The capitol building was completed in 1928.

The State Capitol Museum on W. 21st Avenue is in a beautiful Spanish-style mansion that was originally the private residence of Olympia Mayor Clarence Lord. The museum traces the history of Washington, its government, pioneer settlements and Northwest coastal Indians. The museum is handicap-accessible. Admission charged; phone (360) 753-2580 for hours.

In 1853 a bed of tiny oysters was found in Budd Inlet, and the Olympia oysters, still grown in this area, are considered one of the world's rarest delicacies.

Olympia's largest industry is known worldwide: Olympia Brewing Co., now Pabst Brewing Co., located at the Tumwater exit (see **Mile 410.5**). For guided tour information phone (360) 754-5177. Oyster farming, mushroom growing and dairying along with logging and timber production are important economic mainstays in Olympia.

♿ MP 105 EXIT 105

Mile 412.5 (172): Southbound Exit 105A

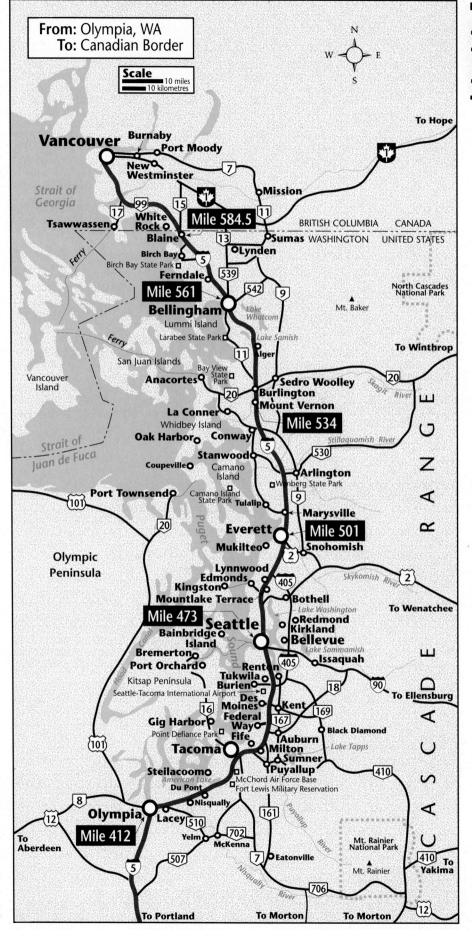

From: Olympia, WA
To: Canadian Border

Scale
10 miles
10 kilometres

leads to the capitol and museum; Exit 105B to Plum Street and the Port of Olympia. Major-chain motels and 24-hour gas are available at this exit.   EXIT 105

Mile 414 (170.5): Exit to Pacific Avenue. Family restaurants, fast-food outlets, 24-hour gas, diesel and food mart at this exit.
MP 107 EXIT 107

Mile 415 (169.5): Exit to Sleater-Kinney Road South, College Street and Sound Center. Food, gas and shopping are available at this exit.   EXIT 108

Mile 416 (168.5): Exit to Martin Way, Sleater-Kinney Road North, Evergreen State College, St. Martins College, LACEY (pop. 21,290) city center and access to Amtrak, state patrol, hospital and Thurston County Fairgrounds. Motels, major-chain fast-food outlets, family restaurants and gas at this exit.   MP 109 EXIT 109

Mile 419 (165.5): Exit for **junction** with Washington Highway 510 to Yelm and Marvin Road. Family restaurants, deli cafe, pizza, 24-hour gas and RV park are available at this exit.

Access to Tolmie State Park, a day-use area with underwater park for divers. Handicap-accessible facilities.   MP 112 EXIT 111

Mile 421 (163.5): Exit to Nisqually and Old Nisqually. Gas, RV park and fast-food outlet are available on the east side of the highway. View to the west of the tide flats on Puget Sound that are part of Nisqually National Wildlife Refuge, located 8 miles west of this exit. The refuge offers foot trails, bird-watching platform and interpretive center. No pets or bikes allowed. Admission charged; phone (360) 753-9467.   MP 114 EXIT 114

Mile 422 (162.5): Nisqually River.

Mile 424 (160.5): Exit to Mounts Road and Old Nisqually. Camping 4 miles east of exit.
MP 117 EXIT 116

Mile 425 (159.5): Weigh station and phone (northbound).

Mile 427 (157.5): Exit to Du PONT (pop. 585), Fort Lewis Military Museum, and northbound access west to Steilacoom and Western State Hospital. The Fort Lewis Military Museum catalogs the military history of the Pacific Northwest from the Lewis and Clark expedition of 1803 to present-day Fort Lewis. The military museum, which can be seen on the west side of the highway, is open to the public Tuesday through Sunday, noon to 4 p.m.; phone (206) 967-7206.
STEILACOOM (pop. 5,700), pronounced still-ah-come, is one of the oldest settlements in the state. Founded in 1854, several historic structures are preserved there. Many buildings are listed on the National Register of Historic Places, including the state's first library, courthouse, territorial jail and Protestant church. The Roman Catholic Immaculate Conception Church, built in 1856, is one of the oldest churches still in use in Washington. The original volumes in Washington Territory's first library are a prized collection at the Steilacoom Historical Museum, located on Main Street in the basement of the town hall.
A ferry leaves Steilacoom for McNeil

Island in Puget Sound, home of a Washington state correctional facility. The McNeil Island facility, formerly a federal penitentiary, is the only island prison still operating in the United States.   EXIT 119

Mile 428 (156.5): Exit to FORT LEWIS (pop. 17,000), North Fort Lewis and Fort Lewis Military Museum. Fort Lewis is I Corps headquarters and the 4th largest employer in the state. No services available. Tourist information center.   MP 120 EXIT 120

Mile 430.5 (154): Exit to Madigan Army Hospital and Camp Murray. Gas and fast-food outlets available at this exit.   MP 123 EXIT 122

Mile 431 (153.5): Exit to Thorne Road in Tillicum and access to American Lake, a favorite fishing, waterskiing and general recreation lake for the Tacoma area. Boathouses, rental boats, boat launches, bait available.   EXIT 123

Mile 432 (152.5): Exit to Gravelly Lake Drive and access to Ponders, VA Hospital and Pierce College. Gas.   EXIT 124

Mile 433 (151.5): Exit to Lakewood, Lakewood Mall and McCHORD AFB (pop. 16,289), home for C-141s. Easy access to major-chain fast-food outlets. Hospital, visitor information, gas and diesel at this exit. The McChord Air Museum, 1 mile east, offers vintage aircraft and aviation memorabilia from the 1930s to 1960s. Free, phone (206) 984-2485 for hours. MP 126 EXIT 125

Mile 435 (149.5): Exit for **junction** with Washington Highway 512 east to Puyallup. This is the access to S. Tacoma Way and Pacific Lutheran University, Northwest Trek via Highway 161, and Mount Rainier via highways 7 and 706 (see Mount Rainier National Park in the MAJOR ATTRACTIONS section).

Northwest Trek, a 635-acre wildlife park, is 6 miles east via Washington Highway 512 and 17 miles south on Highway 161. One-hour, naturalist-guided tram tours offer viewing of North American animals in their natural habitat. Special events in summer. Species include moose, bears, wolves and birds of prey. Open daily March through Oct.; open Friday through Sunday and holidays the rest of the year. Admission charged; phone (360) 832-6116 (recording) or 832-6117. Handicap-accessible.
PUYALLUP (pop. 23,900), pronounced pew-AL-up, offers 7 motels and 18 family and fast-food restaurants, an RV park and all visitor services. Puyallup was founded in 1877 by Oregon Trail pioneer Ezra Meeker. The Meeker Mansion, built in 1890, was a showplace for social and political events. It is a national historic landmark and is open to the public Sunday from 1–5 p.m. It is located at 321 Pioneer Ave.
Puyallup is also the home of the Pettinger-Guiley Astronomical Observatory, the largest amateur-owned-and-operated observatory in western Washington. It is open for the public to view the night sky at no charge. Operated through the Tacoma Astronomical Society, phone (206) 537-2802 for a recorded message on public programs and special TAS programs at the observatory.
Puyallup is also home to one of the largest passion plays in the United States. "Jesus of Nazareth" at the amphitheatre takes place every Friday and Saturday night

from July to Sept. Phone (206) 848-3411 for more information.
In April, Puyallup celebrates the coming of spring with the third largest floral parade in the United States, making use of the thousands of bulb flowers grown in the valley.
Pioneer Days/Meeker Days is held in Pioneer Park in downtown Puyallup the third weekend in June. A Farmer's Market is held at Pioneer Park every Saturday from 9 a.m. to 2 p.m. from May to Sept. Phone the Chamber of Commerce at (206) 845-6755 for more information.
In September, Puyallup welcomes more than 1.3 million visitors to the Western Washington State Fair (1 of the 10 largest in the United States).   EXIT 127

Mile 436 (148.5): Exit to S. 84th Street (northbound only). All services available at this exit including major-chain and 24-hour family restaurants, gas and diesel. EXIT 128

Mile 437 (147.5): Exit to S. 72nd Street, southbound access to S. 84th Street. Food and lodging on the east side of the highway including major-chain motels and fast-food outlets, espresso, pancake restaurant. Southbound access west to Western State Hospital and Steilacoom (see description at **Mile 427**).   EXIT 129

Mile 438 (146.5): Exit to S. 56th Street and access to Tacoma Mall shopping center; gas, food and lodging.   EXIT 130

Mile 440 (144.5): Exit to S. 38th Street, Sprague Avenue, **junction** with Highway 16 west to Gig Harbor and Bremerton via Tacoma Narrows Bridge. Access to Fircrest-Ruston, Point Defiance Park, South Tacoma, Tacoma Mall, University of Puget Sound, Cheney Stadium, Tacoma Community College and city center; family restaurants, hospital.
The Tacoma Narrows Bridge is one of the world's largest suspension bridges. The existing structure replaced "Galloping Gertie," the original suspension bridge, which collapsed in high winds some 4 months after construction in 1940.
Point Defiance Park contains an excellent zoo and aquarium, logging camp museum, Fort Nisqually, Never Never Land and also hiking trails, picnic facilities, boat rentals, scenic drives, a short line ride on a steam locomotive, playgrounds and public beach areas. The waters near Point Defiance are popular fishing grounds for salmon and bottom fish. Handicap-accessible facilities.
EXIT 132

Mile 441 (143.5): Exit to TACOMA (pop. 176,700) city center. Access to Tacoma Dome, Highway 705, Washington State Historical Society Museum (315 N. Stadium Way) and Highway 7. Tacoma has all visitor facilities including major-chain motels. For more information, see description of Tacoma in the MAJOR CITIES section.
CAUTION: Winding road, heavy traffic congestion.   MP 134 EXIT 133

Mile 442 (142.5): Exit to Portland Avenue (northbound only) and Amtrak.   EXIT 134

Mile 443 (141.5): Exit for **junction** with Washington Highway 167 (River Road) to Puyallup and Western Washington Fairgrounds. Southbound access to Portland Avenue via Bay Street and the Tacoma Dome.

Interstate 405—The Eastside
Renton • Bellevue • Kirkland • Redmond • Bothell

Interstate 405 provides access to communities along the east side of Lake Washington. It joins Interstate 5 at its south end at **Mile 462** (Exit 154) and at its north end at **Mile 490** (Exit 182). Ongoing construction at the south end of I-405 and heavy commuter traffic to eastside businesses make this route as heavily congested as I-5 during rush hours. Diamond lanes are restricted to transit and carpool as posted.

Distance from the south junction with Interstate 5 is followed by distance from north junction with Interstate 5.

Mile 0 (30): South **junction** with Interstate 5 (Exit 154). Southbound access to Southcenter shopping mall.

Mile 1 (29): Exit 1 to Tukwila, West Valley Highway, Washington Highway 181 south. Major motel south off exit. Access to Southcenter shopping mall. Former access to Long-acres Racetrack, once noted for its attractive grounds as well as its horse racing. The racetrack was torn down in 1994.

Mile 2 (28): Exit 2 to Washington Highway 167 south to Kent and Auburn, and north to Rainier Avenue and Renton. Major motel, fast-food outlet, shopping and movie theatre north off exit. Valley Medical Center hospital 2.2 miles south of exit via Highway 167. **RENTON** (pop. 45,090) is home to the Boeing Co. plant that does the final assembly of 737s and 757s, the smaller commercial airplanes. (Larger planes are assembled in Everett.) Flight testing is done at Boeing Field (see **Mile 466** in INTERSTATE 5 section). No tours are available at Renton; tours are offered at the Everett Boeing plant, located 3.5 miles west of Exit 189 off I-5 (phone 206/342-4801 for information).

Renton's train station is the departure point for the *Spirit of Washington* dinner train, which takes diners up the eastside to Columbia Winery; phone 1-800-876-7245.

Mile 4 (26): Exits 4A and B to Renton, Maple Valley Road, Washington Highway 169 south to Enumclaw, and Washington Highway 900. 24-hour restaurant, gas and lodging off exit. Camping 3 miles east from Exit 4A at Aqua Barn Campground.

CAUTION: In traffic reports, this winding section of Interstate 405 is referred to as the "S-curves." Drive carefully.

Mile 5 (25): Exit 5 to Park Avenue N., Sunset Boulevard NE and Washington Highway 900 east to Issaquah and Highway 169. Access to the Renton Boeing Plant. Exit west off freeway and follow signs 0.5 mile to Renton's Coulon Beach Park on Lake Washington; food pavilion, very pop-ular log boom beach, swimming, picnicking, boat launch (fee charged) and playground.

Mile 6.5 (23.5): Exit 6 to NE 30th Street; gas station west off exit.

Mile 7 (23): Exit 7 to NE 44th Street. Major motel and fast-food outlet, 24-hour restaurant, at exit.

Mile 9 (21): Exit 9 to 112th Avenue SE, Newport Hills, Lake Washington Boulevard. Park and Ride; phone. Access to Newcastle Beach Park (follow signs, 0.9 mile west from freeway) on Lake Washington; dock, swimming, bathhouse with showers, picnic tables, bike trail.

Mile 10 (20): Exit 10 to Coal Creek Parkway, SE Newport Way. Access to the Factoria Square shopping mall east off freeway 1.1 miles via Coal Creek Parkway; turn north on SE Newport Way.

Mile 10.5 (19.5): Exit 11 is **junction** with Interstate 90 west to Interstate 5 and Seattle via Mercer Island Floating Bridge and east to Spokane (see INTERSTATE 90 section).

Mile 12.5 (17.5): Exit 12 to SE 8th Street. Access to major-chain motel, food and gas to west. This exit also accesses Kelsey Creek Park, a wonderful nature park with farm animals and trails. To reach the park, exit east through the traffic lights and turn left at stop sign at 128th; go 1 block north, turn right onto SE 4th and continue to park entrance.

Mile 13 (17): Exits 13A and B to NE 4th and NE 8th to downtown Bellevue. **BELLEVUE** (pop. 89,710), the Eastside's remarkably fast-growing metropolis, has all visitor services including a number of major motels, restaurants and shopping west off exits 13A or B. Overlake Hospital, fast-food outlets and shopping east off Exit 13B. One of the big attractions at this exit for shoppers is Bellevue Square (Bell Square for short), west on NE 8th (Exit 13B). This 2-story mall has 200 shops, restaurants and department stores. Bellevue Art Museum is located on the 3rd floor of Bellevue Square. Also accessible via Exit 13B is the Museum of Doll Art (phone 206/455-1116), a wonderful collection of dolls, teddy bears, toys, doll houses and miniatures housed in a glittering marble mansion. To reach the Doll Museum go west on NE 8th then

north on 108th Avenue NE and continue to 112th NE. The large modern building to the east of the museum is the excellent Bellevue Regional Library (206/450-1760). For more shopping, Crossroads Shopping Center and Public Market is located about 4 miles east of I-405 via NE 8th. Crossroads has more than 60 shops

One of the many highrises that define the skyline of fast-growing Bellevue. (© *Barbara Harn*)

and services and features 21 international restaurants plus live entertainment. Bellevue's Meydenbauer convention center (206/637-1020) is accessible via Exit 13A. Go west on NE 4th to 112th NE; go north on 112th NE to NE 6th. The convention center is located at the corner of NE 6th and NE 112th. The visitor information center (206/455-1926) is located across the street from Meydenbauer Center.

Mile 14.5 (15.5): Exit 14 to Washington Highway 520 west to Seattle and Interstate 5 via the Evergreen Point Floating Bridge and east to Redmond. **REDMOND** (pop. 38,000) has all facilities. Computer software giant Microsoft is headquartered in Redmond. The Microsoft "campus,"
(Continued on next page)

Nintendo and other high-tech firms are located off Washington Highway 520. Downtown Redmond is also accessible via Washington Highway 908 west from Exit 18. Access this exit to Marymoor Park, which has picnicking, playfields and the Northwest's only velodrome (bicycle racetrack). Marymoor Park accesses the Sammamish River Trail to Woodinville and Bothell. This flat 9.5-mile paved trail is used by cyclists, joggers, walkers and roller skaters. Follow Highway 520 east 5.5 miles to reach Marymoor Park.

Mile 16 (14): Entering Kirkland northbound.

Mile 17 (13): Exit 17 to NE 70th Place, which becomes NE 68th west to Kirkland Park and Ride to east. Gas (diesel), food, grocery and convenience stores 0.5 mile west.

Mile 18 (12): Exit 18 to Highway 908 (NE 85th) east to Redmond, Central Way west to Kirkland. 24-hour gas stations, convenience stores, fast-food outlets, supermarket, warehouse store and other services east off exit. Kirkland Parkplace shopping mall and theatre complex 1 mile west. **KIRKLAND** (pop. 42,000) town center is located at the bottom of the hill to the west on Lake Washington. This busy community is noted for its waterfront location, restaurants, outdoor cafes, art galleries and public art. Several examples of art can be seen at the city parks along Lake Washington Boulevard. The parks offer views across Lake Washington, grassy picnic areas and whimsical bronze sculptures of chil-

dren by artist Prince Monyo Mihailescu. Houghton Beach Park, less than a mile south from town center along the boulevard, has a wading beach and playground. Continue past Houghton Beach on Lake Washington Boulevard for Carillon Point, a private waterfront development of offices, boutiques, restaurants, marina and hotel. Lake Washington Boulevard accesses Washington Highway 520 and the Evergreen Point Floating Bridge across Lake Washington to Interstate 5 and Seattle. Cruises of Lake Washington are available from the tour boat dock at Kirkland's Marine Park at town center; phone (206) 623-1445 May to Oct.

Mile 20 (10): Exits 20A and B to Totem Lake Boulevard, NE 116th and NE 124th. Major-chain motels, fast-food outlets, 24-hour restaurant, shopping, supermarket and gas stations off these exits. Totem Lake shopping mall east off Exit 20B. Park and Ride to west. Access to Fairfax Hospital (west) and Evergreen Hospital (east). Juanita Beach Park 1.6 miles west of Exit 20A via 116th NE; dock, swimming, playground, ballfields.

Mile 22.5 (7.5): Exit 22 to NE 160th Street, Juanita–Woodinville Way NE. Gas station and food east off exit.

Mile 23 (7): Exit 23 to Washington Highway 522 west to Bothell and Seattle, and east to Highway 202, Woodinville, Monroe and Highway 2 to Stevens Pass and Wenatchee. **WOODINVILLE** (pop. 9,407) is a horsey community with 3 wineries (Chateau Ste. Michelle, Columbia Winery and

French Creek Cellars) and Molbak's, one of the largest greenhouses and nurseries in the state. Woodinville is also the end of the Sammamish River Trail (visible from the interstate). **BOTHELL** (pop. 24,530) along the Sammamish River west of I-405 has all services. The 12.5-mile Burke-Gilman Trail, which begins in Seattle, connects with the Sammamish River Trail at Bothell Landing.

Mile 24 (6): Exit 24 to Beardslee Boulevard, NE 95th. Access to major motels and business park. *Seattle Times* printing plant offers tours (phone 206/489-7000).

Mile 25 (5): Entering King County southbound, Snohomish County northbound.

Mile 26 (4): Exit 26 to Washington Highway 527 (Bothell–Everett Highway). Supermarkets, gas stations (diesel), fast-food outlets, restaurants and shopping south off exit. Major fast-food outlet and business park north off exit. Follow Highway 527 south approximately 1 mile for Lake Pleasant RV park and Country Village, a popular shopping mall with a country theme. Highway 527 continues south to Bothell and Kenmore; North, this busy 2-lane highway passes many strip malls and accesses Mill Creek.

Mile 30 (0): **Junction** with Interstate 5 north to Everett and Vancouver, south to Seattle. Turn to **Mile 490** INTERSTATE 5 section for log of that highway. Continue west on Washington Highway 529 for Alderwood Mall shopping center turnoff and Mukilteo.

Crossing the Puyallup River, a major steelhead and salmon river that is heavily fished by commercial Indian nets and sportsmen. The Puyallup originates on Mount Rainier and is discolored by glacial silt during the summer. In the winter, when the glaciers refreeze, the river clears. Fishing areas can be reached by traveling east on the river road. ☞ MP 135 EXIT 135

Mile 444 (140.5): Exit to the Port of Tacoma and 20th Street E. Northbound Exit 136A is access to 20th Street E., and Exit 136B is to Port of Tacoma. Major-chain motels are available this exit. MP 136 EXIT 136

Mile 444.5 (140): Wapato Creek.

Mile 445 (139.5): Exit for **junction** with Highway 99 to **FIFE** (pop. 4,300) and **MILTON** (pop. 5,075). Gas stations are east of the exit; fast food, a 24-hour restaurant and major-chain motels are west of the exit. EXIT 137

Mile 446.5 (138): Hylebos River.

Mile 448 (136.5): Weigh station and rest area (northbound only).

Mile 450 (134.5): Exit 142A to **AUBURN**

(pop. 34,500), North Bend, and Washington Highway 18 east and access to highways 167 and 164. Access to Seattle International Raceway and Supermall of the Great Northwest, a 160-store mall. Highway 18 joins Interstate 90 east of Issaquah, bypassing the downtown Seattle corridor. Travelers planning on driving east on I-90, turn to the INTERSTATE 90 section. Highway 164 junctions with Highway 410 to Mount Rainier National Park.

Half-a-mile east of Exit 142A is the Pacific Rim Bonsai Collection, a 1-acre facility housing more than 50 bonsai trees from the United States, Canada, Japan, Korea, China and Taiwan. Some of the trees are more than 500 years old. The collection was established as a symbol of the importance of Pacific Rim trade relations. Free. Phone (206) 924-5206.

Exit 142B for **junction** with Highway 161 to Puyallup and Mount Rainier. Access to Enchanted Village children's amusement park and Wild Waves Water Park west off exit. Major-chain motels and major-chain 24-hour family restaurant, fast-food outlets, hospital access from this exit. EXIT 142

Mile 451 (133.5): Exit to **FEDERAL WAY** (pop. 72,350) and S. 320th Street and SeaTac Mall. Access to major-chain motels, shopping facilities, gas, diesel, major-chain

restaurants and fast-food outlets west of exit. EXIT 143

Mile 454.5 (130): Exit to S. 272nd Street. Grocery store and fast-food outlet at exit. EXIT 147

Mile 457 (127.5): Exit is the southbound **junction** with Highway 516 east to **KENT** (pop. 40,300), offering 4 motels and numerous restaurants. Also access to **DES MOINES** (pop. 17,300), Midway and Highline Community College, motels and major-chain fast-food outlets, restaurants.

Northbound Exit 149A is access to Kent and Washington Highway 516 east. Just north is Exit 149B, the **junction** with Highway 516 west to Des Moines. Food, gas and lodging west off exit. EXIT 149

Mile 459 (125.5): Exit to S. 200th Street and Military Road. Access to gas, food and major-chain lodging. MP 152 EXIT 151

Mile 460 (124.5): Exit to Orillia Road and S. 188th Street. This is the northbound access to Seattle-Tacoma (Sea-Tac) International Airport via Highway 99; all services available. Three miles east on Orillia Road is The Boeing Co.'s Kent (Boeing Space Center) plant, where the vehicle that was driven and abandoned on the moon was manufactured. Campground, gas, major-chain motels, fast-food outlets at this exit. ▲ EXIT 152

Mile 461 (123.5): Exit (northbound only) to **TUKWILA** (pop. 14,650), Southcenter Parkway and Interstate 405. Tukwila calls itself the Northwest's "Crossroads of Commerce," where I-405 and I-5 meet. Attractions include Southcenter shopping mall, featuring 4 major department stores and more than 100 retail, dining and service facilities; Parkway Plaza—the West's largest concentration of home furnishing outlets; and Pavilion Mall outlet center, the Northwest's first factory outlet mall. Other attractions are Foster Municipal Golf Course, Fort Dente Park and the Christensen Trail near the Green River. EXIT 153

Mile 462 (122.5): Exit to Seattle-Tacoma International Airport and **BURIEN** (pop. 27,610) via Washington Highway 518 west, Southcenter shopping mall and Interstate 405 east to Renton and Bellevue.

I-405 goes up the east side of Lake Washington and intersects with Interstate 90 between Bellevue and Renton. It junctions with Interstate 5 north of Lynnwood at **Mile 490.** See INTERSTATE 405—THE EASTSIDE log this section. EXIT 154

Mile 464 (120.5): Exit to Tukwila, W. Marginal Way, Interurban Avenue and ITT Technical Institute. Major-chain 24-hour restaurant and gas stations are available to the west. Lodging available to the east. Good view northbound of city of Seattle. EXIT 156

Mile 465 (119.5): Exit for **junction** with Highway 900 west, Martin Luther King Way, Empire Way and Renton. EXIT 157

Mile 466 (118.5): Exit to Pacific Avenue, Airport Way, E. Marginal Way; access to hospital, gas, food and lodging west of exit. Also access to Boeing Field and the Museum of Flight. The premier aviation museum on the West Coast, the Museum of Flight features dozens of planes in the 4-story Great Gallery, an impressive glass structure. Exhibits are also housed in the Red Barn, the original Boeing manufacturing plant. A full-size theater presents films on flight. Handicap-accessible facilities. Open daily, 10 a.m. to 5 p.m.; Thursday until 9 p.m. Admission fee. Phone (206) 764-5720. ᕝ★ EXIT 158

Mile 468 (116.5): View of Boeing Development Center and Boeing Field to the west.

Mile 469 (115.5): Exit to Swift Avenue, Albro Place. View to the west of the Port of Seattle. EXIT 161

Mile 470 (114.5): Exit to Corson Avenue, Michigan Street (center lane exit northbound) and access to South Seattle Community College. EXIT 162

Mile 471 (113.5): Exit 163A is the southbound exit to Spokane Street, Columbia Way and access to the Kingdome, West Seattle and cross-sound ferries to Bremerton and Winslow. Good view northbound of the city of Seattle, the Kingdome and Port of Seattle.

Exit 163B is a southbound exit to 6th Avenue S. and Forest Street. Exit 163 is northbound access to these points. EXIT 163

Mile 472 (112.5): Exit for **junction** with Interstate 90 east to Ellensburg, James Street, Madison Street and access to Seattle University and Seattle Central Community College. It is also the southbound access to the Kingdome, Dearborn Street, Airport Way and 4th

Avenue S. I-90 east crosses Lake Washington via the Lacey V. Murrow Floating Bridge (locally referred to as the Mercer Island bridge).

Travelers headed east on I-90 should take this exit and turn to the INTERSTATE 90 section for highway log. MP 164 EXIT 164

Mile 472.5 (112): Express lane northbound entrance (center lane). The reversible express lanes bypass most downtown Seattle exits and end at about Exit 173, where traffic rejoins Interstate 5. The lanes are generally open for southbound traffic in the morning and northbound traffic in the evening.

Mile 473 (111.5): Exit 165 is a northbound access to Seneca Street, the Washington State Convention and Trade Center, and to downtown **SEATTLE** (pop. 522,000). Exit 165A is southbound access to Columbia and James streets. Exit 165A accesses Seattle University and Seattle Central Community College. Exit 165B is southbound access to Union Street, 7th Avenue and the Convention and Trade Center (which spans the freeway here). For description of Seattle, see the MAJOR CITIES section. EXIT 165

Mile 474 (110.5): Exit to Olive Way, Denny Way and Stewart Street. MP 167 EXIT 166

Mile 475 (109.5): Exit to Mercer Street and Fairview Avenue. Center lane exit (northbound) for the Seattle Center and the Space Needle. EXIT 167

Mile 476 (108.5): Exit to Lakeview Boulevard, Roanoke Street and Boylston Avenue.

Just north is Exit 168B to Bellevue, Kirkland and Interstate 405 via Highway 520 east over the Evergreen Point Floating Bridge across Lake Washington.

Northbound, the highway crosses the Ship Canal. View of University of Washington to the northeast. Lake Union is to the west. MP 168 EXIT 168

Mile 477 (107.5): Exit to NE 45th Street and NE 50th Street. This is the access to the University of Washington campus and the University District to the east via NE 45th Street. Access to Seattle Pacific University and Woodland Park Zoological Gardens to the west. (The University of Washington and Woodland Park Zoo are 2 of Seattle's major attractions; see the description of Seattle in the MAJOR CITIES section for more details.) ★ MP 169 EXIT 169

Mile 478 (106.5): Exit to Ravenna Boulevard and NE 65th Street. MP 170 EXIT 170

Mile 479 (105.5): Exit to **BOTHELL** (pop. 13,220), Highway 522, Lake City Way, NE 71st Street and NE 65th Street. EXIT 171

Mile 480 (104.5): Exit to N. 85th Street, NE 80th Street and Aurora Avenue N. (Highway 99). MP 172 EXIT 172

Mile 480.5 (104): Express lane

A spectacular sunset silhouettes Seattle's Space Needle. This view is southbound on Interstate 5 near Milepost 167. (© J. Peery)

southbound entrance (center lane).

Mile 481.5 (103): Exit to Northgate Way, 1st Avenue NE. Access east to hospitals and Northgate shopping center (the first developed shopping mall in the United States). Access west to North Seattle Community College. Express lane northbound exit.

Southbound: On a clear day, you can see 14,410-foot Mount Rainier.   EXIT 173

Mile 482 (102.5): Exit (northbound only) to NE 130th Street, Roosevelt Way and hospital.
            EXIT 174

Mile 483 (101.5): Exit to NE 145th Street and 5th Avenue NE. Exit to Washington Highway 523. Access Shoreline Community College, gas, food and major motel east off exit.
            MP 175 EXIT 175

Mile 484 (100.5): Exit to NE 175th Street and Aurora Avenue N. (Highway 99) and Shoreline Community College.   EXIT 176

Mile 485 (99.5): Exit to **LAKE FOREST PARK** (pop. 3,402), Edmonds, Kingston ferry and northbound access to **MOUNTLAKE TERRACE** (pop. 19,820). Follow Washington Highway 104 west 4.5 miles for Edmonds–Kingston ferry and connections west to the Olympic Peninsula. Gas available east and west of the exit.

EDMONDS (pop. 30,231) is a quiet, bedroom community located on Puget Sound, 4.5 miles west of the interstate, with a dramatic view of the Olympic Mountains on the peninsula to the west. Edmonds has a fishing pier, marina and public beaches. Brackett's Landing Beach, next to the ferry dock, has an underwater park (evidenced by the large number of scuba divers who are usually gathered on the beach here). Edmonds hosts an arts and crafts festival mid-June; the Edmonds Art Festival is the second largest juried art show in Washington. The town prides itself on its slow lifestyle and beautiful, flower-lined streets. Old Milltown is a renovated shopping mall in the downtown area that offers a unique blend of pioneer artifacts, local history and small retail shops. The Edmonds Museum, which served as a library and city hall, is listed on the National Register of Historic Places. All services available including motel, gas, restaurants, banks, post office and supermarkets.   MP 177 EXIT 177

Mile 486.5 (98): Exit to 220th Street SW and Mountlake Terrace. Access Mount Baker–Snoqualmie National Forest Headquarters, west off exit; information on hiking, skiing and road conditions from Mount Baker to Snoqualmie Pass.   EXIT 179

Mile 488 (96.5): Exit to 44th Avenue W., Lynnwood, Washington Highway 524, and access to **BRIER** (pop. 5,855) and Edmonds Community College. **LYNNWOOD** (pop.

Cherry trees bloom in "the Quad" on the University of Washington campus. (David Ovens)

29,580) has all visitor and shopping facilities.
            MP 180 EXIT 181

Mile 490 (94.5): Exit for **junction** with Interstate 405 south to Bellevue and Renton and Washington Highway 525 north to Highway 99. Access west to Alderwood shopping mall (largest covered shopping mall in the Northwest), food and gas. This is the northbound access to U.S. Highway 2 to Stevens Pass and Wenatchee via I-405 and Washington Highway 522. (See INTERSTATE 405—THE EASTSIDE log this section.)
            MP 182 EXIT 182

Mile 491.5 (93): Exit to 164th Street SW (Martha Lake Road), Washington Highway 525 to Highway 99, Alderwood Boulevard and **MILL CREEK** (pop. 8,270). Mill Creek is one of Washington's newest communities, offering motels, family restaurants and gas stations (visitor center at top of eastbound freeway ramp). It was incorporated Sept. 30, 1983.   EXIT 183

Mile 494 (90.5): Exit to 128th Street SW and Post Road west to Paine Field. Paine Field is the site of the Washington State International Air Fair, held in mid-August. Motels, major-chain 24-hour restaurant, fast-food outlets and gas stations west of exit. Camping 2 miles west. Motel and gas station east of exit.   ▲ MP 186 EXIT 186

Mile 496 (88.5): Weigh station. Rest area southbound (handicap-accessible). ♿ MP 188

Mile 497 (87.5): Exit to Washington highways 526 west and 527 south, 99 south, and Broadway Street, Everett Mall Way and access via Highway 526 west to The Boeing Co.'s Everett plant and the Mukilteo–Whidbey Island ferry. Motels, restaurants and fast-food outlets available at this exit. Everett Mall, west off exit, has major department stores and a theatre complex. View to east of the Snohomish River Valley and the Cascade Range.

The Boeing Co.'s main assembly building for 747s, 757s, 767s and 777s is 11 stories tall and covers 62 acres. By volume, it is the world's largest building. Eight 747s and 8 767s can be on the final assembly line at one time. Material and parts for the airplanes are moved to the factory along a 3-mile railroad spur that climbs 600 feet from the main track—the second steepest standard-gauge rail line in the United States. More than 900 planes have been built at this facility since 1968. A 90-minute free tour of the assembly bay and a film are offered several times daily. Children under 12 are not allowed on the tour. To reach the center, go west 3.5 miles past Airport Road exit on Highway 516 and follow signs to tour center parking lot. For schedules and information call Boeing Tour Center at (206) 342-4801.   ★ EXIT 189

Mile 500 (84.5): Exit to South 3rd Avenue, Broadway Street and Everett city center (center lane exit northbound). Major-chain motels and major-chain fast-food outlets at this exit.   MP 192 EXIT 192

Mile 501 (83.5): Exit to Pacific Avenue and **EVERETT** (pop. 79,000) city center. Access to hospital. All services are available including 15 motels, major-chain 24-hour family restaurant and numerous other restaurants at this exit.

Everett, "Great Little City by the Bay," dates from the 1890s when Eastern industrialists Charles Colby, principal owner of the Wisconsin Central Railroad, Walter Oakes of the Northern Pacific and John D. Rockefeller were contacted by their friend Henry Hewitt Jr. about establishing industrial plants in an ideal Western location. With the additional help of timber barons, lumberjacks, mariners and prospectors, Everett (named for Colby's son) became a boom town with a strong industrial base. In 1893, the last spike was driven completing the first transcontinental railroad into Everett.

Built on Port Gardner Bay, many of Everett's industries and pleasure centers are on the waterfront. The Everett Marina Village, at the foot of 18th Street, offers food items from ice cream and muffins to fine dining on steaks and seafood. There are gift shops, souvenirs, fishing charters and sightseeing cruises on the sound. Highly recommended is a trip out to Jetty Island, a 2-mile-long by 200-yard-wide island that is home to many birds. Free ferry from Everett Marine Village; phone (206) 259-0304 for schedule and season. Strolling the promenade deck and enjoying the sea lions offshore are some of the other pleasures of the Everett waterfront. The historic schooner

Equator is also at the Marina Village.

Downtown Everett features the Everett Community Theater, offering theater, dance and musical events from around the world, as well as highlighting regional talent. Located at 2710 Wetmore Ave.; phone (206) 259-8888.

Everett is proud of the Everett Giants, its Class A professional baseball team, an affiliate of the San Francisco Giants. They play other major league affiliate teams in the Memorial Stadium.

A major transportation hub on Puget Sound, Everett has 2 transcontinental railroads, Amtrak, 10 auto freight lines, ocean shipping facilities at the Port of Everett, Snohomish County Airfield at Paine Field and the Everett plant of The Boeing Co., where construction of 767s, 747s and the new 777s provides transportation to the world.

MP 193 EXIT 193

Mile 502 (82.5): Exit for **junction** with U.S. Highway 2 east to Snohomish, Stevens Pass and Wenatchee. Watch for fog in the river valley. Also access to Lake Stevens and Granite Falls via Washington Highway 92. Travelers headed east on U.S. Highway 2 turn to the U.S. HIGHWAY 2 section for log.

The city of **SNOHOMISH** (pop. 6,650) was founded in 1854 and is situated on the Snohomish River 6 miles east of Everett. All services are available including bed-and-breakfast accommodations and many restaurants. The antique shops along 1st Street are a major attraction here: Follow signs for historic district. Snohomish is named after the local Indian tribe. Notice that several place names of Indian origin end in "ish." The suffix means "people." MP 195 EXIT 194

Mile 503 (81.5): Exit (northbound only) to the Port of Everett (see **Mile 506.5**), Marine View Drive, Everett Community College and state patrol. EXIT 195

Mile 504 (80.5): Snohomish River. Union Slough. MP 197

Mile 506 (78.5): Steamboat Slough. MP 198

Mile 506.5 (78): Southbound exit to North Broadway, the Port of Everett and Washington Highway 529 south. Access hospital west of exit. Portside attractions include Marina Village shops and waterfront restaurants. The hulk of Robert Louis Stevenson's *Equator* is on display with an interpretive center. Everett Marina, adjacent to the village, has all marine services and is second in size only to Marina Del Ray, CA. EXIT 198

Mile 507 (77.5): Exit to **MARYSVILLE** (pop. 13,030), the Tulalip (too-LAY-lip) Indian Reservation and Washington Highway 528 east. Easy access to motels, gas stations, family and fast-food restaurants on either side of the freeway. Marysville has 3 motels and 13 restaurants.

For an interesting side trip through the reservation and resort lakes, turn west onto Tulalip/Marine Drive. Tulalip Bingo and Casino, operated by the Tulalip Indian tribe, is located 0.3 mile west of the exit. Open daily, food available. Phone (360) 653-7395 or 1-800-631-3313 (toll free in Washington) for details on bingo sessions and the casino hours.

A fish hatchery that breeds 4 species of salmon can be seen via a 2.5-mile-long dirt road, which leaves the main drive at approximately Mile 5. Kayak Point County Park, with public boat launch, pier fishing, picnic sites and Puget Sound beaches, is at Mile 13.5. Across the road is 18-hole Kayak Point public golf course.

Several lakes are accessible via Lake Goodwin Road, which junctions with Tulalip/Marine Drive. They are Martha, Howard, Crab Apple, Goodwin, Ki and Glissberg Twin lakes. Fishing is fair to good in most for cutthroat and stocked rainbow.

Access to Wenberg State Park on Lake Goodwin with tent and camper sites. The total loop is 25 miles and can be taken in reverse by southbound travelers by taking Exit 206 west at Smokey Point.

🚻🎣▲ MP 200 EXIT 199

Mile 507.5 (77): Southbound access to visitor information center.

Mile 510 (74.5): Exit to 116th Street NE. Truck stop, gas. State patrol.

MP 202 EXIT 202

Mile 514 (70.5): Exit to Washington Highway 531, Lakewood, Smokey Point and Wenberg State Park (7 miles west), which offers 65 tent sites, 10 RV sites with hookups, boat launch and swimming. This is also the exit to Arlington airport, gas, diesel, family restaurants, fast-food outlets and motor inn. ▲ MP 206 EXIT 206

Mile 515 (69.5): Rest area northbound (handicap-accessible). A large, hollow tree is on display that is large enough for several people to stand inside. Free coffee is frequently dispersed by volunteers at this stop.
♿ MP 207

Mile 516 (68.5): Exit to Darrington, Silvana, Arlington and access to North Cascades Highway (Washington Highway 20) via Washington Highway 530. There is a gas station and hospital east off this exit. Highway 530 is a scenic alternative for travelers heading east on Highway 20, winding through sparsely settled river valleys on the apron of the North Cascade mountains. It intersects with Highway 20 at Rockport and is a pleasant, shorter alternative to the freeway hum. Motor inn, restaurant and gas at this exit.

MP 208 EXIT 208

Mile 517.5 (67): Stillaguamish River (a popular fishing destination) offers cutthroat trout, king and coho salmon and steelhead. Summer fly-fishing only. Check state regulations before tackling this river. 🎣

Mile 518 (66.5): Exit to 236th Street NE. MP 210 EXIT 210

Mile 520 (64.5): Exit to Washington Highway 532 west, Stanwood, Camano Island. Access to Camano Island State Park, located 19 miles west with 87 campsites, showers, handicap-accessible, boat launch and dump station. Gas available at exit.
♿▲ EXIT 212

Mile 523 (61.5): Exit to 300th Street NW. Gas station to the west.
MP 215 EXIT 215

Mile 526 (58.5): Exit to Starbird Road.
MP 218 EXIT 218

Mile 527 (57.5): Good view of Skagit River Valley northbound.

Mile 529 (55.5): Exit to Washington Highway 534 east, Conway and Lake McMurray with rainbow fishing and resort facilities. Northbound access to La Conner. There is a gas station east of this exit.

La CONNER (pop. 700) is located

Every spring the Skagit Valley's popular Tulip Festival attracts many visitors to view the daffodil, tulip and iris fields. (L. Linkhart)

11 miles northwest of the exit. Good opportunity to see Skagit Valley flowers in the spring. The valley is famous for producing tulip and daffodil flower bulbs, which are grown in large fields and in the spring create a blanket of color on the valley floor. A late-19th-century fishing port, the town of La Conner is on the national historic register. It has several museums and historic buildings, including a log cabin built in 1869 by Magnus Anderson, one of the area's first settlers. La Conner also offers shopping, quaint bed and breakfasts, a historic hotel, modern motels and restaurants. Sightseeing cruises through the channel and to Deception Pass; fishing charters also available. La Conner is located near the mouth of the Skagit River and at the head of the Swinomish Channel.

Also take this exit to Skagit Wildlife Area, used by hunters from Oct. to Jan., and by bird-watchers the rest of the year. A trail from the parking area leads out to Skagit Flats, where thousands of snow geese and swans stop in winter and spring. Exit west off the interstate and follow Fir Island Road to first major side road south (watch for easy-to-miss signs indicating public hunting access).   ➤ MP 221 EXIT 221

Mile 532 (52.5): Exit to South Mount Vernon. Airfield to west just south of exit. Food, gas, diesel.   MP 224 EXIT 224

Mile 533 (51.5): Exit to Anderson Road. Food, gas, diesel.   MP 225 EXIT 225

Mile 533.5 (51): Martha Washington Creek.

Mile 534 (50.5): Exit to Washington Highway 536 west, Kincaid Street and access to Mount Vernon city center, hospital and fairgrounds. **MOUNT VERNON** (pop. 20,000) is county seat and trade center for Skagit County; all services available. It is one of the largest commercial bulb-growing areas in the country. Thousands of visitors come to view the daffodil, tulip and iris fields in the spring. Best access to the flower fields is off the road to La Conner (Exit 221) or from this exit follow Highway 536 (Memorial Highway) west across the Skagit River to McLean Road. A number of country roads cross McLean and lead to more flower fields. The Skagit Valley Tulip Festival takes place in April. Contact the Mount Vernon Chamber of Commerce, Box 1007, Mount Vernon, WA 98273, or phone (360) 42-TULIP, for more information.   MP 226 EXIT 226

Mile 535 (49.5): Exit to College Way, Washington Highway 538 east and access to Clear Lake, Skagit Valley College and state patrol. Easy access to gas, 24-hour restaurant, motel and shopping mall (visitor information center behind mall) east of this exit; fast-food outlets, restaurant, gas and camping west of this exit.   ▲ EXIT 227

Mile 536.5 (48): Skagit River, the largest drainage into Puget Sound with 2,989 named tributary streams. Fishing guides work the river, and in the fall and winter the river hosts large numbers of bald eagles attracted by the thousands of salmon carcasses washed ashore in the wake of the spawning run. The river offers fishing every month of the year. Check with sporting goods dealers in Mount Vernon to see what's biting where.   ➤

Mile 537 (47.5): Exit to George Hopper Road. Access east off exit to Cascade Mall and Pacific Edge Outlet Center.   MP 229 EXIT 229

Mile 538 (46.5): Exit for **junction** with Washington Highway 20 east to **BURLINGTON** (pop. 4,690), Sedro Woolley and North Cascades Highway, and west to La Conner, **ANACORTES** (pop. 12,000), Deception Pass and Whidbey Island. Travelers headed for the San Juan Islands or ferry connections to Canada should take this exit and travel west 16 miles to Anacortes. Highway 20 continues southwest from the Anacortes turnoff to spectacular Deception Pass bridge and down Whidbey Island. Gas, diesel, food and lodging on both sides of the interstate.

Burlington calls itself the retail center for the county, with most major-chain retail stores located on Burlington Boulevard (east then north from this exit). Southbound access this exit to Cascade Mall and Pacific Edge Outlet Center. Burlington city center via Burlington Boulevard north to Fairhaven.

Anacortes is the southernmost of the San Juan Islands, located on Fidalgo Island, and the gateway to both the San Juans and the Gulf Islands of Canada (see THE ISLANDS section). The Washington State Ferry terminal is located west of town via Oakes Avenue (follow signs). Skagit County's primary industrial and shipping center, Anacortes has all services, including camping at Washington Park. Attractions include the *W.T. Preston*, a 163-foot wooden stern-wheeler, and the historic Railway Depot. The annual Blessing of the Fleet takes place in Anacortes in May during the Anacortes Waterfront Festival. For more information, contact the chamber of commerce, (360) 293-3832.

The North Cascades Highway (Washington Highway 20 east) traverses the spectacular North Cascades National Park. The highway is closed in winter. See description of North Cascades National Park in the MAJOR ATTRACTIONS section. Travelers headed east on Washington Highway 20 turn to NORTH CASCADES HIGHWAY section for log of that route.   EXIT 230

Mile 539 (45.5): Exit to Highway 11 north (Chuckanut Drive), Bow-Edison, Burlington and access to Bay View State Park, which offers 76 campsites.

Washington Highway 11 (Chuckanut Drive) is a scenic 2-lane roadway that winds north along the shoreline of Samish Bay, provides access to Larrabee State Park (61 tent sites, 26 RV sites and boat launch) and rejoins Interstate 5 in approximately 21 miles at Exit 250. This drive is winding and narrow in places and is not recommended for oversized vehicles.   ▲ EXIT 231

Mile 540 (44.5): Exit 232 to Cook Road and access to Sedro Woolley. Access to private campground and hospital.   ▲ EXIT 232

Mile 542 (42.5): Northbound, the highway leaves the Skagit River valley.

Mile 544 (40.5): Exit to Bow Edison and Bow Hill Road. Restaurant.   EXIT 236

Mile 545.5 (39): Rest area (handicap-accessible).   ♿ MP 238

Mile 549 (35.5): Exit to Alger. The northbound interstate begins winding through the Lookout Mountains. Lodge and gas.   MP 241 EXIT 240

Mile 550 (34.5): Exit to Nulle Road and South Lake Samish.   EXIT 242

Mile 551 (33.5): Lake Samish to the west, popular with water-skiers and windsurfers during the summer. Summer fishery for silvers, crappie, largemouth bass and perch. There are resort facilities and a public boat launch. Several years ago a mudslide washed down from Interstate 5 and into the lake, blocking traffic and badly discoloring and silting the lake.   ➤ MP 245

Mile 554 (30.5): Exit to North Lake Samish and access to Lake Padden Recreation Area, a Bellingham community park (day use only). Lake Padden offers fair fishing. Gas available off exit.   ➤ MP 246 EXIT 246

Mile 558.5 (26): Exit to Highway 11 south (Chuckanut Drive), Valley Parkway, Old Fairhaven Parkway, Bellingham's Fairhaven Historical Site and Larrabee State Park. The state park is located 7 miles west of the exit and offers 61 tent sites and 26 RV sites. There are gas stations and services to the west. Scenic Highway 11 (Chuckanut Drive) leads south along Samish Bay and rejoins Interstate 5 at Exit 231. Driving distance is 21 miles (see **Mile 539**). Restaurants, drive-in and coffee shop available here.

Fairhaven Historical Site encompasses 10 historic sites and buildings spread over an 8-block area, including a residential section of Victorian homes. The district preserves what remains from one of the Northwest's great booms in 1889. Picnic grounds and 12-acre rose garden at Fairhaven Park.

Access to Alaska state ferry at Bellingham Cruise Terminal at the foot of Harris Avenue. The Alaska Marine Highway moved its southern terminus from Seattle to Bellingham in October 1989. The Alaska state ferries sail year-round to mainline ports in Southeast Alaska. Shuttle service and sightseeing cruises to the San Juan Islands are also available from this terminal.   ⏚▲ MP 251 EXIT 250

Mile 560 (24.5): Exit to Samish Way, College Park Way and access to Western Washington University. The university's outdoor sculpture collection may be viewed free by the public; drive 1 mile northwest of exit via Bill McDonald Parkway to E. College Way. Gas, diesel, motels, pizza, fast-food outlets available at this exit.   MP 252 EXIT 252

Mile 560.5 (24): Exit to Lakeway Drive and city center. Major-chain motels, pizza, cafe, fast-food outlets and gas stations available.   MP 253 EXIT 253

Mile 561 (23.5): Exit to State Street, Ohio Street, Iowa Street and Bellingham city center. **BELLINGHAM** (pop. 54,580) has a large port and also relies on forestry and agriculture. Downtown shopping area includes historic Fairhaven district (see **Mile 558.5** Exit 250). All services available. Phone the Bellingham/Whatcom County Visitors Bureau at (360) 671-3990 or 1-800-487-2032 for more information.

The Whatcom Museum of History and Art is on the National Register of Historic Places as an outstanding example of Victorian art. Originally the city hall, its 3 floors include permanent exhibits on Northwest birds, the logging industry, Northwest coastal Indians and Eskimos. Collections range from 30,000 photographic prints and negatives to Eskimo, Aleut and Northwest Indian artifacts, plus contemporary regional art. The museum is open noon to 5 p.m., closed Monday. For information write the Whatcom Museum of History and Art, 121 Prospect St., Bellingham, WA 98225, or call (360) 676-6981. Gas and fast-food outlets at this exit. MP 254 EXIT 254

Mile 563 (21.5): Exit to Sunset Drive and Washington Highway 542 east to Mount Baker. Hospital off exit. Impressive cone-shaped Mount Baker (elev. 10,778 feet) can be seen from many directions in northwestern Washington. Mount Baker Ski Area is 60 miles northeast from here via Highway 542, a winding road (up to a 2-hour drive); limited facilities along the road. Good spring skiing. MP 255 EXIT 255

Mile 564 (20.5): Exit to Meridian Street, Bellis Fair Mall (125 stores) and Washington Highway 539 to Lynden. Easy access to food, gas, lodging and shopping east off exit. Access to Sumas and Canada border crossing via Washington highways 539, 546 and 9. Inns, motels, major-chain 24-hour restaurant, fast-food outlets and state patrol are located at this exit. EXIT 256

Mile 565 (19.5): Exit to Northwest Avenue and access to Whatcom Community College. Access to motels and gas. EXIT 257

Mile 566 (18.5): Exit to Bakerview Road and Bellingham airport. Southbound access to Bellis Fair Mall Parkway, Whatcom County Sports Arena, gas, diesel, truck stop and lodging. MP 258 EXIT 258

Mile 568 (16.5): Exit to Slater Road, Lummi Indian Reservation and Lummi Island. Food, gas and casino available. MP 260 EXIT 260

Mile 568.5 (16): Highway crosses the flat Nooksack River valley northbound. Good view to east of the Cascade Range and to the north the Coast Range in Canada.

Mile 570 (14.5): Exit to **FERNDALE** (pop. 6,420), Axton Road and Main Street. There is a truck stop with gas and a fast-food outlet to east, and a motel to west of exit.

The lumbering, fishing and agriculture that were once mainstays of Ferndale's economy have been joined by 2 major oil refineries and an aluminum plant.

Pioneer Park has several old cabins that were moved here and preserved as an early village.

Hovander Homestead, 1 mile south via Hovander Road at 5299 Nielsen Road, is a National Historic Register farmhouse built in 1901–03. The park complex includes the house (with antique furniture) and barn (with vintage equipment), gardens, picnic area, interpretive center and children's farm zoo. The grounds are open daily, the house is open Thursday through Sunday; admission fees charged. Phone (360) 384-3444 for hours. Next to Hovander is Tennent Lake Natural History Interpretive Center. A trail system and bird-watching tower overlook

200 acres of marsh near the banks of the Nooksack River. EXIT 262

Mile 571 (13.5): Nooksack River. Exit to Portal Way, southbound exit to Ferndale. Gas stations with diesel to east. Access to Blaine via Portal Way. The Nooksack is a marginal fishing stream, often discolored by silt sloughing off glaciers in the headwaters. Camping. ▲ EXIT 263

Mile 574 (10.5): Exit to Custer, Washington Highway 548 and Grandview Road; northbound access to Birch Bay. For Birch Bay State Park, follow Grandview Road west to Jackson Road; turn north on Jackson to Helweg Road and state park entrance. The state park has 147 tent sites, 20 RV sites with hookups, hot showers and a picnic area on the beach. Handicap-accessible facilities.
MP 266 EXIT 266

Mile 575.5 (9): Rest area; handicap-accessible restrooms.

In the fall, turning maple leaves add color to the green hillsides along I-5. (David Ovens)

Mile 578 (6.5): Exit to Lynden, Custer and **BIRCH BAY**. Birch Bay resort area has water sports and a giant water slide. Follow Birch Bay–Lynden Road west. Northbound access to Semiahmoo Resort via Birch Bay–Lynden Road (4 miles), right on Harborview then left on Lincoln Road. Access to back entrance to Birch Bay State Park via Birch Bay Drive along the water. Camping, gas and lodging available.

LYNDEN (pop. 5,700) is the home of the Northwest Washington Fair and the annual Tractor Pull Contest held in August. The

annual International Horse Drawn Plowing Match is held here in April. All visitor services. A major stop on the way to or from the Sumas border crossing. Lynden Pioneer Museum features restored buggies and wagons, antique autos and Indian artifacts.
▲ MP 270 EXIT 270

Mile 582 (2.5): Exit to Blaine via Loomis Trail Road, Blaine Road and Peace Portal Drive. Also access to Semiahmoo Resort. Food, gas, lodging and camping available.
▲ MP 274 EXIT 274

Mile 583 (1.5): Exit for **junction** with Washington Highway 543 north to the Canada (truck) customs and access to Highway 15 north to Trans-Canada Highway 1 via Cloverdale. (See TRANS-CANADA HIGHWAY 1 section for log of that route.) Gas and diesel available. EXIT 275

Mile 584 (0.5): Exit to Washington Highway 548 south, Blaine city center and Peace Arch Park. *THIS IS THE LAST EXIT BEFORE BORDER.* There are a restaurant, gas station, visitor information and lodging available at this exit.

Peace Arch State Park lies on the boundary between the United States and Canada. One-half of the Peace Arch rests in each country. The only arch of its kind in the world, the Peace Arch was dedicated in 1921 and commemorates the lasting peace between the 2 nations. An annual Peace Arch celebration is held the 2nd Sunday in June. Open daily until dusk; picnic areas, playground, kitchen shelter and gardens.

BLAINE (pop. 3,860), just west of Interstate 5, has all services available. Good view from main street of Drayton Harbor and Semiahmoo Spit. Semiahmoo Spit is the site of the former Alaska Packers Assoc. cannery, once the largest salmon cannery in the Northwest. The restored cannery buildings are open to the public as a museum.

The recently developed Semiahmoo Resort encompasses nearly 5 miles of the spit's shoreline. The 200-room convention hotel centers around a golf course designed by Arnold Palmer.

For access to Semiahmoo Spit follow Peace Portal Drive to Bell Road, which turns into Blaine Road; turn right on Drayton Harbor Road, left on Harborview Drive and right on Lincoln Road; follow Semiahmoo Resort signs. From Blaine Road, there is also access to Birch Bay resort area and Birch Bay State Park (follow signs). Blaine offers 6 hotels and motels and 24 restaurants. The town's nearby resort area, Birch Bay, offers 7 hotels and motels and 11 restaurants.
MP 276 EXIT 276

Mile 584.5 (0): U.S.–Canada international border. Customs and immigration open 24 hours a day. (See Customs Requirements in the GENERAL INFORMATION section.) If you are headed to Vancouver, BC, continue straight on Highway 99.

CANADA HIGHWAY 5

Coquihalla and Yellowhead Highways
Hope to Tete Jaune Cache, BC
(See maps, pages 69 and 71)

Boston Bar Creek runs along a portion of this scenic highway. (Liz Bryan)

Canada Highway 5 combines the Coquihalla Highway and Yellowhead Highway 5 to connect Hope, Kamloops and Tete Jaune Cache in British Columbia. This south-north route also connects 3 trans-provincial highways: Crowsnest Highway 3 at Hope, Trans-Canada Highway 1 at Kamloops, and Yellowhead Highway 16 at Tete Jaune Cache.

The Coquihalla section of Highway 5 connects Hope at the junction of highways 1 and 3 with Kamloops on Trans-Canada Highway 1. As an alternate route to the Interior of the province (and to points east and north), it is shorter and faster than Highway 1 because it bypasses the older, twisting Fraser Canyon section. The road is a marvel of modern road-building: 4 lanes, with extra passing lanes for trucks, carved through the Cascade Mountains and Nicola Plateau. Beginning close to sea level at the confluence of the Coquihalla and Fraser rivers at Hope, the Coquihalla Highway was built in 2 stages: the first 70 miles/112 km up the Coquihalla River and Boston Bar Creek valleys, then down the Coldwater River drainage to the town of Merritt. This first stage was completed in a rush for Expo '86, and it is one of the most scenic stretches of highway in southern British Columbia.

The second stage of the highway north from Merritt climbs even higher onto the shoulders of the Nicola Plateau before plunging again into the Thompson River valley at Kamloops. While the second part of the highway lacks the alpine grandeur of the first, it compensates by providing easy access to some of the high-country lakes south of Kamloops, famous for their fighting rainbow trout.

The Coquihalla Highway is British Columbia's only toll road. The 1 central toll booth is located near the summit of the Hope–Merritt section, and fees are $10 for passenger cars, light trucks and campers, more for oversize and commercial vehicles. Tolls are payable in cash or by VISA and MasterCard. Permitted driving speed is 65 mph/110 kmph, the highest in the province. It is a limited-access freeway: no U-turns except where indicated.

The Yellowhead section of Highway 5, which begins at Mile 126, connects 2 major east-west routes: Trans-Canada Highway 1 and Yellowhead Highway 16. Yellowhead Highway 5 is logged south to north, from Kamloops to Tete Jaune Cache. The route is not a particularly scenic one, but it gives access to one of British Columbia's largest and most attractive wilderness parks, Wells Gray.

Yellowhead Highway 5 begins in dry belt country, with ponderosa pine park lands and sagebrush, but it very soon passes into the Interior wet zone and runs through thick forests most of the way north. In places, the forest has been cleared for the hay fields of cattle ranches and, in the area around Vavenby, for some of the largest sheep farms in the Interior.

Canada Highway 5 Log

Distance in miles from Hope is followed by distance in miles from the junction with Highway 16 at Tete Jaune Cache. Equivalent distances in kilometres are indicated by Km.

Mile 0 (333.5) Km 0 (537): Junction of Highways 3 and 1, just east of Hope. (For information on Hope see **Mile 438** in the TRANS-CANADA HIGHWAY 1 section.) Highways 5 and 3 follow the same alignment eastbound for several miles.

Mile 4.5 (329) Km 7 (530): Highway 5 strikes north across Nicolum River bridge, one of the engineering wonders of this route. A 5-lane, 4-span bridge with 240-foot-/71-m-long steel box beams passes 160 feet/48m above the river channel. Just beyond the bridge, the road swings into the Coquihalla River valley; the river is west of the highway.

Mile 7.5 (326) Km 12 (525): Othello Road

exit to Kawkawa Lake and Coquihalla Canyon Provincial Recreation Area. Here the focus of interest is the abandoned Kettle Valley Railway, which forced a route through the tortuous canyon by means of 5 rock tunnels linked by bridges over the river. This stretch of railway has been restored as a walking trail, through 3 of the tunnels and across bridges, with spectacular views of the high canyon walls and the rushing water. Restrooms and an information shelter are located at the parking lot near the old station of Othello. Farther along the road is Kawkawa Lake, a great place for family picnics, swimming, boating; commercial and Hope municipal campgrounds nearby. Peers bridge across the Coquihalla just to the north was named for Hudson's Bay Co. clerk Henry Newsham Peers, who in 1847 laid out the Brigade Trail up Peers and Sowaqua creeks over Hope Pass, and a year later built the first Fort Hope.   🏕🏞▲ EXIT 183

Mile 9.5 (324) Km 15.5 (521.5): Orange-and-white checkered buildings mark the start of aerial tramway to microwave station on Mount Jarvis, to the east.

Mile 11 (322.5) Km 18 (519): Ten Mile Creek bridge.

Mile 11.5 (322) Km 18.5 (518.5): Deneau Creek bridge.

Mile 12 (321.5) Km 19.5 (517.5): Large turnout by Coquihalla River, east side of highway, well used by fishermen. The river offers Dolly Varden in spring and fall, coho in fall, and steelhead in the upper reaches in summer, lower reaches in winter. Fly-fishing only; river closures, catch and bait restrictions are posted here. Access to old Coquihalla Road for the serious fisherman. There are several river turnouts north of here, accessible to northbound traffic only.   🐟

Mile 13 (320.5) Km 21 (516): Coquihalla River bridge at Sowaqua Creek near the Kettle Valley station of Jessica.   EXIT 92

Mile 15.5 (318) Km 25.5 (511.5): Dewdney Creek; exit via Carolin Mines (an operating gold mine) Road. Northbound travelers make U-turn to Coquihalla River Provincial Recreation Area, located southwest of the highway. Access is easier for southbound traffic. Recreation area has picnic tables, fishing and hiking. In winter, watch for road closure barriers as highway crews remove potential avalanche and rock fall dangers. Sign advises caution due to sudden weather changes.   🏕🏞🐟 EXIT 194

Mile 17 (316.5) Km 27.5 (509.5): Ladner Creek bridge, a gently curving 6-span structure 840 feet/257m long and 130 feet/40m high. Old railway right-of-way loops to cross creek high upstream.

Mile 18 (315.5) Km 29 (508): Shylock Road overpass (to gravel pit) and U-turn route for southbound traffic. Nearby is a stop of interest marker about the Kettle Valley Railway. This marks the approximate location of the station of Portia. Highway leaves the Coquihalla River and veers northwest into the valley of its tributary, Boston Bar Creek, looping around Needle Peak. Immediately one can notice a difference in topography: The highway begins a steep climb, with rock

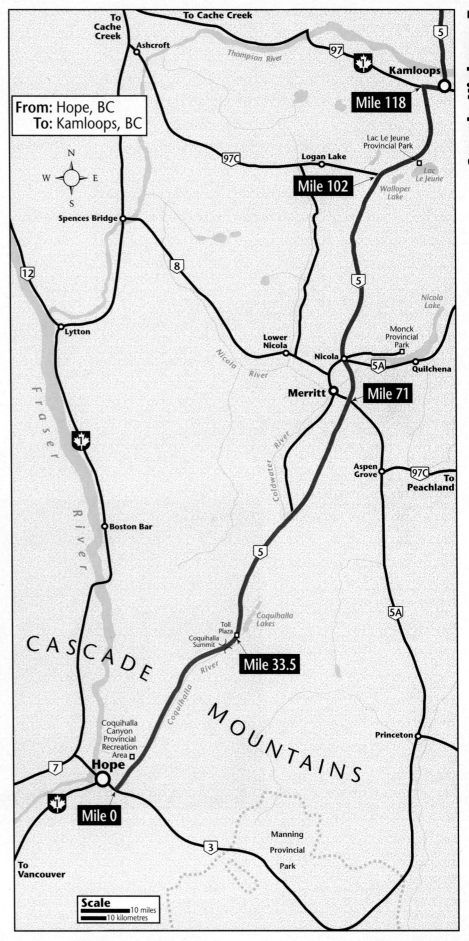

From: Hope, BC
To: Kamloops, BC

faces to the west of the highway carrying a series of waterfalls. EXIT 202

Mile 19.5 (314) Km 32 (505): Chain-up area for northbound vehicles. Snow lingers on the slopes here well into June.

Mile 21 (312.5) Km 34 (503): Portia bridge over Boston Bar Creek.

Mile 21.5 (312) Km 35 (502): Road closure barrier. Start of avalanche protection devices, including earthworks and the first of 12 gun emplacements.

Mile 22.5 (311) Km 36 (501): Cassio Miranda avalanche control ropeway, 1 of 2 in the area. The other is just north of the Great Bear avalanche track and snowshed. Ropeways deliver explosive charges to avalanche trigger zones; charges are detonated by remote control. *WARNING:* Critical accident zone for next 12.5 miles/20 km north. Reduce speed.

Mile 24 (309.5) Km 38.5 (498.5): Impressive Box Canyon on west side of highway, an excellent example of glacial scouring. The stretch of highway north from here to the summit is the most avalanche-prone; 11 major avalanche tracks cross the highway alignment. Box Canyon holds the record for the deepest snowfall of the route: 15 feet/4.6 km in March of 1976.

Mile 25.5 (308) Km 41 (496): South portal of Great Bear snowshed, which shields highway from major avalanches. The shed is among the world's longest at nearly 100 feet/30m. Concrete lintels are decorated with incised figures of bears. A mile north of the snowshed, Boston Bar Creek nears its headwaters (it rises to the west under Zupjok Peak) and the highway veers east back toward the upper Coquihalla Canyon.

Mile 27 (306.5) Km 43.5 (493.5): Viewpoint and rest area under the towering rock slab of Zopkios Ridge and the peaks of Yak, Nak and Thar, all names of Alpine ruminants from the Himalayas. Facilities on west side of road include a heated waiting room, useful for winter emergencies. Access for northbound travelers is through steel "armadillo" culvert underneath highway. This area is within the Coquihalla Summit Provincial Recreation Area, which extends north to just beyond the toll booth; further development is expected. Brake-testing area for southbound traffic.

Mile 28.5 (305) Km 46 (491): Rest area, Boston Bar Creek summit above Romeo railway stop; access to west side of highway via tunnel.

Mile 30 (303.5) Km 48.5 (488.5): Coquihalla Highway Summit (elev. 4,084 feet/1,244m) and Provincial Recreation Area. This pass is not high by British Columbia's standards, but it has a decidedly Alpine feel to it, perhaps because the surrounding peaks are rock slabs, not forested slopes. To the east, good views out across the Coquihalla Upper Canyon.

Mile 31 (302.5) Km 50 (487): Exit for Falls

Lake picnic area, also within Coquihalla Summit Recreation Area; access to old logging road for hiking up Fallslake Creek to the lake; Bridalveil Falls are downstream, behind the last remaining wooden trestle of the Kettle Valley Railway. The falls and trestle may be reached by driving the old pipeline road downstream from Coquihalla Lakes—well worth a detour. Last exit before toll booth. EXIT 221

Mile 32 (301.5) Km 51.5 (485.5): Dry Gulch bridge, a great steel arch 580 feet/175m high over 300-foot-/90-m-deep gulch. (The glacially scoured gulch is misnamed: A small creek does flow through it.)

Mile 33.5 (300) Km 54 (483): Toll plaza; 14 lanes wide, with brake-testing area for southbound traffic, generous gravel turnouts and views across Coquihalla Canyon to the mountains beyond. Tolls, payable in cash or by VISA and MasterCard, are $10 for passenger cars, light trucks and campers. Public telephone.

Mile 35 (298.5) Km 56.5 (480.5): Exit for Britton Creek rest area (heated waiting room) and picnic tables in trees north of Coquihalla Lakes, headwaters of the Coquihalla River. Access to lakes south along Coldwater Road; resort provides cabin rentals, boat launching and camping. South of the resort, Coldwater Road provides access to Bridalveil Falls and KVR trestle, and on to Portia (**Mile 21**). Coquihalla Lakes are stocked with rainbow trout to 2¼ lbs.; fly-fish or troll. Access to Merritt north on Coldwater Road. EXIT 228

Mile 35.5 (298) Km 57 (480): Coldwater River bridge. The Coldwater, a tributary of the Nicola River, rises just to the north of Zopkios Ridge. The highway north crosses the Coldwater several times in the next 10 miles/16 km. Note the high fence beside the highway to keep out deer and ranging cattle.

Mile 41.5 (292) Km 66.5 (470.5): Bridge over Juliet Creek; exit north of bridge for Coldwater River Provincial Recreation Area; fishing and picnicking beside the river. Coldwater has small rainbow and Dolly Varden to 5½ lbs., some steelhead; best fishing July to Nov. You are now in the Interior dry belt, characterized by its lodgepole pine trees.

Mile 49 (284.5) Km 78.5 (458.5): Larson Hill exit, forestry access. EXIT 250

Mile 49.5 (284) Km 79.5 (457.5): Begin 6 percent downhill grade northbound. Despite the ruggedness of the terrain, highway engineers were able to maintain a steady grade, with 6 percent being the steepest incline.

Mile 51.5 (282) Km 82.5 (454.5): Exit Coldwater Road, alternate backcountry route north to Merritt with access southeast to the old railway settlement of Brookmere and Kane Valley Road, a well-maintained backcountry route leading to Highway 5A. Fishing, camping and excellent cross-country ski trails. EXIT 256

Mile 64.5 (269) Km 104 (433): Comstock Road exit; access to Iron Mountain Road, mine ruins, Gwen Lake. EXIT 276

Mile 68.5 (265) Km 110 (427): Good view northbound of the city of Merritt and the Nicola Valley, some of British Columbia's best ranchland.

Mile 71 (262.5) Km 114 (423): Exit to Merritt; rest area by tourist information office in grand log chalet. Also exit to Highway 5A South,

Zopkios Ridge towers above the viewpoint and rest area at Mile 27. (Liz Bryan)

Highway 97C (see HIGHWAY 97C side road log on page 74) and Highway 8. EXIT 286

MERRITT (pop. 6,500) has all visitor services, including campgrounds, motels, restaurants and shops. Logging and mining are the major industries here, and the city is also at the centre of 3 large, historic cattle ranches:

the Nicola Ranch, the Quilchena Cattle Co. and the famous Douglas Lake Cattle Co., Canada's largest. Tourism has become more important to Merritt because of Highway 5, and the city continues to restore its heritage core. An excellent example is the renovated 1908 Coldwater Inn with its balconies and 4-story turret crowned by a red cupola. Nicola Valley museum on Jackson Avenue features the human history of the area, including the native Indians, mining and ranching; open daily.

Merritt, at the confluence of the Nicola and Coldwater rivers, is surrounded by hills dotted with lakes, many with resorts, most of a rustic nature. The fishing for rainbow trout (known locally as Kamloops trout) is exceptionally good.　　　　　　　🎣▲

Mile 72.5 (261) Km 116.5 (420.5): Nicola River bridge. The Nicola rises in Douglas Lake cattle country, flows through Nicola Lake and empties into the Fraser at Spences Bridge on Highway 1. River is fished for rainbow and Dolly Varden trout, whitefish, steelhead and salmon; river is closed below Nicola Lake March through May, above lake Jan. through June. Check restrictions. The valley here is semiarid: Notice the sagebrush and yellow pines.　　　　🎣

Mile 73 (260.5) Km 117.5 (419.5): North exit for Merritt; also exit for Highway 5A north to Nicola, Quilchena, Monck Provincial Park and Kamloops.

The town of **NICOLA** was once the supply centre of the valley; it still has an impressive courthouse, a renovated Victorian mansion and a jaunty little church. Several miles north of Nicola is the Quilchena Hotel, built in 1908 and still providing accommodations in elegant guest rooms, restaurant and bar, tennis courts, boats, riding stables and golf course. Store and gas station adjacent. Across Nicola Lake is Monck Provincial Park; 71 campsites, fishing, swimming, boating. Indian paintings are nearby. Nicola Lake has whitefish, kokanee, burbot and rainbow. *WARNING:* Boaters be prepared for sudden winds.

🎣▲ EXIT 290

Mile 76 (257.5) Km 122.5 (414.5): Chain-up area; highway north starts a long, steady climb up Clapperton Creek into the high forests of the Nicola Plateau. Good view northeast toward the blue twinkle of Nicola Lake and covered black fields of ginseng. Note tunnel under road for cattle and wildlife.

Mile 84 (249.5) Km 135.5 (401.5): Summit (elev. 4,741 feet/1,445m).

Mile 89 (244.5) Km 143.5 (393.5): Helmer Road exit to Helmer Lake.　　　EXIT 315

Mile 92.5 (241) Km 148.5 (388.5): Tiny Quaint Lake tucked into the forest.

Mile 96.5 (237) Km 155.5 (381.5): Begin 6 percent downhill grade for next 3 miles/4.5 km northbound.

Mile 102 (231.5) Km 164.5 (372.5): Meadow Creek Road exit; westbound to Logan Lake and Ashcroft; eastbound to string of fishing lakes, including Walloper, Lac Le Jeune, Stake and McConnell.

LOGAN LAKE (pop. 2,600) lies 9 miles/15 km west, a service centre for mine workers in

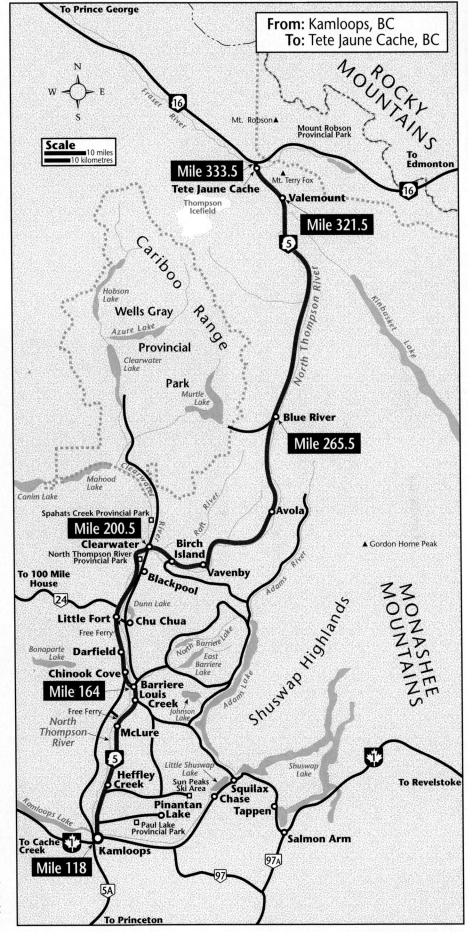

the Highland Valley, known for its rich copper deposits. Highland Valley Copper, North America's largest open-pit copper mine, is open for tours May through Sept. Check at tourist offices in Merritt or downtown Logan Lake. Full tourist facilities.

Walloper Lake and Lac Le Jeune provincial parks and Stake/McConnell Lakes Provincial Recreation Area (15 campsites) all provide excellent fishing for rainbow trout. Lac Le Jeune provides 144 campsites (fee), beach, boat launch, archaeological sites and visitor programs; handicap-accessible. Private resort on lake provides meals, accommodations, boat rentals and a small store with some groceries and fishing tackle. The resort is famous for its cross-country ski trails and also runs a small Alpine ski area. Stake/McConnell also has an extensive network of ski trails (used for mountain biking in the summer).

For a more leisurely and prettier route north, keep on the Le Jeune road all the way to Kamloops. It joins Highway 1 just east of the Highway 5 junction. ☕⛽🚻▲ EXIT 336

Mile 107.5 (226) Km 173 (364): Highway north begins its descent from the plateau into the Thompson Valley; 6 percent downgrade; brake-check area.

Mile 113.5 (220) Km 183 (354): Exit for Inks Lake; U-turn route. EXIT 355

Mile 116 (217.5) Km 187 (350): Visitor centre, turnout for northbound travelers; open summers only.

Mile 117 (216.5) Km 188 (349): Kamloops city limits.

Mile 118 (215.5) Km 190 (347): Junction with Trans-Canada Highway 1 west (also Canada Highway 97) at **KAMLOOPS**, B.C.'s fourth largest city, offering all tourist facilities. Turn to **Mile 273** in the TRANS-CANADA HIGHWAY 1 section for log of that route. EXIT 362

Mile 120.5 (213) Km 194 (343): Copperhead Road to Lac Le Jeune. EXIT 366

Mile 121 (212.5) Km 195 (342): Exit for Highway 5A south to Merritt and Princeton. EXIT 367

Mile 122.5 (211) Km 197 (340): Columbia Street exit for downtown Kamloops. EXIT 369

Mile 125.5 (208) Km 202 (335): Highway 5 exits north to Jasper. **Junction** with Highway 1 East. North of the Thompson River, Highway 5 is known as the Yellowhead Highway because it strikes north to meet Highway 16 which crosses the Rocky Mountains through Yellowhead Pass. EXIT 374

Mile 126 (207.5) Km 203 (334): Former Kamloops Indian residential school (opened in 1890) now houses the Secwepemc Museum of the Shuswap Nation's Kamloops Indian band, and serves as an Indian Education Centre; displays of historical and archaeological artifacts and old photos. Native Heritage Park features prehistoric winter village site and reconstructions showing housing changes from 3000 B.C. to the 19th century. Displays and demonstrations of Native fishing, dancing, story-telling, arts

and crafts. Traditional salmon barbecue. Guided walks. Site of annual August powwow, with dancers from across the continent. Nearby St. Joseph's Church dates from 1880s. **Junction** with road east along the north shore of the South Thompson River to Chase on Highway 1.

Mile 128.5 (205) Km 207 (330): Junction with road east to Harper Mountain Ski Area and Paul Lake Provincial Park (11 miles/18 km). Park has 111 campsites, camping fee, sani-station, picnic area, swimming, fishing (rainbow to 9 lbs.) and hiking. Also access to Pinantan Lake (another 4 miles/6.5 km); fly-fishing and trolling for rainbow. Accommodations and boats at lake. ☕🏕🚻⛽▲

Mile 133.5 (200) Km 215 (322): Northern boundary of the Kamloops Indian Reserve. To the east lie the Dome Hills.

Mile 134 (199.5) Km 216 (321): Kamloops suburb of Aspen Park; store.

Above—*Helmcken Falls, located in the Wells Gray Provincial Park, is Canada's 4th largest waterfall. The park is a vast wilderness area that offers hiking trails, abundant wildlife and camping.* (Courtesy of BC Parks) ***Right***—*Helmcken Falls is as beautiful in winter as in summer.* (Liz Bryan)

Mile 138.5 (195) Km 222.5 (314.5): Old highway to Heffley Creek sawmill.

Mile 139.5 (194) Km 224.5 (312.5): Access road to small settlement of Heffley Creek.

Mile 141 (192.5) Km 227 (310): Road east to Sun Peaks Ski Area (formerly Tod Mountain). Also to Big and Little Heffley lakes (11.5 miles/19 km), with cabins, boats, camping and fishing for rainbow. 🐟⛵▲

Mile 151.5 (182) Km 244 (293): Small community of **McLURE**; coffee shop and campground. ▲

Mile 154 (179.5) Km 248 (289): Road west to McLure Ferry, free transportation across the North Thompson River to Westside Road, which goes south to Kamloops or north to meet Highway 5 at Barriere. The ferry is on call between 7 a.m. and 6:45 p.m., and has room for 2 cars and 10 passengers. Ferry does not operate in high water (early to late June) and during freezeup.

Mile 157 (176.5) Km 253 (284): Fish Trap rest area overlooks Fishtrap Rapids, where Indians used to trap spawning salmon.

Mile 160 (173.5) Km 257.5 (279.5): Thompson River overlook. The North Thompson River rises in the Cariboo Mountains and flows southward to meet the South Thompson at Kamloops. The route was made famous by a small group of Overlanders, led by Thomas McMicking, who turned south at Tete Jaune Cache and headed for Fort Kamloops on their way to the Cariboo goldfields in 1862. (The rest of the Overlanders went down the Fraser.) It took the McMicking group (a party of 32 men, a pregnant woman and her 3 small children) almost a month to reach the civilization of the fort, where the following day Mrs. Catherine Schubert delivered her fourth child, Rose, the first white girl born in the British Columbia Interior. The story of their trip is one of incredible privation and courage.

Every year, a raft race on the Thompson from Clearwater to Kamloops, the quieter section of the river, honours the bravery of the Overlanders, many of whom settled in the Kamloops area.

Mile 161.5 (172) Km 259.5 (277.5): Louis Creek bridge.

Mile 162 (171.5) Km 261 (276): Small community of **LOUIS CREEK** (unincorporated) is supported by a large lumber mill. Gas and food are available. A road leads southeast from here to Forest Lake (13.5 miles/22 km) and Johnson Lake (25 miles/40 km). Both lakes have rainbow; boats and accommodations on Johnson. Road continues to Agate Bay on Adams Lake (north of Squilax on Highway 1). ◂

Mile 164 (169.5) Km 264 (273): Tourist information booth and gas station at south end of loop road to community of **BARRIERE** (area pop. 5,000). Full tourist facilities, small museum in town centre. Large sawmill at north edge of town.

Roads from Barriere lead northeast to Barriere lakes (North Barriere Lake 13.5 miles/ 22 km; East Barriere Lake 20 miles/32 km) and north to Chu Chua and Dunn and Halamore lakes via east side of Thompson River, rejoining Highway 5 at Clearwater. Ferry crossing to Little Fort via Windpass Road.

Mile 164.5 (169) Km 265 (272): Barriere River bridge.

Mile 165.5 (168) Km 266 (271): North end of loop road to Barriere, just south of Thompson River bridge.

Mile 166 (167.5) Km 267 (270): Access to Westside Road, which leads down the west side of the Thompson River 40.5 miles/65 km to Kamloops.

Mile 167.5 (166) Km 269.5 (267.5): Chinook Cove rest area; pleasantly shaded picnic area. **CHINOOK COVE** is a small community by the river. ⋔

Mile 170.5 (163) Km 274 (263): Rest area with picnic tables. Drinking water is piped from a spring. ⋔

Mile 177 (156.5) Km 285 (252): Unincorporated community of **DARFIELD**, with a sawmill and cluster of old buildings. The valley is irrigated for corn and hay.

Mile 182.5 (151) Km 294 (243): Community of **LITTLE FORT** (pop. less than 200) takes its name from a Hudson's Bay Co. fur-trading post that was located here. Food, gas, accommodations available. Rest area.

Junction with Highway 24, which leads west 60 miles/96.5 km to Highway 97 near 100 Mile House. This road gives access to great rainbow fishing in many lakes, including Bridge and Sheridan lakes.

A free ferry connects Little Fort with Dunn

Lake Road up the east side of the Thompson River south to Barriere (see **Mile 164**) and north to Clearwater. Reaction ferry operates on call between 7 a.m. and 6:45 p.m. ◂

Mile 191.5 (142) Km 308 (229): Highway parallels the North Thompson River, with several turnouts and fishing spots among the cottonwoods. Rainbow, Dolly Varden and whitefish are caught here. ◂

Clearwater Lake offers beautiful scenery as well as good fishing for rainbow, Dolly Varden and mountain whitefish. (BC Parks)

Mile 196 (137.5) Km 315.5 (221.5): Gas and store at the **junction** with Old North Thompson Road. West to Clearwater business district.

Mile 198 (135.5) Km 319 (218): North Thompson River Provincial Park, 61 campsites, visitor centre, sani-station, picnic area and fishing at the mouth of the Clearwater River. Camping fee. Cross-country ski trails in winter. This was once the site of a Shuswap Indian camp, and many kekuli holes (remains of semisubterranean dwellings) can still be found. ⋔◂▲

Mile 199 (134.5) Km 320.5 (216.5): Clearwater River bridge. The Overlanders named this river after its crystal-clear waters that contrasted strongly with the muddy Thompson. The Clearwater rises in the glaciated Cariboo Mountains at the north end of Wells Gray Provincial Park.

Mile 200.5 (133) Km 323 (214): Junction with access road to village of **CLEARWATER** (pop. 7,000). A tourist information office is located at the junction. This striking wood building also serves as the information centre for Wells Gray Provincial Park. Turn west for tourist facilities (motels, RV parks, restaurants, gas stations, shopping centre), Dutch Lake public beach, airstrip, Star and Lolo lakes. Fishing is good for rainbow and Dolly Varden in both lakes and the Clearwater River. Turn east for old village centre and bridge over the Thompson River to connect

with road along the east side to Clearwater ski hill, Blackpool, Dunn and Halamore lakes and the ferry to Little Fort.

Just to the north is **junction** with Clearwater Valley Road west to Yellowhead Museum (open by appointment, phone 604/674-3660), Spahats Creek Provincial Park (6 miles/10 km), Trophy Mountain Recreation Area (7.5 miles/12 km) and Wells Gray Provincial Park (21.5 miles/35 km). At Spahats Creek Park there are 20 campsites and a picnic area. Camping fee. The park's chief attraction is impressive Spahats Falls.

Wells Gray Provincial Park is a magnificent wilderness in the Cariboo Mountains containing 5 large lakes and 3 rivers which, on their steep descent to the Thompson, cascade over many spectacular waterfalls, including Helmcken Falls on the Murtle River at 460 feet/140m. There are more than a dozen trails in the park leading to the major scenic attractions.

The park contains such interesting geological features as extinct volcanoes, lava beds, glaciers, mineral springs and warm gas flows, though it is chiefly known for the rugged, unspoiled beauty of its lakes, rivers and mountains. There is abundant wildlife, including moose, deer, caribou, mountain goat and bear. The southeastern half of the park is the Murtle Lake Nature Conservancy Area, where no roads and no tampering with the natural resources are allowed.

It is possible to make a 63-mile/102-km circuit by boat of Clearwater and Azure lakes. The lakes also provide good summer fishing for rainbow, Dolly Varden and mountain whitefish.

There are 4 campgrounds in Wells Gray, with a total of 154 campsites. They are Dawson Falls, Clearwater Lake, Falls Creek and Mahood Lake (reached from 100 Mile House on Highway 97). Camping fee. There are picnic sites at Helmcken Falls, Clearwater Lake and along park roads. Boat-launching ramps are located at Mahood and Clearwater lakes. Powerboats are prohibited on Murtle Lake, considered to be one of the most beautiful wilderness lakes in British Columbia.

Just outside the park boundary is Helmcken Falls Lodge, a 1948 log building with accommodations, meals, store and canoe rentals. Make sure you fill your gas tank in Clearwater; there is no gas on the road to the park.

Mile 202.5 (131) Km 326 (211): Candle Creek Road west to cross-country ski and snowmobile trails.

Mile 204 (129.5) Km 328.5 (208.5): Raft River bridge. Side road leads upriver 22 miles/37 km to Silence Lake; fishing for rainbow. Just north of bridge is Clearwater Forestry Office. Check here regarding backcountry road conditions.

Mile 207.5 (126) Km 334 (203): Birch Island rest area and viewpoint over the Thompson River valley. Just south is a road leading east to the small community of **BIRCH ISLAND**; store, public phone available.

Mile 216 (117.5) Km 348 (189): Road east to community of **VAVENBY**, centre of valley sheep farming. Visitors welcome at Molliet sheep farm, one of Canada's largest.

Mile 225.5 (108) Km 362.5 (174.5): Mad River bridge. The river gives its name to the rapids in the river below, where the weary Overlanders had to portage their rafts.

Highway 97C — "The Coquihalla Connector"
Merritt to Peachland

Just as the Coquihalla Highway drastically reduced traveling time between Vancouver and Kamloops, Highway 97C between Merritt (**Mile 71**) and the Okanagan Valley snips a couple of hours from the driving time between Vancouver and Kelowna.

Conservationists and wildlife lovers were concerned when the highway route was proposed because what lay between the Nicola and the Okanagan valleys was the Douglas Plateau, a huge, untrammelled wilderness breached only by a few forestry or cattlemen's tracks. Nevertheless, the highway went through (or rather over, for it's a super high route), carefully planned and fenced all along the route to keep wildlife and range cattle safely at bay, and humans out of the delicate high forest and fragile lakes.

It is a road for automobiles, not for people. Once the controlled-access freeway begins some 17.5 miles/28 km from Merritt, there are no rest areas, picnic spots or viewpoints. It's as if the highway planners just want you to stay in your car and sail across the jackpine sea as quickly as possible (the speed limit is 70 mph/110 kmph). Apart from chain-up areas and 1 travel infocentre (at the Okanagan end), there are only 3 exits in 52.5 miles/85 km, and only 1 with tourist comforts—the lovely Elkhart log cabin lodge and restaurant, with a gas station nearby.

The most scenic sections of the trips are at both ends, the old part of the route from Merritt to the Aspen Grove turnoff, before the freeway, and the exhilarating hill down to the Okanagan at Peachland, with views of the long, blue lakes.

In summer, the high (5,741 feet/1,750m), fast route is a breeze. Winter brings problems: early snowfall that stays late (and lots of it) and thick fogs which roll up from the warm Okanagan Lakes. Travel advisories should be heeded.

Distance in miles from Merritt is followed by distance in miles from the junction with Highway 97 near Peachland. Equivalent distances in kilometres are indicated by Km.

Mile 0 (71) Km 0 (114): **Junction** with Highway 8, Merritt city centre.

Mile 1.5 (69.5) Km 2.5 (111.5): Coldwater Road leads off to the south, a back road which follows the river and connects with the Coquihalla Highway at several exits. For the first 17.5 miles/28 km, Highway 97C shares the same alignment as Highway 5A; first as a 4-lane (up hill), then as a winding 2-lane.

Mile 2.5 (68.5) Km 4 (110): **Junction** with Highway 5 near the big log tourist information centre. Highway climbs steadily out of the Nicola Valley.

Mile 5 (66) Km 8 (106): Welcome to Merritt sign for westbound travelers.

Mile 7.5 (63.5) Km 12 (102): Brake check for westbound trucks. Good view westbound down hill to Merritt in valley below.

Mile 8.5 (62.5) Km 13.5 (100.5): Road to Marquart and Lundblom lakes, north. Two forestry campsites on Lundblom, good fishing and backroads. Snowmobile reserve in winter.

Mile 11 (60) Km 17.5 (96.5): Iron Mountain Road. Silver, lead and zinc were once mined here; tailings of interest to rock collectors.

Mile 12 (59) Km 19 (95): Road leading southwest to Kane Valley is a delightful backcountry route with a string of little fishing lakes and excellent cross-country skiing trails. Forestry campsite at Harmon Lake.

Just east on Highway 97C are Corbett Lake and lodge. Unfortunately, the enormous increase in people that the new highway brought severely strained the fish stocks of this productive little lake. Now fishing is strictly curtailed until fish stocks recover. Enquire at Corbett Lake Lodge.

Mile 13.5 (57.5) Km 22 (92): Courtney Lake; similar fishing restrictions apply.

Mile 17.5 (53.5) Km 28.5 (85.5): Highway 97C veers east, leaving Highway 5A to continue south to Princeton. Road becomes 4-lane, controlled-access freeway, fenced on both sides. The 60 miles/100 km of chain-link fencing, put up at a cost of $10.5 million, is North America's longest stock fence. There are 25 underpasses and 1 overpass (unique in North America) to allow deer and other ungulates to cross the highway safely.

Mile 26 (45) Km 41.5 (72.5): Pothole Creek.

Mile 26.5 (44.5) Km 43 (71): Chain-up area. Sign alerts motorists to extreme winter conditions of snow, ice and fog.

Mile 27.5 (43.5) Km 44 (70): Loon Lake Road exit. Access on back roads to Kentucky–Alleyne Provincial Recreation Area; 61 campsites, picnic area, boat launch, beach, trails. Blue lakes set in meadows make this a popular camp spot. Visitor program summer weekdays.

Mile 35.5 (35.5) Km 57.5 (56.5): Elkhart Road exit; food, lodging and gas.

Mile 43 (28) Km 69.5 (44.5): Sunset Main exit. Seasonal logging road; access north to Sunset and Pennask lakes; south to Headwaters and Peachland lakes. Pennask Lake is famous for a superior strain of rainbow trout. It has become the principal source of eggs for the fisheries restocking program.

Mile 49.5 (21.5) Km 80 (34): Pennask Summit (elev. 5,669 feet/1,728m), the second-highest paved highway pass in British Columbia. (Highest is Kootenay Pass on Highway 3.) Eastbound travelers may see a line of snowpeaks ahead. These are the Monashees.

Mile 50.5 (20.5) Km 81.5 (32.5): Turnout for brake check. Highway begins swift descent to Okanagan. As the highway descends, view of old Brenda Mines tailings to south. Copper mine closed in 1990.

Mile 62 (9) Km 99.5 (14.5): Chain-off area. A generous turnout; stop here to stretch your legs.

Mile 64.5 (6.5) Km 103.5 (10.5): U-turn route, the one and only. Also a garbage stop.

Mile 66 (5) Km 106.5 (7.5): Ungulate overpass.

Mile 67 (4) Km 108 (6): Trepanier Creek and Trepanier Bench Road overpass (no access).

Mile 68.5 (2.5) Km 110 (4): Okanagan/Similkameen Travel Information Centre, open mid-May to Sept. Access for eastbound traffic only. View from parking lot. Better view from highway curve as you drive east.

Mile 71 (0) Km 114 (0): Exits for Highway 97 north and south. Seclusion Bay Road through overpass tunnel. Highway interchange is 5 miles/8 km north of Peachland (see **Mile 67.5** in CANADA HIGHWAY 97 section).

Mile 231.5 (102) Km 373 (164): McMurphy rest area to west. On the cliffs south of picnic tables are Indian pictographs. 🪧

Mile 233.5 (100) Km 376 (161): Wire Cache rest area beside Thompson River.

Mile 242.5 (91) Km 390 (147): Road west to community of **AVOLA**, named after a town in Sicily. All services available. In the centre of town is an old log inn, now a neighborhood pub, and a small log schoolhouse, now the library.

Mile 245.5 (88) Km 395 (142): Marshy lakes, west side of road. Look for beaver lodges, south of Tum Tum Creek.

Mile 252 (81.5) Km 405.5 (131.5): Rest area beside Finn Creek.

Mile 253 (80.5) Km 407 (130): Access road leads 2 miles/3 km to Little Hell's Gate Regional Park and view of Porte d'Enfer, or Hell's Gate canyon, below the highway. Road open May to Oct., not accessible to trailers. The Thompson River turns abruptly through a narrow canyon and emerges south into tempestuous whirlpools. Here the Overlanders had to abandon their rafts (after a member of the party and all the horses were drowned) and go around the rapids on foot. It took them 3 days to make the 8.5-mile/14-km walk.

Mile 253.5 (80) Km 408 (129): Messiter Summit (elev. 2,411 feet/735m) with view south of the U-shaped North Thompson River valley with the Monashee Mountains to the east, the Cariboo Mountains to the west. The old highway is visible on the canyon side across the river.

Mile 260 (73.5) Km 418.5 (118.5): Highway crosses Froth Creek, just south of Thompson River bridge.

Mile 265.5 (68) Km 427.5 (109.5): Community of **BLUE RIVER** (area pop. 1,000). Begun as a divisional point on the Canadian National Railway, today Blue River is also supported by logging and tourism. Blue River is a jumping-off point for helicopter skiing in the Monashee and Cariboo mountains. All services are available, including camping at Eleanor Lake, which also offers swimming and fishing in summer.

Just north of town is **junction** with 15-mile/24-km gravel road west into the Murtle Lake Nature Conservancy area of Wells Gray Provincial Park. ▲

Mile 268.5 (65) Km 432 (105): Mud Lake Forestry Road. Fishing is good for rainbow in Mud Lake, a short distance east from the highway. 🐟

Mile 272 (61.5) Km 438 (99): Whitewater Creek.

Mile 275.5 (58) Km 443.5 (93.5): Rest area by Thunder River, a tributary of the Thompson River.

Mile 280 (53.5) Km 451 (86): Bone Creek Forestry Road.

Mile 284.5 (49) Km 458 (79): Pyramid Falls, east side of valley, drains from lake on Mount Cheadle.

Mile 289 (44.5) Km 465 (72): Chapel Creek snowmobile area.

Mile 293.5 (40) Km 472.5 (64.5): Thompson River bridge. The highway leaves the valley of the Thompson, which turns west, and follows the Albreda River north almost to its source. The Thompson River rises in the Cariboo Range of the Columbia Mountains, its headwater streams draining the Rausch Glacier.

Mile 300.5 (33) Km 483.5 (53.5): Allen Creek snowmobile area.

Mile 309 (24.5) Km 497.5 (39.5): Good view southbound of Albreda Glacier. Northbound, the highway enters the Rocky Mountain Trench.

Mile 314 (19.5) Km 505.5 (31.5): Camp Creek rest area and stop of interest sign telling about British Columbia's first tourists, Viscount Milton and Doctor Cheadle, who came this way the year after the Overlanders and had an equally terrifying time. Camp Creek is one of the headwater streams of the Canoe River, and was named for an 1871 survey party that wintered here. Cross-country ski trails.

Mile 316.5 (17) Km 509.5 (27.5): Canoe River bridge. At the confluence of this river and the Columbia, explorer David Thompson built canoes for his travels downriver.

Mile 317.5 (16) Km 511 (26): Road east 16 miles/26 km to the northern tip of Kinbasket Lake, impounded behind Mica Dam on the Columbia north of Revelstoke. Boat launch; good fishing for rainbow, Dolly Varden, freshwater ling and whitefish, mainly by troll. 🐟

Mile 318 (15.5) Km 512 (25): Railway underpass.

Mile 320 (13.5) Km 515 (22): Cranberry Marsh, Robert W. Starratt Wildlife Sanctuary. The diked reserve has nesting islands for migrant birds and trails for bird watchers. The marshes, remnant of a prehistoric flat-bottomed lake, are in the Rocky Mountain Trench migration corridor where the Thompson and Columbia valleys meet. It is prime habitat for waterfowl, beaver, muskrat and moose. Cross-country ski trails in winter.

Mile 321.5 (12) Km 517 (20): Tourist information office at the south entrance to village of **VALEMOUNT** (pop. 1,200). Village is well named, for it is indeed in a wide valley surrounded by high mountains: the Selwyn Range of the Rockies to the east and the Premier Group of the Cariboo Mountains to the west. Heavily dependent on tourism, the community has excellent facilities. It is the nearest centre for Mount Robson, the highest mountain in the Canadian Rockies, and its provincial park, east along Highway 16 from Tete Jaune Cache.

Mile 322 (11.5) Km 518 (19): North entrance to Valemount. On west side of road is George Hicks Park, where chinook salmon spawn in Swift Creek in August. Access to spawning grounds is on foot, and there is a footbridge for viewing the salmon. Picnic tables. 🪧

Mile 323 (10.5) Km 519.5 (17.5): North limits of Valemount; road east to airport. Peak directly south is Canoe Mountain.

Mile 326 (7.5) Km 524.5 (12.5): Mount Terry Fox viewpoint and rest area. The peak and nearby undeveloped provincial park were named in 1981 for the young Canadian who started an epic run across Canada on 1 leg to raise funds for cancer research. Before a recurrence of cancer took his life midway through the run, Fox raised some $25 million. In 1985, another young Canadian, Steve Fonyo, who had also lost a leg to cancer, completed a cross-Canada run.

Mile 330 (3.5) Km 531 (6): Jackman Flats Cross-country Ski Area.

Mile 333 (0.5) Km 536.5 (0.5): Turnoff east to small community of **TETE JAUNE CACHE** (pronounced Tee John Cash). *Tete Jaune* is French for "yellow head." Reputedly, a fair-haired trapper regularly cached his furs here in the 18th century. During construction of the Canadian Northern Railway (now the Canadian National), Tete Jaune was a brawling camp, supplied by river steamer from Prince George. Today, it has a store, gas and limited accommodations. The main CNR north line junctions with the east-west line here.

Mile 333.5 (0) Km 537 (0): Fraser River bridge and **junction** with Yellowhead Highway 16. Riverside rest area just north of bridge.

To travel northern Canada and Alaska highways, travelers should obtain a copy of *The MILEPOST® All-the-North Travel Guide®*, the Northern companion guide of *Northwest Mileposts®*.

U.S. HIGHWAY 12

Missoula, MT, to Interstate 5 Junction
(See maps, pages 77, 80 and 83)

U.S. Highway 12, between Missoula, MT, and its junction with Interstate 5 just south of Centralia, WA, is one of the most historically rich and scenically diverse routes in the Pacific Northwest.

It follows the historic path across Lolo Pass and down the valley of the Lochsa and Clearwater rivers taken by the Lewis and Clark expedition heading for the Pacific in 1805 and returning to the Mis-souri River in 1806. It touches the land of the Nez Perce and parallels the tragic route of retreat of Chief Joseph and his band in 1877.

In Idaho and southeastern Washing-ton, U.S. Highway 12 winds through the hills and small towns of the Palouse, the richest wheat-growing region in the United States. From Walla Walla through the Yakima Valley, vineyards dot the hill-sides and roadside stands offer a bounty of fruits and vegetables. The route climbs the east side of the Cascades, crosses White Pass and descends through logging country to the lush green valleys of west-ern Washington.

U.S. Highway 12 Log

Distance from Missoula, MT, is followed by distance from the Interstate 5 junction.

Mile 0 (583): Crossing the Clark Fork River in Missoula. See **Mile 390** in the U.S. HIGH-WAY 93 section for description of Missoula. U.S. highways 12 and 93 share a common alignment south to Lolo; mileposts on this stretch of highway reflect distance from Montana–Idaho border via U.S. Highway 93.
MP 94

Mile 1 (582): Memorial Rose Gardens, hon-oring Montana WWII and Vietnam veterans.

Mile 4 (579): Crossing the Bitterroot River.

Mile 10.5 (572.5): LOLO, **junction** of U.S. highways 12 and 93. Turn west onto U.S. 12. Mileposts reflect distance from Montana–Idaho border via U.S. Highway 12. This small town has gas stations, restaurant, gro-ceries and a private campground.   ▲

Mile 11 (572): Turnout and information sign about Lolo Trail. This route over Lolo Pass was an Indian trail used for at least 200 years before Lewis and Clark passed this way in 1805. The Nez Perce Indians came east to reach the buffalo country east of the Conti-nental Divide, and the Flathead Indians used it to reach the salmon and steelhead fishing grounds along the Clearwater River. The pres-ent highway across the Bitterroot Mountains was completed in 1961.

Mile 12 (571): Cattle ranch on north side of highway raises Texas longhorn cattle. Stream to south is Lolo Creek; trees adjacent to the creek are cottonwoods with pines growing on the drier hillsides.   MP 31

Mile 14.5 (568.5): Gas and food to south.

Mile 15 (568): Fort Fizzle. Lolo National Forest picnic area with shaded tables and handicap-accessible pit toilets. Fort Fizzle was a log fort constructed on the hillside by the Army's 7th Infantry regiment in an aborted attempt to stop the flight of Chief Joseph and Nez Perce in 1877. The Indians detoured around the fort without firing a

A footbridge crosses the Lochsa River to a hiking trail south of the highway.
(L. Linkhart)

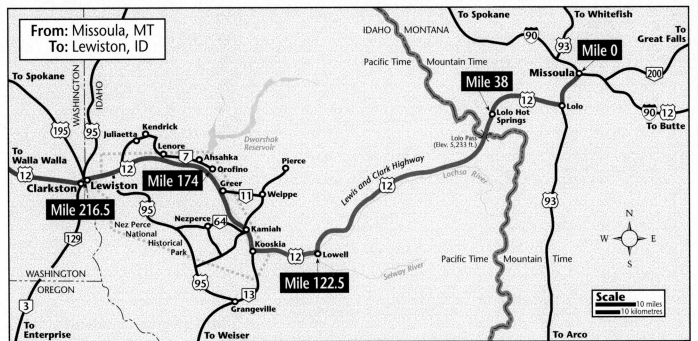

From: Missoula, MT
To: Lewiston, ID

Mile 0
Mile 38
Mile 174
Mile 216.5
Mile 122.5

shot, thus the name. &☂ MP 28

Mile 17 (566): Grocery store. MP 26

Mile 18 (565): Anderson Gulch. Lewis and Clark camped here on Sept. 11, 1805. Cattle ranches line both sides of the valley. Sign on north side of highway points out Lolo Peak (elev. 9,097 feet).

Mile 24 (559): Narrow winding road westbound. MP 19

Mile 26 (557): Lewis and Clark Campground, Lolo National Forest; open May to Sept., 17 sites, trout fishing in adjacent Lolo Creek. ☛▲ MP 17

Mile 27 (556): Graves Creek Road. Gravel road leads 1.5 miles north to restaurant, phone, private campground with 10 sites. ▲

Mile 31 (552): Howard Creek National Park with picnic tables and hiking trails. 👫☂

Mile 36 (547): Historical marker. Lewis and Clark camped here on Sept. 12, 1805. "Party and horses much fatigued."

Mile 38 (545): LOLO HOT SPRINGS. Lewis and Clark stopped here on Sept. 13, 1805, and in June 1806. They soaked in the hot springs on both occasions, noting in their journals that the Indians steamed themselves in the springs, then plunged into the icy waters of Lolo Creek. Facilities today include a private campground (open April to Nov.), grocery, restaurant, casino, gas, and indoor and outdoor pools fed by thermal springs at 140°F. ▲

Mile 39 (544): Lee Creek Campground, Lolo National Forest, open May to Sept., 22 sites, will accommodate trailers up to 22 feet. ▲ MP 6

Mile 40.5 (542.5): Chain-up area.

Mile 42 (541): Highway twists and climbs steeply westbound with deep ravines on the south side. Clumps of white beargrass, the Montana state flower, are visible in early summer. MP 3

Mile 45 (538): Lolo Summit (elev. 5,233 feet) marks the Montana–Idaho border and the division between Mountain and Pacific time zones. Set watches back 1 hour westbound, forward 1 hour eastbound.

Lolo Pass Visitor Center, operated by the Forest Service, is open 9 a.m. to noon and 1–4 p.m. (Pacific time) daily, Memorial Day to Labor Day, weekdays in winter. The chinked log cabin has interpretive displays, maps, brochures and guidebooks for sale. There are picnic tables and pit toilets adjacent. A gravel road leads 1 mile south to Packer Meadows, where blooming camas give the meadows the appearance of a blue lake in summer. The camas root, much like an onion, was a staple of the Indian diet.

From the pass west, U.S. 12 parallels the route of Lewis and Clark. Some parts of the original trail are no longer intact, but you can follow remnants of it as it descends the western slope to the north of U.S. 12. The Lolo Motorway (Forest Road 500) was constructed in the 1930s by the Civilian Conservation Corps on or adjacent to much of the original trail. Normally snowbound from Oct. to late July, the trail can be driven by 4-wheel-drive vehicles and some cars in August and September with high clearance. Check with the ranger at the Lolo Pass Visitor Center for current road conditions and specific directions on this route. ☂

Mile 45.5 (537.5): Westbound, the highway drops steeply down a 6 percent grade with sweeping views of the Lochsa Valley and the snowcapped Bitterroots. Mileposts reflect distance from Idaho–Washington border. MP 174

Mile 48.5 (534.5): Historical marker. Site of the Lolo Trail crossing. Lewis and Clark camped here June 29, 1806. In fall the larch (tamarack) on the sides of this steep canyon turn brilliant gold against a background of evergreens. The larch is the only deciduous conifer in the Northwest.

Mile 50 (533): Highway crosses Crooked Fork Creek.

Mile 51 (532): Turnout to south. Lochsa River flows beside highway. The Lochsa is popular with fishermen after cutthroat, rainbow and steelhead trout. ☛

Mile 53 (530): Highway passes through stands of old-growth cedar. Few specimens as good as these are left anywhere in the Northwest. This entire route through Idaho has been designated a Wild and Scenic River Corridor. MP 167

Mile 55 (528): Bernard De Voto Memorial Grove. De Voto (1897–1955) was a prominent conservationist, author and historian, winner of the Pulitzer Prize and National Book Award, who camped in this grove of old-growth western red cedar while studying the journals of Lewis and Clark. His ashes were scattered here in 1955 and the grove was dedicated in 1962. Pit toilets, campground directory showing current status and large-scale recreation map of the entire Lewis and Clark Highway are located on the north side of the road. MP 165

Mile 56.5 (526.5): White Sounds Campground with 6 sites. ▲

Mile 58 (525): Powell Junction. Powell ranger station (open 8 a.m. to 4:30 p.m., weekdays) is 0.6 mile south on paved road. Access to Powell Campground, Clearwater National Forest, with 29 sites.

Rustic Lochsa Lodge, just south of the highway, has been a landmark on this route since it was built in 1929 by Andrew Erickson as a commercial hunting lodge for sportsmen who braved the primitive road from Missoula and Kooskia, ID. The lodge makes a good stopping place for a cup of coffee or a meal in a dining room decorated with goat, moose, fox, bear and other animal trophies. It's open every day of the year; meals served 6 a.m. to 9 p.m. There are

7 cabins and 5 motel units available; gas, groceries and playground.

Forest Service maintains 35 miles of cross-country ski trails and 83 miles of snowmobile trails in the area. The next gas station westbound is 64 miles. Winding road next 66 miles westbound. ▲★

Mile 60.5 (522.5): Papoose Creek.

Mile 61.5 (521.5): Whitehouse Campground, Clearwater National Forest; 13 campsites, 3 picnic tables. Whitehouse Pond historical marker. Lewis and Clark stopped here Sept. 15, 1805, after camping 4 miles upstream at Powell. ⊼▲

Mile 62 (521): Wendover Campground, Clearwater National Forest; 27 campsites, 3 picnic tables. ⊼▲

Mile 68.5 (514.5): The highway and Lochsa River share a narrow, twisting canyon with massive rock face on the north side. A footbridge crosses the river on the south side of the highway to a mile-long trail that leads up Warm Springs Creek to Jerry Johnson Hot Springs (thermal pools). ⋔ MP 151

Mile 69.5 (513.5): Jerry Johnson Campground, Clearwater National Forest; 15 sites. Jerry Johnson was a Prussian who, with a partner, built a cabin and prospected along the river in 1893. ▲

Mile 72 (511): Point of interest: Colgate Licks Elk Trail on north side of road. A 0.6-mile loop trail climbs from the parking lot to warm springs where salt and other mineral deposits attract deer, elk and sheep. The spot is named for George Colgate, the cook of an ill-fated hunting party, who died near here during the winter of 1893. Parking, handicap-accessible pit toilets. ⅁⋔ MP 148

Mile 73 (510): Historical marker describes the meaning of Lochsa as "rough water." This is a popular river for rafters. The floating season normally extends from May to Aug. Professional boatmen consider the Lochsa a hazardous river requiring heavy equipment and technical knowledge. In the section of the river between Powell ranger station and Lowell, about 65 miles, there are 63 named rapids, the majority of them Class IV.

Mile 77 (506): Wooden suspension bridge to south.

Mile 82 (501): Turnout with river access.

Mile 84.5 (498.5): Wooden bridge to south. Clouds of white syringa, the Idaho state flower, along the road in early summer.

Mile 86 (497): For the next mile the river presents a particularly dramatic series of rapids; turnouts provide good vantage points for watching rafters. Access to Eagle Mountain Trailhead. MP 134

Mile 92 (491): The forest on both sides of the road is typical of second growth, with trees tightly spaced and of nearly uniform size. MP 128

Mile 97 (486): Wilderness Gateway Campground; 89 sites, playground, amphitheater, summer campfire programs, facilities for trail stock. One of the primary gateways to

the Selway-Bitterroot Wilderness to the south. ▲

Mile 98 (485): Lochsa Historical Ranger Station (open daily 9 a.m. to 5 p.m., Memorial Day to Labor Day) dates from the 1920s; the first road reached the station in 1952. The site consists of 8 stops on a self-guided walking tour including 2 ranger dwellings, woodshed, root cellar, Boulder Creek station, barn and corral and other buildings. The small museum is probably the finest exhibit on the Forest Service in the Northwest. ★

Mile 99.5 (483.5): Fish Creek trailhead and river access to north. ⋔

Mile 102 (481): Point of interest. View into Selway-Bitterroot Wilderness.

Mile 103.5 (479.5): A particularly beautiful stretch of highway with steep canyon walls, overhanging rocks and the river dropping on a steep gradient. All of this area is part of the Idaho batholith, a geological form covering approximately 14,000 square miles of granite 80 million years old, one of the largest bodies of granite in the world. Look for distinctive igneous and metamorphic rocks in the highway cuts. MP 116

Mile 104.5 (478.5): Horsetail Falls Creek, where waterfalls spill into the river from a rocky slot in the mountain. MP 115

Mile 108 (475): Split Creek Trail heads south over a wooden suspension bridge across the Lochsa River. ⋔

Mile 112 (471): Major Fenn picnic area; 5 tables, handicap-accessible pit toilets. Fenn was the first supervisor for Clearwater National Forest. ⅁⋔

Mile 113 (470): Deadman Creek. In 1908 a man's skeleton was found 3 miles up this creek. The man was never identified, and the creek was named after him.

Mile 115 (468): Apgar Campground, Clearwater National Forest; 7 sites. Just west of here the U.S. government established a prison work camp in 1935 to aid in construction of the highway. In 1943 Japanese were relocated from the West Coast and interned here. ▲

Mile 123 (460): LOWELL (pop. 23), at the confluence of the Lochsa and Selway rivers, which now form the Middle Fork Clearwater. Two bridges cross the river into town. Gas, groceries, motel and cafe available. Float and horse pack trips depart from here. Resort and private campground offers cabins, 55 campsites and RV hookups.

Forest Service Road 223 heads south along the Selway River for 19 miles to Selway Falls. Eight Forest Service campgrounds along this road have a total of 67 campsites. Steelhead trout and chinook salmon hatch in the Lochsa and Selway rivers and their tributaries and migrate to the ocean 550 miles downstream. They return to spawn after 2 years, weighing as much as 30 lbs. ⬅▲ MP 97

Mile 124 (459): Wild Goose Campground, Clearwater National

Forest; 6 campsites, 2 picnic tables. ⊼▲

Mile 125 (458): Three Devils picnic area; 7 tables, water. The "three devils" were 3 boulders that blocked the center of a section of the Middle Fork. Only when the river was at its highest could logs being floated down the river pass unharmed. In 1918 the boulders were blasted, solving that problem. ⊼

Mile 129.5 (453.5): SYRINGA; gas, cafe, groceries and private RV campground with 35 sites. The town is named for the syringa shrub. The Nez Perce Indians used the softened syringa's leaves for soap and its stems for bows. It is Idaho's state flower. Westbound the river broadens and the highway levels out beyond Syringa. ▲ MP 90

Mile 132 (451): Leaving Clearwater National Forest westbound.

Mile 134.5 (448.5): Resort lodge. Small ranches and homes on the north side of the highway; Clearwater River to south.

Mile 138 (445): Bed and breakfast.

Mile 140 (443): Dramatic cliffs of columnar basalt from an ancient lava flow. U.S. Highway 12 enters Nez Perce Indian Reservation westbound. MP 79

Mile 142.5 (440.5): Tukaytesp'e picnic area with handicap-accessible facilities. ⅁⊼

Mile 143 (440): Historic site. In the Nez Perce War of 1877, General Howard's infantry attacked Chief Looking Glass' band here, even though the Indians had said they were not warlike and wanted to live peacefully. Subsequently, Looking Glass and his followers, formerly neutral, joined Chief Joseph and the other Nez Perce fleeing to Montana. MP 76

Mile 144 (439): KOOSKIA (pop. 692) city center is south of the highway across the Clearwater River. The town sprawls across the valley and has a frontier Western appearance with false-front buildings, small sawmill and other photogenic structures. Limited visitor services include gas, several cafes and 1 motel. Kooskia ranger station is open 8 a.m. to 4 p.m., weekdays. Kooskia National Fish Hatchery, 2 miles southeast (turn left at south end of bridge into town), raises chinook salmon; self-guiding tour daily, 7:30 a.m. to 4 p.m.

Junction with Idaho Highway 13 from Grangeville. Together with U.S. 95 the highways form a loop of about 400 miles that stitches together the 24 sites of Nez Perce National Historical Park. Most of the park sites involve the Lewis and Clark expedition, the Nez Perce Indians or early missionaries and pioneers in central Idaho.

The nearest site on Highway 13 is Clearwater Battlefield, about 7 miles south of Kooskia. Here, on Oct. 11, 1877, Army

troops met the Nez Perce in battle with inconclusive results and the Indians withdrawing to the east.

Mile 148 (435): Gas station and restaurant. MP 71

Mile 150 (433): Handsome gray and yellow Indian Presbyterian Church, founded in 1871, stands on the north side of the highway. Historic graveyard adjacent.

Mile 150.5 (432.5): Nez Perce National Park site, Heart of the Monster, legendary birthplace of the Nez Perce tribe and "comparable to the Garden of Eden as a place of reverence, respect and awe." Here, Coyote slew a great monster. The Nez Perce and other tribes came forth from the parts of the monster that fell to the ground. An interpretive exhibit explains the tale and a 0.2-mile trail leads to the basaltic formation that is the heart. Restrooms. Private full-service RV park on north side of highway.

Mile 152 (431): National Park historic site. Lewis and Clark's Long Camp, where for 6 weeks in 1806 they waited for the snow to melt in the Bitterroots, one of the longest stops on their journey. Nearby is the site of the Asa Smith Mission, established in April 1839 and abandoned 2 years later. MP 65

Mile 153.5 (429.5): KAMIAH (pop. 1,157). Bridge crosses Clearwater into town; gas, restaurants, motels. The town's name comes from the Nez Perce word for the plant dogbone, kamo. The Indians used this plant to make rope, kamia, and the word "kamiah" means literally "place of rope litter." **Junction** with Idaho highways 162 and 64.

Mile 156 (427): The highway hugs the south bank of the Clearwater, flowing broad and flat between treeless foothills. The Camas Prairie Railroad runs along the north side. The Charles Bronson movie *Breakheart Pass* was filmed along another portion of this same railroad near Grangeville.

Mile 168 (415): GREER (pop. 30) at **junction** with Idaho Highway 11; limited visitor services. Highway 11 extends 18 miles through the hills to Weippe Prairie and another 17.5 miles to Pierce. Weippe Prairie is the location of the first meeting between Lewis and Clark and the Nez Perce on Sept. 20, 1805. During the 1877 War, the Nez Perce came here after the Battle of the Clearwater and held a council to decide what to do.

In the fall of 1860 E.D. Pierce, an Irish immigrant and the first man to have climbed California's Mount Shasta, discovered gold at what is now Pierce. The brief gold rush that followed lasted little more than 2 years, but Pierce managed to survive on subsequent lumbering activities and the branch line of the Camas Prairie Railroad that now runs through town. Photogenic old buildings remain, including the Pierce courthouse, Idaho's oldest public building, several pioneer stores and cabins and a Chinese cemetery.

Mile 172.5 (410.5): Historical marker showing the site of an Indian trail across the Clearwater that took Lewis and Clark closer to navigable waters.

Mile 176 (407): U.S. Highway 12 widens to 4 lanes at **OROFINO** (pop. 2,900); full tourist services include automobile repair, several restaurants, motels and 2 RV campgrounds. Orofino is a lumber, cattle and farming center for Orofino Creek where it enters the Middle Fork Clearwater River. The town has the distinction of recording Idaho's highest temperature, 118°F on July 8, 1934. The Clearwater County Museum (open 1–4 p.m., Tuesday through Saturday) has some pioneer displays of mining and lumbering history.

Junction with Idaho Highway 7. Follow Highway 7 for 0.5 mile to the Clearwater National Forest office; a tree section imprinted with Chinese ideograms, found in 1939, is on display in the lobby. Three miles from Orofino on Highway 7 is the Dworshak National Fish Hatchery, at the confluence of the North Fork and Middle Fork Clearwater rivers. The largest steelhead trout hatchery in the world, it offers self-guiding tours of the rearing ponds, fish ladder and other facilities that produce annually about 3 million steelhead, 1.5 million rainbow trout and 1 million chinook salmon. Open daily 7:30 a.m. to 4 p.m.

Nearby Dworshak Dam, one of the highest straight-axis-concrete gravity dams in the world, has a visitor center and guided tours of the dam daily, 10 a.m. to 6 p.m., from mid-May to Sept.; Saturday and Sunday, 8 a.m. to 5 p.m., the rest of the year. Dworshak Reservoir extends 54 miles behind the dam providing 6 campgrounds, boat-launching ramps, fishing, hiking trails, picnic facilities and water recreation. Marinas offer houseboat and powerboat rentals. Dworshak State Park, Idaho's newest, opened in May 1989 and features 1,000 acres of wooded land along the shore of the reservoir with 101 campsites and handicap-accessible facilities. It's located 26 miles northwest of Orofino. MP 44

Mile 180 (403): National Park Historic Site, Canoe Camp, north side of highway. Lewis and Clark camped here beside the Clearwater from Sept. 26 to Oct. 7, 1805, while constructing 5 canoes for the remainder of their journey down the Snake and Columbia rivers to the Pacific. A motel and RV campground are located here. The highway follows the south bank of the Clearwater for the next several miles westbound, twisting and turning with each bend in the river. MP 40

Mile 192 (391): Historical site and rest area with sheltered picnic tables, barbecue grills and handicap-accessible toilets. This was the location of Slaterville, a steamboat port on the Clearwater supplying the gold rush that began at Pierce in 1860. Tricky boat handling conditions here above Big Eddy caused the steamship company to relocate their landing at the confluence of the Clearwater and Snake rivers, establishing Lewiston and leading to the collapse of Slaterville.

Indians have lived here next to good fishing for at least 10,000 years. Archaeological digs at the Lenore site uncovered oval pit houses occupied from about 900 B.C. to about 1300 A.D., as well as evidence this was an important gathering place as early as 8000 B.C. This is one of the oldest prehistoric sites in the Northwest.

Mile 205 (378): Junction with Idaho Highway 3 to Juliaetta and Kendrick. The Potlatch River empties into the Clearwater here.

Mile 206 (377): Spalding Mission Historical Site. Marks the grave of Henry Harmon Spalding who, along with Marcus Whitman, led Presbyterian missionaries west in 1836 to answer a Nez Perce call for teachers.

Mile 207 (376): National Park historic site. Indian legend of the ant and the yellow jacket relates how Coyote tried to settle an argument between them. When they refused to be pacified, he turned them to stone, which is the large basalt formation visible on the south hillside. MP 11

Mile 207.5 (375.5): Junction of U.S. Highway 12 and U.S. Highway 95 south (turn to **Mile 430** in the U.S. HIGHWAY 95 section). Turn south onto U.S. 95 to reach the Nez Perce National Historical Park Visitor Center, 1.5 miles from here. Perched atop a knoll, the center has an excellent small museum devoted to Indian culture, several audiovisual programs, literature and interpretive walks and programs. During the summer, Nez Perce men and women demonstrate pitching a teepee, weaving, beadwork and other skills. Indian arts and crafts are for sale. The center is open daily 8 a.m. to 6 p.m., June to Labor Day; 8 a.m. to 4:30 p.m. the rest of the year. Handicap-accessible. MP 8

Mile 210 (373): National Park historical marker. Another of the Nez Perce tales of the all-powerful Coyote relates an encounter with a bear while fishing. The Coyote threw both bear and fishnet high on the hillsides on opposite sides of the river and turned them to stone. Both are visible from this marker. Clearly visible downstream and across the river is the large pulp and sawmill complex of the Potlatch Corp.

Mile 215 (368): Junction with U.S. Highway 95 north and U.S Highway 195. (Turn to **Mile 438** in the U.S. HIGHWAY 95 section.)

Mile 216 (367): LEWISTON (pop. 28,082), named for Meriwether Lewis; complete visitor facilities including 14 motels and 85 restaurants. (U.S. Highway 12 detours the downtown area, routing noisy truck traffic away from the town's lodgings, most of which are situated in the heart of downtown.) This bustling town at the confluence

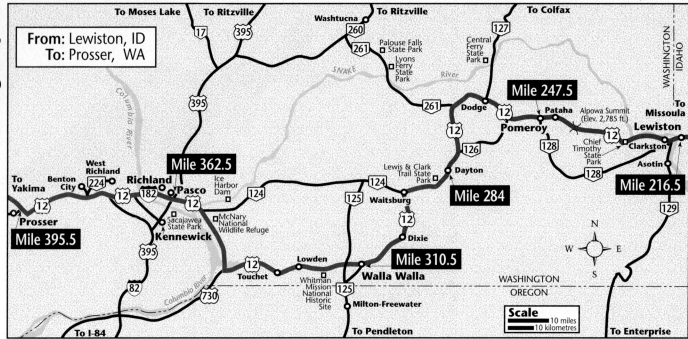

of the Clearwater and Snake rivers is Idaho's only seaport.

Attractions include the Luna Museum, which features Indian and pioneer exhibits (9 a.m. to 5 p.m., Tuesday to Saturday). Hells Gate State Park, 4 miles south on Snake River Avenue, has a marina open all year; trout, bass and steelhead fishing; swimming; sheltered picnic tables; 93 campsites, hookups for RVs, hot showers and flush toilets. The marina is the departure point for jet boat trips that go up the Snake River into Hells Canyon, the deepest gorge in North America. Passengers are welcome on the Hells Canyon mailboat, which departs on Wednesdays to deliver the U.S. mail to isolated ranches as far as the head of navigation, 90 miles upstream from Lewiston. The trip takes 2 days with an overnight at a comfortable cabin camp in the canyon.

Mile 218 (365): Idaho–Washington border. Crossing the Snake River.

Mile 218.5 (364.5): CLARKSTON (pop. 6,903), named for William Clark, has complete visitor facilities including 14 motels, 27 restaurants. Six-thousand-year-old petroglyphs are accessible from River Road; inquire at the Clarkston Chamber of Commerce, 502 Bridge St., phone (509) 758-7712. **Junction** with Washington Highway 129 to Asotin and Oregon border. The Snake River upstream from Clarkston has a reputation for excellent sturgeon fishing.
⚓ MP 434

Mile 220 (363): Junction with Washington Highway 128.

Mile 220.5 (362.5): Highway parallels Snake River on south bank past Port of Whitman (north side) where barges are often being loaded at the grain terminal. For several miles steep basalt bluffs hem the highway to the south. The waters of the Snake are placid in Lower Granite Lake, an impoundment of Lower Granite Dam. Big day-glo red triangles at water's edge are navigation markers for tugs.
MP 432

Mile 226.5 (356.5): Silcott Road. Turn north across bridge for Alpowai Interpretive Center (open 1–5 p.m., Wednesday to Sunday) and Chief Timothy State Park. The center details local Indian history and that of the town of Silcott, which existed here from the late 1880s until the 1920s. Nez Perce chiefs Timothy (the first man to be baptized by Reverend Spalding) and Red Wolf lived here in the 1860s. The state park has 33 hookup campsites, 17 pull-through sites, 16 tent sites, handicap-accessible facilities, boat launch, playground, swimming beach, bathhouse, concession stand, picnic shelters and barbecue grills.
♿🍴▲

Mile 239 (344): Alpowa Summit (elev. 2,785 feet). Rest area with toilets, picnic tables and sweeping view of Garfield County to the west.
🍴

Mile 243 (340): Historical marker. Three Forks Indian trails; Lewis and Clark camped near here May 3, 1806.
🚶

Mile 246 (337): Pataha (meaning Indian brush, also briefly named Waterstown and Favorsburg) is a tiny settlement with cafe.

Mile 247.5 (335.5): POMEROY (pop. 1,415) is the county seat of Garfield County. It was named for Joseph M. Pomeroy, who platted the town in 1878. Big grain elevators shoulder against Villard Street (U.S. Highway 12) in this long, narrow town squeezed down between hills on either side. Visitor services include 1 motel, several restaurants and gas stations. The handsome white county courthouse with its statue of Justice holding her scales is particularly photogenic. There is a small pioneer museum at the Umatilla National Forest ranger station. **Junction** with Washington Highway 128, which makes a loop south into the Blue Mountain foothills before returning to Clarkston (partially gravel).
MP 405

Mile 254.5 (328.5): Junction with Washington Highway 126. This route rejoins U.S. Highway 12 5 miles north of Dayton. High-

way 126 is steep, narrow and winding, with about 5 miles unpaved. U.S. 12 continues to follow the valley, lush with fields of grain, and an abandoned 1-room schoolhouse surrounded by tall stands of wheat. Wheat harvest generally begins here in mid-July when you may see the combines specially designed for these hills at work cutting the wheat. It's wise to be especially alert when driving these winding roads through the Palouse; you're likely to encounter slow-moving farm vehicles around the next bend.

Mile 261.5 (321.5): Tiny cluster of buildings known as Dodge used to be a major stagecoach transfer point on the route to Lewiston. **Junction** with Washington Highway 127. Central Ferry State Park is located on the Snake River 10 miles north. The park has a beach, boat launching, picnic shelters, 60 campsites with hookups and handicap-accessible restrooms. Excellent fishing here for smallmouth bass, channel catfish and summer run steelhead.
♿🍴⚓▲

Mile 270 (313): Junction with Washington Highway 261 to Starbuck and Washtucna. Lyons Ferry State Park, 15 miles northwest at the confluence of Palouse and Snake rivers, has 50 campsites, swimming beach, marina, boat launch, fishing, picnic facilities and handicap-accessible restrooms. Six miles beyond Lyons Ferry is Palouse Falls State Park, where the Palouse River plunges over the rim of the plateau to thunder 190 feet into a rocky basin in a spectacular display of spray and rainbows. A primitive state park with picnic tables, but no other facilities, perches on a promontory overlooking the falls.
♿🍴⚓▲★

Mile 270.5 (312.5): Private campground. ▲

Mile 271 (312): Cafe. MP 381

Mile 271.5 (311.5): Crossing the Tucannon River, Nez Perce for "break root creek."

Mile 276 (307): Pasture land with grazing cattle punctuates fields of grains. The high-

Above—A summer sunset at Lyons Ferry State Park, located at the confluence of the Palouse and Snake rivers. *Right*—Palouse Falls State Park is located 6 miles past Lyons Ferry; turn off at Mile 270 for both parks. *(Photos by L. Linkhart)*

way is following the old Walla Walla–Colville wagon trail, over which thousands of settlers and miners traveled when land north of the Snake River was opened to development in 1858.　　　　MP 376

Mile 279 (304): Highway crests top of hill for sweeping views in all directions.　MP 373

Mile 279.5 (303.5): Junction with Washington Highway 126, which rejoins U.S. Highway 12 east of Dodge.

Mile 284 (299): DAYTON (pop. 2,470); motel, cafe, grocery, gas, limited services. The county seat of Columbia County and a busy agricultural center, Dayton sits at the end of a Union Pacific Railroad spur line that formerly ran as far as Pomeroy. Fruit and vegetable packing houses here keep the railroad busy. Settled in 1859, Dayton has 63 homes and 7 buildings listed as National Historic Places. The Columbia County Courthouse (1887) and Dayton Historic Depot (1881) are the oldest existing in the state and have been restored. The courthouse is open for tours during business hours, and the depot is open Tuesday through Saturday from 10 a.m. to 5 p.m.

The Weinhard Hotel in Dayton has the original high ceilings, heavy doors and Victorian moldings it had when it opened in 1889 as the Weinhard Saloon and Lodge Hall. Today it offers 15 rooms and a Victorian roof garden cafe. Dayton also boasts the only 4-star French restaurant east of the Cascade Mountains. The Patit Creek is open for lunch and dinner, Tuesday through Saturday; reservations recommended, phone (509) 382-4932.　　　　MP 368

Mile 290 (293): Lewis and Clark Trail State Park has 30 campsites nestled in a grove of big trees, firepits, picnic tables and summer campfire programs relating to the Lewis and Clark expedition. Campsites are on the north side of the road, picnic area on south side. ⊼▲ MP 362

Mile 291.5 (291.5): Airfield north side of highway.

Mile 294 (289): Junction with Washington Highway 124 to Prescott. **WAITSBURG** (pop. 1,015); gas stations, restaurants, 1 motel. One of the most picturesque towns in the Palouse, Waitsburg was settled in 1859 around a flour mill built by Sylvester M. Wait. The town retains much of its 19th century character. Detour off U.S. 12 to residential streets (especially Main Street) shaded by huge overhanging trees and lined with gingerbread Victorian homes and turn-of-the-century brick business buildings. Bruce Memorial Museum, in one of the vintage homes, displays historical memorabilia and is open 1–4 p.m., Friday and Saturday. Vistas of Oregon's Blue Mountains on the horizon to the south.

Mile 304.5 (278.5): DIXIE; gas and groceries available. Settled in the 1860s by 3 Kershaw brothers who were known for their dancing and singing performances and especially the tune Dixie, thus the name. Turn south at Biscuit Ridge Road and drive 0.8 mile through vineyards to Biscuit Ridge Winery, open for tasting daily 10 a.m. to 5 p.m.
　　　　MP 348

Mile 310.5 (272.5): Business exit for Walla Walla; Isaacs Avenue to Walla Walla Community College, Dietrich Dome.

WALLA WALLA (pop. 28,520) has complete visitor services including 12 motels and 36 restaurants. It is the primary city in the Walla Walla Valley. Local wags say this is the city they liked so much they named it twice. As an agricultural center it is important in the growing and marketing of wheat, alfalfa, wool, potatoes, dry peas and lentils, asparagus, apples, peaches, pears and the Walla Walla sweet onion for which the valley is famous.

The site of the city has always been an important crossroads in the affairs of the Pacific Northwest. In prehistoric times it lay astride an important Indian trail and gathering place. In 1836 Marcus and Narcissa Whitman arrived to set up a mission (see **Mile 322**). The Indian wars of 1855–58 resulted in Fort Walla Walla being built here, an important garrison for military establishments in other parts of the territory and, later, the terminus of the Mullan Military Road from Fort Benton, head of navigation on the Missouri River.

The Fort Walla Walla Museum Complex features 14 pioneer buildings. It is the largest horse-drawn-era agricultural museum in the West. Open Tuesday through Sunday, 10 a.m.–5 p.m., April to Sept.; Saturday and Sunday, 10 a.m.–5 p.m., in October. Old Fort Walla Walla is now the Veterans Medical Center with many of the buildings intact. See also the scenic campus of Whitman College on the north side of town.

Mile 311.5 (271.5): Walla Walla airport exit.

Mile 313.5 (269.5): Wilbur Avenue exit; access to major-chain fast-food and restaurants.

Mile 314.5 (268.5): Exit to Waitsburg Road and Clinton Street.

Mile 315.5 (267.5): Exit to Rees Avenue, Whitman College.

Mile 316 (267): Walla Walla city center, 2nd Avenue, fairgrounds exit; access to major-chain motel at exit.

Mile 317 (266): Freeway ends westbound. **Junction** with Washington Highway 125 to Prescott, Pendleton and Milton–Freewater, OR.

Mile 318 (265): College Place; Walla Walla College.

Mile 322 (261): Gose Road; Waiilatpu (means "place of the people of the rye grass") historical marker describing Whitman Mission. A short distance west of the marker, turn south 0.5 mile for Whitman Mission National Historic Site. In 1836, the American Board of Commissioners of Foreign Missions (representing Congregational, Presbyterian and Dutch Reformed churches) sent Reverend N.H. Spalding and Dr. Marcus Whitman to establish missions in the region. Against the advice of Dr. John McLoughlin, Hudson's Bay factor at Fort Vancouver and the most important and experienced leader in the area, Spalding went to Lapwai and Whitman settled here west of present-day Walla Walla. Whitman and his wife, Narcissa, a former New York teacher, established their mission and an Indian school.

During the following years the mission became relatively prosperous with fields of cultivated vegetables, wheat, corn and potatoes, cattle and other domestic animals surrounding several wood and adobe buildings adjacent to Mill Creek. Gradually the differences between the Whitmans and the Indians led to distrust and hostility. The Indians blamed a devastating outbreak of measles on the white intruders and in 1847 killed the Whitmans and 11 others.

The visitor center, shaded by large trees and surrounded by a split rail fence, details the missionary period in Northwest history, the mission itself and pioneer immigration along the Oregon Trail. In summer there are demonstrations of pioneer skills and interpretive programs. A mile-long trail leads to mission sites and the hilltop memorial monument. Picnic tables, handicap-accessible. Open daily 8 a.m. to 6 p.m., June to Aug.; 8 a.m. to 4:30 p.m. other months. Admission

fee charged.

Mile 323 (260): McDonald Road. Turn south 2.5 miles for Waterbrook Winery, open by appointment (phone 509/522-1918). MP 329

Mile 324 (259): Stone marker commemorates the site of St. Rose Mission (1850–1900) and the location of an 1855 Indian skirmish. MP 328

Mile 327.5 (255.5): Little settlement of Lowden, named for pioneer Francis M. Lowden. This was one of the first farm communities in the Walla Walla Valley. No services. Woodward Canyon Winery, just west of Lowden, is a small, family-owned winery specializing in Cabernet Sauvignon, Chardonnay and Riesling; open for tasting.

Mile 332 (251): Touchet, at the confluence of the Walla Walla and Touchet rivers; gas and cafe.

Mile 341 (242): Highway leaves cultivated farmlands and begins to wind through sagebrush-covered hills westbound. Remnants of the old Walla Walla & Columbia Railroad, one of the first in the Washington Territory, are visible. MP 311

Mile 344.5 (238.5): Junction with U.S. highways 730 and 395 to Pasco and Umatilla; gas and cafe. U.S. 12 turns north beside the Columbia River. The area is known as the Big Bend of the Columbia, or just Big Bend. Visible immediately to the south is Columbia Gap, also known as Wallula Gap, where the Columbia has sliced through the hills flanking the river, creating dramatic palisades of rock. Weigh station and rest area.

Mile 345 (238): Madame Dorion Memorial Park. Madame Dorion was an Iowa Indian and the second woman to come west over land. She came with her husband and 2 children to set up trading posts along the Columbia. In 1812, after arriving in Wallula, her husband and the other men in the party were killed by Bannock Indians while on a trapping expedition. Dorion and her children lived out the winter in the Blue Mountains. Dorion later remarried and lived in the Willamette Valley until her death on Sept. 3, 1850. The park has picnic tables, a boat launch and handicap-accessible facilities. MP 307

Mile 346.5 (236.5): Historic marker commemorates the site of Fort Nez Perce, also called Fort Walla Walla, which served as a fur-trading post. The post was abandoned in 1855, but its employees stayed on and became some of the first permanent settlers in the area.

Mile 347.5 (235.5): Boise Cascade's Wallula pulp and paper mill to west. The long strings of railroad cars arrive on the Union Pacific from Spokane and Oregon points and on the Burlington Northern from western Washington and Spokane loaded with wood chips to be converted into pulp. Freight cars depart

loaded with corrugated paperboard and corrugated containers. The unpleasant odor is typical of these plants; it is caused by chemicals used in the pulping process.

Mile 352 (231): McNary Pool, a good spot to observe pelicans, cranes, geese and other waterfowl. MP 300

Mile 355.5 (227.5): Gas station and restaurant.

Mile 356 (227): McNary National Wildlife Refuge, 3,600 acres of wetland that are home to thousands of Canadian geese and duck species including mallards, wigeons, pintails, shovelers, canvasbacks, ringnecks and lesser scaups.

Mile 357 (226): Junction with Washington Highway 124. Ice Harbor Dam and Locks on the Snake River (tours available) lie 5 miles east via Highway 124 then 3 miles north. Chateau Gallant Winery lies at the end of Gallant Road, 1 mile east off Highway 124. The winery specializes in Chardonnay and Sauvignon Blanc and is open for tasting noon to 5 p.m., Monday through Saturday. Hood Park on the Snake River has 69 campsites, electrical hookups, handicap-accessible facilities, swimming beach, boat dock, fishing and playground.

Mile 358 (225): The Snake River. Turn south 2 miles for Sacajawea State Park, interpretive center on Lewis and Clark expedition, water sports, swimming, fishing, picnic area and snack food concession.

Mile 359 (224): Turnoff for Pasco Industrial Route and Port of Pasco.

Mile 359.5 (223.5): Lewis Street. MP 293

Mile 361.5 (221.5): Oregon Avenue and **junction** with U.S. Highway 395 north to Spokane (turn to **Mile 419.5** in the U.S. HIGHWAY 395 section). All services available. EXIT 14

Mile 362 (221): U.S. Highway 12 merges with Interstate 182 for 14 miles westbound. Burlington Northern Railroad yards.

Mile 362.5 (220.5): Exit to Pasco city center, 4th Avenue. **PASCO** (pop. 20,840), has all services. According to *Washington State Place Names*, Pasco was named by railroad surveyors who, "suffering from the flatland heat, named it in contrast after Cerro de Pasco, a mining town in the cool atmosphere of a 15,000-foot-high mountain in Peru." Annual Northwest Wine Festival, held in November, is a major event in the city; contact the Pasco Chamber of Commerce, phone (509) 547-9755, for more information. Sightseeing includes the Franklin County Historical Museum. EXIT 13

Mile 363 (220): Exit to 20th Avenue, Columbia Basin College, Tri-Cities Airport. MP 13 EXIT 12B

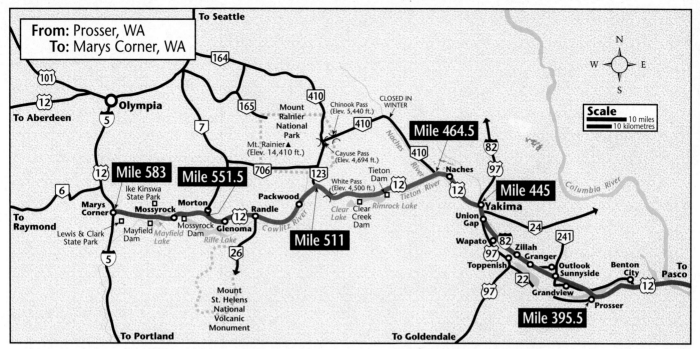

From: Prosser, WA
To: Marys Corner, WA

Mile 583

Mile 551.5

Mile 511

Mile 464.5

Mile 445

Mile 395.5

Scale
10 miles
10 kilometres

Mile 364 (219): Exit for U.S. Highway 395 south to Kennewick and Umatilla. (Turn to **Mile 409.5** in the U.S. HIGHWAY 395 section.) Interstate 182 becomes 6-lane divided highway.   MP 12 EXIT 12A

Mile 367.5 (215.5): Exit to Road 68; no services.   EXIT 9

Mile 369 (214): Exit to Road 100; no services.   EXIT 7

Mile 370 (213): Crossing the Yakima River.

Mile 371 (212): Exit to Richland city center, George Washington Way, hospital. Major-chain motels, restaurants and gas stations at exit. **RICHLAND** (pop. 34,385) was 1 of 4 primary sites (along with Oak Ridge, TN, Los Alamos, NM, and Argonne Laboratory in Chicago) for the development of the atomic bomb in WWII and, until recently, has been a major facility for the development of atomic energy at its Hanford plant. Hanford Science Center, operated by the U.S. Dept. of Energy, has hands-on exhibits, computer games and interpretive films. Open 8 a.m. to 5 p.m. weekdays, 9 a.m. to 5 p.m. Saturday. Located next to the Federal Bldg.; phone (509) 376-6374.   EXIT 5B

Mile 371.5 (211.5): Exit for Washington Highway 240 east to Kennewick.
                                MP 5 EXIT 5A

Mile 372.5 (210.5): Exit for Washington 240 west to Wellsian Way and Vantage. No services.   EXIT 4

Mile 373 (210): Crossing the Yakima River.

Mile 373.5 (209.5): Keene Road and Columbia Drive. No services.   EXIT 3

Mile 376.5 (206.5): U.S. Highway 12 merges with Interstate 82, sharing a common alignment westbound to Yakima.   MP 102

Mile 381.5 (201.5): Exit for Washington highways 225 north and 224 east to Benton City and West Richland. **BENTON CITY** (pop. 1,910) was originally named Giezentanner after the town's first postmaster. There are a family restaurant and private RV park. Fishing in the Yakima River is fair to good for large- and smallmouth bass, crappie and channel catfish.

Three wineries lie east of Benton City off Highway 224. Oakwood Cellars is located 0.5 mile east, then north 1 mile on Demoss Road. Tasting room open noon to 6 p.m. weekends. Farther east on Highway 224, turn north onto Sunset Road 1 mile to Kiona Vineyards and Blackwood Canyon Vintners. Both are open 10 a.m. to 6 p.m. weekends.
                              ☞ EXIT 96

Mile 384.5 (198.5): Yakitat Road exit; no services.   EXIT 93

Mile 389.5 (193.5): Gibbon Road exit; no services.   EXIT 88

Mile 395.5 (187.5): Exit to Mabton and Patterson via Washington highways 22 and 221, and Prosser. Three motels, 5 restaurants, Benton County Historical Museum adjoining the city park (picnic tables) and hospital. **PROSSER** (pop. 4,325) was named for Col. William Prosser, who established

a trading post here in 1882. Prosser has the largest concentration of wineries in the Yakima Valley. The Yakima Valley is the richest fruit and vegetable producing region in the Pacific Northwest and grows substantial quantities of everything from apples to zucchini. A detailed list of the crops, when they are harvested and where to get them, is available from the Yakima Valley Convention and Visitors Bureau, P.O. Box 124, Yakima, WA 98907, or by writing Farm Products Map, 1731 Beam Road, Granger, WA 98932.

Washington State University's Irrigated Agriculture Research and Extension Center here is open to the public and is a fine source of information for home gardeners on growing techniques.

Chinook Wines, Hogue Cellars, Hinzerling Winery and Yakima River Winery are located off Exit 82. Turn east onto Wine Country Road then south onto Wittkopf Road for Chinook, a small winery that specializes in Sauvignon Blanc, Chardonnay, Merlot and sparkling Riesling, open for tasting noon to 5 p.m., Friday through Sunday. Hogue, one of the largest wineries in the state, producing a variety of reds and whites, is about 0.5 mile beyond Chinook on Lee Road; hours are 10 a.m. to 5 p.m. daily. Hinzerling is located in the opposite direction off Wine Country Road near 10th, open 10 a.m. to 5 p.m., Monday through Saturday; 11 a.m. to 3 p.m. Sunday. Yakima River Winery is off Wine Country Road, 1.5 miles west on North River Road; open 10 a.m. to 5 p.m. daily. Also access this exit to Columbia Crest Winery, south 24 miles on Highway 221.   ☞ EXIT 82

Mile 396 (187): Crossing the Yakima River.

Mile 398 (185): Gap Road. Gas, fast food, major motel and rest area with picnic tables and handicap-accessible facilities.
                          ♿☞ EXIT 80

Mile 400 (183): On a clear day westbound travelers have great views of Mount Rainier to the northwest and Mount Adams to the southwest.

"Rodeo" mural in Toppenish is one of more than 2 dozen historically themed murals decorating the downtown buildings. Painted by Western artist Newman Myrah, the mural recalls the rodeo tradition of this region. (Nina R. Zutler, courtesy of Toppenish Chamber of Commerce)

Mile 401.5 (181.5): The tall pole and wire frames standing in fields to the north of the highway are frames for growing hops. The Yakima Valley is the largest hop producer in the country and supplies most U.S. breweries with their domestic hops.   MP 77

Mile 403.5 (179.5): Exit to Grandview County Line Road; gas, groceries, RV park. **GRANDVIEW** (pop. 7,380) is named for the splendid views from here of snowcapped 12,307-foot Mount Adams and 14,411-foot Mount Rainier. Chateau Ste. Michelle's Grandview winery is located at West 5th and Avenue B, 1 mile west. This is the state's oldest operating winery and it specializes in reds such as Merlot and Cabernet Sauvignon. Open 10 a.m. to 4:30 p.m. daily.

A map and directions for touring all these Yakima Valley wineries are available from the Yakima Valley Wine Growers Assoc., P.O. Box 39, Grandview, WA 98930.
▲ EXIT 75

Mile 405.5 (177.5): Exit to Stover Road, Yakima Valley Highway and Wine Country Road; cafe. Vineyards on both sides of the highway. Tucker Cellars, featuring Riesling, Gewurztraminer, Chenin Blanc, Chardonnay, Muscat Canelli and Pinot Noir, is located on Ray Road off Wine Country Road, 1.5 miles west. Winery and tasting room are combined with a fresh fruit market. Open 9 a.m. to 6 p.m. daily.   MP 73 EXIT 73

Mile 409.5 (173.5): Exit for **junction** with Washington Highway 241 to Sunnyside and Mabton. Several major-chain fast-food restaurants, motels, RV park, hospital and gas at the exit. Note the large fruit-packing shed north of the highway.   ▲ EXIT 69

Mile 411.5 (171.5): Midvale Road and Port of Sunnyside exit. Go south on Midvale to Alexander Road, then east, for the Yakima Valley Cheese Co. specializing in Gouda, Edam, cumin and Havarti cheese. Tours, viewing and sales room open 9:30 a.m. to 5 p.m., Monday through Saturday. Exit north for **SUNNYSIDE** (pop. 11,370), known for its asparagus crop. Sightseeing includes pioneer Ben Snipes' cabin (circa 1859) and the Sunnyside Wildlife Refuge for waterfowl.
EXIT 67

Mile 414.5 (168.5): Exit for the small settlement of Outlook.   MP 64 EXIT 63

Mile 419.5 (163.5): Exit for Washington Highway 223 south to **GRANGER.** Gas and RV park. Union Pacific Yakima branch parallels highway on the north. Turn south toward Granger for Stewart Vineyards; follow Outlook Road up the hill until it becomes Cherry Hill Road. Open 10 a.m. to 5 p.m., Monday through Saturday; noon to 5 p.m., Sunday.   ▲ EXIT 58

Mile 424 (159): Exit to Yakima Valley Highway and **ZILLAH** (pop. 1,960), named for Miss Zillah Oakes, daughter of the president of the Union Pacific Railroad. Local restaurant here, El Ranchito, is famous for its Mexican food; tortilla factory in rear. Teapot Dome Service Station Historic Site south of exit was built in 1922 and looks just like its name implies. Named after the Wyoming Oil Lease scandal under President Harding, the service station is still in full operation. Turn east on Yakima Valley Highway to Punkin Corner, then north 0.5 mile on Gurley Road to reach Eaton Hill Winery, featuring Riesling and Semillon. Open 10 a.m. to 5 p.m., weekends. Horizon's Edge Winery (Chardonnay, Pinot Noir, Cabernet Sauvignon, Muscat Canelli) is located nearby on East Zillah Drive. Open 10 a.m. to 5 p.m., daily.   EXIT 54

Mile 426 (157): Exit for Zillah Road; gas and fast food. Five wineries—Zillah Oakes, Bonair, Hyatt, Covey Run and Portteus—are located north of the highway. Zillah Oakes is immediately adjacent to the exit.   EXIT 52

Mile 428 (155): Exit to U.S. Highway 97 to Goldendale and Washington Highway 22 south to **TOPPENISH** (pop. 7,000); all services. This is headquarters for the vast million-acre Yakima Indian Nation that stretches westward as far as the summit of Mount Adams. Powwows take place the second weekend in June, July 4th weekend (includes rodeo) and third weekend in Sept. They feature ceremonial dancing, stick games and storytelling. The cultural center here has excellent dioramas and exhibits of Yakima culture. Fort Simcoe State Park, a preserved frontier military post of the 1850s, is 27 miles west of Toppenish via Washington Highway 220. Five original buildings around a parade ground include 2 blockhouses, barracks and neat, white officers' quarters; picnicking.

The town of Toppenish has become known for its historic murals painted on buildings throughout downtown. Beginning in 1989, the town commissioned several murals a year depicting the region's history from 1850–1920, and now there are 29 murals in all. Maps to the town's murals are available at the visitor center.   ⊼ EXIT 50

Mile 429.5 (153.5): Tall groves of cottonwood trees to the southwest have their roots in the waters of the Yakima River.   MP 49

Mile 434 (149): Exit south to **WAPATO** (pop. 3,790); gas, groceries, fresh fruit and vegetable stand. The tall barn on the northeast side of the exit is a typical hop barn where long strands of hops are hung from the rafters to dry.   EXIT 44

Mile 438 (145): Exit to Thorpe Road, Parker Road and Yakima Valley Highway. Stanton Hills Winery, one of the valley's older wineries, is located on Gangi Road about 1 mile northeast of the exit. Open 11 a.m. to 5:30 p.m., Tuesday through Sunday.   EXIT 40

Mile 440 (143): Exit to **UNION GAP** (pop. 3,110), formerly Yakima City, named for the obvious gap between segments of Ahtanum Ridge. Except for the stubbornness of local landholders back in the 1880s, Union Gap might well be the major city in the valley instead of Yakima. When the Northern Pacific Railroad built through here on its way over Stampede Pass to Tacoma, Union Gap landholders refused to provide concessions to the railroad for yards, station and other facilities, thinking they'd hold out for large profits. The railroad created a new town, North Yakima (now Yakima), 4 miles north, and offered Yakima City residents free property and to move their buildings to the new location. During the winter and spring of 1884–85, more than 100 buildings were moved to the new town.   EXIT 38

Mile 441 (142): Exit to U.S. Highway 97.
     EXIT 37

Mile 442 (141): Exit to Union Gap, Valley Mall Boulevard, Yakima air terminal, state patrol offices, Perry Technical Institute. 24-hour gas station, numerous restaurants and chain motels at exit.   EXIT 36

Mile 443.5 (139.5): Exit to Moxee Nob Hill Boulevard, the Yakima County Fairgrounds, Yakima Valley Museum, Yakima Valley Community College and Washington Highway 24 to Moxee City. Go east on Highway 24 for 1 mile to Keyes Road, then north for private campground on the Yakima River. Just beyond is Yakima Sportsman State Park with 28 tent sites, 36 hookup sites, swimming, fishing and picnic shelters.
     ⚎⚎▲ MP 35 EXIT 34

Mile 445 (138): Exit for business route, historical district, Yakima Avenue and Mall, convention center, Terrace Heights and city center. **YAKIMA** (pop. 58,690), the largest and most important city in central Washington, is a transportation and market center for the surrounding agricultural lands. The Central Washington Fair takes place here in late Sept. Complete visitor services available, with about 40 motels and 150 restaurants. More than 20 local wineries offer tours and tastings.

Downtown features the Capitol Theatre, an original vaudeville house built in the 1920s and faithfully refurbished in 1977. Track 29, also in the city's core, is a unique shopping center housed in 21 train cars transformed into a gallery of shops. The Yakima Arboretum, on the east side of town, features 46 acres of gardens that include an elaborate Japanese garden, 435 species of woody plants, 3 fountains and the tallest living Christmas tree in eastern Washington. Jewett Cultural Center, with a gift shop and horticulture library, is also in the arboretum. Free; open sunrise to sunset. On the outskirts of town is the Yakima Valley Museum, with the country's most comprehensive collection of horse-drawn vehicles and a tribute to former Supreme Court Justice William O. Douglas, a longtime Yakima resident.
     EXIT 33

Mile 446.5 (136.5): Exit here for U.S. Highway 12 west to Naches and White Pass, N. 1st Street, Chinook Pass. Numerous motels, restaurants along N. 1st Street, large RV park.
     ▲ EXIT 31

Mile 448 (135): Exit to 16th Avenue, Yakima Valley Community College, Yakima Valley Museum, Perry Technical Institute. Food, gas and lodging. Highway crosses Washington Central Railroad and Yakima Trolley line.

Mile 449 (134): N. 40th Avenue, Fruitvale Boulevard. Gas, market, cafe, Yakima airport.

Mile 451 (132): Naches River Valley, heart of the Yakima apple country, highway lined with apple-packing sheds. Twin bridges cross Naches River. Highway changes to 4-lane divided with local access westbound. Note the columnar basalt cliffs. The flume high up on the cliff is used to carry water to orchards.

Mile 451.5 (131.5): Selah Road, Old Naches Highway. Gas, market, restaurant, fruit stands.   MP 198

Mile 453 (130): Small town of Gleed; gas, grocery and restaurant.

Mile 454 (129): Historic marker commemorates the site of the junction of a major Native American trail network and the site of Fort Naches, constructed in 1855 to protect Col. Wright and his 9th Infantry. The fort was abandoned in 1856 and has become known as "The Basket Fort" because of its shape in the hillside.

Mile 456 (127): Highway narrows to 2 lanes westbound and is flanked by Umtanum and

There are more than 20 wineries in the Yakima Valley. The Yakima Appellation is 1 of 3 district wine-growing regions in Washington. (L. Linkhart)

Cleman mountains.

Mile 456.5 (126.5): NACHES (pop. 645), an Indian name meaning "plenty of water." Wenatchee National Forest ranger station. Gas, groceries, numerous fruit stands on both sides of the highway. *NOTE*: Next gas westbound is 58 miles from here.

Mile 459.5 (123.5): The big propellers on both sides of the highway are activated during the cold weather to keep the air moving and prevent the orchards from freezing.

Exit on to Highway 410 at Mile 464.5 for Chinook Pass and east entrance to Mount Rainier National Park. *(L. Linkhart)*

Mile 464.5 (118.5): Junction with Washington Highway 410, which leads 51 miles west to 5,440-foot Chinook Pass (closed in winter) and the east entrance to Mount Rainier National Park. U.S. 12 turns west to follow the Tieton River.

Mile 465 (118): Sign on north side marks Oak Creek Game Range, 94,718 acres between the Tieton River and the Wenas Valley, bisected by the Naches River. This is elk winter range with elk, deer, chukar partridge and grouse along 28 miles of stream bank. Established in 1939.

Mile 466 (117): Examples of columnar basalt on the south side of the river. This type of formation, common to eastern Washington, occurs when molten lava cools in huge crystals, the facets of which form regular columns that look like giant pillars.
MP 184

Mile 466.5 (116.5): Elk-viewing area and small exhibit area. During the winter months motorists can often view elk here that have come to this lower elevation to feed. The highway climbs gradually westbound. There are frequent slow-vehicle turnouts to accommodate slow-moving trucks, RVs and sightseers and not impede traffic. The Tieton River is a prime fishing stream all the way from its origin at Rimrock Lake to its confluence with the Naches River.

The Washington Dept. of Game stocks the river with rainbow trout. ⚓

Mile 471 (112): Highway enters Wenatchee National Forest. Westbound, pine trees begin to appear on the hillsides as the road gains elevation.
MP 179

Mile 472.5 (110.5): Windy Point Forest Service campground has 15 sites, pit toilets. Open April to Nov. ▲

Mile 477 (106): Lodge and motel beside the river, cafe and groceries.
MP 173

Mile 479.5 (103.5): Willows Forest Service campground; 16 sites, pit toilets, open April to Nov. ▲

Mile 480 (103): Wild Rose Forest Service campground; 9 sites, pit toilets, open mid-May to mid-Sept.

Most of the pines are lodgepoles (needles in pairs and asymmetric cones). The large red-barked pines are Ponderosas. ▲ MP 170

Mile 481 (102): River Bend Forest Service campground; 8 sites, pit toilets, open mid-May to mid-Nov. ▲

Mile 481.5 (101.5): Haus Creek Forest Service campground; 42 sites, handicap-accessible pit toilets, nature trails, open mid-May to mid-Nov. ♿⚓▲

Mile 482 (101): Highway crosses Soap Creek.

Mile 484.5 (98.5): Tieton Dam to south. This earth-fill dam is 220 feet high and dams the Tieton River and its tributaries to form 6-mile-wide Rimrock Lake, used primarily for irrigation storage. A spur road branches south from U.S. 12 and leads around the southern shore of the lake. Three resorts, boat launches, campgrounds and other recreation facilities ring this popular lake. Fishing is excellent for large kokanee from mid-May through the fall. ⚓▲

Mile 486 (97): Silver Cove resort, restaurant.
MP 164

Mile 487.5 (95.5): Restaurant, recreation facilities, RV park. ▲

Mile 490 (93): Silver Beach lake resort, marina, restaurant, RV campground, groceries, swimming, boat rentals, fishing and hiking trails. Splendid views southwest across the lake into the rugged Goat Rocks Wilderness.

Just west of the resort is Indian Creek Forest Service campground with 39 sites, pit toilets, groceries, swimming, rental boats, fishing and boat ramp. ⚓⚓▲

Mile 490.5 (92.5): Indian Creek Corral offers trail rides, pack trips. MP 159

Mile 491 (92): Tieton Road circles the lake on the south shore. Mixed forest of fir, hemlock and cedar here is an excellent example of second-growth timber. Note uniform size of the trees and dense branching nearly to the ground.

Mile 493.5 (89.5): Westbound, the highway climbs and twists along the mountainside on its way to White Pass. Magnificent views across the valley to the south with numerous talus slopes of loose rock. Note the paths of avalanches down the mountainsides that have swept all of the trees from steep, narrow chutes. MP 156

Mile 496 (87): Turnout to south with view of Clear Creek Falls.

Mile 496.5 (86.5): Road to Clear Lake 2 miles south and west; Forest Service campground with 26 sites, pit toilets, boat ramp and fishing for rainbow and brook trout. ⚓▲

Mile 497 (86): Dog Lake to north offers some fishing for rainbow and brook trout early in the summer. Forest Service campground with 9 sites, pit toilets and boat launch. ⚓▲

Mile 498.5 (84.5): White Pass (elev. 4,500 feet), White Pass winter-recreation complex, lodging, groceries, restaurants, gas. Visitor facilities are open year-round.

The ski area has 4 chair lifts, 1 poma and 1 rope tow, rentals and a ski school. One of the chairs operates during the summer for mountaintop sightseeing. There are 12 kilometers of groomed cross-country trails, rentals and lessons. The world and Olympic champion ski twins, Phil and Steve Mahre, train on these slopes. Highway begins a 6 percent downgrade westbound. ⛷ MP 151

Mile 501.5 (81.5): For the next several miles westbound the south slope of 14,411-foot Mount Rainier is visible from time to time looming above and to the north. In its winding descent the highway hugs the mountainside and passes through several groves with magnificent examples of old-growth fir towering more than 150 feet in the air.
MP 148

Mile 508.5 (74.5): Scenic viewpoint on south side of road of Palisades Rock Formation, another excellent example of columnar basalt. From mid-September, vine maple, willow, big leaf maple and other trees provide splendid autumn color along this section of road. MP 141

Mile 511 (72): Junction with Washington Highway 123. This route leads north to the south entrance to Mount Rainier National Park, 5,440-foot Chinook Pass and 4,630-foot Cayuse Pass. There is an information bulletin board at the intersection that provides current information on camping, trail and road conditions in the national park. It is 2.5 miles north from here to the park entrance and Ohanapecosh, location of a visitor center, nature trails, interpretive programs and a 205-site campground. (See also Rainier National Park in the MAJOR ATTRACTIONS section.)

Mile 511.5 (71.5): La Wis Wis Forest Service campground has 100 sites, flush toilets, fishing and nature trails.

Highway descends westbound. The Cowlitz River is visible to the north. The Washington Game Dept. plants this river with rainbow. MP 138

Mile 514.5 (68.5): Gas station and groceries. MP 135

Mile 517.5 (65.5): PACKWOOD was named for pioneer settler William Packwood. It's a logging town and the primary supply and jumping-off spot for backpackers, anglers, campers and outdoor recreationists heading into Gifford Pinchot National Forest, Mount Rainier National Park, Mount St. Helens National Volcanic Park or the Goat Rocks Wilderness. Complete visitor services including several motels and an RV park. Several outfitters and guides operate out of Packwood. ▲ MP 132

Mile 522 (61): Private recreation area offers horse rides.

Mile 522.5 (60.5): Christmas tree farm, one of many in this area.

Mile 524 (59): Motel.

Mile 526 (57): Private RV park and large picnic area along the Cowlitz River. Handicap-accessible facilities.

Mile 526.5 (56.5): Bridge over Cowlitz River. The broad Cowlitz Valley opens up on either side of the highway and leads past stump ranches and patches of woodland.

The "stump" ranch is a phenomenon peculiar to western Washington and Oregon. Typically it denotes a relatively small subsistence-type farm where the trees have been felled and removed, but the stumps remain. The land between the stumps has not been cultivated and is usually used for grazing. Historically, the landowner paid less tax on land that had not been cleared than on land under cultivation.

Mile 532.5 (50.5): RANDLE is another small logging town and one of the access points to Mount St. Helens National Volcanic Monument. Gas, groceries, restaurants and 4 motels are available. Gifford

Pinchot National Forest ranger station in the middle of town on U.S. Highway 12 has information on Mount St. Helens. Turn south on Cispus Road for Mount St. Helens and large full-service private RV campground 0.3 mile south. Access road to Mount St. Helens has 7 Forest Service campgrounds with a total of 210 sites. ▲

Mile 534.5 (48.5): Junction with Washington Highway 131 to Mount St. Helens and Spirit Lake viewpoint.

Mile 538 (45): Restaurant, gas station.

Mile 542.5 (40.5): GLENOMA; groceries, 9-hole golf course, gas and RV park. ▲

Mile 544.5 (38.5): Road to Riffe Lake, the impoundment behind Mossy Rock Dam. Riffe Lake was named after the early community of Riffe, founded in 1898. The original site of the town is now about 225 feet below the lake's waters. The lake is 23 miles long and is excellent for rainbow trout fishing. Boat launches. ⚓

Mile 546.5 (36.5): Access road south to Riffe Lake Recreation Area. MP 103

Mile 551.5 (31.5): Junction with Highway 7 north and access to Morton Airport. MORTON (pop. 1,135) is a typical logging town where the main street is often lined with big logging trucks. There's a chain saw sculpture of a logger at the entrance to town. Complete visitor services including several motels and restaurants. This is the southern terminus of the Mount Rainier Scenic Railroad steam train excursions that operate during the summer from the little town of Elbe, to the north on Washington Highway 7.

The town's big celebration of the year is the Morton Logger's Jubilee, held in mid-August. In addition to the traditional lumberjack competitions—tree topping, speed chopping, ax throwing, chain saw and hand saw bucking, and log rolling—the celebration features an unusual contest: riding lawnmower races. It's a zany event. For more information, contact the Morton Chamber of Commerce, phone (509) 496-6086.

Mile 555 (28): Mount St. Helens viewpoint 1 mile north atop Hopkins Hill. The mountain

is about 25 miles south from here. MP 94

Mile 556.5 (26.5): Viewpoint of Mount St. Helens and Cowills Valley.

Mile 559 (24): Viewpoint of Mossyrock Dam. MP 90

Mile 561 (22): Highway crosses Cowlitz River. MP 88

Mile 561.5 (21.5): MOSSYROCK (pop. 498). Gas, restaurant, groceries and motels.

Mile 562 (21): Turn off to Mossyrock Dam. Ike Kinswa State Park, 4 miles north on Mayfield Lake, offers 101 campsites, 41 hookups, concession stand for groceries, camping and fishing supplies, fishing, swimming and boat launch. There are 2 private full-service RV resorts on the lake. The 13-mile-long lake has excellent fishing for rainbow and cutthroat trout, crappie and bass. Blueberry picking in summer. ⚓▲ MP 87

Mile 563.5 (19.5): Mossyrock Trout Hatchery; open 9 a.m. to 5 p.m., weekdays.

Mile 565.5 (17.5): Mayfield Lake County Park, boating, picnicking, fishing. ⚓

Mile 566 (17): Gas station.

Mile 566.5 (16.5): Road to south leads to lakeside resort with 138 campsites, 100 hookups, showers, grocery, swimming, fishing, boat rentals. ⚓▲

Mile 567 (16): Highway crosses Mayfield Lake.

Mile 568.5 (14.5): Gershick Road to Mayfield Dam; gas, restaurant, motel.

Mile 569 (14): Junction with Washington Highway 122.

Mile 570.5 (12.5): Cowlitz Salmon Hatchery to south; open 9 a.m. to 5 p.m., weekdays.

Mile 575 (8): Gas and groceries. MP 74

Mile 576 (7): Small town of Ethel; gas, grocery. Cowlitz Trout Hatchery Road.

Mile 576.5 (6.5): County road leads south to Toledo.

Mile 580.5 (2.5): MARY'S CORNER; groceries. Jackson Highway leads south 0.2 mile to Jackson House Historic Site. This old log cabin (circa 1844) pioneer home was also used as a courthouse. Open 2–4 p.m., daily. Lewis and Clark State Park is 1.5 miles south along this road. The park has 25 campsites, an old-growth forest exhibit, nature trails and structures built by the Civilian Conservation Corps (1933– 42). There's a restaurant near the park entrance.

Mile 583 (0): Junction with Interstate 5. Gas, restaurant, fruit stand. Turn to **Mile 376** in the INTERSTATE 5 section.

U.S. HIGHWAY 20

Ontario to Newport, OR
(See maps, pages 89 and 92)

U.S. Highway 20 is one of the few highways that spans the breadth of the United States. It is also a major east-west, border-to-border route through central Oregon. Cross-state motorists using U.S. 20 will experience the contrasting environment of deserts, mountains and sea coast, as the highway travels from the wide-open spaces, sagebrush, high buttes and dry washes of eastern Oregon, to the alpine lakes, thick forests, meandering rivers and quiet farmlands of western Oregon.

Indians once chipped arrowheads from a mountain of glass on this route. Fur traders, wagon trains, cattle barons and sheepmen also left their mark, recorded for modern travelers by roadside plaques and gravesites. There is also much history to be found in small communities and way stations on U.S. 20, many of which began as stagecoach stops.

The *Northwest Mileposts* log of U.S. 20 starts at Ontario on Interstate 84 and follows Highway 201 south to begin U.S. 20 at Cairo Junction, continuing west 437 miles to Newport on the Oregon Coast. There are 5 sets of highway mileposts along U.S. 20. They begin at Newport, Corvallis, Albany, Sisters and Bend. With the exception of mountain passes, where it widens to 3 lanes, U.S. 20 is a 2-lane highway. From Ontario to Sisters, it is straight with long, flat stretches. Slow down for winding road through the Cascades, Willamette Valley and Coast Range.

U.S. Highway 20 Log

Distance from Ontario, OR, is followed by distance from Newport, OR.

Mile 0 (440): ONTARIO (pop. 9,750), located at the **junction** of Interstate 84 and Oregon Highway 201. Follow Highway 201 south 3 miles for U.S. Highway 20. Ontario is the eastern gateway to Oregon and the largest city in Malheur County. All visitor facilities available. Ontario began as a cattle shipping center named for the Canadian province where one of its founders was born. With the construction of reservoirs plus an extensive pipeline and canal network, the city and county became Oregon's major row crop producer.

Ontario is the major agricultural retail center for 7 Oregon and Idaho counties. Local companies store, sort, package, and ship cattle, potatoes, sugar beets, peppermint and an assortment of seeds. Ontario ships more fresh onions than any place in the nation.

The Snake River, 0.5 mile east of Ontario, contains largemouth and smallmouth bass, crappie and bluegills, plus catfish weighing up to 35 lbs. The Malheur River, at the town's edge, is a popular channel catfishing spot. ✦

The Oregon Trail runs through the hills north of Ontario. (L. Linkhart)

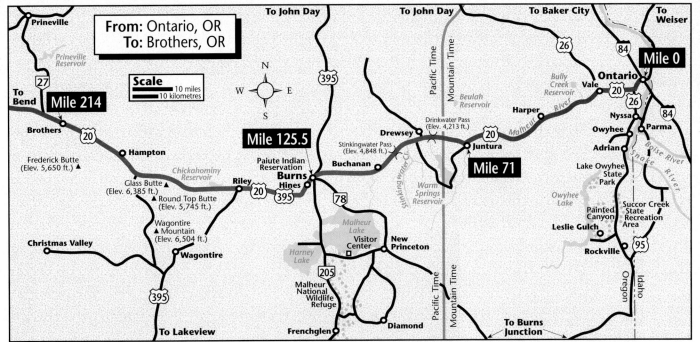

Mile 3 (437): CAIRO JUNCTION. Junction of U.S. Highway 20 and Highway 201, which leads north 3 miles to Ontario, and south 8 miles to Nyssa (description follows).

NYSSA (pop. 2,820) was chosen by the Oregon Short Line in 1883 because it was a convenient point to establish a railroad station. Sugar beets, introduced in 1906, are the mainstay of a diversified agricultural economy. Amalgamated Sugar Co., processors of White Satin Sugar, is the largest employer.

Nyssa is the "thunder egg capital of Oregon" and a rock hound's hot spot. Succor Creek State Recreation Area, approximately 35 miles south of Nyssa via Highway 20 and Succor Creek Road, is known for its abundance of thunder eggs plus petrified wood, agates and jasper. Succor Creek State Park has 19 primitive campsites and a picnic area.

Leslie Gulch and Painted Canyon, south and west of Succor Creek, offer moss agates, jasper and quartz crystal plus spectacular scenery. Area roads are rough clay dirt and should be avoided following heavy rains. Four-wheel drives and high-centered vehicles are recommended as many roads are deeply rutted. Inquire locally for directions.

Lake Owyhee, 33 miles southwest of Nyssa, fills 53 miles of canyon forming Oregon's largest reservoir lake. Often called the "most overstocked and underfished lake in America," it yields excellent catches of crappie and bass. Lake Owyhee State Park has 10 RV sites with hookups, 30 tent sites, picnicking, boating and a dump station. The reservoir's 310 miles of shoreline include lakeside resorts, a marina, cabin rentals and boat rentals. Before forming the state's largest reservoir, the Owyhee River runs through a 1,000-foot-deep canyon. It is a prime spring whitewater rafting destination.   ⚓⛟▲

Mile 4 (436): Oregon State University's Malheur Experiment Station researches weed control, sugar beets, onions, soybeans, spearmint, sweet corn and dry beans. Fields producing some of these crops line the highway between the Experiment Station and Vale.

Mile 5 (435): Potatoes grow south of the highway, sugar beets and onions to the north. Ore-Ida and Simplet are the largest potato contractors here.   MP 256

Mile 7 (433): North of the highway is Malheur Butte, the neck of an extinct volcano. Indians once used it as a lookout.   MP 254

Mile 8 (432): Scenic vista, overlooks Nevada Ditch and onion fields.

Mile 9 (431): Nevada Ditch. This irrigation channel was dug by hand in 1881 and continues to serve local residents. Onions and alfalfa grow north of the highway. To the south are grain and sugar beets.   MP 252

Mile 10.5 (429.5): Bean fields north of the highway and sugar beets to the south.

Mile 12.5 (427.5): Weigh station south side of highway.   MP 249

Mile 13.5 (426.5): VALE (pop. 1,605) is the Malheur County seat. Malheur Crossing, at the town's eastern edge, was an important stop on the Oregon Trail. Here, immigrants bathed and laundered in the hot springs that empty into the river. Original wagon ruts, an Oregon Trail exhibit and pioneer grave can be seen on Lytle Boulevard south of town.

In 1854, Stephen Meek led a wagon train west from here in search of a shortcut to the Willamette Valley. They became lost in a maze of ridges and canyons. More than 70 people perished. Survivor Ezra Meeker retraced the route in 1906, placing markers at significant points. Several are in Vale. Today, water from Vale's hot springs is used to grow 3.5 million lbs. of mushrooms plus heat greenhouses, a mushroom packing house and a slaughterhouse. Tours available by appointment. There is an RV park 2 blocks north of the highway.   ▲ MP 247

Mile 14.5 (425.5): Information center with history of the area. Picnic tables, trash cans and drinking water.   ⛟

Mile 15 (425): Western city limits of Vale.

Mile 16 (424): Bully Creek Road. Bully Creek Reservoir, approximately 8 miles west of Vale, is popular with swimmers and waterskiers. Good fishing for crappie, bass, trout and perch.   ⛟ MP 245

Mile 19 (421): Thirty-five miles of dirt road to the south ends at Dry Creek, which empties into Lake Owyhee.

Mile 22.5 (417.5): Access to Bully Creek Reservoir, 9 miles.

Mile 23 (417): Crossing the Malheur River, which heads into the Strawberry Mountains and flows 165 miles east to the Snake River at Ontario. Peter Skene Ogden and a group of French fur trappers named the river in 1826. Ogden's party left a cache of furs hidden on the banks. When they returned, the pelts had been stolen. Ogden christened it "Riviere Au Malheur," which translates as "unfortunate" or "unlucky river." The section of river paralleling U.S. 20 between Vale and Juntura is unlucky for sportsmen, as it contains mostly trash fish.

Westbound from Vale, the landscape changes from flat, fertile fields to rolling hills of sagebrush—unbroken save for isolated juniper trees.

Mile 30.5 (409.5): LITTLE VALLEY is an unincorporated community with an estimated area population of 150 people. Pay phone. Local farms and ranches grow corn, radishes and dill seed. Excellent hunting for pheasant; good for chukar, quail, deer and antelope.

Mile 34.5 (405.5): Cottonwood Creek, good early spring trout stream.   ⛟

Mile 37 (403): Harper Junction. HARPER, 1 mile north of the junction, was named for the Pacific Livestock Co.'s Harper Ranch. The service station here has the last gas westbound for 34 miles. No accommodations. Pay phone.

Mile 43 (397): Crossing Squaw Creek, a tributary of the Malheur River. Turnout with drinking water. The highway meanders through 1.5 miles of switchbacks created by rolling ravines. *CAUTION:* Gusty winds.

MP 217

Mile 60.5 (379.5): Pass Pole Creek.

Mile 63.5 (376.5): Turnouts south of highway with good views of the Malheur River. At this point, the Malheur is a shallow, slow-moving stream separated into 2 channels by several small islands.

Mile 68.5 (371.5): Historical marker south side of highway tells of Peter Skene Ogden's Oct. 10, 1828, encampment. This was Ogden's fifth and final expedition into the Snake River country. From here he journeyed south to the Humboldt River and east to the Great Salt Lake. The highway crosses the North Fork Malheur River just west of historical marker.

Mile 71 (369): JUNTURA (pop. 55) has a combination gas station/restaurant, 22-site campground (hookups and hot showers) and a 9-unit motel. Last gas westbound for 33 miles. The name Juntura is derived from a Spanish word meaning "to join," and was applied to this area because the north and south forks of the Malheur River merge here. From the turn of the century into the 1930s, Juntura was a trade and shipping center for cattle and sheep. Its decline came with the passage of the Taylor Grazing Act, which prohibited driving sheep over federal lands and shipping them in trucks.

Area rockhounding digs yield agates and poor quality but plentiful quantities of petrified wood. Beulah Reservoir, 15 miles north, is fished for crappie and rainbow natives, best in May, June and October. The Malheur River and Butte Reservoir offer trout, perch and catfish. ◄▲ MP 189

Mile 72 (368): Tent camping and a boat launch 0.5 mile south of highway. ▲

Mile 79 (361): Burns District Bureau of Land Management headquarters north of highway.

Mile 80 (360): Crossing the Malheur/Harney County line and the division between Mountain and Pacific time zones. Westward motorists set watches back 1 hour; eastbound motorists set watches ahead 1 hour.

With 10,228 square miles of land, Harney County is the largest county in Oregon and the third largest county in the nation. It exceeds the combined size of Massachusetts and Rhode Island. Created Feb. 25, 1889, it was named for William S. Harney, a veteran of the Indian, Mexican and Civil wars. The county's economy centers around lumbering and ranching. A short growing season combined with the possibility of frost in any given month inhibits crop production. Average snowfall is 37 inches and precipitation averages 8 inches per year.

Despite its size, Harney County has less than 8,000 people. MP 180

Mile 82 (358): Drinkwater Pass Summit (elev. 4,213 feet). Turnout. Start of a 3-mile-long, 6 percent downgrade.

Mile 84 (356): Malheur River.

Mile 86 (353): Drewsey Junction. DREWSEY, 2 miles north, post office. This ranching community was originally called Gouge Eye (after a popular frontier method of settling arguments) and attracted cattlemen, outlaws, gamblers and miners during its 1880s heyday. The name honors a local rancher's daughter, Drewsey Miller.

Mile 88 (351): Access road to Warm Springs Reservoir, 14 miles south. The unpaved road is not maintained. The reservoir, built in 1919, was dry in 1994. MP 171

Mile 91 (348): Stinking Water Creek and the Stinking Water Mountains; named for the area's hot springs. MP 168

Mile 114 (326): Historical marker on south side of highway recounts the history of Fort Harney, from its establishment on Aug. 10, 1867, to March 2, 1889, when the last 320 acres were restored to the public domain. The fort, named after Gen. William S. Harney, who commanded the Oregon Military Dept., was located 2.5 miles north of the marker. MP 145

Mile 123.5 (316.5): Junction with U.S. Highway 395, major south-north route that extends from California to the Canadian border. U.S. Highway 20 and U.S. 395 share a common alignment from here west 27 miles to Riley. Turn to **Mile 158.5** in the U.S. HIGHWAY 395 section for log.

Egrets are a common sight at the Malheur Wildlife Refuge. (© George Wuerthner)

Mile 93 (347): Highway 20 becomes 3 lanes westbound as it ascends Stinking Water Mountain (elev. 4,948 feet). The mountains are a good source of petrified wood, belvadee jasper, agates and fossils.

Mile 97.5 (342.5): Unpaved access road leads 28 miles south to Warm Springs Reservoir.

Mile 103 (337): Roadside marker on north side of Highway 1 defines this point as the farthest northern edge of The Great Basin. From mid-Feb. to late April, bald eagles are often seen along the highway between Buchanan and Riley. Between Buchanan and Burns, sagebrush fades into lowland meadows. Rest area on south side of highway is open April 1 to Nov. 1. Restrooms, picnic tables, water and trash cans. ♯

Mile 104 (336): BUCHANAN is a combination store and gas station with repair service and 24-hour towing. Free museum and gallery with excellent small collection of Indian artifacts, crystal and firearms. Named for settler Thomas Buchanan, this was originally a stagecoach stop. MP 155

Mile 124.5 (315.5): Weigh station, motel and restaurant.

Mile 125.5 (314.5): BURNS (pop. 2,920), all visitor facilities available. The Harney County seat, Burns was named for poet Robert Burns. It became the administrative headquarters and the modern livestock center of Oregon with the passage of the Taylor Grazing Act in 1936.

The Burns–Hines communities form a transportation hub and business center for Harney County. Recreation centers around bird watching, hunting and rock collecting, much of it taking place at Malheur National Wildlife Refuge south of Burns. Malheur Lake, one of the state's largest bodies of water during high water, is the centerpiece of the 183,000-acre refuge, a major feeding stop on the Pacific flyway. Spring migrations bring waterfowl, shorebirds and songbirds and usually peak during mid-March to mid-April. To reach the refuge visitor center from Burns, drive east 2 miles on Oregon Highway 78, then south 25 miles on Oregon Highway 205, then east 9 miles on county road (gravel). The refuge visitor center is on the south shore of Malheur Lake; open 8 a.m. to

4:30 p.m. weekdays. The refuge museum, located at the visitor center, is open 6 a.m. to 9 p.m. daily. Refuge roads extend south from the visitor center about 35 miles to **FRENCHGLEN**; camping and historic motel. Frenchglen is 60 miles south of Burns via Highway 205. Facilities at the refuge include concealment blinds for photographers and bird-watchers. Other activities are boating, canoeing, hiking, cross-country skiing and cave exploration. During fall, the refuge has 8,000 acres open to waterfowl and upland game hunting. For rock hounds, refuge grounds yield good petrified wood, bog agates, arrowheads and opalite. There are no services within the refuge; carry gas and water. For more information write: Malheur NWR, P.O. Box 245, Princeton, OR 97721; phone (503) 493-2612.

Mile 126 (314): Junction with access road, which leads 1 mile north to **PAIUTE INDIAN RESERVATION** (pop. 160). The reservation is governed by a Tribal Council and maintains its own police department. The tribe operates a processing plant that freeze-dries onion rings. Burns City Park, located at the junction, has picnic tables and playground equipment. Just west of the junction is Harney County Historical Museum and Visitor Information Center. The museum building and grounds have served as a brewery, laundry and wrecking yard. It has an extensive photo collection, women's gowns, thunder eggs, arrowheads, gun, saddles and a waterfowl exhibit. Open June through Sept., 9 a.m. to 5 p.m., Tues-

day through Friday, 9 a.m. to noon on Saturday. Admission fee.

Mile 128 (312): **HINES** (pop. 1,490), developed by the Edward Hines Timber Co., is designed around an oval park from which most streets extend. The police reserve sponsors an annual Obsidian Days gem and mineral show, which attracts dealers from Washington, Idaho, California and Arizona. Snow Mountain Pine, one of the state's largest ponderosa pine sawmilling operations, is located here. All services available.

Mile 129 (311): Valley Golf Club Road leads north to a public 9-hole course.

Mile 129.5 (310.5): Ochoco National Forest Ranger Station.

Mile 130 (310): Access to Delintment Lake, 58 miles northwest of Hines, in Ochoco National Forest.

Mile 131 (309): Western city limits of Hines. Westbound motorists enter Oregon's high desert country, a land of sagebrush flats, dry alkali lake beds and creek bottoms. In spring, the landscape is brightened by wildflowers and green grass.

Mile 136 (304): Bureau of Land Management Wild Horse Corrals. This is the major facility for managing wild horses on Oregon public lands. Since 1974, when the program was started, BLM has processed more than 9,000 wild horses, placing 75 percent with

private individuals. Wild horse herds increase an average of 20 percent per year. Tours are available by prior arrangement.

Mile 142.5 (297.5): Access road to Moon Reservation and Harney Lake.

Mile 144 (296): Rest area with covered picnic tables, water and nature trail. The 0.5-mile Sage Hen Nature Trail takes you through sagebrush and western juniper to scenic viewpoints. Self-guiding brochure is available at the trailhead.

Mile 153 (287): Junction with U.S. Highway 395 south at **RILEY** (est. pop. 4), named for rancher Amos W. Riley. The first post office was established in Riley in 1880.

U.S. 395 leads south from here to Klamath Falls, Lake View, and Reno, NV. Southbound travelers turn to **Mile 127.5** in the U.S. HIGHWAY 395 section for log.

Mile 154.5 (285.5): Historic marker tells of a Bannock, Snake and Paiute uprising in 1878 in protest of white occupation of treaty lands. They were defeated by the First U.S. Cavalry in a battle at nearby Silver Creek.

Mile 158.5 (281.5): Chickahominy Reservoir is stocked with trout and is a popular fishing spot and sometime windsurfing area. Boat ramp, dock and informal camping (water, camping fee).

Mile 162.5 (277.5): Turnoff to north for Silver Valley.

Mile 163 (277): Northern Great Basin Experimental Range, established 1936, dedicated to research on the ecology and management of range lands. Operated jointly by the Agricultural Research Service of the U.S. Dept. of Agriculture and Oregon State University agriculture experiment station.

Mile 173.5 (266.5): Lake County boundary.

Mile 180 (260): The best access road to Glass Buttes rockhounding area, 6 miles south. See feature this page. ★ MP 77

Mile 182.5 (257.5): Dirt road north of highway leads to Buck Creek and G.I. Ranch. Rough dirt road south to Glass Buttes has deep ruts and should be attempted only by 4-wheel-drive or heavy-duty high-suspension vehicles.

Mile 183 (257): Glass Buttes (elev. 6,385 feet), a mountain of volcanic glass beneath a sagebrush and juniper cover. MP 74

Mile 186 (254): An extremely rough dirt road winds south 35 miles around the slopes of Round Top Butte (elev. 5,745 feet) and Wagontire Mountain (elev. 6,504 feet) to junction with an all-weather road that leads to U.S. Highway 395 and west to Christmas Valley. For 4-wheel-drive and high-suspension vehicles only.

Mile 188 (252): Entering Deschutes County westbound.

Mile 193.5 (246.5): **HAMPTON** (est. pop. 9), named for Hampton Butte (elev. 6,333 feet), has a cafe, store, RV hookups and gas station. Only gas between Hines, 65 miles east, and Brothers, 21 miles west. ▲

Glass Buttes

Approximately 4,900,000 years ago, eastern Oregon rumbled and shook with volcanic activity. Rhyolite, with a high silica content, spewed from one of the vents. The thick flow cooled very quickly, and instead of spreading over the bedrock in a thin layer, it formed a mountain around the vent. When the volcanism subsided, Glass Butte had risen 2,000 feet above the surrounding countryside to an elevation of 6,385 feet. It is literally a mountain of glass, and may be the world's largest obsidian outcropping.

Indians discovered the Glass Buttes and turned it into a virtual factory for production of spear points, arrowheads, skin scrapers, axes and chisels. An implement made of Glass Buttes obsidian was a prized possession, as well as a prime trading commodity. Some have been found as far east as the mounds of Ohio.

Today, Glass Buttes obsidian is much sought after by rock hounds, who come from all over to dig in the valley between Glass Butte, which together comprise Glass Buttes. The total rockhounding area covers approximately 7,000 acres.

While most obsidian is jet black, Glass Buttes has a distinctive irridescence and comes in a variety of colors: gold, silver, rainbow, red and brown. Fire obsidian is also found here. Rock shops in Burns (**Mile 125.5**) have maps of the area that pinpoint where the dif-

ferent varieties have been found.

Recreational rock hounds may take 25 lbs. of obsidian out of Glass Buttes per day up to a total of 250 lbs. per year. To make digging easier, bring shovels, picks, rock hammers and crowbars. Explosives and power equipment are not permitted.

While highway signs point to Glass Buttes, access roads are not marked. The only access road that should be attempted with the family car lies about 30 feet west of Milepost 77 (See **Mile 180**). It is in reasonably good condition, and leads south 3 miles to the start of the digging areas, where there is also an open space for informal camping and a natural reservoir that serves as a waterhole for cattle from surrounding ranches. Several more miles of dirt road continue through the prime rockhounding sites.

There are other maintained dirt roads leading from U.S. 20 to the diggings. An occasional muffler, exhaust pipe and other auto parts offer silent testimony to the inadvisability of trying them with anything except a 4-wheel-drive or high-centered vehicle.

There are no facilities at Glass Buttes. Bring water and food as the nearest services are at Hampton, 9 miles west (**Mile 193.5**). Although there are no developed sites, overnight camping is permitted.

Glass Buttes is administered by the Bureau of Land Management for amateur and recreational rockhounding.

Mile 204 (236): All-weather road leads 21 miles north to Camp Creek, which empties into the Crooked River.

Mile 207 (233): Dirt road leads south 11 miles to Frederick Butte (elev. 5,650 feet) and Benjamin Lake.   MP 50

Mile 214 (226): BROTHERS (elev. 4,640 feet) has gas, bar, cafe and store. The area has been a center for ranching since 1873. Several fraternal family groups settled here, and the community was named for the many homesteading brothers. Rest area east of the store has 5 covered picnic shelters, drinking water and restrooms.   ⚲ MP 43

Mile 221 (219): Junction with Oregon Highway 27, which leads north to Prineville Reservoir and Crooked River.   MP 36

Mile 230.5 (209.5): Pine Mountain Observatory, 9 miles south on graded dirt road, has received worldwide recognition as a major astronomical facility. Open Friday and Saturday, viewing begins at dusk. Special tours Thursday and Sunday by appointment; phone (503) 382-8331.

Mile 231 (209): MILLICAN is often called the "one-man town." It has a store and is the last gas stop westbound before Bend.   MP 26

Mile 234 (206): Limited-use road south to Millican Valley, closed in winter.

Mile 235.5 (204.5): Summit of Horse Ridge (elev. 4,292 feet).

Mile 236 (204): Geologic marker tells of a large prehistoric river that drained an ice age lake. The lake's escaping water cut through lava, creating a rocky gap called Dry River, which flowed north into Crooked River. Evidence indicates that the ancient river was once the scene of many Indian encampments.

Mile 237 (203): Viewpoint with good view of the Cascades to the west.

Mile 242 (198): Turnouts on both sides of highway.

Mile 243.5 (196.5): Large turnouts; parking for 10 vehicles.

Mile 250.5 (189.5): County road leads north 3 miles to Bend Airport, 18 miles to Powell Butte and 30 miles to Prineville.

Mile 252.5 (187.5): Access to 27th Street, golf course and hospital.

Mile 253.5 (186.5): Deschutes National Forest headquarters south of highway.

Mile 254 (186): Pilot Butte State Park and Bend city limits. A 1-mile paved road spirals to the top of Pilot Butte (elev. 3,400 feet). Visible from the summit are: Mount Hood (elev. 11,205 feet), Mount Jefferson (elev. 10,495 feet), Three Fingered Jack (elev. 7,848 feet), Mount Washington (elev. 7,802 feet), Middle Sister (elev. 10,053 feet), Broken Top (elev. 9,165 feet) and Mount Bachelor (elev. 9,075 feet).

Mile 256 (184): Information center south side of highway.

Mile 257 (183): South **junction** of U.S. 20 and U.S. Highway 97, both of which become 3rd Street from downtown to northern city limits. **BEND** (pop. 18,700) is the county seat of Deschutes County and a center for year-round outdoor recreation, in particular skiing in winter and golf in summer.

Mount Bachelor, 22 miles west of town via Cascade Lakes Highway, is known for its powder skiing. Ski season begins in November and can run into July. The summit chair lift operates in summer for sightseers. There are several major motels in Bend and resort lodging at Mount Bachelor.

The High Desert Museum, 6 miles south on U.S. 97, is a participation-oriented facility with indoor and outdoor exhibits on art, history, nature and science. Interpretive talks and demonstrations. A "walk through time" depicts the opening of the American West. Hours: April 1 to Sept. 30, 9 a.m. to 5 p.m.; Oct. 1 to March 31, 9 a.m. to 4 p.m., except Thanksgiving, Christmas and New Year's. Fee.

Lava Butte and Lava Lands Visitor Center, 11 miles south on U.S. 97, has displays, a slide show, interpretive trails and naturalist talks; paved road to top provides outstanding view of Cascades. Open daily, mid-March to Oct.

Lava Cast Forest, 14 miles south of Bend via U.S. Highway 97, has the world's largest lava mold trees. Self-guided nature trail.   ⚲👣★ MP 0

Mile 259 (181): North **junction** of U.S. Highways 20 and 97. Highway 20 continues northwest to Sisters, and Highway 97 north to Redmond (see **Mile 140** in the U.S. HIGHWAY 97 section for log).

Mile 260 (180): Deschutes River. The Deschutes heads into the Cascades and flows 240 miles north and northeast to empty into the Columbia River 12 miles east of The Dalles. North of Bend, it is fished for brown, rainbow and some brook trout, best in June.   ➤ MP 18

Mile 261 (179): Access south to Tumalo State Park on the Deschutes River; 20 RV sites with hookups, 68 tent sites and group picnic shelter.   ⚲▲ MP 17

Mile 267.5 (172.5): Viewpoint.

Mile 275 (165): Sisters rodeo grounds and private campground.   ▲

Mile 276.5 (163.5): Sisters city park picnic area, playground and Squaw Creek. The creek has fair fishing for native rainbow and cutthroat, best May through June.   ⚲➤

Mile 277 (163): SISTERS (pop. 780) was established in 1885 as an outpost for Company A of the First Oregon Volunteers. Its economy is based on small business, wood products and tourism. Sisters also has the largest llama breeding ranch in the world.

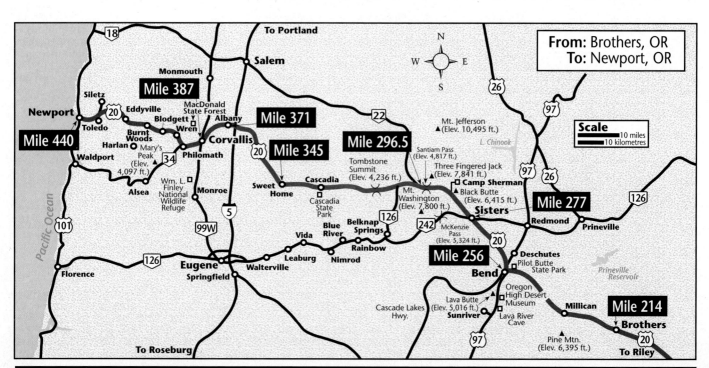

Fishermen use Sisters as a base for angling the McKenzie, Deschutes, Metolius and Crooked rivers. Mule deer hunters, hikers and skiers find it convenient for excursions into the pasture lands and Cascades. All visitor facilities. Last gas westbound for 50 miles.   MP 100

Mile 277.5 (162.5): Junction with Oregon Highway 242 to McKenzie Lava Beds, McKenzie Pass (elev. 5,324 feet), and Oregon Highway 126 to Eugene and Springfield. Dee Wright Memorial, 24 miles west on Highway 242 at McKenzie Pass, offers a spectacular

Above—*The main street of Sisters offers visitors a taste of the Old West.*
Left—*Sisters boasts the largest llama breeding ranch in the world.*
(Photos courtesy of Sisters Chamber of Commerce)

view of the Cascades. A 0.5-mile nature trail leads through portions of the 8-mile-long lava flow at the lava beds. Highway 242 is open late June to Oct., closed in winter. Not recommended for trailers or motorhomes; combinations of more than 50 feet prohibited. Travelers can rejoin U.S. 20 by continuing west on Oregon Highway 242 to Mile 37 and north on Highway 126 for 18 miles.

Mile 278 (162): Entering Deschutes National Forest westbound. Historical marker tells that in this vicinity early Indian trails converged, one coming in from Tumalo Creek to the southeast, one from Sparks and Green lakes to the southwest, one the Scott Trail (as later known) from the west and one from The Dalles to the north.

Mile 281 (159): Cold Springs cutoff and west access to Graham Carroll.

Mile 282 (158): Indian Ford Road, Green Ridge Road, Indian Ford Campground and High Cascades Riding Stables. Indian Ford USFS campground with 24 sites. High Cascades Stables operates hourly, half-day, all-day and overnight wilderness pack trips. Riders of all ages and skill levels welcome. ▲

Mile 284 (156): Black Butte Ranch and Golf Course.

Mile 286 (154): Camp Sherman junction and access to Metolius River headwaters, 5 miles north of junction via paved Forest Ser-

vice Road 14. The Metolius flows from huge underground springs and empties into the Deschutes River. Some 35,000 fish are planted annually in the Metolius. The first 9 miles of the river are limited to fly-fishing with barbless hooks and a wildfish throw-back system. Wildfish populations include brook, browns, rainbow, Dolly Varden, kokanee and whitefish. Whitefish are so plentiful that there is no bag limit. Hiking trails, restrooms, observation point and marked trail. There are several Forest Service campgrounds north of Camp Sherman store.

CAMP SHERMAN, 5 miles north of junction, is a resort community of approximately 300 people. Visitors have a choice of 7 resorts, motels, RV parks, riverside cabins, lakeside lodges, bed and breakfasts, or kitchenettes. Gas, store and stables. MP 91

Mile 286.5 (153.5): Jefferson/Deschutes County line.

Mile 288.5 (151.5): Scaling station and access to Camp Tamerack, Santiam Pass Winter Recreation Area and westbound chain-up area. The Santiam Pass Winter Recreation Area extends west to Highway 126 and the Mount Jefferson Wilderness, and south to the Mount Washington Wilderness. It contains more than 70 miles of snowmobile and Nordic trails.

Mile 289 (151): Junction with Forest Service Road 12 to Mount Jefferson Wilderness Trail Headquarters and Jack Lake Road. Access to

Jack Creek picnic area, which features a self-guiding nature trail.

Mile 290 (150): Access to Blue Lake Resort, 3 miles south of highway. This 300-foot-deep lake is stocked with rainbow trout and also holds kokanee, German brown and brook trout. Link Creek, which empties Blue Lake into Suttle Lake, is a spawning stream that is off-limits to fishing. Best fishing is May through June. Resorts at Blue Lake offer a full range of accommodations and campgrounds. There are also a restaurant, store, marina, boat launches, hiking trails, stables, a Nordic ski center, and playgrounds for children.

Mile 290.5 (149.5): Turnoff for Suttle Lake. Marina, Forest Service campgrounds, lakeside resort. Good fishing for rainbow, German brown, eastern brook, whitefish and kokanee.

Mile 292.5 (147.5): Mount Washington viewpoint, one of several along the south side of the highway.

Mile 293.5 (146.5): Access to Elliott R. Corbett Memorial State Park, 1.3 miles south, and Corbett Sno-Park to the north. The state-funded winter parking areas require a Sno-Park permit in season. Permits may be purchased locally. Corbett State Park is for day use only with picnicking and a 0.5-mile hiking trail.

Mile 296.5 (143.5): Santiam Pass Summit (elev. 4,817 feet), Jefferson/Linn County line and Willamette, Deschutes National Forest boundaries. Approximately 10 percent of all timber cut in national forests comes from the 1.6-million-acre Willamette National Forest.

Mile 297 (143): Turnoff south for Hoodoo Ski Area, Ray Benson Sno-Park and Big Lake Road. Santiam Sno-Park to north and access to Pacific Crest Trail. Hoodoo Ski Bowl has 3 lifts and rope tows in the alpine area, plus a separate Nordic center with groomed trails operated in conjunction with the Forest Service. Full-service lodge with bar. Warming huts at Benson Sno-Park area and access to snowmobile trails.

The Pacific Crest Trail winds north-south along the length of Santiam Pass. A portion marked for winter travel starts here and ends 3.2 miles south.

Mile 299 (141): Brake check area and start of 4-mile steep downgrade westbound.

Mile 300.5 (139.5): Lost Lake lies in a lava basin surrounded by meadows. Nearby are craters and lava fields of the McKenzie flow. It is fished for stocked rainbow and native brown trout.

Mile 302 (138): Junction with Oregon Highway 22 northwest to Salem. U.S. 20 shares a common alignment with Oregon Highway 126 from here east to Sisters.

MP 75

Mile 304.5 (135.5): Sawyers Ice Cave parking for unmarked trail to ice cave.

Mile 305.5 (134.5): Junction of U.S. 20 and Oregon Highway 126, which leads southwest to Springfield (75 miles) and Eugene (78 miles).

For the next 16 miles westbound on U.S. 20, a series of small creeks tumble out of the Cascades, flow under the highway, and empty into the Santiam River. Most hold native brook trout and offer good fishing during June and July. The creeks are: Toad, Speckie, Echo, Slide, Snow, Ram, Sheep and Easy Creek, Storm and Soda.

Mile 309.5 (130.5): Historical marker tells of naming Lost Prairie in 1859. Some expedition members felt the group was lost. To prove they were not, leader Andrew Wiley climbed a tree and by doing so became the first white man to see Santiam Pass from the west side of the mountains. Lost Prairie USFS Campground. ▲

Mile 310 (130): Echo Creek Road, hiking trail. 🏕 MP 67

Mile 313 (127): Tombstone Pass Summit (elev. 4,236 feet); Sno-Park parking. Brake test area and start of 6 percent downgrade westbound that extends for 11 miles.

Mile 313.5 (126.5): Junction with Jump Off Joe Road. *CAUTION:* Slides next 7 miles, winding road next 3 miles westbound.

Mile 322 (118): House Rock USFS campground; 17 sites. ▲

Mile 324 (116): Mountain House Restaurant. Starting in 1868, there have been 4 Mountain Houses here. The first 2 were destroyed by fire. The current one was built in 1940.

Mile 325 (115): Fernview USFS campground; 10 sites. ▲

Mile 327.5 (112.5): Yukwah Campground. ▲

Mile 328 (112): Turnout trailhead and Trout Creek USFS campground (21 sites). The Santiam River parallels the highway westbound. 🏕▲

Mile 330 (110): Bridge crossing Santiam River. MP 47

Mile 332 (108): Western boundary of Willamette National Forest.

Mile 333 (107): Canyon Creek.

Mile 334 (106): Wolf Creek.

Mile 335 (105): Dobbin Creek.

Mile 335.5 (104.5): CASCADIA. During the 1930s, this area attracted many vacationers because of its mineral springs. Today it has a store, post office and gas.

Mile 336 (104): Cascadia State Park; 26 campsites, group picnic shelter, soda water spring, 2-mile trail to Soda Creek Falls, and fishing in Santiam River. A covered bridge, built in 1945, spans the Santiam River just off the highway. 🏕⛽🍴▲

Mile 343.5 (96.5): Junction with road north to Foster Lake and Green Peter Lake reservoirs managed by the U.S. Army Corps of Engineers; fishing, boating, swimming, camping and picnicking. Quartzille Road to Green Peter Lake also provides access to the Quartzille Recreation Corridor. The Quartzille Mining District has been the site of both hardrock and placer mining for gold since the mid-1800s. 🍴⛽▲

Mile 345 (95): SWEET HOME (pop. 7,005), Foster Lake viewpoint and information center, food, gas and lodging. Industry headquartered here includes Slip-N-Snip Scissors, manufacturers of folding scissors; White's Metal Electronics, which makes the world's largest line of mineral and metal detectors; and Sweet Home, Inc., the nation's largest manufacturer of wood stoves. White's Electronic Metal Detector museum is open weekdays from 8 a.m. to 5 p.m. Rock hounds will find the Sweet Home area a good place to dig for petrified wood. The Quartzille Mining District is open to recreational mining (see description at **Mile 343.5**).

Mile 345.5 (94.5): Junction with road north to Foster Dam and fish hatchery; Foster Dam Site. Restrooms, scenic viewpoint, fish viewing and tours. Hatchery is open 8 a.m. to 5 p.m.

Mile 346 (94): Wiley Creek Road.

Mile 347.5 (92.5): Sweet Home Ranger Station, Willamette National Forest.

Mile 348 (92): Access south to Weddle Covered Bridge.

Mile 349 (91): Junction with Oregon Highway 228 west to Brownsville and Halsey. MP 26

Mile 349.5 (90.5): Access to McDowell County Park, 8 miles east; 2 waterfalls and picnic area. ⛽

Mile 357.5 (82.5): Access to Waterloo County Park; hiking and nature trails, boat ramp and playground. 🏕

Mile 358 (82): Pineway public golf course; 9 holes, driving range, restaurant and lounge.

Mile 360 (80): Sodaville Road. Turnoff for

Mountain Home and Sodaville.

Mile 360.5 (79.5): LEBANON (pop. 10,485) is a center for lumber and agriculture. Food, gas and lodging available. The area is rich in agates, petrified wood, jasper, opals and thunder eggs. Seven covered bridges are situated northeast of the city, and can be toured with a self-driving map available from the Lebanon Chamber of Commerce, 1040 Park St., phone (503) 258-7164.

Mile 369.5 (70.5): Junction with Oregon Highway 226 north to Crabtree, Scio and Lyons.

Timber Linn Memorial Park, site of the annual Albany Timber Carnival held July 4 weekend. The carnival features championship and amateur competition in ax throwing, log chopping and other events, drawing contestants from throughout the Pacific Northwest.

Mile 371 (69): U.S. 20 passes over Interstate 5 and through Albany city center to Milepost 10 at the junction with Oregon Highway 99E. After merging with Highway 99, U.S. 20 goes north, across the Willamette River, then turns west.

ALBANY (pop. 28,060) is the county seat and largest city in Linn County. All visitor facilities are available. Albany is an important manufacturing center for rare metals, food processing, grass seed and timber.

The town dates to 1848, and was named for the founder's home, Albany, NY. The 350 homes in the historic district feature every major architectural style popular in the United States since 1850. Self-guiding tour brochures of the historic district and 10 covered bridges are available at the Albany Visitors Assoc., 300 SW 2nd St., phone (503) 928-0911.

Mile 378 (62): Spring Hill Road, Albany Golf Course and Benton–Linn County line.

Mile 379.5 (60.5): Access road to Springhill Cellars, 2 miles.

Mile 381.5 (58.5): Junction with Independence Road north to Adair Village (4 miles), Game Management Area (5 miles) and Buena Vista (10 miles). During WWII, Camp Adair spread across 50,000 acres and became the second largest city in Oregon. Infantry, artillery and engineering units were trained here. Later, it became a U.S. Naval hospital and a prisoner of war camp for Italians and Germans.

Mile 387 (53): CORVALLIS (pop. 43,715) means "heart of the valley." All visitor facilities are available. Oregon State University and Hewlett Packard Corp. are major employers. Agriculture, electronics, engineering and wood products anchor the economy's base.

More than 30 buildings, dating from the late 1850s to 1917, are covered in a self-tour brochure available from the chamber of commerce.

Mile 388 (52): Oregon State University and **junction** with Oregon Highway 99 West to Monmouth and Junction City. The university was founded in 1858 as Corvallis College and is Oregon's oldest state-supported institution of higher education. As one of 28 land and sea grant universities in the nation, it is Oregon's major institution for basic research in forestry, agriculture, fisheries, engineering, electronics and other sciences.

Horner Museum, near the university, highlights natural sciences, history and world culture. Open year-round.

Peavy Arboretum, 8 miles north on Highway 99 West, is maintained by the university. The 40-acre site has 2 interpretive hiking trails and a picnic area. Nearby McDonald State Forest is popular with hikers, birdwatchers, and horseback and bicycle riders.

William L. Finley National Wildlife Refuge, 11 miles south on Highway 99 West, is a stopover for ducks, geese, ruffed grouse, ring-necked pheasants and California quail. Self-guiding trail; hunting from late Aug. to mid-Jan.

Area wineries situated along the Highway 99 West corridor include Arlie Winery, Alpine Vineyards, Serendipity Cellars and Tyee Wine Cellars.

Mile 388.5 (51.5): Turnoff to north for Western Stadium–OSU Coliseum, Horner Museum and **junction** with Highway 99 West south to Junction City and Eugene.
MP 55

Mile 389 (51): Access to Oregon State University's Parker Stadium.

Mile 391 (49): 53rd Street and fairgrounds north of highway.

Mile 392 (48): PHILOMATH (pop. 2,675) means "love of learning," and was derived from 2 Greek words. The United Bretheran Church chartered a coeducational liberal arts and ministerial school in 1865. It ceased operations in 1929, and today forest, truck and tree farming are economic mainstays.
MP 52

Mile 394 (46): The Philomath College Building, on the register of historic landmarks, houses the Benton County Historical Museum. Exhibits cover Camp Adair, timber, local Indians, displays of native basketry, tools and household utensils. Open Tuesday through Saturday, 10 a.m. to 4 p.m.; Sunday 1–4:40 p.m.

Mile 394.5 (45.5): Junction with Oregon Highway 34 south to Alsea and Waldport. The Alsea River is heavily fished weekends from Sept. through Nov. for salmon and steelhead. Services at Alsea, 18 miles south, are 2 cafes, gas, sport shop and market.

Mile 395.5 (44.5): Mary's River.

Mile 398 (42): WREN. Harris Covered Bridge, 2.5 miles west of Wren, was built in 1929 and is still in use.
MP 46

Mile 398.5 (41.5): Junction with King's Valley Highway (Oregon Highway 223). The King's Valley Community Church, 8 miles north, is representative of rural gothic style churches built locally during the late 1800s.

Mile 399 (41): Mary's River.
MP 45

Mile 401 (39): Highway begins ascent westbound into Coast Range.
MP 43

Mile 404 (36): BLODGETT, established in 1888 and originally called Ernerick. It was renamed after pioneer settler William Blodgett. Gas and county store.

Mile 406 (34): Old Blodgett Road.

Mile 408 (32): Lincoln County/Benton County line.

Mile 409 (31): BURNT WOODS has a store with gas. RV park on north side of highway. A 2-lane paved road leads 8 miles south to Harlen Junction and the northern boundary of Siuslaw National Forest.
MP 35

Mile 411 (29): H.D. Elmaker State Park, day-use park with picnicking and handicap facilities.

Mile 412 (28): Cline Hill Summit (elev. 770 feet).

For the next 12 miles westbound, trees line the road's edge, forming a natural canopy over the highway. This section has a quiet beauty that can be enjoyed as sharp curves reduce speeds to 35 and 40 mph.

Mile 417 (23): Little Elk Store. Little Elk Creek meanders beside the highway and through a narrow canyon on its way to the Yaquina River.
MP 10

Mile 419 (21): EDDYVILLE. Isreal Eddy was a storekeeper and grist mill operator who provided overnight accommodations for travelers. Lincoln County's oldest cemetery is located near the town. The Yaquina River, which U.S. 20 follows from Eddyville to the coast, is one of the area's best streams for salmon, steelhead, rainbow trout, native and stocked cutthroat.

Mile 424.5 (15.5): Chitwood Covered Bridge on south side of highway.

Mile 427 (13): Elk City junction. **ELK CITY,** 5 miles south, was platted in 1868. It was the first town in Lincoln County and became the overland stage and mail terminus. Free boat launch and dock. Elk City Store has 5 RV hookups. Camping is also available at the county park along with barbecue pits and water.

Mile 428 (12): Pioneer Mountain loop, east entrance.

Mile 429.5 (10.5): Pioneer Mountain Summit (elev. 337 feet).

Mile 430.5 (9.5): Pioneer Mountain loop, west entrance.

Mile 432 (8): Turnoff for business district of **TOLEDO** (pop. 3,200), named after Toledo, OH. The seat of Lincoln County, its economy is based on wood products and oysters. During WWI, the world's largest spruce mill was built here to supply wood for aircraft. The war ended before the plant was completed. All wood for Howard Hughes' "Spruce Goose" came from Toledo.

A pioneer block-

house, built [...] Indian atta[...] modern man[...] turesque wa[...] local history.

Mile 433 (7[...] course and [...] good catche[...]

Mile 434 (6[...] way 229, [...] **SILETZ** (po[...] The Siletz River is a top fall steelhead and good summer trout stream.

Mile 439 (1): NEWPORT (pop. 8,710). A long sandy beach, a wealth of seafood, lively waterfront, and a mixture of scientific and historic sites make Newport a prime recreation area. The town has a wide range of accommodations available, plus private RV parks. Camping also at South Beach State Park south of town (reservations available). Picnicking at South Beach, Agate Beach and Yaquina Bay state parks. Yaquina Bay State Park is also the location of Yaquina Bay Lighthouse, built in 1871; open in summer.

Yaquina Bay is a major producer of clams, oysters and Dungeness crab. Salmon, bottom fish, perch and steelhead can be caught in season from riverbanks, shore, or charter boat. Area rivers and streams are fished for trout in summer and steelhead during winter.

In addition to equipment rentals and charters, Newport's waterfront is filled with boutiques, restaurants and specialty shops. It also has "Ripley's Believe It Or Not" Museum, the Wax Works Museum and Undersea Gardens.

Visit Hatfield Marine Science Center, where displays explain the properties of the ocean, and specimens of Oregon's fishes and invertebrates are on exhibit. Open daily in summer.

Lincoln County Historical Museum, 579 SW 9th, houses Siletz Reservation artifacts, plus logging, farm and maritime exhibits.

Mile 440 (0): Junction with U.S. Highway 101 (South Coast Highway). Turn to **Mile 210** in the U.S. HIGHWAY 101 section for log.

The Yaquina Bay Lighthouse at Newport is open to visitors in the summer. (Susan Eitsgaard, Courtesy of Newport Chamber of Commerce)

Interstate 84 is one of the most heavily used highways in the Northwest. It has been a heavily traveled route since the Oregon Trail opened 150 years ago. The *Northwest Mileposts®* highway log starts at the junction of interstates 205 and 84 in Portland, OR, and leads 551 miles southeast to the junction with U.S. 93 at Twin Falls, ID.

A highway of contrasts, Interstate 84 travels through the historic and beautiful Columbia Gorge, past rugged vistas of the Cascade Range and high desert of eastern Oregon. In several areas, the interstate parallels the Oregon Trail, and many of the communities have museums and historic sites dedicated to that major westward movement of the 19th century.

While driving this comfortable route, imagine the peril of traveling in Conestoga wagons across the rugged volcanic terrain, fording streams and rivers, slowly breaking trail through snowy mountain passes.

Interstate 84 Log

Distance from Portland, OR, is followed by distance from Twin Falls, ID.

Mile 0 (551): Junction with Interstate 205 at Portland. Interstate 205 is an alternate route to Interstate 5 and skirts Portland city center. For further information on Portland, see the MAJOR CITIES section.

Mile 3 (548): 122nd Avenue in Portland.
EXIT 10

Mile 6 (545): Exit 13A to U.S. Highway 26 and Exit 13B to Fairview, Gresham, 181st Street (Portland) and Blue Lake Park. The park, located at the corner of NE 233rd and Marine Drive, offers picnic sites, restrooms, fishing, swimming, archery range, play area, trails, bathhouse and concessions. Day-use fees are $3. ⚼⚘⚓ EXIT 13

Mile 9 (542): Exit to hospital, Multnomah Kennel Club, Mount Hood Community College, Gresham (pop. 68,200) and Wood Village (pop. 2,920). All traveler services available. You are in the outer perimeter of the Portland metropolitan area.
EXITS 16A and B

Mile 9.5 (541.5): Exit for Marine Drive, **TROUTDALE** (pop. 7,800) and eastbound entrance to Columbia River Scenic Highway. Factory outlet mall south of freeway. All services at exit. Troutdale has 2 large RV parks. The 24-mile-long Columbia River Scenic Highway provides access to a number of

sights, including Crown Point State Park, Bridal Veil Falls and Multnomah Falls. It rejoins Interstate 84 at Exit 35. See feature on page 98. ▲★ EXIT 17

Mile 10 (541): Cross Sandy River.

Mile 10.5 (540.5): Exit to Oxbow County Park and the Lewis and Clark State Park with

Horsetail Falls is one of many waterfalls in the side canyons along the Columbia River Scenic Highway. (© George Wuerthner)

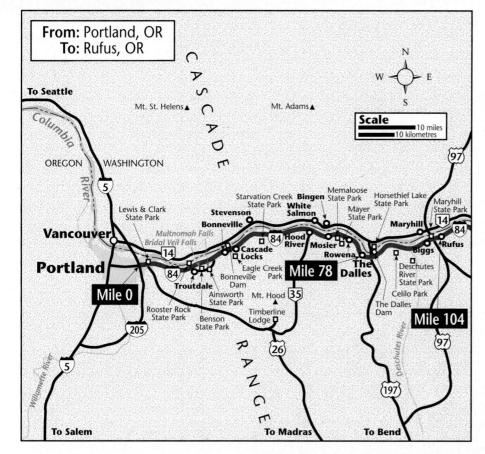

From: Portland, OR
To: Rufus, OR

Mile 35 (516): Exit to Eagle Creek Park and fish hatchery. The park offers 19 campsites and 78 picnic sites. ☂▲ EXIT 41

Mile 37 (514): Eastbound exit to **CASCADE LOCKS** (pop. 900); all services. The city was named for the series of locks built in 1896, which were submerged with construction of the Bonneville Dam in 1938. Marine park with remnants of old locks, rigging area and beach for windsurfers, marina, museum, visitor center, boat launch, picnic area and playground.

The stern-wheeler *Columbia Gorge* operates 2-hour narrated tours from here daily from mid-June to late Sept. The 600-passenger boat is a replica of the stern-wheelers that cruised the Columbia at the turn of the century. Well worth the trip. Phone (503) 223-3928 or 374-8427 for more information.

The Bridge of the Gods is a toll bridge that spans the Columbia River at Cascade Locks. It connects with Washington Highway 14, a 2-lane road connecting Interstate 5 (40 miles west) with U.S. Highway 395 (140 miles east). Access to Stevenson, WA, and Beacon Rock State Park, which has camping and fishing. ☂➤▲ EXIT 44

Mile 38.5 (512.5): Exit (westbound only) to Cascade Locks (see preceding milepost). EXIT 44

Mile 42.5 (508.5): The steep sides of the hills make this a slide area. Drive carefully.

Mile 44 (507): Exit to Wyeth. The Wyeth Campground has 17 sites, swimming and fishing. ➤▲ EXIT 51

Mile 48 (503): Starvation Creek State Park and rest area (eastbound only); 20 picnic sites, restrooms and phone. ☂

Mile 49.5 (501.5): Exit to Viento State Park, which offers 63 campsites and 28 picnic sites. ☂▲ EXIT 56

Mile 51 (500): Exit to the Mitchell Point Overlook. Look for the long train tunnels on the Washington side of the river. EXIT 58

Mile 55.5 (495.5): Exit to West Hood River, Westcliff Drive, the Columbia Gorge Hotel Historic Site and the Hood River Winery. Major motels off exit. Tucker Park county campground (with tent sites and showers) is accessible from this exit. Follow Highway 281 to 13th Street and turn south; 13th Street becomes Tucker Road.

The elegant Columbia Gorge Hotel is a historic site. Built in 1921–22 by

20 picnic sites, restrooms and a boat ramp. ☂ EXIT 18

Mile 14.5 (536.5): Exit to Corbett. Food and RV park. ▲ EXIT 22

Mile 16 (535): Crown Point Lookout visible to south above highway.

Mile 17 (534): Exit to Rooster Rock State Park on the Columbia River; 195 picnic sites, restrooms, boat launch, rigging area for windsurfers, sandy beach, plenty of parking. ☂ EXIT 25

Mile 20.5 (530.5): Exit (eastbound only) to Bridal Veil Falls, a series of 2 falls that drop about 150 feet collectively. EXIT 28

Mile 22 (529): Exit (westbound only) to Dalton Point. EXIT 29

Mile 23.5 (527.5): Benson State Park (eastbound only). The park has 100 picnic sites, restrooms and a boat launch. ☂

Mile 24 (527): Exit to Multnomah Falls Historical Site and tourist information center for pedestrians. (Vehicle access via the Columbia River Scenic Highway from exits 17 and 35.) Park between the interstate lanes and walk underneath the highway via a pedestrian walkway to the falls and the beautiful old stone Multnomah Lodge.

Multnomah Falls, the highest falls in Oregon and the fourth largest in the United States, is the most famous of the Columbia Gorge area. The top falls plunge 542 feet and the lower falls drop an additional 92 feet. A trail leads to a bridge and viewpoint over the falls.

The historical marker at the base of the falls

relates the story of the Indian maiden who threw herself off the cliffs to save her lover. If you are a hopeless romantic and have an imagination, legend claims that the maiden's face can be seen in the upper waterfall.

Souvenirs and food are available at the lodge. ★ EXIT 31

Mile 28 (523): Turnoff for Ainsworth State Park (45 trailer campsites) and westbound access to the 24-mile-long Columbia River Scenic Highway. This scenic route provides access to Multnomah Falls, Bridal Veil Falls and Crown Point State Park. It rejoins Interstate 84 at Exit 17. See COLUMBIA RIVER SCENIC HIGHWAY on page 98. ▲ EXIT 35

Mile 30 (521): Exit (westbound only) to Warrendale and access to scenic loop and Vista House. EXIT 37

Mile 32 (519): Moffett Creek.

Mile 33 (518): Exit to the Bonneville Dam, fish hatchery and information center. Bonneville Dam was the first hydroelectric dam built on the Columbia River. It was completed in 1938 and a second powerhouse was added in 1981. Visitors can watch migrating fish through underwater windows at the Bonneville Regional Visitors Center or the fish-viewing building on the Washington shore. The Oregon Deptartment of Fish and Wildlife operates a fish hatchery on nearby Tanner Creek. EXIT 40

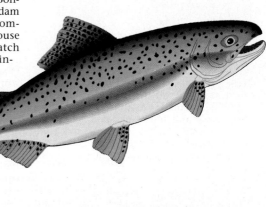

Columbia River Scenic Highway

The Columbia River Gorge is one of our great natural treasures, a 70-mile-long landscape of extraordinary drama and beauty now protected from development as a national scenic area. The first highway through the gorge was begun in 1913 and completed 2 years later. A plaque at Crown Point says of Chief Engineer Samuel C. Lancaster, "His genius overcame tremendous obstacles extending then replacing the early trail through the gorge with a highway of poetry and drama so that millions could enjoy God's spectacular creations."

The construction of Interstate 84 eliminated sections of the old highway, but one 24-mile chunk in the heart of the gorge (plus another farther east) has been preserved as Columbia River Scenic Highway. The detour is well worthwhile as it gives you a chance to savor the beauty and the subtler moods of the gorge better than you can from the interstate, and it provides the best vantage points for photographs.

Eastbound, leave I-84 at Troutdale

Wahkeena Falls (L. Linkhart)

(Exit 17). Watch carefully for the brown-and-white "Scenic Highway" signs. The 2-lane road meanders through dense stands of fir and alder, crossing the Sandy River, past Dabney State Park (picnic tables) and U-pick berry farms, a private RV park, and Portland Women's Forum State Park, an overlook on Chanticleer Point with splendid views upriver including distinctive Crown Point. A short distance beyond you'll come to Crown Point State Park. Here, Vista House perches 733 feet above the river for a commanding 30-mile vista of the gorge. The handsome stone building, built in 1916, houses a visitor center and craft gallery open May 1 to Oct. 15.

Some of the lovely subtleties of the gorge that elude freeway travelers are the grotto-like side canyons. Carpeted with moss and ferns, they often harbor a waterfall bathed in cool green light filtering through the trees overhead. There are numerous places to pull off and explore; signed trails lead from the scenic highway into these side canyons.

Beyond Crown Point the road twists and turns through an overhanging canopy of trees. In places the old stone arched guard wall from the original highway remains, covered in a patina of rust and green moss and lichen. The road gradually descends to river level, past Latourell Falls, Shepperds Dell, Bridal Veil, Coopy, Mist and Wahkeena falls.

Multnomah Falls Lodge is nearly as well known as the gorge itself. Travelers have been stopping here for a snack or a meal since 1925. The massive stone building nestles beneath the fourth highest waterfall in the United States. Two separate cascades have a vertical drop of 620 feet. An easy footpath leads to a footbridge between the upper and lower falls. Beyond, the highway passes the Oneonta Gorge Botanical Area and 176-foot Horsetail Falls before returning to I-84.

for a lesson. For a close-up look at this sport, visit the Hood River Sailpark (see Exit 64).

The Mount Hood Railway offers scenic train rides to Odell and Parkdale from spring through fall. Phone 1-800-872-4661 or (503) 386-3556 for reservations and information. The railway trips depart from the Hood River Depot. Take Exit 63 and turn left on Cascade.

Hood River is also known for its spring water. First tapped in 1928, the city water supply, without chlorination or filtration, has been rated third best in the nation. Contact the Hood River County Chamber of Commerce, Port Marina Park, Hood River, OR 97031, phone (503) 386-2000, for more information on the area. EXIT 63

Mile 58 (493): Major-chain fast-food restaurants, motel and gas stations south off exit. This exit provides access to several attractions and travel routes: Oregon Highway 35 to Mount Hood; White Salmon, Bingen and Washington Highway 14; and Hood River Sailpark. (Descriptions follow.)

Oregon Highway 35 (Mount Hood Loop Highway) leads 40 miles south to Mount Hood Ski Area and Timberline Lodge. Turnoff at Odell on to Highway 281 for access to Tucker County Park (camping).

Cross the interstate toll bridge for access north to Washington Highway 14, a good 2-lane road that connects Interstate 5 (63 miles west) and U.S. 395 (117 miles east). Across the river on Highway 14 is **BINGEN** and **WHITE SALMON**, WA, (2,600) which has an inn, bakery, and a marina with a large grassy rigging area and a long sandy beach for windsurfers.

North off this exit turn left for the Port of Hood River development, which includes the Hood River County Historical Museum, Hood River visitor information (phone 503/386-2000 or 1-800-366-3530), Port offices, and the popular Hood River Sailpark and marina. Hood River windsurfing shops hold their lessons at the sailpark, and it is a popular spot for practicing waterstarts, short board planing and jibes. (Windsurfers who venture across the river here face deep swells, strong currents and barges, and they sometimes end up at Bozo Beach, a steep rocky slope on the Washington side.) This is an excellent spot to view this colorful sport, which has grown so dramatically in recent years. Facilities at the sailpark include restrooms with showers, parking and food concession stands. ㅠ▲★ EXIT 64

Mile 63 (488): Junction of U.S. Highway 30 to **MOSIER** (pop. 250) and a 9-mile scenic loop. All services. The loop runs from Mosier to Rowena and on a high bluff overlooking the river is the Rowena Crest viewpoint. It is adjacent to the Tom McCall Preserve, a refuge for several native plants, many of which are rare and endangered. EXIT 69

Mile 66 (485): Rest area and access to Memaloose State Park (westbound access only; eastbound travelers use Exit 76). Memaloose Park offers 67 tent campsites, 43 trailer sites, 18 picnic sites, drinking water and a historical site.

Memaloose Island in the Columbia River is an ancient Indian burial ground. The island was set aside by the U.S. Land Office as a burial ground for the Warm Spring Indians until Victor Trevitt, one of Oregon's early pioneers, was buried there in 1883.

Simon Benson, pioneer lumberman, it sits high on the Columbia Gorge and offers unequaled views of the river, cliffs and surrounding terrain. It was built for the Roaring '20s crowd and soon became a favorite of the Jazz Age. Rudolph Valentino and Clara Bow were among the frequent guests. The hotel has been restored to its original condition. Phone (503) 386-5566. ▲★ EXIT 62

Mile 57.5 (493.5): Exit south to **HOOD RIVER** (pop. 4,600); hotel, several bed and

breakfasts, many restaurants, 24-hour supermarket and numerous windsurfing shops.

This formerly quiet little lumber and fruit-growing (apples, pears) town is now the mecca for the windsurfing world. The strong and steady winds that howl through the Columbia River Gorge from spring until fall, combined with the strong and opposing river current, make this one of the hottest windsurfing spots in the world. Visitors can stroll through dozens of windsurfing shops downtown to check out the gear or sign up

Above—A view from White Salmon of Hood River with Mount Hood in the distance. *(© John Barger)*

Right—Windsurfing is popular at "the gorge."

Before the high water of 1894, several Indian houses on the island contained the bodies of Indians with their bows, arrows, guns and other artifacts.　　　　　　　　🚻▲

Mile 70 (481): Exit to Rowena, Memaloose State Park (eastbound access only) and Mayer State Park. Mayer Park has 36 picnic sites, water, boat ramp, restrooms, windsurfing and swimming.　　　　🚻 EXIT 76

Mile 76 (475): Exit to the Chenoweth area, a residential suburb of The Dalles. Gas and fast-food restaurants available. *CAUTION:* Watch for gusty winds in this area. EXIT 82

Mile 77 (474): Exit west to The Dalles. All traveler services and many seasonal fruit stands at this exit.　　　　　　EXIT 83

Mile 78 (473): Exit to **THE DALLES** (pop. 11,100) city center. All services are available in The Dalles. Although historians disagree about the exact origin of the name, The Dalles is a derivation of a French term meaning "the steps" or "the trough," both referring to the Columbia River.

The Dalles is proud of its history, which is depicted in a series of downtown murals. St. Peter's Church, on the National Register of Historic Places, located at Third and Lincoln, is just one of many historic buildings in town. The red brick Gothic church has a 176-foot steeple. The Fort Dalles Museum displays early relics and pictures of The Dalles, housed in a picturesque surgeon's quarters of historic Fort Dalles. This unusual building was part of Fort Drum, built during the Yakima Indian wars of the 1850s. The rock fort constructed by the Lewis and Clark expedition is visible on the bank of the Columbia River. Admission fee charged;

phone (503) 296-4547 for hours.

The original Wasco County Courthouse, the seat of government for the largest county ever formed in the United States, still stands at 406 W. 2nd St. It is open from April through Oct., free; phone (503) 296-4798. Wasco County originally encompassed some 130,000 square miles from the Cascades to the Rockies, including the Grand Tetons and part of Yellowstone Park. Wasco County is significantly smaller now, but The Dalles is still the county seat.

Self-guiding walking tour maps are available from The Dalles Convention and Visitors Bureau, 901 E. 2nd St., The Dalles, OR 97058; phone (503) 296-6616 or 1-800-255-3385.
　　　　　　　　　　　　EXIT 84

Mile 79 (472): Exit east to The Dalles, Riverfront Park, Columbia Gorge Community College, The Dalles airport and The Dalles bridge.　　　　　　　　EXIT 85

Mile 81 (470): Junction with U.S. Highway 197 north to The Dalles bridge and The Dalles Dam and south to Dufur and Bend. Access to The Dalles Dam Tour Train (503/296-9778); turn right on Bret Clodfelter Way. North on Highway 197 is Horsethief Lake State Park in Washington. The park lies on the edge of the Columbia River surrounded by huge rock formations where ancient Indian petroglyphs can be seen; 12 camp-

sites with kitchens and tables are available. There are primitive sites for sailboaters, hikers and bikers. Horsethief Lake is a small lake separated from the river by railroad tracks. It has a swimming beach and boat launch.　　　　　　　　▲ EXIT 87

Mile 82.5 (468.5): Exit to The Dalles Dam. The enormous 0.5-mile-long powerhouse has 22 generating units producing 1.8 million kilowatts. Visitors can take a small tour train from the visitor center on the Oregon shore to the fish ladder and powerhouse for a guided tour. The visitor center and train operate daily, 9 a.m. to 6 p.m., Memorial Day through Labor Day; Wednesday through Sunday, 10 a.m. to 3 p.m. during April and the rest of September. From Oct. through March, visitors can visit the powerhouse and observe the petroglyphs. Hydropower exhibits in the powerhouse explain the operation of the dam and the petroglyphs carved nearby. South of the dam on U.S. Highway 197 is the Celilo Converter, the largest converter station in the United States. Celilo converts power from The Dalles Dam for transmission over an 853-mile power line to California. EXIT 88

Mile 91 (460): Junction with Oregon Highway 206 to Celilo Park, the Deschutes River State Park and Fulton Canyon.

Celilo Park offers 33 picnic sites, drinking water, flush toilets, boat ramp, museum, play area and a protected swim area. It is situated on the banks of Lake Celilo, the backwaters of The Dalles Dam. Celilo Falls, now inundated by the reservoir, was the site of the Ancient Indian Fishing Grounds where Native Americans gathered to harvest the plentiful salmon as the fish headed upstream to spawn. The reservoir has a strong current and on-shore wind for good high-wind sailing for the experienced sailor.

Deschutes River State Park offers 34 campsites, 41 picnic sites, water, toilets and fishing.　　　　　　🚻◄▲ EXIT 97

Mile 94 (457): The Deschutes River is one of the world's top trout producers, and native summer-run steelhead are plentiful. The Deschutes River is one of the most intensively managed rivers in the Northwest with strict catch-and-release regulations for specific species in specific areas. Before wetting your line, obtain a copy of the Oregon sportfishing regulations by calling 1-800-ASK-FISH.

Whitewater enthusiasts also find the Deschutes a popular stream, and this sport is also strictly regulated. For a copy of these regulations, contact the Oregon Parks Dept. at (503) 378-6305.　　　　　　🐟

Mile 98.5 (452.5): Junction with U.S. Highway 97 south to Biggs, and north across the Columbia River to Maryhill, WA. (Travelers heading north or south on U.S. 97 turn to **Mile 275** in the U.S. HIGHWAY 97 section for log.)

Worth a side trip for Interstate 84 travelers is the Maryhill Museum, a replica of a Flemish chateau perched high on the wall of the Columbia Gorge. Built as a mansion for wealthy Sam Hill and dedicated by Queen Marie of Romania in 1926, it now is a museum featuring a large collection of antique chess pieces, Indian artifacts, Faberge eggs, and Queen Marie's throne and court gowns. It is open March 15 to Nov. 15. Picnicking is permitted on the museum grounds.

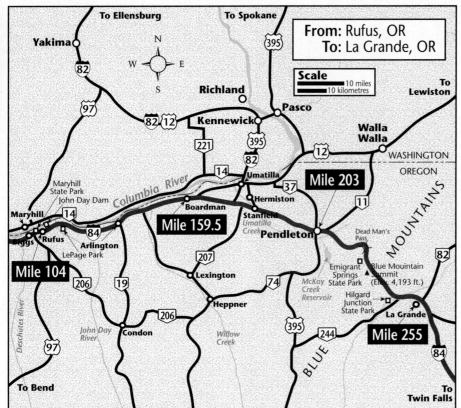

Two miles east of Maryhill is Stonehenge, a copy of the druid temple of England, also built by Sam Hill in memory of soldiers from Klickitat County who died in WWI. It is part of the Maryhill museum complex.

Maryhill State Park on the north side of the river offers 50 campsites, a swimming area, picnic areas and a boat launch.
⚲▲ EXIT 104

Mile 104 (447): Exit to the John Day Dam and **RUFUS** (pop. 380); gas, food and lodging.

The John Day Lock and Dam stretches more than a mile across the Columbia River. The facilities include a navigation lock, a powerhouse, spillway and fish passage facilities. Free self-guiding tours are available daily; phone (503) 296-1186. The John Day Dam is one of the largest producers of power in the world, producing some 2.2 million kilowatts, enough to meet the electrical needs of 2 cities the size of Seattle. Four more units are planned.

The lock on the Washington shore provides passage for more than 8 million tons of commercial traffic each year, in addition to recreation boats. One of the highest single-life locks in the world, it lifts the vessels 113 feet between Lake Celilo (the backwaters of The Dalles Dam) and Lake Umatilla. Its downstream gate is also unusual in that it opens vertically, raised by large cables extending from tall towers.

On the Oregon shore, underwater viewing of the fish ladder is provided. A guide to public recreation areas on Lake Umatilla is available at the project office and guided tours of the powerhouse may be arranged by writing or calling The Dalles–John Day Project, U.S. Army Corps of Engineers, P.O. Box 564, The Dalles, OR 97058.

The reservoir behind John Day Dam is called Lake Umatilla, and is a favorite small-mouth bass and walleye fishing area for Oregon and Washington anglers.
➤ EXIT 109

Mile 105 (446): Rest area and viewpoint.
EXIT 112

Mile 108.5 (442.5): Rest area. Exit to the John Day River Recreation Area. The John Day River crosses under the interstate at this point. LePage Park offers 71 campsites, picnic area, fishing, boating, handicap access, swimming and restrooms.

The lower portion of the John Day River below Kimberly is a major steelhead water area from Aug. through April. Check locally for specific regulations and catch limits.
♿⚲➤▲ EXIT 114

Mile 118 (433): Exit to Philippi Canyon.
EXIT 123

Mile 124 (427): Exit to Blalock Canyon.
EXIT 129

Mile 125.5 (425.5): Exit to Woelpern Road, eastbound exit only, with no eastbound return to freeway.
EXIT 131

Mile 132.5 (418.5): Junction with Oregon Highway 19 at **ARLINGTON** (pop. 470). All services are available at this exit. Arlington has a city park on the water with a picnic area, playground, swimming and boat launch.
⚲ EXIT 137

Mile 142 (409): Junction with Oregon Highway 74, which leads 27 miles south to Ione and 45 miles south to **HEPPNER** (pop. 1,375). Highway 74 to Heppner and Ukiah is part of the Blue Mountains Scenic Byway route. The 130-mile drive takes approximately 5 hours; paved, 2-lane road.
EXIT 147

Mile 146.5 (404.5): Exit to Threemile Canyon. Eastbound travelers are now leaving the Columbia Gorge.
EXIT 151

Mile 154.5 (396.5): Exit to Tower Road.
EXIT 159

Mile 156 (395): Rest area with phone and travel information center.

Mile 159.5 (391.5): Exit to **BOARDMAN** (pop. 1,480) with all traveler services. Boardman Marina Park has 63 campsites with hookups, a boat launch, swimming area, fishing and windsurfing. Boardman is on the edge of the fragmented 29,370-acre Umatilla National Wildlife Refuge, parts of which are in Oregon and Washington, flanking both sides and several islands in the Columbia River system. Up to 90,000 Canada geese and 250,000 ducks winter here, along with bald and golden eagles, peregrine falcons and hundreds of shorebirds. Mule deer, coyotes, beaver, badger, raccoons and muskrats are fairly common at the refuge.
➤▲ EXIT 164

Mile 160.5 (390.5): Blowing dust next 40 miles may cause hazardous driving conditions.

Mile 161 (390): Exit to the Port of Morrow.
EXIT 165

Mile 163 (388): Junction with U.S. Highway 730 north to Umatilla and Irrigon. EXIT 168

Mile 166 (385): Exit to Patersen Ferry Road.
EXIT 171

Mile 173.5 (377.5): Exit to the Umatilla Army Depot.
EXIT 177

Mile 174.5 (376.5): Exit to McNary Dam, I-82 north to Kennewick and Yakima.
EXIT 179

Mile 176 (375): Exit to Westland Road, Hermiston and Umatilla.
EXIT 180

Mile 178.5 (372.5): Junction with Oregon Highway 207 north to Hermiston and south to Lexington. Gas, food, campground, hospital available this exit.
▲ EXIT 182

Mile 183 (368): Rest area with phone and horse exercise area.

Mile 185 (366): Crossing the Umatilla River. **Junction** with U.S. Highway 395 north to Stanfield, Hermiston, McNary Dam and the Umatilla bridge, continuing north through the Tri-Cities. Turn to **Mile 375** in the U.S. HIGHWAY 395 log for description of that route. Interstate 84 and U.S. Highway 395 share a common alignment here south to Pendleton.
EXIT 188

Mile 189 (362): Exit to Echo Road. No services available.
EXIT 193

Mile 194 (357): Exit to Lorenzen Road and McClintock Road.
EXIT 198

Mile 195.5 (355.5): Exit to Stage Gulch and Yoakum Road.
EXIT 199

Mile 199 (352): Exit to Barnhart Road. All services are available at this exit. EXIT 202

Mile 201 (350): Blue Mountains visible in

distance as highway descends to Pendleton.

Mile 203 (348): Junction with U.S. Highway 30 to Pendleton airport, Pendleton city center and historic district, and Blue Mountain Community College. **PENDLETON** (pop. 15,100) has all services, including 13 motels and about 40 restaurants and 5 RV parks. Perhaps Pendleton's biggest claim to fame is the Pendleton Round-Up, the major Professional Rodeo Cowboy Assoc. (PRCA) sanctioned rodeo held the 2nd full week of September. Motels and campgrounds fill to capacity as thousands of visitors converge on the seat of Umatilla County for this 4-day event. Contact the Pendleton Chamber of Commerce, 25 SE Dorion St., Pendleton, OR 97801, phone (503) 276-7411 or 1-800-547-8911, for more information.

Another hallmark for the city of Pendleton is the Pendleton Woolen Mills (Exit 210), one of the most renowned woolen mills in the nation. Guided tours are available weekdays; phone (503) 276-6911. The Pendleton Woolen Mills began using Northwest wool in Pendleton in 1909. Since that time, the company has expanded and its headquarters are now located in Portland. Wool blankets are still produced here.

Pendleton has a self-guided walking tour of its compact historic area. The tour starts at the Umatilla County Historical Society Museum, 108 SW Frazer Ave. There's also a tour of Pendleton's historical underground tunnels; phone (503) 276-0730 for details.

Eastbound travelers note: If the weather is bad or night is approaching, it is a good idea to stop for the night in Pendleton. The Blue Mountains southeast of town can be a driving challenge, especially in winter. ▲ EXIT 207

Mile 205 (346): Umatilla River, a good trout and steelhead stream. The river is well stocked with rainbow. Check at Mission before fishing on the Umatilla Indian Reservation east of Pendleton. ◄

Mile 205.5 (345.5): Junction with U.S. Highway 395 south and Oregon Highway 37 north through Pendleton to Cold Springs. Travelers southbound on U.S. 395 turn to **Mile 354** in the U.S. HIGHWAY 395 section and read log back to front.

Turnoff for McKay Creek Reservoir, a refuge area with good fishing, located 4 miles south. ◄ EXIT 209

Mile 207 (344): Exit to Pendleton and junction with Oregon Highway 11 north to Milton–Freewater and Walla Walla. EXIT 210

Mile 209 (342): Entering Umatilla Indian Reservation eastbound.

Mile 210 (341): Westbound-only exit to Pendleton city center (see **Mile 203** for city description). EXIT 213

Mile 212 (339): Exit to Milton–Freewater and Walla Walla. Gas and food. EXIT 216

Mile 215 (336): Anticipate a steep ascent eastbound from Pendleton as you enter the Blue Mountains. *CAUTION*: Truck traffic on this hill is heavy. Large tractor-trailer rigs travel very slowly up and down this 6 percent grade. Drive with caution. Expect all types of weather at all times. Dense fogs can occur here.

Mile 217.5 (333.5): Viewpoint of the Pendleton Valley from Emigrant Hill.

Mile 221 (330): Poverty Flat Road and the Old Emigrant Hill Road. EXIT 224

Mile 225.5 (325.5): Dead Man's Pass and rest area. This is a chain-up area in winter. You are now at the top of Emigrant Hill. EXIT 228

Exit 261 to Oregon Highway 82 leads northeast to Wallowa Lake. (L. Linkhart)

Mile 230 (321): Exit to Emigrant Springs State Park and Meacham. Emigrant Springs State Park offers 18 full-hookup campsites and 33 tent sites. Sheltered picnic sites, showers and visitor information available. ⤢▲ EXIT 234

Mile 233.5 (317.5): Exit to Meacham and Kamela. EXIT 236

Mile 237 (314): Summit of the Blue Mountains (elev. 4,193 feet).

Mile 239 (312): Exit to Mount Emily Road and Kamela. EXIT 243

Mile 244 (307): Exit to Spring Creek Road. Blue Mountain Crossing Interpretive Center, located 2.5 miles from the interstate, via gravel road, preserves traces of the original wagon trail. Check with the U.S. Forest Service (503/963-7186) for season and hours. EXIT 248

Mile 248 (303): Junction with Oregon Highway 244 to Ukiah. Hilgard Junction State Park, 9 miles west of the interstate, offers 18 tent sites. The park has picnic sites, fishing, handicap facilities and dump station. ♿⤢◄▲ EXIT 252

Mile 248.5 (302.5): Five Point Creek. The Oregon Trail followed this creek west to Meacham.

Mile 252 (299): Perry, a small agricultural community. No services available. EXIT 256

Mile 254.5 (296.5): Crossing Grande Ronde River.

Mile 255 (296): Junction with U.S. Highway 30 to La Grande and Eastern Oregon State College. **LA GRANDE** (pop. 11,800) takes its name from the Grande Ronde River and valley. The city is the seat of Union County and is situated at the foot of the Blue Mountains, where many Oregon Trail immigrants decided to settle in 1861. Today, La Grande has a diversified agricultural base. It is also the home of Eastern Oregon State College. All services are available. For more information, contact La Grande/Union County Chamber of Commerce, phone (503) 963-8588.

Birnie Park, located on C Avenue, is a good place to stretch your legs with a walk through ceramic columns created by local artists to commemorate the immigrant experience.

Above La Grande, the Grande Ronde River offers good trout fishing. La Grande is also the gateway to the Wallowas and Wallowa Lake. ◄ EXIT 259

Mile 258 (293): Junction with Oregon Highway 82, which leads north 20 miles to **ELGIN** (pop. 1,600); gas, food, lodging and hospital. The restored 1912 Elgin Opera House is on the National Register of Historic Places. The 2-story colonial-style brick building shows first-run movies on Fridays, Saturdays and Sundays. Highway 82 continues east as a scenic route 45 miles to **ENTERPRISE, JOSEPH** (pop. 1,100); and Wallowa Lake. Wallowa Lake Tramway, one of the steepest tram rides in the United States, operates May to Sept. Joseph is the gateway to Hells Canyon National Recreation Area (see MAJOR ATTRACTIONS section). EXIT 261

Mile 261 (290): Junction with Oregon Highway 203 to La Grande and **UNION** (pop. 1,895). Gas, food and RV park. Union County Museum (503/562-6003) on Main Street traces the history and geology of the area. Highway 203 is a little-used 52-mile route linking La Grande and Baker City. It accesses the Eagle Cap Wilderness and Catherine Creek State Park (picnicking and fishing). ⤢◄▲ EXIT 265

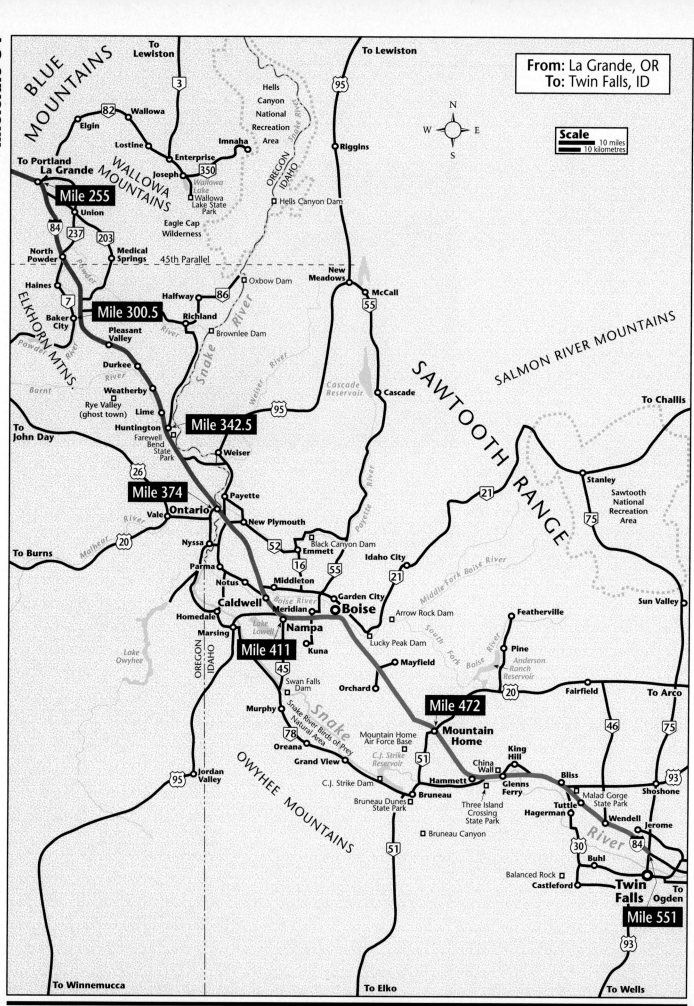

From: La Grande, OR
To: Twin Falls, ID

Mile 264 (287): Exit to Foothill Road. Watch for posted notices concerning weather and road conditions.   EXIT 268

Mile 265 (286): Rest area.

Mile 266.5 (284.5): Exit to Ladd Creek Road (eastbound only). No return to freeway eastbound.   EXIT 270

Mile 270 (281): Exit to Ladd Canyon.
                                                        EXIT 273

Mile 273.5 (277.5): Exit to Clover Creek Road.   EXIT 278

Mile 280 (271): Exit to Wolf Creek Road.
                                                        EXIT 283

Mile 282 (269): Junction with old U.S. Highway 30 and Oregon Highway 237, an alternate route to La Grande through Pyles Canyon to Union. Access to **NORTH POWDER** (pop. 480), **HAINES** (pop. 430) and Anthony Lakes Ski Area; gas, food, lodging at exit. This old section of U.S. Highway 30 leads past farms and ranches 8 miles southwest to Haines, then 11 miles south to Baker City.

Anthony Lakes Mountain Resort ski area (elev. 7,100 feet), located 18 miles west of the interstate via county road, boasts the highest base elevation in Oregon; skiing Thursday through Sunday only from Nov. to April. Day lodge, 1 double chair, 1 poma; phone (503) 963-4599, snow conditions (503) 856-3277.

The Elkhorn Mountain Range is visible on the southwest and is broken by a series of peaks (from south to north): Elkhorn Peak (elev. 8,922 feet); Rock Creek Butte (elev. 9,097 feet); Hunt Mountain (elev. 8,232 feet); Red Mountain (elev. 8,920 feet); and Twin Mountains (elev. 8,920 feet). The Wallowa Mountains are visible to the northeast.
                                                        EXIT 285

Mile 284 (267): The 45th parallel. You are now halfway between the equator and the North Pole.

Mile 285.5 (265.5): Powder River, named for the volcanic ash that lines its banks.

Mile 291 (260): Rest area.

Mile 295 (256): Junction with Oregon Highway 203 to the Baker airport and Medical Springs (18 miles). Access to Balm Creek Reservoir.   EXIT 298

Mile 299 (252): Junction with Oregon Highway 86 and access to North Baker; all services. The National Historic Oregon Trail Interpretive Center at Flagstaff Hill is located 5 miles east of this exit. Open daily throughout the year, the popular BLM site offers interpretive trails, a replica hard-rock mine and the interpretive center, with its living history exhibits on the famous westward trek. Original wagon ruts may be seen. The center is free; phone (503) 523-1843 for more information.

This is also the exit to Oxbow Dam and Hells Canyon via Oregon Highway 86. **RICHLAND** (pop. 170), 41 miles east, has a motel and camping east of town at Hewitt Park on Brownlee Reservoir; **HALFWAY** (pop. 320), 53 miles east of the exit, has a motel and restaurants. About 9 miles north

Oregon Trail

In 1841, the route between Independence, MO, and the Oregon Territory involved traveling more than 2,000 miles across desolate sagebrush-covered plains, raging rivers and steep mountains. But despite the prospective hardships of the trip, more than 300,000 Americans made the journey.

In honor of the Oregon Trail's 150th anniversary in 1993, much has been done to preserve the historic trail sites of this great westward migration. Interstate 84 parallels much of the pioneer trail throughout Oregon and Idaho, and offers numerous side trips and stops for interested modern-day travelers. Following are a few highlights. For more information on exploring the Oregon Trail, contact the Bureau of Land Management, National Historic Oregon Interpretive Center, P.O. Box 987, Baker City, OR 97814, phone (503) 523-1843.

• Southeast of Twin Falls, ID, the California Trail split off the Oregon Trail and traveled through the City of Rocks into Utah and Nevada. Marks and "graffiti" left by pioneers writing with axle grease can still be seen in the City of Rocks National Reserve. Take Exit 208 to Idaho Highway 27 south to Oakley. The City of Rocks is 4 miles west of Almo. Just east of Twin Falls is the Stricker Store Rock Creek Station near Hansen (take Exit 182). Built in 1865, it was one of the first far-west trading posts on the Oregon Trail. Just north of Twin Falls 1.5 miles, wagon-wheel ruts are clearly visible to visitors.

• Just west of Glenns Ferry was the treacherous Three Island Crossing of the Snake River. Emigrants had to make a difficult choice: ford the river here for an easier route on the other side, or take the longer but drier southern route to avoid the river crossing. A re-enactment of the river crossing is staged every August at Three Island Crossing State Park (**Mile 497**, Exit 120).

• The pioneers left the Snake River behind them at Farewell Bend (see **Mile 350**, Exit 353) and began their climb into Oregon Territory. Cresting Flagstaff Hill east of present-day Baker City, OR, the weary travelers could see the Blue Mountains in the distance and rich valleys ahead of them. Today, Flagstaff Hill is the site of the Oregon Trail Interpretive Center (**Mile 299**, Exit 302). This facility recreates life on the trail with multi-media presentations and realistic scenes featuring pioneer figures and authentic wagons and household goods. Outside the center, 4.2 miles of interpretive trails crisscross portions of the Oregon Trail and wagon ruts have been preserved.

• At The Dalles (**Mile 78**, Exit 84) on the Columbia River, many wagon trains officially ended their journeys. With winter approaching, families had to decide for themselves whether to float down the wild river or travel around Mount Hood on foot. Their history is depicted on large murals painted on downtown buildings in The Dalles. The community has a historic walking tour that visits important Oregon Trail sites, such as Fort Dalles, the pioneer cemetery and Pulpit Rock.

of Halfway a forest road leads through Hells Canyon National Recreation Area (see MAJOR ATTRACTIONS section), or continue 8 miles to Oxbow, which has a motel, RV park and jet boat trips up the canyon.
                                                        EXIT 302

Mile 300.5 (250.5): Junction with Oregon Highway 7 south to the city center of **BAKER CITY** (pop. 9,100). All services are available including motels, RV parks, restaurants, gas stations and shopping. For more information, contact the Baker County Visitor and Convention Bureau, or stop by their visitor center just off this exit at 490 Campbell St., Baker City, OR 97814; phone 1-800-523-1235 or (503) 523-3356.

The city of Baker City is located on the banks of the Powder River at the base of the Elkhorn Range to the west and the Wallowa Mountains to the northeast. It has a downtown historic district, which includes the Oregon Trail Regional Museum. Operated by the Baker County Historical Society, the museum features period clothing, artifacts and photos from the early days of Baker County, and has an outstanding collection of rocks, minerals and semiprecious stones. The museum is located 0.5 mile west of Exit 304 on Campbell Street. Open daily, May

through Oct.; admission fee charged. Oregon's largest collection of gold nuggets may be seen at the U.S. National Bank of Oregon at 2000 Main St.

The Powder River is heavily stocked with rainbow for good fishing from Baker City to Philips Reservoir. Philips Reservoir (16 miles southwest via Highway 7) is also a good place to troll for rainbow and coho salmon. There are 2 campgrounds at the lake offering more than 50 sites.

If you have the time, take a 45-minute, 29-mile drive south of Baker City to the frontier town of **SUMPTER** in the Elkhorn Mountains along the Powder River. The drive is pleasant and the scenery is fantastic. (Highway 7 and connecting roads to Granite and back to Baker City via Anthony Lakes and Haines make up the 106-mile loop known as the Elkhorn Drive National Scenic Byway.) Sumpter itself was a wild mining community in the late 1800s and many of the mining relics remain.

The Sumpter Valley Railroad is also a major attraction. The restored steam engine takes visitors on a 40-minute tour through Sumpter Valley on weekends and holidays during the summer months. Those riding the train can view the mine tailings from which some $10 million was produced between

1913 and 1954. Wildlife is often visible from the train as it passes through a wildlife preserve. The train boards at both Sumpter Depot and the Dredge Depot. Phone (503) 894-2268 for train schedule and fares. ➡▲ EXIT 304

Mile 302.5 (248.5): Junction with Highway 30 to Baker.
EXIT 306

Mile 309.5 (241.5): Turnoff to **PLEASANT VALLEY** (eastbound only), a valley named by the immigrant wagon train of 1878 that used the area as a resting place. No services are available.
EXIT 313

Mile 312.5 (238.5): Alder Creek.

Mile 322 (229): Pritchard Creek.

Mile 324 (227): Exit to **DURKEE**; gas and food available. Fire opals may be found along the Burnt River near Durkee.
EXIT 327

Mile 327 (224): Exit to Plano Road and Cement Plant Road. The factory on the south side of the highway is the Durkee plant for Ash Grove Cement West Co. At night, the lights on the buildings may startle the unsuspecting driver. The plant is a good distance from any major city.
EXIT 330

Mile 332.5 (218.5): Rest area and exit to Weatherby. No services available. EXIT 335

Mile 334.5 (216.5): Exit to Lookout Mountain (elev. 7,120 feet). The highway crosses the Burnt River at this point. The rugged, parched mountains in this area are the Burnt Mountains.
EXIT 338

Mile 337 (214): Exit to Rye Valley, a farming and ranching valley. No services available. Gravel road climbs to a pass overlooking Mormon Basin; phone the BLM in Baker City for road conditions (503/523-6391).
EXIT 340

Mile 339 (212): Exit (eastbound only) to Lime. No services available at this exit.
EXIT 342

Mile 342.5 (208.5): Junction with U.S. Highway 30 to **HUNTINGTON** (pop. 540). Food available. The Oregon Trail crossed the Burnt River here and followed on top of the eastern ridges to Flagstaff Hill, east of Baker City, a distance of about 40 miles. Snake River Road (narrow, winding, steep gravel) connects Huntington with Richland to the north.
EXIT 345

Mile 348 (203): Mountain–Pacific time zone line. If you are headed east, set your watch ahead 1 hour. If headed west, turn your watch back 1 hour.

Mile 350 (201): Exit to Farewell Bend State Park and U.S. Highway 30 north to Huntington. Gas, lodging and camping available at exit. Farewell Bend gets its name from the pioneers who turned northwest from the Snake River and took a pass through the Burnt Mountains to the present site of Huntington on the Burnt River. Interstate 84 fol-

This gold dredge is one of the many mining relics to be seen at Sumpter. (L. Linkhart)

lows the same route.

Farewell Bend State Park is open year-round and offers 53 electrical campsites, 43 primitive campsites, picnic tables, a dump station, camp showers, a visitor exhibit, boat launches, swimming areas and fishing. Access to Brownlee Reservoir, a popular spot with boaters and fishermen. ⚲➡▲ EXIT 353

Mile 353 (198): Exit to Weiser and **junction** with Oregon Highway 201.
EXIT 356

Mile 359 (192): Moores Hollow Road exit.
EXIT 362

Mile 368.5 (182.5): Exit to Stanton Boulevard.
EXIT 371

Mile 372 (179): Junction with U.S. Highway 30 and Oregon Highway 201 north to Weiser and south to Ontario and U.S. Highway 20 (see U.S. HIGHWAY 20 section). Lodging, gas and access to campgrounds.
▲ EXIT 374

Mile 374 (177): Junction with U.S. Highway 30 to Ontario, OR, and Payette, ID. Exits 376A and 376B to **ONTARIO** (pop. 9,400), an agricultural community on the banks of the Snake River offering all traveler services, including 16 motels and 35 restaurants. It is the home of Treasure Valley Community College and has close ties to cities in the Treasure Valley: Boise, Nampa and Caldwell.

South of Ontario is Lake Owyhee, Oregon's largest lake. It is 53 miles long and has 310 miles of shoreline in the midst of the Owyhee Mountains.
EXIT 376

Mile 375.5 (175.5): The Snake River marks the border of Idaho and Oregon.

Mile 376.5 (174.5): Rest area and information center.

Mile 378.5 (172.5): Junction with U.S. Highway 95 south to Parma and north to Payette and Weiser. Travelers using U.S. 95

turn to **Mile 183** in the U.S. HIGHWAY 95 section for log.
EXIT 3

Mile 385 (166): Junction with U.S. Highway 30 to **NEW PLYMOUTH** (pop. 1,313) and Idaho Highway 52 to **EMMETT** (pop. 5,000) and Black Canyon Dam. Emmett has food, gas and lodging, and hosts a Cherry Festival in June to celebrate the annual cherry harvest; phone (208) 365-3485. The 183-foot-tall concrete dam backs up water for Black Canyon Reservoir, an important agricultural and recreational resource. Pumps in Black Canyon Reservoir irrigate the famous fruit-growing fields in the Emmett Irrigation District.
EXIT 9

Mile 388.5 (162.5): Junction with Black Canyon Road. Gas, lodging and 24-hour restaurant.
EXIT 13

Mile 393 (158): Exit to Sand Hollow, a small agricultural valley. Food and gas. EXIT 17

Mile 400.5 (150.5): Junction with Idaho Highway 44 to **MIDDLETON** (pop. 1,851), named because it was located midway between Boise and Keeny's ferry on the mouth of the Boise River.
EXIT 25

Mile 401.5 (149.5): Junction with U.S. highways 20 and 26 west to Notus and Parma, small agricultural communities. No services available.
EXIT 26

Mile 402.5 (148.5): Junction with U.S. Highway 30 and Idaho Highway 19 to Caldwell, Homedale, Greenleaf and Wilder. The Boise River crosses below the interstate at this point. The Boise is heavily stocked with rainbow and is a popular fishing area. Gas available at exit.
➡ EXIT 27

Mile 403.5 (147.5): 10th Avenue exit to Caldwell city center. All services available.

CALDWELL (pop. 18,600) is the seat of Canyon County and shares the agricultural distinctions of Nampa. All services available. Caldwell is the home of the College of Idaho, and among other things, Crookham Seed Co., the largest hybrid seed corn company in the world. The Caldwell Ponds are stocked with bluegill, smallmouth bass and rainbow trout. Major event here is the Caldwell Night Rodeo, held in August; phone (208) 459-7493.

Wineries are one of Idaho's newest agricultural industries and the Caldwell–Nampa area boasts 4—2 of which offer tours. Also in Caldwell is the Snake River mini-brewery with a tasting room.
➡ EXIT 28

Mile 404.5 (146.5): U.S. Highway 20 and U.S. Highway 26 east to Boise and Franklin Road. Access to Albertson College, Simplot Stadium. Food, gas and RV park.
▲ EXIT 29

Mile 411 (140): **Junction** with Idaho Highway 55 south and Nampa Boulevard to Nampa, Northwest Nazarene College, Karcher Mall and Marsing (19 miles). Karcher Mall is one of the largest shopping complexes in Idaho. Highway 55 south also accesses Weston Winery, Hells Canyon Winery and Ste. Chapelle Winery.

NAMPA (pop. 28,500) was named after Shoshoni Indian Chief Nampuh, a huge man whose name means "big foot." The town has all visitor facilities, including several motels and dozens of restaurants.

Nampa and the rest of Canyon County pride themselves on their seed crops. Idaho produces more farm crop seeds than anywhere else in America, and Canyon County is the center of that production. Idaho produces 50 percent of the nation's onion and pea seed, 85 percent of the snap bean seed and 90 percent of the sweet corn seed. In addition to the quantity of seed crops, Canyon County farmers produce some 80 different crops, more than any other county in America.

Nampa is the home of the Snake River Stampede, one of the top rodeos in the country, held the 3rd week of July. Phone (208) 466-8497 for more information.　　EXIT 35

Mile 412 (139): Exit to Franklin Boulevard. All services. Access to Pintler Cellar Winery (phone 208/467-1200).　　EXIT 36

Mile 414 (137): **Junction** with U.S. Highway 30 and Garrity Boulevard. Food and lodging.　　EXIT 38

Mile 420.5 (130.5): **Junction** with Idaho Highway 55 north to McCall and Idaho (see PAYETTE RIVER SCENIC ROUTE this page). Highway 69 south to **MERIDIAN** (pop. 8,700) and **KUNA** (pop. 2,300). Meridian is connected to Boise via Fairview Avenue, a busy commercial thoroughfare. All services are available including 2 motels, 9 restaurants and 7 fast-food outlets.

The Kuna area features the Kuna Cave, a 1,000-foot-long lava tube discovered in 1890, and one of the area's most renowned landmarks. Also accessible from this exit is the Snake River Birds of Prey Conservation Area, a reserve of nearly 500,000 acres that hosts the densest population of breeding raptors (birds of prey) in the world. About an hour's drive south on gravel road. Guided boat tours of the canyon are available. For more information contact the BLM, (208) 334-1582.　　EXIT 44

Mile 425.5 (125.5): **Junction** north with Interstate 184 to **BOISE** city center. For more detailed information on Boise, turn to the MAJOR CITIES section.　　EXIT 49

Mile 426.5 (124.5): Exit to Overland Road and Cole Road. Exit for Wild Waters theme park and the Church of Jesus Christ of Latter-day Saints temple. The World Center for Birds of Prey is located 6 miles south on Cole Road; tours by appointment, phone (208) 362-8687.　　EXIT 50

Mile 428.5 (122.5): Orchard Street and the exit to Gowen Field.　　EXIT 52

Mile 429 (122): Exit for Vista Avenue, Boise International Airport. Vista Avenue N. passes by the historic Union Pacific Railroad Depot where it turns into Capitol Boulevard and continues straight to the capitol building. RV park at exit.　　▲ EXIT 53

Payette River Scenic Route, Idaho Highway 55

As you drive east on Interstate 84 through southwestern Idaho, the mountains lie always in sight to the north, distant above Caldwell and Nampa, close behind Boise. There are few paved highways that penetrate these mountains, but one that does, Idaho Highway 55, is a beautiful drive that traverses tall pine forests, roaring mountain rivers and clear mountain lakes.

The tour begins on Highway 44 out of Boise, heads northwest for a few miles to Highway 55 and continues north. It ends at New Meadows, where it junctions with U.S. Highway 95.

Because of the cold winters in this area, recreational facilities are seasonal. Many campgrounds are only open May 15 to Oct. 1. Call the Idaho Travel Council at 1-800-847-4843 for a campground directory.

Mile 0 (117): The trip begins at Front Street and South 15th in Boise, where Idaho Highway 44 begins, heading north.

Mile 1.5 (115.5): Turn west on State Street.

Mile 7.5 (109.5): Turnoff north on Highway 55 at junction with Highway 44 to Payette Scenic Route. RV park 1 mile north.

Mile 11 (106): Shadow Valley Golf Course. A spot of green in an otherwise dry area.

Mile 12 (105): Roadside sign, "Payette River Scenic Route," points out and locates areas of interest and historic value.

Mile 22 (95): Overlook of the canyon downward to the north at Horseshoe Ranch Vue. Sign points to Bread Loaf Rock across the way. Very steep (elev. 4,242 feet) and many switchbacks on the north side.

Mile 25 (92): HORSESHOE BEND (pop. 643). Gas, groceries, food. Horseshoe Bend Historical Site. In 1862, gold was discovered in the Boise Basin to the east and gold miners came through here by saddle, train and stage coach.

Mile 26 (91): Junction to the west on Idaho Highway 52 to Emmett.

Mile 27 (90): Highway parallels Payette River along canyon floor. Frequent fishing and river rafting pullouts.

Mile 31.5 (85.5): Small unincorporated community of Gardena. No services.

Mile 32 (85): Wildlife chainsaw carvings on display.

Mile 33 (84): The Payette River is very popular for trout fishing, but even more so for river rafting. Only small rapids through here, and anyone can try it. Stream edge is thick with pines.

Mile 37 (80): Unincorporated small community of Banks. Gas, motel, restaurant, RV park.

Mile 39 (78): Boundary of Boise National Forest.

Mile 40.5 (76.5): Banks National Forest campground. Pit toilets, 5 day-use spots along the river and 10 rustic overnight spots along the steep bank above, with picnic area along river.

Mile 41.5 (75.5): Banks service station, cafe, store. River trips available.

Mile 42 (75): Crossing South Fork Payette River. At this point the North and South Forks unite to form the Payette River. North Fork has high rapids continually northward for many miles. Most guided raft trips are on the upper reaches of the South Fork. Turnoff to east along South Fork to Crouch, Garden Valley, Lowman. From Banks to Cascade, the North Fork Payette River is a turmoil of rapids, sink holes and thundering spray; it drops 1,700 feet in 15 miles.

Mile 43 (74): Steady climb northbound to the summit from the point, still following the North Fork of the Payette. Road is very winding and narrow.

Mile 51 (66): Swinging Bridge National Forest Campground on side away from the river. 11 sites, water, pit toilets. Swinging bridge over the river.

Mile 54 (63): Big Eddy National Forest Campground. Primitive river sites, sandy beach, water, pit toilets

Mile 55 (62): Boundary of Boise National Forest.

Mile 58 (59): SMITHS FERRY (pop. 75), a small farm and mountain community. Gas and lodging available. Turnoff west to High Valley, Sage Hen Reservoir and Ola.

Mile 71 (46): Private RV camp, restaurant, motel.

Mile 74 (43): Cascade airfield. No services.

Mile 75 (42): Turnoff to Cabarton Park 'n Ski Area.

Mile 78.5 (38.5): Small lumber community of **CASCADE** (pop. 1,070). All services. Cascade is a popular recreational area for those who come to hike, horseback ride, camp, fish, golf, sail and boat. There are 15 campgrounds in the area, 3 RV parks, 1 guest ranch and 5 motels. In the winter the frozen reservoir is a favorite spot for ice fishing and snowmobiling. Boise Cascade Timber and Wood Products mill is the main industry.

Mile 79 (38): Turnoff west to Cascade lake. Historical marker.

Mile 79.5 (37.5): Crossing North Fork Payette River.

Mile 80 (37): Junction with Warm Lake Highway. Turnoff east to Warm Lake, Yellow Pine, Stanley. Warm Lake is 26 miles northeast and has public

Mile 431 (120): Exit for Broadway Avenue, Boise State University and Boise Convention Center. EXIT 54

Mile 433 (118): Junction with Idaho Highway 21 to Idaho City and Stanley Basin, and Gowen Road. Factory outlet mall at exit. EXIT 57

Mile 438 (113): Blacks Creek rest area.

Mile 439.5 (111.5): Junction of Blacks Creek-Kuna Road. Access to Bonneville Point Interpretive Site (follow signs). EXIT 64

Mile 447 (104): Exit to Mayfield and Orchard. Food and gas are available at truck stop at exit, but no services are available at either of the 2 communities. EXIT 71

Mile 450.5 (100.5): Junction of Simco Road, an unimproved cutoff to the Grand View Highway and C.J. Strike Reservoir. EXIT 74

Mile 467 (84): Junction with U.S. Highway 30 to Mountain Home. At the center of town, Idaho highways 67 and 51 lead to Bruneau (limited services), Bruneau Dunes State Park and Mountain Home Air Force Base (10 miles southwest of town). Services near exit. EXIT 90

Mile 472 (79): Exit to **MOUNTAIN HOME** (pop. 8,900) and the **junction** with U.S. Highway 20 to Fairfield and Fun Valley. This is also the turnoff to Mountain Home Air Force Base, Bruneau, Grand View and C.J. Strike Reservoir. To the north is Anderson Ranch Dam and the popular resort community of Fun Valley along the South Fork Boise River, a popular fishing stream. Fun Valley in Sawtooth National Forest includes the communities of Pine, Paradise Resort and Featherville. Along the South Fork Boise River are remains of early mining efforts. Several ghost towns in and above Fun Valley add flavor to the area. Fly-fishing is popular here during the summer.

Mountain Home is the seat of Elmore County. Unlike most southern Idaho communities, its economy is based largely on the military, rather than agriculture.

Mountain Home was originally a "home station" for the stage route and was located 10 miles northeast of its present location. Upon completion of the railroad in 1883, the townsite was moved south to become a major shipping point for agricultural products.

In 1944, the military installation called Mountain Home Army Air Field was opened. It was later designated Mountain Home Air Force Base and today it is the only active military installation in the state of Idaho.

South of Mountain Home is C.J. Strike Reservoir, which offers sailing, power boating, waterskiing, fishing and camping along its banks. EXIT 95

Mile 476 (75): Bennett Road exit and the **junction** with U.S. Highway 30 to Mountain Home. EXIT 99

Mile 488.5 (62.5): Junction with U.S. Highway 30 to **HAMMETT** (pop. 200), an unincorporated agricultural community where gas and food are available. At Hammett is the junction with Idaho Highway 78 to the Bruneau Dunes State Park and Bruneau Canyon, a popular spot for river rafters on the Snake River.

The Bruneau Dunes are unique in the western hemisphere in their formation and are in vivid contrast to the surrounding plateaus. Other dunes in the Americas form the edge of a natural basin; these form near the center. They include the largest single landlocked sand dune in North America, whose peak is 470 feet above the surface of a nearby desert lake. The 2 prominent dunes cover 600 acres. Temperatures at the dunes range from 110°F/43°C in the summer to 0°F/-18°C in the winter.

Bruneau Dunes State Park offers 48 campsites with electric hookups, firepits, showers, water hookups and picnic areas. There are fees for camping and day use. EXIT 112

Mile 494.5 (56.5): The retention wall visible to eastbound travelers is referred to locally as the China Wall. It is 40 feet tall and nearly 4,500 feet long, holding back the steep canyon in this area called The Narrows. The China Wall is made of pre-cast concrete slabs connected with overlapped slip joints. The wall was constructed between 1977 and 1979. MP 117

Mile 497 (54): Exit to Glenns Ferry, eastbound only. Access to Carmela Vineyards winery and Three Island Crossing State Park. All services. The state park offers 50 campsites, water, electrical hookups, toilets, a dump station, a group picnic center and an information center. The park is the site of a much-used pioneer trail across the Snake River. The perilous crossing is re-enacted every August. Buffalo from Montana's National Bison Range and longhorn cattle are on display at the park. There are fees for camping and day use. Open year-round. Carmela Vineyards next to park. EXIT 120

Mile 498 (53): Exit (eastbound only) to Glenns Ferry, King Hill and Three Island Crossing State Park. **GLENNS FERRY** (pop. 1,300), an agricultural community, has all traveler services, including groceries, gas and motel. The town was named for Gustavus Glenn, who started a ferry on the Snake River in 1863. Glenns Ferry is the home of the Elmore County Fairgrounds. EXIT 121

Mile 502 (49): Snake River and exit to Paradise Valley. No services available. EXIT 125

Payette River Scenic Route, contd.

campground, boat ramp and private lodges. Park 'n Ski nordic areas 4 and 8 miles west.

Mile 88 (29): Descend into a wide, irrigated valley with Cascade Lake along its west border. The lake, 17 miles long, has nearly 50 miles of clean sandy shore, fishing, 12 campgrounds, 8 boat ramps, restrooms and water.

Mile 94 (23): Crossing Gold Fork River.

Mile 95 (22): Small farming and lake community of **DONNELLY** (pop. 135). All services. Rainbow Point Campground 4 miles west. Valley County Historical Museum 1 mile east.

Mile 102 (15): LAKE FORK (pop. 100). Groceries.

Mile 104.5 (12.5): McCall Airport. The airport is the base for the McCall unit of the elite smoke jumper corps of the U.S. Forest Service. The 7 National Forests surrounding this core base annually average 1,000 fires. Tours of their facility are welcome.

Mile 105 (12): McCALL (pop. 2,488). Resort community on beautiful Payette Lake. Elegant lakeside homes and resort accommodations line the southern shore. During summer weekends tourists come by the thousands to take advantage of the recreational opportunities on the lake. Downtown McCall has all kinds of shops for vacationers. There are 16 restaurants, gas stations, motels and private RV parks. Several marinas and a public swimming beach are close by. Ponderosa State Park is 2 miles east. The park has 170 campsites, water, hookups, fishing, boat launch, swimming day-use area and group picnic shelter. Lakeshore Drive leads 20 miles around the lake for superb views. McCall is known for its popular winter carnival in late January when the whole town turns out for snowmobile races, snowshoe baseball and ice sculpture exhibits.

Mile 106 (11): Payette Lake Public Beach with restrooms. Also the turnoff to the McCall Fish Hatchery and the crossing of the North Fork Payette as it leaves the lake.

Mile 107.5 (9.5): Warren Wagon Road provides access to the west side of the lake and farther north to Upper Payette Lake. Also boundary of Payette National Forest.

Mile 109 (8): Turnoff to Brundage Ski Area, 4 miles east, and several National Forest campgrounds. Brundage has 1 triple chair, 2 double chairs and a platter tow. Day lodge, restaurants, ski rentals; phone (208) 634-4151.

Mile 112 (5): Steep downgrade along a narrow valley northbound.

Mile 113 (4): Last Chance National Forest campground 2 miles to the east. Dirt road. 23 sites, handicapped access. Water.

Mile 114 (3): Monument to Packer John's Cabin 0.5 mile north, built in 1862. The first Democratic Territorial Convention was held in his cabin in 1863. Now it is part of Packer John's Cabin State Park with 8 primitive sites, pit toilets. No water available. At this turnoff is Goose Creek Store and an RV park.

Mile 115 (2): Meadows, a small unincorporated community. When New Meadows was built, the town was relocated there. Colonial-style house and old brick school speak of times gone by.

Mile 117 (0): NEW MEADOWS (pop. 600). Highway ends at **junction** with Highway 95. Food and gas.

Mile 505 (46): Exit to King Hill.   EXIT 129

Mile 510 (41): Rest area and weigh station.

Mile 514 (37): Exit to Bliss and Thousand Springs Scenic Route (U.S. Highway 30); see Exit 141.   EXIT 137

Above—Shoshone Falls, a 212-foot waterfall, is just 5 miles east of downtown Twin Falls. *(L. Linkhart)*

Right—The Snake River winds past Twin Falls. *(© Lee Foster)*

Mile 517.5 (33.5): Exit to Bliss and U.S. Highway 30 (Thousand Springs Scenic Route) to Hagerman, Buhl and Twin Falls. **BLISS** (pop. 500) has restaurants, gas stations and a motel. **HAGERMAN** (pop. 600) has restaurants, gas stations, a motel and several campgrounds along the river. The Hagerman Valley is the site of Hagerman Fossil Beds National Monument, where more than 125 prehistoric horses have been excavated. The fossil beds are located on the west side of the Snake River near Hagerman. The National Monument headquarters is located in Hagerman, where a visitor center offering exhibits and guided tours is open daily, June through Sept. Rose Creek Winery is located in the basement of a 100-year-old stone building at the south end of town. Southeast of Hagerman via U.S. Highway 30 is Thousand Springs, where natural springs gush from basalt cliffs above the Snake River. Pri-

vate hot springs resorts are located nearby. **BUHL** (pop. 4,000), the next town along Highway 30, is home to the world's largest trout farm, operated by Clear Springs Food. Both commercial and state-operated fish farms line the banks of the Snake River. Local fish farms produce more than 80 percent of the trout commercially grown in the United States. Buhl has gas, food, lodging and camping.

Follow signs from Buhl to Castleford, then drive 6 miles northwest through farmland to see Balanced Rock. The 40-foot-tall rock is balanced on a 1-by-3-foot rock stem. From Buhl to Twin Falls is approximately 12 miles via U.S. Highway 30.
▲ EXIT 141

Mile 523.5 (27.5): Pass over Snake River and Malad Gorge (see Exit 147).

Mile 524 (27): Exit to **TUTTLE**; gas, food and groceries available, and Malad Gorge State Park (follow signs). The park offers picnicking, fishing, sightseeing, photography and nature study. The gorge was named in 1824 by a troop of 37 Hudson Bay trappers led by Alexander Ross. The gorge is 2.5 miles long and 250 feet deep. The falls at Devils Washbowl is 140 feet wide and 60 feet in height.

Malad Gorge is difficult to see until you are right upon it, and its obscurity made it a good hiding place for outlaws. In 1880, 3 escapees from the Boise Territorial Prison evaded law officers for a month by hiding in the gorge.

Upstream from Devils Washbowl, faint remains of the Malad Way Station can be seen. From 1869 to 1879, this way station was 1 of 19 stops along the Kelton Road, a freight wagon route from Kelton, UT, to Boise, ID.   ⚓◀ EXIT 147

Mile 532 (19): Exit to Wendell.

Mile 534 (17): Junction with Idaho 46 to **WENDELL** (pop. 1,963). Gas and food available.   EXIT 157

Mile 543 (8): Junction with Idaho Highway 25 to **JEROME** (pop. 6,529), with all services available including 2 motels and several restaurants. The North Side Canal irrigation project was completed in 1909, which allowed the irrigation of thousands of acres of arid desert on the north side of the Snake River and made the settling of Jerome possible.
EXIT 165

Mile 546 (5): Exit to Jerome and **junction** with Idaho State Highway 79. Services at exit.   EXIT 168

Mile 549.5 (1.5): Rest area with phone for eastbound traffic only.

Mile 551 (0): Junction with U.S. Highway 93, which leads south to downtown Twin Falls and north to Shoshone. For log of Highway 93, turn to the U.S. HIGHWAY 93 section.

TWIN FALLS (pop. 27,590) offers all traveler services, including 22 motels and numerous restaurants. Gas available at exit. All other services 5 miles south. There are 6 RV parks and private campgrounds in the area.

Twin Falls is the hub of the Magic Valley, one of the most productive agricultural areas in Idaho. Since 1905, the waters of the Snake River have been used to irrigate the arid desert of the Twin Falls area. The river is the lifeblood of the region, providing water not only for agriculture, but for fishing, boating and hunting. The Magic Valley is rich with trout lakes and is also well known for its excellent upland bird and waterfowl hunting.

One of the premier attractions of the Twin Falls area is Shoshone Falls, a 212-foot waterfall on the Snake River 5 miles east of downtown Twin Falls (follow signs along Falls Avenue). A breathtaking view of the Snake River can be seen from Perrine Memorial Bridge, site of Evel Knievel's ill-fated attempt to jump the canyon in a rocket-powered motorcycle in 1974. For additional information on the Twin Falls area, refer to the beginning of the U.S. HIGHWAY 93 log.
⚓▲ EXIT 173

INTERSTATE 90

Seattle, WA, to Missoula, MT
(See maps, pages 109 and 113)

Interstate 90, the northernmost western arterial in the federal interstate highway system, is also a major east-west route within the Northwest. Except for a few short stretches of 2-lane road, I-90 rolls across the west as a multiple-lane freeway linking nearly all of the major cities in the northern tier states.

Northwest Mileposts® logs the highway from Seattle, WA, east to Missoula, MT. Physical mileposts along the interstate (and corresponding exit numbers) reflect distances from the Interstate 5 junction (Milepost 0) within Washington; the Washington–Idaho border at the Spokane River, within Idaho; and the Idaho–Montana state line at Lookout Pass, within Montana.

Interstate 90 Log

Distance in miles from I-5 junction in Seattle, WA, is followed by distance in miles from Missoula, MT (Exit 105).

Mile 0 (481): Junction with Interstate 5. Exit 2B to Dearborn Street. Turn to **Mile 472** in the INTERSTATE 5 section for log of that route.   EXIT 2

Mile 0.5 (480.5): Exit 3A to Rainier Avenue S. (Washington Highway 900) and Exit 3B to Rainier Avenue N.   EXIT 3

Mile 1.5 (479.5): Entering Interstate 90 tunnel eastbound. "Portal to the Pacific" is carved above the tunnel's east entrance.

Mile 2 (479): Referred to as "I-90's Last Link," the floating bridge carrying westbound traffic across Lake Washington between Mercer Island and Seattle was completed in 1989. The old Lacey V. Murrow floating bridge, which it replaced, was under renovation to form the eastbound lanes of the new crossing when part of it sank during a November 1990 storm. The LVM replacement pontoon bridge was completed in 1993. Twenty-mile-long Lake Washington is the largest lake in western Washington.

Mile 3.5 (477.5): Exit to W. Mercer Way on **MERCER ISLAND** (pop. 21,210). This residential community occupies an island 5½ miles long and 2½ miles wide at its widest point. Median value of homes on Mercer Island is $464,500.   EXIT 6

Mile 4 (477): Westbound exit to 76th Avenue E. Eastbound Exit 7A to Mercer Island business district and 77th Avenue SE, and Exit 7B to Island Crest Way.   EXIT 7

Spectacular 268-foot Snoqualmie Falls is easily reached from Exit 27 or 31. This popular tourist attraction is adjacent to Salish Lodge. (Lee Foster)

Mile 5.5 (475.5): Exit to E. Mercer Way.   EXIT 8

Mile 6 (475): Crossing Lake Washington via the East Channel bridge.

Mile 6.5 (474.5): Exit to Lake Washington Boulevard, Bellevue Way.   EXIT 9

Mile 7 (474): Junction with Interstate 405 north to Bellevue, Kirkland, Bothell and Everett; south to Renton, Kent, Tukwila and Tacoma. (See log of I-405 in the INTERSTATE 5 section.) Exit 10A to I-405, Exit 10B to Richards Road and Factoria.   EXIT 10

Mile 9 (472): Exit 11A and 11B to 148th Avenue SE, 150th Avenue SE, 156th Avenue SE, state patrol, Eastgate shopping center, Bellevue Community College and 161st Avenue SE. Easy access to 24-hour restaurant, major-chain motel and gas stations. EXIT 11

Mile 10.5 (470.5): Exit to Newport Way and Sammamish Road to Redmond.   EXIT 13

Mile 13 (468): Exit to Washington Highway 900 to Renton and eastbound access to Lake Sammamish State Park. Easy access to major-chain motel, fast-food outlets, 24-hour restaurant, gas station and supermarket south off exit.

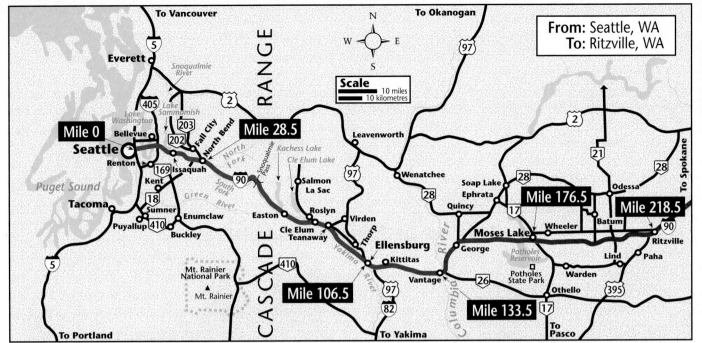

From: Seattle, WA
To: Ritzville, WA

Turn north at exit for Lake Sammamish State Park. After crossing interstate to stop sign by soccer fields, turn west on Lake Sammamish Parkway and drive 0.4 mile to park entrance. This popular day-use area on Lake Sammamish has handicap-accessible facilities, a boat launch, waterskiing, swimming, picnicking, dump station and dock.

Exit south on Issaquah–Renton Road, then turn west on Newport Way and follow it uphill to SE 54th for Washington Zoological Park (watch for signs!). One of 5 zoos in Washington state, the park features primarily threatened and endangered species, especially birds, although cheetahs, cougars, reindeer and primates are included in the collection. Admission fee charged; phone (206) 391-5508 for hours. ⟨ MP 16 EXIT 15

Mile 14 (467): Exit to Front Street, East Sammamish Road and Issaquah. Westbound access to Highway 980 and Lake Sammamish State Park: Follow East Sammamish Road north 0.8 mile to second stoplight; turn west on Lake Sammamish Parkway and drive 1.1 miles to state park entrance. Day-use park with handicap-accessible facilities, showers, a boat launch and swimming. Gas and deli on East Sammamish Road; **junction** with Issaquah–Fall City Road.

Front Street leads south to **ISSAQUAH** city center (pop. 8,175). Originally called Gilman in its days as a coal-mining community for workers of nearby Squak Mountain, its name was changed in 1899 to Issaquah, a Duwamish Indian word meaning "snake." This is the home of the Edelweiss Chalet (visible from Interstate 90), maker of Boehms chocolates. Tours are available, phone (206) 392-6652. The popular Gilman Village in Issaquah is a collection of renovated houses and buildings from the town's early days, converted into a quaint shopping center with about 40 specialty shops. Located just west of Front Street on Gilman Boulevard, the shops are open Monday through Saturday 10 a.m. to 6 p.m., Sunday 1–5 p.m.

The state salmon hatchery on Sunset Way offers self-guiding tours; phone (206) 392-3180. Issaquah's annual celebration, "Salmon Days," held the first weekend in October, has a parade, food and crafts booths, music and many activities for children. The Village Theatre on Front Street presents regional productions of Broadway musicals and plays. ⟨ MP 17 EXIT 17

Mile 15 (466): Westbound only exit to Issaquah, E. Sunset Way. EXIT 18

Mile 17 (464): Exit to High Point Way, access to Tiger Mountain State Forest. Interstate 90 travelers can't help but notice the long lines of cars parked on the High Point frontage road. The explanation is the remarkable popularity of the Tradition Lake–West Tiger Mountain trailhead. The hiking area has become one of the state's most popular. Trails are also used by mountain bicyclists. ⟨ MP 20 EXIT 20

Mile 19.5 (461.5): Exit to Preston and Fall City on the Snoqualmie River; access to Washington Highways 202 and 203. An attraction at this exit is The Herbfarm, a nursery dedicated to herbs. The Herbfarm also offers classes, a country store, tours and special luncheons and dinners. From the exit follow Preston–Fall City Road north approximately 3 miles; turn west across the green bridge over the Raging River (SE 238th); and follow signs 0.5 mile to The Herbfarm. It is open daily in summer.

There is a gas station at Preston. Groceries and gas available in Fall City. This exit provides access to Washington Highway 203, which connects Fall City with Monroe on U.S. Highway 2 (25 miles north), and Washington Highway 202 (Redmond–Fall City Road), which connects Fall City with North Bend (9 miles) and Redmond (15 miles). These backcountry roads are scenic routes through the Snoqualmie River valley. EXIT 22

Mile 22 (459): Junction with Washington Highway 18 west to Auburn and Tacoma. Access to Echo Glen. Highway 18 merges with Interstate 5 at Federal Way. EXIT 25

Mile 23.5 (457.5): Short stretch of highway with 4 lanes, wide shoulders and lightposts. MP 26

Mile 24.5 (456.5): Eastbound exit only to Snoqualmie and North Bend; access to Snoqualmie Winery. To return to the highway, eastbound travelers must follow North Bend Way 4 miles to North Bend and then follow signs to Interstate 90 at Exit 31.

From exit follow signs 0.5 mile uphill to Snoqualmie Winery. The winery has a tasting room open daily 10 a.m. to 4:30 p.m. Handicap-accessible. Beautiful view!

To reach Snoqualmie Falls from exit, follow 4-lane paved road (SE North Bend Way) north 1 mile and turn at sign for falls; follow winding road (Washington Highway 202) approximately 2 miles to stop sign and turn west; continue about another 2 miles through the town of Snoqualmie to public parking area for Snoqualmie Falls Park. Handicap-accessible. There are an overlook and gift shop at the park; food and lodging available at Salish Lodge adjacent. This magnificent waterfall is a not-to-be-missed attraction.

The community of **SNOQUALMIE** (pop. 1,530) has most visitor services. The Puget Sound and Snoqualmie Valley Railroad operates from a depot on Washington Highway 202 in town. The antique train offers a 7-mile round-trip between Snoqualmie and North Bend; phone (206) 746-4025 for schedule and more information. ⟨★ EXIT 27

Mile 28.5 (452.5): Westbound exit to Snoqualmie and Snoqualmie Falls (see description at **Mile 24.5**) via Washington Highway 202 and North Bend. Major-chain fast-food outlets and gas station at exit. Visitor information booth located about 0.5 mile north of interstate exit. **NORTH BEND** (pop. 2,610) has all services. The dominating monolith north of the highway is Mount Si (elev. 4,167 feet). An improved hiking trail leads up the timbered southeast side to the top; spectacular view, moderately strenuous hike. This is a popular hiking trail for Puget Sound residents. To reach the trailhead, follow ranger station signs from the interstate through North Bend city center. Stop at the ranger station for more information, or continue on to Mount Si Road and follow it 2 miles to signed parking area. ☂★ EXIT 31

Mile 30.5 (450.5): Exit to 436th Avenue SE, North Bend. A popular rock climbing area, there is a North Bend climbing guide entitled "Exit 32." EXIT 32

Mile 32.5 (448.5): Exit to Edgewick Road; food and gas. EXIT 34

Mile 34 (447): Crossing the South Fork Snoqualmie River.

Mile 36 (445): Exit to fire training center. EXIT 38

Mile 39.5 (441.5): Entering Mount Baker/Snoqualmie National Forest eastbound.

Mile 40 (441): Exit to Tinkham Road, McClellan Butte trail. Tinkham Road leads to Tinkham Campground; 45 sites, water, camping fee. ▲ EXIT 42

Mile 43 (438): Bandera airfield, Lookout Point Road, Talapus Point Trail. EXIT 45

Mile 45 (436): Denny Creek, Asahel Curtis, Tinkham Road, chain-removal area. Denny

Creek campground has 32 campsites, picnic area and water. Asahel Curtis day-use area has 26 picnic sites and water. ⇞▲ EXIT 47

Mile 50 (431): Exit to Alpental Road, west summit Snoqualmie Pass Recreation Area. Gas, food and major motel. To return to eastbound 90 continue south off the exit to Exit 53. EXIT 52

Mile 50.5 (430.5): Snoqualmie Pass Summit (elev. 3,022 feet). This is the lowest highway pass across Washington's Cascade Range.

Mile 51 (430): Exit to Snoqualmie Pass Recreation Area. Major alpine ski areas at "the

You're in Bigfoot Country

The Pacific Northwest is reported to be the traditional stomping grounds for one of the 20th century's most mysterious and elusive creatures: Bigfoot.

Indian legends tell of a huge manlike creature roaming the Cascade Range, a powerful animal the Indians called soss q'atl, "wild man of the woods," from which the term Sasquatch has its origin. Modern reports of Bigfoot found their way to the public's eye as early as the 1920s, but it wasn't until Roger Patterson returned with a film he claimed was of Bigfoot that the mystery was taken seriously by scientists.

Patterson and a friend claimed they had filmed a female Bigfoot in the Bluff Creek valley of northern California in the fall of 1967. Authorities who examined the film said the figure was between 6¹/₂ and 7 feet tall and weighed from 300–350 lbs. Special-effects technicians who created the movie *King Kong* examined the film and were asked if they could reproduce such a film using a human actor. Their response was, "We could try, but we would have to create a completely new system of artificial muscles and find an actor who could be trained to walk like that. It might be done, but we would have to say that it would be almost impossible."

Since that time, Bigfoot has been reported hundreds of times, but as of yet, no one has been able to capture another film of the creature. Hair and scat samples have been submitted as being of Bigfoot origin, many of which were identified as belonging to other big game species. However, a few hair samples were found to have both human and nonhuman characteristics and have been termed "unidentified in origin."

Bigfoot is believed to be related to the Asian Yeti, the Abominable Snowman sighted in the eastern Himalayas. A similar animal, called the Almas, is reported in Mongolia and a third Asian creature, called the Chuchunaa, has been reported in a limited area of northeast Siberia.

Cliff Crook of Bothell, WA, is a Northwest Bigfoot expert and operates the Bigfoot Hot Line, collecting reports of Bigfoot sightings every year. Crook describes the average Bigfoot as a large primate with a height of about 7 feet 6 inches. After sifting through thousands

of reports, Bigfoot appears to be solitary, nocturnal and omnivorous. Much like a bear, Bigfoot prefers vegetable matter but will eat almost anything. Reports of Bigfoot are consistent in stating that the animal has broad shoulders, a short neck, a flat face, a sloping forehead and is uniformly hairy, although some reports indicate that the hair on the animal's head is slightly longer than on the rest of the body.

Bigfoot is serious business in the Northwest, and in at least 1 county it is a protected species. The county commissioners of Skamania County in Washington passed an ordinance in 1969 that makes it a felony for "any premeditated, willful and wanton slaying of any such creature," punishable by a $10,000 fine and/or imprisonment for up to 5 years in the county jail.

Crook firmly believes Bigfoot is alive and speculates that the population of the species could exceed 200 in the Pacific Northwest. After investigating hundreds of sightings, interviewing the frightened and shaky witnesses, examining footprints and actually hearing the scream of Bigfoot, Crook believes it is just a matter of time before Bigfoot will be identified as a real creature.

Crook is quick to note that most reported sightings are not valid. "Sometimes, people mistake a bear for what they think is Bigfoot," Crook said. Even footprints can be deceiving. Crook said that when a bear steps in his own print, it creates a print that could be confused with a large human footprint. "But once you've taken a close look at it," Crook says, "it's easy to tell if it's a bear."

Crook is also aware that the world is filled with pranksters willing to create

Photo of Bigfoot taken by Daniel Adams Oct. 4, 1992 in North Cascades. (Courtesy of Cliff Crook)

tracks and phony sightings for fun or notoriety. He believes these people set back actual research and muddy the waters for people like he and Dahinden who are seriously studying this mystical creature.

Often, people who believe they have seen Bigfoot refuse to report a sighting for fear of ridicule. That's why Crook has established Bigfoot Central and the Bigfoot Hot Line. "There are people out there who have seen, or believe they have seen Bigfoot, but who are afraid to come forward. Now, all they have to do is call the hot line and report what they have actually seen. They want someone to take them seriously, someone to listen to them."

The Bigfoot Hot Line number is (206) 483-4007 in Bothell, WA. For those who would like to report their sightings in writing, or who would like more information on Bigfoot research or the *Bigfoot Trails* newsletter, write to Cliff Crook, Bigfoot Central, P.O. Box 147, Bothell, WA 98041.

Pass" are: Alpental, Snoqualmie, Ski Acres and Hyak. Food, gas and phone available. Entering Kittitas County eastbound.   EXIT 53

Mile 52.5 (428.5): Exit to ski areas. Hyak is located at the east end of the Milwaukee Railroad tunnel. The 2-mile-long tunnel was built in 1914–15.   EXIT 54

Mile 54 (427): West end of Keechelus Lake.

Mile 54.5 (426.5): Lighted chain-up areas both sides of highway.   MP 56

Mile 56 (425): Good view across Keechelus Lake of snowsheds protecting railroad line.

Mile 59 (422): East end of Keechelus Lake and Keechelus Dam, which regulates the flow of the Yakima River. Keechelus Lake is severely drawn down during summer for irrigation of the Kittitas and Yakima valleys.

Mile 59.5 (421.5): Snow-Park parking on north side of highway.

Mile 61 (420): Exit to Stampede Pass, Kachess Lake and Snow-Park parking. Stampede Pass was discovered in 1881 by Virgil C. Bogue while surveying a route for the Northern Pacific Railroad across the Cascade Range. Scenic Kachess Lake, a few miles north of the interchange via a paved road, has USFS campgrounds, picnic area, swimming beaches and 2 boat ramps. Filled to capacity on summer weekends.   EXIT 62

Mile 62 (419): Exit to Cabin Creek Road. Snow-Park parking.   MP 64 EXIT 63

Mile 66.5 (414.5): Leaving Wenatchee National Forest eastbound.

Mile 68 (413): Exit to Easton, Sparks Road, Lake Easton State Park, Snow-Park parking. Food and gas available. Lake Easton has 145 campsites, hookups, dump station, picnic tables, stoves, showers, boat launch and fishing for planted rainbow; snowmobiling and cross-country skiing in winter.
    MP 70 EXIT 70

Mile 69 (412): Crossing the Yakima River.

Mile 69.5 (411.5): Exit to EASTON (pop. 200); food and gas. Access to Iron Horse State Park (day-use only); John Wayne Trail.
    EXIT 71

Mile 72 (409): Exit to West Nelson Siding Road.   MP 74 EXIT 74

Mile 76 (405): Exit to Golf Course Road.   MP 78 EXIT 78

Mile 77.5 (403.5): Weigh station (closed). Paved turnout with pay phone.

Mile 78 (403): Exit to Roslyn, Salmon la Sac and Ronald via Washington Highway 903. ROSLYN (pop. 875) dates back to 1886 and has many interesting historic buildings. This Western mining town is home of the oldest operating tavern in Washington—The Brick, established in 1889. The Roslyn Museum on Pennsylvania Avenue displays historic documents and photographs highlighting the town's coal-mining days. Roslyn is the mythical community of Cicely, Alaska, on the television series Northern Exposure. Wash-

ington Highway 903 also provides access to Wenatchee National Forest campgrounds along the Cle Elum River and Alpine Lakes Wilderness.   MP 80 EXIT 80

Mile 81.5 (399.5): Exit to Cle Elum, South Cle Elum. Hospital. Lodging, food and 24-hour gas station at exit. CLE ELUM (pop. 1,900) grew up with the coal-mining industry that developed on the east side of the Cascade Range. Logging is a primary industry today; a chipping plant is located nearby. A telephone museum and carpentry museum are downtown. All services available.   EXIT 84

Mile 82.5 (398.5): Exit to Washington Highway 970 (Sunset Highway) east to Wenatchee and Highway 903 west to Roslyn. Gas station north off exit. Access to Washington Highway 10 and Teanaway Valley Road. Highway 970 junctions with U.S. Highway 97.   EXIT 85

Mile 86.5 (394.5): Summit of Indian John Hill (elev. 2,141 feet), and Indian John Hill rest areas both sides of interstate. These are large rest areas with handicap-accessible restrooms, picnic tables, dump station and good views of the Cascades on a clear day.
    MP 89

Mile 89.5 (391.5): Summit of Elk Heights (elev. 2,359 feet).

Mile 90.5 (390.5): Exit to Elk Heights Road and Taneum Creek; no services.   EXIT 93

Mile 98.5 (382.5): Exit to Thorp Highway. Diesel gas south off exit. Thorp was named for Milford A. Thorp, an early settler here.
    EXIT 101

Mile 100 (381): Crossing the Yakima River. The highway parallels the upper Yakima River west to Keechelus Lake, the source of the river in the Cascade Range. The Yakima River is possibly the best trout river in Washington. Best fishing in fall from inflatables or drift boats. Bait is prohibited in the Ellensburg area and upstream almost to Cle Elum.

Mile 103.5 (377.5): Junction with U.S. Highway 97 north, exit to Ellensburg via Interstate 90 Business Loop. Motel, restaurant, gas station and fast-food outlet north off exit. This 4-mile business loop leads through west Ellensburg to town center. (Travelers heading north on U.S. Highway 97 turn to Mile 396 in the U.S. HIGHWAY 97 section for log.)   EXIT 106

Mile 106.5 (374.5): Exit to Canyon Road, Ellensburg. Easy access to major-chain motels, fast-food outlets and gas stations north off exit. Canyon Road leads south to Washington Highway 821.
    ELLENSBURG (pop. 12,440) is the hub of the Kittitas Valley, which was once a neutral area where the Wenatchee, Nez Percé and Yakima Indians, who were normally hostile toward one another, hunted and fished together in peace. The town, which was originally named Robber's Roost, after a store in the area, is now the seat of Kittitas County, a major food-processing, stock-raising and agricultural region. All services are available.
    Ellensburg is also the home of Central Washington University. The 350-acre

campus has an enrollment of more than 8,000 students.
    Downtown Ellensburg (easily accessible north from this exit) has many fine old restored Victorian buildings, most found within the 5-block Ellensburg Historic District. Unusual architecture and memorabilia on local history may also be found at the Kittitas County Historical Museum, E. 3rd Avenue and Pine Street. The museum also has an extensive gem and mineral collection. The Clymer Art Museum at 416 N. Pearl St., featuring the work of Western artist John Clymer, is an attraction here. Open daily, admission charged.
    The biggest annual event in Ellensburg is the Ellensburg Rodeo and Kittitas County Fair, held every Labor Day weekend. The rodeo is one of the premier rodeos in the Northwest, and each year attracts many of the top cowboys in the country. It is important to get tickets and to make reservations for accommodations early. For information, contact the Ellensburg Rodeo ticket office, P.O. Box 777, Ellensburg, WA 98926, or phone (509) 962-7831. Information is also available from the chamber of commerce, phone (509) 925-3137.   EXIT 109

Mile 107.5 (373.5): Junction with U.S. Highway 97 south and Interstate 82. Travelers headed south on U.S. Highway 97 turn to Mile 391 in the U.S. HIGHWAY 97 section for log.   EXIT 110

Mile 112.5 (368.5): Exit to Kittitas; gas station with diesel fuel north off exit. Access to Olmstead Place State Park Heritage Site, where visitors may see a log cabin, farm buildings and equipment from the original homestead established in 1875. KITTITAS (pop. 945) is an agricultural community.
    NOTE: Next exit eastbound is 21 miles.
    EXIT 115

Mile 123.5 (357.5): Ryegrass rest area with picnic tables and handicap-accessible restrooms at Rye Grass Summit (elev. 2,535 feet). Eastbound, the highway descends "Vantage Hill" the next 10 miles to the Columbia River.   MP 126

Mile 133.5 (347.5): Exit to Vantage, Huntzinger Road. VANTAGE (est. pop. 130) was one of many towns along the Columbia River that had to be moved to higher ground when the dams were built. Campground, motel and gas station.
    Follow Huntzinger Road south about 3 miles for Wanapum State Park; 50 campsites, hookups, swimming, picnicking, fishing and boat launch.
    One mile north of this exit is Ginkgo Petrified Forest State Park, which includes several thousand acres of fossilized trees. There are interpretive trails, a museum (open Wednesday through Sunday in summer), picnic area and boat launch.
    Westbound travelers begin 10-mile ascent of the "Vantage Hill." Next exit westbound is 21 miles.   EXIT 136

Mile 134.5 (346.5): Bridge across the Columbia River. Interstate 90 crosses Wanapum Lake, which is in the impound area of Wanapum Dam. CAUTION: Strong cross winds.   MP 137

Mile 135 (346): Junction with Washington Highway 26 east to Othello and Pullman and Washington Highway 243 south. Drive south 5 miles on Highway 243 for Wanapum Dam and visitor center. Self-guiding tours of fish ladders and powerhouse. The visitor center has displays and diagrams on local history. The center is open from April to Oct., 9 a.m. to 5 p.m. daily. Picnic area and restrooms. ⊼ EXIT 137

Mile 137 (344): Access to scenic viewpoint of the Columbia River. Eastbound viewpoint has a view of "Grandfather Cuts Loose the Ponies." The 250-foot-long sculpture by David Govedare is of 18 horses spilling from a 36-foot-high basket. The life-size, 2-dimensional weathering-steel project represents the Great Spirit putting horses on Earth. The work is in progress.

Mile 140 (341): Entering Columbia Basin Federal Reclamation Project eastbound. This New Deal project created a network of canals to irrigate the arid lands of central Washington using water from Grand Coulee Dam.

Above—Miles of wheat fields and old barns make for peaceful scenery. (L. Linkhart) Right—The Moses Lake Centennial Theater hosts summer concerts. (Courtesy of Moses Lake Parks & Recreation)

Mile 141 (340): Exit to Champs de Brionne Winery Road. Follow signs 10 miles for the winery, which is open daily year-round. A summer concert series is presented at the Gorge between May and Sept. Contact the Quincy Valley Chamber of Commerce, phone (509) 787-2140, for more information. Access to the Gorge at George outdoor amphitheater this exit. EXIT 143

Mile 147 (334): Exit to **GEORGE** (pop. 327) and **junction** with Washington Highway 281 north 10 miles to **QUINCY** (pop. 3,800) and 40 miles to Wenatchee. George was founded in 1957 by Charles Brown, the developer who bought the townsite from the U.S. Bureau of Reclamation and became the town's first mayor. The streets are lined with cherry trees and are named after different

types of cherries. The Martha Inn in George is a popular truck stop. Gas, diesel and dump station available. Food, camping and lodging available in George, Quincy, Ephrata and Soap Lake area. ▲ EXIT 149

Mile 148.5 (332.5): For the next 14 miles the crops along the interstate are identified with signs in the fence line.

Mile 149 (332): Exit to Washington Highway 281 north to Quincy and Washington Highway 283 north 20 miles to **EPHRATA** (pop. 5,300) and 30 miles to **SOAP LAKE** (pop. 1,100). EXIT 151

Mile 152 (329): Exit to Adams Road. EXIT 154

Mile 159.5 (321.5): Winchester Wasteway rest areas with handicap-accessible restrooms, covered picnic tables and dump station, both sides of highway. Winchester Wasteway is an irrigation canal that drains Winchester Reservoir. ⑤⊼ MP 162

Mile 162 (319): Exit to Dodson Road. This is an access road to Winchester Wasteway. Private RV park. ▲ EXIT 164

Mile 167 (314): Exit to Hiawatha Road. Columbia Potato. Potatoes are a major product of the area, with shipping, warehousing and manufacture of potato products (granulated potatoes, french fries, hash browns,

etc.) taking place locally. EXIT 169

Mile 172 (309): Exit to Mae Valley and Hanson Road. Access north off exit to Moses Lake State Recreation Area (day-use only) with picnic tables and swimming. Gas station with diesel at exit. Private RV park and off-road vehicle park to south. ⊼▲ EXIT 174

Mile 173 (308): Westbound-only access to Mae Valley, Westshore Drive and Moses Lake State Recreation Area. EXIT 175

Mile 173.5 (307.5): Exit to Moses Lake (see description at **Mile 176.5**) and Interstate 90 Business Loop. The lake upon which the town lies is the third largest natural body of water in the state of Washington. It has more than 120 miles of shoreline. Moses Lake is famous for producing giant white crappie and rainbow. Fishing from the I-90 bridge, accessible from the adjoining state park. ← EXIT 176

Mile 174.5 (306.5): The interstate crosses Marsh Island in the arm of Moses Lake known as Pelican Horn. MP 177

Mile 176.5 (304.5): Exit to Othello and Moses Lake, and **junction** with Washington Highway 17. Major-chain motel, restaurants, 24-hour gas stations with diesel and fast-food outlets north off exit. Access to Big Bend Community College and Grant County Airport. *NOTE:* Next services eastbound 42 miles.

MOSES LAKE (pop. 11,530) is the largest city in central Washington, the commercial hub of the Columbia Basin and the center of Big Bend country (so-called for its location on a bend in the Columbia River).

Travelers on Interstate 90 may be surprised to see a 747 jumbo jet with the Japan Air Lines (JAL) insignia on the tail move across the sky above Moses Lake. Moses Lake is the site of a Japan Air Lines training center, located at Grant County Airport, one of the largest civilian airports west of the Mississippi. The Boeing Co. also uses the airport to flight-test new planes.

The city of Moses Lake operates the Adam East Museum, which contains a large collection of regional Indian artifacts. The collection originally belonged to local businessman Adam East, who left it to the city so that it would remain in the area.

Big Bend Community College in Moses Lake is an accredited 2-year school that offers a variety of technical, vocational and adult education programs. It has an enrollment of about 2,000 students.

Washington Highway 17 leads north 21 miles to Soap Lake and 42 miles to junction with U.S. Highway 2. Washington Highway 17 leads south 11 miles and west 7 miles to Potholes State Park on Potholes Reservoir, site of the Columbia Basin Project Interpretive Center. Potholes State Park is the most popular water recreation area in the Columbia Basin region. It has 66 tent and 60 RV sites, handicap-accessible facilities, a boat launch and showers. ⑤▲ EXIT 179

Mile 180 (301): Exit to Wheeler, Sieler

Siding and O Road NE/SE. EXIT 182

Mile 182 (299): Exit to Q Road NE/SE, Raugust Siding. Simplot plant to south. EXIT 185

Mile 186 (295): Exit to Warden and U Road NE/SE. MP 189 EXIT 188

Mile 187 (294): Leaving Columbia Basin Federal Reclamation Project eastbound. In summer, the break between the irrigated fields of the Columbia Basin and the area of dryland wheat farming is sharply evident. The wheat fields in the Moses Lake–Ritzville area support one of the most dense ringneck pheasant populations in the country. MP 190

Mile 189 (292): Entering Adams County eastbound, Grant County westbound. MP 192

Mile 194 (287): Exit to Deal Road, Batum and Schrag. MP 197 EXIT 196

Mile 195 (286): Schrag Rest Area both sides of highway with handicap-accessible restrooms, picnic area, dump station and phone. ♿🍴 MP 198

Mile 204 (277): Junction with Washington Highway 21, which leads 18 miles north to Odessa and south to Lind. MP 207 EXIT 206

Mile 212 (269): Exit to Paha and Packard. No services. MP 215 EXIT 215

Mile 217 (264): Junction with U.S. Highway 395 south to Pasco, state patrol and Ritzville. Cafe and gas station north off exit. Travelers headed south on U.S. Highway 395 turn to **Mile 494** in the U.S. HIGHWAY 395 section for log. Interstate 90 and U.S. 395 share a common alignment east to Spokane from here. MP 220 EXIT 220

Mile 218.5 (262.5): Exit to Ritzville and Washington Highway 261 south to Washtucna. Easy access to major-chain motel and gas station north off exit.

RITZVILLE (pop. 1,730) has all services. Ritzville is the county seat of Adams County, which ranks number 1 in wheat acreage in production among Washington counties. Cattle is also a major industry here. The town was named after Philip Ritz, who homesteaded here in 1878. It was predominantly cattle country until the 1890s, when local farmers realized the area's wheat farming potential.

Ritzville has several historic buildings on the National Register of Historic Places, including the Andrew Carnegie Library, the Nelson H. Green House and the Dr. Frank R. Burroughs Home. MP 222 EXIT 221

Mile 224 (257): Exit to Coker Road (Ritzville truck access route). EXIT 226

Mile 229 (252): Exit to Tokio weigh station to north. Gas station with restaurant, phone and convenience store south off exit. EXIT 231

Mile 239.5 (241.5): Entering Lincoln County eastbound, Adams County westbound.

Mile 242 (239): Sprague Lake rest area both sides of highway with handicap-accessible restrooms, picnic tables and dump station. ♿🍴 MP 242

Mile 245 (236): Exit to Sprague and **junction** with Washington Highway 23 north to Harrington (22 miles) and south to Steptoe on U.S. Highway 195 (44 miles).

SPRAGUE (pop. 425) is located just to the south of Interstate 90; all services available. Incorporated in 1883, Sprague was named after Gen. John W. Sprague, the director of the Northern Pacific Railroad. Sprague's Roman Catholic church, Church of Mary Queen of Heaven, has a beautiful white gothic revival spire built in 1902.

Sprague Lake, visible from I-90, has numerous fishing resorts. A shallow, heavily silted lake, it was poisoned in 1985 to remove an overpopulation of scrap fish. (The treatment turned up a 7-foot-long white sturgeon, much to the surprise of fish biologists.)

The lake is being restocked with rainbow and brown trout, walleye, smallmouth and large-mouth bass and other game fish. ← EXIT 245

Mile 254 (227): Exit to Fishtrap Lake. Fishing in early spring, heavily stocked with rainbow. Private campground.
←▲ MP 254 EXIT 254

Mile 255.5 (225.5): Entering Spokane County eastbound, Lincoln County westbound.

Mile 257 (224): Exit to Tyler, **junction** with Washington Highway 904 to Cheney (11 miles). Access to the 15,468-acre Turnbull National Wildlife Refuge; good bird watching. Also access to Badger Lake, one of the best trout lakes in the Spokane region.
← EXIT 257

Mile 264 (217): Exit to Salnave Road, Cheney and Medical Lake. EXIT 264

Mile 270 (211): Exit to Washington Highway 904 to Four Lakes and Cheney (6 miles). **CHENEY** (pop. 7,880) is the home of Eastern Washington University, which has more than 8,000 students enrolled. Originally known as Desert Springs, the name Cheney was adopted to cultivate the favor of Benjamin P. Cheney, a founder of the Northern Pacific Railroad. EXIT 270

Mile 272 (209): Junction with Washington Highway 902 north to Medical Lake (7 miles). The community of **MEDICAL LAKE** (pop. 3,780) grew with the reputation of the lake's alkaline waters as a cure for rheumatism. From 1905 until the 1920s, passenger cars on the electric railway line from Spokane to Medical Lake were crowded with people seeking the cure. One of the developers of a Medical Lake health resort, Lord Stanley Hallett, built an unusual home for himself known as "The Castle," which still stands at E. 623 Lake St. EXIT 272

Mile 276 (205): Exit to Geiger Field, West Spokane and Interstate 90 Business Loop.

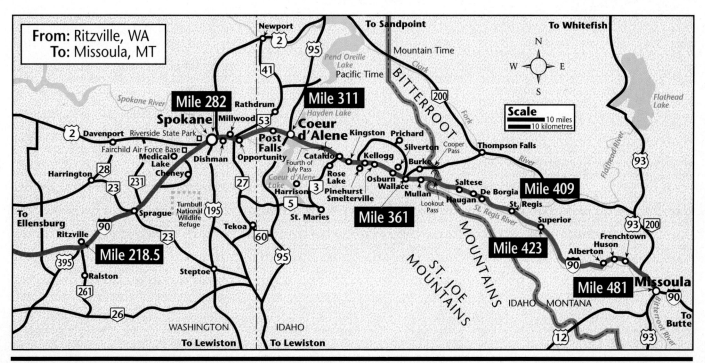

Access to state patrol, Worden's Winery and to private RV park south off exit. ▲ EXIT 276

Mile 277 (204): Exit 277A to Garden Springs. Exit 277B is the **junction** with U.S. Highway 2 to Fairchild Air Force Base, Coulee Dam and Wenatchee. (Exit 277 westbound accesses these points.) Access to Spokane Falls Community College. Fairchild AFB is a Strategic Air Command base. Travelers turning west on to U.S. Highway 2 turn to **Mile 136.5** in the U.S. HIGHWAY 2 section.   EXIT 277

Mile 279 (202): Junction with U.S. Highway 195 south through the scenic Palouse country of eastern Washington to Colfax and Pullman (see log in the U.S. HIGHWAY 195 section).   EXIT 279

Mile 280 (201): Exit to Lincoln Street, Maple Street bridge, Amtrak and VA hospital.   EXIT 280

Mile 281 (200): Division Street exit is also the **junction** with U.S. Highway 2 north to Newport and U.S. Highway 395 north to Colville. (U.S. Highways 2 and 395 share a common alignment north for several miles.) Division Street is a heavily traveled thoroughfare, lined with shopping malls and services; stay on Division Street for both highways. Access to hospital, Gonzaga University and Whitworth College.

Travelers headed north on U.S. Highway 2 turn to **Mile 132.5** in the U.S. HIGHWAY 2 section. Travelers headed north on U.S. Highway 395 turn to **Mile 494** in the U.S. HIGHWAY 395 section.   EXIT 281

Mile 282 (199): Exit to Washington Highway 290 east, Trent Avenue, Hamilton Street and downtown **SPOKANE**, third largest metropolitan area in Washington. See description of Spokane in the MAJOR CITIES section.   EXIT 282

Mile 283 (198): Exit 283A to Altamont Street. Exit 283B to Freya Street and Thor Street; access to Spokane Community College (drive north on Freya to Desmet, turn left on Desmet and right on Ralph Street, continue to Greene Street and Mission Avenue). Easy access gas.   EXIT 283

Mile 284 (197): Westbound-only exit to Havana Street. Spokane city limits. EXIT 284

Mile 285 (196): Exit to Sprague Avenue; access to Felt Field Municipal Airport. This busy airport caters primarily to private aircraft. Go east on Sprague to Fancher, and take Fancher north 1.5 miles to reach the airport.   EXIT 285

Mile 286 (195): Exit to Broadway Avenue and access to Spokane Interstate Fairgrounds.   EXIT 286

Mile 287 (194): Exit to Argonne Road. Access to communities of **MILLWOOD** (pop. 1,665) and **DISHMAN** (pop. 10,169). Access north to Mount Spokane State Park (12 tent sites) and downhill ski area.   ♿⛵▲ EXIT 287

Mile 289 (192): Junction with Washington Highway 27 south to Pullman, Pines Road and the town of **OPPORTUNITY** (pop. 21,241). Valley General Hospital south off exit. Two miles north off exit is the Walk In the Wild

Zoo, which features Alaskan brown bears, lions, tigers, peacocks, flamingos and more. Handicap-accessible. Open 10 a.m. to 3:30 p.m. daily. Admission is $3.75 for adults, $3.25 for seniors and children ages 13–17, $2.25 for children ages 3–12 and free for children under age 3. For special events and other information, call (509) 924-7220. ♿ EXIT 289

Mile 291 (190): Exit to Sullivan Road, Veradale, Trentwood Industrial Area and Spokane Industrial Park. Gas, food and lodging.   MP 292 EXIT 291

Mile 293 (188): Exit to Barker Road. Food, gas and lodging at exit. Access to private campgrounds.   ▲ EXIT 293

Mile 294 (187): Westbound-only exit to Sprague Avenue and interstate business route.   EXIT 294

View of Carlin Bay on Lake Coeur d'Alene. This popular lake offers more than 100 miles of shoreline for water recreation. (© George Wuerthner)

Mile 295 (186): Exit to Otis Orchard and Liberty Lake; public beaches, swimming, fishing, boating and camping.   ⛵▲ MP 296 EXIT 296

Mile 299 (182): Exit to State Line Village, Washington Port of Entry and Spokane River rest area with handicap-accessible facilities. State visitor information center. No eastbound re-entry from rest area.   ♿ EXIT 299

Mile 300 (181): Washington–Idaho state line, crossing the Spokane River. The Spokane River drains Lake Coeur d'Alene and flows west to the Columbia River.

Mile 302 (179): Exit to Post Falls, Pleasant View Road; access to The Greyhound Park, Factory Outlet Mall, RV park and 18-hole golf course. Major-chain fastfood outlet, gas station and motel at exit. Major-chain motel, restaurants and gas stations also in Post Falls.   ▲ EXIT 2

Mile 305 (176): Exit to Spokane Street and access to Post Falls city center. Major-chain motel and gas station at exit. **POST FALLS** (pop. 11,000) is located on the Spokane

River and is named for Frederick Post, who arrived here in 1871. He purchased the site for the town from the Indian Chief Seltice of the Coeur d'Alenes, and established a sawmill here. Treaty Rock Historical Site commemorates the land exchange. A half-mile from I-90 is Falls Park; picnic area, playground, handicap-accessible trails to view falls where Post built his first sawmill.

Daily sternwheeler tours depart Templin's marina on the Spokane River. Q'emilin Riverside Park, 1 mile off I-90, has a picnic area, a playground, beach, boat launch and hiking trails.

Logging and agriculture are mainstays of the local economy. Jacklin Seed Co., one of the world's leading marketers of bluegrass seed, is also located here. I-90 travelers may see grass fields being burned off; this helps control insects and return minerals to the soil.   ♿⛵⚓ EXIT 5

Mile 307 (174): Exit to Seltice Way and **junction** with Idaho Highway 41 to Rathdrum and Spirit Lake. Food, gas and lodging.   EXIT 7

Mile 308 (173): Visitor center and rest area with handicap-accessible restrooms and pay phone.   ♿ MP 8

Mile 311 (170): Exit to Northwest Boulevard, Coeur d'Alene city center. Access to motels, RV park, North Idaho College and Kootenai Memorial Hospital. **COEUR d'ALENE** (pop. 24,561) was originally the site of a fort on the old Mullan Road. General William Sherman chose the north shore of the lake for a military post in 1877, the year of the Nez Perce War. Gold, silver and lead discoveries encouraged miners to arrive in 1883–85. The town was incorporated in 1887 and steamers began plying the lake. Excursions along the lake became a favorite activity for many of the Idaho and Washington residents.

Summer cruises on Lake Coeur d'Alene are still popular for residents and visitors. Cruises depart daily from Coeur d'Alene Resort on the waterfront in downtown.

The name Coeur d'Alene translates to mean "heart of the awl." The term was originally applied by French traders to the Indians of the area who, upon refusing to exchange their expensive pelts for the Frenchmen's trinkets, were seen as hard hearted or, in the Frenchmen's vernacular, sharp as an awl.

Coeur d'Alene is a major recreation destination for the Inland Empire. All facilities are available. Attractions include the North Idaho Museum at 15 Northwest Blvd., which features exhibits on mining, logging and the pioneer life of Kootenai County. The city park at Independence Point, on the lake next to the museum, provides a good view of the lake and has picnic tables. The visitor information center is located on the corner of 2nd and Sherman Avenue near the waterfront.

North Idaho College, which was founded as a private school in the early 1930s, occupies the site of old Fort Sherman, the military post built here in the late 1800s. ⊼▲ EXIT 11

Mile 312 (169): Junction with U.S. Highway 95 north to Sandpoint, Moscow and Canadian border; access to hospital and airport. Major-chain motel, fast-food outlet and gas station at exit. U.S. Highway 95 travelers turn to **Mile 546** in the U.S. HIGHWAY 95 section for log of that route. EXIT 12

Mile 313 (168): Exit to 4th Street in Coeur d'Alene. Access to 24-hour restaurant and gas stations at exit. EXIT 13

Mile 314 (167): Exit to 15th Street in Coeur d'Alene. EXIT 14

Mile 315 (166): Exit to Sherman Avenue. Gas station.

Just east of this exit, travelers get a good view of Lake Coeur d'Alene as the highway hugs the northeastern shore. The lake has more than 100 miles of shoreline and is one of the most popular resort areas in Idaho and eastern Washington for water recreation. Voted one of the 10 most beautiful lakes in the world, it is 25 miles long and has an average depth of 90 to 120 feet. EXIT 15

Mile 316 (165): Silver Beach, moorage. Gravel turnouts overlooking lake.
CAUTION: High head-on collision rate this stretch of road. *Drive carefully!* MP 16

Mile 317.5 (163.5): Bennett Bay and Mullan Trail Road. Restaurant north side of interstate.

Mile 322 (159): Exit to Idaho Highway 97 south to Harrison and St. Maries. Highway 97 is a scenic drive along the east shore of Lake Coeur d'Alene. Access to Wolf Lodge area, private campground and to Beauty Creek Forest Service campground (2.5 miles south and 1 mile east). ▲ MP 22 EXIT 22

Mile 323 (158): Entering scenic Cedar Canyon for 4 miles eastbound. *CAUTION:* Watch for black ice and snow in winter. Chain-up area eastbound. Winding road and 5 percent upgrade eastbound to Fourth of July Summit. MP 23

Mile 324.5 (156.5): Entering Idaho Panhandle National Forest eastbound.

Mile 328 (153): Fourth of July Summit (elev. 3,070 feet). Fourth of July Pass Recreation Area; snowmobiling north side of highway, cross-country skiing south of highway, in winter.

Mullan Tree Historical Site and Mullan Statue. Capt. John Mullan, the builder of the Mullan Military Road from Fort Walla Walla, WA, to Fort Benton, MT, camped near the Mullan Tree on July 4, 1861, while rerouting a 30-mile stretch of the military road along the north shore of Coeur d'Alene (approximately following the current route of Interstate 90). He and his men stopped here to rest and celebrate, marking the occasion by blazing the inscription "M.R. July 4, 1861" on the tree. Though badly weathered, the "y 4" of the inscription is still discernible. The tree was damaged by a windstorm in 1962, and all that remains is the base of the tree. EXIT 28

Field daisies are a common spring bloom in northern Idaho woods. (L. Linkhart)

Mile 328.5 (152.5): Turnout eastbound (elev. 3,069 feet). *CAUTION:* Watch for black ice in winter. Winding road and 5 percent downgrade eastbound through Fourth of July Canyon.

Mile 332 (149): Weigh station (abandoned) north side of highway. The poplar trees along this stretch of highway provide a wonderful display in fall. End downgrade and winding road eastbound. *CAUTION:* Westbound travelers watch for black ice in winter. Chain-up area westbound. Winding road and 5 percent upgrade westbound to Fourth of July Summit. MP 32

Mile 334 (147): Exit to Rose Lake, St. Maries and **junction** with Idaho Highway 3. Gas station with diesel. Highway 3 is part of the 83-mile-long White Pine Scenic Route from Rose Lake to Potlatch, which passes through one of the largest stands of white pine timber in America. MP 34 EXIT 34

Mile 339 (142): Exit to Cataldo Mission, the oldest standing building in Idaho. Built between 1848 and 1853, it is the centerpiece of the Old Mission State Park, which includes the church and surrounding grounds. A 0.5-mile trail walk, which takes about 25 minutes, leads past historical sites on the mission grounds. Picnic grounds and information center (handicap-accessible facilities). ♿⊼ EXIT 39

Mile 340 (141): Crossing the Coeur d'Alene River. Exit to community of **CATALDO** (pop. 100); food and gas. EXIT 40

Mile 343 (138): Exit to **KINGSTON**. Access to the old mining town of Prichard via gravel road north. (It is also accessible from Wallace, farther east.) EXIT 43

Mile 345 (136): Exit to **PINEHURST** (pop. 1,722); gas station and private campground. This community marks the western end of the Coeur d'Alene Mining District's Silver Valley. The hills in this valley, once completely denuded of vegetation by pollution from the smelters, are showing signs of recovery. ▲ EXIT 45

Mile 348 (133): Exit to **SMELTERVILLE** (pop. 464) and Shoshone County airport. Visible on either side of the interstate are old mine tailings. Before modern environmental regulations were passed, the tailings (waste rock left over after the ore was mined) were dumped into the South Coeur d'Alene River. Current regulations require tailings and other mining wastes be held in impoundment areas to prevent leakage of toxic agents. EXIT 48

Mile 349 (132): Eastbound exit to Bunker Avenue, Silver Mountain Recreation Area and business route 90 through Kellogg. To the south are the 715- and 610-foot chimneys of the Bunker Hill Co. The lead smelter, with the taller chimney, operated from 1917 to 1981. The zinc smelter operated from 1928 until 1981. Milo Gulch extends up through the mountainside behind the plant. The tourist information center building, shaped like a miner's hat, is located just off the exit; restrooms and phone.

South of this exit is Silver Mountain Ski and Summer Resort. From Silver Mountain's base village, 1/4 mile off the interstate, to the Mountain Haus upper terminal, Silver Mountain's gondola is the longest single stage gondola ride in the world. The 8-person carriages travel 3,400 vertical feet in 3.1 miles (a 19-minute ride). ⛷ EXIT 49

Mile 350 (131): Exit to **KELLOGG** (pop. 2,591); food, gas and lodging available. A former mining town, Kellogg has been transformed into a Bavarian theme village.

Kellogg was originally known as Jackass. It was Noah Kellogg's jackass, according to popular legend, that discovered the Bunker Hill Mine in Milo Gulch in 1885. Historians dispute the story of Noah and his pack animal, but the mine was discovered nonetheless, and it proved to be one of the greatest lead, silver and zinc deposits ever located. The mine operated from 1885 until 1981, producing more than 35 million tons of ore, with about 130 miles of tunnels and shafts reaching almost a mile below the earth's surface.

When the mine and smelter shut down in 1981, some 2,000 men were thrown out of work. The mine was subsequently sold. The new owners continue to pump thousands of gallons of water a minute from the mine to keep the shafts from flooding, in anticipation of the mine opening again with a rise in metal prices. The Shoshone County Mining and Smelting Museum chronicles the history of Bunker Hill and other mines in the region. EXIT 50

Mile 351 (130): Westbound exit to business route 90 through Kellogg; Division Street. Access to Wardner and Silverhorn Ski Area.

Wardner, an old mining town founded in 1885, is a short distance south of Kellogg. It was named for James F. Wardner, an early-day miner and one of the promoters of the Bunker Hill and Sullivan Mine. EXIT 51

Mile 354 (127): Exit to Big Creek Historical Site. Just off the exit ramp is a memorial erected in honor of the 91 men who died in the 1972 Sunshine Mine disaster. The tragedy was the worst hardrock mine accident in the United States since 1917. EXIT 54

Mile 357 (124): Exit to business route 90 and **OSBURN** (pop. 1,579), an unincorporated community and home of the valley's only radio station, KWAL-AM 620. Gas station and private campground off exit. ▲ EXIT 57

Mile 360 (121): Exit to **SILVERTON** (pop. 800). Hospital north off exit. The U.S. Forest Service Wallace Ranger District Office, located next to the hospital, has detailed information on recreation in the region. EXIT 60

Mile 361 (120): Exit to **WALLACE** (pop. 1,010), which has all facilities, including major-chain motel, restaurants and gas station with diesel. Prior to completion of the freeway bypass here in 1991, Interstate 90 travelers slowed down as the highway wound through downtown Wallace. A stoplight halted the flow of interstate traffic so that people could get from one side of town to the other. It was the only stoplight on the coast-to-coast I-90, which connects Seattle and Boston. The new section of freeway on the edge of town was dedicated on Sept. 12, 1991, and the last stoplight was removed on Sept. 14, 1991. The community held The Last Stoplight Celebration to commemorate the event.

Wallace was founded by Col. W.R. Wallace, a cousin of Lew Wallace, author of the epic book *Ben Hur*. The city grew up at a strategic trading place where 5 canyons meet, and became an important supply center for the mining industry. The city was incorporated in 1888, and in the 1890s Wallace was the third largest city in Idaho. During the great forest fire of 1910, 1/3 of the buildings of Wallace, on the eastern edge of the city, were destroyed.

Despite the losses suffered in the fire, Wallace has numerous historic buildings, and it is well worth the time to take the 45-minute, self-guided walking tour of the city. The walking tour brochure is available from the Wallace District Mining Museum. Because of its large number of important historical structures, where whole blocks remain intact, the town is listed as a historic site on the National Register of Historic Places. Among the attractions are buildings such as the former Northern Pacific depot, which was built in 1901 out of brick imported from China, with its distinctive cupola.

The Sierra Silver Mine Tour will give you a good idea of a silver miner's life underground. A trolley takes visitors a mile out of town to the Sierra Silver Mine, where, after being equipped with hard hats, they are conducted by an experienced miner through the mine's 1,000-foot tunnel and can see how it operates. The tour departs every 30 minutes during the summer from May to mid-Oct.; $6.50 for adults, and $5.50 for children 4–15 years and senior citizens. There is also a family rate of $25 for 2 adults and 2 children. The tour ticket office is located at 420 5th St.; phone (208) 752-5151.

On Nine Mile Canyon Road, just past the handsome old Northern Pacific depot, is the Miners' Cemetery, with the graves of many of the men who died in the mines.

Another attraction in the Wallace area is the old mining town of Burke, which is 6 miles up Idaho Highway 4 along Canyon

Creek. Burke was once featured in *Ripley's Believe It or Not*, because the town was in such a narrow valley that the main street, railroad tracks and a creek all occupied the same space. ★ EXIT 61

Mile 362 (119): Exit to Idaho Highway 4 to Wallace and Burke. EXIT 62

Mile 364 (117): Exit to Golconda District, the site of another formerly rich mine, the Golconda Mine, which produced 300,000 tons of silver, lead and zinc ore from the late 1920s to 1950. The Golconda Mill was torn down in 1980. EXIT 64

Mile 365 (116): Exit to the Compressor District. The name for this district came about when the Morning Mine installed a large air compressor plant at the mouth of Grouse Creek in 1900, with 3 large waterwheels turning out 1,000 horsepower. EXIT 65

Mile 366 (115): Exit to Gold Creek. EXIT 66

Mile 367 (114): Exit to the Morning District. The Morning Mine, near Mullan, was the second-greatest all-time producing mine in the Silver Valley. Since its discovery in 1884, it has yielded more than 18 million tons of lead, zinc and silver ore. Mining on the property ended in 1982. EXIT 67

Mile 368 (113): Exit to **MULLAN** (pop. 821); all services available. This old industrial mining town has numerous historical buildings. It was named for Capt. John Mullan, who built the famous Mullan Road from Fort Walla Walla, WA, to Fort Benton, MT, in the 1850s. An active mine in Mullan is the Lucky Friday Unit of the Hecla Mining Co. The mine was first located around the turn of the century and continues to produce silver, lead and zinc concentrates. EXIT 68

Mile 369 (112): Exit to east Mullan. Good view of headframe and mine, north side of highway.
CAUTION: Highway begins 6-mile climb with 6 percent grade eastbound to Lookout Pass. Chain-up area in winter. EXIT 69

Mile 372 (109): Lead Silver Mines Historical Marker. Discovered in 1884, these mines supplied more than $5 billion in lead and silver.

Mile 372.5 (108.5): Westbound turnout. Beautiful view westbound of valley below to the north. The interstate is climbing the Bitterroot Mountains eastbound.

Mile 374 (107): Exit to Lookout Pass (elev. 4,725 feet), Idaho–Montana state line. No services available. This is a winter ski area with a chair, rope tow, day lodge, cafeteria and rentals; phone (208) 752-1221. Entering Lolo National Forest eastbound.
Eastbound travelers are entering Mountain time zone and should turn watches ahead 1 hour. Westbound travelers are entering Pacific time zone and should turn watches back 1 hour.
CAUTION: No center concrete divider makes winter driving hazardous on next stretch of downhill road eastbound. Truckers use low gear westbound; 6 percent downgrade next 5 miles. ✦ EXIT 0

Mile 378 (103): Rest area and chain-removal area for eastbound traffic. MP 4

Mile 379.5 (101.5): Exit to Taft area, chain-up area for westbound traffic. Named for President William Howard Taft, Taft began as a construction camp on the Milwaukee Railroad during construction of the 8,750-foot tunnel through the mountains. When the tunnel was completed in 1909, the community disappeared.
St. Regis River to the south. Interstate 90 follows the St. Regis River east to the Clark Fork River. EXIT 5

Mile 384.5 (96.5): Exit to **SALTESE**; all services available. Gas station at exit. Saltese is an old mining town on the St. Regis River, and was named for Chief Saltese of the Nez Perce Indians. The St. Regis River was named by Father DeSmet in 1842 in honor of St. Regis de Borgia. EXIT 10

Mile 389 (92): Weigh station.

Mile 390 (91): Exit to **HAUGAN**; phone, food, gas and silver gift shop. The town was established as a "pusher station" for trains ascending the mountain grade. It was named for H.G. Haugan, an official with the Milwaukee Railroad. EXIT 16

Mile 393 (88): Exit to **DeBORGIA**; gas, grocery and restaurant. DeBorgia was a station on the Northern Pacific Railroad.
MP 19 EXIT 18

Mile 397.5 (83.5): Exit to Henderson, a logging town in the early 1900s. Fishing access to the St. Regis River. Access to Cabin City Forest Service Campground, 2 miles northeast via Mullen Pass Road then north on Twelvemile Road. ✦▲ EXIT 22

Mile 401 (80): Exit to Drexel; no services. EXIT 25

Mile 401.5 (79.5): Eastbound exit to Ward Creek Road; no services. EXIT 26

Mile 405.5 (75.5): Exit to Two Mile Road; no services. Fishing access to the St. Regis River. More of a stream than a river, the St. Regis is easily waded and fished from shore. It is heavily fished in the easy-access areas, but still produces fair action for cutthroat and brookies up to 14 inches. ✦ MP 30 EXIT 30

Mile 409 (72): Exit to **ST. REGIS**; major-chain motel, gas stations and food at exit. **Junction** with Montana Highway 135 to Paradise. St. Regis is a well-known shipping center for the logging and wood products industry, and is a popular truck stop. It is located at the confluence of the Clark Fork and St. Regis rivers. EXIT 33

Mile 409.5 (71.5): Crossing the Clark Fork River. The highway crosses the Clark Fork several times from here to east of Missoula. The Clark Fork is a major fishing and recreational river, as well as one of the major drainages in western Montana. It flows west to the Columbia River. Rainbow are the dominant species for fishermen. Because of its wide breadth and meandering flow, it is a favorite for float fishing from inflatables, canoes or drift boats. ✦ MP 34

Mile 412.5 (68.5): Exit to Sloway area; no services. Access to Sloway Forest Service Campground; 19 sites, fishing. ✦▲ EXIT 37

Mile 419 (62): Exit to Dry Creek Road; no services. Access to Sloway Forest Service Campground. ▲ EXIT 43

Mile 423 (58): Exit to Highway 257 and **SUPERIOR** (pop. 1,054), all services including a motel. Gas station with diesel and minimart at exit. Superior is the county seat of Mineral County. It was named for Superior, WI, and was once the site of numerous productive mines. This is a popular hunting and fishing area.

The Clark Fork River bisects Superior, and it is well worth a drive across the bridge on River Street to appreciate the town's setting. Downtown businesses line Mullan Road on the north side of the river.

Camping at Trout Creek Forest Service Campground, 7 miles south of town in Lolo National Forest; 12 sites. Trout Creek is heavily fished for cutthroat, Dolly Varden and some whitefish. Best fishing is above the falls and in the canyon below the falls.   ◄▲ EXIT 47

Mile 424.5 (56.5): Cedar Creek.   MP 49

Mile 430.5 (50.5): Exit to Lozeau and Quartz; gas available.   EXIT 55

Mile 433 (48): Rest area with handicap-accessible facilities and access to campground in pine forest along interstate. Quartz Flat Forest Service campground has 52 sites, flush toilets, phone, picnic tables, drinking water and a nature trail. Access to Clark Fork for fishing.

NOTE: The next rest area westbound is 55 miles from here.   ♿🎍🚻◄▲

Mile 437 (44): Exit to **TARKIO**, the site of a station on the old Milwaukee Railroad; no services.   EXIT 61

Mile 442.5 (38.5): Exit to Fish Creek Road, which leads up Fish Creek Canyon. There is a small camping and fishing spot on Fish Creek 10 miles south of the interstate; excellent fishing for cutthroat and rainbow. This is also a popular camping spot during fall hunting season. Rustic lodge, restaurant and outfitter farther up Fish Creek Canyon.   ◄▲ EXIT 66

Mile 445 (36): Exit to Cyr, formerly a station on the Northern Pacific. No services available.   EXIT 70

Mile 446 (35): Scenic turnout eastbound.

Mile 447.5 (33.5): Rest areas both sides of highway. Picnic tables.   🎍 MP 72

Mile 450.5 (30.5): Exit to **ALBERTON**, an old railroad town; gas, food and camping.   ▲ MP 75 EXIT 75

Mile 452.5 (28.5): Missoula County line. Exit to Petty Creek Road and **junction** with Montana Highway 507. Petty Creek is fished for small cutthroat, brookies and white fish. Access to the Clark Fork.   ◄ EXIT 77

Mile 457.5 (23.5): Exit to Nine Mile Road. The

Tree-lined Brooks Avenue in Missoula comes alive with vibrant fall colors. (© George Wuerthner)

settlement of Nine Mile was named for George Brown's Nine Mile Roadhouse, which was located that distance from Frenchtown. The Nine Mile ranger station, 4.5 miles north of Interstate 90, was a famous "remount station," where for 32 years Forest Service mule teams set out into the backcountry to resupply men in the field.

An exposure of silt and sediment on both sides of the interstate near here was left by glacial Lake Missoula.   MP 82 EXIT 82

Mile 460.5 (20.5): Exit to **HUSON**, named for a Northern Pacific Railroad engineer. Gas, restaurant and phone.   MP 85 EXIT 85

Mile 464.5 (16.5): Exit to **FRENCHTOWN**; gas station and grocery at exit. French Canadians settled here around 1864. A gold stampede brought 3,000 prospectors in 1869. Access to Frenchtown Pond State Park.   EXIT 89

Mile 468 (13): Weigh station. Travelers may note the odor of hydrogen sulfide emitted from the Champion Paper Mill to the south. The wood products industry is a leading employer in this region.

Mile 472 (9): Junction with U.S. Highway 93 north to Flathead Lake, Kalispell and Glacier National Park. Access to Montana Highway 200. Food, major-chain motels and a 24-hour truck stop (diesel) are located at this exit.   EXIT 96

Mile 477 (4): Exit to Business 90 route (U.S. Highway 93) to Missoula and Hamilton. Gas station at exit, major-chain motels south off exit. Access to Reserve Street and U.S. Highway 93 south (also U.S. Highway 12); Montana Highway 430, Snow Bowl Ski Area; Smokejumpers Center and Johnson Bell (Missoula) Airport.

Travelers bound for U.S. Highway 93 south can bypass downtown Missoula by exiting here and going south on Reserve Street. Turn to **Mile 385.5** in the U.S. HIGHWAY 93 section for log of that route. For U.S. Highway 12 west, turn to the beginning of the U.S. HIGHWAY 12 section for log.   EXIT 101

Mile 480 (1): Exit to Orange Street. Gas station at exit. Access to hospital and major-chain motels.   EXIT 104

Mile 481 (0): Exit to Van Buren Street. Gas station south off exit. Access to major-chain motels, downtown Missoula (description follows), University of Montana and business loop.

MISSOULA (pop. 42,900), the seat of Missoula County, is a pleasant city at the confluence of 3 major rivers: the Clark Fork, Bitterroot and Blackfoot. Missoula has all facilities, including good shopping in the well-maintained downtown area, along with shopping centers on the city center arterials. Missoula is also the home of the University of Montana, a 181-acre campus serving some 11,000 students.

Greenough Park provides a beautiful 1-mile drive through a wooded area beside Rattlesnake Creek. The park, donated from the Greenough estate to the city of Missoula, features a landscaped picnic area and wading pool.

Fort Missoula Historical Museum, at the corner of South Avenue and Reserve Street, was established in 1877 as one of the first military posts in Montana. It now serves as the home for National Guard and Reserve units. Displays on the 28-acre reserve depict the industrial development of the West from 1880 to 1920. The Indoor Gallery has a schedule of changing exhibits. The complex is open from noon until 5 p.m. daily, except Monday. For more information, call (406) 728-3476.

The Memorial Rose Garden on Highway 93 was established in 1947 by the American Rose Society and maintained as a memorial to the casualties of WWII and the Vietnam War. More than 2,500 rose plants are maintained at the garden.

One of the unique facilities of Missoula is the Smokejumpers Center, located at Johnson Bell Airport, Highway 10 West. Here, smokejumpers are trained for the dangerous and difficult task of forest fire suppression. The Northern Forest Fire Laboratory is also located here. Scientists study the nature and characteristics of forest fires to better understand and help aid in the suppression of forest fires. The complex is open for visitors from May 15 through July 1, 8 a.m. to 4 p.m. weekdays; and from July 1 through the end of Sept., 9 a.m. until 5 p.m. daily.

The beautiful St. Francis Xavier Church, located at 420 W. Pine, was built in 1889, the year Montana became a state. It features a graceful steeple, stained-glass windows and mural paintings by a Jesuit brother, Joseph Carignano, a kitchen helper, unschooled in art but later recognized as a master. Carignano also painted the 58 murals and frescoes at the famous St. Ignatius Catholic Mission south of Polson.

The paintings of another muralist, Edgar Samuel Paxson, may be viewed at the Missoula County Courthouse from 8 a.m. until 5 p.m. weekdays. The artist is perhaps most famous for his painting of "Custer's Last Stand," completed in 1899. Eight murals, painted between 1912 and 1914, decorate the walls of the courthouse.   EXIT 105

U.S. HIGHWAY 93

Twin Falls, ID, to Missoula, MT
(See maps, pages 118 and 121)

From Twin Falls, ID, U.S. Highway 93 traverses the Snake River plain, passes the volcanic wasteland of central Idaho, climbs the Rocky Mountains and runs below the jagged peaks of the Bitterroot Range as it leads north into Montana.

Take along your trout rod, camera and binoculars because Highway 93 touches some fine fishing holes, big game areas and scenic mountain country. North of Twin Falls, ID, it follows the Little Wood River, a nice trout stream, then leads north along the headwaters of the famous Salmon River—legendary "River of No Return"— and through the Lost River Mountains, home to mule deer, elk and bighorn sheep. It crosses into Montana over the backbone of the beautiful Bitterroot Mountains, moving north along another trout and float fishing river, the Bitterroot.

Because of the mountainous terrain, Highway 93 can often be hazardous to travel in the winter. Be sure to carry snow tires and/or tire chains. It's also wise to carry a few blankets during the cold season in the event you become stranded by snow and have to spend some time in your vehicle before help arrives.

Even during the balmy nights of summer, the weather can be a bit brisk at the higher elevations. Prepare for the trip accordingly and plan to take your time as you travel along one of the most scenic routes in the Northwest.

U.S. Highway 93 Log

Distance from Twin Falls, ID, is followed by distance from Missoula, MT.

Mile 0 (390): TWIN FALLS (pop. 26,209) offers all traveler services. It is the hub of the Magic Valley, one of the most productive agricultural areas in Idaho. Since 1905, the waters of the Snake River have been used to irrigate the arid desert of southcentral Idaho, and wildlife and recreational opportunities abound on the lakes and reservoirs around Twin Falls. It is a land of curious rock formations and lava flows, rich in history.

Among the attractions of the Twin Falls area are Shoshone Falls, Balanced Rock, the City of Rocks and the Snake River canyon.

For additional information on the Twin Falls area refer to **Mile 551** in the INTER-STATE 84 highway log.

Junction with U.S. Highway 30 west to Buhl, ID, and Wells, NV. Regional Medical Center located south of U.S. Highway 93.

Mile 3 (387): Turnoff to Shoshone Falls,

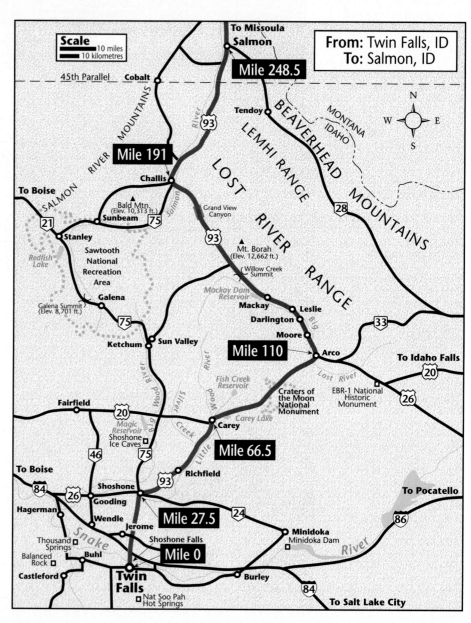

52 feet higher than the famous Niagara Falls. It is best to see the falls in spring, when the Snake River waters are high.

Mile 4.5 (385.5): Scenic overlook of the Snake River canyon and historical site. This is the Perrine Memorial Bridge, 1,500 feet long and 480 feet above the Snake River. It is the longest span bridge in America.

At the north end of the bridge is a road that leads east to the site of stunt man Evel

Knievel's ill-fated attempt to jump the Snake River canyon on a jet-powered motorcycle in the fall of 1974.   MP 50

Mile 6.5 (383.5): Historical marker about the Emigrant Road.

Mile 7.5 (382.5): Junction with Interstate 84 west to Boise and east to Ogden and Pocatello, via Interstate 86. Travelers intending to travel Interstate 84 turn to **Mile 551**

in the INTERSTATE 84 section for the log of that route.   MP 53

Mile 12.5 (377.5): Junction with Idaho Highway 25 to **JEROME** (pop. 6,891). All services available.

Mile 24.5 (365.5): Notch Butte fire lookout.

Mile 27.5 (362.5): SHOSHONE (pop. 1,242), the seat of Lincoln County, is named after the Shoshone (sometimes spelled Shoshoni) Indians. The word means "Great Spirit." All services are available.

Junction with Idaho Highways 75 and 24. Six miles north on Highway 75 is Mammoth Cave, a cooled lava cave that stretches 1 mile deep into the desert floor. North of Mammoth Cave is another cave known as Shoshone Indian Ice Cave. The condensation of moisture and wind draft creates a natural refrigerator in an arid lava desert. Tours available May–Sept.

Idaho Highway 75 also leads to the world-famous ski resort community of Sun Valley. See the log of Highway 75 in the SAW-TOOTH VALLEY SCENIC ROUTE section.

U.S. Highway 93 shares a common alignment with U.S. Highway 26 north to Arco.

Mile 37 (353): Turnoff to **DIETRICH** (est. pop. 100), a small agricultural community with limited services, 6 miles east.

Mile 39.5 (350.5): Little Wood River, a nice trout stream.   ◄

Mile 43.5 (346.5): RICHFIELD (pop. 290), a small agricultural community. Its heyday was in the 1930s when settlers filed on some 40,000 acres of farmland. Food, gas available.   MP 182

Mile 51.5 (338.5): Pagari Bridge turn-off.
MP 190

Mile 54.5 (335.5): Taylor Bear Tracts, Williams public-use area.

Mile 56.5 (333.5): Turnoff to Preacher Bridge.

Mile 59.5 (330.5): Silver Creek Road. The highway crosses Silver Creek, one of the top trout-producing streams in Idaho. Silver Creek is a broad spring creek nationally renowned for its fly-fishing. Special restrictions apply, including catch-and-release sections, and current Idaho Fish and Game fishing regulations should be consulted.   ◄

Mile 62 (328): Littlewood River.   MP 200

Mile 65.5 (324.5): Junction with U.S. Highway 20 to Magic Reservoir, Sun Valley, Fairfield and Mountain Home. Magic Reservoir is one of the most productive rainbow fishing lakes in the state.   ◄

Mile 66 (324): Turnoff to Little Wood Reservoir (11 miles).

Mile 66.5 (323.5): CAREY, a small crossroads community. Food, gas. Carey Lakes Wildlife Management Area to east of highway.   ◄

Mile 71.5 (318.5): Turnoff to Carey on the Kimama Desert Road.

Mile 73.5 (316.5): Turnoff to Fish Creek Reservoir.

Mile 80 (310): Historical marker about Goodale's Cutoff.

Mile 89 (301): Border of the Craters of the Moon National Monument. The volcanic activity in this area gives a moonlike appearance to the ground.

Mile 90 (300): Scenic overlook of the Craters of the Moon National Monument landscape.
MP 228

Park rangers lead tours of Craters of the Moon National Monument. (L. Linkhart)

Mile 90.5 (299.5): Scenic overlook.

Mile 91 (299): Headquarters and entrance to the Craters of the Moon National Monument. The 83-square-mile park was established in 1924 and until that time had been avoided by early settlers. The rough, jagged lava outcroppings were nearly impossible to traverse, totally unsuitable for farming or ranching and lacking mineral wealth. Water was available only in very limited quantities and, as a whole, the area offered little to the settlers.

Visitors to Craters of the Moon often look in vain for a solitary volcano that could be responsible for the desolate terrain, but no single peak erupted here. Rather, the earth split open along an area called the Great Rift, spewing magma, ash and cinders over an area that covered hundreds of square miles. The volcanic activity began about 15,000 years ago and ended just 2,000 years ago. Scientists predict that the area will be subject to volcanic activity sometime again in the future.

A 50-site campground is located near the monument headquarters.

For further information on Craters of the Moon National Monument, see the MAJOR ATTRACTIONS section.   ▲★

Mile 91.5 (298.5): Scenic overlook. An easy 0.2-mile walk out to the point provides a much better view.

Mile 92.5 (297.5): Northern border of the Craters of the Moon National Monument.

Mile 107.5 (282.5): Airport. No services.

Mile 108.5 (281.5): Big Lost River. This river flows along the surface, then disappears among the volcanic crevices at Big Lost River

Sink east of Howe. The river is believed to reappear at the Snake River canyon near Hagerman in what is called Thousand Springs. The Big Lost is a favorite with trout fishermen during the summer. Good access.

Mile 109 (281): Atoms for Peace Historical Site describes the first peaceful use of atomic energy. On July 17, 1955, during an experimental project by the Atomic Energy Commission, Arco became the first town in the free world to be served by electrical energy developed from the atom. The energy was produced at the National Reactor Testing Station, now the Idaho National Engineering Laboratory (INEL), 23 miles east of Arco (see next milepost).

Above—*View of the Lost River Range above Big Lost River. The range includes Borah Peak, elev. 12,662 feet, the highest point in Idaho.* (L. Linkhart) **Right**—*Rafting the Salmon River.* (Lee Foster)

Mile 110 (280): Junction with U.S. Highways 20/26. ARCO (pop. 1,016) is a small agricultural community named (depending on who is telling the story) after a town in Austria; a Count Arco who was visiting in Washington, D.C., at the time; or an early resident, Arco Smith. It is the seat of Butte County, and all services are available including 2 restaurants, 2 fast-food outlets and 2 private campgrounds.

Access to the Idaho National Engineering Laboratory, 23 miles southeast via Highways 20/26. Located at INEL is the Experimental Breeder Reactor No. 1. The first atomic reactor to produce usable amounts of electricity, EBR-1 opened in December of 1951. It is now a national historic landmark. Tours of EBR-1 are available 7 days a week, 8 a.m. to 4 p.m., from Memorial Day weekend through Labor Day weekend. Guided and self-guided tours, movies and demonstrations. Fifty-two nuclear reactors have been built at INEL; 12 reactors are still operational. ▲

Mile 116.5 (273.5): Big Lost River.

Mile 117.5 (272.5): MOORE (pop. 210). Gas and food available.

Mile 121 (269): Turnoff to Antelope Road.

Mile 121.5 (268.5): Challis National Forest access.

Mile 123.5 (266.5): DARLINGTON, a small agricultural community. Food, gas available.

Mile 126 (264): Big Lost River. In springtime, flooding often occurs, so travelers may need to watch for detours in case of road washouts.

Mile 128.5 (261.5): Leslie, unincorporated village. No services available.

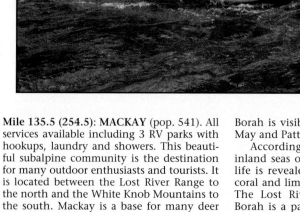

Mile 135.5 (254.5): MACKAY (pop. 541). All services available including 3 RV parks with hookups, laundry and showers. This beautiful subalpine community is the destination for many outdoor enthusiasts and tourists. It is located between the Lost River Range to the north and the White Knob Mountains to the south. Mackay is a base for many deer and elk hunters in the fall heading into the Lost River Mountains, and the Sawtooth National Recreation Area at the headwaters of the Salmon River. ▲ MP 109

Mile 140.5 (249.5): Turnoff to Mackay Dam.

Mile 141 (249): Turnoff to Mackay Dam Reservoir and campground. Pit toilets, covered picnic tables, boat launch. Good summer fishing. ⩪⛵⚓

Mile 142.5 (247.5): Turnoff to Mackay Reservoir and Battle Ground cemetery.

Mile 143 (247): Upper Cedar Creek Road. Sportsman access to Mackay Reservoir.
MP 115

Mile 146 (244): Historical marker describes the discovery of the Lost River. Called Goddin's River after the fur trapper who explored the river in 1819–20, the Lost River was renamed by settlers because it sinks into the lava rocks of the desert area west of Idaho Falls. Also turnoff to Mackay Fish Hatchery 5 miles west.

Mile 147.5 (242.5): Lone Cedar Road.

Mile 150 (240): Trail Creek Road.

Mile 156.5 (233.5): Turnoff to Mount Borah (elev. 12,662 feet), the highest mountain peak in Idaho. The peak was named in honor of Idaho's popular Republican Sen. William Borah, "Lion of Idaho," who served as senator from 1907 until his death in 1940.

Mile 158.5 (231.5): Interpretive signs describe earthquake fault and Mount Borah. **Junction** of a paved/gravel road west to Stanley, the Sawtooth National Recreation Area and Sun Valley; Mount Borah is visible to the east. Turnoff east to May and Patterson.

According to geologists, as many as 12 inland seas once covered this area. The sea life is revealed in a layer of bones, shells, coral and limestone thousands of feet thick. The Lost River Range, of which Mount Borah is a part, is the result of an upward thrust in the earth's crust, exposing the sea floor and the fossils within it.

Mile 163.5 (226.5): Sage Creek turnoff.

Mile 166.5 (223.5): Willow Creek Summit (elev. 7,161 feet).

Mile 169 (221): Turnoffs to Sheep Creek and Broken Wagon Creek.

Mile 171.5 (218.5): Turnoff on Spar Canyon Road to the East Fork Salmon River, a small, high-country cutthroat stream spilling from the Sawtooth National Recreation Area.

Mile 176 (214): Highway 93 passes through a small but beautiful gorge called Grand View Canyon.

Mile 186 (204): Turnoff to Challis Hot Springs private campground on the Salmon River; open April to Oct.; 24 sites, swimming pool, hookups, showers, dump station.
▲ MP 159

Mile 187 (203): Salmon River.   MP 160

Mile 187.5 (202.5): Junction with Highway 75 to Stanley, the Sawtooth National Recreation Area, the Sawtooth Wilderness Area and Sun Valley. See the SAWTOOTH VALLEY SCENIC ROUTE section.

Mile 191 (199): Turnoff to **CHALLIS** (pop. 1,290) city center. All services available. Challis was a trading center for the mining communities of the Stanley Basin and Salmon River, but as the mines petered out, ranching became the major economic base for Challis.

In the mid-1960s, Challis experienced another boom with the discovery of the mineral molybdenum (an alloy in the manufacturing of steel) southwest of the city. Cyprus Mines Corp. operates the mine and is the major employer in the area.

Challis is a major hunting, fishing and river rafting center for the Salmon River headwaters, Idaho Primitive Area and Lost River Range. The primitive road to Sunbeam from Challis, around 10,313-foot Bald Mountain, makes a scenic summer side trip that is likely to be interrupted with big game and scenery viewing stops. The Stanley/Challis area is tailored for the outdoorsman, who should allow plenty of time for stream and lake fishing, day hikes and big game photography. Check locally for current conditions.

Mile 194.5 (195.5): Challis Creek.

Mile 198 (192): Morgan Road, turnoff to Cobalt, Blackbird and Leesburg on a gravel road. All 3 were mining communities and none offer services to today's visitor. Cobalt and Blackbird were producers of the mineral cobalt, used as a high-temperature alloy for steel. Leesburg, established in 1866, was a gold-mining camp that hosted as many as 7,000 miners. By the time the gold rush ended in 1870, Leesburg and two other towns, Smithville and Summit City, had produced an estimated $16 million in gold.

Mile 205.5 (184.5): Cottonwood recreation area. Picnic tables, restrooms.   ⊼

Mile 207.5 (182.5): Community of Ellis, no services available. Ellis is located at the mouth of the Pahsimeroi River where it joins the Salmon River. This is also a turnoff to May and Patterson.

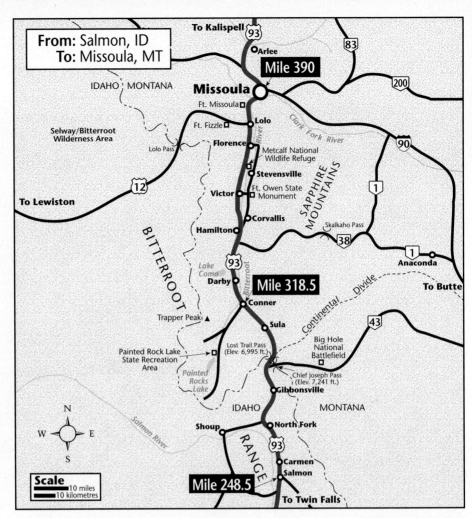

From: Salmon, ID
To: Missoula, MT

Mile 209 (181): Hat Creek Road sportsman's access.

Mile 217.5 (172.5): McKim Creek Road.

Mile 225 (165): Iron Creek Road and Cabin Creek Road.

Mile 226 (164): Community of Elk Bend. You are now in the Salmon River gorge. Food, gas, restaurant, motel, 3 private RV parks with hookups. The Lemhi Mountain Range is visible on the east and the Salmon River Mountain Range is on the west.

The Salmon River was first explored by the Lewis and Clark expedition in 1805. The Shoshoni Indians, who were recruited to help the explorers, referred to the stream as "The River of No Return," and warned the explorers that the river was not navigable. Only after attempting to travel downstream did the explorers decide the Indians were right.

Today the Salmon River offers some of the best whitewater rafting in the nation, with world-class rapids attracting thousands of boaters each year. Contact the Salmon Chamber of Commerce (phone 208/756-2100) for a list of outfitters for day trips and extended trips on the Middle Fork and main Salmon River. The river offers some of the best salmon and steelhead fishing in Idaho. The early Indians called the river Tom-Agip-Paw, "Big Fish Waters."

The Salmon River valley, including the Middle Fork, comprises one of the most cele-brated sportsmen's destinations in the Northwest, and the largest and most remote roadless wildernesses in the Lower 48, the Frank Church River of No Return Wilderness Area.

Mile 230.5 (159.5): Turnoff to Rattlesnake Creek.   MP 286

Mile 235.5 (154.5): Crossing the 45th parallel, halfway between the Equator and the North Pole.

Mile 243.5 (146.5): Turnoff to Williams Lake, Cobalt and the Shoup Bridge Recreation Site. Williams Lake (elev. 4,500 feet) is 15 miles from the town of Salmon and is open from May to Oct. Food, lodging and boat rentals available. Campground with picnic tables, drinking water and a boat launch. Shoup Bridge Recreation Site has picnic tables, toilets, fishing, and shade.

Mile 245.5 (144.5): Turnoff to Salmon Hot Springs, 3 miles.

Mile 248 (142): Junction with Idaho Highway 28 to Leadore and Idaho Falls through the scenic Lemhi Valley.

Mile 248.5 (141.5): SALMON (pop. 3,308), the headquarters for many guides and outfitters and the recreational hub for the River of No Return area. All visitor services are available in Salmon, including a private RV park and several large motels. Salmon is a year-

Idaho guest ranches in the Salmon River valley offer horseback riding in the remote and roadless River of No Return wilderness. (Lee Foster)

round recreation town offering hunting and fishing, whitewater rafting, mountain climbing, snowmobiling and skiing. Steelhead fishing is very good in this area and incredibly popular. Local sporting goods stores provide solid information. Salmon thrives on its tourism industry, but ranching, logging and mining also have a significant impact on the community.

The Lemhi County Museum in Salmon has an extensive collection of Indian and early settler items. Some belonged to Chief Tendoy of the Lemhi Indians and others to Sacajawea's family. Tourist information is available at both ends of the business district. ◄

Mile 253.5 (136.5): Highway crosses the Salmon River. Lemhi County Fair and Rodeo Grounds.   MP 309

Mile 254.5 (135.5): Unincorporated community of **CARMEN** has limited services. High-

way crosses Carmen Creek. A historical marker here describes Fort Bonneville. On Sept. 26, 1832, Capt. B.L.E. Bonneville established a winter fur-trading post in a grove of cottonwoods across the river. Flathead and Nez Perce Indians regularly camped near the fort.

Mile 260 (130): Recreation area, picnic tables, toilets, fishing.

Mile 260.5 (129.5): Highway crosses Tower Creek.

Mile 264 (126): Sportsman's access.

Mile 266 (124): Turnoff to Fourth of July Creek.

Mile 269 (121): Entering Salmon National Forest.

Mile 269.5 (120.5): Wagonhammer Springs day-use area (elev. 3,700 feet) on the banks

of the Salmon River is open from March to Nov. Picnic sites, drinking water, restrooms and fishing.

Mile 271.5 (118.5): Crossing the North Fork Salmon River. U.S. Forest Service information station and entering the unincorporated village of **NORTH FORK**. All services available, including campground, lodging and restaurants. Lewis and Clark historical marker recalls the expedition's attempt to float the churning Salmon River in 1805. ▲

Mile 272 (118): North Fork Salmon River.

Mile 275.5 (114.5): Box Springs Loop Road and turnoff to Indian Peak (elev. 7,763 feet) and Cummins Lake.

Mile 277 (113): Turnoff to Hughes Creek.

Mile 277.5 (112.5): Hughes Creek Field Station for the Salmon National Forest.

Mile 279 (111): Turnoff to Sheep Creek toward Stein Mountain (elev. 8,555 feet). Nearly all of these small creeks offer fair to excellent fishing for native trout.

Mile 281.5 (108.5): Turnoff to Granite Mountain (elev. 6,354 feet).

Mile 282 (108): Crossing Dahlonga Creek and entering the village of **GIBBONSVILLE**, an old gold-mining camp established in 1877 and named after Col. John Gibbon, the man who led the ill-fated attack on Chief Joseph's band of Nez Perce Indians on the Big Hole River in Montana during the Nez Perce War.

Gibbonsville is now an unincorporated village with phone, gas, groceries and campground available.   ▲ MP 337

Mile 288 (102): North Fork Salmon River and turnoff to Twin Creek Campground (elev. 5,100 feet); open June to Oct.; 40 sites, picnic areas, drinking water, toilets with disabled access, fishing and hunting access, camping fee. The campground is located on the historic Lewis and Clark Trail and is open from June to Oct.

Mile 290.5 (99.5): Lewis and Clark historical marker.

Mile 295.5 (94.5): Crossing the Idaho–Montana border and passing through Lost Trail Pass (elev. 6,995 feet) and the turnoff to the Lost Trail Ski Area. This is the **junction** with Montana Highway 43 east to the Big Hole National Battlefield, an impressive national monument that recalls that portion of the Nez Perce War. The Big Hole National Battlefield is approximately 15 miles east, and it is one of the best roadside attractions of its kind in the Northwest. If you're not pressed for time, make a point to visit it. On the way there, you will cross Chief Joseph Pass (elev. 7,241 feet).

You are now at the southern end of the Bitterroot Valley, passing between the Bitterroot Mountains to the west, the Beaverhead Mountains to the southeast and the Anaconda Range to the northeast.

The name Bitterroot refers to a plant that, as one might suspect, has a bitter-tasting root. The Flathead Indians (also called Salish Indians) had discovered that the plant grew in abundance along the Bitterroot River and called the stream Spet-Im-Seulko, or "the water of the bitter-root." Lewis and Clark also encountered the plants and gave the name Bitterroot to the mountain range, valley and river.   ★ MP 351

Mile 297.5 (92.5): The skeleton trees on the west side of the highway are the victim of the mountain pine beetle. The beetles killed approximately 57 million trees on more than 1.3 million acres in the Big Hole Valley and surrounding area between 1926–38. To avoid infestations now, the Forest Service acts promptly when the insects are discovered and all over-mature trees are harvested as quickly as possible.   MP 1

Mile 302.5 (87.5): Turnoff to Indian Trees Campground, 1 mile southeast of the highway; 17 camp units; camping fee; open May to Sept.; historic Indian trees; fishing, hiking, water, toilets, garbage facilities. Walking distance to commercial hot springs. Accessible to larger RVs.   ⛺🍴◄▲

Mile 306.5 (83.5): Sula Creek ranger station, Bitterroot National Forest. **Junction** with Reimel Creek Road.
                                   MP 11

Mile 308.5 (81.5): Ross Hole Historic Site and Recreation Area. On March 12, 1824, Alexander Ross of the Hudson's Bay Co. brought 55 Indian and white trappers, 89 women and children, and 392 horses to camp near this spot en route from the Spokane House to the Snake River country. The group camped nearly a month here while attempting to break through the deep snow to the Big Hole, and because of their hardships, Ross called this basin "The Valley of Troubles."

Entering the town of **SULA**; food, gas, campground. This area is best known as the spot where the Lewis and Clark expedition met the Shoshone Indians.   ▲

Mile 311 (79): East Fork Bitterroot River and turnoff to the town of Sula and to Spring Gulch Campground, open June to Sept., camping fee, 10 sites, fishing, hunting, hiking, swimming, water, toilet, and garbage facilities. Accessible to larger RVs. Southwest of the highway via a side road are Warm Springs Campground, open May to Sept., camping fee, 14 units and picnic areas, fishing, swimming, hiking, water, toilet, and garbage facilities; and Crazy Creek Campground, open May to Sept.; no fee, 6 upper units for gen-

eral camping, 5 lower units for campers with horses. Tie racks and watering trough at lower level area. Fishing, hiking, water, toilets, backcountry trailhead. Lewis and Clark historical marker here.

Private campground at the junction.
                              ⛺🍴◄▲

Mile 313.5 (76.5): Highway crosses the east fork of the Bitterroot River. Laird Creek fishing access.

Mile 315 (75): A 400-year-old ponderosa pine tree on the curve of the river has been the subject of an Indian legend that indicates the tree is a Medicine Tree. This location is sacred to Native Americans and is deliberately not marked. There is a wide spot in the road.

Mile 318.5 (71.5): Junction with road west to **CONNER** (a small community with all services available), Boulder Creek Forest Service Campground and the Painted Rocks State Recreation Area. Boulder Creek Campground, 13 miles southwest of Conner, has 11 campsites, a picnic area, trailer space, toilets and fishing access.

Painted Rocks State Recreation Area, 20 miles southwest, is located on Painted Rocks Lake. The Slate Creek Campground there has 32 campsites, picnic areas, trailer space, drinking water, boat launch, swimming and fishing access.

Painted Rocks Lake, also called the West Fork Bitterroot Reservoir, was drawn almost dry in 1973, but the fishery is reviving and several thousand cutthroat trout have been

Mountain goat kids are usually born in May and June. Despite their name, mountain goats are not true goats but are related to the antelope. Both male and female adults have horns. (L. Linkhart)

planted in recent years.

Private campground is also at the junction.
                                   🍴◄▲

Mile 321.5 (68.5): Rye Creek. Just north of Rye Creek is the turnoff for Hannon Memorial fishing access on the Bitterroot River. There are several public fishing access points along the Bitterroot River in this stretch of highway. The West Fork Bitterroot River joins the main Bitterroot just north of Conner.   ◄ MP 26

Mile 322 (68): Junction with road southwest to Painted Rocks State Recreation Area (see **Mile 318.5**). Trapper Peak Conservation Corps Center and West Fork Road. Highway crosses the Bitterroot River.

Mile 322.5 (67.5): Trapper Peak (elev. 10,157 feet) is visible to the west. It is the highest peak in the Selway-Bitterroot Wilderness Area.

Mile 325.5 (64.5): DARBY (pop. 679), a small resort/ranching community on the banks of the Bitterroot River. All services are available. Darby was established as the terminus of the Northern Pacific Railroad and named after postmaster James Darby in 1889.

Darby has survived 3 fires that destroyed its main street. One of the premier attractions of this small, friendly community is the Darby Pioneer Memorial Museum in Council Park, which shows the early settlement of Darby from 1800 to 1888.   MP 30

Mile 330.5 (59.5): Turnoff to Lake Como, about 3 miles to west; 1 campsite, 9 picnic sites, trailer spaces, drinking water, toilets, boat launches and fishing. Before the irrigation season Lake Como is one of the most pristine lakes in Montana. Wally Crawford fishing access to east.
                            🍴◄▲ MP 35

Mile 331 (59): Durland Park (day-use area) on Lick Creek. Fishing access east of highway.
                                    🍴◄

Mile 332 (58): Lick Creek Campground.   ▲

Mile 333 (57): Lost Horse Creek.

Mile 338.5 (51.5): Junction with Montana Highway 531 West to several cross-country ski trails, Lost Horse Creek, Twin Lakes, Mud Lake.

Bear Creek Pass Campground, 18 miles west, offers 7 campsites and toilets. Open July 15 to Sept. 15.   ▲

Mile 340 (50): Bitterroot River. U.S. Highway 93 crosses the Bitterroot several times on its way to Missoula.

Mile 340.5 (49.5): Turnoff to Anaconda via Montana Highway 38 over Skalkaho Pass. This becomes a narrow, winding gravel road and, although scenic, is not a major thoroughfare.

Skalkaho Wildlife Viewing Area, 27 miles east; elk, mountain goats, moose, black bear; road closed to motor vehicles Oct. 15 to Dec. 1, but open to bicycling. Cross-country skiing opportunities. Only first 10 miles plowed in winter.

Mile 341 (49): Skalkaho Creek.

Mile 343 (47): Junction of Montana Highways 269 and 531 to several ranches and **HAMILTON** (pop. 3,023). Hamilton is the county seat of Ravalli County; a beautiful little town that serves as the business center for the Bitterroot Valley. All services are available including 9 motels and 25 restaurants.

The "Copper King," Marcus Daly, who was responsible for the development of much of western Montana, was also responsible for the development of Hamilton. He built a mansion, complete with a swimming pool and a stocked lake. The stables he constructed were called Tammany Stables after one of his race horses. The mansion is still privately owned and not available for public tours. Daly was instrumental in having the county seat moved from Stevensville to Hamilton.

The architecturally unique courthouse now houses the Ravalli County Museum with 2 floors of excellent Indian and mining exhibits, along with many of Daly's personal holdings on display.

Hamilton is the home of the Rocky Mountain U.S. Public Health Laboratory, the facility that developed the vaccine for Rocky Mountain spotted fever, and is currently working on AIDS research.

Another research facility, the Ribi Immuno Chem Research Center, a privately funded cancer research facility, is also located here.

Mile 344.5 (45.5): Bitterroot National Forest headquarters west of highway.

Mile 345 (45): Bitterroot River.

Mile 346 (44): Blodgett Creek.

Mile 348 (42): Junction with Montana Highway 373 to **CORVALLIS**, a small, rural farming community. Corvallis was originally settled a few miles from its present site by Elija and Margaret Chaffin, who came to the Bitterroot Valley in 1864. They wintered here and then moved to Oregon, but returned in 1866 to the present townsite and named the community Corvallis, which means "center of the valley."   MP 52

Mile 350.5 (39.5): Mill Creek.

Mile 352 (38): Tucker Crossing fishing access. There are many log home manufacturing sites along the highway between here and Missoula.   ⬢ MP 56

Male wood duck has distinctive white striping on head and neck, and bright red at base of bill and around the eye. The female is generally drab brown with a noticeable white patch around the eye. (© John Barger)

Mile 353 (37): Bear Creek.

Mile 354 (36): North Fork Bear Creek.

Mile 355 (35): VICTOR, a small community with gas, food and campground. Originally named Garfield, after the president, it was renamed for Chief Victor of the Salish tribe. The town was first settled in the mid-1860s.
▲ MP 59

Mile 355.5 (34.5): Sweet House Creek.

Mile 357 (33): Junction with Montana Highway 370, which leads to a rural area east of Victor, and fishing access to Big Creek and the Bitterroot River.   ⬢

Mile 357.5 (32.5): Big Creek. Bell Crossing fishing access to east.   ⬢

Mile 359 (31): Trailhead access to St. Mary's Peak.

Mile 362 (28): McCallum Creek.

Mile 362.5 (27.5): Junction with Montana Highway 269 to **STEVENSVILLE** (pop. 1,340); St. Marys Mission, Montana's first Christian mission (founded by Father DeSmet); and Fort Owen State Monument. All services in Stevensville. Metcalf National Wildlife Refuge is located east of town.

Mile 364 (26): Kootenai Creek trail, which leads to North, Middle and South Kootenai lakes (a 12-mile walk on a good trail). Fishing for brook trout in South Kootenai Lake; rainbow in North Kootenai.   🐾⬢

Mile 366 (24): Bass Creek fishing access.   ⬢

Mile 366.5 (23.5): Dr. Charles Waters Recre-ation Area, named in honor of the man who studied the life history and control of forest tree diseases on this site.

The recreation area, 2 miles west of the highway, includes Charles Waters Memorial Campground and the Larry Creek day-use area, with 10 picnic sites. The campground is open May 25 to Sept. 10 and has 20 sites (5 pull through), hunting, fishing, hiking, water, garbage, handicap-accessible toilets, nature trail, fitness trail and access to Selway-Bitterroot Wilderness. Accessible to larger RVs. Fishing in Larry Creek is fair for small rainbow and cutthroat trout.   ♿🏕🚻⬢▲

Mile 367.5 (22.5): Poker Joe fishing access to the Bitterroot River on the north end of the Lee Metcalf Wildlife Refuge. The refuge has nesting osprey and Canada geese as well as mallards, wigeon, teal, redheads, scaup and wood ducks. Marsh birds, including the great blue heron, are common during the summer. Wildlife includes deer, muskrat, fox, mink, beaver, raccoon, skunk and an occasional bear and moose.

Fishing is not permitted within the boundaries of the reserve, but hunting is permitted in portions of the reserve, subject to federal and state regulations. Hunters are required to check in and out at hunter check stations.   ⬢

Mile 370 (20) Entering the village of **FLORENCE**; food, gas, restaurant. The highway is flanked by the Bitterroot Mountains to the west and the Sapphire Mountains to the east.

Junction with Montana Highway 203 across the Florence bridge spanning the Bitterroot River.

Mile 373 (17): Chief Looking Glass fishing access to the Bitterroot River and recreation

area offering 3 picnic areas, drinking water and toilets.

Mile 378 (12): Travelers Rest Historical Site. Lewis and Clark camped here on Sept. 9–10, 1805, as they prepared to cross the Bitterroot Mountains via Lolo Pass. As they secured venison for the trip, the explorers were told of an Indian road up Hells Gate leading to the buffalo country east of the main Rocky Mountain Range.

On their return trip, they again camped here from June 30 to July 3, 1806, and Lewis decided to take the Indian "Road to the Buffalo," while Clark and his men headed east via the Big Hole, Beaverhead, Jefferson and Gallatin valleys and the Yellowstone River. The 2 parties reached their rendezvous at the mouth of the Yellowstone within 9 days of each other.

Mile 380 (10): Junction with U.S. Highway 12 at **LOLO**. All services available. U.S. Highways 12 and 93 share a common alignment to Missoula. (See U.S. HIGHWAY 12 section for log.)

Mile 386 (4): Crossing the Bitterroot River. Highway 93 northbound follows Reserve Street and bypasses downtown Missoula.   MP 90

Mile 390 (0): Crossing the Clark Fork River in **MISSOULA** (pop. 42,918), the seat of Missoula County, with all services available.

Missoula is a pleasant city located at the confluence of 3 major rivers: the Clark Fork, Bitterroot and Blackfoot. It is the home of the University of Montana, a 181-acre campus serving more than 9,000 students in 47 buildings.

Other attractions in Missoula include the Greenough Mansion, located at 102 Ben Hogan St., built in 1897 by Thomas Greenough. It was moved from its original location and is now the home of the Leisure Highlands Golf Course Clubhouse and a restaurant. The house is constructed of tamarack, native to Montana.

Greenough Park provides a beautiful 1-mile drive through a wooded area beside Rattlesnake Creek. The park, donated from the Greenough estate to the city of Missoula, features a landscaped picnic area and wading pool.

Fort Missoula Historical Museum, at the corner of South Avenue and Reserve Street, was established in 1877 as one of the first military posts in Montana. It now serves as the home for National Guard and Reserve units. Displays on the 28-acre reserve depict the industrial development of the West from 1880 to 1920. The Indoor Gallery has a schedule of changing exhibits. The complex is open from noon until 5 p.m. daily, except Monday.

The Memorial Rose Garden on Highway 93 was established in 1947 by the American Rose Society and maintained as a memorial to the casualties of WWII. More than 2,500 rose plants are maintained at the garden.

One of the unique facilities of Missoula is the Smokejumpers Center, located at Johnson Bell Airport on U.S. Highway 93. Here, smokejumpers are trained for the dangerous

The 181-acre campus of University of Montana in Missoula serves more than 9,000 students. (© George Wuerthner)

and difficult task of forest fire suppression. The Northern Forest Fire Laboratory is also located here. Scientists study the nature and characteristics of forest fires to better understand and help aid in the suppression of forest fires. The complex is open for visitors from May 15 through July 1, 8 a.m. to 4 p.m. weekdays; and from July 1 through the end of Sept., 9 a.m. until 5 p.m. daily.

The beautiful St. Francis Xavier Church, located at 420 W. Pine, was built in 1889, the year Montana became a state. It features a graceful steeple, stained-glass windows and mural paintings by a Jesuit brother, Joseph Carignano, a kitchen helper, unschooled in art but later recognized as a master. Carignano also painted the 58 murals and fres-coes at the famous St. Ignatius Catholic Mission south of Polson.

The paintings of another muralist, Edgar Samuel Paxson, may be viewed at the Missoula County Courthouse from 8 a.m. until 5 p.m. weekdays. The artist is perhaps most famous for his painting of "Custer's Last Stand," completed in 1899. Eight murals, painted between 1912 and 1914, decorate the walls of the courthouse.

After crossing the Clark Fork River, northbound travelers turn west on Broadway for continuation of Highway 93. (Travelers may also access Interstate 90 west via Orange Street or Reserve Street and take Exit 96 for continuation of U.S. Highway 93 north.)   MP 94

CANADA HIGHWAY 93

Includes Icefields Parkway
U.S. Border to Jasper, AB
(See map opposite page)

Canada Highway 93 takes travelers through some of the most spectacular scenery on the continent. From the headwaters of the Northwest's mighty Columbia River, the highway climbs into the Canadian Rockies, famous for picture-postcard views of ruggedly beautiful scenery.

The stretch of Highway 93 between Lake Louise and Jasper is known as the Icefields Parkway. This scenic 140 miles/225 km of road traverses Banff and Jasper national parks in the central Canadian Rockies.

Canada Highway 93 begins at the U.S.–Canada border near Roosville, where U.S. Highway 93 ends. (Turn to the U.S. HIGHWAY 93 section for log of that route.)

Canada Highway 93 Log

Distance in miles from the U.S. border is followed by distance in miles from Jasper, AB. Equivalent distances in kilometres are indicated by Km.

Mile 0 (362) Km 0 (582.5): Crossing the U.S.–Canada international border and the Pacific–Mountain time zone line. Turn your watch back 1 hour if you are headed north; forward 1 hour if you are headed south.

Border crossing open 8 a.m. to midnight. For details on crossing the border, see Customs Requirements in the GENERAL INFORMATION section.

Mile 4.5 (357.5) Km 7 (575.5): Community of **ROOSVILLE**. All services available.

Mile 9 (353) Km 14.5 (568): GRASMERE, a small agricultural and timber centre. Limited services.

Mile 14.5 (347.5) Km 23 (559.5): Elk River bridge near the river's mouth on Lake Koocanusa.

Mile 25 (337) Km 40.5 (542): Junction with Highway 3 just west of the community of ELKO, limited services.

BC Highway 93 and Crowsnest Highway 3 share a common alignment the next 35 miles/55 km westbound to the junction with BC Highway 95 at **Mile 60.**

Travelers heading east on Highway 3 turn to **Mile 53** in the CROWSNEST HIGHWAY 3 section for log of that route.

Mile 26.5 (335.5) Km 42.5 (540): Road south to Baynes Lake (2.5 miles/4 km); fishing for eastern brook trout. Also access to Kikomun Creek Provincial Park (7 miles/11 km) on Lake Koocanusa, a man-made lake created by the building of the Libby Dam across the Kootenai River in Montana. The provincial park has 104 campsites, sani-station, picnic area, swimming, fishing, hiking trails and boat launch.

Mile 29 (333) Km 47 (535.5): Caithness Creek rest area.

Mile 33 (329) Km 53.5 (529): Canadian Pacific Railway station and sawmill at community of **GALLOWAY.**

Mile 35.5 (326.5) Km 57 (525.5): Gravel road north to Rosen Lake (just off highway); rainbow and cutthroat trout. Gas and food at junction.

Mile 36 (326) Km 58 (524.5): Unincorporated community of **JAFFRAY**, south of highway. Road to Tie Lake Regional Park, 2.5 miles/4 km; day use only. Also access south to Kikomun Creek Provincial Park (see description **Mile 26.5**).

Mile 42.5 (319.5) Km 68.5 (514): Wardner-Fort Steele Road leads 4 miles/6.5 km north to Kootenay trout hatchery. Station raises rainbow, eastern brook, kokanee, lake and cutthroat trout for stocking lakes throughout the Kootenay and Cariboo areas. Aquarium displays of native fish. Open year-round, 8 a.m. to 4 p.m.

This road also provides access to old lumber town of **BULL RIVER** (with a great old pub) and to Norbury Lake Provincial Park (10 miles/16 km). The park has 46 campsites, picnic area, fishing, swimming, boat launch (no powerboats). Hiking trails and spectacular views of The Steeples, serrated rock peaks of the Hughes Range. Interpretive display explains the Sun Dance of the Kootenai Indians. Fee charged, May to Sept.

This side road continues north 10.5 miles/17 km to junction with Highways

The Steeples, part of the Hughes Range, are reflected in Peckham's Lake in the Norbury Lake Provincial Park.
(Liz Bryan)

93/95 at Fort Steele (see **Mile 63.5**).

Mile 43.5 (318.5) Km 70 (512.5): Kootenay River bridge at the north end of Lake Koocanusa. West of the bridge, a side road leads to the small community of **WARDNER**, a boom town during construction of the CPR's Crowsnest Pass line. Its benefactor, James Wardner, also established a town in Idaho.

Also access to Wardner Provincial Park on the west side of Lake Koocanusa; picnicking, swimming, and fishing for Dolly Varden, cutthroat and whitefish.

Mile 48 (314) Km 78 (504.5): Turnout and stop of interest marker describing the days of steamboating on the Kootenay River between Fort Steele and Jennings, MT.

Westbound, the highway climbs out of the Kootenay Valley.

Mile 57 (305) Km 91.5 (491): Rampart rest area.

Mile 60 (302) Km 95.5 (487): Junction with Highways 95 and 3. Highway 93 shares a common alignment with Highway 95 north to Radium Hot Springs and with Highway 3 the next 35 miles/55 km eastbound. Highway 3 (Crowsnest) leads west to Hope. Westbound travelers turn to **Mile 87.5** in the CROWSNEST HIGHWAY 3 section for log of that route.

Mile 63.5 (298.5) Km 102 (480.5): Kootenay River bridge. North, old waterwheel marks location of **FORT STEELE. Junction** with Wardner-Fort Steele Road and access west to Fort Steele Heritage Town, a restored and reconstructed turn-of-the-century mining town and North West Mounted Police post. The park is open dawn to dusk, daily year-round, but park activities are scheduled only during summer months. From June to Sept., park staff wear period dress, and visitors can watch them baking, spinning, weaving, blacksmithing and performing other skills. Join the North West Mounted Police for flag ceremonies. There is a museum and tea room, theater with live vaudeville, period shops, and stagecoach and steam-train rides. Large visitor centre. Admission fee charged in summer.

Wildhorse cemetery and ghost town site of Fisherville can be reached by a short drive up Wardner Road, then a hike.　★

Mile 66 (296) Km 106.5 (476): Campbell Lake/Meyer rest area. Large, secluded site in forest. Lake is aerated in winter to prevent winter kill. Good rainbow fishing. Watch for painted turtles.　🐟

Mile 69.5 (292.5) Km 111.5 (471): Gravel turnout with litter bins provides good viewpoint over the Kootenay River valley and nearby marshes. Mountains in the background are the Purcells.

Mile 70 (292) Km 112.5 (470): Bummers Flats Wildlife Reserve, 3 marshes, dike trails. Excellent waterfowl viewing; migrating sandhill cranes. Foot access only. Consult map at dike entrance.

Mile 74 (288) Km 119 (463.5): Wasa Slough Provincial Wildlife Sanctuary.

Mile 75 (287) Km 121 (461.5): Road east to community of **WASA** (gas, food and lodging) and to Wasa Provincial Park on the east side of Wasa Lake. Park has 104 campsites, sani-station, picnic area, excellent beaches, swimming, waterskiing, fishing, boat launch and nature trails.　🚴🏕🛶▲

Mile 77 (285) Km 123.5 (459): Road north to Wasa Lake.

Mile 78 (284) Km 126 (456.5): Kootenay River bridge. North of the bridge is the **junction** with Highway 95A south to Kimberley and Cranbrook. To the east, the ragged peaks of the Rockies.

Mile 79 (283) Km 127.5 (455): Wasa rest area beside the Kootenay River.

Mile 83 (279) Km 134 (448.5): Road west to pulp mill at Skookumchuk. This road also goes to Tamarac Lake; rainbow to 3½ lbs.

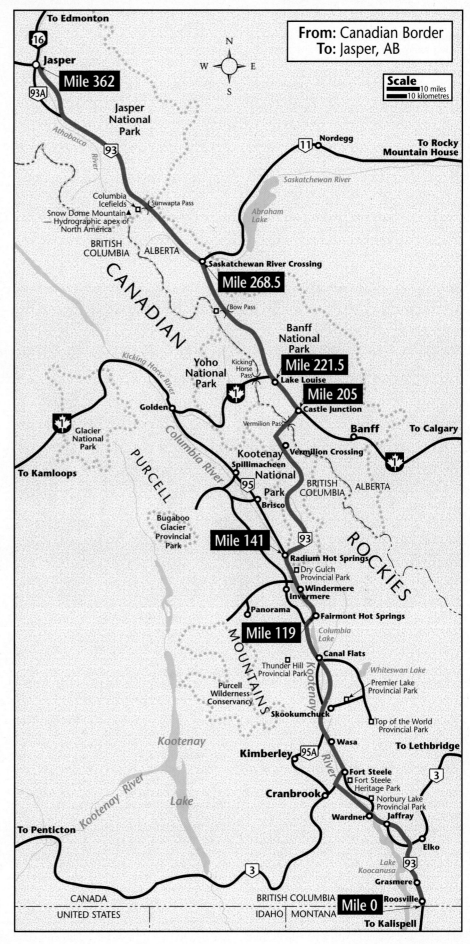

(artificial flies only). ☙

Mile 86.5 (275.5) Km 139 (443.5): Just north of Kootenay River bridge, the settlement and railway station of **SKOOKUMCHUCK** on the Skookumchuck River. Skookumchuck is Chinook jargon for "strong water." Good fishing here for cutthroat and Dolly Varden, best late summer to fall. South access road to Premier Lake Provincial Park, 8.5 miles/14 km in the Hughes Range of the Rocky Mountains. Good place to see Rocky Mountain bighorn sheep, elk and deer. The provincial park has 55 campsites, picnic area, boating, fishing and boat launch (no waterskiing). Premier Lake and 3 others within the park have a good reputation for rainbow and eastern brook trout. Eggs from Premier Lake fish are collected for the Kootenay fish hatchery near Wardner; an interpretive display near fish trap explains the procedure. ⊼☙▲

St. Peter's Church in Windermere, at Mile 129, is called the "stolen" church.
(Liz Bryan)

Mile 87 (275) Km 140 (442.5): Gravel turnout to north with good view of pulp mill.

Mile 87.5 (274.5) Km 141 (441.5): North access to Premier Lake Provincial Park and Sheep Creek Road to undeveloped Ram Creek hot springs. Watch for elk.

Mile 100 (262) Km 161.5 (421): Road east to Whiteswan Lake Provincial Park, 11 miles/17.5 km, and Top of the World Provincial Park, 34 miles/55 km. Road is rough, used by logging trucks; extreme caution is advised.

Whiteswan Lake Park has 87 campsites, picnic areas, fishing, swimming and boat launch. Camping fee. Both Alces and Whiteswan lakes are kept well-stocked with rainbow trout. (Alces Lake, no powerboats, and fly-fishing only.)

Lussier Hot Springs is located at the park's western end. Springs are undeveloped, but rated as excellent, with a pool built from logs and a small bathhouse. Water temperature is 109°F/43°C.

Top of the World Provincial Park has wilderness walk-in camping only (road stops at park boundary). High in the Kootenay Ranges of the Rockies, the park encompasses superlative alpine areas, with a network of trails to the high meadows and mountain peaks. Fishing in well-stocked Fish Lake for cutthroat and Dolly Varden is a prime attraction. Small cabin at Fish Lake provides limited accommodation; fee charged. Access road is usually passable only from late May to mid-Nov.; check locally. Park hut is open May to Oct. ⋀⊼☙▲

Mile 103 (259) Km 166 (416.5): Kootenay River bridge. Road east to sawmill community of **CANAL FLATS** (pop. 700), with gas station, restaurant and food store. Access through town 2.5 miles/4 km to east side of Columbia Lake and Canal Flats Provincial Park; picnic area, swimming, boat launch. ⊼

Mile 105.5 (256.5) Km 169.5 (413): Stop of interest marker commemorating Baillie-Grohman's canal. In 1886 William Baillie-Grohman conceived a grand scheme to connect the Kootenay and Columbia rivers by means of a canal. The canal and 1 lock were built, but only 2 ships made the passage. Not only was the canal too narrow and shallow, but it caused flooding of the Columbia Valley. The canal was abandoned. Traces of it and the lock can still be found in the scrub brush west of the highway.

Mile 106 (256) Km 170.5 (412): Findlay Creek Road leads west to Blue Lake and Thunder Hill Provincial Park; 25 campsites on hillside overlooking Columbia Lake. Listen for saw-whet owls at night. Nearby are remnants of tramway to the Thunder Hill lead and silver mine. ▲

Mile 113 (249) Km 181.5 (401): Coy's Hill rest area to east with picnic tables and good view of Columbia Lake. Interpretive sign tells of the East Kootenay Colonization

Road, built in 1886–89 from Fort Steele to Golden in anticipation of settlement on Baillie-Grohman's land holdings beside the Kootenay River. ⊼

Mile 116.5 (245.5) Km 187.5 (395): Narrow bridge over Dutch Creek by spectacular hoodoo cliffs of yellow sandstone. Look for white-throated swifts. Good fishing in Dutch Creek for Dolly Varden, cutthroat, rainbow and whitefish. Tourist facilities here include camping, gas, food. ☙▲

Mile 117 (245) Km 188.5 (394): West Side Road, an alternative back road to community of Invermere, goes north along west side of Windermere Lake.

Mile 118.5 (243.5) Km 190.5 (392): Columbia River bridge.

Mile 119 (243) Km 191.5 (391): FAIRMONT HOT SPRINGS, a resort community with hot mineral pools, 2 golf courses, downhill and cross-country skiing, tennis courts, airplane sightseeing trips and trail rides. Community has an RV site, villa and lodge accommodations, food, gas and post office. The first resort was the Fairmont Hotel, built in 1888. The mineral springs do not contain sulfur. ⋖▲

Mile 125 (237) Km 201 (381.5): To the east, Indian mission church.

Mile 129 (233) Km 208 (374.5): Junction with loop road to **WINDERMERE** (pop. 800), a resort settlement on the east shore of Lake Windermere. Settlement dates from about 1887, the steamboat era. Kokanee spawn in Windermere Creek in September and October, a feast for hordes of bald eagles. Look for St. Peter's Church on Victoria Avenue. The church was built in 1887 and was "stolen" 10 years later from the semi-deserted town of Donald, 200 km north, and transported intact on the railway.

Mile 133.5 (228.5) Km 214.5 (368): Chamber of commerce tourist information chalet, open May to Sept. **Junction** with road west around north end of Windermere Lake to James Chabot Beach Provincial Park, Invermere and Panorama ski resort. (Opposite the junction is a fine example of Tyrolean architecture: the Black Forest Restaurant.)

James Chabot Beach Provincial Park , 1 mile/2 km west, on the north shore of Windermere Lake, has picnic tables and a fine beach for swimming and water sports.

INVERMERE (pop. 2,000) 2 miles/4 km west, is a lively summer resort community, with public beaches at Dorothy Lake Park and Kinsmen Beach Park. Full tourist facilities; good shopping, food and services.

The first fur-trading post west of the Rockies was established on Lake Windermere by David Thompson in 1807. Known as Kootenae House.

PANORAMA, 11 miles/17.5 km west of Invermere via Toby Creek Road, is the site of Panorama Resort. A year-round resort community, it is known for its heli-skiing and downhill skiing in winter.

Hikers may wish to drive 20 miles/32 km up Toby Creek Road from Invermere to the start of the historic Earl Grey Pass Trail in the Purcell Wilderness Conservancy. The trail follows Itamill Creek to Kootenay Lake south of Argenta, climbing to 7,400 feet. Hike takes about 3 days. ⋖⋀⊼

Mile 138.5 (223.5) Km 223 (359.5): Road east to Dry Gulch Provincial Park; 25 camp-sites on the lower slopes of the Stanford Range of the Rockies. Landscape is generally arid, but despite its name there is a creek in Dry Gulch. Rocky Mountain bighorn sheep winter in the park and surrounding area. ▲

Mile 140 (222) Km 225 (357.5): Stop of interest sign commemorating James Sinclair, who led 200 Red River settlers from Fort Garry (today Winnipeg) across the Rockies and down the Columbia to Oregon in an attempt to hold the territory for Great Britain in 1841. Three viewpoints along west side of the road give good views of Rocky Mountain Trench and Columbia River. Notice the white silt deposits eroded into hoodoo formations along the hillsides.

NOTE: Safer access for viewpoints is for southbound traffic.

Mile 140.5 (221.5) Km 226 (356.5): Access to Redstreak campsite in Kootenay National Park; 242 sites, shelters, showers, sani-sta-tion. Hiking trails and nature programs. Open mid-May to Sept. ▲

Mile 141 (221) Km 227 (355.5): **RADIUM HOT SPRINGS** (area pop. 1,000). This resort community spreads out alongside the high-way; full tourist services. Chief attractions include hot mineral pools, a luxury golf resort (open April to Oct.), river rafting on the Kootenay and Kicking Horse rivers, a water slide and a children's playland. On the hillside, the Queen of Peace Shrine attracts many visitors.

Highway 95 continues north along the Rocky Mountain Trench to Golden; High-way 93 goes east into the Rockies. Highway 93 travelers continue with this log. (See feature on BC HIGHWAY 95 between Radium Junction and Golden in this section.)

Mile 142 (220) Km 228.5 (354): Kootenay National Park gate. Visitors planning to stay overnight in any of the national parks should have a permit: $5 for 1 day; $10 for 4 days; $30 all year. Park information office and restrooms are just east of the gate.

Turnout north side and beginning of Juniper trail, a 2-mile/3-km walk leading through Sinclair Canyon and on to the hot springs. Park here and walk up the road to photograph Sinclair Canyon.

Mile 142.5 (219.5) Km 229 (353.5): Sinclair Canyon. Highway passes through narrow cleft in high, vertical limestone walls.

Gap was cut by action of gushing Sinclair Creek. There are viewpoints north and south of the canyon; best time for photos is late afternoon.

Mile 143 (219) Km 230.5 (352): Radium Hot Springs resort facilities on both sides of the road, with 2 outdoor hot mineral pools, steam rooms, plunge baths, changing rooms and adjacent restaurant. Pools open daily, afternoons only in winter; restaurant open only in the summer. This section of road is full of pedestrians in summer; drive with care.

Springs gushing from the Redwall Fault at the base of Redstreak Mountain daily pour mineral water at temperatures between 95°F/35°C and 116°F/47°C into the pools. The water contains calcium, sodium, magnesium, potassium and other minerals. The springs were originally called Sinclair, but the name

Invermere, a lively resort community, viewed from across Lake Windermere. (Liz Bryan)

was changed to Radium in 1915 because of the water's relatively high radioactivity.

Large parking area just north of pools faces cliffs of limestone and dolomite breccia stained red by iron oxides in the mineral water. In spring and fall, bighorn sheep are often seen on the north side of the canyon here. Trails to aquacourt and Redstreak Creek, a short hike along the creek's canyon. North-bound the highway goes through a short tunnel known as the Iron Gates, then follows fast-flowing Sinclair Creek up to the pass. 肌

Mile 146.5 (215.5) Km 236 (346.5): Kimp-ton Creek trail, a 2.8-mile/4.8-km hike through the forest, provides good views of avalanche slides. 肌

Mile 147.5 (214.5) Km 237.5 (345): Picnic area beside Sinclair Creek. ⚲

Mile 148.5 (213.5) Km 239 (343.5): Kinders-ley Pass trail leads west to the divide on the Brisco Range and on through high alpine meadows to connect with Sinclair Creek trail, a 7-hour circuit. 肌

Mile 149 (213) Km 239.5 (343): Picnic area by well-named Olive Lake. Trail leads up Sin-clair Creek to alpine meadows. 肌⚲

Mile 149.5 (212.5) Km 240.5 (342): Sinclair Pass Summit (elev. 4,875 feet/1,486m). Brisco Range to the west, Stanford Range to the east.

Mile 151 (211) Km 243 (339.5): Cobb Lake trail. Fishing for eastern brook, cutthroat and rainbow trout. Fishermen should obtain a fishing permit and a copy of national parks regulations. 肌⚲

Mile 151.5 (210.5) Km 243.5 (339): View-point overlooking the Kootenay River valley and the long ridge of the Mitchell Range with its prominent horizontal strata. The highway here turns abruptly north and begins a long descent to the Kootenay River.

WARNING: Trucks use low gear.

Mile 154 (208) Km 247.5 (335): Settler's Road southeast to park boundary; connects with forest road that continues down the

Kootenay River to Canal Flats. This is the route by which pioneer priest Father Jean de Smet is believed to have crossed the Rockies on his way east to do missionary work among Alberta's Blackfoot Indians. Logging and ore trucks exit this way; drive with care.

Mile 156 (206) Km 251 (331.5): Kootenay River picnic site. Good views of Mitchell and Vermilion ranges to the east; Brisco Range to west. Nixon Creek trail is an easy hike to small forest lake. 肌⚲

Mile 158 (204) Km 254 (328.5): McLeod Meadows picnic area. Trail leading 1.5 miles/2.4 km to Dog Lake begins here. Just north on Highway 93, there is a campsite with 98 sites, 5 kitchen shelters, sani-station and nature program; open late June to early Sept. 肌⚲▲

Mile 159 (203) Km 256 (326.5): Viewpoint of Mount Harkin. Mountain is the most prominent in the Mitchell Range to the east and was named for the first commissioner of national parks. Columbia ground squirrels have a colony here.

Keep a sharp lookout for elk along this stretch of the Kootenay River valley. An esti-mated 300 of the large animals range in Kootenay National Park throughout the year; they are most often at river level in spring and fall.

Mile 163.5 (198.5) Km 263.5 (319): Dolly Varden picnic area with rustic kitchen shel-ters. Dolly Varden River joins the Kootenay near here. ⚲

Mile 168 (194) Km 270 (312.5): Roadside turnout with signs commemorating the opening of the first road from Banff to Win-dermere in 1923.

Mile 170 (192) Km 273.5 (309): Kootenay River bridge at Kootenay Crossing. Kootenay Pond picnic area to the north. Pond is believed to be a kettle, formed by a stranded block of glacial ice buried in the gravels. When the ice block melted, gravels slumped to form a deep-sided pond. Highway turns into the Vermilion River valley for its climb up to Vermilion Pass.

Mile 170.5 (191.5) Km 274 (308.5): Hector Gorge viewpoint. Turnout provides splendid view into the gorge of the Vermilion River, with the Mitchell Range to the east, the Vermilion Range to the west. The gorge was named for Dr. James Hector, a geologist who explored the area in 1858.

Mile 171.5 (190.5) Km 276 (306.5): Hector Gorge picnic area. Rocky Mountain goats are often seen just above the highway here on the lower slopes of Mount Wardle. Their white coats make identification easy. River beside road is milky green with glacial sediment.

Mile 174 (188) Km 280.5 (302): Wardle Creek picnic area.

Mile 175 (187) Km 282 (300.5): Roadside turnout with drinking water from a major freshwater spring.

Mile 176 (186) Km 283.5 (299): Monument to George Simpson, governor of the Hudson's Bay Co., who came down the Simpson and Vermilion rivers in 1841 searching for a better, more southerly route for his fur traders to cross the Rockies. He found the way impractical for the brigades.

Just south is an animal lick. Moose, elk and deer come down to the river here for mineral salts from the river's mud banks. Best times for viewing are early morning and evening.

Mile 177 (185) Km 284.5 (298): Viewpoint. Bridge across river leads to the Mount Shanks fire lookout and Simpson River trail. The Simpson River trail provides access to isolated Mount Assiniboine Provincial Park.

Just north on Highway 93, if the weather is clear, you might catch a glimpse of Mount Assiniboine, known as the Matterhorn of the Rockies. Look southeast; at 11,870 feet/3,618m, it is one of the highest peaks in the Rockies.

Mile 180 (182) Km 290 (292.5): Community of **VERMILION CROSSING**; lodge, gas, groceries, food. Picnic area near river bridge. Start of Verdant and Verendrye Creek trails. Nearby is a viewpoint of Mount Verendrye (elev. 10,124 feet/3,086m) and the craggy cliffs of the Rockwall.

Mile 185 (177) Km 298 (284.5): Trails to Floe Lake, 6 miles/10 km west, and Hawk Creek to Ball Pass, east. Floe Lake is named for the small blocks of ice that break off from Floe Glacier and float on the lake like small icebergs.

Mile 190 (172) Km 306 (276.5): Access road west across the river to Numa picnic area and trail up Numa Creek. North of the bridge, Vermilion River tumbles into picturesque falls.

Mile 193 (169) Km 311 (271.5): Paint Pots nature trail crosses river to area of brightly colored earth along Ochre Creek. Here red and yellow clays have been stained by deposits of iron from cold mineral springs. Indians from both sides of the Rockies used to come here to collect the ochre clay for body paint and for pictographs. Later, the ochre was mined and shipped to Calgary for use as a paint base. Traces of mining activity remain.

Mile 195 (167) Km 313.5 (269): Marble Creek Campground; 62 sites, 2 kitchen shelters, sani-station. Start of 1-mile/2-km return hike along rim of Marble Canyon, a deep gorge worn by Tokumm Creek into gray-and-white limestone rock. In several places, the limestone has been changed by pressure into marble, best seen at the upper end of the canyon where the waterfall gushes over a marble slab.

Ranger station located near campground. Stop here for information or to register for trails. Trails to Tumbling Glacier and Ottertail Pass begin at bridge.

Mile 197 (165) Km 317 (265.5): Trail to Stanley Glacier, 3 miles/4.8 km. The 4-hour hike leads to a spectacular hanging valley and alpine glacier.

The highway north from here leads through the site of the Vermilion Pass forest fire started by a lightning strike in 1968. Notice the young lodgepole pines, the first to return after the fire.

Mile 199 (163) Km 320 (262.5): Vermilion Pass (elev. 5,382 feet/1,640m) on the Great Divide of the Rocky Mountains. Waters east flow into the Bow River and thence to Hudson Bay; waters west flow into the Columbia River and the Pacific Ocean. The pass is the boundary between British Columbia and Alberta, and Kootenay and Banff national parks.

Fireweed nature trail leads in a short loop through a section of the burn area, provid-

B.C. Highway 95
Radium Hot Springs to Golden

Highway 95 splits off Highway 93 at Radium Hot Springs (**Mile 141**) and continues north through the Rocky Mountain Trench to Golden on Trans-Canada Highway 1. Bird-watchers will love this route. The Columbia River valley is a major migration flyway, and the unspoiled wetlands provide nesting grounds for many kinds of water birds. There are probably more osprey here than anywhere else in the province, and eagles are fairly common. Nesting platforms have been built for geese, and there are colonies of great blue herons. Deer, elk and moose are most often seen in spring and fall, and there are beaver and muskrat. The best way to see the wildlife is to travel down the river by canoe.

Mile 0 Km 0: **Junction** of Highways 93 and 95 at Radium Hot Springs.
Mile 2 Km 3.5: **Upper Ranch.** Exquisite large Victorian gingerbread house. Notice Christmas tree plantations in area.
Mile 6.5 Km 11: **Junction** with loop road to Edgewater, a small community with accommodations, food, gas, pub.
Mile 8.5 Km 14: Luxor Creek, crossed on high embankment. Near the mouth of the creek is Luxor whistlestop on the Canadian Pacific Railway. Paddle-steamers at one time provided the only transportation through the valley from the CPR line at Golden south to the end of Columbia Lake. The first steamboat to navigate this route was the *Duchess* in 1886.
Mile 11 Km 18: Deadman's Creek. Northbound, watch for the "Cauliflower Tree," a Douglas fir distorted by witches broom virus.
Mile 15.5 Km 25: Community of **BRISCO**; general store. Access to Bugaboo Creek forestry road (rough; logging trucks), which leads 1 mile/1.8 km to Columbia Wildlife Area and 28 miles/45 km west to Bugaboo Glacier Provincial Park and Alpine Recreation Area. The park is undeveloped. Strenuous hike in. A favorite for rock climbers.
Mile 16 Km 26: A great blue heronry in river poplars. The Upper Columbia Valley supports 300 pairs of this stately bird.
Mile 18 Km 29: In a meadow to the east is tiny log church of St. Mark. Built in 1896, it is the oldest church in the East Kootenays.
Mile 22 Km 34.5: Spillimacheen rest area.
Mile 22.5 Km 36: Small settlement of **SPILLIMACHEEN**; post office, gas, gift shop, restaurant and old-fashioned trading post. Access to Bugaboo Park and West Side Road to Invermere.
Mile 28.5 Km 46.5: Community of **HARROGATE**; general store.
Mile 32 Km 52: **CASTLEDALE** community under the slopes of Castle Mountain.
Mile 34 Km 55: Large turnout with good view of Columbia Valley. Notice the nesting boxes erected on stilts above the water to keep Canada goose nests safe from predators. Bed-and-breakfast accommodations nearby.
Mile 40.5 Km 65.5: **PARSON**, a sawmill and logging community; gas, store, community hall. Gold panning in Canyon Creek is said to be worthwhile.
Mile 46.5 Km 75: Braisher Creek rest area.
Mile 55.5 Km 89.5: Loop road to community of **NICHOLSON**, today mostly a suburb of Golden.
Mile 61 Km 98.5: Reflection Lake wildlife viewing area. Waterfowl habitat.
Mile 62 Km 100: Kicking Horse River Bridge and Golden town centre. Golden is an important junction point for the Canadian Pacific Railway: Its main east/west line is joined by a north/south line up the Columbia from the Crownest area of the Kootenays. The Crownest cars carry coal from the open-pit mines. As many as 20 long coal trains a day lumber through Golden on their way to the deep-sea coal ports at Roberts Bank, south of Vancouver.
Mile 63.5 Km 102: **Junction** with Highway 1. For information on Golden, see **Mile 44.5** in the TRANS-CANADA HIGHWAY 1 section.

ing a good chance to see forest self-regeneration at work. Wildflowers here are excellent.

Mile 200 (162) Km 322 (260.5): Vista Lake viewpoint. Good views of Storm Mountain (elev. 10,370 feet/3,161m) to the south, and Vista Lake in the valley. Trail starts from the viewpoint down to Vista Lake, a 1-hour hike, and up the flanks of Storm Mountain to Arnica Lake, 3.3 miles/5.3 km and Twin Lakes, 4.7 miles/7.6 km. East from the viewpoint are Castle Mountain and the Sawback Range. Ď

Mile 200.5 (161.5) Km 322.5 (260): Boom Creek picnic area in a stand of spruce/fir forest that escaped the big fire. Trail to Boom Lake, 3.1 miles/5.1 km, begins here. Cross-country ski trails. Ď─

Mile 202 (160) Km 325 (257.5): Storm Mountain Lodge, built in 1923 as a Canadian Pacific Railway hostelry. Sold to private interests and modernized, it retains much of the rustic charm of earlier times. The viewpoint across the road provides excellent views of Castle Mountain to the north and the Vermilion Pass burn to the south. Highway northbound begins steep descent into the Bow River valley; trucks use low gear.

Mile 205 (157) Km 330 (252.5): Castle Junction. **Junction** with Trans-Canada Highway 1. Highways 1 and 93 share a common alignment between Castle Junction and Lake Louise. Turn north on Highway 93 for Lake Louise and Icefields Parkway. Turn south on Trans-Canada Highway 1 for Calgary.

Also access at this junction to Highway 1A, a scenic alternate route between Lake Louise and Banff, which also provides access to Johnston Canyon, Castle Mountain and Protection Mountain campgrounds.

Mile 210.5 (151.5) Km 338.5 (244): Taylor Creek picnic area and 3.9-mile/6.3-km trail to Taylor Lake. The highway is bordered by dense, even stands of lodgepole pines, trees that grow first after a forest fire. West of the picnic area, the original spruce forest remains. Ď─

Mile 216.5 (145.5) Km 348.5 (234): Rest area by the Bow River.

Mile 217.5 (144.5) Km 350 (232.5): Lake Louise overflow campsite. ▲

Mile 219.5 (142.5) Km 353 (229.5): Bow River bridge.

Mile 221.5 (140.5) Km 356.5 (226): Exit to **LAKE LOUISE** village and visitor information office. Access to Highway 1A and Protection Mountain Campground; 89 campsites. ▲

Mile 222 (140) Km 357.5 (225): Hiking and cross-country ski trail up Pipestone River. Ď

Mile 222.5 (139.5) Km 358 (224.5): **Junction** with Trans-Canada Highway 1. Highways 1 and 93 share a common alignment between Lake Louise and Castle Junction. Jasper-bound travelers turn north on Highway 93.

The slab of reddish slate at the junction is among the park's oldest formations, dating from 600 million years ago.

This stretch of Highway 93 is known as the Icefields Parkway and is perhaps the most scenic and certainly the most popular

Aptly named Castle Mountain viewed from near Storm Mountain Lodge.
(Liz Bryan)

of all the roads in the Canadian Rockies. Keeping just to the east of the Great Divide, the highway climbs 2 passes, Bow Summit and Sunwapta, to take motorists to the edge of alpine terrain. The parkway is well-named, for more than 100 glacial remnants of the last ice age are visible along its route.

NOTE: During summer, the next gas northbound is 46 miles/74 km in Saskatchewan Crossing. During winter, when facilities in Saskatchewan Crossing are closed, next gas northbound is 140 miles/224 km in Jasper.

Mile 224 (138) Km 360.5 (222): Herbert Lake, with picnic area at north end. Surrounding forest is lodgepole pine. Good views south from the lakeshore of Mounts Temple, St. Piran, Niblock and Whyte. The lake is known as a "sink" because it has no visible outlet. Unlike other mountain lakes, it warms in summer to reasonable temperatures and is popular for swimming. ─

Mile 230.5 (131.5) Km 371 (211.5): Hector Lake viewpoint, named for Dr. James Hector, geologist of the Palliser expedition, who was the first white man up this valley in 1858. Above the lake is the Waputik Range (Indian for "white goat") with its glacier mantle. Pulpit Peak (elev. 8,940 feet/2,725m), which rises above the lake's north end, is forested with alpine larch, the most northerly stand of this deciduous conifer in the Rockies. Look for glacially carved cirques (bowl-shaped depressions) high on the mountains' flanks. Trail to lake begins just north on Highway 93. Ď

Mile 233 (129) Km 375 (207.5): Mosquito Creek Campground; 32 sites, kitchen shelter and a youth hostel. Across the Bow River, the sandstone cliffs of Bow Peak (elev. 9,409 feet/2,868m) are visible; Mount Hector (elev. 11,135 feet/3,394m) is to the southeast. Across the highway from the campsite,

Mosquito Creek trail leads 6.2 miles/10 km up to Molar Pass. Ď▲

Mile 241 (121) Km 388 (194.5): Crowfoot Glacier viewpoint. To the west, Crowfoot Mountain is hung with blue ice. At the turn of the century, this glacier had 3 tongues or toes, hence its name. Today, as the glacier retreats, only 2 remain. Park panorama points out the mountains within view. Across the highway, trailhead for Helen Lake (good wildflowers in July), 3.7 miles/6 km; Katherine Lake, 5 miles/8 km; and Dolomite Pass, 5.5 miles/8.9 km, where Banff's only woodland caribou can sometimes be seen.

Dark green rock beside the road is part of the formation known as the Crowfoot Dike, the only known occurrence of igneous rock in Banff National Park. The dike was formed by molten lava forcing its way up through the sedimentary rock. Ď

Mile 241.5 (120.5) Km 389 (193.5): Bow Lake viewpoint and picnic area. Bow Lake, in summer a brilliant turquoise, is headwater for the Bow River; it is ice-covered until June. At the north end of the lake is red-roofed Num-ti-jah Lodge, built in the 1920s by pioneer guide Jimmy Simpson. The mountain above the lake was named after him. ─

Mile 243.5 (118.5) Km 392 (190.5): Road to Num-ti-jah Lodge, which provides meals and accommodations year-round. Good view of the icefalls of the Bow Glacier at the head of the valley. Trail starts here to the lodge and on to Bow Glacier Falls, 3 miles/5 km, which tumble 492 feet/150m over a wall of sandstone below the foot of the glacier. Packhorse trips from the lodge into the mountains are operated by Peyto Tours; inquire at the lodge. Ď

Mile 245.5 (116.5) Km 395 (187.5): Bow Summit (elev. 6,788 feet/2,069m). **Junction** with short road west to Peyto Lake viewpoint. The glacial meltwater lake, a brilliant turquoise from suspended glacial sediments pouring in from Peyto Glacier, lies some 787 feet/240m below the viewpoint. Short but steep trail leads from viewpoint to lakeshore. Mistaya Valley north of the lake is U-shaped, scoured by ancient glaciers. The highway follows this valley until the river flows into the North Saskatchewan River.

Mile 249 (113) Km 400.5 (182): Peyto Glacier viewpoint. To the southwest, the tongue of the Peyto Glacier falls from the Wapata Icefield, flanked by Mount Thompson and Peyto Peak. Trail leads down to Peyto Lake from opposite side of road. Signs explain the formation of cirques. ⚏

Mile 250.5 (111.5) Km 403 (179.5): To the west, Snowbird Glacier tumbles down the face of Mount Patterson. Notice the prominent morainal ridges, marking the glacier's former limits.

Mile 253 (109) Km 407 (175.5): Silver Horn Creek overflow campsite. ▲

Mile 255.5 (106.5) Km 411 (171.5): Viewpoint for Upper Waterfowl Lake; Mount Chephren (elev. 10,715 feet/3,266m), the abrupt pyramid to the north; and Howse Peak (elev. 10,794 feet/3,290m). Notice the 2 very prominent cirques in the rock wall of the Great Divide. Watch for moose in the braided river marshes at the lake's southern end.

Mile 256 (106) Km 412 (170.5): Waterfowl Lakes Campground; 116 sites, 7 kitchen shelters, sani-station, amphitheater. Trail to Cirque and Chephren lakes, in the glacially carved cirques above, starts at the rear of the campsite.

The highway runs beside Lower Waterfowl Lake, and there are several good turnouts for photography and wildlife observation. ⚏▲

Mile 264.5 (97.5) Km 426 (156.5): Viewpoint with mountain markers for the 3 Kaufmann peaks, Mount Murchison (elev. 10,935 feet/3,333m) and Mount Wilson (elev. 10,630 feet/3,240m). Turnout and trail to Mistaya Canyon. Here the river has worn a deep, twisting gorge into the limestone bedrock, and tumbling boulders have eroded round potholes. Bridge crosses gorge, and trail continues 16 miles/26 km to Howse Pass. David Thompson of the North West Co. crossed the Rockies this way in 1807 to set up a trading post west of the mountains (near today's Invermere). The pass was the main fur-trading route across the Rockies for 5 years until blockaded by Peigan Indians. The pass was named after Thompson's rival, Joseph Howse, who later came this way for the Hudson's Bay Co. ⚏

Mile 266.5 (95.5) Km 429 (153.5): Saskatchewan River Park warden station.

Mile 268 (94) Km 431 (151.5): Viewpoint over the Mistaya and Howse river valleys. Both rivers flow into the Saskatchewan near here.

Mile 268.5 (93.5) Km 432 (150.5): **SASKATCHEWAN CROSSING**; all services available (some only in summer). **Junction** with Highway 11 (David Thompson Highway), which follows the North Saskatchewan River east through the mountains to the old mining town of Nordegg, now a Provincial Historic Site; Rocky Mountain House (pop.

5,600), 112 miles/180 km east, with all amenities and Fort Rocky Mountain House National Historic Site; and Red Deer, 160 miles/257 km east.

Mile 269 (93) Km 433 (149.5): Trail to Glacier Lake, 5.5 miles/9 km. ⚏

Mile 275 (87) Km 443 (139.5): Rampart Creek Campground, open June to Sept.; 50 sites, 4 kitchen shelters and a youth hostel. The highway follows the North Saskatchewan River. Watch for moose. ▲

Mile 276.5 (85.5) Km 445 (137.5): Viewpoint of Mount Amery (elev. 10,941 feet/3,335m), Mount Saskatchewan (elev. 10,964 feet/3,342m) and tiny Cleopatra's Needle on the ridge. The needle, also known as the Lighthouse Tower, is a dolomite pinnacle.

Mile 278.5 (83.5) Km 448 (134.5): Trailhead to Sunset Pass and Sunset lookout. ⚏

Mile 279 (83) Km 449.5 (133): Viewpoint of the Castelets, well-named cluster of small castle crags on the western horizon.

Mile 283.5 (78.5) Km 456 (126.5): Viewpoint of the North Saskatchewan River as it flows through a narrow gorge.

Mile 284.5 (77.5) Km 458 (124.5): Cirrus Mountain Campground; 16 sites, kitchen shelter. Open June to Sept. ▲

Mile 286 (76) Km 460 (122.5): Weeping Wall viewpoint. Water from melting snowfields high above the Cirrus Mountain cliffs finds its way through cracks in the wall and emerges as a series of graceful waterfalls. Even in midsummer the limestone wall is dark with water; in winter, it is coated with ice. To the northwest is a good example of synclinal folds in the strata of Nigel Peak.

Mile 288 (74) Km 465 (117.5): Nigel Creek canyon. Turnout by highway bridge over gorge cut into dolomite bedrock by Nigel Creek.

To the west, a short trail leads to tumbling waterfalls (about a half-hour hike). Branch trail follows old gravel road to foot of Saskatchewan Glacier, source of the Saskatchewan River (about a 2-hour hike). ⚏

Mile 289 (73) Km 465.5 (117): *CAUTION:* Hairpin bend and steep climb northbound up the "Big Hill." Drive with care.

Mile 289.5 (72.5) Km 466 (116.5): Viewpoint, North Saskatchewan River canyon and the Castle Mountain syncline, a giant U-shaped bend in the strata that runs from Banff to Jasper. Cliffs to the east form base of Cirrus Mountain. Breathtaking view of mountain scenery and highway snaking south. Good view of Bridal Veil Falls.

Mile 291 (71) Km 468.5 (114): Viewpoint, Cirrus Mountain and short trail to Panther Falls. ⚏

Mile 291.5 (70.5) Km 469 (113.5): Viewpoint, Nigel

Peak (elev. 10,535 feet/3,211m) to the northwest with its synclinal (downfolded) strata and the Nigel Creek trail, which follows the river up to Nigel Pass and down into the Brazeau River.

Mile 292.5 (69.5) Km 470.5 (112): Highway warning sign for possible poor visibility; there are often fog and clouds at this high elevation. Steep downgrade southbound.

Mile 293 (69) Km 472 (110.5): Parker Ridge viewpoint and trail, 1.8 miles/3 km round-trip, through the subalpine forest into alpine tundra. Mountain goats and ptarmigan. A short distance along the trail is a fossilized coral reef with fossils of mollusks and large-coiled cephapods. The alpine flowers in mid-June and July are splendid. Trail crosses the ridge to reach a grand viewpoint of the Saskatchewan Glacier, source of the river. Stay on the trail. Alpine terrain is delicate and should not be disturbed. Hilda Creek youth hostel nearby. ⚏

Mile 296.5 (65.5) Km 477 (105.5): Sunwapta Pass (elev. 6,676 feet/2,035m). This high point on the Icefields Parkway is the divide between North Saskatchewan waters flowing south and east to Hudson Bay and the Athabasca River flowing north to the Arctic Ocean. The pass is also the boundary between Banff and Jasper national parks.

Sunwapta is Stoney Indian for "turbulent river." The Sunwapta River drains from the Athabasca Glacier and flows into the Athabasca River some 36 miles/50 km north. Highway 93 follows the river valley.

Mile 297.5 (64.5) Km 479 (103.5): Wilcox Creek Campground; 46 sites, sani-station, interpretive events. Good views of Mount Athabasca (elev. 11,453 feet/3,491m) and Nigel Peak. Hiking trail leads to good viewpoint of the Columbia Icefields. ⚏▲

Mile 298 (64) Km 480 (102.5): Columbia Icefield Campground; 33 sites, tents only. Hiking. ⚏▲

Mile 299.5 (62.5) Km 482 (100.5): Columbia Icefield Chalet provides accommodations, food and gas (gas during summer only). Good views from parking lot of Dome and Athabasca glaciers. Across the road from the chalet, a road leads west to a parking lot beside Sunwapta Lake and the toe of Athabasca Glacier. Along this road are markers that show the extent of the retreating glacier in previous years. In 1890, the glacier was almost beside the highway.

Private road that climbs right onto the glacier is access road for snowmobile tours, available mid-May through Sept.; inquire at the chalet. *CAUTION:* Watch out for very tame bighorn sheep panhandling in the parking lots. (Do not feed them!)

Parks Canada Icefield Information Center, open late May to first week in Oct. The centre has good view windows with markers, permits and maps, an audiovisual presentation on glacier formation and a scale model of the Columbia Icefield area.

The glaciers visible from

Visitor centre in Jasper National Park. (© George Wuerthner)

the road are merely fingers of the giant Columbia Icefield, which covers 241 square miles/389 square km at an average elevation of 8,497 feet/2,590m. Mount Athabasca and Mount Kitchener (elev. 11,397 feet/3,474m) are the dominant peaks. ★

Mile 301.5 (60.5) Km 485 (97.5): Sunwapta Canyon viewpoint. From the viewpoint, the highway descends steeply northbound to the river valley, with sharp corners signposted for 30 mph/50 kmph. Watch for Rocky Mountain bighorn sheep. They are accustomed to people and will approach quite close. Do not feed them; human food is bad for them.

Mile 302 (60) Km 486 (96.5): Tangle Creek. Small roadside picnic area and view of Tangle Falls, tumbling over limestone cliffs. ⚲

Mile 304.5 (57.5) Km 490 (92.5): Picnic area and viewpoint of Stutfield Glacier and its twin icefalls tumbling down Stutfield Peak. ⚲

Mile 310 (52) Km 499 (83.5): Beauty Creek youth hostel. Watch for roadside woodland caribou late fall to spring.

Mile 310.5 (51.5) Km 500 (82.5): Roadside turnout with mountain markers for Mushroom and Diadem Peak and Tangle Ridge.

Mile 315.5 (46.5) Km 508 (74.5): Jonas Creek Campground; 37 campsites. ▲

Mile 317 (45) Km 510 (72.5): Bright pink boulders beside the road are quartz sandstone that fell from the high ridge to the east.

Mile 318.5 (43.5) Km 513 (69.5): Poboktan Creek Park warden station and trail into the Brazeau Lake wilderness region. ⚹

Mile 326 (36) Km 525 (57.5): Bubbling Springs picnic site. ⚲

Mile 329.5 (32.5) Km 530 (52.5): Short access road to parking lot at Sunwapta Falls,

where the river changes course abruptly from northwest to southwest and has eroded a deep, smooth canyon with 30-foot/9-m falls. Short trail from parking lot. Accommodations, food and gas nearby in summer.

Mile 330.5 (31.5) Km 532 (50.5): Short access road east to Buck and Osprey lakes.

Mile 332 (30) Km 534 (48.5): Honeymoon Lake Campground by shore of lake; 36 sites, interpretive events. Across lake is a good view of the Endless Chain Ridge.

Just north on Highway 93 is viewpoint with mountain signposts for the Winston Churchill Range and an excellent view of the Athabasca Valley and its ancient moraines. ▲

Mile 333.5 (28.5) Km 536.5 (46): Ranger Creek Campground. Tent sites for 25 people only. ▲

Mile 334.5 (27.5) Km 538 (44.5): Viewpoint, Mount Christie (elev. 10,180 feet/3,103m) and Athabasca River, which here makes a tight horseshoe loop.

Mile 337.5 (24.5) Km 543 (39.5): Mount Christie picnic area beside the river. ⚲

Mile 340 (22) Km 547 (35.5): Picnic area and viewpoint by popular animal lick. Finely ground glacial deposits here contain mineral salts, which attract mountain goats, sheep and other animals. Fantastic view down the Athabasca Valley and its panorama of high peaks. North of the gap created by the Whirlpool River is the snowy crest of Mount Edith Cavell (elev. 11,033 feet/3,363m), one of the highest in the Rockies. ⚲

Mile 341.5 (20.5) Km 550 (32.5): Mount Kerkeslin Campground; 42 sites. Watch for Canada geese on the river flats. ▲

Mile 343.5 (18.5) Km 553 (29.5): Jasper Park warden station and Athabasca Falls. Youth

hostel nearby.

Mile 344 (18) Km 554 (28.5): **Junction** with Highway 93A, alternate route north for 15 miles/24 km on west side of Athabasca River. A short way along this road is a viewpoint for magnificent Athabasca Falls (a must stop), which drops 40 feet/12m from a sandstone lip to thunder down a short, narrow canyon. Road continues to Wabasso Campground; 238 sites, 6 walk-in sites, sani-station, playground and interpretive events. Also access to Cavell Lake at the base of Mount Edith Cavell and the Angel Glacier; trailhead for the famous Tonquin Valley. Also on Highway 93A is Marmot Basin, Jasper's downhill ski area. ⚹⚹▲★

Mile 346 (16) Km 557 (25.5): Turnout and parking for short trail to Horseshoe Lake under the cliffs of Mount Hardisty. ⚹

Mile 348 (14) Km 560 (22.5): Viewpoint, Mount Edith Cavell. Between this peak and Whirlpool Peak to the south lies the valley of the Whirlpool River. Early fur brigades left the Athabasca River and followed the Whirlpool up to Athabasca Pass.

Mile 355 (7) Km 571 (11.5): Trail to Wabasso Lake and on to Shovel Pass and the Maligne Valley. ⚹

Mile 357 (5) Km 575 (7.5): Trail to Valley of the Five Lakes. ⚹

Mile 359 (3) Km 578 (4.5): Athabasca River bridge. Highway 93A rejoins route just north of bridge. Jasper National Park entrance gate for southbound travelers.

Mile 360 (2) Km 581 (1.5): Wapiti Campground; 340 campsites (40 with electrical hookup), sani-station, hot showers, interpretive events. Wapiti winter campground has 28 trailer sites and 10 walk-in sites. Wapiti is another name for elk, which frequent this valley in fall and winter, often feeding on the bark of the aspen trees. ▲

Mile 361 (1) Km 582 (0.5): **Junction** with road west to Whistlers Campground; 780 sites (77 with full hookups, 43 with electricity only), 24 walk-in sites, sani-station, hot showers, playground and interpretive events. Road continues to the Jasper Tramway, which whisks tourists up Whistler Mountain to the 7,496-foot/2,285-m level. The tramway is open late March to mid-Oct. At the top of the lift is a restaurant, an interpretive area describing life in the alpine zone, and a trail to Whistler Summit. Whistler is the local name for the hoary marmot. ▲

Mile 362 (0) Km 582.5 (0): **Junction** with Highway 16 at west end of **JASPER** (pop. 3,500) townsite, park headquarters for Jasper National Park. All facilities available, with accommodations ranging from bungalows to luxury lodges. A popular ski area in winter, Jasper also offers a variety of summer attractions, including museums, fishing, hiking, boat excursions on Maligne Lake, sky tram rides for aerial views of the park, and river raft trips.

Northwest Mileposts® travelers using Yellowhead Highway 16 refer to *The MILEPOST®* *All-The-North Travel Guide®*, which covers highways to and in Alaska. ⚹⚹⚹

U.S. HIGHWAY 95

Nevada–Oregon Border to Canadian Border
(See maps, pages 134, 136 and 139)

Beginning in the sagebrush-covered high desert of northern Nevada, U.S. Highway 95 passes through rich farming and ranching territory, runs parallel to the Hells Canyon National Recreation Area, and winds through the evergreen forests of northern Idaho and British Columbia. Antelope, mule and white-tailed deer, bighorn sheep and elk inhabit the wooded country and rolling sagebrush regions. The highway crosses numerous good fishing streams plus several major rivers including the Snake, Salmon and Clearwater.

There are many historical points of interest along Highway 95 that reveal the colorful events leading to the settlement of the West. Before attempting to take Highway 95 in the winter, contact the state police or Transportation Dept. for road conditions. Towns are few and far between, particularly in the southern section, so be sure to check your gas gauge as you pass through the communities.

U.S. Highway 95 Log

Distance from Nevada–Oregon border is followed by distance from the Canadian border.

Mile 0 (659): Nevada–Oregon border. **McDERMITT** straddles the border. No sales tax on the Oregon side. All services available. RV park with 16 sites, full hookups, showers and laundromat. Next gas northbound 55 miles. ▲

Mile 18.5 (640.5): Snow zone begins (northbound). Blue Mountain Pass lies ahead. During winter months it is advisable to check with the Oregon or Nevada State Patrol before attempting to cross this pass. MP 103

Mile 21.5 (637.5): Blue Mountain (elev. 7,439 feet) is visible to the west. MP 100

Mile 23 (636): Summit of Blue Mountain Pass (elev. 5,293 feet).

Mile 29.5 (629.5): Entering **BASQUE STATION** (elev. 4,650), Dept. of Transportation maintenance station, picnic table. No services available. Snow zone begins southbound. ⊼ MP 92

Mile 34 (625): **Junction** with Whitehorse Ranch Road. Steens Mountain is visible to the west and is home for pronghorn antelope, bighorn sheep and mule deer. Also popular chukar and Hungarian partridge area.

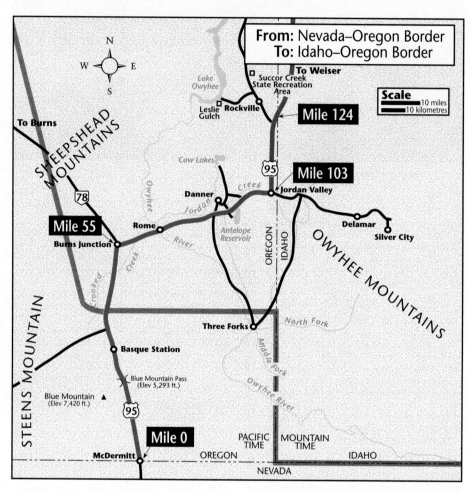

From: Nevada–Oregon Border
To: Idaho–Oregon Border

Mile 42 (617): Conical building east of highway is an aircraft navigation omni-ranging station.

Mile 43 (616): Pacific–Mountain time zone. Set your watches ahead 1 hour if you're headed north, back 1 hour if you're headed south.

Mile 48 (611): Crooked Creek. MP 73

Mile 55 (604): **BURNS JUNCTION**; weigh station. **Junction** with Highway 78 to Burns. MP 66

Mile 55.5 (603.5): Burns Junction Guard Station.

Mile 61 (598): Rest area with picnic tables and drinking water. Historical marker tells of the last major Indian uprising in the Pacific Northwest, the Bannock War of 1878. ⊼

Mile 68 (591): Crossing the Owyhee Canyon at **ROME**. RV park, 10 full hookups, propane, food and gas available. The town

derived its name from the sandstone formations along the Owyhee River just north of the highway, which resemble the columns of Rome. The Owyhee River flows more than 200 miles from the Owyhee Mountains of Nevada through the scabland of Idaho and Oregon. Popular float fishing and whitewater rafting area with Class 4 rapids. Downstream from Rome the river is classified as a scenic waterway. Rafting and fishing guides are available locally. BLM boat launch site 0.4 mile south of the crossing; pit toilets, picnic tables, barbecue. ⊼➰▲ MP 53

Mile 69 (590): Geological monument describes the Owyhee River and surrounding terrain. MP 52

Mile 70.5 (588.5): Entering Soldier Creek Resource Conservation Area.

Mile 82 (577): Rock Creek.

Mile 84 (575): Turnoff north to **DANNER**; no services. Graded dirt road leads 3.6 miles from highway to Charbonneau Historical Marker and Inskip Station, a hostel founded in 1863. No direction signs. Ignore yellow arrow at Mile 2 and go straight across cattle guard. Monument is 1.5 miles past cattle guard. The fortified dwelling at Inskip Station often served as refuge during Indian raids. This is also the burial place for Jean Baptiste Charbonneau, the youngest member of the Lewis and Clark expedition, born to Sacajawea and Toussaint Charbonneau in 1805. Baptiste was educated in Europe and returned to the West to become a mountain man, magistrate, interpreter and '49er for nearly 4 decades. He died of pneumonia at this spot on May 16, 1866, en route to a new gold strike in Montana.

The dirt road continues another 8.5 miles north to Cow Lakes. Only Upper Cow Lake offers any sportfishing, with a fair population of brown bullhead catfish and crappie. Best fishing is near the west end lava beds, which has a BLM campground and boat launch. ☞▲

Mile 85 (574): Turnoff south to Indian Canyon and Three Forks. Popular Owyhee River access and launch at Three Forks. MP 36

Mile 90.5 (568.5): In 1960, under the authority of the Taylor Grazing Act, the Bureau of Land Management began an experimental program of rehabilitating 4.5 million acres of desert rangeland in this area. Called the Vale Project, the program was intended to test new concepts in rangeland rehabilitation and restore the land to productive use. The project was a success, and now some 220 livestock operators graze 82,000 cattle and 6,000 sheep on the project area.

Mile 92 (567): Jack Creek.

Mile 92.5 (566.5): Turnoff south to Antelope Reservoir, which offers a BLM campground. There is no fishing in Antelope Reservoir due to mercury contamination. This is also the turnoff to Antelope School and the Charbonneau Historical Marker. ▲

Mile 99 (560): Jordan Creek and turnoff north to Cow Lakes; 14 miles to Cow Lakes campground, boat launch, pit toilets. ▲

Mile 103 (556): JORDAN VALLEY (pop. 390). All services are available. This is a good area to test the Basque cuisine. Originally from northwest Spain, the Basque people are culturally and ethnically unique. Many Basques immigrated to the United States during the early part of the 20th century and worked as sheepherders. They brought with them their ancient culture and unique lifestyle, which is prominent in the Great Basin area of Oregon, Idaho and Nevada. The first Basques came to Jordan Valley in 1898.

Originally a gold-mining area, the Jordan Valley today is primarily a ranching community for beef cattle. It lies within Oregon's Malheur County, which leads the nation in acres of sugar beets, onions, and alfalfa hay and seed.

Mile 111.5 (547.5): Turnoff west to the Jordon Craters, a Federal Research Natural Area. The rugged lava flows of the Jordan Craters cover some 36 square miles, which are inhabited by 60 species of waterfowl and 120 species of other birds, including eagles, hawks, falcons, quail and grouse. The roads into the area are maintained by the BLM and are purposely left undeveloped to discourage large influxes of visitors.

Mile 113 (546): Cow Creek.   MP 11

Mile 115 (544): Turnoff east to the historic mining camps of Delamar and Silver City. Rich silver mines produced millions of dollars worth of ore during the 1860s. Silver City became a major territorial community and acquired the first telegraph service in the territory in 1866. Idaho's first daily newspaper, the *Idaho Avalanche*, made its home in Silver City. The original press is on display in Homedale (**Mile 155**) in front of the *Owyhee Avalanche* newspaper office. Today, Silver City is an unrestored ghost town. The Owyhee Cattlemen's Assoc. holds its annual convention there in August.

Mile 122 (537): Turnoff to Leslie Gulch and Succor Creek State Recreation Area. Succor

Baling hay in the Jordan Valley, primarily a ranching community for beef cattle. Alfalfa hay, onions, sugar beets and seed are also raised here. (L. Linkhart)

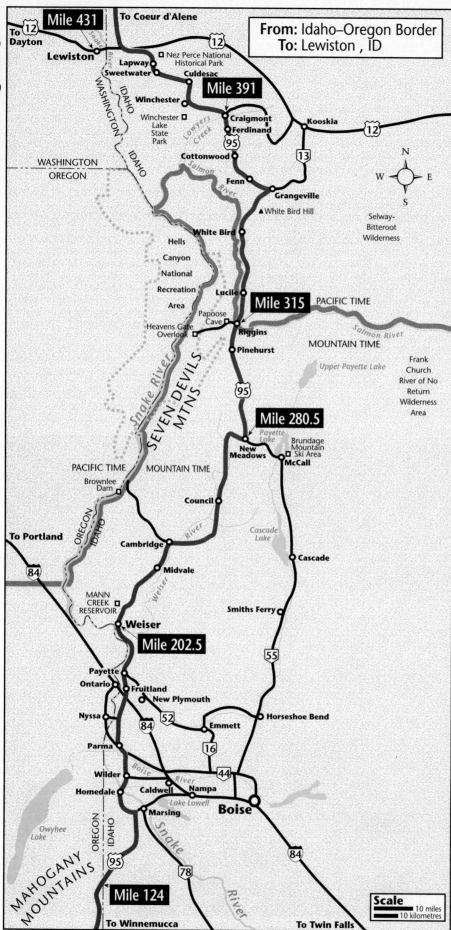

From: Idaho–Oregon Border
To: Lewiston , ID

Creek crossing. The park is located 25 miles north on this unimproved road and offers camping and picnicking facilities. There is also a viewpoint with hiking trails. Leslie Gulch provides access to 40-mile-long Owyhee Reservoir, once rated as southeastern Oregon's premier fishing lake but now has a mercury advisory, recommending only limited consumption of fish caught in the reservoir. (Best access to Owyhee Lake is via Oregon Highway 201 and Lake Owyhee Road south from Nyssa.)　　MP 2

Mile 124 (535): Oregon–Idaho state border.

Mile 129 (530): Turnoff west to Leslie Gulch.

Mile 138 (521): Scenic overlook and historical marker. You are in Owyhee Country, a misspelling of the word Hawaii. In 1818, Donald MacKenzie brought a brigade of Hawaiian fur hunters to this area to trap. He sent several Hawaiians to the Snake River valley. They never returned. Since that time, the county, mountain range and surrounding area have been called the Owyhees.

Six percent grade next 3.5 miles northbound.

Mile 148 (511): Junction with Idaho Highway 55. A short drive east on Highway 55 will bring you to Lake Lowell (sometimes identified as Deer Flat Reservoir), which provides fair to good fishing. This is a popular recreation area for residents of Boise, Caldwell and Nampa.

Mile 152 (507): Jump Creek.

Mile 153.5 (505.5): Sportsman access east 12 miles to Snake River.

Mile 155 (504): HOMEDALE (pop. 1,963), a farming and ranching community. All services are available. On the way through town, stop to see the printing press for the first Idaho territorial daily newspaper on display in front of the *Owyhee Avalanche*. **Junction** with Idaho Highway 19 west to Oregon. MP 34

Mile 156.5 (502.5): Snake River. Dams create a series of giant, productive fishing lakes on this famous river.

Mile 160.5 (498.5): WILDER (pop. 1,350) and the **junction** with Idaho Highway 19 east to Caldwell. Wilder Air Force Station 3 miles west. Notice the vineyards and hop fields near the highway. Idaho wine is becoming a significant economic resource in this area. MP 39

Mile 166 (493): Boise River. Stocked with rainbow trout and good for whitefish.

Mile 167 (492): South **junction** with U.S. Highways 20 and 26 east connecting route to I-84.

Mile 167.5 (491.5): Old Fort Boise Historical Marker. Two miles west of this point, on the bank of the Snake River, an important Hudson's Bay Co. fur-trading post was established in 1834.

Mile 169.5 (489.5): PARMA (pop. 1,597), a small ranching and farming community. All traveler services available. This is the home of the Old Fort Boise Park. A replica of Old

Fort Boise is located in the park; open afternoons Wednesday to Saturday during the summer. The park has a campground with 8 full-hookup sites, showers, restrooms, picnic tables and dump station. ⅋▲

Mile 170 (489): Turnoff west to Roswell, a small farming community.

Mile 176 (483): North **junction** with U.S. Highways 20 and 26 connecting route northwest to main highway near Ontario; access to Nyssa, OR. (See U.S. HIGHWAY 20 section.)

Mile 183 (476): U.S. Highway 95 crosses Interstate 84. Travelers heading east or west on I-84 turn to **Mile 378.5** in the INTERSTATE 84 section for log of that route.

Mile 183.5 (475.5): **Junction** with U.S. Highway 30 to New Plymouth. MP 62

Mile 185.5 (473.5): FRUITLAND (pop. 2,559). All services available.

Mile 186 (473): **Junction** with U.S. Highway 30 to Ontario, 2 miles west; major shopping, motels, restaurants. MP 65

Mile 187 (472): Payette River. Annually stocked with trout, the river also offers native and warm-water fish. ⇔

Mile 188.5 (470.5): Highway 95 business route passes through the town of **PAYETTE** (pop. 5,592) while main Highway 95 goes around the town. They join north of the city. Payette offers motels, restaurants and all traveler services. Payette is named after Francois Payette, a fur trader and the first postmaster at Old Fort Boise. The town boasts Killebrew Stadium, a large sports complex located at the high school, which was named in honor of Payette native and Baseball Hall of Fame member Harmon Killebrew.

Mile 189.5 (469.5): **Junction** with Idaho Highway 52 to Emmett. When traveling in these rural farming communities, be cautious when approaching slow-moving farm vehicles on the highway.

Mile 190 (469): Turnoff east to airport.

Mile 202.5 (456.5): WEISER (pop. 4,571) and the Weiser River. Weiser (Wee-zer) is billed as the "Gateway to Hells Canyon," the deepest gorge in North America, but the actual turnoff is at Cambridge, 32 miles north. Weiser is the home of the National Old-Time Fiddlers Contest, held the third full week of June each year. Contact the Weiser Chamber of Commerce; phone (208) 549-0450, for more information. The town and river were named after Peter Weiser, a Revolutionary War veteran and later a sergeant, cook and hunter for the Lewis and Clark expedition of 1804–06. One of the interesting landmarks of Weiser is the Pythian Castle, a nearly perfect replica of a castle that still exists in Wales. Weiser River and its forks are planted with trout each spring.

Mile 214 (445): Mann's Creek. Road leads northwest to Mann's Creek Reservoir. Campground and fishing. ⇔▲

Mile 216 (443): Chain-up area and turnout. Six percent grade next 2 miles northbound.

Idaho offers great fishing.

Mile 218 (441): Midvale Summit (elev. 3,326 feet).

Mile 221.5 (437.5): Rest area and historical marker explaining the prehistoric rock quarry where natives fashioned a variety of stone tools some 3,000 to 5,000 years ago. Restrooms, covered picnic tables and a beautiful overlook to the north of the Weiser River valley below. ⅋ MP 101

Mile 225.5 (433.5): MIDVALE (pop. 110), a small farming and ranching community. Limited services. MP 105

Mile 228.5 (430.5): The scenic Weiser River valley parallels the highway to the east.

Mile 234 (425): CAMBRIDGE (pop. 324), a small farming and ranching community. Most services. Turnoff to Brownlee Dam, Hells Canyon. MP 113

Mile 234.5 (424.5): Weiser River.

Mile 245 (414): Turnoff east to Indian Valley.

Mile 250.5 (408.5): Middle Fork Weiser River, stocked with rainbow. ⇔

Mile 255.5 (403.5): COUNCIL (pop. 917). Early Indians held periodic councils at an area near the present location of the town. National Forest information center located here. MP 134

Mile 256 (403): Turnoff east to hospital.

Mile 257.5 (401.5): Chain-up area and turnout.

Mile 260 (399): Turnoff west to Fruitvale. No services.

Mile 265 (394): Payette National Forest boundary.

Mile 266 (393): Weiser River. This area is a beautiful, thickly wooded drive. Use the slow-vehicle turnouts if 3 or more vehicles are behind you.

Mile 269 (390): Evergreen Forest Service campground (elev. 3,800 feet); fee charged June 1 to Sept. 10, 12 sites, water, pit toilets. ▲ MP 149

Mile 271.5 (387.5): Payette National Forest boundary.

Mile 272.5 (386.5): Forest Route 089 west to Lost Valley Reservoir; Cold Springs campground 2.5 miles, 31 sites, timbered setting, picnicking, water, toilets, fee charged. Slaughter Gulch campground, 6 miles, 18 sites, picnicking, pit toilets, no fee. ⅋▲

Mile 273.5 (385.5): TAMARACK, a small unincorporated village. No services available. Lumber mill spans highway.

Mile 280 (379): Crossing Little Salmon River.

Mile 280.5 (378.5): NEW MEADOWS (pop. 600). Gas, food and lodging available. Ranger station. Several structures here were built by town founder Colonel Heigho. Picnicking at city park. ⅋ MP 159

Mile 281 (378): **Junction** with Idaho Highway 55 to McCall (11 miles southeast) on beautiful Payette Lake, and to Cascade Reservoir (38 miles south), one of the most popular fishing spots in the state. During winter there is downhill skiing at Brundage Mountain Ski Area, just outside McCall. The McCall area is a year-round vacation destination with many resort and camping facilities. For information, contact the McCall Chamber of Commerce; phone (208) 634-7631. ⋇⇔▲ MP 355

Mile 283 (376): You are crossing the 45th Parallel, the halfway point between the North Pole and the equator. Travel information kiosk. Kimberland Meadows Resort Community.

Mile 285.5 (373.5): Zim's Hot Springs turnoff.

Mile 292 (367): Little Salmon River. Travelers on U.S. Highway 95 will cross this river several times in the next few miles northbound.

Mile 302 (357): PINEHURST, a small unincorporated village with motel, RV park, groceries, gas and cafe. ▲ MP 182

Mile 309 (350): Sheep Creek shaded rest area; restrooms, covered picnic tables, barbecues, water. ⋔

Mile 311 (348): Crossing the Rapid River at **RAPID RIVER**, a tiny community in the river canyon; groceries, RV park. A salmon hatchery is located 3 miles west. ▲ MP 191

Mile 314 (345): Turnoff to Seven Devils Mountains and Heavens Gate overlook (elev. 8,400 feet). Heavens Gate overlook, 19 miles west, is open from July through Sept. and offers photographic opportunities. The turnoff from Highway 95 also leads to Papoose Cave, the largest limestone cave in Idaho and one of the most spectacular in the Northwest. It is one of the 10 deepest caves in the United States, with a maximum depth of nearly 945 feet. A locked gate keeps spelunkers from entering this very dangerous cave. For tour information contact: David Kasner, Gem State Grotto Assoc., 12567 W. De Meyer St., Boise, ID 83704.

Hells Canyon National Recreation Area District Office is on the west side of the road. Hells Canyon is the deepest river gorge in the world at 6,600 feet and is the last free-flowing section of this spectacular river. Float trips through the canyon's legendary rapids are regulated to minimize impact. The recreation area encompasses 652,488 acres of Idaho and Oregon straddling the Snake River.

Mile 315 (344): RIGGINS (pop. 500) offers all traveler services including 3 RV parks and 2 motels. "Gateway to the River of No Return," Riggins lies in a T-shaped canyon at the confluence of the Salmon River and the Little Salmon River. Many outfitters, guides and river raft trips may be arranged for in Riggins. Hunting and fishing opportunities are excellent. Local sport shops provide timely information. The Salmon River Jet Boat Races are held each April.

There is a roadside picnic area with restrooms at the north end of town.
⋔ ⊷▲ MP 195

Mile 317 (342): Race Creek.

Mile 317.5 (341.5): Crossing the Salmon River and the Mountain–Pacific time zone line. Turn your watches back 1 hour if you are headed north, ahead 1 hour if you are headed south. Gold dredges mounted on floating rafts working the riverbed are sometimes visible.

Mile 319 (340): Lightning Creek.

Mile 320 (339): Chair Creek.

Mile 320.5 (338.5): Fiddle Creek.　MP 200

Mile 323.5 (335.5): Lucile Recreation site; boat launch, 1 campsite, pit toilet. ▲

Mile 325 (334): LUCILE, a small unincorporated village. Food available. RV park with 25 sites on river, water and electricity. Gold panning—you keep the gold! ▲

Mile 325.5 (333.5): Hilo Creek. Historical marker explains the city of Florence, a gold-

The Salmon River offers float trips and jet boat rides. Riggins, at Mile 315, is the area's whitewater capital for river trips. (Lee Foster)

mining town 14 air miles east of this point, which produced millions of dollars in gold during a 1-year period.

Mile 328.5 (330.5): John Day Creek.

Mile 330.5 (328.5): RV park with 32 sites, 9 pull through, 8 full hookups, showers, beach, gift shop. Open all year. ▲

Mile 331.5 (327.5): Salmon River canyon geological site.

Mile 334.5 (324.5): Slate Creek ranger station and Slate Creek. No services.

Mile 335.5 (323.5): Slate Creek Recreation Area; boat launch, dump station.

Mile 336.5 (322.5): Rest area.　MP 215

Mile 338.5 (320.5): Sportsman access.
MP 218

Mile 339.5 (319.5): Skookumchuck Creek and roadside rest area; restrooms, picnic tables. ⋔ MP 219

Mile 342.5 (316.5): Hammer Creek Recreation Area.　MP 222

Mile 343 (316): Cafe and RV park. ▲

Mile 344 (315): White Bird Junction and White Bird Creek. The small town of **WHITE BIRD** has all services available. You are about to ascend White Bird Hill; 7 percent grade next 8 miles northbound.

Mile 347.5 (311.5): Nez Perce War Historic Site and valley overlook. Near the base of White Bird Hill is a battleground where the Nez Perce soundly defeated a much larger force of cavalry soldiers on June 17, 1877. That marked the beginning of the Nez Perce War.　MP 228

Mile 350.5 (308.5): Turnoff to White Bird Battlefield auto tour.

Mile 351.5 (307.5): Historical marker about the Salmon River.

Mile 352 (307): Summit of White Bird Hill (elev. 4,245 feet). This highway, completed in 1975, replaced the treacherous 16- to 18-

foot-wide highway that wound its way up the hill. The old highway had so many switchbacks that a car would make the equivalent of 37 complete circles in 22 miles. The new highway cut the driving distance in half.

Mile 354 (305): Camas Prairie Historical Site. The Camas Prairie is named after the camas plant, the root of which was a staple in the Indian diet. In this area, the Nez Perce Indians met to hunt, fish and gather camas roots for the winter.

Mile 360 (299): GRANGEVILLE (pop. 3,666), Idaho County seat, largest county in Idaho at 5.4 million acres. Logging, mining and agriculture are the major industries in this area. Wild scenic rivers, forest wilderness and ski areas nearby. All services available.

Junction with Idaho Highway 13 to U.S. Highway 12 at Kooskia (26 miles). See U.S. HIGHWAY 12 section.   MP 240

Mile 362.5 (296.5): Junction with road to Nezperce. Limited services available. MP 242

Mile 366.5 (292.5): Lawyer's Creek. MP 246

Mile 367.5 (291.5): The small, unincorporated village of Fenn. Groceries available.

Mile 373 (286): Turnoff to the ancient Weis rock shelter (7 miles off the highway) and a historical marker (0.5 mile north) that explains the old native dwelling and battle with Nez Perce. Roadside tables are available.

Mile 375.5 (283.5): Turnoff to **COTTONWOOD** (pop. 941) and the Priory of St. Gertrude. The historic convent, established in 1919, is the only "motherhouse" in the Idaho Catholic diocese. St. Gertrude's Museum (3 miles west) is a fascinating study of Western history and is well worth the visit. Cottonwood is also the home of the North Idaho Correctional Institution.

Mile 377 (282): Turnoff for Cottonwood Butte Ski Area, 5 miles west; day lodge, rentals, 1 T-bar and 1 rope tow.

Mile 379 (280): Nez Perce Indian Reservation boundary.

Mile 383.5 (275.5): FERDINAND (pop. 160). Cafe.   MP 264

Mile 386.5 (272.5): Lawyer's Creek.

Mile 388 (271): Historical markers; Lawyer's Canyon and Railroad Trestles.

Mile 391 (268): CRAIGMONT (pop. 600), named after the first permanent white settler in Idaho, Col. William Craig. All services. This is also the **junction** of Idaho Highway 62 to Nezperce.

Mile 397 (262): Turnoff to Winchester Lake State Park and city of **WINCHESTER**, 2 miles south. Winchester Lake State Park is a forested campground with 75 sites on a small trout lake. No gas motors are allowed on the lake. Boats with electric motors, kayaks, canoes, etc., are permitted. The 418-acre park is open year-round and offers picnic sites, water, toilets, fishing, trails and a boat ramp. Camping fee $9. Winter activi-

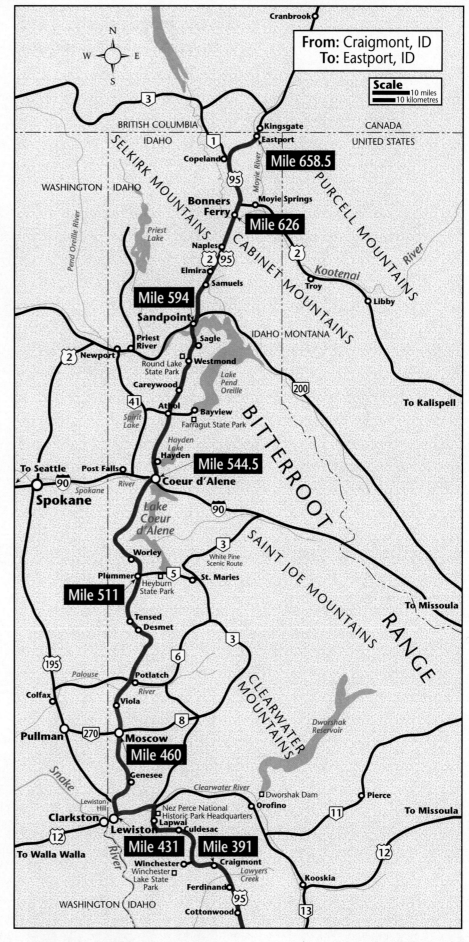

U.S. Highway 195
Lewiston to Spokane

Wheatfields and farms characterize the countryside along U.S. Highway 195. (George Wuerthner)

U.S. Highway 195 is a 93-mile stretch of mostly 2-lane highway through the scenic Palouse country of eastern Washington. A vaguely defined area measuring roughly 85 by 100 miles, the rolling wheatfields of the Palouse straddle the Washington–Idaho border. U.S. Highway 195 is an important north-south connector route between U.S. Highways 95 and 12 at Lewiston, ID, and Interstate 90 at Spokane, WA.

Mile 0 (93): Idaho–Washington state line, approximately a half mile west of the U.S. Highway 95 junction.

Mile 2.5 (90.5): Northbound travelers get their first glimpse of Palouse country. The term "palouse" is derived from a French word early settlers used to describe the distinctive rolling hills of the area. Today, this corner of Washington is a prime producer of soft wheat, which is used in crackers, cookies and other pastry items. (Bread requires hard wheat.) Much of this soft wheat is shipped to the Orient for use in noodles.

Planting of the wheat is done in October. Harvesting takes place in August. Watch for huge combines working the fields well into the night during harvest time.

Mile 5 (88): UNIONTOWN; market and gas station. There's a charming little St. Boniface church here with handsome twin wooden bell towers and stained-glass windows.

Mile 8 (85): COLTON; market, liquor store and post office.

Mile 20 (73): **Junction** with Washington Highway 27 (Grand Avenue) to PULLMAN (pop. 23,579), the largest city in Whitman County, offering several hotels and motels, an RV park and numerous restaurants. The town was named Pullman in 1881 after George Pullman, the Chicago industrialist who invented the Pullman sleeping car.

Pullman's economy revolves around agriculture and Washington State University. Established as a land-grant college in 1890, the university today has about 17,000 students. It is home to the Cougar football team. WSU offers free campus tours on weekdays. Ferdinand's Dairy Bar is the retail outlet for the college's dairy operations and serves "real" ice cream and Cougar Gold cheddar cheese.

Mile 22 (71): **Junction** with Washington Highway 194 west.

Mile 22.5 (70.5): **Junction** with Washington Highway 270 (Davis Way) east to Pullman and Moscow, ID. See description at **Mile 20.**

Mile 28.5 (64.5): Turnoff for Klemgard County Park, a grassy day-use area on Union Flat Creek; interpretive trails, playground, picnic sites.

Mile 34.5 (58.5): COLFAX (pop. 2,500); 2 motels, RV park, restaurants, shopping and hospital. This compact and bustling community was first settled in the late 1860s. It became county seat for Whitman County in 1871. Whitman County is the nation's leading producer of soft wheat, dry peas and lentils. It is also one of the state's largest cattle and swine producing regions.

Mile 35.5 (57.5): **Junction** with Washington Highway 272 east to Palouse.

Mile 36.5 (56.5): **Junction** with Washington State Highway 26 west to Washtucna and Vantage.

Mile 43 (50): Turnoff for Steptoe Butte State Park picnic area. A winding drive leads to the top of Steptoe Butte (elev. 3,612 feet) and a panoramic view of surrounding farmlands.

Mile 45.5 (47.5): Steptoe Butte historical marker, named after Lt. Col. E. J. Steptoe of the U.S. Cavalry.

Mile 46 (47): Entering town of Steptoe and **junction** with Washington Highway 23 west to St. John.

Mile 58.5 (34.5): Rest area.

Mile 60.5 (32.5): **Junction** with Washington Highway 271 to Oakesdale. Access to Steptoe Butte State Park (see **Mile 45**).

Mile 62 (31): Historical marker for Steptoe Butte.

Mile 64 (29): Turnoff for ROSALIA (pop. 650), which has a main street with a gas station, cafe, 2 banks and shops. There's also a classic old street clock that dates from the 1905 Lewis and Clark Exposition in Portland, the turreted Howard House, and the Harthill Clock Museum.

Leaving Whitman County, entering Spokane County, northbound. Whitman County was named in honor of Dr. Marcus Whitman, who established a mission near present day Walla Walla in 1836. Whitman, his wife Narcissa, and 11 others were killed by Indians in 1847.

Mile 69 (24): Turnoff for Plaza.

Mile 76.5 (16.5): Turnoff for SPANGLE; gas and food.

Mile 78 (15): At Milepost 80, U.S. Highway 195 becomes a divided freeway.

Mile 93 (0): U.S. Highway 195 (Inland Empire Way) **junctions** with Interstate 90 on the western edge of Spokane. (See description of Spokane in the MAJOR CITIES section; turn to **Mile 279** in the INTERSTATE 90 section for log of that route.)

ties include ice skating, ice fishing, sledding and cross-country skiing.   ♨🎿⛵⛰ MP 278

Mile 405 (254): Historical marker, railroad tunnels.

Mile 406 (253): Lapwai Creek.   MP 286

Mile 409.5 (249.5): Turnoff to the small unincorporated village of **CULDESAC** (pop. 262); groceries, bank.   MP 291

Mile 412 (247): Turnoff to St. Joseph's Mission (4 miles west). This restored church was built in 1874 under the direction of Father Joseph Cataldo as the first Catholic mission for the Nez Perce Indians. It is part of the Nez Perce Historical Park.

Mile 413 (246): Mission Creek.

Mile 414.5 (244.5): William Craig Historical Site. In 1850, William Craig filed for a 640-acre tract of farmland here. When the original Nez Perce Indian Reservation was established by the Treaty of 1855, Craig was allowed to keep his acreage after requests were made by his friends, the Nez Perce.

Mile 416 (243): Turnoff to Lewiston Orchards, 15 miles.   MP 297

Mile 416.5 (242.5): Sweetwater Creek. Turnoff to town of **SWEETWATER**, small community on the Nez Perce Indian Reservation. No services available.

Mile 418.5 (240.5): Turnoff to **LAPWAI** (pop. 932) city center, Northern Idaho Indian Agency and grounds of old Fort Lapwai (Nez Perce National Historical Park Site). Groceries, gas, restaurant.

Mile 419.5 (239.5): Historical marker, Lapwai Mission.

Mile 421.5 (237.5): Lapwai Creek.

Mile 422.5 (236.5): Headquarters for Nez Perce National Historical Park and site of the Spalding Mission (1838–47). The visitor center has exhibits on Nez Perce Indian culture, a 23-minute film on Nez Perce history and a 5-minute slide show. Cultural demonstrations in summer. Self-guided tour of Spalding Mission site. Open year-round.

Turnoff to Lewiston Wildlife Preserve and crossing the Clearwater River. Excellent steelhead fishing in season. Dworshak National Fish Hatchery upstream on U.S. Highway 12 is the largest trout hatchery in the world. Tours are available.   ➥ MP 303

Mile 423 (236): Sportsman access.

Mile 426 (233): Nez Perce Indian Reservation boundary. Hatwai Creek.

Mile 430 (229): Junction with U.S. Highway 12 west to Clarkston and Walla Walla, WA. (See **Mile 207.5** U.S. HIGHWAY 12 section.) Highway 95 veers north and you begin to ascend Lewiston Hill. The "Lewiston Grade" is 6 percent. Potlatch paper mill to the southeast. The route you are traveling replaced the old Lewiston Grade, a twisting 2-lane highway that climbed nearly 2,000 vertical feet. The old route, although in disrepair, is still passable and is considered a scenic drive. MP 312

Mile 431 (228): LEWISTON (pop. 27,986). All services are available in Lewiston including 16 motels and 71 restaurants. The Lewiston–Clarkston Valley, ancestral home of the Nez Perce Indians, is at the confluence of 2 major river systems, the Snake and the Clearwater. It was also a camp for the Lewis and Clark expedition of 1804–06. Lewiston began as a steamboat landing in 1861. Steamboats operated from Lewiston until 1940. With completion of the Lower Granite Dam on the Snake River in 1975, Lewiston became an inland seaport, 464 miles from the Pacific Ocean. It is the river gateway to Hells Canyon. Numerous outfitters offer jet boat or float trips down the canyon. Hells Gate State Park is 4 miles south of Lewiston on Snake River Avenue, and the Hells Canyon National Recreation Area headquarters is located in the park.

Mile 435.5 (223.5): Viewpoint, accessible to southbound traffic only.

Mile 436.5 (222.5): Viewpoint and historical markers; Lewis and Clark College, McKenzie Post. Accessible to southbound traffic only.

Mile 437.5 (221.5): Dramatic, scenic overlook of Lewiston and Clarkston. Worth the stop. Seven percent grade next 6 miles southbound.   ★

Mile 438 (221): Junction with U.S. Highway 195 to Pullman and Spokane, WA. See U.S. HIGHWAY 195 log on opposite page.

Mile 439 (220): Entering Palouse country, one of the largest wheat-producing areas in the United States.   MP 320

Mile 451 (208): Turnoff east to **GENESEE** (pop. 810); groceries, cafe, gas.

Mile 453 (206): Turnoff to Uniontown, WA, 8 miles west.

Mile 459 (200): Historical marker, University of Idaho.

Mile 460 (199): MOSCOW (pop. 18,519), pronounced mos-coe, was first settled in 1871. It is the home of the University of Idaho, which has an enrollment of 10,000 students. It is a commercial, service and agri-

Administration building at the University of Idaho in Moscow. (L. Linkhart)

cultural center. (Bumper stickers here read "wear wool, eat lamb.")

Mile 461 (198): Junction with Idaho Highway 8 east to Troy and Highway 270 west 8 miles to Pullman, WA. Between Moscow and Pullman is the Appaloosa Horse Museum. The Appaloosa was indigenous to the Nez Perce Indians; its name is derived from "a Palouse horse." More than 250,000 horses are registered at the museum, which contains a number of excellent Nez Perce artifacts.

Mile 461.5 (197.5): Junction with Idaho Highway 8 west to Pullman, WA.

Mile 469 (190): Fourmile Creek. Large grain elevators to west.

Mile 469.5 (189.5): Fourmile Creek. Turnoff to Viola.

Mile 471 (188): Turnoff to Palouse, **junction** with Idaho Highway 66.   MP 358

Mile 476.5 (182.5): Palouse River. Brown and rainbow trout fishing. **Junction** with Idaho Highway 6 west to Palouse and Colfax, WA.   ⊷

Mile 478 (181): Crossing Deep Creek. **Junction** with Idaho Highway 6 east to Potlatch and St. Maries and the White Pine Scenic Route. Potlatch ranger station. The 83-mile scenic route from Potlatch to Rose Lake via Highways 6 and 3 brings you near the largest stand of white pine timber in America. The highway intersects Interstate 90 east of Coeur d'Alene.

Mile 486.5 (172.5): Rest area with picnic tables, barbecues, restrooms and phone.   ⊼

Mile 487.5 (171.5): Coeur d'Alene Indian Reservation boundary.

Mile 495 (164): Sheep Creek.

Mile 497.5 (161.5): Hangman Creek and turnoff to **DESMET.** The Desmet Mission was the third of the Sacred Heart Missions established by Father Pierre DeSmet in the 1800s. The new homes built next to the mission buildings are tribal housing for the Indian reservation. No services.   MP 381

Mile 498 (161): TENSED (pop. 90), gas and food available.

Mile 503.5 (155.5): Junction with Idaho Highway 16 to Tekoa, WA.

Mile 505 (154): Moctileme Creek.

Mile 506 (153): Turnoff to Minaloosa Valley.

Mile 511 (148): PLUMMER (pop. 804), a lumber town; gas and food. Large lumber mill west of highway. **Junction** with Idaho Highway 5 east to St. Maries, west to Fairfield, WA. Heyburn State Park, the Pacific Northwest's oldest state park, is located off Highway 5 east on the south shore of Lake Coeur d'Alene. Camping, hiking, picnicking, boating.   ⛺⊼⊷▲

Mile 514.5 (144.5): Rock Creek.

Mile 515.5 (143.5): WORLEY (pop. 206), named after the Coeur d'Alene Indian Agency superintendent in 1909. All services

available. Turnoff south to Conklin Park.
          MP 402

Mile 521 (138): Coeur d'Alene Tribal Bingo Center.

Mile 521.5 (137.5): Junction with Idaho Highway 58 west to Rockford and Spokane, WA.

Mile 525 (134): Small community of Setters. No services available.

Mile 526.5 (132.5): Lake Creek.

Mile 527.5 (131.5): Recreation area with picnic tables, toilets (seasonal).   ⊼

Mile 530.5 (128.5): Fighting Creek and boundary of Coeur d'Alene Indian Reservation.

Mile 531.5 (127.5): Turnoff east to Rockford Bay on Lake Coeur d'Alene.

Mile 536.5 (122.5): Mica Creek. Turnoff east to Mica Bay on Lake Coeur d'Alene.

Mile 538.5 (120.5): Turnoff to Kidd Island Bay on Lake Coeur d'Alene.

Mile 541.5 (117.5): Cougar Creek.

Mile 542.5 (116.5): Turnoff west to Cougar Gulch and Meadowbrook.   MP 427

Mile 544 (115): Turnoff to Harbor Island and Green Ferry.   MP 429

Mile 544.5 (114.5): Crossing the Spokane River and entering the city of **COEUR d'ALENE** (pop. 24,561). The Interstate 90 business route loops through the city. Coeur d'Alene (CORR-duh-LANE) is the largest city in Idaho's panhandle and is a popular resort town with motels, restaurants and shops. The city has been described as "an Outdoor Paradise." It is located on the north shore of Lake Coeur d'Alene with more than 100 miles of forested shoreline. Boating, sailing and fishing are especially popular, and there are nearly 30 resorts, campgrounds and public docks available to campers, boaters and fishermen. The world famous Coeur d'Alene Resort with luxury facilities and upscale shopping is located on the southwest edge of downtown. The Coeur d'Alene Resort Golf Course has the world's only floating golf green, anchored offshore in Lake Coeur d'Alene just east of town.

Idaho's oldest building, the Cataldo Mission, is east of the city on I-90 at Exit 39. The Coeur d'Alene Mining District features an underground tour at the Sierra Silver Mine. ⊷▲

Mile 546 (113): Junction with Interstate 90 East to Kellogg, Mullan and Lookout Pass Ski Area on Montana border. Westbound on I-90 to Spokane. Kootenai Medical Center, a regional medical facility, is located on U.S. 95 just south of the junction with I-90.

Travelers turning onto I-90 refer to **Mile 312** in the INTERSTATE 90 section for log of that route.

Mile 549 (110): HAYDEN (pop. 3,744); gas, food, store. The town was named for Matt Heyden, who in 1878 won the right to name the lake during a poker game. The spelling eventually was corrupted. Turnoff to city

center and to Hayden Lake, a popular fishing lake, plus water sports and recreational facilities.   ⊷

Mile 559.5 (99.5): Junction with Idaho Highway 53 west to Rathdrum.   MP 439

Mile 560.5 (98.5): GARWOOD, a small community with limited services. Country store and RV park, open all year; 25 sites, hookups, showers.   ▲ MP 440

Mile 563 (96): Small community of **CHILCO,** site of a large Louisiana Pacific sawmill; no services available.

Mile 567 (92): Silverwood Theme Park recreates a turn-of-the-century mining town with period buildings and furnishings. A 3.2-mile narrow-gauge steam train ride, Norton Antique Aircraft Museum, children's zoo and carriage rides are featured attractions. Restaurant; RV park with 125 sites, hookups, laundry, showers, propane; coffee shop.   ▲★

Mile 569 (90): ATHOL (pop. 312); gas, restaurant, RV park. **Junction** with Idaho Highway 54 west to Spirit Lake and Twin Lakes resort areas and east to Bayview and Farragut State Park on Lake Pend Oreille (pon-doe-RAY). Pend Oreille is a corruption of the name *pen d'orielle,* a name given to the lake by French mountain men that means "shape of the ear."

Farragut, formerly a Naval Training Station, was the site of the 1967 World Boy Scout Jamboree and since that time has hosted more than 130,000 Boy and Girl Scouts.

Farragut State Park, 4 miles east, offers campgrounds for both tents and trailers (a total of 212 sites), restrooms, showers, a visitor center and park museum, picnic areas, swimming (lifeguard on duty), hiking trails, bicycle routes, a boat launch and dock, rifle range, fishing and horseback riding. During the winter, snowmobiling, sledding, snowshoeing and cross-country skiing on groomed trails are popular.   ⛺⊼⊷▲

Mile 573 (86): Rest area (seasonal). Turnoff to Granite Lake and Kelso Lake, offering fair trout fishing.   ⊷

Mile 576.5 (82.5): CAREYWOOD; food. Turnoff to Cape Horn and Bayview (7 miles from the highway).   MP 456

Mile 577 (82): Cocolalla Creek.

Mile 582 (77): Cocolalla Lake is on the west side of the highway. Food.   MP 462

Mile 584 (75): Small community of **WESTMOND** and turnoff to Talache. Food and gas.

Mile 586 (73): Turnoff to Round Lake State Park, 2 miles west and Priest River, 19 miles west. The 142-acre park, which surrounds a small lake, has 53 campsites. Facilities include picnic sites, water, toilets, swimming, fishing, trails, a boat ramp, central water, a dump station, vault toilets and restrooms with showers. The area is open for ice skating, ice fishing, sledding and cross-country skiing. An information center is available and interpretive programs are scheduled.   ⛺⊼⊷▲

Mile 589 (70): Small community of **SAGLE;** restaurant, gas, RV park. Turnoff to Garfield

Osprey, also known as fish hawks, may be seen nesting on top of poles and trees near the lakeshore. (George Wuerthner)

Bay recreation area on Lake Pend Oreille (8 miles east); campgrounds, resort, boat launch. ▲

Mile 591.5 (67.5): Turnoff to Bottle Bay on Lake Pend Oreille. This giant natural lake is a major recreational attraction. Fishing available. Kamloops and kokanee are the prime attractions. Surrounding area is excellent for viewing white-tailed deer and elk, with moose and black bear occasionally spotted. Fishing guides and rental boats are available at nearly all developed areas. ⊷ MP 471

Mile 592 (67): Turnoff to Springy Point Recreation Area just south of bridge across Lake Pend Oreille at the osprey nest viewpoint. Osprey often nest on the southwest shore of the lake. Springy Point has 36 campsites, picnic facilities and boat launch.

The bridge is the fourth one built at this crossing. The first bridge, constructed on 1,540 cedar pilings, was nearly 2 miles long, which made it the longest wooden bridge in the world when it was built in 1910. ⊼▲

Mile 594 (65): SANDPOINT (pop. 5,023); all services, 2 information centers (south and north ends of town). Originally a fur-trading camp and later a mining camp, Sandpoint is now a popular resort community on the shores of Lake Pend Oreille. The first week of October brings the International Draft Horse Competition, and the Festival at Sandpoint presents world-famous musical entertainment for a full month during the summer. Sandpoint is also known as "The rail fan's dream," because major rail lines converge at the town, allowing viewing and photographing of trains and locomotives.

Junction of U.S. Highway 95 with U.S. Highway 2; turn to **Mile 56.5** in the U.S. HIGHWAY 2 section for log of that route. Highways 95 and 2 share a common alignment from here north to Bonners Ferry.

Mile 596 (63): **Junction** with Idaho Highway 200.

Mile 597.5 (61.5): Turnoff to Bonner County Fairgrounds and Schweitzer Basin Ski Area, which has become the darling of ski magazines around the world for its lodging, top-notch restaurants, 48 named ski runs, 6 chair lifts (including 1 quad lift) and spectacular views of 3 states and Canada. Summer at Schweitzer offers llama hiking, mountain biking and musical and cultural events. The Great Escape Quad lift operates daily, from July 1 to Sept. 5, carrying visitors to the summit. ⚐

Mile 606 (53): Pack River. Good fly and light tackle trout fishing. ⊷

Mile 606.5 (52.5): Small community of SAMUELS. No services available.

Mile 610 (49): Small town of ELMIRA. Gas and food available. MP 490

Mile 613.5 (45.5): McArthur Lake is on the west side of the road. Sportsman's access. A scenic wildlife refuge for nesting Canadian geese and other birds. Fishing. ⊷ MP 492

Mile 617.5 (41.5): NAPLES, so-named for the Italian workers who labored vigorously on the railroad here. Gas and food available.

Mile 618.5 (40.5): Blue Lake private campground; 34 sites, hookups, showers, laundry. ▲

Mile 621.5 (37.5): Turnoff west to Pleasant Valley, east to Paradise Valley.

Mile 624 (35): Geologic marker explains the glacial action that formed this valley, Lake Pend Oreille and Lake Coeur d'Alene. A second marker tells of the thousands of miners who came through this valley on the way to the gold fields at Wild Horse, BC, in 1864–65.

Mile 624.5 (34.5): Turnoff west to Snow Creek Recreation Area. Ranger station on west side of highway.

Mile 626 (33): BONNERS FERRY (pop. 2,193), named after Edwin Bonner who, in 1864, operated a ferryboat transporting miners and their pack animals across the Kootenai River. All services available. One of the world's largest lumber mills, Bonners Ferry Lumber Co., is located here.

There is a visitor center at the south end of Kootenai River bridge. The Kootenai National Wildlife Refuge is nearby in a wetlands area. Take Riverside Street near the Kootenai River bridge to reach the refuge. MP 506

Mile 630 (29): Historical marker commemorating David Thompson's passage. The famous map maker and trader for the Northwest Co. explored this area in 1808.

Mile 630.5 (28.5): Junction with U.S. Highway 2 east to Moyie Springs and Kalispell, MT; turn to **Mile 16** in the U.S. HIGHWAY 2 section for log of that route. Highways 95 and 2 share a common alignment from here south to Sandpoint.

Mile 632.5 (26.5): Side road to Smith and Dawson lakes. Limited camping May to Oct.▲

Mile 643 (16): Small community of COPELAND and **junction** with Idaho Highway 1, which follows the Kootenai River northwest to the Canadian border along the river's east side. West Side Road goes up the west shore and provides the best access to the Selkirk Mountains. The Selkirks are home to the only herd of woodland caribou remaining in the Lower 48.

Near the junction of Highways 1 and 95, Brush Lake is stocked with kokanee and trout. ⊷

Mile 647.5 (11.5): Round Prairie Creek. Numerous small creeks drain this region and offer fair to surprisingly good fishing. ⊷

Mile 648 (11): Miller Creek.

Mile 652 (7): Robinson Lake Campground; fee area; May 1 to Oct. 31; 10 sites, water, pit toilets, boating, fishing. Wildlife viewing area. ⊷▲

Mile 652.5 (6.5): Monks Creek.

Mile 654.5 (4.5): Private campground. ▲

Mile 655 (4): Meadow Creek Forest Service Campground 10 miles south via a gravel road. Fee area; May 15 to Oct. 1; 23 sites, water, pit toilets. ▲

Mile 657.5 (1.5): Moyie River. Copper Creek Forest Service Campground; May 1 to Oct. 31; 16 sites, water, pit toilets. ▲

Mile 658.5 (0.5): EASTPORT (pop. 64; elev. 2,580 feet).

Mile 659 (0): U.S.–Canada international boundary at Kingsgate. Canadian customs.

Read through the GENERAL INFORMATION section for details on travel in Canada. Use of seat belts is compulsory in British Columbia. Seven miles north is the junction of Crowsnest Highway 3. Turn to **Mile 138.5** in the CROWSNEST HIGHWAY 3 section.

U.S. HIGHWAY 97

Klamath Falls, OR, to Canadian Border
(See maps, pages 145, 147 and 150)

U.S. Highway 97 passes through some of the Northwest's most dramatic desert, ranching and orchard scenery. It runs the length of Oregon and Washington, hugging the eastern foothills of the Cascade Range after crossing it in a low spot north of Weed. Then it crosses into British Columbia to run the full length of the province (see CANADA HIGHWAY 97 section for log of that portion). It is a 2-lane blacktop all the way except for an occasional 4-lane section near a city.

Highway 97 offers the traveler a pleasant and very scenic alternative to the interstate system. You will go through towns instead of cities, past farms instead of shopping centers, along rivers with many scenic turnouts, and past lakes of all sizes, from the vast Upper Klamath Lake to small ponds.

U.S. Highway 97 Log

Distance from Klamath Falls, OR, is followed by distance from the Canadian border.

Mile 0 (611): KLAMATH FALLS (pop. 18,085) offers all visitor services including 26 motels and numerous restaurants. It is the business and recreational center of southcentral Oregon. The town has a beautiful setting with the vast Upper Klamath Lake serving as its western boundary, and to the west of the lake is the dramatic Mountain Lakes Wilderness recently carved out of the Rogue River National Forest. The city is at a relatively high elevation, 4,100 feet, which gives credence to the catchall description of eastern Oregon as high desert country.

Klamath Falls has a number of visitor attractions, including an old-time trolley that operates in the downtown area during the summer months. There are also several successful museums in town, including the Favell Museum of Western Art and Indian Artifacts, one of the best privately owned museums of its kind. The town also features the 800-seat Ross Ragland Theater which highlights local talent as well as national traveling shows. Because the lake is right at the door, several marinas and RV parks are available.

Junction with Oregon Highways 140 and 39. ▲ MP 275

Mile 1 (610): Oregon Avenue and Lakeshore Drive. Gas station.

Mile 2 (609): Oregon Institute of Technology. Hospital and fast food. MP 273

Mount McLoughlin can be seen across Upper Klamath Lake. (L. Linkhart)

Mile 3 (608): Weigh station.

Mile 12 (599): Hagelstein County park with 10 RV and 5 tent sites, boat launch, fishing and restrooms available. ⚓▲ MP 263

Mile 14 (597): Klamath Lake Historical Marker on west side of highway. MP 261

Mile 16 (595): A beautiful viewpoint that shows the mountains across the lake, dominated by Mount McLoughlin (elev. 9,495 feet) and Pelican Butte (elev. 8,036 feet).

Upper Klamath Lake is the largest lake in Oregon; shallow with an average depth of less than 25 feet and prone to developing vicious winds and dangerous wave action. It is a popular fishing lake. The upper end of Upper Klamath Lake is in the federal refuge system and attracts thousands of waterfowl, including bald eagles and white pelicans.

A natural canal connects Upper Klamath Lake with Agency Lake, a brown and rainbow trout-producing lake. ⌐

Mile 17 (594): MODOC POINT, no services, but an intersection for a lake access road. The highway swings away from the lake here. MP 258

Mile 19.5 (591.5): Turnout with sign pointing out Mount McLoughlin across the lake.

Mile 23 (588): Williamson River and the town of **WILLIAMSON.** Restaurant, motel, camping and gas available. ▲ MP 252

Mile 25 (586): Crater Lake **junction** with Oregon Highway 62. It is 37 miles to Crater Lake National Park from here. For more information on Crater Lake National Park see the MAJOR ATTRACTIONS section.

Mile 28 (583): Exit to **CHILOQUIN** (pop. 690), a farm and ranching town about 3 miles east off the highway. Limited services (6 motels); Forest Service campground and ranger station north of town. Also exit to Fort Klamath. ▲

Mile 29 (582): Chiloquin exit. Access to Oregon Highway 61 and Fort Klamath. MP 248

Mile 31 (580): Thunderbeast Park. Gas available. MP 234

Mile 32 (579): Collier Memorial State Park and Logging Museum. Named for the family that gave the original 146 acres, the park has grown over the years as the family donated more and more land and logging equipment for a museum. The campground at the state park offers 50 RV and 18 tent sites, showers, fishing, hiking trails and picnic tables. 🎣🏕⌐▲ MP 244

Mile 36 (575): Spring Creek Forest Service campground with 48 sites to west. ▲ MP 243

Mile 47 (564): Klamath Forest Wildlife Refuge is 7 miles east. Silver Lake, a small town, 52 miles east. MP 228

Mile 48 (563): Sand Creek. Store and gas available. MP 227

Mile 62 (549): Junction with Oregon Highway 138 (N. Umpqua Highway), which leads west 15 miles to the north entrance to Crater Lake National Park and on to Umpqua, Diamond Lake and Roseburg. The north entrance to Crater Lake is closed in the winter; access at **Mile 25.** Gas and restaurant at junction. For more information on Crater Lake National Park see the MAJOR ATTRACTIONS section. MP 213

Mile 66.5 (544.5): BEAVER MARSH, a community with a small airport, market and motel.

Mile 68.5 (542.5): Rest area with handicap-accessible restrooms. ♿

Mile 71.5 (539.5): CHEMULT, a small community with 8 motels and 5 restaurants.

Mile 74 (537): Turnoff west 12 miles to Miller Lake and Forest Service campground. ▲

Mile 75 (536): Coral Springs Forest Service campground; 7 sites. ▲

Mile 80 (531): Junction with Oregon Highway 58. A scenic drive, Highway 58 heads northwest through the mountains to Oakridge, Eugene and Interstate 5. Travelers using Highway 58 to Interstate 5 turn to **Mile 188** in the INTERSTATE 5 section for continuation of that route. MP 195

Mile 88 (523): Deschutes National Forest land ends, and almost immediately housing developments along the Deschutes River begin. This fork of the Deschutes headwaters is small and streamlike and is identified as the Little Deschutes. The Deschutes flows north through the timber and desert to enter the Columbia River at Celilo. From this modest beginning it grows into one of Oregon's mightiest and most important recreational rivers, offering wild white water, quality steelhead and native rainbow fishing, and wilderness float trips. ⌐ MP 187

Mile 90.5 (520.5) RV park with propane. ▲

Mile 91 (520): CRESCENT, a small community with store, motel and gas available.

Mile 92 (519): GILCHRIST. Reputed to be the "last company·town in America," the

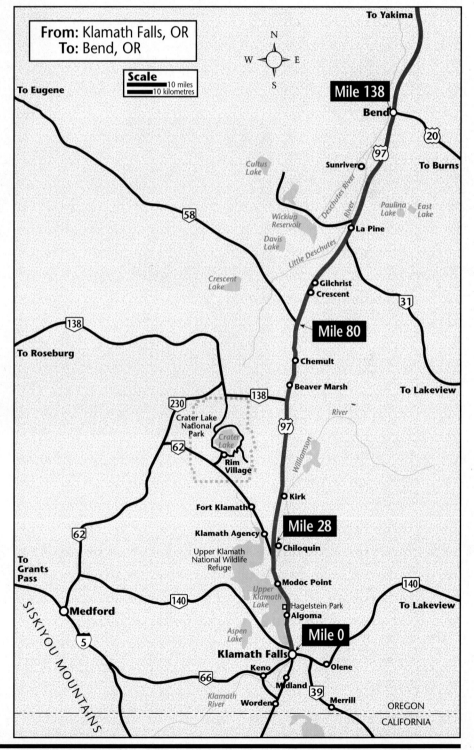

town has been owned by the Gilchrist family of the Gilchrist Lumber Co. since the turn of the century. State police.

Mile 99.5 (511.5): Public phone and mini-market with food and gas.

Mile 105 (506): Junction with Oregon Highway 31, which heads southeast to Silver Lake, Paisley and Valley Falls on U.S. Highway 395. Turn to **Mile 38** in the U.S. HIGHWAY 395 section for log of that route. It is approximately 120 miles from here to U.S. 395 via Highway 31.   MP 170

Mile 108 (503): LA PINE is a small town with all traveler services. Travel 20 miles east on Finley Butte Road to ice caves out in the lava beds that characterize most of the region.   MP 168

Mile 110 (501): Turn west on county road to Wickiup and Crane Prairie reservoirs, major fishing, hunting and camping areas. Wickiup is a shallow, rich lake with excellent fishing. Forest Service campgrounds, resorts, boat launches are accessible from a paved road that nearly encircles the lake. Many smaller lakes are also accessible from this road, including Twin, Odeil, Davis and Crescent lakes.

Crane Prairie Reservoir, just north of Wickiup, is considered one of the best trophy trout producers in the state. Three Forest Service campgrounds, boat launches and an excellent resort with rental boats and local fishing know-how are available.

Crane Prairie Wildlife Management Area includes the entire lake, and travelers can expect to see elk, black-tailed deer, otter, ospreys, bald eagles, geese and ducks and possibly a sandhill crane. This is an extremely popular recreational area.
                                            ←←▲ MP 165

Mile 113 (498): Turnoff on county road to Newberry Crater in Newberry National Volcanic Monument, 19 miles east. The crater, measuring 5 miles across, is an ancient caldera of a vast volcano that collapsed into itself. The crater area offers beautiful scenery, hiking trails, 5 Forest Service campgrounds and Newberry Visitor Center. Remnants of the volcano rumblings are visible throughout the area, with lava cones and basalt boulders littering the steep hillsides.

Two of Oregon's finest fishing lakes, East Lake and Paulina Lake, fill the twin craters of an extinct volcano. Both lakes are more than 6,000 feet in elevation, and you can expect to encounter snow into June. There's a resort with excellent fishing information, boats and supplies on East Lake. Paulina Lake is a fishing lake with 3 Forest Service campgrounds, Little Crater, Paulina and Chief Paulina, on the lakeshore. There are 2 boat launches, a resort with rental cabins and a restaurant. For Paulina Lake Resort, phone (503) 536-2240, for East Lake Resort, phone (503) 536-2230.
                                            ⋈←←▲ MP 162

Mile 115 (496): La Pine State Recreation Area 4 miles west of the highway has 145 campsites, showers and boat launch, and is a major outdoor recreation area, straddling the Deschutes River in an area with good rainbow and brook trout fishing.←←▲ MP 160

Mile 119.5 (491.5): Junction to Fall River, which is 13 miles west of the highway, and Cascade Lakes Highway, which is 25 miles west.

Mile 122 (489): SUNRIVER, a resort development, has a mixture of permanent residents, condominiums owned by time-sharing organizations, many private homes, all the amenities of a first-class resort, and a good transportation system to Mount Bachelor, the nearby mecca for alpine skiers.

Across the highway from the Sunriver entrance is a gravel road that leads 9 miles east to the Lava Cast Forest. It is the largest forest of lava cast trees in the world.
                            MP 153

Mile 124.5 (486.5): Lava River Caves State Park contains a lava tube nearly a mile long that was formed when flowing lava cooled on top to form a crust, while the lava continued flowing beneath the surface until it left the tube. The tunnel, discovered in 1889, is 20 to 35 feet wide and about the same height. No overnight camping facilities.

Mile 125.5 (485.5): Lava Lands Visitor Center. The center is your best introduction to the history of volcanism and the geology of the area. The complex includes interpretive displays, 3 short trails, 1 of which leads to nearby Lava Butte, a 500-foot-high cinder cone and the site of 2 volcano spouts and a magnificent view of the surrounding area.

The visitor center is open 9 a.m. to 5 p.m. daily, phone (503) 593-2421.   ⋈

Mile 130 (481): The High Desert Museum, on 20 acres with trails throughout, is one of the best natural history museums in the region. Outdoor features include otter, porcupine and bird-of-prey exhibits as well as trailside information on stream and pond habitat. Indoors, the museum traces the his-

Above right—Great horned owl is part of the birds-of-prey exhibit at the High Desert Museum at Mile 130. **Above**—Mount Bachelor, elev. 9,065 feet, is a popular ski area in winter. The mountain lies within Deschutes National Forest. *(Photos by Lee Foster)*

tory of the West with walk-through dioramas and Native American and pioneer artifacts. In addition to the static exhibits, the staff and volunteers bring in desert wildlife such as owls, rattlesnakes and other wildlife to show visitors what life is like in the desert. Open daily 9 a.m. to 5 p.m. Admission fee charged. Handicap-accessible.
                                            ♿⋈★ MP 145

Mile 132.5 (478.5) Gas and food.

Mile 138 (473): BEND (pop. 27,555) is the major city in the central Oregon desert, and one of the fastest growing. It was discovered several years ago by Hollywood as an excellent place for movie-making because of its clean air and dramatic scenery. Bend has all services including 37 motels, 4 RV parks and over 50 restaurants.

Until recreation became such a big factor in its economy, Bend was primarily a ranching and farming town. Today it is a mecca for artists and writers, skiers, backpackers and real estate investors taking advantage of the area's rapid growth.

This is also the jumping-off point to the Mount Bachelor Ski Area and the scenic Cascade Lakes. Access is via either Division Street at the north end of the city or Franklin Avenue in south Bend.

There are several parks in the area, including 2 state parks. Pilot Butte is located within Bend's city limits and offers a view of the surrounding area; and Tumalo State Park, 5 miles northwest of town on U.S. Highway 20, has 88 campsites. ▲ MP 137

Mile 140 (471): Junction with U.S. Highway 20, a major cross-state highway that connects Newport on the Oregon coast with Corvallis, Albany, Lebanon, Bend and Burns. It joins U.S. Highway 395 at Riley and Interstate 84 at Ontario. Turn to **Mile 259** in the U.S. HIGHWAY 20 section for log.   MP 135

Mile 142 (469): Northern Bend city limits.   MP 133

Mile 145 (466): Tumalo junction, a local road that leads west to the town and Tumalo State Park, which has 88 campsites, swimming and nature trails. ▲

Mile 146.5 (464.5): Peterson Rock Garden, 3 miles west.

Mile 149.5 (461.5): RV park and store. ▲

Mile 152 (459): Yew Avenue and Redmond Air Center. U.S. Forest Service fire suppression, management and smoke jumper center for Oregon and Washington is located here.   MP 123

Mile 154 (457): Redmond and **junction** with Oregon Highway 126 west to Eagle Crest Resort (5 miles) and Sisters (20 miles), and east to Prineville (20 miles).

REDMOND (pop. 8,365), a twin city to Bend because they are only 15 miles apart and the regional airport is in Redmond. It has all services including 6 motels, 22 restaurants and an RV park. The river flowing through town helps cool it off when it's so hot the desert heat reflects off the pavement back into your face. ▲ MP 121

Mile 159 (452): TERREBONNE, a small, unincorporated town with a market, gas station and restaurant. Turnoff for Smith Rocks State Park (3 miles east). The park is noted for its beautiful canyon topography and multicolored rock formations and is popular with rock climbers. No camping.   MP 116

Mile 162 (449): Jefferson/Deschutes county line. Peter Skene Ogden scenic wayside is a small rest area overlooking the Crooked River Canyon, which at this point is a sheer-walled chasm carved out of basalt hundreds of feet deep. The Crooked River in this area above Lake Billy Chinook offers smallmouth bass fishing. The rest area has handicap-accessible facilities. ♿ MP 113

Mile 164 (447): Turnoff for Crooked River

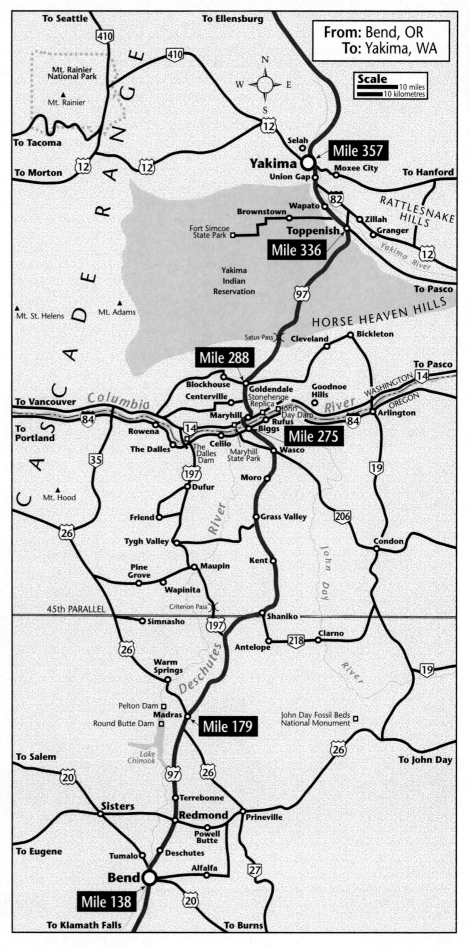

From: Bend, OR
To: Yakima, WA

Ranch, 7 miles west, a resort community with golf course and RV park. ▲

Mile 169 (442): Junction with road west to **CULVER.** Access to The Cove Palisades State Park, named for the vertical cliffs surrounding Lake Billy Chinook. The park has 272 campsites. Observatory and picnic area at Round Butte Dam. 床▲

Mile 170 (441): Side road leads 0.5 mile east to Haystack Reservoir; private campground.
▲ MP 105

Mile 175.5 (435.5): Side road leads west 2 miles to **METOLIUS,** a small community with 2 markets, restaurant and gas station. A french fry factory is located here.

Mile 178 (433): Junction with Oregon Highway 26 southeast to Prineville and Grizzley.
MP 97

Mile 179 (432): MADRAS (pop. 3,820) offers all traveler services. Madras is a very familiar name to travelers en route to the Deschutes River for the trout fishing, and others headed down to Bend for skiing or fall hunting trips. Madras is a main support town for the Warm Springs Indian Reservation. Cattle, potatoes and mint are the main crops in this area.

Southbound access via county road to The Cove Palisades State Park (see **Mile 169**).

Mile 180 (431): Junction with Oregon Highway 26 northwest through Warm Springs Indian Reservation. The town of Warm Springs (15 miles west) is the administrative center for the reservation's various concerns, including Kah-nee-ta Resort north of town. MP 95

Mile 192 (419): Turnoff to east for Richardson's Recreational Ranch (3 miles), home of the Priday Agate Beds. Rockhounding for agates and thundereggs. MP 81

Mile 195 (416): Hay Creek.

Mile 198 (413): Antelope turnoff. The small ranching town of **ANTELOPE** (pop. 35) (14 miles east) was taken over by a religious sect headed by Bhagwan Shree Rajneesh. The disciples of the cult established themselves in Antelope and changed the name to Rajneesh, in honor of their patriarch. The Bhagwan was eventually deported to his native India; most of the commune members left and their possessions were auctioned to pay some of the debts. Control of the town and the name of Antelope was returned to the local residents in 1987. The Bhagwan died in January 1990. MP 75

Mile 204 (407): Rest area with handicap-accessible restrooms. ♿ MP 69

Mile 206 (405): U.S. Highway 197 swings off to the northwest to **MAUPIN** and The Dalles. It can easily be an alternate route to the Columbia River since it emerges at the river about 20 miles west of Highway 97's crossing at Biggs. Maupin sits high above the Deschutes River and is a favorite place for river rafters to put in to shoot the rapids all the way to the Columbia.

Mile 213 (398): A snowcap identifier is on the west side of the highway. This is a round concrete slab with brass nameplates and photo-engravings showing the major, snow-capped mountain peaks of the Cascade Range that can be seen from this site on clear days.

Mile 216 (395): 45th parallel line, the point where you are halfway between the equator and the North Pole.

Mile 218 (393): SHANIKO (pop. 25), at the **junction** with Oregon Highway 218 to Antelope (see **Mile 198**) and John Day Fossil Beds National Monument (see MAJOR ATTRACTIONS section). This is one of the most photographed ghost towns in the Northwest because it is on a busy highway that goes through the center of town. It was founded as a railroad siding and named for August Scherneckau (the local Indians pronounced his name Shaniko), and was a construction headquarters when 2 opposing railroad companies were racing each other up opposite sides of the Deschutes Canyon. It was also an important station on the stagecoach line that went through the desert. But hard times came when the railroad was completed and the stagecoaches abandoned. Services now

Neat orchards at Maryhill, WA. There is a state park on the Columbia River here. (L. Linkhart)

include a refurbished hotel, mini-market and gas station.

Mile 234 (377): Kent is mainly a grain elevator and a few houses. No services.　　MP 41

Mile 246.5 (364.5): Junction with Oregon Highway 216 to Sherars Bridge (22 miles) and Tygh Valley, 29 miles to the west. Junction is just south of the town of **GRASS VALLEY** (pop. 160). Excellent fly-fishing in the Deschutes throughout this area. Inquire at local tackle dealers for current fishing information. Small RV park in town.　　🛶▲

Mile 256.5 (354.5): MORO (pop. 310) is the county seat of Sherman County and a typical grain and cattle country small town with a motel, 2 restaurants, market, hardware store and a nice park with a stream running through it. No gas available. Sherman County Museum and Sherman County Fairgrounds are located here.

Mile 260 (351): DeMOSS SPRINGS and county park. The town was named for a family of that name who were local entertainers and called themselves the Lyric Bards. They performed when their services weren't required on the wheat farms. They also operated an amusement park on the site of the present park.　　MP 14

Mile 265 (346): A roadside marker points out Oregon's Mount Hood (elev. 11,245 feet), almost due west, and Mount Adams (elev. 12,307 feet) across the river to the west-northwest in Washington.

Mile 266 (345): Junction with Oregon Highway 206 to Fulton Canyon and **WASCO** (pop. 400), 1 mile east. Wasco has a market and restaurant. No gas available.　　MP 9

Mile 275 (336): Junction with Interstate 84, U.S. Highways 30 and 97 at **BIGGS** on the Columbia River. Most services available in Biggs. The highway crosses the Columbia River into Washington. The slackwater here is Lake Celilo behind The Dalles Dam. Upstream a short distance is the John Day Dam with the Lake Umatilla slackwater. This area of the Columbia River is generally regarded as the best trophy walleye water in Washington and Oregon. Information is available in Biggs and guides can be arranged. Deschutes State Park with 34 campsites, hiking, and boat launch is west of town.

Travelers headed west to Portland or east to Pendleton on Interstate 84 turn to **Mile 98.5** in INTERSTATE 84 section for log. 🐾🛶▲

Mile 275.5 (335.5): Washington–Oregon border.

Mile 276 (335): MARYHILL, founded as an agricultural community in 1907 by Samuel Hill, who built the International Peace Arch at Blaine and the Columbia River Scenic Highway. Maryhill State Park is located on the river with 50 campsites, all with electrical and water hookups, handicap facilities, swimming area and boat launch. The topography along the river is largely columnar basalt. Lava often cooled and hardened into these forms that are common along the Columbia River east of the Cascades.　　👤▲

Mile 277 (334): Junction with Washington Highway 14, west to Vancouver and east to Kennewick. One mile east on Highway 14 is

the access road to Stonehenge replica, built by the famous Sam Hill as a memorial to those from Klickitat County killed in WWII. It is part of the Maryhill Museum complex. Three miles west on Highway 14 is the Maryhill Museum. This is one of the most eccentric sites in the Northwest and one of the most dramatic buildings along the Columbia River. Built as a mansion for wealthy Sam Hill, it was dedicated by Queen Marie of Rumania in 1926 and now houses a large collection of antique chess pieces, one of the largest collections of Rodin sculpture, Queen Marie's throne and court gowns, and several display cases of Indian artifacts. Admission fee charged. A free picnic area complete with peacocks is available, and there is a marker pointing out sites to be seen over the gorge. The museum is handicap-accessible.　　👤🍴★

Mile 278 (333): Gas and food.

Mile 283 (328): From the west side of the highway you have a view of several of the Northwest's most prominent mountain peaks. Their elevations and distances are: Mount Hood (elev. 11,245 feet) 50 miles; Mount St. Helens (elev. 8,365 feet) 70 miles; Mount Adams (elev. 12,307 feet) 45 miles; and Mount Rainier (elev. 14,408 feet) 85 miles.　　MP 7

Mile 288 (323): Junction with Washington Highway 142. **GOLDENDALE** (pop. 3,360) is the county seat of Klickitat County. It has all services and a good county museum in a Victorian home. The highway bypasses the town. Before leaving Goldendale northbound, check your gas as there are no services for 38 miles.

Above Goldendale on a high hill is the Goldendale Park Observatory, with the world's largest public telescope. It is open year-round and has facilities to handle up to 25 guests. Along with the telescopes, the observatory offers complete darkroom facilities and a science library. Special programs are offered as well as lectures and tours. For further information, write to the Goldendale Park Observatory, Route 1, Box 67, Goldendale, WA 98620.

For a really different experience, visit the tiny, rural community of **BICKLETON** (pop. 90), about 30 miles northeast of Goldendale via dirt road. It is the "Bluebird Capital of

America," with some 1,500 birdhouses erected by residents. Also in the Bickleton area is the Whoop-N-Holler Ranch & Museum (509/896-2344), a private collection of curios, antiques and old cars, and the Bluebird Inn (509/896-2273), considered one of the oldest taverns in the state.

Mile 290 (321): The Little Klickitat River borders the highway north of Goldendale and is a fair light-tackle stream for pan-sized rainbow.　　🐟

Mile 300 (311): Brooks Memorial State Park, with 45 campsites, facilities for the handicapped, hiking trails and fishing areas. This is in a forested area along the Klickitat River and near Satus Pass only a short distance along the road. The pass (elev. 3,149 feet) is the crest of the Horse Heaven Hills and has limited skiing in the winter. The Yakima Indian Reservation's southern border is on the north side of the pass. All hunting and fishing on the reservation requires tribal permits.　　👤🎿🐾🛶▲

Mile 302.5 (308.5): Satus Pass summit, elevation 3,149 feet.　　MP 27

Mile 329 (282): The 8-mile-long downgrade into the fertile Yakima Valley begins northbound.　　MP 54

Mile 332 (279): Toppenish National Wildlife Refuge. There are 2 viewing platforms next to the parking area from which to see some of the area's 233 species of birds. Interpretive center and nature trail; phone (509) 865-2405 for hours.　　🐾

Mile 336 (275): TOPPENISH (pop. 7,000) is an agricultural center known for its crops of apples and other produce. The town has also become known for its historic murals painted on buildings throughout downtown. Beginning in 1989, Toppenish commissioned several murals a year depicting the region's history from 1850 to 1920, and now there are 29 murals in all. Maps to the town's murals are available at the visitor center. All services available in Toppenish. No more services for 38 miles southbound. Intersection with Washington Highway 22, which goes east to Prosser and west to Wapato and Yakima.　　MP 61

Mile 337 (274): Junction with Washington Highway 220 to White Swan (21 miles) and the Yakima Nation Cultural Center. The cultural center is a combination museum, library, meeting hall and restaurant established by the Yakima tribe. Admission charged; phone (509) 865-2800.

Highway 220 west leads 27 miles to Fort Simcoe State Historical Park. From 1856–59, the fort was a U.S. Infantry Advance Post. Original officers' homes, reconstructed and original block houses, a small museum and picnic facilities are available. Handicap-accessible and open year-round; phone (509) 874-2372.　　👤🍴 MP 62

Mile 343 (268): WAPATO (pop. 3,790) is one of the many towns that grew up along the Yakima River and the highway as irrigated agriculture developed in the valley. All services available.

Mile 348 (263): Parker.　　MP 73

Mile 349.5 (261.5): Lateral A—southbound

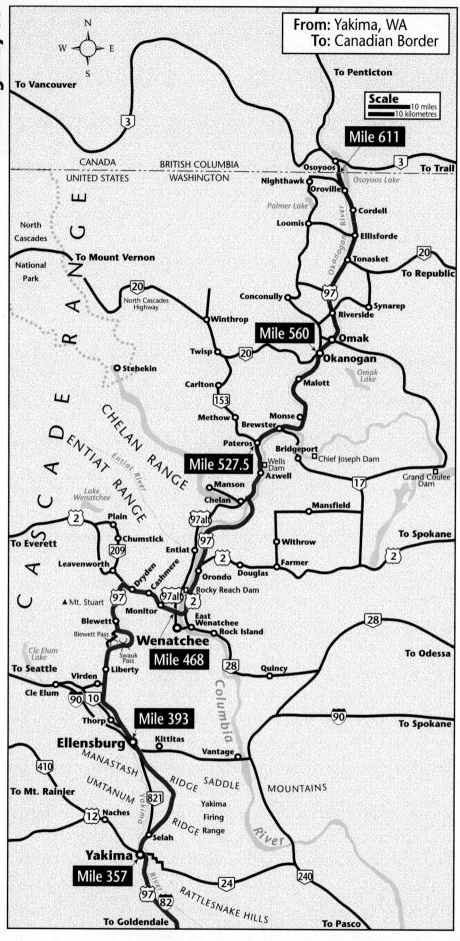

From: Yakima, WA
To: Canadian Border

Scale
10 miles
10 kilometres

Mile 611

Mile 560

Mile 527.5

Mile 468

Mile 393

Mile 357

only—leads south 11 miles to junction with Washington Highway 220.

Mile 351 (260): Southbound only. Yakima Indian War Historical Marker and southbound entrance to Yakima Indian Reservation. MP 76

Mile 352 (259): Yakima and Union Gap exits. UNION GAP (pop. 3,110) is a suburb of Yakima with all services available. Union Gap, formerly Yakima City, was named for the obvious gap between segments of Ahtanum Ridge. Except for the stubbornness of local landholders back in the 1880s, Union Gap might well be the major city in the valley intead of Yakima. When the Northern Pacific Railroad built through here on its way over Stampede Pass to Tacoma, Union Gap landholders refused to provide concessions to the railroad for yards, station and other facilities, thinking they'd hold out for large profits. The railroad created a new town, North Yakima (now Yakima), 4 miles north, and offered Yakima City residents free property and to move their buildings to the new location. During the winter and spring of 1884–85, more than 100 buildings were moved to the new town.　　EXIT 38

Mile 355 (256): Union Gap exit. Here Interstate 82 and U.S. Highway 97 merge with U.S. Highway 12 south to Prosser and the Tri-Cities area.

Mile 356 (255): Exit to Moxee Nob Hill Boulevard, the Yakima County Fairgrounds, Yakima Valley Museum, Yakima Valley Community College and Washington Highway 24 to Moxee City. Go east on Highway 24 for 1 mile to Keyes Road, then north for private campground on the Yakima River. Just beyond is Yakima Sportsman State Park with 28 tent sites, 36 hookup sites, swimming, fishing and picnic shelters.
　　　　　　　MP 35 EXIT 34

Mile 357 (254): Exit to Yakima business district, mall and Convention Center.

YAKIMA (pop. 58,690) is a major city in southcentral Washington with a thriving downtown core, strong arts and cultural offerings, and abundant produce and fruit. Complete visitor services available, with about 40 motels and 150 restaurants. The Yakima Appellation is located here, 1 of 3 distinct wine-growing regions in Washington. Most of the 20 local wineries offer tours and tastings of the varietal wines including Riesling, Chardonnay, Cabernet Sauvignon and Merlot. Downtown features the Capitol Theatre, an original vaudeville house built in the 1920s and faithfully refurbished in 1977. Track 29, also in the city's core, is a unique shopping center housed in 21 train cars transformed into a gallery of shops. The Yakima Arboretum, on the east side of town, features 46 acres of gardens that include an elaborate Japanese garden, 435 species of woody plants, 3 fountains and the tallest living Christmas tree in eastern Washington. Jewett Cultural Center, with a gift shop and horticulture library, is also in the arboretum. No fee, open sunrise to sunset. On the outskirts of town is the Yakima Valley Museum, with the country's most comprehensive collection of horse-drawn vehicles and a tribute to former Supreme Court Justice William O. Douglas, a longtime Yakima resident.

Yakima hosts the Central Washington Fair in late September.　　EXIT 33

Mile 359 (252): Junction with U.S. Highway 12 west, which leads west to Naches, then across White Pass to White Pass Ski Area and Mount Rainier National Park. Travelers headed west on Highway 12, turn to **Mile 446.5** in the U.S. HIGHWAY 12 section for log.

For more information on Mount Rainier National Park turn to the MAJOR ATTRACTIONS section.   EXIT 31

Mile 360 (251): Northbound exit to **SELAH**, a small agricultural community with gas stations, fast-food outlets and other services.

Southbound Exit 30A to Selah and 30B to Rest Haven Road.   EXIT 30

Mile 361 (250): Exit to East Selah Road.
                    MP 29 EXIT 29

Mile 364 (247): Exit to Canyon Road, Yakima Training Center and **Junction** with Washington Highway 821.

Mile 367 (244): Fred G. Redmond Memorial Bridge. Note the windsock that flies there to remind drivers of the strength of the side wind coming across the bridge. This is a long, steep grade, and vehicles low on coolant fluid are prone to overheat on the climb. A rest area is at the south end of the bridge for southbound traffic; on the north end for northbound; both are handicap-accessible.
                    ♿ MP 24

Mile 370 (241): Summit of South Umptanum Ridge (elev. 2,265 feet).   MP 21

Mile 372 (239): Burbank Creek.   MP 19

Mile 374 (237): Summit of North Umptanum Ridge (elev. 2,315 feet). Watch for mule deer and occasional desert bighorn sheep in the sagebrush west of the highway.

Mile 380 (231): Entering the military reservation, which includes the Yakima Firing Range. Admission prohibited.   EXIT 11

Mile 383 (228): Viewpoint of the Kittitas Valley far below. At night the view of the valley is spectacular. Crossing the summit of Manastash Ridge (elev. 2,672 feet).

Mile 388 (223): Exit to Thrall Road and Washington Highway 821 south.
                    MP 3 EXIT 3

Mile 391 (220): Junction with Interstate 90. U.S. Highway 97 shares a common alignment with I-90 westbound for next 5 miles. Travelers headed east to Spokane, turn to **Mile 107.5** in the INTERSTATE 90 section for log.

Mile 393 (218): Exit to Canyon Road, Ellensburg. Easy access to major-chain motels, fast-food outlets and gas stations north off exit.

ELLENSBURG (pop. 12,440) is the hub of the Kittitas Valley which was once a neutral area where the Wenatchee, Nez Perce and Yakima Indians, who were normally hostile toward one another, hunted and fished together in peace. The town, which was originally named Robber's Roost, after a store in the area, is now the seat of Kittitas County, a major food-processing, stock-raising and agricultural region. All services are available.

Ellensburg is also the home of Central Washington University. The 350-acre campus has an enrollment of more than 8,000 students.

Downtown Ellensburg (easily accessible north from this exit) has many fine old restored Victorian buildings, most found within the 5-block Ellensburg Historic District. Unusual architecture and memorabilia on local history may also be found at the Kittitas County Historical Museum, E. 3rd Avenue and Pine Street. The museum also has an extensive gem and mineral collection. The Clymer Art Museum, at 416 N. Pearl St., featuring the work of Western artist John Clymer, is an attraction. Open daily, admission charged.

The biggest annual event in Ellensburg is the Ellensburg Rodeo and Kittitas County Fair, held every Labor Day weekend. The rodeo is one of the premier rodeos in the Northwest. For information, contact the Ellensburg Rodeo ticket office, P.O. Box 777, Ellensburg, WA 98926, or phone (509) 962-7831. Information is also available from the chamber of commerce, phone (509) 925-3137.   EXIT 109

Mile 396 (215): U.S. Highway 97 north leaves Interstate 90 and makes a series of turns before joining Washington Highway 10 for a short distance. Travelers headed west to Seattle turn to **Mile 103.5** in the INTERSTATE 90 section for log. Gas, food and lodging at exit.   EXIT 106

Mile 411 (200): The first of a series of pretty views northbound across the Teanaway Valley as the highway climbs into the foothills. On the northwest side of the Teanaway Valley are the sharp spires of the Stuart Range. Tallest peak is Mount Stuart (elev. 9,415 feet).   MP 147

Mile 414 (197): Intersection with Washington Highway 970 to Cle Elum.

Mile 417 (194): Liberty Road intersection. **LIBERTY** (pop. 130) is 2 miles off the main highway and is a ghostly remnant of the gold rushes that brought people to the area over the decades. When the price of gold shot up in the 1970s, Liberty became repopulated and the old claims are being worked again. Mines are visible from the Liberty Road and it makes an interesting side trip.   MP 153

Mile 420 (191): Mineral Springs Road and Forest Service campground. There is a nice, lodge-style restaurant and local recreation information available here. Mule deer and elk are frequently spotted from the highway. Cross-country skiing is popular in the Swakane Range east of Mineral Springs.
                    ▲ MP 156

Mile 423 (188): Chain-up area at base of Swauk Pass, and Old Blewett Pass Road intersection. This road, slightly maintained by the Forest Service for its historical value, is one of the most beautiful drives in the region and offers a glimpse back into the early days of motoring when cars were slow and the curves steep and extremely sharp. This route is a nice alternative to whizzing over the pass at top speed. It rejoins U.S. Highway 97 at **Mile 436.5** near the old Mining Arrastra rest area.   MP 159

Mile 428 (183): Summit of Swauk Pass (elev. 4,102 feet). This is also a Snow-Park area for cross-country skiers.   MP 164

Mile 433 (178): Bonanza Forest Service campground with 5 sites.   ▲ MP 169

Mile 436.5 (174.5): Intersection with Old Blewett Pass Road.

Mile 438 (173): Mining Arrastra historic site. This relic of the mining days is a stone grinding wheel used to pulverize ore. It was used from 1861 to 1880.   MP 174

Mile 449 (162): Junction with U.S. Highway 2. Highways 97 and 2 share a common alignment eastbound via a 4-lane stretch of highway through the Wenatchee River valley.

Travelers continuing west on U.S. Highway 2 turn to **Mile 310** in the U.S. HIGHWAY 2 section.   MP 185

Mile 450.5 (160.5): Crossing the Wenatchee River.

Mile 451 (160): DRYDEN is a small fruit-growing town with gas, food and groceries available.

Mile 451.5 (159.5): Private lodge and RV park.   ▲

Mile 453.5 (157.5): Peshastin Pinnacles State Park, a popular spot with rock climbers. Picnic tables.   ⛱

Mile 456 (155): CASHMERE (pop. 2,560) has 1 motel and 9 restaurants. It is probably best known as the home of Aplets and Cotlets, a confection made with apples, apricots and walnuts by Liberty Orchards. Free tours of the candy factory are offered; phone (509) 782-2191 for times. The Chelan County Museum here is noted for its pioneer village with 19 restored buildings and Indian artifacts collection.   MP 111

Mile 460 (151): Small town of **MONITOR**, and Wenatchee River County Park. The park is in a beautiful setting between river and highway with 40 full hookups, 24 with water and electric. Picnic shelter, play areas and restrooms available. The river is fished in summer for trout and in fall and early winter for steelhead and salmon.   ⛱⇆▲ MP 115

Mile 468 (143): Access to city of **WENATCHEE** (pop. 22,710) to south; complete visitor facilities available. Travelers continuing east on Highway 2 turn to **Mile 295** in the U.S. HIGHWAY 2 section for log of that route and description of Wenatchee.

Junction with Highway 97 Alternate route, which follows the west side of Lake Entiat north to Chelan. Highway 97 continues its common alignment with U.S. Highway 2 from Wenatchee north to Orondo on the east side of Lake Entiat, rejoining 97A at Chelan.   MP 119

Mile 469 (142): Crossing the Columbia River on Richard Odebasion Bridge. MP 120

Mile 470 (141): Junction with Washington Highway 28 (Sunset Highway), which leads south 4 miles to East Wenatchee. Access to central Wenatchee via Columbia River bridge from East Wenatchee.

Mile 474 (137): For the next several miles, northbound travelers will be driving through the beautiful and famous apple orchards of Wenatchee along Lake Entiat.

Mile 474.5 (136.5): Lincoln Rock State Park and Rocky Reach Dam. The park offers 66 RV and 28 tent sites, picnic areas, boat launch and handicap-accessible facilities. Steelhead and trout are fished for along the bank of Rocky Reach Dam.
⌖ 木 🛥▲

Mile 482 (129): Junction with U.S. Highway 2 to Spokane and Waterville. Travelers continuing on Highway 2, turn to **Mile 281** in the U.S. HIGHWAY 2 section for log.

The small town of **ORONDO**, at this junction, was named for Indians of the same name who worked the copper mines near Lake Superior. It is a major orchard town and you will see thousands of trees—apple, cherry, peach, etc.—along the roadside, stands selling the fresh fruit and fresh vegetables in season, and mountains of picking bins. The rugged hill to the east of the highway is Badger Mountain (elev. 3,500 feet), a landmark for the Wenatchee area. MP 213

Mile 484.5 (126.5): Orondo Park, which offers camping, picnic areas and boat launch. 木▲

Mile 488.5 (122.5): Daroga State Park. A beautiful waterside park with 25 RV and tent sites, large playfields, swimming, picnic tables, boat launch and handicap-accessible facilities. ⌖ 木▲

Mile 503.5 (107.5): Beebe Bridge Park. Camping, picnic and swimming areas, boat launch and handicap-accessible facilities. ⌖ 木▲

Mile 504 (107): Junction with Washington Highway 150 which leads 3 miles to the town of Chelan and Lake Chelan Recreation Area.

Mile 508 (103): CHELAN (pop. 3,070), a popular recreation area on one of the state's most beautiful and most heavily used lakes, Lake Chelan—the largest natural lake in Washington. The city offers 22 motels, 3 bed-and-breakfast facilities, 3 uplake resorts, 6 campgrounds and 27 restaurants. The narrow lake is 50 miles long and runs northwest deep into North Cascades National Park. At its far end is the isolated town of Stehekin, a popular resort area for people who want to get away for awhile. No roads lead in; a daily boat from Chelan brings in passengers and freight. The south end of Lake Chelan is a very popular spot for waterskiing and windsurfing. There is an excellent campground on the southwest shore.

Lake Chelan Recreation Area has 163 campsites, showers and a boat launch. This has been called the most popular campground in Washington, so expect a crowd. A second state campground, Twenty-five Mile Camp, provides 85 sites, a boat launch and a swimming beach. A private facility also offers camping. (See also Lake Chelan Recreation Area in the MAJOR ATTRACTIONS section.)
▲★ MP 233

Mile 509 (102): Highway 97 Alternate rejoins Highway 97. MP 241

Watch for roadside stands selling local produce.

Mile 516 (95): Chelan airport. No scheduled flights.

Mile 520 (91): Town of Azwell and Wells Dam. Visitor facilities, exhibits, fish viewing and fish hatchery are open to the public. Indian pictographs are located at the vista point overlooking Wells Dam.

Mile 527 (84): Washington Highway 153. The road follows the beautiful Methow River valley northwest to Twisp and Highway 20 (31 miles), the popular North Cascades Highway (see NORTH CASCADES HIGHWAY section for log). Another popular drive is the "Loup Loup" Highway, following Highway 153 from Pateros to Twisp, then Highway 20 from Twisp to Okanogan. A scenic loop for U.S. Highway 97 travelers.

The road to Alta Lake State Park is located 3 miles north on Highway 153. A very scenic spot, the lake is popular for boating and swimming and has 164 tent sites, 16 full-hookup sites, handicap facilities. A private lodge is on the north end of the lake.
⌖▲★

Mile 527.5 (83.5): PATEROS (pop. 570). Gas, lodging and food available.

Mile 534 (77): BREWSTER (pop. 1,645) and Washington Highway 173 to Bridgeport and Chief Joseph Dam on the Columbia River (see **Mile 539**). All services available in this orchard community. Brewster was built at the confluence of the Okanogan and Columbia rivers and was for decades a transfer point between the 2 rivers when river navigation was the major transportation system.

Mile 537.5 (73.5): Brewster airport. No scheduled service.

Mile 539 (72): Junction with Washington Highway 17 south 8 miles to Chief Joseph Dam, **BRIDGEPORT** (pop. 1,045) and Bridgeport State Park. Chief Joseph Dam on the Columbia River was completed in 1958 and impounds Rufus Woods Lake. There is a visitor center at the dam. Bridgeport State Park, 2 miles upstream of the dam, offers swimming, boating, picnicking and camping. Fishing for walleye on Rufus Woods Lake. Bridgeport, downstream of the dam, has boat launch to Columbia River, stores, fast-food outlets, restaurants and lodging.

Fort Okanogan State Park, just east and south of this junction, has an interpretive center displaying artifacts from the fur-trading days and from the Colville Confederated Tribes. Open in summer; phone (509) 923-2473. 木 🛥▲

Mile 541.5 (69.5): MONSE junction, an unincorporated community across the Okanogan River west of the highway. No services available. The Okanogan River is lightly fished, but can provide fair smallmouth bass and trout fishing.

The large dish and cluster of dishes on the hilltop to the west are part of the National Radio Astronomy Observatory Very Long Baseline Array. It is 1 of 10 sites spread across the United States to allow astronomers to make detailed studies of celestial objects. Used simultaneously, the 10 sites function as a single antenna 5,000 miles wide. They can measure image detail of better than a thousandth of a second of arc, which is equivalent to being able to see a football on the surface of the moon. 🛥

Mile 552 (59): MALOTT junction, an unincorporated community on the west side of the river with 2 markets, restaurant and gas station. This was the home of Johnny Appleseed.

Mile 556 (55): Cariboo Trail Historical Marker. Picnic tables, no water available. 木

Mile 559.5 (51.5): Junction with Washington Highway 20, the North Cascades Highway, to North Cascades National Park. If you are heading west on Highway 20, see **Mile 174.5** in the NORTH CASCADES HIGHWAY section. For more information on the North Cascades National Park, turn to the MAJOR ATTRACTIONS section.

Mile 560 (51): OKANOGAN (pop. 2,395) is the county seat of the county with the same name, and is near Omak, its twin city. Okanogan offers all traveler services including 11 restaurants, 4 motels and 4 campgrounds. Okanogan began as a trading post on the Okanogan River, and only barely survived until the advent of orchards just after the turn of this century. Both Okanogan and Omak are on the edge of the vast Colville Indian Reservation. The Okanogan airport has no scheduled service. ▲

Mile 561 (50): Omak Lake Road, a local

gravel road to the popular fishing areas. Fishing and hunting privileges on the reservation are controlled by the Colville tribe and permits are required. Inquire in Omak.

Mile 564.5 (46.5): Omak exit and **junction** with Washington Highway 155. **OMAK** (pop. 4,130) is a bit larger than Okanogan and has more services. Omak offers 6 motels, 1 campground and 15 restaurants. It is best known for the annual rodeo called the Omak Stampede. The controversial suicide race is its main event, and involves racing horses down a very steep hill into and across the Okanogan River. The suicide course is visible from the highway, looking west across the river, appearing like a washed-out slash in the hillside. For more information about the rodeo, contact the Omak Chamber of Commerce; phone (509) 826-1880. Highway 155 goes through the heart of the Colville Indian Reservation to Nespelem and Grand Coulee Dam. ▲

Mile 566.5 (44.5): Old Riverside Highway and Omak Airport. No scheduled services.

Mile 573 (38): RIVERSIDE (pop. 250), a small agricultural community with grocery and cafe. Turnoff to Conconully State Park, 15 miles west. Located between 2 lakes, the park is popular with swimmers, boaters and fishermen. Facilities include 0.5-mile nature trail, 65 tent sites, 10 hookups with water and 6 primitive sites; boat launch.

🛶➤▲ MP 299

Mile 578.5 (32.5): Cross South Pine Creek and pass turnoff west to Fish Lake.

Mile 584.5 (26.5): Crossing Okanogan River.

Mile 589 (22): TONASKET (pop. 960) has food, gas, motel and hospital available. Tonasket has a number of special events—including the Tonasket Rodeo in June and the Sagebrush Loggers Tourney in August. **Junction** with Washington Highway 20 east through the famed Okanogan Highlands 24 miles to Wauconda and 40 miles to Republic. **REPUBLIC** (pop. 1,050) is the site of Stonerose Interpretive Center and Fossil Dig. You can dig 50-million-year-old plant and insect fossils in the center's fossil beds; register at the center. Phone (509) 775-2295 for more information. The Republic area is also a longtime gold-mining area. Turnoff from Tonasket east 15 miles for Sitzmark ski area at Havillah for downhill and cross-country skiing. ⛷ MP 315

Mile 594 (17): ELLISFORDE has gas, food and overnight hookups available. Turnoff to Many Lakes Recreation Area, which has fishing, tents, camping and lodging.

Old Okanogan Mission Historical Marker and Indian cemetery are located behind Ellisforde's church. The site also includes the original church bell and headstones, which date to the 1880s. ➤▲

Mile 604.5 (6.5): Okanogan River.

Mile 606 (5): OROVILLE (pop. 1,505). Mostly an orchard town, Oroville is the last town before entering Canada and is at the south end of Osoyoos Lake, which straddles the international border. Oroville has all traveler services. Osoyoos is an excellent smallmouth bass lake. The Osoyoos Lake Recreation Area is on the south end of the lake and provides 86 campsites, handicap-accessible showers and toilets, swimming beach and a boat launch. The lake is a major wintering area for geese and ducks. The area is also heavily mined, and the amount of mining conducted at any given time is almost directly related to the price of gold.

♿➤▲

Mile 611 (0): U.S.–Canada international border. Open 24 hours daily. The highway mileage ends for the southern section of U.S. Highway 97 and begins anew at the international border. Northbound travelers should turn to CANADA HIGHWAY 97 section for log of that route. For details on crossing the border, see Customs Requirements in the GENERAL INFORMATION section.

The more populated south shore of lower Lake Chelan. Lake Chelan is the largest natural lake in Washington. (L. Linkhart)

CANADA HIGHWAY 97

U.S. Border to Prince George, BC
(See maps, pages 155 and 161)

Canada Highway 97 is an extension of U.S. Highway 97, running from the international boundary between Osoyoos, BC, and Oroville, WA, to Prince George, BC.

Travelers along this route will sample 2 of British Columbia's prime vacation areas: the Okanagan and the Cariboo. The Okanagan Valley, with its string of long lakes, is in the Interior dry belt and enjoys more than 2,000 hours of sunshine a year. It is Canada's premier fruit-growing area; orchards stretch from Osoyoos in the south to Vernon in the north, making the valley a tourist destination from spring blossom time through fall harvest. Water recreation plays a large part in an Okanagan holiday because of the warm waters and sandy beaches.

The Cariboo is far less populated than the Okanagan. It is also rougher and wilder, home to cattle ranchers rather than orchardists. Here visitors will find dude ranches, excellent fishing and gold rush history. No visitor will want to miss a side excursion from Quesnel along B.C. Highway 26 to the restored gold rush town of Barkerville.

Canada Highway 97 Log

Orchards around Osoyoos Lake produce cherries, apricots, peaches, plums, apples and grapes. *(Liz Bryan)*

Distance in miles from the U.S. border is followed by distance in miles from Prince George, BC. Equivalent distances in kilometres are indicated by Km.

Mile 0 (504) Km 0 (811.5): U.S.–Canada border; customs open 24 hours.

Mile 1 (503) Km 1.5 (810): Haynes Point Provincial Park, situated on a sand spit jutting into Osoyoos Lake. Day-use area for swimming, waterskiing and fishing (bass and rainbow); 41 campsites on beach, boat launch, hiking trail. A park naturalist program is offered during July and August. Camping fee. A very popular campground in summer.

Throughout the Okanagan Valley, motorists will see signs urging control of Eurasian milfoil, a weed that is growing out of control and gradually choking the lakes in the area. Boaters should remove all weeds from their boats before and after launching. ⚑⛵▲

Mile 1.5 (502.5) Km 2 (809.5): Access road east to **OSOYOOS** (pop. 3,000), offering all traveler services. (For more information on Osoyoos, see **Mile 377.5** in the CROWSNEST HIGHWAY 3 section.)

Mile 2.5 (501.5) Km 4.5 (807): **Junction** with Crowsnest Highway 3 (see CROWS-NEST HIGHWAY 3 section). British Columbia government information trailer at junction is open mid-May to mid-Sept.

Mile 5.5 (498.5) Km 8.5 (803): Side loop road east to site of first customs house, built in 1861 with John Haynes in charge. A Canadian government historic site cairn marks the spot. During the Cariboo gold rush, miners traveled up the Okanagan on the Fur Brigade trail from Oroville, WA.

Mile 6 (498) Km 10 (801.5): Good bird watching at end of lake marshes.

Mile 7.5 (496.5) Km 12 (799.5): Road 22 leads east across meadows and crosses Okanagan River to desert. Road branches beyond bridge: Turn left (north) for road through vineyards to Oliver, turn right for pedestrian access to Osoyoos Oxbows Fish and Wildlife Reserve. ★

Mile 8 (496) Km 13 (798.5): Rest area at Desert Oasis Picnic Park beside south end of Deadman Lake. The lake is a glacial pothole, home to nesting Canada geese. Map of Oxbows Reserve. ⚶

Mile 11.5 (492.5) Km 19 (792.5): Okanagan Vineyard Winery to west.

Mile 12.5 (491.5) Km 20 (791.5): Divino and Gehringer Bros. estate wineries to west. View to the east of Mount Baldy, a local ski hill.

Mile 14.5 (489.5) Km 23.5 (788): **OLIVER** (pop. 3,700) with all traveler services. The town was named for Premier John Oliver, who encouraged a soldier settlement and irrigation scheme here in 1919 that turned the dry sagebrush slopes into rich orchards. Turn east on 7th Avenue (traffic lights) for Mount Baldy ski area and Tuc-el-nuit Lake, swimming, camping, boating (no motors); west for viewpoint of old Fairview gold-mining town, marked by cairn and cross. Fairview jail is now beside Oliver Heritage Museum on 6th Street; open weekdays. Travel infocentre in former Canadian Pacific Railway Station. Hikers/bikers can travel 12.5 miles/20 km along Okanagan River dike trail, a section of the proposed International Peace Park trail through Washington's Okanogan and British

Columbia's Okanagan.

Mile 16 (488) Km 25.5 (786): Quarry above road to west is an abandoned silica mine.

Mile 19 (485) Km 30.5 (781): Okanagan River bridge. Today mostly canalized for flood control and irrigation, the Okanagan River is a tributary of the Columbia River. Access to Bright's Winery and Inkaneep Provincial Park at north end of bridge. The park has 7 campsites, swimming and fishing. Camping fee May to Oct.

Mile 21 (483) Km 34 (777.5): Gallagher Lake, east of highway but hidden by trees, has a resort, private campground and swimming. Opposite is Ye Olde Welcome Inn, an authentic-looking English pub.

Mile 21.5 (482.5) Km 35 (776.5): McIntyre

Creek, named for an early settler. The highway to the north passes McIntyre Bluffs, vertical cliffs that rise 820 feet/250m high, site of an Indian battle between the Shuswaps and Okanagans.

Mile 23 (481) Km 37 (774.5): South end of Vaseux Lake, a federal wildlife sanctuary; resort and beach. British Columbia's largest herd of California bighorn sheep makes its home in the rocky hills. They often come down to the lake for water in the evenings and early mornings, and in winter are fed in roadside fields.

The highway north of here is narrow and very winding along the lake. Recommended speed is 25 mph/40 kmph.

Mile 25 (479) Km 40 (771.5): Vaseux Lake Provincial Park; 9 campsites, swimming and fishing (largemouth bass, rainbow, perch

and whitefish). No motors allowed on the lake. Camping fee May to Sept.

Mile 25.5 (478.5) Km 41.5 (770): Vaseux Wildlife Center; interpretive panels, trails and bird blind. Excellent waterfowl watching. Cliffs to east are home to Canada's largest colony of white-throated swifts. Also look for canyon wrens and calliope hummingbirds. Just to the north is Oliver Ranch Road to Wild Goose Winery. Alternate route to Okanagan Falls.

Mile 28 (476) Km 45 (766.5): OKANAGAN FALLS (pop. 1,700), a small resort community at the south end of Skaha Lake that has recently become known for its antique shops and flea markets. All services available. Heritage Bassett House (1909), at the south end of town, is worth a visit. Christie Memorial Provincial Park on Skaha Lake has a picnic

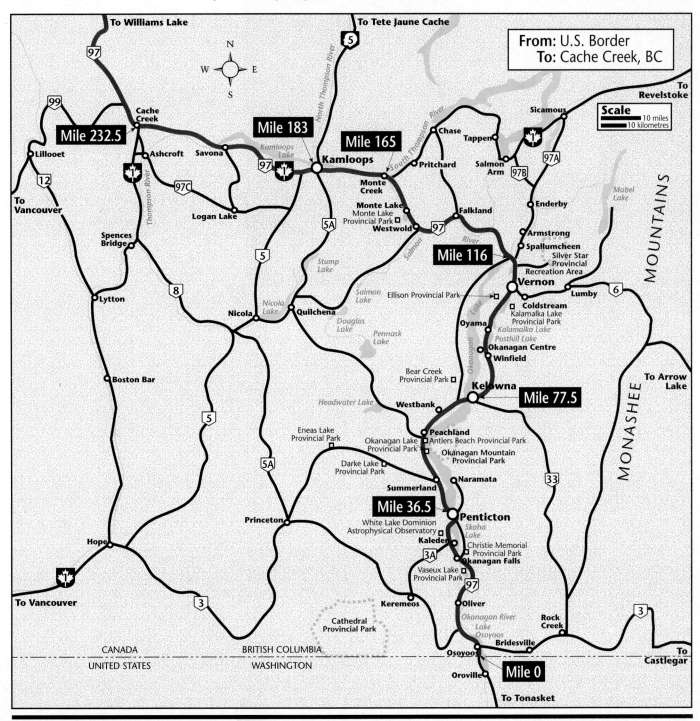

Soaring fibreglass sail sculpture in Kelowna. (Liz Bryan)

area, swimming and fishing for rainbow and kokanee. Skaha (Indian for "dog") Lake stretches 12 miles/20 km north to Penticton.

Mile 29 (475) Km 46.5 (765): Okanagan River bridge. Original falls south of bridge have been dammed for irrigation purposes. Turn south on Green Lake Road for Okanagan Falls Provincial Park; 20 campsites in the trees by the river. The park is known for its variety and number of bats. Le Comte Estate Winery in converted historic log ranch is 3 miles/5 km south on road. ▲

Mile 30.5 (473.5) Km 49.5 (762): Road west to St. Andrews by the Lake golf course and White Lake Dominion Astrophysical Observatory (4 miles/7 km). The observatory visitor centre is open year-round with displays and explanations. Guided tours are given Sunday afternoons from 2–5 p.m. in July and August only. (*NOTE:* Automobiles must be parked at the gate, enter on foot only.) Road continues to Oliver (via Fairview Road) and Okanagan Falls (via Green Lake Road). White Lake itself, in huge sagebrush bowl, has great bird watching.

Mile 31 (473) Km 50 (761.5): **Junction** with

Highway 3A to Keremeos, a shortcut to Crowsnest Highway 3 for westbound travelers.

Mile 32 (472) Km 51 (760.5): Steep side road east to lakeshore community of **KALEDEN**; resort facility, food (in famous 1912 restaurant), gas.

Mile 32.5 (471.5) Km 52 (759.5): Okanagan Game Farm to the west is a major area attraction. Drive or walk to see 130 species of native and exotic animals. Open year-round, 8 a.m. to dusk, except December and January. Late afternoon feeding time is best.

Mile 33.5 (470.5) Km 53.5 (758): Seasonal tourist infocentre and viewpoint overlooking Skaha Lake. This deep blue lake was originally part of the much larger Okanagan Lake to the north; it was cut off by delta deposits from creeks on the east and west side.

Mile 34 (470) Km 55 (756.5): Viewpoint with picnic table and sign about the founding of Penticton by rancher Tom Ellis. Today, orchards cover the old ranch lands. ⼻

Mile 36 (468) Km 58 (753.5): North end of Skaha Lake with a public beach on the south

side of the road. Penticton airport road to north.

Mile 36.5 (467.5) Km 59 (752.5): Canada Highway 97 turns north for Kelowna and Vernon, bypassing the city of Penticton. For city centre continue straight on the old highway beside the lake.

PENTICTON (pop. 27,000) is a centre for fruit packing and canning, but equally important is tourism. With excellent beaches on 2 lakes (Skaha and Okanagan), fine scenery and dependable hot summer weather, Penticton is a major tourist destination and retirement haven. It is also becoming famous as the venue of the Ironman Canada Triathlon, held in late August. Penticton has all visitor facilities with more than 70 hotels, motels and campgrounds and many restaurants. Tourist infocentre on Lakeshore Drive. Activities include floating the 3.8-mile-long Penticton River Channel between Skaga and Okanagan lakes; parasailing; winery tours; golf at 4 area courses; Okanagan Amusements centre (mini-golf, Go Karts, arcade); and a variety of water activities at the Skaha Lake or Okanagan Lake marinas. Attractions include a reptile zoo on Riverside Drive; the R.N. Atkinson Museum on Main Street has local history; the Old West and Ghost Town Museum on W. Eckhardt Avenue has mining and ghost town paraphernalia; and numerous art galleries display local, regional and national artists. The SS *Sicamous*, largest of the lake stern-wheelers, is berthed on Okanagan Lake beach, where it is being restored.

Highway 97 continues along Channel Parkway city bypass, which runs beside the channel of the Okanagan River. A favorite summer pastime is to float down the river on inner tubes or air mattresses from the bridge at the north end of town down to Skaha Lake—2 hours of cool relaxation. A tour company provides rentals and transportation. A bike path parallels the channel. ▲

Mile 38.5 (465.5) Km 62 (749.5): Road west to Apex Mountain Provincial Recreation Area with hiking trails, but no other facilities. Access to Apex Resort; alpine skiing, 45 downhill trails, snowboarding, quad lift, cross-country trails, resort hotel, restaurants, bars and shopping; phone (604) 292-8111. ⼻

Mile 39.5 (464.5) Km 63.5 (748): **Junction** with old highway connecting Canada Highway 97 with Penticton city centre and resort community of Naramata on the east side of Okanagan Lake. Access to lakeshore resorts and services.

Mile 40 (464) Km 64.5 (747): Okanagan River bridge. Put-in point for rafters floating down to Skaha Lake (2 hours).

Northbound the highway runs beside Okanagan Lake. Prominent features of this area are the high clay banks, eroded into miniature hoodoos.

Mile 43 (461) Km 69.5 (742): Kickininee Provincial Park; 14 picnic sites on lake. Kickininee is the local name for kokanee, a species of landlocked salmon abundant in the lake. ⼻

Mile 43.5 (460.5) Km 70 (741.5): Soorimpt picnic area; 10 sites, boat launch. ⼻

Mile 44 (460) Km 71 (740.5): Pyramid picnic area; 16 sites. The highway here has cut through several ridges in the white silt cliffs forming prominent pyramids.

Mile 45 (459) Km 72.5 (739): Sun-Oka Beach picnic area with one of the best swimming beaches in the Okanagan. Site of summer sand castle contests and the Jan. 1 Polar Bear Swim. Boat launch.

Mile 46 (458) Km 74 (737.5): Trout Creek bridge and Summerland Agricultural Research Station, 1.2 miles/2 km west, open to the public for tours in July and August. Gardens are open daily for picnics from 8 a.m. to 8:30 p.m., May 1 to Oct. 31. Trout Creek Canyon is spanned by the high steel girders of the Kettle Valley rail bridge, visible from the gardens. The bridge is 262 feet/80m high and 1,640 feet/500m long.

Mile 46.5 (457.5) Km 74.5 (737): Prairie Valley Road west to Giant's Head Park for picnics, walks and great views (summit is 3,000 feet/900m). The large Tudor-style building about halfway up, built in 1916 as a Baptist College, is now a resort. Access to Darke Lake (10 miles/16 km gravel) and Eneas Lakes provincial parks (12 miles/20 km rough gravel); 5 campsites at Darke, wilderness walk-in sites only at Eneas; good fishing for rainbow and brook trout.

Mile 47.5 (456.5) Km 76.5 (735): Turnoff east to lower Summerland, lakeshore. Peach Orchard Municipal Campground, 90 sites. ▲

Mile 48.5 (455.5) Km 78.5 (733): Turnoff west for **SUMMERLAND** (pop. 9,000); all services available. Travel infocentre just north of junction. The first commercial orchard in the Okanagan was planted here in 1890, and Summerland, a small but busy village with a mock-Tudor look, is still dominated by the fruit industry.

Visit Summerland fish hatchery, which raises rainbow and eastern brook trout for stocking Okanagan lakes and streams; open year-round.

Tour Summerland Sweets on Canyonview Road, which manufactures fruit candy, jams and syrups. Tours 9:30 a.m. to 4 p.m., weekdays only in July and August. Beavan Orchard Cannery on Hespler Road, one of the valley's largest, is also open for summer tours.

Mile 50 (454) Km 81 (730.5): Sumac Ridge Estate Winery, golf course and restaurant.

Mile 51.5 (452.5) Km 83 (728.5): Viewpoint over lake with sign commemorating J.M. Robinson, the father of the fruit industry here, founder of orchards in Peachland, Summerland and Naramata.

Mile 55.5 (448.5) Km 89.5 (722): Okanagan Lake Provincial Park offers 161 campsites, picnic tables, sani-station, fishing, swimming and boat launch. A shady oasis with a great beach. Camping fee April to Oct. Across the lake is Okanagan Mountain Provincial Park, a wilderness area accessible only on foot (trailheads north of Naramata, south of Kelowna).

Mile 59 (445) Km 95 (716.5): Viewpoint with sign pointing out the legendary home of Ogopogo, the Okanagan's resident lake monster, on Squally Point on the opposite shore. Below the point is Rattlesnake Island.

Mile 60 (444) Km 96.5 (715): Antlers Beach Provincial Park; picnicking, fishing, swimming. Just north of the park the highway crosses Deep Creek bridge. A good trail leads up the creek 15 minutes to Hardy Falls. In late September and early October the creek is crimson with spawning kokanee.

Mile 62.5 (441.5) Km 100.5 (711): Picnic tables with small swimming beach. **Junction** with road east to **PEACHLAND** (area pop. 3,500), a small fruit-growing settlement founded by J.M. Robinson in 1898. The community grew with the opening of the

Brenda molybdenum and copper mine in the hill behind. All services available.

Visit United Church (1916); March house (a 1907 log cabin) on Trepanier Bench Road; Greata fruit-packing house (1920); and the library and museum, housed in an octagonal-shaped Baptist church (1910).

Turn west (uphill) for Silver Lake Forestry Centre, an open-air museum of the logging industry (10 miles/16 km), and Headwaters Lake fishing camp (17 miles/27 km). Road also provides access to Pennask Lake Provincial Recreation Area (34 miles/55 km rough gravel); no park facilities but excellent fishing.

Mile 64 (440) Km 102.5 (709): North entrance to Peachland.

Mile 64.5 (439.5) Km 103.5 (708): Highway crosses Trepanier Creek and **junctions** with Trepanier Bench Road, west to Chateau St. Claire and Hainle Vineyards estate wineries. Tours and tastings.

Mile 67.5 (436.5) Km 108.5 (703): Drought Hill Interchange with Highway 97C, the Okanagan Connector to Merritt and Highway 5.

Mile 68.5 (435.5) Km 110 (701.5): Glenrosa Road leads west to Crystal Mountain downhill and cross-country ski areas.

Mile 69.5 (434.5) Km 111.5 (700): Next 4 exits northbound for **WESTBANK** (pop. 6,100), a booming suburb of Kelowna with all services available, including several beachside resorts. A cairn marks the old Hudson's Bay Co. Fur Brigade trail, which passed through the Okanagan Valley on the west side of Okanagan Lake. Much of the land in the area is Tsinstikeptum Indian Reserve.

Mile 70 (434) Km 112.5 (699): Exit east for lakeshore resorts and Boucherie Road scenic drive, which leads to Mission Hill and Quail's Gate wineries; tours and tastings available.

Mile 74.5 (429.5) Km 120 (691.5): Road east to Butterfly World and Parrot Island tourist attractions.

Mile 75.5 (428.5) Km 121.5 (690): **Junction** with Westside Road, which goes up the west side of Okanagan Lake to north of Vernon (49.5 miles/80 km). Bear Creek Provincial Park, 4 miles/7 km from junction, has 80 campsites, picnic tables, sani-station, swimming, fishing and hiking. Kokanee spawn in creek in mid-September.

Mile 76 (428) Km 122.5 (689): The highway starts down long hill to 3-lane floating bridge, which crosses Okanagan Lake at Siwash Point, site of an ancient Indian settlement. The bridge, opened in 1958 by Princess Margaret, is the only one of its kind in Canada. The centre portion is made from floating concrete pontoons anchored to the lake bottom. A section of the span can be lifted to allow large boats through. The centre lane is reversible for traffic control. Shelter Bay marina is at the south end of the bridge.

Mile 77.5 (426.5) Km 124.5 (687): Southern limits of the fast-growing city of **KELOWNA** (pop. 80,000), the largest of the Okanagan communities, with 20 miles/32 km of lake frontage. With a backdrop of rugged hills

Picnic area on Okanagan Lake at turnoff for Peachland. (Liz Bryan)

and orchard-covered benches, Kelowna provides much in the way of tourist attractions. Its central business area is compact, sandwiched between Highway 97 and the lakeshore, but its suburbs sprawl pleasantly to the north and east. It offers excellent accommodations, from luxury resorts to campgrounds, many restaurants and good shopping. Tourist information centre on Highway 97 (Harvey Ave.).

Settlement started here in 1859 when Oblate missionaries Father Charles Pandosy, Father Richard and Brother Sorel founded a mission on a creek at L'Anse au Sable (Sandy Bay). The priests built a tiny church and a school and planted apple trees and vines.

Apart from a few pack trails, settlers depended on the lakes for transportation and shipment of supplies. With the completion of the Canadian Pacific Railway to Kamloops in 1885 and its later spur line to Okanagan Landing near today's Vernon, lake steamer service grew in efficiency and importance. When a townsite was surveyed at L'Anse au Sable in 1892, it planted its feet firmly beside the lake, not back in Mission Valley, and the new town was called Kelowna after the Indian word for "grizzly bear."

Today its burgeoning economy is based on fruit growing (a third of Canada's fruit exports come from this area), manufacturing (Crown Forests plywood plant, Western Star tractor trucks), tourism and retirement.

Kelowna has 10 golf courses and more than 60 parks, one of them the focus of the downtown waterfront. Visit the city park (a blaze of flowers at the foot of Bernard Avenue) downtown to swim at Hotsands Beach, rent paddleboats and windsurfers, play tennis and go lawn bowling. Or dine at the MV *Fintry Queen*, an authentic lake paddle wheeler, now a cruise ship and floating restaurant. Nearby are the soaring white sails of a 40-foot-/12-m-high fiberglass sculpture and a reminder of the Kelowna Regatta, held each August. Nearby, the real sails at the boat harbor emphasize the water sport possibilities of this resort city. There's also a statue of the legendary lake monster, Ogopogo.

Commercial tourist attractions include Flintstones Bedrock City, Old MacDonald's Farm, Appleberry Farm, Wild Waters and Wild n' Wet Waterslide Park.

Drive up Knox Mountain Nature Park (north on Ellis Street) for easy hiking trails and bird's-eye view of city.

Scuba enthusiasts can explore Paul's Tomb diving park at the foot of the mountain, complete with underwater model of Ogopogo.

Visit Guisachan Heritage Park at Cameron Avenue and Gordon Drive, the stately home (built in 1891) of former Governor General of Canada; perennial gardens; restaurant.

Tour the Sun-Rype fruit-processing plant at Ethel Street and Vaughan Avenue; tours Monday to Friday, 9 a.m. to 3 p.m., summer months only. Visit Calona Winery on Richter Street, the valley's oldest and biggest winery, and "newcomers" Cedar Creek Estates and St. Hubertus vineyards.

Drive southeast (follow signs on Richter or Ben-

voulin) to reach Father Pandosy's mission at Benvoulin and Casorso roads in Okanagan Mission. This provincial heritage site includes hand-hewn log buildings that served as mission chapel, living quarters and school, plus 2 pioneer homes that have been moved to the site. Outdoor display of early farm implements and picnic tables under the willows make this a good family spot. Mission is open from 8 a.m. to dusk, April to Oct.; no admission charge. Nearby is Pioneer Country Market: great food, crafts, preserves.

Mile 81.5 (422.5) Km 131 (680.5): Junction with BC Highway 33 south to communities of Rutland, Beaverdell and Rock Creek on Crowsnest Highway 3. Access to Big White ski area.

Mile 86 (418) Km 138.5 (673): Kelowna airport. Travel Infocentre.

Mile 87.5 (416.5) Km 141 (670.5): Road east to Postill Lake (9.5 miles/16 km); accommodations, boat launch and camping. Good fishing for rainbow. Good cross-country skiing in winter.

Mile 88.5 (415.5) Km 142 (669.5): South end of Duck Lake, warm and shallow, good spot for waterskiing. There are several turnouts along the lake with trash bins.

Mile 91 (413) Km 146.5 (665): Community of **WINFIELD. Junction** with road west to **OKANAGAN CENTRE**, an orchard community on Okanagan Lake, and east on Beaver Lake Road to Hiram Walker Distillery, second largest in Canada. Tours May through Aug. No children under 12.

Mile 91.5 (412.5) Km 147.5 (664): Junction with Berry Road west for Gray Monk Cellars; tours and tasting.

Mile 92.5 (411.5) Km 149 (662.5): South end of Wood Lake. Turn east for lakeside resorts. Highway narrows to 2 lanes and winds along lakeshore; several generous turnouts. Good fishing for rainbow and kokanee.

Mile 97.5 (406.5) Km 157 (654.5): OYAMA, a small resort and fruit-packing community on the isthmus between Wood and Kalamalka lakes. Gas is available at the junction.

Mile 101 (403) Km 162 (649.5): Viewpoint of overlooking Jade Bay on Kalamalka Lake, named after the son of an early settler from Hawaii who later became chief of the Okanagan Indians. The lake is noted for its brilliant colors, ranging from green in the shallows to deep blue.

New highway here cuts higher above lake. Old highway, known as Crystal Waters Road, is quieter, more scenic and allows for more photo stops.

Mile 107 (397) Km 172.5 (639): View-

point overlooking Coldstream Valley across the lake. Homesteaded in 1864 by Forbes and Charles Vernon (after whom the city of Vernon, just to the north, is named), the ranch was later subdivided into orchards, a move that helped foster fruit-growing in the Okanagan.

The mountains to the east are the Monashees. Across the lake is Cosens Bay and the ranch lands of Coldstream Valley.

Mile 108 (396) Km 173.5 (638): Turnoff east at head of lake to Coldstream and Kalamalka Lake Provincial Park; swimming, hiking, picnicking. *CAUTION:* Watch for rattlesnakes.

Mile 108.5 (395.5) Km 174.5 (637): To the west is a weather station; to the east, a government forest research station.

Mile 109.5 (394.5) Km 176 (635.5): Stop of interest sign about Camp Vernon; gravel turnaround on west side. The Okanagan Cavalry first mustered here in 1908 and the site grew into the largest military camp in British Columbia, where soldiers received basic training for 2 world wars. Today, only summer cadets train here.

Mile 110 (394) Km 177 (634.5): Southern limits of **VERNON** (pop. 22,000), situated between Kalamalka and Okanagan lakes, with beach frontage and parks on both. The city, with its parks and recreation facilities and its emphasis on cultural events, is a popular tourist destination. It offers a wide range of tourist facilities and shopping.

Incorporated in 1892, Vernon is the Okanagan's oldest city, settled in 1867 by Luc Girouard, who became the area's first postmaster. His original cabin is preserved in Polson Park. As head of the Okanagan Lake paddle-wheeler service, Vernon grew in importance with the construction of a branch line of the Canadian Pacific Railway. Later, irrigation made commercial agriculture possible, with orchards, vegetable farming and dairying being added to the area's cattle ranching and forestry base.

Visit Polson Park, on the east as you enter town, a green oasis lined with weeping willows and with a unique floral clock. See the historic turn-of-the-century courthouse now surrounded by a flowery courtyard and waterfalls.

Swim at Kalamalka Lake Provincial Park (also good birding and wildflowers) or Kinsmen beach on Okanagan Lake. Drive up to Silver Star Provincial Park (see **Mile 112**) and ride the chair lift to the alpine meadows. Great views and hiking trails, and an amazing down-the-mountain bike trail.

Tour Okanagan Springs brewery, 27A Avenue. At the first intersection when you enter Vernon from the south, turn east on Highway 6 to Lumby and the Arrow Lakes; turn west for Okanagan Lake, **OKANAGAN LANDING** and Ellison Provincial Park (9.6 miles/16 km). Ellison Provincial Park has 54 campsites, picnicking, swimming, archaeological sites and hiking trails. It also has British Columbia's only freshwater marine diving park for scuba and snorkeling.

Mile 110.5 (393.5) Km 177.5 (634): Exit east along old highway for Kekuli Bay Provincial Park; picnicking, boat launch.

Mile 111 (393) Km 179 (632.5): Begin bypass northbound that eliminates former zigzag route through north end of Vernon.

Mile 112 (392) Km 180 (631.5): Junction with road east to Silver Star Provincial Park Recreation Area, primarily a ski resort but the chair lift operates in summer for access to alpine meadows. The summer attraction here is biking: There is a mile-high, 15.5-mile/25-km descent from the summit. Prime cross-country skiing at Sovereign Lake in winter. Accommodation on the mountain year-round in "Wild West" village. Also access to Cedar Hot Springs, with 4 mineral pools and camping. ⚞▲

Mile 112.5 (391.5) Km 181 (630.5): Tourist information centre near the south end of Swan Lake, a bird sanctuary bordered by marshes. Fishing for rainbow, eastern brook trout and ling; boat launch (no motors). ⚞

Mile 116 (388) Km 187 (624.5): Junction with B.C. Highway 97A to Armstrong (7 miles/12 km) and Sicamous on Trans-Canada Highway 1 (39 miles/65 km). Attractions in **ARMSTRONG** (pop. 3,000) include historic hotels; the Olde Schoolhouse (1884), now a teahouse; Armstrong Cheese Factory, open Monday, Thursday and Saturday; Canoga Carriage Co., where visitors can watch the restoration of horse-drawn carriages; and Rogers Flour Mills, open for tours in summer, where visitors bag their own flour in the old-fashioned mill store.

Canada Highway 97 turns west for Kamloops and heads across the north end of Swan Lake. Travelers headed north on B.C. Highway 97A to Trans-Canada Highway 1 turn to **Mile 180** in the TRANS-CANADA HIGHWAY 1 section for log of that route.

Mile 116.5 (387.5) Km 187.5 (624): Old Vernon Road goes south to Vernon along west side of Swan Lake.

Mile 119 (385) Km 191.5 (620): Spallumcheen golf course and O'Keefe Ranch, heritage site and stop of interest. One of the earliest cattle empires in British Columbia, this spread was staked in 1867. Soon the ranch grew into a regular village, complete with store, blacksmith's shop, flour and sawmills, church and manor house.

Several of the ranch buildings, including St. Anne's Church, which dates from 1886, the original log cabin and a fascinating general store, have been restored and are open to the public daily, May to Oct. Restaurant, gift shop and picnic facilities. ⚞

Mile 119.5 (384.5) Km 192.5 (619): Junction with Westside Road, which goes south on the west side of Okanagan Lake to Westbank.

Mile 125.5 (378.5) Km 202 (609.5): Round Lake, east of highway.

Mile 127.5 (376.5) Km 205 (606.5): Salmon River, which flows north into Shuswap Lake at Salmon Arm. **Junction** with Salmon River Road, a quiet backroad route to Armstrong, Enderby and Salmon Arm.

Historic O'Keefe Ranch at Mile 119 was one of the earliest cattle empires in British Columbia. (Liz Bryan)

Mile 131 (373) Km 211 (600.5): Una rest area.

Mile 137 (367) Km 220.5 (591): Silvernails Road east to Bolean, Spa and Arthur lakes; rainbow trout, on fly or by troll. Public campground and fishing camp with full facilities are at Bolean Lake, 6.5 miles/11 km. The lakes are high, so summer fishing is good. ⚞▲

Mile 137.5 (366.5) Km 221 (590.5): FALKLAND (pop. 500), small ranching community. All services available. There is an old gypsum mine on the hill above. Falkland is home to a 2-day stampede each Victoria Day weekend (around May 24) when its population swells to nearly 10,000, and also hosts International Sled Dog Races in January.

At the north end of town is the **junction** with road to Pillar Lake, 6.5 miles/11 km, Paxton Valley and Trans-Canada Highway 1 near Chase. Pillar Lake takes its name from a rock hoodoo capped by a giant boulder. Resorts, camping and boat launch are available and fishing for rainbow is good. ⚞▲

Mile 144 (360) Km 231.5 (580): Road west to Pinaus, Ladyking and Square lakes, 6.6 miles/11 km. Accommodations and boats on Pinaus; good fly-fishing for rainbow. ⚞

Mile 146.5 (357.5) Km 235.5 (576): WESTWOLD, a small farm community, with food and gas available. The wide valley, first called Grande Prairie by French Canadian fur traders, was changed by the post office to avoid confusion with the Alberta town.

The highway crosses the Salmon River bridge and junctions with a gravel road southwest to Salmon Lake (25 miles/42 km), Douglas Lake and on to BC Highway 5A at Quilchena.

Mile 151.5 (352.5) Km 244 (567.5): South end of Monte Lake. The highway runs along the east shore, hemmed in by basalt cliffs. Rock hounds find agates in outcrops here. There are resort facilities along the lake. Boat launch, swimming and fishing for rainbow. **MONTE LAKE** community has a rock and gem store, gas and food. ⚞

Mile 154 (350) Km 248 (563.5): Road east to Paxton Valley.

Mile 159 (345) Km 256 (555.5): Rest area with travel information board. Road east to Barnhardtvale.

Mile 164 (340) Km 264 (547.5): Monte Creek rest area.

Mile 165 (339) Km 266 (545.5): Junction with Trans-Canada Highway 1 at **MONTE CREEK**; store and gas station. Canada Highway 97 shares a common alignment with Trans-Canada Highway 1 west to Cache Creek.

Travelers headed east to Revelstoke, Banff and Jasper national parks, turn to **Mile 250** in the TRANS-CANADA HIGHWAY 1 section and read log back to front.

Mile 166.5 (337.5) Km 268 (543.5): Bostock Road leads east to pioneer St. Peter's Church, well worth a photo stop. Road winds back to highway just west.

Mile 169 (335) Km 272 (539.5): Stop of interest on a gravel turnout on the north side of the highway near Monte Creek railway station explains the "Great Train Robbery." The robbery took place near here in 1906. Bill Miner and his gang held up a Canadian Pacific Railway express but netted only $15. Miner was successfully tracked by a mounted police posse and sent to jail for life. His story was made into a movie, *The Grey Fox*.

Notice the eroded clay hoodoos north of Thompson River.

Mile 169.5 (334.5) Km 273 (538.5): Kamloops city limits.

Turn off at Mile 239.5 for Hat Creek Ranch, a restored Cariboo heritage site with working blacksmith shop. (Liz Bryan)

Mile 171 (333) Km 275 (536.5): Turnoff for wildlife park and museum with petting farm and picnic areas; open in summer. Waterslide and RV park adjacent. ⊼▲

Mile 181 (323) Km 291.5 (520): Exit for Highway 5 north to Tete Jaune Cache on Yellowhead Highway 16 (see CANADA HIGHWAY 5 section for log). From here to **Mile 189**, Highways 1, 97 and 5 have a common alignment on controlled-access freeway which bypasses the city of Kamloops.

Mile 183 (321) Km 294.5 (517): Exit 369 (eastbound) and 370 (westbound) for city of **KAMLOOPS** (pop. 68,000); see **Mile 266.5** in the TRANS-CANADA HIGHWAY 1 section for description of city.

Mile 184.5 (319.5) Km 297 (514.5): Junction with BC Highway 5A south to Merritt and Princeton. This is now one of the least traveled highways in southern British Columbia, having been supplanted by the Coquihalla section of Highway 5. Exit 367 westbound, and Exit 368 eastbound.

Mile 186.5 (317.5) Km 300 (511.5): Junction with road south 18 miles/29 km to Lac le Jeune Provincial Park; 144 campsites, excellent swimming and fishing for medium rainbow trout. ⊷▲ EXIT 366

Mile 189 (315) Km 304.5 (507): Freeway continues south to Merritt and Hope as Highway 5. Westbound travelers follow Highways 1 and 97 to Cache Creek. EXIT 362

Mile 192 (312) Km 309 (502.5): Tailings of the Afton copper mine are visible on the south side of the highway. Mining operations are spread for some distance along the highway. On the north side of the highway, notice the range rehabilitation project in which sagebrush semidesert has been cultivated and seeded to grass.

Mile 194.5 (309.5) Km 313 (498.5): Greenstone Mountain Road leads to several high fishing lakes. ⊷

Mile 198 (306) Km 319 (492.5): Cherry Creek Ranch, one of the pioneer ranches in the area.

Mile 205.5 (298.5) Km 331 (480.5): Turnout and viewpoint over Kamloops Lake (a widening of the Thompson River). Geologists believe that the lake may be an ancient volcanic crater, the source of the area's lava outcrops. A stop of interest sign recalls the days of lake steamboats, and display board illustrates the types of Indian shelters on the interior plateau. Sign identifies the different types of noxious knapweed, which in some areas of British Columbia are taking over the rangeland.

Across the lake are Battle Bluffs, their red color attributed to legendary blood stains from an Indian battle fought on top. ⊼

Mile 207.5 (296.5) Km 334 (477.5): Turnoff north to Savona Provincial Park for swimming and picnics. **SAVONA** is a small trading community at the narrow west end of Kamloops Lake; limited facilities. ⊼

Mile 210.5 (293.5) Km 339 (472.5): Bridge over South Thompson River.

Mile 213 (291) Km 342.5 (469): Bridge over Deadman River. Pacific salmon spawn here in the fall. The river was named for an early Hudson's Bay Co. trader who was found murdered here.

Mile 213.5 (290.5) Km 344 (467.5): Turnoff on gravel road north to Deadman River valley, an attractive ranch valley with a spectacular multicolored volcanic canyon (good rockhounding for agates and petrified wood) and rock hoodoos (ask for permission and directions at Deadman Creek Ranch). Also accesses a string of fishing lakes and Vidette gold mine. ⊷

Mile 218.5 (285.5) Km 352 (459.5): Turnoff south to a bridge over the Thompson River and the small community of **WALHACHIN**. When nearby orchards flourished, so did Walhachin; today a desert of prickly pear cactus and sagebrush has ousted the fruit trees and the settlement is almost a ghost town. No services available.

Mile 221 (283) Km 356 (455.5): Juniper Beach Provincial Park beside Thompson River; 30 campsites, sanistation, fishing. An oasis in the dry belt desert. Remains of an irrigation flume are visible on the north side of the highway. ⊷▲

Mile 223 (281) Km 358.5 (453): Stop of interest sign commemorates the orchard settlement of Walhachin. On the river flats east of here pioneers planted apple orchards, building dams in the hills and miles of irrigation flumes to bring water. By 1913, these dry benches were covered with sturdy young trees. But when all but 10 of the eligible males of the area enlisted for service in WWI, the irrigation flumes were breached by floods and landslides and the thirsty orchards shriveled. Today there are still a few phantom trees among the sagebrush and cactus. The flumes are merely rotting streaks of wood along the hillsides.

The climate, too dry for orchards, is ideal for cattle, but few are to be seen from June to Sept. because they are sent to the forested hills to graze. There are huge cattle-feeding stations just east of Cache Creek.

Mile 232.5 (271.5) Km 374.5 (437): Junction of Highway 97 and Trans-Canada Highway 1 at **CACHE CREEK** (pop. 1,200). Travel information centre just north of highway junction. All visitor services offered. Gas stations, motels and restaurants line both sides of the highway. The settlement grew up around the confluence of the creek (named after a reputed cache of gold) and the Bonaparte River. The Hudson's Bay Co. opened a store to benefit from trade at the intersection of trails east and north. Cache Creek became a major supply point on the Cariboo Wagon Road. Today, the junction is still very much a traveler's way station. The area is famous for jade; visit the Cariboo Jade Shop to see stone being cut and polished.

Travelers continuing on Trans-Canada Highway 1 to Hope, turn to **Mile 318.5** in the TRANS-CANADA HIGHWAY 1 section for log of that route.

Mile 235.5 (268.5) Km 379 (432.5): Indian village of Bonaparte with its lumber covered log church dating from 1894 and impressive cemetery gates.

Mile 236.5 (267.5) Km 380.5 (431): Bonaparte River bridge.

Mile 238.5 (265.5) Km 384 (427.5): Good view west across fields to Hat Creek House (see description next entry).

Mile 239.5 (264.5) Km 384.5 (427): Junction with Highway 99 to Lillooet (46.5 miles/75 km) and Vancouver (209 miles/336.5 km); see SEA TO SKY HIGHWAY section for log. A short distance west is Hat Creek Heritage Ranch, one of the last of the Cariboo trail roadhouses, and a section of the original trail. Open daily mid-May to mid-Oct. Working blacksmith shop, saddle maker, wagon rides and tours of roadhouse. Also, trail rides on ranch horses. Phone (604) 457-9722 for more information.

Mile 242 (262) Km 389.5 (422): Gravel turnout with sign commemorating the "BX," the British Columbia Express Co. stage line founded by Francis Barnard, which linked the goldfields of the Cariboo with the outside world for nearly 50 years. Starting point was originally Yale, then Ashcroft, and the red-and-yellow stage coaches made the 270-mile/450-km journey in 4 days.

Across the valley to the west brilliant orange and yellow sulfur-stained cliffs mark the location of the Maggie Mine, founded in 1885, which yielded $500,000 worth of gold.

Mile 246 (258) Km 396 (415.5): Junction with Loon Lake Road, which leads east to Loon Creek fish hatchery and Loon Lake Provincial Park (15.5 miles/26 km); 14 campsites, rainbow fishing. ⇔▲

Mile 246.5 (257.5) Km 397 (414.5): Maiden Creek bridge.

Mile 249 (255) Km 401 (410.5): Carguile rest area.

Mile 251 (253) Km 403.5 (408): Several shallow alkaline lakes along the highway for the next 5 miles/8 km, including Four Mile and Five Mile lakes; gravel turnouts, fair fishing for rainbow and eastern brook trout. ⇔

Mile 256 (248) Km 412.5 (399): Junction with Pavilion Mountain Road west to Pavilion via Kelly Lake at south edge of Clinton. Built in 1861 from Lillooet, this road was the first Cariboo Wagon Road. A stone cairn marks the junction of this route with the later one from Yale in the Fraser Canyon. From Kelly Lake unpaved road goes north to Jesmond, Dog Creek and Alkali Lake, the original River Trail to the Cariboo.

Downing Provincial Park on Kelly Lake where pavement ends, 11 miles/18 km west, has 25 campsites, picnicking, swimming and fishing for rainbow. ⛺⇔▲

Mile 256.5 (247.5) Km 412.8 (398.7): The village of **CLINTON** (pop. 900) has all services. It was originally the site of the 47 Mile Roadhouse (mileage was calculated from Lillooet), a supply settlement at the junction of the 2 gold rush trails. It was later renamed Clinton in honor of the Colonial Secretary and was the centre for freighting on the Cariboo Road. There are several guest ranches in the area. Tourist office in 1915 Pollard House, open June to Sept.

Traces of gold rush days still to be found include Robertson's General Store (1864), with its wagon-wheel veranda; the museum, housed in a red brick building that served as the first school (1892), then as a courthouse;

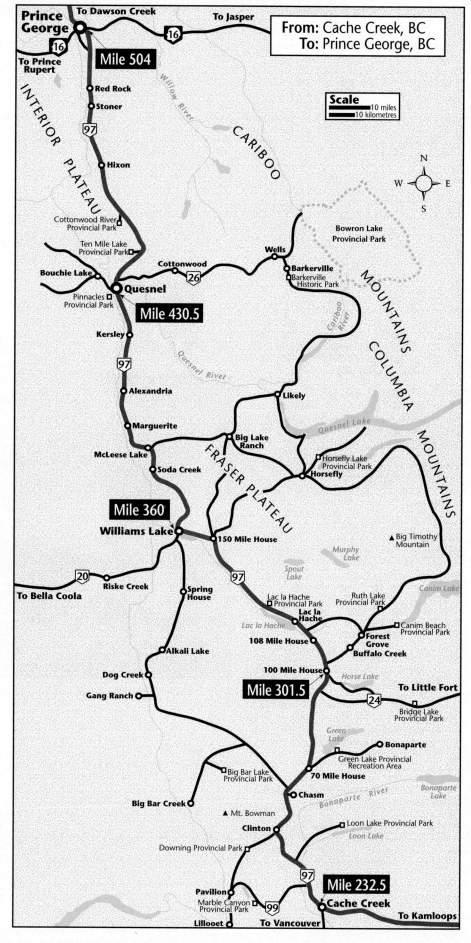

From: Cache Creek, BC
To: Prince George, BC

and the pioneer cemetery just north of town. The present Cariboo Lodge, built of logs, is on the site of the famous old Clinton Hotel, which dated from the 1860s and burned in 1958. The Clinton Ball, held yearly in May, is the oldest continual annual celebration in British Columbia. It began in 1868 and usually lasted for several days, non-stop.

Mile 263 (241) Km 423 (388.5): Junction with a gravel road west to Big Bar Lake Provincial Park (21 miles/34 km), 33 campsites, picnicking, swimming, boat launch and fishing for rainbow. Road accesses 37 miles/60 km of cross-country ski trails, used by hikers and bicyclists in summer. Trails are also accessible from Clinton. Clinton Lookout and Big Bar rest area just north of this junction.

Mile 266.5 (237.5) Km 429 (382.5): Junction with loop road east to Painted Chasm (3 miles/5 km) and marker explaining its geology. The box canyon, some 394 feet/120m deep, was cut into volcanic bedrock by the eroding action of a glacial meltwater stream. The canyon walls are striped with the multicolored layers of different lava flows. A provincial picnic area is on the canyon lip. Chasm road rejoins Highway 97 4.5 miles/7.5 km north of here.

Mile 267.5 (236.5) Km 430.5 (381): Junction with gravel road east to Meadow Lake, Canoe Creek and Cariboo River Trail back road. Roads are rough but drivable by ordinary automobiles.

Mile 276.5 (227.5) Km 444.5 (367): 70 MILE HOUSE settlement, site of a Cariboo roadhouse built in 1862, has food, gas and lodging. **Junction** with North Bonaparte Road east to Green Lake Provincial Park (7.5 miles/12 km), 121 campsites at 5 separate locations, picnic area, sani-station, swimming, boat launch and fishing for rainbow. Accommodations, boats and services are available on lake. Green Lake is named for its color, attributed to algae growth.

Road provides access to several other fishing lakes, including Tin Cup, Round, Little Green and Watch, and connects with BC Highway 24 to Little Fort north of Kamloops.

Mile 278 (226) Km 447 (364.5): Loch Lomond, the largest of several lakes along the highway.

Mile 287.5 (216.5) Km 463 (348.5): 83 Mile Creek, site of 83 Mile House, built in 1862 and later owned by the BX Co., which kept horses here. Road goes up creek 7 miles/11 km to Green Lake.

Mile 289 (215) Km 465 (346.5): Lookout Road to forestry tower on summit of Mount Begbie (elev. 4,186 feet/1,276m).

Mile 297 (207) Km 478 (333.5): Junction with BC Highway 24 east to Lone Butte Bridge Lake and Little Fort on Yellowhead Highway 5 north of Kamloops. Bridge Lake Provincial Park (31 miles/50 km) has camping, swimming, boat launch and fishing. Many resorts and dude ranches are in the area.

Mile 300.5 (203.5) Km 483.5 (328): Road east to 99 Mile Hill cross-country ski area.

Mile 301.5 (202.5) Km 485.5 (326): South edge of **100 MILE HOUSE** (pop. 1,900), a thriving town in the centre of ranching and lumbering activities, where the emphasis is on the manufacture of pre-cut log homes. All tourist facilities are available, including dude ranches in the area.

The first building here was Bridge Creek House, which predated the gold rush, catering to fur traders and early ranchers. The settlement turned out to be exactly 100 miles from Mile 0 on the Cariboo Road at Lillooet, so the roadhouse changed its name and its clientele from ranchers to miners. Bridge Creek Ranch was bought by the Marquis of Exeter in 1912 and the family still owns the holdings. Little remains of the old days except for one of the stagecoaches in the parking lot of the Red Coach Inn, built on the site of the first roadhouse.

Local special events include the 30-mile/50-km Cariboo Cross-Country Ski Marathon, the first Saturday of February, and the Great Cariboo Ride, a 6- to 8-day trail ride across the Fraser plateau in August.

Mile 302 (202) Km 486.5 (325): Junction with gravel road east to Horse Lake, restocked with kokanee, and other fishing lakes of the high plateau.

Mile 302.5 (201.5) Km 487 (324.5): Tourist information log cabin (open May to Sept.) by 100 Mile Marsh, a bird sanctuary with nature trail. The 39-foot-/12-m-long skis beside the cabin are a reminder of 100 Mile House's place as an important cross-country ski centre.

Mile 303 (201) Km 488 (323.5): Road west to Exeter Station on B.C. Railway. Access to Moose Valley chain of 12 lakes; canoeing.

Mile 304.5 (199.5) Km 489.5 (322): Side road east to Ruth, Canim and Mahood lakes, all endowed with resorts and famous for fishing. Ruth Lake Provincial Park (18 miles/30 km), has picnicking, swimming and a boat launch. Canim Lake (21 miles/35 km), 22 miles/37 km long, has lake trout, rainbow and kokanee fishing. Canim Beach Provincial Park (26 miles/43 km) has 16 campsites, swimming and fishing. Good area for moose. Road also provides a secondary access to Wells Gray Provincial Park (see CANADA HIGHWAY 5 section).

Between Canim and Mahood lakes are spectacular Canim and Mahood falls. From Canim Lake, gravel road leads to community of Hendrix Lake, built by Noranda for the workers at its Boss Mountain molybdenum mine.

Mile 309 (195) Km 498 (313.5): 108 MILE RANCH, now a recreational community with health spa, cabins, golf course, tennis courts, riding stables, hiking and cross-country ski trails, lodge and restaurant.

Mile 310.5 (193.5) Km 500 (311.5): 108 Mile airstrip.

Mile 311 (193) Km 501 (310.5): Rest area beside 108 Mile House Lake. Alongside is the 108 Heritage Site, with some of the original log buildings from 108 Ranch (including a huge 1908 log barn) and others relocated from 105 Mile. Guided tours, open May to early Sept. Sucker Lake Road (opposite side of highway) is good spot for June/July wildflowers.

Mile 108 Heritage Site, at Mile 311, has some of the original buildings from the 108 Ranch. (Liz Bryan)

Mile 314 (190) Km 505.5 (306): Road east to Spring and Dempsey lakes by 111 Mile Creek.

Mile 318 (186) Km 512 (299.5): South entrance to **LAC LA HACHE** (pop. 400), a small community on a lake of the same name, so-called because a French Canadian settler lost his ax here while chopping a waterhole in the ice. Small museum in 1930s log schoolhouse beside highway. Lakeside resorts offer full tourist facilities and camping.

The lake is 11.5 miles/19 km long; good fishing for rainbow, kokanee, large lake trout. Excellent ice fishing in winter.

Mile 318.5 (185.5) Km 513 (298.5): Road east to Timothy, Spout, Murphy and other fishing lakes, also to Mount Timothy ski area.

Mile 327 (177) Km 526 (285.5): Lac La Hache Provincial Park offers 83 forested campsites, picnic area, sani-station, swimming, hiking trail, fishing and boat launch. 🏕🏕🅿🟦

Mile 328 (176) Km 527.5 (284): Cariboo Provincial Nature Park, accessible to foot traffic only: Beaver activity on San Jose River; bird watching at Frog Lake.

Mile 335 (169) Km 539.5 (272): Stop of interest sign commemorating the miners, traders and adventurers who came this way to the Cariboo goldfields in the 1860s.

Mile 340 (164) Km 547.5 (264): 140 Mile House (unincorporated).

Mile 341 (163) Km 549 (262.5): Highway warning: Strong crosswinds in this area.

Mile 341.5 (162.5) Km 549.5 (262): Knife Creek Road to Spout and Murphy lakes.

Mile 346 (158) Km 557 (254.5): Mission Road leads west to site of St. Joseph's Mission, founded in 1867 by Oblate Father James McGuckin, who built a chapel, residence and school, and started a cattle ranch whose OMI brand was the first registered brand in the Cariboo. Only a small cemetery and farm buildings remain.

Mile 348 (156) Km 560 (251.5): 148-Mile Marsh, wetlands conservation project sponsored by Ducks Unlimited. Good spot to see waterfowl.

Mile 349.5 (154.5) Km 562 (249.5): **150 MILE HOUSE**, once an important roadhouse and junction on the Cariboo Road (one of the original trails to the gold camps of the Cariboo), now a small service community with a hotel, restaurant, pub, store and gas station.

Road northeast to Quesnel and Horsefly lakes and to communities of Likely (50 miles/80 km) and Horsefly (35 miles/56 km). Provincial park at Horsefly Lake has 22 campsites, boat launch, beach and hiking trails. 🏕🏕🔺

Mile 353.5 (150.5) Km 569 (242.5): South end of Williams Lake; good rainbow fishing. Named for Chief William of the nearby Sugar Cane Reserve. Scenic back road through the reserve rejoins the highway at Mile 346. 🐟

Mile 360 (144) Km 579 (232.5): **WILLIAMS LAKE** (pop. 18,000). All services available. Tourist information located along the highway at south entrance to town.

Virtually bypassed by the Cariboo gold rush, Williams Lake was originally an overnight camp for the Hudson's Bay Co. fur brigade. It later became a farming community, then a centre for ranchers working the Chilcotin country. The advent of the Pacific Great Eastern Railway (now the B.C. Railway) in 1919 made the town the cattle marketing and shipping centre for the whole Cariboo–Chilcotin. Today the city has the largest and most active cattleyards in the province. Lumber and mining for copper-molybdenum are the mainstays of the economy.

Williams Lake is famous for its rip-roaring 4-day stampede held in July.

At the south end of town is the **junction** with BC Highway 20, which goes west across the Chilcotin to Bella Coola on the coast (see the CHILCOTIN HIGHWAY section for log of Highway 20).

Visit Scout Island Nature Center (accessible off Highway 20), located on 2 small islands at the north end of the lake; interpretive centre, nature trails, picnic area, boat launch and beach.

Cariboo Friendship Center on South 3rd Avenue has native crafts for sale. Local arts and crafts are also on display at the Stationhouse Gallery in the historic train station on Oliver Street. 🏕🏕

Mile 369 (135) Km 594 (217.5): Road to Bull Mountain cross-country ski area.

Mile 372.5 (131.5) Km 599.5 (212): Mountain House Road to Likely Road and 150 Mile House.

Mile 375.5 (128.5) Km 604 (207.5): Rest area.

Mile 378.5 (125.5) Km 609.5 (202): Side road leads west 2.5 miles/4.5 km to tiny settlement of **SODA CREEK** on the banks of the Fraser. Soda Creek Emporium at junction provides food and beverage service. The original wagon road to the goldfields ended here and miners went the rest of the way to Quesnel by river steamboats. Soda Creek became an important transfer point for men and supplies until the railway went through in 1920. Soda Creek was so named because the creek bed is carbonate of lime and the water bubbles like soda water.

Mile 385.5 (118.5) Km 620.5 (191): **McLEESE LAKE**; gas, food, stores, motel and a private campground. There is a small but pretty rest area on the lake beside the highway; picnic tables, toilets, litter barrels. Fishing is good for small to medium rainbow. There are resorts around the lake.

Junction with road to Beaver Lake and on to Likely. Historic Quesnelle Forks, a heritage site with a Forestry campsite, is located near Likely. Travelers may continue north from Likely to Barkerville and rejoin Highway 97 at Quesnel. 🅿🏕🟦

Mile 390 (114) Km 628 (183.5): Large turnout and stop of interest sign about the paddle wheelers that provided transport on the Fraser for 390 miles/650 km north of Soda Creek. Good view of river.

Mile 391 (113) Km 629.5 (182): Road west to McAlister and Soda Creek.

Mile 396.5 (107.5) Km 638 (173.5): Marguerite rest area; viewpoint upriver to Marguerite reaction cable ferry across Fraser. Ferry crossing takes 10 minutes; 2 cars and 10 passengers can be accommodated. Ferry runs on call, 7 a.m. to 6:45 p.m., with breaks for lunch and dinner. No charge. On the far side of the river is a gravel road that goes north to Quesnel, south to meet BC Highway 20 near Riske Creek.

Mile 398.5 (105.5) Km 641 (170.5): East of highway an outcropping of basalt columns creates a formation known as the Devil's Palisades.

Mile 399 (105) Km 642.5 (169): Stone cairn commemorates Fort Alexandria, the last North West Co. fur-trading post established west of the Rockies, built in 1821. The actual site of the fort is across the river. Cairn also marks the approximate farthest point reached by Alexander Mackenzie in his descent of the Fraser in 1793.

Mile 400.5 (103.5) Km 645 (166.5): Old barn, house and assorted buildings of Lansdowne Farm, run by the Moffats in the gold rush era.

Mile 403 (101) Km 649 (162.5): Prominent pioneer church and cemetery on top of river bluffs to east.

Mile 404 (100) Km 650.5 (161): Notice prominent clay cliffs along the river, remnants of glacial deposits.

Mile 409.5 (94.5) Km 659 (152.5): Australian rest area, named for nearby Australian ranch, founded in 1863.

Mile 417 (87) Km 671 (140.5): Small community of Kersley (unincorporated); gas and food.

Mile 424.5 (79.5) Km 683 (128.5): South end of loop road east to Dragon Lake; rainbow fishing. 🐟

Mile 430.5 (73.5) Km 693 (118.5): North end of loop road east to Dragon Lake along Quesnel River to old mining centre of Hydraulic and to Beavermouth Forestry Recreation Area; swimming, picnicking, boat launch. 🅿

Mile 433 (71) Km 697 (114.5): Hilltop view of **QUESNEL** (pop. 8,145), which calls itself the "Gold Pan City." The city provides good shopping and full tourist facilities. At the confluence of the Quesnel and Fraser rivers, the town was originally called Quesnelle Mouth to distinguish it from the gold camp of Quesnelle Forks upriver. (The river was named by Simon Fraser in 1808 for his lieutenant, Jules Quesnelle.) From a small fur-trading outpost, Quesnel burgeoned during the Cariboo gold rush, when paddle wheel boats from Soda Creek brought in men and supplies. Other gold rush towns have faded away but Quesnel grew to become the commercial hub of the North Cariboo, its economy centered on the forest industry, with 5 sawmills and planer mills, a plywood plant and 2 pulp mills.

Downtown beside the river is a Cornish waterwheel used in the gold mines; the relics of the SS *Enterprise*, one of the gold rush steamers; and a stone cairn commemorating the building of the Collins Overland telegraph, an ambitious scheme to link America with Asia across the Bering Strait. The scheme was abandoned when a transAtlantic cable was successfully laid from Ireland to Newfoundland.

The old road bridge across the Fraser (built in 1929, now a pedestrian bridge) here has been replaced by a modern one downstream. Across the street from the waterwheel is the restored Hudson's Bay Co. store, built in 1867, now a restaurant.

The museum in LeBourdais Park displays old gold-mining equipment and a collection of native and gold rush artifacts. Pioneer cemetery, flower gardens and tourism information office are adjacent.

A hiking and bike trail starts at the footbridge and goes along Quesnel River. Boat trips are available. Panning for gold is permitted at the confluence of the Fraser and Quesnel rivers (no mining license required).

Highway 97 loops around the town and

BC Highway 26 to Barkerville

The 51.5-mile/82.5-km road from Quesnel to Barkerville is the most historic in British Columbia, for it was here in the 1850s that the gold rush miners converged, on foot, on horseback, by wagon and stage, lured by the promise of riches from the Cariboo creeks. At road's end was Barkerville, the largest and lustiest of all the gold camps, and in its hectic heyday the biggest city west of Chicago and north of San Francisco.

Barkerville is today a provincial historic park, its buildings and boardwalks faithfully restored or reconstructed in period style. The shops and restaurants are open; there are performances at the opera house; and horse-drawn carriages rattle down the main streets.

Today Highway 26 follows the route of the original wagon road, built in 1865. No travelers on Highway 97 should miss this side trip into history.

Mile 0 Km 0: **Junction** with Highway 97 at **Mile 434.5** near Quesnel. Highway 26 climbs steeply up through the jackpine forests of Mouse Mountain, then descends to the Cottonwood River.

Mile 1 Km 1.5: Barlow Creek residential area; grocery, food and fuel. Eastbound, Highway 26 accesses local roads. Watch for deer.

Mile 13 Km 21: Rest area and interpretive trails to south. Wooden rail "snake" and wire fences with wooden top rail allow deer and moose to safely jump them, while penning domestic livestock.

Mile 15 Km 24.5: Cottonwood River bridge. The river is named for the black cottonwood trees growing alongside it.

Mile 16.5 Km 27: Cottonwood House, one of the original roadhouses on the Cariboo Road, is now a provincial historic park. The log house, built in 1864, has been faithfully restored and furnished, along with surrounding barns and outbuildings. The former chicken shed is a small museum and interpretive centre. From the end of May until Sept. there are guides in period costume and stagecoach rides along an original stretch of wagon road. Picnic tables are available.

The John Boyd family operated the roadhouse for more than 80 years, and the account books and diaries (34 volumes) are priceless historical records.

Mile 20 Km 32.5: Side road leads to Lightning Creek Forest Service recreation site; free camping, 14-day limit. *CAUTION:* Active logging road, drive with headlights on.

Mile 21.5 Km 34.5: Lover's Leap viewpoint to south. Also view of Mex-

ican Hill Summit, one of the steepest grades on the original Cariboo Wagon Road.

Mile 27 Km 43.5: Historical stop of interest marker for Charles Morgan Blessing's grave. Blessing, from Ohio,

Old-fashioned general store in Barkerville. (Liz Bryan)

was murdered on his way to Barkerville in 1866. His killer, John Barry, was caught when he gave Blessing's keepsake gold nugget stickpin, in the shape of a skull, to a Barkerville dance-hall girl. John Barry was the only white man hanged in the Cariboo during the gold rush.

Mile 37.5 Km 60: Stanley Road and Boulder Gold Mines (active claim). Stanley Road is a 1.9-mile/3-km loop road that leads past the gold-rush ghost towns of Stanley and VanWinkle, the old Lightning Hotel, and gold rush-era gravesites. A worthwhile sidetrip.

Mile 38.5 Km 62: Stanley (Loop) Road, Chisholm Creek.

Mile 40 Km 64.5: Devil's Canyon paved turnout to south. This was the highest point on the Cariboo Wagon Road.

Mile 43 Km 69: Slough Creek, site of much hydraulic mining activity after Joe Shaw discovered gold here in 1870.

Mile 45 Km 72: Jack o' Clubs Lake; fishing for rainbow, lake trout and Dolly Varden. There are several rest areas and turnouts along the lake.

Mile 47 Km 76: **WELLS** (pop. 300)

offers all visitor facilities, including motels, restaurants, liquor outlet, groceries and gas. Wells dates to the 1930s when the Cariboo Gold Quartz Mine, promoted and developed by Fred Wells, brought hundreds of workers to this

valley. The mine closed in 1967, but the town has continued as a service centre and attraction for tourists. There are numerous art galleries and gift shops, some housed in refurbished 1930s-style buildings. Guided and self-guided tours of the town are available. A museum with displays of local mining history is open daily from June to Sept.

Recreation in the area includes hiking, skiing, curling and snowmobiling. The local Legion hosts horseshoes and bocci tournaments, has a pub, and offers potluck suppers throughout the year.

Mile 49 Km 79: Reduction Road, alternate route to Barkerville; accesses Barkerville Cemetery and returns to Highway 26 at **Mile 51**.

Mile 49.5 Km 80: Barkerville Provincial Park Forest Rose Campground to north. Lowhee Campground to south; 170 campsites, picnic areas and dump stations.

Mile 50 Km 80.5: Gravel road leads north 18 miles/29 km to Bowron Lakes Provincial Park, noted for its interconnecting chain of lakes and the resulting 72-mile/116-km canoe circuit which takes from 7 to 10 days to complete. Visitor information available at registration centre next to main parking lot where canoeists must register and pay circuit fees. Reservations recommended in July and August (required for 7 or more people); phone (604) 992-3111.

Airfield at junction with 2,500-foot/762-m paved runway, elev. 4,180 feet/1,274m.

There are 2 private lodges at the north end of the lake with restaurants, a general store and canoe rentals. Provincial park campground has 25 sites, water, pit toilets, firewood and a boat launch. Swimming, fishing, canoeing, kayaking and hiking.

Mile 50 Km 81: Entrance to Barkerville; admission charged.

Mile 50.5 Km 81.5: Former site of Cameronton, named for John A. "Cariboo" Cameron who found gold in this area. Also in this area is Williams Creek, a rich gold-producing creek during the gold rush.

Mile 51 Km 82: Turnoff on 1.8-mile/2.9-km Reduction Road for gold rush cemetery and Government Hill Campground (0.2 mile/0.4 km), New Barkerville (0.4 mile/0.7 km), and Grubstake Store (0.7 mile/1.1 km).

Mile 51.5 Km 82.5: **BARKERVILLE**, a provincial historic town; open year-round, phone (604) 994-3332. Visitor information at Reception Centre.

Barkerville was named for miner Billy Barker, who struck gold on Williams Creek. The resulting gold rush in 1862 created Barkerville. Virtually a ghost town when the provincial government began restoration in 1958, today Barkerville's buildings and boardwalks are faithful restorations or reconstructions from the town's heyday. Visitors can pan for gold, shop at the old-time general store, watch a blacksmith at work, or take in a show at the Theatre Royal. It is best to visit between June 1st and Labour Day, when the Theatre Royal offers performances and all exhibits are open.

The Theatre Royal is extremely popular with visitors. The half-hour spring show plays daily (except Saturdays) at 12:45 P.M. from mid-May to mid-June. Regular season begins in late June, with 1800s-style musical dramas playing daily (except Fridays) at 1 and 4 P.M. Between July 1 and Labour Day there is an 8 P.M. show on Saturdays and Sundays that is fashioned after a 1930s-style radio show. Admission is charged at all shows.

History comes alive at Barkerville thanks to interpreters and street performers who represent actual citizens of the town in 1870, discuss "current" events with visitors, conduct tours and stage daily dramas throughout the summer.

Beyond Main Street, the Cariboo Wagon Road leads on (for pedestrians only) to Richfield, 1 mile/1.6 km, to the courthouse of "Hanging" Judge Begbie.

swings north along Front Street (turn east for downtown shops). **Junction** with road across new Fraser River bridge to west Quesnel and on to the ranch community of Nazko (60 miles/96 km, unpaved road) and Puntchesakut Lake Provincial Park (21 miles/35 km), with picnicking, swimming and boat launch.

Nazko Road provides access to the Alexander Mackenzie Heritage Trail to Bella Coola. The trail is presently being restored; it can be hiked in sections. The complete 260-mile/420-km route takes about 3 weeks. Contact the BC Parks office at 640 Borland St., Williams Lake, BC V2G 1R8, for more information.

Pinnacles Provincial Park, 5 miles/8 km west of Highway 97, has picnic areas and hiking trails among distinctive eroded sandstone pillars.

Mile 433.5 (70.5) Km 697.5 (114): Quesnel Forest Industry Observation Tower overlooks 4 lumber mills and 2 pulp mills; free, open year-round.

Mile 434.5 (69.5) Km 699 (112.5): **Junction** with BC Highway 26 to Wells and historic Barkerville (see feature this section). Giant gold pan at junction marks north entrance to Quesnel.   ★

Mile 438.5 (65.5) Km 706 (105.5): Ten Mile Lake Provincial Park; 142 campsites, picnic area, sani-station, hiking trails, swimming, fishing for rainbow and boat launch. Cross-country skiing in winter. Highway warning: Watch for moose.

Mile 442.5 (61.5) Km 712 (99.5): Cottonwood River bridge; at the south end, a turnout and stop of interest sign describes the railway bridge seen upriver. This high trestle was built in 1952. The deep canyon of the Cottonwood presented such difficulties for the Pacific Great Eastern Railway (now B.C. Rail) in the 1920s that rail construction halted here for more than 20 years.

Mile 446.5 (57.5) Km 719 (92.5): Hush Lake rest area; boat launch for canoes and row boats, fishing for rainbow and brook trout.

Mile 457.5 (46.5) Km 736.5 (75): Strathnaver (unincorporated); no services.

Mile 459 (45) Km 739 (72.5): *CAUTION:* Steep 7 percent downgrade for northbound traffic.

Mile 467.5 (36.5) Km 752 (59.5): Small community of **HIXON** (pop. 1,500) has a post office, 2 motels, gas stations, grocery stores, 2 restaurants, a pub and private campground.   ▲

Mile 474 (30) Km 763 (48.5): Woodpecker rest area with picnic tables. To the north is a road to Woodpecker Landing, one of the old paddle-wheeler docks on the Fraser River.

Mile 477.5 (26.5) Km 769 (42.5): Sign for southbound travelers: Entering the Cariboo.

Mile 483 (21) Km 777.5 (34): Stone Creek forestry road, east.

Mile 483.5 (20.5) Km 778 (33.5): Stoner (unincorporated); mini-mart, ice, gas station

with diesel, pay phone.

Mile 488 (16) Km 785.5 (26): Red Rock (unincorporated); mini-mart, ice, gas station with diesel, pay phone.

Mile 494 (10) Km 795 (16.5): Road to Buckhorn and St. Marys lakes. Buckhorn Lake is a bird sanctuary with a Forest Service campsite and fishing for small rainbow. St. Marys also has small rainbow and a campsite.

Mile 495.5 (8.5) Km 797.5 (14): Tabor Creek.

Mile 500 (4) Km 804.5 (7): Road east to Prince George airport. Bypass road to Yellowhead Highway 16 East. Northbound, the highway descends a 5 percent grade to Fraser River.

Mile 503 (1) Km 810 (1.5): Fraser River bridge. At the north end, Queensway leads east to Prince George city centre.

Mile 504 (0) Km 811.5 (0): **Junction** with Yellowhead Highway 16 at **PRINCE GEORGE** (pop. 71,000), fourth largest city in British Columbia. All visitor facilities are available.

In the early 1800s, Simon Fraser of the North West Trading Co. erected a fur-trading post here at the confluence of the Nechako and Fraser rivers. He named it Fort George in honor of the reigning English monarch. In 1906, survey parties for the transcontinental Grand Trunk Pacific Railway (later Canadian National Railways) passed through the area, and with the building of the railroad a great land boom took place. The city was incorporated in 1915 under the name Prince George. Old Fort George is now a park and picnic spot and the site of Fort George Museum. The new (1994) University of Northern B.C. has its main campus on the outskirts of the city.

Visitors can walk the 6-mile/10-km Heritage River Trail along the Fraser and Nechako rivers; visit Cottonwood Island and Hudson Bay Slough nature parks; ride a narrow-gauge steam train in Fort George Park; drive up to Connaught Hill for views of the city; or visit Forests for the World Park, on the western escarpment, a large view park with nature trails and a forest education program.

The Railway Museum here includes a station and rolling stock from the days of steam trains. The Regional Museum tells the story of transportation from Indian dugouts to railways. The Native Art Gallery has Indian arts and crafts for sale.

Prince George is primarily an industrial centre, fairly dependent on the lumber industry, with 3 pulp mills, sawmills, planers, dry kilns, a plywood plant and 2 chemical plants to serve the pulp mills. Oil refining, mining and heavy construction are other major area industries. The Prince George Forest Region is the largest in the province.

Prince George is roughly the geographical heart of British Columbia. It is also the hub of major highways (Highway 97 and Yellowhead Highway 16) and railways (B.C. Rail and Canadian National Railways).

Yellowhead Highway 16 and other northern highways are logged in *The MILEPOST®*, available in bookstores or from Vernon Publications Inc. (phone 1-800-726-4707).

S. HIGHWAY 101

ornia–Oregon Border to Olympia, WA
(See maps, pages 166, 169, 173, 176 and 182)

U.S. Highway 101 is one of the world's most popular vacation roads. *Northwest Mileposts*® logs this 2-lane trail from the Oregon–California border, curving past Oregon's mountainous sand dunes, black cliffs and white beaches and winding through the soft green cushion of Washington's Olympic Peninsula rain forest.

Highway 101 weaves through several national parks and recreation areas, innumerable historic sites and scenic areas of international fame. Visitor centers in each community provide a wealth of informational pamphlets. Motels, resorts, campgrounds and other facilities are plentiful along all but 1 section of the highway. North of Aberdeen, WA, to Crescent Lake, where Highway 101 winds inland, there are numerous campgrounds and turnouts, but resorts and motels are scattered and may be filled to capacity during the summer tourist season.

Allow more time than you think you'll need to travel this route, drive slowly and stop often.

U.S. Highway 101 Log

Distance from Oregon–California border is followed by distance from the U.S. Highway 101 junction with Interstate 5 at Olympia, WA.

Mile 0 (712.5): Oregon–California border. California agricultural inspections are in the southbound lanes. All fruits, vegetables and plant material must be declared and are subject to inspection. A myrtlewood factory is located here.

Mile 0.5 (712): Crossing the Winchuck River. Winchuck Campground (13 sites) is 14 miles east on Winchuck Road.　　▲

Mile 2.5 (710): Largest Monterey Cypress in the world. Chetco Valley Museum has local artifacts, documents and photographs.

Mile 4.5 (708): Information center, private RV parks, major-chain motel, restaurant, shopping center and gas station.　　▲

Mile 5.5 (707): Loeb State Park, 8 miles to the northeast, has 53 campsites, 21 RV sites, swimming, fishing and boat launch.　 ◄▲

Mile 6 (706.5): BROOKINGS (pop. 4,300) is a major recreational area famous for fishing,

hunting, beaches and fields of hybrid lilies and azaleas (the town produces more than 75 percent of the Easter lilies grown in the United States). Resorts, major-chain motels and restaurants are available. The area is also noted for its sheep and wool. Ninety percent of all wool sold to the paper-making industry comes from Curry County because of the wool's special "felting quality."

In May, Azalea State Park is a blaze of color. Town facilities include picnic sites, a boat launch, Coast Guard marina, rentals, fishing charters and tackle shops. Guides are available. This is a favorite coastal area for small boaters. Beaches offer good clamming, while the harbor is good for crabs and shrimp.

The Chetco River offers good access to

salt- and freshwater fishing (steelhead, chinook, cutthroat, rainbow). Gray whales are often visible offshore in the spring and fall. During March, a whale-watch program operated by Oregon State Parks is in full swing. Volunteers are visible at nearly every viewpoint along the coast, counting migrating whales and educating the public. ⚓◄ MP 357

Mile 7.5 (705): Harris Beach State Park offers exceptionally scenic sea stacks, cliffs and beach. The Goat Island Bird Preserve offshore is the southernmost part of the Oregon Islands National Wildlife Refuge. Full-hookup campsites and picnicking available at the state park. On the east side of the highway, a state visitor center provides phones

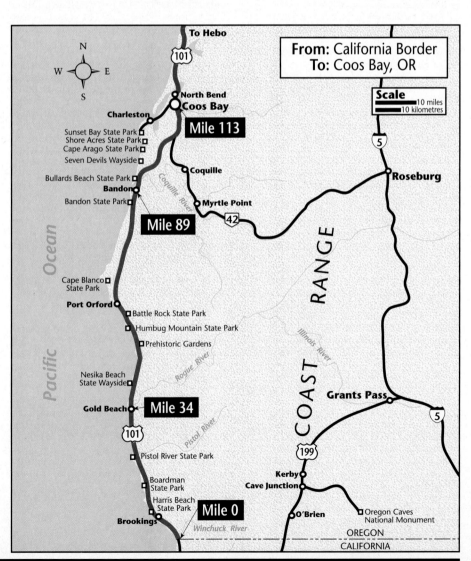

for making campground reservations. ⊼▲

Mile 9 (703.5): The west shoulder of U.S. Highway 101 affords 11 named viewpoints in the next 9 miles northbound, providing often-spectacular views of cliffs, sea stacks and beach access. The viewpoints are included in 11-mile-long Boardman State Park, a network of day-use areas that includes hiking trails, beach access and picnic areas. One of the viewpoints, Thomas Creek Bridge, is the highest bridge in Oregon at 530 feet, spanning 970 feet. Viewpoints include (from south to north) Rainbow Rock, Lone Ranch Beach, Cape Ferrelo, House Rock, Whalehead Viewpoint, Whalehead State Park (no RV turnaround), Indian Sands Trail, Thomas Creek Bridge, Natural Bridge, Spruce Island and Arch Rock. ⋙⊼

Mile 21 (691.5): Northern boundary of Samuel H. Boardman State Park. Hiking on Oregon Coast Trail. ⋙

Mile 24 (688.5): Pistol River State Park with beach access and fishing for steelhead, salmon, trout and ocean perch. The river mouth is often sand-bound during the summer. There are no nearby camping facilities. Battle of Pistol River Historical Site from the Rogue Indian War of 1856. Good beachcombing. ⬱

Mile 25.5 (687): Beach access. Steep grade begins next mile northbound.

Mile 28 (684.5): Cape Sebastian viewpoint. This point was discovered and named by the Spanish explorer Sebastian Vizcaino in 1603.

Mile 32.5 (680): Hunter Creek Beach area. Good year-round fishing. The best salmon action is in tidewater and lower river near U.S. Highway 101 bridge. ⬱

Mile 34 (678.5): GOLD BEACH (pop. 1,585) at the mouth of the Rogue River. A USFS ranger station and visitor center is located here, as well as major-chain motel and other traveler services. Also available are RV parks, a hospital, an airstrip, fishing guides and resorts. Whitewater jet-boat trips up the Rogue River (64, 80 and 104 miles round-trip) are available. Agates are found on the beach areas. There is excellent salt- and freshwater salmon and steelhead fishing in the Rogue River and offshore from the protective jetties that offer easy access to the ocean for small-boat fishermen. Jetty fishing for salmon is popular during the summer. Flood tides bring chinook into the bay to feed during August. ⬱▲

Mile 35.5 (677): Rogue River bridge. Rogue River Road to east.

Mile 36.5 (676): Rogue River viewpoint. Beach access.

Mile 40.5 (672): Giesel (Ge-sell) Monument State Park, commemorating the Indian massacre of the Giesel family in 1856; picnicking. (Difficult access for RVs.) ⊼

Mile 41 (671.5): Nesika (Ness-ih-ka) Beach wayside offers beachcombing, agate hunting, gas, food and RV park. Public access to beach at end of Nesika Road, but no RV turnaround. ▲

Mile 44 (668.5): Honey Bear Beach access

and rest area. Surf fishing, picnicking, beach walking and travel information are available. ⊼⬱ MP 319

Mile 50 (662.5): Prehistoric Gardens, a private exhibit featuring life-size replicas of dinosaurs and other prehistoric animals, also includes an arboretum.

Mile 50.5 (662): Narrow, winding road with no shoulder.

Mile 55 (657.5): Humbug Mountain day-use area with picnic facilities. ⊼ MP 308

Mile 56 (656.5): Humbug Mountain State Park has 30 campsites with full hookups, 75 tent campsites, showers and picnic sites. The primary feature is Humbug Mountain, which rises 1,750 feet sheer above the ocean. Food and lodging available. Access to excellent beach is under the highway. ⊼▲ MP 307

Mile 61 (651.5): PORT ORFORD (pop. 1,000) has the distinction of being the oldest townsite on the Oregon coast (established in 1851) and the westernmost incorporated city in the Lower 48 states. All services are available, including an RV park. There are fish-buying stations and an urchin-processing plant on the pier, as well as a boat launch and public showers. Port Orford provides an excellent "barless" boat harbor for fishing for salmon and bottom fish during August, September and October just offshore. There are no charter or rental boats available. In late summer, cartop boats are used to fish the protected waters and the ocean during windless periods. A few commercial fishing boats work from the public dock. A heavy-duty hoist lifts both recreational and commercial vessels from dock to ocean. It is the only Oregon port where commercial fishing vessels are hauled out of the water and stored on trailers each night. Port Orford Head offers whale watching in the spring and fall migration seasons. Port Orford Heads Wayside just north of town is the site of a Coast Guard lifeboat station and has picnicking and pit toilets. Battle Rock State Park Historic Site with beach access is a day-use-only area with picnic facilities. ⊼⬱▲

Mile 62 (650.5): Garrison Lake public boat landing.

Mile 65.5 (647): Elk River Road **junction**; fish hatchery, camping. ▲

Mile 66.5 (646): Cape Blanco State Park (closed in winter; 5 miles to beach) has 58 tent/RV campsites and dump station. The lighthouse on the cape is the farthest western point that a vehicle may be driven in the Lower 48 states. The cape was discovered on Jan. 19, 1603, by Spanish explorer Martin De Augilar. Scenic cliffs and a waterfall are visible. Secluded campsites and picnic areas offer beautiful ocean views. Fishing and nature trails are available. Blanco reef and Orford reef are both part of the Oregon Islands National Wildlife Refuge. ⋙⊼⬱▲

Mile 67.5 (645): Sixes River bridge.

Mile 71.5 (641): Private campground and RV park. ▲

Mile 73 (639.5): Floras Lake Road, public

boat landing and fishing for trout, flounder and bass. Popular lake for windsurfing. Camping at Boice-Cope County Park. ⬱▲ MP 290

Mile 74 (638.5): Alternate route to Floras Lake boat launch. MP 289

Mile 75.5 (637): Town of **LANGLOIS**. Originally called Dairyville, it was confused with a town in Ohio, so they named it after the postmaster, a Frenchman named Langlois. RV park, food and gas available. ▲

Mile 81.5 (631): Westcoast Game Park, private exhibit featuring walk-through wildlife safari. There are many myrtlewood shops found in the next few miles northbound. MP 282

Mile 85 (627.5): Bradley Lake public boat launch. MP 278

Mile 85.5 (627): Scenic Beach Loop Drive, a 3.6-mile drive following the coastline north to Bandon with access to Bandon State Park (day use only). Limited ocean views from road; motels, private campground and a restaurant are found along this loop; beach access, scenic overlooks; access to Face Rock viewpoint; picnicking, horse rentals, golf, beachcombing and surf fishing for perch. ⊼⬱▲ MP 274

Mile 87.5 (625): Face Rock viewpoint with wayside facilities. Alternative turnoff to Scenic Beach Loop Drive. Good photo opportunities.

Mile 89 (623.5): BANDON (pop. 2,490) has all visitor services, including a hospital, shopping center and RV park. Many of Bandon's accommodations are located on Beach Loop Drive. Motels, shops, art galleries and visitor information center are located in the Old Town area on the Coquille River. The self-proclaimed "Cranberry Capital of Oregon," Bandon has a picturesque harbor and an Old Town shopping area. The area offers excellent river, bay and ocean fishing as well as cranberry bogs, myrtlewood factories and a cheese factory. The Bandon cranberry festival is held in September. Phone the chamber of commerce at (503) 347-9616 for more information. ⬱▲

Mile 92 (620.5): Coquille River Lighthouse (built in 1896) and Bullards Beach State Park. The lighthouse sits at the river's mouth across the water from Bandon. A paved jetty juts out beyond it, offering close-up views of seals and crashing waves. The park, open year-round, offers 92 full-hookup spaces for RVs, 100 tent/RV sites, showers, picnic facilities, nature trails, playground, viewpoint, boat ramp, beach access and swimming area. Equestrian trails and a horse-camping area are available. Fishing in the river is open year-round. Information is available at sporting goods stores in Bandon.

Mile 94 (618.5): Seven Devils Wayside viewpoint with picnicking, beach access, beachcombing for agates and driftwood, and surf fishing at Whiskey Run Beach.

Mile 98.5 (614): Westbound turnoff to Charleston area recreation facilities. These include Seven Devils Wayside, a day-use-only area; South Slough Estuarine Sanctuary with canoe launch to lake, hiking, bird watching; Bastendorff Beach County Park with 81 campsites; Cape Arago State Park day-use area with picnicking, hiking, fishing, viewpoint and sea lions; Sunset Bay State Park, with overnight camping for 75 tents, 34 electric-hookup sites, 29 full-hookup sites, showers, picnicking, hiking, boat ramp, swimming, fishing on rocks, and viewpoints; and Shore Acres State Park day-use area for picnics, enclosed observation building for ocean viewing, interpretive center, summer workshop information, hiking, striking natural rock carvings, photography and fishing. Included in Shore Acres State Park are the exceptional landscaping and Oriental gardens on the former estate of lumber baron Louis J. Simpson. The park charges a summer entry fee.   MP 253

Mile 106.5 (606): Davis Slough. **Junction** with Oregon Highway 42 to Coquille, Roseburg and Interstate 5.   MP 245

Mile 113 (599.5): COOS BAY (pop. 15,100), world's largest lumber-shipping port. Coos Bay has all visitor services including a large number of motels and restaurants, and a hospital. This is a major recreation area with numerous state parks, beach access, bay and river fishing, crabbing and clamming, House of Myrtlewood factory tours, and one of the largest Coast Guard stations on the Oregon coast. Fishing charter boats available daily from Coos Bay at nearby Charleston, where travelers will also find motels, services,

Storm waves strike a sandstone formation at Shore Acres State Park. (© John Barger)

restaurants and oyster farms.

Coos River is a major striped bass fishing area. Clamming is good at low tide in the boat basin at Charleston and nearby beaches. Most recreational features are found in nearby Charleston, including state parks, charter boats, boat ramps, and bait and tackle stores. The turnoff for ocean beaches, via Charleston, is found at city center and is clearly marked. The local fishing situation varies seasonally. Check with local fishermen for latest conditions and where-to-go information.

Mile 116 (596.5): NORTH BEND (pop. 8,850) is a major commercial shipping port. The tri-city complex of Coos Bay, Charleston and North Bend, with about 32,000 residents, forms the metropolitan center serving the central Oregon coast and has all services. Alternate route to Sunset Bay State Park is clearly marked at city center. There is a visitor information center at the north city limits for local tour and fishing information; phone (503) 756-4613, fax (503) 756-0142.

Coos County Historical Society Museum is located here.

Mile 117.5 (595): C.B. McCullough Bridge across the Coos River.

Mile 118 (594.5): McCullough Wayside and boat launch.

Mile 118.5 (594): Southern boundary of Oregon Dunes National Recreation Area in the Siuslaw (sigh-OOS-law) National Forest. For more information on the Oregon Dunes National Recreation Area see the MAJOR ATTRACTIONS section. Horsfall Dune and Beach Access Road to 4 camping areas, ORV area, fishing and dunes. Wild Mare Campground provides horse corral at each site. Hiking trail to Sandpoint and Horsfall lakes.

Mile 122 (590.5): Myrtlewood factory, RV park and ORV rentals.

Mile 123.5 (589): Public boat launch.

Mile 125.5 (587): Clear Lake east side of highway.   MP 226

Mile 127 (585.5): Spinreel Campground (37 sites, flush toilets), access road to a boat ramp, fishing and ORV access. ORV rentals are available.   MP 224

Mile 128.5 (584): LAKESIDE (pop. 1,425) offers resort facilities, access to Camp Easter Seal, South Eel campgrounds and Tenmile Lakes Recreation Area. Fee camping at South Eel (no beach driving is permitted). Tenmile Lakes area is 2 major lakes, North and South Tenmile, offering some of the finest largemouth bass fishing in Oregon. North Lake Resort on North Tenmile Lake offers the only camping facilities, plus a boat launch, boat rentals, RV hookups and access to both lakes.

Mile 129 (583.5): North Eel Campground with 52 tent/RV sites, flush toilets and hiking trails. Fee.

Mile 130 (582.5): Eel Lake and William M. Tugman State Park on the southwest end of the lake. Tugman includes 115 tent/RV sites, dump station, picnicking, swimming beach, fishing and a boat ramp on Eel Lake.

Mile 132.5 (580): Clear Lake is closed to fishing and recreational use. This lake is the water supply for Reedsport.

Mile 134.5 (578): Umpqua Lighthouse State Park; 22 RV hookup sites, 42 tent sites, fishing, boating, hiking trails, whale-watching station and dune access. The picturesque lighthouse marks the mouth of the Umpqua

Spring flowers at Shore Acres State Park botanical gardens.
(Dick Burmeister, courtesy Coos Bay Area Chamber of Commerce)

River and was rebuilt in 1892 on the bluff, replacing a beach lighthouse destroyed by flood in 1857. ♨✦▲

Mile 135.5 (577): WINCHESTER BAY, a small commercial sportfishing community at the mouth of the Umpqua River, has the largest sportfishing marina on the Oregon coast at Salmon Harbor. Winchester Bay has motels, restaurants and gift shops. No gas. A favorite destination for scuba divers. Viewed from sea, the lighthouse guarding the mouth of Winchester Bay is the only one on the Oregon coast with a red light beam. Salmon-fishing charter-boat facilities usually close for the season in late September. This is a large harbor with marina docking area, boat launch, RV camping and cannery services. Crabbing is done in the harbor, and ring traps are available for rent.

Windy Cove County Campground is accessible from marina area on County Road 251; 97 tent sites, 64 RV sites, flush toilets, fishing, crabbing, whale watching, beach and dune access, fee. ✦▲ MP 216

Mile 140 (572.5): REEDSPORT (pop. 5,030), at the **junction** with Oregon Highway 38; all services available, major-chain motel, fast food, RV parks. Headquarters for Oregon Dunes National Recreation Area is located at the northern end of town (see MAJOR ATTRACTIONS section). At the confluence of the Smith and Umpqua rivers, this area was first mentioned in 1578 in the account of Sir Francis Drake's exploration in the North Pacific seeking the mythical Strait of Anian. There are boat ramps onto the Umpqua River and Scholfield Creek, a major tributary. The Dean Creek Elk Viewing Area is home to a herd of 60 to 100 Roosevelt elk. It is located on Road 38, upriver from the Umpqua River bridge. The Umpqua is the second largest river on the Oregon Pacific coast, behind the Columbia, and is a major sportfishing attraction (coho, chinook, perch, searun cutthroat, steelhead, sturgeon, striped bass, shad). Some type of fishing is available all year, but run peaks vary seasonally. Many sporting goods stores, guides and charter facilities provide local seasonal fishing information. ✦

Mile 140.5 (572): Jedediah Smith Historical Marker, commemorating the massacre of his companions and his narrow escape.

Mile 141 (571.5): Smith River bridge.

Mile 142 (570.5): GARDINER, founded in 1841 by the shipwrecked crew of a Boston fur-trading company, is located at the mouth of the Smith River, next to a large paper mill. There is a public boat ramp. Clamming is excellent.

Mile 143 (569.5): Threemile Road 247 corridor to beach. This is recommended for 4-wheel-drive units only.

Mile 147 (565.5): Elbow Lake, fishing for yellow perch and largemouth bass; stocked with rainbow trout. ✦

Mile 147.5 (565): Tahkenitch Lake offers camping, swimming, boating and year-round fishing. The brushy shoreline requires a boat. There are boat launches at Tahkenitch Campground and Tahkenitch Landing Campground (limited RV access). Hiking

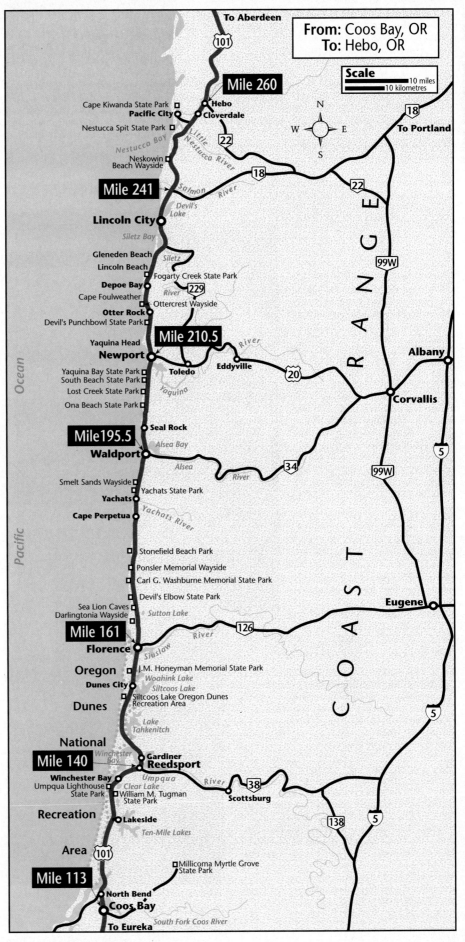

From: Coos Bay, OR
To: Hebo, OR

and dune access (dunes are closed to vehicles in this area year-round). The resort offers rental boats and a boat ramp. This is a very popular summer recreation area.
☵☖➳▲ MP 203

Mile 150.5 (562): Oregon Dunes overlook with access to the ocean beach and dunes trail system. Drinking water, restrooms and dunes information are available. ☖ MP 201

Mile 152 (560.5): East Carter Lake boat launch.

Mile 152.5 (560): Carter Lake Campground has fishing, hiking trail designed for those with disabilities, and drinking water. Lake is stocked with rainbow trout. ♿☖➳▲ MP 199

Mile 153 (559.5): Siltcoos Lake Oregon Dunes National Recreation Area (see MAJOR ATTRACTIONS section). Siltcoos Dune and Beach Access Road to Driftwood II, Lagoon, Lodgepole and Waxmyrtle campgrounds; drinking water, hiking trails, beach access. Small freshwater lagoons and ponds provide fishing. Siltcoos Lake adjoins U.S. Highway 101 on the east. This lake is rated as one of the most productive fishing lakes in Oregon, with stocked rainbow trout, bass, perch, coho, steelhead and bluegill. There are resorts on the lake near U.S. Highway 101 with groceries, boat launches, rental boats, bait, tackle and fishing information. ☖➳▲

Mile 154.5 (558): DUNES CITY (pop. 1,090). Tyee Campground. RV Park. Oregon Dunes National Recreation Area. ▲ MP 197

Mile 155.5 (557): Woahink Lake. There are 2 boat ramps, RV parks and state park campground. Seaplane rides available. Fishing, waterskiing and other water sports are popular here. Myrtlewood factory. ➳▲

Mile 156.5 (556): Sand Dunes Frontier, a private exhibit offering the only commercial sightseeing trips into the Oregon Dunes National Recreation Area on giant custom-built dune buggies. They also have ATV rentals for dune riding, trout pond, miniature golf and a gift shop. MP 195

Mile 158 (554.5): Honeyman State Park has camping with 66 full hookups, 75 electrical only, 241 tent sites, a dump station, firewood, picnic facilities, groceries, restaurant, hiking trail, swimming, fishing, boat rentals, boating and swimming at Cleawox Lake, and easy dune access. Access to Woahink Lake to the west. ☖⊼➳▲

Mile 159.5 (553): GLENADA; restaurant, gas (diesel), motel, food. South Jetty Dune and Beach Access Road west to jetty at the mouth of the Siuslaw River; also Siuslaw Vista, Goose Pasture and South Jetty ORV areas. Rentals available. A crabbing and fishing dock is located at the end of the road.

Mile 160 (552.5): Northern boundary of Oregon Dunes National Recreation Area.

Mile 160.5 (552): Crossing the Siuslaw River bridge. This is a major sportfishing area. There are no charter boat operations, however rental boats are available at marinas and a few fishing guides work the river. Boat launches are located on the north side of the bridge and at several upriver points off Oregon Highway 126, which leads to Mapleton and Eugene. Gas, food, lodging available. 🐟

Mile 161 (551.5): FLORENCE (pop. 5,705) is a recreational resort town, midway on the

Top—Old pilings at Florence, OR, at the mouth of the Siuslaw River. *(George Wuerthner)* **Above**—Scenic sand dunes photographed in Oregon Dunes National Recreation Area. *(Lee Foster)*

Oregon coast, and is at the northern boundary of the Oregon Dunes National Recreation Area (see MAJOR ATTRACTIONS section). All traveler services available, including diesel, hospital, airstrip and public boat landing. It has an Old Town shopping area, Coast Guard station, the pioneer museum and a rhododendron festival in May. Phone the chamber of commerce at (503) 997-3128 for more information. MP 188

Mile 162.5 (550): Harbor Vista County Park with 26 campsites, flush toilets, beach access and playground. ▲

Mile 164 (548.5): Heceta (Ha-SEE-ta) Beach road access area. There is a scenic loop, motels, RV park and resorts. ▲

Mile 165.5 (547): Indian Forest, private exhibit walk-through of an Indian village replica, live buffalo and deer and a trading post.

Mile 166 (546.5): Sutton Lake is stocked with rainbow trout. Sutton Creek USFS Campground has 79 sites, swimming, nature trails and a boat launch. A quarter mile north is the Darlingtonia Botanical Wayside and its rare, cobra-like insect-eating plants. ☖➳▲

Mile 167.5 (545): Alder Dune Campground at Alder Lake; camping, fishing, picnicking and hiking. Private campground. ☖⊼➳▲

Mile 169 (543.5): Access to Oregon Coast Horse Trail System. Trail rides available.

Mile 170 (542.5): Steep, winding ascent northbound, with cliffside turnouts and sweeping views.

Mile 172 (540.5): Sea Lion Caves, private exhibit featuring one of the world's largest sea caves and the only mainland home of the Steller sea lion. Hundreds of sea lions can be seen inside a massive sea cave (accessible by elevator to a viewing area) and lounging on rocks near cormorant nesting areas. The Sea Lion Caves are a must stop for travelers on U.S. Highway 101. Viewpoint of picturesque Heceta Head Lighthouse to north. ★ MP 179

Mile 173 (539.5): Devil's Elbow State Park is a day-use area only, with beach access. Heceta Head picnic area, the lighthouse and marine gardens are attractions. Highway takes a sharp curve just to the north. ⊼

Mile 174 (538.5): Southern boundary of Carl G. Washburne Memorial State Park, which offers 58 full RV hookups, 8 tent sites, a picnic area, fishing, hiking trails and beach access. ☖⊼➳▲

Mile 176 (536.5): Ponsler Memorial Wayside day-use area. Water is available. Narrow access road.

Mile 177 (535.5): USFS Rock Creek Campground with 16 sites and flush toilets. ▲

Mile 177.5 (535): Ocean Beach picnic area. Difficult RV turnaround. ⊼ MP 174

Mile 178.5 (534): Day-use-only beach access. Lodging.

Mile 180 (532.5): Stonefield Beach Park, day

use only. Ten-mile Creek. RV park and motels. ▲

Mile 181 (531.5): Bob Creek Wayside. No facilities.

Mile 182 (530.5): Strawberry Hill viewpoint.

Mile 182.5 (530): Neptune State Park with day-use area, picnicking and restrooms. ⚲

Mile 184 (528.5): Cape Perpetua Visitors Center has a movie relating the history of the Oregon coast, and offers a self-guided auto tour and hiking trails to the beach and forest. Cape Perpetua Campground has 38 sites and flush toilets. Excellent viewpoint from this 800-foot tower named by English explorer James Cook on March 7, 1778. Cape Perpetua is the highest point on the Oregon coast. ⚲▲

Mile 184.5 (528): Devil's Churn viewpoint, a trough carved into rock where the tides churn; picnicking, hiking trails (including Trail of the Restless Water) and tidepools. ⚲⚲

Mile 187 (525.5): YACHATS (pop. 635), a resort town at the mouth of the Yachats (Ya-HOTS) River, is famous for the July-to-Sept. run of smelt that triggers the annual July Smelt Fry Festival. Smelt are caught at night with seines, nets and mesh-framed rakes between Yachats and Beachside State Park about 4 miles north. The area also offers agate-hunting beaches, surf fishing, swimming, clam digging and beach walking. Motels and gas station. Little Log Church by the Sea Museum.

The Yachats Ocean Wayside offers access to the beach on the southern edge of town, and another wayside overlooks the river mouth from the north. ⚲

Mile 187.5 (525): Smelt Sands Wayside (day use only). Smelt dipping is popular during late summer.

Mile 191 (521.5): USFS Tillicum Beach Campground with 57 tent/RV sites, fee. Fishing. ⚲▲

Mile 192 (520.5): Beachside Campground with 60 tent and 20 RV sites. Fishing. ⚲▲

Mile 194 (518.5): Governor I.L. Patterson State Park, day-use area with beach access, picnicking and restrooms. ⚲

Mile 195.5 (517): Junction with Oregon Highway 34 to Corvallis and Interstate 5. Alsea Recreational Area. WALDPORT (pop. 1,610), a resort town at the mouth of the Alsea River, has all services, including RV parks, and a ranger station. Waldport was settled in the late 1870s by Germans (wald meaning "forest" in German). David Ruble was the first to establish a permanent community, laying out streets and establishing a townsite. The townsite is an old Indian burial ground, and Chief Yaquina John of the Alsea tribe is buried just south of town. Although commercial fishing has had an impact on the community, its mainstay is still logging. Two of the town's biggest celebrations are Beachcomber Days held each June, and an annual salmon derby held the first part of October during the fall salmon run on the Alsea River. Dungeness crab are found in the bay. ⚲▲

Mile 196 (516.5): Alsea Bay bridge.

Seagulls rest on the rocks at Seal Rock state wayside, Mile 200. (© John Barger)

Mile 198 (514.5): Driftwood State Park, with beach access, picnicking and restrooms. ⚲

Mile 200 (512.5): SEAL ROCK; state wayside offers beach access, surf fishing and picnic tables. Groceries available. ⚲⚲ MP 151

Mile 201 (511.5): Sea Gulch, a private exhibit built around an Old West town populated with humorous, life-sized chain-saw sculptures and carvings.

Mile 202.5 (510): Ona Beach State Park, with beach access, picnicking, restrooms. ⚲ MP 149

Mile 204 (508.5): Lost Creek State Park with beach access, picnicking, restrooms. RV park. ⚲▲

Mile 208 (504.5): South Beach State Park Campground, 257 sites all with electrical hookups, showers, picnic areas, beach access, hiking trails and fishing. ⚲⚲⚲▲

Mile 209 (503.5): Oregon State University's Mark O. Hatfield Marine Science Center features aquariums, marine pool displays and an estuary trail. The center attracts some 250,000 visitors each year. Seasonal hours,

donation suggested; phone (503) 867-0226. The nearby Oregon Coast Aquarium features animals native to the Oregon coast, including sea lions, otters and giant Pacific octopus. Outdoor tide pools allow a close-up look at marine life. Open year-round, admission fee; phone (503) 867-3474. ♿

Mile 209.5 (503): Yaquina Bay bridge.

Mile 210.5 (502): NEWPORT (pop. 8,685) offers all services including excellent hotels, motels and restaurants. Newport is the largest port on the central Oregon coast and is famous for shrimp, crab and sport fisheries, all celebrated during the annual wine and seafood festival. More bottom fish are caught from Newport boats than from any other Oregon port. There is excellent jetty and boat fishing in Yaquina Bay. Numerous fishing charter boats are available. Oyster farms, scuba diving, surfing and agate beds are located here.

Other attractions include the Yaquina (Ya-kwin-a) Bay Coast Guard Station, Undersea Gardens, The Wax Works, Ripley's Believe It or Not and the Lincoln County Historical Society Museum. Yaquina Bay State Park offers picnicking, fishing, beach access and a lighthouse museum. Phone the chamber of commerce at (503) 265-8801, or fax (503) 265-5589, for more information. U.S. Highway 101 **junctions** with U.S. Highway 20 to Corvallis and Interstate 5 (see U.S. HIGHWAY 20 section). MP 140

Mile 212 (500.5): Agate Beach Wayside.

Mile 213.5 (499): Yaquina Head Outstanding Natural Area; fishing, picnicking. RV park.

Mile 215.5 (497): Moolack Beach area.

Mile 217 (495.5): Beverly Beach State Park, one of the more popular oceanside parks; offers camping with 52 RV hookups, 75 electrical, 152 tent sites and showers. There also are trails, a playground, picnicking, fishing and beach access by way of an underpass. Grocery store.

Mile 218 (494.5): Otter Rock, Otter Crest day-use and resort area, with beach tidal pools. Devil's Punch Bowl State Park has picnicking and restrooms and features a remnant of a collapsed sea cave that creates the Devil's PunchBowl.

Mile 218.5 (494): Alternate route to Otter Rock.

Mile 219.5 (493): Cape Foulweather overlook. Otter Crest Viewpoint, perched 500 feet above the sea, offers an excellent view of Otter Crest and the beach area. Winds here sometimes reach 100 mph. The small gift shop here is registered as a county historical site. Sea lions, cormorants, murres and other seabirds abound. Migrating whales are often spotted during fall and spring. Cape Foulweather was named by Capt. James Cook in 1778.

Mile 221.5 (491): Northern end of Otter Crest Loop Road. Also Rocky Creek State Park, with beach access, picnicking and restrooms.

Mile 222 (490.5): Whale Cove. Whales have been seen inside this small bay. Lodging available.

Mile 223.5 (489): DEPOE BAY (pop. 865); cafe, major-chain fast food, lodging and RV park. Depoe Bay has the world's smallest boat harbor, a 6-acre lagoon accessible by a narrow (less than 50 feet wide) natural opening through a rock wall. Depoe Bay has all services and offers charter boat fishing for salmon and bottom fish, whale-watching, a small aquarium, oceanfront resorts, saltwater-taffy making and a mid-September Indian salmon bake. Depoe Bay is the site where actor Jack Nicholson was filmed stealing a charter boat in the movie *One Flew Over the Cuckoo's Nest.*

Mile 225 (487.5): Boiler Bay Wayside, named for a steam boiler that exploded and sank the boat *J. Marhoffer* here in 1910. It is sometimes visible at low tide. Picnicking and restrooms available.

Pillar Rock and distant Pyramid Rock from Cape Meares State Park. (© John Barger)

Mile 226 (486.5): Fogarty Creek State Park (day use only) offers picnic sites. Food, RV park and lodging available. MP 125

Mile 226.5 (486): Lincoln Beach offers surf fishing and swimming. RV park.

Mile 229 (483.5): Gleneden Beach area has picnic sites, fishing, swimming, an airstrip (scenic flights available) and a golf course.

Mile 229.5 (483): Salishan Lodge Resort is well-known for its beautifully landscaped grounds and luxury accommodations. The resort has 205 rooms, dining room, 18-hole golf course, tennis courts both inside and out, indoor pool, exercise room, beach access, conference rooms and a nearby airport. Gas, shopping center.

Mile 230 (482.5): Junction with Immonen Road. Drive east 0.5 mile to Mossey Creek Pottery Co. and Art Gallery. Alder House glassblowing, one of the oldest glassblowing operations in the Northwest, is located here

and visitors are welcome.
 MP 121

Mile 231 (481.5): Siletz River and **junction** with Oregon Highway 229 southeast to Kernville. Fishing for surfperch; boat launch at bridge. RV park.

Mile 235.5 (477): East Devil's Lake Road encircles Devil's Lake, a narrow, 5-mile-long weedy lake where many world boating-speed records have been set. There is a state park campground (West Devil's Lake) with 32 full hookups and 68 tent sites, and a boat ramp at the south end of the lake. Sand Point County Park is a day-use area. The Roads End Wayside offers picnicking and restrooms. MP 112

Mile 236.5 (476): LINCOLN CITY (pop. 6,280). All traveler services available. Southernmost city in Oregon's famous 20 Miracle Miles area of art galleries and craft shops. Factory outlet stores are also abundant. Known as the Kite Capital of the World, this is a major recreational area with 7¹/₂ miles of beaches, clamming, mussel harvesting, crabbing, fishing, whale watching and resorts. A resident population of sea lions is visible on sandbars at the mouth of the Siletz River. Other attractions include kite flying, the North Lincoln County Historical Museum and a wayside at the "world's shortest river," the D River (approximately 120 feet long), which is actually the mouth of Devil's Lake. Contact the Lincoln City Visitor and Convention Bureau for more information; phone (503) 994-8378, fax (503) 994-2408.

Mile 241 (471.5): Junction with Oregon Highway 18 to Portland and Interstate 5, and crossing the Salmon River bridge. Although small, the Salmon River is an excellent fall and winter salmon and steelhead producer. The fish are unusually large and bank access is plentiful from roads along both banks.

Sunset at Cape Kiwanda State Park silhouettes familiar Haystack Rock. (© John Barger)

Mile 242.5 (470): Steep 2-mile grade begins northbound.

Mile 244 (468.5): Siuslaw National Forest boundary.

Mile 247 (465.5): Siuslaw National Forest boundary.

Mile 247.5 (465): Junction with Slab Creek Road scenic drive.

Mile 248.5 (464): Neskowin Beach Wayside day-use area has fishing, beach access and resorts. RV park, campground, groceries and golf.   ⊶▲ MP 99

Mile 251.5 (461): Viewpoint with wheelchair access.   ♿

Mile 253.5 (459): Little Nestucca River. October chinook and coho fishing, and Dec. to Feb. steelheading is good. Boat launch. ⊶

Mile 255 (457.5): Junction with Brooten Road (Three Capes Scenic Loop), a 39-mile scenic drive to Tillamook that provides access to the resort and fishing community of **PACIFIC CITY**, Cape Kiwanda State Park, the community of **OCEANSIDE**, Cape Lookout and Cape Meares.

Pacific City's famous fleet of fishing dories launches from the hard-packed sand beach at Cape Kiwanda, inside Haystack Rock, just north of Pacific City. Spectacular views, sandstone cliffs and beautiful beach make Cape Kiwanda a popular day-use area for beachcombing. Hang gliders launch from the cape headland.

The road continues north along the coast to Cape Lookout State Park (2.5-mile hike to cape) and then through Oceanside (motel, restaurant) to Cape Meares State Park on the southern point of Tillamook Bay. Several public beaches, dune-buggy-riding areas and nature trails are available.

Camping facilities are available at Sandbeach (101 sites), Cape Lookout State Park (250 sites, full hookups, showers), Happy Camp Resort, Bay Shore and Island County Park.

Three Arches Rock, a National Wildlife Refuge, is located off Oceanside. Thousands of birds nest on the rocks offshore, and sea lions and seals can be seen playing in the surf much of the year.

Cape Meares has a historic lighthouse that is open to the public, picnicking and a 2-mile segment of the Oregon Coast Trail. A photo museum featuring Oregon lighthouses and their histories, and the Octopus Tree—an oddly-shaped giant Sitka spruce measuring 50 feet around, are attractions here.   🚻ᴛ⊶▲★

Mile 257.5 (455): **CLOVERDALE**, a small farming community. Food, gas.

Mile 260 (452.5): Community of **HEBO**. **Junction** with Oregon Highway 22 to Salem and crossing the Nestucca River bridge. This is a large river (heavily stocked with cutthroat).

There is good fishing from boat or bank and several boat launches. Food and laundry facilities are available. Local sporting goods stores offer guide services and shuttles for drift boats.   ⊶ MP 85

Mile 262.5 (450): Wayside by Nestucca River.

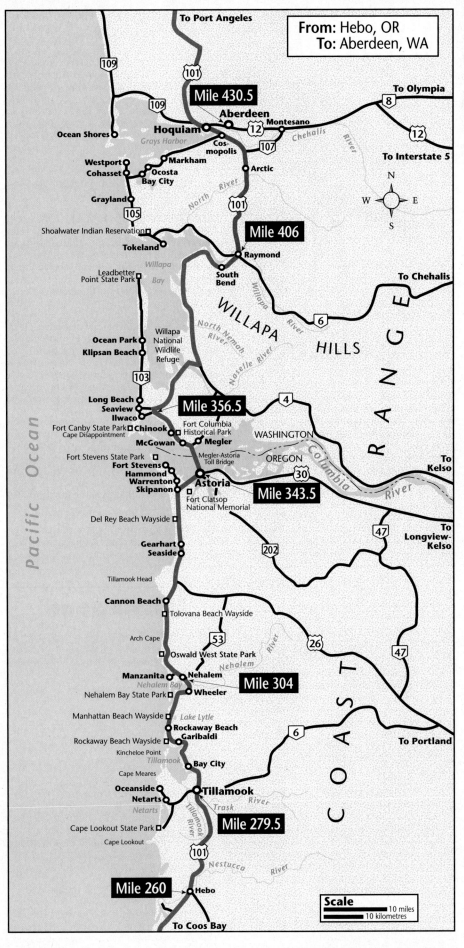

From: Hebo, OR
To: Aberdeen, WA

Mile 265 (447.5): Town of **BEAVER**; grocery, deli and gas stations (diesel). Access to Upper Nestucca River Recreation Area.

Mile 268 (444.5): Community of **HEMLOCK**. Artichoke farm, RV park, private campground. ▲

Mile 268.5 (444): Access to Cape Kiwanda State Park with sand dunes, fishing, marina, hiking, scenic viewpoints, tide pools and wave-sculptured sandstone cliffs. ⋈⋘

Mile 272 (440.5): Community of **PLEASANT VALLEY.** Turnoff to Munson Creek Falls County Park, about 9 miles east. *NOTE:* Road sign for park is at turnoff, no advance warning. MP 73

Mile 273.5 (439): Turnoff to Trask River, which has good seasonal fishing. It is stocked heavily in spring with hatchery trout. ⋘

Mile 274.5 (438): Oregon highway rest area west of highway. ⅙

Mile 279.5 (433): TILLAMOOK (pop. 4,000), famous for its cheese. All traveler services available. Free self-guided tours of the largest cheese factory in the West are available at Tillamook Cheese Factory (open daily, 8 a.m. to 8 p.m. in summer, wheelchair accessible) on the northern edge of city along U.S. Highway 101; phone (503) 842-4481. The Blimp Hangar Museum, located in the world's largest wooden clear-span building, features historic photographs and memorabilia depicting the history of lighter-than-air craft. Open 10 a.m. to 6 p.m. daily in summer; admission fee. Phone (503) 842-2413. **Junction** with Oregon Highway 6 to Portland and Interstate 5. Northern access to Three Capes Scenic Loop. Tillamook Bay, the largest bay on the Oregon coast, is fed by 9 major rivers and offers fishing, clamming and crabbing. Local sporting goods stores provide current information. ⋘

Mile 282 (430.5): Kilchis River Junction and public golf course.

Mile 285 (427.5): BAY CITY (pop. 1,005), offering full services. Gas, RV park. ▲ MP 60

Mile 286.5 (426): Viewpoint.

Mile 287 (425.5): Historical marker on Capt. Robert Gray. MP 58

Mile 289 (423.5): GARIBALDI (pop. 1,060) has all tourist services (chamber of commerce, phone 503/322-0311). It is a major fishing port, offering charters for salmon and bottom fish. A county park is located north of the bayfront. Jetty fishing, Fisherman's Wharf, launch ramps, boat rentals, fresh seafood stands, tours of fish- and shrimp-processing plants, and oyster shucking are attractions. Blue herons may be spotted standing in tide flats. ⋘

Mile 290 (422.5): Viewpoint of bay with picnic facilities. ⋔ MP 55

Mile 291.5 (421): Barview Jetty County Park and viewpoint of the often stormy entrance to Tillamook Bay. Camping with RV hookups, beach access and shellfish harvesting are available. Groceries. ▲

Mile 294 (418.5): ROCKAWAY BEACH (pop. 1,000) with beach access, surfperch fishing and adjacent Twin Rocks resort area. Gas, lodging, RV park. ⋘▲ MP 51

Mile 295 (417.5): Lake Lytle offers boating, fishing, a public dock, waterskiing and windsurfing. It is connected to Crescent Lake, a trout and bass lake surrounded by sand dunes. ⋘

Mile 296.5 (416): Manhattan Beach Wayside with beach access and restrooms.

Mile 297.5 (415): Marinas, RV parks and boat rentals next 2 miles northbound. ▲

Mile 302 (410.5): WHEELER (pop. 350) has a public dock, marina, RV park, motel,

Myrtlewood

Southwestern Oregon and Northern California are the heart of myrtlewood country. Every city, town and hamlet has gift shops filled with myrtlewood salt and pepper shakers, chip and dip bowls, clocks, boxes and cutting boards. Along U.S. 101, myrtlewood factories stand in isolation, manufacturing an assortment of bowls, plaques, goblets, napkin holders and other souvenirs.

While pioneers used myrtlewood for furniture and oxen yokes, the souvenir industry dates only to the 1930s. During the Depression, woodworkers who had lost their jobs survived by making figurines, jewelry boxes and bowls.

Colors of the hard, fine-grained wood vary with each tree. Shades of white, yellow, brown and black are often mottled. Each piece is different and cannot be duplicated. The widely held belief that myrtlewood grows only near the Oregon–California border adds to its appeal as a memento unique to the area.

The Oregon myrtlewood tree is actually a California laurel. It grows between Coos County, OR, and Baja, CA, and from the Pacific Coast to the Sierra Nevada Mountains.

It takes about 100 years for a tree to grow 100 feet tall and 14 to 16 inches in diameter. Each souvenir requires 15 to 17 steps and an average of 3 months processing time from start to finish. Approximately 6 weeks are spent in drying the wood, which has a 40 percent water content. The process cannot be hurried, for myrtlewood that is not dried properly will crack and warp. Without rooms of 85°–100°F circulating heat and without dehumidifiers, the drying would take from 1 to 3 years. Because of the processing time, products are fairly expensive. A plain 10-inch bowl retails for around $50. Button-sized earrings cost $5 to $10.

Souvenirs in the typical myrtlewood gift shop are the products of many craftsmen. Most are specialists who operate out of their homes or backyard shops. The products they make are dictated by the machinery required to manufacture them.

Most jewelry is made in San Francisco by a company with equipment to manufacture small beads and marble-sized balls. A factory in Grants Pass, OR, mass produces flying seagulls, and another near Roseburg specializes in bear figurines. Bowls, goblets and round trays come from lathe-equipped shops.

Myrtlewood's unique properties are limiting. Because of the wood's tendency to buckle, a huge demand for myrtlewood mantles remains unfilled. Several yo-yo makers have tried in vain to balance the wood and fill another void. Its hardness makes ornamentation difficult, time consuming and costly. Very few souvenirs are intricately detailed.

Meanwhile, the myrtlewood industry is doing just fine, thanks to the growing numbers of travelers who are more than happy with the handsome wood and the simple design. For them, it is enough to have an attractive souvenir that is clearly identified with an area they visited.

restaurant, grocery and laundry. ▲ MP 49

Mile 303 (409.5): Junction with Oregon Highway 53 North to U.S. Highway 26 to Portland (84 miles).

Mile 304 (408.5): The town of **NEHALEM** (pop. 240) has shops and galleries. Tours of Nehalem Bay Winery and the Old Fishing Village available. Public dock and restrooms. Nehalem River bridge and bay. This area offers fall coho and chinook salmon runs, winter steelhead, cutthroat, perch, rockfish, numerous boat launches, clamming, crabbing areas, resorts and fishing guides. ← MP 45

Mile 305.5 (407): Nehalem Bay State Park has 291 campsites with electrical hookups, 17 sites with horse corrals, showers, ocean beach access, clamming, crabbing, surf fishing, boat ramp and picnic areas. Gas (diesel) and private camping available. ⊼← ▲

Mile 313.5 (399): Northern boundary of Oswald West Park. Community of **ARCH CAPE** with lodging, grocery and deli.

Mile 315 (397.5): Cannon Beach Historical Marker, and cannon that washed ashore here from a Columbia River bar shipwreck in 1846.

Mile 315.5 (397): Hug Point State Park (day use only) has picnic sites, fishing and beach access. ⊼← MP 33

Mile 317 (395.5): Arcadia State Park (day use only) has picnic sites and fishing. ⊼←

Mile 318 (394.5): Tolovana Loop Road to Tolovana Wayside with beach access, picnicking and restrooms. South access to **CANNON BEACH** (pop. 1,284), all traveler services. Cannon Beach was named for a cannon that washed ashore in 1846 from the wreck of the schooner *Spark*. The area has 7

Mile 324.5 (388): RV park, lodging, restaurants. ▲

Mile 328 (384.5): **SEASIDE** (pop. 5,400) has all traveler services including major-chain motels and fast food. Seaside is the home of the Lewis and Clark Trail turnaround. Lewis and Clark stopped here to make salt from seawater, and it is now a historical site open to visitors. Seaside offers a 2-mile concrete promenade with swimming, beach resorts and the Seaside Aquarium (503/738-6211), one of the few places where visitors can feed seals. This is a very popular spot, especially for youngsters. An annual jazz festival draws crowds in February. Seaside is the largest beach resort city in the Pacific Northwest.
MP 20

Mile 330.5 (382): **GEARHART** (pop. 1,090) is a resort town with clamming and swimming beaches, major-chain fast-food outlets, motels, golf course and RV park. ▲

Mile 332 (380.5): Del Rey Beach Wayside (day-use beach area). No facilities are available.

Mile 335.5 (377): Access to Cullaby Lake and Carnahan County parks to east.

Mile 337.5 (375): Junction with side road to **HAMMOND** and Warrenton, and Fort Stevens State Park (5 miles northwest), which is the largest state park and one of the most popular recreational areas in Oregon. Fort Stevens has 261 tent sites, 130 electric hookups, 213 full hookups (RVs up to 69 feet). Also available are beaches, freshwater and saltwater fishing (sea perch, ling cod and salmon) and access to Columbia River beaches. The park was built on the site of historic Fort Stevens, constructed in 1864 to guard the entrance to the Columbia River. Gun emplacements and underground tunnels still exist. The fort was fired upon by a Japanese submarine in 1942. Wreck of the schooner *Peter Iredale* is visible on the beach. ←▲

Mile 339.5 (373): Fort Clatsop. A reconstructed fort in which Lewis and Clark spent the winter of 1805–06. The area is administered by the National Park Service, and includes a visitor center, the fort, trails and examples of the equipment used by the party.

Mile 340.5 (372): North access to **WARRENTON** (pop. 2,535), most services including private campground and motel-restaurant. ▲

Mile 343.5 (369): **ASTORIA** (pop. 10,100) has all major tourist services including motels, bed-and-breakfast facilities and restaurants. Astoria is the first permanent American settlement on the Pacific Coast, established in 1811 as a fur-trading post. The city's Victorian architecture reflects this heritage. The 4.1-mile-long Megler-Astoria Bridge across the Columbia River is the longest continuous truss bridge in the world (1,232 feet long). The Astoria Column, built in 1926, is 125 feet high and has 166 steps to the top. Astoria is port-of-call for several cruise ships on the Columbia River.

Junction with U.S. Highway 30 east to

Remains of the Peter Iredale, *wrecked in 1906, are visible at low tide at Fort Stevens State Park at Mile 337.5.* (L. Linkhart)

Mile 306 (406.5): MANZANITA (pop. 555) is a resort area with motels, restaurants, gift shops, lots of coffee shops, and golf. Of note are the 7 miles of open sandy beach; Neahkahnie Mountain, a 1,700-foot mountain viewpoint; and a wrecked Spanish galleon believed to be the source of beeswax occasionally found on the beach. There are legends of buried Spanish treasure here.
MP 43

Mile 306.5 (406): Neahkahnie Beach. Begin steep grade northbound.

Mile 308 (404.5): Southern boundary of Oswald West State Park, which offers fishing, picnic area, beach access, clamming. There are 35 primitive hike-in (a quarter mile) campsites at Short Sand Beach. ⋔⊼←▲

Mile 310 (402.5): Parking area for Oswald West day-use and camping areas. ▲

miles of sandy beach, a resort area, music and art programs, galleries, kite flying, fishing and clamming. The beaches are magically transformed during the annual sandcastle-building contest held in June. (Phone the information center at 503/436-2623 for more information.) Haystack Rock Wildlife Refuge offshore is 235 feet high and is one of the most photographed monoliths in the world. Look for tufted puffins April to Aug. ⊼←

Mile 320 (392.5): North access to Cannon Beach and Ecola State Park. Picnicking, fishing, Tillamook Head hiking trail. ⋔⊼←

Mile 321.5 (391): Historical marker. Ecola is the site where William Clark of the Lewis and Clark expedition bought whale meat from the Indians. MP 28

Mile 324 (388.5): Junction with U.S. Highway 26 to Portland.

Longview, WA, and Portland, OR.

Mile 347 (365.5): Crossing the Megler-Astoria Bridge over the Columbia River.

Mile 347.5 (365): Washington–Oregon state border. North end of bridge, **junction** with Washington Highway 401 to Longview via Washington Highway 4. Rest area to west.

Mile 348 (364.5): Historical marker commemorating the discovery of the Columbia River by Capt. Robert Gray in 1792. RV park. ▲ MP 1

Mile 349.5 (363): Lewis and Clark historical campsite.

Mile 350 (362.5): Fort Columbia Historical State Park and viewpoint. Picnic area and interpretive center. Gun battery emplacements are visible. ⊼ MP 3

Mile 352 (360.5): Community of **CHINOOK.** Most tourist facilities are available here, including a county park with 50 tent sites and 50 RV sites, beach access, picnicking, playground and restrooms, and a Port of Chinook boat launch. ⊼▲

Mile 354 (358.5): Chinook River. MP 7

Mile 356.5 (356): Junction with bypass to U.S. Highway 101 and Raymond. Continue west 1.5 miles to **ILWACO** (pop. 800), a fishing town for commercial and charter boat fleets working the Columbia and offshore waters. Ilwaco has lodging, gas (diesel), a hospital, RV park and heritage museum. Three miles southwest of U.S. Highway 101, Fort Canby State Park offers 250 campsites, beach access, fishing, boat launch and the Lewis and Clark Interpretive Center. Also access to North Head Lighthouse (built in 1898); Cape Disappointment Lighthouse (built in 1856), the oldest lighthouse in the Pacific Northwest; and Cape Disappointment Coast Guard Station, home to one of Washington's largest search and rescue operations. Cape Disappointment's treacherous sand bar earned it the sobriquet "Graveyard of the Pacific." Washington Highway 103 leads north up the Long Beach Peninsula to Leadbetter Point. **LONG BEACH** (pop. 1,200), at the southern end of the peninsula, is a popular vacation area offering lodging, restaurants and a kite museum. Long Beach hosts the International Kite Festival in August and the World's Longest Beach Run and Walk in June. The Long Beach Peninsula is known for its 28 miles of hard sandy beaches, oyster farms and migratory birds. Willapa Bay National Wildlife Refuge encompasses more than 11,000 acres of the bay and tidelands. ⊼ ➤ ▲

Mile 359 (353.5): Picnic area at WWII and Coast Guard memorial markers. ⊼ MP 12

Mile 360 (352.5): SEAVIEW, with services, motels and beach access. Gateway to Long Beach.

Mile 363 (349.5): Willapa Bay with famous oyster-farming areas, tours available. Created by the Long Beach Peninsula, Willapa Bay is home to more than 180 species of migratory birds. Good crabbing and perch fishing. **Junction** with alternate Highway 101. Beginning of 13 miles of curvy roadway. ➤

Mile 371 (341.5): Willapa National Wildlife Refuge with canoe/kayak put-in.

Mile 373.5 (339): Bridge across Naselle River.

Mile 376 (336.5): Junction with Washington Highway 4 to Longview-Kelso and Interstate 5.

Mile 382.5 (330): North Nemah Road, turn east to see the state salmon hatchery. Cafe.

Mile 389.5 (323): Bush Pioneer County Park offers camping and picnicking on Willapa Bay. Palix River has spring and fall fishing. Food, private camping available. ⊼ ➤ ▲

Mile 391 (321.5): Niawiakum River.

Mile 393 (319.5): Historical marker on Bruce Port. The deserted site is 1 mile north at Willapa Bay and was once the county seat. The crew of the oyster schooner *Robert Bruce* settled here in December 1851 after their ship burned. They built cabins and named the settlement Bruceville. This site recalls the oyster industry of 1851–80 when enormous quantities of oysters were gathered and shipped to San Francisco.

Mile 395.5 (317): BrucePort County Park and public fishing. Hiking, camping. RV park. ⚌ ➤ ▲

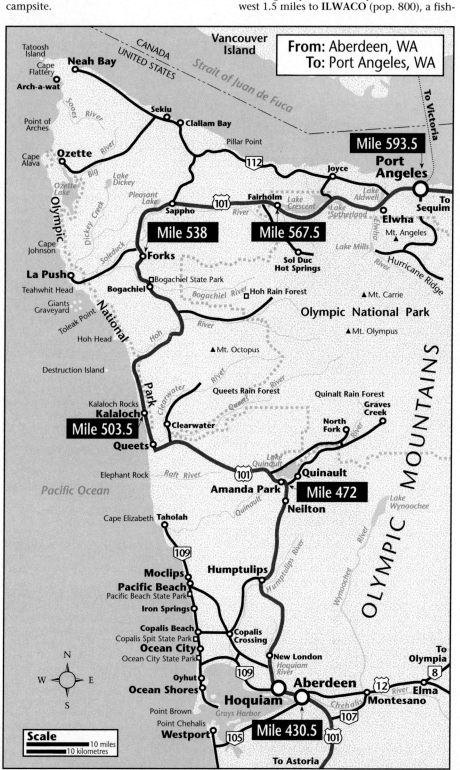

From: Aberdeen, WA
To: Port Angeles, WA

Mile 400.5 (312): SOUTH BEND (pop. 1,600), the "Oyster Capital of the World," has most traveler services, including diesel. Oyster processing plants and excellent steelhead fishing on the Willapa River. Pacific County Historic Courthouse and Museum. Public park with picnicking and restrooms. ⊼⛵

Mile 404 (308.5): Port of Willapa Harbor.
MP 57

Mile 405.5 (307): Golf course and south fork of Willapa River. **Junction** with Washington Highway 6 east to Chehalis and Interstate 5.
MP 58

Mile 406 (306.5): RAYMOND (pop. 2,870) is a logging community with mill operations. All services available, including major-chain fast food.

Mile 406.5 (306): Junction with Washington Highway 105 west to **NORTH COVE, TOKELAND, GRAYLAND** and **WESTPORT** (pop. 1,900). The highway follows the north shore of Willapa Bay to Cape Shoalwater, then heads north along the coast to Westport before turning inland along Grays Harbor to Aberdeen and back to U.S. Highway 101. Sometimes called "the Cranberry Coast" for the acres of cranberry bogs near Grayland, the area offers coastal camping, razor clam beaches, fishing and miles of beaches. The North Cove–Tokeland area has a hotel, RV park, marina and local stores. Westport offers several motels, restaurants and other services. Westport is noted for its beach and charter boat fishing and whale watching. It is approximately 33 miles from this junction to Westport, and about 20 miles from Westport to Aberdeen via Highway 105. ⛵▲

Mile 408 (304.5): Battle Creek picnic area. ⊼

Mile 408.5 (304): Heavily forested area. *CAUTION:* Winding road, 40 mph.

Mile 421.5 (291): North River bridge, community of **ARCTIC**. Excellent sea-run cutthroat fishing, fair steelhead, salmon. This is a popular deer-hunting area. RV park and restaurant. ⛵▲

Mile 423.5 (289): Junction with Washington Highway 107 to Montesano (Montasayno). Start of 2-mile stretch of steep, winding roadway.

Mile 427.5 (285): COSMOPOLIS (pop. 1,545) has all services and a lumbermill. Cooney Mansion is listed as a national historic site. Good sturgeon and salmon fishing in Chehalis River. There is a launch ramp at the Weyerhaeuser mill. ⛵

Mile 430.5 (282): ABERDEEN (pop. 16,600) has all major tourist facilities. Aberdeen received its name from Scottish settlers who gave the name of their home town, Aberdeen, Scotland, to this new area. It is appropriate since Aberdeen is the Gaelic word meaning "the meeting of 2 rivers." Many present residents of Aberdeen are descendants of the original immigrants who came to log the greatest stand of Douglas fir trees in the Pacific Northwest. Today the town relies on lumbering, fishing and related industries. Grays Harbor is the only deep-water port on the Pacific coast north of San Francisco. The area's maritime heritage is celebrated at the Grays Harbor Historical Seaport, home to *Lady Washington*, a 170-ton replica of the tall ship that discovered the harbor. Tours are available when the ship is in harbor. **Junction** with U.S. Highway 12 east to Olympia and with Washington Highway 105 west to Westport.

Mile 434.5 (278): HOQUIAM (HO-Kwee-um) (pop: 9,000) is the twin city of Aberdeen. The communities share geographical and political ties. All services are available. This deep-water port of Grays Harbor is heavily used in transporting lumber and related products. This is one of the gateways to the spectacular Olympic Peninsula, Olympic National Forest and Olympic National Park. An attraction of particular interest is Hoquiam's Castle, a 20-room mansion built in 1897 by lumber tycoon Robert Lytle.

Junction with Washington Highway 109, a 2-lane highway leading west 20 miles to **OCEAN SHORES** (pop. 2,400), the second most visited destination city in the state with 20 motels and 20 restaurants (phone 1-800-76-BEACH for more information). Ocean City State Park, located 1 mile north of Ocean Shores, has 150 tent sites, 29 RV sites, full hookups, swimming beach and surf fishing. Highway 109 continues north along the coast to **OCEAN CITY, COPALIS BEACH, MOCLIPS** (all with lodging and RV parks) and Cape Elizabeth. Highway 109 ends at the south border of the Quinault Indian Reservation, where restrictions and special travel regulations are required for nontribal travelers. (Contact the Quinault Indian Nation, P.O. Box 189, Taholah, WA 98587; phone 360/276-8211.) Highway 109 offers more direct ocean beach access than any other section of U.S. Highway 101 in Washington, with numerous beachfront resorts.

The coastal shoreline here is dominated by wide, sandy beaches, low brush and small fir trees.

These beaches are very popular for razor clam digging and surfperch fishing during peak seasons. Check locally for razor clam digging regulations. This area also boasts 20 miles of freshwater lakes and canals. ⛵▲★

Mile 435.5 (277): Little Hoquiam River bridge. This is a small tidal stream with brushy roadside access and minimal recreational opportunities. Access to ocean beaches via Washington Highway 109 north.

Mile 438.5 (274): Bernard Creek bridge, cafe. **Junction** with 2-lane road leading west to Copalis Beach and coastal resort areas. Washington Highway 109 at **Mile 434.5** junction provides better access to the same area. MP 92

Mile 441 (271.5): West fork of the Hoquiam River parallels and crosses below the highway. The alder, Douglas fir and Sitka spruce forests are heavily clear-cut in this area, and early morning or evening travelers frequently spot black-tailed deer.

Mile 447 (265.5): First views of Olympic Mountains northbound.

Mile 455.5 (257): The highway crosses the Humptulips River, a major steelhead, searun cutthroat and salmon producing river, at the crossroads community of **HUMPTULIPS**. RV park and cabins, and gas are available at the bridge crossing. Ide[...] Recreation Area, seve[...] available on Hansen [...] bridge and off of Kirkpatr[...] also leads to Copalis Cross[...] beaches and the Copalis Natio[...] Refuge in the Washington Island[...] ness Area. The refuge and wildern[...] extends north along the Quinault In[...] Reservation. This is a very popular wint[...] steelhead fishing area with most of the action concentrated below the highway. Current fishing information may be available at the store in Humptulips. There is also a salmon hatchery nearby. ⛵▲ MP 109

Mile 459 (253.5): Promised Land Park (closed in winter) along the west side of the highway offers restrooms, shelter house, shaded picnic tables and a small pond. Nearby Donkey Creek Road leads to the Humptulips ranger station, and 46 miles to Wynoochee Lake Recreation Area; campground, picnicking, boat launch, hiking trails, camping fee charged. ⚞⊼▲

Mile 464.5 (248): Boundary of Olympic National Forest and turnoff to Quinault Ridge Road and Neilton Point. MP 118

Mile 466.5 (246): Junction with Moclips Road, which leads 20 miles southwest to Moclips and ocean beaches. Four miles west of the junction is the Quinault National Fish Hatchery, visitors welcome.

Mile 469.5 (243): NEILTON, a small community with groceries and post office. This area is the heart of the Olympic Peninsula cedar shake industry, and many small working mills are along the highway. Shakes are split from large bolts of wood, which are often carried out of the mountains by helicopter.

Mile 472 (240.5): Junction with the South Shore Road, which winds around Lake Quinault in the southwest corner of Olympic National Park. (See Olympic National Park in the MAJOR ATTRACTIONS section.) South Shore Road junctions with North Shore Road, which connects with U.S. Highway 101 at **Mile 475.5**. The loop drive around the lake is 27.5 miles, mostly well-maintained gravel. One of the most impressive lakes on the Olympic Peninsula, Lake Quinault is a favorite vacation destination, and one of the world's wettest areas with approximately 160 inches of rainfall annually. The road hugs the south shore, which supports most of the lake's development. Lake Quinault is 4 miles long, 2 miles wide and up to 300 feet deep. Recreational use of the lake is regulated by the Quinault Indian Nation.

There is a national park walk-in campground (no fee) on the North Shore Road at July Creek that has 31 primitive sites. Three USFS campgrounds, Falls Creek (31 sites), Willaby (22 sites), and Gatton Creek (5 sites) are on the South Shore Road. Overnight RV parking at Willaby and Gatton Creek campgrounds (trailer length to 16 feet). All offer picnicking, drinking water, restrooms, hiking trails, self-guided nature tours and boat launches. There are also some very pleasant lakeside picnic areas. Several resorts, restaurants, a post office, mercantiles and gas (diesel) can be found about midlake at **QUINAULT**, where a ranger station is located. Lake Quinault Lodge, built in 1926 and visited by Franklin D. Roosevelt, is adja-

Olympic Rain Forests

tified as the Humptulips
ral boat launches are
road south of the
ick Road, which
ng, the ocean
al Wildlife
s Wilder-
ess area
dian
er

.S. Highway 101

... and ...s sit ... side ...Park. ...of the ...rain

...cover the ...Here, mild temperatures and an annual precipitation of more than 140 inches combine to create giant coniferous trees, moss-draped maples and a forest floor covered with ferns. Most of the rain falls during winter, leaving a comparatively dry summer with many clear and sunny days.

The 3 river valleys were formed by glacial action some 2,000 years ago. Broad and flat, they gain only 600 feet in elevation in 20 miles and are about a mile wide. Virtually every square inch of ground is covered by vegetation, ranging from tiny mosses to giant 300-foot spruce trees. There are more than 300 species of plants, 71 mosses, 30 different liverworts and 70 separate lichens.

Sitka spruce and western hemlock dominate an environment characterized by large numbers of giant trees. Douglas fir, western red cedar, big-leaf maple and vine maple are second-class citizens. The varied wildlife ranges from the often-seen Roosevelt elk and black-tailed deer to the reclusive black bear and cougar. Bobcats, coyotes, beaver and otter inhabit forests and riverbanks.

While virtually interchangeable in plants and topography, the 3 forests are diverse in terms of services and facilities.

The Hoh is the most famous and easily accessible. An 18.5-mile paved road leads east from **Mile 524.5** Highway 101 to a visitor center, evening campfire programs, guided walks and campground.

A quarter-mile trail is easily walked by children and accessible to the disabled. Signs explain "lower story" plants, moss-draped boughs, the giant Douglas fir, Sitka spruce and hemlock. The "Hall of Mosses" is the most photographed and popular of all rain forest interpretive trails. Less than a mile long, it is lined with dramatic draperies of club moss and the largest old-growth trees. The 1-mile Spruce Trail meanders through a variety of vegetation and topography, including the present Hoh riverbank and former streambeds. For an extended hike, there is the 17-mile Hoh River Trail. It starts at the visitor center, winds through the river valley and ends with Blue Glacier

Moss-draped trees, such as these in the Quinault Valley, characterize Olympic rain forests. (© John Barger)

and the park's highest peak, Mount Olympus (elev. 7,965 feet).

For $8 per night, visitors can camp beside the Hoh River. It is a premier fishing stream for winter steelhead, midsummer chinook salmon, and fall runs of salmon, steelhead and trout.

Quinault is often called the most beautiful of the rain forests. Situated on the shores of Lake Quinault, it offers a choice of accommodations with its lodge, private resort and several campgrounds.

The rain forest can be seen from cars on a 25-mile loop road that includes the scenic lake, farms and views of the Olympic Mountains. Seasonal attractions are Roosevelt elk, flocks of swans, spring rhododendrons and hydrangea. Several trails begin at the lake. They range from short rain forest hikes to paths leading to remote wilderness areas and distant park borders.

Lake Quinault is frequented by swimmers, boaters and fishermen seeking Dolly Varden, steelhead and cutthroat trout. Fishing is regulated by the Quinault Indian Nation.

Quinault Lodge was built in 1926 and lists Franklin D. Roosevelt as one of its distinguished guests. It contains most of the original furnishings. The full-menu dining room is open year-round along with rooms in the main lodge, annex and new lakeside addition. A heated indoor pool, saunas and therapy spa are available to guests.

At Rain Forest Resort Village, cabins are set along a creek and on the lakefront. The full-service restaurant and lounge specializes in local seafoods and Washington wines. To reach Lake Quinault, leave U.S. 101 at **Mile 472** and travel 3 miles northeast to the lake, lodge and campgrounds.

The Queets River rain forest is for those who want to get away from people and are content with a minimum of services. Facilities are limited to a boat ramp and 26-unit, no-fee campground situated on the riverbank. A ranger is on duty during the summer.

For most of the year, hiking is limited to the 3-mile-long Sam's River Loop Trail. It starts at the campground, winds along the river and continues through beautiful fern and moss displays. Because Queets attracts fewer people, elk frequently feed in 2 meadows along the loop.

During low-water months, hikers ford the stream and take the 16-mile-long Queets River Trail. Highlights are one of the park's largest Douglas fir trees, abandoned fields and buildings. The latter are relics from the 1880s to the 1940s when the valley was heavily homesteaded by Europeans. A generator house, settlers cabin and classic barn still stand.

From Dec. to April, the Queets River is heavily fished for steelhead. It is known for its runs of wild salmon, fall chinook and summer Dolly Varden. Floaters, rafters and boaters use the river during spring and summer. Potential hazards are log jams and sweepers—trees that have fallen into the river and are too low to get under and too high to go over.

Queets access is via 14 miles of good dirt road from **Mile 491** Highway 101.

cent to the ranger station. The historic lodge offers lodging all year; phone (360) 288-2571, or fax (360) 288-2415.

Beyond the lake the South Shore Road becomes gravel and winds up the Quinault Valley along the upper river through the Quinault segment of the famous rain forest, ending at Graves Creek NPS ranger station and campground, 45 sites with a 21-foot maximum length. No fee at this campground, which also serves as a trailhead to the Enchanted Valley region of the Olympic National Park, a 13.5-mile hike along the East Fork Quinault River. A few miles before Graves Creek the road forks and the left turn bridges the Quinault River to connect with the North Shore Road, which provides access to the North Fork NPS ranger station and campground, 8 sites (no trailers), no fee and a trailhead for hikers heading up the North Fork Quinault River trail to Low Divide ranger station.

Mile 473.5 (239): AMANDA PARK at the outlet of Lake Quinault; gas (diesel), food, lodging and post office. U.S. Highway 101 bridges the Quinault River and turns west toward the coast. Except for a 1-mile section near Prairie Creek, the highway is bordered on both sides by the Quinault Indian Reservation. All recreational land and water use in this area is regulated by the Quinault Indian Nation, and permits are required. Inquire at the general store in Amanda Park for permits and regulations.

Mile 475.5 (237): Junction with the North Shore Road (see **Mile 472**). Resort, motel, grocery, gas (diesel).

Mile 477.5 (235): Olympic National Forest boundary.

Mile 488.5 (224): Views of Mount Olympus (7,965 feet).

Mile 491 (221.5): Olympic National Park boundary. **Junction** with the Queets Valley Recreation Area Road to Queets rain forest. The road parallels the south bank of the Queets River, popular for commercial rafting and an excellent winter/summer steelhead, sea-run cutthroat and salmon fishing river outside of the tribal jurisdiction. Two boat launches are found on the river. A ranger station and primitive campground (26 sites, no services, unsuitable for trailers) are located 14 miles upriver in the rain forest area. The Queets rain forest is the middle of the 3 official rain forest areas, flanked by the Quinault to the south and the Hoh to the north. ⌖▲ MP 145

Mile 493.5 (219): Junction with Clearwater River Recreation Area Road (gravel), which follows the Clearwater River upstream. A rough boat launch and 2 primitive campgrounds are along the river (no camping fee). This pretty river offers fair steelhead fishing in December and January and cutthroat fishing from July through Oct., plus hiking access into Olympic National Park.
⌖▲

Mile 498.5 (214): QUEETS, a small tribal town located on the Queets River.

Mile 500.5 (212): Northern boundary of Quinault Indian Reservation and southern coastal segment of Olympic National Park. South Beach camping area is a graveled parking lot-style area best suited for RVs (no hookups), although some beachcombers pitch small tents in primitive spots on nearby bluffs or along the beach. (*NOTE:* Very little advance notice provided for west turnoff.) No drinking water, but restrooms are available. Very popular RV area with excellent beach access and acres of giant driftwood logs. Some surf fishing for perch and swimming for those tough enough to brave the cold ocean waters. Ashenbrenner picnic day-use area adjoins the camping stretch on the south on a brushy, picturesque bluff overlooking miles of sandy beach. A fine place to stop for a travel break. ⌖⌖▲ MP 154

Mile 502 (210.5): Beach access with pit toilets. MP 156

Mile 503.5 (209): KALALOCH (Ka-Lay-Lock) comprises the Kalaloch ranger station, Kalaloch Lodge and Kalaloch Campground. The ranger station has maps and current information on Olympic National Park facilities. Kalaloch Lodge is a private resort with rental cabins and beach access. The lodge also has a small grocery store, restaurant, gas station and gift shop.

Kalaloch Campground, within Olympic

Turnoff at Mile 508.5 between Kalaloch and Ruby Beach for side road to giant western red cedar.
(David Ovens)

National Park, is the largest coastal beach campground on the Olympic Peninsula. It has 179 campsites, picnicking, clamming, swimming and hiking. A popular camping area, likely to be full during peak summer travel periods. Excellent beach access, with a view to the northwest of Destruction Island.
⌖⌖▲ MP 158

Mile 506.5 (206): Beachfront picnic and day-use area. Beach access. ⌖

Mile 507 (205.5): Beach access with pit toilets.

Mile 508.5 (204): Unmarked gravel road 500 feet after sign leads east 0.3 mile to the site of a giant cedar tree. Once thought to be the world's largest western red cedar, it was later found to be slightly smaller than the 183-foot-high record holder located a little north of here in the Hoh River valley. A pleasant beach access area is about 0.5 mile north on the west side of the road. MP 162

Mile 510 (202.5): Destruction Island Historical Marker, commemorating the slaughter of 13 sailors. (*NOTE:* Sign for marker appears at turnoff, with no advance warning.) In 1775 Spanish explorer Bodega y Quadra anchored in the lee of the island and sent 7 sailors ashore for wood and water. They were killed by Indians, and Quadra named the island Isla de Delores, "the island of sorrow." In 1787, a Capt. Barkley also anchored in the protection of the island and sent 6 sailors ashore for supplies. They too were killed by Indians and the captain named the nearby river Destruction River. Later the name was given to the island and the river returned to its native title of Hoh.

Mile 511 (201.5): Ruby Beach day-use area; excellent beach trails, picnicking and restrooms. Ruby Beach gets its name from sands of garnet found on certain parts of the beach. Offshore rock is named Abbey Island and is part of the Quillayute Needles National Wildlife Refuge set aside as a reserve in 1907 by President Theodore Roosevelt. In 1970 the refuge was made part of the Washington Islands Wilderness Area, which extends 100 miles and includes some 870 islands, rocks and reefs between Copalis Beach and Cape Flattery at the entrance to the Strait of Juan de Fuca. Only the islands have refuge status and are important sanctuaries for sea lions, harbor and fur seals, shorebirds, waterfowl and land birds.

The main purpose of this refuge is to provide protection for nesting seabirds, including common murres, cormorants, Cassin's and rhinocerous auklets, tufted puffins, Leach's and fork-tailed petrels, and gulls. These birds nest in large colonies on the high cliffs of predator-free coastal islands. The islands are closed to the public to protect these nesting birds from human disturbance. During peak periods an estimated 1 million birds use the area. The area is frequented by porpoises, piked whales, Pacific right whales, gray whales, humpback

The scenic Sol Duc River (also spelled Soleduck). Sol duc is an Indian term meaning "sparkling water," referencing the water's magical medicinal qualities.
(L. Linkhart)

whales and sometimes sea lions and otters. Highway 101 leaves the coast at this point and swings east through the lower Hoh River valley.

Mile 513.5 (199): Olympic National Park boundary.

Mile 514 (198.5): Hoh Tribal Center. This is both the smallest reservation and the smallest tribe on the Olympic Peninsula. The reservation is only 1 mile square.

Mile 522 (190.5): RV camping, gasoline, groceries.

Mile 523.5 (189): Hoh River bridge and Hoh River Oxbow Recreation Area, which includes 12 primitive campsites (no fee), no water and rough boat launch to the river. The Hoh is the largest and best known of the Olympic Peninsula steelhead and salmon fishing rivers, flowing from the flanks of Mount Olympus to the Pacific Ocean. Guided trips can be arranged at many of the local resorts, tackle or grocery stores. The river is famed for its large salmon and steelhead and is also popular with rafters. There are numerous access points and boat launches on this glacial river. Upriver sites are reached via paved road to the Hoh rain forest, while downstream sites are along the Oil City Road.

Mile 524 (188.5): Turnoff to the Cottonwood Recreation Area leading downstream to Hoh River areas. The Cottonwood campground offers 7 campsites, a boat launch and picnic area. MP 177

Mile 524.5 (188): **Junction** with Hoh River Road, which runs east 18.5 miles along the river to the Hoh rain forest, and Olympic National Park Hoh Rain Forest Visitor Center (phone 360/374-6925). A small drive-in and general store/fruit stand combination are located a few miles down the road before entering Olympic National Park, but despite an informational sign at the highway, there is no resort lodging along this road. The primary campground is at the visitor center near the river and offers 95 excellent sites for RVs (no hookups) and tents. The visitor center is the hub for numerous hiking trails through the rain forest ranging from less than a mile to more than 26 miles to Mount Olympus.

One of the most popular short hikes is the Hall of Mosses 0.8-mile walk through a cathedral of towering Sitka spruce and broad-leaved maples draped with cloaks of club moss. An interpretive center, amphitheater and narrated nature walks operate seasonally. This is one of the most well-known areas of the peninsula rain forests and a picturesque campground. Be warned, the Hoh registers more than 140 inches of rainfall a year. For more information on Olympic National Park turn to the MAJOR ATTRACTIONS section. MP 179

Mile 531.5 (181): Public fishing. MP 185

Mile 532 (180.5): Bogachiel River State Park and resort. The state park has 42 campsites, showers, a beach area, boat ramp and river fishing, and is a popular camping spot for summer vacationers and winter steelhead fishermen. MP 186

Mile 538 (174.5): FORKS (pop. 3,000), largest town on the western side of the peninsula, providing a full complement of services and outdoor recreational facilities. Timber, sportfishing and tourism are the major economic influences on this community, which lies within a few miles of 6 major steelhead and salmon rivers, in a thickly timbered cedar and spruce woods that nearly destroyed the town in 1951. A forest fire roared down the Calawah River valley and forced the evacuation of the town. Thirty-two buildings were destroyed in Forks along with 30,275 acres before the fire was controlled.

Logging and the timber industry are still major, although somewhat depressed, economic factors here, and the heritage of this industry is interestingly displayed at the Forks Timber Museum on the southern edge of town.

Forks is the hub for the Olympic Peninsula's world-famous steelhead and salmon fishing rivers, and is in prime elk, black-tailed deer, black bear and grouse country. Dozens of fishing and hunting guides are based here during the seasons. The river guides fish from McKenzie-style drift boats, a high-sided rockerbottomed craft specifically designed for the white water.

Mile 539.5 (173): **Junction** with La Push Road, which leads west about 15 miles to Olympic National Park's Pacific Coast Beach Area (beach walking and hike-in beach camping, no facilities at First, Second and Third Beaches), Quileute Indian Reservation and the town of **LA PUSH**. Accommodations are available in La Push, which also has charter services for saltwater fishing and a great beach. La Push is also the trailhead for hiking trails to remote wilderness beaches within Olympic National Park.

Branching off from the main La Push Road, Mora Road gives access to Leyendecker County Park (picnic area, boat launch); fishing at the confluence of the Sol Duc, Bogachiel and Quillayute rivers; camping at Mora Campground (91 sites); and Rialto Beach day-use area, a popular spot for watching sunsets. MP 193

Mile 541 (171.5): Sol Duc River bridge. The Sol Duc is an excellent summer and winter steelhead and fall salmon fishing river, and because it is followed much of the way by U.S. Highway 101 there is abundant bank access. Drift boats float fishermen down the river in winter, but it takes an experienced hand on the oars to navigate the treacherous boulder drops and rock gardens. ◄

Mile 542.5 (170): Olympic National Forest and National Park ranger station. A good source for maps of the national forest and national park. (See the MAJOR ATTRACTIONS section for more information on Olympic National Park.) MP 196

Mile 547 (165.5): Community of **BEAVER. Junction** with access road to Pleasant Lake; boat launch. A small grocery store, plus gas and restaurant are at the junction. RV park. ▲

Mile 549.5 (169): Crossing Sol Duc River. Tumbling Rapids State Park (day use). Salmon hatchery and interpretive center.

Mile 550 (162.5): The small community of **SAPPHO**, with services and grocery.

Junction with 10-mile connector road to Washington Highway 112, which leads to **SEKIU, CLALLAM BAY** and **NEAH BAY**—all popular sportfishing areas with food, gas, lodging, camping, boat rentals and fishing charters. Neah Bay is an Indian village and the site of the Makah Cultural and Research Center museum, where one of the finest collections of Indian art in the Northwest is on display. At road end west of Neah Bay, a 0.5-mile walk leads to Cape Flattery, the most northwestern point of the continental United States.

West of Sekiu, Washington Highway 112 junctions with the 19-mile Hoku River Road to Ozette Lake; camping, resort cabins, fishing, hiking trails and site of former archaeological digs.

Washington Highway 112 rejoins U.S. Highway 101 at **Mile 589**.

Mile 552.5 (160): Bear Creek-Albin Wahlgren Washington Dept. of Natural Resources Recreation Site. Free camping, 10 sites, no hookups, nice forested picnic areas and good water. This site is on the Sol Duc River, but the bank is high and steep and there is no boat access. Motel, RV park and restaurant. ⋔▲ MP 206

Mile 555.5 (157): Boundary of Olympic National Forest.

Mile 558 (154.5): Highway crosses Sol Duc River. USFS Klahowya Campground and boat launch with 55 campsites, no hookups. There are picnic tables and hiking trails with fishing access to the Sol Duc River. ⋔⋔◄▲ MP 212

Mile 565.5 (147): Boundary of Olympic National Forest. **Junction** with Sol Duc Valley Road, which winds nearly 12 miles through forested hills to Sol Duc Hot Springs resort and campground (open April through Oct. for swimming; phone 360/327-3583). The hot springs are incorporated into the resort, which includes a freshwater and 3 mineral swimming pools, motels, cabins, RV park, restaurant facilities and a grocery store. The resort, rebuilt on the site of an elegant 1912 spa, is adjacent to Sol Duc Hot Springs National Park Service Campground providing 84 campsites, amphitheater, trailers up to 21 feet, nature trails. There is a camping fee. This is also the trailhead for the Seven Lakes Basin Area of Olympic National Park. An interesting stop is at Cascades Falls on the Sol Duc River, where in September you can watch a run of summer coho salmon climb the white water. ⋔⋔▲ MP 219

Mile 567.5 (145): Lake Crescent Campground and store (closed in off-season) at **FAIRHOLM** on the western end of Lake Crescent, the largest lake in Olympic National Park. Campers will find 87 sites at Fairholm, plus a boat launch, dock, store and amphitheater. Daily camp fee.

U.S. Highway 101 follows the twisting shoreline of 9-mile-long Lake Crescent, providing excellent views of 3,000-foot Pyramid Mountain on the north shore at the elbow in the lake and the jagged 4-peak summit of 4,500-foot Mount Storm King downlake. Lake Crescent has numerous resorts, boat rentals and launches, and its clear 624-foot-deep waters are home to Crescenti cutthroat and Beardslee rainbow trout (very rare subspecies), plus Montana black spot cutthroat, steelhead and landlocked silver salmon. The lake is entirely within the Olympic National Park, and a fishing license is not required. *CAUTION:* The highway, which is grooved in places, is narrow, twists from one curve to the next along the lake and carries a heavy load of logging truck and vacation trailer traffic, a hazardous combination that demands attention. ◄▲

Mile 570 (142.5): La Poel picnic area with 590 feet of lakeshore. The access road is narrow with sharp bends unsuitable for trailers. There are pleasant picnic sites, water and restrooms. ⋔

Mile 574.5 (138): Barnes Point is the peninsular location of one of the lake's major developed recreation areas, including Olympic National Park ranger station, boat launch (steep and unsuited for large boats), dock, Lake Crescent Lodge (open May to Sept.) and 0.8-mile hiking path leading to 90-foot Marymere Falls. (*NOTE:* Steep final ascent to viewpoint next to falls.) Picnic tables and restrooms are near the visitor

Rialto Beach, off the La Push Road at Mile 539.5, is a popular spot for watching sunsets. (Lee Foster)

center. The resort, built in 1937, offers 30 cottages or lodge rooms, 20 motel units, a dining room specializing in seafood, boat rentals and craft shops. ⋔⋔ MP 228

Mile 578.5 (134): Turnoff to north to East Beach-Piedmont Recreation Area, resort, private camping, picnic and boat launch area. The resort is open year-round, located 3.5 miles north of the highway, and offers cabins, campground with full hookups, showers, laundromat, dining room, rental boats, launch ramp, groceries and swimming beach. Nearby the Park Service maintains a picnic area with restrooms, 600 feet of lakefront fishing and swimming area. ⋔◄▲

Mile 579.5 (133): Restaurant, store and resort with food and camping. ▲

Mile 581 (131.5): Access road turns southwest off U.S. Highway 101 to Lake Sutherland, where unusually warm summer temperatures attract heavy waterskiing, swimming and boating pressure. A couple of resorts offer restaurants, RV park, camping, cabins, swimming pool, grocery store and tackle. The lake reportedly holds some of the largest cutthroat in Washington, with 5-pounders not uncommon, for fishermen trolling small plugs. Most of the fishing effort is directed at kokanee salmon. Several local resorts provide current fishing information and boat rental. The road parallels the residentially developed south shore of the lake. A free public boat launch is provided by the Dept. of Game. ◄▲

Mile 582 (130.5): Motel and cafe. MP 235

Mile 585.5 (127): ELWHA. Entering the Indian Creek Recreation Area providing access to Lake Aldwell and the upper Elwha River Recreation Area and trailhead. There is a Dept. of Game boat launch and primitive camping area on Lake Aldwell, an undeveloped impoundment on the Elwha River that can provide some very satisfying light spin and fly-fishing. A resort located at the bridge on Highway 101 provides rustic cabins, RV sites, tackle, groceries, current fishing information and can book raft trips on the river.

A road runs south from the highway, paralleling the Elwha River for 3 miles to the Elwha Campground, 41 campsites, picnic, shelter, water, restrooms, naturalist program and hiking trail access. The river is a fine fly-fishing stream. One mile south of Elwha Campground is the Altaire Campground with 29 campsites, picnic area, water, restrooms and trails. Both campgrounds have a fee. The road forks at Altaire, the west fork going 12 miles up Boulder Creek. The east fork runs south along the shoreline of 2-mile-long Lake Mills. Public boat launch near the dam, fishing for brookies, Dolly Varden and a few rainbow and cutthroat. The best fishing is found in the upper lake near the canyon walls of the Elwha River during late summer and fall. A few primitive campsites are at the upper end of the lake. ⋔⋔◄▲ MP 240

Mile 589 (123.5): Junction with Washington Highway 112, which runs west along the Strait of Juan de Fuca through Joyce, Clallam Bay, Sekiu and Neah Bay, ending on the Makah Indian Reservation. Travelers leaving U.S. Highway 101 to follow this loop road west can rejoin Highway 101 at Sappho (see

From: Port Angeles, WA
To: Olympia, WA

Mile 593.5
Mile 628
Mile 652.5
Mile 677.5
Mile 683.5
Mile 691.5
Mile 712.5

couver Island and Mount Baker from the end of the hook can be exceptional on a clear day.

Port Angeles is also the northern portal to Olympic National Park and spectacular Hurricane Ridge. Overlooks on the road to Hurricane Ridge offer dramatic views of the Strait of Juan de Fuca, Dungeness Spit and Vancouver Island. From U.S. Highway 101 turn south on Race Street and continue to the Olympic National Park Visitor Center at the park boundary. Heart O' The Hills Campground has 105 sites, nature trail, amphitheater and fishing in small Lake Dawn. The 17-mile road to the ridge is paved and follows the contour of the mountains up to a 5,200-foot elevation and a visitor center, lodge and interpretive area with a spectacular view of the jagged snowcapped Olympic peaks, including glacier-bound Mount Carrie (elev. 6,995 feet) and Mount Olympus (elev. 7,965 feet), the glaciated centerpiece of the park beyond. Paved nature trials close to the visitor center are wheelchair-accessible. For more information about Olympic National Park turn to the MAJOR ATTRACTIONS section.

Mile 599.5 (113): Junction with Deer Park Road, which leads 17 miles south to Deer Park Campground, a small site with only 18 campsites and no trailer facilities. A ranger station is manned from June through Sept., and several hiking trails originate here. The road is very scenic and passes through mountain Alpine country but is not safe for motorhomes, trailers or campers.

Mile 602 (110.5): Private campground 0.5 mile east. ▲ MP 255

Mile 606.5 (106): Boundary of the Dungeness Recreation Area, an extremely popular camping and recreational destination adjacent to Dungeness National Wildlife Refuge (phone 360/457-8451), commonly called Dungeness Spit, a 7-mile-long, curving peninsula that has been designated as the world's longest natural sand spit. Dungeness Recreation Campground is located on the bluffs overlooking the spit and offers 65 sites with water, full-service restrooms, showers, playground and kitchen facilities. Fee.

A lighthouse, first built in 1857 and replaced in 1927, marks the tip of Dungeness Spit and is open for tours Thursday through Monday afternoons. The strip of sand is maintained in a roadless wilderness state, with excellent winter clamming on the beaches, tossed rows of salt-seasoned driftwood sculptures, shells and agates, and more than 275 species of birds including black brant (a species of goose) that winter on the vast eelgrass beds and were the reason the area was first designated as a wildlife sanctuary in 1915.

Hiking, boating, fishing, clamming, crabbing, wildlife observation and horseback riding are available. (Horses allowed on weekdays only from April to Oct.) No fires, camping, pets or hunting are allowed on the spit. Open daily, daylight use only, with a small entry fee per family (children under 16 free). The spit forms a 556-acre bay bisected by a finger of sand known as Graveyard Spit, once the site of an Indian massacre and now used as a picnic area. Steep bluffs overlook the spit. A boat launch ramp is provided on Marine Drive, near Cline Spit. Black-tailed deer, elephant and harbor seals are frequently spotted, plus there is good crabbing and salmon fishing in the area around the spit.

Mile 550). Many of the best salmon and bottom fish fishing areas along the strait are located along Highway 112. RV park, services and groceries. ▲

Mile 591.5 (121): Fairchild International Airport.

Mile 593.5 (119): Western city limits of **PORT ANGELES** (pop. 19,000), largest city on the peninsula north of Aberdeen/Hoquiam, headquarters of Olympic National Park and a major summer vacation area. All major traveler services are offered.

Protected by the natural curved peninsula of Ediz Hook, the harbor is a major shipping port. Black Ball Transport Inc. provides daily year-round passenger and automobile ferry service to Victoria, BC, from downtown Port Angeles; phone (360) 457-4491. Victoria

Rapid Transit offers passenger-only ferry service from May to Oct.; phone (360) 452-8088. Arrangements may be made here for tours of Victoria and Butchart Gardens. The chamber of commerce operates a visitor information center next to the ferry terminal; phone (360) 452-2363.

The Clallam County Museum, in the old courthouse building at the intersection of Lincoln and 4th, is an interesting source of regional history and artifacts. The Marine Laboratory on the city pier has an excellent collection of marine life and exhibits with touch tanks. Marine Drive on the west end of downtown's Front Street passes through the giant Daishowa mill and runs along the narrow backbone of Ediz Hook to a Coast Guard station, picnic area and a public boat launch on the tip of the peninsula. The view of the Olympic Mountains, the harbor, Van-

(*NOTE:* No established picnic areas, tables, water, etc., exist on the refuge. There is a trail for handicapped visitors from the joint recreation/refuge parking lot to the bluff on the refuge for a scenic overlook of the spit.)

Mile 607.5 (105): Sequim Valley Center, a small shopping area providing food, gas, RV park and lodging near the Dungeness River bridge. The river provides some seasonal fishing (check state regulations for restrictions). There is a state fish hatchery upstream, and a primitive USFS campground with 9 sites 4.5 miles south on County Road 9537 and 3 miles southwest on Forest Service Road 2958. Four more miles brings you to a second USFS 9-site campground. No fees.

ping up to 200 inches of rain in the Hoh and Queets river valleys, producing an umbrella effect that shelters the downslope northeast of the mountains. Some years Sequim gets as little as 10 inches of rain, aridity comparable to San Diego.

The Sequim-Dungeness Museum, 175 W. Cedar, exhibits cultural artifacts of the area and displays of 19th century living.

West Sequim Bay Recreation Area, east of town, includes the John Wayne Marina on property donated to the public by the famous Western movie star, who often anchored his yacht in Sequim Bay. Picnic facilities, boat launch, fishing charter boats, showers

Above right—Black-tailed deer fawn in Olympic National Park. (© John Barger) Above—Building a driftwood house at Dungeness Spit, accessible from Mile 606.5. (L. Linkhart)

Mile 608.5 (104): Large, red-barked Pacific madrone trees begin to appear at roadside, the only broad-leaved evergreen tree growing in any numbers north of the Oregon border. These curious trees only grow in mild oceanic areas, preferably rocky, and shed their thin bark annually revealing a smooth reddish covering. The largest known madrone, also called madrona, is 10 feet thick with a crown spread of 126 feet.

Mile 609.5 (103): Northern city limits of **SEQUIM** (pop. 3,600), a popular community for retirees because of its proximity to the mountains, salt water and most important its lack of rainfall. The town receives at least some sunshine 306 days a year. Full services are available in Sequim including nearby waterfront resorts on the Strait of Juan de Fuca.

Sequim (Skwim) is in a unique belt of sunshine so dry that in pioneer days cactus plants flourished, and even today irrigation is required for farming (within sight of the famous rain forest less than 30 miles away). The phenomenon is created by the Olympic Mountains, which obstruct Pacific rain squalls moving in from the southwest drop-

and RV sites are at the marina. Private resort facilities are located near the marina.

The Olympic Game Farm, located on Ward Road (follow signs from Sequim), offers walking and driving tours through wildlife areas that include tigers, wolves, grizzly bears, cougars, lions and other exotic animals. Many of these animals are movie stars, appearing in Hollywood and Walt Disney productions. Phone (360) 683-4295 for hours; admission fee charged.

Mile 613.5 (99): Access to John Wayne Marina east 0.5 mile. Boat launch.   MP 267

Mile 615.5 (97): Sequim Bay State Park provides 26 RV campsites with full hookups and 60 tent sites. There are 3 kitchen areas, plus showers, tennis courts, environmental learning center, boat launch and a lodge area.
▲ MP 269

Mile 617 (95.5): Junction with access road to the South Sequim Bay Recreation Area, state park and marina. Tent and trailer camping, trailer dump station. Tribal center.
▲

Mile 617.5 (95): The small crossroads community of **BLYN**. Native American art gallery. No facilities are available.

Mile 621 (91.5): Access road to Diamond Point at the head of Discovery Bay (unmarked eastbound). Just offshore, at the mouth of Discovery Bay, is Protection Island National Wildlife Refuge and a major nesting area for eagles and seabirds (21,000 pairs, roughly 70 percent of all the nesting seabirds in the Puget Sound area, nest here). They share the island with up to 300 harbor seals and approximately half of the rhinoceros auklet breeding population in the United States. The 400-acre island is 1.8 miles long and is closed to public entry. Boats are required to stay at least 200 yards offshore. The island was named by the explorer Capt. George Vancouver and was given refuge status in 1982.

Mile 622 (90.5): GARDINER, a small recreational community where travelers will find a grocery store, RV park and a public boat launch to Discovery Bay. A historical marker at roadside denotes the May 2, 1792, exploration of the bay by English explorer Capt. George Vancouver during his legendary search for the Northwest Passage. Vancouver named the bay in honor of his sailing sloop, *Discovery*.   ▲

Mile 628 (84.5): The small community of **DISCOVERY BAY** is located at the scenic southern end of the inlet, marked by an abandoned mill and the **junction** with Washington Highway 20. Food and lodging available. Highway 20 runs 12 miles north along the east bank of Discovery Bay to **PORT TOWNSEND** and Fort Worden (see feature on page 184), where a Washington state ferry links Highway 20 to Whidbey Island. Highway 20 eventually merges with Interstate 5 at Mount Vernon.

Mile 631 (81.5): Junction with Washington Highway 104, the primary arterial between the northern Olympic Peninsula region and Puget Sound's metropolitan regions of Seattle-Tacoma-Bremerton. Highway 104 crosses Hood Canal on a floating bridge, merges

Port Townsend

Historically rich Port Townsend (pop. 7,750) has a wealth of attractions. Visitors may take a guided tour of Victorian homes; wander through the downtown area of 19th-century brick and stone buildings, or the restored military encampment of Fort Worden (now a state park); or visit the busy waterfront. Port Townsend offers 5 motels, 6 hotels, 17 bed-and-breakfast facilities and 45 restaurants.

The first log cabin in Port Townsend was built in 1851. As the town's importance as a shipping capital grew, the population rose to 7,000. Hopes of Port Townsend becoming the terminus for the railroad were never realized, and the town struggled along until the 1920s, when Crown Zellerbach opened a kraft paper mill and the economy stabilized.

Today, a kraft paper mill, marine-oriented businesses and tourism are the mainstays of Port Townsend.

A recommended first stop for visitors is the Port Townsend Chamber of Commerce at 2437 E. Sims Way, on the southwest edge of the business district. Free maps are available locating the points of interest, including a self-guided auto tour of Victorian home sites, some providing tours and/or offering bed-and-breakfast facilities.

Included in Port Townsend's Victorian collection is the Manresa Castle, built in 1892 by a Prussian baker and patterned after castles built along Germany's Rhine River. The Rothschild House, a New England style house, was built in 1868 by one of the town's first merchants. It is one of Washington's smallest state parks at just 50 by 200 feet. Daily tours during the summer (by appointment in off-season).

The Jefferson County Historical Museum is in City Hall on Water Street, between Madison and Monroe streets. It features nautical artifacts, an antique hearse and fire engine, glassware, machinery and Victorian clothing.

The Jefferson County Courthouse, built in 1891, is one of the oldest jails in the state. On the first floor is the Hall of Honor, which pays tribute to early pioneers.

The starch-white buildings at Fort Worden, at the foot of Point Wilson, are where *An Officer and a Gentleman* was filmed in 1981. The fort was constructed between 1897 and 1911 around a battery of cannons designed to defend against enemy naval invasion through the Strait of Juan de Fuca to cities farther down Puget Sound. Registered as an historic landmark and historic district, the buildings have been restored, the grounds neatly manicured and a self-guided loop path marked through the historic barracks, gun emplacements, parade grounds and officers' housing areas.

The fort is owned by the State Parks Commission and includes conference facilities, a restaurant, a campground with 80 sites (50 year-round), showers, concrete boat ramp, beach access, tennis courts, an underwater scuba diving park and beachfront picnic areas.

Campers will find a 40-site campground 3 miles south of Port Townsend at Old Fort Townsend Recreation Area, open during the summer only. There are also showers, tables, beach access, buoy moorage and the remnants of an 1859 fort.

---

with Washington Highway 3 on the east bank with direct access to cross-sound ferries from Kingston and Bremerton. The bridge earned national notoriety in the late 1970s when it broke apart and was partially sunk by an exceptionally savage storm. The Kingston ferry lands at Edmonds between Everett and Seattle, while the Bremerton ferries provide service to downtown Seattle. A public clamming and crabbing beach is open on the west shore of Bywater Bay just north of the bridge's west end. On the east side there is a public boat ramp at Salsbury Point County Park.

Mile 632.5 (80): Crocker Lake borders the east shoulder of the highway. There is a boat launch and portable restroom. ⊷

Mile 635.5 (77): Access road to Lake Leland leads to a county park, picnic facilities, small campground (22 sites) and public boat launch. ⋏▲ MP 289

Mile 641.5 (71): Full services (including diesel) are provided in the quaint community of **QUILCENE**, a town famous for its oyster production and seafood. A 2-mile side trip down Linger Longer Road leads to the marina at Quilcene Bay and a close-up view of oyster farming at the largest oyster hatchery in the world. Tours are available by appointment. A shop of chainsaw wood sculptures is also in this area. Quilcene ranger station office for the Olympic National Forest provides maps and information on current recreational opportunities in the park.

Mile 643 (69.5): Bridge crosses the Quilcene River. The Quilcene national fish hatchery is just west on Fish Hatchery Road. MP 295

Mile 644.5 (68): Boundary of the Olympic National Forest and the turnoff to Falls View Campground, a wooded 35-site camp overlooking the Quilcene River gorge and a falls. The site is open from May through Oct. only. There is a nightly fee. ▲ MP 298

Mile 646 (66.5): Turnoff, on the east side of the road, to a gravel road (closed in winter) that leads 5 miles into the woods to the Mount Walker viewpoint (elev. 2,750 feet) with Hood Canal, Puget Sound, Seattle, the Cascade Mountains and the Trident nuclear submarine base at Bangor to the east and the Olympic Mountains to the west. This view is worth the drive, but the road is unsuitable for trailers and motorhomes. To the west of highway is Rainbow Campground with 10 tent/camper sites. ▲

Mile 649.5 (63): Southbound travelers will find the highway leaves the Douglas fir and rhododendron forest for the shoreline of Hood Canal's Dabob Bay. The Point Whitney Shellfish Research Laboratory and Camp Parsons Boy Scout Camp are accessible from the 2-lane road intersecting from the east (no advance warning; sign is at turnoff). Dabob Bay is an extremely productive shellfish area, rich with oysters, clams, shrimp and Dungeness crab. The U.S. Navy also uses these deep waters to test torpedoes. A small beach, adjacent to the lab, is open to clam digging and oyster-gathering. A boat launch at the shellfish lab provides boat access to 2 public shellfish beaches: a Dept. of Fisheries beach north of the lab and a Dept. of Natural Resources beach just inside Pulali Point near Camp Parsons. Both beaches are accessible by water only. A tour through the shellfish lab is an interesting side trip. Restrooms available. RV park and groceries. ▲

Mile 652 (60.5): Seal Rock Campground adjacent to the highway is open from May until mid-Oct. Camp fee is $6 to $8 with 40 sites. There is 100 feet of beachfront with swimming, fishing, picnicking and restrooms. The beach can yield good oyster-gathering. For those with boats, excellent shrimping is available just offshore from Seal Rock during the spring season. Salmon and bottom fishing are also productive in this area throughout the year. Boundary of Olympic National Forest. ⋏⊷▲

Mile 652.5 (60): The small resort, timber and fishing community of **BRINNON** has rhododendron gardens, an RV park and all visitor services. It is the access point for the Dosewallips Recreation Area. ▲

Mile 653.5 (59): Dosewallips State Park offers 127 campsites, including 40 with full hookups. The park is on both sides of the highway, giving campers access to fresh water in the Dosewallips River and salt water on Hood Canal. ▲ MP 307

Mile 656.5 (56): Duckabush Recreation Area and Pleasant Harbor Marine State Park day-use area. The Duckabush River is paralleled by a road along the north shore and has a reputation for good fall sea-run cutthroat action. There is a small USFS campground 2 miles from the end of the river road often used by fishermen and deer and elk hunters. The Duckabush delta area is good for shrimp and crab pots. ⊷▲ MP 310

Mile 660.5 (52): Triton Cove is located inside Triton Head and hosts a private RV park and boat launch into Hood Canal. Oyster farm. ▲ MP 314

Mile 664 (48.5): Private campground and lodging. ▲

Mile 664.5 (48): Olympic National Forest Hamma Hamma Recreation Area, 6.5 miles west on the Hamma Hamma River, provides fishing, camping (15 sites) and hiking, and private resort facilities. Hamma Hamma is an Indian word meaning "stinking fish."

Mile 665.5 (47): At **ELDON**, near the Hamma Hamma River bridge, a cafe and gas station serve the tiny community.

Mile 666 (46.5): Crossing Hamma Hamma River. Seafood store and oyster farm. Picnic area. ⌐ MP 320

Mile 672.5 (40): Eagle Creek Recreational Tidelands public beach access, open to clamming and crabbing during season.

Mile 673 (39.5): Lilliwaup Recreational Tidelands, just north of Lilliwaup Bay, is open to public harvest of oysters and shellfish, and just offshore you will find good shrimp and crab trapping. The highway crosses the back of the bay in a sharp switchback. Motel, grocery, gasoline and private resort campground south of the bay. Lilliwaup (Lily-wop) is an Indian word meaning "inlet." ▲

Mile 677 (35.5): RV park and motel. ▲

Mile 677.5 (35): HOODSPORT is the largest community on the west side of Hood Canal and unofficial headquarter community for outdoor recreation in the southern Hood Canal area. Full tourist services include diesel, motels, restaurants overlooking the canal, gift shops, sporting goods stores, beach access, winery, public docks and the Finch Creek-Hood Canal salmon hatchery, the only state hatchery equipped for both salt- and freshwater fish. Near the mouth of Sund Creek is a marina, RV campground and private boat launch.

Both Olympic National Park and Forest maintain a year-round ranger and information station in Hoodsport, at the **junction** of the Lake Cushman Road. For more information on Olympic National Park turn to the MAJOR ATTRACTIONS section.

Lake Cushman, an 8.5-mile-long impoundment on the Skokomish River, is a major recreational and camping area. The lake is developed only on the east bank where a full-service resort, vacation cabins and a large public campground look cross-lake at the Prospect Ridge mountains or north to the 6,000-foot peaks inside Olympic National Park.

Lake Cushman State Park is at midlake providing 80 campsites, 30 with full hookups, showers, a boat launch and trailheads for the Olympic hiking system. There is a daily fee and the camp has limited winter hours. At the north end of the lake, literally at the base of the Olympic Mountains, is Staircase Campground, open from May to Sept. only, with 63 standard sites but no hookups or showers. Fee charged. The Staircase area is a popular base for fishing the upper Skokomish River and jumping-off point for Olympic National Park trails. Cartop boats can be launched here, but there is no developed ramp.

Lake Cushman offers anglers a big variety of catches. Boat rentals and launches are available at the resort on the southeast end of the lake, along with current fishing conditions.

Mile 680 (32.5): POTLATCH, a small residential community named for a Skokomish Indian word meaning "to bestow valuable gifts and feast." The town is on the site of an ancient tribal house. MP 334

Mile 681 (31.5): Tacoma City Light-sponsored day-use area is on the east side of the highway, providing an extremely steep boat ramp into Hood Canal, swimming, picnicking and fishing. There are crabs and shrimp to be trapped offshore. On the west side of the highway, enormous water pipes carry water from Lake Cushman (see **Mile 677.5**) to the Tacoma City Light electrical generating plant at the highway. Cafe, motel, RV park.

Mile 681.5 (31): Potlatch State Park encompasses both sides of the highway, covering 57 acres with 35 campsites, including 18 RV sites with hookups, showers, picnic tables, boat moorage buoys and a beach for shellfishing and swimming. Fee. This neat, well-maintained state park is popular during the summer. Private marina and RV park adjacent. ⌐▲

Mile 683.5 (29): Junction with Washington Highway 106, which swings east to parallel the southern shore of Hood Canal, while U.S. Highway 101 continues south and inland. Highway 106 leads, via intersecting highways, to Bremerton and the only bridge crossing Puget Sound at the Tacoma Narrows.

Twanoh State Park is adjacent to Highway 106 (about 7 miles east of junction) and includes 182 acres with 39 campsites, 9 with full hookups, showers, moorage buoys, fishing, a boat launch, pier, shelter house, tables, hiking trails and shellfish beaches for clams, crabs and oysters. The park has limited winter hours. There is also a boat launch and small beach area in the community of Union.

Mile 684.5 (28): Public fishing.

Mile 685 (27.5): The Skokomish River bridge crosses the largest Hood Canal river, a prolific producer of salmon, steelhead and sea-run cutthroat trout. Although heavily netted by tribal fishermen, the Skokomish is a good producer for sportfishermen. A tribal fishing permit is required. Access to Olympic National Forest Skokomish River Recreation Area with tenting, fishing and hiking and state salmon and trout hatcheries, 4 miles west of the highway.

Mile 685.5 (27): The Skokomish Indian Tribal Center office and reservation administration offices. Store. Recreational opportunities on the reservation, plus cultural and tribal information is available here. Much of the nearby Skokomish River is on tribal land.

The Great Bend Area of Hood Canal is famed for crabbing on the Skokomish delta flats in Annas Bay, shrimping in the deeper water, plus fishing for salmon, sea-run cutthroat near shore and bottom fish from Ayres Point north to Dewatto Bay. ⌐ MP 339

Mile 688 (24.5): Junction with Washington Highway 102 west to the community of Dayton and on to Nahwatzel Lake Recreation Area. Excellent waterskiing and fishing. There is a public boat ramp on the lake and a resort with restaurant, cabins and RV hookups.

Port of Shelton Entry Industrial park, airport, county fairgrounds, motel, RV park and hospital. ⌐▲ MP 342

Mile 691.5 (21): Off-ramp to **SHELTON** (pop. 7,530), the only incorporated city in Mason County, nationally known as Christmastown in recognition of its burgeoning Christmas tree industry. All services are available, with gas and major-chain fast food available at exit. Shelton draws its economic base from the shellfish, fishing and timber industries. One of the community highlights is the Washington State Oyster Shucking and Seafood Festival held the first weekend of October. The city is located on the westernmost inlet of Puget Sound and provides access to state parks on Squaxin Island and Jarrell Cove on Hartstene Island, as well as 200 freshwater lakes. Among Shelton's attractions are the Grisdale House, a turn-of-the-century mansion owned by a timber baron, a steam engine and caboose listed on the National Historic Register and 3 city parks.

Mile 693 (19.5): Access to national historic sites at Shelton and Matlock and to visitor information.

Mile 695.5 (17): Junction with Washington Highway 3 to Bremerton. Motels, RV park, fast food and 24-hour gas station. ▲ MP 349

Mile 698.5 (14): Junction with 2-lane Washington Highway 108 west to McCleary and Aberdeen, coastal beach and resort areas, and Squaxin Island Tribal Center. Food, gas (diesel). MP 353

Mile 705.5 (7): Gas and grocery at junction with road to Steamboat Island and Hunter Point. MP 360

Mile 707 (5.5): Junction with Washington Highway 8, a multiple-lane freeway that is the main arterial between Interstate 5 and the ocean beaches at Aberdeen. U.S. Highway 101 shares a common alignment with Highway 8 eastbound to Olympia.

Mile 707.5 (5): Access to Evergreen State College. MP 362

Mile 710.5 (2): Exit to the residential area of West Olympia and the recreational area at Black Lake, providing good rainbow trout, largemouth bass, panfish and catfish. Waterskiing is popular and there are resort facilities for boat rentals. A free boat launch is located at midlake on the east side. Full services are available at this exit. ⌐ MP 366

Mile 712.5 (0): U.S. Highway 101 ends with the cloverleaf **junction** to Interstate 5 south of Olympia near **TUMWATER** (pop. 10,000), the southernmost reach of Puget Sound and the terminus of the Oregon Trail. Near this junction the first American community was established on Puget Sound, a sparse encampment known as New Market. The Deschutes River tumbles down a picturesque waterfall into Budd Inlet within sight of the junction.

Travelers joining Interstate 5 at this junction turn to **Mile 411** in the INTERSTATE 5 section and continue with that log if northbound for Seattle, or read log back to front if southbound to Portland.

U.S. HIGHWAY 395

California–Oregon Border to Canadian Border
(See maps, pages 187, 191 and 193)

U.S. Highway 395 is one of the original Three Flags Routes, so designated because they ran from Mexico, north across the United States and into Canada. Highway 395 originally started at the Mexican border near Tijuana. From San Bernardino it heads north through the desert to Bishop, on the east side of Yosemite National Park, into Nevada to Reno before heading back north through California to junction with Canada's Crowsnest Highway 3 at the international border northwest of Spokane, WA.

Northwest Mileposts® logs U.S. Highway 395 from the California–Oregon border to the Canadian border. Physical mileposts along U.S. 395 in Washington are very straightforward: They reflect distance from the Oregon–Washington border. However, in Oregon there are several sets of mileposts along U.S. 395 reflecting distance from various points too confusing to explain or to be of much help to the motorist.

U.S. Highway 395 Log

Distance from California–Oregon border is followed by distance from the Canadian border.

Mile 0 (666): NEW PINE CREEK (elev. 4,845 feet; pop. 260) straddles the California–Oregon border. The small community offers limited services including a store, post office and gas. **Junction** with Lake County Road 119.

Mile 0.5 (665.5): Turnoff to Goose Lake State Park, open April through Oct. 3. The park has 48 sites with electrical hookups, showers, swimming, boat ramp and phones. ▲

Mile 7.5 (658.5): North end of Goose Lake. Like many Northwest desert lakes, its level has been fluctuating a great deal during the past few years, so the shoreline changes. However, fishing for bass, crappie and perch is still the sport of choice. The lake was dry in the summer of 1926 and from 1929 through 1934. ◄

Mile 13.5 (652.5): LAKEVIEW (pop. 2,750) has all traveler services, including a hospital. For the convenience of the traveler, the U.S. Forest Service, BLM, and Fish and Wildlife Service have combined into 1 visitor center, located on N. F Street and 2nd. This attractive small town is the county seat of Lake

Abert Rim, seen along U.S. 395 north of Lakeview, is one of the highest fault scarps in the United States. (L. Linkhart)

County, one of those enormous eastern Oregon counties with a lot of scenery and very few people. At 4,800 feet, it is one of Oregon's highest towns. It is a busy town for its size, not only from the recreational traffic but because it is the only town of any size in an area larger than most New England states. Because of the excellent thermals in the surrounding mountains, Lakeview has become a mecca for the sport of hang gliding. A hang gliding festival is held in the area every Fourth of July. This is also a popular rockhounding area for thunder eggs, sunstones, fire opal and petrified wood.

Oregon Highway 140 from Klamath Falls **junctions** with U.S. Highway 395 in Lakeview. It shares a common alignment northbound with U.S. Highway 395 for a short distance.　　　　　　　　　　　　MP 145

Mile 15 (651): The Schminck Memorial Museum at 128 S. E St. features a collection of fashions of the 1880s. Open Feb. through Nov., Tuesday through Saturday, 1–5 p.m. Closed holidays.

Mile 17 (649): Lakeview Ranger District offices.

Mile 17.5 (648.5): Oregon's only geyser is 1 mile north of Lakeview's city center on the grounds of the currently closed Hunter Hot Springs. The geyser shoots 60 feet in the air every 90 seconds. Gas, RV park. ▲

Mile 20 (646): Junction with Oregon Highway 140 east to Adel. Highway 140 provides access to a pair of prime recreational areas. Warner Canyon Ski Area, ideal for family skiing; 14 runs and moderate 730-foot drop with facilities for downhill and cross-country skiing. Ski lodge, restaurant, 0.5-mile Hall T-bar and 17 weeks of uncrowded skiing. The other area of interest is the 270,000-acre Hart Mountain National Antelope Refuge, 65 miles northeast. The refuge protects one of North America's largest pronghorn antelope herds and was established in 1936 to preserve, manage and study pronghorn antelope and other wildlife. Camping is permitted on the refuge at the Hot Springs Campground, and backpack camping is permitted with a Special Use Permit.

Rockhounding is permitted, but samples must not exceed 7 lbs. per person per day. A trip into the Hart Mountain Refuge is also the first leg of one of the BLM's National Back Country Byways Systems. The Lakeview to Steens Back Country Byway travels via State Highway 140 for 41 miles on paved and 50 miles on gravel roads ending at State Highway 205, south of Frenchglen and the Malheur National Wildlife Refuge. The gravel road is suitable for passenger cars, but rough on trailers and RVs. ⚓▲

Mile 32.5 (633.5): Chandler Wayside, a small rest area with picnic tables. ⚟

Mile 35 (631): Chandler Station Historic Ranch. MP 124

Mile 38 (628): VALLEY FALLS, a 1-store town with a gas station at the **junction** with Oregon Highway 31, which heads northwest to La Pine and Bend on U.S. Highway 97. The town was named for some low falls nearby on the Chewaucan River, which is rated one of the finest trout rivers, as well as the largest, in Fremont National Forest. The stream is heavily stocked with rainbow trout, especially in the upper reaches near Bly. The lower river is fished for catfish. Next gas northbound 40 miles. ⬅ MP 90

Mile 41.5 (624.5): South end of Lake Abert, one of Oregon's largest lakes, with an average area of 60 square miles. The water is unusually salty. The lake was first chronicled by the John Work party in 1832 and he called it Salt Lake, but when John C. Fremont came through in 1843, he named it for his chief, Col. J.J. Abert of the U.S. Topographical Engineers. MP 87

Mile 43.5 (622.5): Wildlife viewing area where bighorn sheep, pronghorn antelope (depending on the migration season) and dozens of bird species can be seen.

Mile 47.5 (618.5): Abert Rim roadside sign. The rim, seen along the highway, is 2,500 feet above the valley floor and is one of the highest fault scarps in the United States. It was formed when the lava that covered the region was fractured, then tilted by forces in the earth. Abert Rim is the western edge of one, while the lake lies atop another one. MP 91

Mile 58.5 (607.5): North end of Lake Abert is a broad expanse of salt flats. MP 68

Mile 65.5 (600.5): Hogback Summit (elev. 5,033 feet).

Mile 67.5 (598.5): Rest area. MP 61

Mile 78.5 (587.5): Alkali Lake. A small cafe, gas station (24-hour diesel) and highway department maintenance station. Next gas northbound 22 miles, southbound 39 miles. MP 51

Mile 80.5 (585.5): Backcountry road to Juniper Mountain (elev. 6,679 feet).

Mile 91 (575): Junction with county road that leads to Christmas Valley off to the west. Travelers are in the middle of the great eastern Oregon high desert with virtually no population and where ranches are measured

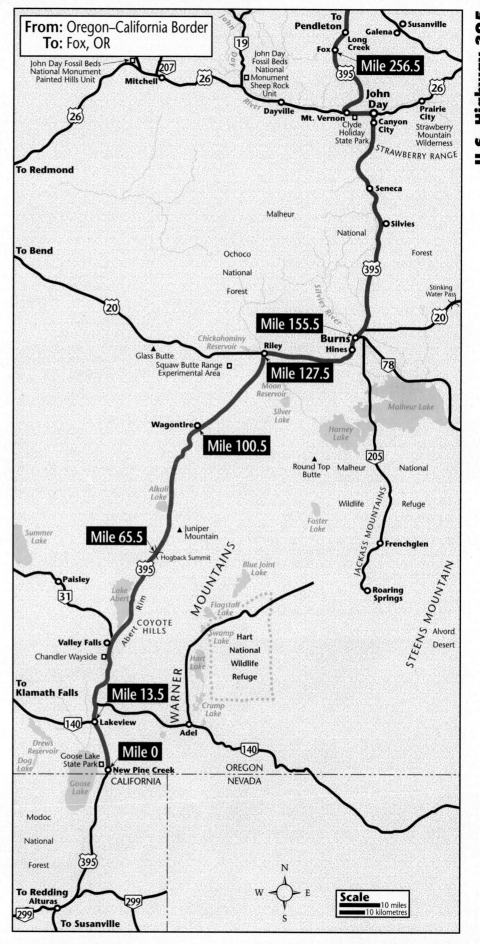

in thousands of square miles.

Mile 95.5 (570.5): Highway leaves Lake County northbound and enters Harney County, at 10,132 square miles the largest county in Oregon, and one of the largest counties in America. It was named for William Selby Harney, who was in command of the Dept. of Oregon of the U.S. Army.

Mile 100.5 (565.5): WAGONTIRE. A sign painted on the store gives the population of 2; elev. 4,725 feet. A 16-unit motel, trailer park (10 sites, full hookups), cafe/store, gas station and landing strip make up the town. There are probably few towns as small, known by so many people, in part because it is so remote that hardly anything else shows on the map, and also because of its unusual name. It came by the name because for many years an old wagon tire lay beside the road up Wagontire Mountain. The mountain lies a short distance to the northwest and is 6,510 feet high.   ▲ MP 27

Mile 117 (549): Squaw Butte/Northern Great Basin Experimental Range, built in 1936. The range is dedicated to research on the ecology and range land. It is operated jointly by the Agricultural Research Service of the U.S. Dept. of Agriculture and the Oregon State University Dept. of Agriculture Experiment Station. It includes 16,000 acres of land, and is located here because vegetation is representative of plants from central Oregon to Nevada, Idaho, Utah and California. Five to 6 different species of sagebrush grow here that are typical of those in the Great Basin region. Research centers on forage management, revegetation and food additives.   MP 10

Mile 127.5 (538.5): RILEY, no services except a post office. **Junction** with U.S. Highway 20, one of the major east-west routes across Oregon (see **Mile 153** in the U.S. HIGHWAY 20 section for log). U.S. Highway 395 shares a common alignment with U.S. Highway 20 for the next 27 miles east.   MP 105

Mile 138 (528): Rest area with covered picnic tables and water. The 0.5-mile Sage Hen Nature Trail here takes you through sagebrush and western juniper to viewpoints. Self-guiding brochure at trailhead.

Adjacent to the rest area, Sage Hen Hill Road (well-maintained gravel) leads east 30 miles past Moon Reservoir and along the shoreline of Harney Lake. It is part of the Malheur National Wildlife Refuge; however, it is off the beaten path from the usual visitor viewing areas. Sage Hen Hill Road intersects U.S. Highway 20 north of the refuge headquarters. If you are planning a side trip to Malheur National Wildlife Refuge, Sage Hen Hill Road is a nice way to begin. ⚑⚑ MP 115

Mile 145.5 (520.5): Burns District Bureau of Land Management Wild Horse Corrals, a major facility for managing wild horses on Oregon public lands. Since 1974, when the program was started, BLM has processed more than 9,000 wild horses, placing 75 percent with private individuals. Wild horse herds increase at an average of 20 percent per year. Tours are available by prior arrangement.   MP 122

Mile 152.5 (513.5): HINES (pop. 1,445) is a sawmill town named for Edward Hines, who owned the lumber sawmill and logging railroad. All services, a BLM office and a private campground with full hookups.   ▲

Mile 153.5 (512.5): Valley golf course.

Mile 155.5 (510.5): BURNS (pop. 2,835). All traveler services. This desert town (elev. 4,148 feet) is the Harney County seat. It was named in 1883 for the Scottish poet Robert Burns by George McGowan, the founder, who was a merchant.

Burns is the gateway to most of Harney County's attractions, such as the Malheur National Wildlife Refuge, at 183,000 acres one of the largest wildlife refuges in the nation. See feature this section.   ★

Mile 156 (510): Burns City Park with picnic tables and playground. Access to **PAIUTE INDIAN RESERVATION** (pop. 160), 1 mile north. The tribe operates a processing plant that freeze-dries onion rings.   ⚑

Mile 157.5 (508.5): Weigh station and 24-hour deli and gas.

Mile 158.5 (507.5): Junction with U.S. Highway 20, which heads east to Ontario. U.S. Highway 395 continues north. See **Mile 123.5** in the U.S. HIGHWAY 20 section for log of that route.   MP 134

Mile 169 (497): This is the first northbound and last of several boundaries southbound that U.S. 395 crosses of the 1,457,457-acre Malheur National Forest.   MP 56

Mile 172.5 (493.5): Idlewild Forest Service campground; 26 sites, covered picnic area.   ⚑▲ MP 53

Mile 173 (493): Devine Ridge Summit (elev. 5,340 feet).

Mile 177.5 (488.5): Malheur National Forest boundary.   MP 49

Mile 183.5 (482.5): Crossing Harney/Grant County line.

Mile 187 (479): SILVIES is a 1-building town set in a wide valley. There is a general store. The Silvies post office was founded in 1892. The Silvies River parallels the highway northbound. The beautiful Silvies Valley is high plateau open range land where at any time you could come upon a cattle drive moving slowly down the middle of the road. The 120,000-acre Ponderosa Cattle Co. and Guest Ranch is headquartered in Silvies.   MP 39

Mile 191 (475): Rock Springs Forest Service campground 6 miles east of highway.   ▲

Mile 201.5 (464.5): SENECA (pop. 290) is an unincorporated former sawmill town with a store, tavern, church, gas station and several picturesque older buildings.   MP 25

Mile 207.5 (458.5): Malheur National Forest boundary.   MP 19

Mile 209.5 (456.5): Junction with road that leads west to Izee (24 miles) and Paulina (55 miles).

Mile 210.5 (455.5): Starr Forest Service campground (elev. 5,152 feet); 14 self-service primitive campsites, picnic area.   ⚑▲ MP 16

Mile 215.5 (450.5): Primitive rest area. Along this section of highway, the views of the Strawberry Mountain Wilderness area to the east are spectacular. This rest area marks the beginning of a steep downgrade northbound to Canyon City.   MP 11

Mile 216 (450): Malheur National Forest boundary.

Mile 222.5 (443.5): CANYON CITY (pop. 665) city limits, services include gas and food. Airport west of highway. The town is so named because it sits in a narrow canyon between steep walls. It was built during the 1862 gold rush to Whiskey Flat 0.5 mile north of town toward John Day.

Joachin Miller, the self-proclaimed poet of the Sierras, spent some time in Canyon City and built a house above town. Miller, in fact, was the first judge of Grant County when it was formed in 1864. His cabin still stands, but not on the original site. It is beside Grant

An adopted Kiger Mustang at Steens Mountain Resort came from the BLM Wild Horse Corrals at Mile 145.5. (Dennis Carpenter)

Malheur National Wildlife Refuge

When Peter French came to eastern Oregon in 1872, he arrived with little more than a herd of cattle. By the time he was murdered by a rival homesteader in 1897, he had become the region's most powerful rancher, his empire covering almost 200,000 acres. Today, French's ranch is part of the 183,000-acre Malheur National Wildlife Refuge, a worthwhile side trip for U.S. Highway 395 (and U.S. Highway 20) travelers located 40 miles south of Burns, OR (**Mile 155**).

Often called "an island of life in the desert," Malheur National Wildlife Refuge includes Oregon's largest natural lake, numerous small ponds and a river. Bullrushes, flooded meadows, and uplands of sagebrush and prairie grasses are ideal habitats for nesting birds. A total of 300 species of birds and 58 mammals have been seen here.

In the early 1900s, the millinery trade decimated the swan, heron and grebe populations, and exterminated the entire egret population here for their plumes. An enraged Theodore Roosevelt made Malheur, Harney and Mud lakes a migratory bird sanctuary in 1908.

Malheur is a stopover on spring and fall migrations. In mid-February, concentrations of pintail ducks, greater sandhill cranes, great horned owls, and golden eagles congregate here. March brings lesser sandhill cranes, whistling swans, snow geese and Canada geese.

May and August are prime months for viewing songbirds. Newborn waterfowl are common throughout the summer.

September and October see the return of greater sandhill cranes, Canada geese, mallards, warblers, whistling swans and hawks. From mid-Nov. through Jan., trumpeter swans, ducks, geese and bald eagles have the refuge to themselves.

Touring should begin at the refuge office and visitor center, where you can get the latest information on viewing hotspots. To reach the center

from Burns, take Highway 78 east 2 miles then Oregon Highway 205 south 25 miles. At the marked county road, travel east 9 miles to the visitor center (these are all paved roads). The

Peter French's long barn and willow stockade. (Dennis Carpenter)

visitor center includes a museum with 200 species of birds beautifully mounted. Museum hours are sunrise to sunset daily. Refuge office hours are 7 a.m. to 3:30 p.m. weekdays. The visitor center has maps for a self-guided auto tour.

For best photo opportunities, stay in your car or hike along the tops of some of the 200 miles of man-made dikes. So many people tour Malheur by automobile that birds are not afraid of cars.

Allowing ample time will give you the opportunity to enjoy the area's other highlights. Near the visitor center a self-guided tour of Diamond Craters will give you the opportunity to view a diverse array of volcanic formations, craters and lava flows. While you are still at the north end of the refuge, Peter French's unusual round barn which was built in the 1880s is another "must." It was constructed from local rocks and native juniper trees and is an architectural wonder. When you reach the south end of the refuge you will have the opportunity to view another of the last remaining remnants of the Peter French Cattle Dynasty, the P Ranch.

All that remains is a long barn and the chimney of the ranch house that burned to the ground many years ago.

There are no services

within the refuge, but the uniqueness of many of the nearby facilities almost requires that you stay over at least 1 night. The south end of the refuge is also known as the "Gateway to the

Oregon Outback," with access to the spectacular 52-mile gravel Steens Mountain Loop (usually snow-free and open July through Oct.). There are 3 BLM campgrounds on the Loop. The Steens Mountain Resort, located at the southern end of the refuge, has a complete RV park, rentals, horse stalls and guided tours of the area.

Also at the south end of the refuge, Oregon State Parks operates the Historic Frenchglen Hotel, built in 1914. Originally known as P Station and part of the P Ranch of the French's cattle empire, when the hotel was built, the town was renamed for Peter French and his father-in-law Dr. Hugh Glenn who financed French's move to the Malheur region in the mid-1800s. Open from March through Nov., the Frenchglen Hotel offers lodging, and their family-style ranch house dinner is so popular, reservations are a must. To the northeast is the old Western town of Diamond. The Diamond Hotel, built in 1898, is again open to serve the modern traveler. (The Diamond Hotel is just south of the Diamond Craters, the round barn and the refuge visitor center.)

For more information contact: Malheur National Wildlife Refuge, HC-72, Box 245, Princeton, OR 97721, phone (503) 493-2612; National Back Country Byway, BLM, Burns District Office, HC-74, 12533 Hwy. 20 W., Hines, OR 97783, phone (503) 573-5241; State Historical Waysides, Frenchglen Hotel, Frenchglen, OR 97736, phone (503) 493-2825; Steens Mountain Resort, Steens Mountain Loop Road, Frenchglen, OR 97736, phone (503) 493-2415.

A total of 300 species of birds have been seen at Malheur National Wildlife Refuge. (© John Barger)

County Historical Museum on the highway in the center of town. The museum is open daily from June 1 to Sept. 30.

OxBow Trade Co., a large wooden building at the south edge of town, has a collection of horse-drawn vehicles and many other "buggy-era items." Open most days; phone (503) 575-2911.

Mile 224.5 (441.5): Grant County Oliver Historical Museum. Joachin Miller's cabin stands beside the museum.

Mile 226.5 (439.5): JOHN DAY (pop. 2,075) has all services, including a hospital and the area's first drive-through espresso establishment, on the corner of U.S. Highway 395 and SE 1st. The Malheur National Forest office is in the middle of town. John Day was named for a member of John Jacob Astor's overland expedition to Astoria in 1811. For reasons not completely clear, his name has been left all over the region—on the town, 2 rivers, more recently a dam, and one of the most interesting national monuments in the Northwest.

Of special interest is the Kam Wah Chung & Co. museum in the city park. It pays tribute to the Chinese laborers who were brought to the area during the gold rush of 1862–64. The central portion of the building went up in 1867, and it was alternately a herb doctor's office, an assay office, a store and a social club. There is a 20-minute narrated tour. Open May to Oct. For information, phone (503) 575-0028. Admission fee.

From John Day, Highway 395 shares a common alignment with U.S. Highway 26 for about 10 miles west along the John Day River to Mount Vernon. U.S. Highway 26 continues west 30 miles to the Sheep Rock Unit of John Day Fossil Beds National Monument (see MAJOR ATTRACTIONS section). ★

Mile 229 (437): Mountain View Country Club and Golf Course.   MP 160

Mile 234 (432): Clyde Holliday State Park and John Day River. Holliday Park has 30 sites with electrical hookups, tent sites, dump station, $15 camping fee, hiker/biker sites $4.   ▲ MP 155

Mile 235 (431): MOUNT VERNON (pop. 560), a small town at the junction with U.S. Highway 26, set in a pretty valley beside the John Day River. Limited services. From Mount Vernon north, the highway begins climbing through pine forests.   MP 120

Mile 245 (421): Malheur National Forest boundary.

Mile 251 (415): Malheur National Forest boundary.

Mile 252.5 (413.5): Beach Creek Summit (elev. 4,687 feet) is at the top of a long, winding climb through timber. The summit has some abandoned buildings in the rocky clearing.

Mile 256.5 (409.5): FOX (unincorporated) is a small, picturesque town on the high

The Cant Ranch House serves as a visitor center for John Day Fossil Beds National Monument. It is located in the Sheep Rock Unit west of John Day. (Dennis Carpenter)

plains with a post office, houses and trailers, but no services. From the hill north of town it looks almost like a Western movie set. Fox Creek flows through and feeds into the John Day River.

Mile 259.5 (406.5): Long Creek Summit (elev. 5,101 feet) offers great views as you descend northbound.

Mile 260.5 (405.5): Malheur National Forest boundary.

Mile 261 (405): A primitive rest area on a sharp curve on the east side of the highway.

Mile 263.5 (402.5): LONG CREEK (pop. 255) was named for the creek that flows through it. At one time locals believed the creek was the longest in the state, but the claim has been modified to the longest in the general area. The town has all traveler services.

Mile 273.5 (392.5): Begin steep 4-mile downgrade northbound.   MP 81

Mile 277 (389): Middle Fork John Day River. Access road to Ritter Hot Springs, 10 miles west of highway; current status unknown.

Mile 283.5 (382.5): Meadow Brook Summit (elev. 4,127 feet) and Umatilla National Forest boundary. Store, gas and RV park. ▲

Mile 290 (376): DALE (unincorporated). A small logging town with service station, cafe, laundromat, etc.   MP 66

Mile 291.5 (374.5): Junction with road east to Olive Lake (29 miles). Camping is available 1 mile from this junction along a gravel road at Tollbridge Campground; primitive, 14-day limit, on the North Fork John Day River. ▲

Mile 293 (373): 45th parallel line marker, which is the halfway point between the equator and the Arctic Circle. This region is the Bridge Creek Wildlife Game Wintering Area.

Mile 304.5 (361.5): Ukiah Dale Forest Wayside on Camas Creek with primitive camping; fee charged.   ▲ MP 51

Mile 306 (360): Junction with Oregon Highway 244, which goes east to La Grande. **UKIAH** (unincorporated; pop. 250), named after the town in California, is a short distance east on Highway 244. It has the Umatilla National Forest North Fork John Day ranger station, gas, store and showers.

Lehman Hot Springs is 16 miles east of Ukiah on Highway 244. Discovered in 1871, it is one of the Northwest's largest hot springs pools. You can enjoy the hot therapeutic mineral water while relaxing in the beautiful Blue Mountains. There is hiking, fishing in nearby streams, RV parking, primitive campsites and overnight accommodations. This facility is open year-round. Call ahead for specific times and more information: (503) 427-3015.   ♨ ⊷◂▲ MP 50

Mile 313.5 (352.5): Junction with road east to Albee (6 miles).   MP 42

Mile 315.5 (350.5): Summit of Battle Mountain (elev. 4,270 feet). The name commemorates a battle in 1878 between whites and Indians that is said to be the last such fight in the region. It occurred when Gen. O.O. Howard out of Fort Vancouver defeated Chief Egan and his Paiute band by chasing them down the Malheur River and out of Oregon.

Mile 316.5 (349.5): Battle Mountain State Park, day use only. The park has one of the grandest views of the region with the towns, farms and ranches laid out below almost as though you are in a small plane.

Mile 331.5 (334.5): Junction with Oregon Highway 74 west to Heppner (37 miles) and Condon (81 miles).

Mile 339 (327): PILOT ROCK (pop. 1,605) is a sawmill and agricultural town. The town has all services and a nice city park. Pilot Rock was named for a basalt butte above town.   MP 16

Mile 346 (320): Pendleton golf and country club.

Mile 349 (317): McKay Creek Reservoir and McKay National Wildlife Refuge, established in 1927. Bird sightings here include bald eagles, great blue and black crowned night herons, long-billed curlews and American avocets. Waterfowl and game bird hunting in season. A near-record bass was caught in the reservoir along with Oregon's record catfish, which weighed 36 1/2 lbs. Perch also thrive here. Two boat ramps. Closed from the first Monday after waterfowl season until March 1.

Mile 353 (313): PENDLETON (pop. 15,100) has all services, including 13 motels and about 40 restaurants and 5 RV parks. Perhaps Pendleton's biggest claim to fame is the Pendleton Round-Up, the major Professional Rodeo Cowboy Assoc. (PRCA) sanctioned rodeo held the second full week of September. Motels and campgrounds fill to capacity as thousands of visitors converge on the seat of Umatilla County for this 4-day event. Contact the Pendleton Chamber of Commerce, 25 SE Dorion St., Pendleton, OR 97801, phone (503) 276-7411 or 1-800-547-8911, for more information.

Another hallmark for the city of Pendleton is the Pendleton Woolen Mills (Exit 210), one of the most renowned woolen mills in the nation. Guided tours are available weekdays; phone (503) 276-6911. The Pendleton Woolen Mills began using Northwest wool in Pendleton in 1909. Since that time, the company has expanded and its headquarters are now located in Portland. Wool blankets are still produced here.

Pendleton has a self-guided walking tour of its compact historic area. The tour starts at the Umatilla County Historical Society Museum, 108 SW Frazer Ave. There's also a tour of Pendleton's historical underground tunnels; phone (503) 276-0730 for details.
▲ MP 3

Mile 354 (312): Junction with Interstate 84 in Pendleton. U.S. Highway 395 shares a common alignment with Interstate 84 west for the next 20 miles. Turn to **Mile 205.5** in the INTERSTATE 84 section.

Mile 355.5 (310.5): Exit to airport, west Pendleton and Blue Mountain Community College.   MP 208 EXIT 207

Mile 358.5 (307.5): Sign warns of blowing dust for the next 40 miles westbound.

Mile 359.5 (306.5): Exit to Stage Gulch and Barnhart Road. Cafe, motel, truck stop and gas at exit.   MP 203 EXIT 202

Mile 363.5 (302.5): Exit to Yoakum Road.   MP 200 EXIT 199

Mile 364.5 (301.5): Exit to Lorenzen Road and McClintock Road.   MP 198 EXIT 198

Mile 370 (296): Exit to Echo Road and Lexington. Original trail ruts can be seen at Echo, 2 miles south of the highway, along with many buildings erected prior to 1915. The Echo Museum is on the National Register of Historic Places and contains pioneer and Indian artifacts.   MP 194 EXIT 193

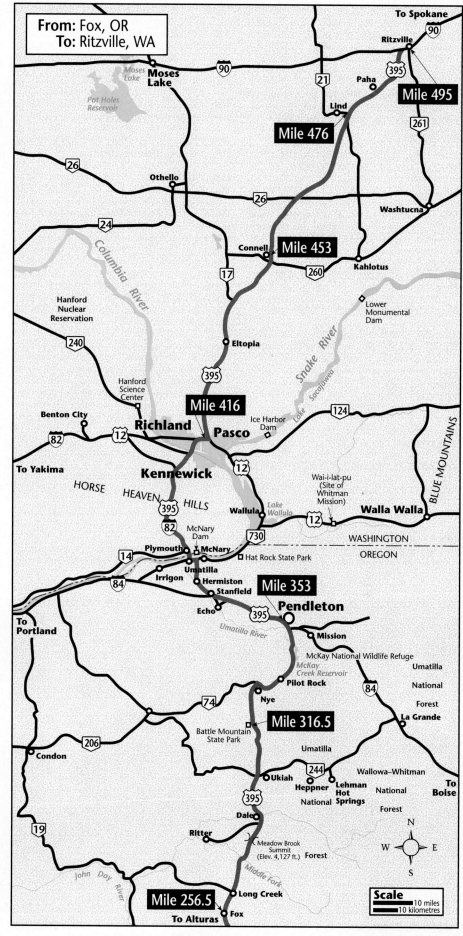

Mile 375 (291): Exit here for continuation of U.S. 395 north to Stanfield and Hermiston; all services and RV park. Interstate 84 continues west. Turn to **Mile 185** in the INTERSTATE 84 section for log of that route.
▲ EXIT 188

Mile 376 (290): STANFIELD (pop. 1,620) is a farming town with grain elevators, seasonal fruit stands and most visitor services.
MP 189

Mile 379.5 (286.5): HERMISTON (pop. 10,000) is one of the major towns in agricultural Umatilla County. The area is noted for pioneer "wind farms," where windmills have been tested for electrical power generation, and the nearby Army depot where chemicals have been stored in concrete bunkers. Hermiston has 5 motels and numerous restaurants.

Mile 380.5 (285.5): Hermiston municipal airport.

Mile 381.5 (284.5): Oregon visitor center.

Mile 384 (282): Doll and Toy Museum on U.S. 395 at 1315 N. 1st, Hermiston. Housed in a railroad car, this museum documents dolls and toys from the 1850s to the 1980s. Included is the first ever patented doll in America (1853). Open May to Oct., 10 a.m. to noon and 1–5 p.m. Admission fee.

Mile 386 (280): Power City Wildlife Management Area.

Mile 387 (279): Power City.

Mile 388 (278): Junction with U.S. Highway 730 west to Umatilla, and east 7 miles to Hat Rock State Park, a day-use area on Lake Wallula, the backwaters of the Columbia River formed by McNary Dam. Also at the junction is the entrance for the Oregon visitor center to the McNary Dam. From this center visitors have access to the Oregon fish-viewing windows and the powerhouse. The Pacific Salmon Visitors Information Center is also located at the Oregon visitor center. Another feature is Spillway Park with complete day-use facilities. Free, open daily April to Sept., 8 a.m. to 5 p.m.

Mile 388.5 (277.5): U.S. 395 merges with Interstate 82 north to Yakima and Kennewick.

Mile 389 (277): The Columbia River, Oregon–Washington state line.

Mile 390 (276): Exit 131 **junction** with Washington Highway 14 west to Plymouth and Vancouver. Easy access east to McNary Dam. The dam is named for Sen. Charles L. McNary of Oregon, who spearheaded efforts to construct it. Construction began in 1947 and was completed in 1953. Visitor facilities include a 300-acre wildlife park with a wildlife interpretive trail and displays, fish-viewing windows, navigational locks and powerhouse galleries. Open daily, April to Sept., 8 a.m. to 5 p.m. Guided tours for groups and organizations by prior arrangement. Free.

Washington Highway 14 is a good 2-lane road, almost empty of traffic, which leads west from Plymouth 180 miles to junction with Interstate 5 at Vancouver. Columbia Crest Winery, the largest winery in Washington, is located 14 miles west in Paterson.

U.S. 395 shares a common alignment with Interstate 82 north through the Horse Heaven Hills.
EXIT 131

Mile 391 (275): Weigh station. MP 131

Mile 399 (267): Exit to Coffin Road.
MP 123 EXIT 122

Mile 407.5 (258.5): Exit to Locust Grove Road.
MP 115 EXIT 114

Mile 409.5 (256.5): Exit here for continuation of U.S. 395 north, Kennewick and Pasco.

24-hour restaurant and gas stations at exit. Kennewick, Pasco and Richland make up the Tri-Cities area. With a regional population of approximately 150,000 people, this is Washington's fourth largest metropolitan area.

The region's development came in 3 stages. In 1880, the Northern Pacific Railroad reached Pasco, which became an important railway maintenance and division point. In 1892, the Northern Pacific Irrigation Co. plotted the Kennewick townsite and later imported settlers from the Midwest. In 1942, the completion of Grand Coulee Dam greatly expanded the agricultural potential of the area. Grand Coulee's vast supplies of hydroelectric power and cold water also led to the building of Hanford Atomic Energy Plant and the booming of Richland.

Long growing seasons and fertile soil return more than $300 million annually from crops of apples, asparagus, alfalfa, hay, dry beans, wheat, corn, cherries, onions, potatoes and a variety of seed crops. Climate and land have also made the Tri-Cities the heartland of Washington's wine country. More than 30 wineries are situated within a 50-mile radius of the Tri-Cities. EXIT 113

Mile 410.5 (255.5): KENNEWICK (pop. 37,180) is derived from an Indian word meaning "winter paradise." Its sunny climate and proximity to the Columbia and Snake rivers make it the departure point for a variety of water-based activities. Oasis Waterworks, at 6321 W. Canal, has a 5,000-square-foot swimming pool and 11 water slides; open mid-May through Labor Day.

RICHLAND (pop. 34,385), 10 miles north via Highway 240 West, was an irrigation boomtown until 1943, when it became "Atomic City" with the building of Hanford, the first plant to produce plutonium for the world's first nuclear weapons. Hanford plutonium was used in the world's first nuclear detonation at Alamogordo, NM. Of interest here is the Hanford Science Center next to the Federal Bldg. at 825 Jadwin, which features displays on Hanford programs, a public document room and hands-on exhibits. Films on energy are shown on request. Free, open Monday through Friday, 8 a.m. to 5 p.m., and Saturday, 9 a.m. to 5 p.m. Phone (509) 376-6374.

Plant 2 visitor center is 10 miles north at 3000 George Washington Way. It offers video tour, interactive exhibits and informational displays that show the working of a nuclear power plant and the process of splitting the atom. Open Thursday through Friday, 11 a.m. to 4 p.m., and Saturday and Sunday, noon to 5 p.m. Phone (509) 372-5860.

The Fast Flux Test Facility (FFTX), 11 miles north of Richland, is a sodium-cooled 400-megawatt thermal reactor that tests fuels and materials for fast breeder reactors. A visitor center overlooking the facility has models and audiovisual presentations explaining the process. Free, open Thursday and Friday, 11 a.m. to 4 p.m., and Saturday and Sunday, noon to 5 p.m. Phone (509) 376-6374.

Mile 415.5 (250.5): Highway 395 crosses the Columbia River via the Blue Bridge, dedicated in the early 1980s by then Governor Dixie Lee Ray. To the

Hat Rock at Hat Rock State Park, a day-use area on Lake Wallula, 7 miles east from Mile 388. (L. Linkhart)

east is the Intercity Bridge, one of America's longest cable-stayed bridges with a continuous concrete girder of 1,794 feet.

Mile 416 (250): PASCO (pop. 20,840) is the Franklin County seat. The wine industry is important to Pasco's economy, and each year in November the Northwest Wine Festival officially celebrates the grape. The city was named by a railroad surveyor because heat, rust and sandstorms reminded him of the Peruvian city of Cerro de Pasco. Major employers include Burlington Northern, Green Giant and Universal Frozen Foods.

Sacajawea State Park, 2 miles southeast of Pasco on U.S. Highway 12, was an important Indian meeting place. An artifacts room features a large collection of Indian implements found along the riverbanks. Exhibits emphasize the role of Sacajawea in the Lewis and Clark expedition, which camped here on October 1805. Boat launch, mooring buoys, docks, picnic tables and stoves.

Mile 419.5 (246.5): Exit here for U.S. 395 north to Ritzville and Spokane.   EXIT 14

Mile 421.5 (244.5): Quarry Lake Vintners, 2520 Commercial Ave., has been a Washington winemaker for 2 decades. Wines made from grapes grown here have received top honors. Tours by appointment only; phone (509) 547-7307.

Mile 425.5 (240.5): Turnoff to east for Preston Wine Cellars, cafe at junction. Washington's largest family-operated winery. Tasting room and self-guided tours available daily 10 a.m. to 5:30 p.m.   MP 27

Mile 430.5 (235.5): Weigh station.

Mile 435 (231): ELTOPIA. A grain elevator beside the railroad track.

Mile 444 (222): **Junction** with Washington Highway 17, which leads north to Mesa and Moses Lake (45 miles). This agricultural area was created by the Columbia Basin irrigation project. It is mostly wheat-farming country.   MP 46

Mile 453 (213): CONNELL (pop. 2,375) is an agricultural center serving both the Columbia Basin irrigation farms, and those still farming without irrigation (dryland farming). Connell has all services and a restaurant near the highway that serves enormous country breakfasts. It is also the **junction** with Washington Highway 260, which leads east to Washtucna.   MP 55

Mile 458 (208): The Milepost 60 cafe; deli/mart and truck stop with gas.   MP 60

Mile 464 (202): **Junction** with Washington Highway 26, which runs from Vantage across the wheat country to Colfax. This is the favorite route for students and families between the coast and Washington State University in Pullman. There is a modern rest area at this intersection.   MP 67

Mile 476 (190): Exit to LIND, a farming town about 4 miles to the west. A welcoming sign invites: "Drop in. Mount St. Helens did," a reference to the load of ash the southwestern Washington volcano dropped on this area during the eruption in 1980,

which for some reason was worse here than anywhere else. Grayish traces of the ash fall can still be seen beside the road and on barren, uncultivated hillsides.

Mile 479.5 (186.5): **Junction** with Highway 21 south to Kahlotus.   MP 82

Mile 480.5 (185.5): **Junction** with Highway 21 to Lind. All traveler services.   MP 83

Mile 481 (185): PAHA, another town that appears on most maps but is only a grain elevator.

Mile 494 (172): **Junction** with Interstate 90 at Ritzville; all services at the intersection and a hospital off the exit. I-90 and U.S. 395 share a common alignment east to Spokane. Travelers headed west on I-90 turn to **Mile 217** in the INTERSTATE 90 section. Tune your radio to 530 AM for visitor and road information.

Mile 495 (171): Exit to Washington Highway 261 to Washtucna (27 miles) and RITZVILLE (pop. 1,845); 2 restaurants, 2 motels and an RV park. Ritzville dates to 1878, when Philip Ritz staked the first claim near here. He secured a subcontract from the Northern Pacific Railroad, the town was platted, and by 1882 it numbered about 150 people. Wheat was planted in 1879, but played a secondary role to cattle ranching until bumper crops in 1897 and 1898 established the dominance that continues today. Ritzville's Carnegie Library was 1 of 33 funded by the Carnegie Institute in Washington State. It is thought to be the third-oldest Carnegie building still used as a

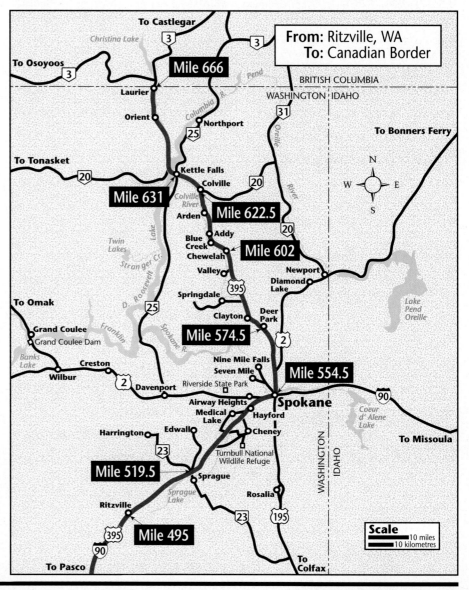

From: Ritzville, WA
To: Canadian Border

library in the state. ▲ EXIT 221

Mile 499.5 (166.5): Exit to Coker Road.
EXIT 226

Mile 504.5 (161.5): Exit to Tokie weigh station, food and lodging. EXIT 231

Mile 513 (153): RV campground on a lake with all services. ▲ MP 239

Mile 516 (150): Rest area on bluff overlooking Sprague Lake. The 6-mile-long lake is a popular fishing hole that yields trout, crappie and bass. Following a 1985 poisoning to remove trash fish, the 1,800-acre lake was restocked with rainbow, brown trout, walleye, smallmouth and largemouth bass.
← MP 241

Mile 519.5 (146.5): Exit north for Washington Highways 23 and 231, exit south for **SPRAGUE** (pop. 462), named for General John W. Sprague, director of the Northern Pacific Railway. This exit has all services.

Sprague is situated in basalt "seablands," which are unique to the area. The geological phenomenon was created by flood waters from Lake Missoula leaving a landscape of canyons, deep ravines, towering mesas and rock formations. ▲ MP 245 EXIT 245

Mile 528 (138): Exit to Fishtrap. Camping available. ▲ MP 253 EXIT 254

Mile 532 (134): Exit to Tyler and east 10 miles via Washington Highway 904 to **CHENEY** (pop. 7,700), home of Eastern Washington University. Cheney has a motel and RV park. Its agricultural-based economy produces multimillion-dollar annual wheat crops. Peas, oats, barley, beef and dairy products are also marketed. Trout and bass fishing are enjoyed on "50 lakes within 50 miles." Cheney has all services.

Turnbull National Wildlife Refuge, southwest of Cheney, is a stopover for migrating ducks and geese. As many as 50,000 can be seen during fall. Redheads, diving ducks and Canadian geese nest here. Open daily, dawn to dusk; $2 per vehicle. Phone (509) 235-4723.
▲ EXIT 257

Mile 538.5 (127.5): Exit south to Cheney and north to **MEDICAL LAKE** (pop. 3,705). Camping available. The salty waters of the lake were thought to have medicinal value, hence the name of the town. It was once a lively resort with trains bringing vacationers from Spokane to dance halls and shoreline camps. ▲ MP 264 EXIT 264

Mile 543.5 (122.5): Exit south to Four Lakes and Washington Highway 904 to Cheney; 6 miles for food mart, gas, camping and motels. Four Lakes was the site of the Battle of Four Lakes, fought Sept. 1, 1858, by 700 U.S. Army troops and 5,000 Indians. ▲ MP 270 EXIT 270

Mile 547 (119): Exit north for Washington Highway 902 to Medical Lake. RV camping and motels. ▲ MP 272 EXIT 272

Mile 550.5 (115.5): Exit to Interstate 90 business loop, Spokane and Geiger Field; state patrol, food, gas, diesel and RV park. Access to Spokane's first winery, Worden's Washington Winery. The tasting room and gift shop are open daily, noon to 5 p.m.
▲ MP 276 EXIT 276

Mile 551.5 (114.5): Exit 277A under contruction to Garden Springs and Spokane Falls Community College; motels.

Mile 552 (114): Exit 277B to **junction** with U.S. Highway 2 west, Spokane Airport and Fairchild Air Force Base. MP 278

Mile 552.5 (113.5): Spokane city limits.

Mile 553 (113): Exit to U.S. Highway 195 South to Colfax and Pullman.
MP 279 EXIT 279

Mile 553.5 (112.5): Exit to Maple Toll Bridge, Lincoln Street and **SPOKANE** city center. (See Spokane in the MAJOR CITIES section.) MP 280 EXIT 280

Mile 554.5 (111.5): Exit here for continuation of U.S. 395 north, which shares a common alignment with U.S. Highway 2 through Spokane, where they become Division Street. Interstate 90 continues east into Idaho and Montana. This is also the exit to Whitworth College, Gonzaga University, Riverside Park, the Museum of Native American Cultures and city center. All services plus a hospital. Visitor information center, left off Division Street onto Sprague.
MP 281 EXIT 281

Mile 555.5 (110.5): Crossing the Spokane River. View of Riverside Park, built for the 1974 World's Fair. The park includes a carousel, spacious lawns, an IMAX theater, an opera house and railroad station clock tower. Restaurants, fast food and restrooms.

Mile 556 (110): Access east to Gonzaga University. Gonzaga's library was a gift from its 1924 alumnus, Bing Crosby. The Crosby-ana Room contains his Oscar for "Going My Way."

Mile 558 (108): **Junction** with Washington Highway 291 to Nine Mile Falls; access to Riverside State Park on the Spokane River. Spokane House Interpretive Center at the park has exhibits on the fur-trading post established here in 1810. Hiking trails at the park lead to Deep Creek Canyon's fossil beds, Indian rock paintings, and to volcanic outcroppings that form the "bowl and pitcher" on the river. The park also offers equestrian trails, horse rentals, a 600-acre ORV area, 100 campsites, fishing, boat launch and beach access. ⚹←▲

Mile 559 (107): **Junction** of U.S. 395 with U.S. 2, which continues northeast to Idaho. Turn to **Mile 126.5** in the U.S. HIGHWAY 2 section for log of that route.

Mile 560.5 (105.5): Access west to Whitworth College. Rated among the West's best small universities, Whitworth has approximately 2,000 students.

Mile 561.5 (104.5): Pine Acres golf course.

Mile 562.5 (103.5): Wandermeer public golf course, lounge and restaurant.

Mile 563 (103): Little Spokane River.

Mile 570 (96): Dragoon Creek Campground, west of the highway; 22 campsites, 5 picnic sites, water and restrooms. ⚹▲

Mile 574.5 (91.5): **DEER PARK** (pop. 2,445)

is 0.5 mile east of the highway. The Great Northern Railroad constructed a branch line from Spokane to this area in 1884. Large deposits of clay, kaolin and mineral pigment were found near the town, and eventually lumber companies and settlers cut the timber back to the mountains. Deer Park's annual winter festival features a frostbite fun run, snowshoe volleyball and baseball. All services, fairgrounds, hospital and community airport. MP 179

Mile 575.5 (90.5): Airport east of highway.

Mile 579.5 (86.5): **CLAYTON**, 0.5 mile west of highway, was established in 1889 and named for nearby deposits of clay. Gas and food service. Many of Spokane's buildings were made of brick from the Clayton area, as were ceramics, terra cotta, fire brick and flower pots.

Mile 584 (82): One-mile-long Loon Lake attracts fishermen, boaters and sailboarders.←

Mile 585.5 (80.5): Access to **LOON LAKE** and west 6 miles to Springdale via Washington Highway 292. Facilities at Loon Lake include a marina, resort, public campgrounds, picnic areas, hiking trails, store, restaurants and boat rentals. ⚹⚹←▲ MP 190

Mile 588 (78): Deer Lake, 4 miles east, is a favorite summer fishing and swimming spot and autumn duck and deer hunting area. Mackinaw trout reach 30 lbs. Resort, campgrounds, restaurant, boat rentals, boat ramp and picnic areas at Deer Lake. ⚹←▲

Mile 593 (73): Jump Off Joe Lake, west of highway, is a resort area with RV campgrounds, showers, boat launch and rentals.
▲ MP 198

Mile 593.5 (72.5): **VALLEY** (unincorporated) at the **junction** with Washington Highway 232 West to Waitts Lake Recreation Area. Waitts attracts water-skiers and has a beach for swimming and sunbathing. Washington's largest rainbow trout was caught here. Excellent fishing for brook, brown and cutthroat trout, largemouth bass and yellow perch. Resort with 6 cabins and 55 RV spaces, also public campgrounds, store, marina and boat rentals at lake. ←▲

Mile 597.5 (68.5): Access to Valley and Washington Highway 231 south 8 miles to Springdale. A 1908 fire virtually destroyed Springdale, which is a mix of false-front buildings, vintage frame and newer brick structures. MP 202

Mile 602 (64): **CHEWELAH** (pop. 2,212) appears little changed from 40 years ago when it was a large manufacturer of Thermax Board. Stone used in terrazzo, cement and stucco was also quarried here. Today, Northwest Alloys, Inc., which produces magnesium products, is the largest employer. Other resources include wood products, marble and silica sand.

Chewelah was a Hudson's Bay trading site and a military post in the 1860s. The local museum preserves more than a century of relics.

All visitor services available, including 2 motels and a private campground. The Chewelah area is popular with deer hunters. In town, the community golf course is one of northeastern Washington's most scenic and challenging courses. There is an airport adjacent to the golf course.

Chewelah also hosts an annual Chataqua outdoor summer arts festival.

Chewelah Mountain is the location of 49 Degrees North, a nationally ranked ski resort that caters to families. Situated 9 miles east of town, it offers day and night skiing from mid-Nov. to mid-April, a day lodge, restaurant and rentals.　⚐▲

Mile 607 (59): BLUE CREEK was once a logging and mining area and a shipping point for farm products, copper and dolomite.

Mile 608.5 (57.5): ADDY is a small farming community, just west of the highway. Services on U.S. 395 include the Old Schoolhouse Trading Post and Emporium.　MP 216

Mile 615.5 (50.5): ARDEN. A scattering of homes and small businesses stretch along 2 to 3 miles of U.S. 395. RV park, gas and food.　▲ MP 228

Mile 622.5 (43.5): COLVILLE (pop. 4,360) is the Stevens County seat and its largest town. Its primary industries are agriculture, manufacturing, timber and tourism. All services available, including an RV park, hospital, county fairgrounds and the Colville National Forest ranger station.

David Thompson of the Northwest Fur Co. explored the area in 1911. Within a year, 11,000 lbs. of furs were shipped from here, and by 1840 the number grew to 18,000 annually.

In 1859, Fort Colville was built. Four companies of U.S. Infantry were stationed here. When the fort was abandoned in 1882, the town was founded. During the 1890s gold rush, Colville became a wide-open frontier town with more than its share of brawling, robberies and murders.

U.S. 395 forms Colville's main street. Other streets are unusually wide, and were originally designed to allow 16-horse teams to turn around wagons loaded with logs.

Recreation in the Colville area includes camping, horseback riding, swimming, boating and hunting the state's largest population of white-tailed deer. The local fish hatchery, which produces trout, is open for tours.　▲

Mile 623 (43): Junction with Washington Highway 20 east. From Colville to the Columbia River, U.S. 395 and Highway 20 share a common alignment. Access to Keller House and Stevens County Historical Society Museum. Situated at Keller Historical Park, 700 N. Wynne, museum exhibits cover Indians, guns, the Hudson's Bay Co., prominent pioneers and founding fathers. Free; open Monday through Saturday, 10 a.m. to 4 p.m., and Sunday, 1–4 p.m., June through Sept.; daily, 1–4 p.m., in May.

Keller House is an example of early 20th century architecture and the Craftsmen Movement in interior design. Open 1–4 p.m., Wednesday through Saturday.

Mile 624.5 (41.5): Williams Lake Drive leads

Kettle Falls Bridge crosses the Columbia River at upper Lake Roosevelt. (L. Linkhart)

north 16 miles to Williams Lake campground; 8 campsites, 2 picnic sites and drinking water.　⛺▲

Mile 631 (35): KETTLE FALLS (pop. 1,382). Prior to 1941, Kettle Falls was situated 4 miles west on the banks of the Columbia River and was called Meyers Falls. Meyers Falls was the site where the first patented flour was milled in the United States. With the building of Grand Coulee Dam, Kettle Falls was one of several towns that were submerged by the backwaters or moved.

French trappers called the area Los Chaudieres, meaning "The Kettles," when they saw water churning in holes ground in rock along the Columbia's shores. The original town and the falls lie buried under the waters of Lake Roosevelt. During spring drawdown, the streets and remains of the original town are above water and can be visited.

The falls were an important meeting, trading and fishing spot for Indians. It was settled in 1826 when Fort Colville was built by the Hudson's Bay Co.

Logging, wood products, farming orchards and tourism are major industries. All visitor services are available, including motels and campgrounds.　▲

Mile 632 (34): Junction with Washington Highway 25 south to Davenport and north to Northport.

Mile 634 (32): Kettle Falls Campground; 89 campsites, picnic areas, swimming beach, amphitheater programs, drinking water, boat dock, ramp and fuel.

East of the highway is St. Paul's Mission. It was built in 1845 by Father Anthony Raville and was made of hand-hewn logs and wooden pegs. In 1951, it was restored and given to Washington state as a memorial park. Interpretive center details the importance of the falls as an Indian meeting place.　⛩▲

Mile 634.5 (31.5): Kettle Falls Bridge over the Columbia River. Backed up by Grand Coulee Dam, the Columbia forms 150-mile-long Lake Roosevelt. The Coulee Dam National Recreation Area includes approximately 75 percent of the reservoir and shoreline. The remaining area is part of the Colville and Spokane Indian reservations.

Mile 636 (30): Northbound, U.S. 395 and Highway 20 common alignment ends. Highway 20 continues west to Tonasket and Whidbey Island. Continue north on U.S. 395.

Mile 640 (26): East of highway is Kamloops Island, Coulee Dam National Recreation Area Campground; 14 campsites, picnic area, boat dock and water.　⛩▲ MP 245

Mile 641.5 (24.5): Private RV park with laundromat, showers and full hookups.　▲

Mile 643 (23): Kettle River Coulee Dam National Recreation Area campground; 20 sites, boat dock, picnic area and water.　⛩▲ MP 248

Mile 648 (18): Kerry Hill Lake.

Mile 652 (14): Begin 1 mile of sharp switchbacks northbound.　MP 257

Mile 655 (11): ORIENT started as a mining camp in 1902 and was originally called Morgan. It was renamed for a local mine, and when the price of gold increased in 1935 it enjoyed a second boom. A medical clinic, gas station, store, restaurant, laundry with showers and bed and breakfast are located here.

To reach Pierre Lake Forest Service campground, drive through Orient over the new bridge and up into the Colville National Forest to Pierre Lake Road. The campground has 15 campsites, 10 picnic sites, water, fishing, boating and hiking.　🎣⛩⛵▲

Mile 665.5 (0.5): LAURIER is largely a residential and service community for customs personnel. During the 1890s gold rush, it was a stopping point for wagon and pack trains. At its peak, it had a population of more than 2,000 people.

Mile 666 (0): U.S.–Canada border. Turn to **Mile 288** in the CROWSNEST HIGHWAY 3 section.

CHILCOTIN HIGHWAY

BC Highway 20
Williams Lake to Bella Coola, BC
(See map, opposite page)

BC Highway 20, known as the Chilcotin Highway, is one of only 3 roads that reach the British Columbia coast. The road west to the coastal settlement of Bella Coola from the town of Williams Lake, on BC Highway 97 (Gold Rush Trail), is a long and lonely road, one that used to be a test of endurance because nearly all of its 282 miles/454 km was rough gravel—in summer a maelstrom of choking dust, with potholes as big as your car.

But the bad times on Highway 20 are all gone—or nearly so. Today more than half is paved, 3 separate sections of pavement with well-maintained gravel sections between. There are just enough settlements so that gas, supplies and even accommodations en route are in good supply. However, if you make the drive through on a Sunday, don't depend on the smaller settlements for gas. Several service stations (and general stores) are open on weekdays only. The scenery is superb, from the grasslands and forests of the rolling Chilcotin country, through the mountain wilderness of Tweedsmuir Provincial Park to the rain forests and pastoral valleys of the coast.

But there is still "The Hill," a nerve-wracking switchback descent from the top of Heckman Pass (elev. 5,000 feet/1,524m) down to the forests of the Bella Coola Valley at just above sea level. This enormous drop is engineered in just 12 miles/19 km of narrow, mostly 1-way track, much of it at 18 percent grade. This section of the route is not for timid drivers, and autos should be in good repair, particularly brakes. Trailers and large RVs will have difficulty negotiating some of the hairpin bends.

The drive down the big hill will be exhilarating to say the least—and remember, since Bella Coola is a dead end with no ferry connections out, after your stay you will have to drive up it. Engines can quickly overheat on the steep grades. The locals know the highway as Freedom Road, as it is their only road connection with the rest of the world, and in fact they built it themselves. In 1950, tired of waiting for government promises, volunteers from both sides of the mountain barrier bulldozed their way through in 3 years.

Chilcotin Highway Log

Distance in miles from Williams Lake is followed by distance in miles from Bella Coola. Equivalent distances in kilometres are indicated by Km.

Mile 0 (282) Km 0 (454): **Junction** of Highways 20 and 97 at Williams Lake (see description of Williams Lake at **Mile 360** in the CANADA HIGHWAY 97 section).

Mile 1.5 (280.5) Km 2.5 (451.5): Road south to Alkali Lake, Dog Creek and south via old Goldrush River Trail to Pavilion and Lillooet.

Westbound, Highway 20 climbs high onto plateau, then drops steeply down a 5 percent grade to the Fraser River.

Mile 15 (267) Km 24.5 (429.5): Viewpoint at the eastern end of Sheep Creek bridge over Fraser River. Begin steep 6 percent grade westbound up to plateau level.

Mile 17.5 (264.5) Km 28 (426): Just east of bridge is a turnout with a map of Chilcotin Wildlife Viewing Areas and information on the Chilcotin grasslands.

Mile 20 (262) Km 32 (422): Top of river trench. Eastbound: Begin steep downgrade; watch for slow-moving loaded logging trucks. The great Fraser Plateau spreads to the west, with snowcapped peaks of the distant Coast Range visible on the horizon. The country west of the Fraser is known as the Chilcotin, taking its name from the river that cuts through the plateau. The country is chiefly rangeland for cattle, though forestry is also important.

Mile 21 (261) Km 33.5 (420.5) Gravel road north to Forest Service picnic area on McIntyre Lake, the small community of Meldrum Creek and on to Quesnel along the west side of the Fraser River. Sweeping grasslands here are known as Becher's Prairie, strewn with large glacial boulders. Notice the nesting boxes set up at regular intervals along the fences here. Boxes are sited in pairs; this allows bluebirds to nest in one box, and the far more numerous tree swallows in the other. Both bluebirds and swallows are encouraged because they eat vast quantities of mosquitoes. 🕊

Mile 21.5 (260.5) Km 35 (419): Canadian Coastguard Service Loran-C tower, part of long-range navigation system shared by British Columbia, Alaska and Washington.

Mile 28 (254) Km 45 (409): Gravel road south to the Indian village of Toosey, Farwell Canyon on the Chilcotin River and on to the ranch community of Big Creek. A sidetrip down the sinuous road and across the spectacular canyon bridge (10 miles/16 km) is recommended. River cliffs have been eroded into statuesque hoodoos and pinnacles; area at the confluence of the Fraser and Chilcotin rivers has been set aside as a

The Atnarko River, accessible at Mile 235.5, is one of several good fishing spots on the Chilcotin. (Liz Bryan)

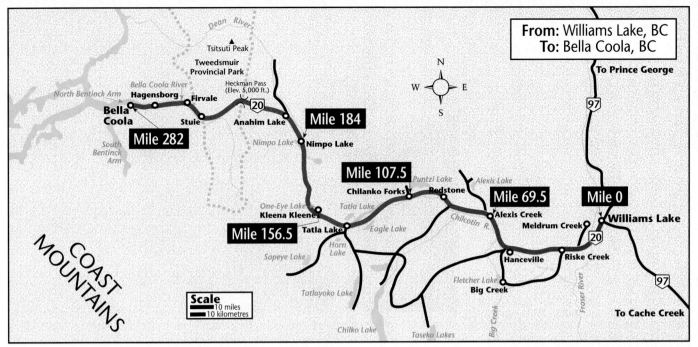

From: Williams Lake, BC
To: Bella Coola, BC

To Prince George

Mile 0

Mile 69.5

Mile 107.5

Mile 184

Mile 156.5

Mile 282

To Cache Creek

reserve for a band of 500 California bighorn sheep. Road can be driven as a 30-mile/50-km loop, returning to Highway 20 at Lee's Corner at **Mile 56**.

Mile 29 (253) Km 46.5 (407.5): Small community of **RISKE CREEK**. Gas, food, accommodations and general store. Note old log cabins painted bright yellow behind gas pumps.

Mile 29.5 (252.5) Km 48 (406): Stack Valley Road to historic Chilcotin Lodge, a capacious log structure, just north of the highway.

Mile 30.5 (251.5) Km 49 (405): Forest Service recreation area at Becher Pond; fishing for small rainbow; picnic tables. Highway here is flanked by lodgepole pines and aspens.

Mile 36 (246) Km 58 (396): Riske Creek recreation complex, including rodeo grounds. Stampede held in mid-June.

Mile 42 (240) Km 68 (386): Gravel road north to Forest Service recreation area on Raven and Palmer lakes; fishing; boat launch.

Mile 47 (235) Km 76 (378): Good stretch of snake fence. Farther west, example of Russell fence, 2 of several traditional Cariboo designs.

Mile 51.5 (230.5) Km 83 (371): Viewpoint and rest area south of highway and start of 9 percent downgrade westbound. Historic marker commemorates the epic and ill-fated Yukon cattle drive of Norman Lee, a local pioneer rancher who drove 200 head of cattle 1,500 miles through the mountain wilderness in an attempt to get beef to the Klondike goldfields in 1898.

Mile 56 (223) Km 90.5 (359.5): Lee's Corner, on site of Norman Lee's ranch house and Hanceville post office. Gas, groceries and food in old-fashioned general store. Turnoff south for old settlement of Hanceville, named for Tom Hance, the original settler, and the TH guest ranch.

This side road continues south, crossing the Chilcotin River (a favorite with river

rafters), to Fletcher Lake Forest Service Recreation Area for canoeing and fishing and the community of Big Creek. (Road loops back to the highway at **Mile 28**.) Also access to Taseko Lakes Road and Ts'yl-os Provincial Park, which includes Chilko and Taseko lakes (undeveloped).

Mile 63.5 (218.5) Km 102 (352): Steepled church and houses of Anahim Reserve, the largest of 6 Indian reserves in the Chilcotin. Highway follows the Chilcotin River, out of sight to the south.

Mile 69.5 (212.5) Km 112 (342): Village of **ALEXIS CREEK** (pop. 1,200), largest settlement of the east Chilcotin. Gas, groceries, hotel, stores, outpost hospital and administrative offices for forestry, fish and wildlife, and highway departments. Pigeon's General Store is a link with pioneer days.

Nearby, Stum Lake Road leads northeast to network of cross-country ski trails and on to forestry recreation areas at McKill and Palmer lakes for fishing and boating. (Final access to McKill is on foot only.) In the area is White Pelican Provincial Park, a sanctuary for white pelicans. It is the only known pelican nesting area in British Columbia. Visitors wishing access must contact the B.C. Parks Cariboo office, RR 1, Lac La Hache, BC V0K 1T0.

Mile 73.5 (208.5) Km 118.5 (335.5): Westbound, road goes steeply downhill; view of Chilcotin River and rock cliffs.

Mile 75 (207) Km 121 (333): Bull Canyon Provincial Recreation Area; picnic tables and 20 campsites in aspen forest beside Chilcotin River. No fee. River is turbulent and colored a bright gray-green from glacial silt. Kayaking, rafting and fishing are popular. Explore canyon walls for caves.

Mile 77.5 (204.5) Km 125 (329): Gravel road north up Alexis Creek to forestry recreation areas on Two and Alexis lakes (16.5 miles/27 km).

Mile 84 (198) Km 135 (319): Rough road

leads deep into the Chilcotin wilderness; follow Chilko River valley south to Ts'yl-os Provinical Park (see **Mile 56**), which encompasses Chilko Lake, one of the largest in the area. Motorboats are allowed on Chilko Lake. *WARNING:* Boaters, beware of sudden high winds. The Chilko River is a famous whitewater stream popular with kayakers and rafters.

Mile 88 (194) Km 142 (312): Chilcotin River bridge; gravel road north to tiny ranch settlement of Chezacut (30 miles/48 km). Just to the west is the scattered community of **REDSTONE** at the confluence of the Chilcotin and Chilanko rivers. Highway west follows the Chilanko River southwest; Chilcotin River comes in from the northwest.

Mile 92.5 (189.5) Km 149 (305): Redstone Indian cemetery, crammed with white painted picket fences and crosses. Indians west of the Fraser are Carrier and Chilcotin tribes, members of the northern Dene nation. Beyond the cemetery the Chilcotin River lies in a deep trench.

Mile 103.5 (178.5) Km 167 (287): Redstone's steepled church (painted bright blue), general store and gas.

Mile 105 (177) Km 169 (285): Stunning view west of snowcapped Coast Mountains.

Mile 107 (175) Km 172 (282): Road north up Chilanko River leads to Puntzi Lake (4.5 miles/7 km), well stocked with rainbow and kokanee, and 5 resorts and a private campground. White pelicans feed on the lake. Access to Chilanko Marsh Wildlife Area for bird watching, beaver, muskrat, deer and moose.

Mile 107.5 (174.5) Km 173 (281): Community of **CHILANKO FORKS**; gas, store, accommodations.

Mile 113.5 (168.5) Km 183 (271): Gravel road south to Pyper Lake Forest Service Recreation Area with picnic tables and fishing.

Pavement ends; all-weather gravel road continues. Use headlights in dusty conditions.

Mile 116 (166) Km 187 (267): Gravel turnout and viewpoint north to the long, deep valley of Tatla Lake.

Mile 130 (152) Km 209 (245): Pollywog Marsh, a wetlands conservation project of Ducks Unlimited. Rest area with picnic tables beside small lake.

Mile 131.5 (150.5) Km 212 (242): Gravel road north to Tatla Lake Forest Service Recreation Area; fishing (kokanee to 2 lbs.); boat launching (motors allowed). To the west, road leads south to Eagle Lake.

Mile 134.5 (147.5) Km 216.5 (237.5): Road south to Pinto Lake Forest Service Recreation Area with picnic tables and boating.

Mile 136 (146) Km 219 (235): Road **junction.** Highway 20 goes north to community of Tatla Lake. Road leads south over the divide to Tatlayoko Lake in the Homathco Valley (21.5 miles/35 km), jumping-off point for expeditions to Mount Waddington (elev. 13,100 feet/3,994m), the highest peak in the Coast Range. Resort on lake, plus Forest Service recreation area for fishing, hiking, boating (powerboats allowed). Road branches to Sapeye, Horn and Bluff lakes, all popular fishing spots with several lodges, resorts and dude ranches.

Mile 137.5 (144.5) Km 221 (233): Community of **TATLA LAKE,** southwest of the long lake itself, sits on the north shore of a small lake with a magnificent view south toward the mountains. Old Graham Hotel (food, accommodations) commemorates the name of first settlers, Robert and Margaret Graham. Settlement has gas, store, restaurant, motel, post office and clinic.

Mile 146.5 (135.5) Km 236 (218): Klinaklini River bridge. River is closed to fishing April 1 to June 30. Notice rusty-red pine trees, a sign of pine beetle infestation.

Mile 153 (129) Km 246 (208): Road north to Forestry Service recreation area on One Eye Lake; fishing, boating.

Mile 156.5 (125.5) Km 252 (202): Tiny community of **KLEENA KLEENE,** with general store (may not be open) and post office. Highway now goes almost due north.

Mile 158.5 (123.5) Km 255.5 (198.5): Road south to Clearwater Lake Forest Service Recreation Area with picnic tables, fishing and boating.

Mile 163 (119) Km 262 (192): Bridge over McClinchie Creek, Dean River tributary.

Mile 177.5 (104.5) Km 286 (168): Road south to Charlotte Lake (12 miles/20 km), rainbow to 4 lbs. Near here is one of the very few Indian pictograph sites in the Chilcotin painted on a single block of granite. One glyph clearly depicts the horns of a bighorn sheep. Ask for directions at Kleena Kleene or Nimpo Lake.

Mile 184 (98) Km 296 (158): NIMPO LAKE community marked by the beginning of

"The Hill," which begins at Mile 223, descends in switchbacks. Narrow, with 18 percent grades, motorists need to keep their eyes on the road! (Liz Bryan)

pavement and a wide view of mountain peaks above the forest. All basic services and several fishing resorts. The area is often quite noisy with floatplanes taxiing on the 7.5-mile/12-km lake that lies just to the west of the settlement. The lake contains choice rainbow, also crossbred trout with both rainbow and cutthroat characteristics.

From Nimpo Lake to Anahim Lake, Highway 20 (paved) follows the upper reaches of the Dean River, famous for its fishing. The river is managed as a special fishery and a permit is needed to fish certain sections. Check British Columbia fishing regulations.

Mile 187 (95) Km 302 (152): Bridge over Dean River; Forest Service recreation site; canoeing and fly-fishing. Historical marker on west side of bridge commemorates the Chilcotin War that prompted the abandonment of Waddington's Road to the goldfields. The road was pioneered by Victoria merchant Alfred Waddington as a shortcut to the Cariboo gold rush. The marker is about 65 miles/104 km north of where the incident took place in 1864, but apparently the Indian war party also killed members of a pack train here at the river crossing known as The Fishtrap, spreading terror throughout the Chilcotin.

Mile 195.5 (86.5) Km 315 (139): ANAHIM LAKE community, home of a large and boisterous stampede in mid-July. Settlement grew in size in 1940 when scattered communities of Ulkatcho Indians relocated here. All major services located on north loop road. Airstrip with daily connections to Vancouver and Bella Coola. Above lake is the ancient volcanic plug of Anahim Peak.

From Anahim Lake, a gravel road leads north along the Dean River valley to Lessard Lake (11 miles/18 km), and beyond for 37 miles/60 km. Access to abandoned Indian villages of Iluak and Ulkatcho and to the mountains of the Rainbow Range. Also access to the Alexander Mackenzie Heritage Trail (see **Mile 251.5**) and to historic Home Ranch, scene of *Grass Beyond the Mountain.*

The lodge, old log house and barns built by Pan Phillips and writer Richard Hobson are deserted, but worth a visit. Highway leaves the Dean Valley west of the lake and heads, unpaved, up to Heckman Pass. The climb west is easy and effortless.

Mile 199 (83) Km 320 (134): Road to Little Anahim Lake Forestry Recreation Area with picnic tables, swimming and boating.

Mile 216.5 (65.5) Km 348.5 (105.5): Road closure gate and bridge over Tsulko River, a tributary of the Dean. Road climbs more steeply, with good views to the north of the Rainbow Range, fragmented shield volcanoes, stained purple, yellow and red with minerals. The highest is Tsitsutl Peak (elev. 8,200 feet/2,500m), site of prehistoric obsidian quarries. Natives used the rock to make spear points and arrowheads.

Mile 218.5 (63.5) Km 352 (102): Eastern entrance to Tweedsmuir Provincial Park and summit of Heckman Pass (elev. 5,000 feet/1,524m). The pass is kept open year-round. Campgrounds and picnic areas are open only from the end of May to the first snowfall. The largest park in British Columbia, much of it is inaccessible except on foot, on horseback or by floatplane to remote lakes. Along Highway 20, the park has 5 picnic sites and 2 campgrounds with a total of 42 campsites, and a sani-station. Prime attractions are hiking and fishing.

Mile 222.5 (59.5) Km 358 (96): Rainbow Range trailhead and East Branch picnic site.

Mile 223 (59) Km 359 (95): Brake check area. Beginning of the notorious descent to the Bella Coola Valley. "The Hill," much of which is at 18 percent grade, descends in 2 stages, with switchbacks around steeply falling Young Creek, which the road crosses twice. It is difficult to take your eyes off the road to view the scenery as the road is narrow (in places single track) and traverses unstable rock slopes. Passengers will appreciate the excellent view of the rugged Coast Mountains. Trailers and large RVs drive with care!

Mile 226 (56) Km 364 (90): Bridge over Young Creek. Space at the creek to pull off and take a break. Highway west climbs up again before final descent.

Mile 228 (54) Km 367 (87): Beginning of 5.5-mile/9-km steep descent requiring very cautious driving. *WARNING:* The mountainside is steep, the road very narrow, and there are no guardrails. Watch for rock slides and extremely tight hairpin bends. Use low gear to prevent brakes from overheating.

Mile 235 (47) Km 378 (76): Road closure gate. Suddenly the road is bordered with coastal cedar and hemlock. Young Creek bridge and picnic ground. Atnarko Tote Road leads south to the upper Atnarko River valley and the Turner Lakes chain, a subalpine canoe route and spectacular Hunlen Falls (18 miles/29 km), which drops 853 feet/260m in a single cascade. Lonesome Lake, 18.5 miles/30 km south, was immortalized in *Crusoe of Lonesome Lake*, a book about Ralph Edwards, who homesteaded there in 1912 and created a winter sanctuary for trumpeter swans.

Begin paved road westbound; in summer there's a roadside sign with information about park services and warning of grizzly bears that frequent the rivers, particularly in spring and fall, around the salmon hatcheries farther downstream.

Mile 235.5 (46.5) Km 379.5 (74.5): Atnarko River Campground; 28 campsites just east of the park headquarters; sani-station; fee charged. The Atnarko and Bella Coola rivers are famous around the world for their fish: steelhead, cutthroat, Dolly Varden and 5 varieties of salmon. Conservation regulations are in effect—both rivers have "special" status and are subject to special regulations and closures. Check with the B.C. Freshwater Fishing Regulations Synopsis, or with park officials.

Mile 242.5 (39.5) Km 390 (64): Big Rock picnic area in the tall cedars. Rock is a giant fallen boulder. Across the road a 1-hour loop trail circles Kettle Pond.

Mile 243.5 (38.5) Km 392 (62): Atnarko River Spawning Channels in former bed of river. Centre provides spawning channels for 50,000 pink salmon and also rearing channels for chinook salmon for Snootli Creek Hatchery downstream. There is a trail system along the banks of the old river channel and beside spawning and rearing beds. Best time to see the pinks spawn is August and September. Grizzly bears have discovered the easy fishing of the spawning beds and often the trails will be closed because of bear danger.

Mile 244 (38) Km 393 (61): Small resort community of **STUIE**. Nearby, ancient Indian burial ground and smokehouse. Nearby is historic Tweedsmuir Lodge, for 50 years run by the Corbould family, famous for its hospitality and the surrounding fishing and hiking opportunities.

Mile 244.5 (37.5) Km 395 (59): Fisheries Pool Campground; 14 campsites, fee, boat launch and picnic area beside Atnarko River. Salmon spawning channels and viewing pool.

Mile 248.5 (33.5) Km 400 (54): Horsetail Falls Creek. Falls drop from high overhanging cliffs to provide a long gush of water like a horse's flowing tail. Best view from the highway, just west of bridge.

Mile 251.5 (30.5) Km 405 (49): Burnt Bridge. Heritage McKenzie/Grease trailhead and picnic area. This 1- to 1½-hour loop trail leads to a good viewpoint of the river and Stupendous Mountain (elev. 8,800 feet/2,700m).

West of the bridge a sign commemorates the Alexander Mackenzie Heritage Trail.

Explorer Mackenzie of the North West Co. was the first white man to cross the North American continent. In 1793 he and his party left Lake Athabaska to find a trade route to the Pacific, a 72-day trek through 1,200 miles/2,000 km of unmapped territory. The 260-mile/420-km trail from Quesnel has been retraced and is being restored in a joint federal, provincial and regional project. The land trail terminates at the Burnt Creek bridge where Mackenzie first came into contact with the coastal Natives. He went the rest of the way to the Pacific by canoe.

Mile 256.5 (25.5) Km 412.5 (41.5): Tweedsmuir Provincial Park west entrance and small settlement of **FIRVALE**; gas available.

Mile 261 (21) Km 420 (34): Bridge across Bella Coola River.

Mile 273.5 (8.5) Km 440 (14): Community of **HAGENSBORG** (pop. 600), all basic services available. Hagensborg was settled in 1894 by Norwegians from Minnesota, who found the country similar to the fjords of their home country. The valley floor here is flat and fertile, the mountains high and sheer.

Mile 274.5 (7.5) Km 441.5 (12.5): Road to Bella Coola airport.

Mile 275 (7) Km 442.5 (11.5): Snootli Creek Fish Hatchery. Each September, eggs from Atnarko chinook salmon are brought here for fertilization and incubation; fry are raised here for 8 to 10 weeks, then transferred to the Atnarko rearing channels.

Mile 278.5 (3.5) Km 448.5 (5.5): Road south up Thorsen Creek. Up this road lies a large and important Indian petroglyph site with more than 100 glyphs. Ask locally for directions.

Mile 279.5 (2.5) Km 450 (4): Acwsalcta, School of the Nuxalk Nation, constructed of cedar with Indian graphic designs and carvings; well worth a stop. Native cemetery across highway.

Mile 282 (0) Km 454 (0): **Junction** at entrance to town of **BELLA COOLA** (pop. 700). All tourist services. Town is home to the Bella Coola Band of the Nuxalk Nation; look for totems outside the band office and the traditional house replica next to the church. Alexander Mackenzie was the first white man to visit this settlement at the head of north Bentinck Arm in 1793. The Hudson's Bay Co. established a trading post here in 1869 (the factor's house by the river still remains). The museum is in a schoolhouse that dates from the 1800s and displays Hudson's Bay Co. relics and items brought by Norwegian settlers. Attractions include charter flights, fishing charters and boat trips to Alexander Mackenzie Historic Park in Dean Channel, where the explorer left a record of his momentous journey: "From Canada by Land, 22nd July, 1793" inscribed on a rock.

Paved road continues around the tidewater flats at the head of the inlet for 1.2 miles/2 km to the government wharf and the fishing harbor. No scheduled ferry.

Indian designs and carvings at School of the Nuxalk Nation at Mile 279.5. (Liz Bryan)

NORTH CASCADES HIGHWAY

Washington State Route 20
Burlington to Okanogan, WA

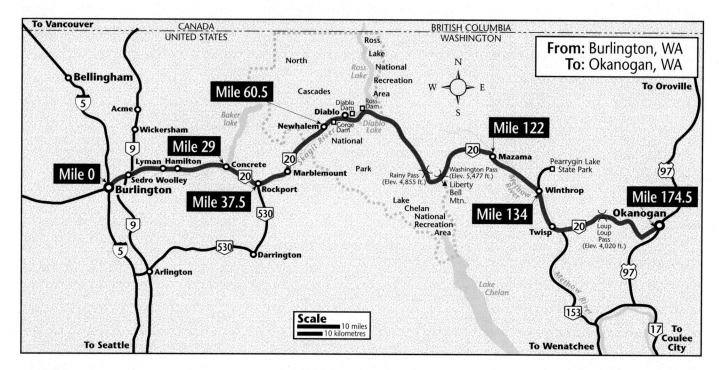

In 1859, Henry Custer described the North Cascades wilderness this way: "No where do the mountain masses and peaks present such strange, fantastic, dauntless and startling outlines as here. Whoever wishes to see nature in its primitive glory and grandeur, in its almost ferocious wilderness, must go and visit these mountain regions."

Efforts to build a highway across the rugged North Cascade mountains began as early as 1893, when Washington state appropriated $20,000 for 200 miles of road. A year later, construction crews were defeated by washouts and massive landslides. Travelers waited through the first half of the 20th century before construction was started again in 1960. When the project was completed in 1972, State Route 20 spanned the state from Anacortes in Puget Sound to Newport on the Idaho border.

The *Northwest Mileposts*® log begins on the edge of the Skagit Valley at Interstate 5 and Burlington. It proceeds east through the highest and wildest mountains in Washington on a route that has been called one of America's great drives. After winding through the Methow Valley recreation area, it ends in the fruit country of Okanogan, near the site of the first permanent settlement in Washington Territory.

The North Cascades has been designated a grizzly-bear ecosystem and recovery area by the U.S. Fish and Wildlife Service. There

were once more than 50,000 grizzly bears in the Western United States, but today there are fewer than 1,000. The service estimates there may be only 10 to 20 bears in the U.S. portion of the North Cascades, and because grizzly bears are the second-slowest-reproducing land animals in North America (after the musk ox), it will take decades before the North Cascades has a healthy grizzly bear population.

The North Cascades Highway is closed in winter between Colonial Creek Campground (Mile 71) on the west side of the Cascades and Mazama (Mile 122) on the east side. The highway is open from about mid-April through Nov., depending on snow conditions. Chains or traction devices are sometimes required. Travelers should check with ranger stations or the State Patrol. In Washington, motorists may call (206) 455-7700 for winter pass conditions, (206) 434-PASS outside Washington.

North Cascades Highway Log

Distance in miles from Burlington, WA, is followed by miles from Okanogan, WA.

Mile 0 (174.5): Junction with Interstate 5 at Exit 230 to **BURLINGTON** (pop. 4,690), which proclaims itself Skagit Valley's hub

city. Scenic Chuckanut Drive to Bellingham begins in northern Burlington (see **Mile 538** INTERSTATE 5 section). All services are available in Burlington, including several family restaurants, drive-ins, private campground, gas, golf course and hospital. The city's 3-day celebration in June features 2 local products (strawberries and dairy) at the annual Berry-Dairy Days. The chamber of commerce can provide visitor information, (360) 755-9382.

Although a logging camp was established in 1882, Burlington was not platted until 1890. With the arrival of the Great Northern Railroad in 1891, the community became the hub of an extensive rail system. Today, its economy is linked to field crops, dairy farming, boat building and chemical manufacturing. ▲

Mile 4.5 (170): Sedro-Woolley western city limits.

Mile 5.5 (169): SEDRO-WOOLLEY (6,330) city center, park. All services are available and there is a private RV park. Sedro (Spanish for cedar) was founded by Mortimer Cook in 1884. In 1889, P.A. Woolley started a community at the Great Northern and Northern Pacific railroad crossing junction nearby and gave it his name. The 2 rival towns eventually merged in 1898 to become 1 town. Downtown buildings display murals depicting Sedro-Woolley's past. The Loggerodeo, held around the July 4 weekend, celebrates its timber heritage with tree rigging and topping, wood splitting, ax throws and other

Concrete High School, which spans a local road, is a tourist attraction in this town of 800 residents. (Michael Dill)

HAMILTON (pop. 220); tavern, deli, liquor store, groceries, laundry, post office, public phone, pottery store and boat launch. Hamilton, founded in 1872, and incorporated in 1891, was settled around the homestead of William Hamilton. It grew to 1,500 people, 4 saloons, a general store, bank, newspaper, large hotels and a school. The town was plagued with economic problems and floods. During high water, merchants wired wooden sidewalks to hitching posts to keep them from floating away. Both Hamilton and Lyman have town councils and mayors. Hamilton mayor's office: (360) 826-3938.

Mile 22.5 (152): Gas station.

Mile 23.5 (151): Baker Lake Highway is a paved Forest Service road that leads 20 miles north to the Baker Lakes area. See feature on page 202.
 Access to private RV park to north.
▲ MP 82

Mile 24 (150.5): Birdsview is an unincorporated area linked to agriculture and timber. It offers an inn, gas, ice, grocery, public phone, and fast-food outlet. Private RV park north and east of town. ▲ MP 83

Mile 24.5 (150): Access south to lodging.

Mile 26 (148.5): Watch for elk crossing next 2^1/2 miles eastbound. During fall, winter and spring, resident herds graze in fields along highway in early morning and evening.

Mile 27.5 (147): Sign marks the Skagit River.

Mile 28.5 (146): Shopping center with groceries, family restaurant, motel, auto parts store, automatic teller machine, fax. North Cascades Inn restaurant is filled with antique firearms, tools and other collectibles.

Mile 29 (145.5): CONCRETE (pop. 800) western city limits and airport road. All services are offered, including several restaurants, cafes, gas stations, motel and medical clinic. The movie *This Boy's Life*, based on Tobias Wolf's autobiographical account of growing up in Concrete, was filmed here in 1992. Tourist attractions include Concrete High School, built in the air space over a local road. Drive ^{1}/4 mile east from the "Entering Concrete" sign to Superior Street on the south side of highway. School is immediately visible. Situated near the banks of the Skagit and Baker rivers, Concrete attracts steelhead, salmon and trout fishermen. A public boat launch is located at the mouth of the Baker River. From Milepost 89 drive 0.5 mile to Everett Avenue, which is just west of the Eagle's Nest Motel. Turn south on Everett and go 0.2 mile to first turnoff on right. RVs exercise caution: Dirt lane starts with deep ruts and boulders before leveling out to good, flat launching area. Everett Avenue also provides access to hard-to-find Shannon Lake in the Baker Lake area. See BAKER LAKE AREA sidebar, this section, for more information.
 From the early 1900s to 1968, a Portland Cement plant was the dominant industry. Following several devastating fires prior to the

events. In addition to logging, the economy is based on manufacturing and wood production. For more information, phone the Sedro-Woolley Chamber of Commerce, (360) 855-1841.
 The North Cascades Institute based in Sedro-Woolley offers more than 70 adult, field-based programs, covering such topics as photography, forest ecology, geology, archaeology, backpacking, birds, butterflies, writing, basketry and marine mammals. It also offers youth programs and mountain camps. For more information, phone (360) 856-5700, ext. 209.
 Sedro-Woolley is the gateway to the North Cascades. On the highway near the western city limits, a caboose serves as a visitor information center; phone (360) 855-0974. It is generally open late spring through the summer. Also located on the highway are the offices of Mount Baker-Snoqualmie National Forest, (360) 775-9702, and North Cascades National Park, (360) 856-5700. See also North Cascades National Park in the MAJOR ATTRACTIONS section. ▲

Mile 5.6 (168.9): Junction with Washington Highway 9, which leads south 21 miles to Arlington and north to Wickersham, Acme and Deming. Highway 9 and Highway 20 run jointly for 1^1/2 miles before Highway 9 goes north at Mile 7.
 The Lake Whatcom Railway in Wickersham operates a 1-hour scenic trip in antique Northern Pacific passenger cars pulled by an early-20th-century steam engine. The ride through the countryside goes alongside picturesque Mirror Lake on Tuesdays and Saturdays, 11 a.m. and 1 p.m., mid-June to the end of August. If they inform the railway in advance, riders may board the 11 a.m. train and take a ^{1}/2-mile dirt-road hike at the end of the tracks to Lake Whatcom for swimming, then catch the 1 p.m. train back. There are no restrooms or changing facilities at the lake, although the railway can pre-

range facilities and picnic tables for groups. The railway also offers special holiday rides by reservation. Fee: Adults, $10; juniors 17 and under, $5; children under 2 are free. Phone (360) 595-2218.

Mile 6.5 (168): Rodeo grounds.

Mile 7 (167.5): Turnoff for Highway 9 north. Sedro-Woolley eastern city limits.   MP 66

Mile 8.5 (166): Crossing Haven Creek, which is a protected salmon spawning stream.

Mile 10 (164.6): Watch for elk crossing highway next 5 miles eastbound.

Mile 11 (163.5): Crossing Coal Creek, a protected salmon stream.

Mile 11.5 (163): Wiseman Creek.

Mile 14 (160.5): An Indian art museum and gift shop on south side of road features collector-quality soapstone sculptures, jewelry, rugs and artifacts. Open daily.   MP 73

Mile 15 (159.5): Restaurant, gas, grocery and hardware store north of highway. Access to downtown **LYMAN** (pop. 310) via a side road south of the main highway. Restful and rural, Lyman, platted in 1884, was once a busy railroad town. Anticipated industrial growth never materialized. A reroute of State Route 20 and business closures turned Lyman and its neighbor Hamilton into quiet towns now questioning how much development is welcome. Lyman city clerk: (360) 826-3033.
 Some of the early buildings still stand. The Birdsey Minkler House, built in 1891, is on the National Register of Historic Places. It is still used as a residence and not open for tours.   MP 74

Mile 18.5 (156): Access road south to

early 1920s, most subsequent structures were made of concrete. A chamber of commerce visitor information office (phone 360/853-8400, hours variable) is in the community center north of the highway. Turn north onto "E" Street just west of Milepost 89, where sign says, "Concrete City Center," then make an immediate right onto a small lane paralleling the railroad tracks and ending at the center. Saturday markets, featuring local handicrafts and products, are held at the community center in the summer.

Concrete Municipal Airport, accessed via Superior Street, has a 2,600-foot runway and is used by glider, experimental and antique airplane clubs for fly-ins. There is no fee for using the facility. ☛ MP 89

Mile 29.5 (145): Crossing Baker River. A unique Puget Power fish-transfer operation can be seen directly east of the bridge. Migrating salmon are diverted into holding tanks, and a 1,000-gallon tank truck "fish taxi" transports them to Baker Lake spawning grounds. A visitor center features a large topographical map of the Mount Baker area, displays and mounted fish. Open weekdays 7 a.m. to 3:30 p.m. year-round. Fish-holding tanks are open to the public 24 hours a day.

Indian craft shop off highway.

Mile 30 (144.5): Concrete eastern city limits.

Mile 35.5 (139): Forest Service Road No. 1030 on left eastbound goes 7 miles to short spur road leading to Sauk Mountain Trail No. 613. The trail offers a sweeping view of the Skagit River valley toward snow-clad peaks, and is a prime area for wildflower viewing from mid-July through Aug. Colorful wildflowers visible on the mountain's east face include lupines, columbines, Indian paintbrush, tiger lilies, phlox and Sitka valerian. The strenuous hike is 4 miles round-trip. From the ridge, a spur trail leads 1.5 miles to Sauk Lake. ☛

Mile 36 (138.5): Rockport State Park (purchased from a timber company in 1935 for $1), phone (360) 853-8461; 50 full hookups, 8 walk-in tent sites and 4 Adirondack-type sleeping shelters with bunk beds; group camp, large picnic area, handicap-accessible toilets, firepits, water and showers. Open mid-April to mid-Nov. Approximately $15 for full hookups, $10 tents, and $13 for Adirondack shelters. County park 1 mile away provides boat-launch area and access to Skagit River. Some 5 miles of trails lead through stands of timber (some trees are 300 feet tall and several hundred years old) and marshy bogs to sunlit viewpoints. Stands of old-growth Douglas fir and hemlock are maintained as a natural forest. ☛♨📷▲ MP 96

Mile 37.5 (137): ROCKPORT, a small com-

Baker Lake Area

"Quietening the mind, deep in the forest, water drips down."—Hosha.

This verse on an interpretive marker along the Shadow of the Sentinels trail in the Baker Lake Area provides some feeling for the allure of the area. It is one of the most beautiful regions in Washington state, with quiet places for contemplation, as well as areas for boating, sailing, swimming, fishing, hiking and camping. It is also one of the wettest places in the state. Lightning generally starts forest fires every 50 to 60 years, but the west slope of the Cascades forest is so wet, fires burn only every few hundred years.

The lakes in the area were created by construction of 2 dams on the Baker River. Lake Shannon, with views of Mount Baker and Mount Shuksan, backs up for 10 miles behind the Lower Baker Dam (completed in 1925). The Upper Baker Dam, built farther upstream and completed in 1959, created Baker Lake, which stretches northward for another 10 miles.

The Baker Lake Highway (Forest Service Road No. 11) to the recreation area junctions with State Route 20 just west of Concrete near Milepost 82 (see **Mile 23.5** in the main log) and heads 20 miles north into the Baker Lake area. En route to the Mount Baker-Snoqualmie National Forest and Baker Lake, the road passes Grandy Creek and Lake, Vogler Lake, Tyee Lake and Lake Shannon. From the Baker Lake Highway, several Forest Service side roads offer many opportunities for picnicking, hiking and photo stops. Watch for logging trucks on weekdays.

Access to Lake Shannon is extremely limited. Most of the surrounding land is privately owned or state forest, with many roads blocked and gated. Best access is from the North Cascades Highway just east of the Lowell Peterson Bridge on the eastern edge of Concrete (see **Mile 29** in the main log). Turn north on Everett Avenue and go to E. Main Street. Drive west to Baker River Road just before concrete bridge. Follow Baker River Road north to primitive gravel boat-launch area on Lake Shannon. *NOTE:* These directions should not be confused with the directions to the Baker River boat launch, for which you turn south onto Everett Avenue, in the main log at **Mile 29.**

Stumps and submerged logs in Lake Shannon make powerboating and water-skiing hazardous. Major activities are canoeing, fishing, and watching Washington's largest flock of ospreys. Biologists are studying the ospreys, sometimes called fish hawks, when they return from Mexico and Southern points each spring to nest on Lake Shannon and Baker Lake. As many as 11 active nests are found in the area representing about 22 adult osprey. The nests are built of sticks on top of snags surrounding the lakes, and biologists have installed additional bowl-shaped nesting sites on tall poles in hopes of encouraging the osprey to nest.

The recreation area is also home to the Pacific giant salamander, woodpeckers, red-backed voles, chickadees, the red-breasted sapsucker, flying squirrels and, during spring and summer, lots of flying insects. Wear insect-repellent or long-sleeves when hiking.

Fishing: Each year Baker Lake is stocked with 50,000 rainbow trout. Whitefish, landlocked king salmon, steelhead, silver trout and Dolly Varden to 10 lbs. are caught here. Boat launches are available at Horseshoe Cove Campground near Upper Baker Dam, at Panorama Point Campground, and at Kulshan Campground near Shannon Creek Campground and at Baker Lake Resort.

Hiking: Hikes range from 0.2 mile to several-day backcountry trips and climbs of Mount Baker (elev. 10,778 feet). The Shadow of the Sentinels trail, about 14 miles from the State Route 20 turnoff, is an easy 0.5-mile-loop hike on a wheelchair-accessible boardwalk through the giant, moss-draped trees (some more than 600 years old) from which the trail takes its name. There is a handicap-accessible restroom at the trailhead, and a reasonable parking area.

Rainbow Falls Viewpoint, 18 miles up Baker Lake Highway, then 5 miles up Road 1130 to the left, is worth a drive. Rainbow Creek cascades down a steep gorge over a 100-foot drop, and on sunny days, a rainbow is visible at the base of the falls. Trail is a short 400 feet to the viewpoint. Use extreme care and do not go beyond the viewpoint barriers.

Other area attractions accessible by trail are Mount Baker Wilderness and Mount Baker National Recreation Area trails, and agate and jasper beds at Swift Creek. The Baker River trail leads through the high passes and into the North Cascades National Park. Backcountry permits are required for overnight stays.

Adjacent to Upper Baker Dam is Glover Mountain Observation Point, offering a view of Baker Dam and nearby Lake Shannon. There is a short nature hike available here.

Camping: Baker Lake has numerous campgrounds along its shoreline. Kulshan and Maple Grove do not require a camping fee. Starting Jan. 1, reservations are taken for the summer at various Baker Lakes campgrounds; call (800) 280-CAMP(2267). There are ample parking opportunities for self-contained RV vacationers. There are no hookups except at Baker Lake Resort. Baker Lake Resort operates 2 campgrounds with 47 hookup sites, 100 sites with water and electricity, plus modern and semimodern cabins. Other services are boat rentals, 40 moorage sites, store, and boat launches. Phone (360) 853-8325.

For more information on the Baker Lake area, contact the information desk at the North Cascades National Park complex and Mount Baker Ranger District offices, Mount Baker R.D., 2105 State Route 20, Sedro-Woolley, WA 98284-9393, (360) 856-5700.

Wildflowers in the North Cascades.
(L. Linkhart)

munity less than 0.5 mile south of the highway, was named for the rocky shores of the Skagit River where boats docked. Gas, restrooms, ice, small store.

Rockport was overshadowed for several years by rival Sauk City. With the decline of Monte Cristo Mining and the panic of 1893, Sauk City became a ghost town, but Rockport survived when the general store was moved across the river to serve several shingle mills. Rockport became a railroad terminus, and in 1928 Seattle City Light chose it as a departure point for overnight trips to Newhalem and Diablo Dam. Tours now begin in Diablo, some 20 miles east; (206) 684-3030.

Mile 38 (136.5): Rockport eastern city limits. **Junction** with Washington Highway 530 to the right eastbound, which leads south to Howard Miller Steelhead Park, (360) 853-8808, and Darrington (20 miles). Howard Miller park includes an 1881 restored cabin, Indian dugout canoe, and the Rockport ferry, which transported passengers across the Skagit until 1981. The 13-acre park bills itself as one of the best fishing areas on the Skagit River and a good bald-eagle viewing area. It has handicapped-approved campsites; 13 tent sites, $8; 80-plus RV sites, $12; 2 Adirondack-type shelters with 8 bunks each, $12; dump station, flush toilets, showers, play area, firepits, a boat launch, and 3¹/₂ miles of walking trails. Reservations accepted 1 calendar year in advance, $2 fee. Boat launch is the start of an annual raft race each July in which contestants race handcrafted rafts to Concrete, and celebrate with an oyster and beer feed.

The Nature Conservancy's Skagit River Bald Eagle Natural Area is a 1,500-acre preserve. In winter, large populations of bald eagles gather along the streams to feed on chum salmon. Scenic float trips from Marblemount to the park are scheduled during the eagle-watching season. ⅋⅋◥▲ MP 98

Mile 40 (134.5): Rest area, south of the highway, is one of the best places to watch bald eagles. During the peak months of Jan-

uary and February, approximately 500 eagles congregate on the Skagit and the Nooksack rivers. Cougars, lynx (declining populations) and bobcats also live in the Cascade Range. Dubbed the "ghost cat of the Cascades" by the National Park Service, the cougar used to range across North America but is now extinct in most of its former range. The nocturnal cats are seldom seen, but if you encounter a cougar, do not run, turn your back or play dead. Instead, avert your gaze; speak in a calm voice; hold your ground; or back away slowly. Spread your arms and open your coat to do all you can to enlarge your image. If the cougar acts aggressively, wave your arms, shout, and throw rocks or sticks. If you're attacked, fight back. MP 100

Mile 41 (133.5): Local farm's roadside produce stand (seasonal).

Mile 43 (131.5): RV park, motel, restaurant and lounge, laundromat. Crossing Corkendale Creek. ▲ MP 103

Mile 44 (130.5): River cabins, 35-unit RV park with hookups and cafe/museum. ▲

Mile 45.5 (129): MARBLEMOUNT. All services available. Blackberry pie is an area specialty. Chamber of commerce: (360) 873-2250. Check your gas gauge as this is the last available gas until you reach Mazama on the east side of the mountains about 75 miles from here. Gas is available there only during daytime hours and may not be available evenings, Sundays or holidays. The next available gas is 13.5 miles farther at Winthrop, some 90 miles away. Likewise, be prepared to wait for food as there are no restaurants available until Mazama or Winthrop.

Marblemount got its name from its proximity to nearby Marble Mountain and the talc and marble in the area. The Log House Inn, built in 1890, has a restaurant and lounge and 5 rooms that rent for around $30 per night (360/873-4311). Gas and campground available. Just past the Log House Inn, Highway 20 swings sharply to the north, following the Skagit River eastbound.

The Cascade River joins the Skagit River in Marblemount and is a base for river rafters to launch their craft for float trips. Inquire locally about commercial river rafting firms. Informal launching area is across the bridge that is just east of The Log House Inn. After crossing bridge, take first dirt road, Cascade River Road, to left. Road goes back under bridge to launching area. No parking allowed. The Cascade River Road continues for 23 miles on mostly rough gravel to the Cascade Pass trailhead, a drive which takes about 3 hours and offers a pleasant side trip. Two campgrounds are located along the middle section of the road. At the end of the Cascade River Road, a 3.7-mile hike up a well-graded trail takes you to the pass.

Hiking another 5.5 miles takes you through the Stehekin Valley. Where the trail meets the Stehekin Valley Road, a National Park Service shuttle can take you 22 more miles into Chelan. The shuttle service is available spring through fall (exact dates depend on snowfall). It is run out of the Goldenwest Visitor Center, located in Stehekin. Shuttles run twice a day, at 8 a.m. and 2 p.m. Reservations are strongly recommended; phone

(360) 856-5700.

The Cascade River Road also provides access to Forbidden Peak, rated 1 of the 50 classic climbs in North America by the authors of a Sierra Club book. Two of the area's resources for climbing information, instruction and guide services are the American Alpine Institute, Bellingham, (360/671-1505), and Mountain Madness in Seattle, (206/937-8389).

Another source of information is the North Cascades National Park Marblemount Ranger Station. Access to the station, which is 1 mile north of the highway, is approximately 0.2 miles into town eastbound. Free backcountry permits are available. Mountain climbers should register here if they did not register in Sedro-Woolley. In summer, phone (360) 873-4500, ext. 33 or 35; if no answer/and in winter, (360) 856-5700. ⅋▲ MP 105

Mile 51 (123.5): Crossing Skagit River. The highway follows the Skagit River (designated a Wild and Scenic River) from Marblemount to Diablo Dam and travels along the power lines coming from the dam area to Seattle.

Mile 52 (122.5): The highway enters Ross Lake National Recreation Area (see MAJOR ATTRACTIONS section). The recreation area divides North Cascades National Park into 2 units. Its 107,000 acres include 3 Seattle City Light power projects. Food, lodging, boat and motor rentals, tackle and basic camper supplies can be obtained in the area. MP 111

Mile 54 (120.5): Several turnouts with good views next several miles.

Mile 55.5 (119): The highway crosses Damnation Creek.

Mile 57 (117.5): Entering Whatcom County eastbound.

Mile 58 (116.5): Exit west to Thornton Creek Road and access to the Thornton Lakes trailhead. First 5.3 miles offer a steep and rigorous day hike. Backcountry use permits are required for camping along the trail. Wood fires are prohibited. ⅋ MP 117

Mile 60 (114.5): Goodell Creek Campground (phone 360/856-5700), with 20 tent/trailer-camper sites, drinking water, pit toilets and boat launch area for river rafters. No hookups. No showers. $7; open all year. The campground is a launching spot for whitewater rafting down the Skagit to Bacon Creek. The

route can be safely run by experienced rafters, kayakers and whitewater canoeists. The first 6 miles are Class II. The latter part is Class III.

▲ MP 119

Mile 60.5 (114): Highway crosses Goodell Creek and enters the Seattle City Light village of **NEWHALEM**; store, parks with playground, post office, Seattle City Light visitor center. Newhalem houses City Light employees who maintain the operation of the powerhouse and dams. Also some highway and National Park Service personnel reside in Newhalem.

Entering Newhalem from the west, a paved lane to the right provides access to the North Cascades Visitor Center and Newhalem Creek Campground. The Sterling Munro Trail, a handicap-accessible boardwalk, takes visitors to the center 300 feet into the woods and to a view of Pinnacle Peak and Mount Terror in the Picket Range. The center features a 20-minute slide show, A Meditation on Wilderness, complete with state-of-the-art sound and spectacular photography. It's shown on the hour, or by request during the off-season. A display for children allows them to touch items ranging from wild Oregon horse lettuce and mountain goat fur to old-man's-beard lichen. There are also 3-D natural history maps, a large stone fireplace, benches, restrooms, and a book and map shop, as well as bound collections of information on local camping, accommodations, activities, trail reports and descriptions. The center is open daily during summer and weekends during winter; phone (360) 386-4495.

Newhalem Creek Campground has 129 tent/RV sites, drinking water, flush toilets and dump station.

The highly recommended Ladder Creek Loop Trail Gardens and Falls starts at the Gorge Creek Powerhouse just off the highway at the east end of Newhalem. Gravel parking area accommodates RVs. Cross the powerhouse bridge by foot to reach the trailhead. The trail is a $^1/_2$-mile loop with steep steps and hand rails, but it's well worth the effort, offering a visual play of yellow and green mosses, emerald trees and brilliant white water churning rapidly over rocks. The trail is lit at night; flashlight advised, however. The second verse of a poem posted near the beginning of the trail may best reflect its mood and purpose: *Let me dream my dreams in a garden fair/With a beauty fragrance everywhere/With a place to dip in crystal springs/The opening heart of lovely things.* ♿ MP 120

Mile 63 (111.5): Highway passes through a 500-foot-long tunnel. Grated deck precedes tunnel entrance eastbound.

Mile 64 (110.5): Turnoffs and parking areas 0.1 mile apart on both sides of highway for viewing the Gorge Creek waterfalls and Gorge Lake. Walk across the steel bridge for the best views; a spectacular sight and photo opportunity. Many waterfalls dot the cliffs along the next 40-plus miles of highway eastbound. MP 123

Mile 64.5 (110): Highway passes through 200-foot-long tunnel.

Mile 65.5 (109): Beautiful view of Gorge Lake as you round curve of highway.

Mile 66.5 (108): Junction with road north to Seattle City Light village of **DIABLO** and tour center for Skagit Tours. Seattle City Light, a municipal utility, has been offering tours of its Skagit River dams since 1928. The 4$^1/_2$-hour Skagit Tour is a popular attraction with visitors. Beginning at the tour center, the guided tour includes a ride up Sourdough Mountain on an antique incline railway, a boat cruise across Diablo Lake to Ross Dam powerhouse and back, and a family-style meal at Diablo. The cost is $24.50 for adults, $22 for seniors above 62 years and $12.50 for children 6 to 11. Children 5 and under are free. Reservations are strongly advised. The tours are offered at 10 a.m., 12:30 p.m. and 3 p.m., from mid-June to the beginning of Sept. No tours Tuesday and Wednesday. One tour a day on fall weekends through early October. Reservations are accepted starting in mid-April. A 90-minute tour featuring the incline railway and a slide show is $5 for those 12 and over; 11 a.m., 1:15 p.m. and 3:45 p.m. For reservations and information phone Seattle City Light's Skagit Tour desk at (206) 684-3030.

Diablo is the trailhead for the Sourdough Mountain hike, which gains 5,200 feet in 5 miles and culminates in spectacular views of the North Cascades, Mount Baker and southern Canada. ♿★ MP 126

Mile 67.5 (107): Pyramid Lake trailhead, near physical Milepost 127. Trail gains 1,500 feet in 2.1 miles. ♿ MP 127

Mile 68 (106.5): Diablo Dam Road turnoff north to Ross Lake Resort; Seattle number, (206) 386-4437. The road ends at a parking lot where tugboats transfer passengers to the floating resort at 8:30 a.m. and 3 p.m. daily mid-June through Oct. Approximately $10 per person. Allow 1$^1/_2$ hours each way from parking lot to resort. Hiker can take a 1-mile downhill trail from the Ross trail parking lot (see **Mile 74.5**), and use phones at end of gravel road to call for water-taxi service—50¢ a person each way. The resort has 10 cabins, 3 bunkhouses built on log floats, full marina services with boat, canoe and kayak rentals, water taxi for backpackers and hikers, and boat launch. Fishing for native rainbow trout July–Oct. Single barbless hooks may be required. There is no store or restaurant at the resort; bring your own food. ♿

Mile 71 (103.5): Colonial Creek Campground and trailhead for Thunder Creek

The lush Ladder Creek Loop Trail at Mile 60.5 offers a refreshing break for motorists. (Michael Dill)

trail. The campground is the largest along the highway with 162 tent/trailer sites (RVs to 22 feet), flush toilets, dump station and boat launch. No hookups. No showers. Docks, fish-cleaning station, nature walks. Fee: $10 per night. Generally open mid-April to Nov. 1, the main campground is often filled to capacity and additional campsites may be available in the annex located across the highway. The lake is good for swimming, canoeing, kayaking, rafting, fishing and all water-related activities. Nature programs and campfire programs are offered during the summer months. The 19-mile Thunder Creek Trail is fairly flat and easy to the 10-mile mark, where it divides and connects to other trails, passes through a variety of vegetation, and ascends Park Creek Pass (elev. 5,400 feet). Here, the trail becomes Park Creek Pass Trail and descends 8 miles into the Stehekin Valley.

The highway may be closed from here east in the winter. ♿ MP 130

Mile 72.5 (102): Diablo Lake overlook. Eastbound, turn into parking area is via separate turn lane and a sharp left. The lake appears jade green due to rock particles, ground into dust by glaciers, which stay suspended in the water. Light reflected off the particles changes the lake's color.

Besides breathtaking views of the lake and mountains, the lookout features abundant and gregarious chipmunks. Don't get too close to the chipmunks. The state of Washington is one of several Western states that have issued warnings about rodents carrying a potent respiratory virus, the hantavirus, which can be spread through the air. Although the virus is typically found in deer mice, it's best to be safe. Also watch for pikas.

Numerous interpretive signs and displays at the lookout include a rock garden identifying the various rocks in formations along the highway.

A plaque notes that the North Cascades National Park is dedicated to former Washington senator Henry M. Jackson "in recognition of his leadership in establishing the North Cascades National Park system." The Jackson bill to create the park was signed into law in 1968 after a 6-year debate.

Numerous turnouts are available in the next 2 miles east to the Ross Lake overlook; they offer pulloff space, and some have photo exhibits pinpointing the mountains, valleys and highlights in the viewing area.

Mile 74 (100.5): John Pearce waterfall.

Mile 74.5 (100): Ross Dam trailhead and parking for approximately 40 cars. The trail leads north for numerous hike-in camping areas along Ross Lake. There are facilities for loading and unloading stock for horseback and llama trips into the mountains. ⚲ MP 134

Mile 75 (99.5): Happy Creek Interpretive Trail is a 0.3-mile boardwalk with 13 informational panels that leads into an old-growth forest. Handicap-accessible. Pit toilet at trailhead. ♿⚲

Mile 76 (98.5): Two Ross Lake viewpoints offer the only views of Ross Lake from the highway. The viewpoints are not well-marked on the highway. An interpretive sign at one points out the 5 sharp horns of Mount Prophet. The horns, which line up like teeth on a saw, were created by ages of glacial sculpting. Impounded by Ross Dam, Ross Lake covers what in 1906 was a small Ruby Creek Mining Co. settlement on the bank of the Skagit River just below the viewpoint. Ross Lake is 24 miles long, covers some 12,000 acres and reaches north into Canada. The lake level can drop as much as 100 feet in winter. The lake was named for J.D. Ross, the Seattle City Light superintendent who conceived and promoted the Skagit Project. MP 135

Mile 79 (95.5): Large parking area for the East Bank trailhead for hiking and horses; bridge over Panther Creek. ⚲

Mile 80 (94.5): Highway enters Okanogan National Forest. Land management changes from the National Park Service to the Forest Service at this point. MP 139

Mile 81.5 (93): Sign marks eastern boundary, Ross Lake National Recreation Area. MP 141

Mile 82 (92.5): The 15.5-mile Chancellor trail begins at Canyon Creek, north of the highway, and takes hikers through the historic mining town of Chancellor (9 miles) where old buildings remain. The trail then enters the Pasayten Wilderness where it eventually connects with the Devils Ridge trail. *NOTE*: The bridge on the connecting

Rowleys Chasm trail was washed out, making it impassible and dangerous. ⚲

Mile 85.5 (89): Ample parking for East Creek trailhead. Trail is open July to Sept. and begins with a short wind down to a bridge over Granite Creek, then climbs for a mile through timber to a boulder field with good views. The trail continues for 7 more miles before ascending meadow areas south of Mebee Pass. May be difficult to follow in places beyond the Gold Creek mine at the 4-mile mark. The first ford of East Creek can be difficult during periods of high water. Use caution. ⚲ MP 145

Mile 86 (88.5): Entering Skagit County eastbound.

Mile 89 (85.5): Highway passes over Granite Creek. MP 148

Mile 92.5 (82): Easy Pass trailhead and parking area to south. ⚲

Mile 94.5 (80): Swamp Creek winter chain-up area for eastbound traffic. MP 154

Mile 97 (77.5): Crossing Porcupine Creek. Highway eastward begins steep 0.7-mile climb. MP 156

Mile 98.5 (76): Summit of Rainy Pass (elev. 4,855 feet). Picnic area, restrooms and trailheads for Rainy Lake, Lake Ann and Maple Pass Loop trails. The mile-long Rainy Lake Trail is an easy, handicap-accessible paved trail with no elevation gain. Fishing is allowed at both Rainy Lake and Lake Ann. Views along the challenging 7.5-mile Maple Pass Loop Trail are spectacular. The trail travels over both Heather and Maple passes and is only for the experienced hiker.

The Pacific Crest Trail crosses the highway at Mile 98.5, with connections north to Hart's Pass and Canada. The first 5 miles of the trail provide an easy day hike to Cut-throat Pass. ♿⚲◀▲

Mile 99 (75.5): Bridge Creek trailhead. Paved parking area with ample room for RVs north of highway, and handicap-accessible pit toilet at trailhead. Access to the Pacific Crest Trail southbound.

Mile 102 (72.5): Turnout with view of Whistler Mountain (elev. 7,790 feet). A spectacular photo stop. MP 161

Mile 102.5 (72): Blue Lake trail, south of highway, and beginning eastbound of steep 3-mile grade. The trail is a gradual 3-mile slope to Blue Lake, with beautiful views along the way of Cutthroat Peak, Early Winter Spires and Liberty Bell Mountain. Hills painted red and gold in fall. Open late July through Sept. ⚲

Mile 103.5 (71): After a steep climb, the highway crests the more dramatic Washington Pass (elev. 5,477 feet). This is the highest point on the North Cascades Highway, and is slightly over a mile above sea level. Open when snow is cleared. A turnoff leads 0.2 mile to overlook access. There is ample parking, picnic areas and restroom facilities. The nearby overlook (handicap-accessible) provides a breathtaking view of the rugged Cascades and 7,720-foot Liberty Bell Mountain. Also visible from here are the Early Winter Spires (elev. 7,807 feet) and the highway's hairpin curves below. Excellent photo opportunities. Picnic area. The short overlook loop trail winds across an outcrop of Goldenhorn granite, the only true granite that has been identified in the north Cascades. Pink mountain heather and mountain hemlock are along the trail.

In the next couple of miles eastbound the highway descends the east side of the Cascades in hairpin curves as it follows the mountainsides. Notice the snow avalanche chutes that are the cause for closure of the

Diablo Lake overlook at Mile 72.5. The lake lies within Ross Lake National Recreation Area. (Michael Dill)

highway pass in the winter months.

&⚐ MP 162

Mile 105 (69.5): Turnout south of highway with excellent views of Silver Star Mountain.
MP 164

Mile 108 (66.5): Cutthroat Creek Road. One mile to trailhead and small campground with hitching rack, truck parking and water for stock. The access road is worth driving just for the view of snow-covered peaks it provides. The 1.7-mile trek to Cutthroat Lake, an alpine lake cradled in a high-walled cirque, is considered an easy day-hike. Trail continues another 3.8 miles to a connection with the Pacific Crest Trail at Cutthroat Pass, where mountain goats are often seen. In summer, be sure to have adequate water before going on to pass from the 1.7-mile mark. Trail open July to Sept.   ⚐▲ MP 167

Mile 109.5 (65): Lone Fir Campground, an Okanogan National Forest campground with pit toilets, firepits and 27 rustic campsites. Handicap-accessible toilet, drinking water. Open Memorial Day to Labor Day; fee $6 per night. Phone (509) 996-2266.   &▲

Mile 112 (62.5): Silver Star Creek turnout area.

Mile 115.5 (59): Steep descent for trucks and large RVs next 1.5 miles.

Mile 116.5 (58): Klipchuck Forest Service Campground; 6 tent sites, 46 tent/RV sites, handicap-accessible toilet, water. Fee: $6 per night. Fishing and hiking trails. Rattlesnakes occasionally seen near area. Open Memorial Day to Labor Day; phone (509) 996-2266.
&⚐◕▲ MP 175

Mile 117 (57.5): Cedar Creek trailhead access via forest road. Trail begins near the southeast end of gravel pit at end of road. A gentle hiking and horse trail leads 2 miles to Cedar Falls. Challenging for mountain bikers. The creek pours from pool to pool then drops 50 to 60 feet in a series of falls. Area around falls is precipitous, and there are no barriers. Open May to early Nov.   ⚐

Mile 118.5 (56): Okanogan National Forest boundary.

Mile 119 (55.5): Early Winters Campground sites are south and north of the highway. Thirteen sites, RVs to 16 feet, handicap-accessible toilet, water available Memorial Day to Labor Day, fee $6; phone (509) 996-2266.
&▲ MP 177

Mile 119.2 (55.3): National Forest Service Early Winters Visitor Center (509/996-2534), has information, maps, brochures and hiking trail information. Closed in winter.   MP 178

Mile 122 (52.5): MAZAMA offers an inn, restaurant, phone, gas and store. Bed and breakfast, lodge and resort with cabins nearby. Rental horses for trail rides are available; inquire at Mazama Country Inn, phone (509) 996-2681. Mazama is also a base for heli-skiing operators; phone (800) 494-Heli.

Mile 125 (49.5): Rocking Horse Ranch operates trail rides and overnight pack trips. $20 per person for 1½ hours, $10 per person for each additional hour. Lunch and special rides can be arranged. Phone (509) 996-2768 for reservations. Private campground with 12 full hookups and pull-throughs for trailers/tents, showers, flush toilets, water, firewood. Tent sites on Methow River. Open mid-May to early Sept.; $10 per night for tents, $13 full hookups, $12 partial hookups.   ▲ MP 184

Mile 134 (40.5): Entering **WINTHROP** (pop. 350), offering all services including gas, family restaurants, fast-food outlets, lodging, parks and more than 15 campgrounds within 8 miles. For lodging in the Methow Valley, phone Central Reservations at 1-800-422-3048.

The bridge into main street Winthrop eastbound takes travelers over the copper-colored Chewuch; the bridge out of downtown eastbound takes travelers over the calm, blue Methow River. The Western-style town of Winthrop is well worth a stop to investigate. It is a good chance to stretch your legs, enjoy a meal or snack, visit one of the many local businesses, see a working blacksmith shop or stop in at the visitor center. The Chamber of Commerce visitor center is open every day 10 a.m. to 5 p.m. May to Sept. (509/996-2125) and offers publications, brochures, hand-outs and information on the Methow Valley, Lake Chelan, Grand Coulee Dam and other travel destinations. A second visitor center at Winthrop Park on Highway 20 has public restroom facilities.

In May, Winthrop hosts the Washington State Chili Cookoff, the 49er Days, the Mountain Man Convention and the Winthrop Rodeo. The town's July Rhythm and Blues Festival draws music lovers from all over, and September features an antique auto rally.

For 9,000 years Indians lived along the banks of the Methow, Twisp and Chewuch rivers, digging camas root, picking berries, fishing and hunting. In 1883 the lure of gold brought the first white settlers to the area. In 1891, Guy Waring opened a store and post office at the forks of the Methow and Chewuch rivers. He named it after a friend, Theodore Winthrop, a Yale graduate who toured the Northwest in the early 1850s. Another friend, Owen Wister, visited in 1898 and may have been inspired by the town and setting for parts of his novel, *The Virginian.*

Winthrop's false-front buildings and Western theme date to 1972 and were a conscious effort to attract visitors. Original buildings include The Last Trading Post, which was the first trading post, and a post office. Waring's Duck Brand Saloon has been a restaurant, pool hall, school, church, community hall and hospital. It is currently a city hall. Waring's log cabin is the Shafer Museum and is on the National Register of Historic Sites. After crossing the bridge into town eastbound, continue straight up Bridge Street; turn south onto Castle Avenue and go approximately ½ block to the museum. Admission by donation.

With more than 300 days of sunshine per year, Winthrop is frequented by campers, photographers, hikers, fishermen and watersports enthusiasts.

There is excellent fishing in area lakes, including Patterson Lake, Twin Lakes and Pearrygin Lake within minutes from Winthrop. Ice-fishing enthusiasts visit Davis Lake in the winter. For more information, call the Winthrop Chamber of Commerce at (509) 996-2125.

Pearrygin Lake State Park, about 5 miles northwest, is open to boaters, wind surfers and swimmers. It has 30 full hookups, 27 water only, and 26 tent sites. Boat launch, jet ski and boat rentals, fishing for rainbow trout. Go-cart track nearby. Campground open mid-April to Nov. 1. Reservations required and taken after Jan. 1 for camping Memorial Day to Labor Day, (509) 996-2370. Peak-season fee $16 per night for full hookups; $11 all other sites.

The 12-mile Pearrygin Lake loop is a scenic, relatively easy (800-foot gain) moun-

A gas station in Winthrop, like many of the town buildings, has a Western-style exterior.
(Michael Dill)

tain-bike loop. From Winthrop follow the signs to the state park. Where the paved entrance road turns right, go straight up the hill on Pearrygin Lake Road. Pedal the dirt road 2 miles. At the "T" intersection at the Methow Wildlife Range Ranch, turn right and coast down to the valley floor. The dirt road turns to pavement as it passes the Bear Creek Golf Course. At the valley floor turn right for a 3-mile road back to town. Good area paved-road rides include the 18-mile Twin Lakes loop, the 14-mile Chewuch loop and the 19-mile Winthrop–Twisp loop.

The Methow Valley is a top Washington snowmobiling and Nordic ski area. In the summer, horseback riding trips are available from numerous area outfitters, as are river rafting trips. The Methow River whitewater season usually lasts from early May into July, with many runs of varying difficulty. A popular easy run is between Winthrop and Carlton. Carlton to Methow has moderate rapids, and Methow to the Columbia River is for those in search of adventure.

More than 130 species of birds are found in the Methow Valley during the spring. The Twisp, Chewuch and Methow rivers draw great blue herons, dippers, merganser, gold-eneye and belted kingfishers. Pearrygin Lake, Twin Lakes and Patterson Lake near Winthrop are popular with Western grebe, piebilled grebe, eared grebe, osprey, and tundra swans. Sullivan's Pond, north and east of Winthrop, features ducks and marsh birds, as well as hawks and golden eagles on nearby cliffs. A loop trail at the pond's north end provides a 10-minute hike in which meadowlarks and woodpeckers may be visible. The Sunnyside trail around Sun Mountain is a good place to see hummingbirds.

Maps and information on bird watching from the car are available from the Winthrop and Twisp offices of the Methow Valley Ranger District.

The Winthrop ranger district office (509/996-2266), can provide information on hiking trails, campgrounds, cross-country ski trails, highway conditions and secondary roads to streams and lakes. ᛉ╼▲★ MP 193

Mile 134.5 (40): Access, before crossing the Methow, to base for smoke jumpers—firefighters who jump out of airplanes to put out wildfires. Winthrop began experimenting with smoke jumping in 1939 and is considered the birthplace of U.S. smoke jumping. Tours available. To reach the base go straight on Eastside County Road; do not cross bridge. Road leads approximately 3 miles to private golf course with open-play policy and then 1 more mile to the base; phone (509) 997-2031.

Mile 134.7 (39.8): First eastbound access to Sun Mountain Lodge, Twin Lakes and Patterson Lake. Sun Mountain Lodge, 8 miles north of the highway, has 50 rooms, 2 heated pools, tennis courts, a golf course, trout fishing, mountain biking, horseback riding, more than 50 miles of hiking trails and cross-country skiing. ᛉ╼

Mile 135.5 (39): Private campground, with RV sites, on riverbank. Fishing onsite. ╼▲ MP 194

Mile 137 (37.5): First westbound access to Sun Mountain Lodge. MP 196

Mile 141 (33.5): Private campground with RV sites. ▲

Mile 142 (32.5): TWISP (pop. 900), name derived from an Indian word for "yellow jacket." Since its founding in 1899, Twisp's fortunes have rested on mining, ranching and agriculture. It has survived several fires, floods and freezing cold that destroyed fruit crops. The coldest temperature ever recorded in Washington state was at Twisp in 1968, when the thermometer plunged to -48°. Between 2 and 2¹/₂ feet of snowfall can be expected in the Twisp area in winter. There is a Freeze Yer Buns Run every January. Twisp offers all traveler services including gas stations with towing and repair service, restaurants, motels, 2 medical clinics, pharmacy, private RV parks, Twisp Information Center (509/997-2926), and Ranger Station (509/997-2131), which provides information on activities, as well as near the highway. Farmer's market 9 a.m. to noon on Saturdays at the community center parking lot. Area recreation encompasses fishing, hiking, horseback riding, rafting, snowmobiling and cross-country skiing. More than 100 birds are indigenous to the area. ᛉ╼▲ MP 201

Mile 143 (31.5): Access to Twisp River Recreational Area, dump station, fishing. ╼

Mile 143.5 (31): Golf course. Alternate access to smoke jumper base (see **Mile 134.5**).

Mile 144 (30.5): Twisp eastern city limits. The section of the highway between Twisp and Okanogan is called the Loup Loup Highway.

Mile 145 (29.5): Junction with Washington Highway 153, which heads south 31 miles to join U.S. Highway 97 at Pateros. Going straight puts travelers on Highway 153. Highway 20 turns north. Airport road is to the north of the highway. MP 204

Mile 150 (24.5): Dept. of Game sign marks Methow Wildlife Area—10,302 acres dedicated to the production and harvest of wild game. The area was acquired primarily as a winter range for mule deer, and also ensures a permanent population of grouse and pheasants. The Methow Valley has the largest mule-deer herd in the state.

Mile 151.5 (23): Okanogan National Forest boundary. Established in 1897, the Okanogan is one of the nation's oldest national forests. It features more than 1,500 miles of trails and spreads from here to the Okanogan–Ferry county line, and from the Canadian border to the Methow–Chelan divide. Morel mushrooms tend to grow on lands burned the previous year; guide available for a fee from the Okanogan National Forest, phone (509) 826-3275. Tick season begins in spring in the forest. Take precautions. Okanogan is a Salish Indian word meaning "rendezvous." MP 210

Mile 155.5 (19): J.R. Campground; 6 tent/RV sites, water, handicap-accessible pit toilets. Open mid-May to mid-Sept. $5 per night. ♿▲ MP 214

Mile 155.8 (18.7): Loup Loup Pass Summit (elev. 4,020 feet) and Summit Road. Snow parking for cross-country skiing and snowmobiling.

Mile 156 (18.5): Turnoff north for Loup

Loup Ski Bowl and Loup Loup Creek Campground. The ski bowl offers 4 primary runs and a vertical drop of 1,200 feet, 2 lifts and 2 rope tows, half pipe for snow boarders, 20-plus km of groomed cross-country trails, and in summer, hiking and mountain biking. A day lodge, cafeteria, equipment rentals, snowmobiling and cross-country and telemark lessons are available in winter; phone (509) 826-2720.

Loup Loup Creek. Campground near the creek has 11 picnic sites, 25 tent/RV sites, water and pit toilets. Open mid-May to Sept.; phone (509) 997-2131. $5 per night. ⊰ᛉ⊼▲ MP 215

Mile 157 (17.5): Watch for rocks.

Mile 164.5 (10): Dirt access road north to Rock Creek DNR Campground with 6 sites, group shelters, water, pit toilets, no fee; phone (509) 684-7474. ▲

Mile 164.7 (9.8): Little Loup Creek and campground. ▲

Mile 165.5 (9): Leader Lake DNR Campground; 16 sites, boat launch, fishing, pit toilets, no water, no fee; phone (509) 684-7474. ╼▲ MP 224

Mile 166 (8.5): Watch for hikers next 2 miles.

Mile 169 (5.5): Junction with road leading south to Malott and Brewster.

Mile 170 (4.5): Historical marker commemorates confrontation between cattlemen and sheepmen near here in the early 1900s. From marker, road winds downward, with view of valley farmlands, orchards and hills below. MP 229

Mile 174.5 (0): Okanogan eastern city limits. **OKANOGAN** (pop. 2,395) straddles the Okanogan River in the dry, sunny Okanogan Valley, an area of sage-covered foothills rimmed by mountainous pine forests. It is located approximately 20 miles west of the first American settlement in Washington, Old Fort Okanogan. The present town began as a trading post in 1886. It includes the former settlements of Alma and Pogue. Until 1906, when an irrigation system was built, Okanogan was little more than a river landing and general store. Local orchards grow cherries, apricots, peaches, pears and apples. The city celebrates Okanogan Days in early summer with a street fair, a parade and a fly-in at its airport. The Okanogan county Balloon Rendezvous takes place in September. Okanogan is the county seat and headquarters for Okanogan National Forest (phone 509/826-3275), plus several other government agencies and county offices. Landmarks include the 75-year-old courthouse. Visitor information center is at Legion Park, (509) 422-1541. The park also offers camping. Okanogan offers motels, gas, restaurants and most facilities, including windshield repair, while its sister city, Omak, 4 miles north, serves the area as the commercial center and offers all visitor services.

At Okanogan, Washington Highway 20 offers a junction with Washington Highway 215 and U.S. Highway 97 business loop. Highway 20 and U.S. 97 merge at Okanogan and continue as a joint highway north to Tonasket. Turn to **Mile 559.5** in the U.S. HIGHWAY 97 section for log of that route. ⊼▲

SAWTOOTH SCENIC ROUTE

Idaho Highway 75
Shoshone to Challis, ID

In its 170-mile northward journey from Shoshone to Challis, Idaho Highway 75—dubbed the Sawtooth Scenic Route—introduces the motorist to some of the finest mountain scenery and outdoor recreation in the West. This is where railroad baron Averell Harriman chose to locate America's first ski resort, Sun Valley, in the 1930s. Over the next several decades most of the big Hollywood stars managed to make at least one trip to Sun Valley to see and be seen. Sun Valley is still one of the top winter sports resorts in the country and also has an extensive summer season.

Just to the north, Sawtooth National Recreation Area (NRA) was one of the West's last great mountain treasures to be discovered by the traveling public. Though popular with Idahoans, it has only recently become known as a vacation destination. Nearly the size of Yosemite National Park, it was seriously considered for national park status in the 1960s. See Sawtooth NRA description in the MAJOR ATTRACTIONS section.

Mileposts along Idaho Highway 75 reflect distance from the Idaho–Nevada border via U.S. Highway 93 South.

Sawtooth Scenic Route Log

Distance from Shoshone, ID, is followed by distance from Challis, ID.

Mile 0 (170): SHOSHONE (pop. 1,249); has all services, including 1 motel and 6 restaurants. A railroad town and supply point on the east-west line of the Union Pacific Railroad, it was once the connecting point where transcontinental passengers boarded trains for Sun Valley. The wide main street is split by the railroad tracks and lined with old brick and false front buildings that make it look like a set from a Western movie. MP 74

Mile 4 (166): Groceries and gas available.

Mile 8 (162): Side road west to Mammoth Cave, 1.5 miles (gravel road). Mammoth Cave is a 0.2-mile-long lava tube discovered in 1902. A museum there has a large collection of mounted bird specimens. Admission is charged.

Mile 8.5 (161.5): Mammoth Cave Civil Defense Shelter 1.5 miles west.

Mile 15 (155): Clear view of the distinctive

shape of the Sawtooths to the north. Sparse sagebrush here barely covers broad fields of lava. View of 1,499-foot Kinzie Butte to the east. MP 89

Mile 15.5 (154.5): County road to Richfield, 16 miles east.

Mile 16 (154): Cafe on east side of highway. Side road leads west to Shoshone Ice Caves, lava tubes with ice formations caused by cool air passing through. Museum has fossil

exhibits; admission fee is charged. MP 90

Mile 16.5 (153.5): Highway crosses a good example of exposed lava flow. View of 1,458-foot Black Butte Crater to the northwest.

Mile 17 (153): Magic Dam historical marker. Magic Dam was completed in 1910 to store water for 89,000 acres of irrigated farms near Shoshone and Richfield. It is now a fishing and recreational area. ✒

To Salmon

93

N
W   E
S

Challis

Custer
Bald Mountain
(Elev. 10,313 ft.)

Bonanza

McKay Creek

Custer Lookout
(Elev. 9,753 ft.)

Mile 170

21

Sunbeam

Clayton

75

Salmon River

Mile 148

Stanley

Stanley Lake

Mile 115.5

Sawtooth

21

75

National

To Lowman

Redfish Lake

Sawtooth

Castle Peak
(Elev. 11,815 ft.)

East Fork Salmon River

93

Recreation

Galena Peak
(Elev. 11,170 ft.)

Ryan Peak
(Elev. 11,795 ft.)

Challis

Mackay

Alturas Lake

Galena Summit
(Elev. 8,701 ft.)

Area

75

National

93

Sun Valley

Mile 54

Ketchum

PIONEER MOUNTAINS

Arco

20

Wilderness

Hailey

Forest

Craters of the Moon National Monument

SAWTOOTH RANGE

Bellevue

26

LOST RIVER RANGE

To Mountain Home

20

Hill City

Magic Reservoir

20

93

Carey

Lava Beds

Shoshone Ice Caves

26

To Boise

30

Big Wood River

75

Richfield

Mammoth Cave

Shoshone

Mile 0

84

93

Jerome

Scale
10 miles
10 kilometres

Cattle graze below the Sawtooth Mountains in Sawtooth National Recreation Area near Stanley, Mile 115.5. (© George Wuerthner)

Mile 18 (152): Crossing Big Wood River. Side road leads west 10 miles to Magic Reservoir.

Mile 19 (151): Highway crosses Richfield Canal and begins gradual ascent into the foothills northbound.

Mile 24.5 (145.5): Side road leads west 5 miles to Magic Reservoir.

Mile 27 (143): Highway crests hill and begins descent into the Big Wood River Valley farmland northbound.   MP 101

Mile 28 (142): Rest area at **junction** with U.S. Highway 20, an alternate route across the Camas prairie through Fairfield to Interstate 84 at Mountain Home. Access to Magic Reservoir; good fishing for rainbow and brown trout, waterskiing, windsurfing, sailing, 1 resort and RV park with 60 sites.
⬥▲ MP 102

Mile 37 (133): BELLEVUE (pop. 1,500); all services, including 1 motel and 4 restaurants. Private RV park with 31 sites, 25 with hookups, is open April through Nov.

Founded as a mining town when rich silver-lead deposits were discovered in the nearby hills in 1880, Bellevue now serves surrounding farms. Topographical features in this area have fascinating names dating from the mining era—Cowcatcher Ridge, Minnie Moore Gulch, Poverty Flat. In the spring and fall it is not unusual to encounter Basque shepherds driving flocks of hundreds of sheep along this road accompanied by a bread-loaf-shaped wagon and a couple of skillful border collies. The railroad right-of-way on the east side of the highway for the original line that caused Sun Valley to be built is now the Wood River Bike Trail, connecting Bellevue, Hailey, Ketchum and Sun Valley.   ▲

Mile 39 (131): Wood River Mines historical marker. Lead and silver strikes beginning in 1879 made this, for a time, Idaho's leading mining region. Hailey had Idaho's first phone service in 1883 and 3 daily newspapers; a Ketchum smelter pioneered electric lighting in Idaho.

Mile 41 (129): HAILEY (pop. 2,920), offers all services, including 8 restaurants and 4 motels. Hailey was also a mining town and now serves primarily vacationers. The main street has been gentrified with a number of the old buildings spruced up with new paint and fixtures. Blaine County Historical Museum (N. Main and Galena) occupies an 1882 brick building and features pioneer artifacts and a collection of political campaign memorabilia. Ezra Pound was born in Hailey in the house on the northeast corner of 2nd Avenue and Pine Street.

Friedman Memorial Airport, used by both private and commercial aircraft serving Sun Valley.   MP 115

Mile 48.5 (121.5): Highway crosses Big Wood River. Both the Big and Little Wood rivers, often fished by Ernest Hemingway, are excellent trout streams. Scores of elegant new homes and ranchettes on both sides of the highway reflect the major influx of affluent migrants to this valley in the last couple of years.   ⬥

Mile 51 (119): Private RV park with 46 sites, 44 with hookups, showers and laundry facilities.▲

Mile 52.5 (117.5): Highway crosses Big Wood River.

Mile 53 (117): Elkhorn Road leads 3 miles east to Elkhorn Village. RV campground beside river on west side of highway has 78 sites, 32

hookups, showers, laundry, groceries, mini-golf, recreation room and swimming pool.   ▲

Mile 54 (116): KETCHUM (pop. 2,523) and **SUN VALLEY** (pop. 660) have 58 restaurants, 21 motels and resorts, and 3 RV parks with 125 hookups. Sun Valley/Ketchum Central Reservations handles reservations and information for the whole area; phone 1-800-786-8259 or (208) 622-4111.

Though the towns are actually about a mile apart, Ketchum and Sun Valley are thought of as one, and restaurants and accommodations spill across the boundaries between the 2 communities. Sun Valley (and nearby Elkhorn Resort) winter sports facilities are focused on Bald Mountain and Dollar Mountain. The resort has 66 downhill runs with a vertical drop of 3,400 feet serviced by 12 chair lifts. It was here that James Curran, a Union Pacific engineer, invented the chair lift and installed the first of them on Dollar and Proctor mountains in 1936. Today the resort offers a complete range of winter activities including cross-country skiing, sleigh rides, helicopter skiing, ballooning, ice fishing, snowmobiling and snowshoeing.

Elegant old Sun Valley lodge is worth a visit whether or not you stay there. Built in 1936 of formed concrete disguised to look like wood, the lodge sits surrounded by gardens, ponds and an ice skating rink where world champions perform in summer ice shows. Hundreds of photos of the rich and famous who have visited Sun Valley adorn a hallway wall adjacent to the lobby. Hemingway wrote *For Whom the Bell Tolls* in room 206 at the lodge. Nearby, the Sun Valley Opera House shows the Sonja Henie film *Sun Valley Serenade* every day of the year.

In summer, the resort offers a host of activities including bicycling, golf, tennis, riding, fishing, trap and skeet shooting, hiking, river rafting, archery, soaring and several music and arts events. Fly-fishing is superb and some area streams such as Silver Creek (pronounced "crick" by Idahoans) are world famous. Lessons and guides are available from several shops in Ketchum. ⬥⛺⬥▲★

Mile 55.5 (114.5): Ernest Hemingway is buried here in the Ketchum cemetery.
MP 130

Mile 57 (113): Sun Peak picnic site beside Big Wood River.   ⊼

Mile 58 (112): Lake Creek trailhead.   ⋔

Mile 61 (109): Crossing Big Wood River. The highway will cross this river several times on this route.   MP 135

Mile 62.5 (107.5): Headquarters to the Sawtooth NRA. Visitor center has free tape tour for playing in your car, several audio-visual programs, literature and restrooms. Open 8 a.m. to 5:30 p.m. daily.

Sawtooth NRA stretches north and west from this point, covering 756,000 acres (about the size of Rhode Island) and 3 mountain ranges—the Sawtooths, White Clouds and Boulders—with 40 peaks reaching 10,000 feet or more.

Mile 63 (107): North Fork NRA campground has 39 sites, pit toilets and fishing. Groceries 1 mile south.

Mile 64.5 (105.5): Wood River NRA campground has 32 sites, flush toilets, swimming, fishing and nature trails. Groceries 2 miles south. Mountains to the southwest are the Smokeys, to the northeast are the Boulders.

Mile 68.5 (101.5): Small store and commercial hot springs with pool and showers. Easley NRA campground has 10 sites, water, toilets, fishing and swimming.

Mile 69 (101): Note the aspen thickets along the Big Wood River. This route is carpeted in wildflowers by early July. Alexander Ross and Hudson's Bay Co. trappers discovered the Sawtooth Valley in 1824.   MP 143

Mile 69.5 (100.5): Boulder View NRA campground has 8 sites, fishing and swimming. **Junction** with Baker Creek Road.

Mile 73 (97): Prairie Creek undeveloped NRA campground.

Mile 74.5 (95.5): Crossing Wood River.

Mile 77 (93): Large volcanic rock outcroppings. Road on east side leads to Galena Pioneer Cemetery. Miners made their first strike of lead ore (galena) here in 1879. Picnic area.   MP 151

Mile 77.5 (92.5): Galena Stage Stop offers trail rides.

Mile 78 (92): Galena Lodge has horseback riding, hiking and mountain biking in summer and cross-country skiing in winter. Food service and equipment rental.

Mile 79.5 (90.5): Terraces on sides of the steep hills ahead were cut to reduce erosion by grazing sheep. Highway begins its steep and winding climb northbound to Galena Summit.

Mile 82.5 (87.5): Overlook to Boulder Mountains and Alexander Ross historical marker.

Mile 84 (86): Galena Summit (elev. 8,701 feet).

Mile 85 (85): Overlook provides splendid views of the Sawtooth Mountains, Sawtooth Valley and the Salmon River drainages. Gouged by glaciers, the valley below is 30 miles long by 5 miles wide. Dozens of pika, chipmunks, ground squirrels and bold Clark's jays live around the overlook and often approach tourists looking for a handout.

Mile 87 (83): Historical marker on the Salmon River.

Mile 88.5 (81.5): Road to south leads to headwaters of the Salmon River and an undeveloped campground.

Mile 89 (81): Crossing the Salmon River for the first time northbound.

Mile 89.5 (80.5): Crossing Frenchman Creek. Large glacial moraines, the deposits of rock and debris left by retreating glaciers, lie on both sides of the road.

Mile 90.5 (79.5): Historical marker, mining community of Vienna. Turnoff 3 miles east to historic Pole Creek Ranger Station, first ranger station in the Sawtooth Wilderness. Paved interpretive trail, toilet.

Mile 91.5 (78.5): Sawtooth City, a small corridor of private land within the National Recreation Area. Residents named it after the historic mining town nearby.   MP 165

Mile 92 (78): Restaurant and gas available. Crossing Smiley Creek.

Mile 92.5 (77.5): Groceries and gas station.

Mile 93 (77): Gas and groceries (seasonal). Turnoff southwest 3 miles to Sawtooth City (circa 1879), an early mining community.

Meadows on east side of the road are spring nesting grounds for sandhill cranes, one of the tallest birds in the world.

Mile 94.5 (75.5): Road to west leads 2 miles to Alturas Lake, which has 3 campgrounds with 60 sites, picnicking, boat launches, sandy beaches and fishing. Cross-country skiing in winter.

Mile 97.5 (72.5): Road leads west 1 mile to Pettit Lake, a small quiet lake with timbered shoreline and an undeveloped campground with trailhead access to the Sawtooth Wilderness Area.

Mile 99 (71): Crossing the Salmon River.

Mile 100 (70): Crossing Champion Creek. The White Cloud peaks are coming into view to the east for northbound travelers.
          MP 174

Mile 101 (69): Fourth of July Creek.

Mile 102.5 (67.5): Fisher Creek.

Mile 104.5 (65.5): Sessions Lodge offers accommodations, cafe, gas, groceries, 16 RV spaces with hookups. Obsidian found in this area is a black, glassy volcanic rock made when lava cools quickly.

Mile 105.5 (64.5): Crossing Williams Creek.

Mile 106 (64): Idaho Rocky Mountain Ranch, another guest ranch and restaurant that offers fishing, watersports, hiking and horseback riding. The handsome log lodge, built in 1929 and said to be one of the best log structures in the West, was the former retreat of the president of Frigidaire, Winston Paul.

Mile 106.5 (63.5): Crossing Gold Creek.

Mile 109.5 (60.5): Sawtooth Fish Hatchery, open 8:30 a.m. to 5 p.m.

Mile 111 (59): Junction with road to Redfish Lake. The largest lake in the Sawtooths, Redfish is named for the sockeye that come here to spawn. Fishing in both the lake and nearby streams is outstanding. The resort here has boats for rent, restaurant, cabins, horseback riding, swimming, sightseeing excursions on the lake, hiking trails and stunning views of the Sawtooths. Gas, groceries and 10 NRA campgrounds with 138 sites are available. Trailhead access to the Sawtooth Wilderness Area.

Redfish Lake Visitor Center has nature exhibits, audio-visual programs, map, interpretive programs, self-guided nature trail, guided nature walks, hiking and auto tours. Cross-country skiing and snowmobiling in

Brightly-colored heather grows at 8,800 feet in the Sawtooth Wilderness Area. (L. Linkhart)

winter. Open 9 a.m. to 6 p.m., late June through Labor Day. ⚏⚏▲ MP 185

Mile 111.5 (58.5): Highway crosses the Salmon River and slices through a glacial moraine.

Mile 112 (58): Stanley ranger station, open weekdays year-round, 8 a.m. to 5 p.m.

Mile 115.5 (54.5): STANLEY (pop. 140), offers all visitor services, including 7 motels/lodges, 5 restaurants, 1 gas station and 3 private RV campgrounds. Stanley has the unenviable reputation of being the coldest town in the state, where -50°F has been recorded. It is also one of the primary outfitting spots for rafting trips down the Salmon River, including single-day excursions from Stanley, and horsepacking and guided hiking trips into the surrounding mountains. For information on these services, contact Idaho Outfitters and Guides Assoc., P.O. Box 95, Boise, ID 83701; phone (208) 342-1438. Scenic flights over the Sawtooths and White Clouds are available from the Stanley airport. In winter local dealers rent snowmobiles.

The Ponderosa Pine Scenic Route, Idaho 21, enters Stanley from the west and offers the opportunity (with Interstate 84 and Idaho Highway 75) for a loop trip through this whole region from Boise. The highway follows the whitewater Payette River, climbs over 2 summits of more than 6,000 feet and passes through the gold rush relic town of Idaho City. From Stanley to the outskirts of Boise it is 130 miles. ⚏⚏▲

Mile 116 (54): Lower Stanley; gas, lodging, groceries and cafe. Idaho 75 is designated the Salmon River Scenic Route north from here. The highway follows the river closely as it swings almost due east for most of the way to Challis, threading through narrow canyons between the mountains.

Mile 119.5 (50.5): Salmon River NRA campground has 32 sites, pit toilets, laundry facilities and fishing. ⚏▲

Mile 121 (49): Riverside NRA campground offers 18 sites, pit toilets and fishing. ⚏▲

Mile 121.5 (48.5): Mormon Bend NRA campground has 17 sites, pit toilets and fishing. ⚏▲

Mile 123 (47): Basin Creek campground offers 13 sites, pit toilets, fishing. The highway and river wind along the bottom of the canyon with mountains rising nearly a thousand feet on either side. Note the thickly wooded north-facing slopes and the open sagebrush terrain on the south slopes due to temperature and rainfall variations. ⚏▲

Mile 127 (43): Sunbeam Hot Springs. Hot water bubbles from the slope on both sides of the road; there is a small unused rock bathhouse and interpretive sign.

Mile 128 (42): SUNBEAM has gas, cafe, groceries and float trips available. The remains of Sunbeam dam jut into the river below the highway. Built in 1909–10 to supply electricity to Sunbeam mine and mill, it is the only dam ever built on the Salmon River. In 1934, after years of controversy because it blocked the salmon and steelhead runs, the

dam was dynamited. Interpretive and information signs.

A gravel side road leads 9 miles north to the ghost town of Bonanza, 1 mile farther to the Yankee Fork gold dredge and another 2 miles to the mining relic town of Custer and the Custer museum. The gold rush really got under way here on Yankee Fork in 1875. Both towns peaked during the late 1800s when the combined population reached about 5,000, then faded and finally folded in 1910.

A few cabins are all that remain of Bonanza; Custer is somewhat better preserved. A pioneer cemetery is situated on a hillside about a mile beyond the Bonanza Forest Service guard station. The massive Yankee Fork gold dredge operated between 1939 and 1952, and it now sits beached on piles of rock waste at the mouth of Jordan Creek. It is open for tours daily, June through Labor Day, from 10 a.m. to 5 p.m. The Custer Ghost Town Museum has a collection of historic mining equipment and other pioneer memorabilia.

Crossing Yankee Fork and Salmon River. Turnouts along here provide good vantage points for watching the many rafters and kayakers who float this river in summer.

Mile 129 (41): Elk Creek float boat access. Parking, toilet.

Mile 130.5 (39.5): Indian Riffles; salmon spawning beds. Interpretive signs and toilet.

Mile 133.5 (36.5): Crossing Peach Creek. MP 208

Mile 134.5 (35.5): Snyder Springs picnic area. Highway crosses Gardner Creek. ⚏

Mile 136 (34): Burnt Creek Inn offers cabins, RV park with 17 sites, hookups, cafe and groceries. Torrey's float boat access. Parking, toilet. ▲

Mile 138.5 (31.5): Crossing Slate Creek.

Mile 139 (31): Highway crosses the Salmon River.

Mile 139.5 (30.5): Mill Creek. MP 214

Mile 141 (29): Thompson Creek. Leaving Sawtooth National Recreation Area eastbound.

Mile 142 (28): Small, unnamed residential community with handsome old log barn on the north side of the highway.

Mile 142.5 (27.5): Yankee Fork ranger station, Challis National Forest. MP 217

Mile 143.5 (26.5): French Creek.

Mile 146 (24): Crossing the Salmon River. Note colorful green lichen on the rocks on the south side of the river.

Mile 148 (22): CLAYTON (pop. 43) has a cafe, groceries and gas. Clayton was founded

Rafting the Salmon River. Stanley is a primary outfitting spot for river raft trips. (L. Linkhart)

in 1881 as the site of a smelter for nearby mines. The smelter closed in 1904. Several mines in the adjacent mountains are still active, producing primarily silver.

Mile 152.5 (17.5): Crossing East Fork Salmon River; picnic area with tables and pit toilets. ⚏ MP 227

Mile 161.5 (8.5): Domestic buffalo graze on the south side of the highway. Valley is dotted with hay and cattle ranches. The ghost town of Bayhorse is located 2.5 miles up Bayhorse Creek.

Mile 162.5 (7.5): Bayhorse Recreation Site on the north side of the highway adjacent to the river, has picnic tables, pit toilets and fishing access. ⚏⚏ MP 237

Mile 164 (6): Crossing Salmon River.

Mile 167 (3): Bighorn sheep crossing sign.

Mile 169.5 (0.5): Land of the Yankee Fork Visitor Center. Exhibits show the area's mining legacy. The visitor center is modeled after 19th century mining buildings. It is open 8 a.m. to 6 p.m. during summer, 9 a.m. to 5 p.m. in winter.

Shoshone Indians used the steep bluff just to the north as a buffalo jump. Buffalo would be driven over the cliffs so the Indians could harvest the meat and hides.

Mile 170 (0): Junction with U.S. Highway 93. Challis is 2.5 miles north.

For more information on Challis, turn to **Mile 191** in the U.S. HIGHWAY 93 section.

SEA TO SKY HIGHWAY

BC Highway 99
Vancouver to Junction with Highway 97

Highway 99 north from Vancouver to Squamish along the shore of Howe Sound has long been known as a scenic drive, one of the "don't miss" attractions for Vancouver visitors. Skiers know the highway well: It's the only road access to the giant ski hills of Whistler and Blackcomb. But only fairly recently could Highway 99 claim to be a viable route to the British Columbia Interior, part of the province's interlocking highway system.

With the paving of a 62-mile/100-kilometre stretch of logging road between Pemberton and Lillooet, it is now possible to drive to the Cariboo and points north or east without first driving up the Fraser Valley to Hope. Promoted as the "Sea to Sky Highway," the new route encompasses a range of scenery, from islands and coastal fjords through glaciated mountains, arid semi-desert and Cariboo forest.

Highway 99 Log

Distance in miles from Vancouver is followed by distance in miles from junction with Highway 97. Equivalent distances in kilometres are indicated by Km.

Mile 0 (209) Km 0 (336.5): North end of Lions Gate Bridge. The bridge crosses Burrard Inlet and joins Vancouver with the North Shore (North and West Vancouver). It was built as a private venture by the British Guinness family (yes, the famous brewery people) to provide access to their new swank housing development, British Properties. It was named for the Lions, the double-peaked mountain that overlooks Vancouver. Until 1955, when the B.C. government bought it for $6 million, this elegant suspension bridge was a toll bridge. Commuters find its 3 lanes a bottleneck in rush hour. Take West Vancouver exit lane.

Mile 0.5 (208.5) Km 1 (335.5): After crossing the Capilano River, Highway 99 turns right, off Marine Drive to climb steeply up Taylor Way.

Mile 1 (208) Km 2 (334.5): **Junction** with Highway 1 West, the Upper Levels Highway. Highways 1 and 99 share a common alignment from here to Horseshoe Bay.

Mile 4 (205) Km 6.5 (330): Exit for Cypress Provincial Park and 10-km paved road to viewpoint and ski hill. Picnicking, alpine hikes, cross-country and downhill skiing.
🚶🏕️🏔️ EXIT 8

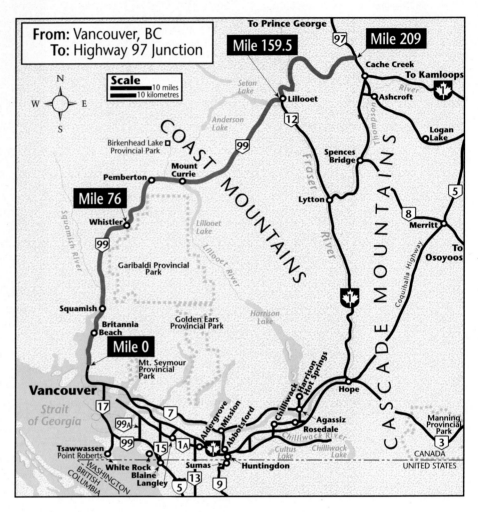

Mile 6 (203) Km 10 (326.5): Cypress Creek. Notice the Arbutus trees on the mountain slopes and, in spring, the yellow English broom.

Mile 8 (201) Km 13 (323.5): Nelson Creek. Westbound turnout and mandatory truck brake check at top of steep downgrade to ferry dock. Follow signs for ferry lineup. There are often 2 or 3 ferry waits on summer holiday weekends.

Mile 9 (200) Km 15 (321.5): Exit for **HORSESHOE BAY VILLAGE** (pop. 1000), a bedroom community with tourist facilities, marina and boat rentals, dominated by a huge BC Ferries terminal. Ferry access for southbound traffic.

This is the official start of the "Sea to Sky Highway." Highway 99 turns north to run along the east shore of spectacular Howe Sound, a coastal fjord, with dramatic views of mountains and islands. The road is mostly narrow and winding, but there are several places to stop and admire the scenery. Keep in mind that this road can be extremely hazardous, subject to rock falls and avalanches, icy winter conditions and bridge washout due to roaring mountain streams. Observe posted cautions.

Mile 10 (199) Km 16.5 (320): Viewpoint overlooking boat and ferry harbor at Horseshoe Bay. Large island opposite is Bowen.

Mile 13.5 (195.5) Km 22 (314.5): Lawrence Way, access to marina and restaurant. *CAUTION:* Debris Torrent Hazard. Do not stop on creek bridges.

Mile 16.5 (192.5) Km 26.5 (310): Community of **LIONS BAY** (pop. 1,400), named for Vancouver's distinguishing mountain landmark, The Lions (elev. 5,400 feet/1,646m). The mountain faces Vancouver to the south, Lions Bay to the north.

Mile 18.5 (190.5) Km 30 (306.5): Picnic area and Howe Sound overlook for southbound traffic only. 🅰

Mile 22 (187) Km 35.5 (301): Viewpoint and stop of interest about the building of the Pacific Great Eastern Railway, now B.C. Railway.

Mile 23.5 (185.5) Km 37.5 (299): Howe Sound Crest and Deeks Lake trailhead.

Mile 25 (184) Km 40 (295.5): Porteau Cove Provincial Park; 44 campsites, 14 walk-in sites, picnicking, swimming, boat launch, wharf. This park is particularly appealing to scuba divers: There is an underwater wreck and lots of sea life, as well as hot showers. The cove is one of the few areas between Horseshoe Bay and Squamish with water access. Across the sound is Woodfibre Pulp Mill. ⛺▲

Mile 26.5 (182.5) Km 42.5 (294): Furry Creek Golf and Country Club; restaurant open to public.

Mile 29.5 (179.5) Km 47.5 (289): Thistle Creek at south entrance to **BRITANNIA BEACH** (pop. 300), once a busy copper-mining town, now known for the B.C. Museum of Mining underground train rides into old copper mine and concentrator (a national historic site). Open Wednesdays through Sundays, May to early Sept.

The community has several restaurants, a pier, old customs house/gallery and Native arts and crafts shop.

Mile 30 (179) Km 48 (288.5): Britannia Creek. Highway climbs steeply northbound.

Mile 31 (178) Km 50 (286.5): Folger Creek. South entrance to Squamish.

Mile 32 (177) Km 51.5 (285): Murrin Provincial Park on Petgill Lake; good swimming, fishing, hiking and picnicking. Steep but low cliffs are popular with rock climbers. 🧗⛺🐟

Mile 32.5 (176.5) Km 52.5 (284): Six percent downgrade northbound and good view of Mount Atwell (usually snow-covered) in Garibaldi Park to the north, and the squat, sheer bluff of the Stawamus Chief (see **Mile 35.5**).

Mile 34.5 (174.5) Km 56 (280.5): Ferry to Woodfibre Pulp Mill. No public access.

Mile 35 (174) Km 56.5 (280): Shannon Falls Provincial Park. The falls plunge 1,099 feet/335m; viewing platform at base. Picnicking and hiking. 🧗⛺

View of Shannon Falls at Mile 35. The falls plunge 1,099 feet. (Liz Bryan)

Mile 35.5 (173.5) Km 57.5 (279): Picnicking area and viewpoint of Stawamus Chief. The world's second largest granite outcrop, "the Chief" (elev. 2,139 feet/652m) is known internationally for its challenging rock climbing. There are more than 180 routes on the face. From the viewpoint you can watch climbers in progress.

Mile 37 (172) Km 60 (276.5): Town of **SQUAMISH** (pop. 12,000) across Mamquam Blind Channel at the head of Howe Sound. All tourist services. Squamish was first a logging town, and the woods industry is still important. There is a thriving port. From a recreation point of view, Squamish is becoming known around the world as a mecca for rock climbing (the Chief and Smoke Bluffs) and windsurfing (the Squamish winds are fierce because of the narrowing fjord and rock cliffs). Scuba diving, horseback riding, bird watching and hiking are other activities available here.

Squamish Valley museum, located in a heritage home, is open Wednesdays to Sundays. Sta-wa-mus Native Cultural Centre, on Highway 99, has carvings and jewelry. Air services at Squamish airport offer glacier tours.

Squamish estuary has the largest concentration of bald eagles in the world, as many as 1,500 in winter. The dikes provide good viewing. Access is from downtown (3rd and Vancouver streets); watch for sign with map of dike walks.

Mile 39.5 (169.5) Km 63.5 (273): Mamquam River. Watch for bald eagles in trees along the river.

Mile 40.5 (168.5) Km 65 (271.5): Mamquam Road to Diamond Head, one of several entrances to Garibaldi Provincial Park. Hikes to alpine meadows and cross-country ski trails. Garibaldi Highlands, a bedroom community, has some tourist facilities. 🧗

Mile 42 (167) Km 68 (268.5): Depot Road to **BRACKENDALE** (pop. 1,000), home to annual B.C. Wildlife Bald Eagle Count. Good eagle viewing from the dike near Government Road. Access to Lake Lovely Water Provincial Park in the Tantalus Mountains on the north side of the Squamish River. No road or bridge access; wilderness camping.

Mile 43.5 (165.5) Km 70.5 (266): Cheekeye Road west to Tenderfoot Fish Hatchery; chinook, coho and steelhead rearing, open year-round. East to Alice Lake Provincial Park, an idyllic mountain lake surrounded by forest and meadow; 88 campsites, picnicking, swimming, canoeing, fishing; cross-country skiing. ⛺🐟▲

Mile 44.5 (164.5) Km 71.5 (265): Cheekeye River. Good fishing for steelhead, spring, coho and Dolly Varden. ⚓

Mile 47 (162) Km 76 (260.5): Brohm Lake Recreation Site, a B.C. Forest Service day-use area with picnicking and fishing. ⛏⚓

Mile 49.5 (159.5) Km 79.5 (258): Viewpoint to south for northbound traffic only; good view of Tantalus Mountains. Viewpoint to north for southbound traffic only overlooks Cheakamus Canyon.

Mile 56 (153) Km 90 (246.5): Canyon overlook and picnic site for southbound traffic only. ⛏

Mile 59.5 (149.5) Km 95.5 (241): Hiking trail leads 2.7 miles/4.5 km up Rubble Creek to Taylor Campground on Garibaldi Lake, the most popular camping spot in Garibaldi Provincial Park. Garibaldi Park is extensive, with lots of lakes, glaciers, trails, alpine flowers, and 196 wilderness walk-in campsites. 👣▲

Mile 61.5 (147.5) Km 99.5 (237): Cheakamus River at the south end of Daisy Lake, created by damming the river; boat launch; good fishing for rainbow, Dolly Varden and kokanee. ⚓

Mile 64.5 (144.5) Km 104 (232.5): Brandywine Falls Provincial Park; 15 campsites, picnicking, swimming, fishing, hiking. The falls are 217 feet/66m high, and a 10-minute walk from the road. Good views of mountains in Garibaldi Provincial Park. 👣⛏⚓▲

Mile 67.5 (141.5) Km 109 (227.5): Mad River cross-country ski area. Note basalt columns on east side of road.

Mile 70.5 (138.5) Km 114 (222.5): Whistler Museum and Archives; logging tools, ski gear and Whistler memorabilia. Trailhead to Cheakamus and Garibaldi lakes. Scenic Cheakamus Lake is a 1.8-mile/3-km walk from end of short road. 👣

Mile 72.5 (136.5) Km 116.5 (220): Road to west side of Alta Lake. Residential area, some tourist facilities on lake.

Mile 74 (135) Km 119 (217.5): Whistler Wayside Park; picnicking, swimming, boating, kayaking and windsurfing. ⛏

Mile 75.5 (133.5) Km 121.5 (215): Singing Pass trailhead and golf course. 👣

Mile 76 (133) Km 122 (214.5): **WHISTLER** (pop. 4,500), east side of highway, is classed as a 4-season world-destination resort. The village lies between 2 famous ski hills, Whistler and Blackcomb, and attracts the international ski set to its huge hotels, fancy condos, shops and restaurants. In summer, visitors are whisked up the mountains for wildflower hikes and glacier viewing. Recreation includes horseback riding, golf, tennis,

whitewater rafting, jet boating and other water sports in the valley's 5 lakes, connected by a 9-mile/15-km bike trail. Blackcomb is the only ski hill in North America to offer summer skiing. Pedestrian traffic–only in the cobblestone village centre, with its flower beds and outdoor cafes. A slick cosmopolitan resort amid wilderness splendor.

In winter, there are 27 ski lifts and more than 200 runs on the 2 mountains, including the longest and the second-longest lift-serviced vertical runs in North America—a skier's paradise.

All tourist facilities open all year, including the huge Chateau Whistler, the largest (and at $50 million the most expensive) hotel built in Canada since the turn-of-the-century glory days of the Canadian Pacific Railway's great Chateaux. ⛷👣★

Mile 78 (131) Km 125.5 (211): River of Golden Dreams and access to the Valley Trail.

Mile 79.5 (129.5) Km 128 (208.5): Green Lake. Good waterfowl watching and views of ski slopes from gravel turnout. Boat launch to north.

Mile 83 (126) Km 134 (202.5): Wedgemount trailhead into Garibaldi Provincial Park. 👣

Mile 94.5 (114.5) Km 152 (184.5): Nairn Falls Provincial Park, 88 campsites, fishing, hiking. A 3-mile/5-km round-trip walk leads to the falls, which plummet 197 feet/60m into Green River. 👣⚓▲

Mile 95.5 (113.5) Km 154 (182.5): One-Mile Lake: picnicking and boardwalk among the waterlilies and waterfowl at southern edge of Pemberton. Infocentre beside highway is open daily, July and August. **PEMBERTON** (pop. 500) is an agricultural village fast

changing into an outdoor recreation centre for hiking, biking, boating, fishing and mountain adventures. Pemberton Museum, open July and August, features the gold rush and native culture. 👣⛏⚓

Mile 96 (113) Km 155 (181.5): **Junction** with road to Pemberton Meadows, Meager Hotsprings and the unpaved forestry road over Hurley Pass (summer only) to Bridge River north of Lillooet. Gas available.

Mile 98 (111) Km 157.5 (179): Lillooet River, flows east into Lillooet Lake.

Mile 100.5 (108.5) Km 162 (174.5): Community of **MOUNT CURRIE** (pop. 1,400), headquarters of the Lil'wat group of the Stl'atl'imx nation. Some interesting old log houses, food and limited accommodations. Site of the famous Whoop-it-up Rodeo held holiday weekends in May and September. Highway 99 turns east at the edge of town and continues (unpaved) through the Indian reserve. **Junction** with road North to Birken, Devine and D'Arcy at the south end of Anderson Lake.

WARNING: No fuel for next 60 miles/96 km northbound.

Mile 102.5 (106.5) Km 165 (171.5): Road north to new native village of Xit'olacw, 1.8 miles/3 km. Store open daily. The road parallels the Lillooet River.

Mile 106.5 (102.5) Km 172 (164.5): Crossing the Lillooet River in the delta (one of the world's fastest growing). Notice the old steamboat landing pilings at lake end. Beyond the bridge, the road is paved again and junctions with a forestry road south to Lillooet Lodge and along the east side of Lillooet Lake to Skookumchuk and Harrison.

Jade-green Seton Lake. B.C. Hydro has a picnic area on the lake at Mile 156. (Liz Bryan)

Bridge of the 23 Camels at Lillooet, Mile 159.5, replaced an older suspension bridge upstream that is now used by pedestrians only. (Liz Bryan)

Highway 99 turns sharply up a steep hill into the Cayoosh Range of the Coast Mountains. *CAUTION:* A former logging road, this section of Highway 99 is steep and narrow in places, with several hairpin turns.

Mile 115.5 (93.5) Km 186 (150.5): Joffre Lakes Provincial Recreation Area; picnic tables and Forest Service campsite. The 3 blue alpine lakes in the chain can be reached by a 3-mile/5-km trail, with an elevation gain of more than 1,300 feet/400m (4 to 6 hours round-trip).

Mile 118 (91) Km 190 (146.5): Cayoosh Creek. Good view of Joffre Peak.

Mile 125.5 (83.5) Km 202 (134.5): Duffey Lake, through trees on west side of road, is ice-covered until late in the year.

Mile 128 (81) Km 206 (130.5): B.C. Forest Service Recreation Site at north end of Duffey Lake; boat launch, rainbow fishing.

Mile 130 (79) Km 209 (127.5): Kane Creek waterfalls. Road follows Cayoosh Creek to Lillooet, crossing the river several times on narrow 1-lane bridges. There are Forest Service recreation areas at Roger and Gott creeks at Km 224 and 226, and at Km 233 and 237. On its final descent, road grade steepens to 13 and 14 percent grades.

Mile 153 (56) Km 246 (90.5): Large viewpoint by hairpin turn.

Mile 154 (55) Km 248 (88.5): *WARNING:* 14 percent downgrade northbound and sharp hairpin bend. Truck brake check.

Mile 156 (53) Km 251 (85.5): B.C. Hydro Seton Lake Recreation Area; picnic site on high sagebrush viewpoint overlooking the jade-green lake. Trail and road down to boat launch and swimming. Look for mountain goat on steep mountainsides. Turn west 1 km to view Hydro dam on Seton Creek.

Mile 157 (52) Km 252.5 (84): Seton Dam campsite, B.C. Hydro. Lower Spawning Channel of Seton Creek Salmon Project. Pink salmon return to spawn here in odd-numbered years.

Mile 159.5 (49.5) Km 256.5 (80): Turnoff for Sheep Pasture Golf Course (4 miles/6 km), dual purpose meadows where munching sheep provide additional hazards. Great views. Town of **LILLOOET** (pop. 1,800) straight ahead. In 1863, when the town was the start of everyone's dreams of Cariboo gold, Lillooet's population exceeded 15,000. Its main street was made wide enough to turn a full team of oxen, transportation of men and goods being the town's chief livelihood.

Tourism is the town's second gold rush, with 15 historic points of interest, a fine museum in the old church, a hangman's tree, gold panning, jade for rock hounds and full tourist facilities. The town is perched high above the Fraser River at its confluence with Cayoosh Creek. In summer it's hot. In fact Lillooet boasts the highest temperature ever recorded in Canada: 111.9°F/44.4°C, in July 1941.

North from Lillooet, Highway 99 veers east (bypassing the town centre) to cross the Fraser River on the Bridge of the 23 Camels, built to replace the former narrow suspension bridge upriver. (The old bridge is still intact, passable only by foot traffic.) Just west of the bridge is Cayoosh Creek Park, with camping, fishing and gold panning. From the bridge there's a good view downstream where the clear blue waters of Cayoosh Creek meet the muddy Fraser.

The gold rush trail followed the route of Highway 99 as far as Pavilion. West from the north end of town, Bridge River Road (Highway 40) leads 65 miles/105 km to Gold Bridge and Bralorne, both home to resorts featuring wilderness activities.

Mile 162 (47) Km 260.5 (76): Junction of Highways 12 and 99. Highway 12 goes south along the Fraser 40 miles/65 km to Lytton and Trans-Canada Highway 1.

Mile 162.5 (46.5) Km 261.5 (75): View of old suspension bridge.

Mile 170 (39) Km 274 (62.5): The highway plays hopscotch with the B.C. Railway, with underpasses and overpasses at times bringing highway speeds down to 30 kmph.

Mile 178.5 (30.5) Km 287 (49.5): Fields of ginseng grown under tarpaulins of black plastic mesh. The dry area of the southern Cariboo grows most of the world supply of North American ginseng, an Asian medicinal root crop.

Mile 183 (26) Km 295 (41.5): Pavilion General Store and post office, an oasis in the high desert, one of the oldest buildings in British Columbia still on its original site and a welcome landmark for travelers.

Mile 183.5 (25.5) Km 295.5 (41): Junction with Pavilion Mountain Road, the original gold rush trail to Clinton (19 miles/31 km northeast via Kelly Lake). Native settlement of **PAVILION** (now known as Tswayaxw) has fine old Catholic mission church with crimped turret roof.

Mile 185 (24) Km 298 (38.5): Road enters scenic Marble Canyon, towering cliffs of red and yellow limestone.

Mile 186.5 (22.5) Km 300.5 (36): Pine-forest-rimmed Pavilion Lake extends east for 5 miles/8 km; good trout fishing.

Mile 188 (21) Km 303 (33.5): Lakeside rest area under towering marble cliffs.

Mile 191.5 (17.5) Km 308.5 (28): Marble Canyon Provincial Park on Crown and Turquoise lakes; 34 campsites on Crown Lake; good swimming and fishing; hiking trail to Teapot Rock and waterfall. Nearby is Marble Canyon Demonstration Forest.

Mile 194 (15) Km 312 (24.5): Limestone mine and crusher.

Mile 196.5 (12.5) Km 316 (20.5): Hat Creek Road, a roundabout backroad to Trans-Canada Highway 1 near Ashcroft Manor.

Mile 208.5 (0.5) Km 335.5 (1): Hat Creek Heritage Ranch on bypassed section of original Cariboo wagon road. The ranch dates from 1861, and contains one of the few remaining roadhouses in existence. Acquired and restored by the B.C. Heritage Trust, the ranch has a working blacksmith, saddle maker, original barns, sheds and gardens, furnished roadhouse (guided tours); also trail rides on ranch horses and wagon rides along Cariboo road. Staff in period costume. Open daily 10 a.m. to 6 p.m., mid-May to mid-Oct. Phone (604) 457-9722.

Mile 209 (0) Km 336.5 (0): Bonaparte River and **junction** with Highway 97 north of Cache Creek. Turn to **Mile 239.5** in the CANADA HIGHWAY 97 section.

Major Cities
BOISE

City of Trees

Boise (BOY-see), the largest city in Idaho with a population of 130,000, is also the capital and hub of the state's political activity. "The City of Trees" received its name from French fur trappers who, after crossing a hot, sage-brush-covered desert, discovered the Boise River flowing through a wooded valley. The river was named *la riviere boise*, "the wooded river," and when the town was platted in 1863, it was named for the river.

As a fort along the Oregon Trail, Boise soon prospered and in 1864, took the territorial capital status away from Lewiston in northern Idaho. Boise was named the state capital in 1890 when Idaho became a state.

With excellent transportation routes, Boise soon became a major commerce city in the Northwest. Huge corporate giants sprung from the valley, including Boise Cascade, the J.R. Simplot Co., Albertson's (supermarkets) and construction giant Morrison-Knudsen, all of whom have their world headquarters here.

Today, the greenbelt of the Boise River still plays a large role in the capital city's identity. Its beautiful parks, golf courses and zoo are all sheltered beneath the trees for which the desert oasis was named.

Union Pacific Depot is probably the most photographed building in the city. An elegant, mission-style building sitting atop a hill and surrounded by lush Platt Gardens, the depot today is still in use as an Amtrack station.

Boise State University, Idaho's largest university with an enrollment of 13,500 students, is itself located in the greenbelt. The school, founded in 1932, now offers 9 schools of instruction with majors in 29 different areas. The university is the site of the Morrison Center for the Performing Arts, where national touring companies come to perform opera, theatre, ballet and music. In addition, the BSU Multi-Purpose Pavilion seats 12,500 at sports and entertainment events. The university offers public tours.

The Broncos, BSU's athletic source of pride, consistently pack the 23,000-seat open-air Bronco Stadium during the football season.

For brochures and travel information, contact the Boise Convention and Visitors Bureau, 168 N. 9th St., Suite 200, Boise, ID 83702; phone (208) 344-7777 or toll free (800) 635-5240 (out of state).

Attractions

Julia Davis Park, located between the capitol and the Union Pacific Depot, contains some of Boise's premier attractions, including Zoo Boise, the Discovery Center of Idaho Science Museum, the Idaho State Historical Museum, and Boise Art Museum.

Zoo Boise offers a look at more than 100 animal species and a children's section of baby farm animals. The first animal on display at the zoo was a monkey that had escaped from a traveling circus in 1916. Since then, the zoo has collected nearly 250 individual animals for display. Hours for the zoo are 10 a.m. until 5 p.m. daily (open until 9 p.m. on Thursday in summer). Admission is $3 for adults, $1.25 for children, $1.50 for senior citizens. Children under age 4 are admitted free. Thursday rates are half price.

The Discovery Center of Idaho is a hands-on science museum for all ages. There are more than 100 exhibits. Open daily except Monday, year-round. Phone (208) 343-9895 for times. Admission charged.

The Idaho State Historical Museum has excellent displays of Idaho's yesteryears including the old Overland Saloon; artifacts from the early Chinese miners; and artifacts of the Native Americans who made this region home long before settlement. Next to the museum is Pioneer Village with several preserved pioneer cabins. Admission to the museum is free, but donations are accepted. Open Monday through Saturday, 9 a.m. to 5 p.m., and Sunday, 1–5 p.m.

Near the historical museum, the Boise Art Museum offers quality Idaho art and prestigious traveling exhibits throughout the year. It is home to the Janss Collection of Realism. Behind the gallery is the Memorial Rose Garden, each bush providing a tribute to a loved one.

Other attractions at Julia Davis Park include Big Mike, a 1920-series Mikado locomotive donated by the Union Pacific Railroad; The Fun Spot, with amusement rides and miniature golf; tennis courts; and boat rentals for those wishing to paddle the shallow lagoon system among the ducks and geese.

Old Idaho Penitentiary: At the end of beautiful Warm Springs Avenue is the historic territorial prison, later the early-day state penitentiary. Self-guided tours of this facility are available from noon until 4 p.m. daily, with an 18-minute slide show. The first inmates moved into the unfinished prison in 1872 and the prison was completed the following year. As the penitentiary grew, virtually all of the expansion work was done by prisoners who quarried the stones on the nearby hills. A member of the Butch Cassidy gang, Butch Meeks, spent time within these walls.

A major riot in the 1970s caused Idaho to construct a new penitentiary (near Gowen Field southeast of town), and the old prison was placed on the National Register of Historic Places in 1974. The self-guided tour allows access to the prison cells and punishment block, referred to as "Siberia" in its time, as well as Death Row and the gallows. The rose garden and grounds are maintained as they were first developed in the early 1900s. On display are pictures of famous inmates and lawmen, stories of escapes and examples of punishment in the early days of Idaho.

Also located at the penitentiary is the Transportation Museum, where stagecoaches, buggies and a 1903 steam fire pumper are on display. The nearby Electricity Museum features early generating devices, radios and TVs. Also on the grounds is the Printing Museum containing the original pressroom of the pioneer Idaho newspaper, *Owyhee Nugget*.

The Old Idaho Penitentiary is open daily (except holidays) and admission is $3 for adults, $2 for seniors and children.

Visitors can see the mighty peregrine falcon at the World Center for Birds of Prey. (© Lee Foster)

The Idaho Capitol in Boise is a smaller version of the U.S. Capitol in Washington, D.C. (© Lee Foster)

The Idaho Botanical Garden, located near the penitentiary, features 7 gardens in bloom from late April to mid-Oct. Self-guiding nature trail and educational displays. Open 10 a.m. to 5 p.m., Tuesday through Sunday. Admission charged. Phone (208) 343-8649 for more information.

Capitol Building: The state capitol is Boise's most impressive public building. It lays claim to being the only state capitol building to be heated with hot water. A smaller version of the nation's capitol in Washington, D.C., construction began in 1905. It was completed in 1920 using native sandstone quarried from nearby Table Rock and marble from Alaska, Georgia and Vermont. A replica of the Winged Victory of Samothrace, a gift from the city of Paris, is of particular interest. Agriculture, timber products and minerals are on display on the lower levels.

The building is located on the corner of Jefferson Street and 8th Street. A guided tour is offered. The capitol is open from 8 a.m. until 5 p.m., Monday through Saturday. Metered parking is available around the capitol building.

The Basque Museum is located in Boise's oldest brick home. Located at 607 Grove St., it details the culture of Idaho's Basque population. Hours are 10 a.m. to 3 p.m., Tuesday through Saturday, and 11 a.m. to 2 p.m. on Sunday.

Boise Train Tour is a 1-hour tour aboard open-air cars pulled by an 1890s locomotive replica. The tours depart from Julia Davis Park and travel through the historic neighborhoods, central business district and other sites of interest. Admission for the narrated tour is $6 for adults, $5.50 for senior citizens and $3 for children age 12 and under. From June 1 through Labor Day, the tour train operates Monday through Saturday 10 a.m. to 3 p.m. Friday and Saturday an evening tour is offered at 7 p.m. Sunday tours are available from noon to 5 p.m. Limited hours in May, September and October.

Eighth Street Marketplace: While many towns are suffering the effects of aging downtown areas, Boise has countered with the creation of the South 8th Street Marketplace, a renovated portion of the old downtown resembling San Francisco's famed Ghirardelli Square. The converted warehouse district includes galleries, theaters, restaurants and delis and several specialty shops.

Les Bois Race Track: One of the Boise area's premier attractions during the summer months is the parimutuel horse racing at Les Bois Race Track, located at the Western Idaho Fairgrounds. Horses are running for more than 50 days from May through Aug.

The Western Idaho Fairgrounds is the site of year-round sports events, concerts, celebrations and expositions. The Western Idaho

Fair begins the last weekend of A[...]

The Boise River winds right th[...] town. A greenbelt along the water [...] allows escape to a quiet place without [...] leaving the city. Thirteen miles of paved paths attract joggers, bicyclists, skaters and walkers and link 6 city parks. The river provides many recreational opportunities, including fishing from its banks in the middle of town. During the summer, tubing the Boise is a favorite diversion. Transportation to Barber Park, a popular place to put in, may be easily arranged. It's a 5-mile float trip from Barber Park to Ann Morrison Park, past pastureland, cottonwoods and corporate headquarters. Inner tubes and rafts are available for rent.

World Center for Birds of Prey: The world's headquarters for The Peregrine Fund (an organization founded to prevent the extinction of the powerful peregrine falcon). Boise was selected, in part, because of its close proximity to the Snake River Birds of Prey Natural Area along the Snake River, where the densest population of breeding birds of prey (raptors) exists.

Raptors have hooked beaks and sharp, curved talons for catching and holding their prey. Species include hawks, eagles, harriers and ospreys in the *Accipitridae* family, and falcons in the family *Falconidae.*

Visitors can see the inner workings of an endangered species program while touring the World Center for Birds of Prey. Large windows look into the monitor, incubator and brooder laboratories. Tours are conducted throughout the year, but are most memorable during the breeding season (April through June) when visitors see the birds courting and feeding chicks (through video monitors), eggs hatching in incubators and chicks clamoring for food in the brooder laboratory. Visit the center and see rare falcons and eagles from a few feet away. Tours last about 1 hour. Phone (208) 362-8687 for tour information. The center is located at 5666 W. Flying Hawk Lane, Boise, ID 83709. Take Exit 50 off I-84, go south on Cole Road approximately 6 miles to Flying Hawk Lane.

Bogus Basin: Though Idaho may be famous for Sun Valley, Boiseans are rightfully proud of Bogus Basin Ski Area, just 16 miles north of town. The area offers a vertical rise of 1,800 feet with 2,000 acres of skiable terrain. The maximum trail is 1.5 miles and the average midseason snow depth is 8 to 10 feet. There are 6 double-chair lifts (uphill capacity of 6,700 skiers per hour) and 2 rope tows guiding skiers to 54 designated runs.

The area offers 2 lodges, meals, overnight rooms, a ski school, day care for youngsters and cross-country facilities.

Ste. Chapelle Winery. Idaho's wine growing country is on the same latitude as the famed regions of France, and local winemakers are producing award-winning vintages on Sunny Slopes above the Snake River. Ste. Chapelle Winery, located 35 miles west of Boise in Caldwell, offers free tours and tasting. On Sunday afternoons from mid-June through July there are jazz concerts on the grounds, perfect for an afternoon picnic lunch. The winery is open Monday to Saturday 10 a.m. to 5 p.m. and Sunday noon to 5 p.m. Tours are given on the hour and samples of wine are offered for tasting in the retail room. Ste. Chapelle is located off Exit 35 on Interstate 84. Call ahead for tour information and directions at (208) 459-7222.

The ... se City

The city's history began in 1843, when Asa Lovejoy landed his canoe on the riverbank where the Willamette meets the Columbia. Lovejoy figured this would be a good location for a port city. Lewis and Clark had landed at the same point in 1806, and before them, the Chinook Indians inhabited the area.

Lovejoy and his compatriot, Francis W. Pettygrove, cleared a townsite and erected the first building in 1844. The name of Portland was decided by the flip of a coin. Francis Pettygrove was from Portland, Maine, and Asa Lovejoy was from Boston, Massachusetts. Pettygrove won the toss. In its early years, Portland was also called "Stumptown," because after a few years of clearing and building there were so many tree stumps littering the streets.

Now a major metropolis of the Northwest, Portland is today one of the nation's leaders in the export of wheat and lumber products, and its freshwater port ranks third in total tonnage on the Pacific Coast.

Portland, the "Rose City," is home to the nation's oldest continuously-operated rose test gardens. Portland's major festival is the Portland Rose Festival, held annually since 1909.

Many people consider Portland one of the West Coast's most progressive cities, citing its urban planning, post-modern architecture, mass transit system and beautiful setting.

The downtown's retail core has been revitalized. A light rail train zooms passengers from the city to nearby communities in just 30 minutes. And the banks of the Willamette River, which for years were scrap metal junkyards, are now beautiful parks with broad walkways.

Portland's farsighted founders left plenty of elbow room, with bountiful space set aside for parks. Forest Park, which sprawls over 4,700 acres, is the largest urban wilderness within an American city. More than 70 miles of hiking trails, ponds and lakes, and a variety of wildlife in this serene setting are within footsteps of city dwellers. The newest addition to Portland's list of parks is also its smallest—Mill Ends Park, a tiny 24 square inches.

A green ribbon runs through the city, thanks to the Park Blocks, established in 1852. This urban greenway spans 25 blocks and offers pleasant relief from buildings and asphalt in the midst of the city.

The city administration building is graced by Portlandia, *a hammered-copper incarnation of the figure adorning Portland's city seal.* (Courtesy of Portland Oregon Visitors Assoc.)

Another favorite Portland retreat is the 107-acre densely forested park donated to the city by Donald Macleay, who requested that no wheeled vehicles be allowed to enter. The city honored his wishes. Macleay Park remains a haven for hikers, photographers, bird-watchers and other nature lovers.

Portland has long been known for its many lush green parks. But confirmed urbanites are taking notice of the city landscape as well.

Architecturally, Portland is compelling, from the Oregon Convention Center—with its dramatic 150-foot-tall glass and steel twin spires—to the Post-Modern city administra-

tion building, designed by Michael Graves and built in 1983, adorned in blue tile and concrete garlands. The building is home to *Portlandia,* a giant hammered-copper incarnation of the goddess-like figure on Portland's city seal. This 34-foot, 6.5-ton sculpture is the second largest hammered copper statue in the world, after the Statue of Liberty. She kneels above the entrance of the Portland Building. Discussion over these additions to the Portland cityscape has brought international attention to the city.

But it is not just intriguing new buildings that make downtown Portland an enjoyable city for a stroll. There are bronze drinking

A revitalized retail core attracts visitors to downtown Portland. City lights reflect on the Willamette River, which divides Portland into east and west halves. (Courtesy of Portland Oregon Visitors Assoc.)

fountains, cast-iron street lamp fixtures, floral displays and artwork, cobblestones and brick sidewalks.

Portland is a sports-minded city. The Portland Trail Blazers professional basketball team and the Winter Hawks hockey team make their home here. One of 2 greyhound race tracks in the Northwest is located near Portland at the Multnomah Greyhound Park. Mount Hood, the Cascade Range and the accessibility to lakes, streams, rivers and the ocean provide plenty of recreational opportunities for city dwellers and visitors.

Portland is an easy city to explore. The Metropolitan Area Express (MAX) is a sleek light rail train that glides from downtown through neighborhoods on the east side of the city to the growing suburb of Gresham. The light rail departs every 15 minutes for the 15-mile trip. Stops along the way include Lloyd Center, Oregon's oldest major shopping center, and the 500,000-square-foot convention center. Fares for the MAX vary; phone (503) 238-RIDE for information.

Avid walkers find Portland a great city to explore by foot. The blocks are just 200 feet—about half the size of the average city block. There are fountains, parks and street musicians. And if you get tired of walking, Portland's bus system, called Tri-Met, offers a bus on line 63 that leaves from SW Washington Street at 5th Avenue. The route stops at Washington Park and the International Rose Gardens, Japanese Gardens, Washington Park Zoo, Oregon Museum of Science and Industry (OMSI), the World Forestry Center and Hoyt Arboretum. For bus fares and schedules, call Tri-Met's information number, (503) 238-RIDE.

The Willamette River runs through Port-land, dividing the city east-west. Traffic flows constantly across the Willamette on the 11 bridges that span the river. The Morrison Bridge is illuminated at night. The Columbia River borders Portland on the north and 2 bridges cross that river into Washington state.

At the river's edge, the stern-wheelers *Columbia Gorge* and *Cascade Queen* offer a variety of excursions on the Willamette River. Phone (503) 223-3928 for more information. For more information on the city, contact Portland Oregon Visitors Assoc., 26 S.W. Salmon St., Portland, OR 97204; phone (503) 222-2223 or 1-800-345-3214.

Attractions

The Waterfront. In the past decade, Portland's waterfront has been transformed from a string of dilapidated warehouses and metal salvage yards to a beautiful park-like setting with sidewalk cafes, fountains, pleasure boat docks and sidewalks. Called Tom McCall Waterfront Park, this is now an extensive greenway for joggers and walkers. RiverPlace Promenade, which features a marina, stores and restaurants, is located here. Front Avenue, which parallels the waterfront park, is the site of Mill Ends Park (the world's smallest city park) and the visitor information center (at the foot of Salmon Street). Salmon Street Springs, a fountain with 100 jets of water, is located across from the visitor center.

Pioneer Courthouse Square. Situated on one of the most historic blocks in Portland is Pioneer Courthouse Square between Broad-way and 6th avenues and Morrison and Yamhill streets. Pioneer Courthouse is across 6th Avenue from the square. The first public school was started here in 1858, and was later the site of the Portland Hotel, which hosted every president from Benjamin Harrison to Franklin Roosevelt.

Today, the square is an urban park with waterfalls, amphitheaters, fountains and over 35,000 bricks bearing the names of local citizens who helped fund its construction. There's even a weather machine. Designed by Terence O'Donnell, this earth-shaped sphere on a 25-foot column announces the weather each day at noon. With a musical fanfare and sprays of mist, a stylized sun (for clear days), dragon (for storms) or blue heron (for changeable weather) appears. The complex also includes the Portland Hotel's original wrought iron gate and a series of handmade bronze tiles depicting scenes from the earth's and Portland's past. Visitors may see musical performances, exhibits, festivals, debates, poetry readings and other public gatherings. The city's light rail also runs alongside the square, located at 701-6th Ave. in downtown Portland. For information call (503) 223-1613.

The Old Church. Listed on the National Register of Historic Places, the Old Church, built in 1883, is a striking example of Carpenter Gothic architecture. The interior is rich in detail and the exterior is characterized by ornate window traceries, archways, buttresses and spires. Windows of leaded stained and frosted glass reflect several types of glassmaker's art. While on the self-guided tour, note the hand-carved pews, late Victorian furniture and a pipe organ donated by one of the founders. Baroque organ concerts are presented each Wednesday at noon.

Top—Among the attractions at the Oregon Museum of Science and Industry are laser light shows and an OMNIMAX theater. **Above**—Exhibits in OMSI's USS Blueback submarine, docked in the Willamette River, demonstrate undersea exploration. (Photos courtesy of Portland Oregon Visitors Assoc.)

to 9 p.m. with free admission after 4 p.m.

Admission is $5 for adults, $3.50 for seniors, $2.50 for students and free for museum members and children under 5. On Thursdays, admission is free for seniors.

The Oregon Historical Center Museum, located across the street from Portland Art Museum, offers permanent and changing exhibits on the history of Oregon and the West. This is also home to a renowned regional research library. A *tromp l'oeil* mural of Western themes by Richard Hass faces the Park Blocks. Free admission, phone (503) 222-1741 for hours.

The American Advertising Museum is one of the first of its kind in the nation. The museum showcases and preserves the history of advertising with exhibits dedicated to radio, television and print advertising and most memorable ad campaigns. Special exhibits are featured. The museum also produces a quarterly called *It's History*, which examines themes and problems in the industry. The museum is located at 524 NE Grand Ave. Phone (503) AAM-0000 for more information.

Portland Center for the Performing Arts is the heart of Portland's performing arts companies. Dedicated in 1987, the center is made up of 4 theatres, 3 located together at SW Broadway and Main. Together with the Portland Civic Auditorium on SW Clay, the 4 stages offer classic and contemporary theater, music and dance performances attracting top performers. The Oregon Symphony, 2 ballet companies and Portland Center Stage, a resident company of the Oregon Shakespeare Festival, make their permanent home in the arts center. For schedule and ticket information, call (503) 248-4496 or the 24-hour Portland area events hot line at (503) 222-2223.

Oregon Museum of Science and Industry (OMSI). As one of the country's best science centers, OMSI offers interactive exhibits on life, space, earth, computer and information sciences. The museum features 6 main exhibit halls, astronomy and laser light shows, live demonstrations, a special education and entertainment area for young children, tornado and earthquake simulations, computer games, a family-style cafeteria, a science store, classes, summer camps and other special attractions and events.

Two of OMSI's main attractions are its 2 theaters. The 330-seat OMNIMAX Theater features a 5-story domed screen and a 16,000-watt sound system; see below for admission prices. The Murdock Sky Theater offers planetarium and laser light shows; admission is $4.50 for adults, $4 for seniors and $3.50 for youths.

A special feature is the USS *Blueback* submarine, docked in the Willamette River next to the museum. The submarine, which features exhibits on undersea exploration, was active in the U.S. Navy from 1961 through 1990 and is perhaps most famous for its appearance in the movie *The Hunt for Red*

Admission is free. The church is located at 1422 SW 11th.

Pittock Mansion. The French Renaissance-style mansion was built in 1914 by Henry Pittock, founder of the *Daily Oregonian* newspaper. His wife, Georgiana Pittock, was instrumental in the campaign to plan rose gardens throughout the city. Standing 1,000 feet above the city, the mansion holds many antiques and furnishings, including a grand marble staircase, art from the 17th, 18th and 19th centuries, a Turkish smoking room, Tiffany tiles and a shower of Mr. Pittock's own design. The mansion is the focal point of the Pittock Acres Park, a 46-acre park commanding some of the best views of the city, the Willamette and Columbia rivers and the Cascade Range. The mansion and park are open from noon to 4 p.m. daily. Admission is $4 for adults, $3.50 for seniors, $1.50 for children ages 6–18 and free for children ages 5 and under. The Mansion is located at 3229 NW Pittock Dr.; phone (503) 823-3624.

The Portland Art Museum, facing the South Park Blocks, houses one of the finest collections of Native American art in the country. It is also known for its outstanding holdings of Asian art, 20th century American and European sculpture, works by Picasso, Degas and Renoir, and Pre-Columbian and West African art. Phone (503) 226-2811 for hours.

The museum is 1 of 3 facilities that make up the Oregon Art Institute, housed in a refurbished complex designed by Pietro Belluschi. Also in the complex is the Northwest Film and Video Center, which offers screenings of films you'll likely never see at the neighborhood movie house. Screenings generally are held from Thursday through Sunday in the Berg Swann Auditorium.

In addition to the museum and the film center, the Art Institute operates the Pacific Northwest College of Art, the first fully accredited school of fine arts on the West Coast.

The Institute is located at 1219 SW Park; phone (503) 226-2811. Hours are Tuesday through Saturday 11 a.m. to 5 p.m. and Sundays from 1 to 5 p.m. The first Thursday of each month, the gallery is open from 11 a.m.

October. Admission is $3.50 per person.

The museum is located at 1945 SE Water Ave. It is open daily (except Dec. 25) from 9:30 a.m. to 5:30 p.m. On Thursdays and Fridays, the museum remains open until 9 p.m. Admission to the museum and the OMNIMAX Theater is $7 for adults, $6 for seniors and $4.50 for youths. Combination prices are available at a discount for 2 or more exhibits.

For tickets 24 hours in advance, call (503) 797-4600 or toll free at (800) 955-6674. For show times and other information, call (503) 797-4000.

Washington Park Zoo. This modest-sized zoo has gained a national reputation for its successful breeding program of the endangered Asian elephant. Since 1962, 26 of the pachyderms have been born, so there's a good chance of a visitor seeing a little one scurrying around with 10 adults in the herd. Another endangered species delightful to watch is the Humboldt penguin. Nearly 25 of these South American birds torpedo at speeds of up to 22 mph in an exhibit that replicates the warm, rocky shoreline of Peru.

In the Cascade exhibit, visitors can see beavers, otters, trout, trillium and many other plants and wild animals native to the Pacific Northwest. Visitors can then travel to the wild, remote Alaskan Tundra to see animals that survive in the extreme environment. Other unique exhibits include underwater viewing of the polar bears, an African rain forest exhibit and an insect zoo. The reptile and birds of prey shows, during which visitors can see free-flight demonstrations of eagles and hawks, are free with admission from mid-June to early Sept. Gate hours are 9:30 a.m. to 4 p.m.; you can stay in the zoo until 5 p.m. Admission is $5.50 for adults and children over 11, $4 for seniors, $3.50 for children ages 3 to 11, and free for ages 2 and under. The zoo is located at 4001 SW Canyon Road; phone (503) 226-7627.

Railroad buffs and children enjoy the authentic 1/5-sized steamer train that brings visitors through the zoo, over the wooded hills of Washington Park to the famed International Rose Test and Japanese gardens. From here, visitors have a sweeping view of Portland, the Willamette Valley and majestic Mount Hood. For an added treat, visitors can attend jazz concerts on Wednesday and bluegrass concerts on Thursday evenings throughout the summer. Concerts are not included with zoo admission.

Washington Park. This is Portland's oldest park, with fantastic vistas of the city and mountains. You may tour the park by car by following the "Scenic Drive" signs, or put on walking shoes to walk to the Rose

The weather machine in historic Pioneer Courthouse Square displays a sun for clear days, dragon for storms, and blue heron for changeable weather. (Courtesy of Portland Oregon Visitors Assoc.)

Gardens or Japanese Gardens within the park. Also within the park are tennis courts, picnic facilities and Alice Cooper's 1905 sculpture *Sacajawea*.

The Rose Gardens include 500 varieties of roses, most of which are marked at their borders. A Shakespeare Garden with traditional herbs, flowers and shrubs named in Shakespeare's plays, and the Sunken Garden Theatre, which stages summer theatrical performances, are also located in the Rose Gardens.

The Japanese Gardens, a 5.5-acre garden in Washington Park, is regarded as one of the most authentic outside of Japan. The gardens were designed by Professor P. Takuma Tono, an internationally renowned authority on Japanese landscaping. Five traditional gardens and an authentic pavilion recapture the mood of the Orient. Admission is $5 for adults, $2.50 for students and seniors and free for children under age 6. The gardens are open daily year-round except for Thanksgiving, Christmas and New Year's Day. Hours are 10 a.m. to 6 p.m., April through May; 9 a.m. to 8 p.m., June through Aug.; 10 a.m. to 6 p.m. in September and 10 a.m. to 4 p.m., Oct. through March.

World Forestry Center. Forest and timber products are the top industry in Oregon, and you can see how this business works—from Douglas fir seedling to finished plywood. The self-guided tour through the exhibit hall takes approximately 1 hour. The World Forestry Center itself is a stunning example of wood construction. The landscaped grounds feature an 1890 Shay steam locomotive and a set of high wheels, both used to haul logs. Admission is $3 for adults, $2 for seniors and students. The center is open daily 10 a.m. to 5 p.m. at 4033 SW Canyon Road; phone (503) 228-1368.

Powell's Books, at 10th and Burnside, calls itself the "City of Books," and with 30,000 square feet and nearly 1 million volumes in stock, the title is appropriate. New and used books, hardbound and paperback books, are shelved by subject in Michael Powell's cavernous bookstore (a store map is available for first-timers). Readings and autograph parties are held in the Anne Hughes coffee room, also a popular gathering place for book lovers, theater-goers, students and Powell's employees. Powell's is open daily from 9 a.m. to 11 p.m. Monday through Saturday, and 9 a.m. to 9 p.m. on Sundays and holidays.

Saturday Market. Local artisans, chefs and entertainers gather every weekend for the Saturday Market, where handcrafted candles, belts, stained glass and jewelry are hawked in a festive open-air market.

The market is held on W. Burnside, under the Burnside Bridge, in what is considered "Old Town."

The market opens on weekends only from March to Christmas. More than 500 vendors are on the selling list, but only 300 are allowed to sell at any one time. The covered food area has 26 chefs, many of them ethnic specialists. Each weekend, they prepare their own specialties.

Saturday Market is known for its entertainment, streetside jugglers, dancers, singers and mimes.

Market hours are from 10 a.m. to 5 p.m. on Saturday and 11 a.m. to 4:30 p.m. on Sunday. For more information, call (503) 222-6072.

Triangle/Pearl District. Art galleries, antique furniture shops, jazz clubs, bookstores, theater companies and microbreweries make up a lively 15-block stretch of renovated warehouses and storefronts just north of downtown and west of the riverfront Old Town.

Oregon Vietnam Veteran's Living Memorial. Located just north of the World Forestry Center in Washington Park, the memorial was erected in November 1987 to honor Oregonians who died in the Vietnam War and those who are still missing. The black granite memorial is wheelchair accessible.

Major Cities
SEATTLE

The Emerald City

With its major role in the Asia Pacific Economic Cooperation (APEC), its renowned music scene, its jets, its rain and its coffee, Seattle and its style command global attention. Visiting Jet City, however, is more like traveling through several distinctive small towns rather than one bustling municipality.

From the historic buildings of Pioneer Square, to the thrift stores and public art of Fremont, to Capitol Hill's celebration of cultural diversity, Seattle's neighborhoods exude a character all their own and give this metropolis its unique take on big city life.

Before the discovery of Puget Sound by white explorers, several Indian tribes inhabited the lush green mountains and valleys surrounding Puget Sound. Capt. George Vancouver was the first European to sail into and map Puget Sound in 1792. He described it as "the most lovely country that can be imagined."

The first settlement was by the Denny party in 1851 at Alki Point (now West Seattle). Because of poor weather, northern exposure and shallow water, the settlers sought a deeper harbor at Elliott Bay. The first buildings were built on mudflats in what is now Pioneer Square. As Seattle began to grow, it became evident that something had to be done about the steep, impractical streets. After a fire in 1889 destroyed downtown Seattle, the ensuing renovation project included leveling the hills and raising the lower areas to give Seattle a more consistent profile. It was a major undertaking, but it worked and today Seattle continues to benefit from that turn-of-the-century idea.

Seattle is bordered on the west by Puget Sound and on the east by Lake Washington. Lake Union, just north of downtown, and the ship canal that joins Lake Washington and Puget Sound, create something of an obstacle course for the flow of traffic. Three floating bridges connect Seattle to its eastside neighbors. And several bridges, including 2 drawbridges, span the waters that bisect the city. A city map is helpful if you expect to do a lot of driving about the city. If possible, avoid the freeways and floating bridges during rush hours.

It is relatively easy to get around downtown without a car. The Pike Place Market and the shopping area around Westlake Mall (5th Avenue and Pine Street) are only a few blocks apart. You can ride Metro buses for free in the area bordered by the Waterfront, the freeway, Jackson Street to the south and Battery Street (near the Seattle Center) to the north, so it's an easy ride to Pioneer Square. Or hop the Monorail to Seattle Center. Visitors can be surprised by some daunting downtown hills, however.

Seafair, a citywide festival that begins in mid-July, has been a summer event since 1950. Seattle's ethnic communities, neighborhoods and suburban communities join in the celebration with parades, milk carton races on Green Lake, salmon bakes and other festivities climaxing with hydroplane races held on Lake Washington. Another major highlight is the annual Torchlight Parade, held the final week of Seafair and featuring the Seafair Pirates.

There are hundreds of attractions in the Puget Sound area. For specific information, write to the Seattle Convention and Visitors Bureau, 520 Pike St., #1320, Seattle, WA 98101, or call (206) 461-5840. For hotel reservations and information, call the Seattle Hotel Hotline, 1-800-535-7071.

Attractions

The Pike Place Market, the oldest farmer's market in the United States, is a favorite place for both visitors and locals. It opened in 1907 as a place where farmers could sell their produce directly to their customers, and by 1927 more than 400 farmers sold produce at the height of the growing season. The market deteriorated in the years after WWII and almost succumbed to urban renewal in the 1970s. It was saved by a citizen's referendum and today is a bustling, thriving marketplace overlooking Elliott Bay with spectacular views of the water and distant Olympic Mountains.

Shoppers can browse through covered stalls and find local produce, fresh-cut flowers, fresh fish, meats and cheeses, and many creations of local artisans and craftsmen. Antique stores, specialty shops, galleries, bakeries and restaurants are also located in the market area. Street musicians, mimes and puppeteers compete for sidewalk space with fishmongers and shopkeepers along the main arcade and enhance the visual delight of the place. Fresh ground coffee and baking cinnamon rolls further tantalize the senses.

The Pike Place Market is located at the end of Pike Street off 1st Avenue and is open 7 days a week. The number and location of vendors changes daily. On-street parking can be difficult to find, so plan on using one of several parking garages on the perimeter of the market. Do not attempt to drive directly in front of the market. It is crowded,

Since its opening in 1907, shoppers have enjoyed the fresh produce at Pike Place Market. (© Lee Foster)

Above—The Fremont troll is a favorite landmark in this neighborhood. *(Sam Smith)*
Right—The cupola-topped Smith Tower was once the tallest building west of the Mississippi. *(Nancie J. Wood)*

congested and used primarily by pedestrians. It is better to find a parking garage within 2 or 3 blocks and walk in.

Pioneer Square. This is Seattle's birthplace. When Seattle's pioneers abandoned Alki Point (now West Seattle) for a more sheltered site, they came here to start their town. Built on mud and stilts, the whole downtown area was constructed almost entirely in wood, and in 1889 it burned down. A massive rebuilding took place immediately, this time in brick, and the result is an architecturally coherent district. The original Skid Road is here. Yesler Way was once used for skidding logs off the hillside and into the waters of Elliott Bay. The hills were logged off, the city grew and moved north, and the area became rundown and the model for the corrupted term "Skid Row." Almost a victim of urban renewal, Pioneer Square was declared a historic district in the 1970s. Today, many of the renovated buildings house art galleries, restaurants, unique shops, bookstores, museums and night spots.

For a narrative and anecdotal history of Seattle's early pioneers, Underground Tours takes you underneath the streets of Seattle. Underground passageways are the result of the rebuilding effort following the Great Seattle Fire, in which the streets were raised and sidewalks were built at the 2nd story level. For a while, storekeepers kept their business open on the ground floor, forcing their customers to climb the stairs. This was soon abandoned, and the 2nd stories became street level, leaving underground passageways. The tours begin at Doc Maynards Public House at 610 1st Ave. Call (206) 682-1511 for tour times and general information.

The Klondike Gold Rush National His-toric Park at 117 S. Main St., phone (206) 553-7220, together with its sister unit in Skagway, AK, is the only site in the national park system that commemorates a major American gold rush. On July 17, 1897, the coastal steamer *Portland* arrived in Elliott Bay and unloaded 2 tons of gold. Seemingly overnight, the city became the point of departure for fortune-seekers. The city's boosters successfully promoted Seattle as the gateway to the North, outfitters provisioned those bound for the Klondike, and Seattle became forever linked with Alaska's history. (The Seattle unit interprets the city's role as the dominant West Coast staging area for the Yukon gold rush of 1897–98.)

The park has a visitor center with historic photos and exhibits of hardware, gold mining artifacts, and the mandatory "ton of goods" that miners were required to have before entering the Yukon. Gold panning demonstrations are available. Guided group museum tours are by advance arrangement.

Also in the Pioneer Square district is Elliott Bay Book Co. at 101 S. Main, one of the region's best bookstores. Its creaky wooden floors and inviting stacks of books make it a wonderful place to browse. There's a cafe downstairs and monthly readings by local and national authors.

The Waterfront. Although Seattle's waterfront has moved south toward Harbor Island, and the downtown waterfront is filled with tourist-oriented shops, restaurants, fish and chip bars and harbor tour operators, it's still worth a visit. You can gaze out into the harbor to watch loaded container ships and ferry boats move across Elliott Bay and imagine the beauty that drew the first settlers here. The waterfront promenade extends from Pier 48 at the foot of Main Street in Pioneer Square north to Pier 70 and Myrtle Edwards Park. If you get tired, you can hop the Waterfront Trolley, which runs along Alaskan Way from Main Street to Myrtle Edwards Park with stops in between. A ride costs $1 end to end, and 1-hour Metro bus transfers are issued and honored.

The Seattle Aquarium on Pier 59 is the waterfront's biggest draw. There are no performing animals here; the Aquarium's innovative displays re-create coastal and intertidal habitats. A huge viewing dome shows life underwater in Puget Sound with sharks, eels and octopi swimming in and out of view. A fish hatchery and salmon ladder explain the migration of anadromous fish, and playful seal and sea otter tanks can be viewed from above and below. Admission is $6.95 for adults; $4.50 for ages 6–18; $5.50 for seniors; $2.25 for children ages 3–5. Call (206) 386-4320 for information.

If you've been watching the ferries glide across the water and have been tempted to take a ride, the Washington State Ferry terminal is at Pier 52 at the foot of Marion Street. For some salt air and an easy, short trip, walk on the ferry to Bainbridge Island. The ride takes about 35 minutes one way, and you can either stay on for the round-trip or make a stop at the small town of Bainbridge Island (formerly Winslow), which is within walking distance of the ferry terminal. The ferries run frequently; call (206) 464-6400 for schedule information.

For a different perspective of Seattle, take a sightseeing cruise. Argosy (206/623-4252) offers 3 tours: a 1-hour narrative tour of Elliott Bay that leaves from Pier 55, a 2 1/2-hour cruise along Seattle's waterfront through the locks into Lake Union, which leaves from Pier 57, and a 90-minute cruise on Lake Washington that leaves from Kirkland's Marina Park. The *Spirit of Puget Sound*

(206/443-1442) offers 2- and 3-hour cruises on Elliot Bay with a buffet lunch or dinner and live entertainment. Departs from Pier 70.

A 1-hour narrated cruise to Blake Island and Tillicum Village departs Pier 56 daily from May to Oct. The village features a Northwest Coast Indian longhouse, tribal dancing and baked salmon dinner. Phone (206) 443-1244 for times and cost. Also access to Blake Island Marine State Park (206/731-0770); beach, hiking trails, camping and picnicking.

Another Seattle institution, Ivar's Acres of Clams on Pier 54, is famed not so much for its cuisine, but for its founder, the late civic booster and raconteur Ivar Haglund. Some say the clam nectar isn't what it used to be, but it's a local institution. Outdoor seating makes it a pleasant lunch stop.

At the waterfront's north end, Myrtle Edwards Park provides a patch of green and a place to picnic and watch lunchtime joggers go by.

The Seattle Center, a legacy of the 1962 World's Fair, is today the cultural, arts and entertainment center of the city. The 74-acre urban park with its landscaped grounds, fountains and hidden sculptures, hosts a number of special events in addition to the restaurants, exhibits, museums and shops open year-round. Three major festivals take place here during the summer that draw tens of thousands of visitors to sample local food, music and crafts. The Folklife Festival opens the summer season during Memorial Day weekend with one of the largest gatherings of musicians and craftspeople of its kind. In July, the city's restaurants entice festival-goers with their favorite culinary delights in a giant food festival called the Bite of Seattle. And Bumbershoot, held during Labor Day weekend, attracts top performers in music, dance and literary arts.

Though outdoor festivals are popular summer pastimes, the Pacific Science Center at the south end of the Seattle Center is a great place to go with kids on a rainy day. A 5-building complex surrounded by shallow pools and futuristic arches, the Pacific Science Center (206/443-2001) is nationally recognized for its family-oriented activities and hands-on approach to discovering science and math. There are high-tech simulations, labs and classes, a Starlab Planetarium, environmental exhibits, Sea

Seattle's Space Needle

Monster House, and replica of a Northwest Indian ceremonial house. Admission is $6 for adults, $5 for seniors and children ages 6 to 13, and $3.50 for children 2 to 5. An IMAX theatre is also featured; phone (206) 443-4629 for schedule and admission fees.

Also for children is the Children's Museum, located in the lower level of the Center House. The upper levels of the Center House are filled with specialty shops, ethnic restaurants and fast food vendors. A few steps from the Center House is Fun Forest, a sort of permanent carnival.

Seattle's Opera House, Playhouse and Bagley Wright Theater on the grounds are home to Seattle's opera, ballet, symphony, and 2 repertory companies. The acclaimed Seattle Children's Theatre is also here, located between the Science Center and Flag Pavillion.

The dominant feature of the Seattle Center is, of course, the Space Needle. Two revolving restaurants and an observation deck at the 500-foot level can be reached by a glass-enclosed elevator. The cost ($5.50 for adults, $3 for children) is steep, so make sure the day is clear before going up for the views. The ride is free for restaurant patrons.

Another holdover from the World's Fair is the Monorail that connects the Seattle Center with the Westlake Mall downtown. The trip takes 90 seconds and costs 90¢ for adults and 70¢ for youth one way.

The Hiram M. Chittenden Locks (3015 NW 54th St.). The spectacle of watching boats float up and down, and the fact that it's free, make this one of the most-visited spots in Seattle. More than 100,000 commercial and pleasure vessels a year pass through the locks that join freshwater Lake Washington and Lake Union to the salt water of Puget Sound. The original idea for connecting the navigable waters was developed as early as 1853. The channel between Lake Washington and Lake Union was completed in 1880, and lowered Lake Washington by 8 feet in the process. It was Major Hiram M. Chittenden, a Seattle district engineer for the Corps of Engineers, who was responsible for the design and completion of the locks in 1917.

A popular leisure sport is watching the

Houseboats rim Lake Union. Sailboats travel between Lake Union and Lake Washington via the Montlake Cut. (Nancie J. Wood)

different kinds of boats that pass through the locks, a trip that takes 10 to 25 minutes. A visitor center at the locks has displays on the history and operation of the locks. The locks are open 7 a.m. to 9 p.m. daily, year-round.

Across the waterway in Commodore Park, the fish ladder provides a unique opportunity to view anadromous salmon fighting their way from the Sound into freshwater spawning grounds. Completed in 1976, the fish ladder has 21 steps leading fish around the spillway dam. An underground viewing area lets visitors watch the fish struggle against the current in their upstream migration. The best time for viewing migrating sockeye salmon is June and July; August for chinook salmon; late September for coho; and January for steelhead.

Around the locks, the Carl S. English Jr. Ornamental Gardens feature more than a thousand species of trees, shrubs and flowers on a 17-acre site. English spent 34 years cultivating and expanding the garden's exotic plants. This is a fine place to picnic on a summer's day.

Washington Park Arboretum. One of the most beautiful places to walk in Seattle, especially on a spring day when trees and flowers are bursting into bloom, is the Washington Park Arboretum, located just south of the University of Washington. The University maintains a botanical research facility here, and you can see more than 5,000 varieties of trees, plants, shrubs and flowers by walking any of the paths that crisscross the park.

Especially popular is the Japanese Garden (206/684-4725), a secluded garden of pools, waterfalls, rockeries and formal arrangements of Japanese trees, shrubs and flowers. The Japanese Garden is located just off Lake Washington Boulevard E., which runs through the Arboretum. A formal tea ceremony is performed in the Japanese teahouse on every third Sunday of the month, April through Oct. Admission to the Japanese Garden is $2 for adults and $1 for seniors and children and it is open daily.

There are several trails in the park. Azalea Way winds through azaleas, flowering cherry and dogwood before ending at the Arboretum's visitor center. The Waterfront Trail follows the shore of Lake Washington and connects to Foster Island Nature Walk, a 1.5-mile round-trip walk over marshes and bogs that ends at the Museum of History and Industry parking lot. Plaques along the way describe the interrelationships between marsh plant and animal life. There are benches for sitting and water-gazing along the way.

University of Washington. More than 34,000 students attend the University of Washington (U-Dub) Seattle campus. The University's park-like setting with views of Lake Washington and the mountains, and its fine examples of diverse architectural styles make it a city treasure. The main entrance is located at NE 45th Street and 17th Avenue NE. There you can obtain a map of the campus and park your car to explore the campus on foot.

Notable campus buildings are: the Suzzallo (SUE-Za-low) Library, the main research library, with ornate stained-glass windows and gothic features; Denny Hall, the oldest building on campus; Drumheller Fountain and Mount Rainier vista; Red Square, an expansive public square surrounded by old and new campus buildings; and the Sylvan Theater, a beautiful, hidden natural theater that incorporates 4 columns from the original University building.

The Burke Museum (206/543-5590) is located at the northwest end of campus. It houses a fine collection of Northwest Coast Indian artifacts and anthropological exhibits. The museum is free, though admission is charged for special exhibits. Soak up some campus atmosphere with espresso and carrot cake in The Boiserie coffeehouse downstairs.

Down the street from the Burke—at 15th Avenue NE and NE 41st Street on campus—is the Henry Art Gallery, featuring changing exhibits of contemporary and historical art. Phone (206) 543-2280.

Off campus, just south of the university, the Museum of History and Industry provides a visual record of Seattle's first 100 years. The main gallery has changing exhibits highlighting Seattle and Pacific Northwest history. Permanent exhibits include a re-created 1880s Seattle street, an aviation wing and information on the development of flight, and a maritime wing with history of water transportation in the Pacific Northwest. Open daily, 10 a.m. to 5 p.m. Admission is $5.50 for adults, $3 for seniors and children ages 6–12, and $1 for ages 2–5. Call (206) 324-1125 for more information.

Although it has lost some of its bohemian energy in the last few years, The Ave, as it's known (really University Way NE), is the University's shopping, eating and movie theater district. The Ave is crowded with ethnic fast food, espresso and ice cream shops, bakeries, bookstores and boutiques. Smoky coffeehouses can still be found in the University District, and The University Bookstore (4326 University Way NE) is one of the largest bookstores on the West Coast.

Smith Tower. A Seattle landmark, and the state's first notable structure, the Smith Tower was completed in 1913. Originally called the L.C. Smith Building, the 42-story struc-

ture was the tallest building west of the Mississippi River for many years. Located on 2nd Avenue at Yesler Way, the observation deck is open to the public daily; there is a charge of $2 for adults, $1 for seniors and children under 12.

The International District. Once known as Chinatown, the International District is both a collection of distinct Asian cultural and ethnic groups and a cohesive melting pot. The area, growing and vibrant with the influx of new immigrants, is located in the area between S. Weller Street and Washington Street, between 2nd Avenue S. and 12th Avenue. It's a neighborhood of colorful grocery stores, small shops, cultural centers, museums and a wonderful variety of restaurants.

The Wing Luke Asian Museum traces the history of Seattle's Asian community since 1860. The museum features Asian folk art and crafts and rotating exhibits. The museum is open Tuesday through Friday, 11 a.m. to 4:30 p.m., and Saturday and Sunday, noon to 4 p.m. Closed Monday. Admission is $2.50 for adults, $1.50 for seniors and students, and 75¢ for children ages 5–12. Admission is free on Thursday. The museum is located at 407 7th Ave. S., phone (206) 623-5124.

For a different shopping experience, try Uwajimaya at 519 6th Ave. S., a Japanese supermarket/department store/emporium with live fish tanks, toys, clothing, books, cookware and more.

Seattle Art Museum. Driving along 1st Avenue through downtown Seattle, visitors will find it very hard to miss the Seattle Art Museum (SAM). The 48-foot-tall Hammering Man kinetic sculpture standing in front of the museum grabs the eye and does not

The 48-foot-tall Hammering Man at the Seattle Art Museum. (© Lee Foster)

let go. The mammoth sculpture was one of the new additions given to SAM when the museum moved from its previous location in Volunteer Park on Capitol Hill to its current location on University Street between 1st and 2nd avenues, just 2 blocks from Pike Place Market. SAM houses internationally renowned collections of Asian, African, Native American and modern art of the Pacific Northwest; its permanent collections number over 19,000 pieces. The museum also has studio art and lecture classrooms, 2 gallery education rooms with hands-on activities, a cafe and an extensive selection of art books in the museum store. SAM's original home reopened as the Seattle Asian Art Museum (SAAM) and highlights some of the 7,000 objects in the museum's Asian collection. SAM is open Tuesday through Sunday 10 a.m. to 5 p.m., Thursday until 9 p.m. Admission is $6 for adults, $4 for seniors and students, and free for children under 12. There is free admission to the museum the first Tuesday of every month. For information on SAM or SAAM, contact the Seattle Art Museum, 100 University St., Seattle, WA 98101-2902; phone (206) 654-3100 for recorded information on hours, directions, and current and upcoming exhibitions.

The Museum of Flight. Though not connected with The Boeing Co., it's hard not to think of the aviation giant. The Museum of Flight is located at Boeing Field, and the Red Barn, Boeing's first plant, is on site. The 6-story glass and steel complex is as impressive as the collection it houses, with 20 full-sized airplanes suspended from the ceiling. The museum brings to life the rich history of aviation in the Pacific Rim region with priceless photos and artifacts. The museum is open daily from 10 a.m. to 5 p.m. (Thursdays until 9 p.m.); admission is $6 for adults, $3 for children ages 6–15. Phone (206) 764-5720.

The Woodland Park Zoo (206/684-4800) is one of the nation's top 10 zoos. The zoo has strived in the last few years to move animals out of barred cages into lifelike representations of their natural habitats. The tropical Rain Forest is a lush, humid environment with over 50 different animal species. A trail leads from the dark forest floor to the sunlit canopy, where tropical birds fly overhead. Leafeating ants, poison dart frogs, snakes, the world's smallest monkeys and ring-tailed lemurs all mingle in this teeming environment. The Asian elephant house is set among tropical plantings and features a luxurious Thai pagoda-style elephant house. The African Savannah is a 5-acre grassland habitat with water holes, dry creek beds, zebras, giraffes, lions, hippos and patas monkeys. A heavily-planted lowland gorilla habitat is considered one of the best of its kind in the world. The gorillas move about in a forest that contains a stream, boulders and climbing trees. You can view them at close range from behind a clear barrier. A nocturnal house turns day into night for viewing those creatures we rarely see. And the family farm has a petting zoo for children, an animal nursery and crafts demonstrations. It's a very pleasant way to spend the day.

Major Cities
SPOKANE

The Lilac City

Spokane (pop. 177,200) is the hub of the Inland Northwest, an area stretching from the Columbia's Big Bend through Idaho's Bitterroot Mountains, and from Canada to Oregon. Before air freight, UPS and fax machines, it was the marketing center for the whole territory.

Spokane was the center of a world unto itself. Isolated by miles and mountains from other market cities, it developed according to its own needs—farms, industries, electricity, minerals, forest products, medical care and education. In fact it was so perfectly isolated that it became an unofficial test market for America's manufacturers. They rightly figured that a new gadget could be market-tested in Spokane with the scientific control of a sealed test chamber. It followed that Spokanites saw more than their share of new cereal boxes, strange soaps and patented widgets.

First were the Native Americans, of course. And then the missionaries and farmers and ranchers and miners, followed by millers, excited by the ready energy of Spokane's falls. Though leveled by the fire of 1889, Spokane didn't slow down or look back after the rails came, for the railroads were Spokane's vital arteries of commerce for the next half-century.

Where rails went, development followed, and so Spokane's development crowded along its rail lines—orchards, for instance. In the early century, the Spokane Valley's favorite crop was apples. Even today, neighborhoods carry the old apple names—Orchard Prairie, Appleway, Otis Orchards. The list goes on.

But the apple era wound down as competition from Yakima and Wenatchee, the Depression and blight took their toll. The fact of the collapse was written in crumbling fruit warehouses ranged along rail sidings.

Before, during and after the apple era, Spokane's biggest-spending benefactor was the Coeur d'Alene mining district. The miners who made it big spent big on the city and endowed its institutions, established its parks, built its tallest buildings and lined Rockwood Boulevard with their mansions. So much silver, gold, lead and zinc came from the ground to fuel Spokane's economy that the city established its own mining stock exchange to channel the investment fever of its citizens.

All through those years the rails prospered. Spokane's youngsters learned reading and geography from boxcars clacking past at crossings—Chesapeake, Wabash, Atcheson Topeka and Santa Fe.

Then came WWII, its warriors and suppliers of war materiel. Spokane jumped into the aluminum business then, thanks to plentiful and cheap power. New plants produced not only the metal, but fabricated aluminum parts for warplanes.

Little Felts Field became a training and jump-off point for new B-25 bombers destined for Russia. A huge new naval ordnance depot was built east of town and a new airfield was laid out on the west side. And the railroads moved even greater loads.

Forest products industries kept a steady work force busy for the half-century ending with the war. But by that time the choice stands of white pine were gone, the city closed around the old mills, and the equipment of newer mills elsewhere had rendered the old-timers obsolete.

By the end of WWII, air travel was an everyday fact, especially among first-class passengers who left rail travel and took to the air. Intercity truck transport also struck at the railroads' customers. Spokane's shippers suddenly found it more convenient to move goods directly to their destinations by truck than to haul them to a rail yard.

For a time, displaced railroad workers found work at Spokane's giant auto-freight docks, patterned after the concept of rail yards. That lasted until the trucking industry woke to the fact that point-to-point transport required no great central forwarding docks, and auto-freight centers went the way of the rail yards.

The postwar years were difficult ones for the region. The mines slowed, the area's wheat was diverted to Columbia River ports. What the city needed was a miracle—which it found in putting on the 1974 World's Fair.

The Opera House rests above Spokane River. (Allen Peery)

The "bowl and pitcher" area in Riverside State Park. (L. Linkhart)

Spokane. How could an isolated town of 172,000 put on a World Exposition? The prescription involved equal parts of daring and vision. First, the old downtown Great Northern and Milwaukee rail yards were ripped up and the terminals razed to make way for the 100-acre development. And once the nay-sayers saw it actually taking shape, the whole city spruced itself up to welcome world travelers. Expo '74 did happen. It was hugely successful and provided Spokane with its finest attraction, Riverfront Park.

One advantage of Spokane's slow growth is that much of the city's early buildings and old homes have not been destroyed by urbanization. The Spokane County Courthouse (on W. Broadway, north of the river), the City Hall building, and some of the Victorian homes in the area west of downtown are visible reminders of Spokane's past wealth.

For more information, contact Spokane Convention and Visitors Bureau, 926 Sprague Ave., Suite 180, Spokane, WA 99204; phone (509) 624-1341, or 1-800-248-3230.

Attractions

Riverfront Park. Everyone votes for Riverfront Park as Spokane's top attraction. Present-day visitors may have difficulty imagining Riverfront Park as the site of bustling Expo '74, a full-fledged world's fair. Today Riverfront Park is a place for strolling on the meandering paved paths beside the river and the footbridges leading to Spokane Falls. You can take the Sky Ride gondola over the cascading lower falls or hop on the 1909 hand-carved carousel. An Imax theater,

winter ice skating at the Ice Palace, and the Eastern Washington Science Center are located in the Pavilion. Free concerts, art shows and other events are scheduled throughout the year. Fresh produce and crafts can be found at the Public Market from May through Oct. near the north entrance to the park.

Visit a Museum. Spokane boasts a number of museums and galleries, but one deserving special note is the Cheney-Cowles Memorial Museum, which displays an outstanding record of Spokane's history. Located at W. 2316 1st Ave., amid the elegant old mansions of Browne's Addition, it is Spokane's most extensive museum. An art gallery, natural history collections, dioramas, historical photos and large Indian and frontier displays portray Spokane the way it was. Admission is $3 for adults and $2 for seniors and children ages 6–16. Open Tuesday through Saturday, 10 a.m. to 5 p.m. and Sunday, 1–5 p.m. Closed Mondays and major holidays.

See Spokane by Air. For an actual overview of the area, take an hour-long charter flight from Felts Field or Geiger Field. Try counting the lakes—they say there are 50 lakes within 50 miles. A scant 22 air miles takes you to Mount Spokane State Park, covering more than 20,000 forested acres with excellent skiing, camping, huckleberry-picking and horseback riding.

To the south, your pilot will point out the fertile dust-dunes that support annual bumper crops of Palouse wheat. To the west, you will pass over scabrock country where chunky basalt formations share space with ponds, pine woods and cattle ranching. The 2 consistent features of your aerial tour are beauty and change. This is a landscape that

begs to be explored.

Visit Wineries. A good start would be Arbor Crest. Headquartered in a Florentine-style mansion perched on a rock promontory 450 feet above Spokane River, Arbor Crest treats visitors to spectacular views east into Idaho and west of Spokane. Even the tennis courts, pool and gardens press at the brink. Definitely not a stop if you're queasy about heights.

An indicator of Arbor Crest quality is their wines' success in foreign markets where their time-tested varietals are earning respect.

To reach Arbor Crest, drive 1 mile east of Pasadena on Upriver Drive. Signs at the junction with Fruithill Road lead on to the winery. The Cliff House, the winery's tasting facility and visitor center, is a national historic landmark and is open daily noon to 5 p.m.

Latah Creek Wine Cellars occupies an attractive Spanish mission-style winery located off Interstate 90 at the Pines Road exit. Mike Conway, owner and host, believes in the "light-touch" approach to winemaking, intruding as little as possible with the natural processes. It must work, since every bit of wall space is covered with prestigious awards won since opening in 1982. The tasting room is open Monday through Saturday, 10 a.m. to 5 p.m. and Sunday, noon to 5 p.m. During winter, it closes at 4 p.m.

Founded in 1980, Worden's Winery is the oldest of Spokane's young wineries. Like Latah Creek, Worden's is family-operated. From humble beginnings in a log cabin and storage shed, Jack Worden's winery quickly grew into new quarters and an annual capacity of 20,000 cases per year.

Visitors will find Worden's Winery at Spokane's west end. Turn off Interstate 90 at Exit 276 and follow the signs to the tasting room where your host might favor you with a taste of his Gold Medal 1985 Chenin Blanc.

Located next to the historic WWP Steam Plant, Knipprath Cellars at S. 163 Lincoln St. gives you a tasting room conveniently downtown. Take I-90's Exit 280 and then go north on Lincoln to the tasting room. It is open Friday through Sunday, 11 a.m. to 6 p.m., and is conveniently located near the visitor information center.

Visit a Nature Park. Among the top choices are Finch Arboretum, Riverside State Park, Turnbull Wildlife Refuge and Walk in the Wild.

Finch Arboretum contains 2,000 specimens in its 65 rolling forested acres. A tumbling stream, quiet trails and many species of birds would make this a gem if only it were easier to find. From city center, go west on 2nd Avenue to Sunset Boulevard. Continue on Sunset past Government Way to just before "F" Street. The entrance to the arboretum is located on the left-hand side of Sunset. Free, open sunrise to sunset daily.

Turnbull Wildlife Refuge deserves attention though it lies some miles out. Located 4 miles south of the town of Cheney (11 miles west of Spokane) on the Badger Lake Road, Turnbull offers unmatched viewing of birds, mainly migratory waterfowl. More than 200 species have been spotted here.

Deer, coyote, beaver, raccoon and muskrat abound and are frequently seen from the 5-mile loop road.

Turnbull, a federal reserve, contains more than 120 lakes and ponds in its 7 square miles of scabrock, grassland, and pine and aspen groves. Numerous trails lead to observation blinds where quiet visitors identify wildlife against checklists provided by the management. Best times for visiting are early mornings in spring or fall. From March through Oct., there is a $2 admission charge per vehicle.

Walk in the Wild is a cageless zoo located on 240 acres overlooking the Spokane River. Exit Interstate 90 at Pines Road (Exit 289) and drive north to Euclid Avenue. Signs lead to the zoo where, for a small fee, visitors follow trails through a variety of habitats. Deer and elk, bison and elephants, peccaries, eagles and several Northwest species are on display. Children will enjoy the look-and-touch farm animals. Open daily, 10 a.m. to 5 p.m., April to Nov. Admission $3.50.

Sports. For the horsey set, Spokane offers expert polo, horse races and mounts to rent for quiet rides through open pine forests.

World-class polo in Spokane? Definitely. The Spokane Polo Club is the undisputed top polo club in the Northwest and a perennial contender for national honors. On 80 lush acres east of the top of Sunset Hill, located west of Spokane on Highway 2, fierce adherents to polo's demanding and dangerous discipline regularly practice and compete. Games played Saturday and Sunday during the summer.

The Playfair Racetrack, the state's oldest, has long been a civic fixture and a magnet to Spokane's devotees of the "Sport of Kings." For casual visitors, a day at Playfair provides unmatched people-watching. Playfair, like all tracks, is a meeting place for that segment of adult society that dares to be different. How different? One has to experience a race crowd to appreciate it.

Race-goers know Playfair as a "bull-ring," a shorter than normal track. Hemmed in as it is by encroaching industrial parks, it has no room to grow. Still, when Playfair came into existence, it was a big step up from the now-forgotten track around Corbin Park.

But if you're not satisfied unless astride a horse yourself, try the Indian Canyon Riding Corrals at South Assembly and West Drive. The corrals, adjacent to Indian Canyon Park, open onto miles of forested and scenic trails.

For those people who like their exercise on a more personal level, the annual Lilac Bloomsday Run could fill the bill. Advertised as the largest timed race in the world, 55,000 runners, walkers and wheelchair racers hit the street each year the first Sunday of May.

The Spokane River Centennial Trail is a new addition to the area. A 39-mile path as much as 12-feet wide will take runners, walkers, hikers and bicyclists from downtown Spokane to the Idaho border. There, it connects to the Idaho Centennial Trail ending in Coeur d'Alene.

Shop the Skywalk. How are Spokane's streets like Venetian canals? Answer: One is forever passing under pedestrian bridges. Crisscrossing streets, they connect the 2nd stories of 13 blocks of Spokane's downtown, and up among the bridges, shoppers browse through block after block of shops and eateries.

The Skywalk was downtown's answer to the growing drain on its business by suburban malls. Spokane's planners, unwilling to concede defeat, came up with their truly extraordinary plan. Their plan became reality, and the Skywalk Mall quickly became the heart of Spokane's downtown shopping area.

Manito Park. Manito Park, on Grand Boulevard between 17th and 25th avenues, hosts more than 100,000 visitors each year and features a conservatory, Japanese garden, perennial and rose gardens, and a formal garden. The Conservatory displays tropical foliage, seasonal flowers, house plant varieties and is of special interest to hobbyists. The center of the dome contains larger tropical plant specimens combined with flowering displays.

The Spokane Nishinomiya Garden, also called the Japanese Garden, is a beautifully designed asymmetrical garden in the park inspiring tranquillity and peace in the Japanese tradition. It was completed in the spring of 1974 and named after one of Spokane's 2 sister cities in Japan. The Japanese Garden is open from 8 a.m. to dusk from May through Oct. There is no admission fee. The flowering season for the perennial and formal gardens is May through Oct.; the rose garden blooms June through Sept.

Cathedral of St. John the Evangelist. This Episcopal cathedral is an architectural masterpiece, built and completed in less than a generation by the members of a congregation. The solid stone structure is a magnificent example of English Gothic architecture. The cathedral is 257 feet tall and seats 1,500 persons. Inside are beautifully intricate stained-glass windows, elaborately carved arches, mouldings and panels, and a 4,094-pipe organ. In the tower is a 49-bell carillon. Carillon concerts are played each Thursday at noon and on Sunday following the main service.

Volunteer guides offer tours of the cathedral each Tuesday, Thursday, Saturday and Sunday noon to 3 p.m.

Higher Education. Spokane and its suburbs offer a breadth and depth of education uncommon for cities its size. The lure of the schools' specialties draws students from far away, and many return to make their homes in Spokane. Industry keeps a close watch on Spokane's educated labor market, taking advantage of the resident pool of talent.

Spokane has 5 colleges: Gonzaga University has 4,722 students; Whitworth College, 1,788; Eastern Washington University, 8,348; Spokane Falls Community College, 5,650; Washington State University, Spokane Campus, 400 master's level.

Walk the lovely campuses. Visit the colleges' libraries or coffee shops. It is always a vibrant experience to rub shoulders with throngs of intelligent young people who are busy shaping their dreams.

A sculpture by local artist Harold Balazs in front of the Clock Tower at Riverfront Park. (Allen Peery)

TACOMA

The City of Destiny

Tacoma, long known for its rail and lumber heritage, has seen a dramatic revitalization since the mid-1980s.

Fueled by a strong sense of civic pride, the city began by building the region's finest arena (the Tacoma Dome) and renovating the magnificent 1911 Union Station. The historic Pantages and Rialto theaters were restored to their former 1918 glory and now, along with the new Theater on the Square, form the Broadway Center for the Performing Arts which attracts national and international performers.

Even though this hard-working, blue-collar city was sometimes scorned by nearby Seattleites who thought of themselves as urbane and sophisticated, the scenic beauty of Tacoma was never in question.

Tacoma is nestled alongside Commencement Bay, a bustling deep-water port. The city has beautiful neighborhoods with tree-lined streets. And the backdrop for the city is the Cascade mountain range, with Mount Rainier towering over the city like a protective parent.

Tacoma, called "The City of Destiny," was the railroad terminus long before tracks reached Seattle 32 miles away.

But before manifest destiny lured explorers West, the beautiful countryside was inhabited by the Puyallup and Nisqually Indian tribes. It wasn't until 1792 that Capt. George Vancouver visited the area. Based on Capt. Vancouver's glowing reports about the area's abundant resources, other explorers soon followed including members of the Hudson's Bay Co. In 1885, the company built a fort and trading post 3 miles north of the Nisqually River.

The Wilkes expedition, headed by Capt. Charles Wilkes, began surveying the waters of Puget Sound on the bay around which Tacoma is now built. Wilkes named his starting point Commencement Bay. The artifacts and documents of the Wilkes expedition would later prove to be the initial collection that convinced Congress to establish the Smithsonian Institution.

In 1852, Nicholas Delin became the first settler in what is now downtown Tacoma, building a sawmill and a cabin. Soon after, Job Carr, Tacoma's first mayor, postmaster and election officer, chose a spot for what he hoped would become the terminus for the Northern Pacific Railroad. Others shared his dream, including General M.M. McCarver, who gave the city its first name, Commencement City. In 1869, the settlement's name was set as Tacoma, a derivation of the Indian Tahoma—their name for Mount Rainier.

Tacoma and the surrounding area grew quickly with the completion of the railroad in 1873. Copper-domed Union Station stands as a reminder of the city's railroad history. Today, Tacoma boasts the sixth busiest port in the United States, the thriving communities of Fort Lewis and McChord Air Force Base, and the seeds of high-tech industries.

Further information on area attractions, activities and points of interest is available from the Tacoma–Pierce County Visitor and Convention Bureau, 906 Broadway, P.O. Box 1754, Tacoma, WA 98401; phone (206) 627-2836, fax (206) 627-8783.

Attractions

Point Defiance Zoo and Aquarium. One of the Northwest's finest parks, 698-acre Point Defiance Park includes trails through forested areas, natural beaches, children's playgrounds, tennis courts, a Japanese garden and lush rhododendron gardens. Also within the park is a reconstruction of Fort Nisqually (originally built in 1833), a railroad village with a working steam engine and views of the Olympic Mountains, Vashon Island and Puget Sound. The world-class, 29-acre zoo and aquarium located in the park focuses on Pacific Rim animals. The zoo is open from 10 a.m. to 4 p.m., except from Memorial Day to Labor Day, when the zoo stays open until 7 p.m. North or south on I-5, take Exit 132 and follow signs that lead to Washington Highway 16 west, toward Gig Harbor; exit on 6th Avenue and follow the signs. For current admission rates, special attractions and other information, call (206) 591-5337.

Broadway Center for the Performing Arts. The **Pantages Theater**, a 1918

The restored Pantages Theater was modeled after Louis XIV's opera house at Versailles. (Courtesy of Tacoma-Pierce County Visitor & Convention Bureau)

Above—*Renovations to the majestic Union Station included a new copper roof.* (Courtesy of Tacoma-Pierce County Visitor & Convention Bureau)
Right—*A statue in front of Union Station.* (Sam Smith)

vaudeville theater, has been painstakingly restored to its original grandeur. It took an 8-year, $6 million restoration to return the theater to the style of Louis XIV's opera house at Versailles, after which it was originally patterned. The theater was built by vaudeville entrepreneur Alexander Pantages—the sixth in a series of showcase theaters that, over the years, provided a stage for Stan Laurel and Bob Hope.

In 1932 it was converted into a movie theater. In 1978 a community project began to restore the theater to its original grandeur. Now it's back offering entertainment by such notables as the Joffrey Ballet and the Boston Pops. To find out what's playing, call (206) 591-5894. The theater is located at 901 Broadway at the corner of Commerce and Broadway.

The equally historic **Rialto Theater** also opened in 1918 with a Beaux Arts decor that was renovated in 1991. The 742-seat theater is now the home of the 250-member Tacoma Youth Symphony, drawing from 85 different regional schools. It performs free to the public several times a year. The theater also hosts the Northwest Sinfonietta chamber orchestra and Rialto Film Guild. Phone (206) 591-5890.

Theater on the Square, the 302-seat home of the Tacoma Actors Guild, opened in 1993. It is adjacent to the Pantages Theater. Founded in 1978, TAG is Washington state's fourth largest professional theater.

The acclaimed theater company draws from classics and new works to produce 6 plays annually ranging from dramas to musicals to comedies. Phone (206) 272-2145.

Ruston Way. Tacoma's busy port and beautiful setting can be enjoyed on a leisurely walk along the Ruston Way waterfront on the south shore of Commencement Bay. On a clear day, you'll see the wide saltwater bay framed by distant islands, snowcapped mountains of the Olympic and Cascade ranges, and towering Mount Rainier. If you get hungry while walking along the 2-mile waterfront promenade, stop at one of the restaurants. Or if you want to savor the view, enjoy one of the parks along the way. Commencement Park at the east end of the waterfront features a large heliochronometer that tells you the time of day by the shadow the sun casts across the numbered bow. An interpretive court surrounding the piece explains the history, geology and other facts of interest about the area.

Pleasure boaters can moor at Old Town Dock, originally built in 1873, or at several other docks along Ruston Way.

Old Town. On a bluff overlooking Ruston Way is Old Town, the original Tacoma settlement area, with many restaurants, galleries and historic buildings, including St. Peter's Episcopal Church. The church is Tacoma's first place of worship, located at N. 29th and Starr streets. Built in 1873, the church's ivy-covered bell tower was a prominent landmark in early Tacoma. The original church bell, weighing 965 lbs., was shipped around Cape Horn. Today it is preserved on a mounted display outside the church.

Ruston Way in Old Town is sometimes referred to as "Restaurant Row" because many of Tacoma's best restaurants are here. Each restaurant features a large deck that makes dining alfresco a popular bayside choice.

Washington State Historical Museum. One of the largest collections of pioneer, Indian and Alaskan artifacts on the Pacific Coast is located at the Washington State Historical Museum. The museum is moving into a new $35.8 million building adjacent Union Station. The new museum building's architecture mimics the massive, arched, Romanesque style of Union Station.

The Stadium District. On the National Register of Historic Places due to the broad spectrum of architectural styles, the area features historic streetlights, brick and cobblestone streets, and stately Victorian mansions.

Points of interest include Annie Wright Seminary, a private school for grades K–12, located at 827 Tacoma Ave., and Stadium High School, located at 111 N. E St., which was modeled after a French castle. This chateauesque structure was designed in 1891 as a luxury hotel for the Northern Pacific Railroad. A depression in 1893 halted construction, however, and in 1906 it was adapted for use as a high school.

Stadium Bowl, located behind the high school, was the first stadium built on the Pacific Coast and one of the first built in the country. Constructed in "Old Woman's Gulch," which provided a natural amphitheater for its tiered concrete design, the stadium has hosted such dignitaries as Theodore Roosevelt, Warren Harding, Franklin Roosevelt, Babe Ruth and Jack Dempsey.

Tacoma Art Museum. Long a top-rated museum, Tacoma Art Museum is currently looking for a larger home in the downtown area for its collection of Northwest artists, impressionists, and classics by Renoir, Chagall and Dali. Museum hours are 10 a.m. to 5 p.m., Tuesday through Saturday, and noon to 5 p.m. on Sunday; closed Monday. On the third Thursday of every month, the museum remains open until 8 p.m. General admission is $3 for adults, $2 for students and seniors, and $1 for children ages 6–12. For current exhibits and other information, call (206) 272-4258. Located at the corner of 12th Street and Pacific Avenue.

Union Station. Once fallen into disuse and disrepair, Union Station at 1713 Pacific Ave. has been restored. The city of Tacoma purchased this majestic building and performed a complete renovation that included the installation of a new copper roof. The station opened in 1911 as the western terminus of the Northern Pacific Railway. It was vacated in 1983 when Amtrak moved its operations. Listed on the Register of Historic Buildings, Union Station was designed by the architects who created New York's Grand Central Station. Today it houses the Federal Courthouse and is also home of the largest single exhibit of sculptured glass art by Dale Chihuly. The lobby with the glass exhibit is open weekdays, 10 a.m. to 4 p.m.

Wright Park. Tacomans take great pride in their parks and with good reason—a century-old tradition of guarding and preserving

Connecting Tacoma and Gig Harbor, the Narrows Bridge was rebuilt in 1950 after it collapsed in a violent wind storm only 4 months after its 1940 completion. Mount Rainier in background. (Courtesy of Tacoma-Pierce County Visitor & Convention Bureau)

open spaces for public use has left Tacoma with a legacy of one of the finest park systems in the country. Wright Park, in the heart of Tacoma (6th and Yakima), offers 27 acres for rest and recreation. Frequently the site for outdoor concerts in the summer, the park also features the Seymour Botanical Conservatory, which is on the National Register of Historic Places. The conservatory has an extensive permanent collection of trees, ferns, cacti and orchids. Other activities include lawn bowling, horseshoes, putting greens and play areas.

Fireman's Park. Overlooking the Port of Tacoma, Fireman's Park is built on a "lid" over Schuster Parkway. A popular brown bag lunch spot, this downtown park is often the site of outdoor concerts. The park's focal point is a 105-foot-tall totem pole carved by Alaska Indians depicting the legend of the Eagle Tribe.

Tacoma Dome. Looking something like a huge waylaid spaceship, the Tacoma Dome is 530 feet in diameter and 15 stories high—the largest wood-domed arena in the world. Completed in 1983, this $44 million facility has excellent acoustics and in 1985 was voted the top performing arena by recording artists nationally. The facility is used for concerts, home shows, rodeos, religious crusades and motorcross races. The Tacoma Dome is on Interstate 5 adjacent to the freeway at Exit 133.

The Narrows Bridge. In the summer of 1940, pious civic leaders stood on the newly-completed Tacoma Narrows bridge and proclaimed, "This bridge will stand for all time. It is the ultimate conquest of nature."

Four months later, the bridge lay at the bottom of the water, a victim of ill-conceived engineering and a violent wind storm. Rebuilt in 1950, the 5,979-foot structure is 187 1/2 feet above water and links Tacoma with the quaint fishing town of Gig Harbor. To get there from I-5, take Exit 132 and follow Washington Highway 16 west to the bridge.

Major Cities
VANCOUVER, BC

Gateway to the Pacific

Below the mountains that rise north of Burrard Inlet, Vancouver spreads out like a 3-dimensional map—from Point Grey in the west to the hump of Burnaby Mountain in the east and south to the gleam of the Fraser River. The forested triangle of Stanley Park and the airy thread of the Lions Gate Bridge draw attention to the downtown office towers and high-rise apartments. Behind them, the grid of city streets stretches for 71 square miles, bound by the waters of Burrard Inlet, English Bay and the river.

In the eyes of history, the glitter and sprawl of today's Vancouver happened overnight. Not much more than 100 years ago, the land between Burrard Inlet and the Fraser River was a thick, virgin forest peopled only with a scattering of Indian villages.

Spanish explorers sailed along the British Columbia coast and anchored briefly off Point Grey in 1791. The following year, Capt. George Vancouver, in search of the elusive Northwest Passage, explored and charted the inlets and took possession of the area for Britain. In 1808, Simon Fraser followed the river (which now bears his name) to the sea, but beat a hasty retreat to the safety of inland fur-trading posts after encounters with the Indians. For the next 50 years, all was quiet.

The Cariboo gold rush of 1858 shattered the peace of the coastal forest as thousands poured into the area from Fort Victoria on their way upriver. Vancouver never became a mining town; when the gold of Cariboo was gone, it was lumber from the thick surrounding forests that was the impetus for settlement.

In 1867, around one of the sawmill communities that had sprung up, "Gassy" Jack Deighton rounded up thirsty volunteers and built a saloon. Deighton House stood at what is now the corner of Water and Carrall streets in Vancouver, and around this jovial center the settlement of Gastown soon grew up.

During the next decade, Burrard Inlet became world famous for its fine lumber. There were often as many as 40 ships waiting to load in the inlet. In 1877, 29 million board feet of lumber were exported.

Then the Canadian Pacific Railway (CPR) chose Coal Harbour on Burrard Inlet as the terminus of its trans-Canada line. By February 1886 there were 100 buildings; in April, a city was incorporated and named for Capt. Vancouver; and by June the number of buildings had jumped to 1,000. In the middle of June, however, disaster struck.

Queen Elizabeth Park offers colorful flowers and great city views. Plantlife displays in the park's Bloedel Conservatory range from desert to tropical. (© Lee Foster)

Twenty minutes of an uncontrolled fire destroyed it all.

Within hours of the fire the rebuilding began. When the first CPR passenger train steamed into the city the following year, there was no trace at all of the fire, only a vibrant new city. With a great harbor at its command, Vancouver prospered. The Canadian Pacific fleet inaugurated trans-Pacific service to Vancouver in 1891. Her port shipped lumber and prairie grain and off-loaded silk and tea from the great clipper ships from the Orient. Trains brought in hordes of immigrants and took supplies to Interior settlements.

Vancouver has never looked back. Today

it is the third largest city in Canada, its population nearing 500,000, and a sophisticated cosmopolitan center for business, shopping and the arts. Its port is one of North America's busiest for dry and bulk cargo, and its diversified industry supplies the province's forestry, mining and fishing resources. Vancouver's moderate, year-round climate and spectacular mountain and maritime scenery have made it an attractive place to live and to visit. And if eating out is your hobby, Vancouver has more than 4,000 restaurants featuring 25 different cuisines.

For more information on Vancouver and its attractions, write to the Vancouver Touristinfo Centre, Plaza Level Waterfront Centre, 200 Burrard St., Vancouver, BC, Canada V6C 3L6, or call (604) 682-2222.

Attractions

Stanley Park. On a downtown peninsula, 5 minutes from the business district, is one of the finest and largest natural parks on the continent. Stanley Park was named for Lord Stanley, the governor general of Canada in 1889.

The park is rimmed by beaches, tennis courts, gold course, cricket fields, rose gardens and a 6-mile/10-km sea-wall promenade, a favorite for joggers, walkers and cyclists. Bicycles, even those built for 2, can be rented near the park's main entrance on Georgia Street. Also encircling the park is a one-way scenic drive that provides access to the various attractions in the park.

Park highlights include: the Children's Zoo and the Vancouver Aquarium (see description following). Admission to Stanley Park is free, but there is an admission fee for the zoo and aquarium.

Lions Gate Bridge links the tip of Stanley Park to the North Shore, crossing the First Narrows of Burrard Inlet. This bridge, named for the twin peaks on the North Shore, is as dramatic and pleasant to look at as San Francisco's Golden Gate. This narrow suspension bridge was built by a private company in 1938 and operated for nearly 20 years as a toll bridge. Since Vancouver's centennial celebrations in 1986, the bridge has been illuminated at night.

Vancouver Aquarium. More than 8,000 beautifully displayed marine and freshwater animals make their appearance at the Vancouver Aquarium, including whales, dolphins, turtles, sea otters, sharks, eels, birds and reptiles. The aquarium, located in Stanley Park, is one of North America's great marine facilities. It is open daily year-round. For current hours, phone (604) 682-1118.

In the Amazon Gallery, spectators are surrounded by the life and color of the Amazon jungle. Exotic birds, South American crocodilians, piranhas and playful marmosets are on display. The H.R. MacMillan Tropical Gallery features sharks, moray eels, angel-fishes, seahorses and more.

The Marine Mammal Complex is one of the most popular features, with killer and beluga whales on display, as well as harbor seals and sea otters. An underwater viewing area is available so spectators can watch as the graceful mammals dive, pitch and roll in their marine habitat.

The British Columbia Hall of Fishes consists of 43 displays of western Canada's saltwater and freshwater sea life.

Gastown. This unique, preserved section

Giant totems surround the University of British Columbia's Museum of Anthropology. (Liz Bryan)

of town is located north of Hastings Street between Hamilton Street and Columbia Street. Its brick alleyways, boutiques, art galleries, antique stores and restaurants provide an exciting shopping experience for visitors.

The steam-powered village clock is the only one of its kind in the world. Built by sculptor and horologist Raymond Saunders, it was unveiled and dedicated in 1977. Weighing in at nearly 2 tons, it is a replica of an 1875 vintage design and has a pinwheel escapement that drives a heavy, gold-plated pendulum. A loud steam whistle sounds-off on the hour. Historic Gastown is one of the most visited areas in Vancouver.

Granville Island. Once the site of aging warehouses and old boat houses, this island adjacent to Granville Bridge is now a popular shopping and culture spot. The huge indoor farmer's market beside the False Creek quay is open daily (closed Mondays during winter) and features fresh produce from Vancouver Island and the Okanagan. Imported specialty items, fresh seafood, spices and baked goods can be found. Outside the market along the cobblestone streets are many specialty craft and gift shops, including a glass-blower.

Other attractions on the island include the Kid's Only Market, a brewery, several good restaurants, a theatre, arts and crafts galleries, and a small but elegant hotel. The walkways and parkland surrounding False Creek provide great views of the city center and the multi-tiered condominium complexes that make False Creek an appealing inner city place to live. Access by car is from 4th Avenue just west of the Granville Bridge. Small passenger ferries ply the waters of False Creek between the island and several ports of call, including the Aquatic Centre, the Maritime Museum, the False Creek Yacht Club and B.C. Place. For information, call Granville Island Information Centre at (604)

The third largest city in Canada, Vancouver boasts one of North America's busiest ports.
(Courtesy of Tourism Vancouver)

666-5784 or Aquabus at (604) 689-5858.

Chinatown. The second largest in North America (San Francisco's is the largest), Vancouver's Chinatown stretches for several blocks between Gore and Carrall avenues along Pender and Keefer streets. It's a colorful, lively quarter. There are authentic Chinese herbalists, butcher shops with pressed duck and live chickens, strange vegetables spilling their color on streetside stalls, shops selling carved ivory and bamboo, brocade dresses and Chinese pastries, and lots of restaurants and curio shops. The street names are written in Chinese, the phone booths have pagoda roofs—even the McDonald's menu is in Chinese.

The Chinese Cultural Centre displays Chinese art exhibits, and behind lies the Dr. Sun Yat-Sen Classical Chinese Garden. A replica of a Ming Dynasty pavilion and garden, this $5 million enterprise was built by artisans from the Chinese city of Suzhou using traditional methods and hand tools. Every rock, plant and pool is symbolic, and together they are designed to create a feeling of complete harmony. The centre is located at 578 Carrall St.; phone (604) 689-7133.

Gardens. This city is crazy about flowers and gardens. Queen Elizabeth Park's quarry garden has colorful carpets of seasonal flowers and great city views. The Bloedel Conservatory, a stunning triodesic dome located in the park, creates a series of mini-climates ranging from tropical to desert with hundreds of flowering and leafy plants, 50 species of birds and a pool with giant carp. The conservatory sits atop Little Mountain, and the surrounding Queen Elizabeth Park's lush gardens are a wonderful place to walk. The park is located off Cambie Street and W. 33rd Avenue. Admission to the conservatory is $3.10 for adults and $1.55 for seniors and children ages 6–18. Phone (604) 872-5513.

The University of British Columbia Botanical Gardens has 16,000 different plants in special gardens, including alpine, native, physic, food and Asian gardens. Also on campus is a rose garden with 1,000 bushes of 100 varieties, and the Nitobe Memorial Garden with traditional Japanese landscaping and an authentic teahouse. For hours, admission prices and other information, call (604) 822-9666.

The Van Dusen Botanical Garden, at 5251 Oak St. and 37th Avenue, houses different types of gardens, including herb, fragrance, winter, medieval maze, Himalayan, a children's garden and more. For more information, phone (604) 878-9274.

Museums. Several museums offer a glimpse into Vancouver's past.

The Museum of Anthropology at the Uni-

Gastown's steam-powered clock.
(© Lee Foster)

versity of British Columbia is known for its stunning modern building designed by Arthur Erickson and its extensive collection of Northwest Indian artifacts. Huge totems and other carvings surround the glass and concrete structure.

A highlight of the museum's contemporary Northwest Coast Indian collection is the massive sculpture carved in yellow cedar, "The Raven and the First Man," by the renowned Haida Indian artist Bill Reid. A new wing houses a collection of European ceramics.

This is Canada's largest university museum, and visitors may ask at the admissions desk for guided gallery walks, lectures, films, crafts, programs, and musical and theatrical events.

The museum is located on the university campus at the tip of Point Grey, 6393 NW Marine Drive. For hours, admission prices and other information, call (604) 822-3825.

The Vancouver Museum, located at 1100 Chestnut St., features Indian art and cultural displays, city history, a trading post, an original Canadian Pacific Railway passenger train and turn-of-the-century rooms. For admission and schedules, call (604) 736-4431.

The Canadian Craft Museum, downtown at 639 Hornby St. (604/687-8266), features historical and contemporary exhibits from across Canada.

The Vancouver Maritime Museum, 1905 Ogdon Ave., features ship models and displays of artifacts and photographs of the British Columbia coast history. The focus of interest is the *St. Roch*, a restored Royal Canadian Mounted Police patrol boat built in Vancouver in 1928. This short, 2-masted schooner was the first vessel to navigate the Northwest Passage in both directions, the first to make the passage in a single season, and the first to circumnavigate the continent of North America. It can be toured in dry dock, inside a special building. Phone (604) 257-8300. Open daily, except Monday, 10 a.m. to 5 p.m. Admission is $5 for adults and $2.50 for children, students and seniors.

Science World, located at 1455 Quebec St. at Terminal Avenue, is an arresting geodesic dome on False Creek. Interactive science exhibits. Kids' heaven! Phone (604) 268-6363 for more information.

The Pacific Space Centre offers a laser light show on a large dome, as well as astronomy exhibits. The Gordon Southam Observatory, next to the planetarium, offers views of celestial events through a large refractor telescope. This facility is open on clear weekends and holidays only. For information, call (604) 738-7827.

Capilano Suspension Bridge, in North Vancouver, is the longest suspension bridge in the world. The swinging footbridge spans a lush gorge in Capilano Park, 230 feet/70m above the river. Open daily, admission charged. Phone (604) 985-7474.

Views. When the scenery is so splendid, it pays to get up high to see it better. Downtown, the observation

deck (the Lookout, phone 604/689-0421) and revolving restaurant (the Top of Vancouver) at Harbour Centre, 555 W. Hastings St., are the place to start. Glass elevators lift you up 553 feet/167m above the city for a bird's-eye view. Also in town is the Vanterm Container Terminal, 1300 Stewart St., with a viewing area where visitors can watch port operations from an overhead walkway and observation deck. Good views of Burrard Inlet. Phone (604) 666-6129 for information.

Canada Place. A legacy of Expo '86, this dramatic complex in the heart of the downtown harbor front is topped by dazzling white Teflon-coated sails. Resembling the bulk and shape of a giant ocean liner, with a restaurant at the prow, the building houses

the Vancouver Trade and Convention Centre, a luxury hotel, the CN IMAX (phone 604/682-IMAX), shops and restaurants. Canada Place is at the north foot of Burrard Street, adjacent to the Waterfront Station and the SeaBus terminal and cruise ship dock. The 3-block-long promenade provides an excellent view of the harbor.

Vancouver's mountain skyline dominates the city, and 3 of the peaks have ski areas. One of the best viewpoints is the top of Grouse Mountain, accessible by a gondola called Superskyride that goes to the 3,700-foot/1,128-m level for paved walking paths, hiking trails, helicopter tours and 2 restaurants. Call (604) 984-0661 for Skyride rates and times.

The Capilano Suspension Bridge is the longest supension bridge in the world.
(Courtesy of Tourism Vancouver)

VICTORIA

Beautiful Butchart Gardens are easily accessible from downtown Victoria by tour bus. (Courtesy of Tourism Victoria)

Victoria, the capital city of British Columbia with a population of 276,000, occupies the southeastern tip of Vancouver Island. The city's European past dates from 1843, when the Hudson's Bay Co. built a fort on the shore of Portage Inlet, which today is Victoria's Inner Harbour. From this tiny outpost, the fur traders controlled the fur trade of the Pacific and established farms nearby to ensure availability of fresh meat and supplies. Vancouver Island became a British Crown Colony, and the townsite of Victoria grew up outside the fort walls.

During the Fraser River gold rush, Victoria boomed as the major supply point, its population swelling to more than 2,000—10 times that of Seattle. The population dwindled when the rush was spent, but Victoria continued to attract English settlers and by 1868, had established itself as the capital of the new colony of British Columbia.

All that is left of the HBC fort are 2 mooring rings in the rocky bluffs below Wharf Street. The grand sandstone and granite parliament buildings, topped by a copper dome, have replaced the old wooden gingerbread capitol buildings known as The Birdcages.

Victoria is a gracious, friendly city, with more than just a touch of merry old England in its ambience. Flower baskets embellish all the old-fashioned street lamps. There are manicured parks and squares; specialty import shops carrying British woolens, china and Irish lace; outdoor cafes; magnificent Victorian houses and Gothic-spired churches; horse-drawn carriages and scarlet double-decker buses.

The city retains its colonial air while continuing to grow larger and more commercial. Behind the Empress Hotel, the modern Victoria Conference Centre has mushroomed, with a glass exterior like a crystal palace, and with a cascading waterfall and 25-foot red cedar totem pole in the lobby. In the heart of town, Eaton Centre features nearly 80 department stores and specialty shops, as well as many food-related businesses. And across the harbour, on the former Songhees Indian lands, is a major development of hotels, condominiums, shopping plazas and parks.

Shopping is a major activity for tourists in Victoria. Government Street between Humboldt and Yates streets is a good place to start. The city is also a great place for walking. Most of the historic places of interest are conveniently located near the Inner Harbour where the Parliament Buildings are lit up at night like a fairy-tale castle.

Stop at Tourism Victoria at the corner of Government and Wharf streets for maps and information on the sights. (This spot is also one of the best for taking photographs of the Parliament Buildings and the Inner Harbour.) Contact the Greater Victoria Visitors and Convention Bureau, 812 Wharf St., Victoria, BC V8W IT3; phone (604) 382-2127.

Attractions

The Empress Hotel, across from the Inner Harbour, is Victoria's elegant dowager, with a definite atmosphere of British gentility. Afternoon tea is served with the traditional finger sandwiches, crumpets, seed cakes and Empress Blend tea. Other signs of "a little bit of England" are fish and chips, dark pubs with dart boards, sweet shops, shops selling Wedgewood and Spode, Scottish tartans and Irish linens, cricket matches in Beacon Hill Park, and lots of roses and formal gardens. Phone (604) 384-8111 for information on tea times and reservations.

Also located in the Empress is Miniature World, a display of 80 miniature scenes drawn from literature and history. Admission is charged. Phone (604) 385-9731.

Crystal Garden, a lovely tropical conservatory located on Douglas Street directly behind the Empress Hotel, has a songbird aviary, streams, waterfalls and tropical plantings. With an expanded mandate, "Preserve and conserve only those birds and animals that are endangered," the Garden hosts 65 species. Open daily, admission varies depending on season; phone (604) 381-1213.

Royal British Columbia Museum, located at Belleville and Government streets, is renowned for its innovative dioramas of British Columbia's human and natural history, its Northwest Coast Indian exhibits and reconstructions of pioneer life. The Indian exhibit includes a replica long house. The museum's state-of-the-art displays are enhanced by evocative sounds and smells. Experience a multimedia tour in a mock submarine at the Open Oceans exhibit, or step foot in a rain forest at the Living Land, Living Sea exhibit. The museum is open daily from 10 a.m. to 5:30 p.m. in winter, and 9:30 a.m. to 7 p.m. July 1 to Sept. 6. Admission is $5.35 for adults, $2.14 ages 6 to 18, and children under 5 are free. Phone (604) 387-3701 for more information.

BC Parliament Buildings. These grand stone buildings overlooking the Inner Harbour and Yacht Basin house British Columbia's Legislative Assembly. Tours are offered daily from June to Sept. and last about 20 minutes; phone (604) 387-3046 for tour times. The buildings were constructed for under $1 million and opened in 1897. A statue of explorer George Vancouver, who first circumnavigated Vancouver Island, stands atop the highest copper dome.

Tour Historic Homes. Helmcken House, built in 1852, is British Columbia's oldest house open to the public. The former home of J.S. Helmcken, a pioneer doctor and first Speaker in the Vancouver Island Legislative Assembly, the house includes one of Canada's finest 19th-century medical collections. Located beside the Royal British Columbia Museum and Thunderbird Park. A stereo taped tour is offered between May 5 and Sept. 26, from 11 a.m. to 5 p.m. daily. Phone (604) 387-1619 for admission fees.

Point Ellice House is an Italianate house dating from 1861 and contains the most complete collection of Victoriana still in its original setting in the province. Its garden is also one of the best examples of a Victorian domestic garden in western Canada. Located at 2616 Pleasant St., near the Bay Street Bridge. Taped tours offered mid-June to mid-Sept.; phone (604) 384-0944 for admission fees and hours.

Carr House is an 1860s Italianate-style residence that was the 1871 birthplace of Emily Carr, one of Canada's foremost artists and authors. It has been restored to reflect the 1890s period. Located at 207 Government St. Phone (604) 387-1619 for admission fees and hours.

The Craigflower farmhouse is a superb example of 1850s Georgian-style achitecture and decor. The site has been restored to its original rural farm appearance and offers special summer programs for children. Pathways allow visitors to walk close to the shore of Portage Inlet. Across the inlet is Craigflower Schoolhouse, the oldest school building in western Canada still standing on its original site. The farmhouse is located at Admirals and Craigflower roads. Phone (604) 387-1619 for admission fees and hours.

Craigdarroch Castle, with its turn-of-the-century furnishings and leaded-glass windows, should not be missed. Coal baron Robert Dunsmuir built this lavish sandstone mansion in 1887–90 to persuade a Scottish wife to come to Victoria. Open daily year-round. Phone (604) 592-5323.

Visit City Parks. Known as the "City of Gardens," Victoria has many parks and gardens. Thunderbird Park, located in the same block as the Royal British Columbia Museum, has a collection of totem poles and an authentic longhouse. During summer months you can sometimes watch Indian carvers working on new totems. Beacon Hill Park, at Douglas and Dallas streets, has won-

derful views of the water and informal gardens. Bicycle rentals are available in Victoria, but there are no established bike lanes.

Butchart Gardens attracts thousands of visitors each year to its 50 acres of beautifully landscaped gardens. Built on a former rock quarry, the gardens are arranged in different international styles and something is in bloom no matter what time of year you visit. During the summer, however, it is best to visit the gardens in the early morning or late afternoon to miss the busloads of tourists. The gardens are located 13 miles/27 km north of Victoria off Highway 17. Open daily, admission fee charged. Phone (604) 652-4422 for hours and fees. There are 2 restaurants at the gardens. If you don't have a vehicle, or don't wish to drive, there are plenty of bus tours from downtown Victoria to Butchart Gardens.

Anne Hathaway's Cottage. Outside Victoria in Esquimalt, Shakespeare's birthplace and the Olde England Inn are part of a recreated 16th-century English village. Admission fee charged. Guided tours daily year-round. Phone (604) 388-4353.

Victoria Butterfly Gardens, 13 miles/17 km north of the city, is an enclosed tropi-

cal garden with a collection of live butterflies and displays on the life cycle of the insects. Open daily, mid-March to Dec. Admission fee charged. Phone (604) 652-3822.

Top right—Street musicians perform near Victoria's Parliament Building. **Above**—*Grand old Empress Hotel is a Victoria landmark and favorite destination for tea drinkers.* (Photos courtesy of Tourism Victoria)

CANADIAN NATIONAL PARKS

In 1985, 4 of the major parks in western Canada—Banff and Jasper national parks in Alberta, and Yoho and Kootenay in British Columbia—were given UNESCO World Heritage Site designations for their scenic beauty and unique geologic features. These 4 wilderness parks are adjacent to one another and are easily accessible via Trans-Canada Highway 1 and Highway 93.

In British Columbia, 2 more mountain national parks, Glacier and Mount Revelstoke, preserve the beauty of sections of the Selkirk Mountains. Both are reached by Trans-Canada Highway 1. Pacific Rim National Park on Vancouver Island in British Columbia, a narrow strip of rugged coast and giant native trees, is the most remote and least developed of these national parks. Pacific Rim National Park is accessible by ferry to Vancouver Island and BC Highway 4 to the north end of the park. Other areas of the park can be reached either by logging roads or by ferry from Port Alberni.

Motorists driving through the Canadian national parks of Banff, Jasper, Yoho and Kootenay and not stopping overnight can do so free of charge; otherwise the fees are $5 a day, $10 for 4 days or $30 for a year's pass. A Park Pass is required for entry to Mount Revelstoke and Glacier national parks. The cost is $3 per day or $21 per year for individuals; a family annual pass costs $50.

All the parks, with the exception of Mount Revelstoke, have campgrounds, the larger ones fully equipped for RV use. Rates vary depending on the time of year and facilities provided. Most backcountry camping is free, though registration and permits are required.

For safety and rescue purposes, climbers and serious backcountry hikers should register with the park warden and check back in upon return. Most park lakes are closed to powerboats, though canoes and rowboats are welcome. A permit is required to fish in the national parks, and anglers should familiarize themselves with regulations, catch limits and closures. Details are available at park information centres and warden offices.

All Canadian national parks are game preserves and as such are excellent places to view wildlife, particularly in the early morning. Canadian parks contain fairly large and stable populations of grizzly and black bear, elk, deer, moose, mountain goat, and bighorn sheep. Though big game may often be seen right beside the highway, remember it is dangerous and illegal to feed them.

The 4 Rocky Mountain national parks, Banff, Jasper, Kootenay and Yoho, were set aside before much destruction of the habitat from logging or mining had taken place. Today, they are magnificent wilderness areas and wildlife reserves, renowned for the textbook examples they provide of mountain formation by geologic upheaval and intense glaciation. The Rockies, in the framework of earth history, are young mountains, formed some 75 million years ago when sedimentary rocks (formed on the bottom of a vast, ancient sea some 600 million years ago) were thrust up, broken along great faults and in some places, strongly compressed.

Since their formation, the mountains and valleys have been slowly eroded by water and wind, but most dramatically by ice. Remnants of the great ice field that covered much of North America during the most recent ice age remain in the Rocky Mountains, most evidently in the huge Columbia Icefield which covers 125 square miles and feeds 6 enormous glaciers and rivers flowing to 3 oceans.

Glacial ice flowing over and down from the mountains scooped out bowl-shaped depressions called cirques, sometimes leaving knife-edged ridges and dramatic horn-shaped peaks. Carrying with it huge amounts of rock rubble, the ice scoured deep U-shaped valleys, and created mountain tarns and hanging valleys where waterfalls tumble. When the glaciers retreated, piles of the rock rubble or glacial debris were left behind, choking the valleys, damming rivers and leaving ridges to mark the glaciers' former extent.

Banff National Park

Banff National Park, in Alberta on the eastern side of the Continental Divide, is accessible by Trans-Canada Highway 1, which runs east-west through the park, or Canada Highway 93, which bisects the park on a north-south route. Refer to the TRANS-CANADA HIGHWAY 1 and CANADA HIGHWAY 93 sections for highway logs.

Canada's first national park, Banff was established in 1885 as a small preserve around the mineral hot springs that, though well known to the Indians for generations,

Picturesque Cirrus Mountain in Banff National Park. (© George Wuerthner)

were first recorded in 1858 by Sir James Hector. With the building of the Canadian Pacific Railway (CPR) through the area in 1883, the tourist possibilities of the mountain scenery and hot springs were realized. By 1887, the reserve was considerably enlarged to become a park, then known as Rocky Mountains Park. Its sole access was of course the railway, and hotels were built by the CPR at Banff and Lake Louise. Cars and buses were not permitted full access into the park until 1915, by which time the scenery of the Canadian Rockies was world famous.

Banff National Park today covers some 2,564 square miles/ 6,641 square kilometres of the Rockies east of the divide, encompassing the valleys of the Bow, Mistaya and North Saskatchewan rivers. It is the most popular of the mountain national parks, hosting more than 3 million visitors a year from all over the world. Because it is so spectacularly scenic and famous, it is crowded—that is, the highways and major tourist centres and attractions are crowded. But the park is immense; hikers and backpackers only have to walk a few miles to find solitude.

There are 2 centres in the park: Banff townsite near the southeastern boundary; and Lake Louise at about the midway point, near the west junction of Highway 93 and Trans-Canada Highway 1. The town of Banff (pop. 5,200) is located 35 miles southeast of Lake Louise via Trans-Canada Highway 1. Granted autonomy from federal jurisdiction in 1990, residents lease their land from the park, and development is strictly controlled.

Both Banff and Lake Louise have information centres. Banff Information Centre is located in downtown on Banff Avenue; phone (403) 762-1550. Lake Louise Information Centre is located on Village Road in Lake Louise. Both townsites also have huge CPR baronial chateaux: Banff Springs Hotel near downtown Banff, and Chateau Lake Louise on the banks of the spectacularly scenic lake of the same name. Lake Louise is looked down upon by the perpetual snow and ice of the Victoria glacier. Both chateaux are built in an architectural style that is a blend of Scottish baronial and French chateau. Both are immense, stately, even luxurious, and are packed solid every summer. Reservations are essential. Both have beautiful grounds and restaurants that are open to the public, and anyone can wander the lobbies of these resorts to get a taste of the interior decor. Besides the chateaux, there are more than 2 dozen lodges and resorts in the park, the majority clustered in the downtown Banff area.

The main attraction in Banff National Park is the mountain wilderness—the high glacially scoured peaks and valleys, the glaciers, lakes, alpine meadows, rushing rivers and wildlife. Main activities, apart from general touring, are hiking, camping and fishing. If you are not an experienced hiker, you'll still enjoy great views from the road, or you can try a gondola ride. The Sulphur Mountain gondola, south of down-

The tilted Mount Rundle rises above forest land and Vermillion Lakes in Banff National Park. (© John Barger)

town Banff next to the Upper Hot Springs, and the Lake Louise Gondola, north of Trans-Canada Highway 1 at the ski resort of the same name, operate in summer.

Another way to experience the scenery is by boat. Cruise boats ply the waters of Lake Minnewanka (about a 15-minute drive from downtown Banff) all the way to Devil's Canyon. You can also rent motorboats at the lake by the hour or day; contact Minnewanka Tours at (403) 762-3473. You may rent canoes and rowboats on Lake Louise and Moraine Lake (which some say is even more beautiful than Lake Louise). Raft trips down the glacial Bow River, which flows through the valley, are available from Rocky Mountain Raft Tours; phone (403) 762-3632.

For a less crowded scenic drive, Highway 1A between Banff and Lake Louise, the original park road, is more narrow and winding but less traveled. It passes scenic Johnston Canyon with its waterfalls and trail to the Inkpots, 7 cold-water springs bubbling into pools of different colors. It passes also the site of the old copper mining town of Silver City. Many nice picnic areas, viewpoints and 2 campgrounds are along this route.

Vermillion Lakes, a chain of little swampy lakes known for their large populations of wildlife, are circumscribed by a scenic road. There are good views of Mount Rundle, the tilted mountain at the back of Banff. Beside the lakes, archaeologists have uncovered remains of early man dating 11,000 years ago.

The Buffalo Paddock, just east of Banff townsite, permits visitors to drive through a small herd of buffalo, remnant of the huge herds of buffalo that once darkened the plains.

You can relax in a hot spring and learn

more about this natural phenomenon at Banff townsite. The historic Cave and Basin Centennial Centre, located on Cave Avenue (turn right after crossing the bridge at the end of Banff Avenue) has an interpretive exhibit around the cave hot springs and basin hot springs. Upper Hot Springs, located on Mountain Avenue about 2 miles from downtown Banff (turn left after crossing the bridge from Banff Avenue), has a hot mineral springs pool for bathing and a great mountain view.

There are easy hikes out from Lake Louise to the Plain of the Six Glaciers and to Lake Agnes. Both have tea houses at their destination points. Longer, more strenuous trips traverse the western shore of Moraine Lake, to Larch Valley, Eiffel Lake and Sentinel Pass. For an overnight trip without a heavy pack, you can hike (or ski in winter) 7 miles/11 km from the trailhead at the end of Temple Fire Road to Skoki Lodge, a historic log chalet and cabins built in 1930 and still in operation. Expect rustic comfort, good food and mountain solitude. Open Christmas to April and June to Sept. Phone the Lake Louise ski area at (403) 522-3555 (fax 403/522-2095) for information and booking for Skoki Lodge. They also provide transportation to the Skoki Lodge trailhead, which is located 2½ miles from the ski resort at the end of a closed fire road.

The 17 campgrounds in Banff National Park are found along the Icefields Parkway (see CANADA HIGHWAY 93 section), in Lake Louise, at Tunnel Mountain near Banff, at Castle Junction and on Highway 1A. Most campgrounds are open by late June and close by the end of September, although limited camping is available the rest of the year.

Northbound from Lake Louise, Highway 93 follows the Bow River to its source, glacier hung Bow Lake with historic Num-Ti-Jah lodge (built in the 1920s) at its northern end. From Bow summit and Peyto Lake, the brightest turquoise of all the Rockies lakes, the highway drops down into the valley of the Mistaya River. The North Saskatchewan River flows south here from its source in the great Columbia Icefield. At Saskatchewan Crossing, the great river turns east, cutting through the side ranges to reach the plains of Alberta. Highway 11 follows the river east to Rocky Mountain House and Red Deer.

Sunwapta Pass below the icefields is the boundary between Banff and Jasper national parks. Here, Highway 93 is known as the Icefields Parkway because of the many glaciers that it passes, especially as it comes close to the toe of the Columbia Icefield itself.

For information, maps and brochures, contact: Banff National Park, Box 900, Banff, AB T0L 0C0; phone (403) 762-1500.

Jasper National Park

Jasper National Park in Alberta adjoins Banff along its northern boundary. It is the largest of the mountain parks, covering 4,200 square miles/10,878 square kilometres, and was set aside as a national park in 1907 when the Grand Trunk Pacific Railway line traversed the country. Most of its beauty and attractions are accessible from Highway 93, the Icefields Parkway (see CANADA HIGHWAY 93 section), and Highway 16, the Yellowhead. The headquarters and only tourist centre in the park is Jasper townsite.

Most visitors experience Jasper's mountain grandeur from Highway 93. From the park boundary at Sunwapta Pass, the highway follows the Sunwapta River north to its confluence with the mighty Athabasca River which, like the North Saskatchewan, flows from the Columbia Icefield. The Columbia Icefield is often called the hydrographic centre of North America because streams from its melting ice feed 3 oceans—the Atlantic, Pacific and Arctic oceans. Just north of Sunwapta Pass, the highway passes close to the receding toe of the icefield.

The Columbia Icefield is the park's principal attraction. It is a great saucer of ancient ice and snow sitting on the Continental Divide, some of which is thousands of feet deep, left over from the ice age. Surrounding this icy remnant are huge mountains. Between these peaks, the ice from the saucer spills down in tongues of glacial ice. This high ice-covered area stretches nearly 150 square miles/388 square kilometres. The main icefield cannot be seen from the road. Special snowcat tour buses venture out onto the glacier nearest to the highway, the Athabasca. This river of ice is today receding, and a line of stakes marks its annual regression.

A visit to the Icefield Interpretative Centre across the road from the glacier provides a far better grasp of the immensity and grandeur of the icefield than the obligatory scramble onto the glacial toe. The centre is open from June to Sept. But take a tour onto the glacier itself by Snowcoach, which operates from about May 1 to early Oct. Phone Brewster Transport in Banff at (403) 762-6735 or in Jasper at (403) 852-3332 for more information. There's a lodge with full tourist facilities right beside the Athabasca Glacier.

Do not miss the drive to Cavell Lake with its reflective views of Mount Edith Cavell and the Angel Glacier. Take Highway 93A, a parallel 14.5-mile/23-km alternative to the main highway. Follow the signs for another 9.5 miles/15 km up the Astoria River. A short hike will take you to the viewpoint. This is also the trailhead for the most popular of the Jasper backcountry hikes—the Tonquin Valley with its beautiful Amethyst Lake and towering Ramparts. It's a 3-day, 26-mile/42-km loop. (For more information on Jasper's many hiking trails, contact the Parks Canada visitor centre on Connaught Drive in Jasper. They have information on short day hikes as well as backcountry trails.)

Highway 93A will also take you to Athabasca Falls and to Marmot Basin downhill ski area.

Another side trip off Highway 93, shortly before the junction with Yellowhead Highway 16, is up Whistlers Road to the Jasper Tramway. The Skytram was Canada's first mountain lift and was designed as a means of access to high alpine country during the summer. From the top terminal on Whistlers Mountain with its breathtaking views, a network of trails and paths invites exploration. And if you hear a whistle, it's

Dammed by a moraine, Peyto Lake is coloured with glacial "flour" in Jasper National Park. (© George Wuerthner)

Above—A scenic view from Trans-Canada Highway 1 just west of Yoho's Kicking Horse Pass. (Liz Bryan) *Right—Radium Hot Springs in Kootenay National Park.* (© Lee Foster)

probably one of the large colonies of whistling marmots from which the mountain got its name. For Tramway times and rates phone (403) 852-3093.

Also on Whistlers Road is Jasper's largest campground, with 781 sites. Jasper National Park has 14 campgrounds in all, most open May to Sept.

Like Banff, the town of Jasper is park headquarters and the centre for lodging, restaurants and other services. Also like Banff, it has a grand old railway hotel, Jasper Park Lodge, built in the 1920s on scenic Lac Beauvert; a glacial river flowing through town (the Athabasca); a hot springs pool; and a beautiful lake nearby with boat rides.

A recommended side trip is the 35-mile/56-km road to Maligne Lake that takes off east of Jasper townsite from Highway 16. This is also the access road to Jasper Park Lodge, where you can stop in for breakfast, play a few holes of golf, and rent horses or boats. Plan to stop at Maligne Canyon, a deep gorge where the river falls 76 feet/23m over a limestone lip. But keep going. At the end of the road is Maligne Lake, one of Jasper's premier attractions and the largest lake in the Canadian Rockies. Here the views are idyllic, especially if you take a cruise to the end of the lake, passing Spirit Island, the photogenic halfway point. Scheduled boat tours depart daily in summer; phone (403) 852-3370. Boat and canoe rentals are also available.

Maligne Lake can also be reached by the 2-day Skyline Trail pack trip (or 3-day hike) from Jasper, with an overnight camp in the Big Shovel meadows. The trail stays above timber most of the way through magnificent wilderness scenery.

Raft trips down the Athabasca River may be arranged in Jasper through Brewster Transport. Phone (403) 852-3332 for details.

Miette Hot Springs, located east of Jasper off Highway 16, has the hottest springs in the Canadian Rockies, which are mixed with cold water in 2 man-made pools to permit comfortable swimming. Miette Hot Springs has a chalet, changing facilities, restaurant, accommodations and picnic grounds. Open daily in summer; phone (403) 866-3939.

For information, maps and brochures, contact: Jasper National Park, Box 10, Jasper, AB T0E 1E0; phone (403) 852-6161.

Kootenay National Park

Kootenay National Park stretches on both sides of the Vermilion and Kootenay rivers and adjoins Banff and Yoho national parks on the west side of the Continental Divide. It is bisected by Highway 93, which follows the main river valleys. Points of interest accessible from the highway, trailheads and the park's 3 highway-accessible campgrounds are noted in the Canada Highway 93 log (see the CANADA HIGHWAY 93 section).

The park is best known for its hot springs, first known as Kootenay, now Radium, at its southern tip. The first development of the spring took place in 1911. The area was set aside as a national park in 1919, and in 1922 the Banff-Windermere Road was completed, the first motor road across the central Canadian Rockies.

The park's chief focus is the hot springs, which bubble up from the Redstreak breccia fault line, itself noteworthy for its towering red cliffs and pinnacles. The hot springs lie just north of a very congested tourist and commercial area outside the park at the town of Radium. All facilities are here.

Hike the trail to Floe Lake, 6 miles/10 km up the Floe River. This pretty alpine lake has miniature icebergs, chunks of ancient ice from Floe Glacier, on its waters. It is one of the very few lakes in the Rockies with this phenomenon.

If you are a sturdy hiker, take the 4-hour hike up to the Stanley Glacier through a spectacularly beautiful valley. If you're looking for more of a gentle stroll, try the Paintpots self-guiding nature trail. It's only a short walk to the ochre beds, which supplied the vermilion used by Indians to paint and decorate their lodges and bodies. The ochre was once commercially mined, and a few traces of the operations still remain. Another gentle walk and spectacular scenery await in Marble Canyon, with a hike along the canyon rim to the waterfall. Trailhead at Marble Creek campground.

For more information, contact Kootenay National Park, P.O. Box 220, Radium Hot Springs, BC V0A 1M0; phone (604) 347-9505.

Yoho National Park

Yoho is the Cree Indian word used to express awe, and visitors tend to agree that the park is well named. Geographically, it encompasses almost the entire watershed of the Kicking Horse River, 507 square miles/1,313 square kilometres of high mountain country. It adjoins Banff Park along the Continental Divide and Kootenay Park to the southwest. The Kicking Horse rises in Wapta Lake near the Great Divide and flows all the way to Golden, where it joins the Columbia River. Just about halfway through the park, the river has carved a natural bridge through the solid rock, one of the more interesting attractions.

Trans-Canada Highway 1 bisects the park, and Yoho's 4 highway-accessible campgrounds are noted in the Trans-Canada Highway 1 log (see TRANS-CANADA HIGHWAY 1 section). These campgrounds are available on a first-come, first-served basis and nightly fees range from $7 to $15 per site, 14-day limit. Chancellor Peak is open from late April to early Oct.; Hoodoo Creek from mid-June to early Sept.; Kicking Horse from mid-May to late Oct.; and Monarch from late June to Sept.

In addition, Yoho operates a walk-in campground at Takakkaw Falls and 6 backcountry campgrounds. A $5 wilderness pass is required for the backcountry campsites, some of which can be reserved in advance.

From a scientific point of view, the most important feature of the park is the Burgess Shale site where, preserved in ancient Cambrian sedimentary layers, are more than 150 species of marine organisms that date back more than 500 million years. The shale is exceptionally fine-grained, and the fossils themselves are so well preserved that scientists can see soft appendages and even some internal organs. The site is a protected area. Hikes to see the fossils are available from licensed guides by reservation (limited to 15 people at a time). Fossil sites are usually snowbound between mid-Oct. and the first week in July. Check with the Yoho-Burgess Shale Research Foundation, phone (604) 343-6321 or fax (604) 343-6724, for information on guided hikes and access to the fossils.

The small railroad town of Field in the centre of the park has the park information centre, park administration offices and basic tourist services. There are 4 lodges and 2 chalets situated in the park. Lake O'Hara Lodge and Lake O'Hara campground are located at the end of an 8-mile/13-km private road that must be walked or skied (cycling is not permitted). Advance reservations must be made for public bus sevice to Lake O'Hara (mid-June through Sept.); phone (604) 343-6433. Various restrictions apply, so phone ahead. Despite the difficulty in getting there, the lodge, lake, campground and trails are very popular. Campground reservations may be made 1 month in advance.

Emerald Lake is also worth the 4.5-mile/ 7-km drive for the view and the hiking trails that surround the lake. Emerald Lake Lodge is located at the lake; phone 1-800-663-6336 or (604) 343-6321. Canoe rentals are available and there are stables with horses for hire. En route you will pass by the famous Natural Bridge.

Another automobile excursion is up the steep and winding Yoho Valley Road (no trailers permitted) east of Field to Takakkaw Falls, at 1,248 feet/380m the second highest falls in British Columbia. Here, water melting from the Daly Glacier and Waputik Icefield plunges over the lip of the main valley into the Yoho River. North of the falls, trails lead to 2 other impressive waterfalls, Laughing Falls and Twin Falls.

Yoho's 249 miles/400 km of hiking trails are described in the Backcountry Guide to Yoho National Park, available for $1 at the information centre in Field.

For more information and a map, contact Yoho National Park, P.O. Box 99, Field, BC V0A 1G0; phone (604) 343-6324.

Glacier National Park

Glacier National Park lies in the Selkirk Range of the Columbia Mountains. Located on the eastern side of the great fault line, the Columbia Trench, these mountains are not sedimentary like the Rockies but are made of metamorphic and igneous rocks that pushed up through older sedimentary beds. The mountains are older than the Rockies and are more resistant to erosion, though they were boldly sculpted by the glaciers of the last ice age.

The park is at the collision point between 2 weather systems, the moist Pacific airflow and the cold, dry Continental. This results in a tremendous amount of precipitation. In summer there is always a 50 percent chance of rainfall, and in winter snow falls almost constantly. Heavy snowfalls feed large and active glaciers—there are more than 100 of them within park boundaries, and more than 10 percent of the park is under perpetual ice. In winter, avalanches are common.

This was the terrain through which the Canadian Pacific Railway chose to route its railroad in 1885. Rogers Pass was the best they could find, even though it was desperately steep and plagued with avalanches. The alpine area of the pass around Mount Sir Donald was set aside as a park preserve in 1886, and the park was extended to its present size in 1930. Access for the casual visitor is limited to areas around Trans-Canada Highway 1, which parallels the route the railroad took. (See the TRANS-CANADA HIGHWAY 1 section for highway log.) In later years, the railway escaped the worst of the Rogers Pass snowfall and avalanche hazards by tunneling under the mountains; the highway goes bravely over the top of the pass.

Located at Rogers Pass Summit is the Rogers Pass Centre. The visitor centre has an indoor theatre, exhibit hall and outdoor computerized information system. Park personnel present special programs in July and August at the centre's theatre. The centre provides excellent interpretation of the park's railway history and the avalanche

One of many beautiful waterfalls to be found in Glacier National Park's steep and avalanche-prone Rogers Pass. (Liz Bryan)

Above—*Glacier National Park is popular among mountain climbers. (K. Webb, courtesy of Parks Canada)* **Right**—*Stores and a bandstand in downtown Revelstoke, headquarters for the national park. (Liz Bryan)*

phenomenon. Children will be delighted by the scale model of the pass, complete with railway lines, tunnels, snowsheds and tiny moving trains. Visitors will also be intrigued to know about the gun positions along the highway that are used to shoot down potential avalanches while they are small and while the highway is closed. Shells are used, and because these do not always explode on impact, hikers are warned not to pick up any strange metal object. Also located at the summit of Rogers Pass is the only hotel in the park, Glacier Park Lodge.

This is a park for mountain climbers and backpackers, although motorists may stand in awe of the rock peaks and the hanging glaciers from the highway picnic areas and on some of the shorter of the park's 18 trails. Recommended walks for the family (all having to do with railway history) include the Trestle Trail to a high bridge viewpoint; the Loop Brook Trail, which follows an abandoned loop of the original railroad grade; the Abandoned Rails Trail at the pass crest, which was abandoned when the first tunnel was built; and the Meeting-of-the-Waters Trail. Details on these and other trails in Glacier and nearby Revelstoke National Park are available at the Rogers Pass Centre.

Guided hikes with a park naturalist are offered in July and August, starting from Illecillewaet Campground, one of Glacier's 2 campgrounds. Illecillewaet is located 2 miles/3 km west of Rogers Pass, and Loop Brook Campground is 3 miles/5 km west of the summit. Both are open from early June until late Sept.

For more information, contact Glacier National Park, Box 350, Revelstoke, BC V0E 2S0; phone (604) 837-7500. For Warden Service at Rogers Pass, phone (604) 837-6274.

Mount Revelstoke National Park

Just west along Highway 1 from Glacier Park is tiny Mount Revelstoke, a 16-square-mile/260-square-km section of rugged territory with impressive icefields and angular peaks. Like Glacier, it is in the Selkirk Range of the Columbia Mountains and enjoys heavy rain and snowfalls. Rain forests just as dank and deep as those along the coast of British Columbia exist here.

Trans-Canada Highway 1 does not penetrate this park—except for a brief few miles around its southeastern edge. But there is a road that leads right up into the high alpine plateau, to a world of sparkling mountain tarns, meadows full of flowers, groves of mountain spruce and balsam, and incomparable views. Mount Revelstoke's Summit Drive turns off Trans-Canada Highway 1 about a half-mile east of Revelstoke townsite. The people of Revelstoke built this road up to the summit in 1910, and the park was established 4 years later. The winding gravel road is 16 miles/26 km long, but the alpine scenery is well worth the trip. There are few places in Canada where you can drive right up to an alpine meadow. Summit Drive is generally open from July to early Sept.

At the end of the road, a network of trails introduces the visitor to the sights and sounds of the high alpine country. Meadows-in-the-Sky Trail begins at the summit parking lot and passes the "Icebox," a place where snow and ice linger to provide ice-cold air even in midsummer. For more serious hiking, the trail to Eva Lake takes about 2 hours. The flowers along this route are so spectacular that in August each year the park organizes an Eva Lake pilgrimage hike.

Other self-guiding park trails (there are a total of 10 trails in the park) introduce visitors to the Interior wetbelt forest. The trailheads for Giant Cedars and Skunk Cabbage trails begin at picnic areas on Trans-Canada Highway 1.

There are no campgrounds in Mount Revelstoke park.

For more information on the park, contact Mount Revelstoke National Park, Box 350, Revelstoke, BC V0E 2S0; phone (604) 837-7500.

Pacific Rim National Park

There is only 1 paved road to Pacific Rim National Park. BC Highway 4 bisects Vancouver Island and leads 87 miles/140 km west from Parksville on BC Highway 19 to the beaches of the wild West Coast, where the waves roll in, uninterrupted, all the way from Japan. The national park includes the rugged and challenging West Coast Trail between the villages of Bamfield and Port Renfrew; the Broken Group Islands, about 100 rocks and islands clustered at the mouth of Barkley Sound; and the most accessible area of the park, Long Beach (named for a 7-mile/11-km stretch of sandy beach), facing the open Pacific along a 25-mile/41-km stretch of Highway 4 between the villages of Ucluelet and Tofino. (See Vancouver Island map in THE ISLANDS section.)

Information centres for the West Coast Trail are at the head of Pachena Bay near Bamfield and at Port Renfrew. The 48-mile/77-km hike, considered one of Canada's toughest, takes veteran backpackers 5 to 6 days to complete. Nevertheless, it attracts more than 5,000 hikers each year.

This is not a route for novices. There are neither established campgrounds nor access roads along the way. All equipment and supplies must be carried.

The trail is as beautiful and wild as it is challenging. It was carved out of dense brush soon after the turn of the century to reach the rugged coast where survivors of frequent shipwrecks were cast.

Most hikers make a one-way trip, beginning either at Port Renfrew (66 miles/106 km west of Victoria via BC Highway 14) or Bamfield (60 miles/100 km southwest of Port Alberni via a gravel logging road).

The Broken Group Islands, accessible only by boat, are popular with kayakers and canoeists. A favorite launching place is scenic Toquart Bay, 22 miles north of Ucluelet at the head of Barkley Sound. It is reached by way of a logging road that runs west from BC Highway 4 at Kennedy Lake. Alternate access to the islands of the Broken Group is from Port Alberni, 29 miles/47 km west of Parksville on Highway 4, at the head of Vancouver Island's longest inlet. From Port Alberni, the 100-foot/31-m passenger and cargo boat MV *Lady Rose* serves Gibraltar Island in the Broken Group Islands, and also Bamfield (for West Coast Trail hikers). Phone the *Lady Rose* at (604) 723-8313 for schedule. Charter boats (primarily those based in Ucluelet) will drop off and pick up those who would like to spend a day playing Robinson Crusoe.

Long Beach is the section of Pacific Rim National Park that draws the overwhelming majority of visitors. Attractions here include hiking, beach walking, wind surfing and camping. There are 8 short, designated walking trails and 1 established campground within the park. The Wickaninnish Centre on Wickaninnish Bay, a few miles from the park entrance, has exhibits and films on the Pacific Ocean, 2 observation decks and a restaurant. The centre is open March to Thanksgiving. There is also an information centre near the park entrance.

Most of the trails at Long Beach are surfaced with wood chips and boardwalks. They include the woodland walks to beaches, a bog walk, a trail through the rain forest, a hike along an old gold mine trail and a series of viewing platforms on a crest overlooking the sweep of Long Beach. There is a daily parking fee of $5 per vehicle charged within the Long Beach unit.

Private campgrounds and motels are available in Ucluelet and Tofino. Each of these villages also has restaurants, stores and such visitor-oriented services as fishing charters and whale-watching

excursions. The annual Pacific Rim Whale Festival is held each spring. Peak season to view migrating gray whales is from mid-March to mid-April. The West Coast Maritime Museum is in Tofino.

For more information on Pacific Rim National Park, contact the Superintendent, Box 280, Ucluelet, BC V0R 3A0; or phone the Long Beach Information Centre from mid-March to mid-Oct. at (604) 726-4212. During the off-season, phone the park administration at (604) 726-7721.

Top—Colourful starfish in the Broken Group Islands. **Above**—Pacific Rim's Broken Group Islands in Barkley Sound are a popular destination for kayakers. (Photos by Joe Hofbeck)

Major Attractions
U.S. NATIONAL PARKS

The 4 U.S. national parks featured in *Northwest Mileposts®* present some of the most dramatic scenery and extraordinary beauty that the Northwest has to offer. The towering rain forests, pounding surf, jagged mountain peaks and alpine glaciers and lakes found in these parks are home to diverse plant and animal life.

Summer is the busiest time of year to visit these parks. Campgrounds fill on a first-come, first-served basis. For more information, contact the individual national parks.

Crater Lake National Park

Crater Lake, in the Cascade Range of southcentral Oregon, is situated in a huge caldera formed by the collapse of ancient Mount Mazama. It is the centerpiece of the 183,180-acre Crater Lake National Park.

The park's 33-mile Rim Drive circles the caldera rim. Other roads in the national park include the spur road to the Pinnacles Overlook in the southeast corner of the park; the south entrance road from Oregon Highway 62; and the north entrance road from Oregon Highways 138/230. (See the map on page 145 in the U.S. HIGHWAY 97 section for location of highways to the park.)

More than one potential visitor to Crater Lake has been disappointed to find the north entrance road and Rim Drive closed by snow in the month of June, when it seems to be summer everywhere else in Oregon. But the Rim Drive—at an average elevation of 7,000 feet—and north entrance to the park may be closed by snow from mid-Oct. to as late as early July. Recorded road and weather conditions are available at any time by calling the park at (503) 594-2211. The south access road from Highway 62 is open all year, as is the paved park road to Rim Village, so off-season travelers can get a look at the lake even if they can't drive around it.

History and Description

At one time the powerful volcano Mount Mazama reached a height of approximately 12,000 feet. Indians in the region some 6,800 years ago who witnessed the violent eruptions believed the volcanic action was the result of a war between 2 gods.

Instead of having just 1 vent at the peak of the mountain, several vents formed, spewing lava and gases, weakening the stability of the mountain. Geologists estimate that in about 4,840 B.C., the mountain collapsed in a thunderous implosion, forming a deep caldera in place of the mountain.

Archaeological evidence indicates that the Indians witnessed the collapse of the mountain. Stories conflict concerning the Indians knowledge and use of Crater Lake following the eruptions. In some stories Indians bathed in it, while in others they avoided it. Tribal shamans in historic times forbade most Indians to view it, and the Indians offered no information about the lake to pioneers who traveled in the area for 50 years without discovering it. A small party of prospectors, among them John Wesley Hillman, accidentally stumbled upon the lake in 1853 while searching for the Lost Cabin gold mine.

Their reports of the deep blue mysterious lake, virtually void of life, prompted exploration by the government. In 1886, a U.S. Geological Survey party carried a boat which weighed nearly 1,000 lbs. up to the lake to explore it. Their depth readings indicated the lake was 1,996 feet deep at its deepest point, amazingly close to the sonar reading recorded in 1959.

Crater Lake is the deepest lake in the United States, the second deepest in the Western Hemisphere and the seventh deepest in the world. Its maximum depth is 1,932 feet.

Wizard Island, a volcanic cone that rises 764 feet above the lake surface, was formed shortly after the collapse of the mountain. When the volcanic activity subsided some 1,000 years ago, springs, snow and rain began to fill the huge caldera with water. As the lake deepened and widened, evaporation and seepage eventually balanced with the incoming flow, causing a constant lake level. The level now fluctuates no more than 3 feet each year. There are no streams into or out of Crater Lake.

Because of its lack of feeder streams, fish are not native to Crater Lake. First stocked by William Steel—who hand-carried buckets of fish from nearby streams—the lake was stocked from 1888 to 1941. The lake is no longer stocked.

The best fishing is near the surface and in

Vibrant-blue Crater Lake, in Crater Lake National Park, fills a caldera left by the eruption of Mount Mazama. (Steve Terrill, courtesy of Oregon Tourism Division)

shallow water, such as the Wizard Island area. No private boats are permitted on the lake, so fishing must be done from the shore areas near Cleetwood Cove or from Wizard Island, which can be reached by concessionaire-operated tour boats. No fishing license is required. Check specific regulations at the park headquarters.

Visitors to Crater Lake immediately comment on the incredible blue color of the lake. Naturalists explain that light is absorbed color by color as it passes through clear water. The first color to be absorbed is red, then orange, yellow and then green. Absorbed last is blue, and only the deepest blue reflects back to the surface from as deep as 300 feet, the natural limit of light penetration. The fact that the lake is so deep and so clear results in its deep, rich blue color. No other lake has light penetration as deep as Crater Lake. Moss grows to depths of 325 feet, the greatest known depth of any freshwater moss in the world.

During the winter each year, the park receives about 500 to 600 inches (45 feet) of snow, yet the lake rarely freezes. Heat from the summer sun, stored in this immense body of water, retards ice formation throughout the winter.

The man responsible for having this area dedicated as a national park was William Gladstone Steel, who as a boy read about the lake in a newspaper in which his lunch was wrapped. Upon discovering its beauty, Steel lobbied for 17 years to have the area set aside. Crater Lake National Park was established on May 22, 1902. Today, it is Oregon's only national park.

Attractions and Activities

Park headquarters and the Steel Information Center are located 3 miles south of Rim Village and both are open daily year-round. Visitor services here include information, first aid, backcountry permits, maps and publication sales. The Rim Village Visitor Center is open June through Sept. Park rangers at Rim Village provide information, assistance and backcountry permits. Services include displays, activity schedules, map and publication sales, and first aid.

A paved walk near the Rim Village Visitor Center leads to Sinnott Memorial, an overlook that is open daily in the summer. Here, you'll find an unobstructed view of the lake from the rock parapet. Inside the exhibit building at the overlook are displays on the history and geology of the area. Open July to mid-Sept.

Rim Drive, the 33-mile road that circles the lake, has excellent views of the lake and geographic formations. The road is closed from about Oct. to July. Trailers are not recommended and trailer drop-off sites are available. From Rim Drive, a spur road leads to the volcanic spires of the Pinnacles area.

For a close-up look at the lake, narrated boat tours are offered by the Crater Lake Lodge Co. and the National Park Service. The 2-hour tour circles the inside of the caldera and stops at Wizard Island, where visitors may hike or relax until the mid-afternoon return trip. The boat leaves from Cleetwood Cove on the northeast side of the lake, 11 miles from Rim Village. There is a steep trail from the parking lot to the dock. Boat tours are available from late June to early Sept. (weather permitting) and reservations, tour times and rates may be obtained at the Crater Lake Lodge front desk at Rim

Village, or by phoning (503) 594-2511.

Some of the more accessible—and shorter—hiking trails leave Rim Drive to ascend Garfield Peak, The Watchman and Mount Scott, providing spectacular views of the lake and surrounding terrain. The Cleetwood Trail to the boat dock is the only access to the lake. Information folders are available for Godfrey Glen, Annie Creek Canyon and Castle Crest Wildflower trails, and may be obtained from the park headquarters, as can details on more strenuous hikes. The Pacific Crest Trail traverses the park and accesses longer connecting trails to more remote corners of the park.

Visitor Services

Rim Village has a visitor center, cafe and restaurant, and Crater Lake Lodge (food and lodging). The park headquarters area south of Rim Village has Steel Information Center and a post office, located in the administration building, that is open weekdays in summer. Mazama Village, on the south entrance road, has a campground, motel, store, and the only gas station in the park.

Crater Lake Lodge at Rim Village was built in 1910. Extensive reconstruction began in 1990 and the lodge opened in May 1995. It offers 71 guest rooms and a restaurant with scenic views of the lake. The lodge also has a gift shop. For information, contact Crater Lake Lodge Co., P.O. Box 128, Crater Lake, OR 97604. For reservations at the lodge or Mazama Village, phone (503) 594-2511.

There is camping at Mazama and Lost Creek campgrounds, or in the backcountry by permit. Mazama Campground, at Mazama Village, has 200 sites, restrooms and a dump station. Fee is $11. Campfire programs are presented at Mazama Campground amphitheater during the summer (topics change nightly), and ranger-led hikes are offered at the campground. Lost Creek, located 3 miles from Rim Village on the Pinnacles Overlook road (no trailers), has 16 sites, water, restrooms and a $5 fee. Campgrounds are open when the snow melts in

early summer and are closed by snow in the fall. There are no showers or hookups and both campgrounds have a 14-day limit. Areas fill quickly. Additional camping is available outside the park on adjacent national forest land.

Season, Fees and Access

The park is open daily year-round, but services, activities and access are seasonal. There are no lodging or camping facilities available during the winter months. Depending on the weather, services are available from May or June through Sept. Rim Drive and the north entrance to the park generally do not open until early July. In winter, vehicle access is available only from Oregon Highway 62 to Rim Village. Winter activities such as snowshoeing are offered; check with park headquarters for details.

There is an entrance fee of $5 per vehicle. Pets must be on leash or in vehicles and are not allowed in public buildings or on trails (except for the Pacific Crest Trail).

Access to the park from the east side is from U.S. Highway 97 north of Klamath Falls via Oregon Highway 62 west 37 miles to the park's south entrance, or via Oregon Highway 138 west 15 miles to the park's north entrance (closed in winter). (See **Mile 25** and **Mile 62** in the U.S. HIGHWAY 97 section.) From the west, access is from Exit 30 on I-5 at Medford via Oregon Highway 62 east 75 miles to the park's south entrance, or from Exit 124 on I-5 at Roseburg via Oregon Highway 138 east 100 miles to the park's north entrance (closed in winter). (See **Mile 30** and **Mile 124** in the INTERSTATE 5 section.)

For more information, contact Superintendent, Crater Lake National Park, P.O. Box 7, Crater Lake, OR 97604; phone (503) 594-2211.

Mount Rainier National Park

Mount Rainier is located southeast of Seattle in the Cascade Range of Washington. At 14,411 feet, the towering mountain is a landmark for Puget Sound communities and the focal point of Mount Rainier National Park (established on March 2, 1899, as the nation's fifth national park). More than 1.8 million visitors travel through Mount Rainier National Park each year to enjoy the misty rain forests, giant old-growth forests, subalpine meadows, glaciers and rocky outcrops, along with the wide diversity of plants and wildlife.

On some days, the mountain seems tantalizingly close to Seattle, but the park is a 2½ to 3 hour drive for most Puget Sound residents.

There are 4 entrances to the park: the Nisqually entrance at the southwest corner of the park; the Stevens Canyon/Ohanapecosh entrance at the southeast corner of the park; the White River entrance at the northeast corner of the park; and the Carbon River entrance at the northwest corner of the park. (The Carbon River road does not connect with any other roads in the park.) Only the Nisqually entrance and the Nisqually-Paradise Road are open year-round; all other park roads are closed in winter.

Lupine meadow in Mount Rainier National Park. (© John Barger)

Hikers enjoy more than 300 miles of trails in Mount Rainier National Park. (L. Linkhart)

History and Description

Mount Rainier is the largest single-peak glacier system in the Lower 48 states and the greatest volcano in the Cascade chain. It is considered a dormant volcano which developed at a weak spot in the earth's crust between 500,000 and 1 million years ago.

There are approximately 75 glaciers in the park, 25 larger ones which have been named and about 50 smaller ones, all on the slopes of Mount Rainier. The glaciers are tracked and measured each year to help determine climatic changes.

A rapid retreat of the glaciers began around 1920, but from 1950 through 1980, a general advance of the larger glaciers was noted. The total retreat of the glaciers until 1950 averaged about one-quarter of their length, but some, like Paradise, retreated drastically. However, Winthrop and Carbon glaciers showed very little change. But since 1980, most glaciers have resumed minor retreat.

Before the discovery of the area by explorers, Indians lived in the lowlands sur-rounding the mountain. During the summer they would move up the slopes of the mountain to hunt and collect berries, bulbs, herbs and beargrass. The native Indians still call it Tahoma, "the highest mountain." In 1792, Capt. George Vancouver was so impressed with this majestic peak that he named it for a friend, Admiral Peter Rainier.

Mount Rainier is often said to create its own weather. It reaches high into the upper atmosphere and interrupts the flow of moist maritime air masses from the Pacific Ocean. The result is great amounts of rain and snowfall. During the winter of 1971–72, a world's record 93.5 feet (1,122 inches) of snow fell at Paradise.

The first recorded ascent of Mount Rainier was made in 1870 by Hazard Stevens and Philimon Beecher Van Trump from the south side of the mountain. Their Indian guide, Sluiskin, warned them of the perils and begged them not to go. Sluiskin then waited in fear at their camp on Mazama Ridge while Stevens and Van Trump com-pleted their climb. The duo returned late the next day, having conquered the summit. Since then, thousands of people have climbed to the summit by several routes.

With hunting prohibited, wildlife abounds in Mount Rainier National Park.

The largest animal to be encountered at Mount Rainier is the elk. September is the best time to listen for the male's bugling call, which can be heard from most high ridges on the east side of the park. Elk are found mostly in the high meadows and sub-alpine forests during the summer, browsing on twigs, bark and shrubs. Some of the best places to see elk are the Cowlitz and Ohanapecosh areas, Shriner Peak and Stevens Ridge. Elk are most often found on the east and north sides of the park, but have been seen in all areas.

The elk, which number about 1,500, are the No. 1 resource management problem in the park. Introduced into the Cascades in the 1920s, the elk migrate into the park each spring and remain until very late fall. With habits like domestic cattle, they selectively over-browse forest and subalpine meadows all summer. They threaten irreversible damage to an ecosystem not designed for elk, according to park officials.

The mountain goat is the only large mammal in the park that remains white year-round. The envy of all climbers, this large animal with its strong legs and soft hooves is specially suited to live among rocky crags. Never far from the snowline, mountain goats venture into alpine mead-ows to feed on grasses and flowers in the early morning and evening. They spend warm afternoons resting in the shade digest-ing their food. Binoculars are usually needed to spot goats high in the meadows. The best times to see goats are early in the morning (until about 10 a.m.) and late afternoon (from 6 p.m. until dark).

Black-tailed deer follow the melting snows up into the high mountains in early summer as the shrubs develop buds and leaves and as huckleberries begin to ripen. In June and July, new fawns may be seen with their does. Their tan color and white spots allow them to effectively blend into their surroundings. Deer can often be seen from the road as you drive through the park in the morning or evening. If you want to watch them, choose a safe place to pull off the road so you will not create a traffic hazard.

Black bears, the only kind found in the park, are not commonly seen. When locat-ed, they are generally spotted in the back-country and again are most visible during the morning and evening hours.

Other mammals common in Mount Rainier National Park include cougar, marten, raccoon, porcupine, beaver, snow-shoe hare, hoary marmot, pika, golden man-tled ground squirrel and the yellow pine chipmunk.

Birds found in the park include geese, ducks, peregrine falcons, red-tailed hawks, osprey, kestrel, golden and bald eagles, herons, gulls and countless other species.

Attractions and Activities

Sightseeing along the 140 miles of park road system, hiking and climbing are the major summer activities in Mount Rainier National Park. The park also is a popular place for winter activities, such as snowshoe-ing, sledding and cross-country skiing.

Details on attractions, naturalist-led hikes and talks, and maps are available at the park's 4 visitor centers. Longmire Visitor Center, located on the Nisqually-Paradise Road, is the park's oldest developed area, first established as a hot spring resort in 1884. Today the original park administrative building houses a museum of park history. The Henry M. Jackson Memorial Visitor Center is at Paradise, a center for park activities in summer and winter. Ohanapecosh Visitor Center near the Stevens Canyon entrance has exhibits on Northwest forests. Sunrise Visitor Center, located approximately 16 miles beyond the White River entrance, is—at 6,400 feet—the highest point in the park reached by road. Exhibits here focus on alpine environments.

With Mount Rainier as its centerpiece, it is no wonder that climbing is a popular activity in the park. The peak itself sometimes seems so tantalizingly attainable that first-time visitors have been known to get out of their cars at Paradise ready to walk to the top in their street shoes.

Each year, about 8,000 visitors attempt to climb Mount Rainier, with more than 4,000 climbers reaching the summit and with more people reaching that goal every year. Climbers must be in top physical condition and have experience in glacial travel, ice ax use and rescue. Climbers must register with a ranger before attempting the climb, and special regulations apply. A guide service at Paradise offers 1-day climbing schools and guided 2-day climbs to the summit. Contact Rainier Mountaineering Inc., 535 Dock St., Suite 209, Tacoma, WA 98402, or phone (360) 569-2227.

Hiking the park's more than 300 miles of trails is a premier attraction. Hiker information centers are open daily during the summer at the Longmire and White River entrances to the park. Hiking season generally extends from mid-July to mid-Sept. in the park, though trails at the lower elevations are open somewhat earlier and remain open later into the fall. The weather is generally best from mid-May to mid-Sept., though the upper elevation trails may not open until mid-July. The number of clear days peaks in July and August though campers should remember that the nights are cool and the weather is unpredictable. Prepare for most any weather condition. Permits are required for overnight backcountry hikes.

Wildflowers are a major attraction in Mount Rainier National Park, but it is against the rules to pick them. You can pick berries in season (look for blueberries in August).

Self-guiding nature trails can be found at Longmire Meadows, Sourdough Ridge, Nisqually Vista, Ohanapecosh, Grove of the Patriarchs and Carbon River. The 93-mile Wonderland Trail completely encircles the mountain. Because many trails leave from Paradise, it is a popular place to start.

Fishing is not exceptional at Mount Rainier, and generally only experienced anglers do well. Rangers report that anglers' success is often less than anticipated. The park waters are not stocked and depend on limited natural reproduction to replenish the fish population. Anglers are encouraged to use barbless hooks and artificial lures and to release uninjured fish. No license is required to fish within the park. The species most sought after include cutthroat, rainbow, brook and Dolly Varden.

Non-motorized boating is permitted on all lakes, except Frozen Lake, Reflection Lakes, Ghost Lake and Tipsoo Lake.

Winter is a popular season in Mount Rainier National Park, with activities taking place in the Paradise area of the park. Snow depth is the factor that determines the start of many winter activities at Paradise. The snowpack must be adequate to protect the fragile alpine plants from being damaged or destroyed. Thus, snow camping begins when the snow depth has reached about 5 feet at Paradise and 2 feet in other areas, and the snow play area cannot be opened until approximately 4 feet of snow covers the ground.

One of the most popular activities at Paradise is inner-tube sliding. Due to the potential hazards of terrain and trees, sliding is permitted only in designated areas north of the large parking lot near the Paradise Inn. Here, 1 long run for adults and 1 shorter run for children are provided. For safety, sliding is permitted only on inner tubes, saucers and other soft sliding devices. Wooden toboggans, metal-runner sleds and other hard devices are not permitted. The sliding runs are maintained and operated on weekends and holidays only throughout the winter and are not maintained or supervised on weekdays. The operation generally closes by mid-April.

Snowshoeing is also a popular pastime at Paradise. Park naturalists lead snowshoe walks to introduce visitors to snowshoeing and explore winter ecology. The walks are presented from Jan. through mid-April, weekends only. Phone the park for details.

When there is sufficient snow, park rangers mark 3 trails in the Paradise area for cross-country ski touring. These trails are the Nisqually Vista Trail, the Narada Falls Trail and the trail from the Valley Road over Mazama Ridge to Reflection Lakes. A map of these trails is available at the Paradise Visitor Center.

Visitor Services

Lodging is available year-round at the National Park Inn at Longmire and from May through early Oct. at Paradise Inn. For accommodations at either, contact Mount Rainier Guest Services, 55106 Kernahan Road E., Ashford, WA 98304; phone (360) 569-2275, fax (360) 569-2770.

Food service can be found at Longmire (year-round), Paradise (in summer and weekends in winter) and Sunrise (summer only). National Park visitor centers are at Longmire (year-round), Paradise (daily, May through mid-Oct., weekends the rest of the year), Ohanapecosh and Sunrise (summer only). Longmire also has a grocery. There is no gas available in the park.

There are 5 campgrounds in the park providing a total of 577 campsites. All are available on a first-come, first-served basis. All have toilets and water. There are no RV hookups. Sunshine Point (18 sites) near the Nisqually entrance is the only campground open year-round. Cougar Rock campground, with 200 sites, is located between Longmire and Paradise. Ohanapecosh is the largest with 205 sites. White River campground, near the White River entrance, has 117 sites. Ipsut Creek campground (29 sites) is located at the end of the Carbon River entrance road. Group camping is also available and may be reserved in advance; phone the park for more information.

Camping permits are required for all backcountry campsites. Campsites in the backcountry are on a first-come, first-served basis.

Season, Fees and Access

Mount Rainier is open daily year-round, although only the Nisqually-Paradise Road is open in winter. Tire chains are frequently required on all vehicles traveling from Longmire to Paradise. Phone the park for recorded information on weather and road conditions.

The fee to enter the park is $5 per vehicle for a 7-day visit. For those entering by commercial bus, it is $3 per person for anyone between the ages of 16 and 62. The fee is $3 for motorcycles and individuals on bikes, walking or otherwise entering the park. Camping fees range from $6 to $10, depending on the campground, and there is a charge for additional vehicles.

Pets must be on leash or in vehicles, and are not allowed in buildings or on trails (except for the Pacific Crest Trail).

There are 4 entrances to the park, although most visitors usually want to end up at Paradise. Following are 5 access routes to Paradise; refer also to the INTERSTATE 5 and U.S. HIGHWAY 12 sections.

Seattle to Paradise (3 hours): Southbound on I-5 take Exit 127 and follow Highway 512 east 2 miles to Pacific Avenue/Parkland Spanaway. Exit onto Pacific Avenue, which merges into Highway 7. Follow Highway 7 to Elbe, then go east on Highway 706 for 13 miles to the Nisqually entrance, then 18 miles to Paradise.

I-405 to Paradise: From I-405 take Exit 4A and follow Highway 169 south to Enumclaw and junction with Highway 410. Take Highway 410 south past the White River entrance to the Stevens Canyon entrance. Follow Stevens Canyon Road west to Paradise.

Portland to Paradise (2 hours): Northbound on I-5 take Exit 68 and follow U.S. Highway 12 east to Morton. Turn north on Highway 7 and continue 16 miles to Elbe. From Elbe go east on Highway 706 13 miles to the Nisqually entrance, then 18 miles to Paradise.

Olympia to Paradise: Northbound on I-5 take Exit 111 to Marvin Road/ Highway 510. Go east on Marvin Road to Pacific Avenue, which becomes Highway 510 to Yelm. Follow Highway 510 through Yelm and turn at the BP gas station onto Highway 702. Follow Highway 702 east 12 miles and turn at the flashing light onto Highway 7. Continue on Highway 7 to Elbe. From Elbe go east on Highway 706 for 13 miles to the Nisqually entrance, then 18 miles to Paradise.

Yakima to Paradise (2 hours): From Yakima on U.S. Highway 12 there are 2 ways to get to Paradise. Follow U.S. Highway 12 northwest 20 miles to junction with Highway 410, which leads 51 miles west to Chinook Pass and Highway 123 south to the Stevens Canyon entrance, then follow Stevens Canyon Road west to Paradise. Or drive west from Yakima 66 miles on U.S. Highway 12 over White Pass to the junction with Highway 123 north to Ohanapecosh. From there it is 3 miles to the Stevens Canyon entrance and the road to Paradise.

For more information, contact Mount Rainier National Park, Tahoma Woods, Star Route, Ashford, WA 98304; phone (360) 569-2211.

North Cascades National Park

North Cascades National Park is located in the wild northernmost reaches of the Cascade Range in northwestern Washington. The mountains of the North Cascades have been called "the North American Alps" for the spectacular beauty of their jagged peaks, hanging glaciers, cascading waterfalls and wildflower meadows. This remote wilderness has giant forests of red cedar, crevass-scoured glaciers, deep valleys and sheer-walled pinnacles that challenge backcountry travelers. Readily accessible areas are heavily visited, but there are areas of the park that have yet to be explored.

The park complex is comprised of 3 adjoining areas: Ross Lake and Lake Chelan national recreation areas and the North Cascades National Park. National forest lands flank the park on the south, east and west. The North Cascades Highway (Washington Highway 20) separates North Cascades National Park into south and north units, cutting across the Cascade Range through Ross Lake National Recreation Area.

History and Description

Exploration of the North Cascades began in 1814 when Alexander Ross crossed the present national park's southern unit. The handful of explorers who followed Ross also commented on the region's rugged, isolated nature. Miners prospected for gold, lead, zinc and platinum here from 1880 to 1910, but because of limited profits and extremely rough terrain, mining was abandoned. Some logging and homesteading occurred around 1900 and the electric potential of the Skagit River was realized, providing more development. Seattle City Light built 3 dams (Ross, Diablo and Gorge) on the Skagit River between 1924 and 1961 for electrical generation.

The North Cascades Highway crosses the park complex through Ross Lake Recreation Area. Forming a large L-shape within North Cascades National Park, Ross Lake National Recreation Area encompasses Ross Lake, Diablo Lake and Gorge Lake. The highway was built along an old rail and truck route originally intended to serve Skagit River power projects. Congress established North Cascades National Park in 1968. The highway was extended after the park was established and the route was dedicated in 1972. It has been called the "most scenic mountain drive in Washington," and it is probably the most visited area of the 505,000-acre park.

Lake Chelan National Recreation Area occupies the southernmost tip of the park complex. Lake Chelan is a natural lake, resting in a glacially carved trough. At 1,500 feet it is one of the deepest lakes in the nation. Its bottom lies 400 feet below sea level. A dam built at Chelan in 1927 raised the water level 21 feet to increase power production.

The destination of many visitors to North Cascades National Park is the wilderness community of Stehekin, which lies at the north end of Lake Chelan within the recreation area. There are no roads to this remote community and visitors must hike, boat or fly in. Most visitors take the 4-hour boat trip from the community of Chelan—outside the park—to Stehekin.

Because of the many wilderness areas and the remote setting of the rugged North Cascades National Park, the area hosts some of the highest populations of big game animals in Washington state. Black-tailed deer are abundant, as are black bear, mountain goats and smaller mammals. Less numerous are the wolverine, marten, lynx, bobcats and cougar. White ptarmigan, blue grouse and countless other smaller birds make their home here. During the winter, large numbers of bald eagles may be viewed feeding on the salmon of the Skagit River.

The beautiful Cascade Range of North Cascades National Park has been called "the North American Alps." **Above**—*Gorge Creek Falls.* **Right**—*Overlook at Diablo Lake.* (Photos by Michael N. Dill)

Attractions and Activities

Many of the park's major attractions are found within the national recreation areas (see Ross Lake National Recreation Area and Lake Chelan National Recreation Area this section). Activities in the national park's north and south units are limited to hiking, climbing and backcountry camping. Stop at the North Cascades Visitor Center in Newhalem on Highway 20 (phone 206/386-4495), the park headquarters/visitor center in Sedro-Woolley (360/856-5700), or the ranger stations in Marblemount (360/873-4590) and in Chelan (509/682-2549).

Hiking the 345 miles of trails within the national park complex is one of the principal activities in North Cascades. Permits, required for all backcountry camping, may be obtained either at the ranger stations in Marblemount or Chelan and at various park and U.S. Forest Service offices.

Most hikers and backpackers enter the national park complex from trailheads along the North Cascades Highway. Several long trails traverse or loop the north and south units of the park and most have campsites spaced every 3 to 4 miles. Day hikes are more numerous in the national recreation areas.

North Cascades Highway traverses Ross Lake NRA. Three other roads bring you near trailheads for hiking into the park. The Cascade River Road, a 23-mile dirt and gravel road out of Marblemount (open during the summer and fall), provides access to the Cascade Pass trailhead. The Stehekin Valley Road, accessible only by passenger ferry from Lake Chelan, is served by a Park Service shuttle to Cottonwood Campground. Highway 542 (Mount Baker Highway) provides access to the park through the Mount Baker-Snoqualmie National Forest at Hannegan Campground.

Nature trails, conducted walks and evening programs are available in the summer at Colonial Creek and Newhalem campgrounds, and at Stehekin, all located within the recreation areas.

Remember that weather in the North Cascades is notoriously changeable. Unless you are taking a brief stroll, take extra clothing, water and supplies along on day hikes.

Pack animals are available for rent at several of the communities, or horsemen may bring their own. Professional guide and pack train services are available. For a list of guides, contact the park headquarters.

Both the north and south units of the national park have many high peaks to challenge the mountain climber. For safety, it is recommended that parties have 3 or more climbers; be equipped with internationally recognized climbing gear; and register names of the party, destination, name of the mountain and the approximate length of stay. Mountain climbers should register in Sedro-Woolley at park headquarters or at the Marblemount Ranger Station or at the Glacier Public Service Center.

A valid Washington fishing license is required to fish in the national park and in both national recreation areas. Besides the 2 large lakes, there are hundreds of small mountain and valley lakes with thousands of streams. Ross Lake is one of the few large lakes left in Washington that depends on its native fishery and is not artificially stocked. The principal game fish is trout, including rainbow, brookies, cutthroat and Dolly Varden.

No hunting is permitted within the boundaries of the national park, but hunting is permitted in parts of both recreation areas.

A valid Washington hunting license is required and all state regulations apply.

Visitor Services

Lodging is available at Ross Lake Resort, a floating resort on Ross Lake off Highway 20, and in Stehekin at the North Cascades Stehekin Lodge. Groceries can be found in Newhalem and just outside the park at Marblemount. Marblemount also has the last available gas before entering the park from the west side. The next gas is at Mazama on the east side of the mountains. There are no restaurants along the highway within Ross Lake NRA.

Major campgrounds along the North Cascades Highway are Newhalem Creek, Goodell Creek and Colonial Creek. Campsites are available on a first-come, first-served basis. Camping fee charged.

Season, Fees and Access

The park is open year-round, although Highway 20 is closed from Nov. to mid-April from east of Diablo to Mazama. There is no entrance fee.

Pets are not permitted on trails or in the backcountry (except on Pacific Crest Trail).

Highway access to the park is via Highway 20 (see NORTH CASCADES HIGHWAY section). Boat access from Chelan on U.S. Highway 97; see Lake Chelan National Recreation Area this section.

For more information, contact North Cascades National Park, 2105 State Route Highway 20, Sedro-Woolley, WA 98284; phone (360) 856-5700.

Olympic National Park

There are 3 separate entities that bear the Olympic name. The first is the peninsula, on which the other 2 are located. The peninsula is bordered on the west by the Pacific Ocean, the north by the Strait of Juan de Fuca and on the east by Hood Canal and the Puget Sound. The impressive Olympic Mountains form the backbone of the park, forest and peninsula. The Olympic National Forest surrounds the park and contains much of the peninsula's area. Inside the boundaries of the forest is Olympic National Park. The forest and park are noted for their marine climate, dense rain forests, rugged mountain terrain and principal big game resident, the Roosevelt elk. U.S. Highway 101, the Olympic Peninsula's major route, encircles the east, north and west sides of the park.

History and Description

Mount Olympus (elev. 7,965 feet) was named in 1788 by a British captain, but the first major explorations of the area didn't happen until 1885–90 when public attention to the area began. President Cleveland set aside half the Olympic Peninsula as a forest reserve in 1897 and President Theodore Roosevelt turned 600,000 acres of the forest into a national monument, but President Franklin Roosevelt signed the bill in 1938 that created the national park. Today, the park encompasses 923,000 acres of wilderness. The park's 57 miles of coastline, added in 1953, comprise the longest primitive stretch of coastline remaining in the contiguous United States.

The land received national park status for 3 basic reasons: (1) to protect and preserve the native wildlife, including the Roosevelt elk, together with sufficient range to perpetuate this and other rain forest species under natural conditions; (2) to preserve a substantial remnant of the dense, virgin rain forests of the Northwest coast type, which elsewhere are rapidly disappearing and; (3) to protect one of the finest scenic and wilderness areas remaining, of which the Olympic Mountains are the climax.

The park hosts the largest remaining herd of Roosevelt elk in the nation (which number more than 5,000). Blacktailed deer, black bear, cougar and other large mammals also inhabit the region. The Olympic marmot is one of the several small animals that are found only in this area. Many species of sea lions, seals and whales live in the water or on the rocks just offshore.

Olympic is synonymous with wet. The Olympic Mountains block and catch the Pacific Ocean storm clouds, causing them to dump their heavy loads of rain on the western slopes. The wettest point in the contiguous United States is Mount Olympus (elev. 7,965 feet), with 200 inches of precipitation per year. The mountain also receives the greatest amount of snow of any place in the contiguous United States.

Three rain forest valleys (the Quinault, Queets and Hoh) exist within the park and each receives between 141 and 161 inches of precipitation per year. Rain forests are noted for the quantity and quality of vegetation. There is hardly a square inch of soil not occupied by plants, which range in size from microscopic to giant Douglas firs up to 298 feet tall. Sitka spruce and western hemlock are the dominant species, but Douglas fir, western red cedar, big-leaved maple, red alder, vine maple and black cottonwood also thrive in the forest. Over a thousand varieties of ferns, mosses and fungi carpet the soggy floor of the rain forest.

Most of the rain received each year falls from late fall to early spring. The summers are comparatively dry with many days of clear, sunny weather. Along with the wet weather comes mild temperatures. Temperatures rarely dip below freezing in the lower elevation valleys and summer highs rarely exceed 80°F. One of the unique environments of the park is the coastal rain forests.

Glacial ice is one of the foremost scenic and scientific values of Olympic National Park. There are nearly 60 glaciers crowning the Olympic peaks. The prominent glaciers are those on Mount Olympus, covering approximately 10 square miles. Beyond the Olympus complex are the glaciers of Mount Carrie, the Bailey Range, Mount Christie and Mount Anderson. In the company of these glaciers are perpetual snowbanks that have the superficial appearance of glacial ice.

The Olympic glaciers are slow moving in comparison to those in Alaska (where glaciers can advance up to 100 feet per day). There is no great advance of these glaciers. Today, they are retreating. Forward surges in glacial flow often occur after a number of very heavy winters and cool summers, but such activity has been relatively infrequent with Olympic glaciers in recorded time.

The movement of glacial ice, past and present, has produced striking geological features in the Olympic Mountains. The lake basins, U-shaped valleys and jagged peaks are the products of massive glacial erosion that occurred many thousands of years ago when the year-round climate was much colder. This erosion process continues today, but on a much smaller scale.

Attractions and Activities

The park offers a wealth of activities—hiking, fishing, mountaineering, river rafting, fishing, beach walking, camping, horseback riding and skiing—and a long list of scenic attractions.

National Park visitor centers are located in Port Angeles (phone 360/452-0330) and Hoh Rain Forest, both open all year, and at Hurricane Ridge, open April to Sept. The Hoh River Visitor Center offers interpretive programs, displays, exhibits and informative publications about the formation and biology of the rain forest. Three trailheads are located at the center for those wishing a closer view of the forest.

Hurricane Ridge, located 17 miles south of Port Angeles via a steep, winding paved road, is one of the most popular—and accessible—spots in the park for motorists to view the mountain scenery of Olympic National Park. Hurricane Ridge Visitor Center offers spectacular views of the Olympics and the Strait of Juan de Fuca. Naturalist programs are offered daily from July through Labor Day. This is also a popular winter-use area for downhill skiing, cross-country skiing and snowshoeing.

Ranger/information stations, open as staffing is available, are located at Storm King (Lake Crescent), Ozette, Mora, Sol Duc Hot Springs, Kalaloch, Quinault and Staircase. A U.S. Forest Service/National Park Service information station is located on U.S. Highway 101 north of Forks and in Hoodsport. Most ranger stations offer maps, brochures and publications; some have naturalist activities.

The park is best known for its rain forests—the Hoh, Quinault and Queets River (see feature on page 178). Of the 3, the Hoh rain forest is perhaps the most popular among visitors. The Hoh River valley and rain forest are accessible from U.S. Highway 101 on the west side of the peninsula via the 18.5-mile Hoh River Road (see **Mile 524.5** in the U.S. HIGHWAY 101 section).

Lake Quinault South Shore Road, which junctions with U.S. Highway 101 at **Mile 472**, leads to scenic Lake Quinault and the historic Lake Quinault Lodge, built in 1926. Beyond the lake, the South Shore Road winds up into the national park through the Quinault River valley to the rain forest, ending at Graves Creek.

Queets rain forest, between the Hoh to the north and Quinault to the south, is located 14 miles up the Queets Valley Recreation Area Road from **Mile 491** on U.S. Highway 101. The access road parallels the Queets River, a popular commercial rafting and fishing river.

Commercial river trips are available on the Elwha, Hoh and Queets rivers in Olympic National Park. For details on the river trips, contact Olympic Raft & Guide Service, 239521 Highway 101 W., Port Angeles, WA 98362; phone (360) 452-1443.

Top right*—The Olympic marmot is one of several small animals found only in the Olympic National Park area.*
Above*—The snow-capped peaks of the eastern Olympic Mountains.* (Photos by © John Barger)

Another commercial boating enterprise within the park is the *Storm King,* a 64-foot-long paddle wheel vessel operating on Lake Crescent. The boat is modeled after the paddlewheelers that ferried people across the lake during the early 1900s. U.S. Highway 101 hugs the twisting south shore of 9-mile-long Lake Crescent—the largest lake in Olympic National Park—some 25 miles west of Port Angeles. The excursion boat operates narrated tours 4 times daily from Memorial Day to Oct. Phone (360) 452-4520 for more information. Shuttle bus service to the boat dock.

No visit to Olympic National Park is complete without experiencing the beaches of the peninsula's west coast. Best beach access is between South Beach (**Mile 500.5**) and Ruby Beach (**Mile 511**). Or take the La Push Road at **Mile 539.5** west about 15 miles to the Pacific Coast Beach Area; beach walking and hike-in camping (no facilities) at First, Second and Third beaches. Watch for trailhead parking areas. It is a very short walk from the trailhead to the beach, which is an unforgettable spot and usually not crowded.

As you hike the beaches and explore the tide pools, be alert to the change in tides along this coast. There can be a difference of 10 feet between the low and high tides. Always be alert to having an escape route on an incoming tide. There are many points of land that jut into the ocean. Several of these headlands are farther around than they appear and should be crossed over rather than trying to walk around their base. If you try to round some of the points at other than the lowest (minus) tides, you may get trapped and find that you cannot continue, your retreat cut off by the rising waters of an incoming tide.

Each year some visitors are trapped on cliff faces (most notably Taylor Point, which is particularly dangerous), and in some cases have been washed from the cliffs to their deaths. Check at the visitor centers or at the coastal ranger stations for information on local hazards before attempting beach hiking.

Since most of the national park is backcountry, it is laced with hiking trails. There are even trails to the park's glaciers. From the Hoh rain forest, the upriver hiking trail leads 18 miles to the snout of Blue Glacier on Mount Olympus. Free permits are required for all overnight stays anywhere in the park's backcountry.

Olympic National Park even has hot springs. The most developed is Sol Duc Hot Springs, 12 miles from **Mile 565.5** on U.S. Highway 101 via Sol Duc Valley Road. There are 3 large outdoor swimming pools, lodging, camping and food available.

The many lakes and streams on the Olympic Peninsula, as well as the surrounding bodies of salt water, offer outstanding fishing. Salmon, steelhead, cutthroat, eastern brook, Dolly Varden and rainbow trout are the most popular game fish on the peninsula. Some of the most famous salmon and steelhead rivers on the peninsula are the Hoh, Sol Duc, Queets, Bogachiel and Humptulips. The Hamma Hamma is a popular stream for sea-run cutthroat, and the mouth

Purple lupine and scattered bistort adorn Olympic National Park. (© John Barger)

of this river is good for steamer clams and Dungeness crabs.

Two subspecies of trout offer unique fishing in Lake Crescent. The state record for the largest Crescent caught in Lake Crescent is 12 lbs. while the record for the largest Beardslee is more than 23 lbs.

The general fishing season begins in April and extends through Oct., but the high lakes (over 4,000-foot elevation) generally don't begin to thaw until mid-June. The Fourth of July holiday is usually the kick-off for the season in these lakes.

No license is required within Olympic National Park, however, a punch card is needed for steelhead and salmon. Always check with park personnel regarding current regulations.

There is a large variety of shellfish on the peninsula, the most popular of which are oysters, razor clams, steamer clams, crabs and the monstrous geoducks (gooey-ducks). The Hood Canal region is popular for its oysters, steamer clams and the delicate spot shrimp (prawns).

With the exception of razor clams, no license is required to harvest the ocean-shore clams. The best time to dig these shellfish is during a minus tide. (Tide charts are available at nearly every resort and sports shop along the coast.)

Visitor Services

Food, gas and lodging are available at communities along U.S. Highway 101 just outside the park's perimeter. Concessions operating within the park are: Kalaloch Lodge (food, gas and lodging), open all year, phone (360) 962-2271; Lake Crescent Lodge (food and lodging), open April through Oct., phone (360) 928-3211; Log Cabin Resort on Lake Crescent (food, lodging, RV park and store), open May to Oct., phone (360) 928-

3245; and Sol Duc Hot Springs (food, lodging, store and mineral pools), open May to Oct., phone (360) 327-3583. Fairholm General Store, on the west end of Lake Crescent along U.S. Highway 101, has snack foods, camping and fishing supplies and vehicle and boat gas. The store is open from April through Oct.

There are 16 established campgrounds within the national park (1 walk-in). Kalaloch Campground is the largest coastal beach campground on the Olympic Peninsula with 177 sites; expect it to be full on summer weekends. Most of the national park campgrounds are open all year. A camping fee of $10 is charged at Altaire, Elwha, Fairholm, Heart O'the Hills, Hoh, Kalaloch, Mora, Sol Duc, Graves Creek, July Creek, and Staircase campgrounds; $8 at Dosewallips; and no fee at North Fork, Deer Park, Ozette and Queets.

Season, Fees and Access

The park is open year-round, although some services are closed in winter. Entrance fees for Olympic National Park are collected at Heart O' the Hills, Elwha, Sol Duc, Staircase and Hoh ranger stations from mid-May through Sept.: $5 per vehicle.

U.S. Highway 101 is the major access to the area as it runs the outer perimeter of the park on the west, north and east sides. Major access roads into the park from U.S. Highway 101 are: Hurricane Ridge, Elwha and Sol Duc roads at the north end of the park; and the Hoh River, Queets River and Quinault roads from the west. There is also access from the east side via Dosewallips Road west of Brinnon and Staircase Road west of Hoodsport.

For more information, contact Olympic National Park, 600 E. Park Ave., Port Angeles, WA 98362; or phone (360) 452-0330.

NATIONAL MONUMENTS

The violent, fiery volcanic eruptions of the Northwest are dramatized in 2 national monuments: Craters of the Moon National Monument in southcentral Idaho and Mount St. Helens Volcanic Monument in southwestern Washington.

A third national monument, John Day Fossil Beds National Monument in central Oregon, is the result of several geological changes over the centuries and today offers one of the most complete fossil records of world history known to man.

Oregon Caves is also noted for its geology. Preserved within this fourth national monument are the fantastic formations created by the relentless movement of water beneath the earth.

A trip to any of these monuments reminds visitors of the great natural power of the earth and its atmosphere, and introduces them to the diversity of the land formations in the Great Northwest.

Craters of the Moon National Monument

The 83 square miles of Craters of the Moon National Monument in southcentral Idaho are covered with a thick mat of volcanic rock, ash and cinders.

For the most part, the barren, rocky surface is void of vegetation, except for sparse bunches of sagebrush, limber pine and springtime floral displays.

History and Description

To the onlooker, this vast, open plain located off U.S. Highway 93 is anything but inviting. It is the result of a series of cracks in the earth's surface (The Great Rift), through which hot lava, ash and steam exploded and shot skyward nearly 15,000 years ago and continued to erupt sporadically until just 2,000 years ago.

The area was virtually unknown until 1921. Early settlers avoided it because the terrain is so difficult to cross. Farmers and ranchers ignored the inhospitable area that would not support a good growth of sagebrush, much less cattle or crops.

In the 1920s, the area was described as a "weird lunar landscape" and many people speculated that the surface of the moon must look much the same as this area. In 1924, 83 square miles were set aside as a national monument.

Craters of the Moon was first explored when Robert Limbert headed into the then unknown lava beds in 1921 with W.L. Cole

and a dog. The trio trekked the lava, which was often so rugged they were unable to sleep for lack of level ground. Cole's feet were blistered and the dog's were so cut to shreds that they carried it. At last they reached smoother flows, but now they lacked water as the porous lava allowed no water to remain on the surface. By following dove flights, they found snowmelt water holes within Great Rift faults. According to a pamphlet issued by the Park Service, Limbert's reports of the expedition and his photographs of the area were instrumental in securing its protection as a national monument.

More than 2,000 species of insects fly, roam and crawl throughout the crevices of Craters of the Moon. In addition, there are 142 bird species, 49 mammals, 8 reptiles and 1 amphibian that survive the rugged terrain. Mule deer pick their way through the cinders in search of feed, and bobcats, great horned owls and other birds of prey hunt for smaller mammals. Although vegetation is sparse, more than 300 species of plants take root in Craters of the Moon, including sagebrush, antelope bitterbrush, rabbitbrush and several wildflowers.

Attractions and Activities

Stop at the visitor center at the park headquarters near the entrance to view a dramatic film about erupting volcanoes. The film explains how lava flowed from fissures in the earth to create the volcanic features within the park. The displays—complete with easy-to-read graphics and samples of various lava rocks—help visitors recognize the formations, wildflowers and animals of the park. Check at the visitor center for information about the conducted nature walks and talks offered during the summer. Evening programs in the campground amphitheatre, often illustrated with slides, are a regular summer feature.

Visitors may take an hour's drive on the monument's 7-mile loop road to see spatter and cinder cones, lava flows, lava tubes and other points of interest. Seven stops along the loop road offer a quick, graphic

explanation of the phenomena that formed Craters of the Moon.

A short trail at the North Crater Flow along the loop road leads to a group of monoliths (crater wall fragments) transported by lava flows. This flow is one of the youngest. Here the Triple Twist Tree suggests, because of its 1,350 growth rings, that these eruptions ceased only 2,000 years ago. Two forms of lava are visible: the crumbly áa (ah-ah), which in the Hawaiian language literally means "hard on the feet," and the pahoehoe (pa-hoy-hoy), meaning "ropy."

The third stop along the loop road is a half-mile self-guiding trail to Devils Orchard, a group of lava fragments standing like islands in a sea of cinders.

A spur road beyond the Inferno Cone leads to the Tree Molds area, Trench Mortar Flats and the Craters of the Moon Wilderness. Tree molds formed where molten lava flows encased trees and then hardened. The cylindrical molds that remained after the

Visitors hike up an inferno cone in Craters of the Moon National Monument. (L. Linkhart)

wood rotted away range from a few inches to just under 1 foot in diameter.

One of the most interesting formations in the park are the lava tubes. When molten lava flowed out of the ground, it behaved like a stream of water working its way downhill. When the surface of the lava stream cooled, it solidified, but beneath the surface the lava continued to flow. The interior lava eventually flowed out of its caselike stream leaving an empty tube which exists today. Check with park rangers before attempting to explore any lava tubes and secure a copy of The Cave Trail, a pamphlet describing the caves and safety guidelines for explorers.

Craters of the Moon offers a land of exploration for even the meekest hiker. Several caves are located off trails on the loop road, but a powerful flashlight or lantern is needed for all except Indian Tunnel. Visitors should wear sturdy boots or shoes and stay on the trails, because lava rocks can be sharp. Never climb on spatter cones or monoliths. Collecting rocks or any natural object is prohibited. The area is being preserved and visitor cooperation is needed.

Visitor Services

The monument's only campground and picnic area is near the visitor center at the monument's entrance. Fifty campsites, water and restrooms are available. Take advantage of them here, because water is not available anywhere else in the park. Waterless restrooms are available at the Tree Molds parking lot, the Devil's Orchard parking lot, and at the Cave Area parking lot on the loop road and its spurs. No hookups are available and there is a $10 fee per night. No wood fires are permitted, but a charcoal grill is located at each site. Any campers planning to stay overnight in the wilderness must secure a camping permit from the visitor center.

Season, Fees and Access

The visitor center is open year-round from 8:30 a.m. until 4:30 p.m. From June 15 to Labor Day, the visitor center has extended hours from 8 a.m. until 6 p.m. The park is most often busy during June, July and August. The 7-mile loop road is closed from Nov to April, depending on snowfall. There is a fee of $4 per vehicle or $2 per bicycle to enter the park.

Access from the west is via U.S. Highway 93/Interstate 84 at Twin Falls, ID. U.S. Highway 93 travels through the Craters of the Moon National Monument. From the east, access is from Interstate 15 and either U.S. Highway 26 or 20 at their junctions with Interstate 15 near Idaho Falls, ID, then west to the junction with U.S. Highway 93 at Arco. See **Mile 110** in the U.S. HIGHWAY 93 section.

For more information, contact Craters of the Moon National Monument, P.O. Box 29, Arco, ID 83213; phone (208) 527-3257.

Above right—Mudflows at the Clarno Unit created these fantastic pinnacles. (L. Linkhart)
Right—Volcanic ash colors the Painted Hills Unit. (© John Barger)

John Day Fossil Beds National Monument

Lying peacefully along the quiet banks of the John Day River in central Oregon is one of the most complete records of natural history in the world, the John Day Fossil Beds National Monument. The monument includes some 14,000 acres split into 3 separate units: Sheep Rock Unit, Painted Hills Unit, and Clarno Unit.

History and Description

Forty million years ago, near tropical forests covered portions of central Oregon. Fifteen million years later, saber-toothed cats prowled a different landscape. Over millions of years, tiny 3-toed horses, camels, rhinoceroses and tapirs inhabited Oregon along with huge animals that have no counterparts in the current animal kingdom. The Oreodont, both sheep- and hog-like, had a grazing lifestyle. Creodonts were primitive meat eaters. Titanotheres evolved from the size of a hog to more than 7 feet high at the shoulder.

The record of this past life is preserved in the rocks of the 3 units of the John Day Fossil Beds National Monument. Collectively, the beds portray a total environment. Each has its unique landscape, attractions and scientific importance.

Calvary patrols and settlers were removing fossilized bones and wood as early as the 1860s. One of the first to recognize the value of this historical resource was Thomas Condon, a frontier missionary and natural history enthusiast—who later became the first professor of geology at Oregon State University—who shared his findings with professional paleontologists and geologists.

In the early 1900s, field paleontologists such as John Merriam began compiling John Day's fossils in geological and chronological order, beginning the preservation movement for the John Day Basin that would culminate in its becoming a national monument in 1974.

Attractions and Activities

The Sheep Rock unit is the best place to begin your introduction to John Day Fossil

Beds National Monument. Spread in 4 sub-units along Oregon Highway 19, Sheep Rock Unit exposes a continuous sequence of evolutionary development spanning 17 million years. A series of short trails branch from parking areas and lead to creeks, fossil beds, a scenic amphitheater, fossil reproductions and magnificent views of the John Day River and valley. Expect to see towering cliffs, rugged mountains and badland colors running from green to red rock.

The first portion of the Sheep Rock unit is the "Overlook," with its view of Picture Gorge, 3,360-foot Sheep Rock, the meandering John Day River and the visitor center just to the north.

The Cant Ranch House Visitor Center, which is the visitor center for all 3 units of John Day Fossil Beds National Monument, displays fossils of many prehistoric animals. They include the entelodont, a rhinoceros, foot bones of a 3-toed horse, and a skull from a sabre-toothed cat. A fossil preparation laboratory is in an 1800s cabin. There are interpretive displays on the 3 units and a history of fossil expeditions in the area. Built in 1917, the Cant Ranch House is on the National Register of Historic Places. One room is furnished with original Cant family antiques. There is a picnic area here.

The next stop in the Sheep Rock Unit is the Blue Basin area a few miles north of the visitor center. The half-mile Island in Time Trail and the more strenuous 3-mile Overlook Trail give visitors a good feel for what the fossil beds have to offer. Continuing north the highway passes the third sub-unit—Cathedral Rock—a huge slump that slid from the high bluffs and came to rest on the valley floor, rerouting the John Day River.

The fourth sub-unit is the Foree area, with a picnic area and 2 short trails: The Flood of Fire Trail and the Story in Stone Trail, which is wheelchair-accessible with touch exhibits for the visually impaired.

Painted Hills Unit, 10 miles northwest of the town of Mitchell, is characterized by dune-like mounds with brilliant bands of chimney red and yellow volcanic ash. Its scientific importance lies in the large numbers of plant fossils preserved in specific layers of the hills. It is known for spring shows of wildflowers which peak in May. One plant, the John Day Chaenactis, grows only here.

Interpretive trails at Painted Hills include the 0.75-mile Carroll Rim Trail with spectacular views of Sutton Mountain and the Painted Hills. The short Painted Cove Trail offers a closeup look at the clay stone of the Painted Hills. Leaf Hill Trail highlights the area's fossilized plant specimens. There is a picnic area at Painted Hills Unit.

Clarno Unit, 18 miles west of Fossil, is the oldest of the 3 units. It dates from 50 million to 35 million years ago. Fossil seeds, nuts and fruits are preserved here, making it unique among geologic sites. Seeds of grapes, magnolia, water lily, bananas and palms have been found at Clarno.

Its most distinctive feature is the Palisades—200-foot cliffs formed by ancient, successive, ash-laden mudflows. Two trails begin at the base of the cliffs: the 0.3-mile Trail of the Fossils and the 0.5-mile Clarno Arch Trail. Both lead to examples of embedded fossils. Nearby is a picnic area. The Hancock Field Station, operated by the Oregon Museum of Science, offers several programs for people interested in the geology, paleontology and ecology of the area. For informa-

Trails in Mount St. Helens monument lead to views of volcanic destruction.
(L. Linkhart)

tion contact Hancock Field Station, Fossil, OR 97830.

When hiking in areas with exposed geological formations, stay on established trails as walking off trails damages the fragile fossil beds.

Plants, fossils, rocks and artifacts within the monument are protected and it is illegal to disturb or remove them.

Visitor Services

The Sheep Rock visitor center is the primary information source for the John Day fossil beds and includes a museum of fossils and interpretive videos.

There are no campgrounds within the monument. State and federal campgrounds are available within the region, however. Check with the information center for campground locations near the monument. Lodging, food, gas and phones are available in the surrounding communities. These services are not available in the park. Water is available at the visitor center year-round and at the picnic areas during the summer. Picnic areas also have restrooms.

Season, Fees and Access

The monument's trails and picnic areas are open all year. The Sheep Rock visitor center is open daily from March through Oct., weekdays only in winter. Hours are 8:30 a.m. to 5 p.m.; to 6 p.m. Memorial Day to Labor Day. There are no entrance fees collected at the monument.

Access to Sheep Rock Unit from U.S. Highway 395 is via U.S. Highway 26 from Mount Vernon 27 miles west through Dayville to the Oregon Highway 19 junction, then 2 miles north on Highway 19 to the Sheep Rock visitor center.

To reach the Painted Hills, continue west on U.S. Highway 26 past the Sheep Rock turnoff through the town of Mitchell to the marked county road that takes you north into the Painted Hills Unit.

The Clarno Unit is located on Oregon Highway 218, 18 miles west of Fossil and 15

miles east of Antelope.

For more information, contact John Day Fossil Beds National Monument, HCR 82, Box 126, Kimberly, OR 97848; phone V/TDD (503) 987-2333, fax (503) 987-2336.

Mount St. Helens National Volcanic Monument

In a blast more powerful than an atomic bomb, Mount St. Helens erupted on May 18, 1980. Some 110,000 acres was set aside as national monument land in 1983. Administered by the U.S. Forest Service, the monument is a graphic example of the power of nature. It is also a vivid example of recent volcanic activity.

History and Description

Scientists began expecting activity at Mount St. Helens on March 20, 1980, when an earthquake that registered 4 on the Richter scale shook the mountain. A week later, the first eruption of steam and ash was reported, and similar explosions continued until about April 22. The mountain was quiet until the week of May 7–14, when steam and ash again belched from the mountain.

The morning of Sunday, May 18, 1980, Mount St. Helens made worldwide headlines. In a powerful, violent explosion following an earthquake, the mountain blew 1 cubic mile of earth into the air, clouding the skies of the Northwest with its fine, abrasive ash. The eruption was accompanied by huge landslides, flooding, heavy ash deposits and devastating mudflows which choked the Toutle River and enlarged the formerly scenic Spirit Lake.

The bodies of 31 visitors, forest workers and government researchers were later found among the debris, and several more

A grim reminder of Mount St. Helen's devastation is the "Miner's Car" on the road to Windy Ridge. (L. Linkhart)

were reported missing. (The final count was 57 people dead.) Virtually all of the campgrounds immediately adjacent to the mountain were wiped out in a matter of seconds.

More than 3 billion board feet of timber was tossed about and demolished by superheated hurricane-force winds spewing from the mouth of the volcano.

Hundreds of miles away, the ash cloud dropped like snow on hundreds of communities, blanketing fields, contaminating watersheds and destroying mechanical equipment. The ominous cloud of ash was accompanied by lightning as it rolled over Washington, Oregon, Idaho and Montana. Millions of dollars were spent cleaning up the ash and recovering from the fury of the mountain.

Today, the land around Mount St. Helens is recovering. Scattered throughout the devastated area, wildflowers are blooming, and regrowth trees have reached heights of 15 to 20-feet. Look for the bright pink of fireweed in ash deposits and along roadsides. Blue lupine can be found on rocky surfaces and on coverings of pumice. Animals that have returned include mountain bluebirds, elk and the seldom-seen pocket gopher.

Attractions and Activities

Before recommending what to see at Mount St. Helens, monument personnel usually query visitors on where they are coming from and how much time they have to spend.

Although not located within the monument, the Mount St. Helens Visitor Center in Castle Rock is a good place for Interstate 5 travelers to visit and learn about the history of the mountain. The visitor center is located next to Silver Lake and across from Seaquest State Park, 5 miles east of Interstate 5 (Exit 49) on Highway 504. Visitors can walk under a relief model of the mountain for an inside view of a volcano in action and learn about the history of Mount St. Helens. The center also has a 22-minute film on the eruption, seismographs, and naturalist talks

and walks. Open daily year-round, except Thanksgiving, Christmas and New Year's, from 9 a.m. to 6 p.m. April to Sept., 9 a.m. to 5 p.m. the remainder of the year. Phone (360) 274-2100.

Visitors with the time to spend can continue 43 miles east on Spirit Lake Memorial Highway 504 up the Toutle River to the Coldwater Ridge Visitor Center, northwest of the monument's border, which offers dramatic viewpoints of Mount St. Helens. The Coldwater Ridge visitor center focuses on the eruption and the region's recovery. Guided walks and interpretive programs are also offered. Open daily year-round, except Thanksgiving, Christmas and New Year's, from 9 a.m. to 6 p.m. April to Sept., 9 a.m. to 5 p.m. the remainder of the year. Phone (360) 274-2131.

Interstate 5 travelers exit onto Highway 503 to Cougar for the principal southern entrance to the monument. This route accesses Forest Service (FS) Road 83, which leads through the southern section of the monument. One mile west of FS Road 83 on FS Road 8303 is Ape Cave geologic site, the longest lava tube in the Western Hemisphere, named for the Boy Scout troop that first explored it in 1946 (the St. Helens Apes). The cave can be explored by those with good sources of light and warm clothes. Ape Cave information station rents lanterns, and is open daily from Memorial Day to Labor Day.

Monument personnel recommend that if visitors have the time, the east side of the monument offers a totally different view of the mountain than the west side. Driving from Yakima, motorists approach Mount St. Helens from the north, turning off U.S. Highway 12 at Randle. Drive south 20 miles via FS Road 25, then 17 miles west on FS Road 99 to the Windy Ridge Viewpoint. (From Cougar at the southern entrance to Windy Ridge viewpoint it is a 58-mile drive.)

Nothing prepares visitors for seeing the devastation for the first time from Windy Ridge. After driving the access roads through

magnificent virgin timber—including 650-year-old Douglas firs reaching more than 200 feet into the sky from the mossy forest floor—the gray and naked landscape of the blast zone is truly shocking.

At Windy Ridge you are within 4 miles of the crater and can see the side of the mountain that was blown away. Forest interpreters conduct information talks at Windy Ridge daily between mid-June and Sept.

The monument offers a number of hiking trails from the northern and southern access roads. On the approach to Windy Ridge, the Meta Lake Trail is a short paved trail to the lake of the same name and a view of trees blown down by the hurricane-force winds of the eruption. A few miles beyond the Meta Lake trailhead, at Mile 12 on FS Road 99, is Independence Pass Trail, a popular hike through downed timber to an overlook that provides a spectacular view of Spirit Lake and Mount St. Helens. For the energetic, the trail extends 2 miles from Spirit Lake to Norway Pass, with outstanding views of the crater and lava dome. The Harmony Trail, off FS Road 99 just 3 miles before the Windy Ridge viewpoint, is a 1-mile walk to Spirit Lake.

At the south end of the monument, the Trail of Two Forests, located 6 miles east of Cougar via FS Road 90, 2 miles north via FS Road 83 and a half-mile west on FS Road 8303, features a boardwalk trail through a forest that has grown on top of an old lava flow.

The Plains of Abraham Trail, which begins at Lahar off FS Road 83, is an 8-mile trail to Windy Ridge traversing the monument.

A hiking guide to monument trails is available for purchase at the visitor centers.

Visitor Services

There are 3 camping areas: Kalama River Horse/Campground on FS Road 81, 9 miles north of Cougar; and Lower Falls Campground and Lewis River Horse/Campground on FS Road 90.

Season, Fees and Access

The monument is open year-round, although access to the northeast side of the monument is closed by snow from Nov. 1 to Memorial Day. There are no entrance fees charged.

Access to the northern end of the monument is via U.S. Highway 12 to Randle, then about a 2-1/2-hour drive south to Windy Ridge via Forest Service roads. Southern access is from Interstate 5 via Washington Highway 503 from Woodland (Exit 21) 30 miles to Cougar and then via FS Roads 83 and 90. Washington Highway 504 from Castle Rock on I-5 (Exit 49) provides access to the Mount St. Helens Visitor Center and Spirit Lake Memorial Highway. See **Mile 329** and **Mile 357** in the INTERSTATE 5 section, and **Mile 532.5** in the U.S. HIGHWAY 12 section.

The Mount St. Helens National Monument Headquarters is located outside Amboy on Highway 503. For more information, contact Mount St. Helens Volcanic National Monument, 42218 NE Yale Bridge Road, Amboy, WA 98601; phone (360) 750-3900 or 750-3903. Maps and information are also available in or near the monument at the ranger station in Randle and information stations in Pine Creek and Iron Creek (open daily from Memorial Day through Labor

Day). It is important to obtain a current map of the monument for information on roads, trails and lookouts in the monument.

Oregon Caves National Monument

From its location on the map—tucked away in the southwest corner of the state—Oregon Caves National Monument may seem remote. It's not. This fantastic geologic treasure is easily accessible to Interstate 5 travelers.

History and Description

The caves were discovered in 1874 by one Elijah Davidson, who was chasing his dog, who was chasing a bear. Tales of the beautiful and mysterious cave brought other visitors, including Joaquin Miller, the poet of the Sierras, in 1907. Interest in preserving what Miller called the "Marble Halls of Oregon" grew, and in 1909, President William Howard Taft created the 480-acre Oregon Caves National Monument.

An automobile road was built to the caves in 1922, and in 1934 a hotel was constructed. Administration of the monument was also transferred to the National Park Service.

The caves themselves are a series of passageways and larger "rooms" decorated with a myriad of calcite formations. The water dripping, flowing and seeping through the caves, along with air movement—or lack of it—help determine the types of formations.

In recent years the National Park Service has concentrated on preservation and restoration of the caves, which were in danger of being destroyed or irretrievably altered by the effects of outside visitors. New tunnels and widened passages created during the 1930s to accommodate visitors changed air flow patterns, which in turn altered the growth of formations in the caves. Lights in the caves promoted the growth of algae, while smoke from torches had blackened other portions. Even the lint from clothing and oil from people's hands that touched the cave walls altered the formations.

Today, artificial tunnels act as airlocks to restore natural cave winds. Visitors cannot touch the cave walls, and passage through the caves is restricted to roped-off walkways.

Attractions and Activities

Looking to all the world like Hollywood special-effects for some fantastic movie, the eerie sculptures covering the walls and ceilings of Oregon Caves are the main attraction. Calcite formations within the caves include flowstone, pillars and stalactites.

To see the caves, visitors must take a guided tour, which leave from near the cave entrance across from the Chateau. The tours are offered several times daily year-round, except Christmas and Thanksgiving. Canes, staffs, walking aids and tripods are not permitted in the cave. Children under 6 years must be over 42 inches in height and able to climb steep stairs. Infants and toddlers are not allowed on cave tours. The guided tours last slightly over an hour and the walk is considered strenuous.

There are also hiking trails outside the caves and within the monument. These offer good views of the surrounding Siskiyou National Forest.

The 6-story Oregon Caves Chateau, which rises among waterfalls and trees near the cave entrance, is also a major attraction.

Refurbished in the early 1990s, the hotel was declared a historic building by the National Park Service in 1987. The lobby, with its massive marble fireplace and original furnishings, is worth a visit, as is the 1930s-style coffee shop.

Visitor Services

Oregon Caves Chateau offers 22 guest rooms, dining room and coffee shop from mid-May through the first week in Sept. During the winter, the Chateau operates a bed and breakfast.

Campgrounds are available in the adjoining Siskiyou National Forest along Highway 26 between Cave Junction and the monument. Gas, food and lodging are also available in Cave Junction.

Season, Fees and Access

Oregon Caves National Monument is open year-round. There is no entrance fee to the monument, although there is a $5.75 fee for adults, $3.50 for children 6 to 12, for the guided cave tour.

Access from Interstate 5 is via U.S. Highway 199 (the Redwood Highway); use Exit 55 near Grants Pass (see **Mile 55** in the INTERSTATE 5 section). It is an easy 34-mile drive to Cave Junction from I-5; Highway 199 is a busy connecting route between I-5 and U.S. Highway 101 on the coast. From Cave Junction, it is 19 miles to Oregon Caves National Monument via Highway 46. This is a winding road with some very sharp switchbacks and a noticeable upgrade; it is not recommended for large RVs and trailers.

For more information contact Oregon Caves National Monument/Oregon Caves Chateau, P.O. Box 128, Cave Junction, OR 97523; phone (503) 592-3400.

Water, air and calcite create the fantastic formations within Oregon Caves National Monument. (© John Barger)

NATIONAL RECREATION AREAS

Recreational pursuits abound in the Northwest, but unusual opportunities exist in the region's National Recreation Areas. These areas have been set aside for their unique recreational attributes, and thousands of visitors walk the trails, fish the rivers and streams, admire the wildlife and photograph the scenic wonders within the boundaries of these areas.

Administered by the U.S. Forest Service or National Park Service, NRAs in the Northwest included here are: Hells Canyon on the Oregon–Idaho border between Lewiston and Weiser, ID; Oregon Dunes, on the central Oregon coast between Florence and Coos Bay, OR; Ross Lake and Lake Chelan, in the Cascade Range of northern Washington; and Sawtooth National Recreation Area, 8 miles north of Sun Valley, in central Idaho.

Hells Canyon National Recreation Area

The name Hells Canyon conjures up visions of frontier ruggedness, impassable obstacles and Western romance. And well it should: Hells Canyon is all that and more. It is generally a remote and undeveloped area with few good roads. Access to the Snake River is limited. It is recommended you plan your trip carefully before entering the area.

History and Description

It was the mild winters that attracted the first human visitors to Hells Canyon. The Native American Indians lived in much of the region, leaving traces of their camps on nearly every terrace. Rock faces are covered with Indian carvings and petroglyphs. Relics of early white settlement have also been discovered, built atop ancient Indian villages because of the lack of flat land.

The canyon formed a natural barrier against white explorers, who were time and again forced to retreat. In 1877, the swift river prevented the Army from following Chief Joseph into Idaho at the start of the Nez Perce War. Chief Joseph, on the other hand, was able to lead his people across the flooding Snake River without losing a single human, horse or cow.

In 1975, 652,488 acres were set aside as the Hells Canyon National Recreation Area (NRA). The Hells Canyon National Recreation Area Act also designated 67 miles of the Snake River as a protected "wild and scenic river." The Snake River divides the 190,000-acre Hells Canyon Wilderness Area within Hells Canyon NRA into 2 distinct natural units. On the Idaho side, canyon slopes ascend to the Seven Devils. On the Oregon side, the river rimrock gives way to grassy benches and timbered regions.

The 71-mile-long canyon, formed by the erosion of the Snake River, is the deepest river gorge in North America, with an average depth of 6,600 feet and the deepest spot 7,900 feet. The 20-mile slot along the Idaho–Oregon border from Spring Creek to Johnson Bar is flanked by the 10,000-foot peaks of the Seven Devils Range in Idaho to the east and the Wallowa Mountains of Oregon to the west. The upper 5 miles of the gorge is inundated by Hells Canyon Reservoir. Below Hells Canyon Dam, the Snake River winds north to Lewiston, a free-flowing wild and scenic river for 67 miles. The river drops more than 11 feet per mile as it thunders over a succession of spectacular rapids, interspersed with placid stretches.

Although the river previously produced trophy-sized trout, the fishery has suffered from nitrogen supersaturation from the dams, and the numbers of trophy fish are down. The most popular fish in the canyon is the smallmouth bass. Smallmouth run from 1 to 3 lbs. and there are a lot of them. The farther downstream from Hells Canyon Dam you get, the better the smallmouth fishing becomes. Crappie are plentiful in the canyon and the sturgeon fishery is a popular target for anglers.

The distance is so great between the top and bottom of the canyon that several ecosystems exist within themselves. The canyon and mountain ranges within the NRA contain the widest varieties of wildlife species in the Northwest, including elk, mule and white-tailed deer, bear, cougar, marten, eagle, mountain goats and bighorn sheep. Many birds of prey roost and nest on the craggy cliffs of Hells Canyon, and the gorge is the premier chukar hunting region in the Northwest. Blue and ruffed grouse also inhabit the canyon.

In the springtime, Hells Canyon shows its beauty with an abundance of grasses, shrubs, trees and colorful wildflowers. As summer approaches and temperatures soar to above 100°F, the perennial grasses and flora dry and bake to form a parched, gray and brown scene. The wind within the canyon is relatively calm, and even in the winter, the canyon bottom has comparatively mild temperatures.

Attractions and Activities

There are 29 points of interest identified in the U.S. Forest Service brochure on Hells Canyon NRA, and access is the key to enjoying most of them. Getting there also has to be considered one of the attractions of Hells Canyon National Recreation Area, since it's not easy. Access to Hells Canyon is by boat, hiking trail and by vehicle.

Seeing the canyon by jet boat or float trip is perhaps the easiest. Numerous outfitters provide jet boat trips down the Snake River from Hells Canyon Dam and upriver from Lewiston. Float trips down the Snake are provided by licensed outfitters. Trips generally last 2 to 5 days, and the usual float season is from the Friday preceding Memorial Day weekend through Sept. 15. Float reservations are required. A list of jet boat operators and float trip outfitters is available by contacting the Hells Canyon NRA headquarters.

Private parties floating the river are required to make reservations and secure a permit. Registration by private boat owners is also mandatory. Obtain information from the Hells Canyon NRA headquarters. Self-issuing permits are available at Pittsburg Landing, Dug Bar and at the mouth of the Salmon River. River guards are available to issue permits at the mouth of the Grande Ronde River and at Hells Canyon Dam during the season. The Forest Service maintains a boat launch site year-round, and an information center (summers only), at Hells Canyon Creek Recreation Site below Hells Canyon Dam. This is the primary launch site for float trips and jet boat tours of the "wild" Snake River. No overnight facilities are available.

There are actually only 3 roads that take visitors to the Snake River within Hells Canyon: Snake River Road, Pittsburg Landing Road, and Dug Bar Road. At the south end of the NRA, the 2-lane, paved Snake River Road connects Oxbow Crossing and Hells Canyon Dam, the center for much of the boating activity within the NRA. Pittsburg Landing Road is a steep, narrow gravel Forest Service road that leads 17 miles southwest of Whitebird, ID, to Pittsburg Landing boat launch on the Snake River. (Pittsburg Landing is also the trailhead for Snake River National Recreation Trail.) Dug Bar Road is a steep and narrow 1-lane dirt road from Imnaha, OR, to the Snake River at the north end of Hells Canyon Wilderness near the confluence of the Imnaha River.

Dramatic views of Hells Canyon are available from 3 viewpoints, all of them a somewhat challenging drive. All are open summer into the fall.

The Hat Point Overlook (elev. 6,982 feet) offers an excellent view of Hells Canyon and the Seven Devils Mountains. The viewpoint is accessible by car on a dirt and gravel road 24 miles from Imnaha, OR. Some of the most rugged and spectacular backcountry in the state of Oregon can be seen on the trip from Imnaha to Hat Point. It is a rough road, and a one-way trip takes 2¹/₂ hours. The road is not recommended for cars with low clearance and those pulling trailers. Camping and picnicking available.

Heavens Gate Overlook, often called the best view into Hells Canyon from the Idaho side, is a 19-mile drive west from Riggins, ID, via a very steep and winding gravel Forest Service road. There is a steep half-mile trail to the overlook. There are no facilities at the overlook and the road is not recommended for RVs, trailers or low-clearance vehicles.

Easiest access to the rim of Hells Canyon is Hells Canyon Overlook on the Oregon side, 30 miles northeast of Halfway or 43 miles southeast of Joseph via Forest Service roads. The Wallowa Mountain Road (Forest Service Road 39), a 5-hour scenic drive through the Wallowa Mountains between Baker City and La Grande, OR, accesses the Hells Canyon Overlook; turnoff onto Forest Service Road 3965 for the overlook.

A second scenic drive recommended by the Forest Service is the Imnaha River Road (Forest Service Road 3955). This road goes south from Imnaha and parallels the Wild and Scenic Imnaha River as it meanders through rims and benches much like those along the Snake River. Continue on to Indian Crossing Campground where you can hike to the "Blue Hole."

Nearly 1,000 miles of trails traverse Hells Canyon NRA, including 2 national recreation trails: the Nee-Me-Poo and the Snake River.

The Nee-Me-Poo National Recreation Trail is a historic trail following the steps of Chief Joseph. The trailhead is at Dug Bar. This 3.7-mile trail is part of the 1,800-mile trek led by Chief Joseph in 1877 just prior to the Nez Perce War. Nearly 700 Nez Perce Indians passed along this trail when they were forced to leave their fertile, lush homeland in the Wallowas. They were en route to the Lapwai Indian Reservation when their relocation movement turned to a historic flight for freedom at the beginning of the Nez Perce War. Their hope of freedom turned to tragedy when the tribe was captured just 30 miles south of the Canadian border in the Bear Paw Mountains of Montana.

The Nee-Me-Poo (means "the real people") National Recreation Trail was set aside in 1968 as a reminder of the nation's history and the tragedy of the Nez Perce people.

For experienced hikers, the 31.5-mile Snake River National Recreation Trail parallels the Snake River on the Idaho side. The trail begins at Granite Creek (access by boat from the Hells Canyon Dam) and ends at Pittsburg Landing. Sections of the trail may be flooded in high water.

Visitor Services

The Wallowa Mountains Visitor Center near Enterprise, OR, has information and displays on Hells Canyon NRA and the Wallowa-Whitman National Forest. There is also an information station open in summer at Hells Canyon Creek Recreation Site below Hells Canyon Dam.

There are approximately 17 Forest Service campgrounds—about half with trailer sites—within the NRA. Most are in remote loca-

Hells Canyon and the Snake River from Hat Point Overlook in Oregon. Three viewpoints offer 3 different dramatic views of the canyon. (L. Linkhart)

tions, accessed by Forest Service roads, and have limited facilities available between June and Nov.

Idaho Power Co. maintains 4 park sites with RV facilities within Hells Canyon NRA: Copperfield Park at Oxbow Crossing; Hells Canyon Park, 7 miles north of Oxbow; McCormick Park, a half mile north of Brownlee Dam; and Woodhead Park near Brownlee Dam. All are open all year and are located on paved roads and have hookups, water, showers and picnic areas.

Food, water, gas and supplies should be obtained in local communities before venturing into Hells Canyon NRA.

Season, Fees and Access

Hells Canyon NRA is open all year, although roads, campgrounds and points of interest are generally open only from June or July to Nov. There are no entrance fees.

Camping fees are charged at the Idaho Power Co. RV parks.

Access to secondary roads leading to Hells Canyon NRA points of interest is from Interstate 84 in Oregon and U.S. Highway 95 in Idaho.

Visitors to Hells Canyon should be aware that fire danger during the summer months is extremely high. The parched cheatgrass and sagebrush are explosively flammable. An open fire closure is in effect annually between July 1 and Sept. 15 in the river corridor.

For more information, contact the Hells Canyon National Recreation Area Headquarters, Wallowa Whitman National Forest, 88401 Highway 82, Enterprise, OR 97828, phone (503) 426-4978; or the Wallowa Whitman National Forest, P.O. Box 907, Baker, OR 97814, phone (503) 523-6391. There are offices in Clarkston and Riggins as well. Write to the Hells Canyon NRA, Snake River Office, P.O. Box 699, Clarkston, WA 99403; or Hells Canyon NRA, P.O. Box 832, Riggins, ID 83549.

Lake Chelan National Recreation Area

Lake Chelan National Recreation Area at the southern tip of the North Cascades National Park is a magnificent scenic wilderness inaccessible by car. The 55-mile-long lake, one of the deepest in the country at 1,500 feet, thrusts up into the North Cascade mountains. At its southern end is the resort area around the town of Chelan which, with 300 days of sunshine a year, is a favorite vacation destination for those wishing to escape the Northwest rains.

History and Description

Lake Chelan National Recreation Area occupies 62,000 acres in the southernmost corner of North Cascades National Park. Only the upper 4 miles of Lake Chelan lie within the recreation area. Most of the lake lies within the boundaries of Wenatchee National Forest. The only settlement within the recreation area is Stehekin, at the head of Lake Chelan.

The Stehekin Valley enjoyed a short-lived fur-trapping, mining and homesteading history during the late part of the 19th century. Many of the descendants of the early homesteaders still live there year-round. The scenic valley's recreational potential was recognized early, and summer cabins and resorts began to appear around the turn of the century. Today, Stehekin remains isolated, and residents must rely on boat service from Chelan for mail and supplies.

Attractions and Activities

Most activities within the recreation area center around Stehekin, which has about 40,000 visitors a year, according to the National Park Service. The Golden West Visitor Center (phone 360/856-5703, ext. 14) in Stehekin offers ranger-led hikes and naturalist presentations, and displays featuring local history. It is open daily from mid-March to mid-Oct.

Hiking and exploring the beautiful remote wilderness is the prime reason for coming here. The Stehekin Valley offers a wide choice of day hikes from several trailheads in Stehekin or near the campgrounds. A National Park Service shuttle bus from the North Cascades Lodge at Stehekin provides transportation to trailheads, campgrounds, fishing holes and scenic areas along the Stehekin Valley Road. Shuttle reservations are required, phone (360) 856-5703, ext. 14.

For a day trip into the recreation area, many people take the round-trip cruise out of Chelan. Lake Chelan Boat Co. offers daily passenger excursion trips between Chelan and Stehekin year-round aboard the *Lady of the Lake* and *Lady Express*. Reservations are recommended; no pets allowed between March 15 and Oct. 31. Phone (509) 682-2224 for recorded message on schedule and fares, or (509) 682-4584 for more information. Stop for lunch at the North Cascades Lodge, or take a scenic side trip to Rainbow Falls before returning to Chelan (check with lodge).

This is a backpacker's paradise. Established trails run north into the national park and high alpine country or follow the shore of the lake. Weather can change abruptly in the Cascades, so be sure to take extra clothing (wool, not cotton) even if you are planning only a short day hike.

Hikers sometimes meet topography head-on, but the rewards of scenic mountain and glacier vistas are many.

A backcountry permit is required for all overnight trips. No camping is permitted on sensitive alpine or subalpine meadows.

Most of the boating activity on Lake Chelan takes place around the south end of the lake at Chelan. Canoes, kayaks and small craft do travel the lake, but powerful north winds can be dangerous. It is recommended that you keep close to the shore and keep an eye on the weather. Rental boats are available at the North Cascades Stehekin Lodge in Stehekin.

Winter is becoming a popular time to visit Stehekin. The lodge grooms trails for cross-country skiing.

Visitor Services

North Cascades Stehekin Lodge, overlooking the lake, has 28 sleeping units and a full-service restaurant. Phone (509) 682-4494 for more information. The concession also has a small convenience store and marina, as well as offering bike and boat rentals. Bed and breakfasts and guest cabins are also available in Stehekin.

The Stehekin Valley Road begins at the boat landing in Stehekin and continues 23 miles up the valley to North Cascades National Park, Cottonwood Campground and Cascade Pass Trail. There are 7 other campgrounds and numerous trailheads along the road. Free camping permits are available from the ranger station at Stehekin. Free shuttle bus service from the lodge.

Season, Fees and Access

Lake Chelan National Recreation Area is open year-round. There is no entrance fee to the recreation area, although if you go in by boat from Chelan, it will cost between $20 and $40 round-trip in summer for the *Lady of the Lake* or *Lady Express* service.

You can fly, hike or boat in, but you can't get to Lake Chelan National Recreation

Left—*Backpackers on shoreline trail at Lake Chelan National Recreation Area.* **Above**—*Boat service is offered year-round from Chelan to Stehekin, at the head of Lake Chelan within the national recreation area.* (Photos by L. Linkhart)

Area by car. Most visitors take the *Lady of the Lake*, the private boat service that travels up the lake to Stehekin. The boat leaves Chelan in the morning, and the 4-hour trip provides shoreline views of private residential and farming development on the lower lake and rugged mid-lake shorelines and national forest lands before reaching the wilderness area. Charter floatplane service is also available in Chelan. Chelan, in central Washington, is located at **Mile 508** on U.S. Highway 97 (see U.S. HIGHWAY 97 section).

Trail access to the national recreation area is available via the Pacific Crest Trail from Rainy Pass off the North Cascades Highway or the shorter Cascade Pass Trail. Pets on leash are allowed on trails.

For more information, contact North Cascades National Park, 2105 State Route Highway 20, Sedro-Woolley, WA 98284; phone (360) 856-5700.

Oregon Dunes National Recreation Area

Visitors to the Oregon Dunes are treated to some of the most scenic stretches of coastline in the world. The sand dunes, among the largest in the world, reach up to 400 feet high and are more than a mile in length. Dunes such as these, associated with the ocean, exist nowhere else in the Northern Hemisphere.

History and Description

Oregon Dunes National Recreation Area lies within Siuslaw National Forest. Of the 31,500 acres between the Coos and Siuslaw rivers on the central Oregon coast that have been set aside as the Oregon Dunes National Recreation Area, more than 14,000 acres are mixed open sand dunes and open to ORVs.

The dunes are the result of 60 million years of changing sea levels, erosion on volcanic bluffs, high ocean winds, glacial movement and 6 major streams emptying into the ocean. The wind continues to shift the sand, changing the size and location of the dunes and creating an eerie, almost mystical atmosphere. A foredune stretches for 40 miles along the eastern edge of the beach. This low, vegetated hill—as high as 30 feet in some places—is formed when wind-swept sand is caught by the beachgrass.

Attractions and Activities

The Oregon Dunes area offers a wide range of activities, including camping, off-road vehicle (ORV) driving, hiking, beachcombing, fishing, horseback riding, canoeing and various hobbies using the wind, including kite flying. Visitors can view a 20-minute film on the dunes at the Oregon Dunes NRA headquarters in Reeds-port.

Only part of the Oregon Dunes National Recreation Area is open to ORV travel. Some beaches are open year-round to ORVs, others are open seasonally, and others are closed. Secure a map of the area before driving in the dune area.

The North Siltcoos area, in the northern portion of the recreation area, is open to ORVers between the Siltcoos Road and the South Jetty access road. There is a small closure around Honeyman State Park/Cleawox

Lake area because of heavy pedestrian traffic. There is also a noise-control buffer strip on the eastern edge.

Just south of Winchester Bay is the High Dunes area in the southern portion of the recreation area. This area is open to ORVs from here to the Douglas–Coos County line, approximately 1 mile south of the last beach parking lot on the bay. The dunes are closed to motor vehicles from this point to Tenmile Creek, where the South Dunes area begins.

The most popular ORV area is in the South Dunes, between Tenmile Creek and Horsfall Road. Here, lakes and forests divide the dunes in half, providing many spots for remote camping. ORVers should be aware that there are some scattered parcels of privately owned land, and the landowners' rights should be respected.

Oregon state law requires all ORVs to be equipped with lights, brakes, flags, roll bars or cages, chain guards and secure fuel tanks and seats. Permits issued by the Dept. of Motor Vehicles are also required. Specific regulations are available at the Oregon Dunes National Recreation Area headquarters, which is adjacent to U.S. Highway 101 in Reedsport.

The Oregon Dunes area offers more than a dozen hiking trails, most rated easy or moderate and ranging in length from 1 to 4-plus miles. The Taylor Dunes Trail is designed to accommodate physically impaired visitors. Pick up a copy of "Hiking Trails in the Oregon Dunes National Recreation Area" at the Reedsport office.

Hiking the dunes can be a challenge. Forest Service officials ask that hikers observe the landmarks around them when starting across the open sand. Stop and look back often, so that you may recognize the area when you return. You can easily become disoriented in the dunes.

Beachcombing for natural and sea-tossed treasures is popular with visitors. Hundreds of species of sea life, or remnants of them, may be found along the beach. Sea shells, driftwood, old bottles, Japanese floats and countless other items are collected by visitors.

Wear lightweight shoes (such as tennis shoes) when hiking the dunes or beach. Other items you might bring along include a windbreaker (wind velocity averages 12 to 16 mph), sunglasses, hat, sunscreen, a light raincoat and a compass. Don't forget your camera. The wind can form spectacular features in the sand, and the creative photographer can have a heyday in this constantly changing environment.

Although 32 freshwater lakes are found in the area, don't drink from them. Carry safe drinking water with you. Some of the

Young visitor experiences the joy of walking on sand dunes. (© Lee Foster)

areas are open to ORVs as well as hikers, and both parties should be aware of and respect the other's presence.

The area in and around the Oregon Dunes NRA is one of the prime fishing spots in the Northwest. The Umpqua is the second-largest river on the Oregon coast and is a major sportfishing attraction, offering striped bass, chinook, coho and jack salmon, steelhead, green and white sturgeon, shad, smelt, perch and sea-run cutthroat.

Tahkenitch Lake offers steelhead, bass, coho, sea-run cutthroat, perch, crappie and bluegill, and is best fished from a boat due to the brushy shoreline. Siltcoos Lake and the 2-mile long Siltcoos River are good for anadromous cutthroat, steelhead and coho salmon. The lake is stocked with rainbow. There is a good resident population of panfish, cutthroat, rainbow, largemouth bass and brown bullhead catfish. Tahkenitch and Siltcoos are considered the best bass fishing lakes in Oregon.

The Siuslaw River and Bay offer Dungeness crab, clamming, the largest sea-run cutthroat fishery in the world, shad, chinook and coho salmon, steelhead, surf smelt, pinkfin perch, lingcod and rockfish. The harbor can be treacherous, but offshore fishing is often good for salmon and bottom fish.

There are hundreds of charter fishing operations along the coastline that offer charter trips, equipment and everything necessary to fish the ocean. Inquire locally.

Visitor Services

Communities along U.S. Highway 101

offer food, gas and lodging, and there are private, state and federal campgrounds available. Some of the 13 national recreation area campgrounds may be reserved; phone 1-800-280-2267. All have a 10-day limit and none have hookups.

There are 6 designated picnic areas, and visitors may also picnic on the beach. Permits are not required for beach fires. Officials ask that fires be built from down, dead wood (not always available) or that you bring your own fuel. Fires should be attended with care and extinguished with water. Sand-covered embers can quickly be uncovered by the wind, and the embers may spread. Do not build fires in or near a standing pile of driftwood.

The NRA has designated 6 ORV staging areas and 3 horse staging areas at campgrounds and parking lots along U.S. Highway 101.

There are boat ramps at Tyee Campground, Carter Lake, Tahkenitch Lake and Spinreel Campground.

Season, Fees and Access

Oregon Dunes National Recreation Area is open year-round. There are no entrance fees to the park. The National Recreation Area stretches along U.S. Highway 101 from a few miles north of Coos Bay to Florence, OR. See **Mile 118.5** to **Mile 161** in the U.S. HIGHWAY 101 section for more information on the location of attractions and services available from the main highway.

For more information, contact Oregon Dunes National Recreation Area, Siuslaw National Forest, 855 Highway Ave., Reedsport, OR 97467; phone (503) 271-3611, TDD 271-3614.

Ross Lake National Recreation Area

Ross Lake NRA divides the North Cascades National Park into 2 units. The 117,500-acre recreation area encompasses 3 power dams impounding 3 lakes (Ross, Diablo and Gorge), and provides a corridor for the North Cascades Highway. Ross Lake is 24 miles long, and its waters are cold. Even during hot summers, activity on Ross and Diablo lakes is confined to boating and fishing.

Attractions and Activities

The North Cascades Visitor Center in Newhalem is open daily during the summer, weekends in winter; phone (206) 386-4495. The center features a slide show, hands-on nature exhibit for children, and maps and information on park activities, trails and camping. Also in Newhalem visitors can view the Gorge Creek Powerhouse and take the scenic Ladder Creek Falls Loop Trail. Hiking is popular in the recreation area, with numerous trailheads along Highway 20, some starting from the campgrounds.

Seattle City Light offers scheduled tours of its hydro facilities at Diablo Lake and Ross Dam. The 4½-hour Skagit Tour begins in Diablo with a presentation and slide show on the history of the Skagit Project and includes a ride on an antique incline railway to Diablo Dam, a boat cruise across Diablo Lake for a tour of the Ross Dam, and a family-style meal upon returning to Diablo. The tours operate mid-June through Labor Day. Tickets cost $24.50 for adults, $22 for seniors over 62 and $12.50 for children 6 to

Gorge Creek Powerhouse at Newhalem within Ross Lake National Recreation Area. (Michael Dill)

11; children under 5 free. Reservations are strongly recommended. Contact Skagit Tours Office, Seattle City Light, 1015 3rd Ave., Seattle, WA 98104; phone (206) 684-3030.

Fishing is popular on Ross Lake and in mountain lakes and streams in the recreation area. Rainbow, Dolly Varden, brook and golden trout are the principal game fish. State fishing regulations apply to fishing in the recreation area, and a Washington license is required.

Visitor Services

Overnight lodging within the national recreation area can be found at Ross Lake Resort (phone 206/386-4437), a favorite destination for canoeists and trout anglers, with 10 cabins, 3 bunkhouses, full marina services, boat rentals, and boat portaging and water taxi service. No food service is available. Take the Diablo Dam Road turnoff north from Highway 20. The road ends at a parking lot where tugboats transfer passengers to the floating resort at 8:30 a.m. and 3 p.m. daily mid-June through Oct. Cost is $5 per person for the 1½ hour round trip

There are developed campgrounds along Highway 20 at Goodell Creek (20 sites), Newhalem Creek (129 sites) and Colonial Creek (162 sites). Nature trails, evening programs and conducted walks take place during the summer at Colonial Creek and Newhalem Creek campgrounds.

There are 17 boat-access camping areas located on Ross Lake, some have docking facilities, others are accessible only to kayaks and canoes. Free backcountry permit required. Picnic tables and pit toilets are at the campsites, but water must be carried in or treated.

The only boat launch facility on Ross Lake is located at the north end of the lake at Hozomeen, accessed via rough gravel road from Canada. Those wishing to transport kayaks and canoes to Ross Lake can launch them at Colonial Creek Campground on Diablo Lake, boat to the base of Ross Dam, and then portage around Ross Dam on a 1-mile gravel road to enter the lake. Gorge Lake has a small ramp near the town of Diablo.

Season, Fees and Access

Ross Lake National Recreation Area is

open year-round, although the area's only highway access—Washington Highway 20—is closed in winter from east of Diablo at the Ross Lake trailhead to Mazama. There is no entrance fee to the recreation area. Pets on leash permitted on trails.

Within the recreation area, Diablo Lake can be reached by car off the North Cascades Highway. Ross Lake is accessible by car only from the north through Canada via a 40-mile gravel road near Hope, BC, to Hozomeen. At the south end, access to Ross Lake is limited to hiking trail and water routes. See the NORTH CASCADES HIGHWAY section for log of Highway 20 through Ross Lake NRA.

For more information, contact North Cascades National Park, 2105 State Route Highway 20, Sedro-Woolley, WA 98284; phone (360) 856-5700.

Sawtooth National Recreation Area

Sawtooth National Recreation Area (NRA) remains one of the West's last great mountain treasures to be discovered by the traveling public. With its magnificent snowcapped ranges, alpine lakes and meadows and whitewater rivers, Sawtooth NRA is fast becoming a vacation destination.

Within the Sawtooth NRA's 756,000 acres (about the size of Rhode Island) are the Sawtooth Wilderness, the White Cloud and Boulder mountains, more than 90 miles of the Snake River and 5 large lakes. Just south of the Sawtooth NRA boundary is the glamorous winter playground of Sun Valley and Ketchum.

History and Description

Two million acres in central Idaho were set aside in 1905 by President Theodore Roosevelt to establish the Sawtooth Forest Reserve, despite the opposition of cattle, sheep, mining and timber interests. National park bills were introduced in Congress in 1913, 1916, 1935, 1960 and 1966, and all were defeated. Finally, a compromise between landowners and preservationists was achieved in 1972 with the establishment of the Sawtooth National Recreation Area "to assure the preservation and protection of the natural, scenic, historic, pastoral and fish and wildlife values and to provide for the recreational values associated therewith."

Some 20,000 acres of the 756,000-acre recreation area remain privately owned and are regulated by Sawtooth NRA. The Sawtooth Primitive Area, established by the Forest Service in 1937, was redesignated the Sawtooth Wilderness Area in 1972.

Attractions and Activities

Sawtooth NRA is a land of exceptional beauty and endless recreational opportunities. You can hike, climb, camp, kayak, water-ski, fish, cross-country ski, backpack or ride the rapids. Many of the activities in Sawtooth NRA are within reach of paved roads. Sawtooth NRA Headquarters Visitor Center is located on Idaho Highway 75, about 9 miles north of Ketchum. It is open daily from 8 a.m. to 5:30 p.m.

Highway 75, the Sawtooth Scenic Route, is one way many visitors experience Sawtooth NRA. There are scenic overlooks and historical markers along the highway. Informational taped tours of the route are available at the Stanley Ranger Station and at the Sawtooth NRA Headquarters Visitor Center outside Ketchum or the Ketchum Ranger Station in Ketchum. The tapes point out natural and historical points of interest, what to do in Sawtooth NRA, and ecological and environmental information.

Grand Mogul rises above Redfish Lake. (L. Linkhart)

In addition to the Sawtooth Scenic Route, 3 scenic byways meet inside Sawtooth NRA at Stanley: the Sawtooth Scenic Byway, the Ponderosa Pine Scenic Byway and the Salmon River Scenic Byway.

There are 750 miles of hiking trails in Sawtooth NRA. Much of Sawtooth NRA, including all of the Sawtooth Wilderness and most of the high country of the Boulder and White Cloud mountains, is accessible only on foot or horseback. You can take a leisurely stroll along Pettit Lake or a mountaineering expedition. Most of the trailheads can be reached by car or a high-clearance vehicle. Forest Service maps, available at Sawtooth Forest ranger stations and at Sawtooth NRA offices, are very useful as road maps to get to the trailheads. Topographic maps are also recommended.

Power boating and waterskiing are popular activities on Alturas, Pettit, Redfish and Stanley lakes. Challenging mountain winds are favored by wind surfers and sailboats on the big lakes, especially Alturas and Redfish. Nonmotorized boats only are allowed on Perkins, Yellow Belly and Little Redfish lakes.

Famous for its stream and lake fishing, good fishing for trout and whitefish is within easy walking or boating distance. Some species of salmon found within the recreation area are either threatened or endangered. Check with the Idaho Fish and Game Dept. for restrictions.

Some of the best native trout fishing can be found in the South Fork of the Payette River near Grandjean, accessible by car. Backcountry fishing in high mountain lakes and streams is within a day's hike or a longer pack trip. The eastern brook trout has been very successfully introduced in high country lakes. Native cutthroat trout are primarily found in the lakes and streams of the White Cloud Peaks. Idaho state fishing regulations apply, and an Idaho license is required. The general trout limit is 6 fish.

The easiest way to float the turbulent waters of the upper Salmon River is through commercial outfitters operating out of Stanley. Not all of the Salmon River is rough and foaming. Low water levels of late summer tame some parts of the river. Then the stretch from Stanley to Basin Creek can be floated safely in almost anything—from a large raft to an inner tube. Keep in mind that Idaho state law requires you to wear a life preserver when floating the river.

For information on outfitters operating the river in Sawtooth NRA, contact the Idaho Outfitters and Guides Associ.,

P.O. Box 95, Boise, ID 83701, phone (208) 342-1438, or the Sawtooth NRA headquarters.

During the winter, Sawtooth NRA is a beautiful winter wonderland. By early December, snow blankets the mountains and forests. Highways 75 and 21 are plowed and open, but all other roads, buildings and campgrounds are closed to automobiles.

Downhill skiing in Sun Valley draws most winter visitors to the area. The winter season is the busiest time for the resort area, but the recreation area remains peaceful and unpeopled.

Winter recreation is the fastest growing activity within Sawtooth National Recreation Area, with more than 55 miles/90 km of groomed cross-country skiing trails. There is limited alpine skiing in the recreation area and then only by helicopter with a guide.

Snowmobiling is also a winter activity in Sawtooth NRA. The Motorized Trail map, available at the headquarters and at rangers stations, provides information on more than 100 miles of groomed snowmobile trails and on areas closed to snowmobiles.

Visitor Services

Within Sawtooth NRA, groceries and supplies can be found in Stanley and Obsidian and at Redfish Lake and Smiley Creek resorts. Stanley also has motels and restaurants; contact the Stanley-Sawtooth Chamber of Commerce at (208) 774-3411 for more information.

Two guest ranches and 3 resorts operate in Sawtooth NRA during the summer. The largest of the resorts is Redfish Lake Lodge, at the north end of Redfish Lake, with cabins and lodge rooms, sailboat rentals, trail rides, pack trips, and a general store and restaurant open to the public.

The Sun Valley resort area is just 9 miles south of Sawtooth NRA and provides a wide range of services. Reservations and information for a number of motels and resorts in the area are available through Sun Valley-Ketchum Chamber Central Reservations, P.O. Box 2420, Sun Valley, ID 83353; phone 1-800-786-8259 or (208) 622-4111.

There are 29 improved campgrounds along the lakes and rivers of the recreation area for a total of 850 campsites. Some have flush toilets and piped water. The most heavily used camps at Redfish, Little Redfish and Alturas lakes fill quickly during the summer.

Public boat ramps are available at all but Pettit Lake. Rental boats, fuel, paddle boats and canoes can be obtained at Redfish Lodge.

Season, Fees and Access

Sawtooth National Recreation Area is open all year. No entrance fees are charged.

Highway access to Sawtooth NRA from Boise over Idaho Highway 21 during summer months is renowned for its scenic beauty. Traveling north from Twin Falls, turn off U.S. Highway 93 at Shoshone on to Idaho Highway 75, then pass through Ketchum and near Sun Valley to reach the Sawtooth NRA boundary. Traveling south from Salmon, turn west off U.S. Highway 93 on to Idaho Highway 75 at Challis and follow the Salmon River west to Stanley. See the SAWTOOTH SCENIC ROUTE section for log of Idaho Highway 75.

For more information, contact Sawtooth National Recreation Area, Star Route, Ketchum, ID 83340; phone (208) 726-7672.

THE ISLANDS

San Juan Islands, Whidbey Island, Vancouver Island, Gulf Islands, Ferries and Cruises

Land meets sea in a flurry of islands along the Northwest Coast. There, where the Pacific Ocean is anything but pacific, lies a cruiser's paradise. The scenic, sheltered waterway called the Inside Passage is "inside" of islands—countless hundreds of them—which take the brunt of the ocean surge and storms. The Northwest's islands range in size from rocks that disappear beneath the highest tides to Whidbey Island, longest in the contiguous United States, and Vancouver Island, the continent's largest on the Pacific Coast.

Ferries serve the major islands, putting them within easy reach. Among those with special appeal to visitors are Washington's jewel-like San Juans, historic Whidbey Island and the lush refuges of Bainbridge and Vashon. The latter 2 are only a half-hour commute from Seattle's urban heart.

Visitors to the Canadian metropolis of Vancouver (on the British Columbia mainland, across the Strait of Georgia from Vancouver Island) are just 2 hours by ferry from Victoria, the provincial capital. That "little bit of England" is just a sample of what Vancouver Island has to offer. Ferries zigzag between the big island, the mainland and the smaller islands in between, including the Gulf Islands.

A triangular route popular with motorists links Seattle, Victoria and Vancouver. Starting in Seattle, drive north to the Washington state ferry terminal at Anacortes. Cruise through the San Juans to Victoria. From Swartz Bay, take a British Columbia ferry through the southern Gulf Islands to Tsawwassen. A drive back to Seattle is the trip's final leg.

Sailing the San Juan Islands is a popular activity in the Northwest. (Jonathon Dodds)

San Juan Islands

The first inhabitants of the San Juan Islands, the Lummi Indians, believed that human life began in a wilderness paradise on San Juan Island and that the land of the islands was truly sacred. In the 1770s and 1780s, Spanish explorers arrived to chart the waters and islands of the archipelago. A look at a map today will establish the importance of these explorers—Lopez de Haro, Jacinto Caamano, Galiano, Valdez, Salvador Fidalgo, Qiumper, Juan de Guemes and others. Later, the English and the Russians began to stake claims in the islands. Finally, with the arrival of George Vancouver in the 1790s to chart the channels and bays, the Russians withdrew.

In 1841, a U.S. expedition led by Capt. John Wilkes established American claim to the islands. British and American rivalry escalated during this period of joint occupancy, culminating in the infamous Pig War which ended with a border settlement in 1872. The islands were finally American.

Today, islanders probably agree with the Lummis that the islands are a wilderness paradise. A moderate climate, friendly people, an easygoing way of life, and lack of hectic traffic (with the exception of the ferry lines) make these tranquil islands an attractive haven for vacationers and sightseers. There are 172 named islands out of 400, (700 islands are counted at high tide), totaling 175 square miles. Fewer than 35 of those are inhabited, and only the 4 biggest—San Juan, Orcas, Lopez and Shaw—can be reached by ferry.

Travelers visit the San Juans via the Washington State Ferry System from Anacortes. Anacortes, on Fidalgo Island, is reached from Exit 230 off Interstate 5 by traveling west about 16 miles on Washington Highway 20 (See **Mile 538** INTERSTATE 5 section). The route to the ferry landing near Anacortes is well marked. Ferries serve Lopez, Shaw, Orcas and San Juan islands as well as Sidney, BC. The islands are a favorite vacation destination, and the ferries can be very crowded during the summer. Long lines and a long wait can be exasperating if you are not prepared. See Ferries and Cruises on page 280 for more information.

A growing number of private tour companies are also offering a variety of cruises to the San Juan Islands. (See Ferries and Cruises this section).

Gray Line of Seattle offers daily bus service from Seattle to the Anacortes ferry terminal. Call (206) 624-5077 for details. Bicycle and car rentals are available on San Juan and Orcas (not located near the ferry docking site).

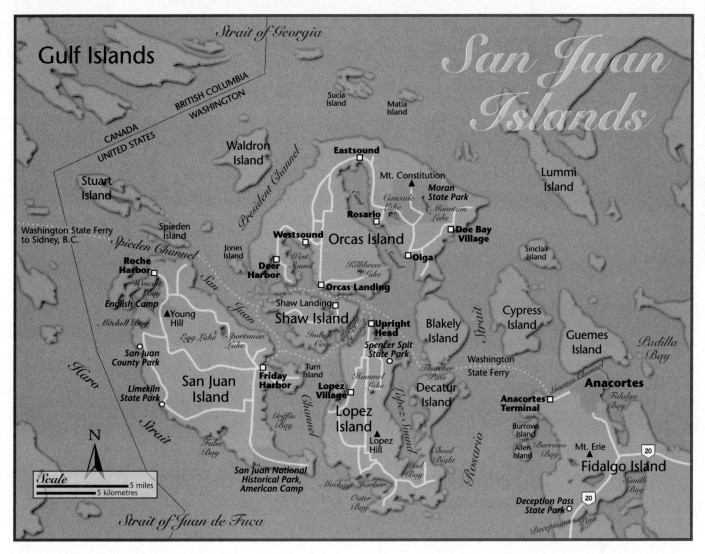

West Isle Air of Anacortes offers direct charters; phone (360) 293-4691. Several others, including Kenmore Air (206/486-8400), connect from major cities such as Seattle and offer inter-island service.

Charters and rentals of private boats may be arranged in Seattle, Anacortes or on the islands themselves for inter-island travel.

Lopez Island

The first stop on the ferry from Anacortes is Lopez Island, a 29-square-mile island of fewer than 3,000 people. Because of its rugged shoreline and lack of good harbors, it is the least visited island among pleasure boaters, but bicyclists find it their favorite because of the rural atmosphere and the lack of tiring hills and busy traffic.

From **UPRIGHT HEAD**, where the ferry lands, it is approximately 1.3 miles to Odlin County Park where there is an old Civil War cannon and a beached boat for kids to play on. The beach is one of the best in the San Juans—great beachcombing.

The hub of activity on Lopez Island is **LOPEZ VILLAGE**, located about 4 miles from the ferry landing. There are stores, the Lopez Village Market grocery, restaurants, a wonderful bakery, a bank, post office, library, medical clinic, pharmacy and a historical museum that features artifacts and photos from Lopez Island's past.

Hummel Lake is a great spot to picnic, swim or fly-fish for stocked rainbow trout. No gas-powered boats are allowed on the lake. Rental bikes are available from two outfits.

Agate Beach is a small public beach on Outer Bay at the south side of Lopez. There are picnic tables, pit toilets and a stairway descending to the beach—a great place to hunt for agates or interesting pieces of driftwood.

Spencer Spit State Park offers the visitor many attractions—clam digging in season (April 1 to June 30, license required), fishing, bicycling, beachcombing, swimming, 25 vehicle-access and 10 walk-in campsites ($11 camping fee, reservations not accepted), restrooms, canoeing and marine views. Spencer Spit is an outstanding example of a sandspit surrounding a saltwater lagoon that has evolved over a long period of time by the action of the wind and surf. There is a sign at the park entrance that explains the geology and ecology of this unique lagoon. The park is closed from Nov. 1 through Feb.; phone (360) 468-2251 for more information.

Lopez Island has a private golf course (located near the airport) open to the public for greens fees.

Shaw Island

The second stop for ferry passengers is Shaw Island, the smallest of the major islands at 8 square miles.

First-time visitors to Shaw Island are surprised to see a nun in her Franciscan habit operating the ferry slip. The nuns also run the island's only store, post office, marina, laundromat and 2 gas pumps. The store is a remarkable old-time general store stocked not only with the usual fare but also with imported cheese, beer and wine, a selection of gifts and baskets, gift wrapping and beautiful greeting cards. It also features herbs and spices grown locally and dried at the Benedictine monastery near the middle of the island.

Shaw is a heavily wooded island with meadows, pastures and orchards. Most of the 17 miles of road are inland, with few views of the water and no access to bays. Because there are no accommodations or restaurants, Shaw gets few visitors.

In the middle of the island where Blind Bay Road intersects with Hoffman Cove Road, there is a "little red schoolhouse." The 1-room schoolhouse with an enrollment of 10 students is listed on the National Register of Historic Places.

Approximately 2 miles from the ferry terminal, at Indian Cove, is Shaw Island County Park, the location of the only public campsites. They are large and situated above South Beach, one of the loveliest sandy beaches in the San Juans. On hot summer days the water of the bay warms enough for swimming.

Landmark Rosario Resort on Orcas Island was built on the Robert Moran estate.

(Courtesy of Rosario Resort)

Orcas Island

The third stop for Washington state ferry passengers, horseshoe-shaped Orcas Island is the largest of the group (56 square miles), though second in population to San Juan Island. The quiet, mood-setting ambiance and the enchanting land and seascape of Orcas Island make this a popular destination for Northwest travelers.

Between the Turtleback Mountains to the west and Mount Constitution rising 2,409 feet to the east are green pastures with sheep and cows, picturesque split-rail fences and rolling hills with forests of fir trees. The 125 miles of saltwater shoreline feature bays and coves with sandy or gravel beaches and sometimes high bluffs. The ferry arrives at **ORCAS LANDING**, a small collection of stores that cater primarily to tourists waiting for the ferry and pleasure boats that stop to fuel up and resupply. Overlooking the ferry landing is the Orcas Hotel, a 3-story Victorian resort built between 1900 and 1904, which is now on the National Register for Historic Places. It was extensively restored in 1985 and once again offers lodging. A bullet hole through one of the veranda posts gives testimony to the escape in the early 1900s of a bank robber who jumped to freedom over the porch railing. Phone (360) 376-4300 for reservations.

An immediate left after debarking from the ferry puts you on the main road of the island, Horseshoe Highway. Follow the highway north 2.5 miles from the ferry landing and turn west on Deer Harbor Road to the community of **WEST SOUND** at the base of 1,500-foot Turtleback Mountain. There is a yacht club, marina and store. Four miles past West Sound is **DEER HARBOR**, a charming town of clapboard buildings that date from the 1890s. The marina, a favorite stopping place for pleasure boaters, provides moorage, fuel, launching, boat rentals, supplies, groceries, gift shops, restaurants, showers, laundry and a swimming pool.

EASTSOUND, located 7 miles from the ferry terminal, has been the main business community of Orcas Island since the 1880s. Some of the original buildings still exist. Outlook Inn, built in 1888, and the beautiful little Emmanuel Episcopal Church, built in 1886, are good examples. Restaurants, shops, galleries, gas stations, a library, bank, theater, medical clinic and lodging are available to the visitor. The Orcas Historical Museum, housed in 6 homestead log cabins, features island pioneer and Indian artifacts collected by Ethan Allan, the county superintendent of schools during the 1900s. The museum is open to visitors Tuesday through Sunday.

Near Eastsound is the turnoff on the right to **ROSARIO**, one of the most outstanding historical landmarks of the San Juans. The estate was built in 1904 by Robert Moran, Seattle mayor and millionaire shipbuilder. When the 47-year-old businessman was told by his doctor that he had 6 months to 2 years to live, he sold everything and bought almost a quarter of the land on Orcas Island and built the mansion. No expense was spared. An organ with 1,972 pipes, installed by Moran, is still used regularly, and visitors can admire the intricate parquet floors, rare hardwood paneling, solid mahogany doors and the imported stained-glass window. All of the original buildings of Rosario are on the National Register of Historic Places. Rosario Resort (phone 360/376-2222) offers 179 rooms in waterfront and hillside villas overlooking Cascade Bay. The 22-acre resort is centered around the historic Moran mansion.

Moran didn't die until age 83. In 1921 he donated 3,600 acres of his land to the state of Washington to be used as a park. Moran State Park is considered one of the finest parks in the state. The park, encompassing nearly 5,000 acres of forest, is open year-round and features 4 campgrounds, 1,800 feet of saltwater shoreline, 5 freshwater lakes, almost 30 miles of hiking trails, 4 waterfalls and the highest peak in the San Juans, Mount Constitution (elev. 2,409 feet). Write ahead for reservations: Moran State Park, Star Route Box 22, Eastsound, WA 98245; phone (360) 376-2326.

Three of the campgrounds are located at Cascade Lake. The lake offers swimming, a boat launch, boat rentals, fishing and windsurfing rentals. There is a picnic area, shelter, ranger station, an interpretive display and a number of hiking trails.

The fourth campground is at Mountain Lake, located off the Mount Constitution Road. It has good trout fishing, boat rentals, boat launch and hiking trails.

Past Cascade Lake less than a mile, a 6-mile-long road ascends to the summit of Mount Constitution. The road is closed after dusk from June through Aug. On the way to the summit is Summit Lake and Little Summit (elev. 2,032 feet) with views that rival the main summit. On top of Mount Constitution is a stone fire lookout and observation tower, built in 1936, which is a reproduction of a 12th century Russian fort. The tower provides spectacular 360-degree views of Canada, the Olympic Mountains, the Cascade Range, the Strait of Juan de Fuca and the San Juan archipelago.

The village of **OLGA** offers the oldest general store on the island, the Olga Cafe, and Orcas Island Artworks Cooperative, featuring work by local artists.

Just south of Olga is Obstruction Pass, 80 acres of Dept. of Natural Resources land that is open to the public. The park offers boating, fishing, hiking, picnicking and beachcombing.

The tiny village of **DOE BAY**, northeast of Olga, offers Doe Bay Village Resort with rustic cabins, camping, store and cafe, mineral-water-fed hot tubs (bathing suits optional) and sauna. The resort is open year-round and reservations are required; phone (360) 376-4755.

Orcas Island also offers a golf course, open to the public for greens fees, located in Crow Valley on the main road between the ferry landing and Eastsound. Eclipse Charters offers charters for whale watching and sightseeing; phone (800) 376-6566. Shear Water Kayaks has several island locations; phone (360) 376-4699.

San Juan Island

Approximately 1½ hours from Anacortes, the ferry calls at Friday Harbor on San Juan Island. (For international sailings, this is the final U.S. stop before sailing on to Sidney, BC, on Vancouver Island.) San Juan Island is the most populated and the "busiest" island in the archipelago. It is an island of forests, meadows, orchards and farmlands that gently slope down to the sea and in some places drop off abruptly from bluffs pounded by the surf.

FRIDAY HARBOR (pop. 1,730) is the county seat of San Juan County. It is also the largest and only incorporated town in the San Juan Islands. A picturesque community of grocery stores, arts and crafts galleries, gift shops, real estate offices, bookstores, fine restaurants, a movie theater and other businesses, Friday Harbor's marina hosts thousands of transient boats each summer from the United States and Canada. In July, the island hosts a 3-day dixieland jazz festival. There are a number of inns and resorts around the town.

Friday Harbor is also the home of the University of Washington Oceanographic laboratories, established in 1903. Scientists from all over the world visit the labs to research marine life in the underwater environment of the islands. The labs also operate a 200-acre biological preserve located on False Bay which is open to the public for walking and beach observation.

There are 2 museums in Friday Harbor. The San Juan Historical Museum is located on Price Street off Spring Street in an 1890s homestead, and is open Wednesday through Saturday from 1 to 4:30 p.m. It features artifacts from pioneer days and the famous Pig War incident. The Whale Museum (62 1st St. N.) is the only museum in the United States strictly devoted to whales. It features a life-size model of an infant humpback and a scale model of an Orca skeleton. There is also a special room for children's activities.

San Juan Island National Historical Park was established to commemorate the settlement of the border dispute between the United States and England in 1872, which was started in 1859 by a shot that killed a pig. It is really 2 separate parks in 2 locations, English Camp and American Camp. Picnic areas and drinking water are available at both camps. There are no campgrounds at either site.

English Camp (520 acres) lies in the tree-sheltered cove known as Garrison Bay, 10 miles northwest of Friday Harbor. The park contains a historic display, a small formal garden and 4 original buildings—barracks, guardhouse, hospital and commissary. Near the barracks is a 300-year-old big-leaf maple, one of the world's largest. A hiking trail starts at the camp and winds up Young Hill past a tiny cemetery where 4 British soldiers are buried. The 680-foot summit provides wonderful views of Haro Strait, Vancouver Island, the Olympic Mountains, the Canadian Gulf Islands, Mount Baker and the Cascade Range.

American Camp (1,222 acres) is on the barren, windswept southeast tip of the island, about 5 miles from Friday Harbor. Two original buildings, an officers' quarters and a laundress' quarters, survive. There is a 0.7-mile interpretive trail starting near the information center that provides a self-guided tour with signs portraying the Pig War history and other features of the park. On some summer weekends there are slide shows, and actors recreate the lives of the soldiers and settlers who lived at the time.

One phenomenon at the park is the extremely large population of rabbits. The loose glacial soil of sand and gravel is ideal for tunneling, and entrances can be seen everywhere. Use caution when walking to avoid stepping into one. Along the interpretive trail the soil has been cut away to reveal the intricate network of tunnels that comprise a rabbit warren. The rabbits, protected from hunting and trapping, are a major food source for the bald eagles, golden eagles, great horned owls and other predatory birds that live on the island.

The only sand dune area in the San Juan Islands is located at Cattle Point. The Dept. of Natural Resources has almost 7 acres with facilities that include toilets, garbage cans, parking lot, and picnic shelter with tables and stove. The Cattle Point Light, a white concrete tower, is perched on the dunes 80 feet above the beach.

ROCHE HARBOR, the one-time site of a Hudson's Bay Co. trading post and the largest lime-producing company west of the Mississippi River, was turned into a first-class resort and marina in the 1950s. One of the largest private pleasure boating marinas in Washington north of Seattle, Roche Harbor attracts thousands of boaters from Canada and the United States. The Hotel de Haro, on the National Register of Historic Sites, hosted many famous people including Presidents Teddy Roosevelt and William Howard Taft. Other points of interest at Roche Harbor include the beautiful formal gardens of the hotel; Our lady of Good Voyage Catholic Church, the only privately owned Catholic church north of Mexico; the Afterglow Vista Mausoleum; the old lime kilns and lime quarry; and the company store which is still in operation. At sunset, there is a traditional flag-lowering ceremony when Canadians and Americans join together to honor their countries.

San Juan Island County Park is located on the west side of the island, 12 miles from Friday Harbor at Smallpox Bay, the site of an Indian village wiped out by smallpox many years ago. The popular 12-acre park is at the head of the bay, with magnificent evening views across Haro Strait to the lights of Vancouver Island. The park has 20 campsites. A tiny log cabin in the campground was built in the early 1900s.

Past San Juan County Park is Lime Kiln Lighthouse, the location of the first Whale Watching Park in the country. Pods of whales passing very near to the rocky shoreline offer whale watchers incredible close-up views. Whale Watch Park is a day-use park with interpretive displays, parking, picnic tables and pit toilets.

Sportsman's Lake (4 miles from Friday Harbor) and nearby Egg Lake are open for swimming and fishing. There is a privately owned campground located at Sportsman's Lake. The marshes surrounding the lakes are ideal for bird watching in the spring.

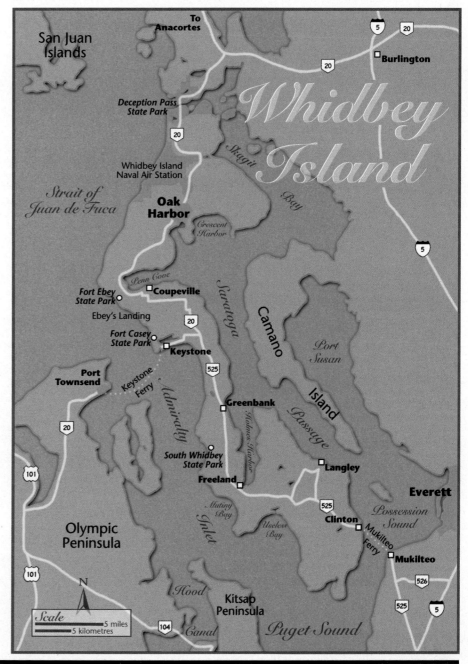

Whidbey Island

It's possible to tour Whidbey Island in one day, but to do so would be a shame. Home to 58,000 people, the longest island in the contiguous United States has much to see: beautiful parks, rich farmlands, bed and breakfast inns, shops for browsing, historical monuments, military installations and a spectacular coastline.

The island lies in the rain shadow of the Olympic range, consequently enjoying more sunshine and less of the rain for which Puget Sound is known. When Capt. George Vancouver visited the island in 1792, he found it densely populated with friendly Skagit Indians. Vancouver named the place for Joseph Whidbey, master of their ship, *Discovery*.

Two Washington state ferry routes serve Whidbey. One runs between Mukilteo (45 minutes north of Seattle) and Clinton, at the island's southern end. The other ferry runs between Port Townsend on the Olympic Peninsula and Keystone, near the island's midpoint. It is possible to tour the island without taking the scenic ferry ride by approaching the island at the north end via Deception Pass bridge on Highway 20.

The main highway that runs the length of the island has 2 designations: Washington Highway 525 between the Clinton ferry dock and the Keystone ferry turnoff (30.5 miles); and Washington Highway 20 from the Keystone ferry turnoff to the north end of the island at Deception Pass (31.5 miles). (Highway 20 begins at the junction with U.S. 101, 13 miles south of Port Townsend. From the Keystone ferry dock to the junction with Highway 525 it is 3.5 miles.) Roads off the main highway invite exploration of coves and beaches. There are several campgrounds on the island and many bed-and-breakfast inns around the island if you want to make more than a day trip out of a visit. For island information, contact the Greater Oak Harbor Chamber of Commerce at P.O. Box 883-11, Oak Harbor, WA 98277; phone (360) 675-3535; or phone the Central Whidbey Chamber of Commerce at (360) 678-5434. For bus service information, phone Island Transit at (360) 678-7771.

LANGLEY (pop. 959), at the southeast end of the island, is known for its small-town atmosphere and upscale shops. The Choochokam arts-and-crafts festival in July and the Island County Fair in August draw crowds, but otherwise Langley is a nice uncrowded place to browse. The elegant Inn at Langley serves gourmet dinners (reservations only) in a beautiful, cedar-shingled building. Open Friday and Saturday nights year-round and Sunday nights the end of May through Sept.; phone (360) 221-3033 for reservations. For those on a smaller budget, the Dog House reputedly has the best burgers on the island. Langley has several bed-and-breakfast inns.

Near Greenback, mid-island, are the red barns of Whidbey's Greenback Farm, the Chateau Ste. Michelle Winery that grows loganberries to make Whidbey's Liqueur.

Adjacent to the Keystone-Port Townsend ferry dock is Fort Casey State Park and the picturesque farmlands of the Ebey's Landing National Historical Reserve just beyond. The Fort Casey area, along with Ebey's Landing and prairie, the town of Coupeville and other sites around Penn Cove (together encompassing more than 17,000 acres), make up the historical reserve. The reserve was named for Colonel Issac Ebey, who was killed by Haida Indians in 1857. Today this reserve provides a living record of the 19th century exploration and settlement of Puget Sound and houses 91 nationally registered historic structures.

Established in the 1890s, Fort Casey became one of the string of gun emplacements that guarded Puget Sound through WWII. The fortifications and underground bunkers are open for exploring. Admiralty Head Lighthouse at the park is now a small museum. From the top of the tower are sweeping views across the inlet and the Strait of Juan de Fuca.

COUPEVILLE (pop. 1,550), the government center for Island County, is the most historically-rich town on the island. Some of its early character is present in the main street's wooden storefronts now filled with souvenir and antique shops, restaurants and boutiques. Perched on the shore of Penn Cove, Coupeville is the second-oldest town in the state and home of the Island County Historical Museum. Many of the town's Victorian homes have been restored. Coupeville also offers hospital services.

OAK HARBOR (pop. 19,421), the largest city on the island, has all traveler services. Two public golf courses are open to visitors. Oak Harbor was named for the many Garry oaks that grew to great size in this area. Many sea captains and their families settled here to be within sight of the water. In the 1850s Irish settlers dominated the area, but in the 1890s Hollanders came from Michigan and the Dakotas. In 1941, the Navy arrived to build the Whidbey Island Naval Air Station, which comprises much of the island's population.

At the north tip of the island on Highway 20 is Deception Pass State Park and Deception Pass bridge. Deception Pass is a treacherous channel separating Whidbey and Fidalgo islands, with tiny Pass Island in the middle of the channel. Swirling water and spectacular views of the sea and distant islands make this a favorite picnic, camping and beach-combing spot. It is also one of the most photographed sites in the state. A good vantage point is afforded by Deception Pass bridge, where there is ample parking and restroom facilities. Deception Pass State Park actually spans the channel, encompassing beaches and forests on Whidbey and Fidalgo islands, with 30 miles of hiking trails and 3 freshwater lakes. The park has 251 campsites, picnic tables, stoves, bathhouse, dump station, handicap-accessible restrooms, fire pits, seasonally-operated concession stands, and swimming, fishing and scuba diving. Phone (360) 675-2417.

North of Deception Pass a spur road off Highway 20 leads 4.5 miles to Anacortes on Fidalgo Island, departure point for Washington state ferries to the San Juan Islands. Main Highway 20 continues east 11.5 miles to junction with Interstate 5 (see **Mile 538**, Exit 230 in the INTERSTATE 5 section) at Burlington. Washington Highway 20 continues east as the North Cascades Highway (see the NORTH CASCADES HIGHWAY section).

Dramatic Deception Pass bridge at the head of Whidbey Island.
(© Jay Peery)

The Gulf Islands

Lying on the windward side of Vancouver Island, the Gulf Islands receive only a third of the rainfall the west coast of Vancouver Island receives. Of the approximately 200 islands, relatively few are inhabited and most do not have ferry service. The most populated islands are Galiano, Mayne, the Penders, Salt Spring and Saturna in the southern Georgia Strait. All may be reached by ferry service from Tsawwassen and from Swartz Bay (see Ferries and Cruises this section).

Other Gulf Islands farther north in the Strait of Georgia are reached from ferry terminals along the east side of Vancouver Island. These include Cortes, Denman, Gabriola, Hornby and Quadra. (See the Vancouver Island map).

The Gulf Islands attract those who welcome a slower pace. Much of island life is water-oriented, but farming is also a mainstay of the economy, and there are miles of rural roads to explore on some islands. A significant percentage of the resident population are retirees, although the people who live here represent a wide variety of occupations and lifestyles.

The larger islands in the southern Gulfs attract day-trippers with bicycles or cars, weekenders who may stay at the seaside resorts or bed-and-breakfast establishments, and vacationers who scatter to the relatively few camping spots on the islands. Many artists and artisans make the islands their home, and a popular pastime is shopping for their wares.

Not all of the islands offer overnight accommodations, and the ferry schedule is complex. Visitors are advised to avoid island-hopping without first determining that they can either stay on the other side or hop back.

Following are some of the more populated islands in the Gulfs, from south to north.

Saltspring Island

Saltspring Island, the largest and most populous of the Gulf Islands, with all tourist facilities available, was the first thriving agricultural settlement in the colony of Vancouver Island. Sheep farming became important, and Saltspring lamb is an internationally known gourmet specialty.

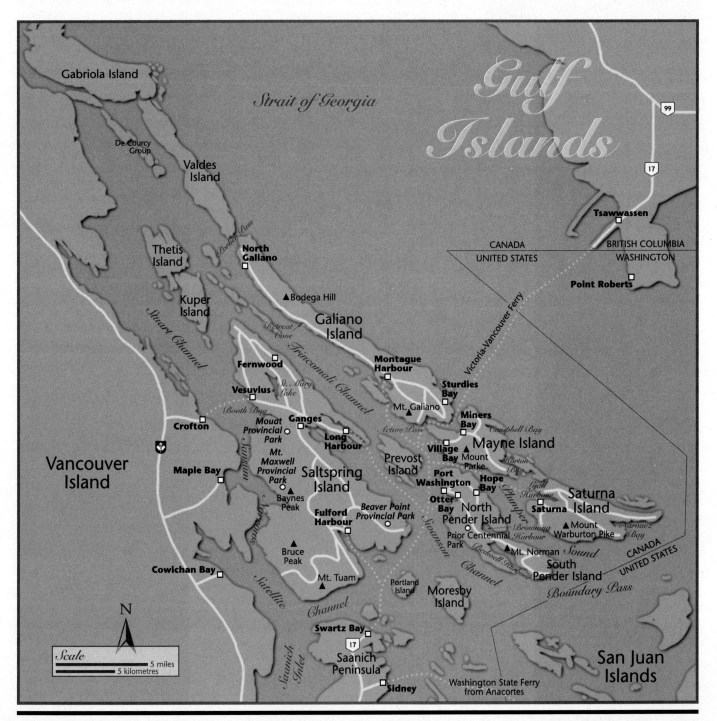

Sheep farming is important on Saltspring Island, largest of Canada's Gulf Islands.

A 40-mile trip around the island can start or end at any of the 3 ferry terminals. Ferries from Tsawwassen on the mainland dock at Long Harbour, outside Ganges, the largest village. Ferries from Swartz Bay (on Vancouver Island near Victoria) dock at Fulford Harbour. Ferries from Crofton (near Duncan on Vancouver Island) dock at Vesuvius Bay, near St. Mary Lake, the largest body of fresh water in the Gulfs.

Attractions on Saltspring include the Farmers' Market in **GANGES** on Saturday mornings, arts and crafts galleries, Hastings House (a well-known luxury inn), and many pleasant resorts on saltwater beaches around St. Mary Lake. The island has many bed-and-breakfast establishments and several English pubs that serve good lunches and snacks. St. Paul's Church in Fulford Harbour was built around 1880, and the second-oldest school in British Columbia still stands in Beaver Point Provincial Park. Beaver Point has camping, hiking and beachcombing.

One of the nicest places to sample the atmosphere of the Gulf Islands is from the meadows of Ruckle Provincial Park, a sheep farm operated by the Ruckle family who homesteaded here in 1872.

The drive up Baynes Peak in Mount Maxwell Provincial Park has great views of the islands and mainland.

Mayne Island

Mayne Island is popular with cyclists because of its quiet, paved country roads and absence of hills. There are about 19 miles of main road on the island. The ferry docks at Village Bay, but Miners Bay is the centre of activity. Named for the throngs of fortune-seekers who stopped there on the way from Victoria to the goldfields, Miners Bay welcomes visitors and pulses with life during the summer pleasure-boat season. The government wharf is a good vantage point for watching marine traffic in Active Pass, a major transportation route through turbulent waters. All tourist facilities are available.

Mayne is a mixture of old and new, with century-old mansions standing side-by-side with homes straight from modern suburbia. Many of the original farms are still in operation, including Hardscrabble Farm with its blue-roofed farmhouse, visible from Fernhill Road. Other attractions are Bennett Bay Beach (the best on this island), and turn-of-the-century buildings that include the Plumper Pass Lockup (1896), now the Mayne Island Museum, St. Mary Magdalene Church (1898) and Active Pass Lighthouse (1885).

Pender Islands

North and South Pender islands are joined by a bridge that spans a canal between Bedwell and Browning harbours. Before the federal government dredged the canal to provide access from one harbour to another, boats had to be carried across a wide neck of land called Indian Portage. In recent years an archaeological dig here unearthed artifacts dating back 10,000 years.

The Penders are known for their many secluded coves and beaches accessible to visitors, and for the number of artists and artisans who live here. A gallery of their work is in an old schoolhouse at the top of the hill as you leave Hope Bay on Bedwell Harbour Road. There is another craft store at Port Washington. Other attractions are the picturesque barns, turn-of-the-century mansions, and country stores. The ferry docks at Otter Bay. Camping is available at Prior Centennial Park. Other accommodations can be found at inns, resorts and bed-and-breakfast homes.

Galiano Island

Scenic Galiano Island is long and slender, sheltering many of the other islands from the winds of Georgia Strait. Nearly ¾ of the land is a tree farm of fir and cedar. Ferries from the mainland, Vancouver Island and other Gulf Islands dock at Sturdies Bay where lodging, stores, gas and an information centre are found. Up the road from the ferry terminal at Sturdies Bay is Bluff Drive, with a good viewpoint for marine traffic in Active Pass. Two miles beyond is Active Pass Road with a small, well-kept cemetery where early settlers are buried. A few feet out from the beach is a marker on Collision Reef where the ferry *Queen of Alberni* ran aground in 1979. Several ancient Indian village sites have been found on this island.

Saturna Island

Saturna Island, the most southerly of the Gulf Islands, is sparsely populated, and accommodations are limited. The BC Ferry terminal is located at Lyall Harbour and is serviced by ferries from Swartz Bay, and Mayne and Galiano islands. There is no direct connection with the mainland. Inter-island connections are infrequent, so check schedules carefully. There are no public campgrounds on the island.

Saturna Island is known for its Lamb Barbecue on the July 1 holiday weekend. An old-fashioned country fair, crafts sale, games and a beer garden keep visitors entertained until the lamb (barbecued whole over an open pit) is served in mid-afternoon. Other attractions include beautiful Winter Cove Provincial Park, the historic East Point Lighthouse (1888), and Mount Wharburton Pike, the second-highest peak in the Gulfs.

Gabriola Island

Accessible by car and passenger ferry from downtown Nanaimo to Descanso Bay, Gabriola is the second largest of the southern Gulf Islands. It is known unofficially as Petroglyph Island because of the large number of ancient Indian stone carvings

Sea kayaking is one way to experience the islands of the Northwest. (Joe Hofbeck)

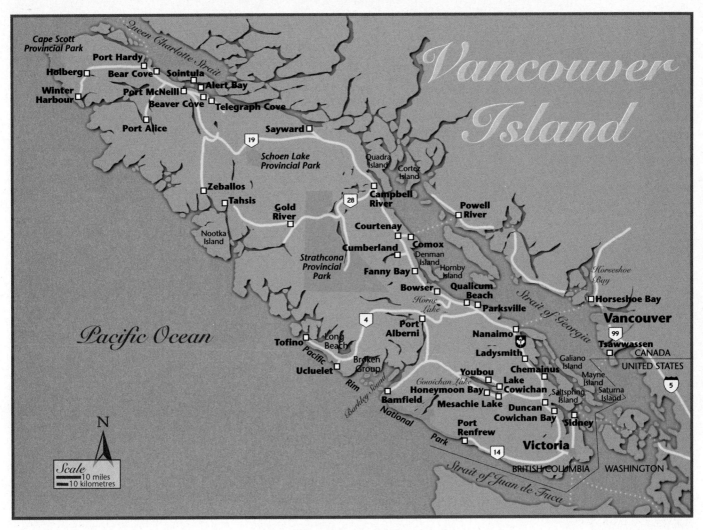

found here. The best-known petroglyph, that of a killer whale, is found by the shore at Degnen Bay. At nearby Weldwood, more than 50 separate motifs have been discovered under a carpet of thick moss. Other petroglyph sites are at Jack Point and Lock Bay. The only sizable community on the island is Gabriola, which has most services.

Gabriola Sands Provincial Park, on the north end of the island, is known for its expansive beaches; nearby are the Malaspina Galleries—wave-washed, eroded sandstone ledges. Drumbeg Provincial Park, on the south end, has a small sandy beach and sandstone shelves. Neither park provides camping.

Quadra Island

Accessible by a short ferry ride from Campbell River, Quadra Island is known for its sportfishing and for the Kwakiutl Museum in Yaculta Indian Village on the Cape Mudge Reserve. Built in the form of a sea snail, the museum houses heritage potlatch goods seized by the government when this traditional ceremony was decreed illegal and only returned to the band in the early 1980s. The totem poles, ceremonial masks and tribal costumes are truly priceless. The museum is open daily, July to Sept., and Tuesday to Saturday the rest of the year. Across from the museum is a small park containing petroglyph boulders moved from their original beach location to protect them

from vandalism and water erosion.

There are 2 settlements on Quadra Island: at Quathiaski Cove, where the Campbell River ferry docks; and at Heriot Bay, where another ferry connects with Cortes Island. There are plenty of accommodations on the island, including commercial campsites, lodges and cottages. Highlights include hiking up Chinese Mountain for the view; visiting the Lucky Jim mine ruins; photographing Cape Mudge Lighthouse; and fishing or canoeing on island lakes or in the ocean.

Rebecca Spit Provincial Park on the east side of Drew Harbour, has fine sandy beaches and plenty of picnic tables, walking trails and a boat launch. Just off the northeast coast of Quadra are the Octopus Islands, a wilderness marine park for fishing, swimming, boating and scuba diving.

Denman Island

Denman Island, separated from Vancouver Island by narrow Baynes Sound, is accessible by ferry from Buckley Bay (about midway between Qualicum Beach and Courtenay on Vancouver Island). The rural, unspoiled island is surrounded by rocky and gravel shores, good for clams, crabs and oysters. The village has a store, gas station, restaurant and guesthouses. Island artists weave, make pottery and other handicrafts.

Accessible on foot during low tides or by boat, Sandy Island Provincial Marine Park is

just off the northwest coast for wilderness beach camping and beachcombing. Near the ferry dock is Fillongley Provincial Park with 10 campsites and a good oyster beach. Walk to Boyle Point for a good view of Chrome Island lighthouse.

Hornby Island

Hornby Island lies just off the southern toe of Denman Island and is reached only by ferry from Gravelly Bay on Denman Island to Shingle Spit on Hornby. A good spot for watching eagles and marine mammals is Helliwell Provincial Park. There are colonies of nesting birds along the cliffs, a 3-mile/5-km hiking trail, and huckleberry picking on forested headland. If you want sandy beaches and safe, warm swimming, try Tribune Bay Provincial Park at the southeast end of the island. No camping allowed in the parks. Supplies and gas are available at the ferry dock, Ford's Cove, and at the co-op store in the island centre. Some accommodations are available in bed-and-breakfast homes.

Cortes Island

Cortes Island, a large island with an intricate shoreline, lies at the entrance to Desolation Sound, perhaps British Columbia's best-known boating destination. The island can be reached by ferry from Heriot Bay on Quadra Island. Roads lead from the ferry

Top—Spirit of British Columbia *serves the Swartz Bay–Tsawwassen ferry route.* (Courtesy of BC Ferries) **Above**—*Whale watching trips are popular off Vancouver Island, as well as in the San Juans.* (Courtesy of Tourism Victoria)

and water service connect major towns and other key points along the coast. The Esquimalt and Nanaimo Railway operates a daily passenger dayliner between Victoria and Courtenay, with 19 stops along the way; phone (604) 383-4324. Island Coach Lines operates buses between Victoria, Nanaimo, Port Alberni, Campbell River and Port Hardy (with connections to the BC ferry *Queen of the North* at Bear Cove); phone (604) 385-4411.

The backbone of the island is the Insular Mountain Range that runs the island's length. Its jagged, snowy peaks punctuate the skyline, contrasting with the greens and blues of forest and sea. The mountains are at their most impressive midway up the island at Strathcona Provincial Park.

West of the mountains the climate is stormy and the coastline rugged. The open ocean, beautiful scenery, picturesque settlements and Pacific Rim National Park are major attractions for visitors here. Settlement has gravitated toward the island's sheltered, sunnier eastern side. Most of the people live in a narrow strip along the east-facing coast, half of them clustered around Victoria. Trans-Canada Highway 1 and BC Highway 19 run north from Victoria to Port Hardy, linking major communities along the way (see THE ISLAND HIGHWAY this section for log). In addition, several very good east-west roads span the island's 62-mile width.

Forestry is a major industry with much of the land under lease to timber companies. Agriculture, fishing and mining (of coal and even gold) were early contributors to the island's development. Farming and fishing remain important, but mining has played out. Now recreation and tourism are significant elements in the economy.

Britain's Capt. Cook, who landed on the island's west shore in 1778, was the first European visitor. Fur traders followed, and Vancouver Island came under the influence of the Hudson's Bay Co. Victoria became the company's headquarters in 1843 and grew to be the economic hub of the region and eventually, capital of British Columbia.

The island today has more than 50 provincial parks; public and private campgrounds abound. A list of hotels, motels, lodges, trailer parks and campgrounds on the island is available free from Tourism British Columbia; ask for the current *Accommodations Guide*. The same agency offers a free *British Columbia Road Map and Parks Guide*, which includes a summary of all provincial park facilities. Phone 1-800-663-6000.

Recreational opportunities on the island range from whale watching to antique hunting, from salmon fishing to sunbathing on sandy beaches, from the most rugged backpacking to the most civilized taking of crumpets and tea.

If you look at a map of Vancouver Island, you can see why most of the settlements and the roads concentrate along the eastern shore. The western side of the island, exposed to the full brunt of the open Pacific, is steep, rugged and tortuous, fretted with long, deep and sinuous fjords that make land access difficult. By contrast, the eastern shore faces the sheltered waters of the Inside Passage, and it is smooth and gently sloped, with miles of sandy beaches.

dock at Whaletown to Manson's Landing and Squirrel Cove, a well-known anchorage facing Desolation South.

Some accommodations, supplies and gas can be found at the 3 settlements. Camping is available at Smelt Bay Provincial Park on the island's southwestern tip where tens of thousands of smelt come to spawn. Manson's Landing Provincial Marine Park has freshwater and saltwater fishing, swimming and a good sandy beach.

Vancouver Island

Beautiful Vancouver Island lies just off the Northwest coast at the border between the United States and Canada, its southern tip extending below the 49th parallel. The rest of its 282-mile length runs northwesterly, sheltering smaller islands on the landward side.

Both ships and planes link Vancouver Island with the mainland. Connecting points in the United States include Seattle (for scheduled air service; Clipper Navigation's *Victoria Clipper*, a jet-propelled passenger-only catamaran; and Victoria Line's *Royal Victorian* vehicle ferry), Anacortes (for Washington state ferries), and Port Angeles (for the *Victoria Express* and Black Ball Transport's MV *Coho*). All dock in or near Victoria. For more information, see Ferries and Cruises, this section.

Air Canada (604/360-9074), Canadian Airlines International (604/382-6111) and Air B.C. (604/360-9074) fly from the mainland to Victoria. Helijet Airways schedules flights between downtown Vancouver and downtown Victoria; phone (604) 273-1414 for reservations. British Columbia ferries run between Tsawwassen (south of Vancouver) and Swartz Bay (just north of Victoria), from Horseshoe Bay (west of Vancouver) to Nanaimo, and from mainland Powell River to Comox. British Columbia ferries also run between Port Hardy (at the north end of Vancouver Island) and Prince Rupert (on the mainland farther north). Pacific Coach Lines (604/385-4411) operates buses between Vancouver and Victoria via BC Ferries.

Within Vancouver Island, rail, bus, air

The Island Highway
Trans-Canada Highway 1/BC Highway 19

Trans-Canada Highway 1 and BC Highway 19 together provide continuous access up the east coast from Victoria to Port Hardy, a distance of about 300 miles/500 km. Considered as a whole, the highway provides a stimulating contrast between the settled and domesticated south and the wilderness of the north. Up the island as far as Campbell River, the road threads its scenic way between a string of resort communities that are famous for recreational fishing and boating in the island-sprinkled waters of the Strait of Georgia. But north of Campbell River, the highway forges away from the coast to provide a lonely, austerely beautiful route through the forested heartland before reaching the north coast communities of Port McNeil and Port Hardy. Port Hardy is the terminus for the BC ferry route to Prince Rupert and points north.

Mile 0 (315) Km 0 (507): **Junction** of Trans-Canada Highway 1 and BC Highway 17, just north of downtown Victoria at Mayfair Shopping Centre. Highway 17 branches off to Saanich and the BC Ferries Swartz Bay Ferry Terminal north of Sidney.

Mile 1 (314) Km 1.5 (505.5): Tillicum Road south; Glanford Avenue north. Take Glanford for an unhurried route to the Dominion Astrophysical Observatory and Butchart Gardens.

Mile 2.5 (312.5) Km 4 (503): View of Portage Inlet. **VIEW ROYAL** (pop. 4,959), incorporated in 1988.

Mile 4 (311) Km 6.5 (500.5): Exit for Highway 1A to Colwood, Fort Rodd Hill, Sooke and along the West Coast Road (Highway 14) to Port Renfrew and the start of the West Coast Trail in Pacific Rim National Park.

Mile 4.5 (310.5) Km 7 (500): Exit to Thetis Lake Regional Park and Nature Sanctuary. A large natural forest park laced with hiking trails. The horseshoe-shaped lake with sandy beaches is popular for swimming, canoeing and fishing for trout and bass. Colorful chart illustrates 32 varieties of wildflowers to look for in the sanctuary.

Mile 6.5 (308.5) Km 10.5 (496.5): District of Langford. Tourist Information Centre. Fun centre (open seasonally).

Mile 9 (306) Km 14.5 (492.5): Sooke Lake Road to Goldstream Provincial Park with 150 vehicle/tent sites, showers, sani-station. There is a fee. Visitor Centre has interpretive programs June through Aug. The forested park is named for the Goldstream River, which witnessed a brief flurry of gold mining activity in 1863. Some of the park trails are old

Inner Harbour in downtown Victoria at the southern tip of Vancouver Island. (Courtesy of Tourism Victoria)

prospectors' paths, and one leads to an old gold mine. The river was important to the native Coast Salish Indians and still supports a large fall salmon run. Naturalists enjoy the diversity of the forest that ranges from the dry Arbutus and Garry oaks at the higher elevations to the near rain forest conditions with 600-year-old Douglas firs and red cedars.

Mile 9.5 (305.5) Km 15.5 (491.5): South end of Malahat Drive, a scenic stretch of highway that climbs high above Saanich Inlet. This road was originally a trail cut across the bluffs to get cattle to the Victoria market. It became a wagon road in 1884 and a narrow paved highway in 1911. It is now a 4-lane superhighway, but the views are still magnificent. Malahat is Indian for "the place where one gets bait."

Mile 10.5 (304.5) Km 17 (490): Finlayson Arm Road to east, entrance to Goldstream Day-Use Picnic Area and Visitor Centre. 0.2 mile/0.3 km to north along highway is trail access to Niagara Falls and canyon. To the east, a good view down to the head of Finlayson Arm.

Mile 16.5 (298.5) Km 26.5 (480.5): Turnoff for the south end of Shawnigan Lake (4.5 miles/7 km), a summer cottage area and provincial park for picnicking, swimming, fishing and waterskiing. Memory Island, accessible by boat only, has good walking trails, picnicking, and excellent bird watching. No camping permitted.

Mile 17 (298) Km 27.5 (479.5): Exit to Spectacle Lake Provincial Park, 1.2 miles/2 km, with picnic tables, hiking trails, fishing for rainbow trout, swimming at small beach. You can hike around the lake in less than 1 hour.

Mile 17.5 (297.5) Km 28.5 (478.5): Malahat Summit (elev. 1,156 feet/ 352m). Parking for view of Saanich Inlet and peninsula and, if it's clear, the mountains on the mainland. The most spectacular peak is Mount Baker in Washington state.

Mile 19 (296) Km 30.5 (476.5): Arbutus rest area.

Mile 19.5 (295.5) Km 31.5 (475.5): Viewpoint with spectacular views.

Mile 21.5 (293.5) Km 34.5 (472.5): North end of Malahat Drive. Look for golden broom in bloom along the road in May and June, a legacy of early British settlers. Exit east to Bamberton Provincial Park overlooking Finlayson Arm. There is a developed sandy beach, swimming, fishing, 50 campsites; fee.

Also south access road to small car ferry across Saanich Inlet to Brentwood Bay. Several sailings daily.

Mile 24.5 (290.5) Km 39.5 (467.5): Community of Mill Bay and a travel information centre. North access road to Brentwood Bay ferry.

Mile 25 (290) Km 40.5 (466.5): Road to Shawnigan Lake, 3 miles/5 km east. Roads encircle the lake and connect with forestry roads to Port Renfrew, west about 40 miles/64 km,

The Island Highway (continued)

The wild west coast of Vancouver Island is accessible from the main highway via 4 different spur roads. (Joe Hofbeck)

and south to Milne's Landing on Highway 14. Check condition and public accessibility of these roads before attempting travel; some of these roads are active logging roads.

Mile 29.5 (285.5) Km 47.5 (459.5): Junction with road west to community of Cobble Hill, founded in 1868 and known for its fall fair; and road east to Cowichan Bay and a section of the Old Island Highway, an alternate route which hugs the shore and returns to the highway at **Mile 34.5/Km 55.5.**

COWICHAN BAY (pop. 3,358) is home to the Cowichan band of the Coast Salish Indians, who are famous for their hand-knit sweaters crafted from local raw fleece with traditional Scottish family crest designs. The Indians were taught how to knit by Scottish settlers who arrived here in 1862. The community is also a prime sportfishing centre providing complete facilities.

Mile 32 (283) Km 51.5 (455.5): Road west to Cowichan Station; east to Cowichan Bay.

Mile 33 (282) Km 53 (454): Whippletree Junction, a collection of 14 restored old buildings, many from Duncan's old Chinatown, reassembled around a village square to form a colourful year-round tourist market with restaurants, antique stores, and souvenir and craft shops.

Mile 34.5 (280.5) Km 55.5 (451.5): Road to Cowichan Bay and bridge over the Koksilah River. Nearby is a farmer's market and stores selling Cowichan Indian sweaters and other crafts.

Mile 35.5 (279.5) Km 57 (450): Koksilah tree nursery of B.C. Forest

Products. Duncan City limits.

Mile 36 (279) Km 58 (449): The Silver Bridge over Cowichan River is famous for its fighting brown trout. Some sections of the river are for flyfishing only. The Cowichan River footpath provides continuous access upstream for 19 miles/31 km. Canoeing and kayaking also on this river. Just north of the bridge is the turnoff west to the Native Heritage Centre, featuring native crafts and demonstrations.

Mile 36.5 (278.5) Km 59 (448): Entering DUNCAN (pop. 4,539), the major business centre for the Cowichan Valley, dubbed the City of Totems. At last count, 22 totems stand alongside the highway and in the downtown area, all the work of local native carvers. The Cowichan Valley Museum displays period memorabilia and books on local history, and is open Monday to Saturday, June through Sept.; Thursday through Saturday, Oct. through May.

Mile 38.5 (276.5) Km 62 (445): BC Forest Museum. Spread throughout 100 acres of woodland and meadows beside Somenos Lake is a living history of the forest industry, complete with a working sawmill and planer mill, blacksmith's shop, logging camp and heavy machinery. Visitors can ride a narrow-gauge steam train that crosses a spindly wooden trestle over the lake. Open May to Sept.

Mile 39.5 (275.5) Km 63.5 (443.5): Junction with Highway 18 east 17 miles/28 km to the community of LAKE COWICHAN (pop. 2,170). Lake Cowichan is at the eastern end of Cowichan Lake, one of the island's largest lakes. Paved roads run north

along the lake to the logging community of Youbou and south to Mesachie Lake and Honeymoon Bay, which has a wildflower reserve. Logging roads complete the lake circuit and continue through the forest to the West Coast communities of Port Renfrew and Bamfield, trailhead for Pacific Rim National Park's West Coast Trail. It is 51 miles/83 km from the west end of Cowichan Lake to Bamfield via unpaved logging road.

Along the road to Youbou is the Teleglobe Canada Satellite Earth Station, 1 of 5 major transmission stations in Canada that pass data back and forth from space. The facility is open to the public from mid-June to early Sept.

Cowichan Lake offers good fishing for rainbow, cutthroat trout or Dolly Varden; also water sports. Gordon Bay Provincial Park, along the lake's southern shore, has 131 campsites (fee April to Oct.), sani-station, boat launch, and excellent swimming beach. Cowichan is the Indian word for "the warm land."

Mile 44 (271) Km 71 (436): Mount Sicker Road to the pulp mill and fishing town of Crofton and the BC car ferry to Vesuvius on Saltspring Island. Ferries run hourly but only until 6:30 p.m. Saltspring, the largest of the Gulf Islands, is also serviced by ferries from Tsawwassen and Swartz Bay. (See Gulf Islands, this section.)

Mile 44.5 (270.5) Km 71.5 (435.5): Chemainus River bridge. Just north of the bridge, the old Island Highway (1A) follows the shore around to the town of Chemainus. The road rejoins Highway 1 just south of Ladysmith.

CHEMAINUS, (pop. 3,900), was a sawmill town until the early 1980s when the mill closed and citizens faced an uncertain future. The town has succeeded in attracting tourists by turning the walls of downtown buildings into an open-air art gallery. Twenty-four huge, colourful murals depict the area's history. Giant yellow footprints painted on the sidewalks provide a walking tour to the various exhibits. Art galleries, craft shops, restaurants and other tourist facilities abound.

Car ferries leave Chemainus for the tiny islands of Kuyper, a native Indian reservation, and Thetis.

Mile 53.5 (261.5) Km 86 (421): LADYSMITH (pop. 4,875) is a town that has the distinction of lying exactly on the 49th Parallel. Once a coal port for the mines at Nanaimo, the town has been restoring its heritage buildings. Transfer Beach Park offers summer swimming, playground and picnicking.

The Island Highway (continued)

Mile 58.5 (256.5) Km 94 (413): Yellow Point Road east for excellent ocean beach access, fine resorts, campgrounds, and the Crow and Gate, an authentic English pub overlooking Stuart Channel. Small Quennell Lake provides good fishing, and its intricate shoreline makes for interesting canoe trips. Roberts Memorial Provincial Park has a sandstone beach, perfect for picnics and glimpses of sea lions in March and April. Yellow Point Road returns to Highway 1 at **Mile 65.5/Km 105.5.**

Mile 59 (256) Km 95 (412): The unincorporated town of Cassidy.

Mile 60 (255) Km 96.5 (410.5): Spitfire Road to Nanaimo Airport.

Mile 60.5 (254.5) Km 97.5 (409.5): Nanaimo River bridge. The river, a favorite with sport-fishermen, is the site of a government salmonid enhancement project. It's also become a favorite spot for the daring sport of bungy jumping, with North America's first Bungy bridge over the Nanaimo River.

Mile 61 (254) Km 98 (409): Roadside rest area.

Mile 61.5 (253.5) Km 99 (408): Exit to South Wellington and the Nanaimo Lakes.

Mile 65.5 (249.5) Km 105.5 (410.5): North end of loop road to Yellow Point and beaches.

Mile 67 (248) Km 108 (399): Petroglyph Provincial Park. Short woodland trail leads to a large area of sloping bedrock covered with native carvings believed to be about 1,000 years old. Park sign indicates location of other petroglyph sites in the vicinity.

Mile 68.5 (246.5) Km 110.5 (396.5): **Junction** to Nanaimo city centre and ferries to Gabriola and Newcastle Islands. **NANAIMO** (pop. 60,129), the second-largest city on Vancouver Island, was originally the site of 5 Indian villages gathered at a place called "Snenymo," which means "big strong people." The Hudson's Bay Co. established a settlement here in 1852 to work the nearby coal deposits, and soon Nanaimo became the largest coal producer on the Pacific Coast. The original Hudson's Bay Co. bastion, erected as a defence against possible Indian raids, still stands near the waterfront and is a well-known landmark. During the summer months at noon every day, the Bastion Guards, in 19th-century uniforms, fire the old cannon.

In the downtown area, a scenic waterfront promenade overlooks the harbour, offering strollers a great view. Nanaimo is an important deep-sea port and its harbour is always a hub of activity. Sportfishing is good for salmon, cod and red snapper.

Nanaimo is well-endowed with parks, including Newcastle Island, accessible by passenger ferry. This island was the site of the first coal mines worked by the Hudson's Bay Co., and it was named for the coal mining town in England. It was later purchased by the Canadian Pacific Railway, which turned it into a pleasure island, complete with teahouse, soccer field, dance pavilion and floating hotels. It was turned over to the city in 1955. Today the island is a nature reserve with abundant bird and animal life. There are campsites, picnic tables, good beaches, boat anchorage and a marvellous network of walking trails. Sea caves along the north and west shores were used for ancient ritual burials.

The third Sunday in July is Nanaimo's big day, the annual Bathtub Race across the 30 miles/48 km of Georgia Strait to Vancouver. The race attracts competitors from around the world. For more information on the community and its events, contact the Nanaimo Infocentre, phone (604) 754-8474, fax (604) 754-6468.

Mile 69 (246) Km 111 (396): South exit for Departure Bay ferry. Car and passenger ferries leave hourly for Horseshoe Bay, north of Vancouver on the BC mainland. Highway 19, the Island Highway, begins here.

Mile 70.5 (244.5) Km 113.5 (393.5): North exit to ferry via Departure Bay Road.

Mile 73.5 (241.5) Km 118.5 (388.5): Rest area beside Long Lake.

Mile 75.5 (239.5) Km 121.5 (385.5): Hammond Bay Road to Piper's Lagoon (good bird watching) and the Pacific Biological Station, established in 1908 for researching the management of the Pacific fisheries.

Mile 76.5 (238.5) Km 123 (384): South end of loop road to Lantzville, a small seaside community with a good sandy beach. Ada Islands offshore are wintering grounds for hundreds of sea lions.

The coastal highway from Nanaimo to Campbell River links together a string of resort communities, each with its own particular appeal. Most have facilities for fishing and boating, comfortable accommodations, including bed-and-breakfast homes and good restaurants. Another British import, the teahouse, is growing in numbers and popularity on this part of the island. All of these serve the traditional English tea of sand-

Nanaimo Bars

No one can verify that these delicious 3-layer confections originated in Nanaimo, BC, but the community's tourism department has claimed them as its own and even hands out an official Nanaimo bar recipe. For those culinary-inclined readers, here is the official Ultimate Nanaimo Bar Recipe courtesy of Tourism Nanaimo. (Substitutes or U.S. equivalents are given in parenthesis courtesy of Northwest Mileposts® reader Shirley Weisgerber.)

The Ultimate Nanaimo Bar Recipe

1/2 C unsalted butter (butter)
1/4 C sugar
5 Tb cocoa (or 1 square bitter chocolate)
1 egg, beaten
1 3/4 C graham wafer crumbs (or 20 squares of graham crackers crushed into crumbs)
1/2 C finely chopped almonds (or walnuts)
1 C shredded coconut
Melt first 3 ingredients in top of a double boiler. Add egg and stir to cook and thicken. Remove from heat. Stir in crumbs, coconut and nuts. Press firmly into an ungreased 8x8 pan. Chill.

1/2 C unsalted butter (butter)
2 Tb and 2 tsp. cream (2 Tb milk)
2 Tb vanilla custard powder (or 2 Tb instant vanilla pudding dry mix)
2 C icing sugar (powdered sugar)
Cream butter, cream (milk) and custard powder (instant pudding dry mix) and powdered sugar together well. Beat until light. Spread over bottom layer and chill.

4 squares swemi-sweet chocolate (1 oz. each)
2 Tb unsalted butter (butter)
Melt chocolate and butter over low heat. When cool but still liquid, pour over second layer and chill.

wiches and cakes in the afternoon, and most also serve lunches. Excellent food is also available at many of the British-style pubs along the road, though these are licensed premises and children are usually not allowed inside.

Mile 78.5 (236.5) Km 126.5 (380.5): North end of Lantzville loop road.

Mile 83 (232) Km 133.5 (373.5): Road to Schooner Cove with its large marina. The small community of Nanoose is site of the Canadian Forces Maritime Experimental and Test Ranges Base.

Mile 83.5 (231.5) Km 134.5 (372.5): Nanoose Creek.

Mile 87 (228) Km 140 (367): Junction with Highway 4 to Port Alberni (29 miles/47 km) and the West Coast communities of Tofino and Ucluelet (87 miles/140 km west). Highway 4 accesses the Long Beach unit of Pacific Rim National Park between Tofino and Ucluelet (see Canadian National Parks in the MAJOR ATTRACTIONS section).

PORT ALBERNI (pop. 20,000), 29 miles/47 km west, is the home port of the MV *Lady Rose,* a steamship that makes day trips to the West Coast towns of Bamfield and Ucluelet, sometimes stopping en route in the islands of the Broken Group. Also in Port Alberni is the Alberni Harbour Quay, a bustling marketplace with stalls selling fresh seafood, produce and local crafts. The Alberni Inlet is well-known for its salmon fishing. Access from Port Alberni via unpaved logging road south 64 miles/102 km to Bamfield.

Mile 88.5 (226.5) Km 142.5 (364.5): Craig Heritage Park is a small collection of pioneer buildings, including a log schoolhouse that has been moved onto this small site to provide a living museum of history. Open early June to early Sept.

Mile 89.5 (225.5) Km 144 (363): Access to Rathtrevor Beach Provincial Park, 1 mile/2 km east. This is a major park with 174 campsites (fee), sanistation, extensive picnic and day-use area, nature displays, interpretive programs and nature house. Its chief appeal is its huge sandy beach where the shallow water is usually warm.

Mile 90 (225) Km 145 (362): Englishman River bridge. Good fishing.

Mile 90.5 (224.5) Km 145.5 (361.5): Village of **PARKSVILLE** (pop. 7,306), a popular seaside resort and retirement community. The beach here is wide and at low tide is perfect for building sandcastles. The

annual Parksville Sandcastle Contest brings entrants from all over the West. In August, the sport switches to croquet, and the championships are taken very seriously. Parksville Community Park (east on Beachside Drive) has picnicking, playground and sports field beside the beach.

Mile 94.5 (220.5) Km 152 (355): Road east to small community of French Creek and the Lasqueti Island ferry; foot passengers only. The island lies 10.5 miles/17 km out in the Strait, and its serrated coastline, offshore islands and reefs invite exploration by canoe or kayak. The island is also popular with cyclists, though the gravel roads are better suited for mountain bikes.

Mile 95 (220) Km 153 (354): Bridge over French Creek. Good steelhead and trout fishing.

Mile 96.5 (218.5) Km 155.5 (351.5): Qualicum Airport.

Mile 97.5 (217.5) Km 157 (350): QUALICUM BEACH (pop. 5,137) is a resort and retirement community.

Mile 98.5 (216.5) Km 158.5 (348.5): Junction with Highway 4A, which links to Highway 4, the route to the west coast of the island.

Mile 101 (214) Km 162.5 (344.5): Little Qualicum River.

Mile 107 (208) Km 172 (335): Horne Lake Road. This gravel road follows the route of the original Indian trail to the west coast at Alberni Inlet. The Hudson's Bay Co. came this way

in 1840 and established a farm on Cherry Creek. Today, the road provides access to Spider Lake (5.5 miles/9 km) for picnicking, swimming and non-motorized boating. Farther down the road is Horne Lake (9.5 miles/15 km), famous for its spectacular limestone caves. Four of the 6 undeveloped caves are open to the public, but anyone venturing inside must be well-equipped and experienced. Guided tours are sometimes given in summer; check at Rathtrevor Beach. Both Spider Lake and the Horne Lake Caves are provincial parks, but there are no camping facilities.

Mile 107.5 (207.5) Km 173 (334): Qualicum River Fish Hatchery is just south of the Big Qualicum River bridge. More than 100,000 salmon return to spawn here every year. Visitors are welcome to tour the self-guiding trails.

Mile 110 (205) Km 177 (330): Nile Creek bridge.

Mile 111.5 (203.5) Km 179.5 (327.5): Village of Bowser. There is a story that in the 1930s the Bowser Hotel had a dog that served beer to the customers. The village was, however, named for a premier of British Columbia.

Mile 116 (199) Km 187 (320): Cook Creek bridge.

Mile 117 (198) Km 188.5 (318.5): Rosewall Creek Provincial Park has picnicking and fishing.

Mile 119 (196) Km 191.5 (315.5): Waterlook Creek bridge.

Mile 120.5 (194.5) Km 194 (313): Coal Creek bridge. The highway runs along the shore of Fanny Bay, with Denman Island off to the east. The beach is shingle, scattered with heaps of oyster shells.

Mile 121.5 (193.5) Km 195.5 (311.5): The old established Fanny Bay Inn (known locally as the FBI) is still open for business near Cougar Creek.

Mile 122 (193) Km 196.5 (310.5): The former cable-laying vessel, the *Brico,* is beached and has been converted to a restaurant.

Mile 123.5 (191.5) Km 199 (308): Buckley Bay Road turnoff to the Denman Island Ferry. From Denman, a second ferry connects to Hornby Island.

Mile 125.5 (189.5) Km 202 (305): Buckley Bay rest area by the beach.

Mile 128 (187) Km 206 (301): At the Union Bay centre, the old jailhouse is now a gift shop, and the post office is in a red Victorian mansion. Union Bay was once the shipping port for the Cumberland coal mines. Now its fortunes rest with oysters. Fanny Bay oysters are considered especially tasty.

A 62-lb. Tyee salmon taken in waters off Vancouver Island. (Roger McDonnell, courtesy of Campbell River Tourism)

Mile 132.5 (182.5) Km 213.5 (293.5): Trent River bridge and community of Royston.

Mile 133 (182) Km 214 (293): Junction with road to Comox Lake and **CUMBERLAND** (pop. 2,396), 3.5 miles/6 km west. Cumberland was an important coal-mining town from the 1880s until the 1930s. Cumberland's Chinatown was the island's largest mine. Today only a few of the old buildings remain, but the museum displays relics of the mining era. Comox Lake Park, just north of the old town, has camping, picnicking, hiking, fishing and watersports.

Mile 136 (179) Km 219 (288): Puntledge River Fish Hatchery.

Mile 136.5 (178.5) Km 219.5 (287.5): Comox Valley Visitor Information Centre at the entrance to the town of **COURTENAY** (pop. 13,984), a logging, fishing, farming and tourist centre. Courtenay is the terminus for the Esquimalt and Nanaimo Railway that runs daily service to and from Victoria. The city is rapidly becoming the ski centre of Vancouver Island, with 2 ski mountains, the older Forbidden Plateau and the newer Mount Washington. Forbidden Plateau, on the lower slopes of Mount Becher, is visible from Courtenay and about a half-hour drive. Mount Washington Ski Area is 19 miles/31 km west of town

Mile 137 (178) Km 220.5 (286.5): Road branches east to Courtenay's twin city of **COMOX** (pop. 10,545), home of a Canadian Forces base. The Comox Valley is fertile and has been farmed since 1862. The old Lorne Hotel (1878) and Filberg Lodge (1890) still survive from the Victorian era. Just north of Comox, BC Ferries provides 4 sailings a day for cars and passengers to Powell River on the BC mainland north of Vancouver.

Mile 139 (176) Km 223.5 (283.5): Junction with road west to Forbidden Plateau and connections to Mount Washington ski area.

Mile 142 (173) Km 228.5 (278.5): Carlton Sheep Farm, operating since 1886.

Mile 146.5 (168.5) Km 236 (271): Community of Merville.

Mile 151 (164) Km 243 (264): Black Creek bridge and Black Creek Country Market; gas.

Mile 153.5 (161.5) Km 247 (260): Miracle Beach Provincial Park, 1.2 miles/2 km east. This is a popular family camping spot beside a long sandy beach with 193 campsites, hiking trails, visitor centre and interpretive programs. Black Creek runs through the park and flows into the sea through a salt marsh. Lots of wildlife in the forest, marine life in tidal pools, spawning coho in the river and wildflowers all summer make this park extremely enjoyable.

Mile 154.5 (160.5) Km 248.5 (258.5): Oyster River bridge and road east to Saratoga Beach, with golf course, marina and boat launch.

Mile 157 (158) Km 252.5 (254.5): Rest area beside the beach on Oyster Bay.

Mile 162.5 (152.5) Km 261.5 (245.5): Roadside sign commemorating Capt. Vancouver, who first sailed up Discovery Passage and Johnstone Strait in 1792 and established that Vancouver Island was an island.

Mile 163 (152) Km 262.5 (244.5): Road to Campbell River airport, which has regularly scheduled flights from Vancouver and Seattle.

Mile 165 (150) Km 265.5 (241.5): Huge glacial boulder on beach. Rocks offshore are popular perches for cormorants; the boulder itself seems to be a popular spot for local graffiti.

Mile 166 (149) Km 267 (240): Sign for the 50th Parallel.

City of **CAMPBELL RIVER** (pop. 26,000) is famous as a world-class fishing centre. The turbulent waters of Discovery Passage with their strong tidal surges stir up bait from the sea bottom, attracting giant salmon. The Tyee Club of British Columbia, organized in 1924, is open to anyone who catches a salmon weighing more than 30 lbs. from an open rowboat and using certain tackle. Many sportsmen come to Campbell River to take up the challenge. The Tyee record, established in 1968, is 71 lbs. The harbour is full of boats of all kinds, and there are many resorts and boat charters for the serious offshore fisherman. But one can fish successfully from 600-foot/182-m Discovery Pier, Canada's first saltwater fishing pier, which has shelters, fish cleaning stations, lots of seats and lighting for night fishing. Fee for fishing from the pier is $1 from May through Sept.; valid sportfishing license required. No fishing fee during off-season, and there is never a fee simply for strolling along the pier and enjoying the waterfront view. Seniors are free.

Primarily geared to visiting sportfishermen, Campbell River is also an important centre for forestry and mining.

The Campbell River Museum and Archives, relocated to 5th and Island Highway, contains a fine selection of Indian artifacts; organized nature tours available. Discovery Park along the downtown waterfront has an Indian longhouse shelter, complete with house totems and canoe.

BC Ferries carries autos and passengers to Quadra Island. It leaves hourly from the terminal just north of Discovery Park for a 15-minute ride across the narrow passage.

Mile 169.5 (145.5) Km 273 (234): Highway 28 west 57 miles/92 km to Gold River, a modern pulp mill community; and Tahsis, a small timber town.

Highway 28 is one of the few highways that cross Vancouver Island east to west. The highway provides access to Elk Falls Provincial Park with 121 campsites, sani-station, swimming and handicap-accessible trails. The falls are spectacular in spring when water is let out of the John Hart hydroelectric dam on Lower Campbell Lake.

Highway 28 passes through Strathcona Provincial Park, British Columbia's oldest park. Strathcona has 2 campgrounds, one at Buttle Lake with 85 campsites, and one at Ralph River with 76 campsites. This huge, rugged mountain wilderness has glaciers, lakes and streams. Within the park are 3 nature conservancies which have been set aside to protect areas of outstanding scenery and natural history. At the south end of the park is Della Falls (no road access), among the world's 10 highest falls.

GOLD RIVER (pop. 2,200) was built in 1965 as an "instant town" and has full traveler services. Gold River is a centre for caving. The local Speleological Assoc. runs regular trips to the deepest vertical cave in North America and to the scenic Upana Caves, located about 10 miles/16 km west of Gold River on the gravel road to Tahsis. Self-guided tours are possible (make sure you check in at the register) and take about 1 hour. You'll need rubber-soled shoes and a good flashlight to explore the 1,500 feet/460m of passageways.

TAHSIS (pop. 1,050), at the head of Tahsis Inlet, is 41 miles/66 km from Gold River. Tahsis is a natural deep-sea port, serving ships from around the world. Excellent saltwater fishing, hiking. Hosts the annual Great Walk held in June. Limited accommodations are available.

Mile 169.5 (145.5) Km 273 (234): Campbell River bridge. North of Campbell River the road becomes the North Island Highway and the country becomes far more wild; settlements are few and far between (fewer than 3 percent of the island's residents live on the north island), and the scenery is mostly forest. Vast stretches of timber have been clearcut and the land is a patchwork of regrowth forest of various ages. Forest companies have provided details of the forest's history on large billboards. Watch for logging trucks and heavy machinery on the 2-lane highway.

Mile 172 (143) Km 277 (230): Elk Falls Pulp Mill on Duncan Bay.

Mile 176.5 (138.5) Km 284 (223): Rest area and Seymour Narrows Lookout. The narrow stretch of water between Quadra and Vancouver Island has tides up to 16 knots, which makes navigation tricky. It used to be even more dangerous because of Ripple Rock, a shallowly submerged hazard that is claimed to have caused the demise of 2 dozen ships and more than 100 lives. In 1958, one of the largest nonatomic explosions in history blasted the double-peaked rock out of the water. Race Point Road, just to the north of the rest area, leads down to the cliffs above the narrows.

Mile 178 (137) Km 286.5 (220.5): Mohun Creek bridge.

Mile 178.5 (136.5) Km 287.5 (219.5): Rough gravel road west 10 miles/16 km to Morton Lake Provincial Park. First 6 miles/9.5 km consists of active logging road. Sign reads "CAUTION: Drive with lights on at all times. Pull over and stop when logging trucks approaching." Park offers 24 campsites, picnic tables, boat launch and beach. The lake is popular for windsurfing and swimming.

Mile 180 (135) Km 289.5 (217.5): Hiking trail to vantage point above Seymour Narrows and site of Ripple Rock.

Mile 189.5 (125.5) Km 305 (202): Roberts Lake rest area with boat launch and fishing.

Mile 194.5 (120.5) Km 313 (194): Road east to Rock Bay and Chatham Point Light Station, about 13 miles/20 km. Just north of the road is Amor de Cosmos Creek. De Cosmos was a former premier of British Columbia, a flamboyant newspaperman who changed his name from William Smith, and in 1858 founded the *British Colonist* newspaper in Victoria, still in existence as the *Victoria Colonist.*

Mile 204 (111) Km 328.5 (178.5): Sayward Valley bee farm has honey for sale.

Mile 206.5 (108.5) Km 332.5 (174.5): Salmon River bridge.

Mile 207.5 (107.5) Km 334 (173): Road east to Sayward and Kelsey Bay, 6 miles/10 km. **SAYWARD** (area pop. 1,200) provides full tourist services. At the east end of the 1-lane bridge, the Cable House Cafe, constructed of tons of used steel logging cable, serves excellent pies.

Mile 208 (107) Km 335 (172): Bridge over Lower Elk Creek canyon.

Mile 211.5 (103.5) Km 340.5 (166.5): Bridge over Upper Elk Creek canyon.

Mile 213.5 (101.5) Km 343.5 (163.5): Rest area on Keta Lake.

Mile 219.5 (95.5) Km 353 (154): Adam River bridge.

Mile 225.5 (89.5) Km 363 (144): Rest area by Eve River.

Mile 238.5 (76.5) Km 384 (123): Tsitika River bridge and entrance to the Nimpkish Valley, one of Vancouver Island's largest watersheds and richest sources of timber. Watch for herds of Roosevelt elk.

Mile 242 (73) Km 389.5 (117.5): Gravel road east to Mount Cain Regional Alpine Park and ski area and Schoen Lake Provincial Park, 7.5 miles/12 km. The road is rough and

Colourful sunset on Vancouver Island. (Dane Simoes, courtesy of Campbell River Tourism)

not suited to trailers. The provincial park, which has 10 campsites (no fee), is one of the best wilderness parks on the island. Hiking is superb, especially when alpine flowers are in bloom. Lots of wildlife, canoeing, fishing, swimming and mountain climbing on Mount Schoen.

Mile 244.5 (70.5) Km 393.5 (113.5): Hoomak Lake rest area.

Mile 248.5 (66.5) Km 400 (107): Road to Woss Camp, a logging community that lies 1 mile/1.6 km to the south. In the centre is an old steam locomotive, used when railways played an important part in island logging. Gravel logging road from Woss leads south to Gold River. Check at Woss for accessibility.

Mile 249.5 (65.5) Km 401.5 (105.5): Gold Creek bridge.

Mile 252 (63) Km 405.5 (101.5): Eagles Nest rest area, with a fine view over Nimpkish valley.

Mile 262 (53) Km 421.5 (85.5): Gravel road to **ZEBALLOS** (pop. 225),

26 miles/42 km south. Zeballos was once a gold and iron mining town. While the mines are not as active now (panning for gold is now a tourist pursuit), its scenic location makes it a popular take-off point for ocean kayakers and fishing charters. Zeballos is served by the *Uchuck III* from Gold River.

A short distance down the Zeballos road from the junction with the highway, Little Hustan Cave Park is an excellent place for first-time cavers. The caves are extensive and remarkable with arches, sinkholes and a huge vaulted entrance. Exercise caution, wear good shoes and carry a dependable flashlight.

Mile 267.5 (47.5) Km 430.5 (76.5): Turnoff to Nimpkish Camp at the south end of Nimpkish Lake. Gas station and store are on the highway.

Nimpkish Lake is long, narrow and windy—a popular place for sailboard enthusiasts who gather in August for the Speed Weekend competitions. The highway follows its 14-mile/22.5-km length high above the eastern shoreline. Nimpkish is the name of the local Indian tribe, named for a mythical monster halibut that is said to cause riptides near the river mouth.

Mile 271 (44) Km 436 (71): Noomas Creek.

Mile 284 (31) Km 457 (50): Road east to Beaver Cove (8 miles/13 km) and Telegraph Cove (9 miles/14.5 km). **BEAVER COVE** is a huge log-sorting ground, with giant machinery that loads logs from railway cars and logging trucks. There's a roadside pulloff that provides a perfect bird's eye view of the hustle and bustle.

TELEGRAPH COVE provides a distinct contrast to Beaver Cove. Here, one of the last existing boardwalk communities on the coast bustles in summer with activity of a different sort. Thousands of tourists come here with canoes and kayaks to launch into the waters of Johnstone Strait to see the killer whales. Others cram into tour boats. At Robson Bight (12 miles/20 km south), the orca whales congregate to rub their bellies on the gravel in the shallow waters at the mouth of the Tsitika River, an area preserved as a government ecological reserve. During the rest of the year, Telegraph Cove is a quiet, idyllic little village, its houses on stilts above the bay and its main street a wooden boardwalk between them.

Mile 285 (30) Km 458.5 (48.5): Nimpkish River bridge.

Mile 288.5 (26.5) Km 464 (43): **Junction** with road to Port McNeill, 1.2 miles/2 km north.

PORT McNEILL (pop. 2,641) provides full tourist services in a neat little town that owes its livelihood to logging and fishing. From its docks, BC Ferries provides a triangular service between Sointula, on Malcolm Island, and Alert Bay on Cormorant Island. **SOINTULA** (pop. 672) was originally established in 1901 as a colony by Finnish miners from Nanaimo who wanted a peaceful place to farm and fish. The colony survived and today is a fishing village of about 1,000 inhabitants.

ALERT BAY (pop. 628) is a thriving settlement with strong Kwakiutl Indian connections. All tourist services are available. Tall totems of the Nimpkish Band tower above the burial ground; the U'Mista Cultural Centre displays potlatch collections and old and contemporary Kwakiutl artifacts in an Indian-style longhouse. The museum is crammed with Indian materials, and local shops sell Indian handicrafts.

The ferry from Port McNeill accommodates cars as well as passengers, but both Cormorant and Malcom islands are small so cars are not needed. Travelers can explore the

Just watching the ocean is a satisfying and popular pastime on Vancouver Island. (Joe Hofbeck)

2 communities on foot, since ferries arrive and depart every 2 or 3 hours during the day.

Mile 294.5 (20.5) Km 474 (33): Cluxewe River bridge.

Mile 296.5 (18.5) Km 477 (30): Johnstone Strait viewpoint.

Mile 299 (16) Km 481 (26): Rest area by lake.

Mile 300.5 (14.5) Km 483.5 (23.5): Keogh River bridge.

Mile 301 (14) Km 484.5 (22.5): **Junction** with road to Port Alice, 36 miles/58 km south. Located in scenic Quatsino Sound, **PORT ALICE** (pop. 1,371) was built in 1965, near the site of a much older townsite. A pulp mill provides the main means of livelihood, although hunting, fishing and boating attract increasing numbers of travelers each year. Forestry roads lead to several good lakes for fishing and picnicking and also to incredible limestone rock formations and caves. Limited service.

Mile 311.5 (3.5) Km 501.5 (5.5): **Junction** with road to Prince Rupert Ferry at **BEAR COVE**, 3 miles/5 km. In the centre of the ferry parking lot is a huge spruce burl and a totem, the remains of an 8,000-year-old native settlement, the oldest known on Vancouver Island. There is a picnic area beside the bay and a travel information centre. From June to Sept., car and passenger ferries leave Bear Cove on alternate days for the 15-hour cruise through the Inside Passage to Prince Rupert; reservations are recommended. Cabins are available for those who want to overnight on board in Prince Rupert and return the next day. In winter the ferry schedule is curtailed.

Mile 312.5 (2.5) Km 503 (4): **Junc**-tion with road south to old whaling port of Coal Harbour (8.5 miles/14 km) on Holberg Inlet; and north to Port Hardy via Hardy Bay Road.

Mile 313 (2) Km 503.5 (3.5): **Junction** with unpaved road west to community of Holberg, 26 miles/42 km; Winter Harbour, 39 miles/62 km; and to Cape Scott Provincial Park at the extreme northwestern tip of Vancouver Island. The park is large, with more than 37,000 acres/15,000 hectares and is accessible only by sea or on foot along a rough trail from the end of a 10-mile/16-km forest track from Holberg. It's a magnificent, rugged wilderness of forest and shore and the site of a defeated turn-of-the-century Danish settlement of which a few relics remain. Trails, some of them historic, range in length from 1 mile/2 km to 19 miles/30 km; some sections are boardwalk. The lighthouse crew at Cape Scott and a few residents of the San Josef Valley are the only human inhabitants, but wildlife abounds.

Mile 315 (0) Km 507 (0): **PORT HARDY** (pop. 5,000), the main community on the north island, is situated on Hardy Bay where the town beach is ringed by parkland and a promenade. Fishing boats line the harbour. Full tourist facilities are available. Activities include fishing, scuba diving and harbour cruises.

At the north end of the waterfront promenade is Carrot Park, its name commemorating the long delay in getting the road north from Campbell River paved. As officials in Victoria kept "dangling the carrot" of paving, residents along the muddy, pot-holed road publicized their plight by holding an annual Pothole Golf Tournament.

Ferries and Cruises

The adventure of visiting the islands of the Northwest begins when you leave the mainland. Transportation to most of these islands is by boat or by air: No roads connect them to the mainland. Visitors must use the ferry system to visit the islands, or one of the growing number of tour boats that cruise these waters.

The ferry ride itself is a popular pastime with Northwesterners. On the shorter routes, many walk-on passengers take a round-trip just to relax and enjoy the view in a hassle-free fashion. Whales, dolphins and other marine mammals are often sighted by ferry passengers. The ferries come in a variety of shapes and sizes, from big, sleek computerized "super ferries" to small vintage craft. The waterways are endlessly fascinating, from the wide open crossing of the Strait of Juan de Fuca, to the zigzag passage through the San Juan archipelago. Visitors will find the ferry system a convenient and memorable way to explore this corner of the Northwest.

The Washington state Legislature has designated ferry routes crossing Puget Sound as state highway routes. The Seattle–Bainbridge Island route is part of State Route 305, which connects Bainbridge Island with the Kitsap Peninsula; the Edmonds–Kingston route is part of State Route 104, which connects Interstate 5 and Edmonds; and the Seattle (Fauntleroy)–Vashon Island route is State Route 339.

On fine summer weekends, ferry lines can be long for passengers with vehicles and the wait for space on the ferry can be several hours on some runs. (Walk-on passengers and cyclists go on ahead of vehicles.) Factor the ferry wait into your travel plans if traveling on summer weekends or holidays.

Washington State Ferries

The southernmost ferry system, serving the islands and peninsulas in and around Puget Sound, is Washington State Ferries, whose vessels ply Puget Sound through the San Juan Islands to Canada's Vancouver Island.

The Washington State Ferry System is the largest in the country, with 26 vessels ranging in length from 86 to 440 feet. Thousands of commuters rely on the ferry system daily to commute from their island homes to their jobs in the Seattle metropolitan area. Heavily-traveled commuter routes include Seattle–Bainbridge Island (formerly Winslow) and Seattle–Bremerton. In addition, Washington state ferries offer service to Vashon Island from 4 different locations and between Fauntleroy in West Seattle and Southworth on the Kitsap Peninsula.

Hundreds of thousands of travelers use other ferry routes connecting the greater Puget Sound area with the Kitsap and Olympic peninsulas and Whidbey Island. Seattle–Bremerton, Fauntleroy–Southworth and Edmonds–Kingston ferry routes all access the Kitsap Peninsula. The Mukilteo–Clinton ferry run connects Whidbey Island with the mainland, while the Keystone–Port Townsend ferry run connects Whidbey Island and the Olympic Peninsula. (The Keystone ferry run is one of the only ferry runs that may be cancelled during stormy weather. Service on this run may also be influenced by tides.)

Washington state ferries are the main mode of transportation for visitors and residents in the San Juan Islands. Departing from the ferry terminal near Anacortes (located about a 2-hour drive north of Seattle), Washington state ferries call at Lopez Island, Shaw Island, Orcas Island and Friday Harbor on San Juan Island on several westbound and eastbound sailings daily in summer. International sailings between Anacortes, WA, and Sidney, BC, via the San Juan Islands are offered twice daily between mid-June and mid-Sept., and once daily off-season. Sailing time is 3 hours between Anacortes and Sidney. Courtesy vehicle reservations are accepted in summer for the international sailings (the only Washington state ferry route that does accept reservations) and are recommended. Call ahead and make sure there will be room for your vehicle on the international sailings to and from Vancouver Island, especially during the busier summer months.

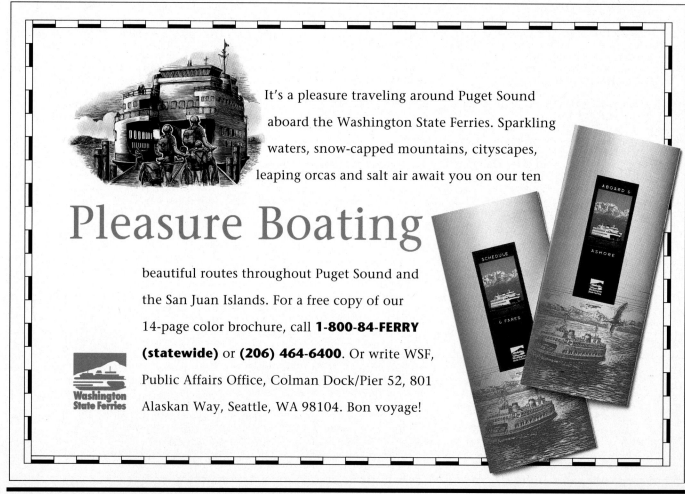

To reach Anacortes from Seattle, take Interstate 5 north 65 miles to Exit 230, then follow Highway 20 west 20 miles to the ferry terminal, which is located 4 miles from Anacortes.

The San Juan Islands are an extremely popular destination. Expect long ferry lines at Anacortes and on Orcas and San Juan islands on summer weekends. Also check at the Anacortes terminal before departing for the islands on campsite availability: "Camp full" signs are posted on the front of the toll-booth.

For more information, contact Washington State Ferries, Colman Dock/Pier 52, 801 Alaskan Way, Seattle, WA 98104-1487; phone (206) 464-6400 or 1-800-84-FERRY.

BC Ferries

The Canadian coast is served by the British Columbia Ferry Corp. Its ships provide passenger and auto service on more than 2 dozen coastal routes, crisscrossing the passage between Vancouver Island and the mainland and sailing north to remote Bella Bella and Prince Rupert.

To reach Vancouver Island from the lower British Columbia mainland, take BC Ferries from either Tsawwassen or Horseshoe Bay. The 3 major route choices are Tsawwassen–Swartz Bay, Tsawwassen–Nanaimo, or Horseshoe Bay-Nanaimo. BC Ferries also depart from Horseshoe Bay for the Sunshine Coast.

Follow Highway 99 through Vancouver for the Horseshoe Bay terminal, 13 miles/21 km northwest of the city, and ferry service to Nanaimo. Or turn off Highway 99 approximately 17 miles/27 km north of the U.S. border for the Tsawwassen terminal and service to Swartz Bay near Victoria (1¹/₂-hour crossing) and to Nanaimo (2-hour crossing). There are a minimum of 16 round- trips daily during the summer between Tsawwassen and Swartz Bay, and 8 round- trips daily year-round between Tsawwassen and Nanaimo. Reservations are not accepted for passengers or vehicles on these routes.

Downtown-to-downtown bus service via the ferry is available between Nanaimo or Victoria and Vancouver, and between the Vancouver airport and Victoria.

BC Ferries, *Queen of the North* sails from Port Hardy, on the north end of Vancouver Island, to Prince Rupert on the mainland farther north. Prince Rupert is the Canadian port for the Alaska Marine Highway System serving Southeastern Alaska ports. The Alaska state ferries offer almost daily sailings in summer north from Prince Rupert. (Bellingham, WA, is the southern terminus for the Alaska Marine Highway System, with Southeast Alaska-bound ferries departing the Bellingham Cruise Terminal every Friday in the summer.)

It is approximately an 8-hour drive between Victoria, on the south end of Vancouver Island, and Port Hardy, on the north end of the island. (See THE ISLAND HIGHWAY this section for log of road.)

Walk-on passengers and cyclists debark Washington state ferries first, followed by vehicles. (© Jay Peery)

For more information, contact British Columbia Ferry Corp., 1112 Fort St., Victoria, BC, Canada V8V 4V2; phone (604) 277-0277 for 24-hour recorded schedule information, or (604) 669-1211 to speak to a customer service representative. In Victoria, phone (604) 656-0757 for schedule information, or (604) 386-3431 for reservations.

Other Services

A growing number of private companies service Vancouver Island and the San Juan Islands, offering either ferry service or cruise tours. Following is a list of some of these services:

Black Ball Transport, 430 Belleville St., Victoria, BC V8V 1W9; phone (206) 622-2222 in Seattle, (360) 457-4491 in Port Angeles, (604) 386-2202 in Victoria. Scheduled passenger and vehicle service aboard the MV *Coho* between Port Angeles, WA, and Victoria, BC (1¹/₂ hour crossing time).

Cruise West, 4th & Battery Bldg., Suite 700, Seattle, WA 98121; phone 1-800-426-7702 or (206) 441-8687. 7-night cruises spring and fall from Seattle to Desolation Sound aboard the *Spirit of Discovery*. 7-night Historic Island Hopping Cruise features islands and historic ports in Washington waters, includes San Juans, Whidbey, LaConner, Port Townsend and South Sound; spring and fall sailings. (Cruise West also operates a number of Alaska cruises and Columbia and Snake river cruises.)

Island Mariner Cruises, 5 Harbor Esplanade, Bellingham, WA 98225; phone (360) 734-8866. Ninety-mile, narrated whale-watching cruise through the San Juan Islands. Operates weekends in June, weekends plus 2 weekdays in July and August. Phone for brochure.

San Juan Island Shuttle Express Inc., phone (360) 671-1137. Daily passenger service (bicycles welcome) from Bellingham Cruise Terminal to Orcas Island and Friday Harbor on San Juan Island; late May through Sept. Overnight packages and whale watching cruises available.

Mosquito Fleet, 1724-F W. Marine View Dr., Everett, WA 98201; phone 1-800-325-ORCA or (206) 252-6800 or 787-6400. Whale watching trips through the San Juan Islands; calls at Friday Harbor. Morning departures from Everett harbor, returns early evening, from mid-May through Oct.

Victoria Line, 185 Dallas Rd., Victoria, BC V7V 1A1; phone 1-800-668-1167 for recorded message, (206) 625-1880 in Seattle for reservations, (604) 480-5555 in Victoria for reservations and information. Daily passenger and vehicle service between Victoria and Pier 48 in Seattle aboard the *Royal Victorian*.

Victoria Clipper, 2701 Alaskan Way, Pier 69, Seattle, WA 98121; phone (206) 448-5000. Passenger-only service between Seattle and Victoria (2¹/₂ hours) daily year-round aboard the *Victoria Clipper* high-speed catamaran. Seasonal trips between Seattle and Friday Harbor on San Juan Island and Rosario Resort on Orcas Island.

Victoria–San Juan Cruises, 355 Harris St., Suite 104, Bellingham, WA; phone 1-800-443-4552 or (360) 738-8099. Narrated passenger boat service to Victoria through the San Juan Islands from Bellingham Cruise Terminal. Day, overnight packages and nature cruises available aboard *Victoria's Star.*

Western Prince Cruises, P.O. Box 418, Friday Harbor, WA 98250; phone (360) 378-5315 or 1-800-757-6722. 4-hour excursions of San Juan Islands out of Friday Harbor.

Yacht Ship Cruise Line, 520 Pike St. #1400, Seattle, WA 98101; phone (206) 623-2735 or 1-800-720-0012. One-day San Juan Islands cruise, round-trip from Seattle, aboard the high-speed catamaran *Spirit of Adventure* in May and October, the *Klondike* from late May to Sept. Calls at Roche Harbor or Friday Harbor.

Inquire at local harbors about seasonal sightseeing and whale watching excursions available.

Another option is to charter a boat and do your own sailing through the islands. Check with any of the major marinas in the Seattle area, Everett, Anacortes or Bellingham.

Guided sea kayak trips of the San Juan Islands, ranging from half-day to 5 days, are available on Orcas Island at Doe Bay and Rosario (phone 360/376-4699), San Juan Island, and out of Seattle (phone 206/281-9694) and Bellingham.

GENERAL INFORMATION

Alcoholic Beverages

The legal drinking age in Idaho, Oregon and Washington is 21. The legal drinking age in British Columbia is 19. The legal drinking age in Alberta is 18.

Fishing and Hunting

BRITISH COLUMBIA

Fishing: A nonresident, non-Canadian annual angler's license costs $40. An 8-day nonresident angler's license may be purchased for $25 and a 1-day license for $10. Licenses are not required for nonresident anglers under 16 years of age who are accompanied by someone with a license. Special permits required for steelhead and for nonresident fishing lakes and streams classified as "Special Water." Freshwater and saltwater fishing licenses are required of all anglers 16 and older; both are renewable on March 31.

To get a license for freshwater fishing, contact the Ministry of Environment, Lands and Parks, Fish and Wildlife Information, Parliament Buildings, Victoria, BC V6V 1X4; phone (604) 387-9688. To get a license for saltwater fishing, contact the Federal Dept. of Fisheries and Oceans, 555 W. Hastings St., Vancouver, BC V6B 5G2; phone (604) 666-3545. Licenses for both salt and fresh water are also available though government agents and at 1,400 sporting goods stores and most marinas and charter outfits in British Columbia. For more information on licenses, fees and regulations, contact the Ministry of Environment, Lands and Parks or the Federal Dept. of Fisheries and Oceans.

A nonresident season **hunting** license (to hunt all game and carry firearms) costs $145. Nonresident licenses, as well as information on fees and regulations, are available through some Regional British Columbia Environment Offices, government agents or the Ministry of Environment, Lands and Parks.

IDAHO

A nonresident season **fishing** license costs $51. A 10-day nonresident fishing license may be purchased for $31, a 3-day license for $16 and a 1-day license for $7. All anglers 14 and older must have a license to fish all Idaho waters. All nonresident children less than 14 must be accompanied by the holder of a valid fishing license when fishing, and their fish must be counted as part of the license holder's daily limit.

Resident children under 14 can fish without a license and need not be accompanied by the holder of a valid fishing license. Idaho licenses are also valid when fishing from boats on the boundary waters of the Snake River between Idaho, Oregon and Washington, and on Bear Lake, which straddles the border with Utah.

Steelhead and salmon fishermen need a general fishing license plus separate steelhead and salmon permits. Children under the age of 14, including nonresidents, are exempt from buying steelhead permits if accompanied by a valid permit holder. The child's catch, however, must be counted against the permit holder's bag limit.

Licenses are available from the Idaho Dept. of Fish and Game offices and more than 500 vendors statewide. For licenses, fees, complete regulations and other information, contact the Idaho Dept. of Fish and Game, 600 S. Walnut St., P.O. Box 25, Boise, ID 83707; phone (800) 635-7820. Nonresidents may also purchase licenses over the phone using a credit card (VISA, MasterCard, American Express or Discover) by calling (800) 55-HUNTS.

A nonresident season **hunting** license costs $101. For licenses, regulations, other fees and other information, contact the Idaho Dept. of Fish and Game.

OREGON

Fishing: An annual nonresident angling license costs $40.50. A 7-day angling license may be purchased for $30.50, a 3-day license for $18.25, a 2-day license for $12.50, and a 1-day license for $6.75. All anglers 14 years old and older need a fishing license for all fish except smelt, shellfish and marine invertebrates. Licenses *are not* required to dig clams, trap crabs or collect mussels. A fishing license is also not required inside Crater Lake National Park, north of Klamath Falls.

Steelhead and salmon fishermen, regardless of age, are required to have a valid unfilled salmon or steelhead tag or daily angling license in possession. Both Oregon and Washington licenses are valid when angling from a boat in the ocean within 3 miles of shore between Cape Falcon, OR, and Leadbetter Point, WA.

Licenses and tags may be purchased directly from the Oregon Dept. of Fish and Wildlife or from any Dept. of Fish and Wildlife agent (most sporting goods stores). For furher information on licenses, fees and regulations, contact Oregon Dept. of Fish and Wildlife, 2501 SW 1st Ave., P.O. Box 59, Portland, OR 97207; phone (503) 229-5403.

A nonresident season **hunting** license costs $53. For licenses, regulations, other fees and other information, contact the Oregon Dept. of Fish and Wildlife.

WASHINGTON

A nonresident state game **fishing** license costs $48 (for the season). A 3-day nonresident fishing license may be purchased for $17. A fishing license is required of all fishermen over the age of 15 while angling in fresh water except in Mount Rainier and Olympic national parks, where unlicensed fishing is allowed (a steelhead permit to fish for steelhead, however, is required).

A fishing license is required to fish in salt water. Persons must also possess appropriate licenses for taking Pacific salmon, food fish, shrimp and razor clams. A valid steelhead permit is required of persons fishing for steelhead in salt water.

Licenses and tags may be purchased through the Washington Dept. of Fish and Wildlife (either the Olympia headquarters or any of the regional offices) or at more than 1,000 sporting goods stores throughout the state. For licenses and more information on fees and regulations, contact the Washington Dept. of Fish and Wildlife, 600 Capitol Way N., Olympia, WA 98501-1091; phone (360) 902-2464 (the walk-in address is 1111 Washington St. SE, Olympia).

A nonresident season **hunting** license costs $150. For licenses, regulations, other fees and other information, contact the Washington Dept. of Fish and Wildlife.

Holidays

New Year's Day	Jan. 1
Martin L. King Jr. Day	3rd Monday in Jan.
Presidents Day	3rd Monday in Feb.
Victoria Day (Canada)	Monday before May 25
Memorial Day	Last Monday in May
Canada Day	July 1
Independence Day	July 4
British Columbia Day	1st Monday in Aug.
Labor Day (U.S. & Canada)	1st Monday in Sept.
Thanksgiving Day (Canada)	2nd Monday in Oct.
Columbus Day	2nd Monday in Oct.
Veterans Day (U.S.)	Nov. 11
Remembrance Day (Canada)	Nov. 11
Thanksgiving Day (U.S.)	4th Thursday in Nov.
Christmas	Dec. 25
Boxing Day (Canada)	Dec. 26

Information Sources

Contact the following state and provincial tourism agencies for free maps and brochures and for travel-related questions:

Travel Alberta, 3rd floor, 10155 102 St., Edmonton, AB T5J 4L6; phone (800) 661-8888.

Discover British Columbia, Parliament Buildings, Victoria, BC V8V 1X4; phone (800) 663-6000.

Idaho Travel Council, Joe R. Williams

Bldg., 2nd Floor, 700 W. State St., P.O. Box 83720, Boise, ID 83720-0093; phone (800) 635-7820 or (208) 334-2470.

Oregon Economic Development Dept., Tourism Division, 775 Summer St. NE, Salem, OR 97310; phone (800) 547-7842 or (503) 986-0000.

Washington State Dept. of Commerce & Economic Development, Tourism Development Division, P.O. Box 42500, Olympia, WA 98501; phone (360) 586-2088, 586-2102 or toll free out of state (800) 544-1800.

National Forests

BRITISH COLUMBIA

British Columbia's forests are divided into 6 forest regions and further subdivided into forest districts. Reservations are not accepted at Provincial Forest campgrounds; they are all first-come, first-served and are user-maintained. For maps and general information, contact the British Columbia Forest Service, Recreation Branch, 610 Johnson St., Victoria, BC V8W 3E7, phone (604) 387-1946, fax (604) 356-5909.

Contact the following regional offices for maps and more detailed information about the forest districts and campgrounds within their regions.

Cariboo Forest Region, 540 Borland St., Williams Lake, BC V2G 1R8; phone (604) 398-4345, fax (604) 398-4380.

Kamloops Forest Region, 515 Columbia St., Kamloops, BC V2C 2T7; phone (604) 828-4131, fax (604) 828-4154.

Nelson Forest Region, 518 Lake St., Nelson, BC V1L 4C6; phone (604) 354-6200, fax (604) 354-6250.

Prince George Forest Region, 1011 4th Ave., Prince George, BC V2L 3H9; phone (604) 565-6100, fax (604) 565-6671.

Prince Rupert Forest Region, Bag 5000, 3726 Alfred Ave., Smithers, BC V0J 2N0; phone (604) 847-7500, fax (604) 847-7217.

Vancouver Forest Region, 4595 Canada Way, Burnaby, BC V5G 4L9; phone (604) 660-7500, fax (604) 660-7778.

IDAHO

To make reservations at National Forest Service campgrounds throughout the United States and for general information, call (800) 280-CAMP (800/879-4496 for the hearing impaired). For maps and information on National Forests in northern Idaho, contact the U.S. Forest Service, Northern Region, Federal Bldg., P.O. Box 7669, Missoula, MT 59807, (406) 329-3511. For National Forests in southern Idaho, contact the U.S. Forest Service, Intermountain Region, 2501 Wall Ave., Ogden, UT 84401, (801) 625-5306.

Contact the National Forests directly for more detailed information:

Boise National Forest, 1750 Front St., Boise, ID 03702; phone (208) 364-4100.

Caribou National Forest, Federal Building, Suite 282, 250 S. 4th Ave., Pocatello, ID 83201; phone (208) 236-7500.

Challis National Forest, Highway 93 N., HC-63 Box 1671, Challis, ID 83226; phone (208) 879-2285.

Clearwater National Forest, 12730 Highway 12, Orofino, ID 83544; phone (208) 476-4541.

Idaho Panhandle National Forest, 3815 Schreiber Way, Coeur d'Alene, ID 83814;

phone (208) 765-7223.

Nez Perce National Forest, Route 2, Box 475, Grangeville, ID 83530; phone (208) 983-1950.

Payette National Forest, 106 W. Park St., P.O. Box 1026, McCall, ID 83638; phone (208) 634-0700.

Salmon National Forest, Forest Service Bldg., Highway 93 N., P.O. Box 729, Salmon, ID 83467; phone (208) 756-2215.

Sawtooth National Forest, 2647 Kimberly Road E., Twin Falls, ID 83301-7976; phone (208) 737-3200.

Targhee National Forest, 420 N. Bridge St. P.O. Box 208, St. Anthony, ID 83445; phone (208) 624-3151.

OREGON

To make reservations at National Forest campgrounds throughout the United States and for general information, call (800) 280-CAMP (800/879-4496 for the hearing impaired). For maps and information on National Forests in Oregon, contact the U.S. Forest Service, Pacific Northwest Region, 333 S.W. 1st Ave., P.O. Box 3623, Portland, OR 97208-3623; phone (503) 326-2877.

Contact the National Forests directly for more detailed information:

Deschutes National Forest, 1645 Highway 20 E., Bend, OR 97701; phone (503) 388-2715.

Fremont National Forest, 524 N. G St., Lakeview, OR 97630; phone (503) 947-2151.

Malheur National Forest, 139 NE Dayton St., John Day, OR 97845; phone (503) 575-1731.

Mount Hood National Forest, 2955 NW Division, Gresham, OR 97030; phone (503) 666-0700.

Ochoco National Forest, 3061 E. 3rd St., P.O. Box 490, Prineville, OR 97754; phone (503) 447-6247.

Rogue River National Forest, 333 W. 8th St., P.O. Box 520, Medford, OR 97501; phone (503) 858-2200.

Siskiyou National Forest, 200 NE Greenfield Rd., P.O. Box 440, Grants Pass, OR 97526, phone (503) 471-6500.

Siuslaw National Forest, P.O. Box 1148, Corvallis, OR 97339, phone (503) 750-7000.

Umatilla National Forest, 2517 SW Hailey Ave., Pendleton, OR 97801; phone (503) 278-3716.

Umpqua National Forest, P.O. Box 1008, 2900 Stewart Parkway, Roseburg, OR 97470; phone (503) 672-6601.

Wallowa-Whitman National Forest, 1550 Dewey Ave., P.O. Box 907, Baker City, OR 97814; phone (503) 523-6391.

Willamette National Forest, 211 E. 7th Ave., Eugene, OR 97401; phone (503) 465-6522.

Winema National Forest, 2819 Dahlia St., Klamath Falls, OR 97601; phone (503) 883-6714.

WASHINGTON

To make reservations at National Forest campgrounds throughout the United States and for more general information, call (800) 280-CAMP (800/879-4496 for the hearing impaired). For maps and information on National Forests in Washington, contact the U.S. Forest Service, Pacific Northwest Region, P.O. Box 3623, Portland, OR 97208, phone (503) 326-2877.

Contact the National Forests directly for more detailed information:

Colville National Forest, 765 S. Main St., Colville, WA 99114; phone (509) 684-3711.

Gifford Pinchot National Forest, 6926 E. 4th Plain Blvd., Vancouver, WA 98661-7299; phone (360) 750-5000.

Mount Baker-Snoqualmie National Forest, 21905 64th Ave. W., Mountlake Terrace, WA 98043; phone (206) 775-9702.

Okanogan National Forest, 1240 S. 2nd Ave., Okanogan, WA 98840-9723.

Olympic National Forest, 1835 Black Lake Blvd. SW, Olympia, WA 98512-5623; phone (360) 956-2300.

Wenatchee National Forest, P.O. Box 811, Wenatchee, WA 98807; phone (509) 662-4335.

Ski Resorts

BRITISH COLUMBIA

Apex Alpine Ski Resort
P.O. Box 1060, Penticton, BC V2A 7N7, phone (604) 292-8111, snow phone 492-2929 (ext. 2000). 56 runs. Lifts: 1 quad, 1 triple, 1 T-bar, 1 beginner tow. Day lodge, cafeteria, restaurants, accommodations, general store, retail stores, skating rink, day care. Open daily, late Nov. to early April. Night skiing Wednesday, Friday and Saturday. Ski rentals/ski school. Cross-country trails. Snowboards permitted. From **Mile 38.5**/Km 62 on CANADA HIGHWAY 97, go west 20 miles/32 km.

Bear Mountain Ski Hill
P.O. Box 807, Dawson Creek, BC V1G 4H8, phone (604) 782-4988. 10 runs. Lift: 1 T-bar. Day lodge, cafeteria, lounge. Open weekends and holidays, early Dec. to late March. Night skiing Wednesday through Saturday and holidays. Ski rentals/ski school. Cross-country trails. Snowboards permitted. From **Mile 504**/Km 811.5 on CANADA HIGHWAY 97, continue north to Dawson Creek.

Big Bam Ski Hill
P.O. Box 6113, Fort St. John, BC V1J 5J6, phone (604) 785-7544, snow phone 789-3366. British Columbia's northernmost ski area. 11 runs. Lifts: 1 T-bar, 1 beginner tow. Day lodge, snack bar, lounge. Open Friday through Sunday, Dec. through March. Night skiing Monday through Wednesday. Ski rentals/ski school. Snowboards permitted. From **Mile 504**/Km 811.5 on CANADA HIGHWAY 97, continue north to Fort St. John.

Big White Ski Resort
P.O. Box 2039, Station R, Kelowna, BC V1X 4K5, phone (800) 663-2772, snow phone (604) 765-SNOW. British Columbia's highest lift-serviced resort at 7,960 feet/2,426m. 51 runs. Lifts: 4 quads, 1 double, 1 platter, 1 T-bar. 3 day lodges, restaurants, accommodations, lounges, grocery store, medical centre, arcade, day care. Open daily, mid-Nov. to Easter. Night skiing Tuesday through Saturday. Ski rentals/ski school. Cross-country trails. Snowboards permitted. From **Mile 81.5**/Km 131 on CANADA HIGHWAY 97, go south on BC Highway 33.

Crystal Mountain
P.O. Box 26044, Westbank, BC V4T 2G3, phone (604) 768-5189, snow phone 768-3753. Family-oriented. 20 runs. Lifts: 1 double, 2 T-bars, 1 rope tow. Day lodge, cafeteria, lounge. Open weekends and holidays in Dec.; Tuesday through Sunday, Jan. through mid-March. Night skiing. Ski rentals/ski school. Snowboards permitted. Located just off CANADA

HIGHWAY 97 at **Mile 68.5**/Km 110.

Cypress Bowl
P.O. Box 91252, West Vancouver, BC V7V 3N9, phone (604) 926-5612, snow phone 926-6007. 24 runs. Lifts: 4 doubles, 1 rope tow. Day lodge, cafeteria, pub, retail store. Open daily, early Dec. to mid-April. Night skiing daily. Ski rentals/ski school. Cross-country trails. Snowboards permitted. From **Mile 527.5**/Km 849 on TRANS-CANADA HIGHWAY 1, continue west; resort located off Highway 1 just north of downtown Vancouver.

Fairmont Hot Springs Resort
P.O. Box 10, Fairmont Hot Springs, BC V0B 1L0, phone (604) 345-6311, snow phone 345-6413. 14 runs. Lifts: 1 triple, 1 beginner tow/platter. Natural hot springs, day lodge, restaurants, lounge, snack bar, pool, golf course, day care. Open daily, mid-Dec. to mid-April. Night skiing on Friday. Ski rentals/ski school. Cross-country trails. Snowboards permitted. Located just off CANADA HIGHWAY 93 at **Mile 119**/Km 191.5.

Fernie Snow Valley Resort
Ski Area Road, Fernie, BC V0B 1M1, phone (604) 423-4655, snow phone 423-3555. 47 runs. Lifts: 1 quad, 2 triples, 2 T-bars, 1 alpine tow, 1 beginner tow. Day lodge, restaurants, indoor swimming pool, day care. Open daily, Dec. to April. Ski rentals/ski school. Cross-country trails. Snowboards permitted. Located just off CROWSNEST HIGHWAY 3 at **Mile 36**/Km 58.

Forbidden
P.O. Box 3268, Courtenay, BC V9N 5N4, phone (604) 334-4744, snow phone 338-1919. 22 runs. Lifts: 1 double, 2 T-bars, 1 handle tow. Day lodge, cafeteria, lounge. Open Thursday through Sunday and holidays, early Dec. to early April. Ski rentals/ski school. Snowboards permitted. Located on Vancouver Island, just off Highway 19.

Grouse Mountain
6400 Nancy Greene Way, North Vancouver, BC V7R 4K9, phone (604) 984-0661, snow phone 986-6262. 22 runs. Lifts: 2-section aerial tramway, 4 doubles, 2 T-bars, 4 beginner tows. Day lodge, restaurant, bar, cafeteria. Open daily, Nov. to early April. Night skiing daily. Ski rentals/ski school. Snowboards permitted. From **Mile 527.5**/Km 849 on TRANS-CANADA HIGHWAY 1, continue west; resort located off Highway 1 just north of downtown Vancouver.

Harper Mountain
2042 Valleyview Dr., Kamloops, BC V2C 4C5, phone (604) 372-2119, snow phone 828-0336. 15 runs. Lifts: 1 triple, 1 T-bar, 1 beginner tow. Day lodge, cafeteria. Open daily, mid-Dec. to mid-March; weekends other months, snow permitting. Night skiing. Ski rentals/ski school. Cross-country trails. Snowboards permitted. Located off CANADA HIGHWAY 5 at **Mile 128.5**/Km 207.

Hemlock Valley Resorts
Comp. 7, Hemlock Valley Site, RR 1, Agassiz, BC V0M 1A0, phone (604) 797-4411, snow phone 520-6222. 34 runs. Lifts: 1 triple, 2 doubles, 1 handle tow. Day lodge, cafeteria, lounge, retail store, day care. Open Friday through Sunday and holidays, Dec. through March. Night skiing Friday, Jan. through mid-March. Ski rentals/ski school. Cross-

country trails. Snowboards permitted. From **Mile 437**/Km 703.5 on TRANS-CANADA HIGHWAY 1, take Highway 7 west.

Kimberley Ski and Summer Resort
P.O. Box 40, Kimberley, BC V1A 2Y5, phone and snow phone (604) 427-4881. 44 runs. Lifts: 2 triples, 1 double, 1 T-bar, 3 beginner tows/platters. Day lodges, restaurant, cafeteria, lounge, gift shop, day care. Open daily, early Dec. to early April. Night skiing Tuesday through Saturday. Ski rentals/ski school. Cross-country trails. Snowboards permitted. From **Mile 91**/Km 146.5 on CROWSNEST HIGHWAY 3, take Highway 95A north 20.5 miles/31 km.

Manning Park Resort
P.O. Box 1480, Hope, BC V0X 1L0, phone (604) 840-8822, snow phone 689-7669. 24 runs. Lifts: 2 doubles, 1 T-bar, 1 rope tow. Day lodge, day care. Open early Dec. to early April (daily in February; days vary other months). Ski rentals/ski school. Cross-country trails. Snowboards permitted. Located in Manning Provincial Park, just off CROWSNEST HIGHWAY 3 at **Mile 492**/Km 793.

Mount Baldy Ski Area
P.O. Box 1528, Oliver, BC V0H 1T0, phone (604) 498-4086, snow phone 498-2262. 15 runs. Lifts: 2 T-bars. Day lodge, cafeteria, lounge. Open Friday through Monday and holidays, mid-Dec. to Easter. Ski rentals/ski school. Cross-country trails. Snowboards permitted. Located off CROWSNEST HIGHWAY 3 at **Mile 355**/Km 571.5.

Mount Cain
P.O. Box 1225, Port McNeill, BC V0N 2R0, phone (604) 949-9496, snow phone 956-CAIN. 17 runs. Lifts: 2 T-bars, 1 beginner tow. Day lodge. Ski rentals/ski school. Cross-country trails. Located on Vancouver Island, just off Highway 19.

Mount MacKenzie
P.O. Box 1000, Revelstoke, BC V0E 2S0, phone (604) 837-5268. 21 runs. Lifts: 2 doubles, 1 T-bar, 1 beginner tow/platter. Day lodge, cafeteria, lounge. Open Thursday through Monday, mid-Dec. to mid-March. Night skiing Friday. Ski rentals/ski school. Snowboards permitted. Located just off TRANS-CANADA HIGHWAY 1 at **Mile 137**/ Km 220.5.

Mount Seymour Resorts
1700 Mount Seymour Road, North Vancouver, BC V7G 1L3, phone (604) 986-2261, snow phone 879-3999. Family-oriented. 25 runs. Lifts: 4 doubles, 1 twin rope tow. Day lodge, pub, cafeteria, gift shop. Open daily, Dec. to late March. Night skiing daily. Ski rentals/ski school. Snowboards permitted. From **Mile 527.5**/Km 849 on TRANS-CANADA HIGHWAY 1, continue west; resort located off Highway 1 just north of downtown Vancouver.

Mount Timothy Ski Hill
P.O. Box 33, 100 Mile House, BC V0K 2E0, phone (604) 395-3772, snow phone 395-7310. 25 runs. Lifts: 1 T-bar, 2 beginner tows/platters. Day lodge, cafeteria. Open Friday through Monday (generally), mid-Dec. to mid-April. Ski rentals/ski school. Snowboards permitted. From **Mile 318**/Km 512 on CANADA HIGHWAY 97, follow signs 14.5 miles/23.5 km east.

Mount Washington
P.O. Box 3069, Courtenay, BC V9N 5N3, phone (604) 338-1386, snow phone 338-

1515. Vancouver Island's largest ski area. 46 runs. Lifts: 1 quad, 2 triples, 2 doubles, 1 handle tow, 1 poma. 2 day lodges, restaurants, day care. Open daily, late Nov. to late April. Ski rentals/ski school. Cross-country trails. Snowboards permitted. Located on Vancouver Island, just off Highway 19.

Panorama Resort
Panorama, BC V0A 1T0, phone (800) 663-2929. Over 50 runs. Lifts: 1 quad, 1 triple, 2 doubles, 2 T-bars, 2 beginner tows/platters. Day lodge, restaurants, accommodations, sleigh rides, miniature golf, skating rink, hot tubs, day care. Open daily, Dec. to April. Ski rentals/ski school. Cross-country trails. Snowboards permitted. From **Mile 133.5**/Km 214.5 on CANADA HIGHWAY 93, go west 12 miles/19.5 km.

Phoenix Mountain
P.O. Box 2428, Grand Forks, BC V0H 1H0, phone (604) 445-6161 (it's a mobile phone; wait for beep, then dial 7745; also serves as snow phone). Family-oriented. 9 runs. Lifts: 1 T-bar, 1 beginner tow. Day lodge, restaurant. Open daily, Dec. through March. Night skiing Wednesday and Friday. Ski rentals/ski school. Cross-country trails. Located just off CROWSNEST HIGHWAY 3 at **Mile 310**/Km 499.

Powder King Ski Village
P.O. Box 2260, Mackenzie, BC V0J 2C0, phone (604) 997-6323. Features the area's highest chair lift. 18 runs. Lifts: 1 triple, 1 T-bar, 1 beginner tow/platter. Day lodge, restaurant, lounge, day care. Open Thursday through Monday, Nov. to April. Ski rentals/ski school. Snowboards permitted. From **Mile 504**/Km 811.5 on CANADA HIGHWAY 97, continue north and turn north onto Highway 39. Resort located just north of Mackenzie.

Purden Lake Ski Village
P.O. Box 1239, Prince George, BC V2L 4V3, phone (604) 565-7777, snow phone 565-SNOW. 13 runs. Lifts: 2 doubles, 1 T-bar. Day lodge, cafeteria. Open Friday through Monday, mid-Nov. to Easter and holidays (generally). Ski rentals/ski school. Snowboards permitted. From **Mile 504**/Km 811.5 on CANADA HIGHWAY 97, take Highway 16 east 38 miles/61 km.

Red Mountain
P.O. Box 670, Rossland, BC V0G 1Y0, phone (604) 362-7700, snow phone 362-5500. Red Mountain has the highest ratio of advanced and expert terrain of any ski resort in British Columbia. 77 runs (30 are marked). Lifts: 3 triple, 2 doubles, 1 T-bar. 2 day lodges, cafeteria, restaurant, day care. Open daily, early Dec. to early April. Ski rentals/ski school. Cross-country trails. Snowboards permitted. From **Mile 257.5**/Km 414 on CROWSNEST HIGHWAY 3, take Highway 3B south 17 miles/28 km.

Salmo Ski Hill
P.O. Box 204, Salmo, BC V0G 1Z0, phone (604) 357-2323, snow phone 357-2656. 4 runs. Lifts: 1 T-bar, 1 beginner tow. Day lodge, concession stand. Open weekends and holidays, Dec. through April. Night skiing daily. Ski rentals/ski school. Cross-country trails. Snowboards permitted. Located just off CROWSNEST HIGHWAY 3 at **Mile 206**/Km 331.5.

Shames Mountain
P.O. Box 119, Terrace, BC V8G 4A2, phone (604) 635-3773, snow phone 638-8SKI. 18 runs. Lifts: 1 double, 1 T-bar, 1 handle tow. Day lodge, cafeteria, bar, lounge, day care. Open daily, Dec. to April. Ski rentals/ski school. Snowboards permitted. From Mile 504/Km 811.5 on CANADA HIGHWAY 97, take Highway 16 west to Terrace; resort is located 21 miles/35 km north.

Silver Star Mountain Resort
P.O. Box 2, Silver Star Mountain, BC V0E 1G0, phone (604) 542-0224, snow phone 542-1745. 80 runs. Lifts: 3 quads, 2 doubles, 2 T-bars, 1 handle tow. Day lodge, restaurants, cafeteria, bars, hotels, conference rooms, exercise rooms, sports medicine clinic, swimming pool, day care. Open daily, Nov. to April. Night skiing Tuesday through Saturday, Dec. to April (generally). Ski rentals/ski school. Cross-country trails. Snowboards permitted. Located adjacent to Silver Star Provincial Recreation Area, just off CANADA HIGHWAY 97 at Mile 112/Km 180.

Ski Smithers
P.O. Box 492, Smithers, BC V0J 2N0, phone (604) 847-2058, snow phone 975-9655. Family-oriented. 18 runs. Lifts: 1 triple, 2 T-bars, 1 beginner tow/platter. Day lodge, restaurant, day care. Open daily, Dec. through late April. Ski rentals/ski school. Snowboards permitted. From Mile 504/Km 811.5 on CANADA HIGHWAY 97, take Highway 16 west to Smithers; follow signs 13.5 miles/22 km west to resort.

Sun Peaks Resort
P.O. Box 869, Kamloops, BC V2C 5M8, phone (604) 578-7222, snow phone 578-7232. 63 runs. Lifts: 2 quads, 1 triple, 1 double, 1 T-bar, 1 platter. 4 day lodges, restaurants, accommodations, ski shop, golf course, day care. Ski rentals/ski school. Cross-country trails. Snowboards permitted. From Mile 141/Km 227 on CANADA HIGHWAY 5, take Tod Mountain Road east 16.5 miles/27 km.

Tabor Mountain
P.O. Box 1570, Prince George, BC V2L 4V5, phone (604) 963-7542, snow phone 564-SNOW. 10 runs. Lifts: 1 triple, 1 T-bar, 1 beginner tow. Day lodge, restaurant. Open daily, Dec. through March. Ski rentals/ski school. Snowboards permitted. From Mile 504/Km 811.5 on CANADA HIGHWAY 97, take Highway 16 east.

Troll Ski Resort
P.O. Box 4013, Quesnel, BC V2J 3J1, phone (604) 994-3200. 14 runs. Lifts: 3 T-bars. Day lodge. Open daily, late Nov. through March. Night skiing on Wednesday. Ski rentals/ski school. Snowboards permitted. From Mile 434.5/Km 699 on CANADA HIGHWAY 97, take Highway 26 east 27 miles/43.5 km.

Whistler Resort
4010 Whistler Way, Whistler, BC V0N 1B4, phone (604) 932-4222. Home of Blackcomb and Whistler mountains, Whistler Resort has won several awards as one of the best ski resorts in North America. Restaurants, accommodations, retail stores, golf course, movie theatre, ice arena, sleigh rides, arcade, conference centre. Cross-country trails. Blackcomb Mountain, 4545 Blackcomb Way, Whistler, BC V0N 1B4, phone (604) 932-3141, snow phone 932-4211. Over 100 runs. Lifts: 1 gondola, 6 quads, 3 triples, 2 T-bars, 1 beginner tow. Day lodges, restaurants, lounges, grocery store, day care. Ski rentals/ski school. Cross-country trails. Snowboards permitted. Whistler Mountain, P.O. Box 67, Whistler, BC V0N 1B0, phone (604) 932-3434, snow phone 932-4191. Over 100 runs. Lifts: 1 gondola, 4 quads, 3 triples, 1 double, 2 T-bars, 3 beginner tows/platters. Day lodge, restaurants. Open daily, Thanksgiving to late April. Ski rentals/ski school. Snowboards permitted. From Mile 527.5/Km 849 on TRANS-CANADA HIGHWAY 1, continue west; north of Vancouver, Highway 1 becomes Highway 99. Resort located just off Highway 99 at Whistler.

Whitetooth Ski Area
P.O. Box 1925, Golden, BC V0A 1H0, phone (604) 344-6114 (also serves as snow phone). 8 runs. Lifts: 1 double, 1 T-bar. Day lodge, cafeteria, day care. Open Friday through Monday and holidays, early Dec. to early April. Ski rentals/ski school. Cross-country trails. Snowboards permitted. Located off TRANS-CANADA HIGHWAY 1 at Mile 44.5/ Km 71.5

Whitewater Ski Resort
P.O. Box 60, Nelson, BC V1L 5P7, phone (604) 354-4944, snow report 352-7669. 27 runs. Lifts: 3 doubles. Day lodge, restaurant, day care. Open daily, Dec. through March. Ski rentals/ski school. Snowboards permitted. From Mile 207.5/Km 334 on CROWSNEST HIGHWAY 3, take Highway 6 north; resort located 12.5 miles/20 km south of Nelson.

IDAHO
Bogus Basin
2405 Bogus Basin Road, Boise, ID 83702, phone (208) 332-5100, snow phone 342-2100. One of the largest night skiing facilities in the United States. 47 runs. Lifts: 6 doubles, 2 rope tows. 2 day lodges, restaurants. Open daily, Thanksgiving to early April. Night skiing daily. Ski rentals/ski school. Cross-country trails. Snowboards permitted. From Mile 425.5 on INTERSTATE 84, continue north 5 miles to the River Street exit.

Brundage Mountain
P.O. Box 1062, McCall, ID 83638, phone (208) 634-4151, snow phone 634-5650. 32 runs. Lifts: 2 triples, 2 doubles, 1 poma, 1 handle tow. Day lodge, restaurant, ski store, day care. Open daily, Thanksgiving to mid-April. Ski rentals/ski school. Snowboards permitted. Located just off IDAHO HIGHWAY 55 at Mile 109.

Kelly Canyon
P.O. Box 367, Ririe, ID 83443, phone (208) 538-6261, snow phone 538-7700. 20 runs. Lifts: 4 doubles. Day lodge, restaurant. Open Tuesday through Sunday and holidays, Dec. through Feb. Night skiing Tuesday through Saturday. Ski rentals/ski school. Snowboards permitted. From Mile 551 on INTERSTATE 84, continue east; take Interstate 86 east 63 miles, Interstate 15 north 42 miles, and Highway 26 east 25 miles.

Lookout Pass
P.O. Box 108, Wallace, ID 83873, phone (208) 744-1392, snow phone 744-1301. 12 runs. Lifts: 1 double, 1 rope. Day lodge, cafeteria, ski shop. Open Thursday through Sunday and holidays, Nov. to early April. Ski rentals/ski school. Cross-country trails. Snowboards permitted. Located just off INTERSTATE 90 at Mile 374 (Exit 0).

Magic Mountain
3367 N. 3600 E., Kimberly, ID 83341, phone and snow phone (208) 423-6221. 20 runs. Lifts: 1 double, 1 poma, 1 rope tow. Day lodge, cafeteria, lounge. Open Friday through Sunday, Dec. to early April. Ski rentals/ski school. Cross-country trails. Snowboards permitted. From Mile 551 on INTERSTATE 84, continue east 8.5 miles.

Pebble Creek Ski Area
P.O. Box 370, Inkom, ID 83245, phone (208) 775-4452, snow phone 775-4451. 24 runs. Lifts: 1 triple, 2 doubles. Day lodge, cafeteria, bar, day care. Open daily, Dec. through Feb.; Wednesday through Sunday, March to April. Night skiing Friday and Saturday, Jan. through Feb. Ski rentals/ski school. Snowboards permitted. Located just off INTERSTATE 15 at Exit 57.

Pomerelle
P.O. Box 158, Albion, ID 83311, phone (208) 638-5599. Family-oriented. 22 runs. Lifts: 1 triple, 1 double, 1 rope tow. Cafeteria. Open Tuesday through Saturday, late Nov. to April. Ski rentals/ski school. Cross-country trails. Snowboards permitted. From Mile 551 on INTERSTATE 84, continue east, then take Highway 77 south 28 miles.

Schweitzer Mountain Resort
P.O. Box 815, Sandpoint, ID 83864, phone (800) 831-8810, snow phone (208) 263-9562. 55 runs. Lifts: 1 quad, 5 doubles. Day lodges, general store, restaurants, cafes, lounge, gift shop, day care. Open daily, Thanksgiving to mid-April. Night skiing Thursday through Saturday and holidays. Ski rentals/ski school. Cross-country trails. Snowboards permitted. Located just off U.S. HIGHWAY 95 at Mile 597.5.

Silver Mountain Resort
610 Bunker Ave., Kellogg, ID 83837, phone and snow phone (208) 783-1111. Features the world's longest single-stage gondola. 50 runs. Lifts: 1 gondola, 1 quad, 2 triples, 2 doubles, 1 surface. Day lodge, food, lounge. Open daily, late Nov. to mid-April. Ski rentals/ski school. Snowboards permitted. Located just off INTERSTATE 90 at Mile 349 (Exit 49).

Snowhaven
225 W. North, Grangeville, ID 83530, phone and snow phone (208) 983-2299. 7 runs. Lifts: 1 T-bar, 1 rope tow. Day lodge, snack bar, ski shop. Open weekends and holidays, mid-Nov. to early March. Night skiing on Friday, Jan. through Feb. Ski rentals/ski school. 1 cross-country trail. Snowboards permitted. From Mile 360 on U.S. HIGHWAY 95, go south 10 miles (follow signs).

Soldier Mountain
Box 465, Fairfield, ID 83327, phone (208) 764-2526. 45 runs. Lifts: 2 doubles, cat skiing. Day lodge, cafeteria, ski shop. Open Wednesday through Sunday and holidays, Dec. through March. Ski rentals/ski school. 1 cross-country trail. Snowboards permitted. From Mile 28 on SAWTOOTH SCENIC ROUTE, take U.S. Highway 20 west to Fairfield, then follow signs north 12 miles.

Sun Valley Resort
Sun Valley, ID 83353, phone (208) 622-4111, snow phone (800) 635-4150. 77 runs.

Lifts: 7 quads, 5 triples, 5 doubles. Lodge, inn, restaurants, banquet rooms, convention center, indoor and outdoor ice skating rinks, indoor pools, bowling alley. Open daily, Thanksgiving to late April. Ski rentals/ski school. Cross-country trails. Snowboards permitted. Located just off SAWTOOTH SCENIC ROUTE at **Mile 54**.

OREGON

Anthony Lakes Mountain Resort
61995 Quail Road, Island City, OR 97850, phone (503) 963-4599, snow phone 856-3277. Highest base elevation in the state (7,100 feet). 23 runs. Lifts: 1 double, 1 poma, snow cat. Day lodge, lounge, retail shops. Open Thursday through Sunday and holidays, Nov. through April. Ski rentals/ski school. Cross-country trails. Snowboards permitted. At **Mile 282** on INTERSTATE 84, take North Powder exit; resort is 15 miles west.

Cooper Spur
11000 Cloud Cap Road, Mount Hood, OR 97401, phone (503) 352-7803 (also serves as snow phone). 10 runs. Lifts: 1 T-bar, 1 rope tow. Day lodge, restaurant. Open weekends and holidays, Nov. through March. Night skiing Thursday through Saturday and holidays. Ski rentals/ski school. Cross-country trails. Snowboards permitted. From **Mile 58** on INTERSTATE 84, take Oregon Highway 35 south 23 miles.

Hoodoo Ski Area
Box 20, Highway 20, Sisters, OR 97759, phone (503) 822-3799, snow phone (800) 949-LIFT. 22 runs. Lifts: 1 triple, 2 doubles, 1 rope tow. 2 day lodges, cafeteria, deli, pizza pub, nordic center. Open daily except Wednesday, Thanksgiving to Easter. Night skiing Thursday through Saturday beginning Dec. 26; in March, night skiing Friday and Saturday only. Ski rentals/ski school. Cross-country trails. Snowboards permitted. Located just south of U.S. HIGHWAY 20 at **Mile 297**.

Mount Bachelor
P.O. Box 1031, Bend, OR 97709, phone (800) 829-2442, snow phone (503) 382-7888. 60 runs. Lifts: 5 quads, 4 triples, 1 double, 2 children's platters. 6 lodges, restaurants, retail center, day care. Open daily, Nov. to July. Ski rentals/ski school. Cross-country trails. Snowboards permitted. From **Mile 138** of U.S. HIGHWAY 97, follow signs to Cascade Lakes Highway; resort is 21 miles from Bend.

Mount Bailey
Mount Bailey Snowcat Skiing, Diamond Lake Resort, Diamond Lake, OR 97731, phone and snow phone (800) 733-7593. Only 12 skiers per day, with guides. Average 5 to 8 runs per day on advanced trails. Lift: snowcat. Resort has restaurants, lounge, grocery store, motels, cabins, laundry service. Open daily, Dec. 1 to April 15, depending on snow conditions. Cross-country trails at resort. Snowboards permitted. From **Mile 62** on U.S. HIGHWAY 97, take Oregon Highway 138 west 22 miles.

Mount Hood Meadows Ski Resort
P.O. Box 470, Mount Hood, OR 97041, phone (503) 337-2222, snow phone 227-SNOW. 82 runs. Lifts: 2 quads, 6 doubles, 1 pony, 1 rope tow. 2 day lodges, restaurants, lounges, sports shop. Open daily, Nov. to May. Night skiing Wednesday through Sunday. Ski rentals/ski school. Cross-country trails. Snowboards per-

mitted. From **Mile 58** on INTERSTATE 84, take Highway 35 south 36 miles.

Mount Hood SkiBowl
P.O. Box 280, Government Camp, OR 97028, phone (503) 272-3206, snow phone 222-BOWL. Largest night ski area in the United States. 64 day runs, 33 night runs. Lifts: 4 doubles, 5 surface. 2 day lodges, restaurants, lounges. Open daily, Nov. to April. Night skiing daily. Ski rentals/ski school. Snowboards permitted. From **Mile 6** on INTERSTATE 84, follow signs to U.S. Highway 26; resort is 30 miles east.

Ski Ashland
P.O. Box 220, Ashland, OR 97520, phone (503) 482-2897, snow phone 482-2754. 23 runs. Lifts: 2 triples, 2 doubles. Day lodge, cafeteria, retail stores, lounge, bar. Open daily, Thanksgiving through mid-April. Night skiing Thursday through Saturday and holidays. Ski rentals/ski school. Snowboards permitted. Located off INTERSTATE 5 at **Mile 5.5** (Exit 6).

Spout Springs Resort
Rt. 1, Box 65, Weston, OR 97886, phone (503) 566-2164 (also serves as snow phone). 11 runs. Lifts: 2 doubles, 2 surface. Restaurant, lounge, day care. Open Wednesday through Sunday, Nov. to March. Night skiing Wednesday, Friday, Saturday. Ski rentals/ski school. Cross-country trails. Snowboards permitted. From **Mile 207** on INTERSTATE 84, take Oregon Highway 11 north, then take Oregon Highway 204 east.

Summit Ski Area
P.O. Box 1215, Welches, OR 97067, phone (503) 272-0256 (also serves as snow phone). Oldest ski area on Mount Hood. 7 runs. Lifts: 1 double, 1 rope tow. Day lodge, restaurant. Open weekends and holidays, Nov. to April. Ski rentals/ski school. Cross-country trails. Snowboards permitted. From **Mile 6** on INTERSTATE 84, follow signs to U.S. Highway 26 east.

Timberline Lodge Ski Area
Timberline Lodge, OR 97028, phone (503) 231-7979, snow phone 222-2211. Has the longest ski season in the state. Timberline Lodge is a National Historic Landmark. 30 runs. Lifts: 1 quad, 1 triple, 4 doubles. Lodge, restaurants, hotel, lounges, gift shop, pool, sauna, spa. Open daily, from Nov. through Labor Day weekend. Night skiing Wednesday through Saturday, Dec. through March (depending on snow conditions). Ski rentals/ski school. Snowboards permitted. From **Mile 6** on INTERSTATE 84, follow signs to U.S. Highway 26; resort is 40 miles east.

Willamette Pass
P.O. Box 5509, Eugene, OR 97405, phone (800) 444-5030, snow phone (503) 345-SNOW. 29 runs. Lifts: 4 triples, 1 double. Open daily, Nov. to April. Night skiing Friday and Saturday. Ski rentals/ski school. Cross-country trails. Snowboards permitted. From **Mile 188** (Exit 188A) on INTERSTATE 5, take State Highway 58 east 60 miles.

WASHINGTON

Alpental, Ski Acres, Snoqualmie, Hyak
7900 SE 28th St., Suite 200, Mercer Island, WA 98040, phone (206) 232-8182, snow phone 236-1600. Largest night skiing facility in North America. Over 65 runs. Lifts: 1 quad, 4 triples, 19 doubles, 1 platter, 11 rope tows. Open daily, mid-Nov. to mid-April.

Night skiing daily. Ski rentals/ski school. Cross-country trails. Snowboards permitted. Located at Snoqualmie Pass, just off INTERSTATE 90 at **Mile 51**.

Crystal Mountain Resort
1 Crystal Mountain Blvd., Crystal Mountain, WA 98022, phone (360) 663-2265, snow phone 634-3771. 54 runs. Lifts: 2 quads, 3 triples and 5 doubles. Open daily, mid-Nov. to mid-April. Night skiing Friday through Sunday. Ski rentals/ski school. Snowboards permitted. From **Mile 450** of INTERSTATE 5, take Washington Highway 18 east to Washington Highway 410 east, go 30 miles to Crystal Mountain turnoff.

49 Degrees North Ski Area
P.O. Box 166, Chewelah, WA 99109, phone (509) 935-6649, snow phone 458-9208. 23 runs. Lifts: 4 doubles. Day lodge, restaurant, day care. Open Friday through Tuesday, mid-Nov. through mid-April. Ski rentals/ski school. Cross-country trails. Snowboards permitted. From **Mile 602** on U.S. HIGHWAY 395, go 9 miles east.

Mission Ridge
P.O. Box 1668, Wenatchee, WA 98807-1668, phone (509) 663-7631, snow phone (800) 374-1693. 33 runs. Lifts: 4 doubles, 2 rope tows. Day lodge, cafeteria, bar, midway cafe, day care. Open daily, mid-Nov. through mid-April. Night skiing daily. Ski rentals/ski school. Snowboards permitted. Located just off U.S. HIGHWAY 2 at **Mile 295**.

Mount Baker
1017 Iowa St., Bellingham, WA 98226, phone (360) 734-6771, snow phone 671-0211. 38 runs. Lifts: 2 quads, 6 doubles, 1 rope tow. 2 day lodges, food, day care. Open daily, mid-Nov. to May. Ski rentals/ski school. Cross-country trails. Snowboards permitted. From **Mile 563** on INTERSTATE 5, take Highway 542 east 60 miles.

Mount Spokane
P.O. Box 159, Mead, WA 99021, phone (509) 238-6281, snow phone 238-6223. 27 runs. Lifts: 5 doubles. Cafeteria, lounge, espresso bar. Open Wednesday through Sunday, late Nov. to May. Night skiing Wednesday through Saturday. Ski rentals/ski school. Cross-country trails. Snowboards permitted. From **Mile 120** on U.S. HIGHWAY 2, take Highway 206 east 20 miles.

Ski Bluewood
P.O. Box 88, Dayton, WA 99328, phone (509) 382-4725, snow phone 382-2877. 23 runs. Lifts: 2 triples, 1 platter. Day lodge, cafeteria, pub, retail shop. Open daily, mid-Nov. to April. Ski rentals/ski school. Snowboards permitted. From **Mile 284** on U.S. HIGHWAY 12, follow signs 21.5 miles southeast.

Stevens Pass
P.O. Box 98, Skykomish, WA 98288, phone (360) 973-2441, snow phone 634-1645. 36 runs. Lifts: 1 quad, 4 triples, 6 doubles. 3 day lodges, food, lounges, retail shop, day care. Open daily, late Nov. to early April. Night skiing daily. Ski rentals/ski school. Cross-country trails. Snowboards permitted. Located just off U.S. HIGHWAY 2 at **Mile 348**.

White Pass
P.O. Box 354, Yakima, WA 98907, phone (509) 453-8731, snow phone 672-3100. 32 runs. Lifts: 1 quad, 3 doubles, 1 rope tow.

Day lodge, cafeteria, restaurant, retail shop, espresso bar, day care. Open daily, Thanksgiving to late April. Night skiing Friday and Saturday, mid-Dec. to early March. Ski rentals/ski school. Cross-country trails. Snowboards permitted. Located just off U.S. HIGHWAY 12 at **Mile 498.5.**

State and Provincial Parks

BRITISH COLUMBIA

B.C. Parks does not accept reservations except for group camping. A group must have 15 or more people; contact the district offices, listed below, for reservations. Camping fees, which vary from park to park, are generally charged between April 1 and Oct. 31. Several parks, though not all of them, are open year-round; however, full facilities and services may not always be available. For general information on all parks, contact B.C. Parks, 2nd Floor, 800 Johnson St., Victoria, BC V8V 1X4; phone (604) 387-5002, or fax (604) 387-5757.

The park system is organized by regions and districts. In addition to arranging group reservations, the district offices (which are located at a park within their district) can provide more detailed information about visitor programs, facilities, services and recreational opportunities found in all parks within their district.

Northern Region (northern and central BC):

Cariboo District, 540 Borland St., Williams Lake, BC V2G 1R8; phone (604) 398-4414, fax (604) 398-4686.

Peace-Liard District, 10003 110th Ave. #250, Fort St. John, BC V1J 6M7; phone (604) 787-3407, fax (604) 787-3490.

Prince George District, Box 2045, 4051 18th Ave., Prince George, BC V2N 2J6; phone (604) 565-6340, fax (604) 565-6940.

Skeena District, Bag 5000, 3790 Alfred Ave., Smithers, BC V0J 2N0; phone (604) 847-7320, fax (604) 847-7659.

South Coast Region (southwestern BC):

Fraser Valley District, Cultus Lake Park, P.O. Box 10, Cultus Lake, BC V0X 1H0; phone (604) 858-7161, fax (604) 858-4905.

Garibaldi/Sunshine Coast, Alice Lake Park, Box 220, Brackendale, BC V0N 1H0; phone (604) 898-3678, fax (604) 898-4171.

Malahat District, Rural Route #6, 2930 Trans-Canada Highway, Victoria, BC V9B 5T9; phone (604) 387-4363, fax (604) 478-9211.

Strathcona District, Rathtrevor Beach Park, Box 1479, Parksville, BC V9P 2H4; phone (604) 248-3931, fax (604) 248-8584.

Vancouver District, Golden Ears Park, Box 7000, Maple Ridge, BC V2X 7G3; phone (604) 463-3513, fax (604) 463-6193.

Southern Interior Region (southeastern BC):

East Kootenay District, Wasa Lake Park, Box 118, Wasa, BC V0B 2K0; phone (604) 422-3212, fax (604) 422-3326.

Okanagan District, Okanagan Lake Park, Box 399, Summerland, BC V0H 1Z0; phone (604) 494-0321, fax (604) 494-9737.

Thompson River District, 1210 McGill Road, Kamloops, BC V2C 6N6; phone (604) 828-4494, fax (604) 828-4633.

West Kootenay District, Site 8, Comp. 5, Rural Route #3, Nelson, BC V1L 5P6; phone (604) 825-4421, fax (604) 825-9509.

IDAHO

Reservations are available at the state parks listed below. You can make reservations by contacting the parks directly. Reservation applications for the summer season are accepted by mail starting the first business day of January; applications received prior to January are returned to sender. After March 31, telephone and walk-in reservations are accepted as well as mail-in reservations. If you're planning on a walk-in reservation, call beforehand to assure that someone will be available. Some parks are open year-round. To find out when a particular park is open for the season, contact the park directly. For a complete list of Idaho state parks or other information, contact the Idaho Dept. of Parks and Recreation, P.O. Box 83720, Boise, ID 83720-0065; phone (208) 334-4199.

Farragut State Park, E. 13400 Ranger Road, Athol, ID 83801; (208) 683-2425.

Hells Gate State Park, 3620A Snake River Ave., Lewiston, ID 83501; (208) 799-5015.

Ponderosa State Park, P.O. Box A, McCall, ID 83638; (208) 634-2164.

Priest Lake State Park, Indian River Bay #423, Coolin, ID 83821; (208) 443-2200.

OREGON

Reservations are available at the state parks listed below, Memorial Day weekend through Labor Day weekend; the rest of the year, campsites are available on a first-come, first-served basis. You can make reservations by completing a reservation application and mailing or delivering it directly to the park. Phone reservations are not accepted. Applications are accepted Jan. 1 or later; those postmarked before Jan. 1 will be returned to sender. For an application, a complete list of Oregon state parks, or other information, contact the Oregon Parks and Recreation Dept., 1115 Commercial St. NE, Salem, OR 97310-1001; phone (503) 378-6305. Applications are also available from the parks, the state police, most Motor Vehicles Division offices and many chambers of commerce.

You can get current information on campsite availability at all Oregon state parks by calling the Oregon State Park Campsite Information Center, (800) 452-5687 or (503) 731-3411. The center is open 8 a.m. to 5 p.m., the first Monday in March to Labor Day weekend. You cannot make reservations through the center, but reservation cancellations are accepted.

All 50 state parks are open mid-April to late Oct., and 21 are open year-round. Most of the year-round parks are located on the coast, where mild winter weather normally prevails. For information on park schedules, contact the Oregon Parks and Recreation Dept. Also, a brochure describing the features and facilities of each year-round park, "Parks for All Seasons," is available from Parks and Recreation.

Beachside State Park, P.O. Box 693, Waldport, OR 97394; (503) 563-3220.

Beverly Beach State Park, 198 NE 123rd St., Newport, OR 97365; (503) 265-9278.

Cape Lookout State Park, 13000 Whiskey Creek Road W., Tillamook, OR 97141; (503) 842-4981.

The Cove Palisades State Park, Route 1, Box 60 CP, Culver, OR 97734; (503) 546-3412.

Detroit Lake State Park, P.O. Box 549, Detroit, OR 97342; (503) 854-3346.

Devil's Lake State Park, 1452 NE 6th, Lincoln City, OR 97367; (503) 994-2002.

Fort Stevens State Park, Hammond, OR 97121; (503) 861-1671.

Harris Beach State Park, 1655 Highway 101, Brookings, OR 97415; (503) 469-2021.

Jessie M. Honeyman State Park, 84505 Highway 101 S., Florence, OR 97439; (503) 997-3641.

Prineville Reservoir State Park, 916777 Parkland Dr., Prineville, OR 97734; (503) 447-4363.

South Beach State Park, 5580 S. Coast Highway, South Beach, OR 97366; (503) 867-4715.

Sunset Bay State Park, 10965 Cape Arago Highway, Coos Bay, OR 97420; (503) 888-4902.

Wallowa Lake State Park, 72214 Marina Lane, Joseph, OR 97846; (503) 432-4185.

WASHINGTON

Reservations are available at the state parks listed below, March 31 through Sept. 30. You can make reservations by completing a reservation application and mailing it directly to the park. Applications are accepted Jan. 1 and later; those postmarked before Jan. 1 will be returned to sender. You can also make reservations in person at the park on or after April 1. For an application, a complete list of Washington state parks, or other information, contact the Washington State Parks Headquarters, 7150 Cleanwater Lane, P.O. Box 42650, Olympia, WA 98504-2650; phone (360) 902-8563. Applications are also available from the state parks and the regional offices: Southwest Region (Olympia), (360) 753-7143; Northwest Region (Burlington), (360) 755-9231; Eastern Region (Wenatchee), (509) 662-0420; and Puget Sound (Auburn), (206) 931-3907.

Most of the state parks are open year-round, but often have limited facilities during the winter. For more information on park schedules, contact the Washington State Parks Headquarters.

Belfair State Park, NE 410 Beck Road, Belfair, WA 98528-9426, (360) 275-0669.

Birch Bay State Park, 5105 Helweg Road, Blaine, WA 98230-9625; (360) 271-2800.

Fort Canby State Park, P.O. Box 488, Ilwaco, WA 98624-0488, (360) 642-3078.

Fort Flagler State Park, Norland, WA 98358-9699, (360) 385-1259.

Grayland Beach State Park, % Twin Harbors, Westport, WA 98595-9801; (360) 268-9717.

Ike Kinswa State Park, 873 Harmony Road, Silver Creek, WA 98585-9706; (360) 983-3402.

Lake Chelan State Park, Route 1, Box 90, Chelan, WA 98816-9755; (509) 687-3710.

Lincoln Rock State Park, Route 3, Box 3137, E. Wenatchee, WA 98802-9566; (509) 884-8702.

Moran State Park, Star Route, Box 22, Eastsound, WA 98245-9603; (360) 376-2326.

Pearrygin Lake State Park, Route 1, Box 300, Winthrop, WA 98862-9710; (509) 996-2370.

Steamboat Rock State Park, P.O. Box 370, Electric City, WA 99123-0370; (509) 633-1304.

Twin Harbors State Park, Westport, WA 98595-9801; (360) 268-9717.

Wineries

The Northwest is fortunate to have almost the perfect climate and conditions for wine grape growing. The result is an abundance of wineries, plenty to choose from when planning your trip or exploring the region. The wineries that follow are categorized by state and province and by the highways they are located near. Since some wineries have infrequent operating hours or only offer tours by appointment, call before you visit.

The following organizations assisted *Northwest Mileposts®* in its research on wineries. Contact them for more information:

British Columbia Wine Institute
1864 Spall Road, Suite 5
Kelowna, BC V1Y 4R1
phone (604) 762-4887

Idaho Grape Growers and Wine Producers Commission
Box 6016
Boise, ID 83707
phone (208) 343-2582

Oregon Winegrowers' Association
1200 NW Front Ave., Suite 400
Portland, OR 97209
phone (503) 228-0713

Washington Wine Commission
P.O. Box 61217
Seattle, WA 98121
phone (206) 728-2252

BRITISH COLUMBIA

Trans-Canada Highway 1

Andres Wines
2120 Vintner St., Port Moody, BC V3H 1W8; phone (604) 937-3411, fax (604) 937-5487. Andres produces Rosé, Sparkling Wine, Sherry, and Red and White Table Wine. From **Mile 517.5** (Exit 44) on TRANS-CANADA HIGHWAY 1, go northeast on Highway 7, west on Highway 7A (which becomes St. Johns), into Port Moody for 2 miles, north on Douglas and west on Vintner.

Domaine De Chaberton Estate Winery
1064 216th St., Langley, BC V3A 7R2; phone (604) 530-1736, fax (604) 533-9687. Claude Violet, winemaker. Tours by appointment only. From **Mile 508.5** on TRANS-CANADA HIGHWAY 1, go south on 200th Street, east on North Bluff Road and south on 216th Street.

Crowsnest Highway 3

St. Laszlo Vineyards
Site 97, C8, Rural Route #1, Highway 3, Keremeos, BC V0X 1N0; phone (604) 499-2856, fax (604) 499-5600. St. Laszlo is located in the heart of the Similkameen Valley, off CROWSNEST HIGHWAY 3 at **Mile 406.5**.

Canada Highway 97

Bella Vista Vineyards
3111 Agnew Road (off Bella Vista), Vernon, BC V1T 6L7; phone (604) 558-0770, fax (604) 542-1221. North America's most northerly cottage winery. Located off CANADA HIGHWAY 97 at **Mile 110**.

Blue Mountain Vineyard and Cellars
Allendale Road, Rural Route #1, Site 3, C4, Okanagan Falls, BC V0H 1R0; phone (604) 497-8244, fax (604) 497-6160. Blue Mountain produces Pinot Blanc, Pinot Gris, Chardonnay, Pinot Noir and Methode Champenoise Sparkling Wine from grapes grown on their 55 acres of vineyards. Completed in October 1993, the winery facility is set amid scenic park land that includes a lake and bird sanctuary. Tours and tastings by appointment. Closed Oct. through April. From **Mile 25.5** on CANADA HIGHWAY 97, go northeast on Oliver Ranch Road.

Calona Wines
1125 Richter St., Kelowna, BC V1Y 2K6; phone (604) 762-3332 or 762-9144, wine information line (800) 663-5086, fax (604) 762-2999. Calona is British Columbia's oldest, largest and most awarded winery. Howard Soon, winemaker. From **Mile 77.5** on CANADA HIGHWAY 97, go north on Richter Street.

CedarCreek Estate Winery
5445 Lakeshore Road, Kelowna, BC V1Y 7R3; phone (604) 764-8866, fax (604) 764-2603. Overlooking Okanagan Lake, CedarCreek offers a tour of the vineyard, lab, cellar and bottling room. CedarCreek produces Chardonnay, Chancellor, Ehrenfelser, Riesling, Dry Riesling, Gewurztraminer and Pinot Blanc. The winery is open daily, May to Nov. Ann Sperling, winemaker. From **Mile 77.5** on CANADA HIGHWAY 97, go south on Pandosy Street, then southeast on Lakeshore Road.

Chateau Ste. Claire Estate Winery
Trepanier Bench Road, Rural Route #2, Site 27, C29, Peachland, BC V0H 1X0, phone (604) 767-3113. British Columbia's first estate winery, Chateau Ste. Claire was established in 1979 under the name of Chateau Marion John. Chateau St. Claire produces Johannisberg Riesling, Muscat, Gewürztraminer, Foch, Ice Wine and Blush. Closed Nov. through March. Located off CANADA HIGHWAY 97 at **Mile 64.5**.

Divino Estate Winery
Road 8, P.O. Box 866, Oliver, BC V0H 1T0; phone (604) 498-2784, fax (604) 498-6518. Wines produced by Divino Estate Winery include Merlot, Cabernet, Pinot Nero, Pinot Grigio and Chardonnay. Although tours are not offered, visitors can taste the wines as well as enjoy picnic lunches and wander through the vineyard's 70.8 acres. Nov. through April, open by appointment only. From **Mile 12.5** on CANADA HIGHWAY 97, go west on Road 8.

Gehringer Brothers Estate Winery
Road 8, Rural Route #1, Site 23, C4, Oliver, BC V0H 1T0; phone (604) 498-3537, fax (604) 498-3510. Gehringer Brothers produces Germanic-style wines ranging from dry to medium and Ice Wine. Tours by appointment. From **Mile 12.5** on CANADA HIGHWAY 97, go west on Road 8.

Gray Monk Estate Winery
1051 Camp Road, P.O. Box 63, Okanagan Centre, BC V0H 1P0; phone (604) 766-3168 or (800) 766-3168, fax (604) 766-3390. Located above Okanagan Lake, the winery is built in the style of a European villa. From **Mile 91** on CANADA HIGHWAY 97, go northwest on Okanagan Centre Road, then west on Camp Road.

Hainle Vineyards Estate Winery
5355 Trepanier Bench Road, Rural Route #2, Site 27A, C6, Peachland, BC V0H 1X0; phone (604) 767-2525, fax (604) 767-2543. Organically certified and family run, Hainle produces vinifera varietals and Canada's first Ice Wine. Tours can be arranged, but the emphasis is on tastings. Located off CANADA HIGHWAY 97 at **Mile 64.5**.

Hillside Cellars
1350 Naramata Road, Penticton, BC V2A 6J6; phone (604) 493-4424, fax (604) 493-4424. Vera Klokocka, winemaker. From **Mile 36.5** on CANADA HIGHWAY 97, go east on Lakeshore Drive, then northeast on Vancouver Road to Naramata Road.

House of Rose
Rural Route #5, 2270 Garner Road, Kelowna, BC V1X 4K4; phone (604) 765-0802, fax (604) 765-0802. A small winery, House of Rose offers tasting and tours. They use grapes from their own vines to produce Verdelet, Chardonnay, Riesling, Perle of Zala and a Red Wine made from a blend of Pinot Noir, Merlot, de Chaunac and Foch. From **Mile 77.5** on CANADA HIGHWAY 97, go north on Garner Road.

Lang Vineyards
2493 Gammon Road, Rural Route #1, Site 11, C55, Naramata, BC V0H 1N0; phone (604) 496-5987, fax (604) 496-5706. Guenther Lang, winemaker. Tours by appointment only. Closed Oct. through April. From **Mile 36.5** on CANADA HIGHWAY 97, go east on Lakeshore Dr., northeast on Vancouver Road, north on Naramata Road, east on Ganne Road and north on Gammon Road.

LeComte Estate Winery
Green Lake Road, P.O. Box 498, Okanagan Falls, BC V0H 1R0; phone (604) 497-8267, fax (604) 497-8073. LeComte produces 10 varieties of white wine and 5 varieties of red. Tours are available July through Oct., and include a visit to a dog cemetery, old wine cellar, the winery, crushing area, bottling area and vineyards. A large patio area is available for picnicking and provides a view of the valley below the mountain vineyard. From **Mile 29** on CANADA HIGHWAY 97, go south on Green Lake Road.

Mission Hill Wines
1730 Mission Hill Road, Westbank, BC V4T 2E4; phone (604) 768-5125 or (604) 768-7611 (for the boutique), fax (604) 768-2044. In addition to various table wines, premium private reserves and specialty dessert wines, Mission Hill also produces California Coolers and Okanagan Ciders. The winery features picturesque picnic areas and gardens as well as a tour and wine tasting. From **Mile 70** on CANADA HIGHWAY 97, go northeast on Boucherie Road, then west on Mission Hill Road.

Nichol Vineyard
1285 Smethurst Road, Rural Route #1, Site 14, C13, Naramata, BC V0H 1N0; phone (604) 496-5962. Established in August 1993, Nichol has already won a gold medal from the Vintners Quality Alliance of British Columbia Nichol produces barrel-fermented white, including the award-winning Ehrenfelser, and barrel-aged red varietals, including Syrah. From **Mile 36.5** on CANADA HIGHWAY 97, go east on Lakeshore Drive, northeast on Vancouver Road, north on Naramata Road and east on Smethurst Road;

winery is 9 miles north of Penticton.

Okanagan Vineyards Winery
Rural Route #1, Site 27, C5, Road 11 W., Oliver, BC V0H 1T0; phone (604) 498-6663, fax (604) 498-4566. Sandor Mayer, winemaker. Located in Canada's only desert, Okanagan Vineyards produces Chardonnay, Cabernet Sauvignon, Merlot, Riesling and Pinot Noir. From **Mile 11.5** on CANADA HIGHWAY 97, go west on Road 11.

Quail's Gate Vineyards Estate Winery
3303 Boucherie Road, Kelowna, BC V1Z 2H3; phone (604) 769-4451, fax (604) 769-3451. The wine shop is housed in a heritage log home. Quail's Gate produces Pinot Noir, Chardonnay, Chasselas, Gewürztraminer, Riesling and Optima. From **Mile 70** on CANADA HIGHWAY 97, go northeast on Boucherie Road.

St. Hubertus Vineyards
5225 Lakeshore Road, Kelowna, BC V1Y 7R3; phone (604) 764-7888, fax (604) 764-0499. St. Hubertus produces Swiss-style wines, including Riesling, Pinot Blanc, Marechal Foch, Bacchus and Gamay Noir. Jan. through Feb., open only by appointment. From **Mile 77.5** on CANADA HIGHWAY 97, go south on Pandosy Street, then southeast on Lakeshore Road.

Sumac Ridge Estate Winery
17403 Highway 97, P.O. Box 307, Summerland, BC V0H 1Z0; phone (604) 494-0451, fax (604) 494-3456. Western Canada's first champagne cellar, Sumac Ridge also offers a restaurant and golf course. Located off CANADA HIGHWAY 97 at **Mile 50**.

Summerhill Estate Winery
Rural Route #4, 4870 Chute Lake Road, Kelowna, BC V1Y 7R3; phone (604) 764-8000, fax (604) 764-2598. British Columbia's first champagne house, Summerhill offers a tour of the Pyramid aging facility. Summerhill produces Methode Champenoise. From **Mile 77.5** on CANADA HIGHWAY 97, go south on Pandosy Street, then southwest on Chute Lake Road.

Vincor International
38691 Highway 97, P.O. Box 1650, Oliver, BC V0H 1T0; phone (604) 498-4981, fax (604) 498-6505. Frank Supernak is the winemaker at one of the largest wineries in North America. Open year-round. Tours available May through Oct. Located off CANADA HIGHWAY 97 at **Mile 19**.

Wild Goose Vineyards and Winery
Rural Route #1, Site 3, C11, Lot 11, Sun Valley Way, Okanagan Falls, BC V0H 1R0; phone (604) 497-8919, fax (604) 497-6853. One of British Columbia's first farm wineries, Wild Goose produces Riesling and Gewürztraminer. Tours by appointment only. Nov. through March, visits by appointment only. From **Mile 25.5** on CANADA HIGHWAY 97, go northeast on Oliver Ranch Road, then northwest on Sun Valley Way.

The Islands

Blue Grouse Vineyards and Winery
4365 Blue Grouse Road, Rural Route #7, Duncan, BC V9L 4W4; phone (604) 743-3834. Dr. Hans and Evangeline Kiltz, winemakers. Located on Vancouver Island, just off BC HIGHWAY 19 at **Mile 35.5**.

Cherry Point Vineyards
840 Cherry Point Road, Rural Route #3, Cobble Hill, BC V0H 1L0; phone (604) 743-1272, fax (604) 743-1059. Wayne and Helena Ulrich, owners. Located on Vancouver Island, just off BC HIGHWAY 19 at **Mile 29.5**.

Venturi-Schulze Vineyards
4235 Trans-Canada Highway 1, Rural Route #1, Cobble Hill, BC V0R 1L0; phone (604) 743-5630, fax (604) 743-5630. Giordano Venturi and Marilyn Venturi (née Schulze) boast that Venturi-Schulze is the smallest winery in British Columbia. Family-owned and operated by organic practices, Venturi-Schultze produces Madeleine Sylvaner, Schönburger, Müller-Thurgau, Ortega, Pinot Auxerrois, Siegerrebe, Pinot Noir and Methode Champenoise Sparkling Wine. Traditional Basalmic Vinegar, which takes 12 years to develop, is also offered. Tours by appointment only. Located on Vancouver Island; from **Mile 29.5** on BC HIGHWAY 19 (Trans-Canada Highway 1), go west to Cobble Hill, then phone for directions.

Vignetti Zanatta Ltd.
5039 Marshall Road, Rural Route #3, Duncan, BC V9L 2X1; phone (604) 748-2338, fax (604) 746-5684. Vignetti Zanatta has been in operation since 1959. All of their wines are produced naturally, using a minimum of sulfites. The winery is adjacent to the original 1903 farm house and includes a small tasting room and wine shop open 1 to 4 p.m. on weekends only. Closed Nov. through May. Located on Vancouver Island, just off BC HIGHWAY 19 at **Mile 35.5**.

IDAHO
Interstate 84

Carmela Vineyards
795 W. Madison, Glenns Ferry, ID 83626; phone (208) 366-2313. One of Idaho's newest wineries, Carmela is owned and operated by the Martell family. A 9-hole golf course winds through the vineyards; the winery includes a tasting room, gift shop and deli. Carmela produces Chardonnay, Cabernet Sauvignon, Merlot, Muscat Canelli, Lemberger, Johannisberg Riesling and Blush. From **Mile 498** (Exit 121) on INTERSTATE 84, follow signs; winery is next to Three Island Crossing State Park.

Hells Canyon Winery
18835 Symms Road, Caldwell, ID 83605; phone (208) 336-2277. Hells Canyon Tasting Room, Mussel's Fish Market, 3107 Overland Road, Boise, ID; phone (208) 336-2277. Founded in 1980 by Steve and Leslie Robertson, Hells Canyon produces Chardonnay and Cabernet Sauvignon. The wines are sold primarily in Idaho, but have also found a niche in the British market. Visits to winery by appointment only. From **Mile 403.5** (Exit 28) on INTERSTATE 84, go south on Highway 55, south on Chicken Dinner Road and west on Symms Road.

Indian Creek Winery
Route 1, 1000 N. McDermott Road, Kuna, ID 83634; phone (208) 922-4791. Owned and operated by the Stowe family, Indian Creek produces Pinot Noir, Chardonnay, White Riesling, Chenin Blanc, White Pinot Noir, Gewürztraminer, Cabernet Sauvignon and light red and white table wines. From **Mile 420.5** (Exit 44) on INTERSTATE 84, go south to Kuna, west on Kuna Road for 3 miles and right on McDermott Road.

Petros Winery
264 N. Maple Grove Road, Boise, ID 83704; phone (208) 322-7474. Petros Wine Shoppe, Boise Towne Square Mall, 350 N. Milwaukee, Boise, ID 83788; phone (208) 322-4739. Owned and operated by Petro and Janet Eliopulos, Petros produces Chardonnay, Cabernet Sauvignon, Merlot, Pinot Noir, Rieslings, Méthode Champenoise Champagnes and Botrytis Affected Late Harvest dessert wines. The winery is not open to the public. From **Mile 425.5** on INTERSTATE 84, take Interstate 184 to Boise city center, then the Franklin exit to the mall.

Pintler Cellar
13750 Surrey Lane, Nampa, ID 83686; phone (208) 467-1200. Situated on the rim of Hidden Valley, Pintler Cellar offers a panoramic view of the Owyhee Mountains and the Boise Valley, as well as annual festivals such as the Mother's Day Wine and Food Festival and the Thanksgiving Barrel Tasting and Open House. Pintler produces Chardonnay, Riesling, Semillon, Chenin Blanc, Cabernet Sauvignon, Merlot and Pinot Noir. From **Mile 412** (Exit 36) on INTERSTATE 84, go south on Franklin Road, southwest on 11th, southeast on 3rd S., southwest on 12th Ave. S. (which becomes Highway 45), west on Missouri Avenue for 4 miles, south on Sky Ranch Road for 2 miles and west on Surrey Lane.

Rose Creek Winery
111 W. Hagerman Ave., P.O. Box 356, Hagerman, ID 83332; phone (208) 837-4413. Located in a century-old, stone building, Rose Creek is owned and operated by three families. Rose Creek produces Chardonnay, Blush, Riesling and Pinot Noir. From **Mile 514** (Exit 137) on INTERSTATE 84, go south on Highway 30 (Thousand Springs Scenic Route); the winery is in the basement of the lava-rock building on State Street.

South Hills Winery
3099 E. 3400 N, P.O. Box 727, Twin Falls, ID 83301; phone (208) 734-6369. One of Idaho's smallest wineries, South Hills is family owned and operated by Frank and Crystal Hegy and their 2 children. All grapes are pressed on an antique Italian press. South Hills produces Riesling, Chenin Blanc, Lemberger, Blush, Gewürztraminer and Chardonnay. By appointment only. From **Mile 551** (Exit 173) on INTERSTATE 84, go south on Blue Lakes Boulevard, then east on 3400 N.

Ste. Chapelle Winery
14068 Sunny Slope Road, Caldwell, ID 83605; phone (208) 459-7222. Ste. Chapelle on the Grove, 801 Main St., Suite 105, Boise, ID 83702; phone (208) 344-9074. Owned and operated by the Symms family, Ste. Chapelle is situated on Winery Hill overlooking the Snake River. Ste. Chapelle produces Chardonnay, Johannisberg Riesling, Fumé Blanc, Blush, Pinot Noir Blanc, Chenin Blanc, Gewürztraminer, Cabernet Sauvignon, Pinot Noir, Merlot, and Champagne (Brut, Pinot Noir, Johannisberg Riesling, Johannisberg Riesling Special Harvest). From **Mile 411** (Exit 35) on INTERSTATE 84, take Highway 55 south for 13 miles, then go left on Lowell Road.

Vickers Vineyards
15646 Sunny Slope, Caldwell, ID 83605; phone (208) 376-7330 (daytime, work phone number for the owner). Kirby Vickers, owner. Located off INTERSTATE 84 in Caldwell.

Weston Winery

14949 Sunny Slope Road, Caldwell, ID 83605; phone (208) 454-1682 or 459-2631. One of Idaho's oldest wineries, and also one of the highest (2,750 feet), Weston produces Johannisberg Riesling, Chardonnay, Pinot Noir, Cabernet Sauvignon, Merlot, Cabernet Franc and Zinfandel. From **Mile 411** (Exit 35) on INTERSTATE 84, take Highway 55 south for 12 miles.

U.S. Highway 95

Camas Winery

110 S. Main St., Moscow, ID 83843; phone (208) 882-0214. Located in a century-old brick building, Camas is owned and operated by Stu and Sue Scott. Camas produces Chardonnay, Cabernet Sauvignon, Riesling, Hot Spiced Wine, Palouse Gold, Hog Heaven Red and White, Lemberger, Blush, Methode Champenoise, Red Table Wine and Mead (wine from honey). Located off U.S. HIGHWAY 95 at **Mile 460**; winery is located near the corner of 1st and Main.

Cana Vineyards

Box 555, Wilder, ID 83676; phone (208) 482-7372. Simultaneously one of the oldest and newest wineries in Idaho, Cana was the original winery of Idaho industry pioneer Lou Facelli. Cana has been revived by the Larry Dawson family and produces White Riesling, Chardonnay, Merlot, Cabernet Sauvignon and Champagne. Tours and tastings by appointment. From **Mile 160.5** on U.S. HIGHWAY 95, go west on Peckham Road.

OREGON
Interstate 5

Ashland Vineyards

2775 E. Main St., Ashland, OR 97520; phone (503) 488-0088, fax (503) 488-5857. Located in the Rogue Valley, Ashland produces Cabernet Sauvignon, Chardonnay, Müller-Thurgau, Sauvignon Blanc and Merlot. From **Mile 14** (Exit 14) on INTERSTATE 5, go east on Highway 66, then north on E. Main Street.

Bridgeview Vineyards

4210 Holland Loop Road, Cave Junction, OR 97523; phone (503) 592-4688, fax (503) 592-2127. Winemaker Laurent Montalieu of Bordeaux, France, creates the Bridgeview wines. The winery produces Pinot Noir, Chardonnay, Riesling, Gewürztraminer and Pinot Gris. From **Mile 58.5** (Exit 58) on INTERSTATE 5, go southwest on U.S. 199 approximately 25 miles, east on Highway 46 and south on Holland Loop Road.

Callahan Ridge Winery

340 Busenbark Lane, Roseburg, OR 97470; phone (800) 695-4946 or (503) 673-7901. Established in 1987, Callahan Ridge is owned by Mary Sykes-Guido, Richard Mansfield, and Kris and Joel Goodwillie. The winery and tasting room is housed in a 110-year-old barn. Callahan Ridge produces Dry Gewürztraminer, Dry Riesling, Chardonnay, Pinot Noir, Cabernet, Red Zinfandel, White Zinfandel, White Riesling and Hot Spiced Wine. From **Mile 245** (Exit 125) on INTERSTATE 5, go west on Garden Valley Boulevard, west on Melrose Road and north on Busenbark Road.

Champoeg Wine Cellars

10375 Champoeg Road NE, Aurora, OR 97002; phone (503) 678-2144. Planted in 1979, the vineyard is one of the oldest wine grape plantings in Oregon. Champoeg produces Pinot Noir, Chardonnay, White Riesling, Müller-Thurgau and Gewürztraminer, and is owned and operated by the Pitterle and Killian families. Closed Thanksgiving, Christmas and New Year's. From **Mile 398** (Exit 278) on INTERSTATE 5, go west on Ehlen Road, north on Butteville Road and west on Champoeg Road.

Chateau Lorane

27415 Siuslaw River Road, Lorane, OR 97451; phone (503) 942-8028. Linde and Sharon Dester planted their 30-acre vineyard in 1984, and opened the winery and tasting room in 1992. Chateau Lorane produces Riesling, Gewürztraminer, Chardonnay, Sauvignon Blanc, Pinot Noir, Late Harvest Sauvignon Blanc, Flora, Melon de Bourgogne, Cabernet Franc, Durif (a.k.a. Petit Sirah), Maréchal Foch, Grand Noir, Baco Noir, Grignolino, Pinot Meunier, Negrette, Cascade and Chancellor. From **Mile 174** (Exit 174) on INTERSTATE 5, go west on Main Street, west on Cottage Grove-Lorane Road and west on Siuslaw River Road.

Cooper Mountain Vineyards

9480 SW Grabhorn Road, Beaverton, OR 97007; phone (503) 690-4681, fax (503) 649-0027. Cooper Mountain, an extinct volcano overlooking Oregon's Tualatin Valley, is home to the 75-acre vineyard and winery. The winery is located on the Cooper Homestead, which was settled in 1865. Cooper Mountain produces Pinot Noir, Chardonnay and Pinot Gris. From **Mile 292** (Exit 292) on INTERSTATE 5, go north on Highway 217 to Beaverton, west on Highway 8, southwest on Farmington Road and south on Grabhom Road.

Elk Cove Vineyards

27751 NW Olson Road, Gaston, OR 97119; phone (503) 985-7760. "For the pure beauty of its setting, no winery in Oregon can match the breath-taking views from Elk Cove's splendid wine-tasting room," said Robert Parker of the *Wine Advocate*. Elk Cove produces Pinot Noir, Dry Riesling, Ice Wine, Chardonnay, Pinot Gris, Gewürztraminer, Cabernet Sauvignon and Late Harvest Riesling. Closed Thanksgiving, Christmas and New Year's. From **Mile 292** (Exit 292) of INTERSTATE 5, go north on Highway 217 to Beaverton, west on Highway 8, south on Highway 47 approximately 6 miles and west on Olson Road.

Foris Vineyards Winery

654 Kendall Road, Cave Junction, OR 97523; phone (503) 592-3752, fax (503) 592-4796. The Pacific Northwest's most Southern winery, Foris Vineyards is located on the back terrace of the Illinois River valley. The winery produces Pinot Noir, Chardonnay, Gewürztraminer, Early Muscat, Cabernet and Merlot. Closed some major holidays. From **Mile 58.5** (Exit 58) on INTERSTATE 5, go southwest on U.S. 199 approximately 25 miles, east on Highway 46, southeast on Holland Loop Road and south on Kendall Road.

Girardet Wine Cellars

895 Reston Road, Roseburg, OR 97470; phone (503) 679-7252, fax (503) 679-5445. Philippe Girardet established the vineyard in 1971 in a picturesque valley reminiscent of his native Switzerland. Girardet produces Pinot Noir, Cabernet Sauvignon, Chardonnay, Riesling, White Zinfandel, Rosé, Vin Blanc, Vin Rouge, Maréchal Foch, Boco Noir and Sayval Blanc. Closed Dec. 20 through Jan. 30. From **Mile 119** (Exit 119) on INTERSTATE 5, go west on Highway 42, then north on Reston Road.

Henry Estate Winery

687 Hubbard Creek Road, Umpqua, OR 97486; phone (503) 459-5120 or 459-3614, fax (503) 459-5146. The vineyard was planted in 1972 on land that the Henry family has owned and farmed for 75 years. The winery produces Gewürztraminer, Chardonnay, Pinot Noir, Cabernet Sauvignon and White Riesling. Closed major holidays. From **Mile 136** (Exit 136) on INTERSTATE 5, go west on Highway 9 past Umpqua.

Hillcrest Vineyard

240 Vineyard Lane, Roseburg, OR 97470; phone (800) 736-3709. Owned and operated by Richard Sommer, Hillcrest produces Riesling, Cabernet Sauvignon and other varietals. Closed major holidays. From **Mile 125** (Exit 125) on INTERSTATE 5, go west on Garden Valley Boulevard, west on Melrose Road, west on Doerner Road, north on Elgarose Road and west on Vineyard Lane.

Hinman Vineyards

27012 Briggs Hill Road, Eugene, OR 97405; phone (503) 345-1945, fax (503) 345-6174. Located in the foothills of the Oregon Coast Range, Hinman produces Pinot Noir, Cabernet Sauvignon, Pinot Gris, Chardonnay, White Riesling, Sauvignon Blanc Semillon, White Pinot Noir, Gewürztraminer and Semi-Sparkling Muscat. Closed Dec. 24 through Jan. 1. From **Mile 194** (Exit 194) on INTERSTATE 5, go west on Highway 126, south on Bertelsen Road for 5 miles, west on Spencer Creek Road and south on Briggs Hill Road.

Honeywood Winery

1350 Hines St. SE, Salem, OR 97302; phone (800) 726-4101 or (503) 362-4111. Established in 1934, Honeywood is the oldest producing winery in Oregon. The winery produces Pinot Noir, Riesling, Chardonnay, Muscat and other varietals as well as fruit wines. Closed Easter, Thanksgiving, Christmas and New Year's. From **Mile 253** (Exit 253) on INTERSTATE 5, go west on Highway 22 (Mission Street), then west on Hines Street.

Houston Vineyards

86187 Hoya Lane, Eugene, OR 97405; phone (503) 747-4681. Steve and Jewelee Houston are the fifth generation of Houstons to be vineyardists. The winery produces Chardonnay exclusively. By appointment only. From **Mile 189** (Exit 189) on INTERSTATE 5, go east on 30th Avenue, north on Frontage Road, southeast on Franklin Boulevard, east on Seavey Loop and south on Hoya Lane.

Kramer Vineyards

26830 NW Olson Road, Gaston, OR 97119; phone (503) 662-4545. Nestled in the hills of northern Yamhill county, the family-run winery produces Pinot Gris, Gewürztraminer, Müller-Thurgau and berry wines. There are also activities for the kids. From **Mile 292** (Exit 292) on INTERSTATE 5, go north on Highway 217 to Beaverton, west on Highway 8, south on Highway 47 approximately 6 miles and west on Olson Road.

La Garza Cellars

491 Winery Lane, Roseburg, OR 97470; phone (503) 679-9654, fax (503) 679-3888.

La Garza Cellars is family owned and operated, as is the Gourmet Kitchen, which serves lunch (dinners by reservation only). La Garza produces Cabernet Sauvignon, Chardonnay, Riesling and Merlot. Closed Dec. 19 through Jan. 31. Dining room closed Oct. through May. Located off INTERSTATE 5 at **Mile 119** (Exit 119).

Laurel Ridge Winery

46350 NW David Hill Road, P.O. Box 456, Forest Grove, OR 97116; phone (503) 359-5436. First chosen as a vineyard site in the 1800s by a German winemaking family, Laurel Hill was replanted in 1966. Laurel Hill produces Pinot Noir, Gewürztraminer, Semillon, Sylvaner, Methode Champenoise Sparkling Wine and Riesling. Closed January. From **Mile 292** (Exit 292) on INTERSTATE 5, go north on Highway 217 to Beaverton, west on Highway 8 and northeast on David Hill Road.

Marquam Hill Vineyards

35803 S. Highway 213, Mollala, OR 97038; phone (503) 829-6677. Located at the foot of the Cascades, Marquam Hill produces Pinot Noir, Chardonnay, Riesling, Gewürztraminer and Müller-Thurgau. Woods surround an 8-acre lake, just as the vineyards surround the winery. From **Mile 271** (Exit 271) on INTERSTATE 5, go west on Highway 214, north on Highway 99 East, west on Highway 211 approximately 15 miles and south on Highway 213 for 5.2 miles.

Momokawa Sake Ltd.

920 Elm St., Forest Grove, OR 97116; phone (503) 357-7056, fax (503) 357-1014. The tasting room offers various imported Momokawa sakes and information on the tradition of rice wine. Production of U.S.-produced sake planned. Closed major holidays. From **Mile 292** (Exit 292) on INTERSTATE 5, go north on Highway 217 to Beaverton, west on Highway 8 and south on Elm Street.

Montinore Vineyards

3663 SW Dilley Road, P.O. Box 560, Forest Grove, OR 97116; phone (503) 359-5012, fax (503) 357-4313. A Victorian mansion graces the 711-acre wine estate. Montinore produces Pinot Noir, Pinot Gris, Chardonnay, White Riesling, Chenin Blanc, Gewürztraminer and Müller-Thurgau. Closed major holidays. From **Mile 292** (Exit 292) on INTERSTATE 5, go north on Highway 217 to Beaverton, west on Highway 8, south on Highway 47, west on Stringtown Road and south on Dilley Road.

Oak Knoll Winery

29700 SW Burkhalter Road, Hillsboro, OR 97123; phone (503) 648-8198, fax (503) 648-3377. Founded in 1970 by the Vuylsteke family, Oak Knoll produces Chardonnay, Pinot Noir, Pinot Gris, Riesling, Gewürztraminer and Raspberry Dessert Wine. From **Mile 292** (Exit 292) on INTERSTATE 5, go north on Highway 217 to Beaverton, west on Highway 8, south on Highway 219 and east on Burkhalter Road.

Orchard Heights Winery

6057 Orchard Heights Road NW, Salem, OR 97304; phone (503) 363-0375, fax (503) 363-0418. Host to frequent musical performances and arts activities, Orchard Heights produces Pinot Noir, Pinot Gris, Gewürztraminer, Riesling, Brut and 2 dessert wines, Late Harvest Gewürztraminer and Sauvignon Blanc. From **Mile 253** (Exit 253) on INTER-

STATE 5, go west on Oregon Highway 22, north on Wallace Road (Highway 221) and west on Orchard Heights Road.

Redhawk Vineyard

2995 Michigan City NW, Salem, OR 97304; phone (503) 362-1596, fax (503) 362-1596. First planted in 1979, Redhawk Vineyard produces Merlot, Cabernet Sauvignon, Cabernet Franc and Red Table Wine. The popular cartoon labels "Chateau Mootom" and "Great White" received "Worst Label" awards from *Decanter* magazine. Other cartoon labels "Jug Wine," "Bear Blanc," "Rat Race Red" and "Winosaurs" have recently been released. Closed Dec. through April. From **Mile 253** (Exit 253) on INTERSTATE 5, go west on Oregon Highway 22, north on Wallace Road (Highway 221) 3.3 miles and west on Michigan City Avenue.

St. Innocent

1360 Tandem Ave. NE, Salem, OR 97303; phone (503) 378-1526. St. Innocent produces Pinot Noir, barrel-fermented Chardonnay, and an aged Methode Champenoise sparkling wine. Open Memorial Day weekend and Thanksgiving weekend; other times, by appointment. From **Mile 260** on INTERSTATE 5, take Salem Parkway west.

Secret House Vineyards Winery

88324 Vineyard Lane, Veneta, OR 97487; phone (503) 935-3774. A small family-owned winery, Secret House is located in the foothills of the Coast Range, and is host to an annual wine and blues festival. Secret House produces Late Harvest Riesling, White Pinot Noir, Chardonnay, Red Pinot Noir, Sparkling Wine and Riesling. Closed Dec. 24 through Feb. 9, and Tuesdays. From **Mile 194** (Exit 194) on INTERSTATE 5, go west on Highway 126, then north on Vineyard Lane.

Shafer Vineyard Cellars

6200 NW Gales Creek Road, Forest Grove, OR 97116; phone (503) 357-6604. The tasting room overlooks the Gales Creek Valley and is decorated with dried flower arrangements, swags and wreaths by Miki Shaker. Shafer produces Chardonnay, White Riesling, Pinot Noir, Pinot Noir Blanc, Gewürztraminer, Müller-Thurgau and Sauvignon Blanc. Closed January and February. From **Mile 292** (Exit 292) on INTERSTATE 5, go north on Highway 217 to Beaverton, west on Highway 8 past Forest Grove and north on Gales Creek Road.

Tualatin Vineyards

10850 NW Seavey Road, Forest Grove, OR 97116; phone (503) 357-5005, fax (503) 357-1702. The tasting room offers a view of Tualatin Valley and the 85-acre vineyard, which was established in 1973. Tualatin produces White Riesling, Gewürztraminer, Chardonnay and Pinot Noir. Closed January and holidays. From **Mile 292** (Exit 292) on INTERSTATE 5, go north on Highway 217 to Beaverton, west on Highway 8 past Forest Grove, north on Thatcher Road, west on Clapshaw Hill Road and west on Seavey Road.

Valley View Winery

1000 Upper Applegate Road, Jacksonville, OR 97530; phone (503) 899-8468. Tasting Room in the Village Gallery, 130 W. California St., Jacksonville, OR 97530. Valley View Vineyard, the Northwest's first winery, was established in 1850 by Peter Britt in the Rogue Valley. More than a hundred years later, in

1971, Valley View Winery was established by the Wisnovsky family in the Applegate Valley, which is in the Rogue Valley. Valley View produces Cabernet Sauvignon, Merlot, Chardonnay and Fumé Blanc, and won 12 gold medals in 1993. From **Mile 27** (Exit 27) on INTERSTATE 5, go west on Highway 238, then south on Upper Applegate Road.

Weisinger's of Ashland

3150 Siskiyou Blvd., Ashland, OR 97520; phone (503) 488-5989, fax (503) 488-5989. Offering a view of the Rogue Valley and Southern Oregon Cascades, Weisinger's produces Cabernet Sauvignon, Chardonnay, Gewürztraminer, Italian Style blend, "Mescolare" and Cabernet Blanc. From **Mile 11** (Exit 11) on INTERSTATE 5, go west 1 mile on Siskiyou Boulevard.

Willamette Valley Vineyards

8800 Enchanted Way SE, Turner, OR 97392; phone (800) 344-9463 or (503) 588-9463. Over 4,000 Oregon wine enthusiasts pooled their resources through public stock ownership to create Willamette Valley Vineyards. The winery produces Pinot Noir, Chardonnay, Riesling, Müller-Thurgau and Pinot Gris, and offers guided and self-guided tours. Closed Thanksgiving, Christmas and New Year's. From **Mile 248** (Exit 248) on INTERSTATE 5, go east on Delaney Road, then south on Enchanted Way.

U.S. Highway 20

Airlie Winery

15305 Dunn Forest Road, Monmouth, OR 97361; phone (503) 838-6013. Airlie Tasting Room at Spindrift Wine & Cheese, 220 S. Columbia, Seaside, OR 97138; phone (503) 838-6013. Established in 1986 by Larry and Alice Preedy, Airlie sits above the Dunn Forest Vineyards. The winery produces Pinot Noir, Chardonnay, Maréchal Foch, Müller-Thurgau, Riesling, Gewürztraminer, and Late Harvest Gewürztraminer. Closed January and February. From **Mile 398.5** on U.S. HIGHWAY 20, go north on King's Valley Highway (Highway 223), east on Maxfield Circle Road and east on Dunn Forest Road.

Serendipity Cellars Winery

15275 Dunn Forest Road, Monmouth, OR 97361; phone (503) 838-4284. Specializing in hearty wines that lack the usual tannic roughness, Serendipity produces Cabernet Sauvignon, Zinfandel, Maréchal Foch, Dry Chenin Blanc and Müller-Thurgau. Closed Tuesdays, March and Christmas Day. From **Mile 398.5** on U.S. HIGHWAY 20, go north on King's Valley Highway (Highway 223), east on Maxfield Circle Road and east on Dunn Forest Road.

Springhill Cellars

2920 NW Scenic Dr., Albany, OR 97321; phone (503) 928-1009. Located in the Willamette Valley, Springhill produces Pinot Noir, Pinot Gris, Chardonnay and Riesling. From **Mile 371** on U.S. HIGHWAY 20, go north on Scenic Drive.

Interstate 84

Edgefield Winery

2126 SW Halsey St., Troutdale, OR 97060; phone (503) 669-8610, fax (503) 665-4209. Located within the historic Edgefield property, formerly the Multnomah County Poor Farm, the winery produced its first wine in 1990. Edgefield produces Pinot Gris, Chardonnay,

Dry Riesling, Pinot Noir, Pinot Noir Blanc, Red Zinfandel, Merlot, Cabernet Sauvignon, Blanc De Noir and Zinfandel Port. From **Mile 9** (Exit 16A) on INTERSTATE 84, go south on 242nd, then east on Halsey Street.

Hood River Vineyards

4693 Westwood Dr., Hood River, OR 97031; phone (503) 386-3772. Established in 1981 by Eileen and Cliff Blanchette, the winery overlooks the Columbia River Gorge and the Hood River valley. Hood River produces Chardonnay, Pinot Noir, Cabernet Sauvignon, White Riesling, Zinfandel, Raspberry and Pear. Closed Jan. through Feb. From **Mile 55.5** (Exit 62) on INTERSTATE 84, go west on Country Club Road, west on Post Canyon Drive and west on Westwood Drive.

Wasson Brothers Winery

41901 Highway 26, Sandy, OR 97055; phone (503) 668-3124. The winery produces Loganberry, Raspberry, Blackberry, Blueberry, Rhubarb, Apricot, Pinot Noir, Chardonnay, White Riesling, Gewürztraminer, Muscat and Sparkling Wine, and offers wine- and beer-making supplies. Closed July 4, Thanksgiving, Christmas and New Year's. From **Mile 9** (Exit 16A) on INTERSTATE 84, go south on 242nd, then east on Highway 26.

Highway 99 West

*A worthwhile side trip for winery seekers is Highway 99 West, a major north-south highway that parallels and is located west of Interstate 5. The wineries listed here are located along Highway 99 between its junction with Interstate 5 at Eugene (**Mile 192** on INTERSTATE 5) and its junction with Interstate 5 at Tigard (**Mile 294** on INTERSTATE 5).*

Alpine Vineyards

25904 Green Peak Road, Monroe, OR 97456; phone (503) 424-5851, fax (503) 424-5891. Located in the foothills of the Coast Range, Alpine produces Chardonnay, Pinot Gris, Pinot Noir, Riesling, Gewürztraminer, Cabernet Sauvignon and White Cabernet. Closed Dec. 24 through Jan. 31. From Highway 99 West, just north of Monroe, go west on Alpine Road, then north on Green Peak Road.

Amity Vineyards

18150 Amity Vineyards Road SE, Amity, OR 97101; phone (503) 835-2362, fax (503) 835-6451. A family-operated winery, Amity produces Pinot Noir, Nouveau, Dry Gewürztraminer, Dry Riesling, Late Harvest Riesling, Gamay Noir, Chardonnay and Blush. Closed Dec. 24 through Jan. 31. From Highway 99 West at Amity, go east on Rice Lane, then north on Amity Vineyards Road.

Argyle (The Dundee Wine Co.)

691 Highway 99 W., Dundee, OR 97115; phone (503) 538-8520, fax (503) 538-2055. The company is a partnership between Australian vintner Brian Croser and Oregon vintner Cal Knudsen. Argyle produces Sparkling Wine, Chardonnay, Dry Riesling, Pinot Gris and Pinot Noir. The winery is housed in a former hazelnut processing plant, and the tasting room is located in a restored Victorian farmhouse. Closed Thanksgiving, Christmas and New Year's. Located off Highway 99 West at Dundee.

Autumn Wind Vineyard

15225 NE North Valley Road, Newberg, OR 97132; phone (503) 538-6931. Overlooking the North Chehalem Valley, Autumn Wind produces Pinot Noir, Chardonnay, Sauvignon Blanc, Pinot Gris and Müller-Thurgau. Open weekends, April through Nov. From Highway 99 West at Newberg, go west on Highway 240, north on Ribbon Ridge Road and west on North Valley Road.

Bethel Heights Vineyard

6060 Bethel Heights Road NW, Salem, OR 97304; phone (503) 581-2262, fax (503) 581-0943. Established in 1984, Bethel Heights is owned and operated by Ted and Terry Casteel, Marilyn Webb and Patricia Dudley. The winery produces Burgundian-style Pinot Noir, Chardonnay, Chenin Blanc, Pinot Gris, Gewürztraminer and Cabernet Sauvignon. Closed Christmas through Feb. From Highway 99 West, just south of Amity, go east on Bethel Road, then north on Bethel Heights Road NW.

Broadley Vineyards

265 S. 5th (Highway 99), Monroe, OR 97456; phone (503) 847-5934, fax (503) 847-6018. Located on the banks of the Long Tom River, Broadley specializes in Pinot Noir. Located off Highway 99 West at Monroe.

Chateau Benoit

6580 NE Mineral Springs Road, Carlton, OR 97111; phone (503) 864-2991, fax (503) 864-2203. The French-style Chateau offers a panoramic view of Yamhill County. Chateau Benoit produces Müller-Thurgau, Sauvignon Blanc, Chardonnay, Pinot Noir, Dry Riesling, Pinot Gris, Dry Gewürztraminer, Dessert Wine and Brut. Closed Thanksgiving, Christmas and New Year's. From Highway 99 West at Lafayette, go north on Mineral Springs Road.

Chateau Bianca Winery

17485 Highway 22, Dallas, OR 97111; phone (503) 864-2291, fax (503) 864-2203. Family owned and operated, Chateau Bianca produces Pinot, Chardonnay, Riesling, Blush, Gewürztraminer, Champagne and Glühwein. Closed Christmas and New Year's. From Highway 99 West, just north of Rickreall, go west on Highway 22 for 10 miles.

Chehalem

703 N. Main, Newberg, OR 97132; phone (503) 538-4700, fax (503) 537-0850. Chehalem, a local Indian word meaning "gentle land," is a small winery dedicated to reflecting what the vineyard has produced, with minimal processing. Stylistically, the wines are bold and intense—in ripeness, fruit, alcohol and spice. Chehalem produces Pinot Noir, Pinot Gris, Chardonnay, and a Gamay Noir-Pinot Noir blend. By appointment only. From Highway 99 West at Newberg, go west on Highway 240 to the intersection of Main Street and Illinois.

Cristom Vineyards

6905 Spring Valley Road NW, Salem, OR 97304; phone (503) 375-3068. One of the Willamette Valley's newest wineries, Cristom produces Pinot Noir and Chardonnay using natural methods, natural yeast and minimal handling. From Highway 99 West, just south of Amity, go east on Bethel Road, east on Zena Road and north on Spring Valley Road.

Cuneo Cellars

9360 SE Eola Hills Road, Amity, OR 97101; phone (503) 835-2782. Located in the Eola Hills, Cuneo overlooks the Willamette Valley and the Cascade Range. Cuneo produces Cabernet Sauvignon, Pinot Noir, Merlot and Riesling. From Highway 99 West at Amity, go east on Nursery Street, south on Old Bethel Road and east on Eola Hills Road.

Duck Pond Cellars

23145 Highway 99 W., P.O. Box 429, Dundee, OR 97115; phone (503) 538-3199, fax (503) 538-3190. Family owned and operated, Duck Pond produced the first vintage in 1989. The winery produces Pinot Noir and Chardonnay. Closed Thanksgiving, Christmas and New Year's. Located off Highway 99 West just north of Dundee.

Ellendale Winery

1 Main St., P.O. Box 89, Rickreall, OR 97371; phone (503) 623-6835. Ellendale Vineyards; phone (503) 623-5617. Ellendale at Rickreall is the tasting room for Ellendale Vineyards, which are located 3 miles west of Dallas. Ellendale produces Methode Champenoise Sparkling Wine, Pinot Noir, Chardonnay, White Riesling, Gewürztraminer, Mead, Niagara, and a blend of berries and cherries. Closed Thanksgiving, Christmas and New Year's. Located off Highway 99 West at Rickreall.

Eola Hills Wine Cellars

501 S. Pacific Highway (Highway 99), Rickreall, OR 97371; phone (503) 623-2405, fax (503) 623-0350. Featuring a large tasting room with an open view of the production area, Eola Hills produces Chardonnay, Pinot Gris, Sauvignon Blanc, Riesling, Gewürztraminer, Blush, White Table Wine, Gamay, Pinot Noir and Cabernet Sauvignon. Located off Highway 99 West just south of Rickreall and Rickreall Road.

The Eyrie Vineyards

P.O. Box 697, Dundee, OR 97115; phone (503) 472-6315, fax (503) 472-5124. Established in 1966 by David and Diana Lett, Eyrie pioneered the premium wine industry of the Willamette Valley. The winery produces Pinot Noir, Chardonnay, Muscat Ottonel and Pinot Meunier. By appointment only. From Highway 99 West at McMinn-ville, go south on Lafayette Avenue, then west on E. 10th Street.

Flynn Vineyards

2200 W. Pacific Highway, Rickreall, OR 97371; phone (503) 623-8683, fax (503) 623-0908. Planted in 1982, Flynn produces Brut and Blanc De Blancs (Sparkling Wines), Pinot Noir, Chardonnay and Pinot Noir Blanc. Located off Highway 99 West, 2 miles north of Highway 22 intersection.

Knudsen Erath Winery

Worden Hill Road, P.O. Box 667, Dundee, OR 97115; phone (800) KEW-WINE, fax (800) 538-1074. Offering a tasting room terrace that overlooks the Willamette Valley, Knudsen Erath produces Pinot Noir, Chardonnay, Cabernet Sauvignon, Gewürztraminer and White Riesling. Closed Easter, Thanksgiving, Christmas and New Year's. From Highway 99 West at Dundee, go west on 9th Street (which becomes Worden Hill Road).

Kristin Hill Winery

3330 SE Amity-Dayton Highway, Amity, OR 97101; phone (503) 835-0850. Family owned and operated, Kristin Hill's vineyard was planted in the spring of 1985 with the help of friends and family. The winery was established in 1990, and the tasting room opened in 1992. Kristin Hill produces Methode Champenoise Sparkling Wine, Gewürztraminer, Chardonnay, Pinot Noir and Riesling. Closed Thanksgiving, Christmas and New Year's. Located off Highway 99 West at Amity.

Lange Winery
18380 NE Buena Vista, Dundee, OR 97115; phone (503) 538-6476. Founded in 1987, Lange Winery produces Pinot Gris, Pinot Noir and Chardonnay. Don and Wendy Lange warn all visitors: "Dry Wine—Dry Humor." From Highway 99 West at Dundee, go west on 9th Street (which becomes Worden Hill Road), north on Fairview Road and east on Buena Vista Road.

Panther Creek Cellars
455 N. Irvine, McMinnville, OR 97128; phone (503) 472-8080, fax (503) 472-5667. The winery features premium Pinot Noir, Chardonnay and Melon. Panther Creek is one of the nation's few producers of Melon—rich with the Muscadet grape's banana, pear and apple flavors. Open daily by appointment. Located just off Highway 99 West at McMinnville.

Ponzi Vineyard
14665 SW Winery Lane, Beaverton, OR 97007; phone (503) 628-1227, fax (503) 628-0354. Portland's closest winery and vineyard, Ponzi has been listed regularly among the Top 100 Wines in *The Wine Spectator; The Wine Advocate* also has recognized Dick Ponzi as one of the top 15 international winemakers. Ponzi produces Pinot Noir, Pinot Gris, Chardonnay and Dry White Riesling. Tours by appointment. Closed January and holidays. From Highway 99 West, go northwest on Beef Bend Road, west on Highway 210, south on Vandermost Road and east on SW Winery Lane.

RainSong Vineyards Winery
92989 Goldson/Templeton Road, Cheshire, OR 97419; phone (503) 998-1786. A small, family-owned winery, RainSong produces small lots of Pinot Noir, Chardonnay, Pinot Meunier and Methode Champenoise Sparkling Wine. Except for seasonal help in the vineyard, all operations are carried out by proprietors Michael and Merry Fix and family and friends. Closed Labor Day weekend. From Highway 99 West, just south of Junction City, go west on Highway 36, then north on Goldson/Templeton Road.

Rex Hill Vineyards
30835 N. Highway 99 W., Newberg, OR 97132; phone (503) 538-0666, fax (503) 538-1409. Offering an elegant tasting room with fireplace, antiques and oriental rugs, Rex Hill produces Pinot Noir, Chardonnay, Pinot Gris, Sauvignon Blanc, Symphony and White Riesling. Their Kings Ridge label designates a lighter style of wine. Rex Hill owns or manages 235 acres of Willamette Valley grapes, including some of the oldest vineyards in Yamhill County. Closed Thanksgiving Day, Christmas and New Year's. Located off Highway 99 West just north of Newberg.

Sokol Blosser Winery
5000 Sokol Blosser Lane, P.O. Box 399, Dundee, OR 97115; phone (800) 582-6668 or (503) 864-2282. The Walk-Through Showcase Vineyard offers visitors a self-guided tour that explains the grape varieties and the different seasons in the vineyard. Founded in 1977 by Bill and Susan Sokol Blosser, the winery produces Pinot Noir, Chardonnay, Müller-Thurgau, Riesling, Gewürztraminer and Pinot Noir

Blanc. Closed Thanksgiving, Christmas and New Year's. From Highway 99 West, just south of Dundee, go north on Sokol Blosser Lane.

Stangeland Vineyards & Winery
8500 Hopewell Road NW, Salem, OR 97304; phone (503) 581-0355. A small family-owned winery specializing in estate bottled wines using traditional methods, Stangeland produces Pinot Noir, Chardonnay, Pinot Gris, Gewürztraminer and Reserve Pinot Noir. Open Memorial Day, Labor Day and Thanksgiving weekends; other times by appointment. From Highway 99 West, north of Rickreall, go east on Zena Road, then north on Spring Valley Road to Hopewell Road.

Torii Mor
18325 NE Fairview Dr., Dundee, OR 97115; phone (503) 538-2279 or (503) 434-1439, fax (503) 538-2239 or (503) 434-5733. One of Yamill County's oldest vineyards, it includes Pinot Noir, Pinot Gris and Chardonnay grapes. Winemaker Patricia Green believes in a Burgundian way, using only French oak barrels. Open weekends and holidays, June through Oct. From Highway 99 West, go west on 9th Street (which becomes Worden Hill Road), then north on Fairview Road.

Tyee Wine Cellars
26335 Greenberry Road, Corvallis, OR 97333; phone (503) 753-8754. Located on a 460-acre, fourth-generation family farm in the foothills of the Coast Range, Tyee is owned and operated by Dave and Margy Buchanan, Nola Mosier and Barney Watson. Tyee produces Pinot Gris, Pinot Noir, Chardonnay, Gewürztraminer, Pinot Blanc and other varietal wines. Closed Jan. through April. From Highway 99 West, south of Corvallis, go west on Greenberry Road.

Veritas Vineyard
31190 NE Veritas Lane, Newberg, OR 97132; phone (503) 636-0836. Established in 1983 by John and Diane Howieson, Veritas produces Pinot Noir, Chardonnay, Riesling, Pinot Gris and Müller-Thurgau. French oak barrels are used in fermentation and storage. Closed Dec. 12 through March 3. Located off Highway 99 West south of Sherwood.

Witness Tree Vineyards
7111 Spring Valley Road NW, Salem, OR 97304; phone (503) 585-7874, fax (503) 362-9765. Named after a surveyor's marker designated in 1854, Witness Tree produces Pinot Noir and Chardonnay. Closed Mondays and January. From Highway 99 West, just south of Amity, go east on Bethel Road, east on Zena Road and north on Spring Valley Road.

Yamhill Valley Vineyards
16250 Oldsville Road, McMinnville, OR 97128; phone (503) 843-3100, fax (503) 843-2450. A family-operated winery, Yamhill Valley's 100-acre vineyard is situated on a 300-acre estate in the foothills of the Pacific Coast range. Yamhill Valley produces Pinot Noir, Pinot Gris, Chardonnay and Riesling. Open June 1 through Thanksgiving weekend. From Highway 99 West, just south of McMinnville, go west on Highway 18, then north on Oldsville Road.

WASHINGTON
U.S. Highway 2

Quilceda Creek Vintners
5226 Old Machias Road, Snohomish, WA

98290; phone (360) 568-2389. Quilceda Creek produces only 1,000 cases of Cabernet Sauvignon a year with grapes from the Columbia Valley vineyards of Kiona, Klipsun and Mercer Ranch. Tours and tastings by appointment. From Mile 410 on U.S. HIGHWAY 2, go north on Highway 9, east on Bunk Foss Road (52nd Street SE), and north on Old Machias Road.

Interstate 5

Di Stefano Wines
1458 Elliott Way E., Seattle, WA 98119; phone (206) 282-6484. Located off INTERSTATE 5 in Seattle.

E. B. Foote Winery
9354 4th Ave. S., Seattle, WA 98108; phone (206) 763-9928. Covey Run produced its first wines in 1982. The winery boasts a view of the vineyard and Mount Adams. Covey Run produces Chardonnay, Lemberger, Riesling and other varietals. From Mile 480 (Exit 172) on INTERSTATE 5, go north on Aurora Avenue (Highway 99), west on S. 96th Street and north on 4th Avenue S.

Johnson Creek Winery
19248 Johnson Creek Road SE, Tenino, WA 98589; phone (360) 264-2100. The grapes grown on the property and brought in from eastern Washington produce the wine that is served at the adjacent Alice's Restaurant. Nearby is the gazebo and a bubbling stream. Wine tasting and tours are offered just before the evening sitting at Alice's. From Mile 396 (Exit 88A) on INTERSTATE 5, go east on Highway 12 for 7 miles, east on Highway 507 for 5 miles and south on Johnson Creek Road.

Manfred Vierthaler Winery
17136 Highway 410 E., Sumner, WA 98390; phone (206) 863-1633. Manfred Vierthaler's Bavarian chalet includes Vierthaler's Restaurant, which offers a wide selection of German dishes, as well as Gewürztraminer, Chablis, Rosé, and White and Red Table Wine. From Mile 450 (Exit 142A) on INTERSTATE 5, go south on Highway 167, then east on Highway 410.

McCrea Cellars
13443 118th Ave. SE, Rainier, WA 98576; phone (360) 458-9463. Recently relocated from Lake Stevens, McCrea produces Chardonnay, Syrah, and a blend of Syrah and Grenache. Tours and tastings by appointment only. From Mile 396 (Exit 88A) on INTERSTATE 5, go east on Highway 12 for 7 miles, then east on Highway 507 to Rainier; call for further directions and appointment.

Mount Baker Vineyards
4298 Mount Baker Highway, Deming, WA 98244; phone (360) 592-2300. The winery and vineyard offer views of Mount Baker from the picnic area and tasting room. Mount Baker Vineyards produces Chardonnay, Pinot Noir, Gewürztraminer, Madeline Angevine, Müller-Thurgau and other varietals. From Mile 563 (Exit 255) on INTERSTATE 5, go east on Highway 542, then north on Hilliard Road.

Salishan Vineyards
35011 N. Fork Ave., LaCenter, WA 98629; phone (360) 263-2713. The Wolvertons planted their vineyard on a hillside in 1971 and produced their first wines in 1976. Salishan produces Pinot Noir, Chardonnay, Cabernet Sauvignon, dry Chenin Blanc and

dry Riesling. Open May through Dec. From **Mile 324.5** (Exit 16) on INTERSTATE 5, go east on NW LaCenter Road, then west on N. Fork Road.

Silver Lake Winery
17616 15th Ave. SE #106B, Bothell, WA 98012; phone (206) 485-2437. Silver Lake was selected as an American Winery of the Year (1992) by *Wine & Spirits Magazine*. From **Mile 491.5** (Exit 183) on INTERSTATE 5, go east on 164th Street, south on Highway 527 (Bothell-Everett Highway) and east on 180th Street SE.

Soos Creek Wine Cellars
20404 140th Ave. SE, Kent, WA 98042; phone (206) 255-9901. Located off INTERSTATE 5 in Kent.

Wilridge Winery
1416 34th Ave., Seattle, WA 98122; phone (206) 325-3051. Located off INTERSTATE 5 in Seattle.

Interstate 405 (in Interstate 5 log)

Cavatappi Winery
9702 NE 120th Pl., Kirkland, WA 98034; phone (206) 823-6533. Peter Dow produces wines ranging from Sauvignon Blanc to Cabernet Sauvignon to Nebbiolo, and serves it in his adjacent Italian restaurant, Café Juanita. Winery tours by appointment. From **Mile 20** (Exit 20A) on INTERSTATE 405, go west on NE 116th Street, north on 97th Avenue and east on 120th Place.

Chateau Ste. Michelle
1 Stimson Lane, Woodinville, WA 98072; phone (206) 488-1133. Established more than 50 years ago, Chateau Ste. Michelle pioneered an entire vineyard region in the Columbia Valley. The winery's cellar is located on the estate of the late Frederick Stimson, a Seattle lumber baron. Performances in the amphitheater take place in the summer. From **Mile 23** (Exit 23) on INTERSTATE 405, go east on Highway 522, west on NE 175th and south on Highway 202.

Columbia Winery
14030 NE 145th, Woodinville, WA 98072-1248; phone (206) 488-2776. Established over 30 years ago, Columbia is located in a Victorian-style building, which features a tasting room, gift shop and banquet room. Columbia produces Cabernet, Merlot, Syrah and Cabernet Franc. From **Mile 23** (Exit 23) on INTERSTATE 405, go east on Highway 522, west on NE 175th and south on Highway 202.

DeLille Cellars/Chaleur Estate
P.O. Box 2233, Woodinville, WA 98072; phone (206) 489-0544. Located off INTERSTATE 405 in Woodinville.

Facelli Winery
16120 Woodlinville-Redmond Road #1, Woodinville, WA 98072; phone (206) 488-1020. Family owned and operated, Facelli produces Merlot, Chardonnay, Fumé Blanc, Semillon and Riesling. From **Mile 23** (Exit 23) on INTERSTATE 405, go east on Highway 522, west on NE 175th and south on Highway 202.

Matthews Cellars
14627 165th Ave. SE, Renton, WA 98059; phone (206) 255-7319. Located off INTERSTATE 405 in Renton.

Paul Thomas Winery
17661 128th Pl. NE, Bldg. C, Woodinville, WA 98072; phone (206) 489-9307. Located off INTERSTATE 405 in Woodinville.

Silver Lake at Country Village
23732 Bothell-Everett Highway, Suite M, Bothell, WA 98021; phone (206) 485-6041. Located just 4 miles south of the Silver Lake Winery, the Country Village includes more than 40 shops. The tasting room also offers gifts and wine accessories. From **Mile 26** (Exit 26) on INTERSTATE 405, go south on Highway 527 (Bothell-Everett Highway).

Silver Lake Sparkling Cellars
17721 132nd Ave. NE, Woodinville, WA 98072; phone (206) 486-1900. From **Mile 23** (Exit 23) on INTERSTATE 405, go east on Highway 522, south on 132nd Avenue NE and east on NE 177th Place.

U.S. Highway 12

Badger Mountain Vineyard
110 Jurupa, Kennewick, WA 99337; phone (800) 643-WINE, fax (509) 627-4986. Located on the south-facing slope in the Columbia Valley, Badger Mountain is one of the first Washington State Certified organic vineyards making estate wines. Tours and tastings by appointment. From **Mile 376.5** on U.S. HIGHWAY 12, go south on Interstate 82, take Exit 109, go north on Badger Road, east on Leslie Road, east on Reata Road, north on Mota, east on Escolar, east on Rachel, east on Clover and north on Jurupa.

Blackwood Canyon
Route 2, Box 2169H, Benton City, WA 99320; phone (509) 588-6249. Blackwood Canyon produces Chardonnay, Semillon, Merlot, Cabernet Sauvignon and Late Harvest wines. From **Mile 381.5** (Exit 96) on U.S. HIGHWAY 12, go east on Highway 224, then north on Sunset Road.

Bonair Winery
500 S. Bonair Road, Zillah, WA 98953; phone (509) 829-6027. The Puryear family, after 10 years of amateur winemaking in California, moved back to their native Yakima Valley and began production in 1985. They call the winery "the little hobby that got out of hand." Bonair produces Chardonnay, Cabernet Sauvignon, Johannisberg Riesling, BFD Riesling, Nouveau Rouge and Blush. From **Mile 426** (Exit 52) on U.S. HIGHWAY 12, go north on Cheyne Road, west on Highland Drive and south on Bonair Road.

Bookwalter Winery
710 S. Windmill Road, Columbia Drive and Windmill Road, Richland, WA 99352; phone (509) 627-5000. Bookwalter produces Cabernet Sauvignon, Merlot, Chardonnay, Riesling, Chenin Blanc, Muscat and red table wine and offers tasting and tours at their Richland tasting room. From **Mile 373.5** (Exit 3) on U.S. HIGHWAY 12, go south on Kennedy, east on Columbia Drive and south on Windmill Road.

Canoe Ridge Vineyard
P.O. Box 684, Walla Walla, WA 99362; phone (509) 527-0885. Located off U.S. HIGHWAY 12 in Walla Walla.

Chateau Gallant
S. 1355 Gallant Road, Pasco, WA 99301; phone (509) 545-9570. Located on the edge of the McNary Game Refuge, Chateau Gallant produces Chardonnay, Sauvignon Blanc, Cabernet Sauvignon, Merlot, White Riesling and Gewürztraminer, and offers a view of the geese and ducks using the sloughs for rest stops on their annual migrations. From **Mile 357** on U.S. HIGHWAY 12, go north on Highway 124, then east on Gallant Road.

Chateau Ste. Michelle
205 W. 5th, Grandview, WA 98930; phone (509) 882-3928. Washington state's oldest wine-making facility, the grapes are crushed and fermented to produce Cabernet Sauvignon, Merlot, Port and other varietals. The wines are bottled at the Woodinville facility. Located off U.S. HIGHWAY 12 at **Mile 403.5** (Exit 75).

Chinook Wines
Wine Country Road, P.O. Box 387, Prosser, WA 99350; phone (509) 786-2725. Owned and operated by Clay Mackey and Kay Simon, Chinook produces Chardonnay, Sauvignon Blanc, Semillon, Merlot and Cabernet Sauvignon. Closed Christmas to Presidents Day. From **Mile 395.5** (Exit 82) on U.S. HIGHWAY 12, go east on Wine Country Road, then south on Wittkopf Road.

Covey Run Wines
1500 Vintage Road, Zillah, WA 98953; phone (509) 829-6235. Offering a view of the vineyard and Mount Adams, as well as a tasting room from which you can view the cellar operations through large windows, Covey Run produces Chardonnay, Lemberger, Riesling and other varietals. From **Mile 426** (Exit 52) on U.S. HIGHWAY 12, go north on Cheyne Road, east on Highland Drive and north on Vintage Road.

Eaton Hill Winery
530 Gurley Road, Granger, WA 98932; phone (509) 854-2508. The 80-year-old Rinehold Cannery Homestead, now turned bed and breakfast and winery, is owned by Dr. Edwin Stear and his wife JoAnn. The winery is located in the cannery building, which is being restored. Eaton Hill produces Rieslings, Semillon, Chenin Blanc and Sauvignon Blanc. From **Mile 424** (Exit 54) on U.S. HIGHWAY 12, go east on Yakima Valley Highway to Punkin corner, then north on Gurley Road.

Gordon Brothers Cellars
531 Levey Road, Pasco, WA 99301; phone (509) 547-6224. The Gordon brothers sell most of their grapes to other wineries; 20 percent of the crop makes up the Chardonnay, Johannisberg Riesling, Sauvignon Blanc, Cabernet Sauvignon and Merlot that are released under the Gordon Brothers Cellars label. From **Mile 359.5** on U.S. HIGHWAY 12, go north on Kahlotus Highway, then east on Levey Road.

Hinzerling Winery
1520 Sheridan, Prosser, WA 99350; phone (509) 786-2163. Yakima Valley's oldest family owned and operated winery, Hinzerling was established in 1976 by the Wallace family. Hinzerling produces Cabernet Sauvignon, Gewürztraminer, Port, Angelica, special late harvest styles. From **Mile 395.5** (Exit 82) on U.S. HIGHWAY 12, go west on Wine Country Road, then south on Sheridan.

The Hogue Cellars
Wine Country Road, P.O. Box 31, Prosser, WA 99350; phone (509) 786-4557. The Hogue Cellars is part of Hogue Ranches, a 1,200-acre farm that produces apples, aspara-

gus, juice grapes, mint and hops. The tasting room/gift shop features preserves as well as Chenin Blanc, Johannisberg Riesling, Blush, Semillon, Dry Johannisberg Riesling, Late Harvest White Riesling, Fumé Blanc, Chardonnay, Brut, Yakima Valley Sparkling Wine, Cabernet Sauvignon, Merlot and 4 reserve designations. From **Mile 395.5** (Exit 82) on U.S. HIGHWAY 12, go east on Wine Country Road, then north on Lee Road.

Horizon's Edge Winery

4530 E. Zillah Dr., Zillah, WA 98953; phone (509) 829-6401. Horizon's Edge tasting room offers a panoramic view of the Yakima Valley, Mount Adams and Mount Rainier. The small, family-owned winery produces Chardonnay, Cabernet Sauvignon, Pinot Noir, Muscat Canelli, White Riesling Dry, Merlot, Champagne and Nouveaux Riche. From **Mile 424** (Exit 54) on U.S. HIGHWAY 12, go west on Yakima Valley Highway, then east on E. Zillah Drive.

Hyatt Vineyards

2020 Gilbert Road, Zillah, WA 98953; phone (509) 829-6333. Sitting among 73 acres of grapes, and offering a view of Yakima Valley and the Cascades, Hyatt Vineyards produces Chardonnay, Sauvignon Blanc, Cabernet Sauvignon, Merlot, Late Harvest Riesling and Ice Wine. Closed January. From **Mile 426** (Exit 52) on U.S. HIGHWAY 12, go north on Cheyne Road, then west on Gilbert Road.

Kiona Vineyards

Route 2, Box 2169E, Benton City, WA 99320; phone (509) 588-6716. Kiona Vineyards on Red Mountain is owned and operated by the Jim Holmes and John Williams families. The tasting room, winery and vineyard are located at the Williams' home, and the tank aging facilities are located at the Holmes residence. Kiona produces Chardonnay, Cabernet, Riesling and Lemberger. From **Mile 381.5** (Exit 96) on U.S. HIGHWAY 12, go east on Highway 224, then north on Sunset Road.

L'Ecole No. 41

41 Lowden School Road, Lowden, WA 99360; phone (509) 525-0940. Located in the cellars of the historic Frenchtown school, L'Ecole No. 41 is family owned and operated. The label features children's artwork. L'Ecole produces Semillon, Merlot and other varietal wines. From **Mile 327.5** on U.S. HIGHWAY 12, go north on Lower Dry Creek Road.

Oakwood Cellars

Route 2, Box 2321, Benton City, WA 99320; phone (509) 588-5332. Owners Bob and Evelyn Skelton toured England, France, Germany and Italy through 1992 to study wine-making techniques. Oakwood Cellars produces Chardonnay, Merlot, Cabernet Sauvignon, Lemberger, Semillon, Riesling and Muscat Canelli. From **Mile 381.5** (Exit 96) on U.S. HIGHWAY 12, go east on Highway 224, then north on De Moss Road.

Patrick M. Paul Vineyards

1554 School Ave., Walla Walla, WA 99362; phone (509) 522-1127. The wines at Patrick M. Paul are oak-aged with a focus on new American oak for its spicy, vanillin qualities. Cabernet Franc, Pinot Noir, Merlot, Cabernet Sauvignon, Chardonnay, and Boysenberry and Concord grape dessert wine. Tours and tastings by appointment only. From **Mile 313.5** on U.S. HIGHWAY 12, go south on Wilbur Avenue, east on Alder Street E. and south on School Avenue.

Pontin del Roza

Route 4, Box 4735, Prosser, WA 99350; phone (509) 786-4449. The Pontin family has been farming in the Roza district for over 30 years; they began harvesting wine grapes in the 1980s. Pontin del Roza produces White Riesling, Chenin Blanc, Chardonnay, Cabernet Sauvignon, Sauvignon Blanc, Blush, Pinot Gris and other limited specialty wines. From **Mile 398** (Exit 80) on U.S. HIGHWAY 12, go north on Gap Road, east on Kingtull Road, and north on Hinzerling Road.

Portteus Winery

5201 Highland Drive, Zillah, WA 98953; phone (509) 829-6970. Paul and Marilyn Portteus planted their 47-acre vineyard in 1982, and began wine production 1984; they now produce Cabernet, Merlot, Chardonnay, Red Zinfandel and Rattlesnake Ridge "Spaghetti Red." Portteus was selected in 1992 as one of Washington's 5 favorite wineries by *Pacific Northwest* magazine. Dec. through Jan. by appointment only. From **Mile 426** (Exit 52) on U.S. HIGHWAY 12, go north on Cheyne Road, then east on Highland Drive.

Seth Ryan Winery

Sunset Road, Route 2, Box 2168D1, Benton City, WA 99320; phone (509) 588-6780. Seth Ryan is owned and operated by the Olsen and Brodzinski families; it produces Riesling, Gewürztraminer, Chardonnay, Cabernet Sauvignon, Cabernet Franc and Merlot. From **Mile 381.5** (Exit 96) on U.S. HIGHWAY 12, go east on Highway 224, then north on Sunset Road.

Stewart Vineyards

1711 Cherry Hill Road, Granger, WA 98932; phone (509) 854-1882. The mailing address is 1381 W. Riverside Ave., Sunnyside, WA 98944. Planted on the Wahluke Slope and in the Yakima Valley, the vineyards offer a blizzard of blossoms in early April and ripe cherries in early June. Stewart Vineyards produces Johannisberg Riesling, Dry Riesling, Chardonnay, Gewürztraminer, Cabernet Sauvignon, Late Harvest White Riesling and Blush. From **Mile 419.5** (Exit 58) on U.S. HIGHWAY 12, go south on Washington Highway 223, then east on Outlook Road (which becomes Cherry Hill Road).

Tagaris Winery

1625 W. A St., Unit E, Pasco, WA 99301. The mailing address is P.O. Box 5433, Kennewick, WA 99336. Owner Michael Taggares created the winery in 1987. Tagaris produces Cabernet Sauvignon, Pinot Noir, Chardonnay, Chenin Blanc and Riesling. Located off U.S. HIGHWAY 12 at **Mile 362.5**.

Tefft Cellars

1320 Independence Road, Outlook, WA 98938; phone (509) 837-7651. The winery offers tastings from the bottle or barrel, and dinners are served to small groups. Tefft produces Cabernet Sauvignon, Merlot, Late Harvest Chardonnay, Late Harvest Sauvignon Blanc and Sweet Nebbiolo and Cabernet Champagne. Located off U.S. HIGHWAY 12 at **Mile 414.5** (Exit 63).

Tucker Cellars

70 Ray Road, Sunnyside, WA 98944; phone (509) 837-8701. Owned and operated by Dean and Rose Tucker and their 4 children, Tucker Cellars produces Chardonnay, Cabernet Sauvignon, Riesling, Muscat and other varietals. The winery is located adjacent to the Tucker Fruit and Produce Market, which offers fresh in-season fruits and vegetables. From **Mile 405.5** (Exit 73) on U.S. HIGHWAY 12, go west on Wine Country Road, then north on Ray Road.

Washington Hills Cellars

111 E. Lincoln Ave., Sunnyside, WA 98944; phone (509) 839-WINE. Housed in the old Carnation facility, a landmark building, Washington Hills produces Cabernet Sauvignon, Merlot, Chardonnay, Johannisberg Riesling, Sauvignon Blanc, Semillon, Muscat, Dry Chenin Blanc and Gewürztraminer. Located off U.S. HIGHWAY 12 at **Mile 411.5** (Exit 67).

Waterbrook Winery

Route 1, Box 46, Lowden, WA 99360; phone (509) 522-1918. Owned and operated by Eric and Janet Rindal, Waterbrook is the largest winery in Walla Walla Valley. It produces Chardonnay, Sauvignon Blanc, Merlot and Cabernet Sauvignon. From **Mile 323** on U.S. HIGHWAY 12, go south on McDonald Road.

Woodward Canyon Winery

Route 1, Box 387, Lowden, WA 99360; phone (509) 525-4129. Owned by Rick Small, as is the grain elevator and machine shop on the other side of Highway 12, Woodward Canyon produces Cabernet Sauvignon, Merlot, Chardonnay and other varietals. Located off U.S. HIGHWAY 12 at **Mile 327.5**.

Yakima River Winery

Route 1, Box 1657, Prosser, WA 99350; phone (509) 786-2805. Founded in 1978 by the Rauner family, the winery produces Cabernet Sauvignon, Merlot, Rendezvous, Lemberger, Dry Fumé Blanc, Semi-Dry Johannisberg Riesling, Dryberry Riesling and Vintage Port. Yakima River hosts educational wine events during July 4th weekend, Thanksgiving weekend and 1 weekend in April. From **Mile 395.5** (Exit 82) on U.S. HIGHWAY 12, go west on Wine Country Road, then west on North River Road.

Zillah Oakes Winery

Vintage Valley Parkway, P.O. Box 1729, Zillah, WA 98953; phone (509) 829-6235. Zillah and Zillah Oakes Winery are named after the daughter of the president of the Northern Pacific Railroad. Her husband, Walter Granger, transformed Yakima Valley from sagebrush land into a fertile valley with his irrigation projects. Located off U.S. HIGHWAY 12 at **Mile 426** (Exit 52).

Interstate 84

Charles Hooper Family Winery

196 Spring Creek Road, Husum, WA 98623; phone (509) 493-2324. The terraced vineyard at Hooper's offers a spectacular view of Mount Hood. The winery produces Riesling, Gewürztraminer, Pinot Noir Blanc, Chardonnay, Merlot and Huckleberry Apple Wine. Open March through Nov., other times by appointment only. From **Mile 58** (Exit 64) on INTERSTATE 84, go east on Highway 14, north on Highway 141 and east on Spring Creek Road.

Mont Elise Vineyards

315 West Steuben, Bingen, WA 98605; phone (509) 493-3001. The Bavarian-style building at Mont Elise houses the tasting room, which offers a view into the operating winery below. From **Mile 58** (Exit 64) on

INTERSTATE 84, go east on Highway 14.

Interstate 90

Arbor Crest Winery
N. 4705 Fruithill Road, Spokane, WA 99207-9562; phone (509) 927-9463. The Arbor Crest Cliff House, located on a rock promontory 450 feet above the Spokane River, is a national historical landmark. It houses the tasting facility and visitor center. From **Mile 287** (Exit 287) on INTERSTATE 90, go north on Argonne Road, east on Upriver Drive and north on Fruithill Road.

Caterina Winery
North 905 Washington, Spokane, WA 99201; phone (509) 328-5069. Located off INTERSTATE 90 in Spokane.

Hedges Cellars
1105 12th Ave. NW, Suite A4, Issaquah, WA 98027; phone (206) 391-6056. Hedges Cellars produces 1 red wine, a blend of Cabernet Sauvignon and Merlot. The Issaquah location houses the tasting room and the aging room. From **Mile 315** (Exit 15) on INTERSTATE 90, go south on Sherman Avenue, east on Gilman Boulevard and south on 12th Avenue NW.

Hunter Hill Vineyards
2752 W. McMannaman Road, Othello, WA 99344; phone (509) 346-2736. The tasting room is located in the original old farmhouse, with a view of the canyons and lakes of the Columbia National Wildlife Refuge. There is a picnic area and RV accommodations. Hunter Hill produces Riesling, Chenin Blanc, Chardonnay, Muscat Canelli and Merlot. From **Mile 176.5** (Exit 179) on INTERSTATE 90, go south on Highway 17, east on Highway 262 and south on Road H.

Latah Creek Wine Cellars
E. 13030 Indiana Ave., Spokane, WA 99216; phone (509) 926-0164. Housed in a Spanish-mission-style structure, Latah Creek produces Chenin Blanc, Chardonnay, Semillon, Merlot and Cabernet Sauvignon. The annual Mayfest features a strawberry-and-herb flavored Maywine. From **Mile 289** (Exit 289) on INTERSTATE 90, go north on Pines Road, east on Indiana Avenue.

Mountain Dome Winery
16315 E. Temple Road, Spokane, WA 99207; phone (509) 928-BRUT. The winery is named for the geodesic dome home of the owner, Dr. Michael Manz. Mountain Dome produces Sparkling Wine. Tours and tastings by appointment only. From **Mile 282** (Exit 282) on INTERSTATE 90, go east on Trent Avenue, north on Evergreen (which becomes Forker Road) and east on Temple.

Snoqualmie Winery
1000 Winery Road, Snoqualmie, WA 98065; phone (206) 888-4000. Snoqualmie Winery offers a gift shop, tasting room and large picnic area where summertime concerts and special events take place. Located off INTERSTATE 90 at **Mile 24.5** (Exit 27).

White Heron Cellars
101 Washington Way N., George, WA 98824; phone (509) 785-5521. Located in an old gasoline station, White Heron produces Dry Riesling, Pinot Noir and Red Table Wine. From **Mile 147** (Exit 149) on INTER-STATE 90, go south on George Washington Way, then west on Montmorency Boulevard.

Worden's Washington Winery
7217 W. 45th, Spokane, WA 99204; phone (509) 455-7835. Spokane area's first winery, Worden's is located in a log cabin in a forest of pine trees. Worden's produces Chardonnay, Cabernet/Merlot, Chenin Blanc, Riesling, Gewürztraminer and others. From **Mile 276** (Exit 276) on INTERSTATE 90, go south on Grove Road, then east on Thorpe Road.

U.S. Highway 97

Columbia Cliffs Winery
8866 Highway 14, P.O. Box 14, Wishram, WA 98673; phone (509) 767-1100. Established in 1985, Columbia Cliffs is bordered on the north side by Basalt cliffs that rise to 400 feet. Closed Nov. through March. From **Mile 277** on U.S. HIGHWAY 97, go east on Highway 14.

Staton Hills Winery
71 Gangl Road, Wapato, WA 98951; phone (509) 877-2112. Offering a panoramic view of the Yakima Valley and Mount Adams, Staton Hills produces Cabernet Sauvignon, Merlot, Pinot Noir, Chardonnay and Brut Rosé. Located off U.S. HIGHWAY 97 at **Mile 343**.

Thurston Wolfe Wines
27 N. Front St., P.O. Box 9068, Yakima, WA 98909; phone (509) 452-0335. A small family winery specializing in dessert and table wines, the winery is located in the old City Hall in the Yakima Historical District. In addition to the dessert wines, Thurston Wolfe also produces Port, Black Muscat, Late Harvest Sauvignon Blanc, Lemberger, Zinfandel, Aligote, Riesling, and Absolute Brut (sparkling wine). Located off U.S. HIGHWAY 97 at **Mile 357**.

U.S. Highway 101

Camaraderie Cellars
165 Benson Road, Port Angeles, WA 98362; phone (360) 452-4964. Located on the Olympic Peninsula and offering views of the Olympic Mountains, Camaraderie began production in 1992 with grapes from eastern Washington vineyards. Camaraderie produces Cabernet Sauvignon. By appointment only. Located off U.S. HIGHWAY 101 at **Mile 593.5**.

Hoodsport Winery
N. 23501 Highway 101, Hoodsport, WA 98548; phone (360) 877-9508, fax (206) 877-9508. Owned by the Patterson family, Hoodsport produces Raspberry Wine, Red Table Wine and other fruit wines and varietal wines. Tours of the Stretch Island vineyard are offered only during the summer. Located off U.S. HIGHWAY 101 at **Mile 677.5**.

Lost Mountain Winery
3174 Lost Mountain Road, Sequim, WA 98382; phone (360) 683-5229. Located in the Olympic foothills, Lost Mountain Winery is owned and operated by Romeo Conca. He uses grapes from eastern Washington, Oregon and California to make red wines in the style of his Italian ancestors. The annual "open winery" takes place the last week of June and the first week of July. Visits by appointment or by chance. From **Mile 607.5** on U.S. HIGHWAY 101, go north on Taylor Cutoff Road, then east on Lost Mountain Road; winery is approximately 6 miles from Highway 101.

Neuharth Winery
148 Still Road, Sequim, WA 98382; phone (360) 683-9652. A dairy barn built in the 1930s is now the home of the Neuharth Winery. The tasting room offers a view of the winery. Neuharth produces Chardonnay, Riesling, Cabernet, Rosé, Merlot and White and Red Table Wine. From **Mile 609.5** on U.S. HIGHWAY 101, go south on Still Road for a quarter mile.

U.S. Highway 395

Columbia Crest Winery
P.O. Box 231, Paterson, WA 99345-0231; phone (509) 875-2061. The largest winery in Washington, the Columbia Crest complex houses more than a million gallons of wine and elegant tourist facilities. From **Mile 390** (Exit 131) on U.S. HIGHWAY 395, go west 14 miles on Highway 14.

Knipprath Cellars
S. 163 Lincoln St., Spokane, WA 99201; phone (509) 483-1926. Located next to the historic WWP Steam Plant in downtown Spokane, Knipprath offers a tour in which visitors may see and sample wines during the various stages of development. From **Mile 553.5** (Exit 280) on U.S. HIGHWAY 395, go south on Lincoln Street.

Preston Premium Wines
502 E. Vineyard Dr., Pasco, WA 99301; phone (509) 545-1990. The Preston family, one of the pioneer grape growers in the Columbia Valley, has seen their vineyard grow from 50 acres to 180 acres. The vineyard features the winery with a tasting room and gift shop and a picnic park with a gazebo and an amphitheater. From **Mile 425.5** on U.S. HIGHWAY 395, go east onto Vineyard Drive.

The Islands

Lopez Island Vineyards
Route 2, Box 3096, Lopez Island, WA 98261; phone (360) 468-3644. A small family-run winery, Lopez Island produces wines with grapes from their own organic vineyard and grapes from eastern Washington. Closed Christmas through March 15. Take the Washington State Ferry from Anacortes to Lopez Island, then go south on Ferry Road, west on Fisherman Bay Road and south to the winery.

Whidbey Island Vineyard & Winery
5237 S. Langley Road, Langley, WA 98260; phone (360) 221-2040. Owned and operated by Greg and Elizabeth Osenbach, Whidbey Island Winery is located in a red barn, and offers a picnic area with a view of the vineyard and an old apple orchard. Take the Clinton Ferry from Mukilteo to Whidbey Island, then go north on Highway 525 and north on Langley Road.

Whidbey's
Wonn Road off Highway 525, Greenbank, WA 98253; phone (360) 678-7700. The farm is surrounded by 125 acres of loganberries, the ingredient in Whidbey's Loganberry Liqueur. The tasting room also offers the wines of Chateau Ste. Michelle, Whidbey's sister winery. Take the Clinton Ferry from Mukilteo to Whidbey Island, then go north on Highway 525 and east on Wonn Road.

INDEX

FIELD EDITOR REPORT

If, during your travels, you find changes along the highways logged in *Northwest Mileposts*®, please let us know by dropping a note to the Editor, *Northwest Mileposts*®, 3000 Northup Way, Suite 200, Bellevue, WA 98004.

We've found that some of our best travel information comes from our readers. So let us know if you find an interesting attraction or new campground not logged in *Northwest Mileposts*®.

Have a fantastic trip ... and let us know how it goes!   – The Editors

On page _____ of *Northwest Mileposts*®, in column _____ (1,2,3), we suggest that you make the following change(s):

_____

_____

_____

On page _____ of *Northwest Mileposts*®, in column _____ (1,2,3), we suggest that you make the following change(s):

_____

_____

_____

On page _____ of *Northwest Mileposts*®, in column _____ (1,2,3), we suggest that you make the following change(s):

_____

_____

_____

Notes and comments: _____

_____

_____

_____

_____